COLLINS WILDLIFE TRUST GUIDES

The Wildlife Trusts are working for a UK richer in wildlife. Their extensive network covers all parts of the countryside and reaches into cities as far apart as Belfast and Ipswich. They care for more than 2,300 nature reserves: from rugged coastline to urban oases, remote islands to flower-rich meadows.

With more than a third of a million members, The Wildlife Trusts provide an unrivalled source of expertise on wildlife and conservation issues, offering advice that helps local landowners and communities care for their local wildlife. This work also includes the implementation of rescue plans for nationally rare species, including the red squirrel, the dormouse and its ancient woodland home, the marsh fritillary butterfly and the otter.

The Wildlife Trusts also campaign for better protection for wildlife at the local, national and international level, and recognise that people are a vital part of the solution to the challenges they face.

Joint projects like this one between The Wildlife Trusts and Collins Natural History are important, not just because they help raise vital funds for wildlife in the UK (for each copy of this book sold 30p will be donated to The Wildlife Trusts), but also because they show people the wonders of the natural world through the medium of first-class photographs, which encourage their interest and commitment to help protect it.

COLLINS WILDLIFE TRUST GUIDE TREES

A photographic guide to the trees of Britain and Europe

Keith Rushforth

Photographs assembled by FLPA

HarperCollins*Publishers*

HarperCollins*Publishers*
77–85 Fulham Palace Road
London
W6 8JB

The HarperCollins website address is:
www.**fire**and**water**.com

First published 1999

2 4 6 8 10 9 7 5 3 1

99 01 03 04 02 00

Titles in this series include:

Birds of Britain and Europe, John Gooders

Butterflies of Britain and Europe, Michael Chinery

Mushrooms of Britain and Europe, Régis Courtecuisse

Night Sky, Mark Chartrand

ISBN 0 00 220013 9

Edit and page make-up by D & N Publishing, UK

Colour origination by Colourscan, Singapore
Printed and bound by Rotolito Lombarda SpA, Milan, Italy

CONTENTS

7 Preface
9 Introduction
11 Plant Naming – Taxonomy and Nomenclature
21 How to Use this Guide
29 Key to the Colour Plates

Part I Colour Plates
33 Key to Flowers and Fruit
38–352 Colour Photographs

Part II Family and Species Descriptions
353–1272

Part III Appendices
1275 Glossary
1283 Picture Credits
1289 Location Photographs
1290 Index
1336 Quick Reference Guide

PREFACE

Trees are some of the most beautiful objects in the natural world. They give character and scale to our countryside and our gardens, to our streets and parks. Areas of cities without trees are often barren and uninviting (unless the architecture is exceptional) whilst those areas with flourishing trees have a tranquillity beyond the mere presence of the trees themselves. Trees are important both in our lives and in our enjoyment of our lives. They provide beauty, food and timber – yes, trees are a source of food, whether it is fruits such as apples, nuts such as walnuts and pecans, or delicacies such as maple syrup and cocoa.

This is a tree-identification book, designed to assist you to recognize and name the overwhelming majority of trees which may be found in all parts of Europe. Identifying a tree will give access to details about its origin, characteristics and relationships, and thereby helping you to learn more about it.

I wish to record my thanks to the many people who have assisted me in learning about and enjoying trees. I would also like to acknowledge the observations of the following on specific parts of the text: Peter Gregory (*Acer*), Kenneth Ashburner (*Alnus* and *Betula*), Dr Hugh McAllister (*Betula* and *Sorbus*), Citrus Centre, Pulborough, Sussex (*Citrus*), Bob Adams (*Cupressus*), Dr Stephen Spongberg (*Magnolia*), Allen Coombes (*Quercus*), Michael Frankis (*Pinus*), John White (*Salix*), Dr Donald Piggot (*Tilia*) and Susyn Andrews (*Zelkova*). I would also like to express my appreciation to the Curator and staff of the Hillier Arboretum, Westonbirt Arboretum, Bedgebury Pinetum, Cambridge University Botanic Garden and the University of Liverpool Ness Botanic Garden who all made available reference material for the written descriptions. I would also like to thank the photographers and staff of the Frank Lane Picture Agency for so many excellent slides, and David Price-Goodfellow and his colleagues at D & N Publishing.

INTRODUCTION

What is a Tree? The definition of a tree used here is a woody plant capable of growing at least 3 m (10 ft) in height. There are no satisfactory ways of distinguishing between trees and the larger shrubs – the character sometimes used that a tree has a single stem is arbitrary, often being broken by plants, whilst all trees start much smaller than 3m in height! I have, therefore, included some species which are more often seen as shrubs, or as climbers.

A Personal Taxonomic Approach The taxonomic account of tree species used here is inevitably a personal one. Other authors will treat some trees in a different way. However, if you look at half a dozen references you will often find two or three taking one approach to a species, and three or four another. Some of these differences cross national boundaries. I have followed the treatments with which I feel most happy. Sometimes this is not the current favoured treatment (but botanical treatments have a habit of changing over cycles of perhaps half a century!), at other times it might be because of recent research which has highlighted a different aspect of a tree's relationships. The index which includes relevant synonyms should allow comparison with other accounts.

The Scope of this Guide The coverage includes the whole of Europe where plants make trees. This ranges from the Mediterranean north to beyond the Arctic circle, and from the Urals to the Atlantic coast and islands. This is a very wide geographical area which experiences a range of different climates. However, trees are adaptable, with many occurring over a wide range of countries.

The coverage includes both native and introduced (or exotic) trees. Almost all the trees native to Europe are featured but they form only part of the full variety of trees which are grown in Europe. Throughout the continent but especially in the more southerly and westerly regions

many exotic or non-native trees flourish.
Some of these are early introductions, such
as the Walnut (*Juglans regia*) which is
probably native to central Asia, the Olive
(*Olea europaea*) which is probably a native
of Arabia, or the Peach (*Prunus persica*)
from China, which were important as
foods and widely transported by our
distant forefathers. Others are European
species which have been spread purely for
their beauty, such as the Horse Chestnut
(*Aesculus hippocastanum*) which was taken
from its restricted native range in the
Balkans in the 15th century.

Nearly 1,200 tree species (plus a
number of prominent cultivars) are
featured in the book, with over 825
illustrated and 750 described in detail.
This includes the vast majority of trees
which are likely to be encountered.
However, this is only a proportion of the
species which could be cultivated. For
instance, there are approximately 450
species of *Quercus* (oaks) and 500 of
Eucalyptus (gums), most of which could
be grown somewhere in Europe.
Specialist collections such as those of
major arboreta or tree collections (e.g. the
Royal Botanic Gardens at Kew) will
contain a number of trees not featured
here. Fortunately, such places tend to be
well labelled, although *no* collection is
always perfectly and accurately labelled!

Many of the trees used in our gardens,
streets and parks are hybrids or garden
selections. These may differ from the parent
species in botanically minor but very
obvious characters, such as coloured foliage,
or larger fruits or flowers. Information on
many of these is included.

PLANT NAMING – TAXONOMY AND NOMENCLATURE

The purpose of taxonomy is to sort out the relationships between entities, whether genera, species or cultivars, thereby making a judgement on the importance of different characters. Nomenclature aims to give the correct name (according to certain botanical and horticultural rules) to the taxonomic entities, but does make a value judgement on the differences. The two, therefore, are related but quite separate.

Plant taxonomy is based on the binomial system. In this the basic units are the genus and the species. The genus contains from one to many species which share certain major characteristics, such as flower or fruit structure. A species consists of many plants sharing similar characters. Examples are *Abies alba*, *Morus alba*, *Acer carpinifolium* or *Zelkova carpinifolia*. In these examples *Abies*, *Acer*, *Morus* and *Zelkova* are the names of individual genera (singular genus). Genera are unique in plant taxonomy. You cannot have two genera with the same name (plant and animal taxonomy are different, and there are a few examples of the same genus name being applied to a plant and an animal group, such as *Pieris* (which in botany refers to a genus of shrubs in the family Ericaceae and related to *Arbutus*, and in Zoology is the generic name for the cabbage white butterflies). Generic names are nouns and always start with a capital letter. They give information about a plant, as related plants will belong to the same genus.

The second basic unit is the specific name or species name. In the above examples, two are *alba*, meaning white, and two are *carpinifolium* or *carpinifolia*, meaning leaves like a hornbeam or *Carpinus*. The specific names are adjectives, they describe a part of the genus. They are always written in the lower case, even when named after a person. The other point is that as the scientific language is Latin, the ending changes depending upon whether the genus is male, female or neuter. In the above example, *Acer* is neuter, so the adjective ends in '-um', whereas *Zelkova* is female, hence it ends '-a'.

Specific names are only unique in a genus. The same descriptive word can be used again in another genus. Sometimes problems arise where further research shows that two genera should be amalgamated. An example is in *Rhododendron* where Linnaeus originally considered *Azalea* a different genus. He named *Rhododendron ponticum* and *Azalea pontica* (both after the Roman name for a region of modern Turkey) but when botanists concluded that two genera could not be maintained, *Azalea pontica* had to have a new name and is now known as *Rhododendron luteum*.

It is often useful to divide a species into two or more elements. The main subdivisions are subspecies, varieties (Latin *varietas*) and forms which are botanical names and are printed in italics. In horticulture there are also cultivars (the abbreviation of *culti*vated *vari*ety), which are printed in Roman text. Note that cultivars are not in Latin but are vernacular nouns. Therefore they have an initial capital as for the genus name, whereas subspecies, varieties and forma do not.

The level of subspecies is used for a degree of variation which is more conveniently treated as belonging to the same species but which has a different geographical or ecological distribution. This means that normally two subspecies will not occur at the same place in an identical ecological zone. Varieties are obvious variants but which can occur together. Forms (Latin *forma*, plural *formae*) are minor variants. An example is the glaucous or blue-leafed forms of Atlas Cedar (*Cedrus atlantica*) which are treated as forma *glauca*.

An important element of the name of a tree (or any plant) is the authority who first named it. The system of a unique combination of a genus and a specific name was started by Carl von Linné, in 1753. Linné was Swedish and worked at Upsalla University. He is better known by the latinized form of his name, Linnaeus. All plants correctly named by Linnaeus have his name after the scientific or Latin name to show that he is the author of that name. As Linnaeus started the system his name is abbreviated to L. However, modern opinion is that Linnaeus was not always correct. For example, in the pine family he treated all the species which he knew as species of *Pinus*. For *Pinus sylvestris* and *Pinus strobus* this is accepted today, so for both of these the authority after the name is Linnaeus, written as *Pinus sylvestris* L. and *Pinus strobus* L. However, no serious botanist today considers Norway Spruce (*Pinus abies* L.) to belong to the genus *Pinus* as presently understood. The genus *Picea* was soon established for the spruces. At first Norway Spruce was given a complete new name in *Picea*, as *Picea excelsa* Link. However, it was soon decided that the interests of clarity require the oldest valid specific epithet is used where possible. This is *abies*, because Linnaeus first named it as *Pinus abies*. The correct name is therefore *Picea abies*, with the authority (L.) Karsten, where (L.) is in brackets to show that the name started with Linnaeus but in a different genus, and that Karsten was the first person to publish the correct combination in *Picea*.

However, another plant which Linnaeus called a pine is the European Larch. Linnaeus called this *Pinus larix*. Miller quickly pointed out that it differed from *Pinus* in so many features that it was a separate genus, using the ancient Latin name *Larix* for the generic name. In botany, saying the same thing twice (tautology) is not allowed (in zoology it is). Miller could not, therefore, call European Larch *Larix larix*. Instead he made a new specific name *decidua*. European Larch is therefore scientifically named *Larix decidua* Miller.

The authority of a name is often shortened and there is a standard way of shortening author's names. However, the average saving of space is about three letters! In the index, the species names are given with authorities (*see* pp.1293–335); the names are cited in full except for L. for Linnaeus.

Hierarchy of Classification

The classification of plants (taxonomy) has an ordered sequence or hierarchy of categories. So although the genus and specific epithet (species name) provide a unique name which defines a plant, the system has both subdivisions of species below the species, and ranks higher than genera.

The primary divisions are classes. There are three classes of plant described and illustrated in the book. The ferns or Pteridophytes (Pteridophyta) do not have seeds but have spores. Only *Dicksonia antarctica* is featured here, *see* p.664. The two principal classes are the seed plants, the Gymnosperms (or Gymnospermae) and the Angiosperms (or Angiospermae). Gymnospermae is the Greek for 'naked seed' and in this group the young seeds or ovules are naked or exposed at the time of pollination. This contrasts with the situation in the Angiospermae (Greek for 'hidden seeds') where the ovules are enclosed in an ovary at the time of pollination. The naked ovules of a Gymnosperm are easily seen under a strong hand lens in the young female cones of *Cupressus* at pollination. The Angiosperm state can only be seen when a flower is cut into sections and viewed.

The Angiosperms are divided into two subclasses. In the Dicots or Dicotyledoneae the germinating seedling or embryo has two cotyledons or seed leaves, contrasting with the single cotyledon or seed leaf of the Monocots (or Monocotyledoneae). Fortunately, there are other differences closely associated with this important but soon lost character (although always initially present). The Dicots have a cambium and can make secondary thickening of the stem (therefore the stem gets thicker with time), the leaves rarely have parallel venation and the flowers have the parts in fours or fives. In the Monocots, the stems are not capable of making secondary thickening, hence a palm tree or bamboo cannot become thicker once it has initially grown, whilst the leaves have parallel veins and the flower parts are in threes.

The next division is into superorders, ending in '-idae', such as Magnolidae and Rosidae, and beneath these are orders, ending in '-ales', such as Coniferales, Rosales and Magnoliales. The next tier is the family, which has an ending '-aceae', as in Rosaceae and Magnoliaceae. Families may be divided into subfamilies and tribes, such as the principal four subfamilies of the Rosaceae which are the Spiraeoideae, Rosoideae, Prunoideae and the Maloideae. All of these end in '-oideae'.

Illustrative Heirarchy of Tree Classification

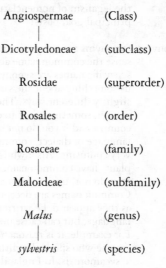

Angiospermae	(Class)
Dicotyledoneae	(subclass)
Rosidae	(superorder)
Rosales	(order)
Rosaceae	(family)
Maloideae	(subfamily)
Malus	(genus)
sylvestris	(species)

Some of the species within a genus may be more closely allied than other species and these groupings help in understanding a genus. Therefore within a genus, there may be two or more subgenera (singular subgenus), sections and subsections, in descending order. Any level within the botanical hierarchy is a taxon (plural taxa).

Knowledge of Superorders and Orders is not important for the purpose of identifying trees, but recognizing families and subfamily groupings can be very helpful as it will allow you to 'recognize' the affinities of a tree you have not previously seen. Even more useful is knowledge of the groupings or alliances within a genus.

It is important always to remember the most important difference between taxonomy and nomenclature. Nomenclature is very legalistic in approach. There are, therefore, correct or legitimate names according to the rules and incorrect or illegitimate ones. By contrast, taxonomy is an art form rooted in scientific fact. Therefore, in absolute terms there are no rights and wrongs, just opinions (although some opinions are better than others). But taxonomy needs the legalism of nomenclature to fix the principal goal posts!

Synonyms   Synonyms are alternative names. In one sense the common name and Latin or scientific names are synonyms as they tell us something about the same tree, albeit in slightly different ways. The common name is local, sometimes just to certain parts of a country and if you do not speak that language or dialect, common names can be very confusing. Also, whilst most native plants have common names, many exotic ones do not, until someone coins one. Common names are deceptive. They appeal as they appear to be written in a familiar language, but can cause untold confusion. For example, it is reasonable to assume that anyone who speaks English will know what a 'sycamore' is. In England, 'sycamore' is a member of the maple genus, *Acer pseudoplatanus*. The same holds true in much of Scotland, although it is also known as 'plane'. In the United States, however, 'sycamore' is not a maple but a member of the plane genus, *Platanus occidentalis*. To add further confusion, in the Bible, the references to 'sycamore' refer to the historically true sycamore, which is a fig, *Ficus sycamorus*. It may seem strange to begin with, but using the Latin or scientific name is more straightforward! At the very least, it tells you whether the tree you are looking at is related to the maples, planes (*Platanus*) or figs!

The Latin or scientific name of a genus and a species as a pair or binomial is universal for any one species and is the international unique name, which is why the Latin names are used in the ordering of the descriptive account of the trees. However, in the following pages you will find synonyms to many Latin names.

There are three main reasons why a name may be relegated to synonymy. Some synonyms are simply duplicate names – the same plant named by two or more botanists on separate occasions. For example, Pax named a maple collected by the British botanist Augustine Henry from west China as *Acer maximowiczii*, after the botanist Maximowicz. One month later, Maximowicz named his copy of Henry's collection (i.e. the same gathering of material) *Acer urophyllum*, because of the resemblance of the leaves to the Uri Maple of Japan (*Acer crataegifolium*). In cases like this, the older name has priority (in this case *Acer maximowiczii* Pax).

Sometimes the oldest name is found to be invalid and has to be replaced by a new name. For example, the Himalayan Blue Pine was first named *Pinus excelsa* by Wallich (although actually published by G. Don, therefore the authority is Wallich ex G. Don) but Lambert had earlier used the name *Pinus excelsa* for the Norway Spruce *Picea abies*. The name *Pinus excelsa* Lambert is therefore a synonym of *Picea abies* (L.) Karsten and under the legalism of nomenclature cannot be used later for a different tree. McClelland then renamed this species of pine after Griffith, as *Pinus griffithii*. Joseph Hooker named a larch *Larix griffithii* after Griffith (the true name for this larch is *Larix griffithiana* Carrière). Unfortunately, Parlatore did not accept *Larix* as a separate genus from *Pinus* and named the larch *Pinus griffithii* Parlatore, which is an older name than *Pinus griffithii* McClelland. Therefore McClelland's name for the pine is invalid. To give it a valid name, Jackson renamed the tree after Wallich (who originally recognized it as a distinct species), as *Pinus wallichiana* A.B. Jackson. This is the correct Latin name according to the rules of nomenclature, but *Pinus excelsa* and *Pinus griffithii* are often used for this same tree and therefore are listed as synonyms.

The second category of synonyms are taxonomic synonyms. These occur when botanist 1 thinks trees 1 and 2 are both species A, whilst botanist 2 thinks they represent two species, A and B. If you consider that botanist 1 was correct, then species B becomes a synonym of species A. An example is *Acer stachyophyllum* Hiern and *Acer tetramerum* Pax. It was first named from the Himalayas by Hiern in 1875. In 1887 Pax named a tree from western China *Acer tetramerum*. It is now usually accepted that they represent the two ends of the range of one species and by this treatment Pax's species becomes a synonym of *Acer stachyophyllum*.

The third main category of synonyms are hierarchical synonyms. These are when the same plant can be treated as a species, subspecies or variety. For example, in the following account I accept *Acer maximowiczii* Pax and *Acer mono* Maximowicz as species. An American botanist Murray has treated *Acer maximowiczii* as a subspecies of *Acer pectinatum*, and *Acer mono* as a subspecies of *Acer truncatum*. Some botanists agree with Murray on his treatment of *Acer maximowiczii* but not of *Acer mono*. However, there is no question but that *Acer maximowiczii* and *Acer pectinatum* ssp. *maximowiczii* are the same plant, one treated as a species, the other as a subspecies.

The listing of synonyms assists in relating to other books, where the treatment may be complimentary but different!

What Makes a Species? A species is the basic botanical (or zoological) unit. However, for something so important there is no really satisfactory definition. The best one 'A species is whatever a competent botanist considers is a species' is both correct, and not very helpful as competent botanists argue vehemently about species! Another one is 'the aggregate of all those individuals which have the same constant and distinctive characters' which is excellent until you consider how many characters and what is a constant character!

I find the most useful approach is that a species differs in a minimum of two (preferably four or more) major and unrelated characters from other related species. Subspecific entities have only a single major character, or perhaps a few minor ones, and a geographical or ecological difference in their habitat. Varieties also differ in one major or a few minor characters but do not have a geographical or ecological separation. Forms often only have a single minor character. For example, the blue forms of Atlas Cedar are horticulturally important but the 'blueness' character is only of minor botanical importance; therefore these are *Cedrus atlantica* forma *glauca*.

Unrelated characters are on different organs. For instance leaf length and breadth are two related characters as leaves longer in length (in cm or inches) tend to be broader in width and the operative character may be the ratio of length to width. But a flower and a leaf character are not assumed to be closely related. For instance, a poplar tree with long ovate leaves and a capsule splitting into three parts (i.e. along three sutures) is generally accepted as a different species from the closely related poplar with ovate to broad ovate leaves and a capsule which splits along two sutures – the first is the Western Cottonwood *Populus trichocarpa*, the second the Balsam Poplar *Populus balsamifera*.

The species concept is both very useful and often artificial. In most genera, some or all of the species will hybridize, if not in the wild then when brought together in cultivation. The species concept, therefore, is often more relevant to us than to the trees! It helps us understand, but as a tool for our understanding we must not push it too far. The best 'species', in that they are constant and uniform, are the apomictic microspecies (*see* the account on *Sorbus* p.1138) which only rarely outbreed. However, these are restricted and not typical. At the other extreme are the birches, most of which have an amazing ability to hybridize.

Informal Keys   The descriptions of the larger genera contain informal keys to assist in distinguishing between the possible species. In a formal key, a series of questions leads to a single species. This is excellent if the specimen you are trying to identify has a full range of characters, but for most trees flowers are not available at the same time as fruits. The informal keys use noticeable characters and list a number of species which have or may have this character. The possible species can be compared with the photographs and text. However, in some cases, there are two or more informal keys, and the process can be repeated with a second (or third) character. This will produce a different listing of possible species. Only one or a small number should be found on both lists, and the photographs and written descriptions of this smaller number can then be compared.

How to Use this Guide

There are several ways to use the book, and it is probable that you will find alternative ones appropriate at different times.

If you have a leafy specimen but do not know or do not recognize the tree, the photographs will assist you in identifying it. However, with about 2500 photographs, there are simply too many just to flick through with any certainty of recognizing a tree. The photographs are laid out in an order, so first turn to p.29 where the sequencing of the photographs is explained according to 'Key' leaf characters.

If you have fruits, look through pp.33–7.

If you know the genus or two or three genera to which you think the tree belongs, turn to the genus introduction and look through this and any informal keys. This should get you to the correct species, or to a small group. Check the features against the photographs and descriptions.

If you know what the tree is called and want to find out more about it, such as where it comes from, or what time of year it flowers, look it up in the index and turn to the relevant pages in the text and colour section.

Generally the photographs will take you to a single tree. However, it is always worthwhile checking the genus introduction as this includes easily accessible characters which cannot be illustrated, such as a scent. (For example, the oil of wintergreen scent in the shoots of many birches *Betula* spp.)

Examples Imagine you are walking through a park and collected six leaves or leafy specimens. How can you set about identifying them?

Specimen 1 has a few pairs of small leaves. A quick examination shows that it is not a piece of a shoot with leaves, as there are no buds in the leaf axils (the junction of the leaf with the stalk) and there is also a single leaf at the end. This rules out a tree with small leaves set tightly on the shoot, such as *Ulmus* and *Ligustrum,* and indicates that the leaf is compound. The specimen, therefore, represents a single pinnate leaf. You can turn to the photographs on pp.306–43 and look through these. However, before doing so, a little more investigation may make the task easier by reducing the number of photographs you have to examine. You look at the tree and note that the pinnate leaves are in pairs on the shoot. This eliminates those trees with pinnate leaves set alternately along the shoot, such as *Sorbus* and *Rhus*. You now have only to check through pp.312–19, as the choice is restricted to *Acer negundo*, *Campsis*, *Dipteronia*, *Eucryphia*, *Fraxinus*, *Lyanothamnus*, *Phellodendron*, *Sambucus* and *Tetradium*.

Specimen 2 is similar, except there are only three leaflets, meaning the plant is trifoliate. Check through pp.306–9. However, observing whether the leaves are opposite or alternate on the shoot will still reduce the number of photographs you need to examine. Possible genera include *Acer*, *Cytisus*, *Jasminum*, *Laburnum*, *Ptela* and *Staphylea*.

Specimen 3 has leaves which have untoothed margins and are simple (i.e. the leaves consist of one leaf blade attached to the shoot by a variable length of stalk with a bud in the angle formed between the base of the leaf stalk and the shoot). Trees with this leaf type are illustrated between pp.122–68. Again, a little more consideration can reduce the number of pages of photographs considerably. Are the leaves more or less identical on both sides? If yes, the tree will probably be a *Eucalyptus*, *see* pp.122–7. If it is not a *Eucalyptus*, the other photographs of simple untoothed leaves are broadly split into two groups on the base of the length to breadth ratio of the leaf, with one group having leaves less than twice as long as they are broad and the second group with leaves more than twice as long as they are broad. Each of these two groups is further divided into two groups on the basis of whether the leaves and buds are set alternately or oppositely along the shoot.

If we suppose our leaf of specimen 3 is just over 10 cm (4 in) in length by 4 cm (1.6 in) in width and has opposite leaves and buds, it will have a leaf width of less than half the length (or a length of more than twice the width), so it should be found on pp.149–51, with possible genera including *Acer*, *Buxus*, *Ligustrum* and *Punica*.

Specimen 4 may also have simple leaves but this one has the margin sharply toothed, but not lobed. Trees fitting this broad description can be found between pp.169–263, a section which is illustrated by some 750 photographs! It is desirable, therefore, to try to reduce the number of pages which have to be consulted and therefore we need to find other characters. For instance, if there are one or two glands towards the top of the leaf stalk or just at the base of the leaf blade, the tree is probably a *Prunus* and pp.220–9 can be consulted. Other foliage characters which might help include making a note of any strong feature, such as are the teeth along the leaf margin regular and even, or is the margin doubly toothed (with small teeth between larger, less frequent teeth), or are the leaf veins few and spaced (e.g. *Malus*), or many and closer together (e.g. *Carpinus*). All of these features will assist in picking out likely trees, or genera.

Nevertheless, it will be helpful to look for other features. At the front of the colour section is a colour key for fruit (pp.33–7). This key only relates to trees which have an obvious fruit feature (and of course the specimen must be in fruit), but referring to this section may save time by reducing the number of spreads through which to look! If, for instance, the fruit is a woody catkin, it will probably be a *Betula* or *Alnus* (pp.178–86). However, let us assume that specimen 4 has opposite leaves and buds. Possible trees on pp.169–76 include *Acer*, *Aucuba*, *Buddleja*, *Cercidiphyllum*, *Clerodendrum*, *Euonymus*, *Laurelia*, *Philadelphus*, *Phillyrea*, *Rhamnus* and *Viburnum* (note that *Maytenus* is also illustrated on p.173. However, it is placed in this group because of its close relationship with, and general similarity to *Euonymus*, but has alternate leaves).

Specimen 5 has rather large leaves which are palmately lobed. This section runs from pp.284–305, but divides into the species with opposite leaves (pp.284–301) and those with alternate leaves (pp.302–5). Assuming specimen 5 has opposite leaves, it will be an *Acer*.

Specimens 1–5 could all belong to *Acer* or the maples. This genus has the most variation in the foliage, although *Quercus* is not far behind! In all there are nearly 200 photographs of *Acer* species – leaves, flowers, fruit, bark, shoots, buds and habits – in five different sections (pp.150, 169, 284–301, 306–7 and 314) because the primary ordering of the photographs has been on leaf characters. To save having to thumb through 23 pages, refer to the introduction to *Acer* on p.412 and the informal key (p.413). The introduction mentions some of the features which are not easily illustrated, for instance the presence of a milky or latex sap which is found in several *Acer* and is easily examined by snapping a leaf off at the stalk.

Now, if when we carried out this simple test on specimen 5 (the specimen with large palmately lobed leaves and opposite buds) and the answer was that the sap is milky white (as compared to clear and translucent), instead of thumbing through pp.284–301, only pp.284–8 need to be consulted.

Specimen 6 is clearly different, having wiry shoots and no obvious leaves. Close examination shows the shoots are covered by small scale leaves which are decurrent, that means they 'run' or extend down the shoot to the next set of leaves. The trees with this type of leaf are mainly conifers of the Cypress family, but includes some odd non-conifers. Look to see whether the leaves are in pairs or are arranged spirally around the shoot, and consult pp.38–51.

A warning, however ...

Some specimens are not easy to assign to one category or another. For instance, does *Liriodendron* have pinnately lobed leaves or palmately lobed ones? For this reason, it is placed between the pinnately lobed oaks and the start of the palmately lobed section, on p.283.

Another difficulty may be because the specimen belongs to an odd form of the species. For instance, if specimen 2 had had alternate leaves, it could be an occasional trifoliate leaf on a single-leafed variant of a normally pinnate-leafed tree. *Robinia pseudoacacia* 'Unifolia' has either leaves reduced to a single large leaflet, or one large leaflet and two small ones, whilst the single-leafed ashes (*Fraxinus excelsior* 'Monophylla' and *F. angustifolia* 'Velthamii') both usually carry a few trifoliate leaves. Just occasionally it will be necessary to thumb through the colour section looking for a match.

Each species description is laid out in the following order:

Size provides information about the scale of the species, with both height and the dimensions of the bole or trunk (at around 1.5 m (5 ft) above the ground level to avoid the effect of buttresses). It does not intend to indicate the maximum size attainable, but the likely range of sizes. This heading is also used to state whether the tree is evergreen or deciduous.

Crown gives an indication of the habit of the tree, whether it has upright branching which forms a narrow crown, or wide spreading or weeping branches.

Bark describes ... the bark. Unfortunately, whilst the bark can be very distinctive, it is the most variable of all characters, usually changing markedly between young and old trees.

Shoot describes the characters of the twigs, from the new shoots in early summer to twigs several years old. Shoot and bud characters are extremely useful in identifying trees.

Buds describes their characters, such as shape, size and number of scales. Also in this section there is information on whether the buds are alternate along the shoot, in opposite pairs, or whorls of three. Buds alternate along the shoot is the commonest and should be assumed unless there is any other character stated. If the buds are alternate (or opposite) then the leaves will be alternate or opposite, as will the shoots which spring from the buds. This feature could be repeated for both shoot and foliage, but is only mentioned once under buds. Within a genus, whether the buds are alternate or opposite is normally constant. It would be possible, therefore, to state in the generic introduction that all maples (*Acer*) have opposite buds and then to assume this in the descriptions. However, if you do not know the genus well, it is infuriating having to keep cross-referencing to the introduction. Thus each description is intended to stand alone, allowing, therefore, for a direct comparison to be made, for instance, between sycamore (*Acer pseudoplatanus*) and Plane (*Platanus* × *hispanica*).

Foliage is the most useful character. For a start it is there for a long period, not quite as long as the shoots and the bark, but for much longer than flowers or fruit (and often fallen leaves can be found in mid winter). The characters described include: leaf shape and size, from the tip to the base, the leaf margin which can be very useful such as untoothed, lobed or sharply and doubly toothed as three examples, texture of the upper and lower surfaces, aspects like hairiness and the venation (veins), the size and shape of the leaf stalk or petiole (including how it is attached to the shoot), whether the tree has any autumn colour and other aspects.

Flowers includes details of how the flowers are arranged – are they single, in racemes or panicles, are they carried with the new foliage, at the ends of the current year's growths or from buds laid down last year, and the characters of the flowers.

Fruit covers colour, shape, whether there are remains of the calyx and petals attached, and other characters.

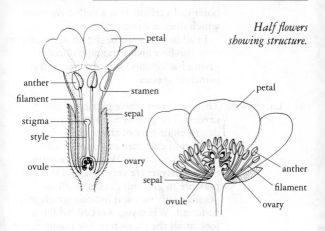

Half flowers showing structure.

Labels (left diagram): petal, anther, filament, stigma, style, ovule, stamen, sepal, ovary

Labels (right diagram): petal, anther, filament, ovary, sepal, ovule

Range gives the native distribution of the tree, i.e. from which countries it is found in the wild.

Habitat describes the type of location in which the tree is found, such as conifer woods, or beside streams, or 'cultivated' if the tree is not native to Europe.

Varieties discusses the variants of the particular tree species. These include the botanical entities, i.e. subspecies and varieties, and also any major or interesting cultivars.

Synonyms gives alternative names by which the species may also be known.

Similar species includes brief descriptions of related similar species (taxa). A few of these are illustrated where it was not possible to get pristine photographs of a slightly more common species but most are only described in the text and related taxa do not feature in the informal keys. There is some overlap between varieties and related taxa, as one botanist may think a tree is better treated as a subspecies (in which case it would be under the 'Varieties' heading) and another as a related species. I have made my judgement, which is why you will find the taxa as treated here, but others are free to take a different view. The word taxa (singular taxon) refers to any level of

botanical variant. It is a collective noun
which does not indicate status.

In addition to all the details above, there
may also be a final paragraph of notes
giving background information on the
principal species.

Limitations   There are areas where particular care is
needed. The photographs and basic
descriptions refer to tree species. A large
number of cultivars and hybrids are
described under the 'Varieties' heading.
Some cultivars are very odd, and it is not
possible to give full details on all the
possible cultivars and hybrids which may
be found. When you meet an 'odd' tree,
look at all the characters. For example, the
Single-leafed Ash (*Fraxinus excelsior*
'Monophylla') has leaves which are simple
not compound and pinnate as in nearly all
ash species. The buds are very similar to
Ash (*Fraxinus excelsior*) and clearly show it
to be a cultivar of this species. In fact the
first true leaves on a seedling Ash are
simple leaves, with the pinnate leaves only
forming as more growth is made. The buds
in opposite pairs on the shoot which is
flattened at the nodes and the winged fruits
should get you to *Fraxinus*. The difference
between the buds will separate *Fraxinus
excelsior* 'Monophylla' from 'Velthamii'
which is the single-leafed form of *Fraxinus
angustifolia*.

KEY TO THE COLOUR PLATES

Needle leaves
scale leaves, mainly conifers pp. 38–51

acicular leaves pp. 52–7, 66–77

main conifer leaves pp. 58–65, 78–102

fascicles of pine leaves
(pp. 103–21)

Simple leaves
simple leaves, unlobed; untoothed, with
pinnate venation

leaves identical on both sides; change from
opposite in juvenile state to seemingly
alternate in adult (*Eucalyptus*) pp. 122–7

leaves less than twice as long as broad;
alternate pp. 128–39

leaves less than twice as long as broad;
opposite pp. 140–8

leaves greater than twice as long as broad; opposite pp.149–51

 leaves greater than twice as long as broad; alternate pp.152–68

 simple leaves, unlobed; toothed pp.169–263

 simple leaves, unlobed; teeth spine tipped to some extent pp.264–7

 simple leaves with lobes; lobes pinnate pp.268–83

 simple leaves with lobes; lobes palmate and buds/leaves opposite on shoot pp.284–301

 simple leaves with lobes; lobes palmate and buds/leaves alternate on shoot pp.302–5

simple leaves, unlobed; untoothed but with parallel veins pp.350–1

fan-shaped leaves (*Ginkgo*) p.352

Compound leaves (and various oddities)

leaves trifoliate pp.306–9

leaves digitate and buds opposite pp.310–11

leaves pinnate and buds opposite pp.312–19

leaves pinnate and buds alternate pp.320–39

leaves bi- (or tri-) pinnate pp.340–3

effectively leafless, but with phyllodes and therefore appearing leafy (these have similarities with simple, unlobed leaves with parallel veins) pp.344–5

Shoots: leafless, green

effectively leafless, i.e. with cladodes pp.346

palms pp.347–9

It always helps to have more than just a single leaf – try to get a piece of shoot with buds. Always check whether you have a leaf or a single leaflet!

Colour Key to Fruits

The photographs (pp.38–352) are ordered on foliage characters. This is convenient as leaves are present for many months or all year round, but sometimes places members of the same genus many pages apart (e.g. *Acer*, *Quercus* and *Sorbus*). The fruit is another reliable character, which is usually present, at least in a developing state, for much of the time. The following key uses fruit types to direct you to the relevant sections. This page illustrates conifer fruits. Pages 34–5 show broadleafed trees with at least somewhat fleshy or juicy fruits, and pages 36–7 show broadleafed trees with dry fruits. The fruit illustrations are examples; for instance with capsules there is more variation than shown, and the fruit is not illustrated for every species.

CONIFERS

CONE with radially arranged scales: *Abies* pp.78–93, *Araucaria* p.56, *Cedrus* pp.66–7, *Cunninghamia* p.98, *Hesperopeuce* p.98, *Keteleeria* p.67, *Larix* pp.99–102, *Picea* pp.68–77, *Pinus* pp.103–21, *Pseudolarix* p.100, *Pseudotsuga* p.94, *Saxegothea* p.60, *Taiwania* p.57, *Tsuga* pp.95–7

CONE with peltate or shield-like scales in pairs or radially set: *Athrotaxis* p.55, *Chamaecyparis* pp.40–1, *Cryptomeria* p.57, *Cupressus* pp.42–5, *Metasequoia*, p.59, *Sciadopitys* p.60, *Sequoia* p.58, *Sequoiadendron* p.58, *Taxodium* p.59

CONE with few pairs of valvate scales, which are hinged at the base: *Austrocedrus* p.47, *Calocedrus* p.47, *Fitzroya* p.49, *Platycladus* p.48, *Tetraclinis* p.47, *Thuja* p.46, *Thujopsis* p.47

CONIFER fruit with a fleshy covering or aril: *Cephalotaxus* p.63, *Juniperus* pp.50–4, *Podocarpus* pp.61–2, *Taxus* pp.64–5, *Torreya* p.65

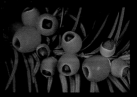

BROADLEAFED TREES WITH FLESHY OR JUICY FRUITS

BERRY fleshy fruit containing one or more seeds set in a pulp: *Arbutus* pp.196–7, *Aucuba* p.170, *Azara* p.177, *Cordyline* p.351, *Diospyros* p.153, *Dracaena* p.351, *Frangula* p.154, *Hedera* p.133, *Hippophaë* p.152, *Idesia* p.200, *Ilex* pp.264–5, *Jasminum* p.309, *Kalopanax* p.303, *Laurus* p.129, *Lonicera* p.145, *Melia* p.343, *Myrtus* p.146, *Nyssa* p.219, *Opuntia* p.346, *Parthenocissus* p.303, *Persea* p.168, *Picrasma* p.320, *Punica* p.151, *Rhamnus* p.176, *Sambucus* p.315, *Sassafras* p.129, *Smilax* p.166, *Umbellularia* p.168, *Yucca* p.351

POME several carpels enclosed in a thick fleshy fruit: *Amelanchier* pp.202–3, *Cotoneaster* pp.156–7, *Crataegus* pp.204–5, 268–71, *Cydonia* p.129, *Eriobotrya* p.206, *Eriolobus* p.263, *Malus* pp.207–11, *Mespilus* p.206, *Photinia* p.155, *Pyrus* pp.158–9, 212–13, *Sorbus* pp.214–18, 272–3, 331–5

FOLLICLE fruit opening along only one suture: *Decaisnea* p.325

HESPERID or citrus fruit: *Citrus* pp.230–2

FIG: *Ficus* pp.132, 303

DRUPE fruit with a hard stony layer surrounded by a fleshy layer, although this may become dry: *Celtis* p.191, *Chamaerops* p.349, *Clerodendrum* p.171, *Cornus* p.144, *Cotinus* p.128, *Davidia* p.238, *Ehretia* p.201, *Elaeagnus* p.166, *Ginkgo* p.352, *Grislinia* p.128, *Halesia* p.233, *Howeia* p.348, *Jubaea* p.348, *Ligustrum* pp.148–9, *Meliosma* pp.236, 320, *Myoporum* p.133, *Myrica* p.152, *Olea* p.147, *Phellodendron* p.312, *Phillyrea* p.175, *Phoenix* p.347, *Pistacia* pp.321–2, *Prumnopitys* p.62, *Prunus* pp.220–9, *Pterostyrax* p.235, *Rehderodendron* p.235, *Rhus* pp.323–4, *Schinus* p.322, *Styrax* pp.233–4, *Swida* pp.142, 144, *Syagrus* p.348, *Trachycarpus* p.349, *Viburnum* pp.141, 175, *Washingtonia* p.349, *Zelkova* p.192, *Ziziphus* p.177

CAPSULE with seeds covered by a fleshy aril: *Euonymus* p.174, *Maytenus* p.173

CLUSTER OF CARPELS separate units contain one or more seeds: *Hoheria* p.236, *Liriodendron* p.283, *Magnolia* pp.134–9, *Michelia* p.139

NUT enclosed in a dehiscent, somewhat fleshy case: *Aesculus* pp.310–11, *Camellia* p.238, *Carya* pp.329–30, *Castanea* p.266, *Chrysolepis* p.160, *Juglans* pp.326–7

BANANA *Musa* p.350

BROADLEAFED TREES WITH DRY FRUITS

CAPSULE dry fruit which opens to scatter seeds: *Abutilon* p.302, *Buddleja* p.170, *Buxus* p.151, *Campsis* p.314, *Carrièrea* p.200, *Casuarina* p.38, *Catalpa* pp.140–1, *Cercidiphyllum* p.171, *Embothrium* p.167, *Erica* p.38, *Eucalyptus* pp.122–7, *Eucryphia* p.173, 313, *Hamamelis* pp.198–9, *Hibiscus* p.302, *Jacaranda* p.342, *Lagerstroemia* p.146, *Oxydendrum* p.197, *Parrotia* p.199, *Paulownia* p.141, *Philadelphus* p.172, *Pittosporum* pp.164–5, *Poliothyrsis* p.201, *Rhododendron* p.130, *Schima* p.239, *Stuartia* p.239, *Syringa* p.147, *Tamarix* pp.38–9, *Tetradium* p.312, *Toona* p.336, *Trochodendron* p.237, *Vitex* p.312, *Zanthoxylum* p.324

LEGUME pod with two sutures: *Acacia* pp.340–1, 344–5, *Albizia* p.342, *Ceratonia* p.340, *Cercis* p.128, *Cladrastis* p.337, *Cytisus* p.308, *Genista* p.346, *Gleditsia* p.343, *Gymnocladus* p.343, *Laburnum* p.309, *Maackia* p.337, *Robinia* p.338, *Sophora* p.339, *Spartium* p.346, *Wisteria* p.339

BLADDER inflated fruit: *Colutea* p.337, *Koelreuteria* p.320, *Staphylea* p.308

LIME tree fruit: *Tilia* pp.256–61

ACHENE dry non-opening fruit: *Clematis* p.314, *Laurelia* p.172

CATKIN fruit with overlapping bracts: *Alnus* pp.178–80, *Betula* pp.181–6, *Carpinus* pp.187–9, *Ostrya* p.189, *Platycarya* p.325, *Populus* pp.244–9, *Pterocarya* p.328, *Salix* pp.250–5, *Tetracentron* p.237

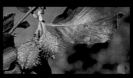

CUPULE bracts united at the base of a fruit or fruits: *Corylus* p.190, *Fagus* p.131, *Lithocarpus* p.160, *Nothofagus* pp.240–3, *Quercus* pp.161–3, 266–7, 274–82

PAIRED WINGED NUTLET or samara: *Acer* pp.150, 169, 284–301, 306–7, 314, *Dipteronia* p.315

SINGLE WINGED NUTLET or samara: *Ailanthus* p.336, *Eucommia* p.154, *Fraxinus* pp.316–19, *Paliurus* p.152, *Ptelea* p.308, *Ulmus* pp.193–5

SYNCARP aggregate fruit containing many carpels: *Benthamidia* p.143, *Broussonetia* p.263, *Cudrania* p.132, *Drimys* p.167, *Liquidambar* p.305, *Maclura* p.132, *Morus* p.262, *Platanus* p.304

NOT SHOWY: *Dicksonia* p.350, *Lyonothamnus* p.314, *Phyllostachys* p.350

She Oak *Casuarina equisetifolia* p.575
1. leaf; 2. habit; 3. bark; 4. fruit

Tree Heath
Erica arborea p.675
1. leaf; 2. habit; 3. flowers

Tamarix africana
p.1196 flower

Tamarix parviflora
p.1197 flower

Tamarix smyrnensis p.1197
1. flower; 2. habit

Tamarix ramosissima
p.1196
habit

Tamarix tetrandra
p.1197
flower

Lawson Cypress *Chamaecyparis lawsoniana* p.598
1. leaf & young cones; 2. leaf underside; 3. habit, various cultivars;
4. male flower; 5. mature cone, blue selected form; 6. bark;
7. golden foliage, 'Winston Churchill'

White Cypress *Chamaecyparis thyoides* p.603
leaf & fruit

Taiwan Cypress *Chamaecyparis formosensis* p.597
1. leaf; 2. fruit

Hinoki Cypress *Chamaecyparis obtusa* p.600
1. leaf upperside; 2. leaf underside; 3. bark; 4. fruit

Sawara Cypress *Chamaecyparis pisifera* p.601 1. leaf
& fruit; 2. bark; 3. habit, 'Filifera Aurea'; 4. leaf, 'Squarrosa'

Arizona Cypress *Cupressus arizonica* p.646
1. leaf; 2. bark

Smooth Cypress *Cupressus glabra* p.648
1. bark; 2. male flowers; 3. habit; 4. fruit

Gowen Cypress *Cupressus goveniana* p.649
1. leaf; 2. bark; 3. fruit

Mexican Cypress *Cupressus lindleyi* p.652
1. leaf & male flowers; 2. fruit

Monterey Cypress *Cupressus macrocarpa (above)* p.653
1. leaf; 2. habit; 3. bark; 4. fruit

Italian Cypress *Cupressus sempervirens* p.656
1. fruit; 2. habit, f. *stricta*

Bhutan Cypress
Cupressus cashmeriana
p.647 1. leaf; 2. habit;
3. bark; 4. male cones; 5. fruit

West Himalayan Cypress
Cupressus torulosa p.657
leaf

Leyland Cypress *Cupressus × leylandii* p.650
1. habit, 'Haggerston Grey'; 2. leaf; 3. habit, 'Castlewellan'

Nootka Cypress *Cupressus nootkatensis* p.654
1. leaf; 2. habit; 3. bark; 4. fruit

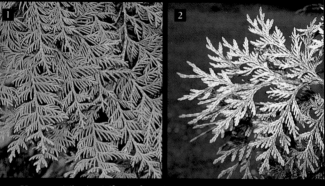

Korean Thuja *Thuja koraiensis* p.1208
1. leaf upperside; 2. leaf underside

White Cedar *Thuja occidentalis* p.1209
1. leaf upperside; 2. leaf underside; 3. fruit

Western Red Cedar *Thuja plicata* p.1210
1. leaf upperside; 2. leaf underside; 3. bark; 4. habit; 5. & 6. fruit

Chilean Cedar *Austrocedrus chilensis* p.516
1. leaf upperside; 2. leaf underside; 3. habit

Incense Cedar *Calocedrus decurrens* p.554
1. leaf; 2. bark; 3. habit; 4. fruit

Hiba *Thujopsis dolabrata* p.1211
1. leaf upperside; 2. leaf underside; 3. bark; 4. fruit

Biota *Platycladus orientalis* p.990
1. leaf & male cones; 2. fruit; 3. bark; 4. habit; 5. fruit

Alerce *Tetraclinis articulata* p.1206
1. leaf; 2. fruit

Grecian Juniper *Juniperus excelsa* p.760
1. leaf; 2. bark; 3. fruit

Stinking Juniper *Juniperus foetidissima* p.761
1. leaf; 2. fruit

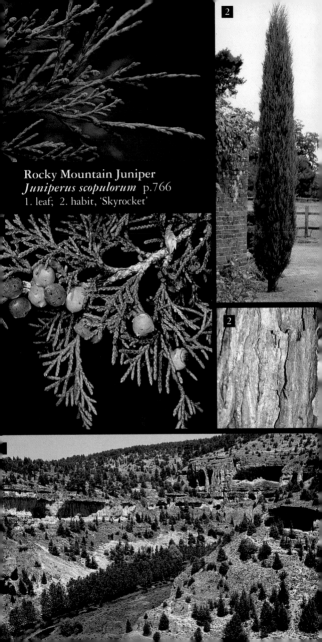

Rocky Mountain Juniper
Juniperus scopulorum p.766
1. leaf; 2. habit, 'Skyrocket'

Chinese Juniper *Juniperus chinensis* p.757 1. juvenile
needle leaf; 2. bark; 3. habit, 'Aurea'; 4. adult scale leaf; 5. fruit

Juniper *Juniperus communis* p.758
1. leaf; 2. habit; 3. fruit

Prickly Juniper *Juniperus oxycedrus* p.762
leaf & fruit

Syrian Juniper *Juniperus drupacea* p.759
1. leaf; 2. habit; 3. fruit

Smooth
Tasmanian
Cedar
*Athrotaxis
cupressoides*
p.513
leaf

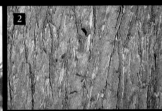

Tasmanian Cedar *Athrotaxis laxiflora* p.513
1. leaf; 2. bark; 3. fruit

King Billy Pine *Athrotaxis selaginoides* p.514
1. bark; 2. leaf & fruit

Monkey Puzzle
Araucaria araucana (*above*)
p.505
1. leaf; 2. bark;
3. habit;
4. male cones

Cook Pine
Araucaria columnaris (*left*)
p.507
1. leaf; 2. habit

Norfolk Island Pine *Araucaria heterophylla*
p.508 1. leaf; 2. fruit; 3. & 4. habit

Fortune Cedar *Cryptomeria fortunei* p.640
1. leaf & male cones; 2. fruit; 3. bark

Japanese Cedar *Cryptomeria japonica* p.641
1. leaf & fruit; 2. habit, 'Elegans'

Redwood *Sequoia sempervirens* p.1133
1. leaf upperside; 2. habit; 3. leaf underside; 4. bark; 5. fruit

Dawn Redwood *Metasequoia glyptostroboides* p.840
1. leaf; 2. bark; 3. habit

Pond Cypress *Taxodium ascendens* p.1198
1. leaf; 2. habit

Swamp Cypress *Taxodium distichum* p.1199
1. leaf; 2. knees & bark; 3. fruit

Japanese Umbrella Pine *Sciadopitys verticillata* p.1132
1. leaf; 2. habit; 3. bark; 4. fruit

Prince Albert's Yew *Saxegothea conspicua* p.1127
1. leaf upperside & male flowers; 2. leaf underside; 3. fruit

Kusamaki *Podocarpus macrophyllus* p.992
leaf

Chilean Totara *Podocarpus nubigenus* p.992
leaf

Willowleaf Podocarp *Podocarpus salignus* p.993
1. leaf; 2. habit; 3. bark; 4. fruit

Totara *Podocarpus totara* p.994
leaf

Andean Plum Yew *Prumnopitys andina* p.1011
1. leaf upperside; 2. leaf underside; 3. bark; 4. male flowers;

Fortune Plum Yew *Cephalotaxus fortunei* p.591
1. leaf upperside; 2. leaf underside; 3. bark; 4. fruit

Plum Yew *Cephalotaxus harringtonia* p.592
1. bark; 2. habit

Yew *Taxus baccata* p.1201 1. leaf upperside; 2. leaf underside; 3. bark; 4. habit; 5. fruit; 6. male cones

Japanese Yew *Taxus cuspidata* p.1203 leaf & fruit

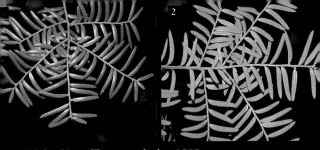

Maire Yew *Taxus mairei* p.1203
1. leaf upperside; 2. leaf underside

Californian Nutmeg Tree *Torreya californica* p.1236
1. leaf upperside; 2. leaf underside; 3. male cones;
4. fruit; 5. habit; 6. bark

Atlas Cedar
Cedrus atlantica (above)
p.582 1. leaf; 2. bark;
3. male flower; 4. fruit

Cyprus Cedar
Cedrus brevifolia (left)
p.584 leaf

Deodar *Cedrus deodara* p.585
1. leaf; 2. bark; 3. habit; 4. fruit

David Keteleeria *Keteleeria davidiana* p.771
leaf & fruit

**Norway Spruce *Picea abies* p.885 1. leaf upperside;
2. habit; 3. bark; 4. open fruit; 5. closed fruit**

**Dragon Spruce *Picea asperata* p.887
1. leaf; 2. bark; 3. fruit**

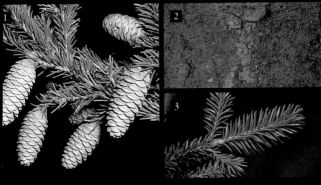

Siberian Spruce *Picea obovata* p.900
1. fruit; 2. bark; 3. leaf

Wilson Spruce *Picea wilsonii* p.911
1. leaf; 2. fruit; 3. bark

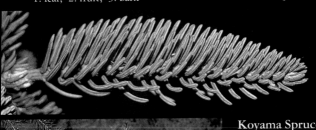

Koyama Spruce
Picea koyamai
(above)
p.895 leaf

Taiwan Spruce
Picea
morrisonicola
p.899 leaf

Schrenk Spruce *Picea schrenkiana* p.906
leaf

Morinda Spruce *Picea smithiana* p.908
1. fruit; 2. habit; 3. bark

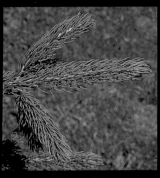

Engelmann Spruce
Picea engelmannii
p.891 leaf

Mexican Spruce
Picea mexicana
p.891 fruit

Colorado Spruce *Picea pungens* p.903
1. leaf; 2. habit; 3. leaf, blue form; 4. bark

Tiger Tail Spruce *Picea torano* p.910
1. leaf; 2. fruit

Hondo Spruce *Picea jezoensis* ssp. *hondoensis* p.894
1. leaf; 2. fruit

Sitka Spruce *Picea sitchensis* p.907 1. leaf upperside &
flushing buds; 2. habit; 3. bark; 4. leaf underside; 5. fruit

White Spruce *Picea glauca* p.892
1. leaf; 2. fruit

Black Spruce
Picea mariana
(above)
p.898
1. leaf; 2. habit;
3. fruit

Alcock Spruce
Picea alcoquiana
p.886
leaf & fruit

Lijiang Spruce *Picea likiangensis* p.897
1. leaf; 2. habit; 3. bark; 4. fruit; 5. male & female flowers

Purple-cone Spruce *Picea purpurea* p.904
1. leaf upperside; 2. leaf underside; 3. bark; 4. fruit; 5. habit

Glehn Spruce *Picea glehnii* p.893
1. leaf; 2. fruit

Caucasian Spruce *Picea orientalis* p.902
1. leaf; 2. bark; 3. habit; 4. young fruit

Serbian Spruce *Picea omorika* p.901
1. leaf; 2. habit; 3. bark; 4. fruit

Sikkim Spruce *Picea spinulosa* p.909
1. leaf; 2. habit; 3. fruit

Sargent Spruce *Picea brachytyla* p.888 1. leaf
upperside; 2. leaf underside; 3. bark; 4. fruit; 5. female flower

Silver Fir *Abies alba* p.357 1. leaf upperside;
2. leaf underside; 3. habit; 4. male cone buds; 5. fruit; 6. bark

Cilician Fir
Abies cilicica
p.365
1. leaf upperside;
2. fruit;
3. leaf underside

Nordmann Fir *Abies nordmanniana* p.389 1. leaf upperside; 2. rachis; 3. habit; 4. leaf underside; 5. bark; 6. fruit

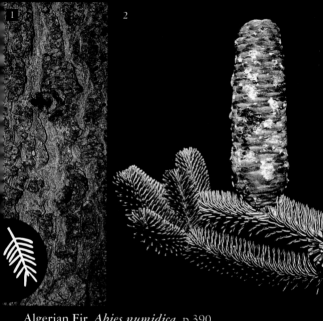

Algerian Fir *Abies numidica* p.390
1. bark; 2. leaf & fruit

Spanish Fir *Abies pinsapo* p.393
1. leaf; 2. habit; 3. fruit; 4. male cone buds clustered on shoot

Red Fir *Abies magnifica* p.384
1. leaf; 2. bark; 3. fruit, var. *shastensis*

Noble Fir *Abies procera* p.394 1. leaf upperside;
2. bark; 3. habit; 4. shoot & leaf underside; 5. fruit

White Fir *Abies concolor* p.366
1. leaf; 2. fruit; 3. bark; 4. bark, var. *lowiana*

Grand Fir *Abies grandis* p.377
1. leaf; 2. habit; 3. bark

Sacred Fir *Abies religiosa* p.397
1. leaf; 2. fruit

Salween Fir *Abies chensiensis* p.364
1. leaf; 2. fruit

Momi Fir *Abies firma* p.373
1. leaf underside; 2. leaf upperside; 3. bark; 4. fruit

Nikko Fir *Abies homolepis* p.379
1. leaf; 2. bark; 3. habit; 4. male cones; 5. fruit

Min Fir *Abies recurvata* p.395
leaf

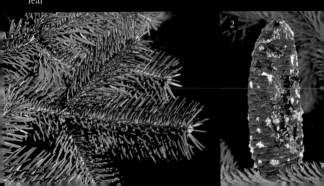

Cheng Fir
Abies chengii
(above) p.363
leaf and young
fruit

Forrest Fir
Abies forrestii
p.374

Delavay Fir *Abies delavayi* (*above*) p.367
1. leaf upperside; 2. leaf underside; 3. habit; 4. male cones; 5. fruit; 6. bark

Sikkim Fir *Abies densa* (*left*) p.369 leaf & fruit

Faber Fir *Abies fabri* p.370
1. leaf upperside;
2. fruit;
3. male flowers;

Farges Fir *Abies fargesii* p.372
1. leaf upperside; 2. bark; 3. leaf underside

Santa Lucia Fir *Abies bracteata* p.360
1. leaf & buds; 2. habit; 3. bark; 4. fruit

Webb Fir *Abies spectabilis* p.400
1. leaf upperside; 2. fruit; 3. leaf underside; 4. rachis

Pacific Fir *Abies amabilis* p.358 1. leaf upperside;
2. fruit; 3. bark; 4. habit; 5. leaf underside & shoot

Maries Fir *Abies mariesii* p.386
1. leaf upperside; 2. leaf underside

Korean Fir *Abies koreana* p.381
1. leaf upperside;
2. leaf underside;
3. habit; 4. bark;
5. fruit, maturing;
6. young female fruit

Khinghan Fir
Abies nephrolepis
(left) p.388 leaf

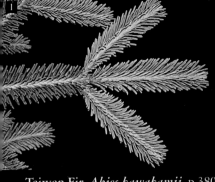 

Taiwan Fir *Abies kawakamii* p.380
1. leaf; 2. bark

Sakhalin Fir *Abies sachalinensis* p.398
leaf

Balsam Fir *Abies balsamea* p.359
1. leaf; 2. bark; 3. fruit

Fraser Fir *Abies fraseri* p.376
1. leaf underside; 2. fruit; 3. leaf upperside

Big Cone Douglas Fir *Pseudotsuga macrocarpa* p.1037
1. leaf; 2. fruit

Eastern Hemlock *Tsuga canadensis* p.1240
1. leaf; 2. habit

Carolina Hemlock *Tsuga caroliniana* p.1242
1. leaf; 2. bark; 3. fruit; 4. habit

Northern Japanese Hemlock *Tsuga diversifolia*
p.1244 1. leaf upperside; 2. leaf underside; 3. habit; 4. fruit

Himalayan Hemlock *Tsuga dumosa* p.1245
1. leaf upperside; 2. bark; 3. leaf underside

Southern Japanese Hemlock *Tsuga sieboldii* p.1248
1. leaf; 2. leaf underside & fruit

China Fir *Cunninghamia lanceolata* p.643
1. leaf upperside; 2. bark; 3. leaf underside; 4. fruit

Mountain Hemlock *Hesperopeuce mertensiana* p.735

European Larch *Larix decidua* p.777 1. leaf; 2. habit; 3. bark; 4. fruit; 5. flower, fruit & almost leafless shoots

**Dahurian Larch
Larix gmelinii p.778**
1. leaf; 2.fruit

**Siberian Larch
Larix sibirica p.785**
leaf & fruit

Japanese Larch *Larix kaempferi* p.781
1. leaf; 2. habit; 3. young & old fruit; 4. shoot and buds

Golden Larch *Pseudolarix amabilis* p.1035
1. leaf, early autumn colour; 2. fruit

Sikkim Larch *Larix griffithiana* p.780
1. habit; 2. habit, autumn colour; 3. female cone; 4. fruit

Tamarack *Larix laricina* p.782
1. leaf, autumn colour; 2. habit; 3. bark; 4. fruit

Scots Pine *Pinus sylvestris* p.971 1. leaf; 2. habit;
3. lower trunk bark; 4. upper-branch bark; 5. male flowers; 6. fruit

Chinese Red Pine *Pinus tabuliformis* p.972
1. leaf; 2. male flower & fruit

Black Pine *Pinus nigra* p.951 1. leaf & fruit; 2. habit, ssp. *nigra*; 3. leaf; 4. bark; 5. habit, var. *pallasiana*; 6. habit, var. *corsicana*

Japanese Black Pine *Pinus thunbergii* p.974
1. leaf; 2. fruit

Bosnian Pine *Pinus heldreichii* var. *leucodermis* p.940
1. leaf & 1-yr fruit; 2. shoot; 3. bark; 4. fruit

Table Mountain Pine *Pinus pungens* p.961
1. leaf; 2. fruit

Calabrian Pine
Pinus brutia
p.923
1. leaf; 2. habit;
3. bark; 4. fruit

Jack Pine *Pinus banksiana* p.922
1. leaf; 2. fruit

Shore Pine *Pinus contorta* p.929
1. leaf; 2. fruit; 3. leaf & fruit; 4. bark; 5. male cones;
6. habit (1. & 2. var. *contorta*, 3.–6. var. *latifolia*)

Maritime Pine *Pinus pinaster* p.956
1. leaf; 2. bark; 3. fruit

Stone Pine *Pinus pinea* p.958
1. leaf; 2. bark; 3. fruit; 4. habit

Shortleaf Pine
Pinus echinata
p.932
leaf

Slash Pine
Pinus elliottii
(below)
p.934
1. leaf; 2. male
flower; 3. fruit

Knobcone Pine *Pinus attenuata* p.918
1. leaf; 2. fruit

Bishop Pine
Pinus muricata
p.950
1. leaf; 2. fruit

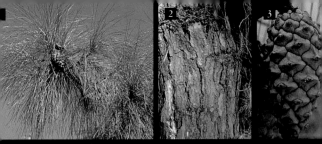

Canary Island Pine *Pinus canariensis* p.925
1. leaf; 2. bark; 3. fruit

Jeffrey Pine *Pinus jeffreyi* p.941
1. leaf; 2. bark; 3. fruit

Coulter Pine *Pinus coulteri* p.930
1. leaf; 2. fruit; 3. habit

Mexican Weeping Pine *Pinus patula*
p.954 1. leaf; 2. bark; 3. habit; 4. fruit

Lacebark Pine *Pinus bungeana* p.924 1. leaf & 1-yr
conelet; 2. bark; 3. habit; 4. mature fruit & 1-yr conelets

Mexican Piñon *Pinus cembroides*
p.927 1. leaf & fruit; 2. bark

Johan Piñon
Pinus johannis p.942
1. leaf; 2. habit

Papershell Piñon
***Pinus remota* (right)**
p.964 leaf

Rocky Mountain Piñon *Pinus edulis* p.933
1. leaf; 2. habit; 3. bark; 4. fruit

Single-leaf Piñon
Pinus monophylla
p.945
1. leaf; 2. habit

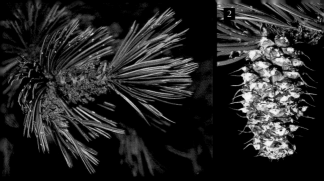

Bristlecone Pine *Pinus aristata* p.916
1. leaf & male cone; 2. fruit

Foxtail Pine *Pinus balfouriana* p.921
1. leaf; 2. fruit

Western White Pine *Pinus monticola* p.948
1. leaf; 2. fruit

Armand Pine *Pinus armandii*
p.917 1. leaf; 2. fruit; 3. bark

**Macedonian
Pine** *Pinus
peuce (above)*
p.955 leaf & fruit

Blue Pine *Pinu
wallichiana*
p.976 1. leaf;
2. bark; 3. mature
fruit; 4. 1-yr
conelet; 5. habit

Mexican White Pine *Pinus ayacahuite* p.919
1. leaf; 2. fruit

Limber Pine *Pinus flexilis* p.936
1. fruit; 2. habit; 3. leaf

Southwestern White Pine *Pinus strobiformis* p.968
leaf

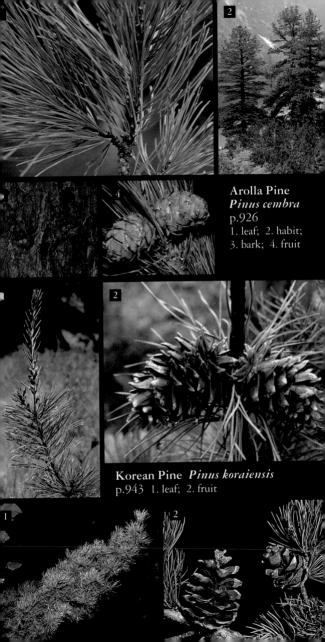

Arolla Pine
Pinus cembra
p.926
1. leaf; 2. habit;
3. bark; 4. fruit

Korean Pine *Pinus koraiensis*
p.943 1. leaf; 2. fruit

Apache Pine
Pinus engelmannii
p.935
1. leaf; 2. bark;
3. fruit; 4. habit

Hartweg Pine *Pinus hartwegii* p.939
1. leaf; 2. habit; 3. fruit

**Montezuma Pine
*Pinus montezumae
(right)*** p.947 leaf

Cider Gum *Eucalyptus gunnii* p.685
1. leaf; 2. habit; 3. juvenile leaf; 4. flower; 5. fruit

Broad-leaved Kindling Gum *Eucalyptus dalrympleana*
p.682 1. leaf; 2. habit; 3. juvenile foliage; 4. bark

Mount Wellington Peppermint *Eucalyptus coccifera*
p.681 1. leaf; 2. juvenile leaf; 3. fruit

Snow Gum *Eucalyptus niphophila* p.687
1. leaf; 2. habit; 3. bark; 4. flower

**Tasmanian
Blue Gum**
*Eucalyptus
globulus
(above)*
p.683
1. leaf;
2. juvenile leaf;
3. bark; 4. habit;
5. fruit

Maiden's Gum
*Eucalyptus
maidenii*
p.687
bark

Johnston's
Gum
*Eucalyptus
johnstonii*
p.686
leaf

Red Gum
*Eucalyptus
camuldulensis
(below)*
p.680
1. leaf; 2. bark;
3. flower bud

Lemon-scented Spotted
Gum *Eucalyptus
citriodora* p.681 bark

Forest Red Gum
Eucalyptus tereticornis
p.690 bark

Tuart *Eucalyptus gomphocephala* p.684
1. bark; 2. fruit

Red Mahogany *Eucalyptus resinifer* p.689
1. leaf & flower; 2. bark; 3. flower

Swamp Mahogany *Eucalyptus robusta* p.690
1. bark; 2. flower; 3. fruit

Judas Tree *Cercis siliquastrum* p.596
1. leaf; 2. bark; 3. habit; 4. flower; 5. fruit

Venetian Sumach *Cotinus coggygria* p.623
1. leaf of purple form; 2. habit; 3. flower; 4. autumn colour

Papauma *Grislinia littoralis* p.726
1. leaf upperside & flower; 2. leaf underside

Quince *Cydonia oblonga* p.658
1. flower; 2. habit; 3. bark; 4. fruit

Bay Laurel *Laurus nobilis* p.787
1. leaf & flower; 2. habit; 3. fruit

Sassafras *Sassafras albidum* p.1126
1. leaf; 2. habit

Gurass *Rhododendron arboreum* p.1095
1. leaf; 2. bark; 3. habit; 4. flower

Korlinga
Rhododendron falconeri
p.1096 1. leaf;
2. flower; 3. bark;
4. habit

Rhododendron
Rhododendron ponticum
p.1097 leaf & flower

Engler Beech *Fagus engleriana* p.702
leaf

2

Oriental Beech *Fagus orientalis* p.703
1. leaf; 2. fruit

Rubber Plant *Ficus elastica* p.707
1. bark; 2. leaf; 3. habit; 4. fruit

Osage Orange *Maclura pomifera* p.805
1. bark; 2. leaf & flower; 3. habit; 4. fruit

Ivy *Hedera helix*
p.733
1. adult leaf;
2. juvenile leaf;
3. habit, growing over tree;
4. fruit;

Myoporum *Myoporum tenuifolium* p.847

Campbell Magnolia *Magnolia campbellii* p.809 1. leaf
upperside; 2. leaf underside; 3. habit; 4. bark; 5. flower; 6. fruit

Sauce Magnolia *Magnolia × soulangiana* p.819
1. leaf; 2. habit; 3. flower

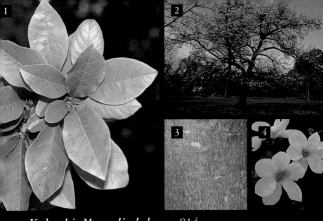

Kobushi *Magnolia kobus* p.814
1. leaf; 2. habit; 3. bark; 4. flower

Loebner's Magnolia ×*Magnolia loebneri* p.815
1. leaf; 2. habit; 3. flower

Cucumber Tree *Magnolia acuminata* p.808
1. leaf; 2. bark; 3. habit; 4. flower

Fraser Magnolia *Magnolia fraseri* p.812
1. leaf; 2. flower

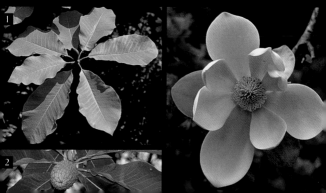

Big-leafed Magnolia *Magnolia macrophylla* p.815
1. leaf; 2. bark; 3. flower

Umbrella Tree *Magnolia tripetala* p.820
1. leaf & flower; 2. flower

Sweet Bay *Magnolia virginiana* p.821
1. leaf upperside; 2. leaf underside; 3. flower

Delavay Magnolia *Magnolia delavayi* p.811 1. leaf upperside; 2. leaf underside; 3. flower; 4. bark; 5. habit

Evergreen Magnolia *Magnolia grandiflora* p.813
1. leaf upperside; 2. habit; 3. leaf underside; 4. flower

Wilson Magnolia *Magnolia wilsonii* p.822
1. leaf; 2. habit; 3. flower; 4. fruit

Michelia *Michelia doltsopa* p.841
1. leaf & flower; 2. habit

Michelia velutina p.842
1. leaf & fruit; 2. flower

Indian Bean Tree *Catalpa bignonioides* p.577
1. leaf; 2. habit; 3. fruit; 4. flower

Hybrid Catalpa
Catalpa × erubescens
p.578 leaf

Northern Catalpa
Catalpa speciosa
p.581 leaf & flower

Yellow Catalpa *Catalpa ovata* p.580
leaf & flower

Farges Catalpa *Catalpa fargesii* p.579
1. leaf; 2. flower; 3. habit

Paulownia *Paulownia tomentosa* p.871
1. leaf; 2. flower; 3. flower buds over winter; 4. fruit

Table Dogwood *Swida controversa* p.1189 1. leaf upperside; 2. leaf underside; 3. flower; 4. habit; 5. fruit

Himalayan Cornel *Benthamidia capitata* p.518
1. leaf; 2. flower; 3. fruit

Flowering Dogwood *Benthamidia florida* p.520
1. leaf; 2. flower; 3. habit

Japanese Cornel
Benthamidia kousa
p.521
1. leaf; 2. fruit;
3. habit; 4. bark;
5. flower

Pacific Cornel *Benthamidia nuttallii* p.522
1. flower; 2. habit

Cornelian Cherry *Cornus mas* p.619
1. flower; 2. habit; 3. leaf; 4. fruit

Dogwood *Swida sanguinea* p.1191
1. leaf; 2. habit; 3. flower

Honeysuckle *Lonicera periclymenum* p.801
1. flower; 2. fruit; 3. habit

Crape Myrtle *Lagerstroemia indica* p.776
1. leaf; 2. flower; 3. habit & bark

Myrtle *Myrtus communis* p.849
1. leaf; 2. flower; 3. fruit

Hungarian Lilac *Syringa josikaea* p.1193
1. leaf; 2. fruit

Lilac *Syringa vulgaris* p.1192
1. leaf; 2. habit; 3. flower; 4. fruit

Olive *Olea europaea* p.862
1. leaf; 2. habit; 3. bark; 4. fruit

Chinese Privet *Ligustrum lucidum* p.790
1. leaf; 2. bark; 3. flower; 4. habit; 5. fruit

Privet *Ligustrum ovalifolium* p.791
1. leaf; 2. flower

Chenault's Privet *Ligustrum chenaultii* p.789
leaf & flower

Wild Privet
Ligustrum vulgare
p.792
1. leaf & young fruit;
2. leaf & fruit

Smoothbark Maple *Acer laevigatum* p.441
1. leaf & flower; 2. flower; 3. leaf & fruit

Phirphiri *Acer oblongum* p.451
1. leaf upperside; 2. bark; 3. leaf underside; 4. fruit

Balearic Box *Buxus balearica* p.552
leaf & flower

Box *Buxus sempervirens* p.552
1. leaf & flower; 2. bark; 3. habit; 4. fruit

Pomegranate *Punica granatum* p.1046
1. leaf; 2. young fruit & flower

Sea Buckthorn *Hippophaë rhamnoides* p.738
1. leaf; 2. habit; 3. bark; 4. fruit

Canary Islands Myrtle *Myrica faya* p.848
1. leaf & fruit; 2. flower

Christ's Thorn *Paliurus spina-christi* p.867

Persimmon *Diospyros kaki* p.665
leaf in autumn colour & fruit

Date Plum *Diospyros lotus* p.665
1. leaf; 2. bark; 3. habit; 4. fruit

Persimmon *Diospyros virginiana* p.666
1. leaf; 2. bark; 3. fruit

Gutta-percha Tree *Eucommia ulmoides* p.693
1. leaf; 2. habit; 3. bark; 4. male flower; 5. fruit

Alder Buckthorn *Frangula alnus* p.709
1. leaf; 2. fruit; 3. habit

Stranvaesia *Photinia davidiana* p.880
1. leaf & flower; 2. fruit

Tree Cotoneaster *Cotoneaster frigidus* p.625 1. leaf upperside; 2. leaf underside; 3. bark; 4. fruit; 5. habit; 6. flower

Cotoneaster *Cotoneaster affinis* p.624
1. leaf & fruit; 2. flower

Almond-leafed Pear *Pyrus amygdaliformis* p.1047
1. leaf & fruit; 2. bark; 3. habit; 4. flower

Oleaster-leafed Pear *Pyrus elaeagrifolia* p.1052
1. leaf; 2. flower; 3. fruit

Snow Pear *Pyrus nivalis* p.1052
1. leaf; 2. bark; 3. habit; 4. flower; 5. fruit

Willow-leafed Pear *Pyrus salicifolia* p.1053
1. leaf & fruit; 2. flower; 3. habit

Golden Chinkapin *Chrysolepis chrysophylla* p.605
1. leaf upperside; 2. leaf underside; 3. bark; 4. habit;
5. fruit & flower

Japanese Stone Oak
Lithocarpus edulis
p.798 leaf

Henry's Stone Oak
Lithocarpus henryi
p.800 leaf

Willow Oak *Quercus phellos* p.1077
1. leaf; 2. bark; 3. habit

Holm Oak *Quercus ilex* p.1069 1. leaf; 2. habit;
3. juvenile leaf; 4. bark; 5. fruit; 6. male flowers

Akagashi *Quercus acuta* p.1055
1. leaf; 2. habit

Kohuhu *Pittosporum tenuifolium* p.983
1. leaf; 2. flower; 3. habit; 4. fruit

Wavy Pittosporum *Pittosporum undulatum* p.985
1. leaf; 2. flower; 3. fruit

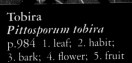

Tobira
Pittosporum tobira
p.984   1. leaf; 2. habit;
3. bark; 4. flower; 5. fruit

Black Mapou
Pittosporum colensoi
p.981   leaf

Karo
Pittosporum crassifolium
p.982   leaf

Pittosporum ralphii
p.982   leaf & flower

Rough Bindweed *Smilax aspera* p.1136
1. leaf & flower; 2. fruit

Akiraho *Olearia paniculata* p.863
leaf & flower

Russian Olive *Elaeagnus angustifolia* p.672
1. leaf & flower; 2. habit; 3. leaf underside; 4. fruit

Winter's Bark *Drimys winteri* p.670
1. leaf; 2. bark; 3. flower; 4. fruit

Fire Bush *Embothrium coccineum* p.673
1. leaf & flower; 2. habit; 3. fruit

Avocado *Persea americana* p.873
1. leaf & fruit; 2. habit

Californian Laurel *Umbellularia californica* p.1258
1. leaf & flower; 2. fruit; 3. bark; 4. habit

Hornbeam Maple *Acer carpinifolium* p.422
1. leaf; 2. fruit

David's Maple *Acer davidii* p.427
1. leaf; 2. bark; 3. fruit; 4. leaf underside; 5. habit

Lime-leafed Maple
Acer distylum
p.429 leaf

Birch-leafed Maple
Acer stachyophyllum
p.473 1. leaf; 2. fruit

Aucuba *Aucuba japonica* p.515
1. leaf; 2. habit, 'Variegata'

Buddleja colvilei p.551
1. leaf & flower; 2. bark

Butterfly Bush *Buddleja davidii* p.550
1. leaf; 2. bark; 3. habit; 4. flower

Katsura *Cercidiphyllum japonicum* p.594
1. leaf; 2. habit; 3. bark; 4. fruit & shoot

Peruvian Nutmeg *Laurelia sempervirens* p.786
1. leaf; 2. habit

Ulmo *Eucryphia cordifolia* p.694
1. leaf; 2. bark; 3. flower

Tasmanian Eucryphia *Eucryphia lucida* p.697
1. leaf upperside; 2. flower; 3. leaf underside

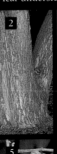

Spindle *Euonymus europaeus* p.699
1. leaf & flower; 2. fruit; 3. habit

Japanese Spindle *Euonymus japonicus* p.700
1. leaf & flower; 2. fruit

Wayfaring Tree *Viburnum lantana* p.1260
1. leaf; 2. flower; 3. habit; 4. fruit

Guelder Rose *Viburnum opalus* p.1260
1. leaf; 2. flower; 3. fruit

Alaternus *Rhamnus alaternus* p.1093
1. leaf; 2. habit, 'Argenteovariegata'; 3. flower; 4. fruit

Small-leafed Azara
Azara microphylla p.517
1. leaf & flowers; 2. bark

Jujuba
Ziziphus zizyphus p.1271
1. leaf & flowers;
2. leaf & fruit

Italian Alder *Alnus cordata* p.492 1. leaf; 2. habit;
3. bark; 4. male (yellow) & female flowers; 5. young fruit; 6. fruit

Grey Alder *Alnus incana* p.495 1. leaf upperside & fruit; 2. bark; 3. leaf underside; 4. & 5. catkins

Red Alder *Alnus rubra* p.497
1. leaf & fruit; 2. bud

Speckled Alder *Alnus rugosa* p.498
1. fruit; 2. leaf

Silver Birch *Betula pendula* p.540
1. leaf & young fruit; 2. habit; 3. bud; 4. bark; 5. catkin;
6. fruit & scales; 7. leaf & shoot, 'Dalecarlica'

Japanese Birch *Betula mandshurica* p.534
leaf

White Birch *Betula pubescens* p.543 1. leaf & fruit;
2. catkin; 3. habit; 4. bark; 5. male catkins in bud; 6. shoot

Maximowicz Birch *Betula maximowiczi* p.536
1. leaf; 2. catkin; 3. bark

Medwediew's Birch *Betula medwediewii* p.537
1. leaf; 2. habit; 3. fruit

Chinese Red Birch *Betula albo-sinensis* p.525
1. leaf; 2. bark

Jacquemont Birch *Betula jacquemontii* p.531
1. leaf; 2. bark; 3. habit

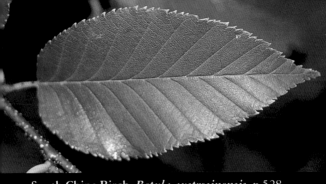

South China Birch *Betula austrosinensis* p.528
leaf

Erman's Birch *Betula ermanii* p.529
1. leaf; 2. habit; 3. bark; 4. catkin

Yellow Birch *Betula alleghaniensis* p.526
1. leaf; 2. habit; 3. bark; 4. catkin; 5. leaf, autumn colour

Hornbeam *Carpinus betulus* p.558
1. leaf; 2. bark; 3. fruit; 4. habit; 5. habit, 'Fastigiata'

Aka-shide *Carpinus laxiflora* p.561
leaf

Chonosuki's Hornbeam *Carpinus tschonoskii* p.562
1. leaf; 2. fruit

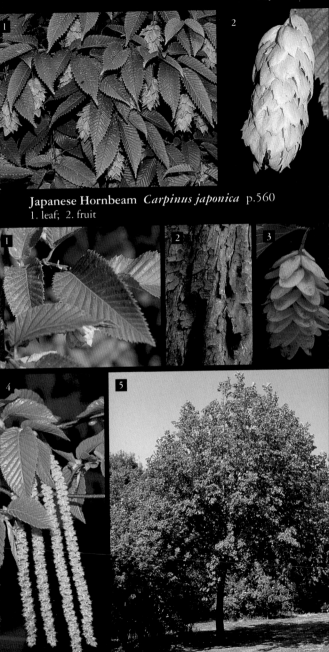

Japanese Hornbeam *Carpinus japonica* p.560
1. leaf; 2. fruit

Hop Hornbeam *Ostrya carpinifolia* p.865
1. leaf; 2. bark; 3. fruit; 4. male catkin; 5. habit

Hazel *Corylus avellana* p.620
1. leaf; 2. catkin

Turkish Hazel *Corylus colurna* p.621
1. leaf; 2. habit; 3. bark; 4. fruit

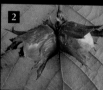

Filbert
Corylus maxima p.622
1. leaf, var.
purpurea;
2. fruit

Nettle Tree *Celtis australis* p.588
1. leaf; 2. fruit; 3. habit

Hackberry *Celtis occidentalis* p.589
1. leaf; 2. bark; 3. fruit

Cretan Zelkova *Zelkova abelicea* p.1268
leaf

Caucasian Elm *Zelkova carpinifolia* p.1269
1. leaf; 2. habit; 3. fruit

Wych Elm *Ulmus glabra* p.1250
1. leaf; 2. habit; 3. bark; 4. fruit; 5. flower

Japanese Elm *Ulmus japonica* p.1252
leaf

English Elm *Ulmus procera* p.1256
1. leaf; 2. & 3. habit; 4. bark; 5. flower

Grey Elm *Ulmus canescens* p.1249
leaf

Smooth Elm *Ulmus minor* p.1254
1. leaf; 2. habit, var. *sarniensis*; 3. bark; 4. fruit

Dutch Elm *Ulmus × hollandica* p.1251 leaf

Fluttering Elm *Ulmus laevis* p.1253
1. leaf; 2. fruit

Chinese Elm *Ulmus parvifolia* p.1255
1. leaf; 2. habit; 3. bark; 4. flower

Siberian Elm *Ulmus pumila* p.1257
1. leaf; 2. habit

Cyprus Strawberry Tree *Arbutus andrachne* p.509
1. leaf; 2. bark; 3. flower

Strawberry Tree *Arbutus unedo* p.511
1. leaf & flower; 2. habit; 3. bark; 4. fruit

Hybrid Strawberry Tree *Arbutus × andrachnoides*
p.509 leaf

Madroño *Arbutus menziesii* p.510
1. leaf; 2. habit; 3. bark; 4. flower; 5. fruit

Sorrel Tree *Oxydendrum arboreum* p.866
1. leaf & flower; 2. leaf, autumn colour

Hybrid Witch Hazel *Hamamelis × intermedia* p.731
1. leaf, early autumn colour; 2. flower

Japanese Witch Hazel *Hamamelis japonica* p.731
1. leaf; 2. flower

Chinese Witch Hazel *Hamamelis mollis* p.730
1. fruit; 2. leaf upperside; 3. habit; 4. flower; 5. leaf underside

Witch Hazel *Hamamelis virginiana* p.732
1. leaf; 2. flower

Goat Horn Tree *Carrièrea calycina* p.564
1. leaf; 2. flower

Ehretia *Ehretia dicksonii* p.671
1. leaf; 2. bark; 3. flower

Poliothyrsis *Poliothyrsis sinensis* p.995
1. leaf; 2. habit; 3. bark; 4. flower; 5. fruit

Snowy Mespilus *Amelanchier × grandiflora* p.501
1. leaf, autumn colour; 2. habit; 3. flower

Snowy Mespilus *Amelanchier laevis* p.502
1. leaf; 2. flower

Snowy Mespilus *Amelanchier lamarkii* p.503
1. flower; 2. habit; 3. leaf, autumn colour; 4. fruit

Snowy Mespilus *Amelanchier canadensis* p.503
leaf & fruit

Snowy Mespilus *Amelanchier rotundifolia* p.502
1. leaf & flower; 2. flower

Cockspur Thorn *Crataegus crus-galli* p.629
leaf, thorn & fruit

Broad-leafed Cockspur Thorn *Crataegus persimilis*
p.635 1. leaf, summer; 2. leaf, autumn; 3. fruit; 4. habit

Downy Hawthorn *Crataegus submollis* p.637
leaf & fruit

Loquat *Eriobotrya japonica* p.676 1. leaf upperside & flower; 2. leaf underside; 3. fruit; 4. bark; 5. habit

Medlar *Mespilus germanica* p.839
1. leaf; 2. habit; 3. bark; 4. flower; 5. fruit

Apple *Malus domestica* p.826
1. leaf & flower; 2. fruit; 3. habit

Crab Apple *Malus sylvestris* p.832
1. leaf upperside; 2. leaf underside; 3. bark, young tree;
4. bark, mature tree; 5. fruit

Siberian Crab *Malus baccata* p.824
1. leaf & fruit; 2. habit; 3. bark; 4. flower

Italian Crab *Malus florentina* p.827
1. leaf & fruit; 2. flower

Hubei Crab *Malus hupehensis* p.830
1. leaf; 2. habit; 3. fruit

Flowering Crab *Malus × floribunda* p.829
1. & 4. leaf & flower; 2. habit; 3. bark

Hall's Crab *Malus halliana* p.829
leaf & fruit

Magdeburg Crab *Malus* '*Magdeburgensis*' p.827
1. leaf; 2. flower

Purple Crab *Malus* × *purpurea* p.831
1. leaf; 2. habit; 3. bark; 4. flower

Common Pear *Pyrus communis* p.1049
1. leaf; 2. bark; 3. flower; 4. habit; 5. fruit (pear)

Callery's Pear *Pyrus calleryana* p.1049
1. flower; 2. habit; 3. bark

Wild Pear *Pyrus pyraster* p.1050
1. leaf; 2. habit; 3. flower; 4. fruit

Whitebeam *Sorbus aria* p.1141
1. leaf upperside; 2. bark; 3. habit; 4. leaf underside; 5. fruit

Folgner's Whitebeam *Sorbus folgneri* p.1154
1. leaf upperside; 2. leaf underside; 3. fruit

Grecian Whitebeam *Sorbus graeca* p.1156
1. leaf upperside; 2. leaf underside; 3. fruit

Hedlund's Whitebeam *Sorbus hedlundii* p.1158
1. leaf upperside & fruit; 2. leaf underside

Tibetan Whitebeam *Sorbus thibetica* p.1172
1. leaf upperside; 2. bark; 3. habit; 4. leaf underside; 5. fruit

Himalayan Whitebeam *Sorbus vestita* p.1177
1. leaf upperside; 2. leaf underside

Alder-leafed Whitebeam *Sorbus alnifolia* p.1140 1. leaf
upperside & flower; 2. leaf underside; 3. habit; 4. bark; 5. fruit

*Sorbus
epidendron*
p.1165
1. leaf upperside
& fruit;
2. leaf underside

Austrian Whitebeam *Sorbus austriaca* p.1146
1. leaf upperside; 2. leaf underside; 3. unripe fruit

Bristol Gorge Whitebeam *Sorbus bristoliensis* p.1146
1. leaf upperside & unripe fruit; 2. leaf underside; 3. fruit

French Hales *Sorbus devoniensis* p.1150
1. leaf upperside & flower; 2. leaf underside; 3. bark; 4. fruit

Service Tree of Fontainebleau *Sorbus latifolia* p.1163
1. leaf upperside & flower; 2. leaf underside; 3. fruit

Mougeot's Whitebeam *Sorbus mougeotii* p.1167
1. leaf upperside; 2. leaf underside; 3. fruit

Balkan Whitebeam *Sorbus umbellata* p.1176
1. leaf upper- & underside; 2. flower in bud; 3. fruit

Chinese Tupelo *Nyssa sinensis* p.860
1. leaf & flower; 2. habit

Gean *Prunus avium* p.1014
1. leaf; 2. bark; 3. flower; 4. habit

Spire Cherry *Prunus × juddii* 'Spire' p.1027
1. leaf; 2. flower; 3. habit

Fuji Cherry *Prunus incisa* p.1020
1. leaf; 2. flower

St Lucie Cherry *Prunus mahaleb* p.1023
1. leaf & young fruit; 2. flower; 3. young fruit

Sargent's Cherry
Prunus sargentii
p.1026
1. leaf; 2. flower; 3. habit

Tibetan Cherry ***Prunus serrula*** p.1029
1. leaf; 2. habit; 3. bark; 4. flower

Apricot *Prunus armeniaca* p.1013
1. leaf; 2. flower; 3. fruit

Rosebud Cherry *Prunus × subhirtella* p.1032
1. leaf; 2. bark; 3. & 4. flower; 5. habit

Briançon Apricot *Prunus brigantina* p.1015
1. leaf; 2. fruit

Naples Plum
Prunus cocomila
p.1018
1. leaf; 2. habit

Peach or Nectarine *Prunus persica* p.1025
1. leaf; 2. fruit; 3. flower

Plum *Prunus domestica* p.1018
1. leaf; 2. habit; 3. bark; 4. fruit; 5. flower

Almond *Prunus dulcis* p.1019
1. leaf; 2. fruit; 3. flower

Myrobalan Plum *Prunus cerasifera* p.1015
1. leaf; 2. habit; 3. bark; 4. flower; 5. fruit; 6. leaf, 'Pissardii'

Bird Cherry *Prunus padus* p.1024
1. leaf; 2. flower; 3. habit; 4. fruit

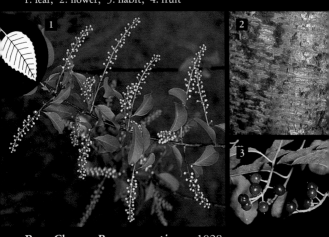

Rum Cherry *Prunus serotina* p.1028
1. flower; 2. bark; 3. fruit

Cherry Laurel *Prunus laurocerasus* p.1021
1. leaf; 2. bark; 3. habit; 4. flower; 5. fruit

Seville Orange *Citrus aurantium* p.610
1. leaf; 2. fruit

Tangerine *Citrus deliciosa* p.606
1. leaf; 2. unripe fruit

Bergamot Orange *Citrus bergamia* p.610
1. leaf; 2. fruit

Ichang Lemon
Citrus ichangensis
p.609 leaf & flower

Sweet Lime
Citrus limetta
p.607 fruit

Shaddock *Citrus grandis* p.609
1. leaf; 2. fruit

Citron *Citrus medica* p.608
1. leaf; 2. fruit

Snowdrop Tree *Halesia monticola* p.728
1. leaf & flower; 2. habit; 3. bark; 4. leaf & fruit

Hemsley's Storax *Styrax hemsleyana* p.1185
1. leaf; 2. habit

Japanese Storax *Styrax japonica* p.1186
1. leaf; 2. habit; 3. bark; 4. flower; 5. fruit

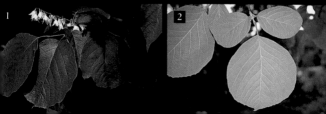

Winged Storax *Pterostyrax corymbosa* p.1044
1. leaf; 2. habit; 3. flower; 4. fruit

Gogun Tree *Meliosma dilleniifolia* p.837
1. leaf; 2. flower; 3. fruit

Trochodendron *Trochodendron aralioides* p.1239
leaf & flower

1

2

3

4

Dove Tree *Davidia involucrata* p.661 1. leaf upperside;
2. bark; 3. habit; 4. leaf underside; 5. fruit; 6. flower

Schima *Schima argentea* p.1129
1. leaf; 2. flower

Deciduous Camellia *Stuartia pseudocamellia* p.1182
1. leaf; 2. habit; 3. bark; 4. flower; 5. fruit

Chinese Stuartia *Stuartia sinensis* p.1183
1. leaf & fruit; 2. bark

Rauli *Nothofagus nervosa* p.856
1. leaf; 2. young tree bark; 3. habit; 4. fruit

Roble *Nothofagus obliqua* p.858
1. leaf; 2. bark; 3. habit; 4. fruit

Antarctic Beech *Nothofagus antarctica* p.852
1. leaf; 2. habit; 3. bark; 4. flower; 5. fruit

Red Beech *Nothofagus fusca* p.854
leaf

Coigüe de Magallanes *Nothofagus betuloides* p.853
leaf

Coigüe *Nothofagus dombeyi* p.854
1. leaf; 2. habit; 3. bark; 4. fruit

Cunningham Beech *Nothofagus cunninghamii* p.856
leaf

Silver Beech *Nothofagus menziesii* p.855
1. leaf; 2. habit; 3. flower; 4. fruit

Mountain Beech *Nothofagus solandri* p.859
1. leaf upperside; 2. leaf underside

White Poplar *Populus alba* p.997 1. & 3. leaf upperside;
2. leaf underside; 4. young tree bark; 5. catkin; 6. habit

Grey Poplar *Populus × canescens* p.1002
1. leaf upperside; 2. mature tree bark; 3. habit; 4. leaf underside

Aspen *Populus tremula* p.1007 1. leaf upperside;
2. bark; 3. habit, autumn colour; 4. leaf underside; 5. flower

Hybrid Black Poplar *Populus × canadensis* p.1000
1. leaf upperside; 2. bark; 3. habit; 4. leaf underside

Balsam Poplar *Populus balsamifera* p.998
1. leaf; 2. habit; 3. bark

Western Balsam Poplar *Populus trichocarpa* p.1009
1. leaf upperside; 2. habit; 3. leaf underside; 4. bark

Berlin Poplar *Populus × berolinensis* p.999
1. leaf; 2. habit

Balm of Gilead *Populus candicans* p.1001 1. leaf;
2. leaf, 'Aurora'; 3. bark with characteristic cankers; 4. habit

Central Asian Balsam Poplar *Populus laurifolia* p.999
leaf

Maximowicz's Balsam Poplar *Populus maximowiczii*
p.1004 1. leaf; 2. bark; 3. habit; 4. fruit

Simon's Poplar *Populus simonii* p.1007
1. leaf upperside; 2. bark; 3. habit, 'Fastigiata'

White Willow *Salix alba* p.1107 1. leaf; 2. leaf, 'Sericea'; 3. habit; 4. bark; 5. flower; 6. habit, var. *britzensis*

Crack Willow *Salix fragilis* p.1115
1. leaf; 2. habit; 3. bark; 4. flower

Salix × *rubens* p.1117
leaf

Chinese Weeping Willow *Salix babylonica* p.1109
1. leaf; 2. shoot; 3. habit

Peking Willow *Salix matsudana* p.1117
1. leaf; 2. habit

Rusty Sallow *Salix cinerea* p.1112
1. leaf upperside; 2. leaf underside; 3. bark; 4. habit;
5. shoot, bark removed showing striations

Purple Osier *Salix purpurea* p.1119
1. & 2. leaf; 3. male catkin; 4. female catkin

Osier *Salix viminalis* p.1122
1. leaf upperside; 2. leaf underside; 3. habit; 4. flower

Hoary Willow *Salix elaeagnos* p.1115
1. leaf; 2. habit; 3. catkin

Dark-leafed Willow *Salix nigricans* p.1110
leaf

Violet Willow *Salix daphnoides* p.1114
1. leaf; 2. bark; 3. habit; 4. flower; 5. shoot

Bay Willow *Salix pentandra* p.1118
1. leaf; 2. habit; 3. catkin

Small-leafed Lime *Tilia cordata* p.1215
1. leaf upperside; 2. leaf underside; 3. fruit; 4. flower; 5. habit

Large-leafed Lime *Tilia platyphyllos* p.1230 1. leaf upperside; 2. leaf underside; 3. bark; 4. habit; 5. flower; 6. fruit

Silver Lime *Tilia tomentosa* p.1233 1. leaf upperside;
2. bark; 3. habit; 4. leaf underside & flower: 5. fruit

Pendent Silver Lime *Tilia × petriolaris* p.1232
1. leaf upperside; 2. habit; 3. leaf underside & flower

Manchurian Lime *Tilia mandshurica* p.1225
1. leaf upperside; 2. leaf underside

Maximowicz Lime *Tilia maximowicziana* p.1226
1. leaf upperside; 2. leaf underside; 3. fruit; 4. habit

White Basswood *Tilia heterophylla* p.1223
1. leaf upperside & fruit; 2. leaf underside

Crimean Lime *Tilia dasystyla* p.1217
1. leaf; 2. shoot

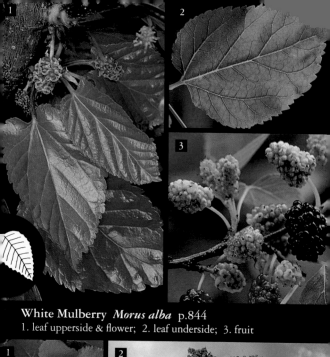

White Mulberry *Morus alba* p.844
1. leaf upperside & flower; 2. leaf underside; 3. fruit

Paper Mulberry *Broussonetia papyrifera* p.549
1. leaf; 2. female flower

Holly *Ilex aquifolium* p.744
1. leaf; 2. juvenile leaf; 3. habit; 4. male flower; 5. female
flower; 6. fruit; 7. fruit, ssp. *flava*

Highclere Holly *Ilex × altaclerensis*
p.743 1. leaf; 2. fruit; 3. habit;
4. leaf, 'Golden King'

Madeira Holly *Ilex perado* p.746
leaf

Perny Holly *Ilex pernyi* p.747
1. leaf; 2. habit

Sweet Chestnut
Castanea sativa p.574
1. leaf; 2. habit; 3. bark;
4. flower; 5. fruit

Asian Chestnut Oak
Quercus acutissima
p.1055 leaf

Golden Oak of Cyprus *Quercus alnifolia* p.1057
1. leaf upperside; 2. leaf underside

Himalayan Oak *Quercus semecarpifolia* p.1086
1. adult leaf; 2. habit; 3. juvenile leaf; 4. leaf underside

Kermes Oak
Quercus coccifera
p.1061
1. leaf; 2. habit;
3. bark; 4. male
flower 5. fruit

Crimean Hawthorn *Crataegus microphylla* p.629
1. leaf; 2. fruit

May *Crataegus monogyna* p.632

Midland Hawthorn *Crataegus laevigata* p.630
1. leaf & fruit; 2. habit; 3. bark; 4. flower

Azarole *Crataegus azarolus* p.627
1. leaf & unripe fruit; 2. flower; 3. ripe fruit

Oriental Hawthorn *Crataegus laciniata* p.639
1. leaf; 2. fruit

Heldreich's Hawthorn *Crataegus heldreichii* p.639
leaf & flower

Black Hawthorn *Crataegus nigra* p.634
leaf

Red Hawthorn *Crataegus sanguinea* p.636
1. leaf; 2. fruit; 3. shoot

Arran Whitebeam
Sorbus arranensis p.1143
1. leaf; 2. habit; 3. flower

Sorbus rupicola p.1143
leaf & fruit

Swedish Whitebeam *Sorbus intermedia* p.1160
1. leaf; 2. habit; 3. bark; 4. flower; 5. fruit

Thuringian Service Tree *Sorbus thuringiaca* p.1174
1. leaf & fruit; 2. habit

Balkan Pedunculate Oak *Quercus pedunculiflora (left)* p.1083
leaf

English Oak *Quercus robur (below)* p.1081
1. leaf upperside; 2. habit; 3. leaf underside; 4. bark; 5. male catkin; 6. fruit

Sessile Oak
Quercus petraea
p.1075 1. leaf upperside;
2. habit; 3. leaf underside;
4. fruit; 5. bark

Balkan Sessile Oak *Quercus polycarpa* p.1076 leaf

Downy Oak *Quercus pubescens* p.1079
1. leaf; 2. fruit

Mirbeck Oak *Quercus canariensis* p.1058
1. leaf upperside; 2. leaf underside; 3. bark; 4. habit; 5. fruit

Portuguese Oak *Quercus faginea* p.1064
1. leaf; 2. fruit

Hungarian Oak *Quercus frainetto* p.1065
1. leaf upperside; 2. leaf underside; 3. bark; 4. habit; 5. fruit

Valonia Oak *Quercus macrolepis* p.1071 1. new leaves & male catkins; 2. habit; 3. bark; 4. germinating fruit

White Oak
Quercus alba (above)
p.1056 leaf

Daimio Oak
Quercus dentata (right)
p.1063 leaf

1

2

3

4

Caucasian Oak *Quercus macranthera* p.1070
1. leaf; 2. bark; 3. habit; 4. fruit

1

2

Turkey Oak *Quercus cerris* p.1059
1. leaf; 2. habit; 3. bark; 4. male catkins/flowers; 5. fruit

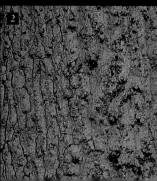

Chinese Cork Oak *Quercus variabilis* p.1089
1. leaf; 2. bark; 3. fruit

Red Oak
Quercus rubra
p.1085
1. leaf, autumn
colour; 2. habit;
3. bark;
4. flowers &
young leaves;
5. fruit

Black Oak
*Quercus
velutina*
p.1090 leaf

Scarlet Oak *Quercus coccinea* p.1062
1. leaf; 2. bark; 3. habit; 4. leaf, autumn colour

Blackjack Oak
Quercus
marilandica
p.1071 1. leaf;
2. gall/oak apple

Pin Oak *Quercus palustris* p.1074
1. leaf; 2. habit

Chinese Tulip Tree *Liriodendron chinense* p.795
1. leaf upperside; 2. leaf underside

Cappadocian Maple *Acer cappadocicum* p.421
1. leaf; 2. leaf, autumn colour; 3. bark; 4. shoot; 5. fruit

Norway Maple *Acer platanoides* p.460
1. leaf; 2. habit; 3. bark; 4. flower; 5. shoot & fruit

Mono Maple *Acer mono* p.448
1. bark; 2. leaf & fruit; 3. habit

Field Maple *Acer campestre* p.419
1. leaf; 2. habit; 3. bark; 4. flower; 5. fruit

Miyabe Maple *Acer miyabei* p.447
leaf

Horned Maple
Acer diabolicum
p.428 leaf

Acer sterculiaceum
p.429
fruit

Oregon Maple *Acer macrophyllum* p.444
1. leaf; 2. bark; 3. flower; 4. habit; 5. fruit

Red Maple *Acer rubrum* p.465 1. leaf upperside;
2. leaf underside; 3. leaf, autumn colour; 4. flower

Silver Maple *Acer saccharinum* p.468
1. leaf upperside; 2. bark; 3. habit; 4. leaf underside

Sugar Maple *Acer saccharum* p.469
1. leaf; 2. bark; 3. leaf, autumn colour

Campbell Maple *Acer campbellii* p.417
1. leaf; 2. fruit; 3. habit

Oliver Maple *Acer oliverianum* p.453
1. leaf; 2. fruit

Wilson's Maple *Acer wilsonii* p.418
leaf

Heldreich's Maple *Acer heldreichii* p.437
1. leaf upperside & flowers; 2. leaf underside & fruit

Sycamore *Acer pseudoplatanus* p.462 1. leaf upperside;
2. bark; 3. habit; 4. flower; 5. shoot; 6. leaf underside & fruit

Red-bud Maple *Acer trautvetteri* p.438
leaf

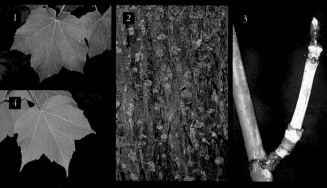

Giraldi's Maple *Acer giraldii* p.432
1. leaf upperside; 2. bark; 3. shoot; 4. leaf underside

Italian Maple *Acer opalus* p.454
1. leaf upperside; 2. habit; 3. leaf underside; 4. flower

Van Volxem's Maple *Acer velutinum* var. *vanvolxemii*
p.479 leaf

Uri Maple *Acer crataegifolium* p.425
leaf

Maximowicz's Maple *Acer maximowiczii* p.446
leaf

Japanese Maple *Acer palmatum* p.455 1. leaf; 2. bark;
3. habit; 4. fruit; 5. habit, autumn; 6. leaf, purple form; 7. shoot

Full Moon Maple *Acer japonicum* p.440 1. new leaf & flower; 2. bark; 3. habit; 4. young fruit; 5. leaf, autumn colour

Keijo Maple *Acer pseudosieboldianum* p.464
leaf

Shirasawa Maple *Acer shirasawanum* p.472
leaf, f. *aureum*

Trident Maple *Acer buergerianum* p.416
1. leaf upperside; 2. leaf underside; 3. habit; 4. mature fruit

Syrian Maple *Acer obtusifolium* p.452
1. leaf; 2. bark; 3. fruit

Spanish Maple
Acer granatense
p.433
leaf & flower

Balkan Maple
Acer hyrcanum (below)
p.439
leaf & fruit

Amur Maple *Acer ginnala* p.431
1. leaf & flower; 2. bark; 3. fruit; 4. habit, autumn colour

Tartar Maple *Acer tataricum* p.475
leaf

Tail Leaf Maple *Acer caudatum* p.423
1. leaf; 2. bark; 3. habit; 4. fruit

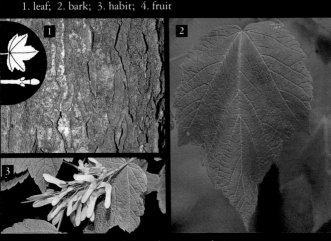

Mountain Maple *Acer spicatum* p.479
1. bark; 2. leaf; 3. fruit

Ukurundu Maple *Acer ukurunduense* p.478
1. leaf; 2. flower

Deep-veined Maple *Acer argutum* p.414 1. leaf & flower;
2. bark; 3. habit; 4. fruit; 5. shoot; 6. leaf, autumn colour

Kyushu Maple *Acer capillipes* p.420
1. leaf; 2. bark; 3. habit; 4. leaf, autumn colour; 5. fruit

Forrest's Maple *Acer forrestii* p.430
1. leaf upperside; 2. leaf underside

Wongka Maple *Acer pectinatum* p.457
1. leaf upperside; 2. leaf underside; 3. bark

Moosewood *Acer pensylvanicum* p.459
1. leaf upperside; 2. leaf underside; 3. bark; 4. fruit; 5. habit

Abutilon × *suntense* p.405
leaf & flower

Chilean Mallow *Abutilon vitifolium* p.405
1. leaf & flower; 2. habit

Fig *Ficus carica* p.706
1. leaf; 2. habit; 3. bark; 4. fruit

Prickly Castor-oil Tree *Kalopanax septemlobus* p.770
1. leaf; 2. bark; 3. shoot

Japanese Creeper *Parthenocissus tricuspidata* p.870
1. leaf, autumn colour; 2. habit, autumn colour; 3. fruit

° **London Plane** *Platanus × hispanica* p.986
1. leaf; 2. bark; 3. fruit; 4. habit

Oriental Plane *Platanus orientalis* p.987
1. leaf; 2. habit; 3. fruit

Chinese Sweet Gum *Liquidambar formosana* p.792
leaf

Oriental Sweet Gum *Liquidambar orientalis* p.793
1. leaf; 2. habit

Sweet Gum *Liquidambar styraciflua* p.794
1. leaf; 2. bark; 3. habit; 4. leaf, autumn colour; 5. fruit

Nikko Maple *Acer maximowicziana* p.445
1. leaf & fruit; 2. bark

Paperbark Maple *Acer griseum* p.434
1. leaf; 2. bark; 3. habit; 4. bark on young stem; 5. fruit

Chosen Maple *Acer triflorum* p.475
1. leaf; 2. bark

Vine-leafed Maple *Acer cissifolium* p.424
1. leaf & fruit; 2. bark; 3. habit

Moroccan Broom *Cytisus battandieri* p.660
1. flower; 2. habit

Hop Tree
Ptelea trifoliata p.1039
1. & 2. leaf & fruit

Bladder-nut *Staphylea pinnata* p.1182
1. leaf & flower; 2. fruit

Wild Jasmine
Jasminum fruticans
p.749 leaf & flower

Winter Jasmine
Jasminum nudiflorum
p.748 leaf

Scotch Laburnum *Laburnum alpinum* p.774
1. leaf & flower; 2. bark

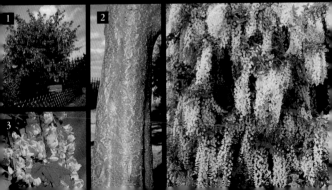

Red Horse Chestnut *Aesculus × carnea* p.481
1. & 2. leaf & flower; 3. habit; 4. bark; 5. fruit

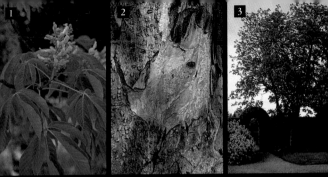

Yellow Buckeye *Aesculus flava* p.483
1. leaf & flower; 2. bark; 3. habit

Indian Horse Chestnut *Aesculus indica* p.486
1. leaf & flower; 2. bark; 3. habit; 4. fruit

Amur Cork Tree *Phellodendron amurense* p.874
1. leaf; 2. bark; 3. fruit

Euodia *Tetradium daniellii* p.1207
1. leaflets; 2. habit; 3. flower

Eucryphia *Eucryphia glutinosa* p.695
1. leaf; 2. habit, autumn colour; 3. flower

Rostrevor Eucryphia *Eucryphia × intermedia* p.696
1. leaf; 2. habit; 3. bark; 4. flower

Nyman's Eucryphia *Eucryphia × nymansensis* p.698
1. leaf upperside; 2. leaf underside; 3. habit; 4. bark; 5. flower

Box Elder *Acer negundo* p.450
1. leaf; 2. fruit; 3. male flower; 4. habit, 'Variegata'; 5. bark

Lyonothamnus
Lyonothamnus floribundus (above)
p.803 1. leaf; 2. bark

Old Man's Beard *Clematis vitalba*
(right) p.613 leaf & fruit

Trumpet Vine *Campsis radicans* p.557
1. leaf; 2. flower

Dipteronia *Dipteronia sinensis* p.667
1. leaf; 2. flower

Elder *Sambucus nigra* p.1124
1. leaf; 2. habit; 3. bark; 4. flower & leaf, f. *laciniata*; 5. fruit

Ash *Fraxinus excelsior* p.713 1. leaf; 2. bark; 3. male
flower; 4. habit; 5. female flower; 6. fruit

Narrow-leafed Ash *Fraxinus angustifolia* p.712
1. leaf; 2. bark

Manna Ash *Fraxinus ornus* p.716
1. leaflets; 2. bark; 3. habit; 4. flower; 5. fruit; 6. shoot & buds

White Ash *Fraxinus americana* p.711
1. leaf upperside; 2. leaf underside; 3. bark; 4. fruit; 5. habit

Oregon Ash *Fraxinus latifolia* p.715
1. leaf; 2. fruit

Pride of India *Koelreuteria paniculata* p.773
1. leaf; 2. bark; 3. habit; 4. flower; 5. fruit

Veitch's Meliosma *Meliosma veitchiorum* p.838
1. leaf; 2. bark; 3. habit; 4. flower; 5. fruit

Large Terebinth
Pistacia atlantica
p.978
habit

Mastic Tree
Pistacia lentiscus (below)
p.979
1. leaf & flower;
2. habit

Pistacio *Pistacia vera* p.980
1. leaf & flower; 2. fruit

Peruvian Pepper Tree *Schinus molle* p.1130
1. leaf & flower; 2. fruit

Sumach *Rhus coraria* p.1100
leaf & fruit

Potanin's Sumach *Rhus potaninii* p.1099
1. leaf; 2. bark

Stag's Horn Sumach *Rhus typhina* p.1100 1. leaf, autumn
colour; 2. leaf; 3. habit; 4. bark; 5. shoot; 6. flower; 7. fruit

Varnish Tree *Rhus vernaciflua* p.1101
1. leaf; 2. bark; 3. habit; 4. fruit

Japanese Toothache Tree *Zanthoxylum ailanthioides*
p.1266 leaf, autumn colour

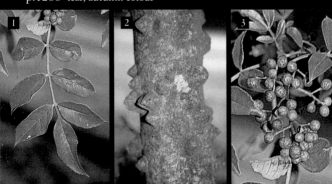

***Zanthoxylum simulans* p.1267**
1. leaf; 2. bark; 3. fruit

Decaisnea *Decaisnea fargesii* p.663
1. leaf & fruit; 2. flower

Japanese Walnut *Juglans ailanthifolia* p.751
1. leaf; 2. male flower; 3. female flower; 4. shoot & pith

Butter Nut *Juglans cinerea* p.752
1. leaflets; 2. shoot

Black Walnut *Juglans nigra* p.753
1. leaf & fruit; 2. habit; 3. bark

Caucasian Wingnut *Pterocarya fraxinifolia* p.1040
1. leaf; 2. bark; 3. flower; 4. habit; 5. fruit

Hybrid Wingnut *Pterocarya × rehderiana* p.1042
1. leaf; 2. flower

Chinese Wingnut *Pterocarya stenoptera* p.1043
1. leaf; 2. fruit; 3. shoot, cut to show chambered pith

Bitternut *Carya cordiformis (above and right)* p.566
1. leaf; 2. bark;
3. shoot; 4. fruit;
5. leaf, autumn colour

Water Hickory *Carya aquatica (left)* p.567
male flower

Shagbark Hickory *Carya ovata* p.571
1. leaf; 2. bark, young tree; 3. habit; 4. fruit

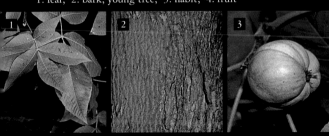

Mockernut *Carya tomentosa* p.572
1. leaf; 2. bark; 3. fruit

Pignut *Carya glabra* p.567
leaf

Pecan *Carya illinoinensis* p.568
1. fruit; 2. leaf

Shellbark Hickory *Carya laciniosa* p.570
1. leaf; 2. bark; 3. fruit

Service Tree *Sorbus domestica* p.1151
1. leaf; 2. bark; 3. habit; 4. fruit

Harrow Rowan *Sorbus harrowiana* p.1156
1. leaf; 2. fruit

Bastard Service Tree *Sorbus hybrida* p.1159
1. leaf & flower; 2. fruit

Rowan *Sorbus aucuparia* p.1144
1. leaf; 2. bark; 3. habit; 4. flower; 5. fruit

Esserteau's Rowan *Sorbus esserteauiana* p.1152
leaf & fruit

Ladder Rowan *Sorbus scalaris* p.1171
1. leaf & fruit; 2. habit

Joseph Rock's Rowan *Sorbus* 'Joseph Rock' p.1162
1. leaf in autumn colour & fruit; 2. habit, autumn colour

Japanese Rowan *Sorbus commixta* p.1149 1. leaf &
flower; 2. bark; 3. habit; 4. fruit; 5. leaf, autumn colour

Sargent's Rowan *Sorbus sargentiana* p.1170
1. leaf, autumn colour; 2. leaf & fruit; 3. shoot in bud

Kashmir Rowan *Sorbus cashmiriana* p.1148
1. leaf & flower; 2. habit; 3. fruit

White-fruited Rowan *Sorbus glabrescens* p.1154
1. leaf & fruit; 2. bark; 3. habit

Kite-leaf Rowan *Sorbus oligodonta* p.1168
1. leaf; 2. fruit

Small-leaf Rowan *Sorbus microphylla* p.1166
1. leaf & flower; 2. fruit

Tsema Rowan *Sorbus rufopilosa* p.1169
1. leaf; 2. flower; 3. fruit

Tree of Heaven *Ailanthus altissima* p.488
1. part of leaf; 2. bark; 3. flower; 4. fruit; 5. habit

Yellow-wood
*Cladrastis
kentukea*
p.611 1. leaf;
2. bark; 3. habit;
4. flower

Chinese Cladrasti
*Cladrastis
sinensis (left)*
p.612 leaf & flower

Bladder Senna
*Colutea
arborescens
(below)*
p.616 1. leaf &
fruit; 2. flower

Rose Acacia *Robinia hispida* p.1104
1. leaf; 2. flower

Robinia *Robinia pseudoacacia* p.1102
1. leaf; 2. bark; 3. habit; 4. flower; 5. fruit; 6. spines on shoot

Pagoda Tree *Sophora japonica* p.1137
1. leaf; 2. bark; 3. flower; 4. fruit; 5. shoot; 6. habit

Wisteria *Wisteria sinensis* p.1264
1. leaf; 2. habit; 3. flower

Silver Wattle *Acacia dealbata* p.407
1. single leaf; 2. habit in flower; 3. flower in bud; 4. bark

Carob *Ceratonia siliqua* p.593
1. leaf; 2. flower; 3. fruit; 4. habit

Opoponax *Acacia farnesiana* p.411
leaf & flower

Karoo *Acacia karoo* p.410
leaf & flower

Green Wattle *Acacia mearnsii* p.408
1. leaf & flower; 2. habit

Pink Siris *Albizia julibrissin* p.490
1. leaf & flower; 2. bark; 3. habit; 4. fruit

Plume Albizia *Albizia lophantha* p.491
1. leaf; 2. flower

Jacaranda *Jacaranda mimosifolia* p.748
1. leaf; 2. bark; 3. flower

Honey Locust *Gleditsia triacanthos* p.724
1. leaf; 2. bark; 3. fruit; 4. habit; 5. flower; 6. spines

Kentucky Coffee-tree *Gymnocladus dioica* p.727
1. single leaf; 2. bark

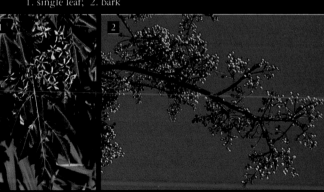

Bead Tree *Melia azedarach* p.836
1. leaf & flower; 2. fruit

Cyclops Wattle
Acacia cyclops (above)
p.409
leaf & fruit

Golden Wattle
Acacia pycnantha (left)
p.411   leaf & flower

Swamp Wattle
Acacia retinodes (above)
p.410   leaf & flower

Golden Wreath *Acacia cyanophylla*
p.406 1. leaf; 2. flower

Sydney Golden Wattle *Acacia longifolia* p.408
1. leaf & flower; 2. habit

Blackwood Acacia *Acacia melanoxylon* p.409
leaf & flower

Mount Etna Broom *Genista aetnensis* p.721
1. bark; 2. fruit; 3. habit in flower; 4. shoot

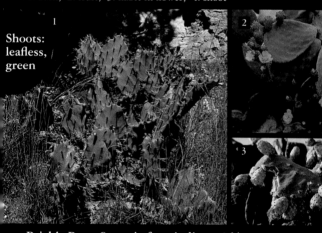

Shoots: leafless, green

Prickly Pear *Opuntia ficus-indica* p.864
1. habit; 2. flower; 3. fruit

Spanish Broom *Spartium junceum* p.1180
shoot & flower

Canary Palm *Phoenix canariensis* p.878
1. bark; 2. fruit; 3. habit

Date Palm *Phoenix dactylifera* p.879
1. fruit; 2. habit

Cretan Palm *Phoenix theophrastii* p.879
1. leaf & fruit; 2. habit; 3. flower

Queen Palm *Syagrus romanzoffiana* p.1192
1. leaf; 2. flower; 3. habit; 4. fruit

Sentry Palm
Howeia forsteriana
(above) p.741
1. leaf; 2. fruit; 3. habit

Chilean Wine Palm
Jubaea chilensis
(right) p.750
habit

European Fan Palm *Chamaerops humilis* p.604
1. leaf; 2. habit; 3. fruit

Chusan Palm *Trachycarpus fortunei* p.1238
1. leaf; 2. bark; 3. habit; 4. flower; 5. fruit

Petticoat Palm *Washingtonia filifera*
p.1263 1. leaf; 2. habit

Tree Fern *Dicksonia antarctica* p.664
1. leaf upperside; 2. bark; 3. habit; 4. leaf underside & spores

Banana *Musa cavendishii* p.846
1. leaf ; 2. fruit

Bamboo *Phyllostachys nigra* p.882
1. leaf upperside; 2. leaf underside; 3. habit

Cabbage Tree *Cordyline australis* p.617
1. leaf & flower; 2. & 3. habit; 4. fruit

Dragon Tree *Dracaena draco* p.668
1. bark; 2. habit; 3. fruit

PART II

FAMILY AND SPECIES DESCRIPTIONS

The number preceding each species description in the following pages corresponds to the page number in the colour section on which that species can be found. Some trees only mentioned in the 'Similar species' and 'Varieties' sections of the main species' descriptions are also illustrated in the colour section. In such cases, a page reference follows their name.

SILVER FIRS, *ABIES*
FAMILY PINACEAE

This is a genus of around sixty species of evergreen conifers from the northern hemisphere, that extends south just into the tropics in Vietnam and Taiwan, but as far south as Guatemala and Honduras in North America. Silver firs occur in two main ecological zones: most species form extensive and often pure forests in the boreal to subalpine belts (at higher elevations towards the south of their ranges); a number of species are characteristic of the warm temperate zone and these tend to occur with or near oaks, and in small groves or as scattered trees. The name silver fir derives from the two bands of stomata on the underside of the leaves. These bands are usually covered by a silvery or glaucous wax, which assists in preventing moisture loss and, in the species coming from areas of highest rainfall, helps to shed moisture, thus allowing the stomata to function. In some species, especially those from the warm temperate zones, the bands are green or grey-green and not silvery.

This character can be used to separate the species. Species which have bright silvery bands on the leaves include *AA. amabilis* (variable in this character), *delavayi*, *densa*, *fabri*, *fargesii*, *forrestii*, *koreana*, *spectabilis* and *veitchii*. Species with only moderately silvery bands on the leaves include *AA. alba*, *amabilis* (variable in this character), *balsamea*, *bracteata*, *cephalonica*, *chengii*, *cilicica*, *fraseri*, *grandis*, *homolepis*, *mariesii*, *nebrodensis*, *nephrolepis*, *nordmanniana*, *religiosa*, *sachalinensis*, *sibirica* and *squamata*. Species with the leaves green or greenish white on the underside, i.e. without silvery bands, or species which are the same bluish green or bluish grey on both sides of the leaf include *AA. bracteata*, *chensiensis* ssp. *salouenensis*, *concolor*, *firma*, *holophylla*, *kawakamii*, *lasiocarpa*, *magnifica*, *pindrow*, *pinsapo*, *procera*, *recurvata* and *vejarii*.

The characters which best separate the species are found in the cones and on the mature branches of the lower outer crown. The foliage on coning shoots tends always to curve upwards much more, and to be short and often sharply pointed. The leaves are flattened to some extent. They are arranged spirally on the shoot, but in most species they are twisted at the short 'leaf stalk' at the base (never a peg-like pulvinus as found in the spruces) to give a pectinate arrangement, at least beneath the shoot. However, in *AA. cephalonica*, *delavayi*, *forrestii* (but not always), *koreana* (but not always), *numidica*, *pinsapo* and *sibirica*, the leaves beneath the shoot are at least partly at right angles to the shoot, i.e. some leaves point straight down. The buds are rounded to bluntly conic, often resinous and sometimes densely so. Only in one species (*A. bracteata*) are they pointed, and not in the manner of *Pseudotsuga* but spindle-shaped and similar to those of *Fagus*.

The female flowers open in the spring from buds laid down in the previous year and are generally only carried on the upper branches. They are erect both at flowering time and as they develop. During development the cones may be violet or purple, or green or yellow-green. They ripen to brown in the first autumn, and then disintegrate, scattering both the seeds and the subtending bract but leaving the stalk or rachis on the branches. The rachis is very narrowly cylindrical (*see* photograph 2 on p.79, *nordmanniana*) in *AA. alba*, *balsamea*, *cephalonica*, *chensiensis* ssp. *salouenensis*, *cilicica*, *firma*, *grandis*, *holophylla*, *koreana*, *lasiocarpa*, *nebrodensis*, *nephrolepis*, *nordmanniana*, *numidica*, *pindrow*, *procera*, *sachalinensis*, *sibirica* and *veitchii*, but in other species it is stout cylindro-conic (*see* photograph 4 on p.89, *spectabilis*) to spindle shaped. As the rachis may be retained on the tree for some time this can be a useful character. Silver firs have a uniform whitish wood of moderate quality. They are used in forestry and also planted as amenity trees.

Informal Key

LEAVES

(i) **soft, not stiff or prickly:** *alba*, *amabilis*, *balsamea*, *chengii*, *cilicia*, *concolor*, *delavayi*, *densa*, *fabri*, *fargesii*, *forrestii*, *fraseri*, *grandis*, *kawakamii*, *koreana*, *lasiocarpa*, *magnifica*, *mariesii*, *nephrolepis*, *nordmanniana*, *pindrow*, *procera*, *religiosa*, *sachalinensis*, *sibirica*, *spectabilis*, *veitchii*

(ii) **hard, sharp or stiff:** *bracteata* (sharp), *cephalonica* (often sharp), *chensiensis* ssp. *salouenensis*, *firma* (with two sharp points on young trees), *holophylla* (sharp), *homolepis*, *nebrodensis* (stiff), *numidica* (stiff), *pinsapo* (stiff and nearly perfectly radial), *recurvata* (sharp, stiff), *squamata* (stiff, sometimes sharp), *vejarii* (stiff and somewhat sharp)

BRACTS

(i) **projecting from the mature cone:** *alba*, *bracteata*, *cephalonica*, *delavayi*, *densa*, *fabri*, *fargesii*, *firma*, *forrestii*, *fraseri*, *koreana*, *nebrodensis*, *nordmanniana*, *procera*, *religiosa*, *sachalinensis*, *squamata*, *veitchii*, *vejarii*

(ii) **enclosed in the mature cone** (for species marked with an asterisk (*) the tips of the cusp may show): *amabilis*, *balsamea*, *chengii**, *chensiensis* ssp. *salouenensis*, *cilicia*, *concolor*, *delavayi* (rarely), *grandis*, *holophylla*, *homolepis*, *kawakamii*, *koreana*, *magnifica*, *mariesii*, *nephrolepis**, *numidica*, *pindrow*, *pinsapo*, *recurvata**, *sibirica*, *spectabilis**

p.78 **Silver Fir** or **European Silver Fir**
Abies alba

Description: Evergreen tree, 15–50 m (50–165 ft) with
a bole to 2 m (6.6 ft).
Crown Conical in young trees, with the
branches in whorls, becoming columnar in
old ones, often with a flat top. *Bark* Grey
or brown-grey, smooth in young trees,
becoming cracked into small thick plates
with pinkish fissures. *Shoot* Moderately
slender, fawn-brown in first winter,
darkening or becoming greyer, with short,
dark-brown hairs in shallow grooves.
Buds Ovoid, bluntly pointed, red-brown,
non-resinous to moderately resinous, to
5 mm (0.2 in). *Foliage* Spreads widely
beneath the shoot and slightly forwards,
then in several ranks becomes more erect
with a definite parting above; on shaded
shoots the upper parting is wider, or the
foliage pectinate. Leaves linear and
grooved above; apex rounded, notched to
acute, and stiff. Upper surface is dark shiny
green without stomata or with a few in a
small spot near the tip; lower surface has
two whitish-green to silvery-green waxy
bands of stomata, 1.5–2.5 cm (0.6–1 in),
to 3.5 cm (1.4 in) on vigorous young trees,
by 1.5–2 mm (0.1 in); crushed foliage is
resin scented. *Flowers* On previous
season's shoots in late spring; male cones
greenish-yellow, 2 cm (0.8 in).
Fruit Cylindrical with projecting reflexed
bracts, tapered at both ends, yellowish
green or green-brown when growing,
ripening in first autumn to brown or
reddish-brown, 10–15 cm × 3.5 cm (4–6 ×
1.4 in); rachis conical; scales fan-shaped, to
3.5 cm (1.4 in) in width.

Range: From the Pyrenees across to the Alps,
southern Germany and the Carpathians
south to the Balkans and Italy.

Habitat: Montane mixed forests, often associated
with beech (*Fagus*) trees.

Varieties: No varieties but several cultivars are often
encountered. These include 'Fastigiata',
which has the branches at an acute angle to
the stem and forms a narrow conical tree,

and 'Pendula', in which the branches are pendulous.

Synonyms: *A. pectinata*, *A. taxifolia*.

Similar species: In the southern Balkans and in northern Greece there are plants which are intermediate between *A. alba* and *A. cephalonica*. These have been named *A. borisii-regis*. It differs from *A. alba* in the sharp pointed leaves with a large spot of stomata on the upper surface near the tip, and from *A. cephalonica* in the dense black hairs on the shoot. It is sometimes treated as a straight hybrid, but it is probably more useful to consider it as part of the gene pool in this group of firs, with genes moving each way.

This tree is an important forest tree over much of Europe, producing a high-quality, yellowish-white timber. It is tolerant of a wide range of sites, preferring cool moist climates on acidic soils. It is frequently naturalized, such as in western Britain. A leaf-sucking aphid (*Adelges nordmannianae*) causes dieback and death and is the reason why it is no longer planted on any scale in British forestry.

p.90 **Pacific Fir** *Abies amabilis*

Description: Evergreen tree, 15–30 m (50–100 ft) with a bole diameter to 1 m (3.3 ft).
Crown Conical when young, becoming columnar or spire-like with slightly pendent branches bearing dense foliage. *Bark* Grey, smooth with resin blisters when young, later corky and scaly, reddish grey or reddish brown. *Shoot* Grey-brown to reddish grey-brown in the first winter, with a dense covering of short brown hairs, becoming darker and hairless in succeeding years, slender, flexible. *Buds* Globose, nearly rounded, densely resinous, whitish-grey, to 3 mm (0.1 in). *Foliage* In pendent dense flat sprays with side shoots filling the gaps and leaves retained for six to eight years. Beneath the shoot widely parted and 75 degrees to the shoot. Above the shoot the foliage becomes progressively more erect, set

forwards and shorter so that inner rank points forwards along the shoot at more or less 45 degrees with a narrow V-parting; leaves linear, rounded and bluntly notched to give a squarish apex, dark green above without stomata, beneath with two silvery white waxy bands of stomata, 2–4 cm (0.8–1.6 in) by 2 mm (0.1 in); crushed foliage with scent of parsley or tangerines. *Flowers* On previous season's shoots in early summer; male cones red, 1–1.5 cm (0.4–0.6 in). *Fruit* Oblong or ovoid-cylindrical with hidden bracts, purple, ripening to brown in first autumn, 8–15 cm (3.1–6 in) by 5–6.5 cm (2–2.6 in); rachis cylindro-conic; scales 2.5–3.5 cm (1–1.4 in) in width, bract scale less than half seed scale.

Range: Western North America from southeast Alaska to west Oregon and with scattered populations in northern California.

Habitat: Cultivated in Europe as an ornamental. In the wild occurring in cool conifer forest in moist mountain valleys.

The scientific name (*amabilis*) means beautiful, which epithet is admirably justified by this tree when growing well. In its luxuriant foliage it resembles *A. nordmanniana* but can be easily distinguished by the resinous globular buds. The buds resemble *A. grandis* but from this it is separated by the dense foliage which rises above the stouter hairy shoot.

p.93 **Balsam Fir** *Abies balsamea*

Description: Evergreen tree 10–15 m (33–50 ft) with a bole diameter to 30 cm (1 ft).
Crown Conical and regularly whorled in young trees, becoming columnar with a pointed apex in old trees. *Bark* Dark grey, smooth with resin blisters in young trees, becoming fissured and scaly. *Shoot* Buff-brown with hairs in grooves in first winter, then yellow-brown or dark brown.
Buds Ovate to globose, bluntly pointed and lumpy, thickly encrusted with purple resin, to 4 mm (0.2 in). *Foliage* Widely parted

below the shoot, spreading at the sides and becoming more curving above, often with a narrow parting; leaves linear, with a rounded notched tip, mid-green above with an incomplete band of waxy white dots of stomata in the groove above, underneath with two silvery white waxy bands of stomata and a pale green midrib, 1.2–2.4 cm (0.5–0.9 in) by 2 mm (0.1 in); crushed foliage balsam resin scented. *Flowers* On previous season's shoots in early summer; male cones yellow and purple, 6 mm (0.25 in). *Fruit* Cylindrical with hidden bracts, ripening from green or purple to brown in first autumn, 5–8 cm (2–3.1 in) by 2–3 cm (0.8–1.2 in); rachis conical; scales fan-shaped, hairy on the exposed portion, 1.4–1.7 cm (0.6–0.7 in) in width.

Range: Eastern North America from Maine to Alberta and south to West Virginia.

Habitat: Cultivated in Europe as an ornamental, in the wild forming extensive forests on acid sands and silty soils.

Varieties: Var. *phanerolepis* covers the plants which have the bract scales projecting. It has been suggested as a hybrid with *A. fraseri* but occurs with the normal form of *A. balsamea* throughout its range. From *A. fraseri* it is distinguished by the long cusp to the bract.

This makes a neat and initially fast growing tree but is not long lived in cultivation. The resin in the bark blisters is the source of Canada Balsam, which is used in laboratory work and as an optical cement.

---

p.89 **Santa Lucia Fir** or **Bristlecone Fir**
Abies bracteata

Description: Evergreen tree to 25 m (80 ft) with a bole to 1 m (3.3 ft).
Crown Conical or columnar-conic, dense with short spreading branches. *Bark* Black-grey or reddish brown, smooth but with resin blisters when young, becoming fissured at the base into small scales in old trees. *Shoot* Olive-brown in first year, maturing to pale grey-brown, slender,

hairless. *Buds* Spindle-shaped, tapered to a pointed apex, light brown, without resin, 1.5–2.5 cm (0.6–1 in). *Foliage* Spreading forwards in three to four ranks either side of the shoot, flat beneath and with a wide V-groove above; leaves linear or sickle-shaped, tapered to the sharp hard pointed apex, rounded at base, dark glossy green above without stomata, beneath with two silver bands either side of a pale green midrib, 3.5–5 cm (1.4–2 in) by 2–3 mm (0.1 in); crushed foliage has a faint grassy scent. *Flowers* On previous season's shoots in early summer; male flowers yellow-brown; female flowers erect on strong shoots. *Fruit* Ovoid with long reflexed bracts holding blobs of whitish resin, ripening from purple green to purple brown, 5–10 cm (2–4 in) by 4–6 cm (1.6–2.4 in); rachis cylindro-conical; scales thin, rounded, hairless, bract scale with extremely long cusp to 3 cm (1.2 in), golden brown.

Range: Santa Lucia mountains of Monterey county, California.

Habitat: Cultivated in Europe as an ornamental. In the wild found on dry mountain slopes or canyon bottoms.

Synonyms: *A. venusta.*

It is unlikely to be confused with any other fir as it is remarkable for the spindle-shaped buds and the very long cusps on the cone's bract scales and uncomfortable to handle because of the very sharp points of the needles. Only species of *Torreya* have similar foliage, although several spruces may be as pungent! In the wild it is restricted to a single mountain range in western California but has proved hardy in cultivation in Britain as far north as Aberdeen.

p.78 **Greek Fir** *Abies cephalonica*

Description: Evergreen tree to 30 m (100 ft) with a bole diameter to 1.5 m (5 ft).
Crown Conical in young trees, becoming columnar; old trees may develop massive side branches which spread forming

secondary leaders and giving a very broad and ragged crown. *Bark* Grey, tinged with pink or brown in young trees and smooth and finely flaky, becoming fissured into small scaly plates in old trees. *Shoot* Brown or red-brown in first winter, hairless, becoming red-brown or orange-brown. *Buds* Ovoid or ovoid-conical, with a pointed apex, pale brown with a thin coat of whitish resin 5 mm (0.2 in).
Foliage Weakly parted beneath or with some leaves below, those at the side slightly forward with rising or erect leaves above the shoot, with or without a parting; leaves linear and tapered to both ends; apex pointed to a short bony tip, base circular or oval on the shoot, above mid to dark glossy green without stomata apart from a small spot at the tip, below with two greenish white waxy stomatal bands and a mid-green midrib, 2–3 cm (0.8–1.2 in) by 1.5–2.5 mm (0.1 in); crushed foliage with a sharp turpentine scent. *Flowers* On previous season's growth in late spring; male cones red, expanding to 1.8 cm (0.7 in) and becoming yellow.
Fruit Cylindrical but tapered to both ends, apex nipple-like or bluntly pointed, with projecting reflexed bracts, green-brown during the growing season, ripening in the first autumn to brown, 10–16 cm (4–6.3 in) by 3.5–4.5 cm (1.4–1.8 in); rachis cylindrical; scales 2–3 cm (0.8–1.2 in) in width and yellow-brown hairy on the exposed part.

Range: Southern Greece from the island of Cephalonica and the Peloponnese and into northern Greece.

Habitat: Mountain slopes on well drained and calcareous soils.

Varieties: No botanical varieties but see *A. borisii-regis* under *A. alba*.

Synonyms: *A. apollinis.*

This fir forms a large tree, with enormous spreading branches in old trees. In cultivation in northern Europe it tends to be susceptible to spring frosts. It grows on a wide range of soils, including chalky ones.

p.86 **Cheng Fir** *Abies chengii*

Description: Evergreen tree 15–20 m (50–65 ft) with a bole diameter to 70 cm (2.3 ft).
Crown Conical in young trees, with spaced whorled branches, older trees broader and denser, with a flat top, branches oval in section, narrower than deep. *Bark* Grey, smooth, becoming cracked at the base and lightly fissured. *Shoot* Red-brown or mahogany, rough, hairless or with a few hairs in grooves, orange-brown in second year, darker in later years, usually paler above, stout. *Buds* Ovoid to conical, apex rounded thickly resinous, brown, 7 mm (0.3 in), bud scales persisting on shoot. *Foliage* On spreading branches with the laterals held rising above the main branch; leaves pointed forward beneath the shoot, a few may point downwards, at the side spreading forwards and may be bent forwards, above the shoot curving upwards at 90 degrees, with a narrow or wide V-parting between the two sides, leaves above the shoot half the length of the side and lower ones, mid glossy green above without stomata, whitish or silvery green beneath on the two waxy bands of stomata, linear, apex rounded with a cleft or bifid notch, 2.5–4 cm (1–1.6 in) by 2.5–3 mm (0.1 in) on old trees, up to 6 cm (2.4 in) on young trees; crushed foliage with a resinous slightly fishy smell. *Flowers* On previous season's shoots, opening in late spring; male cones 2–4 cm (0.8–1.6 in), purplish red, pollen yellow. *Fruit* Ovoid-cylindric, apex dimple-tipped and the bract scales hidden or just projecting at base of cone, violet, ripening in first autumn to brown, 6–9 cm (2.4–3.5 in) by 3.5–4.5 cm (1.4–1.8 in); rachis spindle-shaped, stout; scales wedge-shaped, 2.6 cm (1 in) wide.

Range: Northwest Yunnan, China.

Habitat: Valley slopes.

Synonyms: *A. fargesii* misapplied.

This fir may be a hybrid between *A. forrestii* and *A. chensiensis* ssp. *salouenensis*. It is more tolerant of dry conditions than *A. forrestii* and makes a vigorous tree in cultivation.

p.84 **Salween Fir** *Abies chensiensis*
ssp. *salouenensis*

Description: Evergreen tree to 15 m (50 ft) with a bole
diameter of up to 60 cm (2 ft).
Crown Conical in young trees, later
columnar with a conical apex. *Bark* Grey,
smooth with resin blisters when young,
developing red-brown fissures and scaly
plates. *Shoot* Olive-brown in the first
winter, then fawn-brown and later greyer,
somewhat shiny, hairless, stout.
Buds Conical, pointed, light brown, very
slightly resinous, to 1 cm (0.4 in).
Foliage Spreading widely and forwards
both above and below the shoot in several
ranks, with a wide V-groove above; leaves
linear, slightly wider in the middle, apex
rounded bifid with two bony points, or
rounded notched, dark glossy green above
without stomata, with two whitish-green
waxy bands of stomata below and mid
green midrib and margins, 3.5–7.5 cm
(1.4–3 in) by 3–4 mm (0.1–0.2 in);
crushed foliage with a resin scent.
Flowers On previous season's shoots in late
spring. *Fruit* Cylindrical or conical, with
the bracts included, green or blue, ripening
in first autumn to golden or light brown,
8–10 cm × 4–5 cm (3.1–4 × 1.6–2 in);
rachis conical; scales fan-shaped, 3–3.5 cm
(1.2–1.4 in) in width.

Range: Northern Yunnan across northern Burma to
the extreme east of India.

Habitat: Cultivated in Europe as an ornamental, in
the wild occurring in valley bottom sites.

Varieties: The typical subspecies, Shensi Fir, ssp.
chensiensis, occurs in Shaanxi and Hubei
provinces of China where it is found in valley
bottom sites or below *A. fargesii*. It has
smaller and narrower leaves, usually no more
than 4.5 cm (1.8 in) long (but up to 6 cm
(2.4 in) on young trees) by 2.5–3.5 mm
(0.1 in), which are light or somewhat
yellow-green in colour. They are arranged
widely parted below but the uppermost
ranks curve up to give a U-shaped groove
along the shoot. The buds are smaller, to
6 mm (0.25 in). It is rarer in cultivation.

Synonyms: *A. salouenensis.*

This tree has the largest leaves of any silver fir, up to 11 cm × 5 mm (4.3 × 0.2 in) recorded. It thrives on sheltered and moist sites.

---

p.79 **Cilician Fir** *Abies cilicica*

Description: Evergreen tree to 30 m (100 ft) by 70 cm (2.3 ft) bole diameter.
Crown Conical when young, becoming columnar conic. *Bark* Dark grey, smooth but becoming scaly and fissured with age. *Shoot* Greenish brown to brown in first winter, later pale brown, hairless or faintly hairy at first. *Buds* Ovoid-conical, acute, light brown, non-resinous or lightly resinous, 5 mm (0.2 in). *Foliage* Widely parted beneath the shoot or flat, spreading and pointing forwards at the sides with the upper ranks shorter and pointing forwards and along the shoot, with either a narrow parting or with some crossing over; leaves linear, apex rounded to bluntly pointed, lustrous dark green above without stomata (or a few in a spot at the tip), beneath with whitish-green waxy bands of stomata and an equally prominent pale green midrib, 2.5–4.5 cm × 1.5–2 mm (1–1.8 × 0.1 in); crushed foliage with parsley resinous scent. *Flowers* On last season's shoots in late spring; male cones yellow, 1–1.5 cm (0.4–0.6 in). *Fruit* Cylindrical with included bracts, ripening from yellow-green to pale brown, 16–20 cm (6.3–8 in), rarely to 30 cm (12 in), by 4–6 cm (1.6–2.4 in); rachis conical; scales fan-shaped, 3–4 cm (1.2–1.6 in), hairy on the exposed portions, bract scales around half the length of the seed scales.
Range: Southeast Turkey from the Taurus Mountains to northwest Syria and into the Lebanon.
Habitat: Cultivated in Europe as an ornamental, occurring in the wild on calcareous soils in mountain districts with wet winters and dry summers.

Varieties: Ssp. *isaurica* occurs in the Isaurian Taurus on Turkey's south coast to the west of the main range. It differs in the hairless branches and resinous buds but has been included within the general description above.

This tree is related to *A. nordmanniana* in the foliage, although the cone is more similar to *A. pinsapo* and *A. numidica* in the hidden bracts. It has the largest cones of any Silver Fir.

p.82 **White Fir** *Abies concolor*

Description: Evergreen tree 15–30 m (50–100 ft) with a bole diameter of up to 1.2 m (4 ft).
Crown Conical when young, becoming columnar in old trees, with whorled and spaced branches. *Bark* Light to dark grey and smooth with resin blisters in young trees, but becoming thick, deeply furrowed and corky near the base on old trees.
Shoot Olive-green to olive-brown in first winter, turning pale brown or grey subsequently, hairless, slender.
Buds Globose, or conical on vigorous shoots, whitish brown, thickly encrusted with resin, 4 mm (0.2 in). *Foliage* Lax, not densely set, with the leaves all curved upwards and bowed, none below the shoot; leaves flat, linear, soft, apex rounded, bluntly pointed or notched, grey-green to blue grey-green, concolorous, i.e. much the same colour on both surfaces, with one broad waxy band of stomata above and two beneath, 4–6 cm × 2 mm (1.6–2.4 × 0.1 in); crushed foliage with strong lemon verbena scent. *Flowers* On last season's growths in late spring; male cones red, 1–2 cm (0.4–0.8 in); female cones erect on upper tiers of branches. *Fruit* Cylindrical or elliptic with hidden bract scales, variously coloured from green, olive-green, yellow to pale blue, ripening in autumn to brown, 7–13 cm × 3–4.5 cm (2.8–5.1 × 1.2–1.8 in); rachis narrow conical; scales fan-shaped, to 3.5 cm (1.4 in) wide, exposed part finely hairy, bract scales small.

Range: Western USA from Utah, Arizona, Nevada and New Mexico into northern Mexico with the variety or related species in California.

Habitat: Cultivated as an ornamental in Europe, in the wild forming mixed or pure stands on a wide range of site types.

Varieties: Several cultivars selected for the stronger colour of the foliage are often grown, including 'Candicans', with more silvery white foliage, and 'Violacea', with bright bluish-white leaves.

Similar species: **Low's Fir** is a related taxon. This is variously treated as a species, *A. lowiana* or as a variety of *A. concolor* var. *lowiana*. It comes from California and southwest Oregon. It differs in the foliage which is in flat ranks either side of the shoot. The ranks are either spreading or erect with a wide V- or U-groove. The leaves are usually weakly notched, have somewhat fewer stomata above (five to nine rows, cf. seven to eighteen in *A. concolor*) and the central portion of the leaf on the upper surface is not glaucous. The bark is either black, rough and shallowly fissured or brown and corky with deep fissures. This entity is commoner in cultivation than White Fir and makes a larger tree, to 50 m × 1.5 m (165 × 5 ft). It is intermediate between White Fir and Grand Fir.

This fir makes an attractive tree when well grown with its glaucous grey or bluish foliage. The thin bark gives no protection against forest fires, which are common in its native habitat. Whereas other trees, such as *Sequoiadendron*, have protective thick barks, White Fir relies upon its fecundity to ensure sufficient regeneration.

---

p.87 **Delavay Fir** *Abies delavayi*

Description: Evergreen tree 10–15 m (33–50 ft) in height with a bole diameter of up to 50 cm 1.6 ft.
Crown Conical when young with spaced whorled branches, old trees columnar, with flat tops; branches in section ellipsoid, not

round, with the width smaller than the height, lateral branches with foliage rise above the slightly ascending or horizontal primary branches. *Bark* Grey, smooth but developing red-brown fissures and becoming platy at the base of the bole. *Shoot* Red-brown or orange-brown in first winter, becoming maroon or dark red-brown with age, usually hairless but sometime with blackish hairs in grooves, somewhat shiny, stout with a thick bark. *Buds* Globular or ovoid conic (but massed male cone buds on underside of shoot conic), orange green-brown or red-brown, thickly encrusted with resin which may become whitish over winter, to 7 mm (0.3 in); where there are two side buds with a terminal bud, the side buds are raised above the terminal one. *Foliage* Radial around the shoot but longer beneath and decreasing to the shortest leaves above the shoot, more or less perpendicular to the shoot but those beneath in particular are reverse S-shaped – at base pressed against the shoot then curving away and finally curving forwards, sprays bright to mid green above without stomata, bright silvery white beneath due to the waxy covering over the stomatal bands; leaves linear with a groove and no stomata above, apex rounded, notched, margins down curved, which with the prominent midrib gives an m-shape in fresh cross-section and ∞ when dried, 1.5–3.5 cm × 1–2 mm (0.6–1.4 × 0.1 in); crushed foliage with a strong and distinctive resin scent. *Flowers* On previous season's growth in early summer; male cones violet-blue, expanding to 2.5–3 cm (1–1.2 in) and releasing yellow pollen; female cones on uppermost branches, erect, violet-purple. *Fruit* Ovoid or cylindrical with a dimpled apex and projecting bracts, violet-blue, ripening to brown in first autumn and disintegrating to release the seeds and bracts, leaving the cylindro-conic erect rachis, 6–10 cm × 3.5–5 cm (2.4–4 × 1.4–2 in); scales wedge-shaped with a rounded apex, 1.5–2.5 cm (0.6–1 in) in width, bract scales projecting, erect or reflexed, cusp slender, to 6 mm (0.25 in).

Range: West Yunnan, China to southeast Tibet, across northern Burma and also in northern Vietnam.

Habitat: Cultivated in Europe as an ornamental, in the wild occurring in moist montane forests as the dominant tree, extending to the treeline.

Varieties: The trees referred to this species as varieties in older books are now accepted as species (*see A. fabri, A. forrestii*). Var. *nukiangensis* has cylindrical cones with included bract scales and longer male cones. At least some of the Burmese plants in cultivation belong to this variety.

This is most distinctive in the way the leaf margins are curved down in fresh material and close together to form an infinity sign shape (∞) in dried material. The cones are attractively displayed against the fresh green foliage, especially when seen from above, whilst in early summer the male cones can be very attractive.

p.87 **Sikkim Fir** *Abies densa*

Description: Evergreen tree to 30 m (100 ft) with a bole diameter to 1.5 m (5 ft).
Crown Conical in young trees, later columnar, often with a flat top, with the side branches rising above the level of the main branches. *Bark* Grey, smooth in young trees, in old ones becoming scaly. *Shoot* Pale to fawn-brown in first winter, becoming darker and somewhat shiny, often paler above the shoot, with red-brown hairs in grooves, moderately stout. *Buds* Rounded conic to ovoid, resinous, brown to red-brown, to 5 mm (0.2 in). *Foliage* Parted beneath with the side leaves drooping, less often radial, above the shoot spreading slightly forwards and decreasing in length in several ranks with a wide parting; leaves linear, taper to rounded notched apex, upper surface deep

glossy green without stomata, beneath with two silvery bands of waxy stomata, margins slightly curved down, 2–4 cm × 1.5–2 mm (0.8–1.6 × 0.1 in); crushed foliage with a somewhat citrus resin smell. *Flowers* On previous season's shoots in early summer; male cones violet, 2 cm (0.8 in); female cones ovoid, 1 cm (0.4 in), violet-purple. *Fruit* Cylindrical with projecting bracts, violet-blue, ripening in late autumn to brown, 8–10 cm × 4–4.5 cm (3.1–4 × 1.6–1.8 in); rachis cylindro-conical; scales fan-shaped, 2–2.5 cm (0.8–1 in) in width, exposed portion hairy, bract scales projecting with a short fragile cusp.

Range: Northeast Nepal across Sikkim and Bhutan to northeast India.

Habitat: Cultivated in Europe as an ornamental, in the wild occurring in pure forests up to the treeline.

Synonyms: *A. spectabilis* var. *densa.*

This tree has been confused with *A. spectabilis* from which it differs in the smaller cones with projecting bracts (and usually a more vivid violet-blue colour), the brownish twigs, the leaves with a rolled or recurved margin and the more scaly bark. It occurs along the southern flank of the Himalayan mountains in areas noted for the high monsoon rainfall, and the rolled margin of the leaf is probably a water-shedding device.

---

p.87 **Faber Fir** *Abies fabri*

Description: Evergreen tree 15–20 m (50–65 ft) with a bole to 60 cm (2 ft) in diameter. *Crown* Conical in young trees, columnar to broad columnar with age, often with a flat top; branches spreading and rising slightly with the laterals rising above the main branches. *Bark* Grey, smooth in young trees, developing red-brown fissures and scaly plates. *Shoot* Pale brown or fawn-brown in first winter, then paler and rough in the third or fourth years, hairless or with short red-brown hairs, stout. *Buds* Ovoid, rounded at tip, purplish brown with a thick coat of whitish resin, to 6 mm (0.25 in). *Foliage* Arrangement beneath the shoot parted or with a few leaves pointing forwards, at the side spreading at a wide angle, above the shoot shorter with a narrow parting and a flat plateau; leaves linear, rounded or squarish notched, occasionally pointed, upper surface dark glossy green without stomata, underside with two narrow bright silver bands of waxy stomata and dark green recurved margins and a prominent midrib, 1.5–2.5 cm × 2–2.5 mm (0.6–1 × 0.8–1 in). *Flowers* On previous season's growths in early summer; male cones violet or purple with yellow pollen, 2–3.5 cm (0.8–1.4 in). *Fruit* Broad cylindrical or ovoid, with projecting bracts, violet, ripening to brown, 5–9 cm × 4–4.5 cm (2–3.5 × 1.6–1.8 in); rachis spindle-shaped; scales fan-shaped, to 2 cm (0.8 in), bracts projecting with tip and slender cusp.

Range: Central west Sichuan, China.

Habitat: Cultivated in Europe as an ornamental, in the wild forming extensive forests.

Varieties: Ssp. *minensis* (or *A. minensis* (also called *A. faxoniana* misapplied) differs in the honey-coloured shoots with ovoid purplish buds and foliage which is widely parted beneath the shoot and widely parted and shorter forward-pointing leaves above; the leaves are nearly flat beneath, with whitish-green stomatal bands beneath. It occurs in northern west Sichuan in areas drier than *A. fabri*. At the two extremes, the two taxa are very different but there are intermediates where their ranges meet in west Sichuan.

Synonyms: *A. delavayi* var. *fabri*.

This tree shares the curved down leaf margins and prominent midrib with only two other species. From *A. densa* it is separated by the smaller cones and less grooved and hairy shoots, whilst *A. delavayi* has much more rolled margins and longer, bright green leaves with erect bracts.

p.88   **Farges Fir**   *Abies fargesii*

Description: Evergreen tree to 15–20 m (50–65 ft) with
a bole diameter of up to 50 cm (1.6 ft).
Crown Conical on young trees, becoming
columnar with pendent branches which are
upturned or erect at the tips. *Bark* Buff-
brown, finely flaky in small curls but not
peeling or exfoliating. *Shoot* Purple in the
first winter, becoming red-brown, strong
shoots moderately stout and hairless, weak
shoots red-brown hairy. *Buds* Conical, apex
rounded, resinous, purple or purple-brown,
5 mm (0.2 in). *Foliage* Spreading either
side of the shoot and slightly forwards
below, those above the shoot gradually
becoming more forward pointing as they
become more erect and decrease in size;
leaves linear, apex rounded, notched or
pointed (on strong shoots in the upper
crown all three tips can be found), dark
glossy green above without stomata or with
just a few in a spot at the leaf tip, below
with two silvery white waxy stomatal bands,
1–2.5 cm × 2–2.5 mm (0.4–1 × 0.1 in);
crushed foliage with resinous fishy smell.
Flowers On previous season's growths in
early summer; male cones violet-purple,
2.5 cm (1 in). *Fruit* Ovoid or oblong-ovoid
with projecting bracts, rich purple, ripening
in first autumn to brown, 4–7 cm ×
2.5–3.5 cm (1.6–2.8 × 1–1.4 in); rachis
spindle-shaped; scales fan-shaped, to 2 cm
(0.8 in) in width, bract scales projecting
with a straight or recurved narrow cusp.

Range: West China from Shaanxi and Hubei across
to Gansu and northwest Sichuan.

Habitat: Cultivated in Europe as an ornamental, in
the wild forming extensive montane forests.

Varieties: Var. *faxoniana* differs in the hairier brown
or red-brown shoots. It is found in
northwest Sichuan and southern Gansu,
along with the typical form and may not be
worth distinguishing. The name *faxoniana*
has been misapplied to the tree here listed
as *A. fabri* ssp. *minensis*. Another variety is
var. *tieghemii* from Hubei and Shaanxi,
which has foliage more parted above and
slightly longer, to 3.5 cm (1.4 in).

Synonyms: *A. sutchuenensis, A. fargesii* var. *sutchuenensis.*

This is one of the most attractive firs for its neat habit, purple shoots and cones and foliage which is dark glossy green on the upper surface and bright silvery white beneath. The branch tips often become erect, forming competing leaders.

---

p.84 **Momi Fir** *Abies firma*

Description: Evergreen tree 20–30 m (65–100 ft) with bole diameter of up to 1 m (3.3 ft).
Crown Broad conic, becoming domed in old age, with spaced tiered branches.
Bark Pink-grey and smooth with resin blisters in young trees, becoming thick, corky and ridged in old trees. *Shoot* Olive-brown in first winter, later grey-brown or yellowish brown, hairless, slender.
Buds Conical or ovoid conical, resinous, brown. *Foliage* Dense on side branches which rise above the level of the main laterals; leaves arranged parted either side of the shoot below and either parted above or curving upwards, with or without a V-groove between the two sides; mid yellowish green and sub-shiny above with a few stomata in a spot near the apex; whitish green along the two waxy stomatal bands below; apex on mature trees rounded and bluntly pointed or deeply notched, but on young trees and on epicormic (water) shoots of old trees with two bony divergent spines (bifid); leaves linear but slightly wider in middle, flattened, 1.5–2.5 cm (0.6–1 in) (to 5 cm (2 in) on young trees) by 2–4 mm (0.1–0.2 in); crushed foliage with a faint to mild resin scent. *Flowers* On previous season's shoots in late spring; male cones pendulous, 2–3 cm (0.8–1.2 in), yellow; female cones erect on branches in upper crown. *Fruit* Ovoid-conical with projecting reflexed bracts especially at the base of the cone, apex rounded pointed, yellow-green, maturing in first autumn to yellow-brown, 8–15 cm × 3–5 cm (3.1–6 × 1.2–2 in); rachis narrow conical; scales

broad fan-shaped, about 3 cm (1.2 in) wide, bracts with a triangular yellow or yellow-green cusp.

Range: Japan from central Honshu south to Kyushu and Shikoku.

Habitat: Cultivated as an ornamental in Europe, in the wild normally occurring as a component of mixed coniferous/deciduous forest.

Synonyms: *A. bifida.*

The variation between the rather short leaves of mature trees and the bifid leaves of young trees or on watershoot growths on the bole of older trees is very marked. It grows on a wide range of sites but is susceptible to spring frost damage.

p.86   **Forrest Fir** *Abies forrestii*

Description: Evergreen tree 10–25 m (33–80 ft) with a bole diameter to 70 cm (2.3 ft).
Crown Conical with spaced whorled branches when young, becoming columnar and denser, often with a flat top; branches slightly ascending with the laterals rising above the level of the branch.
Bark Brown-grey, smooth in young trees, in old ones becoming cracked into rectangular plates with red-brown fissures or into small scales. *Shoot* Light red-brown or purplish brown in first winter, becoming redder red-brown and then brown in succeeding seasons, hairless or lightly hairy in lines, moderately stout to stout with a thick phloem/bark over the wood.
Buds Globose (rarely conical or ovoid), red-brown, very thickly encrusted with resin which usually clouds to white as it absorbs water over winter and often obliterates the bud scales, variable in size to 1 cm (0.4 in); male cone buds conical, bluntly pointed, 7 mm (0.3 in). *Foliage* Radial around the shoot and more or less perpendicular, the longest leaves being those below which curve down beneath the shoot, those rising above the shoot shortest and form a flat plateau which may include a V-parting or

in young trees are more parted; leaves linear, apex rounded, notched, upper surface deep glossy green without stomata, lower surface with two white to silver waxy bands of stomata and a narrow green midrib, 1.2–3.5 cm × 2.5 mm (0.5–1.4 × 0.1 in); crushed foliage with a faint to strong orangey resin scent. *Flowers* On previous season's shoots in early summer; male cones violet-purple with yellow pollen, to 4 cm (1.6 in), clustered in the middle portion on the underside of shoots; female cones violet-blue, erect on strong branches. *Fruit* Barrel-shaped (broad ovoid-oblong) to short cylindrical, with projecting bracts, ripens from violet-blue to brown over the first autumn and may persist for some weeks before disintegrating to release the seeds, 8–15 × 4–7 cm (3.1–6 × 1.6–2.8 in); rachis spindle-shaped or, less often, cylindro-conical; scales fan-shaped, to 2 cm (0.8 in) with the exposed portion coarsely hairy, bract scale with a broad rounded blade and a slender cusp to 1 cm (0.4 in), both of which are projecting.

Range: Northwest Yunnan, extending at least as some of the varieties listed below in southern Sichuan and northeast Yunnan, and into northwest Burma and southeast Tibet.

Habitat: Cultivated in Europe as an ornamental, in the wild occurring in cool mountain forests in relatively dry zones.

Varieties: Var. *smithii* has shoots which are densely rusty pubescent and occurs at higher altitudes. It is often called *A. georgei* (or *A. delavayi* var. *georgei*) but this has very different bract scales to the cones and is not in cultivation. Var. *ferreana* also has densely hairy shoots but the cones are smaller, more ovoid and usually less than 9 cm (3.5 in). It occurs into Sichuan and across to southeast Tibet.

Synonyms: *A. delavayi* var. *forrestii*.

This makes an attractive tree for the silvery foliage and the bright violet-blue cones, which are colourful from early summer through to ripening in late autumn and beyond. It will grow on a wide variety of sites, although the best trees are found in areas with cool and not too dry summers. It is related to *A. delavayi* but easily separated by the dark green leaves which are flat below without the curved down margins and are much broader, and the globose buds. From *A. fabri*, the shoot colour and radial leaf arrangement provide the best characters.

p.93 **Fraser Fir** *Abies fraseri*

Description: Evergreen tree 10–15 m (33–50 ft) with a bole diameter to 30 cm (1 ft).
Crown Narrow conical, but may become broader with age. *Bark* Grey or brown, smooth with resin blisters in young trees, becoming fissured and scaly. *Shoot* Grey-brown or yellow-brown, with pale hairs in grooves, becoming brown or red-brown. *Buds* Rounded to globose, bluntly pointed and thickly encrusted with purple or whitish resin, to 70 cm (2.3 ft).
Foliage Widely parted below the shoot, spreading forwards at the sides and becoming more curved upwards above with a narrow parting; leaves linear, apex rounded to a notched tip, mid to dark green above with an incomplete band of waxy white dots of stomata in the groove above, beneath with two pale silvery or greenish-white waxy bands of stomata and a pale green midrib, 1.2–2.6 cm × 1.5–2 mm (0.5–1 × 0.1 in); crushed foliage strongly resin scented. *Flowers* On previous season's shoots in early summer; male cones yellow and red, 1 cm (0.4 in).
Fruit Cylindrical with projecting and reflexed yellow-green bracts, ripening from green or dark purple to brown in first autumn, 4–6 × 2.5–4 cm (1.6–2.4 × 1–1.6 in); rachis conical; scales broad fan-shaped, hairy on the exposed portion, 1–1.5 cm (0.4–0.6 in) in width.

Range: Southern Appalachians from southwest Virginia, western North Carolina and eastern Tennessee.

Habitat: Cultivated in Europe as an ornamental, in the wild forming forests on ridges and mountain tops, usually mixed with *Picea rubens* and other trees.

Initially a fast-growing tree, this is not long lived in cultivation. It is related to *A. balsamea* but can be distinguished by the cones with their broad projecting and reflexed bract scales. The buds are larger, and more softly resinous.

p.82 **Grand Fir** or **Giant Fir** *Abies grandis*

Description: Evergreen tree 20–60 m (65–200 ft) with a bole diameter of up to 2 m (6.6 ft). *Crown* Narrow conical when young, becoming columnar in old trees with short spreading branches and often a flat ragged top once it emerges above the surrounding trees. *Bark* Brownish grey and smooth with resin blisters in young trees, in old trees becoming duller and cracked into small square plates. *Shoot* Olive-green in the first winter, becoming brown or dark reddish brown in succeeding years, covered with very short hairs. *Buds* Globose or rounded conical, brown or purple, encrusted with resin which slowly clouds and becomes white, to 3 mm (0.1 in). *Foliage* Leaves below the shoot widely parted and either at 90 degrees or forwards at up to 45 degrees, those above the shoot half as long and rising and forwards at 45 degrees, giving a very wide to wide parting, on shaded shoots often fully pectinate; leaves linear, with a rounded notched apex, dark lustrous green above without stomata, below with two waxy white or greenish white bands of stomata and a light green midrib, 2–6 cm × 2 mm (0.8–2.4 × 0.1 in); crushed foliage with a fruity orange or aniseed aroma. *Flowers* On previous season's growths in late spring; male cones yellow-green, to 1.8 cm (0.7 in). *Fruit* Cylindrical or cylindrical-elliptic with included bracts scales, green during the growing season but ripening in the first autumn to grey-brown, 7–12 × 3–4 cm (2.8–4.7 × 1.2–1.6 in); rachis conical,

slender; scales fan-shaped, to 3 cm (1.2 in)
in width, hairy on the exposed portion,
with bract scale half length of seed scale.

Range: Vancouver Island south along the coastal
ranges to northern California, inland in the
Cascade Mountains and on the east side of
the Rocky Mountains in southeast British
Columbia to northern Idaho.

Habitat: Cultivated in Europe as an ornamental and
in forestry, in the wild occurring in valleys
and on cool moist mountain slopes.

Varieties: None recorded, but *A. concolor* var. *lowiana*
may be the product of introgression
(hybridization) with genes from *A. grandis*.

This is a very fast growing tree, especially
in the origins from Washington and
Oregon west of the Cascade Mountains.
Origins from the inland part of its range are
much slower growing. It is used in forestry,
where it is a prodigious volume producer
but the timber is light and not of the first
quality. As an amenity tree, it is usually the
tallest tree, emerging above surrounding
plants and then suffering in the increased
wind exposure. The combination of
pectinate or widely spreading foliage on
slender shoots and the globose or conical
very small buds quickly distinguish it.

p.84 Manchurian Fir or Needle Fir
Abies holophylla

Description: Evergreen tree 15–20 m (50–65 ft) with a
bole to 60 cm (2 ft) in diameter.
Crown Conical when young, becoming
columnar in old trees. *Bark* Grey or grey-
brown in young trees, becoming fissured
and platy in old trees, although some trees
develop a buff-coloured bark which
exfoliates in thin papery scales.
Shoot Buff-brown or pink-brown in first
winter, becoming straw coloured in later
years, hairless, stout. *Buds* Ovoid-conic,
pointed, pale brown with thick whitish
resin, 6 mm (0.25 in). *Foliage* On shoots
in full light, all leaves curve upwards
(except a few beneath direct along the

shoot) with a flat plateau along the top of the shoot, but in shade parted above and below; leaves linear and tapered to a sharp bony point, curved, above glossy yellow-green without stomata, below with two pale yellow-green bands of stomata which are scarcely distinguishable from the rest of the leaf, 2–4.5 cm × 2.5 mm (0.8–1.8 × 0.1 in) crushed foliage scentless, although scraped bark still has a resin scent. *Flowers* On previous season's shoots in late spring; male cones 1–1.5 cm (0.4–0.6 in), yellow. *Fruit* Cylindrical with included bracts and a bluntly pointed or truncate apex, green during the growing season, ripening brown, 9–14 × 3–4.5 cm (3.5–5.5 × 1.2–1.8 in); rachis conical; scales fan-shaped, exposed portion hairy, to 3 cm (1.2 in) in width.

Range: Korea, northeast China and adjacent Pacific Russia.

Habitat: Cultivated in Europe as an ornamental, in the wild occurring in a region with wet summers and cold arid winters, forming mixed forest.

This tree has leaves which are virtually always entire with a needle-like point, except on the occasional epicormic shoot. The form with flaky bark does not have quite the quality of the bark of *A. squamata*, although is interesting and makes a larger tree.

p.85 **Nikko Fir** *Abies homolepis*

Description: Evergreen tree to 25 m (80 ft) with a bole to 1 m (3.3 ft) in diameter.
Crown Conical, becoming broad conical or columnar with wide-spreading branches.
Bark Grey or grey-pink, smooth but finely flaky, in old trees broken into scaly plates.
Shoot White, straw or pale brown, becoming yellow-brown, hairless and deeply ridged, moderately slender.
Buds Ovoid, rounded to conic, dark brown with thick resin which clouds to white, to 5 mm (0.2 in); male cone buds globose, resinous. *Foliage* Widely parted beneath

or somewhat radial, at sides spreading perpendicular, above rising or somewhat recurved with a wide parting; leaves linear, apex rounded, pointed or notched, 1.5–3.5 cm × 2 mm (0.6–1.4 × 0.1 in); crushed foliage with a sweet minty resin scent. *Flowers* On last season's shoots in early summer; male cones yellow.
Fruit Oblong-cylindrical, rounded at both ends, with included bracts, violet-blue, ripening to brown, 7–12 × 2.5–3.5 cm (2.8–4.7 × 1–1.4 in); rachis narrow conical; scales fan-shaped, 2.3–2.5 cm (0.8–1 in) wide, bract scales half length of seed scale.

Range: Southern Japan from Honshu and Shikoku.
Habitat: Cultivated in Europe as an ornamental, in Japan growing in mountain forests.
Synonyms: *A. brachyphylla.*

This tree carries the violet cones throughout the crown, whereas in most other silver firs they are restricted to the upper whorls of branches. It is tolerant of a wide range of sites.

---

p.92 **Taiwan Fir** *Abies kawakamii*

Description: Evergreen tree to 15 m (50 ft) with a bole diameter of up to 60 cm (2 ft).
Crown Conical in young trees but soon broad conical with an open habit and often with a flat top; branches ascending.
Bark Bright grey, becoming pink or buff-grey, thick and corky, and fissuring into grey-brown plates. *Shoot* Yellow-brown or orange-brown and shiny in first winter with red-brown hairs in lines, becoming darker brown and matt with blackish hairs, slender. *Buds* Conical or ovoid-conical, purple, resinous, to 4 mm (0.2 in). *Foliage* Generally pointing forwards at about 45 degrees to the shoot, beneath laxer, upper leaves shorter and more curved upwards, with usually a narrow V-parting; leaves linear, rounded notched at apex, dark glossy green, without stomata above or stomata

restricted to a small spot near the apex, beneath with two whitish to pale green bands of stomata and a light green midrib, 1.5–3 cm × 1 mm (0.6–1.2 × 0.1 in); crushed foliage with a fishy scent.
Flowers On previous season's shoots in early summer; male cones yellow, to 2 cm (0.8 in). *Fruit* Ovoid-cylindrical, with a rounded or pointed apex and hidden bracts, violet, ripening in the first autumn to brown, 7–9 × 2.5–4 cm (2.8–3.5 × 1–1.6 in); rachis cylindro-conical or narrowly spindle-shaped; scales fan-shaped, 2–2.5 cm (0.8–1 in), bract scales half to three-quarters length of seed scale.

Range: Taiwan in the high mountains in the centre and north.

Habitat: Cultivated in Europe as an ornamental, in Taiwan occurring in moist montane forest, often in pure stands.

Synonyms: *A. mariesii* var. *kawakamii*.

This tree shares the thick corky bark with *A. lasiocarpa* var. *arizonica*. It grows on the Tropic of Cancer.

p.91 **Korean Fir** *Abies koreana*

Description: Evergreen tree to 10 m (33 ft) with a bole diameter of up to 30 cm (1 ft).
Crown Conical or broad conical, with tiered slightly ascending branches. *Bark* Light grey with a purple or olive tinge, smooth with resin blisters when young, at the base fissuring in old trees into grey-black plates. *Shoot* Fawn, initially shiny, either hairless or with grey or brown hairs, becoming greyer or browner with age, slender. *Buds* Globular, purple with a thick encrustation of whitish resin, 3 mm (0.1 in); female cone buds on top of last season's shoots, conical, 7 mm (0.3 in), otherwise similar. *Foliage* Shoots spaced, leaves radial and perpendicular around the shoot but often thinner below, spaced; leaves slightly broader towards the apex or from the middle, apex rounded notched, on very vigorous shoots may be acute, upper

surface dark shiny green without stomata, lower surface with two broad waxy silver bands of stomata, 1–2 cm × 2–2.5 mm (0.4–0.8 × 0.1 in); crushed foliage with a pleasant resinous aroma. *Flowers* On last season's shoots in early summer; male cones yellow and scarlet or green, 1 cm (0.4 in); female cones erect, purple, red or green-yellow, cylindrical, 1–2 cm (0.4–0.8 in), often clustered on the shoots and carried on small trees. *Fruit* Cylindrical with a rounded or nipple-like tip and projecting bracts, 5–7 × 2.5 cm (2–2.8 × 1 in) wide, ripen in first autumn from purple or greenish purple (rarely yellow-green) to bright light brown; rachis narrow conical, persistent on the shoot; scales fan-shaped, 1.5 cm (0.6 in) in width, bracts just projecting, reflexed, with a short cusp.

Range: Southern Korea and the offshore island of Cheju (Qualpert).

Habitat: Cultivated in Europe as an ornamental, in the wild restricted to subalpine forests.

Varieties: No botanical varieties. Some dwarf or slow growing cultivars are occasionally grown, such as 'Horstmann's Silver' in which the leaves are twisted and curled so as to reveal the silvery underside.

Similar species: **Shikoku Fir** *A. sikokiana* (syn. *A. veitchii* var. *sikokiana*), from the Japanese Island of Shikoku, is a related species which is occasionally cultivated. It is somewhat intermediate between *A. koreana* and *A. veitchii*. It has olive-brown shoots which have dark brown or blackish hairs, globular purple-brown resinous (but not as thickly and not becoming white) buds, narrower leaves 1.5–2 mm (0.1 in) which are more whitish than silver and smaller narrower cones 3–5 × 1.5–2 cm (1.2–2 × 0.6–0.8 in).

This small tree is widely planted as it will produce the attractive cones at an early stage, often on plants less than a metre in height, whilst the silvery underside to the foliage is a year-round feature. It tolerates a wide range of sites, but tends to be short lived.

p.93 **Subalpine Fir** *Abies lasiocarpa*

Description: Evergreen tree 10–20 m (33–65 ft) with a
bole diameter up to 60 cm (2 ft).
Crown Conical, spire-like or columnar in
old trees. *Bark* Dark grey and smooth
with resin blisters in young trees,
ultimately fissured and scaly. *Shoot* Pale
fawn or grey with rust or fawn hairs,
moderately stout but one- and two-year-
old shoots are pliable. *Buds* Globose or
conical, brown but thickly encrusted with
resin, 4 mm (0.2 in). *Foliage* Spreading
widely beneath the shoot, rising above the
shoot at 90 degrees, spaced out; leaves dark
green to bluish grey-green, with a diffuse
band of stomata above and two greenish-
white bands beneath, linear, apex blunt or
notched, 2–4.5 cm × 1.5–2 mm (0.8–1.6 ×
0.1 in); crushed foliage with a pungent
resinous almondy scent. *Flowers* On
previous season's shoots in early summer;
male cones 1.5–2 cm (0.6–0.8 in), purple
with yellow pollen; female cones erect,
purple, on uppermost branches.
Fruit Cylindrical with hidden bracts,
tapered to both ends, dark purple but
ripening brown, 7–10 × 2.5–3.5 cm
(2.8–4 × 1–1.5 in); rachis narrow
conical; scales very yellow-brown hairy on
the exposed portion, 1.3–2.3 cm
(0.5–0.9 in) wide, bract scale shorter than
seed scale.

Range: Western North America in coastal
subalpine forests from Alaska to California,
but see *A. bifolia* below.

Habitat: Cultivated as an ornamental in northern
Europe, in the wild forming extensive
subalpine forests.

Varieties: Var. *arizonica* or the Corkbark Fir is found
at the south of the range in Arizona to
Colorado. It has bluer foliage, smaller cones
and a thick corky white-grey bark. It may
be better placed under *A. bifolia*. It has
given a slow growing form, 'Compacta',
which is often planted and will eventually
make an ovoid tree to 5 m (16 ft).

Similar species: *A. bifolia* (syn. *A. subalpina*) has
traditionally been considered a synonym of

A. lasiocarpa. However, recent research has indicated that it represents a distinct taxon. The best distinguishing characters are in the colour on the bark of the scars from freshly fallen leaves, which in *A. bifolia* are tan coloured but in *A. lasiocarpa* are red, and in the shape of the basal scales of the buds (forming an isosceles triangle and with entire margins in *A. bifolia*, but forming an equilateral triangle with crenate or dentate margins in *A. lasiocarpa*), with further separating data provided by resin and wood anatomy analyses. It is native to the continental subalpine forests from the eastern Yukon south to northern Mexico along the Rocky Mountains. Hybrids with *A. lasiocarpa* are reported where the two meet in a band from central Yukon to northern Washington.

The species is better suited to continental climates, whereas in Britain it is often caught by spring frosts. The lower branches in its native habit are often bent down by snow and roots.

p.81 **Red Fir** *Abies magnifica*

Description: Evergreen tree to 30 m (100 ft) with a stout bole, to 1 m (3.3 ft) in diameter.
Crown Columnar with a conical apex, and short spreading branches. *Bark* Grey and purple in young trees with resin blisters, quickly fissuring to show red-brown, and becoming rough. *Shoot* Red-brown or purple-brown, densely hairy, becoming grey-brown or brown with age, hidden beneath the adpressed leaves from above, stout. *Buds* Globose, red-brown and encrusted in resin which clouds to white, 2–3 mm (0.1 in); male cone buds lumpy, 5 mm (0.2 in). *Foliage* Widely parted beneath the shoot and either flat or down curved, side leaves spreading perpendicular or forwards, upper leaves shorter, pressed against the shoot at base and curved erect; on very strong shoots, all the leaves are twisted at the base and

curved upwards more or less vertically above the shoot; leaves four-sided or rhombic in section (without a narrow groove as in Noble Fir), stiff, apex rounded to a slender sharp bony point, waxy bands of stomata on all four sides giving the leaves a bluish-grey to glaucous grey colour, 1.5–3.5 cm (0.6–1.4 in), rarely to 4 cm (1.6 in), by 2 mm (0.1 in); crushed foliage with an orange or turpentine smell. *Flowers* On previous season's shoots in late spring; male 1.5–2 cm (0.6–0.8 in), scarlet. *Fruit* Broad conical or barrel-shaped with hidden bracts, massive, golden-green or purple-green, ripening in first autumn to yellow-brown or brown, 15–20 × 7–10 cm (6–8 × 2.8–4 in); rachis narrow conic; scales fan-shaped, 3–4 cm (1.2–1.6 in) in width with the exposed portion covered in fine yellow-brown hairs, bract scales somewhat shorter than seed scale.

Range: Southwest Oregon and northwest California and south along the Sierra Nevada to extreme western Nevada.

Habitat: Cultivated in Europe as an ornamental, in the wild occurring on high mountain slopes where the summers are dry and most precipitation is in the form of snow.

Varieties: Selection of the most glaucous foliage forms have been named 'Glauca'. Shasta red fir, var. *shastensis*, is a form with the foliage of *A. magnifica* in which the cones have the bract scales projecting and reflexed, as in *A. procera* but only covering around half the cone surface. This occurs at the northern end of the range of *A. magnifica* and just within the range of *A. procera*. It may be the result of introgression from *A. procera* (i.e. it may have some genes from *A. procera* from past hybridization) but has smaller cones, to only 14 cm (5.7 in), than both *A. magnifica* and *A. procera*.

The tree very quickly makes a stout bole. It is attractive in the glaucous foliage but the mammoth cones are rarely seen in cultivation. The common name derives from the red-brown fissures in the bark.

p.90 **Maries Fir** *Abies mariesii*

Description: Evergreen tree 15–25 m (50–80 ft) with a bole diameter to 70 cm (2.3 ft).
Crown Conical when young, becoming columnar. *Bark* Silvery grey and smooth in young trees, becoming grey and scaly at the base. *Shoot* Covered with rusty brown, pink-brown or orange hairs for one to three years, then dull grey-brown. *Buds* Globose with a thick encrustation of clouded white or milky resin, 2.5 mm (0.1 in). *Foliage* In three or four ranks of decreasing length, widely parted beneath the shoot, spreading or slightly forwards at the sides and arching forwards and curved over to either side of the shoot above, with an indistinct parting; leaves linear, apex rounded, notched, tapers to yellowish base, light glossy green without stomata above, milky white from two wide waxy bands of stomata below, 0.8–2.2 cm × 1.5–2.5 mm (0.3–0.9 × 0.1 in); crushed foliage with a strong resin scent. *Flowers* On previous season's shoots in early summer; male cones yellow, expanding from 1.5–2 × 4–6 cm (0.6–0.8 × 1.6–2.4 in). *Fruit* Ovoid or ovoid-oblong with hidden bracts, dark purple when growing, ripening in the first autumn to blackish purple, apex bluntly pointed, 4–10 × 2–4.5 cm (1.6–4 × 0.8–1.8 in); rachis conical; scales 2–2.5 cm (0.8–1 in) wide.

Range: Northern and central Honshu, Japan.

Habitat: Cultivated in Europe as an ornamental, in the wild occurring on the upper slopes of high mountains, especially on the wetter western side facing the Sea of Japan.

This makes a neat tree with dense foliage. It is closely related to *A. amabilis* from the opposite side of the Pacific, differing in the short and more slender shoots with different coloured hairs. In the wild it occurs in the subalpine zone, either in pure stands or with *Abies veitchii*, *Tsuga diversifolia*, *Picea jezoensis* ssp. *hondoensis* and *Betula ermanii*, with an understorey of dwarf bamboo.

p.78 **Sicilian Fir** *Abies nebrodensis*

Description: Evergreen tree to 15 m (50 ft) with a bole
diameter to 50 cm (1.6 ft).
Crown Conical, becoming columnar or wide
spreading with age. *Bark* Orange, finely
shredding in young trees, in old ones
becoming cracked into irregular flakes.
Shoot Buff-brown and shiny in first winter,
becoming greyer with age, hairless on
strong shoots but with brown hairs in
grooves on weak ones, strong shoots stout.
Buds Conical to ovoid-conical, light brown,
with a coat of white resin covering but not
obliterating the scales, to 8 mm (0.3 in).
Foliage In spaced sprays, leaves beneath the
shoot twisted so that they spread at right
angles and are slightly rising, those above
the shoot assurgent to erect, with or without
a V-parting above; leaves linear, apex
rounded and notched on side shoots to form
a slender sharp bony point on strong shoots,
dark glossy green above with a few stomata
in a spot near the tip, beneath with two
greenish-white waxy bands of stomata,
1.5–2.2 cm × 2.5–3 mm (0.6–0.9 × 0.1 in);
crushed foliage with resin scent.
Flowers On previous season's shoots in early
summer; male cones greenish yellow,
1.5–2 cm (0.6–0.8 in). *Fruit* Cylindro-
conic with projecting bracts, tapering to a
pointed tip, green-yellow, ripening to
brown in first autumn, 8–10 × 3–4 cm
(3.1–4 × 1.2–1.6 in); rachis cylindrical;
scales fan-shaped, to 3.3 cm (1.3 in) wide,
bract scales projecting and reflexed.

Range: Northern Sicily.
Habitat: Dry mountain slopes.
Synonyms: *A. alba* var. *nebrodensis*.

This fir is very rare, at one time being
reduced by deforestation to a mere score of
trees in the wild and grafts from another
one in cultivation. Recent conservation
measures have increased the population. It
is very distinct in the foliage and in the
shoot and unlikely to be confused with *A.
alba*. Despite its Sicilian origin, it is hardy
in southern Sweden.

p.91 **Khinghan Fir** *Abies nephrolepis*

Description: Evergreen tree 15–20 m (50–65 ft) with a
bole diameter to 50 cm (1.6 ft).
Crown Narrow conical, columnar in old
trees, with short branches. *Bark* Grey,
smooth with resin blisters in young trees,
becoming shallowly fissured or fluted and
greyish brown. *Shoot* Fawn and somewhat
shiny with scattered blackish hairs, scarcely
changing with aging. *Buds* Globose to
ovoid or ovoid-conic, with a bluntly
pointed apex, red-brown or brown,
moderately resinous, 4 mm (0.2 in).
Foliage Dense and rather radial and
forwards along the shoot with fewer leaves
beneath and shorter leaves along the top of
the shoot or more widely parted; linear,
tapered to base, apex rounded, notched,
somewhat squarish, dull mid green above
without stomata, with two dull silvery
white to greenish-white bands of waxy
stomata below, 1.5–3 cm × 1.5 mm
(0.6–1.2 × 0.1 in); crushed foliage with a
strong balsam scent. *Flowers* On last
season's shoots in late winter or early spring;
male cones cylindrical, lemon yellow,
1–1.8 cm (0.4–0.7 in). *Fruit* Cylindrical
or ovate-oblong with the tips of the cups
projecting, ripening from reddish purple or
green to dull purple-brown or brown in first
autumn, 4.5–7.5 × 2–3 cm (1.8–2.9 ×
0.8–1.2 in); rachis narrow conic; scales
kidney-shaped, 1.5–1.8 cm (0.6–0.7 in)
wide, bracts with a straight cusp.

Range: Manchuria region of China south to the
Wutai Shan west of Beijing, mainly in the
Greater and Lesser Khinghan (Hinghan)
ranges, also in northern Korea and
adjoining Pacific Russia.

Habitat: Cultivated in Europe as an ornamental, in
the wild forming stands on mountain sides,
either pure or with other conifers.

Varieties: Forma *chlorocarpa* covers plants with
greenish cones. It is mentioned in most
books but is scarcely worth distinguishing,
as most *Abies* (especially in this group of
species) have individuals with green or
greenish cones.

This tree is closely related to *A. veitchii* and *A. koreana*. It differs from these in the duller aspect to the foliage and the stomatal bands and the denser foliage.

---

p.79 **Nordmann Fir** or **Caucasian Fir**
Abies nordmanniana

Description: Evergreen tree 25–40 m (80–130 ft) with a bole diameter to 1.5 m (5 ft).
Crown Conical and dense when young, becoming columnar with declinate branches. *Bark* Grey, smooth, becoming fissured into small square plates.
Shoot Olive-brown with scattered hairs or hairless in first winter, becoming pink-brown or grey-brown. *Buds* Ovoid, light brown, not resinous, 5 mm (0.2 in).
Foliage Widely parted beneath the shoot, at the sides spreading or weakly forwards, more curving upwards and forwards above or with a weak parting, dense and luxuriant; leaves linear, tapering at both ends, apex rounded, notched, upper surface rich glossy green without stomata, below with two silvery white or greenish-white bands of waxy stomata and a deep green midrib, 1.5–3.5 cm × 2 mm (0.6–1.4 × 0.1 in); crushed foliage with light resinous or petrol scent. *Flowers* On last season's shoots in late spring; male cones yellow, 1–2 cm (0.4–0.8 in). *Fruit* Cylindrical with projecting and reflexed bracts, tapering slightly to the rounded apex, pale green but ripening in first autumn to brown, 12–16 × 4–5.5 cm (4.7–6.3 × 1.6–2.2 in); rachis conical; scales fan-shaped, 3–4 cm (1.2–1.6 in) in width.
Range: Northeast Turkey and western Caucasus from Georgia and Abkhazia.
Habitat: Mountain slopes, in pure stands or mixed with *Picea* or *Fagus*.
Similar species: **Bornmueller Fir** *A. bornmuelleriana* differs in the hairless shoot, ovoid conic and resinous buds and the foliage. This tends to be arranged with a wider parting above and the individual leaves 2.5–4 cm (1–1.6 in) have a scattered band of silvery white

stomata above as well as the two silvery bands beneath. It occurs in northern Turkey on the mountains above the Black Sea. *A. equi-trojani* occurs in the Ida range of northwest Turkey, of Trojan horse fame. It is close to Bornmueller Fir, differing in the yellow-brown shoots, broadly ovoid and only slightly resinous buds and the blunt leaves which are only 1.5–2.5 cm (0.6–1 in) (rarely 3 cm (1.2 in)) in length.

Both these taxa are sometimes treated as subspecies of *A. nordmanniana*.

This makes an attractive and densely crowned tree, which tolerates a wide range of sites. It is widely used as a Christmas tree, keeping its needles despite modern central heating systems. The leaves are retained longer than any other *Abies*, usually four to six years but exceptionally up to 25 years (on lower crown shoots in good light).

---

p.80 **Algerian Fir** *Abies numidica*

Description: Evergreen tree to 25 m (80 ft) with a bole diameter of up to 1 m (3.3 ft).
Crown Conical in young trees, becoming columnar, dense. *Bark* Grey with a purple or pinkish tinge, smooth in young trees, becoming fissured into small scaly plates in old trees. *Shoot* Orange-brown in first winter, becoming paler brown or greyer in later years, hairless. *Buds* Conical or ovoid-conical, brown with free scale tips and a slight covering of whitish resin, to 7 mm (0.3 in); male cone buds ovoid, lumpy, more resinous, 5–6 mm (0.2–0.25 in). *Foliage* Leaves radial and perpendicular around the shoot but less dense or with a parting below, those above the shoot somewhat shorter, giving a flat plateau to the arrangement; leaves linear, stiff, with a rounded to slightly notched apex, upper surface grey-green with a broad but incomplete band of waxy whitish-grey stomata, below with two narrow white to whitish-green bands of

waxy stomata and a broad mid green midrib, 1–2 cm × 2.5–3 mm (0.4–0.8 × 0.1 in) (but on shaded shoots or on seedlings the leaves may be pointed, laxer and longer, to 2.5 cm × 2–2.5 mm) (1 × 0.1 in); crushed foliage with a sweet resin scent. *Flowers* On previous season's shoots in early summer; male cones yellow, 1–2.5 cm (0.4–1 in). *Fruit* Cylindrical with a abruptly short-pointed or nipple-tipped apex and included bracts, light green or purple tinged green and ripening in first autumn to light brown, 12–18 × 4–6 cm (4.7–7.1 × 1.6–2.4 in); rachis conical; scales fan-shaped, to 3.5 cm (1.4 in) in width, bract scales hidden, rarely with the cusp showing at the base.

Range: Northern Algeria.

Habitat: Cultivated as an ornamental in Europe, in Algeria occurring on the Algerian Atlas around Mount Barbor on calcareous rocky soils with a north or east aspect.

Varieties: No varieties but cultivars include 'Glauca', with more bluish foliage.

This tree is closely related to *A. pinsapo* and *A. marocana*, differing in the less completely radial arrangement of the foliage and the less resinous buds. Like these species, it thrives on chalky and other sites with reasonable or better drainage.

---

p.85 **Pindrow Fir** or **West Himalayan Fir**
Abies pindrow

Description: Evergreen tree 20–40 m (65–130 ft) with a bole diameter to 1 m (3.3 ft).
Crown Columnar with a pointed apex and short declinate branches. *Bark* Dark grey and rough, becoming shallowly fissured in old trees. *Shoot* Ash grey for the first winter or two (especially above the shoot), smooth and hairless, later becoming straw-yellow. *Buds* Globose to ovoid-conic, thickly resinous, brown but becoming white due to the clouding of the resin, 6 mm (0.25 in). *Foliage* Moderately to widely parted both above and below the

shoot, those at the side in several ranks and pointing forwards, slightly open (not dense); leaves linear, apex bifid (especially on young plants but more weakly on old ones), upper surface glossy green with a groove, lower surface with two narrow whitish-green bands of stomata, 3–5.5 cm (1.2–2.2 in) (occasionally up to 7–9 cm (2.8–3.5 in)) by 2 mm (0.1 in); crushed foliage resin scented. *Flowers* On previous season's growths in spring; male cones yellow, 1–1.5 cm (0.4–0.6 in).

Fruit Cylindrical with included bracts, ripening from violet-blue to brown in first autumn, 10–14 × 5.5–7 cm (4–5.5 × 2.2–2.8 in); rachis conical; scales fan-shaped, 3–4 cm (1.2–1.6) broad, bract scale half length of seed scale, with a short 1 mm (0.05 in) cusp.

Range: Himalayas from Afghanistan to western Nepal.

Habitat: Cultivated in Europe as an ornamental, in the wild occurring on mountain slopes usually with *Picea smithiana* and *Cedrus deodara*.

Varieties: **Gamble Fir** *A. gamblei* (also called *A. pindrow* var. *brevifolia*) is a related species or subspecies. It has more radially arranged foliage which is shorted, with the apex blunt and a broad band of stomata on the upper leaf surface. It occurs in northwest India and appears to be a high-altitude form.

This tree does best in cool moist mountain districts but needs protection from spring frost when young. It is sometimes confused with *A. spectabilis* which occurs in the same forests, although mainly at higher altitude. The smooth and hairless ash-grey shoot of *A. pindrow* (cf. deeply ridged with lines of hairs in the grooves) and the much shorter male cones distinguish it. The buds are also different in shape and texture. *A. pindrow* is more closely related to *A. chensiensis*, especially subspecies *salouenensis*. They are the only two hardy *Abies* with leaves longer than 6 cm (2.4 in), although they are much narrower in *A. pindrow*.

p.80 **Spanish Fir** or **Hedgehog Fir**
Abies pinsapo

Description: Evergreen tree to 25 m (80 ft) with a bole
to 1 m (3.3 ft) diameter.
Crown Conical with open whorled
branches when young, becoming columnar
in old trees. *Bark* Dark grey, smooth but
becoming rough and fissured in old trees.
Shoot Olive-brown in first winter, later
red-brown, smooth, marked by the large
rounded or elliptic leaf bases, of moderate
thickness. *Buds* Ovoid to conical,
rounded, with free triangular scales,
thickly resinous, red-brown, 3–5 mm
(0.1–0.2 in). *Foliage* Nearly perfectly
radial in mature trees with the leaves of
similar length around the shoot; in young
trees, there may be a parting in the
arrangement above the shoot; leaves stout,
stiff, with large rounded or ellipsoidal
sucker-like bases, linear with a bluntly
pointed apex, upper surface blue-green
with a wide waxy band of stomata (or two
bands), lower surface similar or paler with
two waxy bands, 0.8–1.8 cm × 2 mm
(0.3–0.7 × 0.1 in); crushed foliage has a
moderately strong resinous scent.
Flowers On last season's shoots, opening in
late spring; male cones red or violet with
yellow pollen, 7 mm (0.3 in); female cones
on upper branches only. *Fruit* Cylindrical
with a nipple-like projection at the apex
and hidden bract scales, pale green
ripening in first autumn to brown, 10–15
× 3–4 cm (4–6 × 1.2–1.6 in); rachis
conical; scales to 2.5 cm (1 in) wide with
the exposed portion slightly hairy, bract
scale half the length of the seed scale.

Range: Southeast Spain in the mountains around
Ronda where it occurs in three scattered
stands.

Habitat: Dry calcareous rocks.

Varieties: Trees with more strongly blue-glaucous
foliage are cultivated under several clonal
names, including 'Glauca' and 'Kelleriis'.
There are also selections with weeping
foliage and one with golden new foliage
('Aurea').

Similar species: Two related trees from northern Morocco are treated either as varieties or separate species. *A. marocana* has parted foliage and leaves with fewer stomata above and more pointed and larger cones (10–18 × 3–5.5 cm (4–7.1 × 1.2–2.2 in)). *A. tazaotana* has non-resinous buds, lanceolate leaves and still larger cones 16–20 cm (6.3–8 in). Both are rare in cultivation.

This species is unusual in the nearly perfectly radial foliage arrangement. It grows on all well-drained soils as north as northern Scotland but is especially suited to chalk.

p.81   **Noble Fir** *Abies procera*

Description: Evergreen tree 20–50 m (65–165 ft) with a bole diameter of up to 1.5 m (5 ft). *Crown* Conical or narrow conical and open in young trees with pronounced whorls of branches, becoming broad columnar in old trees and often ragged. *Bark* Bright silvery grey and smooth in young trees, then fissuring and cracking at the base, often (especially in dry areas) with drought cracks which show as 1–2 m (3.3–6.6 ft) vertical or slightly spiral bands and 3–5 cm (1.2–2 in) in width. *Shoot* Light red-brown or orange-brown in first winter, becoming darker red-brown, with persistent red-brown to blackish hairs, shoot not visible from above due to the density of leaves pressed on to the shoot, moderately slender to stout. *Buds* Globose or pointed, lumpy, red-brown, rather hidden in leaves, only 2 mm (0.1 in) on side shoots but larger on main shoots. *Foliage* Widely parted beneath the shoot with the leaves curving downwards, at the side, spreading and gradually becoming shorter and more forward pointing so that above the shoot they are pressed against the shoot and curve through 90 degrees to be erect at the tips; leaves linear, apex bluntly pointed or notched, rhombic (four-sided) in section on vigorous shoots but flat with a shallow groove along the upper surface on side shoots, upper surface grey-green to blue-green with a variable band of waxy stomata, below with two whitish to silvery white bands of stomata, from 1–1.3 cm (0.4–0.5 in) above the shoot to 3–3.5 cm (1.2–1.4 in) at the sides, by 1.5 mm (0.1 in); crushed foliage with a pungent somewhat oniony resin scent. *Flowers* On previous season's growths in late spring; male cones 1.5–2.5 cm (0.6–1 in), red with yellow pollen. *Fruit* Cylindrical with a rounded pointed apex, with prominent reflexed bracts, green during the growing season but ripening to brown in first autumn, 15–25 × 5–6.5 cm (6–10 × 2–2.6 in); rachis cylindrical; scales fan-shaped, to 3.5 cm (1.5 in) wide, with the exposed portion hairy, bract scales projecting and reflexed, covering around 90% of the cone surface.

Range: Oregon and Washington states, USA.

Habitat: Cultivated in Europe as an ornamental and in forestry, in the wild occurring in mixed conifer forests on moist mountain sites.

Varieties: Forma *glauca* covers the forms with rich glaucous blue foliage.

Synonyms: *A. nobilis.*

The silvery grey bark, often glaucous foliage and the cones carried on the upper whorls of branches of even young trees make this a very beautiful tree, although unfortunately it will not grow on chalky sites. It is used in forestry, but the tendency to produce drought cracks during dry summers reduces the quality of the timber. In the wild it is currently the tallest growing silver fir, to 85 m (280 ft), beating *A. grandis* by some 15 m (50 ft).

p.85 **Min Fir** *Abies recurvata*

Description: Evergreen tree to 15 m (50 ft) with a bole diameter of up to 30 cm (1 ft).
Crown Conical, dense, with spreading or slightly erect branches. *Bark* Pink-brown

or orange-brown, finely flaky but not peeling. *Shoot* Shiny straw brown, light brown or pink-brown in first winter, then ash white by third year, stout, hairless. *Buds* Ovoid conic, slightly resinous, brown or pink-brown. *Foliage* In dense sprays, with the leaves longest at the base of the shoot and gradually becoming shorter towards the tip; on very vigorous shoots, the leaves are bent back along the shoot, especially those below it; on less vigorous shoots, the leaves beneath the shoot are widely parted and curved up slightly, those above erect, with a parting or more usually forming a flat plateau; leaves linear, apex rounded notched to a slender point, bent, mid green and slightly bloomed above without stomata or with a few in groove near the tip, below with two broad greenish-white bands of stomata, 1–2.8 cm × 2.5–3 mm (0.4–1.1 × 0.1 in); crushed foliage with a pleasant resinous scent. *Flowers* On last season's shoots in early summer; male cones yellow or red, 1–1.5 cm (0.4–0.6). *Fruit* Ovoid-oblong, usually with an abruptly short-pointed apex and hidden bracts, violet-blue, ripening to brown in first autumn, 6–8 × 3–3.5 cm (2.4–3.1 × 1.2–1.4 in); rachis cylindro-conical; scales fan-shaped, 2–2.5 cm (0.8–1 in) in width, bract scale hidden or tip of cusp just projecting at base of cone.

Range: Northwest Sichuan, China in the Min valley.

Habitat: Cultivated in Europe as an ornamental, in the wild it is found in mountain valley forests.

Varieties: Var. *ernestii* is a form from west Sichuan which has more pectinate foliage to 3.5 cm (1.4 in) and more cylindrical cones with a dimpled apex.

The scientific name for this small tree refers to the recurved foliage. In cultivation, this is only shown on the strongest shoots. It makes a small and narrow crowned ornamental tree, which is very tolerant of shade.

p.83 **Sacred Fir** *Abies religiosa*

Description: Evergreen tree 15–30 m (50–100 ft) with a bole to 1 m (3.3 ft) in diameter.

Crown Conical when young, old trees may be narrow conic, columnar or broad conic; branches spreading, curving downwards with upcurved tips and drooping side shoots. *Bark* Grey, smooth, becoming cracked into small plates with reddish fissures. *Shoot* Olive-green for the first winter, slowly becoming brown or red-brown, hairless or with short hairs in shallow grooves, moderately stout to slender. *Buds* Ovoid or rounded, dull blue with a thick coat of whitish resin, 2.5–4 mm (0.1–0.2 in). *Foliage* Below the shoot hanging down like two curtains on either side and gently forwards, side leaves forwards and down, upper leaves forwards at 45 degrees and widely parted, soft; leaves dull green above with none or a few stomata near the rounded pointed bony apex, below with two whitish-green waxy bands of stomata, 2–4 × 2 mm (0.8–1.6 × 0.1 in); crushed foliage with a citrus resinous scent. *Flowers* On last season's shoots in early summer; male cones yellow, 1–1.5 cm (0.4–0.6 in). *Fruit* Conical or oblong-ovoid with projecting bracts, apex acute, purple or green, ripening to brown in first autumn, 8–15 × 4–6 cm (3.1–6 × 1.6–2.4 in); rachis cylindro-conic; scales fan-shaped, to 3.5 cm (1.4 in) in width, bract projecting, erect or reflexed.

Range: Central Mexico.

Habitat: Cultivated in Europe as an ornamental, in the wild forming forests on moist mountain slopes below *Pinus hartwegii*.

Synonyms: *A. hirtella.*

This makes a neat tree which has an open habit, but it is not hardy in cold districts. It is closely related to *A. vejarii*, differing in the longer and softer foliage and the larger cones which have more prominent bract scales.

p.92 **Sakhalin Fir** *Abies sachalinensis*

Description: Evergreen tree 15–25 m (50–80 ft) in
height with a bole diameter to 60 cm (2 ft).
Crown Conical in young trees, then
becoming columnar with a pointed or flat
top. *Bark* Greyish white, smooth in young
trees but becoming shallowly fissured and
somewhat scaly in old ones. *Shoot* Buff or
grey-brown in the first winter with dark or
blackish hairs in shallow grooves, blackish
or dark brown later. *Buds* Ovoid or
globular, red or purple but thickly
encrusted with resin which clouds as it
absorbs water, 3 mm (0.1 in)
Foliage Forward pointing and parted
beneath the shoot with the outer leaves
drooping, upper leaves curving upwards
with a narrow parting, with a steady
increase in leaf length from the top leaves
to the longest at the side; linear, apex
square, notched, upper surface grooved,
without stomata, mid sub-shiny green,
lower surface with two white bands of
stomata and a pale green midrib of similar
width, 2–3.5 × 1 mm (0.8–1.4 × 0.1 in);
crushed foliage with a pungent resin scent.
Flowers On previous season's growths in
spring; male cones yellow, 1 cm (0.4 in).
Fruit Cylindrical or ellipsoidal with shortly
projecting and reflexed bract scales,
ripening in first autumn from green or
violet-blue to brown, 5–8 × 2–2.5 cm
(2–3.1 × 0.8–1 in); rachis narrow conic;
seed scales kidney-shaped, hairy on exposed
portion, to 1.6 cm (0.6 in) in width, bract
scales with only the tip of the cusp or a
short portion of the scale showing.

Range: Hokkaido, Japan, and north along the
Kurile Island chain and in Sakhalin Island
of Pacific Russia.

Habitat: Cultivated in Europe as an ornamental, in
the wild occurring in pure or mixed stands.

Varieties: **Mayr Fir** var. *mayriana* has thinner bark
which does not become fissured on old
trees, and yellowish-green immature cones
which have more strongly projecting and
reflexed bracts. It occurs on Hokkaido
Island. Var. *nemorensis* covers those plants

which have hidden bract scales, and which occur occasionally within the population.

This tree has soft foliage. It is similar in general appearance and feel to *A. sibirica* and *A. lasiocarpa*, from which it can be distinguished by the projecting bracts scales.

p.92 **Siberian Fir** *Abies sibirica*

Description: Evergreen tree 10–25 m (33–80 ft) with a bole diameter to 50 cm (1.6 ft).
Crown Conical when young, becoming columnar conic, with short spreading branches. *Bark* Grey or grey-brown, smooth with resin blisters when young, becoming scaly at the base in old trees. *Shoot* Silvery grey or fawn brown, shiny, hairless or with scattered dark hairs, later matt and dark greyish brown, slender. *Buds* Globose or ovoid-conic, reddish brown, but thickly encrusted with resin which clouds to grey-white, 4 mm (0.2 in). *Foliage* Pointing forwards and rather radial at around 45 degrees to the shoot, generally with a parting both above and below, upper leaves shorter, soft, linear, apex notched, shiny yellowish green above without stomata or with two incomplete bands, with two pale green bands of stomata below, 1–3 cm × 1 mm (0.4–1.2 × 0.1 in); crushed foliage with a strong sweet resin scent. *Flowers* On previous season's growths in late spring; males red with yellow pollen, 1.5 cm (0.6 in). *Fruit* Ovoid-cylindric with hidden bracts, ripening from violet-blue to bluish brown, cinnamon or greenish brown, 5–7.5 × 2.5–3.5 cm (2–2.9 × 1–1.4 in); rachis narrow conical; scales fan-shaped, 2–2.2 cm (0.8–0.9 in) in width.

Range: Northeast Russia west of the Urals across Siberia to the Amur region and south to the Russian–Chinese border.

Habitat: Cold continental regions but with a warm albeit short summer season.

Synonyms: *A. pichta.*

Similar species: *A. semenovii* (syn. *A. sibirica* ssp. *semenovii*) is a related species found in the western Tien

Shan in Kirgizia. It differs in the prominently ridged and grooved shoots which are yellow-brown, in the less resinous buds, in the leaves with more lines of stomata beneath and in the yellow-brown cones.

This tree is well adapted to continental climates with pronounced seasons but in more maritime ones tends to come into leaf at the first sign of warm weather after new year, only to be frosted by the next cold snap. It has beautiful soft foliage and makes a very neat specimen when well grown.

---

p.89 **Webb Fir** or **Himalayan Fir**
Abies spectabilis

Description: Evergreen tree to 30 m (100 ft) with a bole diameter to 1 m (3.3 ft).
Crown Broad conical in young trees, columnar in old trees; in the wild, storms remove the primary branches which are replaced by epicormic shoots growing from buds on the main stem. *Bark* Pink-grey, smooth and finely flaky in young trees, in old trees becoming rough and dull grey with pink or red-brown fissures. *Shoot* Yellow-brown in the first winter, becoming ash grey or pale brown, ridged behind the leaf bases with prominent lines of pale brown hairs in the grooves, moderately stout.
Buds Globose to ovoid, rounded or pointed, red-brown with a thick coating of resin, to 4 mm (0.2 in). *Foliage* Parted beneath the shoot with the foliage drooping at the sides; at the sides, spreading or slightly forwards, becoming more forwards and shorter above the shoot with a wide V-parting; leaves linear, flat on the underside, apex rounded deeply notched or bifid with two bony points, dark glossy green above without stomata, below with two whitish waxy bands of stomata, 2–4.5 cm (0.8–1.8 in), in some forms to 6 cm × 1.5–2 mm (2.4 × 0.1 in); crushed foliage with resin or turpentine scent. *Flowers* On previous season's shoots in late spring; male purplish blue with yellow pollen, to 3 cm (1.2 in);

female cones cylindrical, purple or violet.
Fruit Oblong or ovoid-oblong with
included bracts, violet-blue during the
growing season, ripening in the first autumn
and slowly changing to brown, 7–15 ×
4–7 cm (2.8–6 × 1.6–2.8 in); rachis conical;
scales fan-shaped, 3–3.5 cm (1.2–1.4 in)
wide, hairy on exposed portion, bract scales
just over half length of seed scale.

Range: Eastern Afghanistan along the Himalayas
to east Nepal.

Habitat: Cultivated in Europe as an ornamental, in
the wild forming pure forests on moist but
not too wet slopes.

Varieties: Var. *brevifolia* has leaves with a bluish
bloom but is of uncertain taxonomic status.

Synonyms: *A. webbiana, A. brevifolia.*

This tree, whose scientific name translates
as 'beautiful' can be most impressive when
well grown, for which it requires a moist
climate. It is susceptible to spring frost
damage. A purple dye has been made from
the cone scales.

---

p.88 **Flaky Fir** *Abies squamata*

Description: Evergreen tree to 15 m (50 ft) with a bole
diameter of up to 40 cm (1.3 ft).
Crown Conical in young trees, becoming
columnar with a conic apex.
Bark Mahogany or red-brown, less often
grey-brown or orange-brown, exfoliating in
small papery scales from bole and branches
after four to six years; in very old trees, the
bark may become thick and scaly at the
base. *Shoot* Maroon or purplish red-brown
in first winter, later becoming brown,
usually hairless, moderately stout with a
thick bark. *Buds* Globose or slightly
rounded pointed, brown but thickly
encrusted with resin which becomes whitish
grey over winter, 7 mm (0.3 in). *Foliage* In
spreading, slightly rising sprays; leaves
widely parted beneath the shoot, at the sides
spreading and pointing gently forwards,
above the shoot pressed down at the base
and more or less curving erect to give a flat

plateau due to the leaves above the shoot being shorter; linear, apex rounded notched, on vigorous shoots pointed, upper surface grey-green with an incomplete band of greyish waxy stomata concentrated near the tip, beneath with two whitish-green waxy bands of stomata, 1–2.5 × 2 mm (0.4–1 × 0.1 in); crushed foliage with a slightly orangey resinous scent. *Flowers* On previous season's shoots in early summer; male cones 2–3 cm (0.8–1.2 in).
Fruit Ovoid with projecting bracts, purple, ripening to brown in first autumn, 5–7 × 3–4 cm (2–2.8 × 1.2–1.6 in); rachis spindle-shaped; scales fan-shaped, to 1.5 cm (0.6 in) wide, bracts with a long reflexed cusp.

Range: Border region between China and Tibet (west Sichuan and east Qinghai).

Habitat: Cultivated in Europe, in the wild occurring in pure stands in alpine forests at up to 4500 m (14,750 ft) in cold dry areas.

This rare tree has a remarkable flaky bark. It is closely related to *A. fargesii* and with it shares the median resin canals in the leaves. If a needle is snapped in half and examined under a hand lens, two large blobs of resin will be visible.

p.91 **Veitch Fir** *Abies veitchii*

Description: Evergreen tree 10–20 m (33–65 ft), with a bole to 50 cm (1.6 ft).
Crown Conical or columnar conic, with rather spaced tiers of level branches with rising lateral shoots. *Bark* Smooth grey-brown, with resin blisters, becoming fluted and slightly cracked on old trees.
Shoot Pink brown with dark yellow-brown hairs, becoming buff-brown and shiny, slender. *Buds* Ovoid, resinous, reddish purple, 3 mm (0.1 in). *Foliage* Forward pointing at an angle of about 45 degrees to the shoot, with a narrow groove in the arrangement above the shoot, more spreading beneath; leaves mid to somewhat waxy bloomed green above, with two silvery waxy stomatal bands beneath, linear,

apex squarrish-rounded, notched, 2–2.5 (0.8–1 in) (rarely to 3 cm (1.2 in)) × 1.5–2 mm (0.1 in); crushed foliage with a sweet resinous aroma. *Flowers* In spring on previous year's shoots; male cones in clusters on undersides of shoots, from conical buds, opening to about 1.5 cm (0.6 in), red or purple with yellow pollen; female cones erect on upper side of strong shoots in upper crown, purple or green. *Fruit* Cylindrical, apex rounded or flat with a short nipple, bracts either just projecting or just hidden, 4.5–8 × 2–2.5 cm (1.8–3.1 × 0.8–1 in), violet-purple (rarely greenish brown), ripening to brown; rachis narrow cylindrical; scales 1.5 cm (0.6 in) wide; bracts about as long as the scales.

Range: Japan on the mountains of central Honshu.

Habitat: Cultivated as an ornamental tree in Europe, rarely in forest plots, in the wild forming subalpine forests with other conifers.

Varieties: 'Glauca' is a form with more strongly bloomed foliage than usual, but is rare.

Similar species: *A. nephrolepis* from northeast China, Pacific Russia and northern Korea has minutely hairy shoots which are fawn coloured, leaves which are paler green above with less silvery bands beneath and cone scales which are kidney-shaped. It is only found in specialist collections.

It is an attractive small tree of moderately fast growth and suited to a wide variety of soils. Closely related to *A. koreana* which differs in the broader, shorter leaves which are more glaucous beneath.

p.83 **Vejar Fir** *Abies vejarii*

Description: Evergreen tree to 25 m (80 ft) with a bole to 80 cm (2.6 ft) in diameter.
Crown Conical whilst young, then becoming columnar with short spreading branches.
Bark Grey, smooth in young trees, later silvery-grey and cracking into small square plates. *Shoot* Olive-brown and slightly shiny in the first winter, turning medium brown and matt, moderately stout. *Buds* Globular,

dull purple with a thick whitish coat of resin. *Foliage* Parted beneath the shoot and pointing forwards at about 45 degrees, leaves above the shoot rising at 30–40 degrees, with a narrow V-groove between the two ranks, dark green to vivid blue-green, depending upon the degree of waxy bloom, hard to the touch; leaves linear, tapering to a blunt bony apex, upper surface without stomata or with an incomplete band, lower surface with two whitish bands of stomata, 2–3 × 2–2.5 mm (0.8–1.2 × 0.1 in); crushed foliage with sharp resin scent. *Flowers* On last season's growths in early summer; male cones globular, 5 mm (0.2 in). *Fruit* Cylindrical to ovoid with projecting bracts, violet or purple, ripening brown in the first autumn, resinous, 6–15 × 4–6 cm (2.4–6 × 1.6–2.4 in); rachis cylindro-conic; scales fan-shaped, to 2.5 cm (1 in) in width, bracts with broad erect cusp.

Range: Northeast Mexico from Nuevo Leon, Coahuila and Tamaulipas.

Habitat: Cultivated in Europe as an ornamental, occurring on mountain slopes, usually with *Pinus rudis*, where much of the precipitation comes in the form of fog or cloud.

Varieties: Var. *macrocarpa* covers the forms with cones over 10 cm (4 in) in length.

This Mexican tree is surprisingly hardy and tolerant both of dry acid sands and chalk sites. In the wild, it is extremely variable in the degree of waxy bloom on the foliage, with glaucous blue trees growing beside dull green ones!

MALLOWS OR FLOWERING MAPLES, *ABUTILON*
(SYNONYM: *CORYNABUTILON*)
FAMILY MALVACEAE

This is a genus of around a hundred species, including both woody and herbaceous plants. They mainly come from central and southern America but with one herbaceous member in southern Europe. The flowers have the mallow family character of numerous stamens united into a column which surrounds the style. In *Abutilon*, there are as many lobes to the style as chambers to the ovary.

p.302 **Chilean Mallow** or **Flowering Maple**
Abutilon vitifolium

Description: Deciduous or semi-evergreen large shrub or
small tree 4–9 m (13–29 ft) with a bole
diameter to 25 cm (10 in).
Crown Rounded upright, usually on several
main branches or stems. *Bark* Brown.
Shoot Green in first year, becoming greyish
brown in second year, densely covered in
white star-shaped persistent hairs, with a
thick pith. *Buds* Conical, green, with star-
shaped hairs, 2 mm (0.1 in). *Foliage* Leaves
alternate, round or palmately lobed, with
three or five lobes, main lobe triangular,
acute or with a slender point, side lobes
acute, sinuses broadly acute, base deeply
heart-shaped, margin with rounded
lobulate teeth, upper surface mid matt
green with a light coat of star-shaped hairs,
lower surface whitish green due to dense
covering of star-shaped hairs, midrib and
main veins prominent below, 10–15 ×
8–12 cm (4–6 × 3.1–4.7 in). Leaf stalk
round, to 10 cm (4 in), star-shaped hairy,
green, with two strap-like 5 mm (0.2 in)
stipules at the base. No autumn colour.
Flowers In leaf axils on current season's
growths from May through July, in cymes
of three to five, on a long round star-shaped
hairy green peduncle to 15 cm (6 in); flower
stalks to 5 cm (2 in); flower to 9 cm (3.5 in)
across; calyx lobes three to five, ovate-
triangular, acute, star-shaped hairy, green,
persisting; petals five, obovate, to 4.5 cm
(1.8 in) wide and long, spreading flat,
white to pale purplish blue; stamens
golden-yellow, in a boss clustered on the
short style which bears several stigmas.
Ovary conical, white with star-shaped hairs.
Fruit Capsules with several beaked
segments each containing a single seed.

Range: Chile.

Habitat: Cultivated as an ornamental; in the wild
found in coastal forests.

Varieties: Several colour forms are often grown, such
as 'Tennant's White', with snow white
flowers. *A. × suntense* (p.302) is a hybrid of
A. vitifolium with another Chilean species

A. ochsenii. It has smaller leaves and flowers than *A. vitifolium.* The hairs are a mixture of star-shaped and simple hairs, the latter inherited from *A. ochsenii.* It quickly forms an upright bush or tree to 5 m (16 ft).

Synonyms: *Corynabutilon vitifolium.*

This is very attractive when laden with flowers but is only reliably hardy in warm southern gardens. The stems are stout, soft and pithy, and it is not long lived.

WATTLES AND ACACIAS, *ACACIA*
FAMILY LEGUMINOSAE

The genus *Acacia* contains around 1200 species of trees and shrubs. Acacias are widely distributed across the tropical and warm temperate regions that have a pronounced dry season, but they are not native to Europe. They are especially common in Australia and Africa, making the spreading trees characteristic of the African savannah. The true leaves are bi-pinnate, that is doubly pinnate, and thus feathery. However, many species only produce true leaves as small seedlings, replacing them by phyllodes, or modified shoots. These carry out the functions of leaves but reduce water loss. The shoots may have spines derived from the stipules. The flowers are invariably some shade of yellow, with a rounded knob of many stamens, and are followed by typical legume fruits.

Acacia is used for soil stabilization (as with all members of the Legume family, the roots have a symbiotic relationship with bacteria which allows them to 'fix' atmospheric nitrogen), for timber and as amenity trees. The flowers, especially of *A. dealbata*, are very showy and used in floristry. The species illustrated here may be separated as follows: leaves wholly bi-pinnate *A. dealbata*; leaves both bi-pinnate and with phyllodes (mainly found in young trees) *AA. longifolia*, *melanoxylon*; only phyllodes present (i.e. true leaves absent) *AA. cyanophylla* and *rhetinodes* and in old trees of *longifolia* and *melanoxylon*.

p.345 **Golden Wreath** or **Willow Wattle**
Acacia cyanophylla

Description: Evergreen shrub or small tree to 10 m (33 ft), usually on several stems. *Crown* Dense, rounded. *Bark* Smooth, grey at first, becoming grey-brown and fissuring. *Shoot* Finely ribbed, hairless, flexible and usually pendent. *Buds* Minute. *Foliage* True leaves on very young seedlings only; phyllodes linear to lanceolate, either straight or sickle-shaped, usually pendulous, apex with slender point, wedge-shaped at the base, margin untoothed, dull to shiny green or glaucous with a conspicuous single vein or midrib, usually with a gland on the upper margin near the base, 10–20 × 0.6–3 cm (4–8 × 0.25–1.2 in) but sometimes to 35 × 8 cm (14 × 3.1 in) on suckers. *Flowers* In large heads of up to 70 flowers, set in short pendulous racemes of two to eight 1–1.5 cm (0.4–0.6 in) rounded bright yellow flowers with many stamens, flowering between March and May. *Fruit* Flattened legume which is constricted between the seeds, glaucous when young, ripening brown, 6–12 × 4–8 mm (2.4–4.7 × 0.2–0.3 in); stalk which encircles the seed is short and whitish.

Range: Western Australia.

Habitat: Cultivated as an ornamental and to stabilize sand dunes.

This tree is planted across the Mediterranean region from Portugal to Greece.

---

p.340 **Silver Wattle** or **Mimosa** *Acacia dealbata*

Description: Evergreen tree 6–20 m (20–65 ft) with a bole diameter to 30 cm (1 ft).
Crown Conical in young trees, becoming columnar. *Bark* Blue-green and smooth in young trees, then chocolate brown and later grey or black, often corrugated or fluted. *Shoot* Green, but covered with short silvery hairs, leaf bases decurrent on the shoot, angled. *Buds* Ovoid, small, blackish brown, 1.5 mm (0.1 in). *Foliage* Leaves evenly bi-pinnate, 10–15 × 4–6 cm (4–6 × 1.6–2.4 in), around 25 pairs of pinnate leaflets, 3–4 cm (1.2–1.6 in), with around 50 pairs of oblong linear pinnules (little leaflets) 3–4 mm (0.1–0.2 in); grey-green with a few silvery hairs, young leaves golden-brown; leaf stalk and rachis silvery

hairy. *Flowers* From buds formed in previous summer, opening in late winter, in globose or conical panicles 7–15 cm (2.8–6 in); flowers globose, fragrant, bright yellow, 5–6 mm (0.2–0.25 in) with showy stamens. *Fruit* Legume or pod, ripening in the autumn, blue-white, ripening to brown, compressed between the seeds, $4–10 \times 1–1.2$ cm ($1.6–4 \times 0.4–0.5$ in).

Range: New South Wales, Victoria and Tasmania, Australia.

Habitat: Cultivated as an ornamental and for soil stabilization in Europe.

Synonyms: *A. decurrens* var. *dealbata*.

Similar species: **Green Wattle** *A. mearnsii* (p.341) is a smaller tree, to 15 m (50 ft), which is covered with soft yellow hairs. The leaves have 8–14 leaflets, each with 20–40 pairs of leaflets, with glands on the rachis between the leaflets. The slender legume, 5–7 mm (0.2–0.3 in) in width, is constricted between the seeds and ripens to blackish-brown. This tree is native to southeast Australia and Tasmania and most frequently planted in the Iberian Peninsula, Corsica and Italy. *A. decurrens* is closely allied to *A. dealbata*, differing in the less hairy and rich green leaves which have more widely spaced leaflets.

This tree has become naturalized in parts of southern Europe. It provides the 'mimosa' of florists, but is not a true Mimosa. In colder climates it is cut back by hard winters, but often regrows from the base.

p.345 **Sydney Golden Wattle** *Acacia longifolia*

Description: Evergreen shrub or small tree to 10 m (33 ft). *Crown* Slender in young trees, becoming rounded with age. *Bark* Smooth, dull grey. *Shoot* Stiff, angular, hairless. *Buds* Minute. *Foliage* Phyllodes oblong to oblong-lanceolate, leathery, apex blunt or somewhat pointed, wedge-shaped, margin untoothed, light green with prominent veins running the length of the blade, $7–15 \times 0.8–3$ cm ($2.8–6 \times 0.3–1.2$ in). *Flowers* In large cylindrical spikes 2.5–5 × 0.6–1 cm (1–2 × 0.25–0.4 in), fluffy, yellow and strong scented, in late spring. *Fruit* Legume linear, round in cross-section, constricted between the seeds, straight to curled, maturing to brown, 7–15 × 4–5 mm (2.8–6 × 0.2 in); seeds with a white stalk.

Range: Coastal districts of New South Wales, Australia.

Habitat: Cultivated as an ornamental and for stabilization of sand dunes.

Synonyms: *Mimosa longifolia.*

In flower, this is very easily told by the slender spikes. It is planted in southwestern Europe, elsewhere being used as a conservatory plant.

p.345 **Blackwood Acacia** *Acacia melanoxylon*

Description: Evergreen tree to 25 m (80 ft) with a bole diameter to 80 cm (2.6 ft).
Crown Columnar to tall domed.
Bark Dark grey-brown, becoming rough and furrowed. *Shoot* Angular, downy.
Buds Minute. *Foliage* Mainly phyllodes but true leaves, which are bi-pinnate with leaflets oblong, apex abruptly pointed, 5–7 mm (0.2–0.3 in), are often mixed with phyllodes on young trees but rarely present on old trees; phyllodes lanceolate to oblanceolate, slightly curved like a scimitar, apex bluntly pointed, wedge-shaped at the base, margin untoothed, downy when young, dull dark green with three to five veins, 6–13 × 0.7–2 cm (2.4–5.1 × 0.3–0.8 in). *Flowers* In short axillary racemes, about 1 cm rounded yellow to creamy white flowers with many stamens, flowering in spring.
Fruit Flattened contorted reddish-brown legume, usually curved, 7–12 × 0.8–1 cm (2.8–4.7 × 0.3–0.4 in), with a scarlet stalk around the seed.

Range: Southeastern Australia and Tasmania.

Habitat: Cultivated as an ornamental and for timber.

Similar species: **Cyclops Wattle** *A. cyclops* (p.344) tends to be a low shrub usually only 3 m (10 ft) or

so, which has naturalized on cliffs in
Portugal. The phyllodes have three to six
veins, the flower heads are yellow, 4–6 mm
(0.2–0.25 in), solitary or in clusters of two
or three, and followed by a twisted pod.

This tree is planted both for ornament and
for the valuable timber, from western Britain
south and east to Italy and is occasionally
naturalized in southwestern Europe.

---

p.344   **Swamp Wattle** *Acacia rhetinodes*

Description: Evergreen shrub or tree to 10 m (33 ft)
with a bole diameter to 30 cm (1 ft).
Crown Rounded, low domed.
Bark Smooth, grey, grey-brown in old
trees. *Shoot* Angular, hairless, brown, not
pendent. *Buds* Minute. *Foliage* True
leaves only found on young seedlings;
phyllodes linear to narrowly oblanceolate,
apex blunt or pointed and usually curved,
base wedge-shaped, margin untoothed,
texture thin, with a single main vein and
weak laterals, light green to glaucous,
hairless, 6–12.5 cm (2.4–4.9 in) (rarely to
18 cm (7.1 in)) × 0.3–1 cm (0.1–0.4 in).
Flowers In short axillary racemes with five
to ten rounded pale yellow small, sweetly
scented flowers 4–6 mm (0.2–0.25 in)
across with many stamens, flowering from
spring to autumn but mainly in June–July.
Fruit Legume flattened and straight with
an almost straight margin and only slightly
constricted between the seeds, 10–17 cm
(4–6.7 in); the scarlet stalk to the seed
encircles the seed.

Range: Victoria, Tasmania and South Australia.

Habitat: Cultivated as an ornamental, occasionally
naturalized.

Synonyms: *A. retinodes.*

Similar species: Other shrubby species of Acacia are
sometimes encountered. These include:
Karoo *A. karoo* (p.341) which makes a
deciduous shrub or small tree to 4 m (13 ft).
This species has small bi-pinnate leaves with
leaflets 0.6–1 cm (0.25–0.4 in) and slightly
fragrant yellow flowers in clusters of four to

six. The pod or legume is flattened and constricted between the seeds and 8–13 cm (3.1–5.1 in) long. It is most remarkable for the paired long spines 5–10 cm (2–4 in) on old branches, which are derived from stipules. It is a native of South Africa and is grown both as an ornamental and to make hedges in southwest Europe.

Opoponax *A. farnesiana* (p.341) is similar in size and in the small bi-pinnate leaves but the leaflets are smaller, only 3–5 mm (0.1–0.2 in) and linear-oblong. The fragrant flowers are carried in clusters of two to three mainly above the branches on long flower stalks. The pods are cylindrical, inflated, 5–9 cm (2–3.5 in). This tree also has spines derived from stipules, but only to 2.5 cm (1 in) in length. It is native to Dominica in the West Indies and is planted in southwest Europe for ornament and for perfumery.

Golden Wattle *A. pycnantha* (p.344) from south and east Australia, makes a shrub or small tree to 8 m (26 ft). It has phyllodes which are leathery and usually curved, 8–20 × 1–4 cm (3.1–8 × 0.4–1.6 in) with only a single main vein, glaucous twigs and golden-yellow fragrant flowers in large heads. It is planted in southwest Europe.

The Swamp Wattle is a small tree, hairless in all its parts. It flowers in up to four flushes from spring to autumn, although June–July is the main period. It tolerates a wide range of soils, including limey ones. The scientific name derives from the Greek *Rhetine*, for resin (hence the rhetsina wines), and not the Latin *retina* or net.

MAPLE, ACERACEAE

Family of small to large trees, rarely shrubs, including two genera, *Acer* and *Dipteronia*. The family is characterized by the fruit which has a large wing to aid dispersal. The leaves and buds are in opposite pairs on the shoot. The leaves may be simple, toothed, lobed or pinnate.

MAPLES, *ACER*
FAMILY ACERACEAE

This is a large genus of 120–150 species. Maples are found in the northern temperate regions, especially in China, but extend into the tropics in central America and in southeast Asia (especially in the mountains). Maples form small to large trees, rarely only shrubs. Most species are deciduous, often assuming spectacular autumn tints, but some from the Mediterranean region and Asia are evergreen. The leaves and buds are always in opposite pairs (which readily distinguishes *Acer* from *Liquidambar* and *Platanus*, which both have leaves similar to some maple species). In some species, including *AA. campbellii, japonicum, laevigatum, oliverianum, palmatum, pseudosieboldianum* and *shirasawanum*, the terminal bud is aborted, so the tip of the shoot has only a pair of buds, whereas in other species there will be the terminal bud and a pair of laterals. The number of bud scales can help identification, varying from two pairs up to 10–15 pairs. In some species, the buds are stalked (*see also Alnus* but these have alternately arranged buds). Species with stalked buds (and also two pairs of bud scales) include *AA. argutum, barbinerve, capillipes, caudatum, crataegifolium, davidii, forrestii, grosseri* var. *hersii, maximowiczii, pectinatum, pensylvanicum, rufinerve, stachyophyllum* and *ukurunduense*.

The leaves may be untoothed (entire) or toothed on the margin, and be simple, palmately lobed, trifoliate or pinnate (in *A. negundo; see* the informal key below). In some species, the sap in the leaf stalk is milky (snap the leaf stalk in half and squeeze) but most species have a watery sap. Species with a milky sap include *AA. amplum, campestre, cappadocicum, lobelii, macrophyllum, miyabei, mono, platanoides* and *truncatum*. The flowers open in the spring, sometimes before the leaves, and the fruit ripens in the autumn (except in *AA. rubrum* and *saccharinum* when they ripen in early summer). The flowers may be many together in hanging racemes or panicles, or few in stalkless umbels and corymbs. The fruits are winged nutlets or samaras, arranged as a number of pairs. Dispersal is aided by the helicopter or spiralling motion of the wings. The seeds germinate with two large cotyledons or seed leaves which are raised above the soil surface, except in *A. truncatum*. The bark in most species is variously smooth to furrowed or forming scaly plates, and mainly some shade of brown. However, some species have a persistent green bark which is marked by white striations (*see AA. capillipes, crataegifolium, davidii, forrestii, grosseri* var. *hersii, maximowiczii, pectinatum* (poorly), *pensylvanicum, rufinerve* and *stachyophyllum*). In *AA. griseum* and *triflorum* the bark is flaky with thin flakes. In *AA. rubrum* and *saccharinum* and in young trees of *pseudoplatanus*, the bark is smooth and silvery.

Informal Key

LEAVES

(i)   **simple, untoothed:** *laevigatum, oblongum*

(ii) **simple, toothed:** *carpinifolium, crataegifolium* (lobulate), *davidii* (sometimes lobulate), *distylum, stachyophyllum* (lobulate), *tataricum* (lobulate)

(iii) **three lobed (or with small additional basal lobes):** *barbinerve, buergerianum, capillipes, forrestii, ginnala, granatense, grosseri* var. *hersii, monspessulanum, obtusifolium, pensylvanicum, rubrum, rufinerve, sempervirens, stachyophyllum, wilsonii*

(iv) **palmately lobed, lobes five to seven, margins untoothed or with a few large teeth:** *amplum, campestre, cappadocicum, diabolicum, lobelii, macrophyllum, miyabei, mono, platanoides, saccharum, truncatum*

(v)   **palmately lobed, lobes five to seven, margins with many, often sharp, teeth:** *argutum, campbellii, caudatum, giraldii, heldreichii, hyrcanum, maximowiczii* (sometimes only three lobed), *oliverianum, opalus, palmatum, pectinatum* (sometimes only three lobed), *pensylvanicum* (sometimes only three lobed), *pseudoplatanus, rubrum* (sometimes only three lobed), *saccharinum,* (*spicatum*), *ukurunduense, velutinum* var. *vanvolxemii*

(vi) **palmately lobed, lobes 7–11:** *japonicum, palmatum, pseudosieboldianum, shirasawanum*

(vii) **trifoliate (with three leaflets):** *cissifolium, griseum, henryi, maximowiczianum, triflorum*

(viii) **pinnate, leaflets five to seven (rarely only three):** *negundo*

---

p.285 **Broad Maple** *Acer amplum*

Description: Deciduous tree 10–15 m (33–50 ft) with a bole diameter to 40 cm (1.3 ft).
Crown Broad and spreading on a short bole. *Bark* Smooth, greyish brown, becoming shallowly ridged and furrowed. *Shoot* Light green and hairless at first with a glaucous waxy bloom, becoming darker green, but remaining green for five years or so, then grey-brown. *Buds* In opposite pairs, ovoid, shiny green with rounded acute scales, 5 mm (0.2 in). *Foliage* Leaves usually five lobed and making a rectangle between the four side lobes with the terminal lobe extending forwards, occasionally on fruiting specimens basal lobes weak, lobes very broad ovate with

an abruptly slender tail-like tip ending in a small filament, sinuses very open, base subcordate, margin untoothed, wrinkled or wavy, rather stiff, upper surface matt deep green, sparsely hairy or hairless, underside light green, hairless except for axillary tufts on the raised veins, 8–11 cm × 9–13 cm (3.1–4.3 × 3.5–5.1 in); leaf stalk with a milky sap, grooved with a swollen base, green, 5–9 cm (2–3.5 in); autumn colour yellow. *Flowers* In broad rounded corymbs on a short peduncle of less than 1 cm (0.4 in), yellow-green. *Fruit* Nutlet flattened, 1.5 cm × 8 mm (0.6 × 0.3 in), with wing 3 cm (1.2 in) (making samara 4.5 cm (1.8 in)), with the pairs spreading at an obtuse angle.

Range: China from Sichuan east to Zhejiang and south in Yunnan to the Burma border.

Habitat: Cultivated as an ornamental, in the wild occurring in mixed forests.

Varieties: The common form in cultivation is var. *jianshuiense* which occurs in western Yunnan along the border with Burma. Var. *tientaiense* from the east of the range in Zhejiang has leaves usually only three lobed on fruiting specimens.

Synonyms: *A. longipes* ssp. *amplum*.

Similar species: *A. longipes*, from central China, differs in the leaves being velvety beneath, of thinner texture and more rounded at the base on fruiting specimens (sterile trees of this group of maples tend to have more spreading basal lobes).

This small tree is a close relative of *A. cappadocicum*, differing in the broader leaves with more rounded ovate lobes and the wide inflorescence which is on a peduncle of less than 1 cm (0.4 in).

---

p.299 **Deep-veined Maple** *Acer argutum*

Description: Deciduous tree 6–10 m (20–33 ft) with a bole diameter to 30 cm (1 ft).
Crown Rounded, on several stems and rather shrubby. *Bark* Grey-green, dark with prominent lenticels. *Shoot* Green with

incurved fine white hairs in the first year, maturing to pinkish purple with green striations. *Buds* In opposite pairs, stalked, ovoid, pointed, green or pinkish, 5 mm (0.2 in). *Foliage* Leaves rounded in outline, with five (rarely three or seven) short triangular slender-pointed lobes which extend less than a third of the way to the middle, base more or less truncate, margins sharply doubly serrate with triangular teeth, sinuses scalloped, upper surface blistered (indented at the veins), light to yellow-green with veins raised and hairy, undersurface pale green with prominent raised veins, puckered, with pale brown hairs on the veins and in axillary tufts, 5–10 × 5–10 cm (2–4 × 2–4 in); leaf stalk grooved, pink or green, variable in length from 3–15 cm (1.2–6 in); autumn colour bright yellow. *Flowers* On separate male and female trees, in pendulous 3–6 cm (1.2–2.4 in) racemes in spring, on leafy side shoots. *Fruit* Nutlet green, ripening brown, ridged and flattened, 3 mm (0.1 in), wings 1.5–2.5 cm (0.6–1 in), spreading widely.

Range: Southern Honshu and Shikoku, Japan.

Habitat: Cultivated as an ornamental, in the wild occurring in woods.

This is a very pretty tree in the finely cut foliage which is set on long pink leaf stalks. The leaves have given rise to a variety of descriptive common names, including Sharp-toothed Maple and Pointed-leaf Maple.

p.299 **Bearded Maple** *Acer barbinerve*

Description: Deciduous tree to 10 m (33 ft) with a bole diameter to 25 cm (10 in).
Crown Rounded, domed, often on several stems. *Bark* Green or yellow-green with pale strips for several years, becoming greyish brown. *Shoot* Green or pinky green in the first year, becoming hairless and light green with pale or whitish striations, remaining green for many years. *Buds* In opposite pairs and on a short stalk, ovoid, blunt, green or pink, slightly

hairy, 4 mm (0.2 in). *Foliage* Leaves roundish ovate, with three main lobes from the base but with small variable basal lobes, apex with a slender point, tail-like, base heart-shaped to subcordate, margin irregularly and variably doubly toothed to lobed, sinuses acute, narrow, upper surface matt mid green, somewhat hairy especially on the rounded veins, underside light green to whitish green, softly hairy especially in the vein axils which have bearded tufts, with black dots on the midrib and base of the leaf on both sides, 5–11 × 5–12 cm (2–4.3 × 2–4.7 in); leaf stalk pink or green, grooved, hairy and with black dots, 1.5–8 cm (0.6–3.1 in); autumn colour yellow. *Flowers* On separate male and female trees; in racemes with the new foliage terminating leafy side shoots. *Fruit* In pendent racemes 5 cm (2 in) long, nutlet 1 cm × 8 mm (0.4 × 0.3 in) on a flower stalk 2 mm (0.1 in), sub-globose, ribbed, wing 3–3.5 cm × 1 cm (1.2–1.4 × 0.4 in), the pairs spreading at an obtuse angle.

Range: Northeast China, Korea and adjoining Maritime Russia.

Habitat: Cultivated as an ornamental, in the wild occurring as an understorey tree in woods.

This small shrubby tree is closely related to *A. argutum* and *A. stachyophyllum* and with them belongs to the section *Argutum*. It is geographically intermediate between them, and is in the degree of lobing and toothing of the leaves. Like them, it has stalked buds and striated shoots, but does not belong to the true snake-bark maples.

---

p.295   **Trident Maple** *Acer buergerianum*

Description: Deciduous tree 10–15 m (33–50 ft) with a bole diameter to 50 cm (1.6 ft).
Crown Ovoid, becoming domed, dense.
Bark Buff-brown, becoming scaly with rectangular plates of dark grey, brown or black which flake off to show orange beneath. *Shoot* Hairless or less often

densely white haired, becoming orange-brown in the second year and later buff. *Buds* In opposite pairs, ovoid, chocolate brown, with hairy scales. *Foliage* Leaves trilobed from the base, with three forward pointing lobes above the middle, apices acute with short slender point, sinuses acute, base rounded or wedge-shaped, margins untoothed or obscurely toothed, upper surface shiny green, hairless except for a few hairs along the impressed veins, underside glaucous, initially hairy but most soon lost except along the raised veins, texture hard, 4–8 × 3.5–6.5 cm (1.6–3.1 × 1.4–2.6 in); leaf stalk grooved, green, 3–7 cm (1.2–2.8 in); autumn colour scarlet and green with unchanged leaves. *Flowers* In pendent umbel-like corymbs on a 2 cm (0.8 in) downy peduncle on leafy or leafless shoots, white. *Fruit* In pendent clusters of around ten, nutlet angular, 4 mm (0.2 in), wing 1.5 cm (0.6 in), with the pairs erect and parallel or somewhat overlapping.

Range: China, mainly in the east.

Habitat: Cultivated as an ornamental, in the wild occurring in mixed forests.

Synonyms: *A. trifidum.*

This tree has prominently three-veined leaves with the lobes pointing forwards, as in Neptune's trident. It is native to China but was an early introduction to Japan and has been much employed as a subject for bonsai. Young plants tend to have more laterally spreading side lobes.

p.290 **Campbell Maple** *Acer campbellii*

Description: Deciduous tree 10–15 m (33–50 ft) with a bole diameter to 30 cm (1 ft).
Crown Tall dome. *Bark* Green-brown in young trees, then brown and scaly at the base in old trees. *Shoot* Green or reddish with sparse oval pale lenticels, hairless, rigid, remaining green for several years. *Buds* In opposite pairs, conical, green or reddish green, 5 mm (0.2 in), terminal

buds absent. *Foliage* Leaves rounded in outline with five or seven (rarely nine) deep lobes, lobes lanceolate or oblong with a tapered slender point or tail-like tip, sinuses deep and very narrow, base heart-shaped, rarely truncate or subcordate, margin finely and regularly finely serrate with small forward-pointing bristle-tipped teeth, upper surface mid matt green, hairless with raised veins, underside light green with prominent raised veins which are white haired at first, especially in axillary tufts, 9–15 × 10–20 cm (3.5–6 × 4–8 in); leaf stalk red, round or faintly grooved, enclosing the bud in its enlarged base, 4–8 cm (1.6–3.1 in); autumn colour yellow. *Flowers* In panicles in early summer on leafy side shoots, flowers greenish, floral disc and ovary hairy.
Fruit In pendent panicles, nutlet rounded, 5 mm (0.2 in), wing 2–3.5 cm (0.8–1.4 in), with the pairs spreading almost horizontally.

Range: Himalayas from Nepal eastwards to Yunnan, China.

Habitat: Cultivated as an ornamental, in the wild occurring in temperate broadleaved forests.

Similar species: **Fan-leafed Maple** *A. flabellatum* (syn. *A. campbellii* ssp. *flabellatum*) differs in the leaves which have shallower lobes (thus fan-shaped) and deeply heart-shaped bases, with the margins having slender-pointed but not bristle-tipped teeth, and the floral disk and ovary being hairless. It comes from Sichuan and Hubei in central China but is rare apart from specialist collections. *A. flabellatum* var. *yunnanense* is a form from southern Yunnan which is intermediate between *A. campbellii* and *A. flabellatum*, being closer to the former in the bristle-tipped teeth but having a hairless ovary. It is found in a few collections and makes a tree to 10 m (33 ft).
Wilson's Maple *A. wilsonii* (p.290), from central China, has smaller leaves which are three lobed and rounded at the base, especially on fruiting specimens.

This has made only a small tree in cultivation, but in the warm temperate forests of Bhutan and Sikkim trees 25 m (80 ft) tall are found.

p.287 **Field Maple** *Acer campestre*

Description: Deciduous tree usually 10–12 m (33–39 ft) but sometimes to 15–25 m (50–80 ft). *Crown* Rounded dome with a dense twiggy habit. *Bark* Pale grey-brown, scaly in small squares or flakes, darker in older trees. *Shoot* Initially hairy, brown by first autumn, developing pale striations, subsequently often forming corky ridges. *Buds* In opposite pairs, small, conical, dark brown, 3 mm (0.1 in). *Foliage* Leaves five lobed, sinuses open, acute, margins lobulate, but not toothed, heart-shaped at base, usually hairy on both sides, especially beneath in tufts in vein axils. Leaves around 7 cm (2.8 in) long and wide but up to 16 cm (6.3 in). New foliage in summer often purple or pink. Autumn colour golden-yellow. Leaf stalk hairy, to 5 cm (2 in), sap milky. *Flowers* Inconspicuous after the leaves in few-flowered terminal corymbs, yellow-green. *Fruit* Nutlet flattened, pairs of wings nearly in a straight line, to 2.5 cm (1 in), up to 5 cm (2 in).

Range: England, Wales, central and southern Europe west to Turkey and west Asia, south to North Africa.

Habitat: Hedgerows and broadleafed woodland.

Varieties: No varieties but the following three cultivars are occasionally grown in parks: 'Postelense', in which the new leaves are bright gold; 'Pulverulentum', in which the leaves are flecked with white patches; and 'Schwerinii', with strongly purple new foliage.

This small tree has a good-quality timber, but which is not often available. It is excellent for hedges, tolerating clipping and adding an extra dimension with the brilliant colour of the new summer foliage. It is a tough tree, equally at home on soils derived from chalk, clay or sands.

p.300 **Kyushu Maple** *Acer capillipes*

Description: Deciduous tree to 10–15 m (33–50 ft) with a bole diameter to 40 cm (1.3 ft).
Crown On ascending and arching branches, usually making a low rounded tree.
Bark Olive-green with bright white vertical striations and crossing short buff-brown stripes, usually remaining green to the base. *Shoot* Green and hairless at first, becoming more olive-green in the second year and starting the fissures in the bark which develop as white snake-like striations. *Buds* In opposite pairs, ovoid, pointed, hairless, with two reddish to purple valvate scales, 4 mm (0.2 in), on a short bloomed stalk. *Foliage* Leaves broad ovate and three lobed (or with small additional basal lobes), middle lobe triangular-ovate ending in a short slender point, side lobes forward pointing, short and slender pointed with rounded or scalloped sinuses, base rounded or truncate, margin with irregular broadly triangular acute or abruptly short-pointed teeth, upper surface matt green, hairless apart from a few short sparse brown hairs along the slightly raised veins (although somewhat sunken in folds in the leaf), lower surface light or whitish green, hairless except occasionally for a few whitish hairs in vein axils, veins prominent, often with small peg-like projections in the vein axils, 10–15 × 8–12 cm (4–6 × 3.1–4.7 in); leaf stalk grooved, green or pink, hairless, 4–8 cm (1.6–3.1 in); autumn colour good but variable, from yellow, orange-red or crimson. *Flowers* In slender pendent hairless racemes to 10 cm (4 in) of thirty or so yellow-green flowers on slender flower stalks. *Fruit* Nut pink or yellow-green, 5 mm (0.2 in), with wings 2 cm (0.8 in), pendent on the racemes in pairs with the wings spreading at an obtuse angle, flower stalks 1–1.5 cm (0.4–0.6 in), slender.
Range: Southern Japan from southern Honshu, Kyushu and Shikoku.
Habitat: Cultivated as an ornamental, in the wild occurring in mountain forests.

Similar species: *A. morifolium* from Yakushima Island, off
the southern coast of Kyushu, differs in the
leaves being unlobed or only weakly lobed
and totally hairless.

A. rubescens from Taiwan is also closely
allied, differing in the more reddish green
leaves which are more sharply serrate and
have a more rounded outline with two or
four short side lobes. The bark has a
stronger contrast between the olive-green
and white striations, but it is only hardy in
milder areas.

This is one of the best all-round snake bark
maples, having perhaps the best autumn
colour and keeping a good contrast between
the olive-green and white striations on the
bark. It is allied to *A. davidii*, and in
cultivation the two often hybridize. There
are often, but not always, small peg-like
projections in the vein axils on the
underside along the main vein and at the
base. These are found more strongly in this
tree, but are found in several or all the snake
bark maples. The Latin name is derived
from *capillus*, meaning a hair's width, and
refers to the slender flower stalks.

p.284 **Cappadocian Maple** *Acer cappadocicum*

Description: Deciduous tree 15–25 m (50–80 ft) with a
bole diameter to 80 cm (2.6 ft).
Crown Ovoid in young trees but soon
becoming rounded domed, with suckers
from the roots. *Bark* Grey and finely
roughened. *Shoot* Green with small red-
brown lenticels, hairless but may be
bloomed grey when new, becoming shiny
and remaining green for three or four
seasons, then brown, slender. *Buds* In
opposite pairs, bluntly ovoid, green-brown,
4 mm (0.2 in). *Foliage* Leaves five or seven
lobed, lobes ovoid-triangular with a drawn-
out triangular tip which ends in a fine
filament, sinuses bluntly pointed, base
subcordate and somewhat rounded, margins
untoothed, upper surface mid matt green
with paler raised veins, hairless except in

vein axils at base, lower surface light green
with raised veins, hairless except for a tuft
in the main veins axils at base, broader than
long, 8–12 × 12–16 cm (3.1–4.7 ×
4.7–6.3 in), although on flowering shoots
the last leaves may be smaller and only
three lobed; leaf stalk with a milky sap,
round or shallowly grooved, pink, red or
green, 3–12 cm (1.2–4.7 in); autumn
colour butter yellow, one of the best golds.
Flowers In terminal corymbs on a common
peduncle of 2–3 cm (0.8–1.2 in) after the
leaves, yellow. *Fruit* Pendent, seeds flat,
around 1 cm (0.4 in), with a spreading
wing 2 cm (0.8 in), pairs of fruits widely
spreading or at an obtuse angle.

Range: Eastern Turkey, Caucasus to Iran.

Habitat: Deciduous forests.

Varieties: 'Rubrum' is the commonest form in
cultivation. The new foliage and shoots are
reddish. 'Aureum' is a spectacular small
tree with pale yellow to gold leaves,
greening with age, and with the tips
somewhat reddish. It forms a small tree to
15 m (50 ft). Ssp. *sinicum* is a related taxon
from central and west China. The leaves are
smaller with longer lobes and the bark is
more strongly fissured.

Synonyms: *A. laetum*.

This has one of the best and most reliable of
yellow autumn colours, turning in early to
mid October before most other trees. It is
also unusual amongst maples in that it
suckers from the roots. The persistently
green and thus photosynthetic shoots
distinguish it from *AA. platanoides*, *mono*
and *truncatum*, which also have milky sap. It
is close to *A. lobelii*, which has strongly
bloomed and thicker shoots and leaves with
some marginal toothing.

---

p.169 **Hornbeam Maple** *Acer carpinifolium*

Description: Deciduous tree to 10 m (33 ft) with a bole
diameter 30 cm (1 ft).
Crown Low, spreading with rather arching
and horizontal branching. *Bark* Smooth,

brown. *Shoot* Green with round lenticels and hairless in the first year, becoming light brown or grey-brown, slender.
Buds In opposite pairs, ovoid, rounded, with numerous overlapping green and brown scales, 6 mm (0.25 in).
Foliage Leaves lanceolate-oblong to ovate-oblong, tapering to the acute or slender-pointed apex, base rounded, margin coarsely doubly serrate with ovate-triangular forward pointing teeth which taper to a short point, upper surface light matt green, ribbed with 18–23 pairs of parallel side veins, underside lighter sub-shiny green with raised veins, hairy with long, soft, straight, pale brown hairs on the veins and in the axils, texture thin, 8–15 × 3.5–7 cm (3.1–6 × 1.4–2.8 in); leaf stalk deeply grooved, hairless, 1–1.5 cm (0.4–0.6 in); autumn colour pale yellow.
Flowers In pendulous nearly hairless racemes 5–12 cm (2–4.7 in), with separate male and female trees, flowers not showy.
Fruit Nutlet flattened, the wings 2.5–3 cm (1–1.2 in), with the pairs ascending at a narrow to obtuse angle.

Range: Throughout Japan.
Habitat: Cultivated as an ornamental, in the wild occurring in mountain valleys and ravines.

This maple has leaves which strongly resemble *Carpinus* in their many parallel side veins, but their arrangement in pairs readily distinguish it even when not in fruit. It makes a rather small tree of curious aspect.

---

p.298 **Tail-leaf Maple** *Acer caudatum*

Description: Deciduous tree to 10 m (33 ft) with a bole diameter to 30 cm (1 ft).
Crown Rounded, often on several stems.
Bark Ash grey or brown, finely ridged, becoming flaky and stringy in thin sheets.
Shoot Green with a light covering of sandy white to rusty hairs in the first year with a few raised oval lenticels, in the second year outer layer is grey and peels to reveal green

beneath, later whitish grey. *Buds* In opposite pairs, ovoid, outer pair of scales valvate and light green to reddish brown with brownish hairs at the tip, 4–8 mm (0.2–0.3 in). *Foliage* Leaves rounded in outline with five to seven triangular lobes which are tail-like with a slender point at the apex and 4–6 cm (1.6–2.4 in) long, sinuses broad but acute at the angle, base heart-shaped, margin sharply and irregularly doubly serrate with triangular or rounded slender pointed teeth, upper surface medium matt green with slightly impressed veins and veinlets, with the main veins raised and with a few rufous hairs, underside pale to whitish green, hairless except for sparse hairs on the main veins, 10–15 × 10–15 cm (4–6 × 4–6 in); leaf stalk shallowly grooved, pink or green, with a swollen base, length variable, to 20 cm (8 in); autumn colour yellow. *Flowers* In dense erect panicles. *Fruit* Nutlet dimpled, with acute to parallel ascending wings 2–2.5 × 1 cm (0.8–1 × 0.4 in), on short flower stalks 3–7 mm (0.1–0.3 in).

Range: Himalayas from East Nepal across Sikkim, Bhutan, northeast India to Burma and west China (Yunnan).

Habitat: Cultivated as an ornamental, in the wild mainly occurring in the zone dominated by *Abies densa*.

Synonyms: *A. papilio.*

This small tree is related to *A. ukurunduense* and *A. spicatum*. The pink leaf stalks and deeply cut leaves can be very attractive.

---

p.307   **Vine-leafed Maple** *Acer cissifolium*

Description: Deciduous tree 10–15 m (33–50 ft) with a bole diameter to 40 cm (1.3 ft). *Crown* Wide spreading, rather flat and low. *Bark* Smooth, grey, with large whitish areas. *Shoot* Pink and green, covered at first with long whitish hairs, ash grey in the second and later years. *Buds* In opposite pairs, conical, whitish hairy, with two pairs of dark red scales, 4 mm (0.2 in); enclosed in the leaf-stalk base during the summer. *Foliage* Leaves trifoliate, with forward-pointing ovate to obovate leaflets which are wedge-shaped or rounded at the base, acute at the tip and coarsely toothed with large rounded abruptly short-pointed teeth in the upper part only, upper surface with stiff hairs, matt green, underside shiny light green with hairs, especially on the raised veins, leaflets 4–10 × 2.5–4 cm (1.6–4 × 1–1.6 in); stalk of leaflets red, slender, grooved, 1–2 cm (0.4–0.8 in); leaf stalk pink, enclosing the bud at the base, 3–7 cm (1.2–2.8 in); autumn colour pale yellow. *Flowers* Dioecious, with the single sex racemes pendent at the tips of leafy shoots in May, 10–16 cm (4–6.3 in), yellow-green. *Fruit* Nutlet flattened and dimpled on one side, 7 mm (0.3 in), with narrow wing 1.5–2.5 cm (0.6–1 in), with the pairs spreading at an acute angle.

Range: Hokkaido, Honshu, Shikoku and Kyushu, Japan.

Habitat: Cultivated as an ornamental, in the wild found in mountain forests.

Synonyms: *Negundo cissifolium*.

This tree is similar to *A. negundo*, from which the invariably trifoliate leaves separate it, and more closely to *A. henryi*, which has shoots which are green for several years. Like these two species, it is dioecious with separate male and female trees. In cultivation it is largely represented by a single clone, which has a rather flat habit. The Latin name refers to the resemblance of the leaves to those of *Cissus*, which is a large tropical genus in the vine family.

p.293 **Uri Maple** or **Hawthorn-leaf Maple**
Acer crataegifolium

Description: Deciduous tree to 6–10 m (20–33 ft) with a bole diameter to 30 cm (1 ft).
Crown Often rather shrubby on several stems, or a small slender tree. *Bark* Green

with vertical white snake-like striations. *Shoot* Purplish red or green, smooth and hairless, with minute lenticels, developing green or white striations from the third season, sometimes with a slight glaucous bloom. *Buds* In opposite pairs, elliptic-acute, pointed, purple-red or green, with two outer bud scales, 3 mm (0.1 in), on a short stalk. *Foliage* Leaves ovate triangular, apex tapers to a short slender point, base rounded to subcordate, three lobed below the middle with or without lobules (small rounded lobes), weak basal lobes on young plants and vigorous shoots, side lobes short, broad triangular, acute, sinuses bluntly pointed to just acute, margin sharply serrate with acute teeth, upper surface matt green but often with some purplish bronzing and hairless except for sparse brown hairs on the slightly raised veins, undersurface pale green, hairless or with some sparse rufous hairs on the veins, 5–7 × 4–7 cm (2–2.8 × 1.6–2.8 in); leaf stalk grooved, with a few hairs, pink, red or green, 2–3 cm (0.8–1.2 in); autumn colour purple or dark reddish purple. *Flowers* In short erect racemes of about ten flowers, 3–5 cm (1.2–2 in) in length, petals whitish. *Fruit* Small, with wing 2 cm (0.8 in), in spreading or erect pairs.

Range: Japan, from Honshu, Shikoku and Kyushu.

Habitat: Cultivated as an ornamental, in the wild occurring in woods and thickets at the base of mountains.

Varieties: 'Veitchii' is a selection which has the leaves mottled with white and rose, although a proportion of the leaves are normal green.

The Latin name translates as Hawthorn-leaf Maple. It only makes sense if a suitable hawthorn (genus *Crataegus*) is selected, and even then the resemblance has been termed 'fanciful'! The Japanese name is Uri kaede (maple). It is very close to *A. maximowiczii*, and it is pertinent that a synonym for that tree is *A. urophyllum* (by one month!).

p.169 **David's Maple** *Acer davidii*

Description: Deciduous tree 10–15 m (33–50 ft), with a bole diameter to 40 cm (1.3 ft).
Crown Upright and domed or vase shaped with radiating branches which arch out.
Bark Olive-green with white or glaucous-white snake-like striations, becoming brown, fissured and somewhat corky at the base in some old trees. *Shoot* Green or pink-green, remaining so but developing green or whitish fissures or striations.
Buds In opposite pairs, on a short stalk or projection, ovoid-conic and pressed against the shoot, with two pairs of bud scales, green or red, to 1 cm (0.4 in).
Foliage Leaves rather variable, ovate or oblong with a triangular apex with a slender pointed tip, base subcordate, margin serrate with rounded bluntly pointed teeth, sometimes lobed or lobulate, upper surface sub-shiny, hairless or initially with a few rufous hairs on the veins, underside pale green with raised veins which have a scattering of short rufous or reddish hairs and sometimes with a white bridge or peg, 6–18 × 4–9 cm (2.4–7.1 × 1.6–3.5 in); leaf stalk green or pink, grooved, hairless or shortly rufous haired; autumn colour variable, from pathetic to clear yellow or good red, depending upon form! *Flowers* In pendulous racemes terminating side shoots in late spring, yellow. *Fruit* Nutlets flattened, rounded on one side and dimpled on the other, to 8 mm (0.3in), set on slender flower stalks, wings 2–3 cm (0.8–1.2 in), spreading at a wide angle.

Range: Throughout China except the far west and north.

Habitat: Cultivated as an ornamental, in the wild occurring as an understorey in woods and in thickets.

Varieties: The forms from Yunnan, such as 'George Forrest', are commonest in cultivation. These tend to have ovate or oblong-lanceolate leaves which are rather regularly toothed and unlobed. 'Ernest Wilson', which was collected in Hubei province, has lobulate leaves which are folded along the midrib and rather glaucous beneath. The introduction which Maries made to Veitch's nursery appears to have acquired two names, *A. veitchii* and *A. schwerinii*. It is indistinguishable from 'Ernest Wilson'.

Synonyms: *A. veitchii*, *A. schwerinii*.

This tree is very variable in cultivation, as might be expected with its enormous range across China. It is one of the commonest snake-bark maples, although not one of the best barks. It will grow on most soils, except shallow soils over chalk.

---

p.288 **Horned Maple** or **Devil's Maple**
Acer diabolicum

Description: Deciduous tree 10–15 m (33–50 ft) with a bole diameter to 50 cm (1.6 ft).
Crown Broad domed. *Bark* Smooth, grey-brown or pinkish grey, developing fissures at the base. *Shoot* Green and rather shiny in the first year with scattered oval brown lenticels, initially sparse long, soft, straight white hairs, in second and later years mid brown and finely fissured. *Buds* In opposite pairs in the leaf axils along the shoot but in trees of flowering age, there is a vegetative bud flanked by flower buds, all of which are ovoid-conic with acute free tips to the scales and dark brown with brown hairs, 4–7 mm (0.2–0.3 in). *Foliage* Leaves rather rounded in outline, with three or five shallow lobes which form narrow acute sinuses, lobes with acute tips and broad triangular teeth, base rounded to subcordate, upper surface dark matt green with pale raised veins which have sparse stiff hairs and slightly impressed and net-like tertiary veins, lower surface shiny mid green, veins raised with whitish stiff hairs on all veins, 10–15 × 10–15 cm (4–6 × 4–6 in); leaf stalk round or grooved near apex, green, sparse straight hairs, 3–11 cm (1.2–4.4 in); autumn colour variable, sometimes a good red. *Flowers* In short

pendulous racemes which arise from the lateral buds at nodes on last season's shoots, in spring before the leaves, yellow or red. *Fruit* Nutlet angular with white irritant bristles, on 1–2 cm (0.4–0.8 in) flower stalks, wings erect and oval, to 3 cm (1.2 in).

Range: Honshu, Kyushu and Shikoku, Japan.

Habitat: Cultivated as an ornamental, in the wild occurring in woodlands.

Varieties: Forma *purpurascens* covers the trees with flowers, new foliage and young fruits purple.

Similar species: *A. sterculiaceum* (syn. *A. villosum*) (p.288) is the Himalayan representative of this section and differs in the much larger leaves, to 20 cm (4 in) or more.

The curious name refers to the two styles which persist on the fruit between the two nutlets and look like the devil's horns. When in flower it can be attractive but has been called the least ornamental of the Japanese maples. It is the hardiest member of the section *Lithocarpa*, which extends across China and northern Vietnam to the Himalayas.

---

p.169 **Lime-leafed Maple** *Acer distylum*

Description: Deciduous tree 6–12 m (20–39 ft) with a bole diameter to 30 cm (1 ft).
Crown Broad, with arching branches.
Bark Grey-green, stripped orange.
Shoot Green when young and white to light brown hairy, soon hairless and brown, in the second and later years grey to buff-brown. *Buds* In opposite pairs, narrow long conic and slightly stalked, red with brownish tips to the paired bud scales and covered in short brown hairs, 1 cm (0.4 in).
Foliage Leaves broad ovate to oblong-ovate with a short abrupt triangular tip and very like the leaves of most limes, base heart-shaped, margin unlobed, with rounded forward shallow teeth, upper surface pale or yellow-green, rather crinkled and leathery in texture, lower surface pale with

raised veins, hairless but new leaves buff-
pink with long rusty hairs, 6–17 ×
5–12 cm (2.4–6.7 × 2–4.7 in); leaf stalk
round but grooved near the top, scarlet to
yellow-pink, hairless; autumn colour
golden-yellow. *Flowers* On leafy side
shoots in early summer, in short erect
spikes which are somewhat branched
(corymbose) at the base, with nodding
small yellowish-green flowers.
Fruit Nutlet rounded, 5 mm (0.2 in),
wing 2–3 cm (0.8–1.2 in), the pairs
spreading at a wide angle to nearly erect.

Range: Honshu and Kyushu, Japan.
Habitat: Cultivated as an ornamental, in the wild
occurring on fertile volcanic silts at the
lower elevations on mountains in mixed
deciduous forest.

This is a rare maple with leaves which
uncannily resemble those of Lime or
Linden (*Tilia*). However, their opposite
arrangement and usually non-oblique
bases, plus the erect racemes of maple
flowers and fruits readily distinguish it. It
requires an acidic site and does not tolerate
lime in the soil.

p.300 **Forrest's Maple** *Acer forrestii*

Description: Deciduous tree 6–12 m (20–40 ft) with a
bole diameter to 50 cm (1.6 ft).
Crown Vase-shaped with ascending
branches which arch outwards and spread
horizontally or droop at the tips.
Bark Olive-green with vivid white
striations, becoming brown and shallowly
fissured at the base of old trees.
Shoot Green or pink, hairless with sparse
white oval lenticels, developing green or
white striations in the second and
subsequent years. *Buds* In opposite pairs,
ovoid-conic, on a short stalk, with two
pairs of bud scales, green or pink, 1 cm
(0.4 in). *Foliage* Leaves strongly three
lobed or with small additional basal lobes,
lobes triangular or triangular-ovate and
tapering to a narrow tail-like tip, sinuses

acute, deep, base heart-shaped to rounded, margin doubly serrate with broad triangular teeth which end in a short acute slender point, upper surface light green, matt, with impressed but slightly raised veins, lower surface pale or becoming somewhat glaucous green with raised veins, hairless except for sparse axillary tufts of white or pale hairs, 5–12 × 3–12 cm (2–4.7 × 1.2–4.7 in); leaf stalk grooved, pink, hairless, up to 8 cm (3.1 in); autumn colour yellow. *Flowers* In spreading or pendulous racemes termination leafy shoots in late spring; greenish yellow. *Fruit* Nutlet rounded, 5 mm (0.2 in), with wings 2–2.5 cm (0.8–1 in) which spread at a wide angle or nearly horizontally.

Range: West Yunnan, China and Upper Burma.

Habitat: Cultivated as an ornamental, in the wild found in mixed forest.

Varieties: No cultivars but confused with *A. davidii* in some collections, which has unlobed but sometimes slightly lobulate leaves which are slightly rufous pubescent beneath.

Synonyms: *A. pectinatum* ssp. *forrestii.*

Similar species: *A. laxiflorum* is a related species from Sichuan, China, which has more shallowly lobed leaves, thus more ovate in outline, which are rufous pubescent beneath.

This is one of the most attractive of the snake bark maples with a good olive-green bark which is strongly marked with snaking white striations. The leaves are attractively lobed and a bright light green which contrasts well with the pink leaf stalks. From related species, it is well marked by the almost hairless three-lobed leaves. It thrives best in light woodland, preferably on acid or neutral soils.

---

p.297 **Amur Maple** *Acer ginnala*

Description: Deciduous tree to 10 m (33 ft) with a bole diameter to 30 cm (1 ft).
Crown Often shrubby on several stems with an upright or rounded crown.

Bark Dark grey, smooth, becoming shallowly fissured and ridged in old trees. *Shoot* Olive-brown with small round lenticels in the first year, becoming red-brown. *Buds* In opposite pairs, ovoid, rounded, with dark chocolate brown scales, 3 mm (0.1 in). *Foliage* Leaves ovate in outline with a dominant central lobe but usually strongly three lobed at the base with the lobes ovate to lanceolate with narrow acute sinuses, tip acute, base rounded, central lobe ovate with a coarsely doubly toothed or somewhat lobulate margin (in addition to the basal lobes), teeth triangular, acute, not sharp, texture thin, upper surface matt to glossy deep green, hairless, underside shiny light green with raised veins which have axillary tufts, 4–8 × 3–8 cm (1.6–3.1 × 1.2–3.1 in); leaf stalk pink and green, grooved, 3–5 cm (1.2–2 in); autumn colour red in early autumn. *Flowers* In spreading or erect fragrant panicles in May, flowers yellow-green. *Fruit* Nutlet 1 cm (0.4 in), flattened with striations, wing 1.5 cm (0.6 in), the pairs erect or spreading at a narrow angle.

Range: Throughout Japan, eastern Siberia, Korea and northeastern China.

Habitat: Cultivated as an ornamental, in the wild occurring in thickets in damp localities.

Synonyms: *A. tataricum* var. *ginnala*.

This small tree is one of the first to turn in September, developing a rich if fleeting crimson. It is allied to *A. tataricum*, which has unlobed or scarcely lobed leaves on mature trees, although on saplings and watershoots (basal vigorous shoots) on old trees the leaves are more strongly lobed.

p.292 **Giraldi's Maple** *Acer giraldii*

Description: Deciduous tree 15–20 m (50–65 ft) with a bole diameter up to 60 cm (2 ft).
Crown Domed, spiky in young trees.
Bark Brown, with vertical thin peeling flakes. *Shoot* Green for several years and

stout, initially with a glaucous waxy bloom which is usually rubbed off in the second year, lenticels oval, dark brown. *Buds* Conical or ovate-conical, with several overlapping brown scales, 7 mm (0.3 in). *Foliage* Leaves broader than long, three lobed or with vestigial basal lobes, main lobes broad triangular with a short slender pointed apex, sinuses acute, base heart-shaped, margins with coarse rounded teeth, upper surface matt dark green, veins impressed with short brown hairs, underside glaucous green, veins prominent with white hairs, tertiary veins net-like, 15 × 20 cm (6 × 8 in); leaf stalk purplish-pink or green, with a glaucous waxy bloom; autumn colour yellow or poor. *Flowers* In upright corymbs, greenish. *Fruit* Seed angular, 1 cm (0.4 in), with a wing 2–5 cm (0.8–2 in), with the pairs of fruits spreading at an acute or obtuse angle.

Range: China from Shaanxi in the north across Yunnan to southeast Tibet.

Habitat: Cultivated as an ornamental, in the wild occurring as a component in mixed forests.

Synonyms: *A. caesium* ssp. *giraldii*.

Similar species: *A. caesium* from the northwest Himalayas to western Nepal and in northwest Bhutan is a related species. This differs in the brown, not or scarcely bloomed shoots, the more prominently five-lobed leaves with serrate margins and the thin grey smooth bark.

This tree is very distinct in the thick glaucous bloom on the shoots and leaf stalks. The leaves are similar to *A. pseudoplatanus* but with smaller lobes which are more abruptly slender pointed and less lobed, but the fruits are angular and rather deltoid.

---

p.296 **Spanish Maple** *Acer granatense*

Description: Deciduous tree to 10 m (33 ft) or so with a bole diameter to 60 cm (2 ft).
Crown Ovoid, densely branched.
Bark Smooth, grey-brown. *Shoot* Green-

brown and hairless, with small orange oval lenticels, in the second year light shiny brown and becoming fissured. *Buds* In opposite pairs, ovoid, bluntly pointed, light brown, 5 mm (0.2 in).
Foliage Leaves rather oblong with three to five main lobes, main lobes short oblong-acute with lobulate and coarsely rounded teeth, sinuses narrow, rounded, base deeply heart-shaped, upper surface shiny green, nearly hairless, underside light somewhat glaucous green, hairy or hairless except for pale hairs on the raised veins, 3–7 × 4–8 cm (1.2–2.8 × 1.6–3.1 in); leaf stalk hairless or hairy, pink and green, faintly grooved, with a watery sap, 3–7 cm (1.2–2.8 in); autumn colour yellow.
Flowers In terminal corymbs with the leaves, yellow. *Fruit* Nutlets small, wings spreading.

Range: Southern Spain, and Algeria and Morocco, possibly also in the Pyrenees and southwest France.

Habitat: Mountain forests and hedgerows.

Synonyms: *A. opalus* ssp. *hispanicum*.

This tree has foliage which is very similar in appearance to that of *A. campestre*, differing in the more frilly lobing and in the watery sap. It is closer to *A. hyrcanum*, differing in the smaller and more hairy leaves.

---

p.306 **Paperbark Maple** *Acer griseum*

Description: Deciduous tree 10–15 m (33–50 ft) with a bole diameter to 60 cm (2 ft).
Crown Ovoid, becoming domed or rounded in old trees. *Bark* Unmistakable with thin peeling flakes or small sheets of red-brown, copper or chestnut showing orange and often bloomed bark beneath, starting on branches three to four years old and extending throughout the crown, only tight in poor growing unthrifty trees. *Shoot* Olive-brown and woolly at first but hairless and shiny by autumn, then dark brown to red-brown with a

greyish cast, slender, stiff. *Buds* In opposite pairs, long ovoid-conic, pointed, scales dark chocolate brown with some marginal hairs, 2–5 mm (0.1–0.2 in). *Foliage* Leaves trifoliate, 10 × 14 cm (4 × 5.5 in); leaflets elliptic, ovate-oblong to ovate-lanceolate, acute at the tip, wedge-shaped on the terminal leaflet which has a stalk to 1 cm (0.4 in), oblique and wedge-shaped to rounded on the lateral pairs which are almost stalkless (stalk to 2 mm (0.1 in)), margin ciliate, with two to four pairs of large triangular teeth but usually untoothed on the lower half of the terminal leaflet and on the inner sides of the lateral leaflets, upper surface green slightly net-veined with impressed hairy veins, underside bright glaucous green with raised veins which are hairy, 4–10 × 2–6 cm (1.6–4 × 0.8–2.4 in); leaf stalk round, pink, hairy, clasping bud in the enlarged base; autumn colour brilliant crimson, red or orange. *Flowers* In threes, terminal on spur shoots, yellow.
Fruit Nutlet rounded, green, ripening to brown, densely hairy, with a very thick case, 1 cm (0.4 in), wing parallel, 3 × 1.2 cm (1.2 × 0.5 in), with the pairs spreading at an acute angle.

Range: Central China from Hubei, Hanan, Shaanxi, Gansu and east Sichuan.

Habitat: Cultivated as an ornamental, in the wild occurring in mixed forests as an understorey tree.

Synonyms: *A. nikoense* var. *grisea.*

This tree has the best bark of any maple (better than almost any other trees – *see Stuartia sinensis, Myrtus luma (apiculata), Abies squamata, Rhododendron falconeri, Betula utilis* and some *Eucalyptus* for comparable barks), with the added bonus of excellent autumn colour. It thrives on a wide range of sites, including chalk and limestone. The trifoliate leaves resemble those of *AA. maximowiczianum, mandshuricum* and *triflorum.* The nutlets have a very thick shell. They often form without pollination, and thus are empty.

p.300 **Hers' Maple** *Acer grosseri* var. *hersii*

Description: Deciduous tree to 8–15 m (26–50 ft) with
a bole diameter to 40 cm (1.3 ft).
Crown Rounded, developing branches
which arch out from a short trunk.
Bark Olive-green with bright white
striations, in old trees becoming dull grey-
brown at the base. *Shoot* Pale green,
hairless in the first year, becoming dark
green or olive-green in the second and
later years and developing bright chalky
white striations, remaining green and
striated for many years. *Buds* In opposite
pairs on a short stalk, conical or ovoid-
conic, pointed, green, hairless, with a pair
of valvate outer scales, 6 mm (0.25 in).
Foliage Leaves ovate, usually strongly
three veined from the base with the side
veins terminating in a small triangular
lobe just below the middle (occasionally
also with small basal lobes), apex with
slender point, base rounded heart-shaped,
margin with rounded abruptly short-
pointed teeth, somewhat doubly toothed,
upper surface dull matt green, nearly
hairless, underside pale somewhat whitish
green, with five to seven main pairs of
veins, hairless except for a few rufous hairs
in the vein axils which usually contain a
prominent peg-like projection, 5–12 ×
3–9 cm (2–4.7 × 1.2–3.5 in); leaf stalk
green, grooved, hairless, 2–3 cm
(0.8–1.2 in); autumn colour yellow,
orange or sometimes red. *Flowers* In
racemes with the new foliage terminating
leafy side shoots, yellow. *Fruit* In pendent
racemes to 12 cm (4.7 in), nutlet 7 ×
4 mm (0.3 × 0.2 in), convex, on a flower
stalk 4 mm (0.2 in), wing 2.5–3 cm ×
5 mm (1–1.2 × 0.2 in), the pairs spreading
at a wide angle or horizontally.

Range: Central China.

Habitat: Cultivated as an ornamental, in the wild
occurring as an understorey tree in woods.

Synonyms: *A. hersii*.

Similar species: *A. grosseri* differs mainly in the leaves
being ovate with a tail-like tip and only
weak lateral lobes. It is more widely

distributed in China. *A. hersii* is
sometimes treated as synonymous with *A.
grosseri* and they are both sometimes
treated as *A. davidii* ssp. *grosseri*.

This maple is closely related to *A. davidii*
and *A. capillipes*, differing from both in the
matt green leaves and almost total absence of
any pink or red coloration, from which it has
acquired one common name, Green Bark
Maple. It has one of the best snake-barks.

p.291 **Heldreich's Maple** *Acer heldreichii*

Description: Deciduous tree 15–20 m (50–65 ft) with a
bole diameter to 80 cm (2.6 ft).
Crown Ovoid and spiky in young trees,
becoming an upright dome with age.
Bark Smooth and pink-grey in small trees,
darkening with age but being slow to
become finely fissured. *Shoot* Green or
brown in the first year with fairly dense
narrow elliptic orange lenticels, in the
second year dark brown and starting to
fissure along the lenticels. *Buds* In
opposite pairs, ovoid-conic, pointed, with
numerous overlapping red-brown scales
which leave a ring of circular scars at the
base of each season's growth, 5 mm (0.2 in);
on flowering spur shoots the terminal bud
is often absent. *Foliage* Leaves strongly and
deeply palmately lobed with three large
similar lobes and two small basal ones,
sinuses deep, narrow, reaching five-sixths of
the way to the middle of the leaf, lobes
with two to four rounded teeth, basal lobes
rounded, untoothed, upper surface dark
shiny green, hairless, with deeply impressed
veins, underside pale or glaucous green
with hairs only along the prominent veins,
9–17 × 6–22 cm (3.5–6.7 × 2.4–8.7 in);
leaf stalk oval and stout, hairless, with
lenticels, pink or green, 5–15 cm (2–6 in);
autumn colour yellow. *Flowers* In erect
ovoid corymbs after the leaves, yellow.
Fruit In large clusters, seed hairy,
triangular, 1 cm (0.4 in), wing 2.5–4 cm
(1–1.6 in), erect or overlapping.

Range: Balkans from northern Greece, Albania, Bulgaria, Macedonia, Serbia, Montenegro and Bosnia-Herzegovina.

Habitat: Mountain forests.

Similar species: **Red-bud Maple** or **Trautvetter's Maple** *A. trautvetteri* (p.291) has less deeply cleft leaves, with the sinuses extending only three-quarters of the way to the middle, more coarsely toothed margins and more glaucous beneath with orange hairs on the veins and in the axils. The bud scales are crimson as the new foliage expands, whilst the wings of the seeds are often rosy pink. It occurs in the Caucasus, eastern Turkey and northern Iran and is closely related to *A. heldreichii*, of which some authors treat it as a subspecies (ssp. *trautvetteri*).

This tree is closely related to *A. pseudoplatanus* but is distinguished by the deeply cleft leaves. It is more attractive for the erect flower clusters and has a much superior autumn colour.

p.307 **Henry's Maple** *Acer henryi*

Description: Deciduous tree 10–15 m (33–50 ft), with a bole diameter to 40 cm (1.3 ft). *Crown* Domed. *Bark* Green but becoming brown and lightly fissured. *Shoot* Green, sparsely hairy at first or densely and persistently hairy, remaining green for several years. *Buds* In opposite pairs, ovate, pointed, with a pair of valvate scales which are green or pink, with white hairs, 3 mm (0.1 in). *Foliage* Leaves trifoliate, terminal leaflets largest, elliptic with a slender pointed tip and a wedge-shaped base, margin untoothed or with a few coarse serrations 6–12 × 3–5 cm (2.4–4.7 × 1.2–2 in), on a short 0.5–1 cm (0.2–0.4 in) leaflet stalk, upper surface shiny green and hairy on the veins, lower surface light green, densely hairy on the prominent veins; leaf stalk rounded, slender, red or pink, slightly to densely hairy, 3–7 cm (1.2–2.8 in); autumn colour good red. *Flowers* On separate male and female trees, in pendulous spike-like racemes to 7 cm (2.8 in) on a hairy peduncle, terminating short leafy shoots; flowers yellow, with very short flower stalks. *Fruit* In pendulous racemes to 15 cm (6 in), nutlets 1 × 0.5 cm (0.4 × 0.2 in), flat, with erect parallel wings to 2.5 cm (1 in), at first green or purplish, ripening to yellow-brown, set on short (1 mm (0.05 in)) flower stalks.

Range: Central China (from Henan, Shaanxi, Zhejiang, Jiangsu, Anhui, Hubei, Hunan, Guizhou and Sichuan provinces).

Habitat: Cultivated as an ornamental, in the wild occurring as an understorey in woods.

Synonyms: *A. cissifolium* ssp. *henryi*.

This tree is related to *A. cissifolium*, differing in the very short flower stalks to the flowers and fruit, and the leaves which have a different texture and are generally less toothed. It turns an attractive red in autumn. The forms in cultivation vary in the degree of hairiness. Some are persistently hairy; in most however the hairs are sparse and soon lost.

---

p.296 **Balkan Maple** *Acer hyrcanum*

Description: Deciduous tree 10–15 m (33–50 ft) with a bole diameter to 70 cm (2.3 ft). *Crown* Small and domed, often on several stems in the wild and rather shrubby. *Bark* Brown. *Shoot* Olive-green with small oval pale lenticels, hairless, becoming reddish brown later. *Buds* In opposite pairs, ovoid-conic, pointed, with many overlapping brown scales, 3 mm (0.1 in). *Foliage* Leaves five lobed with fairly even lobes, basal ones occasionally lacking, lobes square with a triangular apex, sometimes constricted at the base in the deep narrow cleft sinuses which reach up to half way to the middle, base heart-shaped, margin with a few large acute teeth, upper surface green with impressed veins, mainly hairless, underside pale glaucous green, variably hairy, especially

along the raised veins, texture hard, 4–6 ×
5–8 cm (1.6–2.4 × 2–3.1 in); leaf stalk
grooved, pink or green, 2.5–8 cm
(1–3.1 in); autumn colour yellow.
Flowers Terminal on short leafy shoots,
petals yellow-green. *Fruit* Seed angular,
9 mm (0.4 in), wing 2–2.5 cm (0.8–1 in),
the pairs spreading at an acute angle.

Range: Balkans east into Turkey, the Lebanon to
Iran and the Caucasus.

Habitat: Dry open hillsides with *Quercus* and
Juniperus.

Varieties: Ssp. *reginae-amaliae* from Greece and
Turkey has much smaller leaves
0.5–1.5 cm (0.2–0.6 in) across which are
thick and tough. It occurs in dry stony
locations and makes a small shrub rather
than a tree.

Synonyms: *A. opalus* var. *hyrcanum*.

This small tree appears in foliage like *A.
campestre* but the watery sap immediately
distinguishes it. Its relationship is with
AA. monspessulanum, obtusatum, opalus and
sempervirens. Several variants have been
named, mainly from Turkey and west Asia.

---

p.294   **Full Moon Maple**   *Acer japonicum*

Description: Deciduous tree 8–15 m (26–50 ft) with a
bole diameter to 40 cm (1.3 ft).
Crown Ovoid, with sinuous branches on a
short bole. *Bark* Grey or grey-green,
smooth. *Shoot* Green or purplish-green,
initially with a few long white hairs,
remaining green or grey-green for several
years. *Buds* In opposite scales, ovoid-conic,
acute, with a pair of red or green valvate
outer scales, hidden in base of leaf stalk,
5 mm (0.2 in); terminal bud absent.
Foliage Leaves rounded in outline, with
nine to eleven (rarely seven) shallow ovate
to slender pointed lobes with deep cleft
sinuses, base deeply heart-shaped, margins
coarsely doubly serrate with acute forward
teeth, upper surface matt green with raised
hairy veins, underside light green with
dense whitish hairs on the prominently

raised veins, 7–12 cm (2.8–4.7 in) long and broad; leaf stalk grooved, densely white shaggy haired, pink or green, with a swollen base which encloses the bud, 3–6 cm (1.2–2.4 in); autumn colour a cacophony of scarlet, orange, yellow and gold. *Flowers* In small drooping corymbs in advance of the leaves on side shoots in spring, purplish red. *Fruit* Nutlet rounded, 7 mm (0.3 in), wings 2–2.5 cm (0.8–1 in), spreading variously from an obtuse angle to ascending.

Range: Hokkaido and Honshu, Japan.

Habitat: Cultivated as an ornamental, in the wild occurring in mountain woods and thickets.

Varieties: 'Vitifolium' is a form with larger leaves, to 15 cm (6 in), which turn brilliant colours in autumn. In 'Aconitifolium', the leaves are deeply cleft, almost to the base, and the lobes themselves divided and sharply toothed. For the small tree called 'Aureum', *see A. shirasawanum*.

This small tree is grown for its beautiful autumn colour, especially of the form 'Vitifolium'. The rounded or circular leaves are likened to the round full moon. From its near relatives, the combination of nine to eleven lobes and hairy shoots distinguish it.

p.150 **Smooth Maple** or **Smoothbark Maple**
Acer laevigatum

Description: Evergreen tree 10–15 m (33–50 ft) with a bole diameter to 50 cm (1.6 ft).
Crown Ovoid, domed. *Bark* Green or bluish green, stripped with pale or white, later brownish at base. *Shoot* Pink or light green and slender in the first year and raised behind the nodes, hairless and almost or without lenticels, persistently mid to bluish green thereafter. *Buds* In opposite pairs, conical, green or pink, with a ring of pale hairs, 2 mm (0.1 in), terminal bud absent. *Foliage* Leaves lanceolate or lanceolate-oblong, tapering to the tail-like or slender pointed tip, base

rounded or wedge-shaped, margin pinkish, untoothed or with widely spaced small forward teeth at irregular intervals and mainly towards the apical half, upper surface with a raised midrib and finely sunk side and tertiary veins which are rather net-like, hairless, sub-shiny and mid to yellow-green, lower surface shiny light green, veins raised, especially the midrib, hairless or with brown axillary tufts, 8–15 × 2–5 cm (3.1–6 × 0.8–2 in); leaf stalk grooved, pink or green, 0.5–1.5 cm (0.2–0.6 in); autumn colour can be yellow, usually leaves lost in cold periods over winter. *Flowers* In corymbose panicles at the end of current season's shoots in early summer, flowers yellowish or red to white. *Fruit* Nutlet rounded to strongly ridged, 6 mm (0.25 in); wings 3–4 × 1 cm (1.2–1.6 × 0.4 in), purple or pink when young, spreading at an obtuse or acute angle.

Range: Himalayas from Nepal eastwards into central China.

Habitat: Cultivated as an ornamental, in the wild occurring in forests and thickets in the warm temperate zone.

Similar species: There are a number of related species found in southern China and south into Vietnam and southeast Asia. Two which are sometimes found in cultivation, mainly in specialist collections, are *A. fabri*, with the leaf stalks 2–3 cm (0.8–1.2 in), and *A. reticulatum*, with the leaves more strongly reticulate or net-veined.

This evergreen tree is only hardy in the milder southern and Atlantic coastal regions of Europe. The Latin name translates as smooth or polished.

p.284 **Lobel's Maple** *Acer lobelii*

Description: Deciduous tree 15–25 m (50–80 ft) with a bole diameter to 60 cm (2 ft).
Crown Columnar, narrow and upright with ascending branches. *Bark* Grey-green in

young trees with vertical strips, as the tree matures becoming shallowly furrowed. *Shoot* Green and covered by a thick glaucous blue waxy bloom, remaining green for several years but the bloom usually rubbing off during the second year. *Buds* Ovoid, pointed, scales several and overlapping, green with hairy brown tips, 5 mm (0.2 in). *Foliage* Leaves broader than long with five lobes which are shouldered and abruptly tapered to the slender-pointed to tail-like apex, base subcordate, margins crinkled, mostly untoothed but sometimes with a few teeth on the main lobes, sinuses narrow, acute, upper surface matt sub-shiny green with slightly raised veins, lower surface shiny light green, rather net-veined, veins prominent, hairless except for obvious axillary tufts of light brown hairs, 6–12 × 6–15 cm (2.4–4.7 × 2.4–6 in); leaf stalk round, with a milky sap, 3–10 cm (1.2–4 in); autumn colour golden yellow. *Flowers* In terminal corymbs of yellow-green flowers on current years growths with the leaves in spring. *Fruit* Flattened nutlet with wide spreading wings, to 2.5 cm (1 in).

Range: Southern Italy.
Habitat: Woodlands, but planted as an ornamental for the narrow upright habit.
Synonyms: *A. cappadocicum* ssp. *lobelii*.

This tree has been confused by some botanists, sometimes being treated as a variety of *A. platanoides* (from which it is distinguished by the shoots remaining green for several years and the few toothed leaves), *A. cappadocicum* (from which it is distinguished by the bloomed shoot, the bark, the leaves having crinkled margins and usually a few teeth and the common peduncle to the inflorescence being less than 1 cm (0.4 in)) or as a hybrid. The differences from these species seem to justify a separate specific rank. Unlike *A. cappadocicum*, it does not sucker, except when *cappadocicum* has been used as a rootstock.

p.288   **Oregon Maple** or **Big-leafed Maple**
Acer macrophyllum

Description: Deciduous tree 15–25 m (50–80 ft) with a
bole diameter to 80 cm (2.6 ft).
Crown Tall to broad dome, with spreading
or drooping branches. *Bark* Dark grey and
smooth, becoming brown and furrowed and
cracking into small square scales.
Shoot Green or green and purple, with small
round lenticels, remaining green for several
years, stout. *Buds* In opposite pairs and
hidden in base of leaf stalk, ovoid, green to
dark red, 5 mm (0.2 in). *Foliage* Leaves
rounded to half-moon shaped, deeply five
lobed, main lobes broadest towards apex
with a pair of large triangular teeth but
otherwise margins untoothed, base
subcordate and somewhat truncate, upper
surface deep matt green, rather rough with
slightly raised veins, lower surface light
green, with raised network of veins
(reticulate), hairy on veins and in vein axils,
10–25 × 13–35 cm (4–10 × 5.1–14 in); leaf
stalk with a milky sap, grooved, pink or
green, with a swollen base which clasps the
bud, stout and variable in length; autumn
colour orange, yellow or russet. *Flowers* In
drooping panicles to 15 cm (6 in) which
terminate leafy side shoots in spring, flowers
yellow, fragrant, 6 mm (0.25 in).
Fruit Nutlet covered with irritant stiff
yellow hairs, rounded-angular, 1 cm (0.4 in),
wings 5–6 × 1.5 cm (2–2.4 × 0.6 in), with
the pairs spreading at a right angle.

Range: Southwest British Columbia along the coast
southwards to southern California and
inland on the Sierra Nevada in California.

Habitat: Cultivated as an ornamental, in the wild
occurring in moist locations near streams
and canyon bottoms.

This tree has very large leaves, with only
A. velutinum having leaves as large. These
two are easily separated in fresh specimens,
as *A. macrophyllum* has a milky sap in the
leaf stalk, whereas it is watery in
A. velutinum, as well as by the deeper lobing
of *A. macrophyllum*.

p.306 **Nikko Maple** *Acer maximowicziana*

Description: Deciduous tree 10–15 m (33–50 ft) with a bole diameter to 40 cm (1.3 ft).
Crown Conical in young trees, becoming columnar and domed in old ones.
Bark Smooth, greenish grey or pink-grey, not peeling. *Shoot* Light greenish brown with a dense covering of whitish hairs in the first year, becoming hairless and red-brown or purple-grey with oval lenticels in the second year. *Buds* In opposite pairs, ovoid-conic, with many overlapping brown, downy, scales, 5 mm (0.2 in).
Foliage Leaves trifoliate, with the leaflets pointing forwards, leaflets stalked to almost stalkless, elliptic to elliptic-oblong, tapered at both ends, margins with a few rounded teeth or untoothed at base, upper surface matt green, sparsely hairy, underside glaucous or bluish green, softly hairy especially on the 10–15 pairs of main veins and the midrib, 4–12 × 2–6 cm (1.6–4.7 × 0.8–2.4 in); leaf stalk densely hairy, round, pink and green, enlarged at the base where it clasps the bud and stem, 3–6 cm (1.2–2.4 in), leaflet stalks similar, 2–3 mm (0.1 in) on side leaflets, to 1 cm (0.4 in) on terminal leaflet. *Flowers* In threes on leafy shoots in late spring, yellow.
Fruit Pendent, nutlet rounded, hairy, woody, 1 cm (0.4 in), with wings 2–4 cm (0.8–1.6 in), with the pairs of fruits erect.

Range: Honshu, Kyushu and Shikoku, Japan, and in central China from Hubei to Anhui.

Habitat: Cultivated as an ornamental, in the wild occurring in mountain forests.

Synonyms: *A. nikoense*.

This tree is closely related to *A. griseum* and *A. triflorum*, but is easily distinguished by the smooth, not flaking or peeling, bark. Like these two trees, the seeds are very woody and often empty, unless several trees are grown together. It is more commonly found in collections labelled as *A. nikoense* (Nikko being located in central Honshu) but this name is unfortunately invalid under the rules for botanical nomenclature.

It is not related to *A. maximowiczii*, which is a graceful snake-bark maple with three-lobed leaves.

---

p.293 **Maximowicz's Maple** *Acer maximowiczii*

Description: Deciduous tree 10–15 m (33–50 ft) with a bole diameter to 30 cm (1 ft).
Crown Upright and usually narrow but arching or spreading on vigorous trees in the open. *Bark* Olive-green with white longitudinal striations, in very old trees becoming brown at base. *Shoot* On strong shoots pinkish green with oval pale lenticels, developing white snake-like striations in the second year and some olive-green, but on weaker or non-extension shoots the shoot is primarily olive-green and only slowly developing white striations. *Buds* In opposite pairs, elliptic-conical with a pointed apex, green and hairless with two outer bud scales, 3 mm (0.1 in), and set on a short stalk. *Foliage* Leaves ovate oblong, usually strongly three lobed and often with weak basal lobes but the side lobes short, slender pointed with acute sinuses, main lobe much longer and tapering to an acute and somewhat slender-pointed apex, base rounded subcordate, margin doubly serrate with rounded abruptly short-pointed teeth and sometimes lobulate (with small lobes), upper surface matt or sub-shiny mid green, hairless apart from some sparse short brown hairs on the raised veins, underside bluish green, matt, hairless apart from tufts of sandy white, or white tipped with red-brown, hairs in the axils of the somewhat prominent veins, 5–8 × 3.5–7 cm (2–3.1 × 1.4–2.8 in); leaf stalk grooved along its whole length, hairless, pink or green, of variable length from 2–8 cm (0.8–3.1 in); autumn colour yellow. *Flowers* In short stiff racemes of 6–15 flowers, petals reddish. *Fruit* In pendent racemes, seed dimpled, 5 mm (0.2 in), wing 2 cm (0.8 in), with the pairs of fruits diverging at a right angle.

Range: Northwest China from Shanxi, Shaanxi,
Qinghai, Hubei, Hunan, Guizhou, Gansu
and northwest Sichuan, with a variety in
Guangxi.

Habitat: Cultivated as an ornamental, in the wild
occurring as an understorey in mainly
mixed woodland.

Synonyms: *A. pectinatum* ssp. *maximowiczii*, *A.
urophyllum*.

This makes an attractive leafy small tree,
and is one of the hardiest of the snake bark
maples. Although associated in some works
with the Himalayan *A. pectinatum* (*see the
above synonym*), it is really quite different.
It is much closer to the Japanese
A. crataegifolium with which it shares the
small three lobed to lobulate leaves, and it
is interesting to note that Maximowicz
named it *A. urophyllum*, i.e. 'leaves like Uri
maple (*A. crataegifolium*)'.

---

p.287 **Miyabe Maple** *Acer miyabei*

Description: Deciduous tree to 15 m (50 ft) with a bole
diameter of 50 cm (1.6 ft).
Crown Ovoid in young trees, becoming
domed with age. *Bark* Grey and brown,
with orange fissures, finely roughened.
Shoot Green with pale oval lenticels in the
first year, usually hairless but sometimes
initially hairy, orange-brown or buff and
finely fissured in subsequent seasons.
Buds In opposite pairs, ovoid, acute, red-
brown, hairy on the scale margins, hidden in
base of leaf stalk during growing season,
2–5 mm (0.1–0.2 in). *Foliage* Leaves five
lobed but the basal lobes may be small, lobes
ovate to oblong triangular, often constricted
at the base of the sinuses which are deep and
acute or U-shaped with a rounded base, with
one or more large teeth especially on the
outer side, tip acute to slender pointed, base
deeply heart-shaped, upper surface matt
green, hairy especially along the flat veins,
undersurface pale green, hairy, with the veins
raised, variable, from 7–20 × 12–20 cm
(2.8–8 × 4.7–8 in); leaf stalk with a milky

sap, weakly grooved, hairy, green, clasping bud at enlarged base, variable, to 15 cm (6 in); autumn colour yellow. *Flowers* In small terminal corymbs on leafy or leafless shoots, petals yellow. *Fruit* Seed flat, 8 mm (0.3 in), downy, with yellow-green wing to 2.5 cm (1 in), pairs spreading at 180 degrees or slightly reflexed.

Range: Hokkaido and northern Honshu, Japan.

Habitat: Cultivated as an ornamental, in the wild occurring as a rare component of moist streamside woods.

This tree is closely allied to *A. campestre* and represents this species in Japan. The leaves appear similar to *A. saccharum* and its allies, and also to *A. hyrcanum* but from these the milky sap in the leaf stalk immediately distinguishes it.

---

p.286 **Mono Maple** *Acer mono*

Description: Deciduous tree 15 m (50 ft) with a bole diameter to 60 cm (2 ft).
Crown Rounded, usually as broad or broader than high. *Bark* Grey-brown, becoming shallowly furrowed and scaly. *Shoot* Initially green and hairless in the first year with raised elliptic lenticels, as it ripens turning brown and in the second and subsequent years grey-brown or yellow-grey with prominent brown lenticels. *Buds* In opposite pairs, ovoid, with few brown outer scales, 5 mm (0.2 in). *Foliage* Leaves rounded to kidney shaped, more or less as long as broad, five to seven lobed and heart-shaped at base, lobes ovate-triangular with a slender-pointed apex, depth of lobing variable but the sinuses are open and frequently scalloped rather than indented, margins entire without teeth but usually somewhat wavy, upper surface matt green, smooth with slightly impressed veins, lower surface shiny green with prominent veins, usually hairless except for basal axillary tufts beneath but in some forms hairy along the veins, 8–15 cm (3.1–6 in; leaf stalk with a milky sap, oval in section, pink or green,

length very variable, up to 18 cm (7.1 in); autumn colour golden or yellow. *Flowers* In terminal corymbs, to 10 cm (4 in) across, with the leaves, usually all male or all female; flowers yellow. *Fruit* Nutlet flattened, 1 cm (0.4 in), with wings 1.5 times nutlet (giving a fruit or samara 2–2.5 cm (0.8–1 in)), with the pairs spreading at an obtuse or right angle.

Range: Central, North and West China across Manchuria to Pacific Russia, Korea and Japan.

Habitat: Cultivated as an ornamental, in the wild occurring in mixed mainly broadleaved forests.

Synonyms: *A. pictum.*

The leaves of this tree are similar to *A. cappadocicum* but the two species can easily be distinguished by the shoots. In *A. mono*, the twigs quickly become brown and cease to be actively photosynthesizing, whereas in *A. cappadocicum* they remain green for several years. The Latin and common name is based on a Japanese name, and does not refer to the Latin word for one. It is sometimes called Painted Maple, which is appropriate to the variegated form called *A. pictum* which was confused with *Kalopanax pictus* by Thunberg.

p.296 **Montpelier Maple** *Acer monspessulanum*

Description: Deciduous tree 10–15 m (33–50 in) with a bole diameter to 70 cm (2.3 ft).
Crown Densely twiggy, upright, becoming domed in old trees. *Bark* Grey or black, becoming finely cracked, sometimes corky. *Shoot* Green with dark brown narrow lanceolate lenticels, hairless, becoming brown or buff-brown in later years. *Buds* In opposite pairs, ovoid, with numerous dark chocolate scales with white hairy margins, 3 mm (0.1 in). *Foliage* Leaves trilobed with the lobes diverging at slightly greater than 45 degrees, lobes ovate, tip rounded, sometimes abruptly short pointed, base wedge-shaped but heart-shaped, margin

untoothed, upper surface sub-shiny deep green, usually hairless, with impressed veins, lower surface rather pale glaucous green with hairs along and in the axils of the raised veins, texture rather hard, 3–6 × 4–7 cm (1.2–2.4 × 1.6–2.8 in); leaf stalk round, green, very slender with a watery, not milky, sap, 2.5–5 cm (1–2 in); autumn colour yellow. *Flowers* In pendulous few flowered corymbs on long slender flower stalks 2–3 cm (0.8–1.2 in), petals greenish yellow. *Fruit* Seed angular, 5 mm (0.2 in), wing 1.5 cm (0.6 in), narrow, the pairs spreading at an acute angle or overlapping.

Range: Shores of the Mediterranean region, north to southern Germany and the Ukraine and east into the Caucasus, Iran and Iraq.

Habitat: Dry open hillsides.

Varieties: Ssp. *microphyllum* is found in Corsica but apparently was described from the Lebanon. It has much smaller leaves, usually only 2.5 cm (1 in) long × 3 cm (1.2 in) wide.

Synonyms: *A. trilobatum*.

This widely spread small tree is quite variable and by some authorities split into a proliferation of forms, especially from Asia Minor.

p.314   **Box Elder** or **Ash-leafed Maple**
Acer negundo

Description: Deciduous tree 10–15 m (33–50 ft) with a bole diameter to 60 cm (2 ft).
Crown Domed or spreading and flat topped. *Bark* Grey-brown, smooth, in old trees becoming dark brown-grey and shallowly fissured and cracked.
Shoot Green, downy or hairless, often bloomed when young, remaining green for two to four years, then becoming grey and brown with shallow fissures. *Buds* In opposite pairs, ovate, silky hairy, small, 3–5 mm (0.1–0.2 in), with two or three pairs of bud scales. *Foliage* Leaves trifoliate or pinnate with five or seven, rarely nine, leaflets, leaf to 20 × 15 cm (8 × 6 in), usually smaller, leaflets stalkless or short

stalked, apex acute or slender pointed, base rounded or wedge-shaped, margin lobulate or coarsely toothed, upper surface light to mid matt green with sparse stiff hairs, lower surface with prominent veins and sometimes softly downy, leaflets to 10 × 6.5 cm (4 × 2.6 in); leaf stalk pink or green, round, downy; autumn colour very poor. *Flowers* On separate male and female trees, males pendent, before the leaves, purple and lacking a perianth, 5–7 cm (2–2.8 in); female flower yellow or pink, 6–8 cm (2.4–3.1 in). *Fruit* On female trees only, in pendent racemes with erect to acute wings, nutlet small, often empty.

Range: Across North America from the east coast to California and south into northern Mexico.

Habitat: Cultivated as an ornamental, in the wild occurring in moist habitats (such as along stream sides) in mixed broadleaved forest.

Varieties: 'Variegatum' has the leaves margined and variegated with pure white. It is inclined to revert and is a female tree. 'Flamingo' has pink in the variegation and is less inclined to throw reversions. 'Auratum' has new foliage rich yellow. Ssp. *californicum* has the shoots and leaves hairy. It is one of several geographical subspecies named to account for the natural variation of this tree.

Synonyms: *Negundo aceroides*.

This is the only maple which has pinnate leaves, although several other maples may also have trifoliate leaves. It is rather common but not endearing, making a poor tree and rarely having sufficient presence to justify its position. It can be tapped for Maple syrup.

p.150 **Phirphiri** or **Flying Moth Maple**
Acer oblongum

Description: Semi-evergreen or deciduous tree to 20 m (65 ft) with a bole diameter to 50 cm (1.6 ft). *Crown* Rounded, domed. *Bark* Red-brown to grey, smooth at first but developing peeling plates in old trees. *Shoot* Dark brown or greenish brown in first winter, then mid to dark brown or grey-brown with paler striations. *Buds* In opposite pairs, long narrow ovoid, light brown with about 10 pairs of scales, to 6 mm (0.25 in). *Foliage* Leaves oblong-elliptic, leathery, slender pointed, base rounded, edge entire with a hyaline or translucent margin, a pair of main lateral veins at the base which extend for one third of the leaf blade and rarely (most frequently in young plants) giving rise to small side lobes, tertiary veins net-like, upper surface mid to dark green, lower surface glaucous light green, initially may have short hairs but later hairless, 5–12 × 3–5 cm (2–4.7 × 1.2–2 in); leaf stalk round, light green, with a swollen base, 2–6 cm (0.8–2.4 in). *Flowers* With or before the new leaves in spring, yellow-green, 15–50 flowers in lax terminal or lateral corymbs to 3–7 cm (1.2–2.8 in) in diameter; petals five, oblong, 5 × 2 mm (0.2 × 0.1 in). *Fruit* Nutlets angular, with wings 2.5–3 × 1 cm (1–1.2 × 0.4 in) which are acute to parallel and ripen brown.

Range: Himalayas from Kashmir across to central China.

Habitat: Cultivated in Europe as an ornamental, in the wild occurring in broadleaf warm temperate forests.

Plants from China are hardy in southern England but the Himalayan forms appear less hardy. The leaves are mainly lost over winter during cold spells.

---

p.295 **Syrian Maple** or **Cyprus Maple**
Acer obtusifolium

Description: Evergreen tree to 10 m (33 ft) with a bole diameter to 50 cm (1.6 ft).
Crown Rounded, domed in old trees and often on several stems. *Bark* Greyish brown, smooth but becoming finely fissured. *Shoot* Green-brown, hairless, becoming dark-brown or grey. *Buds* In opposite pairs, ovoid, acute, brown, 2–5 mm (0.1–0.2 in). *Foliage* Ovate and unlobed to broadly three lobed, thick and leathery, apex bluntly

pointed, base wedge-shaped, rounded or heart-shaped, margins entire to sharply serrate, sinuses bluntly pointed, with three main basal veins forming 45 degree angles, tertiary veins net-like, deeply shiny green above, paler beneath, hairless, (2–)4–6(–10) × (2–)4–6 cm ((0.8–)1.6–2.4(–4) × (0.8–)1.6–2.4 in); leaf stalk 1–4 cm (0.4–1.6 in) (rarely to 6 cm (2.4 in)), green or pinkish. *Flowers* In lax terminal corymbose cymes late winter or early spring, yellow-green. *Fruit* In pairs, seed 7 mm (0.3 in) with papery wing 2–3 × 0.8–1 cm (0.8–1.2 × 0.3–0.4 in), the two fruits with spreading or sub-erect wings.

Range: Cyprus, Syria and Lebanon.
Habitat: Dry rocky hillsides.
Synonyms: *A. syriacum.*

This forms a small evergreen tree. It was originally described as coming from Crete but this was almost certainly due to a mistake in labelling the specimens, as it has not otherwise been recorded on Crete, although common on Cyprus, which Sibthorp (who described it) also visited at the same time.

p.290 **Oliver Maple** *Acer oliverianum*

Description: Deciduous tree to 10 m (33 ft) with a bole to 40 cm (1.3 ft).
Crown Upright or rounded with spreading branches. *Bark* Grey-green or grey-brown, smooth. *Shoot* Shiny green or pinky purple, slender, hairless, showing little change with age. *Buds* In opposite pairs, broad conic, with a pair of green valvate outer scales, 3 mm (0.1 in), terminal bud absent. *Foliage* Leaves palmately three to five lobed, main lobes triangular to slender pointed, spreading, with open sinuses which are obtuse to right angled and extend more or less two-thirds to the middle, basal lobes smaller or absent, may point back, base rounded (especially with three lobes) to heart-shaped (five lobes), margin with a few forward pointing small

teeth, often leathery, upper surface light green, hairless except for soft long hairs on the raised veins, lower surface light shiny green, white or light brown hairy along the slightly raised veins and in the vein axils, 4–8 × 5–10 cm (1.6–3.1 × 2–4 in); leaf stalk round, hairless, pink or green, 3–5 cm (1.2–2 in); autumn colour yellow or brown, not strong. *Flowers* In few flowered corymbs on a slender hairless pink or green stalk to a group of flowers after the leaves. *Fruit* Nutlet squarrish-rounded, 3–4 mm (0.1–0.2 in), wing 2 cm (0.8 in), green or pink when young, pairs of fruits spreading at a wide angle to nearly horizontal.

Range: Central China on both sides of the Yangtse valley from Yunnan to Jiangsi.

Habitat: Cultivated as an ornamental, in the wild occurring as an understorey in broadleaved forests.

Synonyms: *A. campbellii* ssp. *oliverianum*.

Similar species: *A. serrulatum* differs in the more deeply and consistently five-lobed leaves which are hairless and larger. It is native to Taiwan, where it forms a tall tree, up to 20 m (65 ft).

This small maple has neatly lobed leaves and looks very attractive during the summer, especially when carrying the fresh pink winged fruits.

---

p.292 **Italian Maple** *Acer opalus*

Description: Deciduous tree 10–20 m (33–65 ft) with a bole diameter to 1 m (3.3 ft).
Crown Broad low dome. *Bark* Smooth and grey in young trees, becoming pinkish grey to orange-pink and scaling in small squares which reveal orange beneath, in old trees shaggy with large curving plates which peel away at the two ends. *Shoot* Dark chocolate brown with small raised orange lenticels, hairless, becoming grey-brown. *Buds* In opposite pairs, conic to long ovoid-conic, pointed, scales green with brown tips, 8 mm (0.3 in). *Foliage* Leaves wider than long, with five acute, rounded to bluntly pointed lobes and acute to shallow rounded

sinuses (but the basal pair of lobes much smaller), base heart-shaped, margin untoothed or irregularly toothed, upper surface deep green, net-veined and somewhat rugose with impressed veins, underside whitish green with a network of raised veins and veinlets, hairy all over, 7–13 × 5–16 cm (2.8–5.1 × 2–6.3 in); leaf stalk grooved, pink and green, 3–10 cm (1.2–4 in); autumn colour red to brown or yellow, variable. *Flowers* Before the leaves in short stalked pendulous corymbs, good yellow. *Fruit* In drooping clusters, nutlet 1 cm (0.4 in), rounded, wing to 2.5 cm (1 in), ripening brown, with the wings spreading at an obtuse angle.

Range: From the Pyrenees and southeast France east through Corsica, Italy, southern Switzerland and the Balkans to the Caucasus, and in Morocco and Algeria in North Africa.

Habitat: Mountain forests.

Varieties: The name ssp. *obtusatum* is sometimes applied to the forms in which the leaves have shallower rounded sinuses, more rounded and less toothed margins and the flower stalks are hairy, but it is included in the above description.

Synonyms: *A. italicum, A. italum.*

This tree has the best floral display of any maple, with the yellow corymbs hanging below the bare branches before (or sometimes as) the leaves emerge. At other times, the foliage shows its relationship with *A. pseudoplatanus*, but the leaves are much less toothed and more softly lobed and the bark tends to be more coarsely scaling.

p.293 **Japanese Maple** *Acer palmatum*

Description: Deciduous tree 6–10 m (20–33 ft), rarely to 15 m (50 ft), with a bole diameter to 40 cm (1 ft).
Crown Rounded or domed, with a short bole and ascending branches.
Bark Smooth, green-grey and stripped on young trees, becoming brown or grey-

brown in old trees and slightly fissured. *Shoot* Green or pinkish, smooth, hairless and slender, becoming purple or remaining green in second year. *Buds* In opposite pairs, with the terminal bud missing, conical, green, enclosed in the base of the leaf stalk during the growing season, to 3 mm (0.1 in). *Foliage* Leaves fan-shaped in outline with five or seven deep lobes, base rounded to subcordate, lobes narrow ovate to oblong-ovate, with slender pointed tips, sinuses cleft deep into the blade, extending half way or more to the base, margins toothed with sharp forward-pointing serrations with slender pointed tips, upper surface with raised veins and tertiary veins net-like, lower surface shiny pale green, veins prominent, hairless or with some hairs especially in the vein axils, 6–12 × 5–9 cm (2.4–4.7 × 2–3.5 in); leaf stalk slender, grooved, pink or green, hairless, 2.5–5 cm (1–2 in); autumn colour yellow, orange or reds, sometimes spectacular. *Flowers* In small spreading corymbs on a long stalk to a group of flowers which terminate side shoots in late spring, flowers with red or purple sepals and creamy white petals. *Fruit* Rounded nutlet 3–5 mm (0.1–0.2 in) with a wing 1–2 cm (0.4–0.8 in), the wings of the pairs may be erect to spreading almost horizontally.

Range: Throughout Japan and in Korea and northeast China, also reported from central China but this may be a separate species.

Habitat: Cultivated as an ornamental, in the wild occurring as an understorey in woods and in thickets.

Varieties: Ssp. *palmatum*, the typical form, has five- or seven-lobed leaves which are small, only 4–7 cm (1.6–2.8 in) across and doubly serrate, flowers in corymbs of more than ten and seeds with wings 1–1.5 cm (0.4–0.6 in). It occurs in the lowlands and lower mountains of Honshu, Kyushu and Shikoku. Ssp. *amoenum* (syn. *A. amoenum*) has the leaves larger, 6–12 cm (2.4–4.7 in), with seven or nine lobes which are regular serrate and fruits which are larger, with the wings 2–2.5 cm (0.8–1 in). It occurs throughout Japan and is a more montane plant. Ssp. *matsumurae* (syn. *A. matsumurae*) has leaves mainly seven lobed (sometimes five or nine) with the margins doubly or incisely serrate and fruits with wings 1.5–2.5 cm (0.6–1 in). It also is a mainly montane plant from throughout Japan. Most noteworthy of the cultivars or garden selections: The Dissectum group, where the leaves are very deeply lobed, almost digitate in some forms. These are mainly shrubs, rarely small trees. The Atropurpureum group are selections with purple foliage, with 'Bloodgood' being perhaps the best. Some forms of the Dissectum group of cultivars also have purple foliage. 'Senkaki' (syn. 'Sangokaku') has the twigs brilliant coral-red over winter. The leaves are small and turn yellow in autumn. 'Osakazuki' assumes brilliant scarlet and orange autumn colours.

This delightful species consists of three main entities which are probably best considered as separate species under the names in parentheses above. However, as it has given rise to over 250 cultivars, many of which are garden hybrids of the different entities, it is more convenient to treat them as subspecies. The above description broadly covers all these forms. It thrives best on acid or neutral soils and requires a moist location and some shelter from full sunlight and wind or the leaves tend to burn off.

p.301 **Wongka Maple** *Acer pectinatum*

Description: Deciduous tree 10–15 m (33–50 in) with a bole diameter to 30 cm (1 ft).
Crown Erect or on arching branches from a short bole. *Bark* Light brown, rough, slightly scaly and shallowly pitted.
Shoot Light green, hairless but often with an initial waxy bloom, becoming green or purple with white striations developing after the third year. *Buds* In opposite

pairs, ovoid, acute or pointed at the apex, red, to 1 cm (0.4 in), set on a distinct peg or stalk 2–5 mm (0.1–0.2 in), with two pairs of scales. *Foliage* Leaves broad ovate but with two lateral lobes breaking the outline at or above the middle, three lobed or five lobed with small spreading basal lobes, main lobes triangular and ending in a long or short slender-pointed to tail-like tip, base rounded and heart-shaped, margin with small sharp forward-pointing teeth, finely and regularly serrate or weakly doubly serrate especially on young plants and on non flowering shoots, upper surface matt green with raised veins which carry short rufous hairs, underside with raised veins, all veins (including tertiary ones) initially densely rufous pubescent but hairs may only persist in vein axils, 8–15 × 8–11 cm (3.1–6 × 3.1–4.3 in); leaf stalk rufous hairy along the groove, pink, 2–7 cm (0.8–2.8 in); autumn colour yellow. *Flowers* In short pendulous loose racemes, petals pink or green. *Fruit* In racemes to 12 cm (4.7 in) with the pairs of fruits on short flower stalks to 7 mm (0.3 in), seed flattened, dimpled, 8 mm (0.3 in), with the wing to 1.5 cm (0.6 in), spreading at a wide angle.

Range: Himalayas from Nepal east to Burma.
Habitat: Cultivated as an ornamental, in the wild occurring as an understorey element in mainly conifer forests.

This tree is characterized by the rufous pubescence of the veins, the slender pointed forward lobes and the finely serrate leaf margins. The bark is poor for a snake bark maple, often becoming pale brown when only a few years old. It is one of the many trees which does not really have an English common name, with the common name given above deriving from its name in the Bhutanese national language, Dzonka. The Latin or scientific name refers to the fruits which are set spreading either side of the rachis like the teeth of a comb, and the common name Comb-Toothed Maple has been coined for it.

p.301 **Moosewood** or **Striped Maple**
Acer pensylvanicum

Description: Deciduous tree 10–15 m (33–50 ft) with a
bole diameter to 30 cm (1 ft).
Crown Arching branches from a short bole
and erect stems. *Bark* Green to light grey
with short, white striations in shallow
furrows which snake up the trunk and
branches; the grey striated bark usually
persists to soil level. *Shoot* Green in the
first year and hairless, becoming olive-
green or brown above and persisting green
below, developing white striations in the
second year, slender. *Buds* In opposite
pairs, ovoid, acute or pointed at the apex,
red or yellow-brown, to 1 cm (0.4 in), set
on a distinct peg or stalk 2–5 mm
(0.1–0.2 in), with two pairs of scales.
Foliage Leaves variable, on short shoots
(especially flowering ones) large and
trapeziform, strongly three lobed with the
side lobes strongly forwards and nearly as
long as the short broad triangular main
lobe, apices of lobes acute and short
slender points, with scalloped sinuses, base
rounded and heart-shaped, margins finely
serrate with short triangular teeth set in
clusters of four to six, upper surface matt
green with the main veins set in grooves
but raised and having short curly rufous
hairs (at least when young), undersurface
light green with all the veins prominent
and bearing short curly rufous hairs, to
22 cm (8.7 in) across and long; on
extension shoots, the leaves may be ovate-
lanceolate, tapering to an acute apex and
sharply toothed but unlobed, down to 12
× 5 cm (4.7 × 2 in); on shoots of
intermediate vigour, the leaves may be
somewhere between these two extremes;
leaf stalk with a groove in which are
rufous hairs, pink, 6–12 cm (2.4–4.7 in);
autumn colour clear golden-yellow, in
early autumn. *Flowers* In spreading
racemes from short shoots, yellow-green,
to 12 cm (4.7 in). *Fruit* In pendent
unbranched racemes; seed flattened,
usually dimpled on one side, with wing to

2.5 cm (1 in); pairs of fruits making an acute angle.

Range: Eastern North America in a triangle from the Great Lakes across to Nova Scotia and south to Georgia.

Habitat: Cultivated as an ornamental, in the wild occurring as an understorey element in broadleaved forests.

Varieties: 'Erythrocladum' has shoots which are pink and yellow during the first growing season but maturing to salmon-red by the winter.

This tree has one of the best snake barks, so called for the white striations which appear to weave up the stem, and is the only member of the group occurring naturally outside of eastern Asia. It has the boldest foliage of any snake bark maple. The only species with which it might be confused is *A. rufinerve*, which can have similar, albeit usually much smaller leaves, but the flat seeds contrast with the rounded seeds of *A. rufinerve*, and it lacks the glaucous bloom on the shoots, which is usually a feature of *rufinerve*. Moosewood will grow on a wide range of soils, although does not like dry ones or shallow soils over chalk. Linnaeus was responsible for the omission of one 'n' in Pennsylvania!

p.285   **Norway Maple** *Acer platanoides*

Description: Deciduous tree 15–25 m (50–80 ft) with a bole diameter to 1.3 m (4 ft).
Crown Ovoid in young trees, becoming rounded on a short bole or tall domed when grown in woodland. *Bark* Grey or buff-grey and smooth, developing fine folds and in old trees becoming shallowly fissured and ridged. *Shoot* Green during the summer, becoming olive-brown to reddish brown with small lenticels, in the second year somewhat shiny. *Buds* In opposite pairs, ovoid, rounded, green or reddish, with several pairs of scales, 7 mm (0.3 in).
Foliage Leaves five lobed or with weak additional basal lobes, the main three lobes point forwards at 45 degrees with parallel

sides to a pair of large slender pointed teeth which end in a somewhat whiskered tip then scalloped to the slender pointed apex with rounded sinuses which extend between one-third and one-half of the distance to the middle, lesser lobes only partly toothed, base heart-shaped, upper surface matt green with slightly impressed veins, underside light green with prominently raised veins, hairless except for axillary tufts of buff-brown hairs, 7–14 × 8–20 cm (2.7–5.5 × 3.1–8 in); leaf stalk with a milky sap, pink and green, rounded with an enlarged base; autumn colour good butter yellow, only rarely red, 10–20 cm (4–8 in); new foliage often purplish or yellowish. *Flowers* Before the leaves in early spring from buds on last year's shoots in hairy erect corymbs terminating short shoots, yellow-green (but purplish green in some forms), conspicuous for ten days before the leaves enlarge. *Fruit* Nutlet flattened, 1 cm (0.4 in), with a wing 3–4 cm (1.2–1.6 in), with the pairs spreading at a wide angle or nearly horizontally.

Range: From extreme southern Norway and south Sweden across Europe to the Crimea and the Caucasus region.

Habitat: Woodlands, extensively planted in towns.

Varieties: 'Columnare' is one of several narrow crowned forms selected as street trees. 'Drummondii' has the leaves variegated with white or cream, but is inclined to revert. 'Globosum' is a slow-growing form, usually seen as a small mop-headed tree grafted onto a 2 m (6.6 ft) trunk. 'Goldsworth Purple' and 'Crimson King' are two purple forms. The new foliage is attractive, but come mid-summer like most purple foliages they are rather heavy and dull. Best avoided by those with plant sense, although the flowers are more showy, having purple-red petals. 'Lorbergii' has the leaves deeply dissected into lobes which are narrower at the base; as the leaves thus resemble an eagle's claw, it is colloquially known as the Eagle's Claw Maple. 'Dissectum' is similar. 'Schwedleri' is an attractive form in which the new foliage is bright purple-red, as are the flowers.

Unlike 'Crimson King' the leaves do not become dull purple but mature to a fairly normal green.

Norway Maple is one of the showiest maples in flower. It is also an extremely tough tree, adapting to harsh urban conditions. In the wild, however, it is not recorded from the western fringe of Europe. The leaves bear a passing similarity to *Platanus* × *hispanica* and *A. pseudoplatanus*, but a glance at the bark will quickly distinguish it. It is superficially more similar to *A. saccharum* (and its close allies). The best character, and one which separates the group of related species from all except *A. macrophyllum* is the milky sap in the leaf stalk, which can be ascertained by snapping a leaf stalk in half.

p.291 **Sycamore** *Acer pseudoplatanus*

Description: Deciduous tree 15–35 m (50–115 ft) with a bole diameter to 2 m (7 ft).
Crown Conic and spiky in young trees, developing through a phase with rather tiered branches and becoming rounded domed with a majestic broad canopy, especially in cooler and moister mountain areas. *Bark* Smooth and silvery grey in young trees (but sometimes brown), becoming progressively cracked and finally with large peeling scales 10–20 × 5–10 cm (4–8 × 2–4 in) which are pinkish brown to orange-brown. *Shoot* Green-brown to grey-green-brown by autumn, with pale slender lenticels, in the second and later years dark brown to grey-brown. *Buds* In opposite pairs, ovoid, pointed, green with open brown tips to the scales, 0.5–1 cm (0.2–0.4 in). *Foliage* Leaves very variable, palmately lobed with three main lobes and two smaller basal lobes, lobes broad triangular with a short acuminate apex, coarsely toothed margins and narrow acute sinuses, base rounded to heart-shaped, upper surface dull green, finely net-veined with raised tertiary

veins, main veins indented, lower surface glaucous green with raised veins which are downy at their base, 10–20 cm (4–8 in) (sometimes larger on vigorous young trees) by as much in width; leaf stalk round, green or red, 4–17 cm (1.6–6.7 in); autumn colour poor, leaf usually riddled with galls and tar spot by autumn and falling off in shame but occasionally a good yellow is managed, the leaves may flush bright yellow or purplish before turning green. *Flowers* In pendent 6–12 cm (2.4–4.7 in) dense panicles with the new foliage in spring terminating short shoots. *Fruit* In pendent clusters, nutlet ovoid, 0.7–1 cm (0.3–0.4 in), with a wing 2.5–3 × 0.8–1 cm (1–1.2 × 0.3–0.4 in), with the wings spreading more or less at right angles; the fruits are quite often in threes.

Range: Western Europe from France, northern Spain and southern Germany east across Europe to the Crimea and the Caucasus region, but widely naturalized outwith these areas in Britain and northwestern Europe.

Habitat: Forests, woods and field boundaries.

Varieties: Var. *tomentosum* from southern Italy, Sicily and the Dalmatian coast of Croatia has leaves which are downy beneath with coarser teeth. Forma *erythrocarpum* covers the forms with the fruit wings bright red when immature. Many cultivars are also recorded: 'Atropurpureum' has the leaves normal (if slightly darker) green above but purple beneath. It can be most attractive and the colour of the underside changes, depending upon whether sunlight is reflected off the purple or shining through it (when it becomes bright brown). 'Brilliantissimum' and 'Prince Handjery' are two slow-growing selections made for the vivid pink of their new foliage, which then turns through a yellow-green phase before maturing to green. 'Corstorphine' and 'Worleei' are selections with the new foliage golden yellow-green. 'Erectum' is a narrow crowned selection with tight ascending branches. 'Leopoldii' and 'Simon-Louis' have leaves yellow-pink at first, then splashed with yellow and pink on the green background.

This tree is not native to Britain, but behaves as one and is widely naturalized (to the bane of many gardeners as the winged seeds germinate profusely). It is much maligned, but can make a most impressive tree, especially in cooler mountain areas. It does not support the variety of aphids and other species of wildlife as are found on oak, but the quantity is similar, thus providing a valuable resource for predators. Ecologically, it seems to alternate with ash, each regenerating better under the other's canopy than under their own. The timber is good quality, sometimes with a beautiful ripple grain which is prized for violins. The tree may suffer following hot summers from sooty bark disease, which is caused by a fungus (*Cryptostroma corticale*) which originated in eastern North America. This normally occurs harmlessly within the tissues, but during hot summers which put the tree under stress, it can develop and kill trees or large portions of trees, releasing masses of soot coloured spores in autumn or next year.

---

p.294 **Keijo Maple** *Acer pseudosieboldianum*

Description: Deciduous tree 6–10 m (20–33 ft) with a bole diameter to 30 cm (1 ft).
Crown Domed. *Bark* Greenish, becoming grey-brown at the base. *Shoot* Green, hairless, smooth, remaining green for three or more years but becoming purplish on the upper side, sometimes with a glaucous bloom when young. *Buds* In opposite pairs, conic, pointed, scales with silky white hairs, maturing from green to dark red, terminal buds missing, 3 mm (0.1 in). *Foliage* Leaves nearly round, with nine to eleven triangular-ovate to ovate-lanceolate lobes which are acute with coarse sharp doubly serrate pointed teeth, sinuses narrow, acute, extending one-half to two-thirds of the way to the midrib, base heart-shaped, upper surface deep green with

raised veins, underside light green with raised veins, both sides initially densely white pubescent but only remaining so beneath on the veins and vein axils, 6–14 cm (2.4–5.5 in) long and wide; leaf stalk grooved, hairy or hairless, 3.5–6 cm (1.4–2.4 in); autumn colour good red or purple-red. *Flowers* Appearing before the leaves in terminal corymbs, with reddish-purple sepals and creamy petals.
Fruit Nutlet convex, strongly veined, 5–7 mm (0.2–0.3 in), with narrow obovate wings 2–2.5 cm (0.8–1 in), with the pairs spreading widely.

Range: Korea, Pacific Russia and northeast China.
Habitat: Cultivated as an ornamental, in the wild occurring in mixed forests as an understorey tree.
Similar species: *A. sieboldianum* differs in the shoots and leaf stalks having long grey hairs, giving them a hoary aspect, in the smaller leaves 6–8 cm (2.4–3.1 in) and in the pale yellow flowers. It occurs throughout Japan.

This tree has brilliant autumn colours. It is closely related to *A. japonicum*, differing in the doubly incise or sharply toothed leaves which are smaller and more rounded in outline with the lobes reaching at least half way to the middle of the leaf. It is also called Korean Maple.

p.289 **Red Maple** *Acer rubrum*

Description: Deciduous tree to 25 m (80 ft) with a bole diameter to 1 m (3.3 ft).
Crown Ovoid in young trees, becoming columnar-domed in old ones. *Bark* Pale grey or silvery grey, smooth and thin but becoming cracked in old trees into long plates which lift off the trunk at the ends. *Shoot* Red to coppery brown in the first winter, then grey, usually hairless, lenticels small. *Buds* In opposite pairs, ovoid, rounded or pointed, red-brown, scales with hairy margins, 2–3 mm (0.1 in).
Foliage Leaves with three main lobes and often two small basal lobes, lobes triangular

with the veins to the main pair of lobes at an angle of about 45 degrees to the central vein, sinus between the lobes acute, margins coarsely and irregularly toothed to almost lobulate, upper surface dark green to yellow-green and hairless, undersurface silvery white or glaucous blue-white and downy, especially along the veins, 8–10 × 7–11 cm (3.1–4 × 2.8–4.3 in); leaf stalk red on upper surface, yellow-green beneath, 7–9 cm (2.8–3.5 in); young foliage reddish, autumn foliage starts with gold and scarlet and often ends with brilliant reds.

Flowers On previous season's shoots in early spring before the leaves, usually monoecious but some plants dioecious; male flowers in clusters of three to four from the buds, petals 2 mm (0.1 in), scarlet, stamens five, small, chocolate but opening yellow, on filaments 6 mm (0.25 in); female flowers similar, stalkless, with two hairy spreading stigmas 2 mm (0.1 in). *Fruit* Ripens in early summer, red, wings erect to narrowly parted, each 2–2.5 cm (0.8–1 in) long, pendent on long flower stalks.

Range: Eastern North America from Newfoundland south to Florida, west to eastern Texas and north to Ontario.

Habitat: Cultivated in Europe as an ornamental, in the wild occurring in wet or swampy river margins, less often on dry ridges or in mixed hardwood forests.

Varieties: Several cultivars have been named. They include 'Columnare' and 'Scanlon' with narrow upright habits, and 'October Glory', 'Red Sunset' and 'Schlesingeri', with good autumn colour. Var. *drummondii* is a form from Arkansas, Louisiana and Texas which has slightly larger leaves and is generally more downy.

This tree is spectacular when in its full autumn glory. It also make a display in early spring before the leaves as the flowers open. The leaves are similar to *A. saccharinum* in the silvery undersides, but in that species the leaves are larger, more strongly five lobed and with coarser and sharply pointed teeth.

p.301 **Honshu Maple** *Acer rufinerve*

Description: Deciduous tree to 10–15 m (33–50 ft) with a bole diameter to 40 cm (1.3 ft). *Crown* Fan-shaped on a short bole with spreading arching branches. *Bark* Green or grey-green with greyish-white striations, rarely with a hint of pink, becoming brown and slightly fissured at the base in old trees. *Shoot* Green, with a distinct (if sometimes slight) waxy bloom in the first year and hairless, developing whitish fissures in the second or third year and becoming more olive-green. *Buds* In opposite pairs, on a stalk 3–4 mm (0.1–0.2 in), ovoid-conic, pointed, with two valvate outer scales which are green with a thick grey-blue waxy bloom, 1 cm (0.4 in). *Foliage* Leaves ovate, with three ovate-triangular lobes at or around the middle and ending in a slender pointed or tail-like tip, with shallow rounded sinuses, base rounded or somewhat truncate and rarely with small basal lobes, margin coarsely doubly and irregularly serrate with ovate-triangular teeth, upper surface matt green with rufous hairs on the veins, underside light green, more strongly rufous hairy on the prominent veins, especially in the axils, 8–15 × 8–15 cm (3.1–6 × 3.1–6 in); leaf stalk with shaggy long rufous hairs, grooved, pink or green, 3–5 cm (1.2–2 in); autumn colour orange to red. *Flowers* In pendent racemes after the leaves on short leafy side shoots, on a rufous haired stalk to a group of flowers. *Fruit* Nutlet rounded, almost spherical, 5 mm (0.2 in), wings 2 × 1 cm (0.8 × 0.4 in), pairs spreading at an obtuse angle.

Range: Honshu, Shikoku and Kyusho, Japan.

Habitat: Cultivated as an ornamental, in the wild occurring in mountain woods or forests.

Varieties: Forma *albolimbatum* has the leaves variegated with patches or areas of white. It comes moderately true from seed.

Synonyms: *A. pensylvanicum* ssp. *rufinerve*, *A. tegmentosum* ssp. *rufinerve*.

The strongly lobed leaves and the dense rufous hairs on the leaf undersides and the stalks to a group of flowers show a similarity to *A. pensylvanicum*, especially in the forms with larger leaves. However, in fruit the two are very distinct in the rounded fruits of *A. rufinerve*, which resemble lead shot, as compared to the flattened nutlets of *A. pensylvanicum*. The fruit and matt green leaves indicate a closer affinity with *A. grosseri*. The Latin name refers to the rufous hairs on the veins.

---

p.289　**Silver Maple**　*Acer saccharinum*

Description:　Deciduous tree 15–30 m (50–100 ft) with a bole diameter to 80 cm (2.6 ft).
Crown Tall domed with strongly ascending main branches and drooping side branches, with profuse watershoot suckers at the base of old trees. *Bark* Silvery grey, smooth, becoming shallowly fissured and platy at the base in old trees. *Shoot* Green at first but often with pink bands around the nodes and hairless, with slender, linear and rather dense buff-coloured lenticels, in the second and subsequent years maturing to brown or purplish brown. *Buds* In opposite pairs, long ovoid, pointed, slightly angular, usually red but sometimes green, to 1 cm (0.4 in). *Foliage* Leaves rounded in outline but deeply five lobed with narrow deep sinuses which are either rounded or acute, tips of lobes with slender points, margins with coarse, often double, triangular teeth, base broad wedge-shaped, truncate to subcordate, upper surface shiny green with raised veins and fine net-like tertiary veins, underside silvery white or glaucous, with prominent veins, 8–15 × 8–15 cm (3.1–6 × 3.1–6 in); leaf stalk green and/or pink, terete or round, long, 5–15 cm (2–6 in); autumn colour gold, scarlet or crimson. *Flowers* In short dense corymbs or umbels in early spring from leafless shoots, flowers red or greenish red, without petals. *Fruit* Ripening in late spring (May) but rarely formed in cultivation, germinating immediately, fruits with large rounded wings 3–5 × 1.2–2 cm (1.2–2 × 0.5–0.8 in), spreading at an obtuse

angle, on long slender flower stalks 3–5 cm (1.2–2 in).

Range: Eastern North America from Minnesota and southern Ontario east to New Brunswick, south to northern Florida and across to eastern Oklahoma.

Habitat: Cultivated as an ornamental, in the wild occurring in wet valley bottom sites and along streams or at the edges of swamps.

Varieties: Forma *laciniatum* covers those plants with more deeply lobed leaves than typical. The cultivar 'Wieri' is perhaps the best selection of this group, with pendulous branches and leaves with narrow lobes and sharp teeth.

Synonyms: *A. dasycarpum*, *A. eriocarpum*.

Silver maple is closely related to *A. rubrum* and also produces the reddish flowers in spring before the leaves but is easily distinguished by the larger and much more incisely lobed leaves which are a stronger silver beneath. It is a fast-growing tree and much used in amenity plantings. However, the branches are unusually brittle and disfiguring storm damage often occurs. The Latin name translates as 'with sugar', as Linnaeus when he described it thought he was naming the Sugar Maple. It can be tapped for maple sugar but the quantity obtained is small.

p.289 **Sugar Maple** *Acer saccharum*

Description: Deciduous tree 15–25 m (50–80 ft) with a bole diameter to 1 m (3.3 ft).
Crown Ovoid and spiky in young trees, becoming domed in old ones. *Bark* In young trees smooth and grey, as the tree matures developing broad ridges with long fissures and becoming platy.
Shoot Greenish brown or brown, often purplish at the nodes and on the base of the leaf stalk, becoming brown or grey, hairless, slender. *Buds* In opposite pairs, ovoid-conic with the outer scales purplish and overlapping, 5–6 mm (0.2–0.25 in).
Foliage Leaves palmately five lobed (occasionally with small additional basal

lobes) with the lobes extending around half way into the middle of the leaf, main lobes broad with a restricted base, ending in a thread-like whisker, with a few large teeth with rounded or acute tips, sinuses rounded, base heart-shaped or rarely truncate, upper surface dull dark green, hairless, lower surface pale green with prominent veins and usually somewhat hairy at least in the axils, 9–14 × 9–14 cm (3.5–5.5 × 3.5–5.5 in); leaf stalk with watery sap, partially grooved, purplish at the base which encloses the bud, 8–12 cm (3.1–4.7 in); autumn colour gold or scarlet. *Flowers* In spring with the leaves in pendulous clusters on a long slender hairy stalk to a group of flowers, yellow-green. *Fruit* Seed rounded, green but ripening to brown, on long slender flower stalks, 5 mm (0.2 in), wing 2–2.5 cm (0.8–1 in), spreading at an acute angle.

Range: North Eastern North America from the Atlantic coast across to southeast Manitoba and south to northern Georgia and South Carolina.

Habitat: Cultivated as an ornamental, in the wild forming part of extensive broadleaved forests.

Synonyms: *A. barbatum*.

Similar species: Five related species occur in North America, which are sometimes treated as varieties or subspecies of *A. saccharum*.
Black Maple *A. nigrum* often occurs with *A. saccharum*. It has leaves which are usually three lobed, with the lobes broad and long pointed, drooping sides and yellow-green with soft hairs beneath. The twigs are orange coloured, whilst the bark is darker and more furrowed.
Florida Maple *A. floridanum* occurs in the southeast USA in an arc from Virginia through Florida to east Texas. It has smaller leaves only 4–7.5 cm (1.6–2.9 in) which are whitish and hairy below and a light grey bark.
Chalk Maple *A. leucoderme* with a similar distribution to Florida Maple also has small leaves but the main distinguishing feature is the chalk white or whitish grey and smooth bark.

Bigtooth Maple or **Canyon Maple**
A. grandidentatum occurs on the eastern side
of the Rocky Mountains from Idaho
through Arizona and Texas to northern
Mexico. It has leaves 5–8 × 6–11 cm (2–3.1
× 2.4–4.3 in) and red-brown hairless shoots.
Skutch Maple *A. skutchii*, from Guatemala,
has larger 12–16 cm (4.7–6.3 in) leaves
which are glaucous beneath.

The leaf of this tree is perhaps best known
as the stylized symbol on the Canadian flag.
The lobing is very similar to but different to
that of *A. platanoides*, with the teeth
rounded, but these two trees are
convincingly distinguished by snapping a
leaf stalk in half. In *A. saccharum* (and its
relatives) a clear watery sap will form at the
fracture, whilst in *A. platanoides* (and its
relatives) the sap will be milky and
occluded. *A. saccharum* is tapped for maple
syrup. Incisions are made into the bark and
the sap collected. At this stage it contains
around 3 per cent sugar, which is then
reduced by boiling to give maple syrup at
circa 50 per cent sugar. The sap is primarily
collected in spring when rising, although
the autumn flow can be tapped for a lower
yield. *A. saccharum* is not the only maple
which can be tapped for sugar, but it is the
major one and the most prolific. The native
Americans knew to collect the sap. They
did not have iron pans and therefore were
not able to concentrate and thus store the
syrup until the early settlers brought pans
which would withstand prolonged boiling.

p.295 **Cretan Maple** *Acer sempervirens*

Description: Evergreen shrub or small tree to 10 m
(33 ft) with a bole diameter to 30 cm (1 ft).
Crown Rounded, often shrubby.
Bark Dark grey with orange fissures and
developing small scales. *Shoot* Green, stiff,
usually hairless but forms with short down
are recorded, with sparse small round
lenticels, in the second and subsequent
years dull mid brown. *Buds* In opposite

pairs, ovoid, pointed, chocolate brown at tips, small, 1–2 mm (0.1 in).
Foliage Leaves evergreen or tardily deciduous, ovate or ovate-triangular in outline, very variable in shape and lobing but always strongly three veined from the base, with small basal lobes to strongly three lobed and sparsely toothed, margin crinkled, apex bluntly acute, sinuses acute to shallow and rounded, base rounded to broad wedge-shaped, upper surface lustrous deep green and somewhat net-veined, hairless, lower surface mid or light green with raised veins, 1–4 × 1–2 cm (0.4–1.6 × 0.4–0.8 in); leaf stalk grooved with a tuft of hairs in the vein axils at the top, green or pink, very short, 3 mm (0.1 in); no autumn colour. *Flowers* In few flowered pendulous corymbs in spring, flowers greenish yellow. *Fruit* Nutlet with widely spreading wings, to 1.5 cm (0.6 in).

Range: Eastern Mediterranean region, from Greece including Crete and possibly Turkey.
Habitat: Dry rocky hillsides.
Synonyms: *A. creticum*, *A. orientale*.

This tree is closely related to *A. obtusifolium* (which has much larger leaves and is a more robust plant) and *A. monspessulanum* (with thin deciduous leaves which have wide spreading lobes), sharing with them the slender but very stiff branches and the arrangement of the flowers. Although more of a shrub than a tree in its native haunts, where time and adequate moisture are both allowed, it will grow to 10 m (33 ft) or more.

---

p.294 **Shirasawa Maple** *Acer shirasawanum*

Description: Deciduous tree to 10–15 m (33–50 ft) in height with a bole diameter to 50 cm (1.6 ft).
Crown Columnar to domed. *Bark* Grey to brownish grey, becoming shallowly ridged. *Shoot* Hairless, shiny green or purplish green on the upper surface for two years, then shiny buff brown in the third season.

Buds In opposite pairs, conical or ovoid conical, green or purple, with a ring of long white hairs, terminal buds absent, 3 mm (0.1 in). *Foliage* Leaves rounded with a broad heart-shaped base and nine to eleven triangular ovate lobes with short slender pointed tips, sinuses deep and narrow, extending one-third to one-half way to centre of the blade, margins sharply and somewhat doubly serrate with slender pointed, forward teeth, main veins raised on both surfaces, mid matt green above with the tertiary veins slightly impressed, pale green below, hairless except for axillary tufts below, 7–12 cm (2.8–4.7 in); leaf stalk hairless, grooved, pink or green, enclosing the bud in the enlarged base, 3–5 cm (1.2–2 in); autumn colour yellow. *Flowers* In upright corymbs of six to ten flowers appearing with and above the leaves in spring; sepals purple, petals white. *Fruit* Seed rounded, wing 2–3 cm (0.8–1.2 in), spreading at an obtuse angle.

Range: Southern Honshu and Shikoku, Japan.

Habitat: Cultivated as an ornamental, in the wild occurring in montane forests.

Varieties: Forma *aureum* is the main form in cultivation (usually under the synonymous name *A. japonicum* 'Aureum'). It has the leaves opening greenish yellow and maintaining a soft golden colour until turning red and orange in autumn.

Synonyms: *A. japonicum* var. *microphyllum*.

This small tree is not common in cultivation except as the form *aureum*.

---

p.169 **Birch-leafed Maple** *Acer stachyophyllum*

Description: Deciduous tree to 10–20 m (33–65 ft), often on more than one bole, each of which may be up to 30 cm (1 ft) in diameter. *Crown* Conical in young trees, becoming tall domed, arching in old trees, sometimes suckering from the base. *Bark* Green and faintly striped with pale whitish striations for several years, developing large rough brown lenticels in old trees. *Shoot* Green or pink-green and smooth for several years, brittle. *Buds* In opposite pairs, ovoid, on a short stalk, with two or three pairs of bud scales, to 5 mm (0.2 in). *Foliage* Leaves ovate with an acute or slender pointed tip, rounded base and coarsely few toothed or somewhat lobulate margins (but sometimes with three to five short slender pointed lobes especially on young trees and basal shoots), upper surface dark green with impressed slightly hairy veins, lower surface shiny green, with raised somewhat hairy veins, to 12 × 8 cm (4.7 × 3.1 in). Leaf stalk red or pink especially on the upper side, or green, downy, round (terete), very variable in length, up to 12 × 8 cm (4.7 × 3.1 in), clasping bud at base. Autumn colour yellow, not strong. *Flowers* Dioecious, i.e. on separate male and female trees. In pendent yellow-green catkin-like racemes in spring, to 12 cm (4.7 in). Male flowers with four stamens. *Fruit* In pendent racemes of circa 12 fruits, wings spreading at a wide angle, each 2–2.5 × 0.75–1.5 cm (0.8–1 × 0.3–0.6 in), seed ridged, 1 cm (0.4 in).

Range: Eastern Himalayas through to west and northwest China as far east as Shaanxi and Hubei provinces.

Habitat: Cultivated as an ornamental, in the wild occurring in mixed forest or in moist pine forest.

Varieties: Ssp. *betulifolium* has smaller leaves and a more suckering habit but probably best considered as just part of the normal variation.

Synonyms: *A. tetramerum.*

This small tree is very variable in the extent to which the margins are toothed or lobed, and occasionally suckers from the roots. It belongs to the section *Arguta*, which is a small group of species which have several characters of the snake bark maples (section *Macrantha*), such as the stalked buds, striated shoots and bark, but which differs in being dioecious and in the buds having two or three pairs of scales.

p.297 **Tartar Maple** *Acer tataricum*

Description: Deciduous tree 8–12 m (26–39 ft) with a
bole diameter to 50 cm (1.6 ft).
Crown Domed or ovoid, often on several
stems. *Bark* Pale brown, smooth, with
broad flat pink-brown fissures.
Shoot Brown with slightly raised lenticels,
red-brown in the second year, then grey-
brown. *Buds* In opposite pairs, ovoid,
with three pairs of dark chocolate and
loosely fitting scales exposed (but five to
ten pairs in total), 2 mm (0.1 in).
Foliage Leaves broadly ovate or sometimes
almost rounded, apex acute, base heart-
shaped, margin with large coarsely
lobulate double teeth to three lobed with
the central lobe with lobulate teeth, upper
surface shiny green with impressed but
rounded and coarsely hairy veins,
underside light sub-shiny green with six
to eight pairs of raised and variably hairy
veins, 4.5–10 × 4–7 cm (1.8–4 ×
1.6–2.8 in); leaf stalk grooved, pink,
2–5 cm (0.8–2 in); autumn colour orange
to red, but sometimes poor. *Flowers* In
small erect panicles from terminal or
axillary buds, opening with the leaves in
May, pale green or white. *Fruit* Nutlet
flattened, 1.2 cm (0.5 in), together with
rounded wing 3 cm (1.2 in), pairs erect
with the wings overlapping, red or green
when immature, ripening to brown in
September.

Range: Southeast Europe from Austria east to the
Caucasus and Turkey.

Habitat: Open light woods, as an understorey tree.

This small tree is related to *A. ginnala*.

p.306 **Chosen Maple** *Acer triflorum*

Description: Deciduous tree 10–15 m (33–50 ft) with a
bole diameter to 30 cm (1 ft).
Crown Ovoid, rounded in older trees.
Bark Grey-brown or yellow-brown, with
stiff shaggy vertical ridges. *Shoot* Initially
green and slender with sparse spreading

long white hairs with small elliptic raised lenticels, in the second year shiny brown and still hairy, hairless and dark or grey-brown in later years. *Buds* In opposite pairs, ovoid-acute, with numerous overlapping dark chocolate or black scales, 3 mm (0.1 in). *Foliage* Leaves trifoliate, to 15 × 13 cm (6 × 5.1 in) including leaf stalk, terminal leaflet lanceolate, apex with a broad acumen, base rounded wedge-shaped onto the 5–7 mm (0.2–0.3 in) stalk of a leaflet, margin with one or two pairs of spreading broad triangular teeth, upper surface matt green with impressed hairy veins, margin ciliate, undersurface bluish green, veins raised with sparse spreading white hairs, to 10 × 2.5 cm (4 × 1 in), lateral leaflets with short stalks 1–2 mm (0.1 in), oblique with two to three large teeth on the outer side with much smaller or absent teeth on the inner side, to 9 × 4 cm (3.5 × 1.6 in); leaf stalk round except near base, with stiff spreading sparse white hairs, circa 5 cm (2 in); autumn colour orange or golden-yellow. *Flowers* In cymes of three, pendent with a stiff hairy common stalk, petals yellow. *Fruit* Nutlet rounded, fat and hairy, 1 cm (0.4 in); wings acutely angled to parallel and overlapping wings constricted and hooked like a claw, 2–4 cm (0.8–1.6 in).

Range: Northern China across to Korea.
Habitat: Cultivated as an ornamental, in the wild occurring in mixed forests.

This tree is closely related to *A. griseum* and *A. maximowiczianum* but the shredding yellow-brown or grey-brown bark distinguish it. As with these species, the flowers are in threes, and an alternative common name mirrors the scientific epithet, Three-flowered Maple. However, I prefer the one used here, which refers to an old name for the Korean peninsula, which is an important part of its natural range. It thrives best in continental climates, preferring more summer heat and less spring frost than the British climate provides.

p.286 **Shandong Maple** *Acer truncatum*

Description: Deciduous tree 10–15 m (33–50 ft) with a bole diameter to 80 cm (2.6 ft).

Crown Broad domed, usually spreading wider than high. *Bark* Brown, roughly fissured. *Shoot* Shiny green with sparse oval lenticels in the first year, brown by the autumn and becoming rough in the third year, rather slender. *Buds* In opposite pairs, ovoid-conical, with numerous overlapping green or pinkish scales, 5 mm (0.2 in). *Foliage* Leaves fan-shaped in outline, deeply five lobed with triangular or ovate to slender pointed lobes which end in a fragile whisker, truncate across the base of the leaf, margins untoothed but wavy, rarely with a pair of teeth on the main lobe, upper surface deep lustrous green, beneath pale lustrous green, hairless except for some axillary tufts below, veins raised on both sides but especially below, 5–10 × 7–11 cm (2–4 × 2.8–4.3 in), usually broader than long, young leaves often somewhat purplish; leaf stalk rather oval in section, with a milky sap, greenish, clasping bud at base, variable in length, from 3–10 cm (1.2–4 in); autumn colour yellow, brownish reds and purple.

Flowers In terminal corymbs with the new leaves on short leafy shoots, yellow-green. *Fruit* Nutlet flattened, 1.3–1.8 cm (0.5–0.7 in), with a short wing to 2 cm (0.8 in), pairs spreading at an obtuse angle.

Range: Northern China from Gansu to Shandong provinces.

Habitat: Cultivated as an ornamental, in the wild occurring in woods.

Varieties: Several cultivars with white variegations have been named in Japan and are occasionally encountered in specialist collections, usually as shrubs.

Synonyms: *A. laetum* var. *truncatum*.

The neatly cut leaves on their oval leaf stalks tend to flutter in the wind. As the young leaves are usually reddish, this has given rise to an alternative common name, the Purpleblow Maple. This tree is related to *A. cono* and *A. platanoides* but can be separated by the bark and leaf shape. From *A. cappadocicum* and its relatives, the shoots turning brown by the first winter amply distinguishes it. It is the only maple which has hypogeal germination, i.e. the cotyledons remain in the seed coat and a true shoot emerges from the ground, whereas in all other species, the cotyledons are raised above the ground and act as the first leaves.

p.298 **Ukurundu Maple** *Acer ukurunduense*

Description: Deciduous tree to 8 m (26 ft) with a bole diameter to 30 cm (1 ft).
Crown Rounded, somewhat shrubby.
Bark Brown or pale brown, becoming rough and fissuring or peeling slightly when old. *Shoot* Green with a dense covering of golden-brown or yellowish-brown hairs, becoming purple in the second year but remaining hairy, hairless and dark reddish brown in the third year with rounded pale lenticels. *Buds* In opposite pairs, ovoid, pointed, yellow-green with a dense covering of golden-brown hairs on the outer pair of valvate scales, 0.4–1 cm (0.2–0.4 in).
Foliage Leaves rounded in outline with five or seven shallow ovate to triangular lobes with narrow acute sinuses usually only extending one-quarter or one-fifth the way to the midrib but deeper on vigorous extension shoots, base heart-shaped to deeply heart-shaped, margin irregularly and doubly serrate with acute or triangular and slightly bristle-tipped teeth, upper surface matt green, hairless, rugose from the deeply indented veins and veinlets, underside whitish or glaucous green with raised veins and veinlets which are densely covered with yellow-brown hairs, 7–15 × 7–15 cm (2.8–6 × 2.8–6 in); leaf stalk grooved, yellow haired, green or pinkish, 6–12 cm (2.4–4.7 in); autumn colour

yellow. *Flowers* In narrow erect racemes with the new foliage in spring, 10–15 cm (4–6 in), with small yellow flowers.
Fruit In erect racemes but with the pairs of fruits drooping on slender 1 cm (0.4) flower stalks, nutlet dimpled, 5 mm (0.2 in), wing 1.5–2 cm × 7 mm (0.6–0.8 × 0.3 in), green, ripening brown, with the pairs nearly erect.

Range: Northeast China and Manchuria to Korea, Pacific Russia, the Kurile Islands and Hokkaido, Honshu and Shikoku, Japan.

Habitat: Cultivated as an ornamental, in the wild occurring in mountain forests.

Synonyms: *A. caudatum* ssp. *ukurunduense*.

Similar species: **Mountain Maple** *A. spicatum* (p.298) from North America from Saskatchewan across to Newfoundland and south to Georgia along the Appalachian Mountains is closely related with similar erect flowering racemes and impressed leaves but differs in the following characters: the leaves have three or five deeper lobes which point forwards and are much less hairy beneath, the fruits are more rounded with larger wings 2–2.5 cm (0.8–1 in) which are divergent. It tends to be more shrubby, occasionally making a small tree to 7 m (23 ft).

This small tree has leaves which are rugose or blistered above due to the deeply impressed veins. It is related to *A. caudatum*, differing most clearly in the shallowly lobing of the yellow-brown hairy leaves. The name refers to a place in Manchuria, northeast China.

p.292 **Van Volxem's Maple**
Acer velutinum var. *vanvolxemii*

Description: Deciduous tree 15–20 m (50–65 ft) with a bole diameter to 80 cm (2.6 ft).
Crown Low broad dome when grown in the open, on a long bole when closely surrounded by other trees. *Bark* Smooth, green-brown to purplish grey, with prominent branch scars (as in Beech or

Fagus), only becoming scaly at the base of the largest trees. *Shoot* Olive-brown, shiny, with small linear orange lenticels, brown, green-brown or grey-brown with enlarged lenticels on two-year and older shoots. *Buds* In opposite pairs, conic or ovoid-conic, dark brown and green, downy, 5 mm (0.2 in). *Foliage* Leaves rounded in outline, with three or five shallow or deep lobes (extending from one-fifth to one-half way to the centre) which are bluntly pointed to pointed with narrow cleft sinuses, base heart-shaped to subcordate, margin with blunt triangular or rounded teeth, upper surface matt mid green, hairless, beneath glaucous pale green with a prominent network of raised veins, hairless except for axillary tufts, size variable, to 25 cm (10 in) across on young plants but 10–16 × 10–18 cm (4–6.3 × 4–7.1 in) on less vigorous older trees; leaf stalk round, pink or green, very variable up to 25 cm (10 in) but mainly around 10 cm (4 in); autumn colour yellow.
Flowers After the leaves in erect corymbose panicles 7–12 cm (2.8–4.7 in) with many small greenish flowers. *Fruit* Nutlets downy, 1 cm (0.4 in), wings 3–5 cm (1.2–2 in), the pairs spreading at a right or obtuse angle.

Range: Georgia, and in the eastern and central Caucasus region.

Habitat: Cultivated as an ornamental, in the wild occurring in mountain forests.

Varieties: Typical *A. velutinum* has small leaves, rarely more than 15 cm (6 in) across. It is variable in the degree of pubescence on the leaves, generally having a velvety coating beneath, but in var. *glabrescens* (syn. *A. insigne*) they are hairless. It comes from northern Iran and the southern Caucasus.

Synonyms: *A. vanvolxemii*.

This variant, with *A. macrophyllum*, has the largest leaves of any maple, commonly 25 cm (10 in) across in vigorous young trees but a more regular 15 cm (6 in) on older trees. It is allied to *A. pseudoplatanus*, which the leaves closely resemble.

HORSE CHESTNUTS OR BUCKEYES, *AESCULUS* (SYNONYM: *PAVIA*)
FAMILY HIPPOCASTANACEAE

This is a small genus of trees and shrubs. The leaves and buds are in opposite pairs, on stout shoots. The leaves are always palmately compound or digitate, with five to nine leaflets. The flowers are in large terminal panicles, with the petals fused to form an offset tube, and are followed by the large seed. The genus is divided into four sections. In section *Aesculus*, the flowers have five petals, the fruit is spiny and the buds large and very sticky. This subgenus includes only *AA. hippocastanum* and *turbinata*. Section *Pavia* has the flowers with only four petals. The fruits may be smooth or spiny, whilst the buds are non-resinous. This section is restricted to the eastern half of the USA and the species listed here are *AA. flava* and *pavia*. These two sections have been united in the hybrid, *A. × carnea*. Section *Calothyrsus* also has only four petals, but the buds are resinous, and much squatter than those of the rest of the genus. It is the most widely spread section with most species, ranging from California, across Asia from China to northwest India and south into Vietnam, but only *A. indica* is featured here. The fourth section, *Macrothyrsus* includes *A. parviflora* from the southeast USA. This has four or five petals with the stamens longer than the tube and non-resinous buds. It forms a suckering shrub to 3–5 m (10–16 ft) but only with very slender stems, and flowers in July or into August.

Ȧ *Aesculus* is planted mainly as an amenity tree, having a timber with very few uses.

p.310 **Red Horse Chestnut**
Aesculus × carnea

Description: Deciduous tree 15–25 m (50–80 ft) with a bole diameter to 1 m (3.3 ft).
Crown Rounded domed. *Bark* Grey-green with narrow pink-buff vertical fissures and finely roughened with horizontal lenticels, becoming reddish brown, not or only slightly scaly at the base; often with large brown cankers on the bole. *Shoot* Buff-grey, becoming browner and fissured, finely hairy at first, leaf traces kidney-shaped. *Buds* In opposite pairs, ovoid pointed, scales green-brown, only slightly resinous and not sticky, arranged in four rows, giving a rather square cross-section,

0.6–2.5 × 0.4–1.5 cm (0.25–1 × 0.2–0.6 in). *Foliage* Leaves digitate with five or seven leaflets; leaflets obovate or elliptic, apex rounded or with an abrupt short point, base wedge-shaped onto a short stout leaflet stalk, margin coarsely toothed, dark blackish green above and wrinkled on the veins, yellow-green beneath, to 25 × 13 cm (10 × 5.1 in); leaf stalk stout, to 23 cm (9.1 in); autumn colour poor. *Flowers* On panicles 15–20 × 10 cm (6–8 × 4 in) across; flowers rose-red with a yellow central blotch, petals 1 cm (0.4 in) with glandular margins. *Fruit* Rounded, smooth with few or no spines, to 4 cm (1.6 in); seeds mid to dark chestnut brown.

Range: Garden ornamental.

Habitat: Hybrid of garden origin.

Varieties: 'Briotii' has flowers which are a deeper red and leaves which are more glossy.

Similar species: *A. × plantierensis*, is a backcross with *A. hippocastanum*. It has flowers which are softly suffused with pink. It is a sterile triploid, with two sets of chromosomes from hippocasanum and one from pavia, with characters of the two species in about these ratios.

A. × carnea is a hybrid between *A. hippocastanum* and *A. pavia*, from which it inherits the pinky-red flowers. The leaves are larger than the common Horse Chestnut, deeper green and relatively broader, whilst the buds are not sticky and only slightly resinous. The origin of this hybrid is obscure, probably arising in Germany at the beginning of the 19th century. The original trees were sterile diploids. However, at some stage, a doubling of the chromosomes occurred, making the trees tetraploid. This had the effect of making the tree fertile, as the chromosomes could now pair at the formation of the ovules and pollen. However, as the trees are propagated by both seed and grafting, both forms have persisted in cultivation. The diploid tends to have a larger more oblong fruit which is soft and watery inside, and useless for playing conkers!

p.311 **Yellow Buckeye** *Aesculus flava*

Description: Deciduous tree to 25 m (80 ft) with a bole diameter to 1 m (3.3 ft).
Crown Narrow domed. *Bark* Smooth but developing thin scaly plates at the base, pink-grey or red-brown. *Shoot* Grey-green or grey-fawn or whitish, with small rounded buff lenticels, often hairy, stout, becoming light brown in the second year. *Buds* In opposite pairs, ovoid, with a sharp pointed apex, light brown, not resinous, 1.5 cm (0.6 in). *Foliage* Leaves palmate with five stalked leaflets (but only three or four on weak shoots); leaflets obovate to elliptic, tapering to an slender pointed and rather tail-like tip, base wedge-shaped, margin with regular rounded-pointed teeth, upper surface sub-shiny deep green with 15–20 pairs of lightly impressed and hairy veins, underside whitish green to yellow-green and often hairy, veins raised, 10–20 × 4–8 cm (4–8 × 1.6–3.1 in); leaf stalk round but ribbed towards the base, 9–18 cm (3.5–7.1 in), stalks of leaflets circa 1 cm (0.4 in); autumn colour orange-red. *Flowers* In erect panicles 10–15 cm (4–6 in), flowers 3 cm (1.2 in) with four very unequal yellow petals and seven or eight stamens. *Fruit* Ovoid, golden-yellow and warty but without prickles, 5–8 cm (2–3.1 in), splitting along two or three sutures and containing one to three large seeds (circa 3 cm (1.2 in)) which are chestnut brown with a scar or hilium which is half the diameter of the seed and pale buff brown.

Range: Eastern USA from Pennsylvania south to Alabama and Georgia and west to Illinois.

Habitat: Cultivated as an ornamental, in the wild occurring in moist river valley sites in mixed forests.

Synonyms: *A. octandra*.

Similar species: **Ohio Buckeye** *A. glabra* is a similar species, differing in the fruit which is covered with small triangular pimples or warts (thus somewhat intermediate between the smooth fruit of *A. flava* and the strongly spined one of

A. hippocastanum). The leaves are nearly stalkless, with a leaflet stalk of only around 2 mm (0.1 in) and may be in sevens. The bark is fissured pale brown, becoming ash grey and scaly, with the foetid scent of elder. The flowers are smaller, 2–2.5 cm (0.8–1 in), pale yellow to greenish yellow, with four nearly equal petals. It is distributed from Pennsylvania south to Alabama and west to Oklahoma and Iowa, occurring in mixed broadleafed forests.
Texas Buckeye *A. arguta* differs from *A. glabra* in the seven to eleven leaflets which are lanceolate and saw toothed. It is found on sandy soils from Nebraska south to Missouri, Oklahoma and Texas. It is usually only a small tree to 6 m (20 ft).

The name buckeye refers to the pale hilium, which is the plant equivalent of our navel and is the point of attachment of the seed to the placenta; when viewed face on, the fruit resembles a deer's eye, with the hilium representing the iris. Yellow buckeye makes an attractive tree, both in flower and in autumn foliage.

p.310 **Horse Chestnut** *Aesculus hippocastanum*

Description: Deciduous tree 20–35 m (65–115 ft) with a bole diameter to 2.2 m (7 ft).
Crown Ovoid and spiky in winter when young, becoming rounded or tall domed.
Bark Reddish brown to grey-brown, smooth but becoming scaly in large plates, in old trees somewhat shallowly fissured at the base. *Shoot* Dark brown or pink-brown with oval pale lenticels, at first green and densely covered with a loose reddish-brown wool, in later years pale brown to grey-brown with large horseshoe-shaped traces from the fallen leaves. *Buds* In opposite pairs, ovoid, pointed, sharp, very resinous and sticky, to 2.5 cm (1 in). *Foliage* Leaves palmately lobed (digitate), with five or seven stalkless leaflets; leaflets obovate, rounded with a short acute cusp at the apex, base narrow long wedge-shaped,

margin coarsely and doubly serrate, upper surface matt green and rather rugose, initially reddish hairy but soon hairless except for some reddish-brown glands along the impressed veins, underside pale green with parallel raised veins which retain some light brown hairs in the axils, 13–30 × 2–13 cm (5.1–12 × 0.8–5.1 in); leaf stalk rounded, only grooved near the bulbous base, 7–20 cm (2.8–8 in); autumn colour variable from scarlet, gold, orange or yellow, or dropping dull brown. *Flowers* In large terminal panicles to 30 cm (12 in) on leafy shoots in April to May from previous year's buds, flowers with four or five petals which are white with a yellow or red blotch and longer stamens. *Fruit* Globose, ripening in October, case prickly, green but maturing to yellow and opening along three sutures, with one or two flattened globose chestnut brown seeds with a pale brown hilium or scar which covers 50 per cent of one side, 3–5 cm (1.2–2 in).

Range: Albania and Northern Greece, especially in the Pindus Mountains.

Habitat: Mixed woodland, widely planted as a parkland tree.

Varieties: 'Baumanii' is a form with double flowers which does not set seed, thus frustrating small (and not so small) boys.

Similar species: **Japanese Horse Chestnut** A. *turbinata* is very closely related despite the considerable distance and the entire Asian land mass between them. It differs in the leaves being much more regularly toothed, which is readily apparent when they are compared together but not so obvious on its own as the teeth are not perfectly regular. They are also generally larger, with leaflets to 40 × 15 cm (16 × 6 in). The fruits also are often larger, and lack the sharp prickles. It is found on Honshu and Hokkaido.

This is one of the commonest and most majestic of broadleaved trees, regularly bearing masses of large white 'candles', to be followed by the fruits, or conkers which are used in the game of conkers. Chestnuts have a curious cycle of growth, not found in any other broadleaved trees. In many ways, they mimic bulbs like Daffodils and Bluebells in the way they behave. Growth is made from a single burst or flush of activity in the spring, and only rarely, or in young trees, is a further flush made before next spring. If the leaves are lost early due to drought or some other cause, so be it, next spring will arrive in due season. They are also variable in the time of flushing, with some trees in full leaf and flower weeks before others.

p.311	**Indian Horse Chestnut** *Aesculus indica*

Description: Deciduous tree 15–25 m (50–80 ft) with a bole diameter to 80 cm (2.6 ft).
Crown Rounded, domed, rather spiky when young. *Bark* Pink-brown or buff, rough and warty, scaly in old trees at the base only. *Shoot* Green or brown with raised elliptic lenticels, shiny pink-brown in the second year, stout. *Buds* In opposite pairs, rounded with a blunt apex, green or pink, somewhat resinous, to 1.5 cm (0.6 in). *Foliage* Leaves with seven, less often five or nine, stalked leaflets, overall to 40 cm (16 in) across; leaflets obovate to lanceolate, apex rounded or acute with a short slender pointed tip, base wedge-shaped, margin finely and regularly serrate with acute forward teeth, upper surface light to mid green, hairless, undersurface pale to glaucous green, hairless, with circa 20 pairs of prominent veins, 15–30 × 5–10 cm (6–12 × 2–4 in); petiolule 2–3 cm (0.8–1.2 in), leaf stalk rounded, 10–18 cm (4–7.1 in); autumn colour poor. *Flowers* In terminal panicles in June or early July, 25–40 cm (10–16 in); flowers with four petals, white with pink and/or yellow blotches, stamens eight, long projecting. *Fruit* Globose, rough but not spined, with a leathery husk, seed dark glossy chocolate or blackish brown, wrinkled, with a small pale scar where it is attached to the husk, 3–4 cm (1.2–1.6 in).

Range: Northwest Himalayas from west Nepal to Afghanistan.

Habitat: Cultivated as an ornamental, in the wild occurring in mixed valley forests.

Varieties: 'Sydney Pearce' is a selected form which carries abundant panicles of flowers but few fruits.

This tree flowers and fruits some six weeks later than *A. hippocastanum*, and is usually overlooked by those searching for conkers. On the continent, it is often misnamed as *A. chinensis*, a related species from China with smaller leaves and smaller trusses of whiter flowers.

---

p.311 **Red Buckeye** *Aesculus pavia*

Description: Deciduous tree 8–14 m (26–46 ft) with a bole diameter to 50 cm (1.6 ft). *Crown* Rounded, often grafted at 1.5 m (5 ft) onto *A. hippocastanum* in the larger trees. *Bark* Brown-grey to light grey, smooth. *Shoot* Brownish green at first, maturing to pale grey by autumn, with a covering of down and small round buff to pinkish-orange lenticels, grey to brownish grey in later years. *Buds* In opposite pairs, ovate-conic, sharply pointed, with green and brown scales, not resinous, 1–1.5 cm (0.4–0.6 in). *Foliage* Leaves compound, palmate, with five, rarely seven, leaflets, to 15 × 15 cm (6 × 6 in) (excluding leaf stalk); leaflets narrowly elliptic to obovate, tapering to the pointed or short slender pointed apex, base wedge-shaped to narrow wedge-shaped onto a short leaflet stalk of 3–4 mm (0.1–0.2 in), margin with rounded teeth except at the base, upper surface shiny green with the 15–20 pairs of parallel veins impressed with some hairs remaining in the grooves, underside light somewhat whitish green, hairless except for pale hairs along the veins, 5–15 × 3–6 cm (2–6 × 1.2–2.4 in); leaf stalk green, hairy, round at the top but becoming grooved towards the base, 7–15 cm (2.8–6 in); autumn colour yellow.

Flowers In terminal upright narrow panicles 10–20 cm (4–8 in) long in spring with many 3 cm (1.2 in) flowers each with four bright red unequal petals and six to eight stamens. *Fruit* Light brown capsule 4–5 cm (1.6–2 in) across, smooth, without prickles, opening along two or three sutures with one to three shiny brown seeds.

Range: Southeast USA from North Carolina south to northern Florida and across southern Texas and north to Illinois.

Habitat: Cultivated as an ornamental, in the wild occurring in damp sites such as near rivers, and as an understorey tree.

This species is not common in cultivation, having been largely displaced by its more vigorous hybrid (*see A. × carnea*). Although normally red, the flowers can be yellow-red and in the far west of Texas in particular they are yellow.

AGAVE, AGAVACEAE

This is a small, rather inconsistent, family related to the Liliaceae. *Cordyline* (p.617), *Dracaena* (p.668) and *Yucca* (p.1265) are featured here.

TREES OF HEAVEN, *AILANTHUS*
FAMILY SIMAROUBACEAE

This is a genus of half a dozen or so species found from India and China south across southeast Asia to Australia. The leaves are pinnate, and can be enormous, and are provided with extra-floral nectaries. The shoots are similarly stout. Both leaves, shoots and flowers have a somewhat foetid smell. The fruit is a single nutlet located in the centre of a twisted wing.

---

p.336   **Tree of Heaven** *Ailanthus altissima*

Description: Deciduous tree 15–30 m (50–100 ft) with a bole diameter to 90 cm (2.9 ft).
Crown Rounded, on a stout single trunk with radiating branches, often with

suckers in the grass around the tree.
Bark Smooth and grey-brown to blackish brown with white streaks in young trees, becoming shallowly fissured with grey to buff stripes. *Shoot* Stout, greeny brown to coppery brown with a golden tinge and very finely velvety (which can be felt but not seen except under a strong handlens) with small oval orange lenticels, in the second year more red-brown with buff lenticels and large horseshoe leaf traces, matt brown in the third year.

Buds Domed, red-brown, 2×4 mm (0.1×0.2 in). *Foliage* Leaves large, mainly 30–60 cm (12–23.6 in) but up to 90×25 cm (36×10 in), pinnate with 5–20 pairs of stalked leaflets; leaflets ovate to ovate-oblong, tapering to a long tail-like often twisted tip, base heart-shaped, often oblique, with a translucent margin which is untoothed except for one to three large marginal glands on either side near the base, upper surface sub-shiny to glossy deep green with raised veins and midrib, underside pale glaucous green with strongly raised veins with axillary tufts, bruised or handled foliage with a strong foetid smell, $7–15 \times 3.5–6.5$ cm ($2.8–6 \times 1.4–2.6$ in); leaf stalk round with an enlarged base; rachis slightly grooved, leaflet stalks grooved, hairless or hairy, 0.5–1.5 cm (0.2–0.6 in); autumn colour poor, falling without turning. *Flowers* In large greenish clusters terminal on the current year's growths in July, usually with separate male and female trees, greenish white, foul smelling on male trees.

Fruit Clusters expand to 30 cm (12 in) across, composed of many keys or samaras with a round 1 cm (0.4 in) seed set in the centre of the twisted wing which is $3.5–4 \times 1.2$ cm ($1.4–1.6 \times 0.5$ in) and bright red or green prior to ripening brown.

Range: Northern China.
Habitat: Cultivated as an ornamental, in the wild occurring in forests.
Synonyms: *A. glandulosa*.
Similar species: *A. vilmoriniana* is closely related but differs in the young shoots, especially on

seedling trees, being covered with stout spines (which I believe to be a devise to discourage slugs and snails) and very downy leaves. It is sometimes grafted onto *A. altissima*, which is unfortunate as the root stock suckers and the graft is often lost.

This tree has bold foliage with numerous leaflets. It is most impressive in late summer when the female trees are loaded with bright red or yellow-green immature fruits. Male trees are usually avoided in towns as the flowers are atrociously scented, with the foliage of both sexes also having a somewhat foetid aroma. The bark is distinctive with its broad shallow pale grey cracks. The scientific name comes from the Moluccan name for a very tall tree (originally used for the species found in Indonesia) and signifies reaching the heavens, and thus leading to the common name. The glands at the base of the leaves are extra-floral nectaries, designed to dispense nectar to ants who keep the leaves clear of foliage eating insects and caterpillars.

SILK TREES, *ALBIZIA* (SYNONYM: *ALBIZZIA*)
FAMILY LEGUMINOSAE

This is a genus of around 150 species from the warm temperate to tropical regions of the Old World and South America. They form fast-growing trees with a useful timber. The flowers form a rounded knob with many stamens and are similar in appearance to *Acacia*.

p.342 **Pink Siris** *Albizia julibrissin*

Description: Deciduous tree 8–15 m (26–50 ft) with a bole diameter to 50 cm (1.6 ft).
Crown Broad spreading and often rather flat topped. *Bark* Smooth, black or grey. *Shoot* Brown or grey, often angled, hairless, sometimes with conspicuous lenticels. *Buds* Small. *Foliage* Leaves bipinnate, with fern-like leaflets,

15–40 cm (6–16 in) long; leaflets with fine hairs, in 5–12 pairs each with 15–30 pairs of pinnules or leaflets, which are oblong, pale green, hairless above but finely hairy beneath and 0.6–2 × 0.2–0.6 cm (0.25–0.8 × 0.1–0.25 in); leaf stalk channelled above and slightly pilose with a conspicuous gland at the base, 4–10 cm (1.6–4 in). *Flowers* In terminal panicles of ten to many spherical flowers during the summer; flowers composed of many stamens which have silky filaments 2.5–3 cm (1–1.2 in) in length and are rose-pink towards the tip with minute anthers. *Fruit* Long flat oblong pod which ripens yellow-brown but usually remains unopened, 13–16 × 2–3 cm (5.1–6.3 × 0.8–1.2 in), with flattened shiny seeds.

Range: Caspian region of Iran and the Caucasus east to China.

Habitat: Cultivated as an ornamental.

Synonyms: *Acacia julibrissin*.

Similar species: **Plume Albizia** *A. lophantha* (p.342) is a smaller growing tree, usually to only 7 m (23 ft) in height. The leaves are similar, but the rachis is velvety hairy, as is the shoot. The stamens have filaments only 1.3–1.8 cm (0.5–0.7 in) in length, which are creamy white or bright yellow. It is native to southern and western Australia. *A. lebbeck* has the leaves with only two to four (rarely one or five) pairs of leaflets, which in turn have only three to eleven pairs of leaflets (pinnules). The leaflets are much larger, 1.5–4.8 × 0.8–3 cm (0.6–1.9 × 0.3–1.2 in). The flowers are fragrant, greenish white or yellow, with filaments 1.5–3 cm (0.6–1.2 in). The pod is 15–33 × 3–6 cm (6–13 × 1.2–2.4 in). It is native to tropical Asia but cultivated in warm temperate regions.

This makes an attractive tree in its fern-like foliage and pink flowers borne over an extended period of summer. Long cultivated, its original wild origin is unclear but was probably China. The leaves close over night.

ALDERS, *ALNUS*
FAMILY BETULACEAE

Alnus is a genus of around 30 or so species. They are commonly associated with water, such as beside streams or on flood plains ('alder carrs'), but they may also be found in damper spots where water is not apparent on the surface. Some species also tolerate quite dry conditions. The genus is mainly found in the northern hemisphere, in the Old World occurring as far south as northern Vietnam and Taiwan. In the Americas, however, they cross the equator and extend as far south as The Argentine. Generally, alders are not the largest trees, and some species are effectively shrubs, but they have a useful timber. Traditionally, they have provided the wood for clogs, whilst alder made the preferred charcoal for gunpowder. Modern uses, apart from the visual one, include utilization of their association with nitrogen-fixing bacteria. Alders are similar to birches with most species having the male catkins exposed over the winter and expanding in spring before the leaves. However, the female catkins become a woody and thus persistent cone-like structure. Three species, *AA. nitida* and *nepalensis* from the Himalayas to southeast Asia and *A. maritima* from the USA have the male catkins expanding in the autumn. Whilst these are not featured here, they may be found in specialist collections. In most species the buds are stalked with a pair of outer scales, but in the subgenus *Alnobetula* the buds are not stalked and have many spirally set scales. Also the wood in this section does not turn brown if cut and exposed to the air as occurs in the other sections. The leaves are coarsely toothed to lobulate (with small lobes) in *AA. incana*, *rubra* and *rugosa*, but finely to regularly toothed in *cordata*, *glutinosa*, *orientalis* and *viridis*. The leaf base can also help in separating the species: it is heart shaped in *AA. cordata* and *orientalis*, wedge shaped in *AA. glutinosa* and *rubra*, and rounded in *AA. rugosa* and *viridis*, although it can vary from wedge shaped to rounded in *A. incana*.

---

p.178   **Italian Alder** *Alnus cordata*

Description: Deciduous tree 15–30 m (50–100 ft) with a bole diameter to 1 m (3.3 ft).
Crown Conical in young trees, then becoming columnar. *Bark* Grey-brown to dull grey, smooth with blisters, developing fissures at the base. *Shoot* In the first winter grey due to a waxy bloom but where this is lost revealing shiny brown beneath

with raised buff elliptic lenticels, triangular in section, becoming round in section in second and later years, retaining a mixture of bloomed grey and brown. *Buds* Ovoid and rounded, 7 mm (0.3 in), enclosed within two scaly green and white scales, on a scaly green stalk 5 mm (0.2 in). *Foliage* Rounded to broad ovate, apex rounded (Corsican origins) or with an abrupt short point, deeply heart-shaped at base, margin with fine shallow forward teeth except near base, shiny dark green above, paler green beneath with tufts of orange or brown hairs in vein axils and along the midrib, veins weak, not reaching the leaf margin, 3–12 × 4–8 cm (1.2–4.7 × 1.6–3.1 in); leaf stalk 3 cm (1.2 in). *Flowers* From exposed buds at the ends of previous season's shoots, opening in late winter or early spring; male catkins in clusters of (1–)3–5 on a green stalk which has small blackish glands or scales, pendent, to 10 cm (4 in), green with yellow pollen and showy, turning brown when spent; female flowers at the base of the catkins, usually in twos or threes, erect, cylindrical and 1 cm (0.4 in) on scaly green stalks, with purple-red stigmas protruding between the green scales to 1 mm (0.1 in). *Fruit* Woody cone-like structure, erect, ovoid-oblong or egg-shaped, 2.5–3 cm (1–1.2 in), ripening from green with white resin to mid to dark brown in first autumn and persisting on the tree for up to a year after opening.

Range: Corsica, southern Italy and northwest Albania.

Habitat: Damp thickets to drier forest.

Similar species: *A. subcordata* from northern Iran and the Caucasus region differs in the dull leaves which are hairy and in the hairy shoots.

This tree, with its glossy heart-shaped and ovate foliage is more reminiscent of a pear than most alders, but has woody cone-like fruits and long pendulous catkins in spring typical of alders, if somewhat larger than usual. It makes a vigorous tree, capable of growing far further north than its native

origin, such as in southern Scotland. It is
also quite drought tolerant. Most cultivated
plants are of Italian origin and have leaves
which are acute to slender pointed at the
apex and 6–12 cm (2.4–4.7 in) in length;
in the Corsican plants, the leaves are
bluntly pointed or rounded and smaller,
3–7 cm (1.2–2.8 in) in length, and the tree
is much slower growing.

---

p.178   **Alder** or **Common Alder**   *Alnus glutinosa*

Description: Deciduous tree 15–25 m (50–80 ft) in
height with a bole diameter to 1 m (3.3 ft).
Crown Conic or ovoid when young,
becoming broad conic or columnar, often
on several stems where coppiced.
Bark Purplish brown in young trees,
darkening with age to grey-brown with
pale or orange fissures and becoming
cracked, grey and fissured into small
vertical plates in old trees. *Shoot* When
young covered with minute glutinous
glands which show as black dots in the first
winter when the shoot is grey, remaining so
or becoming brown in patches, round and
hairless. *Buds* Oblong, with two bud
scales (perulae) which are covered by grey
scales, curved, 7 mm (0.3 in), on a grey
scaly stalk 5 mm (0.2 in). *Foliage* Broadly
obovate to nearly rounded, base wedge-
shaped, apex rounded, often notched,
margin somewhat wavy with irregular
shallow teeth, upper surface deep shiny
green and initially with glutinous glands,
underside paler with tufts of white hairs in
the axils of the six to eight pairs of veins,
4–10 × 3–7 cm (1.6–4 × 1.2–2.8 in); leaf
stalk 1.5–3.5 cm (0.6–1.4 in), with dark
glandular dots. *Flowers* On catkins formed
on previous season's growths in late winter;
male catkins in clusters of three to five,
purple over winter, pendulous, 2–3 cm
(0.8–1.2 in) in bud but opening to 7 cm
(2.8 in), purple and yellow; female catkins
erect to nodding in clusters of four or five
(but may be two or three clusters together),
ovoid, red-purple, 4–6 mm (0.2–0.25 in).

Fruit Ovoid or globular, ripening from green to blackish brown, woody, 1.2–1.5 cm (0.5–0.6 in).

Range: Throughout Europe except Iceland, Faroes, the Balearic Islands and Crete, extending south into North Africa and west to the Caucasus and northern Iran.

Habitat: Wet situations, especially alongside streams.

Varieties: Var. *barbata* has leaves rounded at the base and often pointed at the apex, with 8–10 pairs of veins, and hairy shoots. It is the form in the Caucasus and Iran. Three cultivars often encountered in parks are 'Aurea', with golden yellow leaves, and 'Imperalis' and 'Laciniata', both with cut-leaves.

This is a common riverside tree, very attractive over winter when the male catkins give a purplish haze. The leaves immediately distinguish it from other *Alnus*, although in catkin it is very similar to *A. incana*. The wood has been used for clogs, whilst the charcoal was preferred as the charcoal for making gunpowder. The Greek populations are tetraploid and perhaps should not be included in *A. glutinosa*. This may also apply to other southerly populations such as in Spain and North Africa. The form wild on Corsica has thin red-brown twigs and small, nearly circular leaves.

p.179 **Grey Alder** *Alnus incana*

Description: Deciduous tree to 20 m (65 ft) with a bole diameter to 60 cm (2 ft).
Crown Conical in young trees, broadening with age, often surrounded by suckers from the roots. *Bark* Dark grey with a greenish tinge, smooth with vertical lenticels, becoming dull grey with fissures at base. *Shoot* Grey or grey-brown with raised round orange lenticels in first winter, initially grey downy and round, then grey and brown. *Buds* Oblong, curved, rounded, with two outer bud scales which are covered with small warty scales, purple-

red, 0.8–1 cm (0.3–0.4 in); on a scaly grey stalk 4–7 mm (0.2–0.3 mm).

Foliage Oval, ovate to obovate, acute at the apex, margins with around six triangular coarse teeth or small lobes with additional small secondary teeth, base wedge-shaped to rounded and without teeth, upper surface dull green, underside greyish with hairs all over or on the 9–12 pairs of veins, 5–10 × 4–6 cm (2–4 × 1.6–2.4 in); leaf stalk 2.5–3 cm (1–1.2 in), rarely longer.

Flowers From exposed buds formed on previous season's growths, opening in early spring; male catkins in clusters of three to six, pendulous, purple-red with yellow pollen, 5–10 cm (2–4 in), on scaly grey peduncles; female catkins at base of male clusters, spreading and nodding, in threes to eights, oval to 5 mm (0.2 in), red-purple, with purple stigmas. *Fruit* Ovoid woody cone-like structure, ripening to dark brown, 1.2–2.2 cm (0.5–0.9 in).

Range: Western Europe (but not Britain) east to the Caucasus.

Habitat: Mountains, especially on damp sites, and riverbanks.

Varieties: 'Aurea' is a selection with golden leaves and reddish yellow twigs. 'Ramulis Coccineus' has much stronger red-coloured twigs. Both form attractive trees, but need moist sites for best effect. 'Pendula' has weeping branches and makes an attractive small weeping tree. 'Laciniata' has the leaves pinnately divided to two thirds the distance to the midrib with six to eight narrow lanceolate, toothed lobes. Forma *angustissima* has the leaves similarly cut nearly to the midrib, but the lobes are prolonged into thread-like points. It is recorded as an occasional tree in Scandinavian populations.

Grey Alder is much used on soil reclamation sites and for protection from frosts and wind in fruit orchards. It tolerates drier soils than most other alders, including chalky ones. It is also unique in suckering, forming a cluster of suckers around the base. It is closely related to *A. rugosa*.

p.179 **Oriental Alder** *Alnus orientalis*

Description: Deciduous tree to 20 m (65 ft) with a bole
diameter to 60 cm. (2 ft)
Crown Slender, pointed to rounded conical.
Bark Grey, becoming fissured with age.
Shoot Slender, hairless. *Buds* Oblong,
blunt, glutinous or sticky, on a short stalk,
4–7 × 3–4 mm (0.2–0.3 × 0.1–0.2 in).
Foliage Leaves ovate to oblong, bluntly
pointed, acute or short slender point at the
tip, base heart-shaped, margin variably
toothed, upper surface mid green, hairless,
underside paler, hairy at first but usually
only remaining so on the veins or in the
vein axils, veins in six to eight pairs,
branched and not reaching the leaf margin,
3–12 × 1.3–6 cm (1.2–4.7 × 0.5–2.4 in);
leaf stalk slender, hairless or thinly hairy,
1–3 cm (0.4–1.2 in); stipules soon falling,
oblong, 4–7 mm (0.2–0.3 in); autumn
colour poor. *Flowers* Male catkins
numerous in clusters of three to six,
pendulous, reddish purple, 4–12 cm
(1.6–4.7 in). *Fruit* Ovoid glutinous cone
2 × 1.5 cm (0.8 × 0.6 in); seeds flattened,
usually with no wing but occasionally
slightly winged.

Range: Cyprus, southeast Turkey, Syria to the
Lebanon.

Habitat: River margins.

This tree is related to *A. cordata*, from
which the wingless or almost wingless
seeds distinguish it. The plants in Cyprus
tend to be more resinous and glutinous
with smaller leaves than those in Turkey.

p.180 **Red Alder** *Alnus rubra*

Description: Deciduous tree 15–25 m (50–80 ft) with a
bole diameter to 60 cm (2 ft).
Crown Narrow conical when young,
becoming broader and domed with age.
Bark Light dull grey to nearly white, with
lines of pale lenticels, becoming ridged and
mottled with black patches in old trees,
smooth or slightly scaly. *Shoot* Green-

brown, shiny with a thin grey layer of wax, sparsely glandular and grey haired at first, angled and often triangular in section.
Buds Stalked, curved, red, resinous.
Foliage Leaves ovate-elliptic to elliptic, apex acute and shortly pointed, base wedge-shaped, margin wavy and decurved or rolled down with double serrate teeth or lobulate to 1 cm (0.4 in), texture rather thick, upper surface dull or somewhat shiny green with 10–15 pairs of parallel strongly impressed veins, underside grey-green with rusty coloured hairs on the veins and midrib, 10–15 × 4.5–7.5 cm (4–6 × 1.8–3 in); leaf stalk 2.5–3.5 cm (1–1.4 in); autumn colour nil. *Flowers* Male catkins in clusters of three to four, yellowish with reddish scales, 10–15 cm (4–6 in). *Fruit* Elliptic cones with many hard black scales, 1.2–2.5 × 1.5 cm (0.5–1 × 0.6 in); seeds flattened, rounded, with two narrow wings.

Range: Western North America from southeast Alaska to central California and east of the Rocky Mountains with a disjunct population along the Clearwater River in north Idaho.

Habitat: Cultivated as an ornamental and in forestry plantations, in the wild occurring on river margins and on land slip sites.

Synonyms: *A. oregona*.

This tree makes very fast initial growth and is useful in forestry, especially as a nurse tree and to add nitrogen to the soil. However, on dry sites it is rather short lived, and in exposed conditions the foliage is somewhat fragile. It is similar to *A. incana*, differing in the soon hairless shoots and the broader leaves having recurved margins and deeper lobes.

p.180 **Speckled Alder** *Alnus rugosa*

Description: Deciduous shrub or small shrubby tree to 6–10 m (20–33 ft) with a bole to 15 cm (6 in).
Crown Rounded, often on several stems.
Bark Grey, smooth. *Shoot* Grey-brown,

slender, slightly hairy when young, triangular in section (especially the pith). *Buds* Ovoid. *Foliage* Leaves elliptic or ovate, broadest around the middle, apex rounded or acute, base rounded, margin wavy and doubly and irregularly serrate, upper surface dull dark green with 9–12 pairs of impressed veins, hairless or hairy, underside whitish green with prominent hairy veins and secondary veinlets, 5–10 × 4–7.5 cm (2–4 × 1.6–3 in); leaf stalk hairy, short; autumn colour poor. *Flowers* Male catkins yellowish, 4–7.5 cm (1.6–3 in). *Fruit* Elliptic cone with hard black scales, 1.2–1.5 cm (0.5–0.6 in); seeds rounded.

Range: North America mainly across Canada from the Yukon and British Columbia to Newfoundland and south into the USA in Iowa, Idaho and along the Appalachians to West Virginia.

Habitat: Cultivated in forestry plantations and occasionally naturalized (such as northern Poland), in the wild occurring on river and lake margins.

This small alder is used as a nurse and pioneer species. It is related to *A. incana*, differing in the more finely toothed leaves which are scarcely or not lobed, the darker grey bark, the less hairy leaves and the cones having projecting scales. The Latin name refers to the deeply impressed veins.

---

p.180 **Green Alder** *Alnus viridis*

Description: Deciduous shrubby 'tree' to 5 m (16 ft), almost always on several stems, with bole diameters up to 25 cm (10 in).
Crown Ovoid with erect branches, becoming wider than high in old trees in alpine regions. *Bark* Brown.
Shoot Brown and strongly ridged below the leaves, shiny and rather viscid and hairless, with oval lenticels, maturing green-brown to purplish brown with pale round lenticels, greyer in the second year. *Buds* Lanceolate, pointed, with imbricate

scales, shiny green or purplish, not stalked towards the tip of the shoot but somewhat stalked at the base of current year's shoots, 1–1.5 cm (0.4–0.6 in). *Foliage* Leaves ovate to rounded oval, apex acute, base rounded, margin doubly serrate with triangular teeth and hairs in the small sinuses, upper surface sub-shiny green with impressed hairy veins, underside light shiny green and viscid, with black dots on the six to eight pairs of raised veins and axillary tufts of pale brown hairs, 2.5–8 × 2–7 cm (1–3.1 × 0.8–2.8 in); leaf stalk grooved, sparsely hairy, green, circa 1.5 cm (0.6 in); autumn colour poor.
Flowers Opening with the leaves in April/May, male catkins yellow, 5–8 cm (2–3.1 in), often white resinous over winter. *Fruit* Four or five together in short racemes from buds on previous season's shoots, ovoid woody cone-like structure, green, ripening to dark brown, 1.2–2 cm (0.5–0.8 in), on slender downy flower stalks to 2 cm (0.8 in); seeds pale, with a wide thin wing.

Range: Central and southeastern Europe.
Habitat: Mountains.
Synonyms: *Betula viridis*, *A. alnobetula*, *Alnobetula viridis*.
Similar species: Related species occur across the northern hemisphere, and are variously treated as separate species or subspecies.
A. *maximowiczii* from Japan is the most distinctive element. It has leaves with a rounded to heart-shaped base and margins with long slender fringe-like teeth.
Sitka Alder A. *sinuata* from the Pacific coast of western North America has rounded to wedge-shaped ovate leaves 7–15 × 4–10 cm (2.8–6 × 1.6–4 in) which are lustrous green beneath and doubly toothed.

This small tree is the representative species of a section of alder, typified by the non-stalked buds, although those at the base of the shoot may develop stalks, with imbricate scales, as opposed to the paired opposite scales of other alders. The seed is different, with a thin wide wing.

Snowy Mespilus or Service Berry, *Amelanchier*
Family Rosaceae

This is a genus of mainly deciduous large shrubs, rather than trees. It is most abundant in North America, but with species in Europe and Asia. They are grown for the showy white flowers with the new leaves in spring, which are followed by the reddish to purple or black small miniature apple-like fruits which ripen in early summer. These can be eaten when slightly over-ripe, although the birds usually get there first. Amelanchiers thrive on a wide range of soils.

p.202 **Snowy Mespilus** *Amelanchier × grandiflora*

Description: Deciduous shrub or small tree to 8 m (26 ft) with a bole diameter to 20 cm (8 in). *Crown* Rounded, often on several stems. *Bark* Smooth and grey-brown, becoming finely ridged and cracked. *Shoot* Olive-brown at first, hairless, becoming pink brown by late summer, brown and grey later. *Buds* Long conic or ovoid-conic, slender, pink-yellow, 6 mm (0.25 in). *Foliage* Leaves ovate to oblong-obovate, apex tapers to a short point, base rounded, margins with sharp triangular aristate teeth, upper surface sub-shiny green with slightly impressed net-like veins, lower surface somewhat glaucous green, initially whitish hairy beneath but most soon lost, 4–7 × 2–5 cm (1.6–2.8 × 0.8–2 in); leaf stalk faintly grooved, yellow-green, hairless, 2–3.5 cm (0.8–1.4 in); autumn colour red and orange, new foliage coppery to purplish with whitish hairs. *Flowers* In crooked (flexuous) racemes 5–7 cm (2–2.8 in) in late spring (late April–May), white or flushed pink, with sepals reflexed soon after the flower is over. *Fruit* Rounded, 0.8–1 cm (0.3–0.4 in), ripening to purplish red or black in June or July, with reflexed sepals.

Range: Hybrid origin.

Habitat: Cultivated and possibly naturalized as an ornamental.

Varieties: 'Rubescens' is a selection with flowers purplish pink, opening to flushed pink.

This is perhaps the showiest *Amelanchier*. It occurs where the two parent species, *A. arborea* and *A. laevis* are found, including in the wild in North America.

---

p.202 **Snowy Mespilus**   *Amelanchier laevis*

Description: Deciduous shrub or small tree to 8 m (26 ft) with a bole diameter to 20 cm (8 in). *Crown* Rounded, often on several stems. *Bark* Smooth, grey-brown. *Shoot* Olive-brown, slender with few small lenticels, becoming dark or chocolate brown in the second year. *Buds* Long conic or ovoid-conic, slender, green, 6 mm (0.25 in). *Foliage* Leaves oblong-ovate to oblong-obovate, apex rounded to an acute tip, base rounded-truncate or rounded, margin with regular triangular serrations which end in a short forward-pointing tip, hairless on both sides, smooth above and dull mid green, below light green with a raised midrib, 2.5–5.5 × 1.5–3.5 cm (1–2.2 × 0.6–1.4 in); leaf stalk faintly grooved, green, hairless, 1–2 cm (0.4–0.8 in); autumn colour red and orange, new leaves bronzy purple. *Flowers* Opening when leaves half formed in spring, in lax racemes with the basal flower stalks 2–5 cm (0.8–2 in), flowers white with five strap-like petals. *Fruit* Globose or ovoid with spreading sepals, ripening from green to red then blackish purple in June or July, juicy and edible, 6–8 mm (0.25–0.3 in).

Range: Eastern North America from Newfoundland south along the Appalachians.

Habitat: Cultivated and naturalized as an ornamental, in the wild occurring as an understorey in broadleafed forests.

Similar species: *A. rotundifolia* (syn. *A. ovalis*, *Mespilus amelanchier*) (p.203) is a native of central and southern Europe east to the Crimea and Caucasus, in Asia Minor south to the Lebanon and in North Africa. It only makes a shrub to 4 m (13 ft), having ovate to obovate leaves which are rounded, notched or pointed at the apex and coarsely toothed. The flowers are in racemes of up to eight, to 4 cm (1.6 in) across with narrow oblanceolate petals. In var. *integrifolia* from Asia Minor across at Iraq, the leaves are untoothed.

---

p.202 **Snowy Mespilus** *Amelanchier lamarckii*

Description: Deciduous shrub or small tree to 12 m (39 ft) with a bole diameter to 30 cm (12 in).
Crown Rounded, often on several stems.
Bark Smooth and grey-brown, becoming finely ridged and cracked. *Shoot* Green at first with many small rounded lenticels, hairless, becoming light brown in the second and later years. *Buds* Long conic or ovoid-conic, slender, green, 6 mm (0.25 in).
Foliage Leaves elliptic, oblong-elliptic or oblong-obovate, apex rounded to a short abrupt point, base rounded or sometimes subcordate, margins finely serrate with small spaced forward teeth, upper surface shiny mid green with slightly impressed net-like veins, lower surface somewhat glaucous green, initially whitish hairy beneath but most soon lost, 4–8 × 3–4 cm (1.6–3.1 × 1.2–1.6 in); leaf stalk faintly grooved, yellow-green, hairless, 1.2–3 cm (0.5–1.2 in); autumn colour red and orange, new foliage coppery to purplish with whitish hairs. *Flowers* In racemes 5–7 cm (2–2.8 in) in late spring (late April–May), with the flower stalks 2–2.5 cm (0.8–1 in) long at the base, decreasing towards the apex of the raceme to circa 1 cm (0.4 in), petals white, oblanceolate to elliptic, 1.5–2 cm × 6 mm (0.6–0.8 × 0.25 in). *Fruit* Rounded, 0.8–1 cm (0.3–0.4 in), ripening to purplish red or black in June or July, with erect sepals.
Range: Naturalized in England, Holland and northwest Germany.
Habitat: Cultivated and naturalized as an ornamental, of uncertain derivation.
Synonyms: *A. × grandiflora* misapplied.
Similar species: *A. canadensis* (p.203) from the eastern North America from Quebec south to Georgia where it makes a multi-stemmed tree to 9 m (29 ft). It differs from *A. lamarckii* in the short racemes 2.5–6 cm (1–2.4 in) with

a hairy rachis, flower stalks and calyx tube
and shorter petals only circa 1 cm (0.4 in).
A. spicata (p.203) is a suckering shrub rarely
to 6 m (20 ft) with flowers in erect woolly
racemes to 5 cm (2 in), downy leaves which
range from broad oval, ovate or obovate and
in the oblong 1 cm (0.4 in) petals.

This is the commonest *Amelanchier* in
cultivation in England, Holland and
Germany. It is an apomictic microspecies,
which has probably arisen in cultivation as
a hybrid between two eastern North
American species. It is particularly
common on acid sandy heaths.

CASHEW NUT, ANACARDIACEAE

This is a mainly tropical family, but with
some warm temperate members. Genera
treated here include *Cotinus* (p.623), *Pistacia*
(p.977), *Rhus* (p.1098) and *Schinus* (p.1130).

HOLLY, AQUIFOLIACEAE

This family include four genera, three of
which are very restricted and not generally
cultivated, leaving only *Ilex* (p.742) as
significant here.

IVY, ARALIACEAE

This large and mainly tropical family is
characterized by the flowers and fruits
being in stalked umbels. The fruits are a
juicy berry or drupe. It includes both trees,
shrubs, climbers and herbaceous plants.
The genera included here are *Hedera* (p.733)
and *Kalopanax* (p.770).

MONKEY PUZZLE, ARAUCARIACEAE

This is a family of three genera, *Araucaria*,
Agathis and *Wollemia* (the latter two not
treated here). Although known now only

from the southern hemisphere, in the Triassic period they were found in both hemispheres. The family is characterized by the single seed which is fused to the bract scale (cf. the two seeds free from the bract in Pinaceae).

MONKEY PUZZLES, *ARAUCARIA*
FAMILY ARAUCARIACEAE

This is a genus of southern hemisphere conifers, from southern South America, eastern Australia, New Guinea and several Pacific Islands. The trees are invariably either male or female. The male cones are in clusters of two to six and are lateral and conical, remaining on the tree for some time. The female cones are globose, falling apart when ripe after 18 months or more. The seeds are large, single and fused to the bract scales. They make excellent eating, preferably roasted like sweet chestnuts. The leaves are spirally set, in most species they are awl-like, slender and curved (*see AA. columnaris* and *heterophylla*), but in *A. araucana* they are flattened, broad and very sharp. The leaves are long persistent, for 10–15 years. The trees are characterized by a very simple branching structure. Laterals are produced in whorls at irregular intervals of time and produce side branches which either do not branch further or only have unbranched laterals, so that no more than three or four orders of branches are produced (cf. the complex branching arrangement of an oak tree).

p.56 Monkey Puzzle or Chile Pine
Araucaria araucana

Description: Evergreen tree 15–30 m (50–100 ft) with a bole diameter to 1 m (3.3 ft).
Crown Conical with open whorls of branches in young trees, developing a domed habit as height growth slows and branches continue to grow, eventually more or less flat topped, branches curving downwards, in moist climates retained to ground level but in dry or polluted atmospheres lower branches lost.
Bark Grey or dark grey, with horizontal wrinkles which have been compared to the hide on an elephant's legs. *Shoot* Green from the decurrent leaf bases for many

years, finally becoming brown, stout, circa 9 mm+ (0.4 in+). *Buds* Hidden in the leaf axils. *Foliage* Radial around the shoot; leaves ovate with a slender pointed sharp bony tip, cupped, grey green with lines of white waxy stomata, showing as white dots, on both sides, 3–5 × 1–2 cm (1.2–2 × 0.4–0.8 in); the leaf base is 7 mm (0.3 in) wide when the leaf is young, but as the shoot expands after a few years, so does the leaf base (but not the leaf blade); crushed foliage with a light resinous scent. *Flowers* On previous season's growths in summer, dioecious; male cones in clusters of one to six, lateral, green when shedding pollen in summer but persisting in a brown state on the tree for several months, 8–15 cm (3.1–6 in) long; female cones small green globes which are terminal on shoots. *Fruit* Globose, golden-green, ripening in second summer and then turning brown, disintegrating to release the brown 4 cm (1.6 in) long seeds.

Range: Chile and adjoining Argentina from 37 degrees south to 39 degrees south.

Habitat: Cultivated in Europe as an ornamental, in the wild occurring on the sides of volcanoes above the *Nothofagus* tree line.

Synonyms: *A. imbricata.*

This is a very distinctive tree and unlikely to be confused with any other. They look better either as single specimens isolated from other trees or, better, as a group. Group planting is also essential if the seeds are to be enjoyed, as the tree is dioecious, i.e. there are separate male and female trees. The story of the original introduction is that Menzies kept some seeds offered at a banquet. This is plausible, as they are edible and reasonably palatable when raw, although like chestnuts considerably improved by roasting. It is tolerant of a wide range of soil and site types, including salt spray. It is vulnerable in the wild as although all the main populations are in nature reserves, they all happen to be volcanoes, supposedly extinct but maybe just dormant. The growth of the tree is in pronounced whorls. In all other trees such whorls represent one year's growth or less (*see* the multi-nodal pines), but in this species, a whorl may represent more than a single season.

---

p.56 **Cook Pine** *Araucaria columnaris*

Description: Evergreen tree 30 m (100 ft) or more (60 m (200 ft) recorded) with a bole diameter to 80 cm (2.6 ft).
Crown Ovoid-conic in young trees with regular whorls of branches, but in old trees becoming narrower and columnar with a broader top as the lower branches are shed and replaced by adventitious shoots.
Bark Dark brown or blackish, outer layers shedding in thin papery layers.
Shoot Green for two to three years, then brown as the decurrent leaf bases die.
Buds Hidden in leaf bases. *Foliage* Leaves arranged radially on the shoot; juvenile foliage awl-like or triangular with wider leaf blades running down the stem base, pointed, green, 1–1.5 cm (0.4–0.6 in); adult foliage densely overlapping and giving the impression of a plaited cord, 4–6 mm (0.2–0.25 in). *Flowers* Male cones in leaf axils, 2.5–6 × 1.2–2 cm (1–2.4 × 0.5–0.8 in). *Fruit* Ellipsoidal, ripening to 15 × 11 cm (6 × 4.3 in), teasel-like when immature due to the terminal appendages on the seed scales.

Range: New Caledonia and New Hebrides.

Habitat: Cultivated in southern Europe as an ornamental, in the wild occurring in coastal lowland forests.

Synonyms: *A. cookii.*

This tree is unusual in the way it loses the lower branches yet reforms the crown from epicormic shoots, thus giving a narrow columnar tree except for a wider tuft of branches at the top. This character appears to be an in-built response to tropical storms. It is similar to *A. heterophylla* but has shorter foliage and a less plumose habit.

p.56 **Norfolk Island Pine**
Araucaria heterophylla

Description: Evergreen tree 30 m (100 ft) or more (60 m (200 ft) recorded) with a bole diameter 1 m (3.3 ft) or more.
Crown Conic with the branches in regular whorls. *Bark* Dark brown, outer layers shedding in thin plates. *Shoot* Green for two to three years, then brown as decurrent leaf bases die. *Buds* Hidden in leaf bases. *Foliage* Leaves arranged radially on the shoot; juvenile foliage awl-like with a blunt soft tip, decurrent on the shoot, bright green, 1.5 cm × 4–6 mm (0.6 × 0.2–0.25 in); adult foliage densely overlapping, incurved and imbricate, broadly ovate, 4–6 × 4–6 mm (0.2–0.25 × 0.2–0.25 in). *Flowers* Male cones in leaf axils, 4–7 × 1–1.7 cm (1.6–2.8 × 0.4–0.7 in). *Fruit* Globose, ripening to 9–11 × 8–10 cm (3.5–4.3 × 3.1–4 in), seed scales with a flat triangular spine.

Range: Norfolk Island, Australia, which is located to the east of Brisbane in the Pacific Ocean between New Zealand and New Caledonia.

Habitat: Cultivated in southern Europe as an ornamental, in the wild occurring in coastal lowland forests.

Synonyms: *A. excelsa.*

This tree will take a few degrees of frost. It tolerates the dry conditions of buildings and is frequently seen as a pot plant.

STRAWBERRY TREES, *ARBUTUS*
FAMILY ERICACEAE

This is a genus of around a dozen species, most abundant in south and west North America and south into Mexico, but with two species in Europe. They make small to large evergreen trees. The white bell-shaped flowers show their affinity to *Erica* and other members of the Ericaceae, but unlike many of these they tolerate lime-rich soils. Most have beautiful peeling barks, although in *A. unedo*, it is stringy. The fruit is a fleshy edible berry, but of insipid taste. The leaves are usually toothed, but in *A. menziesii* they are not toothed except in small seedlings.

p.196 **Cyprus Strawberry Tree**
Arbutus andrachne

Description: Evergreen shrub or small tree to 12 m
(39 ft) with a bole diameter to 60 cm (2 ft).
Crown Domed, often on several stems.
Bark Smooth and reddish, peeling
annually to reveal pale grey or greenish
underbark. *Shoot* Bronze-red when young,
then yellow-green and hairless for first
winter, later peeling to reddish brown.
Buds Small. *Foliage* Broad elliptic to
obovate, apex acute, pointed, base rounded
or broadly wedge-shaped, lustrous dark
green above, glaucous and finely net-veined
beneath, chartaceous (like stiff card),
margins entire or faintly toothed, 4–10 ×
2–6 cm (1.6–4 × 0.8–2.4 in); leaf stalk
shallowly channelled on top, 2–4 cm
(0.8–1.6 in). *Flowers* On previous season's
shoots in late spring, in large terminal
pyramidal panicles, 6–9(–12) × 5–8 cm
(2.4–3.5(–4.7) × 2–3.1 in); flowers dull
white, pitcher shaped, 6 mm (0.25 in).
Fruit Ripens in first autumn to red or
yellow, globose, rough, 1.2 cm (0.5 in).

Range: Eastern Mediterranean region, from
Albania across to the Crimea and Caucasus
and south to Palestine.

Habitat: Woodland or maquis sites, on both igneous
and limestone rocks.

This tree has an attractive red and brown
peeling bark.

---

p.197 **Hybrid Strawberry Tree**
Arbutus × andrachnoides

Description: Evergreen tree 10–15 m (33–50 ft) with a
bole diameter to 30 cm (1 ft).
Crown Domed. *Bark* Ruby red or orange
red, peeling to expose orange-brown areas,
becoming scaly and fissured at base.
Shoot Glandular hairy to a varying extent
when very young, red-brown and green in
the first winter, then shedding the outer
layer to become orange-brown and smooth.
Buds Beaked, ovoid, 1 mm (0.1 in).

Foliage Ovate to broad elliptic but variable, tapered at both ends, margins with forward serrate teeth, shiny green above, pale green and somewhat glaucous beneath with a prominent yellow-green midrib, 4–12 × 2.5–6 cm (1.6–4.7 × 1–2.4 in); leaf stalk green and purple, margins with narrow flanges, 1 cm (0.4 in). *Flowers* At ends of shoots in either autumn (current year's shoots) or spring (previous season's growths); panicles terminal, glandular downy, flowers urn-shaped, white, 6 mm (0.25 in). *Fruit* Smaller globose, smoother than in *A. unedo*, circa 1.2–1.5 cm (0.5–0.6 in).

Range: Where the two parent species meet.

Habitat: Natural hybrid occurring where the parent species meet.

Synonyms: *A. hybrida*.

This tree is a hybrid between *A. andrachne* and *A. unedo*. It is mainly found in Greece but has also been reported from Cyprus. It is fertile and therefore produces a variety of forms, all intermediate to some extent between the parents.

---

p.197 **Madroña** *Arbutus menziesii*

Description: Evergreen tree 15–25 m (50–80 ft) in height with a bole diameter to 1 m (3.3 ft). *Crown* Conical in young trees, becoming tall ovoid with large upswept and sprawling branches. *Bark* Smooth and orange in young trees, then red or yellow-pink and peeling in large sheets, at the base not peeling but becoming dark purple and cracked into small squares. *Shoot* Green for the first winter, hairless, then peeling to become cinnamon or orange-brown. *Buds* Ovoid-conical, pointed and flattened, green and brown, to 1 cm (0.4 in). *Foliage* Oval to broad elliptic, apex rounded to bluntly pointed, often abruptly short pointed, base wedge-shaped and leaf blade growing down the leaf stalk, lustrous dark green above, glaucous pale or chalky green beneath, leathery, margins entire or faintly toothed with a hyaline border, midrib prominent below, 5–17 × 3–8.5 cm (2–6.7 × 1.2–3.3 in); leaf stalk flattened on top, red-purple above with green, to 4 cm (1.6 in). *Flowers* On previous season's shoots in late spring, in large terminal pyramidal panicles, 8–27 × 15 cm (3.1–10.6 × 6 in); flowers dull white, pitcher shaped, 6 mm (0.25 in). *Fruit* Ripens in first autumn to orange-red, 1–1.2 cm (0.4–0.5 in).

Range: Western North America from British Columbia to California, mainly near the coast but inland in the Sierra Nevada of California.

Habitat: Cultivated in Europe as an ornamental, in the wild occurring in canyons and on upland slopes, primarily in oak and pine forest.

Synonyms: *A. procera.*

This is the most attractive Strawberry Tree, with the shiny peeling bark. The flowers and fruits are not as showy as in *A. unedo*. The fruits are edible in small quantities. Like other members of the genus it will grow on limestone and chalk sites, as well as acidic ones. The young trees are rather tender. They also have toothed leaves, although the teeth are usually lost once the tree is a few years old.

p.196 **Strawberry Tree** *Arbutus unedo*

Description: Evergreen tree to 8–13 m (26–43 ft) in height with a bole diameter to 1.2 m (4 ft), or a shrub.
Crown Rounded domed on a short, often leaning bole. *Bark* Dark red, with age shredding and developing scaly grey-brown ridges. *Shoot* Green or pink in the first winter, then brown or fawn-brown, hairless or initially glandular hairy. *Buds* Conic, pink-red, 1 mm (0.1 in). *Foliage* Elliptic or obovate, margins with forward serrate teeth or rarely entire (f. *integerrima*), apex acute, base wedge-shaped, leathery, dark green above with a pale midrib, beneath

light green, veins rather weak, 5–10 × 1.5–4 cm (2–4 × 0.6–1.6 in); leaf stalk pink, 0.7–1 cm (0.3–0.4 in). *Flowers* Bell shaped with reflexed lobes, 6 mm (0.25 in), white or pink, in pendulous clusters of 15–20 flowers from October to December. *Fruit* Globose, strawberry like, rough, 1.5–2 cm (0.6–0.8 in), ripening from green to yellow, orange-red or scarlet, ripening in the autumn, as the next years flowers are opening.

Range: Southwest Ireland across southern Europe to Cyprus and Turkey.

Habitat: Moist acid soils to calcareous hillsides in maquis scrub.

Varieties: Forma *rubra* covers the plants with reddish pink flowers. However, the pink flowers detract from the fruits and are not an improvement on the white flowered normal form.

This tree is at its best in the autumn when covered both with the bell-shaped flowers and the freshly ripened fruit. It grows on a wide range of soils. The fruit looks like a strawberry and is edible. However, the Latin name translates as 'I eat one', referring to the insipid taste and texture.

BLACK SASSAFRAS, ATHEROSPERMATACEAE (SYNONYMS: MONINIACEAE IN PART)

This small family comprises two genera, *Atherosperma* (not treated here, with a single species of evergreen tree from southeast Australia and Tasmania which in cultivation makes a shrub or small tree to 6 m (20 ft)) and *Laurelia* (p.786).

TASMANIAN CEDARS, *ATHROTAXIS*
FAMILY TAXODIACEAE

This is a genus of three species of conifers from Tasmania. The leaves are scale-like in *A. cupressoides*, scale-like but with free tips in *A. laxiflora* and awl-like in *A. selaginoides*, set spirally on the shoots. The male cones are rather large and ellipsoidal in early spring, whilst the cones are ovoid to globose.

p.55 **Smooth Tasmanian Cedar**
Athrotaxis cupressoides

Description: Evergreen tree to 15 m (50 ft) with a bole
diameter to 60 cm (2 ft).
Crown Conical in young trees, becoming
columnar and domed in old trees.
Bark Brownish grey, thin, becoming
slightly shredding. *Shoot* Green for three
or four years, then brown or red-brown as
the scale leaves die and are shed, rounded.
Buds Hidden in scale leaves. *Foliage* In
stiff sprays; leaves scale-like, rhombic,
ridged, apex acute, pressed against stem or
just free at the tip, mid green but with
scattered white dots of stomata at the sides,
2–5 mm (0.1–0.2 in); crushed foliage resin
scented. *Flowers* At the tips of previous
season's growth in early spring; male cones
globular. *Fruit* Globular, ripening in the
first autumn, 1 cm (0.4 in).
Range: Tasmania, in the western mountains.
Habitat: Cultivated in Europe as an ornamental, in
the wild occurring on exposed ridges or at
lake margins.

This is the hardiest of the three species of
Athrotaxis, although less common in
cultivation than *A. laxiflora*. The terete
(rounded) branches with addressed scale
leaves distinguish it from the other two
species.

p.55 **Tasmanian Cedar** *Athrotaxis laxiflora*

Description: Evergreen tree 10–20 m (33–65 ft) with a
bole diameter to 60 cm (2 ft).
Crown Conical or broad conical, in old trees
the branches are generally spaced and the
crown may be more rounded and billowing.
Bark Red-brown, smooth but becoming
fissured into shaggy peeling strips.
Shoot Green for several years from the
decurrent leaf bases, later red-brown.
Buds Hidden in scale leaves. *Foliage* Spirally
arranged around the shoot with scale-like
leaves; free portion triangular with an acute,
incurved bony tip and running down the

shoot at the base, hyaline but untoothed margin, deep green on outer surface with two small patches of stomata, larger pair of silvery waxy stomata on inner abaxial surface, 7–8 × 1.5–3 mm (0.3 × 0.1 in) with a free tip 2.5–3.5 mm (0.1–0.2 in); crushed foliage resin scented. *Flowers* At tips of previous season's growths, in spring; male cones terminate weak shoots, brown, 1 × 4–5 mm (0.4 × 0.2 in); female cones on stronger side shoots, globular, green-brown, 5 mm (0.2 in). *Fruit* Globular but lumpy, yellow-green when growing, ripening to brown in first winter, 2 cm (0.8 in); scales 10–16, with a single erect triangular point or tooth.

Range: Tasmania, in the western mountains.
Habitat: Cultivated in Europe as an ornamental, in the wild occurring in gullies or ridges, usually occurring with either *A. cupressoides* or *A. selaginoides*.

This tree is intermediate between the other two species and as it generally occurs with one or other species, a hybrid origin has been postulated. It is the hardiest and more widely distributed of the three species. It is related to *Cryptomeria* but the cones have only the single central point and lack the ring of pointed appendages which characterize the *Cryptomeria* cone scale. In *Athrotaxis*, these are reduced to small rounded lumps.

p.55 **King Billy Pine** or **King William Pine**
Athrotaxis selaginoides

Description: Evergreen tree to 20 m (65 ft) with a bole diameter to 70 cm (2.3 ft).
Crown Conic, becoming domed with billowing branches in old trees. *Bark* Red-brown, thick and rather spongy, furrowed and peeling in the fibrous strips.
Shoot Green for two or more years, later red-brown. *Buds* Hidden in scale leaves. *Foliage* Radial with the leaves incurved forwards along the shoot but held away from it; leaves awl-shaped, apex acute, margin entire and not translucent, outer

surface rich green, inner surface with two white bands of stomata, 0.6–1.2 × 0.3 cm (0.25–0.5 × 0.1 in). *Flowers* Terminal on previous season's shoots; male cones ovoid, 1 cm (0.4 in). *Fruit* Ripening in the first autumn to globular, orange-brown, 2.5 cm (1 in); scales with a triangular apex.

Range: Western Tasmania.

Habitat: Cultivated in Europe as an ornamental, in the wild occurring in rocky gullies up to 1800 m (5940 ft) above sea level.

This tree has a thick spongy bark similar to that of the redwoods (*Sequoia* and *Sequoiadendron*) but not as thick. As with these species, tree creepers often shape small egg-cup size depressions as roosting sites. This tree is the least hardy of the three *Athrotaxis*, although forming the largest tree in the wild.

AUCUBA, AUCUBACEAE

Monotypic family, sometimes included within the Cornaceae.

AUCUBA, *AUCUBA*
FAMILY AUCUBACEAE

This is a small genus of three or four species, characterized by the opposite, evergreen leaves and the showy red fruits. However, male and female flowers are carried on separate trees and the fruits are only formed when both sexes are present.

p.170 **Aucuba** *Aucuba japonica*

Description: Evergreen shrub to 3–5 m (10–16 ft). *Crown* Rounded. *Bark* Grey-brown. *Shoot* Stout, hairless, fleshy, green. *Buds* In opposite pairs, small, scales hairy at the tips. *Foliage* Narrow oval, leathery, apex acute, base wedge-shaped, margin untoothed except for a few teeth near the apex, glossy dark green on both sides, 7–20 × 4–8 cm (2.8–8 × 1.6–3.1 in); leaf stalk 1.2–5 cm (0.5–2 in). *Flowers* Dioecious on

separate plants; not showy, yellow-green.
Fruit On female plants grown with a male
only; in compact clusters 5–8 cm (2–3.1 in)
across; berries rounded oval, 1.2–2 cm
(0.5–0.8 in), bright scarlet.

Range: Honshu, Kyushu and Shikoku, Japan.

Habitat: Cultivated as an ornamental.

Varieties: 'Variegata' is the common spotted aucuba.
Yuk.

This is a common shrub which just
occasionally attains small tree status. It is
extremely tolerant of shade and pollution.
When both sexes are grown together, it is
attractive in fruit.

CHILEAN CEDAR, *AUSTROCEDRUS*
FAMILY CUPRESSACEAE

Monotypic genus from South America which is related to
Libocedrus and has been included within it. The leaves are in
decussate but very unequal pairs.

---

p.47   **Chilean Cedar** *Austrocedrus chilensis*

Description: Evergreen tree 10–15 m (33–50 ft) with a
bole diameter to 40 cm (1.3 ft).
Crown Columnar, with short ascending
branches. *Bark* Reddish or brownish grey,
smooth but becoming finely and closely
grey scaly. *Shoot* Green, slender for the first
winter, then pale brown and then red-
brown. *Buds* Hidden in axils of scale
leaves. *Foliage* In flat sprays in decussate
very unequal pairs; facial leaves small,
triangular, 1 mm (0.1 in), lateral leaves
5 mm (0.2 in) with long incurved free tips
2 mm (0.1 in); leaves shiny fresh to yellow-
green above and paler beneath, with
patches of glaucous white waxy bands of
stomata on both sides but primarily above;
crushed foliage with a mushroom-like
scent. *Flowers* On previous season's shoots
in spring; male cones ovoid or globose,
3 mm (0.1 in). *Fruit* Oblong-ovoid,
ripening in the first autumn to yellow-
brown, 1.2–1.5 cm (0.5–0.6 in); scales four,

valvate, with a small point; seeds one or two per scale, with two dissimilar wings.

Range: Central Chile and adjoining western Argentina.

Habitat: Cultivated in Europe as an ornamental, in the wild occurring in cool wet forests.

Synonyms: *Libocedrus chilensis*.

This tree is allied to *Calocedrus* but differs in the blunt incurved lateral leaves and the cones with only four fertile scales.

AZARAS, *AZARA*
FAMILY FLACOURTIACEAE

This genus consists of ten species from South America. The flowers lack petals but have showy stamens and are strongly scented. The leaves appear to be in pairs set alternately along the shoot, with one much larger; however, only the large leaf is a true leaf, the smaller one is a leafy-like stipule.

p.177 Small-leafed Azara *Azara microphylla*

Description: Evergreen shrub or tree 10–12 m (33–39 ft) with a bole diameter to 30 cm (1 ft).
Crown Ovoid, upright, narrow.
Bark Light brown, with small scales.
Shoot Slender, with dense dark down, set in flattened sprays. *Buds* Minute, alternate.
Foliage Leaves appearing to be in unequal pairs; the larger leaf obovate, apex rounded, base wedge-shaped, margin more or less toothed, dark shiny green above, paler beneath, 1.2–2.5 cm (0.5–1 in), the second leaf being a stipule which is rounded and much smaller. *Flowers* In leaf axils on the previous year's shoots in late winter to spring; in tiny fragrant clusters which have green sepals, not petals and showy deep yellow stamens, strongly vanilla scented.
Fruit Globose berry, red.

Range: Central Chile and bordering areas of The Argentine.

Habitat: Cultivated as an ornamental, in the wild occurring as an understorey element to *Nothofagus obliqua* forest.

Varieties: 'Variegata' has the leaves with a variable margin of creamy white.

This shrub to small tree has deliciously scented small flowers in late winter. It is hardy over much of Britain, although preferring a warmer climate.

BAMBOOS, GRAMINEAE (BAMBUSAE)

The bamboos are a group of woody grasses. They either form dense tufts, or send rhizomes which bear shoots at intervals. Several genera of bamboo are cultivated, but only *Phyllostachys* (p.882) is described here.

FLOWERING DOGWOODS, *BENTHAMIDIA* (SYNONYMS: *CORNUS* IN PART; *DENDROBENTHAMIA*)
FAMILY CORNACEAE

This is a small genus which is planted as amenity trees. It is often included within *Cornus*. The leaves are in opposite pairs, as in most *Cornus* species. The flowers are in clusters, but are small and insignificant. However, they are subtended by four to six bracts. These form in the autumn and expand in the spring, colouring from green to creamy white, yellow or pink and up to 8 cm (3.1 in) in length. The character of the bracts over winter can assist in identifying the species, as in *BB. capitata, kousa* and *nuttallii* the bracts are spreading over the winter whilst in *B. florida* they cover the flower cluster until expanding in the spring. The bracts are yellow or creamy yellow in *B. capitata*, creamy white (but often fading to pink) in *BB. kousa* and *nuttallii*, whilst they can be creamy white, pink or red in *B. florida*. The fruits are a cluster of single-seeded drupes. In the American species (*BB. florida* and *nuttallii*), the drupes are spaced, but in the Asian species (*BB. capitata* and *kousa*) they coalesce into a compound fruit and these species are sometimes treated as a separate genus, *Dendrobenthamia*.

---

p.143   **Himalayan Cornel**   *Benthamidia capitata*

Description: Evergreen shrub or tree up to 10–15 m (33–50 ft) with a bole diameter to 50 cm (1.6 ft).
Crown Conical or rounded, usually on a single stem but occasionally on several.

Bark Grey or grey-brown, smooth, becoming somewhat scaly in old trees.
Shoot Green and purple in first year with fine grey hairs pressed against the shoot, becoming brown, slender. *Buds* In opposite pairs, linear, with two valvate scales which are pressed together but free at the tips, 1.5–3 mm (0.1 in). *Foliage* Leaves elliptic to elliptic-oblong, tapered to the bluntly acute apex which is often down-curved (to drain water off the leaf), base wedge-shaped, margins untoothed, upper surface dull green, lower surface pale green, both with short grey hairs, leathery, lateral veins in three or four pairs which loop forwards, 5–11 × 2–4 cm (2–4.3 × 0.8–1.6 in); leaf stalk to 1 cm (0.4 in), grooved, pink or green; if a leaf is carefully broken in half fine rubbery threads are drawn out from the veins and these will hold it together.
Flowers Opening in early summer from exposed flower buds which have four small grey-brown bracts; the bracts expand to 3.5–6.3 × 2.3–4.3 cm (1.4–2.5 × 0.9–1.7 in) and are obovate to sub-orbicular, the colour changes from green to creamy white or yellow; within the bracts is the head (0.8–1.5 cm (0.3–0.6 in) across) of small flowers, with yellow petals to 2 mm (0.1 in). *Fruit* Globose, 2–3 cm (0.8–1.2 in) in diameter (occasionally to 5 cm (2 in)), expanding from the cluster of small flowers to form a pendent succulent fruit which ripens to yellow-green, pink or red; seeds surrounded by edible flesh, about 5 mm (0.2 in).

Range: Himalayas from northwest India east (through Nepal, Sikkim, Bhutan, Burma) to southwest China (Yunnan and Sichuan) and northern Vietnam.

Habitat: Cultivated in the milder parts of Europe as an ornamental, in the wild occurring in dry to moist broadleaved forest.

Synonyms: *Cornus capitata.*

This makes a very attractive tree, with open grown specimens neatly conical until old. It tolerates a wide range of soil types but is tender in cold districts. It is surprisingly tolerant of coastal conditions, considering that for most of its native range it does not get to within a 1000 miles of the sea! The fruit is sweet when ripe, and tasty in small quantities.

---

p.143   **Flowering Dogwood**   *Benthamidia florida*

Description: Deciduous tree 6–10 m (20–33 ft) with a bole diameter to 30 cm (1 ft).
Crown Rounded with spreading branches or conical, often on several stems.
Bark Smooth, grey-brown, in old trees reddish brown, becoming rough and scaly.
Shoot Green or whitish grey-green when young, slender, becoming green or purple in the second year and changing to brown in the second and subsequent seasons. *Buds* In opposite pairs, minute. *Foliage* Leaves oval, elliptic, obovate to ovate, apex acute or slender pointed, base rounded to broad wedge-shaped, margin wavy but apparently untoothed but with a hyaline margin which is usually finely toothed when seen under a lens, upper surface matt green with many short stiff white hairs making the leaf feel harsh to the touch, underside light green and somewhat glaucous, similarly hairy, with five to seven pairs of raised curved veins, 6–13 × 4–6 cm (2.4–5.1 × 1.6–2.4 in); leaf stalk yellowish, grooved, 1 cm (0.4 in); autumn colour red. *Flowers* From flower buds which are enclosed by the bracts over winter (not exposed as in *B. nuttallii* and *B. capitata*), the four bracts expanding in early summer to broadly elliptic, white or pink, 4–5 × 3–4 cm (1.6–2 × 1.2–1.6 in). *Fruit* Erect, with a number of shiny red ellipsoidal berries 1–1.5 cm (0.4–0.6 in) containing one or two seeds.

Range: Eastern North America from southern Ontario and Maine south to Florida and eastern Texas.

Habitat: Cultivated as an ornamental, in the wild forming an understorey in mixed hardwood forests.

Varieties: Many selections, especially ones with pink or red bracts, have been named.

Synonyms: *Cornus florida*.

At its best, this is a very striking tree or large shrub but it requires hot humid summers for best effect. In England it is inferior to *B. kousa* and *B. nuttallii*. Apart from eastern North America, this species extends down into eastern Mexico, either as a variety or separate species (*B. pringlei*).

p.143 **Japanese Cornel** *Benthamidia kousa* var. *chinensis*

Description: Deciduous tree 8–12 m (26–39 ft) with a bole diameter to 30 cm (1 ft).
Crown Conical with flat spreading branches which droop down at the ends.
Bark Smooth, grey-brown. *Shoot* Green-brown in first year with short pale hairs pressed against the shoot, brown or grey-brown and hairless in later years, slender.
Buds In opposite pairs, narrow-conic, dark chocolate brown with rufous hairs pressed against the shoot, 4 mm (0.2 in), flower buds at tips of shoots ovoid-conic with a fat rounded base and long tip with a slender point, 1 cm (0.4 in), enclosing the flower.
Foliage Leaves ovate to elliptic, apex with a slender point and often twisted, base rounded to wedge-shaped, margin untoothed but wavy or wrinkled, upper surface glossy lustrous dark green with short stiff pale brown hairs, underside glaucous green with circa four pairs of parallel raised veins which loop around the margin, warty and with scattered rufous hairs, 4–10 × 2–4.5 cm (1.6–4 × 0.8–1.8 in); leaf stalk 1–1.5 cm (0.4–0.6 in), grooved, sparsely haired; autumn colour often red. *Flowers* In globose heads in June carried on a 4–6 cm (1.6–2.4 in) stalk to a group of flowers above the foliage from buds laid down the previous summer, with four creamy white ovate to slender-pointed bracts 4–6 × 2–3.5 cm (1.6–2.4 × 0.8–1.4 in). *Fruit* In rounded heads composed of many single seeded drupes, ripening to pink-red, edible, 2–2.5 cm (0.8–1 in) across.

Range: Hubei, Central China.
Habitat: Cultivated as an ornamental, in the wild occurring as an understorey in woods.
Varieties: Var. *kousa* has smaller (4–7 × 2–2.5 cm (1.6–2.8 × 0.8–1 in)) yellow-green leaves which are rounded at the base and have around three pairs of veins. The shoots tend to be reddish brown when mature, and floral bracts are smaller, 2.5–5 × 1.2–2 cm (1–2 × 0.5–0.8 in). It is native to Honshu, Shikoku and Kyushu, Japan and Korea, and makes a smaller tree usually less than 8 m (26 ft).
Synonyms: *Cornus kousa* var. *chinensis*.

This is a very attractive small tree which is at its best in full sun to light shade on a moisture-retentive soil. From *B. capitata*, it differs in the flower buds being enclosed in bud scales.

---

p.143   **Pacific Cornel** *Benthamidia nuttallii*

Description: Deciduous tree generally to 10 m (33 ft), but up to 25 m (80 ft), with a bole diameter to 0.5 m.
Crown Conical with ascending branches with spreading side branches. *Bark* Dark purple-brown, smooth. *Shoot* Green with whitish fine hairs pressed against shoot in the first year, becoming browner in the second with patches of green, brown or greyish brown in the third year.
Buds Terminal buds conical, green with brownish hairs to 1 cm (0.4 in), bud scales triangular, lateral buds minute.
Foliage Leaves in opposite pairs, narrow elliptic to obovate, apex acute and somewhat slender pointed, base wedge-shaped, margin untoothed but wrinkled, upper surface deep shiny green, with short forward simple teeth all over, veins pale, slightly impressed, underside light green with prominently raised veins, hairy as above but with axillary tufts, 8–18 × 3–6 cm (3.1–7.1 × 1.2–2.4 in); leaf stalk grooved, base enlarged to clasp stem, hairy, green, 1–1.5 cm (0.4–0.6 in); autumn colour can be yellow and scarlet. *Flowers* Flower buds exposed

over winter, rounded, with four to eight small bracts; as the flower opens in the spring, the bracts enlarge to become rounded oval or obovate, 4–7 × 2.5–5 cm (1.6–2.8 × 1–2 in), and white or pinkish white with the rounded head of small insignificant flowers, with four calyx lobes, in the centre.

Fruit Erect rounded head to 3 cm (1.2 in) of fifty or more individual fruits each with one or two seeds, ripening from green to pinkish purple, on a stout stalk, flesh mealy, bitter.

Range: Southwest British Columbia, Washington, west Oregon and south along the mountains to south California.

Habitat: Cultivated as an ornamental, in the wild occurring in woodland.

Synonyms: *Cornus nuttallii*.

This is the largest and grandest of the cornels, capable of making 25 m (80 ft) in the rain forests of the Pacific coast of North America. The bulk of flowering is in May, lasting for around four to six weeks, but there is often a small flush during October.

BIRCH, BETULACEAE

This is a family of six genera, mainly found in the northern hemisphere, with five of the genera treated here. These can be separated as follows: the fruit is a hard ovoid woody and persisting catkin in which the scales open to release the small winged seeds in *Alnus* (p.492); the fruit is a flexible catkin which usually disintegrates to release the small winged seeds in *Betula* (p.524); the fruit is in short pendulous racemes with single nutlets resting on a leafy bract in *Carpinus* (p.558); the fruit is a large rounded nut carried singly or in small clusters in *Corylus* (p.620); the fruit is in short pendulous racemes in *Ostrya* (p.865) but the nutlet is enclosed in a bladder-like leafy structure. (The sixth genus, *Ostryopsis*, is related to *Corylus* but only contains two small shrubs which have small seeds.) The male catkins are formed in the autumn and carried exposed but not expanded over winter in most genera, but in

Carpinus, and in some *Alnus* not treated here, the male catkins are protected in buds over winter. The family contains three subfamilies, which are sometimes treated as separate families, Betuleae with *Alnus* and *Betula*, Coryleae with *Corylus*, and Carpineae with *Carpinus* and *Ostrya*.

BIRCHES, *BETULA*
FAMILY BETULACEAE

This is a genus of perhaps sixty species, including both trees and dwarf shrubs. The commonest birches are easily recognized by the white coloration of the bark, caused by the chemical betulin. This is present in all species to a greater or lesser extent. However, in a large proportion of the genus, the quantity of betulin present is low and, rather than white, the bark is brown or coppery, or occasionally black. Species which do not have white but have coppery to brown barks include *BB. albo-sinensis, allegheniensis, austrosinensis* (sometimes), *grossa, lenta, nigra,* and *utilis,* but young trees of other species, especially *B. pubescens* may also have brown bark. The leaves are always simple, generally ovate in outline and singly to doubly toothed. They are mostly relatively small, and the trees have light crowns. The flowers are wind pollinated, with separate male and female flowers. The male catkins are exposed over the winter period, in clusters of two or three at the ends of the twigs. They expand in early spring, hanging gracefully. The female flowers are carried lower down the twigs, and are erect at the time of pollination. They develop into small cylindrical or ovoid catkins which mostly disintegrate when ripe, scattering the small nutlets and the three-lobed bracts. The mature catkins may remain erect, when they are usually rough and knobbly in outline, in *BB. allegheniensis, austrosinensis, ermanii* (often, but not always), *grossa, lenta, medwediewii, nigra,* and *utilis* (only rarely) or become pendent and usually smooth in the other species. The seed is a nutlet with two wings. In most species the wings are broad (more than the width of the seed) and thin, but in *BB. allegheniensis, austrosinensis, grossa, lenta* and *medwediewii* the wing is thicker and narrower than the seed. The bark of some species contains large quantities of methyl salicylate or 'oil of wintergreen' and this can be detected by scrapping a twig. Species with this character include *BB. allegheniensis, austrosinensis, grossa, lenta, maximowiczii* and *medwediewii.* Birches are not long lived, rarely making as much as a hundred years. Generally, they are trees of open woods or moors, requiring full sunlight and not tolerating shade. They hybridize freely in cultivation, especially but not totally with other species of the same ploidy level. The basic chromosome number is 14, with diploids having 28 chromosomes. However, many species are tetraploid (56 chromosomes), a few hexaploid (84) but up to 168 (with 12 pairs of chromosomes) is known. In species with a peeling bark, it is important not to remove the innermost layer or the result will be a zone of unattractive brown bark. The timber is light and used for furniture and plywood.

p.184 **Chinese Red Birch** *Betula albo-sinensis*

Description: Deciduous tree 10–20 m (33–65 ft).
Crown Narrow columnar or conic when young, becoming domed in old trees.
Bark Orange to orange-red, purple or copper, with some waxy white bloom, successive layers peeling in large thin sheets once trunk 5–10 cm (2–4 in) in diameter.
Shoot Slender, hairless, smooth, only with glands when very immature, purplish green in first year, becoming dark grey-brown, lenticels small, round to elliptic, pale.
Buds Conical or oblong, shiny green to brown, 4–6 mm (0.2–0.25 in).
Foliage Leaves alternate on long shoots, on spur shoots in pairs; ovate to elliptic with a short slender pointed tip, base rounded, margins with simple triangular variable forward pointing teeth; side veins in 9–14 pairs, slightly impressed above, prominent below, minor veins net-like and impressed on both sides, hairless above and below except for tufts at the junctions of the midrib with main veins, glandular beneath when young, upper surface mid sub-shiny green, beneath shiny light green, 5–9 × 2.5–4.5 cm (2–3.5 × 1–1.8 in); leaf stalk grooved above, pink or green, 1–1.8 cm (0.4–0.7 in); stipules ovate, 7 mm (0.3 in), quickly dropping; autumn colour yellow, not strong. *Flowers* Male catkins cylindrical, usually in threes, slender and smooth or somewhat knobbly with slightly embossed scales over winter, expanding to 4–6 cm (1.6–2.4 in) in spring, pendulous, yellow; female catkins erect, single, 2–3 cm

(0.8–1.2 in). *Fruit* Catkins pendent, 2.5–4 × 0.7 cm (1–1.6 × 0.3 in); bracts three-lobed, side lobes rounded, forward at 45 degrees, main lobe strap-like, twice as long as side lobes, glandular on the exposed portion; seed rounded, flat, 2.5 mm (0.1 in), wings as wide as to half as wide as seed.

Range: Northwest China from Hubei, Shaanxi, Gansu to Sichuan.

Habitat: Cultivated as an ornamental, in the wild forming a component of cool temperate mixed or mainly conifer forest.

Varieties: Var. *septentrionalis* has an orange-grey or coppery grey bark with a much stronger wax bloom. The leaves are longer, more oblong-ovate with a short acute tip and deeper irregular, somewhat double, sharp teeth and silky hairs along the full length of the midrib. The shoots are glandular with short hairs, whilst the exposed male catkins have strongly embossed scales. In all these characters it shows at least intermediate status between *B. albo-sinensis* and *B. utilis*; however, it is probably closer to *B. utilis* and would better fit as a northern subspecies of that (the adjective *septentrionalis* means northern), rather than under *B. albo-sinensis*.

Synonyms: *B. utilis* var. *sinensis*.

This is a majestic tree with its bright coppery bark exfoliating in large papery sheets. It is closely allied to *B. utilis*, from which it is distinguished by the hairless and not glandular dark brown or grey-brown shoots, leaves with a more slender-pointed tip and male catkins which are smoother, narrower and cylindrical during the winter period.

---

p.186 **Yellow Birch** *Betula allegheniensis*

Description: Deciduous tree 10–20 m (33–65 ft) with a bole diameter to 60 cm (2 ft).
Crown Ovoid and rather open with radiating branches. *Bark* Yellowish grey or silvery grey, peeling in small papery rolls. *Shoot* Green with dense long hairs and ovate stipules when new, but as they become firm,

they become hairless and change to light brown or grey-brown, scraped bark has a strong oil of wintergreen (methyl salicylate) aroma. *Buds* Ovoid conic, green and brown, 8 mm (0.3 in). *Foliage* Leaves ovate-oblong to obovate-oblong, tapered to a short slender-pointed apex, base rounded to subcordate, margin finely serrate with bristle-tipped teeth which are slightly larger at the vein ends but more coarsely toothed on extension growths, upper surface matt green with long sparse whitish hairs pressed against the shoot, underside sub-shiny, light green with 9–12 pairs of raised veins which are white haired, 7–14 × 3–7 cm (2.8–5.5 × 1.2 –2.8 in); leaf stalk grooved, pilose (with long soft hairs), green, 1–2 cm (0.4–0.8 in); autumn colour excellent bright yellow. *Flowers* Male catkins yellow; female catkins erect, in early spring. *Fruit* Catkins erect, 2–3 × 1.5 cm (0.8–1.2 × 0.6 in), on a stalk 7–8 mm (0.3 in), green until ripening brown in autumn, bract scales with three forward lobes, side lobes obovate, nearly as long as and broader than the lanceolate central lobe, hairy on the margins and both sides, 9 × 7 mm (0.4 × 0.3 in); seed ovate with a narrow wing which is wider at the top, 4–5 × 3–4 mm (0.2 × 0.1–0.2 in).

Range: Eastern North America from Newfoundland across to Manitoba and Iowa and south to Georgia.

Habitat: Cultivated as an ornamental, in the wild occurring close to streams in broadleaved or conifer forests or in mixed secondary forest.

Synonyms: *B. lutea.*

This tree is one of the best for golden yellow autumn colour. It belongs to the group of birches whose sap contains methyl salicylate or oil of wintergreen, which is used as a disinfectant. It is an hexaploid, closely allied to the diploid *B. lenta*, differing from it most clearly in the hairiness of the fruit bract scales which are more woody and persistent, but also in the usually slightly lobed double-toothed leaves which are persistently hairy and the more light coloured bark. It is also allied to *B. grossa*.

p.185 **South China Birch** *Betula austrosinensis*

Description: Deciduous tree 10–20 m (33–65 ft) with a bole diameter to 60 cm (2 ft).
Crown Conic in young trees, becoming domed. *Bark* Smooth and yellow-brown in young trees, becoming rough due to fissures and low ridges in old trees. *Shoot* Grey-brown, with pale pilose hairs, becoming shiny brown with small round lenticels, scraped bark with a strong oil of wintergreen aroma. *Buds* Conic to ovoid-conic, pointed, green or brown, 7 mm (0.3 in).
Foliage Leaves ovate-lanceolate, tapering to a triangular acute apex, more or less rounded at the base, margin with somewhat double toothing with ovate slender forward-pointing teeth, upper surface shiny green, hairless or with pilose hairs on the impressed midrib, underside light green with pilose hairs on the 10–14 pairs of raised veins, 5–15 × 2.5–6.5 cm (2–6 × 1–2.6 in); leaf stalk grooved, grey-green, pilose, 1.2–1.7 cm (0.5–0.7 in); autumn colour yellow; spring and new growths bronze.
Flowers Showy long yellow-green to yellow-brown male catkins which expand to 15–25 cm (6–10 in). *Fruit* Ovoid, erect, persisting over winter, 2.5–6 cm (1–2.4 in); bracts hairy with three nearly equal erect lobes; seed oval, with narrow wings.

Range: Southern China from Sichuan across to Guangxi.

Habitat: Cultivated as an ornamental, in the wild occurring in mixed woodland.

Similar species: *B. jinpingensis* differs in the more slender strobiles (fruits) in which the bract scales have only small lateral lobes. It comes from southern Yunnan, China, and adjacent North Vietnam, and is tolerant of wet, heavy soils. The new foliage may be strongly bronze coloured.

The bark is not colourful but excels in the strong oil of wintergreen (methyl salicylate) scent. It is a decaploid, i.e. it has ten sets of chromosomes, making 140 in all. It is an uncommon tree which was only first introduced in 1985.

p.185 **Erman's Birch** *Betula ermanii*

Description: Deciduous tree to 10–25 m (33–80 ft) with
a bole diameter to 80 cm (2.6 ft).
Crown Ovoid-conic in young trees,
becoming broad conic and in old trees
domed; old trees sturdy and similar to oak in
appearance. *Bark* Young trees with pale
brown peeling bark, as the trees mature
becoming white and peeling in shreds
especially below branches, with the white
bark extending up the branches of the crown;
old trees often with a pinkish hue or buff
orange and scaly, lenticels large, horizontal.
Shoot Light brown with shiny warty glands
and pale buff oval lenticels in the first year,
usually hairless but may be somewhat downy
when young, darker or grey-brown in the
second year with the lenticels enlarging and
becoming round, in the second or third year
the outer layer peeling to reveal shiny mid
brown with the lenticels round or wider than
long. *Buds* Narrow ovoid-conic, pointed at
the apex which is often curved, green and
brown with some hairs on the fringes of the
scales, gummy or resinous, 0.7–1.3 cm
(0.3–0.5 in). *Foliage* Leaves ovate to deltoid-
ovate, apex short slender pointed, base
truncate, shallowly heart-shaped or broadly
rounded, margin doubly serrate with
rounded slender-pointed teeth with the larger
ones terminating each of the 7–12 pairs of
veins, sinuses narrow, acute or rounded and
sometimes with a tuft of hairs, upper surface
sub-shiny green with glands on the slightly
indented veins, underside shiny light green
with glands both on the blade and the raised
veins, tufts in the vein axils and sometimes
on the veins, 5–10 × 4–7 cm (2–4 ×
1.6–2.8 in); leaf stalk grooved, with dark
brown glands, usually hairless, 1–3.5 cm
(0.4–1.4 in); autumn colour golden-yellow.
Flowers Male catkins in threes, 2–3 cm ×
5 mm (0.8–1.2 × 0.2 in) over winter, green,
expanding to yellow in spring; female flowers
on short shoots with two or three leaves.
Fruit Erect or pendent catkin 2–3.5 ×
0.8–1 cm (0.8–1.4 × 0.3–0.4 in) on a stalk to
1.5 cm (0.6 in), bract 6 mm (0.25 in) with

the main lobe lanceolate, side lobes rounded, one-half to one-third as long as the main lobe and spreading at a wide angle, margins finely ciliate under a hand lens, seed ovate, 3 mm (0.1 in), wing narrower than the seed, usually around half as wide.

Range: Honshu, Hokkaido and Shikoku, Japan, extending north along the Kurile Islands and Sakhalin, on mainland Asia in northeastern China, Korea and Pacific Russia as far west as Lake Baikal in Siberia, also on the Kamchatka peninsula.

Habitat: Cultivated as an ornamental, in the wild occurring in mixed forests, often as a dominant long lived tree, or forming open montane forest to the tree line.

Varieties: Var. *japonica* has the veins in 14 or 15 pairs and is one of a number of varieties named to account for the inherent variability of the wild populations. 'Grayswood Hill' is a garden selection for the fine creamy white bark.

This tree develops an interesting bark with a strongly pinkish tinge. It is relatively sensitive to drought, which causes dieback, but tolerant of wet soils. It is unusual for a birch in that it is often dominant and long lived in some parts of its range. It is also extremely variable with a number of varieties described. It is a tetraploid. It is closely allied to *B. utilis* but the more strongly toothed margins of the generally broader leaves and the narrower fruiting catkins of *B. ermanii* and the embossed scales on the male over-wintering catkins of *B. utilis* separate them.

---

p.186   **Japanese Cherry Birch** *Betula grossa*

Description: Deciduous tree 10–20 m (33–65 ft) with a bole diameter to 50 cm (1.6 ft).
Crown Conical when young, becoming rounded on radiating branches.
Bark Yellow-grey, smooth, only peeling in small curls as in cherry, dark grey-brown in old trees. *Shoot* Light yellow-brown and white pilose at first with oval pale lenticels, becoming hairless and fawn-brown in the

second year, then dark grey-brown; scraped twig with a strong oil of wintergreen scent. *Buds* Ovoid, green, shiny, 6 mm (0.25 in). *Foliage* Leaves ovate-oblong, tapered to an acute apex, base subcordate to rounded, sometimes oblique, margin serrate with rounded to slender pointed or acute teeth which are often incurved and somewhat doubly serrate, upper surface dull green with 8–15 pairs of veins which are indented above with a line of pilose hairs, under side light sub-shiny green with raised hairy veins and scattered small black glandular dots, 5–10 × 3–6 cm (2–4 × 1.2–2.4 in); leaf stalk deeply grooved and densely pilose, 1–2.5 cm (0.4–1 in); autumn colour yellow-gold. *Flowers* Male catkins knobbly and often white resinous in bud. *Fruit* Catkins upright, more or less stalkless, ellipsoidal to oblong, 2–2.5 × 1.2–1.5 cm (0.8–1 × 0.5–0.6 in); scales ciliate, with a narrow oblong middle lobe and two ascending elliptic side lobes, 7 mm (0.3 in); nutlet ovate, 2 mm (0.1 in), with slightly narrower wings.

Range: Honshu, Shikoku and Kyushu, Japan.
Habitat: Cultivated as an ornamental, in the wild occurring as a component of mountain deciduous forests.
Synonyms: *B. ulmifolia.*

This tree is similar to *B. lenta* from the eastern North America, differing in the smaller persistently hairy leaves which have black glandular dots on the underside and are thicker in texture, and in the ciliate margins to the seed scales.

p.184 **Jacquemont Birch** or **Himalayan White Birch** *Betula jacquemontii*

Description: Deciduous tree 15–20 m (50–65 ft) with a bole diameter to 70 cm (2.3 ft).
Crown Ovoid with a pointed apex in young trees, becoming domed in old trees on several ascending branches. *Bark* Creamy white with large horizontal pinkish-white lenticels, peeling in large thin sheets, extending

through the crown to all branches over 5 cm (2 in) diameter. *Shoot* Green with long silvery hairs, smooth to rough with warts and linear-elliptic lenticels, in the second year brown or greenish brown and starting to peel. *Buds* Ovoid, pointed, laterally compressed against the shoot, light to mid brown with whitish hairs, 0.8–1.2 cm (0.3–0.5 in). *Foliage* Leaves ovate, tapering to the shortly acuminate apex, base rounded and faintly subcordate, margin coarsely and variable doubly serrate, upper surface matt green, sparsely hairy, lower surface pale or pale glaucous green, hairless except for white or brown hairs on the midrib and 7–11 prominent veins, 7–14 × 6–10 cm (2.8–5.5 × 2.4–4 in); leaf stalk grooved, pink or green, hairy, 1–2 cm (0.4–0.8 in); autumn colour yellow. *Flowers* Male catkins slender with slightly to moderately embossed scales, opening to 10–15 cm (4–6 in), yellow, showy. *Fruit* Catkins pendulous, to 5 × 1.2 cm (2 × 0.5 in); bracts three lobed, side lobes rounded, ear-like, central lobe linear with a rounded abruptly short pointed tip and hairy margins.

Range: Himalayas from eastern Afghanistan to west Nepal.

Habitat: Cultivated as an ornamental, in the wild occurring in pure or mixed forests.

Varieties: 'Inverleith', 'Doorenbos' and 'Jermyns' are clones which may be forms or hybrids of *B. jacquemontii*. They are propagated for their vivid white to creamy white bark, although 'Jermyns' is also showy when the male catkins are expanded. In the extreme western Himalayas from Kashmir to western Afghanistan, *B. jacquemontii* has leaves glandular beneath and buds resinous over winter. These have been separated as ssp. *occidentalis*.

Synonyms: *B. utilis* ssp. *jacquemontii*, *B. utilis* var. *jacquemontii*.

Sometimes considered as a subspecies or variety of *B. utilis*, it can be easily separated by the more ovate leaves and the strikingly creamy-white bark. *B. jacquemontii* is restricted to the western Himalayas, separated from *B. utilis* by the wide and deep Kali Gandaki Gorge which delimitates central and west Nepal. It is a tetraploid and will readily hybridize in cultivation with other tetraploids such as *BB. pubescens, ermanii* and *utilis* and with the hexaploid *B. papyrifera* to produce fertile offspring. Tetraploids can be derived by doubling of a diploid or by the joining of two diploids; either mechanism will give four sets of chromosomes. This provides a possible explanation for both the similarities and distinctions between *B. jacquemontii* and *B. utilis* if they share only one pair of chromosomes, with the other pair coming from unrelated taxa. For instance, with Jacquemont, the second set could derived from the *BB. pendula/szechuanica* series of diploids, thus giving a concentration of the white wax, betulin, in the bark. *B. utilis* could have the second set of chromosomes derived from another diploid species. *B. jacquemontii* is the best of the white barked birches, whilst *B. utilis* is the best of the coppery-brown barked species.

Sweet Birch or **Cherry Birch** *Betula lenta*

Description: Deciduous tree 10–20 m (33–65 ft) with a bole diameter to 50 cm (1.6 ft).
Crown Globose, usually with a rather low radiating crown on a short bole.
Bark Blackish or dark brown, smooth, not papery but in old trees becoming fissured into scaly plates. *Shoot* Green or yellow-green and hairless, but soon becoming olive-brown and shiny, slender, in the second year light to chocolate brown, scraped twigs release a strong aroma of oil of wintergreen (methyl salicylate). *Buds* Ovoid conic, green and brown, shiny, 8 mm (0.3 in).
Foliage Leaves ovate to ovate-oblong, tapered to an acute apex, base subcordate, margin finely serrate with abruptly short-pointed tips to the triangular forward-pointing teeth, rarely slightly doubly toothed, very thin, upper surface matt green with long sparse whitish hairs pressed against the shoot,

underside shiny light green and glandular, with 9–12 pairs of raised veins which are white haired, 7–14 × 3–7 cm (2.8–5.5 × 1.2–2.8 in); leaf stalk grooved, pilose (with long soft hairs) when young, green, 1–2 cm (0.4–0.8 in); autumn colour gold and orange for a brief period. *Flowers* Male catkins yellow; female catkins erect, in early spring. *Fruit* Catkins erect, 2–4 cm × 9 mm (0.8–1.6 × 0.4 in), stalkless, rather smooth, green until ripening brown in autumn, bract scales three lobed, with the side lobes rounded, shorter than the triangular central lobe, hairless, 5 × 4 mm (0.2 in); seed ovate to rhombic with a wing which is wider near the top, 3 × 3 mm (0.1 × 0.1 in).

Range: Eastern North America from southern Maine and southern Ontario south to Alabama and Ohio, mainly along the Appalachians.

Habitat: Cultivated as an ornamental, in the wild occurring in broadleaved or conifer forests but not montane forests, tolerating some shading.

This tree yields a valuable timber in North America but does not tend to make such grand trees in Europe. It is a diploid but is closely allied to *B. allegheniensis* (which is hexaploid), differing in the hairless strobile (fruit) bract scales and the leaves and twigs which become glaucous. The bark is darker and looks like most cherries, in a young state it is sweet to the taste. As with *B. allegheniensis*, scraped twigs have a strong and pleasant aroma of oil of wintergreen (methyl salicylate).

p.182 **Japanese Birch** or **Manchurian Birch**
Betula mandshurica var. *japonica*

Description: Deciduous tree 10–20 m (33–65 ft) with a bole diameter to 70 cm (2.3 ft).
Crown Ovoid, with usually ascending main branches. *Bark* Creamy white, and peeling in small sheets or large flakes, in young trees dark brown. *Shoot* Green-brown or brown in the first year and densely covered with warty glands and with small orange

lenticels which are oval along the branch, initially hairy but this is usually soon lost, in later years grey-brown or brown, with the lenticels expanding laterally, to become oval around the branch. *Buds* Ovoid-conical, acute, green, shiny, 5 mm (0.2 in). *Foliage* Leaves in twos or threes on spur shoots and alternately along extension shoots, ovate with a short acute tip, base rounded to slightly truncate or subcordate, margin sharply but evenly serrate except for the base which is entire, sometimes doubly toothed, wavy on young shoots, upper surface matt mid green, hairless except for hairs along the slightly raised veins, lower surface whitish green, without glandular dots, hairless except for hairs on the five to eight pairs of veins or in the vein axils or at the basal margin, 4–7 × 3–6 cm (1.6–2.8 × 1.2–2.4 in); leaf stalk grooved, pale green, 1.5–4 cm (0.6–1.6 in); autumn colour golden-yellow. *Flowers* Male catkins pendent and yellow, green over winter and 1.5 cm (0.6 in). *Fruit* Catkins pendulous, 2.5–3 × 1 cm (1–1.2 × 0.4 in), the bracts have a short central lobe and spreading obovate side lobes, seed narrow, with wider wings.

Range: Japan from Hokkaido and northern Honshu, Korea, Sakhalin, Kamchatka and the Kurile Islands, but *see* below.

Habitat: Cultivated as an ornamental, in the wild forming extensive forests or groves.

Varieties: Var. *japonica* is the form in general cultivation. Typical var. *mandshurica* differs only in being less hairy or hairless and comes from the mainland of northeast Asia (Pacific Russia, northeast China and Korea). It intergrades with *B. pendula* across Siberia. The white barked diploid birch of Alaska to Manitoba appear very closely related to *B. mandshurica*. If treated as a separate species, this is *B. neoalaskana*.

Synonyms: *B. platyphylla* misapplied, *B. resinifera*.

In appearance it is similar to the better forms of *B. pubescens*, although distinguished by the warty shoots and more evenly rounded leaves. It is a diploid, and more directly related to *B. pendula* and *B. szechuanica*. It is often treated as synonymous with *B. platyphylla*, but this species differs in the hairless leaves (except possibly for some ciliate hairs on the margin). *B. platyphylla* is more fully discussed under *B. pendula*.

p.183   **Maximowicz Birch** or **Monarch Birch**
Betula maximowiczii

Description: Deciduous tree 15–25 m (50–80 ft) with a bole diameter up to 1 m (3.3 ft).
Crown Ovoid to domed with heavy branches. *Bark* Greyish white, smooth and slightly peeling with the lenticels on the bole closely superimposed, but red-brown in young trees. *Shoot* Green with brown warty glands and orange oval lenticels, stout, in later years brown, bruised bark without an oil of wintergreen scent.
Buds Ovoid, pointed, glossy green, 7 mm (0.3 in). *Foliage* Leaves ovate or ovate-oblong, apex acute and short with a slender point, base heart-shaped, margins doubly toothed with aristate oval teeth terminating the main veins and with about five much smaller aristate teeth between, upper surface sub-shiny mid green, veins raised above with hairs, beneath pale green, with 10–12 pairs of prominent veins, 8–15 × 6–12 cm (3.1–6 × 2.4–4.7 in), new leaves coppery purple; leaf stalk grooved, 2–4 cm (0.8–1.6 in); autumn colour yellow.
Flowers Male catkins 10–12 cm (4–4.7 in), yellow. Female catkins in racemes of two to four. *Fruit* Catkins pendulous, 5–9 cm × 8 mm (2–3.5 × 0.3 in); bract scale with long narrow central lobe; seed with broad wing.
Range: Honshu and Hokkaido, Japan and along the Kurile Islands.
Habitat: Cultivated as an ornamental, in the wild occurring as a component in mixed forests.

This tree has the largest and boldest foliage of any birch. It is unusual in the female catkins being in clusters. In nearly all other birches, the male catkins are in clusters but the female ones are single. Compared to the excellent foliage, the bark is nondescript. It is intolerant of drought.

___

p.183 **Medwediew's Birch** *Betula medwediewii*

Description: Shrub or shrubby tree to 6 m (20 ft) with a short bole rarely to 30 cm (1 ft) diameter. *Crown* Rounded flat dome, broader than high. *Bark* Silvery grey-brown or somewhat golden, slightly flaking, on young trees dusty pink. *Shoot* Initially green and hairy, in the second year brown and hairless with oval pale lenticels, bruised bark with an oil of wintergreen (methyl salicylate). *Buds* Narrow ovoid, pointed, shiny green, to 1.2 cm (0.5 in).
Foliage Leaves ovate to rounded, apex acute, base rounded or subcordate, margin with forward-pointing acute teeth, upper surface with 8–11 pairs of impressed veins with bands of long white hairs, underside pale green with prominent hairy veins, 5–10 × 4–7 cm (2–4 × 1.6–2.8 in); leaf stalk grooved, with long white or brown hairs, 1–1.5 cm (0.4–0.6 in); autumn colour golden yellow. *Flowers* Female catkins erect, male catkins pendulous with brown scales subtending 10 yellow stamens, to 8 × 1 cm (3.1 × 0.4 in).
Fruit Erect and long persistent, 2.5–4 cm (1–1.6 in); bract scales woody, to 6 mm (0.25 in), with small side lobes and a long narrow central lobe, lobes obovate, with a truncate tip with long white hairs; seed obovate, wing narrow.

Range: Caucasus region, from Northern Iran to Georgia and Turkey.

Habitat: Cultivated as an ornamental.

This small tree is very distinctive in the buds and glossy shoots and is one of several species with oil of wintergreen in the bark. It is a decaploid, i.e. it has ten sets of chromosomes ($2n = 140$). It is not known to hybridize with any other commonly cultivated species.

p.185   **River Birch** or **Black Birch** *Betula nigra*

Description: Deciduous tree 10–15 m (33–50 ft) with a
bole diameter to 30 cm (1 ft).
Crown Ovoid, pointed in young trees,
becoming rounded, often on several stems.
Bark Soon buff-pink or orange with large
peeling grey or brown papery flakes, in very
old trees becoming reddish or black with
peeling flakes. *Shoot* Green and densely
white hairy at first in the commonly
cultivated forms, in second year grey-
brown, hairs lost in second or third year,
lenticels minute, round, pale.
Buds Conical, green and hairy, 4 mm
(0.2 in). *Foliage* Leaves alternate on long
shoots and in pairs or threes on short
shoots, rhombic or rhombic-ovate, apex
acute, base wedge-shaped, margin weakly
doubly serrate, with around four bluntly
acute teeth in a scallop between slightly
larger triangular teeth, upper surface sub-
shiny dull green, veins in 6–10 pairs,
slightly impressed above with a few hairs,
prominent and white hairy below,
underside pale whitish green, 4–9 ×
2–6 cm (1.6–3.5 × 0.8–2.4 in); leaf stalk
round, densely white hairy, circa 1 cm
(0.4 in), stipules 1 cm (0.4 in), narrow
triangular, soon lost; autumn colour yellow.
Flowers Male catkins 5–8 cm (2–3.1 in),
yellow. *Fruit* Erect, cylindric-ovoid,
ripening in summer, 2.5–4 × 1.2 cm (1–1.6
× 0.5 in), bract with three equal lobes,
hairy, seed rounded, flat, hairy, 4 mm
(0.2 in), with the two broad thin wings to
7 mm (0.3 in) across.

Range: Eastern North America from New England
and the Atlantic coast across to Wisconsin
and south to Eastern Texas.

Habitat: Cultivated as an ornamental, in the wild
often occurring in moist situations or along
river banks.

The commonly cultivated form of this
species has an orange or buff-pink bark, but
most wild trees have a darker reddish or
blackish flaky bark and hairless, copper
coloured twigs.

p.183 **Paper Birch** or **Canoe Birch**
Betula papyrifera

Description: Deciduous tree 10–20 m (33–65 ft) with a
bole diameter to 70 cm (2.3 ft), very rapid
growing vigorous tree.
Crown Ovoid with strongly ascending
branches which spread or droop at the tips.
Bark Creamy white to chalky white, often
with a pinkish bloom when the thin papery
strips have freshly peeled, with prominent
horizontal bands of lenticels, some trees
may take a decade to develop the white
coloration, whilst occasionally it does not
develop, with the bark remaining shiny or
blackish brown. *Shoot* Brown, downy and
sparsely pilose or hairless, warty, slender, by
the third year shiny brown with round
orange lenticels. *Buds* Long conic, slender,
green and brown, sticky, 1 cm (0.4 in).
Foliage Leaves narrow to broad ovate-
triangular, tapering to a pointed apex, base
rounded or subcordate, margin with acute
double teeth, upper surface matt green,
underside light shiny green with black
glands, with 5–10 pairs of raised veins and
light tufts in the vein axils, 5–10 × 3–5 cm
(2–4 × 1.2–2 in); leaf stalk grooved,
glandular and hairy, 1.5–2.5 cm (0.6–1 in);
autumn colour yellow. *Flowers* Male
catkins yellow, pendent, 6–10 cm
(2.4–4 in). *Fruit* Pendent, cylindrical, 4–5
× 1 cm (1.6–2 × 0.4 in), on a 1 cm (0.4 in)
stalk to a group of flowers; bract with a
short rhombic central lobe and two
spreading side lobes, seed with a broad
wing two to three times as wide as the seed
on either side.

Range: Across northern North America from
Alaska to New Brunswick extending south
to New York and Pennsylvania.

Habitat: Cultivated as an ornamental, in the wild
occurring on moist sites, forming extensive
forests.

This tree is a hexaploid with six sets of
chromosomes, i.e. $2n = 84$. It is only
distantly related to the Eurasian white-
barked birches, such as *B. pubescens*

(tetraploid) and *B. mandshurica*, *B. pendula* and *B. szechuanica* (diploids) but will hybridize with these, forming fertile offspring. *B. papyrifera* can be distinguished from these by the combination of ovate-triangular leaves with more than six pairs of veins and occasional long hairs on young twigs, by the black dots on the underside of the leaves and leaf stalks, and the fruiting bract having a diamond (rhombic)-shaped central lobe and erect side lobes. The cultivated clones are planted for the vivid white bark. With such a wide distribution, it shows very great variability.

p.181 **Silver Birch** *Betula pendula*

Description: Deciduous tree usually to 14 m (46 ft) but rarely up to 30 m (100 ft), with a bole diameter to 40 cm (1.3 ft), and rarely to over 1 m (3.3 ft).
Crown Narrow upright with ascending main branches bearing pendulous twigs.
Bark Silvery white in the upper crown, developing black diamond shapes in the lower bole and eventually becoming thick, corky and fissured with black to dark brown knobbly plates and ridges, in young trees shiny red-brown at first. *Shoot* Green-brown with raised whitish warts, becoming purple-brown over winter, then grey-brown to red-brown, slender, only hairy on watershoot or sucker growths.
Buds Ovoid, pointed, shiny green, 4–5 mm (0.2 in). *Foliage* Leaves alternate on long shoots and in pairs on spur shoots, triangular to rhombic ovate, tapering to an acute or short slender-pointed apex, base truncate to rounded or broad wedge-shaped, margin doubly serrate with sharp triangular teeth, upper surface green, hairless but with dotted glands, with around six pairs of raised veins, lower surface pale green, similarly dotted with glands, 3–7 × 2.5–4.5 cm (1.2–2.8 × 1–1.8 in); leaf stalk grooved, hairless, slender, 1.5–2 cm (0.6–0.8 in); autumn

colour golden-yellow. *Flowers* Male catkins shiny green to purple-brown over winter in clusters of two to four, expanding to 3 cm (1.2 in) and becoming pale yellow in spring; female flowers erect.

Fruit Pendulous oblong cylinder, 2–3 × 7 mm (0.1 × 0.3 in); bract rounded in outline, with broad spreading side lobes and a small rounded main lobe, 4 mm (0.2 in); seed obovoid, light brown, 1.5–2 × 1 mm (0.1 × 0.1 in), with wings twice as wide and notched at the apex.

Range: Europe, extending into northern Asia where it intergrades with *B. platyphylla* and *B. mandshurica*.

Habitat: Open hillsides, forests and on sandy heaths, in mountain valleys in the south of its range.

Varieties: 'Dalecarlica' has the leaves deeply cut, making an attractive tree, with its pendulous branching. 'Tristis' is a narrow crowned selection with strongly weeping side branches and a bark which does not develop thick corky fissures. In 'Youngii' the branches all weep and it struggles to make a tree. 'Fastigiata' makes a tall tree but the erect branches have lost all the grace and poise of the species, creating useful firewood! Even worse is 'Purpurea' in which the foliage is deep purple. As the tree has a light crown, the foliage is usually lost and the eye not offended. The only scenario in which it can be attractive is with a golden conifer as a background.

Synonyms: *B. verrucosa*, *B. alba* in part.

Similar species: *B. aetnensis* is doubtfully distinct from *B. pendula*. It is only found on Mt Etna in Sicily. It differs in the leaves being more or less simply toothed and not glandular above, with a shorter slender-pointed tip and smaller, to only around 2.5 cm (1 in). The bark does not fissure at the base. Populations in the Maritime Alps and on Corsica only consist of trees with non-fissuring bark, suggesting a possible relationship with *B. aetnensis*.

B. platyphylla is a related plant from eastern Siberia to the Pacific coast and into Inner Mongolia province of China. The leaves tend to be larger, with a truncate or broad wedge-shaped base, not rhombic in outline as in *B. pendula* although they are similarly hairless (except sometimes for some ciliate hairs on the leaf margin). The fruits are smaller, with narrower wings. It has a smooth white bark, not developing the corky fissured bark typical of *B. pendula*. It has been treated as a variety.

This attractive and common tree can be variable in the habit. At its best, this is graceful and weeping. The key characters are the hairless strongly warty shoots (but less so on shaded branches), the doubly serrate leaves and the bark which becomes fissured with thick corky ridges and no white at the base (in *B. pubescens* the base is persistently pinky white). It is a diploid, with two sets of chromosomes.

p.181 **Grey Birch** *Betula populifolia*

Description: Deciduous tree to 10 m (33 ft) with a bole diameter to 30 cm (1 ft).
Crown Conical, with pendulous branchlets. *Bark* Chalky white or grey-white, smooth, tight, not papery, thin, becoming fissured and scaly at the base. *Shoot* Very slender, densely covered with warty glands but totally hairless, olive-brown, becoming dark brown or grey-brown but remaining warty for several years. *Buds* Very narrow ovoid-conic, resinous, green, 6 mm. *Foliage* Leaves rhombic, tapered to a long tail-like point, base broadly wedge-shaped, margin regularly rather doubly serrate with broad flat triangular teeth which end in a short aristate or bristle point, hairless on both sides, upper surface lustrous dark green, rough with raised veins and warts, underside light green shiny, with copious warts and four to eight pairs of flat veins, 4–7.5 × 3–6.5 cm (1.6–3 × 1.2–2.6 in); leaf stalk grooved along the entire length, slender, warty, 1.5–2.5 cm (0.6–1 in); autumn colour yellow. *Flowers* Male catkins singly or in pairs at branch tips,

green, small and slender, 2 cm (0.8 in), expanding to 5–9 cm (2–3.5 in).

Fruit Pendulous to horizontal cylindrical catkins, slightly tapered towards the rounded tip, small and slender compared to those of other species and often persistent, 2–3 × 7 mm (0.1 × 0.3 in), on a 6 mm (0.25 in) stalk; scales small, T-shaped with two spreading hairy side lobes, a wedge-shaped stalk and a small projecting oblong central lobe, seed elliptic, small, with a broad obovate brown wing.

Range: Eastern North America from Nova Scotia to southern Ontario and south to North Carolina.

Habitat: Cultivated as an ornamental, in the wild occurring on barren uplands and disturbed sites.

This species is rather short lived and does not make a large tree. It is closely related to *B. pendula*, differing especially in the long tail-like tip to the leaves which are covered in warty glands and have more aristate or bristly teeth, the shape of the seed scales and the often stronger wartiness of the shoots.

p.182 **White Birch, Downy Birch** or **Brown Birch** *Betula pubescens*

Description: Deciduous tree 8–14 m (26–46 ft), rarely to 20 m (65 ft), with a bole diameter to 80 cm (2.6 ft).

Crown Ovoid when young, becoming rounded on a short bole with few twisting ascending branches. *Bark* Dull brown in young trees, then grey-white or white and slightly chalky, with a pinkish tinge in the shallow fissures at the base but never thick with black corky ridges with black diamond shapes as in *B. pendula*.

Shoot Brown and velvety downy with spreading pale hairs, small orange oval lenticels and very few or no warts at the base, in the second year grey-brown with few hairs, in the third year dark brown, almost shiny. *Buds* Ovoid-conic, pointed, slightly gummy, green and brown, 4–7 mm (0.2–0.3 in). *Foliage* Leaves broad ovate to rounded-ovate, acute to slightly pointed at the apex, base rounded to very broad wedge-shaped, margin regularly singly toothed or somewhat doubly toothed but never sharply doubly toothed (as in *B. pendula*) with broad triangular spreading teeth and ciliate, upper surface dark sub-shiny green and finely rugose under a hand lens, soon hairless except along the veins which also have some black glandular dots, underside pale whitish or slightly glaucous green with tufts of hairs on the raised midrib and veins and a few black glandular dots, 1.5–5.5 × 1.5–4.5 cm (0.6–2.2 × 0.6–1.8 in), larger on sucker or regrowth shoots; leaf stalk slender, grooved, downy with glandular dots, green or purplish, 1–2 cm (0.4–0.8 in); autumn colour yellow, rather variable. *Flowers* Male catkins expanding to 3–6 cm (1.2–2.4 in), yellow; female catkins erect on short spur shoots with one to three leaves, 2 cm (0.8 in). *Fruit* Pendent on a 1–1.5 cm (0.4–0.6 in) warty stalk, cylindrical, ripening from mid-summer to late autumn and breaking up and scattering seeds over many months, 1–4 × 0.5–1 cm (0.4–1.6 × 0.2–0.4 in); bract with a short bluntly pointed terminal lobe and two rounded ciliate spreading side lobes, circa 4 × 4 mm (0.2 × 0.2 in); seed light brown, elliptic, 2 × 1 mm (0.1 × 0.1 in), with two wings each 1–1.5 times as wide as the seed.

Range: Throughout Europe from Iceland extending in related forms through central Asia.

Habitat: Moorland and montane forests, especially on moist sites, or as a minor component in woodland.

Varieties: Ssp. *carpatica* is a more shrubby mountain form with smaller leaves to 4 cm (1.6 in) and soon hairless shoots, more resinous and warty new growths and more viscid buds. It is the predominant form in the Scottish Highlands. Ssp. *tortuosa* is a shrubby form with a dark bark, small leaves usually only 2.5 cm (1 in) long or less and more densely downy shoots. It is found in Scandinavia, northwest Russia and also reported from the Alps and Scotland.

Synonyms: *B. alba* in part.

Similar species: *B. celtiberica* is a related species from northern and central Spain and northern Portugal. It has the characters of *B. pubescens* except the shoots are glandular and thus similar to *B. pendula*. However, it is a tetraploid.

B. litvinowii is a related doubtfully distinct taxon from the Caucasus and northeastern Turkey. The bark is white or pink and peels, the twigs are both downy and glandular and the leaves are soon hairless, 2.5–5 cm (1–2 in).

This widespread small tree is frequently confused with the more picturesque *B. pendula*. It differs in the consistently downy and only slightly warty shoots, the leaves having more regular and spreading teeth and hairs below, and in the bark colour. This is usually inferior to *B. pendula*, but extends down to ground level and sometimes along exposed roots, never being thick and corky as in *B. pendula*. The habit lacks the graceful pendulous quality of *B. pendula*. However, in all these characters it is variable, and individual trees can sometimes be difficult to assign absolutely to one or other species. Another key difference is that *B. pubescens* is a tetraploid, i.e. it has four sets of chromosomes ($2n = 56$) whilst *B. pendula* is a diploid with 28 chromosomes. Triploid hybrids are known but are rare and generally if you have difficulty determining whether a tree is *B. pendula* or *B. pubescens*, it is *B. pubescens*! As a tetraploid, *B. pubescens* has the same chromosome number as *BB. ermanii*, *jacquemontii* and *utilis*. It will hybridize with all these species in cultivation and with the hexaploid *B. papyrifera*. The ecology is slightly different from *B. pendula*, occurring (especially in the warmer regions) in damper sites and where water lingers, being less common on dry heathlands.

p.182 **Sichuan Birch** *Betula szechuanica*

Description: Deciduous tree 10–20 m (33–65 ft) with a
bole diameter to 60 cm (2 ft).
Crown Ovoid in young trees, becoming
domed or rounded in old trees. *Bark* Young
bark dull brown, but soon becoming white,
creamy white or silvery white, covered with
a generous chalky coat which rubs off on the
hands, tight or lightly flaking.
Shoot Hairless, green and slender in the first
years with many warty glands, grey-brown
to dark brown in subsequent years with
small round lenticels. *Buds* Ovoid, green or
brown, 7 mm (0.3 in). *Foliage* Leaves
alternate, single or in pairs on spur shoots,
triangular ovate or rhombic ovate, apex acute
to very short slender points, base broadly
wedge-shaped or more or less truncate,
margins weakly doubly serrate, upper surface
matt to sub-shiny mid to dark green, lower
surface whitish green, both surfaces with
warty glandular dots, main veins in five to
seven pairs, slightly raised on both surfaces,
hairless (except for a few basal or marginal
hairs), 5–9 × 4–7 cm (2–3.5 × 1.6–2.8 in);
leaf stalk grooved, green or pinkish green,
with glandular dots, to 2 cm (0.8 in);
autumn colour yellow, usually poor.
Flowers Male catkins cylindrical, opening in
spring to 8–10 cm (3.1–4 in), yellow; female
catkins pinkish green, erect.
Fruit Cylindrical, pendent, to 5 cm × 6 mm
(2 × 0.25 in); bracts triangular, lobes
rounded, central lobe not greatly longer or
shorter than the spreading side lobes; seed
oval with a wing narrower to slightly wider
than the seed.

Range: Southeast Tibet, Gansu, west Sichuan and
northwest Yunnan, West China.

Habitat: Cultivated as an ornamental, in the wild
occurring in woodland and on open hillsides.

Synonyms: *B. platyphylla* var. *szechuanica*, *B.
mandshurica* var. *szechuanica*.

The white of many birches is due to the
waxy substance betulin, which is produced
on the bark of this tree to excess, rubbing
off as a chalky coating on the hands. The

Latin and common names denoting the old and current ways of transliterating the name of the Chinese province of Sichuan (Sichuan means 'four rivers'). *B. szechuanica* has been allied to *B. platyphylla* from eastern Siberia to Sakhalin, but this tree appears to be very closely related to (and scarcely to be distinguished from) *B. pendula*. It has also been confused with *B. mandshurica* from northeast Asia and Japan, but this does not have glandular dots on the leaves (but which usually have tufts of hairs). *B. szechuanica*, like *BB. pendula* and *mandshurica*, is a diploid, i.e. it has two sets of chromosomes. It also shows similarity to the tetraploid *B. pubescens* in the whitish green underside of the leaves and in the bark, differing in the hairless shoots, leaves and leaf stalks and the presence of warty glands on the leaves. It is also similar in gross appearance to *B. papyrifera* but differs from this in the absence of hairs and the whitish underside to the leaves.

---

p.184 **Himalayan Birch** *Betula utilis*

Description: Deciduous tree 10–20 m (33–65 ft) in height with a bole diameter to 60 cm (2 ft). *Crown* Ovoid-conic or columnar when young, becoming domed in old trees. *Bark* Red-brown to copper brown or pink-red but rarely almost black, with scarcely or no waxy white bloom, successive layers peeling in large thin sheets. *Shoot* Strongly glandular and at first silky hairy, becoming hairless in the second year, pale green in first year, green-brown in later seasons, peeling in the second year, lenticels small, round. *Buds* Conical, shiny green when immature, dark brown over winter, 4–8 mm (0.2–0.3 in). *Foliage* Leaves alternate on long shoots, on spur shoots singly or in pairs; ovate, tapering to an acute tip, base rounded, cut off abruptly or subcordate, margins with simple triangular small forward pointing teeth; side veins in 9–14 pairs, slightly impressed above, prominent below, minor veins net-like and impressed on both sides, silky hairy above, below hairless except along the midrib and veins, glandular (especially beneath) when young, upper surface mid to dark green, beneath matt or sub-shiny light green, 3–10 × 2–8 cm (1.2–4 × 0.8–3.1 in); leaf stalk grooved above, pink or green, 1–2.5 cm (0.4–1 in); stipules ovate-elliptic, 0.7–1.2 cm (0.3–0.5 in), quickly dropping; autumn colour yellow, not strong.

Flowers Male catkins cylindrical, single or in threes, knobbly over winter with embossed scales, expanding to 6–12 cm (2.4–4.7 in) in spring when showy and pendulous, yellow; female catkins erect, single, 2–3 cm (0.8–1.2 in). *Fruit* Catkins usually pendent (but erect in the forms from the inner dry regions of Bhutan and southeast Tibet), 2–4 × 1–1.5 cm (0.8–1.6 × 0.4–0.6 in); bracts three-lobed, ciliate and hairy, side lobes rounded, erect, main lobe strap-like, two-three times as long as side lobes; seed obovate, flat, 2.5 × 1.5 mm (0.1 × 0.1 in), wings half as wide as seed.

Range: Himalayas from the east side of the Kali Gandaki Gorge in central Nepal east along the Himalayas to southeast Tibet, north Burma, Yunnan and Sichuan in west China.

Habitat: Cultivated as an ornamental, in the wild forming pure forests at the treeline or in moist conifer forest.

Varieties: Var. *prattii* is recorded from Yunnan and Sichuan and in the drier parts of southeast Tibet, where it occurs within the same regions as typical *B. utilis*. The bark is very dark brown but otherwise it appears indistinguishable. *See also B. albo-sinensis* var. *septentrionalis* which may fit better as a subspecies of *B. utilis*.

Synonyms: *B. bhojpattra*.

The Latin name means 'useful', providing timber and firewood, with the foliage making cattle fodder and the thin sheets of bark usable as paper. The best forms have red-brown or mahogany-coloured bark but in parts of the range, such as northern Bhutan, the bark is papery and only brown. It is allied to *B. albo-sinensis* and also to *B. jacquemontii*, q.v.

BIGNONIA, BIGNONIACEAE

This is a large, mainly tropical family, but includes *Campsis* (p.557) and *Catalpa* (p.576).

PAPER MULBERRIES, *BROUSSONETIA*
FAMILY MORACEAE

This is a genus of seven species from east Asia to Polynesia, but only one species is in general cultivation. The leaf stalks contain a milky or latex sap. The male flowers are in pendent heads and have explosive anthers. The female flowers are globose, leading to a syncarp or cluster of orange-red drupelets. The inner bark has been used to make paper, hence the common name.

p.263 **Paper Mulberry** *Broussonetia papyrifera*

Description: Deciduous tree 8–15 m (26–50 ft) with a bole diameter to 50 cm (1.6 ft).
Crown Rounded or spreading dome.
Bark Light grey, smooth, becoming fissured. *Shoot* Grey-green or grey-brown, hairy, soft with a thick pith on strong shoots.
Buds Ovate, with two or three outer scales.
Foliage Leaves ovate or broadly ovate, with three main veins from the base which often extend to give three or more parallel-sided lobes with deep rounded sinuses, apex acute, base heart-shaped, margin with short teeth, upper surface grey-green, scabrid with rough hairs, more strongly softly haired beneath, 9–20 × 6–16 cm (3.5–8 × 2.4–6.3 in); leaf stalk stout, long; autumn colour poor.
Flowers Dioecious; male flowers in pendent catkins to 10 × 1 cm (4 × 0.4 in); female flowers in globose pendent heads circa 1 cm (0.4 in). *Fruit* Globose syncarp 2–2.5 cm (0.8–1 in) across, with many fused drupes each containing a single stone 2 mm (0.1 in), inedible.
Range: China and Japan.
Habitat: Cultivated as an ornamental.
Synonyms: *Morus papyrifera*
Similar species: *B. kazinoki* is more of a shrub, to 6 m (20 ft). It is distinguished by the short male flowers and the hairless shoots.

The origin of this small tree is lost due to its widespread cultivation in the Far East to make paper, which is produced from the inner bark. The leaves are similar to *Morus* (mulberry), but the fruit is hard and inedible.

BUTTERFLY BUSH, BUDDLEJACEAE (SYNONYM: LOGANIACEAE IN PART)

This is a small family which in temperate cultivation is represented by the genus *Buddleja*.

BUTTERFLY BUSH, *BUDDLEJA*
FAMILY BUDDLEJACEAE

This is a large genus of mainly shrubs. The leaves are mainly in opposite pairs, with a stipular ridge between the pair of leaves, with the shoot squarrish in section. The flowers are in terminal or axillary racemes or clusters (except *B. globosa* where they form a tight globe), and have a strong honey scent. The genus is either placed in its own family, or as part of the Loganiaceae.

p.170 **Butterfly Bush** *Buddleja davidii*

Description: Evergreen or semi-evergreen shrub or small tree to 6 m (20 ft).
Crown Rounded, on several stems.
Bark Pale brown, fibrous. *Shoot* Grey and densely woolly, flattened at the nodes and four angled when growing fast, later round and brown. *Buds* In opposite pairs, hidden in new foliage. *Foliage* Leaves lanceolate to linear lanceolate, tapering to an acute apex, base wedge-shaped and stalkless on the shoot, margin toothed, upper surface greyish green with impressed veins, underside silvery haired with raised interlooping veins, up to 30 cm (12 in) in length and 8 cm (3.1 in) in width. *Flowers* In long slender panicles 15–70 cm (6–28 in) on the current season's growths from June until October, purple, but selected forms pink or white,

very fragrant, with a tube circa 1 cm (0.4 in) and four small petals. *Fruit* Erect brown capsule 5–6 mm (0.2–0.25 in), opening along two sutures.

Range: Central and west China, from Sichuan, Hubei, Yunnan and adjoining provinces.

Habitat: Cultivated as a garden shrub but escaping and often forming a large sprawling bush, especially on chalk and gravelly sites.

Varieties: Many colour forms selected.

Synonyms: *B. variabilis*.

Similar species: These include:

B. colvilei (p.170), which may make a small tree. This has much larger blooms in June, to 2 cm (0.8 in) long × 2 cm (0.8 in) wide across the mouth, tinted rose or crimson, and in panicles 15–20 cm (6–8 in) or more. It comes from the eastern Himalayas.
B. alternifolia has much smaller flowers, which are stalkless on the arching shoots. The leaves are alternate, only 3–10 cm (1.2–4 in). It is native to western China, from Gansu (and possibly across to southeast Tibet).

This commonly cultivated shrub is especially useful as a food source for butterflies, in addition to the attractive and honey-scented blooms. It is often coppiced in gardens, to get larger panicles of flowers, but untrimmed plants flower earlier, if not as profusely.

BOX, BUXACEAE

This is a small family, represented in cultivation by *Buxus*, which forms shrubs to small trees, by the purely shrubby *Sarcococca* and the herbaceous *Pachysandra*. The latter two are not treated here.

BOX, *BUXUS*
FAMILY BUXACEAE

This is a genus of around thirty species from the Mediterranean region across Asia and Africa, and in the West Indies and Central America. The leaves are in opposite pairs, leathery and evergreen, and the shoots are squarrish in section. The flowers are monoecious, with a terminal female flower surrounded by male flowers. The fruit has three cells, each with a pair of horns, and are explosive, to scatter the small blackish seeds. The species are used as ornamentals, being especially tolerant of clipping. They have a hard wood with a fine close grain and bony texture. It is especially useful for detailed carving.

p.151 **Balearic Box** *Buxus balearica*

Description: Evergreen tree to 10 m (33 ft) with a bole diameter to 60 cm (2 ft).
Crown Columnar. *Bark* Pinkish brown, pale. *Shoot* Light green or yellow-green for three to four years, then brown, square at first due to the decurrent ridges below the leaves, gradually becoming rounded, initially hairy but soon hairless or almost so. *Buds* In opposite pairs, ovoid-conic to long conic, pale brown, 4 mm (0.2 in).
Foliage Leaves in opposite decussate pairs; elliptic, apex rounded, shallowly notched, base wedge-shaped, margins entire, slightly rolled down, upper surface shiny light or yellow-green, underside matt light or yellow-green, 2.5–5 × 1–2 cm (1–2 × 0.4–0.8 in); leaf stalk flat, 3 mm (0.1 in).
Flowers On previous season's growths in spring from buds in the leaf axils, yellow-green. *Fruit* Three-celled capsule.
Range: Balearic Islands, southwest Spain and Sardinia.
Habitat: Damp rocky localities.

This is related to *B. sempervirens*, differing in the larger leaves which are less glossy and yellow-green, not dark green.

p.151 **Box** *Buxus sempervirens*

Description: Evergreen shrub to small tree 10 m (33 ft) with a bole diameter to 30 cm (1 ft).
Crown Narrow columnar if a tree, otherwise tending to be rather a sprawling shrub. *Bark* Pale or whitish brown, becoming cracked into small squares.

Shoot Green for several years, gradually becoming brownish in patches, square and slightly winged, with two lines of pale hairs in a groove between the decurrent leaf bases. *Buds* In opposite pairs, minute, cylindrical, with two very hairy brown scales, 1–2 mm (0.1 in). *Foliage* In rather flat sprays with the leaves in opposite pairs on either side of the shoot; leaves ovate, oval or oblong, tapering to a rounded or notched apex with a short mucro (peg-like tooth) and wedge-shaped base, margins entire, above glossy mid to dark green with a raised midrib, beneath pale green, 1.2–2.5 × 0.5–1.1 cm (0.5–1 × 0.2–0.4 in); leaf stalk 1–2 mm (0.1 in), flat and finely hairy. *Flowers* In late spring from terminal and axillary buds from last and previous season's growths, in clusters of five to eight male flowers and a single terminal female flower; male flowers pale green with yellow stamens. *Fruit* Sub-globose to oblong with three horns, blue-green, often with a bloom, ripening to grey or brown, 7 mm; the capsules open violently to expel the black, shiny, 5–6 mm (0.2–0.25 in) seeds.

Range: Southern and central Europe to Turkey and Iran, and from Algeria and Tunisia in North Africa.

Habitat: Wide ranging but primarily on dry hills on base rich soils, tolerating dense shade.

Varieties: Many forms selected as dwarf or hedging plants; 'Pendula' has pendulous branches but makes a small tree.

This is frequently used as a hedging plant, withstanding clipping. It has a high quality heavy yellow timber, which is prized for carving, although not available in large sizes!

CACTUS, FAMILY CACTACEAE

The Cactus family is a large one which is confined (with one possible exception) to the New World. The general absence of functional leaves and the spininess of the plants diagnose the family. Only *Opuntia* (p.864) is featured here.

INCENSE CEDARS, *CALOCEDRUS* (SYNONYMS: *HEYDERIA*)
FAMILY CUPRESSACEAE

Genus of three species from western USA, Taiwan and southwest China to Thailand, Burma, Laos and Vietnam. They are related to *Thuja* in the foliage and cone characters, but with the seeds only having one wing. Only one species, *C. decurrens*, is common in cultivation.

---

p.47   **Incense Cedar**   *Calocedrus decurrens*

Description: Evergreen tree to 30 m (100 ft) in height with a bole diameter of up to 1.5 m (5 ft). *Crown* Columnar, occasionally becoming broad and domed with spreading billowing branches. *Bark* Purple and grey, smooth, becoming reddish brown, thick and irregularly furrowed into longitudinal scales which exfoliate. *Shoot* Green for first winter, then becoming dull reddish or purplish brown, flattened and flexible, 2–3 mm (0.1 in) but quickly thickening.
Buds Hidden in axils of the scale leaves. *Foliage* Foliage in flat sprays which are irregularly arranged, with lateral sprays to about 10 × 7 cm (4–2.8 in), with no appreciable difference between the two sides; leaves in whorls of four, due to two pairs being superimposed, apex acute with a bony point, pointing forwards but free at the tip, 1.5–3 mm (0.1–0.1 in) on laterals, to 1.2 cm (0.5 in) on extension growths, facial pairs with a minute scarcely visible resin gland; crushed foliage has a resinous shoe-polish aroma. *Flowers* On previous season's growths in late spring; male cones ovoid, yellow, 3–4 mm (0.1–0.2 in), infrequently carried but when present massed; female cones green. *Fruit* Hanging, spreading or occasionally erect oblong cones which ripen from yellow-green to reddish brown, 2–2.5 cm (0.8–1 in); scales six, woody with a small spine, hinged from the base (valvate) and only the central pair fertile, each with two unequally winged seeds.

Range: West Oregon south through California and western Nevada (USA) into Baja California (Mexico).

Habitat:	Cultivated in Europe as an ornamental, in the wild occurring in mixed coniferous forests on mountain slopes.
Varieties:	No varieties but the cultivar 'Aureovariegata', with unappealing splashes of golden yellow foliage, is occasionally cultivated.
Synonyms:	*Heyderia decurrens*, *Libocedrus decurrens*.

In cultivation this is often a narrow crowned tree, with a remarkably slender crown. In the wild, however, it usually becomes much broader, with spreading horizontal branches. Incense Cedar tolerates a wide range of soils and site conditions. It is valuable in gardens not only for the narrow habit but because it is resistant to honey fungus (caused by species of *Armillaria*) and to *Phytophthora* root rot (caused by yeast-like fungi in the genus *Phytophthora*). The timber is easily worked and aromatic. Because it can be cut in any direction, it is used extensively for pencils.

CAMELLIA, *CAMELLIA* (SYNONYM: *THEA*)
FAMILY THEACEAE

This genus contains over a hundred species and is most famous for containing the tea plant, *Camellia sinensis*, whose new leaves are picked and dried (green tea) or briefly fermented before drying (black tea). The species range from shrubs to medium-sized trees, although tending to be shrubby in northern Europe. The flowers are carried from late autumn to late spring. The petals are attached to the numerous stamens and fall with them. The ovary has three cells and ripens into a woody capsule. The seeds are large and oily, with several species cultivated for the oil which is pressed from the seeds. However, in Europe, America and Australia, the species are cultivated for their showy flowers.

---

p.238 **Camellia** *Camellia japonica*

Description:	Evergreen tree or shrubby tree to 5–15 m (16–50 ft) with a bole diameter to 50 cm (1.6 ft).
	Crown Rounded domed, usually on several stems. *Bark* Smooth, dark grey.

Shoot Mid to dark brown. *Buds* Conical, pointed, green, 1 cm (0.4 in); flower buds ovoid, to 2 cm (0.8 in). *Foliage* Oval to ovate, thick, firm and leathery, persisting for two years, margins with shallow dark brown teeth, apex short with slender point and twisted down, base rounded, hairless, upper surface lustrous dark green with a raised midrib, paler beneath with black or dark brown glandular dots, 5–10 × 3–6 cm (2–4 × 1.2–2.4 in); leaf stalk 1 cm (0.4 in), green. *Flowers* On previous season's growths in late winter and early spring, 6–10 cm (2.4–4 in) in diameter; petals five or more, fleshy, red, pink or white, obovate, to 4 × 3 cm (1.6 × 1.2 in), stamens many in a central erect rounded boss and united at the base, style with three or four lobes. *Fruit* Globular, 3–4 cm (1.2–1.6 in), ripens from green to dark brown in autumn, opening by three sutures to release the large seeds which are round or compressed on one side and 1.5–2.5 cm (0.6–1 in).

Range: Japan including the Liukiu Island archipelago, and Korea.

Habitat: Cultivated in Europe as an ornamental, in the wild occurring as an occasional component of temperate mixed forest.

Varieties: Many different colour forms exist, including a full range of doubles.

Similar species: *C. × williamsii* is a hybrid between *C. japonica* and *C. salouenensis*. It has elliptic leaves and the flowers tend to be cerise pink. The ovary is hairy, a character inherited from the *salouenensis* parent. The flowers are produced over a long period from November to May (depending upon season and individual cultivar) and have the immense advantage that the petals fall off once they are finished, whereas in *C. japonica* they tend to persist and detract from the display.

This is usually seen as a shrub in colder districts but can make a large tree. It is hardy and floriferous, being widely cultivated for the showy flowers. The fleshy petals are easily damaged by spring frosts.

TRUMPET VINES, *CAMPSIS*
FAMILY BIGNONIACEAE

This is a genus of two species, one from China and the
second from the eastern USA but which have hybridized in
cultivation. The leaves are opposite and in pairs, with each
leaf pinnate. The flowers are large and trumpet shaped. They
are carried on the current seasons' growths in late summer.
The two species are climbers, rather than trees.

p.314 **Trumpet Vine** *Campsis radicans*

Description: Deciduous climber capable of growing
10 m (33 ft) or more into a tree.
Crown Depends on support. *Shoot* Hairless,
with two rows of aerial roots. *Buds* In
opposite pairs. *Foliage* Leaves pinnate,
15–38 cm (6–15 in), with 7–11 leaflets;
leaflets ovate, slender pointed at the apex,
margin with coarse angular teeth, upper
surface hairless and dark green, paler and
downy below, especially on the midrib and
veins, 2–10 × 0.6–5 cm (0.8–4 × 0.25–2 in).
Flowers In clusters of 4–12 at the ends of
current season's growths in August–
September; corolla trumpet shaped with five
broad rounded lobes, to 8–10 cm (3.1–4 in)
across, scarlet and orange. *Fruit* Capsule
pod-like, widest in the middle, brown,
10–20 × 2 cm (4–8 × 0.8 in); seeds flattened,
wings transparent and silvery.
Range: Southeastern USA.
Habitat: Cultivated as an ornamental.
Synonyms: *Bignonia radicans.*
Similar species: *C. grandiflora* is the only other species in the
genus and comes from China, although
long cultivated in Japan. The best
distinguishing characters are the
inflorescence being in a panicle and the
leaves hairless. It is less hardy, making its
best floral display in southern Europe. *C. ×
tagliabuana* covers the hybrids between the
two species, with the clone 'Mme Galen'
the commonest form in cultivation.

The flowers are large and flamboyant,
although accompanied by too much foliage
to make a stunning display.

HONEYSUCKLE, CAPRIFOLIACEAE

This family includes 16 genera, with most species shrubs or climbers. The genera treated here are *Lonicera* (p.801), *Sambucus* (p.1124) and *Viburnum* (p.1259), but *Sambucus* is sometimes placed in its own family, Sambucaceae.

HORNBEAMS, *CARPINUS*
FAMILY BETULACEAE (CARPINACEAE)

This is a genus of 30–40 species. The male catkins are enclosed in buds during the winter, expanding in early spring when they become similar to those of *Betula* and *Alnus*. The fruit is a small ribbed nut which is subtended by a large leafy bract. The bract is strongly and equally lobed, showing the nutlet, in *C. betulus*; in *C. laxiflora* the bract is weakly but distinctly lobed; in *CC. orientalis*, *tschonoskii* and *turczaninowii* the bract is not lobed but toothed on one or both sides; in *CC. cordata* and *japonica* the bract is folded over the nutlet, concealing it but not enclosing it as in *Ostrya*. The twigs are generally slender. The leaves are simple, coarsely toothed and usually with many pairs of veins. In *CC. laxiflora* and *turczaninowii*, there are usually 8–10 (but occasionally up to 13) pairs of leaf veins, in *CC. betulus*, *orientalis* and *tschonoskii* there are 10–15 pairs (occasionally only 9) of leaf veins, whilst *CC. cordata* and *japonica* have 15–24 pairs of leaf veins. The bark is rather smooth and beech-like. The timber is hard and the English name, hornbeam, means 'hard tree' in derivation. Hornbeams make useful leafy trees, and usually have good autumn colour.

p.187 **Hornbeam** *Carpinus betulus*

Description: Deciduous tree 15–25 m (50–80 ft) with a bole diameter to 90 cm (2.9 ft).
Crown Ovoid in young trees, becoming rounded. *Bark* Silvery grey, smooth, becoming fluted in old trees but remaining basically thin and smooth. *Shoot* Slender, green with long white hairs, becoming brown and usually hairless. *Buds* Small, ovoid-sharp pointed, adpressed, green-brown, 4–7 mm (0.2–0.3 in). *Foliage* Leaves

oblong-ovate to broad elliptic, tapering to the acute apex, base rounded to subcordate, margin coarsely and doubly toothed with narrow triangular teeth, upper surface matt green slightly hairy with infolded veins, lower surface light shiny green with 10–15 pairs of raised veins, hairless except for light brown hairs in vein axils, 4–9 × 2.5–5 cm (1.6–3.5 × 1–2 in); leaf stalk grooved, yellow-green with sparse long white hairs; autumn colour yellow or old gold. *Flowers* Male catkins hidden in the buds over winter but emerging in early spring, pendulous, 3–5 cm (1.2–2 in); female flowers green, terminating short leafy shoots. *Fruit* In pairs set on a pendulous catkin on a white hairy rachis; each fruit consisting of a large green leafy bract to 2.5–4 cm (1–1.6 in) which has a long oblong middle lobe which is variously toothed and much smaller spreading basal lobes, enclosing a flattened ovoid ribbed seed 7 × 6 mm (0.3 × 0.25 in).

Range: Southeast England across Europe to Asia Minor.

Habitat: Woodlands, especially on heavy soils.

Varieties: 'Fastigiata' is a very widely planted selection. It forms an ovoid or flame-shaped young tree with ascending branches. However, once the mature height for the site is attained, the side branches continue growing and eventually, after a century or so, a domed or fan-shape is reached. 'Asplenifolia', 'Heterophylla' and 'Incisa' are cut-leafed forms.

The bark and the buds are similar to beech but it is a smaller tree. It often grows with beech, but is better adapted to heavy soils derived from clays. It is similarly useful for hedging, with the brown old leaves retained over winter on young or clipped plants. The common name acknowledges the hard ('horn') timber, with beam being derived from the Anglo-Saxon word for tree (*Baüme* in German and *Bomen* in Dutch). Traditionally it was used for chopping boards.

Sawa Hornbeam *Carpinus cordata*

Description: Deciduous tree to 15 m (50 ft) with a bole
diameter to 50 cm (1.6 ft).
Crown Ovoid, becoming rounded.
Bark Grey-brown, becoming scaly and
furrowed. *Shoot* Green-brown sparsely
pilose, with oval orange lenticels, later grey-
brown or brown, slender. *Buds* Ovoid,
acute, shiny green, 4 mm (0.2 in).
Foliage Leaves oval or oblong-ovate, apex
short with slender point, base heart-shaped
to shallowly heart-shaped, margin regularly
serrate with short spreading aristate teeth,
upper surface dull matt green, with
impressed somewhat pilose veins, lower
surface light green with around 15–20 raised
pilose veins and tufts of pale hairs in the vein
axils, 7–11 × 4.5–7 cm (2.8–4.3 ×
1.8–2.8 in); leaf stalk grooved, slender, more
or less hairless, 1.5–2 cm (0.6–0.8 in);
autumn colour yellow. *Flowers* Male catkins
in spring. *Fruit* In pendulous catkins 5–8 ×
2.5 cm (2–3.1 × 1 in), containing 20–30
fruits set in pairs on the rachis with a slender
hairless stalk 2 cm (0.8 in); fruit with a large
leafy bract (to 2.5 × 1.5 cm (1 × 0.6 in))
which is coarsely toothed with a dense tuft of
hairs at the base on the outside and with the
base folded over the nutlet from both sides.
Range: Throughout Japan and Korea, with a
variety in eastern Sichuan, China.
Habitat: Cultivated as an ornamental, in the wild
occurring in woodlands.
Varieties: Var. *chinensis* from east Sichuan differs from
the typical form in somewhat smaller leaves
and more strongly hairy shoots.
Similar species: **Japanese Hornbeam** *C. japonica* (p.189)
shares the folded basal lobes of the fruiting
bract but differs in the narrower leaves
(2.5–4 cm (1–1.6 in) in width) which form
long slender points at the apex and more
rounded at the base with 20–24 pairs of
veins. It comes from Honshu, Shikoku and
Kyushu, Japan, and forms a similar tree to
C. cordata.

This species belongs to a section of the genus
characterized by the basal lobes of the leafy

bract folding over the nutlet. It is, therefore, midway between *Carpinus* and *Ostrya*.

p.188 **Aka-shide** *Carpinus laxiflora*

Description: Deciduous tree to 10–15 m (33–50 ft) with a bole diameter to 30 cm (1 ft).
Crown Domed, leafy with pendent spreading shoots. *Bark* Grey. *Shoot* Very slender, reddish brown, initially with long loose hairs which only persist just above the axillary buds. *Buds* Acute, red, 1–2 mm (0.1 in). *Foliage* Leaves ovate or ovate-elliptic with a slender pointed apex and rounded to subcordate base, margin doubly finely toothed, with scattered long hairs when young, but only persistently hairy in the axillary tufts of the 8–10 pairs of veins on the leaf underside, 4–7 × 2.5–3.5 cm (1.6–2.8 × 1–1.4 in); leaf stalk slender, hairless, circa 1 cm (0.4 in); young foliage reddish; autumn colour yellow.
Flowers Inconspicuous. *Fruit* Clusters to 15 cm (6 in) but lax with spaced fruits, pendulous, hairless stalk to a group of flowers, rarely very finely hairy; leafy bract narrow ovate with two small but distinct basal lobes, toothed on one or both sides, with short hairs, 1–1.8 cm (0.4–0.7 in); nutlet deltoid-ovate, with shallow ridges, hairless or finely hairy, 3 mm.

Range: Hokkaido, Honshu, Shikoku and Kyushu, Japan and Korea.

Habitat: Cultivated as an ornamental, in the wild occurring in woodland.

Similar species: *C. fargesii* is related but differs in the larger and usually ovate leaves to 10 × 4 cm (4 × 1.6 in) which have 12–15 pairs of leaves, shoots which are brown with pale lenticels, and ovoid acute shiny reddish buds to 5 mm (0.2 in) long. The peduncle is hairy and the leafy bract of the fruit is larger, to 2.5 cm (1 in) and narrowly deltoid. It is more often seen labelled under the synonymous name *C. laxiflora* var. *macrostachys*. It makes a small tree 10–15 m (35–50 ft) and comes from central and western China.

This small tree is distinct in the slender-pointed tips to the leaves. It makes a small leafy tree but is uncommon outside of major collections.

---

p.187 **Oriental Hornbeam**   *Carpinus orientalis*

Description: Deciduous tree to 20 m (65 ft) with a bole diameter to 60 cm (2 ft), but occasionally a shrubby bush.
Crown Domed. *Bark* Purplish grey with brown markings. *Shoot* Slender, green with a silky down during the first summer, thereafter dark grey. *Buds* Ovoid, acute, to 3 mm (0.1 in). *Foliage* Leaves ovate to elliptic, apex acute to slender pointed, base rounded, margin sharply and regularly doubly toothed, upper surface dark green, paler beneath, silky down on the midrib and 10–14 pairs of veins on both sides, 2–6 × 1.2–2.5 cm (0.8–2.4 × 0.5–1 in). *Fruit* Clusters 3–6 cm (1.2–2.4 in), on hairy stalks; bract triangular oval or ovate, irregularly and coarsely toothed on both sides but not lobed, 1.5–2 cm (0.6–0.8 in).
Range: Southern Europe from northeast Italy and Sicily east across the Balkans to the Crimea, Asia Minor, the Caucasus region and northern Iran.
Habitat: Woodland or scrub.
Synonyms: *C. duinensis.*

This small tree or shrub is best distinguished from other common hornbeams by the bracts of the fruits being irregularly toothed but not lobed and by the smaller leaves.

---

p.188 **Chonosuki's Hornbeam**
Carpinus tschonoskii

Description: Deciduous tree 15–20 m (50–65 ft) with a bole diameter to 60 cm (2 ft).
Crown Ovoid. *Bark* Grey. *Shoot* Densely hairy and initially maturing to pale buff-brown, in later years becoming silvery grey. *Buds* Rounded ovate, green with

bright red tips. *Foliage* Leaves elliptic to ovate-oblong, slender pointed at the apex, base rounded to broad wedge-shaped, margin jaggedly serrate, often doubly toothed, with the teeth having bristle or aristate points, upper surface deep green with flattened hairs especially along the midrib, underside hairy, especially along the 9–15 veins and in the axils, 4–9 × 2.5–4 cm (1.6–3.5 × 1–1.6 in); leaf stalk densely hairy, to 1.7 cm (0.7 in).
Fruit Pendent, on a loosely silky haired peduncle 1.5–3 cm (0.6–1.2 in); fruiting bract not lobed but toothed on one side, narrow ovate, long hairy, 2–2.5 cm (0.8–1 in); nutlet rounded ovoid, with few striations, hairless or thinly hairy, 4 mm (0.2 in).

Range: Honshu and Shikoku, Japan, Korea and possibly central China.

Habitat: Cultivated as an ornamental, in the wild occurring in mixed forests.

Synonyms: *C. yedoensis.*

The combination of the densely hairy shoots, the sharply toothed leaves and the leafy fruiting bract having no lobes and teeth only on one side should distinguish this species.

---

p.188 **Turczaninow's Hornbeam**
Carpinus turczaninowii

Description: Deciduous tree 10–15 m (33–50 ft) with a bole diameter to 60 cm (2 ft).
Crown Domed. *Bark* Grey. *Shoot* Slender, olive green, usually hairless but sometimes with long hairs, lenticels pale, scattered.
Buds Ovoid, 2–3 mm (0.1 in).
Foliage Leaves elliptic-ovate, apex acute, base rounded, margin doubly serrate with abruptly short-pointed tips, upper surface matt green, net-veined with the 8–13 pairs of veins impressed but the tertiary veins slightly raised, initially hairy but soon hairless, lower surface shiny green, with hairs pressed against the shoot and axillary tufts, 2.5–6 × 1.8–2 cm (1–2.4 ×

0.7–0.8 in); leaf stalk hairy, green above and purple beneath, 0.5–1.2 cm (0.2–0.5 in); stipules narrowly linear, remaining attached to the shoot and persisting through the winter; autumn colour brown or orange. *Fruit* Clusters 3–5 cm (1.2–2 in) with only four to eight fruits, spreading or ascending, stalks hairy, fruiting bract ovate to narrow ovate, oblique, coarsely toothed, 1–1.8 cm (0.4–0.7 in); nutlet broadly ovoid, sparingly hairy, 4 mm (0.2 in).

Range: Northwestern and northern China across to Korea and in Honshu, Shikoku and Kyushu, Japan.

Habitat: Cultivated as an ornamental, in the wild occurring in mixed forests and in scrub.

Varieties: Var. *ovalifolia* from west China has ovate leaves which are more finely and regularly toothed, hairy shoots, larger buds to 4 mm (0.2 in) and less toothed fruit bracts.

This has delightful small leaves and makes a neat slow-growing tree.

CARRIÈREA, *CARRIÈREA*
FAMILY FLACOURTIACEAE

This is a genus of four species from eastern Asia, but only *C. calycina* is found in cultivation, and then only rarely.

---

p.200 **Goat Horn Tree** *Carrièrea calycina*

Description: Deciduous tree to 15 m (50 ft) with a bole diameter to 40 cm (1.3 ft).
Crown Domed, with wide spreading branches. *Bark* Grey, smooth until in old tree it becomes furrowed. *Shoot* Reddish green, maturing to grey-brown with buff lenticels, finely downy when young but mainly hairless by autumn. *Buds* Ovoid-conic to rounded, reddish, finely downy especially on scale margins, 3–8 mm (0.1–0.3 in). *Foliage* Leaves ovate, tapering to a slender tip, base rounded to heart-shaped, margin with coarse rounded teeth, young leaves reddish, maturing to

dark glossy green above, paler beneath, hairless or sparsely hairy on both sides, 7–15 × 4–7 cm (2.8–6 × 1.6–2.8 in); leaf stalk 2–5 cm (0.8–2 in); autumn colour poor. *Flowers* In erect or spreading inflorescences of up to ten yellowish-white to greenish-white flowers; sepals five, heart-shaped, forming a cup 4 cm (1.6 in) long × 2.5 cm (1 in) across; petals absent; central portion composed of a vase-shaped downy ovary with central radiating yellow stigmas and numerous short stamens at the base. *Fruit* Capsule with three sutures, initially green with a furry outer covering which ripens to brown and reflexes, 6–9 cm (2.4–3.5 in); seeds flattened, circa 1 cm (0.4 in).

Range: Western China from western Hubei, Sichuan and northern Guizhou.

Habitat: Cultivated as an ornamental, in the wild occurring in mixed warm temperate woodland.

This tree is very showy when in flower but is uncommon. The common name is based on a translation of the Chinese name, Yang Jiao Shu.

HICKORIES, *CARYA* (SYNONYM: *HICORIA*)
FAMILY JUGLANDACEAE

This genus mainly occurs in Eastern North America but has three or four species in China and Vietnam. It can be distinguished from *Juglans* when leafless by the pith of the one-year twigs being solid, not chambered. The male catkins are in threes (rarely fives). The fruit has a fleshy covering with four valves. Hickories make majestic large trees, having economic value both for the timber (which is springy and widely used for tools and sports equipment) and the tasty nuts (especially in the Pecan, *C. illinoinensis*). However, young trees greatly resent disturbance and they should be planted in their final position whilst still small. The number of leaflets can provide a quick initial means of separating the species, with *C. illinoinensis* having 11–17 leaflets; species with 7–9 leaflets are *CC. tomentosa, cordiformis* and *laciniosa* (although *cordiformis* and *laciniosa* sometimes have only 5 leaflets), whilst *CC. glabra* and *ovata* have mainly 5 leaflets.

p.329 **Bitternut Hickory** *Carya cordiformis*

Description: Deciduous tree to 25 m (80 ft) with a bole
diameter to 1 m (3.3 ft).
Crown Conic when young, becoming
domed. *Bark* Pale grey, smooth in young
trees, then finely fissured and finally
furrowed with narrow forking scaly ridges.
Shoot Olive-brown with slender orange
lenticels in the first year, becoming red-
brown and later grey, with heart-shaped
leaf traces. *Buds* Bright yellow to brown,
somewhat flattened, hairy, to 1 cm
(0.4 in), often superposed with a small one
beneath the prominent lateral bud.
Foliage Leaves 10–35 cm (4–14 in) by up
to 25 cm (10 in) across, pinnate with nine
(rarely five or seven) leaflets with the
terminal five largest; terminal leaflet
elliptic, tapering to an acute tip, abruptly
tapering at the base to long narrow wedge-
shape with a short 3 mm (0.1 in) hairy
stalk to leaflet, margin with small saw-like
triangular teeth with a small acute sinus
between each tooth, upper surface dark
yellow-green to matt green, with scattered
hairs, especially on the narrow but sharply
raised veins and midrib, underside light
grey-green with hairs on the prominent
raised midrib, veins and veinlets, to 15 ×
6.5 cm (6 × 2.6 in); uppermost two pairs
of leaves similar but slightly oblique at
the base and with a hairy stalks to leaflets
of only 1 mm (0.1 in), sometimes curved
forwards like a scimitar; lower two pairs
more rounded or subcordate at the base, as
small as 7 × 3.5 cm (2.8 × 1.4 in); leaf
stalk slightly grooved at base but
otherwise ridged as is the rachis, hairy,
green, 5–6 cm (2–2.4 in); autumn colour
bright gold. *Flowers* In early spring
before the leaves expand; male catkins in
clusters of three, pendent 5–7 cm
(2–2.8 in), each flower with four or five
stamens; female flowers at tip of the shoot,
in clusters of one or two. *Fruit* Nearly
round but with a short point, 2–3 cm
(0.8–1.2 in), green with a thin husk with
yellow spots, splitting along the four

sutures; nut smooth, with a bitter-tasting kernel.

Range: Eastern North America from Minnesota, Quebec to New Hampshire and south to Florida and eastern Texas.

Habitat: Cultivated as an ornamental, in the wild occurring in moist valley sites and on dry hillsides in the north, with other hardwoods.

Synonyms: *Juglans cordiformis, C. amara*.

Similar species: **Water Hickory** *C. aquatica* (p.329) is similar in the bitter-tasting nearly round nut, but can be separated by the 7–13 leaflets which are more lanceolate in shape and the dark reddish-brown winter buds. It comes from southeast USA from Virginia and southern Illinois south to Florida and eastern Texas, occurring naturally in low elevation wetland forests.

The flattened yellow buds, the leaves curved forwards beside the leaf stalk and the small bitter nuts all distinguish this species.

p.330 **Pignut** *Carya glabra*

Description: Deciduous tree 15–25 m (50–80 ft) in height with a bole diameter to 60 cm (2 ft). *Crown* Broad, irregular. *Bark* Light grey or grey-purple, smooth, becoming wrinkled or furrowed and somewhat rough. *Shoot* Browny green and hairless, becoming shiny and red-brown, slender. *Buds* Ovoid, yellow-green to orange-brown, small, only 6–8 mm (0.25–0.3 in). *Foliage* Leaves palmately compound, 20–30 cm (8–12 in), mainly with five leaflets but on weaker shoots only three, occasionally seven, terminal trio largest; leaflets narrow elliptic or narrow ovate, broadest around or just above the middle, apex short slender pointed, base narrow wedge-shaped to rounded on the lower pair, margin finely serrate, texture firm, dark green and rather oily above, hairless except for some tufts in the vein axils beneath, stalkless or subsessile,

7–15(–18) cm (2.8–6(–7.1) in); autumn colour yellow or orange. *Flowers* Male catkins 5–7 cm (2–2.8 in), before the leaves; female flowers two to ten, greenish. *Fruit* Obovoid (pear-shaped) or rounded, 2.5–5 cm (1–2 in); husk only slightly ridged and splitting only to the middle; seed not angled, flesh bitter, protected by a thick shell.

Range: North America from Maine across to south Ontario and Illinois, and south to eastern Texas and central Florida.

Habitat: Cultivated as an ornamental, in the wild occurring in mixed upland broadleaved forests.

Synonyms: *C. porcina*.

Similar species: **Red Hickory** *C. ovalis* is probably a hybrid of *C. glabra* and *C. ovata*. It has sweet nuts in which the husk splits to the base and a more shaggy bark. It is sometimes treated as *C. glabra* var. *odorata*. It has a similar distribution.

This tree has smaller buds and leaves than is usual in hickories. It produces a good timber which is particularly resilient to constant vibration. The name pignut refers to the partiality that hogs have to the fruits.

p.330 **Pecan** *Carya illinoinensis*

Description: Deciduous tree to 30 m (100 ft) with a bole diameter to 1 m (3.3 ft).
Crown Conic when young, developing a broad rounded crown with large spreading branches. *Bark* Light brown or grey, developing deep and irregular furrows and narrow crossing scaly ridges. *Shoot* Covered with star-shaped or fascicled hairs, green-brown at the tip, chocolate brown, shiny and hairless at the base with narrow pale lenticels, in the second year grey-brown, with half-moon to kidney-shaped leaf traces. *Buds* Conic with a bluntly pointed hairy apex, chocolate brown, laterals superposed (in tandem), 3 mm (0.1 in), to 1 cm (0.4 in)

on shoot tip. *Foliage* Leaves 30–50 cm (12–20 in) × up to 35 cm (14 in) across, pinnate with 11–17 leaflets with no great size difference between them but larger in the upper middle portion; leaflets lanceolate to broad lanceolate and usually sickle- or scimitar-shaped, tapering to an acute tip and wedge-shaped base on a short 2–3 mm (0.1 in) hairy stalk (except terminal with a stalk to 2 cm (0.8 in)), margin with irregular small forward pointing saw-like triangular teeth with a rounded and ciliate sinus, upper surface dark matt green, with scattered hairs especially on the narrow but sharply raised veins and midrib, underside pale shiny green with a thin covering of hairs, especially on the prominent raised midrib, veins and veinlets, 5–20 × 3–6.5 cm (2–8 × 1.2–2.6 in); leaf stalk and rachis ridged, hairy, brown and green, 10 cm (4 in); autumn colour yellow. *Flowers* In early spring before the leaves expand; male catkins in clusters of three, pendent, each flower with five or six stamens; female flowers at tip of the shoot, in clusters of two to ten. *Fruit* Oblong, with a short point at the tip and a rounded base, with a thin husk which ripens dark brown and splits to the base along four ridges, 3–5 cm (1.2–2 in); nut light brown with darker markings, smooth with a thin shell and a sweet-tasting kernel.

Range: Central North America from Iowa and Indiana south to Louisiana and Texas and south into Nuevo Leon, northern Mexico.

Habitat: Cultivated as an ornamental and for the tasty nuts, in the wild occurring on well-drained but moist valley sites, with other hardwoods.

Synonyms: *Juglans illinoinensis, C. pecan, C. illinoensis.*

This is the source of pecan nuts, but like other hickories, it also has an excellent timber. It requires a hot summer to ripen the shoots, and thus is not long lived in Britain but grows much better in warmer areas, such as Italy.

p.330   **Shellbark Hickory** *Carya laciniosa*

Description: Deciduous tree to 20 m (65 ft) with a bole
diameter to 70 cm (2.3 ft).
Crown Broad conic when young, becoming
an open, narrow dome. *Bark* Light or dull
grey, becoming rough and shaggy as it
separates into long narrow strips which are
loosely attached and curl away at both ends,
revealing orange. *Shoot* Pale green-brown
at first and hairy but orange to orange-
brown by autumn with long slender slit-
like lenticels, in the second year buff with
rounded lenticels and triangular leaf traces.
Buds Ovoid-conic, green with brown
margins, hairy, laterals superposed,
1.5–2.5 cm (0.6–1 in). *Foliage* Leaves
30–65 cm (12–26) × up to 45 cm (18 in)
across, pinnate with seven (rarely five or
nine) leaflets with the terminal trio largest;
terminal leaflet obovate, rounded at the apex
and tapering to a short slender-pointed tip,
margin with rounded teeth ending in a
short forward curved point, ciliate, base
wedge-shaped onto a short leaflet stalk circa
1.5 cm (0.6 in), upper surface dark matt to
shiny green, nearly hairless, underside light
green with a scattered covering of fascicled
hairs all over and denser on the prominent
midrib, veins and veinlets, to 30 × 15 cm
(12 × 6 in); uppermost pair of leaves similar
but with an oblique somewhat rounded
base and a short leaflet stalk 3 mm (0.1 in);
lower pairs broad elliptic with an oblique
rounded to subcordate base, 10–15 ×
5–9 cm (4–6 × 2–3.5 in); leaf stalk
flattened at base, yellow-green, to 20 cm
(8 in), rachis round; autumn colour yellow.
Flowers In early spring before the leaves
expand; male catkins in clusters of three,
pendent 10 cm (4 in); female flowers at tip
of the shoot, in clusters of two to five.
Fruit Nearly round, 4.5–6 × 4–5 cm
(1.8–2.4 × 1.6–2 in), ripening to brown
with the husk splitting to the base; nut
nearly round, with four to six ridges on the
thick shell, edible.
Range: Eastern USA from Iowa across to Ohio and
Pennsylvania and south to Tennessee and

Oklahoma, rarely in Ontario, New York, Georgia and Mississippi.

Habitat: Cultivated as an ornamental, in the wild occurring in moist valley sites with other hardwoods.

Synonyms: *Juglans laciniosa, C. sulcata.*

This hickory has the largest buds. The bark is similar to *C. ovata* but the strips are smaller and narrower, and the leaves have more leaflets. The Latin name translates as 'with flaps or folds' and refers to the shaggy bark.

---

p.329 **Shagbark Hickory** *Carya ovata*

Description: Deciduous tree to 25 m (80 ft) with a bole diameter to 1.5 m (5 ft).
Crown Broad conic when young, becoming gaunt and irregular on a few large arching branches. *Bark* Pale grey, becoming rough with small shaggy thin plates as a young tree but by the time the tree is around 25 years old, the plates have become large and 50–60 cm (20–24 in) long, loosely attached and curl away at both ends. *Shoot* Dark shiny chocolate brown and soon hairless with slender orange-brown lenticels in the first year with a ring of rufous hairs persisting from the bud scales, in the second year dull, with large kidney-shaped leaf traces.
Buds Long conic, green with brown margins, sparsely hairy, 0.5–1.5 cm (0.2–0.6 in), superposed with a second small one below the prominent one.
Foliage Leaves 20–35 cm (8–14 in) by up to 28 cm (11 in) across, pinnate with five leaflets with the terminal trio largest and pointing forwards; terminal leaflet narrow obovate, tapering to an acute, slightly slender-pointed tip, margin with small flat teeth with a cluster of rufous hairs (especially when young when more generally ciliate), base wedge-shaped onto a short leaflet stalk circa 1 cm (0.4 in), upper surface yellow-green to matt green, smooth and hairless except for a few hairs on the veins and midrib, underside light grey-green with a few hairs on the prominent raised midrib,

veins and veinlets, to 20 × 7 cm (8 × 2.8 in); uppermost pair of leaves similar but narrow elliptic and oblique at the base with one side wedge-shaped and the other rounded, almost heart-shaped, and stalkless on the rachis; lower pair elliptic with an oblique wedge-shaped and rounded to subcordate base, spreading widely, 10–13 × 4–5 cm (4–5.1 × 1.6–2 in); leaf stalk ridged above with an enlarged base, green, to 10–15 cm (4–6 in), rachis ridged; autumn colour yellow.

Flowers In early spring before the leaves expand; male catkins in clusters of three, pendent and 7–13 cm (2.8–5.1 in), each flower with four stamens; female flowers at tip of the shoot, in clusters of two to five.

Fruit Nearly round, 3–6 cm (1.2–2.4 in), green with white spots, ripening to dark brown or black with the thick husk splitting along four sutures to the base; nut elliptic to nearly round, slightly four angled, light brown, edible.

Range: Eastern North America from Quebec across to Maine and south to Georgia, west to Texas and into northeast Mexico.

Habitat: Cultivated as an ornamental, in the wild occurring in moist valley sites and on hillsides with other hardwoods.

Synonyms: *Juglans ovata, C. alba.*

The very characteristic bark is only produced on trees over a quarter of a century in age. The terminal three leaflets point forwards in contrast to the spreading basal pair. The name hickory derives from the Indian name for a food made from pulping the edible nuts with boiling water.

---

p.329 **Mockernut** *Carya tomentosa*

Description: Deciduous tree 15–25 m (50–80 ft) in height with a bole diameter to 60 cm (2 ft). *Crown* Slender, conic in young trees, broadening with age and becoming irregular. *Bark* Smooth and grey in young trees, developing fissures which become narrow forking ridges. *Shoot* Stout, dull brown to brown with persistent short stiff hairs. *Buds* Ovoid, large, to 2 × 1.5 cm (0.8 × 0.6 in); scales whitish green and red-brown, densely haired. *Foliage* Leaves 20–50 cm (8–20 in), with seven or nine leaflets; leaflets elliptic, obovate or ovate, apex tapered to a short slender-pointed tip, base rounded, margin toothed, shiny dark green with down on the midrib above, underside yellowish, glandular and hairy, basal leaflets smallest, sometime only 4 cm (1.6 in), increasing in size towards the terminal trio which may be 20 cm (8 in) in length, subsessile except for the terminal leaflet which is on a slender stalk 2–4 cm (0.8–1.6 in); leaf stalk and rachis yellowish, hairy; autumn colour yellow or gold; foliage aromatic, especially if rubbed. *Flowers* Male catkins dull yellow, to 15 cm (6 in), before the leaves; female flowers two to five. *Fruit* Elliptic to obovoid, maturing to brown, 4–5 cm (1.6–2 in); husk thick, splitting to the middle or beyond; nut thick shelled, slightly angled, round or elliptic; flesh edible.

Range: North America from southern New England across to south Ontario and Iowa, south to east Texas and central Florida.

Habitat: Cultivated as an ornamental, in the wild occurring in mixed moist upland broadleaved forests.

Synonyms: *C. alba*.

The big buds and the hairy undersides to the leaves help distinguish this tree. The foliage is fragrant, especially if rubbed.

SWEET CHESTNUTS, *CASTANEA*
FAMILY FAGACEAE

This is a genus of 10–12 species, deciduous large trees and shrubs from North America, the Mediterranean region, China, Japan and North Vietnam, although only one species is commonly encountered. Sweet chestnuts are similar to *Quercus*, differing in the flowers and fruits. The male flowers are borne in erect long slender showy catkins in July at the ends of the current season's shoots. Some of the catkins have one or two female flowers at the base. The fruits develop into spiny burrs, with up to three sweet nuts ripening in the autumn.

p.266   **Sweet Chestnut** or **Spanish Chestnut**
Castanea sativa

Description: Deciduous tree 20–30 m (65–100 ft) with a
bole diameter to 2–3 m (6.6–10 ft) in old
trees, occasionally up to 10 m (33 ft).
Crown Conical and rather open, whorled
when young, becoming columnar but old
trees with broad domed or spreading
crowns; basal shoots often present.
Bark Grey, smooth in young trees,
becoming ridged and fissured in old trees,
often as a regular spiral up the trunk.
Shoot Stout, brittle, greeny grey-brown and
bloomed in the first year with small pink-
grey lenticels and ridges from the decurrent
leaf stalk bases, often initially hairy,
becoming darker brown and more strongly
ridged in the second year. *Buds* Ovoid,
red-brown or green, with few overlapping
scales, terminal buds lacking.
Foliage Leaves oblong lanceolate, stiff, base
subcordate to wedge-shaped, apex acute,
margin with regular forward-pointing teeth
terminating the lateral veins, dark shiny
green above, paler and finely hairy beneath,
15–20 × 7–10 cm (6–8 × 2.8–4 in); leaf
stalk grooved, pale yellow or reddish,
2.5–3.5 cm (1–1.4 in). *Flowers* At ends of
current season's extension growths in mid-
summer, mass of whitish yellow male
flowers in erect or spreading catkins to
12 cm (4.7 in) and with basal greenish
female flowers (sometimes on short separate
catkins) at the base; male catkins turning
brown and persisting. *Fruit* Pale yellow-
green prickly burr, to 7–8 cm (2.8–3.1 in)
across; prickles branch, sharp, to 1.5 cm
(0.6 in); nuts one to three, chestnut
coloured with persistent styles.

Range: Mediterranean region from Spain and
North Africa east to Turkey.

Habitat: Woods on sands and other acid soils,
planted as far north as Scotland.

This tree is widely grown for the very tasty
nuts. It makes its best growth, and ripens
the best nuts, in hot sunny climates, but
will grow in cooler situations. It thrives on

light sandy soils but does not tolerate shallow chalk or like heavy clays. The timber is similar to oak but of poorer quality. It splits well and is used for stakes and staves. Sweet chestnut will coppice (regrow from the stump) if cut.

SHE OAK, CASUARINACEAE

This is a monotypic family (but up to four genera in a modern treatment). The leaves are in whorls and connate, appearing very similar to those of the horsetail ferns (*Equisetum*). However, they are angiosperms or 'broadleaved' trees, as is indicated by the fruit which is a woody cone with visual similarities to those of *Alnus* (p.492) and *Liquidambar* (p.792).

SHE-OAKS, *CASUARINA*
FAMILY CASUARINACEAE

This genus is mainly Australian in origin but extends into southeast Asia and the western Pacific islands. It comprises around ninety species which are adapted to dry and salty conditions. The leaves are scale-like and in whorls. The flowers are wind pollinated, whilst the fruit is a woody cone which contains a large number of ovaries, with only one seed developing from each.

---

p.38 **She Oak** *Casuarina equisetifolia*

Description: Evergreen tree 15–30 m (50–100 ft) with a bole diameter to 40 cm (1.3 ft).
Crown Columnar, narrow. *Bark* Grey-brown, scaly. *Shoot* Pendulous, green with six to eight ridges from the decurrent leaves, with fine hairs (under a hand lens) in the grooves, later brown or dropping. *Buds* Minute. *Foliage* Leaves scale like, in whorls of six to eight with 0.5–1 cm (0.2–0.4 in) between the whorls, leaf tips acute, 0.3–1 cm (0.1–0.4 in). *Flowers* In autumn; male catkins 1–4 cm × 2–4 mm (0.4–1.6 × 0.1–0.2 in), brown.
Fruit Cylindrical to spherical cone-like

structure, 1–2.4 × 1–1.8 cm (0.4–0.9 ×
0.4–0.7 in), on a stalk 0.3–1.2 cm
(0.1–0.5 in), containing a cluster of single-
seeded cells, remaining on the tree after
seeds shed; seed winged at the apex.

Range: Southeast Asia south to northern Australia
and across Polynesia.

Habitat: Cultivated as an ornamental in the
Mediterranean region, especially suited to
coastal sands and similar dry sites.

Similar species: Several species are occasionally encountered
in addition to *C. equisetifolia* and make
trees.

C. torulosa has the leaves set in whorls of
four, rarely five.

Two species which have the leaves in
whorls of six to eight as in *C. equisetifolia*
but differ in their erect foliage shoots are *C.
cunninghamiana* (with the shoots absolutely
hairless) and *C. littoralis* (with the shoots
minutely hairy along the grooves).
C. glauca has the leaves in whorls of 12–17,
whilst in *C. verticillata* the leaves are in
whorls of 9–13. These are all natives of
various regions of Australia.

This makes a tall tree with an open cypress-
like habit in warm regions. The leaves are
similar to the scale leaves of many conifers
and to *Tamarix*, differing in being in
whorls of at least four, and up to twenty. In
the somewhat similar conifers, the leaves
are either spirally set, in decussate pairs or
in whorls of four but with one pair larger
than the other. In *Tamarix*, the leaves are
spirally set and scale-like without a long
decurrent base. The only plants with really
similar foliage are the horsetails and
marestails (*Equisetum*), which are
herbaceous and unrelated.

BEAN TREES, *CATALPA*
FAMILY BIGNONIACEAE

This is a genus of around ten species, two from North
America and the others in eastern Asia. The leaves are large
and untoothed, although triangular pointed lobes may be
present in *CC. fargesii, ovata* and × *erubescens*. The leaf base is

truncate to wedge-shaped in *C. bignonioides*, rounded in *CC.* × *erubescens* and *fargesii*, and heart shaped or slightly heart shaped in *CC. ovata* and *speciosa*. The leaves are arranged in whorls of three or in pairs on the shoot and are usually thin, making them fragile in exposed situations. The flowers are in terminal panicles and are bell-shaped, like the finger-sized blooms of foxgloves (*Digitalis*). They are white or creamy white with red, purple or yellow markings in most species but in *C. fargesii* the flowers are predominantly pink. The fruit is a long capsule, which hangs down and resembles a cluster of French beans; it contains many small winged seeds.

---

p.140 **Indian Bean Tree** *Catalpa bignonioides*

Description: Deciduous tree 10–15 m (33–50 ft) with a bole diameter to 1.1 m (3.6 ft).
Crown Spreading dome, wider than high. *Bark* Pink and brown, smooth in young trees but soon becoming grey and scaly in thin flat plates. *Shoot* Green with raised orange lenticels, becoming grey-brown. *Buds* In pairs or whorls of three, usually slightly displaced, ovoid, purple-brown, 1 mm (0.1 in). *Foliage* Leaves ovate or broad ovate with an abrupt slender-pointed apex, base truncate to broad wedge-shaped, margin untoothed, matt green above, thin in texture, beneath light green with three basal veins and circa six pairs of secondary veins which are hairy, extra-floral nectaries in vein axils, 12–25 × 10–18 cm (4.7–10 × 4–7.1 in); leaf stalk round, green, shiny, 5–15 cm (2–6 in); autumn colour nil; crushed foliage with an unpleasant odour. *Flowers* In large terminal panicles 20–30 cm (8–12 in) high and wide in July, composed of many tubular white flowers with a brick-red strip and purple dots, with spreading wrinkled lobes, 4–4.5 cm (1.6–1.8 in), in bud round, with two or three calyx lobes. *Fruit* Pod purplish, 15–40 cm (6–16 in).
Range: Georgia, Florida, Alabama and Mississippi.
Habitat: Cultivated as an ornamental, in the wild found at the edges of woods.
Varieties: 'Aurea' is a small growing form which has the leaves rich yellow, becoming greener in

shade but remaining bright in the open.

This tree has a short bole on which the branches spread widely. It is very showy when carrying the large panicles of white and red/purple flowers. The pods have many small winged seeds and hang beneath the tree-like strands of spaghetti. The leaves are thin and very susceptible both to wind damage and also to frost. The leaves remain green until killed by frost in autumn.

p.140   **Hybrid Catalpa**   *Catalpa* × *erubescens*

Description: Deciduous tree to 20 m (65 ft) with a bole diameter of up to 1 m (3.3 ft).
Crown Tall domed to spreading.
Bark Buff-brown, in thin flaky scales, becoming fissured in old trees.
Shoot Green, stout, with oval buff lenticels, grey-brown in the second year with the lenticels raised. *Buds* In pairs or threes but not perfectly together, ovoid, conic, flat, brown, 1.5 mm (0.1 in). *Foliage* Leaves deltoid or broad ovate, occasionally somewhat three lobed, purplish when young, tapering to a tail-like apex, base rounded, margins untoothed except for the lobes if present, texture thin, upper surface light green, net-veined, underside light green with whitish curved hairs on the raised veins, 15–38 × 10–33 cm (6–15 × 4–13 in); leaf stalk green and pink, round, stout, to 18 cm (7.1 in); autumn colour poor. *Flowers* In terminal panicles, corymbs or racemes in tiered whorls of three, in bud like a spinning top, opening to bell-shaped with five frilly petals, flowers white with two yellow areas and purple lines, 3–4 cm (1.2–1.6 in), calyx lobes two, purplish. *Fruit* Pendent pod-like capsule, hanging down from the old inflorescences like strands of spaghetti, to 25 cm (10 in).
Range: Hybrid raised in cultivation.
Habitat: Cultivation only.
Varieties: 'J. C. Teas' is the from described above. 'Purpurea' has the new foliage deep purple

to almost black, with the colour tending to remain on the leaf stalks.

Synonyms: *C.* × *hybrida*.

This tree is a hybrid of *C. bignonioides* and *C. ovata*. It shows hybrid vigour and can have leaves to 60 cm (23.6 in) across and inflorescences with over 300 individual blooms.

---

p.141 **Farges Catalpa** *Catalpa fargesii*

Description: Deciduous tree 10–20 m (33–65 ft) with a bole diameter to 60 cm (2 ft).
Crown Columnar, with short spreading or ascending branches. *Bark* Grey, with yellow-orange beneath, peeling in thin flakes and shaggy. *Shoot* Olive-brown, with oval buff or orange lenticels, becoming chocolate brown in later years. *Buds* In pairs or whorls of three, usually slightly displaced, ovoid, flat, brown, 1 mm (0.1 in). *Foliage* Leaves ovate to slender pointed, apex long tail-like, base rounded, margins untoothed or occasionally with a small acute lobe on one or both sides, texture rather thick and stiff, upper surface hairless, matt green, warty, underside somewhat glaucous green with raised veins which are generally pubescent with star-shaped hairs, with extra-floral nectaries in the vein axils beneath, 8–20 × 4–12 cm (3.1–8 × 1.6–4.7 in); leaf stalk round, green, 4–12 cm (1.6–4.7 in); autumn colour nil. *Flowers* In large terminal panicles 20–30 cm (8–12 in) high and wide in July, composed of many tubular pink flowers which are spotted with brownish red and yellow, lobes frilled, 4 cm (1.6 in). *Fruit* Pod purplish and slender, 30–50 cm (12–20 in).
Range: West China.
Habitat: Cultivated as an ornamental, in China commonly planted beside roads in Yunnan province.
Varieties: Forma *duclouxii* covers the forms which have hairless leaves, instead of the star-shaped hairs found on the typical form.

Synonyms: *C. vestita.*

This tree is the only *Catalpa* to make a
narrow columnar crowned tree. The pink
flowers are also distinct, whilst the bark is
decidedly shaggy.

---

p.140   **Yellow Catalpa**   *Catalpa ovata*

Description: Deciduous tree 10–15 m (33–50 in) with a
bole diameter to 50 cm (1.6 ft).
Crown Spreading dome. *Bark* Smooth
grey-brown, becoming scaly. *Shoot* Green
or browny green with stiff spreading sparse
hairs, becoming dark brown. *Buds* In pairs
or whorls of three, usually slightly
displaced, ovoid, purple-brown, 2 mm
(0.1 in). *Foliage* Leaves ovate or broad
ovate with three or five triangular and
abruptly slender-pointed lobes, base
subcordate, margin untoothed except for
lobes, matt green above with velvety
covering of fine hairs and a number of
purplish extra-floral nectaries in the vein
axils at the base of the leaf, beneath light
green with circa five pairs of secondary
veins and interconnecting tertiary veins,
veins palmate at base, hairy, 12–25 cm
(4.7–10 in) long and wide, leaf stalk round,
purple and green, shiny and warty,
5–15 cm (2–6 in); autumn colour nil.
Flowers In large terminal panicles
20–30 cm (8–12 in) high and wide in
July–August, composed of many tubular
creamy white flowers with yellow strip and
purple dots, 2–2.5 cm (0.8–1 in), in bud
round, with two or three calyx lobes.
Fruit Pod purplish, to 30 cm (12 in).
Range: China and possibly Japan.
Habitat: Cultivated as an ornamental, in the wild
found in woods.
Varieties: 'Flavescens' is a form with deeper yellow
but smaller flowers, to 2 cm (0.8 in).
Synonyms: *C. kaempferi.*

This *Catalpa* differs in the leaves having
three, or less often five, short slender-
pointed lobes, making the leaf rather

pentagonal in outline. The creamy white and yellow flowers are smaller than in other *Catalpa*.

---

p.140 **Northern Catalpa** *Catalpa speciosa*

Description: Deciduous tree 10–20 m (33–65 ft) in height with a bole diameter to 1 m (3.3 ft). *Crown* Conic, becoming rounded at the apex but remaining narrow and dense. *Bark* Dark grey, deeply fissured and cracked into small scaly ridges. *Shoot* Grey-brown, with raised knobbly grey leaf scars. *Buds* In opposite pairs or threes, dark red, flattened, small, terminal lacking. *Foliage* Leaves ovate-triangular, apex with straight sides except for the somewhat slender-pointed tip, base heart-shaped, occasionally rounded, margin untoothed, texture leathery, smooth and deep green above, paler with soft hairs beneath, 15–30 × 10–20 cm (6–12 × 4–8 in); leaf stalk 10–15 cm (4–6 in); no autumn colour, leaves killed by frost and falling black. *Flowers* In broad terminal panicles 15–20 cm (6–8 in) in late June to July, not dense; flowers white with little purple spotting; bell-shaped corolla with frilly lobes, 5 cm (2 in) long and across. *Fruit* Capsule pod-like, dark brown 20–45 × 1.2–1.5 cm (8–18 × 0.5–0.6 in), splitting along two sutures to release the many light brown flat seeds with two papery wings.

Range: Central USA along the Mississippi valley from Arkansas to southwest Indiana.

Habitat: Cultivated as an ornamental, in the wild occurring on moist valley sites near streams.

This makes a much better tree than *C. bignonioides*, and is hardier in cold climates. The flowers are individually larger, although there are fewer of them in the trusses. When rubbed, the leaves do not have the unpleasant odour of *C. bignonioides*. They are also more neatly ovate triangular, without a rounded shoulder.

CEDARS OR TRUE CEDARS, *CEDRUS*
FAMILY PINACEAE

This is a genus of four conifers from the Mediterranean region and the northwest Himalayas. They make two types of growth. Extension shoots have single leaves or needles which are helically arranged along the shoot. A useful nemonic for distinguishing the species is that in *C. deodara* the tips of the shoots are drooping, in *C. libani* (and *brevifolia*!) they are level and in *C. atlantica* they are ascending, but this does not work on the pendulous forms of *C. atlantica*! From the buds that form in the leaf axils, short shoots are formed in subsequent years. These grow very slowly for many years, usually only 1–3 mm (0.1 in) in a season, and rarely branch. The leaves on short shoots are less than 1.5 cm (0.6 in) and in whorls of 15–20 in *C. brevifolia*, mainly 1.5–2.5 cm (0.6–1 in) in length in *C. atlantica* (whorls of 15–25 or more) and *C. libani* (whorls of 10–20), and mainly over 3 cm (1.2 in) (in whorls of 15–30) in *C. deodara*. The flowers terminate short shoots, after which the shoot dies. Male cones are erect, showy and shed pollen in autumn. The female flowers are erect, smaller, and rather difficult to find in the autumn. They remain erect, expanding to 8–12 cm (3.1–4.7 in) by the next autumn when they are fully ripe. The seeds are scattered by the mature fruit breaking apart, which it does over the next two winters, leaving the central stalk or rachis on the tree. Cedars have a good quality, fragrant timber but are mainly grown for their amenity value. They must have light, faring badly if crowded by other trees. Taxonomically, the Mediterranean species are closely related and sometimes treated as subspecies of *C. libani*. This becomes ridiculously complex once quadri-nomials are required and therefore it is rejected here.

---

p.66   **Atlas Cedar**   *Cedrus atlantica*

Description: Evergreen tree 20–35 m (65–115 ft) with a bole diameter to 1.5 m (5 ft).
Crown Broad conical and spiky in young trees with ascending branches, becoming more regular with age, usually remaining conical in some form although old trees with pendent flat dense foliage-laden branches are occasionally spreading or domed. *Bark* Pale grey, smooth in young trees, becoming fissured and eventually into small flaky plates which reveal red-brown underbark. *Shoot* Grey-green or grey-

brown in first winter with blackish hairs, becoming duller and greyer later, slender. *Buds* Globose, dark brown, 3 mm (0.1 in). *Foliage* Radial and pointing forwards on long shoots but deceasing in length towards the tip, on short spur shoots, which are all held above the level of the branch, in whorls of usually 30–45; leaves linear, tapering to a hard bony point, four sided with lines of waxy stomata on all sides, colour varies from bright silvery glaucous due to a dense waxy covering to grey-green, 1.5–2.5 × 1–1.5 mm (0.6–1 × 0.1 in); crushed foliage with weak resinous scent with overtones of rotten eggs.

Flowers Terminating short shoots more than two years old in autumn; male cones cylindrical, erect, opening to 5 cm (2 in), pale brown with yellow pollen; female cones narrow cylindric, 2 cm (0.8 in), pale green. *Fruit* Ovoid or barrel-shaped, green but ripening in autumn twelve months after pollination to brown and purple-brown, apex dimpled, 5–8 × 4–5 cm (2–3.1 × 1.6–2 in); rachis conical; scales fan shaped, to 4 cm (1.6 in) in width.

Range: Atlas Mountains of northern Morocco and northeast Algeria.

Habitat: Cultivated as an ornamental in Europe, in the wild occurring on dry mountain slopes on calcareous soils in mixed or pure forest.

Varieties: Forma *glauca* covers the plants with particularly glaucous foliage. The new foliage is often very silvery. Forma *fastigiata* includes the forms with a narrow crown due to ascending branches, and usually have glaucous foliage as well. Forma *pendula* is the name for those with weeping branches, usually needing training to make a tree.

Synonyms: *C. libani* var. *atlantica*, *C. libani* ssp. *atlantica*.

This tree is probably the most widely planted member of the pine family. It thrives on a wide variety of soils, including on chalk, and only demands good drainage and light. Like other cedars, it is intolerant of shade. The wild populations show some variation in the colour of the foliage, but in cultivation it is nearly exclusively the glaucous forms which are seen and enjoyed. The four taxa of Mediterranean cedars are closely allied and sometimes treated as subspecies of *C. libani*. There is no botanical objection to this arrangement but on a practical note it just makes the names unnecessarily long winded, with the glaucous forms of Atlas Cedar being *C. libani* ssp. *atlantica* f. *glauca*.

p.66 **Cyprus Cedar** *Cedrus brevifolia*

Description: Evergreen tree 15–20 m (50–65 ft) with a bole diameter to 80 cm (2.6 ft).
Crown Narrow conical in young trees, becoming broader and spreading or domed in old trees when growing in the open, remaining narrow and columnar when in groves. *Bark* Silvery grey, smooth in young trees, becoming cracked into small squares in old trees.
Shoot Yellow-brown to grey-brown in first winter, slightly hairy, slender, becoming greyer. *Buds* Globose, small, light brown, 2 mm (0.1 in). *Foliage* On long shoots radial and forwards with a parting beneath the shoot and with short whorls of 6–16 leaves around the buds, on short or spur shoots whorls of 15–20 leaves; leaves linear, apex drawn out to a sharp bony point, four sided, glossy green to bluish green with bands of white stomatal dots on all sides, to 1.2 cm (0.5 in) but up to 2.5 cm (1 in) on young trees by 1–1.5 mm (0.1 in); crushed foliage with a resin scent with a hint of rotten eggs. *Flowers* On short shoots two or more years old in autumn; male cones erect, 3–4 cm (1.2–1.6 in). *Fruit* Narrow ovoid to cylindric-ovoid with a dimple or nipple tip, broadest in lower third, ripening pale brown in autumn 12 months after flowering and breaking up over subsequent winter or spring, 5–9.5 × 4–5 cm (2–3.7 × 1.6–2 in); rachis cylindrical; scales fan-shaped, thin, 3–4 cm (1.2–1.6 in) in width.

Range: Tripylos Mountain in Paphos forest, Cyprus.

Habitat: Dry mountain slopes with *Quercus alnifolia* on andesite igneous rocks.

Synonyms: *C. libani* var. *brevifolia*, *C. libani* ssp. *brevifolia*.

This tree occurs in the wild only in an open forest which extends over both the north and south sides of Tripylos, a modest peak in the Troodos Mountains of western Cyprus. It is often associated with *C. libani* as a variety but is comfortably distinguishable in the smaller cones, shorter foliage and silvery grey bark. Really old trees do not exist, with the oldest perhaps 150 years. There is some variation in the blueness of the foliage.

p.67 **Deodar** or **Deodar Cedar** *Cedrus deodara*

Description: Evergreen tree to 40 m (130 ft) by 1.5 m (5 ft) bole diameter.
Crown Conical on a single bole with a weeping or nodding leader and terminal shoots on the branches, older trees remain conical to broad conical with spreading horizontal branches which retain the drooping tips. *Bark* Smooth and grey in young trees, becoming progressively fissured into wide black to pinkish-grey furrows and short scaly grey ridges.
Shoot Fawn-brown and hairy in first winter, slender and drooping, later grey-brown. *Buds* Ovoid, green or brown, very small, 1–2 mm (0.1 in). *Foliage* Radial and forwards on long shoots, decreasing in length towards the tip, on spur or short shoots in radial whorls of 15–30 leaves; leaves linear, tapered to a sharp bony point in section, flattened and rhombic, not quadrangular, grey-green with pale lines of white dots (stomata) in four bands, 2.5–6 cm (1–2.4 in), mainly 3.5–4.5 cm (1.4–1.8 in), by 1–1.5 mm (0.1 in), with the longest leaves at the base of the extension shoots; crushed foliage with a weak to pungent resin scent. *Flowers* On

short or spur shoots two or more years old
in mid autumn; male cones erect, 6–7 cm
(2.4–2.8 in). *Fruit* Barrel-shaped,
glaucous when young but ripening to
brown 12 months after pollination, 8–12 ×
5–6 cm (3.1–4.7 × 2–2.4 in); rachis
conical; scales fan-shaped, 5–6 cm
(2–2.4 in) in width.

Range: Western Himalayas from eastern
Afghanistan to west Nepal.

Habitat: Cultivated in Europe as an ornamental, in
the wild forming extensive forests in dry
mountain areas where much precipitation
may be in the form of winter snow.

This is the most distinctive of the cedars,
and as a young tree is exquisite with its
slender habit and drooping shoot tips.
However, as an old tree, it does not have the
beauty of a *C. libani*. It tolerates a wide
range of site types.

---

p.66 **Cedar of Lebanon** *Cedrus libani*

Description: Evergreen tree 20–40 m (65–130 ft) with a
bole diameter 1–2 m (3.3–6.6 ft).
Crown Conical when young but old trees
develop a very wide-domed crown with
spreading branches which form flat sprays
in tiers, often on several stems.
Bark Brown or dark grey and smooth when
young, becoming cracked into small scaly
ridges and in old trees usually blackish.
Shoot Coffee-brown or fawn-brown with
short fine hairs, later grey-brown to dark
brown. *Buds* Ovoid to globose, scales with
free tips, dark brown or black, 2 mm
(0.1 in). *Foliage* On long (extension)
shoots and rosettes on short shoots above
the level of the branch; leaves on long
shoots decrease in length along shoot,
radial; leaves on short shoots in whorls of
10–20 leaves (but retained two to three
years so two or three rosettes present);
leaves four sided, grey-green with white
lines of stomata on all four sides,
occasionally more bluish with a stronger
waxy bloom, apex with a bony point, from

1–3 cm (0.4–1.2 in) on long shoots but usually 2–2.5 cm (0.8–1 in) on rosettes; crushed foliage with a resin scent.

Flowers On short shoots at least two years old in late autumn; male cones erect, pale green, expending to brown with yellow pollen, to 5 cm (2 in). *Fruit* Barrel-shaped, broadest at one third and tapering to a bluntly pointed or dimpled apex, grey-green and somewhat resinous, ripening to brown or dark brown in autumn but breaking up over the following year, 8–12 × 5–6.5 cm (3.1–4.7 × 2–2.6 in); rachis conical; scales rectangular fan-shaped, to 5 cm (2 in) in width.

Range: Lebanon north into southeast Turkey in the Taurus Mountains.

Habitat: Dry rocky mountain sides on calcareous soils and with a north aspect.

Varieties: Ssp. *stenocoma* is found in the Cilician Taurus of southern Turkey as far west as Elmali. It differs in the slender ovoid-conic crown, although still becoming flat topped in old trees and in the light blue-grey leaves. It is more tolerant of colder winter temperatures than the other cedar species. There is also a single population on mountains near the Black Sea coast.

This tree is believed to be the tree used by Solomon when he built the temple in Jerusalem. Since those days, extensive felling has reduced its wild population in Lebanon. It has been in cultivation in Europe since the early 17th century, with almost all the old cedars being this species. It is at its best as a mature tree, consequently needing space, being less attractive as a young tree than the other species.

SPINDLE, CELASTRACEAE

This is a large family, characterized by the seeds having a fleshy covering or aril. The two genera described here are *Euonymus* (p.699) and *Maytenus* (p.835). *Celastrus* is a genus of woody climbers not treated here.

HACKBERRIES OR NETTLE TREES, *CELTIS*
FAMILY ULMACEAE

This is a large genus of rather nondescript trees. The leaves are simple and toothed, but sometimes with curious large pointed teeth, and are distinctly three veined at the base. The flowers are insignificant, but are followed by small globose edible drupes, which hang down from the branches and may ripen to green or red. The wood can be used to make a yellow dye.

p.191	**Nettle Tree** *Celtis australis*

Description: Deciduous tree to 10–25 m (33–80 ft) with a bole diameter to 1 m (3.3 ft).
Crown Ovoid in young trees, becoming rounded and domed. *Bark* Smooth with sparse wrinkles, grey, becoming slightly ridged at the base, beech-like in general appearance. *Shoot* Slender, slightly zig-zagged, brown or reddish brown with pale hairs, in the second year brown to grey-brown. *Buds* Narrow long conic, flattened and pressed against the shoot, red-brown with white hairs, 5 mm (0.2 in). *Foliage* Leaves narrow oval to lanceolate with the apex drawn out into a long tail-like or drip tip, base rounded to truncate, oblique, margin regularly serrate with triangular teeth which end in a long straight or curved aristate tip, upper surface shiny deep green, rough due to stiff hairs, veins three from the base, with two or three additional pairs, slightly impressed, underside pale to whitish green with raised veins and long whitish hairs, 10–15 × 2–6 cm (4–6 × 0.8–2.4 in); leaf stalk faintly grooved, green, hairy, 1–2 cm (0.4–0.8 in); autumn colour poor.
Flowers Flowering in May, small and greenish, singly in the leaf axils of the current shoots. *Fruit* Globose to slightly ellipsoidal, ripening from green through yellow to brownish red and finally black, 0.9–1.2 cm (0.4–0.5 in), on a slender green flower stalk 2–2.5 cm (0.8–1 in), containing a single ridged nut 7–8 mm (0.3 in).

Range: Southern Europe from Portugal, France and Spain east to Asia Minor.

Habitat: Thickets, planted as a shade tree.

Similar species: *C. tournefortii* (p.191) from Sicily, Greece, Bulgaria, Serbia and east to Turkey has broadly oval leaves 5–8 cm (2–3.1 in) with only a short tapered apex and a rounded to subcordate base and rounded but aristate teeth, and the fruit is more ovoid and ripens to yellow-brown. It makes a small tree to 6 m (20 ft), or a shrub.

C. caucasica has leaves 3–8 cm (1.2–3.1 in) but rhombic-ovate to oblong-elliptic in outline and with sharp teeth. The fruit ripens to dark reddish brown. It extends from eastern Bulgaria across Turkey and the Ukraine to the Caucasus.

This makes a good shade tree in southern Europe but inclined to suffer from frost damage when planted further north. The fruits are drupe with a flesh which is sweet when ripe. The bark resembles that of beech, but the buds are far smaller.

---

p.191 **Hackberry** *Celtis occidentalis*

Description: Deciduous tree to 10–20 m (33–65 ft) with a bole diameter to 60 cm (2 ft).
Crown Rounded, often broader than tall.
Bark Grey or grey-brown, smooth but with curious raised narrow ridges.
Shoot Slender, shiny brown with sparse stiff hairs, brown in the second year and then grey. *Buds* Narrow long conic, flattened and pressed against the shoot, brown with white hairs, 5 mm (0.2 in).
Foliage Leaves ovate to oblong-ovate, tapering to an acute apex, base rounded to subcordate, margin with forward-pointing broad triangular teeth which end in a short point, upper surface light green, rough with stiff white hairs, three veined from the base with four to six pairs of lateral veins, underside light green with raised veins and stiff white hairs, 5–13 × 4–6 cm (2–5.1 × 1.6–2.4 in); leaf stalk grooved, shiny green slightly hairy, 1–1.5 cm

(0.4–0.6 in); autumn colour yellow.
Flowers Flowering in May, small and greenish, singly in the leaf axils of the current shoots. *Fruit* Globose drupe, ripening from green to orange-red and dark purple, 0.6–1 cm (0.25–0.4 in), on a slender green flower stalk 1 cm (0.4 in), containing a single ridged nut, flesh dry but sweet.

Range: Eastern North America from southern Ontario across to New England, south to Georgia, west to Oklahoma and north to North Dakota, with scattered populations in Manitoba and Quebec.

Habitat: Cultivated as an ornamental, in the wild in mixed hardwood forests.

The curious bark is the most distinctive aspect of this small tree (although it makes 30 m in favoured river valleys sites in the wild). As the tree matures, it develops spaced raised ridges separating the generally smooth and beech-like bark.

PLUM YEW, CEPHALOTAXACEAE

This is a small family containing *Cephalotaxus*. Some authorities also include the genus *Amentotaxus* (not treated here but so called because of the long male catkins or 'aments') here, rather than in the Taxaceae. The female cone is a true cone, with several decussate scales with two ovules, although only one ovule normally develops into a fruit. It is this character which separates the family from the Taxaceae, the species of which have a single terminal ovule.

PLUM YEWS, *CEPHALOTAXUS*
FAMILY CEPHALOTAXACEAE

This is a small group of evergreen conifers which have yew-like foliage and are very shade tolerant. The leaves persist for several years, and have two broad bands of whitish stomata on the lower surface. They are arranged pectinately either side of the shoot, which remains green for five or more years.

The sexes are on separate trees, with male cones short, yellow and carried on the underside of the shoot. The female fruit is an oblong to ovoid fleshy berry.

---

p.63 **Fortune Plum Yew** *Cephalotaxus fortunei*

Description: Evergreen tree to 10 m (33 ft) with bole diameter to 30 cm (1 ft).
Crown Conic when young then columnar, or a spreading bush. *Bark* Red-brown, smooth, in young trees, then becoming shedding in strips or coarse scales.
Shoot Pale green, similar for three or more years, later red-brown, slender.
Buds Globose to ovoid, apex rounded or bluntly pointed, green, with many incurved scales, 2–3 mm (0.1 in).
Foliage Widely parted and pectinate (comb-like) with the leaves spreading at a right angle, rising and arching out; leaves lanceolate, tapering to an acute bony apex and somewhat rounded base and decurrent on the shoot, curved, upper surface yellow-green to pale green with a raised midrib and no stomata, lower surface with two pale greenish or silvery white bands of small stomata, 3.5–9 cm (1.4–3.5 in), occasionally to 13 cm (5.1 in), × 4–5 mm (0.2 in); crushed foliage with a parsley-like scent. *Flowers* On previous season's shoots in late spring, dioecious; males cones in globular heads, 4 mm (0.2 in), carried on short stalks (2–3 mm (0.1 in)) below the shoot; female cones on side shoots.
Fruit Ovoid or elliptic-ovoid, with a single seed enclosed in a fleshy covering, whitish green to yellow-green, ripening brown, 2–2.5 cm (0.8–1 in), on a 2 cm (0.8 in) peduncle.

Range: Eastern and central China as far south as Yunnan.

Habitat: Cultivated in Europe as an ornamental, in the wild occurring in mixed forest in dry zones.

This can make either a small tree on a single slender bole, or a sprawling shrub. It is very shade tolerant.

p.63 **Plum Yew** *Cephalotaxus harringtonia*

Description: Evergreen shrub or tree to 10 m (33 ft)
with a bole diameter to 25 cm (10 in).
Crown Columnar, with spreading branches.
Bark Purplish brown, smooth, later
peeling, revealing cinnamon-brown
beneath. *Shoot* Green for four years, then
red-brown. *Buds* Ovoid to globose, with
free scale-tips, green, to 4 mm (0.2 in).
Foliage Widely parted and spreading or
pointing forwards both above and below
the shoot, pectinate or in three or four
ranks; leaves linear or widest near base,
tapering to abruptly rounded and pointed
or acute apex, base wedge-shaped,
downwards growing on the shoot, dark
shiny green above with a raised midrib,
below with two whitish green waxy bands
of stomata, 3–6 cm × 3–4.5 mm (1.2–2.4 ×
0.1–0.2 in); crushed foliage scented but not
resinous. *Flowers* On previous season's
shoots in late winter or early spring; male
cones in globular heads 8 mm (0.3 in) in
diameter, comprising of 10–15 globose
whitish green catkins, 2 mm (0.1 in).
Fruit Ovoid, ellipsoidal to obovoid with a
rounded and depressed apex, with a fleshy
coat of green or with dark green striped
flesh which ripens to brown, 1.7–3 ×
1.3–2 cm (0.7–1.2 × 0.5–0.8 in), and
containing a single seed.

Range: Japan, Korea and northern China.

Habitat: Cultivated in Europe as an ornamental, in
the wild occurring in mixed thickets as an
understorey element.

Varieties: The type is based on the cultivar
'Fastigiata', which has short erect shoots
with radially arranged leaves. However, this
invariably throws some sports and these are
identical to the var. *drupacea* of literature.

Synonyms: *C. drupacea, C. harringtonia* var. *drupacea*.

Similar species: *C. sinensis* differs in the shorter leaves
(2.5–5 cm (1–2 in)) which are slender with
a bony point and arranged in two rows,
which may either spread pectinately or be
arranged almost upright. The heads of male
catkins are smaller, to 3–4 mm
(0.1–0.2 in), whilst the fruit has a rounded

apex which is shortly pointed. It comes from east and central China.

This small tree tolerates dense shade. It is similar in appearance to *Taxus*, but the drupe-like fruit is a modified cone and does not have a cup-like aril. Like yew, however, it will coppice if cut down.

LOCUST, *CERATONIA*
FAMILY LEGUMINOSAE

This is a genus of two species from Arabia and Somalia, but only *C. siliquastrum* is widely planted and naturalized in the Mediterranean region.

p.340 **Carob** or **Locust** *Ceratonia siliqua*

Description: Evergreen shrub or tree to 10 m (33 ft) with a bole diameter to 60 cm (2 ft). *Crown* Broad rounded dome, sometimes wider than high. *Bark* Dark brown, rough. *Shoot* Grey, slender, hairy when young. *Foliage* Leaves oblong 12–30 cm (4.7–12 in), usually equally pinnate with two to four, less often to six, pairs of leaflets without a terminal leaflet, rarely bi-pinnate; leaflets oblong to obovate, apex blunt to rounded or somewhat emarginate (notched), base rounded or abruptly wedge-shaped, margin untoothed, somewhat wavy, texture leathery, upper surface lustrous green, underside dull, ashy grey with slightly raised veins, 2–8 × 1–4.5 cm (0.8–3.1 × 0.4–1.8 in); rachis thinly hairy, often tinged red, grooved above, 7–15 cm (2.8–6 in); stalk to each leaf less than 5 mm (0.2 in). *Flowers* From July to November, mainly on separate male and female trees, although some hermaphrodite flowers probably produced by female trees; carried on the older branches or off the trunk; in cylindrical inflorescences of 3.5–15 cm (1.4–6 in) (rarely longer) with 20–60 brownish and scarcely showy flowers. *Fruit* Oblong pod 10–30 × 1.5–3.5 cm (4–12 × 0.6–1.4 in), sometimes larger in cultivated trees, initially green (or purplish), ripening to brown but not opening, containing a fleshy sweet glutinous pulp and 10–16 glossy brown very hard ovate-oblong seeds which are somewhat compressed and 0.8–1 cm × 7–8 mm (0.3–0.4 × 0.3 in).

Range: Eastern Mediterranean region, but widely cultivated.

Habitat: Dry hillsides.

This tree has very hard seeds and it was probably this aspect which Linnaeus had in mind when he derived the Latin name from the (Greek) word, *keras*, meaning horn. The seeds are very uniform in weight, which led to their being used as measures. This continues as the carat in which diamonds and precious stones are sold and equates to a fifth of a gram, whilst the purity of gold is measured in carats. The pods are used as food, mainly for animals. They provided the locusts as eaten by John the Baptist. The sweet flesh has a taste of chocolate and is used as a substitute.

KATSURA, CERCIDIPHYLLACEAE

This is a monotypic family.

KATSURA, *CERCIDIPHYLLUM*
FAMILY CERCIDIPHYLLACEAE

This genus contains only two species from Japan and China. It has leaves in opposite pairs on the extension or long shoots, with reddish paired buds. The leaves are ovate and resemble *Cercis* in appearance; they colour beautifully in autumn. The flowers are wind pollinated, and not showy. They are followed by the small, greenish pods.

p.171 **Katsura** *Cercidiphyllum japonicum*

Description: Deciduous tree 10–20 m (33–65 ft), with a bole diameter to 60 cm (2 ft) or more. *Crown* Conical or columnar, becoming domed. *Bark* Smooth, grey, or fawn, becoming shallowly fissured and in old tree scaly with exfoliating plates. *Shoot* Slender, green, becoming grey-purple or grey, studded with short paired side shoots on older shoots. *Buds* In opposite pairs, but sometimes the pairs displaced, conical with a pointed elongated tip, green or pink, 3 mm (0.1 in). *Foliage* Leaves always single, rounded in outline, apex shortly pointed, base heart-shaped, margin toothed with regular rounded teeth, upper surface dark matt green, lower surface beneath somewhat glaucous green with raised veins, 6–10 × 6–10 cm (2.4–4 × 2.4–4 in); leaf stalk pink or green, 2.5 cm (1 in); autumn colour usually good, including yellow, scarlets, crimsons, golds and pinks. *Flowers* On separate male and female trees; not showy. *Fruit* Capsules glaucous green, ripening brown, 1.5–2 cm (0.6–0.8 in).

Range: Southern Japan and Sichuan, and adjacent provinces of west China.

Habitat: Cultivated as an ornamental, in the wild occurring in mixed forests.

Similar species: *C. magnificum* has larger, more kidney-shaped leaves with broader, crenate teeth and the seeds are winged at both ends (in *C. japonicum*, they are winged at one end only). It is restricted to Honshu, Japan, where it occurs in scattered groves.

The new foliage is often damaged by spring frosts but a further flush usually gets away. The leaves are similar to those of *Cercis siliquastrum* but they are in opposite pairs and have rounded teeth. In west China, old trees develop enormous boles.

JUDAS TREES, *CERCIS*
FAMILY LEGUMINOSAE

This small genus contains around ten species native to the eastern Mediterranean region, much of China and North America from Canada to Mexico and west to California. The leaves are unusual in the Leguminosae for being simple and untoothed, with a heart-shaped base (almost all other legumes have pinnate leaves). The flowers are typical pea-shaped flowers, carried in fascicles (except in one species where they are in racemes) and on the old wood in late spring but before the leaves. Flowers are often produced straight out of the trunk and branches. The fruit is a typical legume.

p.128 **Judas Tree** *Cercis siliquastrum*

Description: Deciduous tree generally to 10 m (33 ft) but up to 15 m (50 ft), with a bole diameter to 60 cm (2 ft).
Crown Spreading, rounded domed, often sprawling. *Bark* Smooth or folded, grey-brown, becoming cracked into small brown rough squares. *Shoot* Hairless, green, later dark chocolate brown or red-brown.
Buds Ovoid, rounded or with slender-pointed scales, 3 mm (0.1 in).
Foliage Leaves rounded in outline, apex slightly notched or pointed, base heart-shaped, margin untoothed, slightly sinuous, untoothed, upper surface matt green, beneath somewhat glaucous green with raised veins, 6–10 × 6–10 cm (2.4–4 × 2.4–4 in); leaf stalk pink or green, slightly grooved, base enlarged with a tuft of hairs, 2.5–5 cm (1–2 in); autumn colour poor. *Flowers* Carried in May before the leaves from leafless shoots, often on several year old shoots, flowers pea-shaped, pink or white, 2 cm (0.8 in) across on 2 cm (0.8 in) stalks, in clusters of three to six. *Fruit* Pod or legume 7–12 cm (2.8–4.7 in).

Range: Southeast Europe across to western Asia.
Habitat: Dry open hillsides.

The flowers are carried on naked branches (whereas in most trees they are only found on the new or recent growths) and make the tree attractive and prominent in late spring. It requires a hot dry climate. The common name is often claimed to refer to the tree on which Judas hanged himself but may simply refer to the land of Judea, which is within its natural distribution. The foliage is very similar to *Cercidiphyllum* but the combination of alternate and untoothed leaves and the showy pea flowers distinguish it.

CYPRESSES OR FALSE CYPRESSES, *CHAMAECYPARIS*
(SYNONYM: *CUPRESSUS* IN PART)
FAMILY CUPRESSACEAE

This small genus is closely related to *Cupressus* but is
distinguished by the smaller cones. The cones are
0.5–0.7 cm (0.2–0.3 in) in *CC. pisifera* and *thyoides*,
0.7–1 cm (0.3–0.4 in) in *CC. formosensis* and *lawsoniana*, and
1–1.2 cm (0.4–0.5 in) in *C. obtusa*. The cones ripen in the
first autumn and have only two to five seeds per fertile scale.
C. thyoides has only six cone scales in the cones, the other
species having 8–12 scales. Flowering also occurs in the
period late winter to spring, whereas in *Cupressus* it is from
autumn until late winter. The leaves are scale-like. In *CC.
lawsoniana* and *thyoides* there is a prominent dorsal gland on
the scale leaves, but in *CC. formosensis*, *obtusa* and *pisifera* the
gland is obscure. The species produce a good-quality light
timber, but are mainly planted as amenity trees. The foliage
is also used in floristry.

---

p.41 **Taiwan Cypress** *Chamaecyparis formosensis*

Description: Evergreen tree to 15 m (50 ft) with a bole
diameter of up to 40 cm (1.3 ft).
Crown Broad conical with spreading
branches with pendent shoot tips.
Bark Red-brown, developing shallow
ridges which are slightly peeling.
Shoot Green or bronze-green for the first
winter, then dark red to red-brown,
moderately slender, 1–1.5 mm (0.1 in).
Buds Hidden in axils of the scale leaves.
Foliage In flat open sprays with the side
shoots pointing forwards at an acute angle
to the shoot, one year sprays to 10 × 3–4 cm
(4 × 1.2–1.6 in), mid green, paler beneath;
scale leaves in more or less similar pairs,
dorsal glands very obscure, apex acute,
pointed, incurved but not pressed against
the shoot, leaves on whip-like extension
shoots with free-spreading tips, somewhat
shiny, scales from 1 mm (0.1 in) on short
shoots up to 8 mm (0.3 in) on vigorous
ones; crushed foliage with a cabbage or
seaweed scent. *Flowers* On previous season's
shoots in late winter; male cones ovoid, pale
yellow-brown, 1.5 mm (0.1 in).
Fruit Ellipsoidal to globose, carried above

the level of the foliage, scales 10–12, with a transverse ridge and a small reflexed prickle, green, ripening to light brown in first autumn, to 9 × 8 mm (0.4 × 0.3 in).

Range: Central Taiwan.

Habitat: Cultivated in Europe as an ornamental, in Taiwan forming forests with other conifers in the mountains.

Synonyms: *Cupressus formosensis*.

In Taiwan, this makes an enormous tree, to 60 m (200 ft) in height with bole girths of over 20 m (65 ft) recorded. In Britain, it is often cut back by hard winters and is better suited to the mild and wetter west. It is closely related to *C. pisifera*, differing in the finer foliage, yellow-green male cones and the ripe cones being carried above the general level of the foliage, whereas in *C. pisifera* they are rather lost within it, or are prominent from below.

p.40 **Lawson Cypress** *Chamaecyparis lawsoniana*

Description: Evergreen tree 20–40 m (65–130 ft) with a bole diameter to 1.2 m (4 ft).
Crown Columnar-conic with short spreading branches which have pendulous tips, often forking with narrow crotches, old trees often with erratic spreading branches. *Bark* Grey-green, smooth and somewhat shiny in young trees, becoming dark purple-brown or red-brown and fissured in old trees, with slightly fibrous ridges. *Shoot* Green from decurrent leaf bases for first winter, becoming brown, slender. *Buds* Hidden in axils of the scale leaves. *Foliage* In flat pendent sprays with lateral sprays 15 × 6 cm (6 × 2.4 in); leaves in decussate unequal pairs, facial pair rhombic in outline, with a short free tip and a prominent dorsal gland (more visible from above), to 2 mm (0.1 in), lateral pairs with an acute tip which may be free and spreading at 30–45 degrees or incurved and pressed against the shoot, 3–8 mm (0.1–0.3 in), light to dark green above, beneath with whitish bands of stomata

around the margins where the leaves abut; crushed foliage with a pungent resinous parsley-like aroma. *Flowers* On previous season's shoots in early spring; male cones terminating weak shoots, globular, 1.5 mm (0.1 in) and black or green and black in bud, opening brick red and 4 mm (0.2 in); female cones terminating side shoots at branch tips, grey-blue with acute scales. *Fruit* Globular and wrinkled with four (rarely five) pairs of scales, 7–10 mm (0.3–0.4 in), blue-green when growing, ripening to dull mid brown in first autumn and opening to release the seeds by the scales parting; scales peltate (shield-like on a stalk), with dorsal dimple.

Range: Southwest Oregon and northwest California in a coastal belt and inland on Mount Shasta.

Habitat: Cultivated in Europe as an ornamental, in the wild restricted to ridges and valley sides.

Varieties: No botanical varieties but innumerable cultivars. Many of these are dwarfs and not considered here but there are a number of tree selections. These included: 'Erecta', with the foliage in erect dark green plates; 'Intertexta', which has grey-green stout foliage carried in lax pendulous sprays and develops a columnar crown with branches splaying out; 'Kilmacurragh', which is a very narrow bright green selection; 'Allumii', conical with blue-grey foliage which billows at the base; 'Columnaris', pale blue-grey foliage and tightly columnar habit; 'Pembury Blue', a broadly conical habit with bright blue-grey foliage in pendulous sprays; 'Lane', with golden-yellow foliage on a columnar crown; 'Lutea', a narrow columnar tree with golden yellow foliage in large pendulous sprays; and 'Stewartii', a conical tree with arching sprays of fern-like golden foliage.

Synonyms: *Cupressus lawsoniana*.

In the wild, this tree has a restricted range and is uniform in its characters. In cultivation, it has produced an incredible range of variants, as noted above, and is the most widely planted ornamental conifer. It grows on a wide range of sites, including chalks and clays, and is hardy north to southern Sweden.

p.41   **Hinoki Cypress** *Chamaecyparis obtusa*

Description: Evergreen tree 15–25 m (50–80 ft) with a bole diameter of up to 70 cm (2.3 ft). *Crown* Broad conic with a broadly pointed apex and pendent leader, not dense. *Bark* Red-brown or grey-brown, becoming fissured with long parallel ridges, soft and stringy. *Shoot* Green for first winter, becoming red to red-brown, moderately stout, 1.5–2 mm (0.1 in). *Buds* Hidden in axils of the scale leaves. *Foliage* In flat spreading sprays, side sprays at a wide acute to right angle to the shoot, forming side sprays about 20 × 15 cm (8 × 6 in); leaves with markedly different facial and lateral pairs, laterals thick, 1.5–2 mm (0.1 in), incurved, blunt, coming together below the facial pair, facial pair small, 1 mm (0.1 in), bluntly pointed, on whip-like extension growths; the leaf tips are spreading, acute with free tips 1 mm (0.1 in); dark green with few or no stomata above, below with waxy silvery white stomatal bands at the margins of the scale leaves and otherwise shiny mid green; crushed foliage with resinous scent. *Flowers* On previous season's growths in late winter; male cones globular dark brown dots 1 mm (0.1 in); female cones yellow-green. *Fruit* Globose, with eight to ten scales which have a small central ridge, yellow-green, ripening in first autumn to orange-brown, 1–1.2 cm (0.4–0.5 in).

Range: Central and southern Japan from south Honshu, Kyushu and Shikoku.

Habitat: Cultivated in Europe as an ornamental, in Japan forming mountain forests and widely planted in forestry.

Varieties: It has produced a large number of cultivars, most of which are dwarf forms. Amongst the tree selections are: 'Crippsii' which has foliage bright gold in colour and forms a broad conical tree to 15 m (50 ft), 'Aurea' is similar but not such a good gold, becoming green in shade; 'Tetragona Aurea' has golden-yellow to bronze-yellow foliage and the leaves arranged in four-sided sprays with the distinction between lateral and facial pairs lost, and can make a tree to 10 m (33 ft).

Synonyms: *Cupressus obtusa.*

Similar species: *C. taiwanensis*, a related taxon from northern and central Taiwan, which is also treated as a variety, var. *formosana*. It has rich shiny green foliage and smaller cones. In Taiwan it makes an enormous tree, to 60 m (200 ft) and 6 m (20 ft) in bole diameter.

Hinoki Cypress has a first quality red timber but is grown as an amenity tree in Europe. It is attractive for the flat sprays which have silvery white lines between the scales beneath, and can be easily separated from other *Chamaecyparis* by the blunt and rounded leaf apices.

---

p.41 **Sawara Cypress** *Chamaecyparis pisifera*

Description: Evergreen tree to 20 m (65 ft) with a bole diameter of up to 1 m (3.3 ft).
Crown Conical, relatively open with horizontal spreading branches and a nodding leading shoot. *Bark* Red-brown, occasionally grey, smooth but becoming regularly and deeply fissured with broad ridges which are finely peeling.
Shoot Light or yellow-green for first winter, becoming pale red-brown to brown.
Buds Hidden in axils of the scale leaves.
Foliage In spreading rather flat and crowded sprays, one year lateral sprays to 7 × 3 cm (2.8 × 1.2 in), mid shiny green above, paler with whitish waxy stomatal bands between the scale leaves beneath; leaves with only slight differences between facial and lateral pairs, dorsal glands obscure, apex acute but incurved, not pressed on shoot and usually partly free at tip, 1.5–4 mm (0.1–0.2 in), on whip-like extension shoots with free tips to 2 mm

(0.1 in) and to 8 mm (0.3 in); crushed foliage with a sharp, slightly menthol-like resin scent. *Flowers* On previous season's shoots in early spring; male cones globose black dots, 1 mm (0.1 in). *Fruit* Globose, angular, carried either within the body of the flat sprays or slightly nodding, scales 8–12, dimpled with a minute spine in the centre, 5–7 mm (0.2–0.3 in), green with a waxy white bloom, ripening to bright brown in first autumn.

Range: Japan, from Honshu and Kyushu.

Habitat: Cultivated as an ornamental in Europe, in the wild forming forests in mountain districts.

Varieties: Cultivars include: 'Aurea', with bright gold new foliage. The group, typified by 'Filifera', have whip-like branches which hang down as a weeping loose curtain, with few side shoots. 'Filifera' will make a tree 15–20 m (50–65 ft), with dark green foliage, whilst 'Filifera Aurea' has golden yellow foliage and is slow growing, to 12 m (39 ft). The 'Plumosa' group have partially juvenile foliage, with free tips to the leaves in the range 2–4 mm (0.1–0.2 in). In 'Plumosa' the foliage is yellowish grey-green, and it makes a conic or broadly columnar tree to 20 m (65 ft), with a rounded top. In the 'Squarrosa' group, the foliage remains juvenile, i.e. the leaves are acicular or needle-like (but very soft to the touch in these plants) with free tips 5–7 mm (0.2–0.3 in) long. 'Squarrosa' makes a broad crowned tree to 20 m (65 ft) with blue-grey foliage, only marred by the persistent dead brown old foliage. 'Boulevard' is a sport which is an improvement as a young plant, with silvery blue foliage, but which quickly deteriorates except on moist sites.

Synonyms: *Cupressus pisifera.*

The tree does not like dry sites but requires moist soil and preferably a moist climate; on dry sites, it is apt to lose the old foliage, which becomes brown and mars the appearance of the tree. It has produced a wide range of cultivars, as noted above.

p.40 **White Cypress** or **Atlantic White-cedar**
Chamaecyparis thyoides

Description: Evergreen tree 10–15 m (33–50 ft) with a
bole diameter of up to 60 cm (2 ft).
Crown Conical or spire-like, with short
horizontal branches and pendent shoot
tips. *Bark* Reddish brown or grey-
brown, thin, developing interconnecting
ridges which peel in fibrous strips.
Shoot Green in first winter, then red-
brown and later dull brown, slender,
1 mm (0.1 in). *Buds* Hidden in axils of
the scale leaves. *Foliage* In irregular
sprays, with small fine sprays which are
flat and 4 × 3 cm (1.6–1.2 in) arranged
at an angle of 45–60 degrees to the
shoot, retained for two years and not
covering the shoots; scale leaves with
acute incurved tips and a prominent
dorsal gland, which in old leaves may
become a raised pimple of brown resin,
grey-green, scales on fine shoots
1–1.5 mm (0.1 in), to 1 cm (0.4 in) on
extension shoots. *Flowers* On previous
season's growths in late winter; male
cones globular, brown, 1 mm (0.1 in).
Fruit Globular, bluish purple and very
glaucous, ripening in first autumn to
dark red-brown, with 6 scales each with
a small prickle, 6 mm (0.25 in).

Range: Eastern USA from Maine south to Georgia.

Habitat: Cultivated in Europe as an ornamental, in
the wild found in swamps along the
Atlantic coast.

Varieties: Three cultivars which are often cultivated
are 'Andelyensis', with a tight conical
habit, 'Glauca', similar in habit but more
glaucous foliage, and 'Variegata', in which
there are large patches of yellow in the
foliage.

Synonyms: *Cupressus thyoides*.

Similar species: *C. henryae* is a related taxon found along the
Gulf coast from Florida to Mississippi. It is
also treated as a variety. It differs in the
bark which has shallower fissures more
spirally arranged, the paler green and
longer scale leaves and the larger less-
glaucous cones.

The angled fine sprays are very characteristic.
It is the hardiest of the cypress and tolerates
very boggy conditions. It is, however, slow
growing and rarely makes a large tree.

EUROPEAN FAN PALM, *CHAMAEROPS*
FAMILY PALMAE

This is a monotypic genus which is similar in appearance to
Trachycarpus, sharing with it the fan-shaped leaves and the
fibrous base of the leaf stalk. It differs botanically in the
stamens being united into a tube, whilst in *Trachycarpus*
they are free, and in the leaf stalk being armed with spines.

---

p.349 **European Fan Palm** *Chamaerops humilis*

Description: Evergreen shrub or tree to 5 m (16 ft) with
a bole diameter to 25 cm (10 in).
Crown Shrubby, with several erect
monopodal stems. *Bark* Covered with
reddish brown, white or grey fibres from the
sheaths of the leaves, true bark grey.
Foliage Palmate, round, to 1 m (3.3 ft) in
diameter, with stiff and deeply divided
lanceolate segments with a single rib, held
erect or spreading, green, grey-green or
bluish; leaf stalk long, stout, with
conspicuous spines. *Flowers* Dioecious, but
occasionally with a few flowers of the
opposite sex on the inflorescence which is
subtended by a large basal bract and smaller
bracts at the base of the branches; flowers
single but packed close together, golden-
yellow. *Fruit* Rounded, maturing to
reddish brown with a rancid fleshy covering.

Range: Western Mediterranean region, usually near
the coast.

Habitat: Dry hillsides.

This makes a small shrub, sometimes
forming a distinct tree but usually less than
2 m (6.6 ft). It develops a series of shoots,
unlike most other tree palms which have
only a single growing point. It is similar in
many respect to *Trachycarpus*, which has
only a single stem and less-pronounced
spines on the leaf stalks.

GOLDEN CHINKAPIN OR GOLDEN CHESTNUT, *CHRYSOLEPIS* (SYNONYM: *CASTANOPSIS* IN PART)
FAMILY FAGACEAE

This is a small genus of two species from California and Oregon. It has been placed in *Castanopsis* in the past but does not belong in this large warm temperate Asian genus and is really intermediate between *Castanea* and *Castanopsis*. The leaves are evergreen and golden haired beneath. The fruits are in a cluster of three nuts but with seven free cupule valves, five around the perimeter and one between each pair of nuts. The female flowers are borne at the base of the male catkins, a character which it shares with *Castanea* (there are separate male and female flowers in *Castanopsis*).

p.160 **Golden Chinkapin** or **Golden Chestnut**
Chrysolepis chrysophylla

Description: Evergreen spreading shrub or tree 15–30 m (50–100 ft) with a bole diameter to 1.5 m (5 ft).
Crown Spreading or domed. *Bark* Grey, smooth in young trees, becoming reddish brown and deeply fissuring into plates, with a bright red inner bark.
Shoot Greeny brown and slender for the first winter, initially with a scurfy covering of hairs, then dark reddish brown.
Buds Ovoid to ovoid-conic, with free scales which are light brown where exposed but green where covered (until exposed by expansion in the spring), 1 × 6 mm (0.1 × 0.25 in). *Foliage* Variable in shape from ovate through lanceolate to obovate, tapered at both ends to a slender point or sometimes rounded at the apex, leathery, margins entire, mid glossy green above, golden beneath due to the thick covering of hairs, 5–13 × 1.5–4 cm (2–5.1 × 0.6–1.6 in); leaf stalk light yellow-green 1–1.5 cm (0.4–0.6 in). *Flowers* On current season's growths in mid summer, in upright spike-like catkins to 6 cm (2.4 in) with many whitish male flowers, to 3 mm (0.1 in), and usually two female flowers at the base. *Fruit* Expanding in the second summer to a rounded globose prickly burr 2.5–4 cm (1–1.6 in) across

and golden or yellow-brown, containing three triangular edible nuts, each 1.2–1.5 cm (0.5–0.6 in).

Range: Oregon and California, mainly along the coastal ranges.

Habitat: Cultivated in Europe as an ornamental, in the wild occurring on rock slopes on gravelly soils.

Synonyms: *Castanea chrysophylla*, *Castanopsis chrysophylla*.

This makes a very attractive tree with the golden undersides to the leaves. It is similar to *Quercus alnifolia* but this has toothed leaves which are nearly as broad as long and fruits which are acorns.

CITRUS FRUITS, *CITRUS*
FAMILY RUTACEAE

This is a genus of around 16 species (although one revision has only three species and makes the rest complex hybrids) from warm temperate Asia. They are widely cultivated as citrus fruits. Botanically, these are curious structures, also called 'hesperides'. They have 8–15 segments within the pithy rind. The flesh is juicy due to inflated hair cells (except in one Chinese species which is cultivated for the not particularly edible pith!). The leaves have the translucent glands typical of the Rutaceae. In some species, however, the leaf stalk is strongly winged with a distinct joint where it meets the leaf blade, *see C. paradisii*, but in *CC. deliciosa*, *limon* and *sinensis* it is only narrowly winged and in *C. medica* it is not winged. The flowers have 20 stamens in *CC. deliciosa* and *sinensis*, and more than 20 stamens in *CC. limon*, *medica* and *paradisii*.

---

p.230 **Tangerine** or **Mandarin Orange**
Citrus deliciosa

Description: Evergreen small tree to 8 m (26 ft). *Crown* Low, spreading. *Shoot* Green, slender, with axillary spines. *Buds* Small. *Foliage* Leaves narrow elliptic, apex acute, base wedge-shaped, margin wavy, lustrous dark green above, underside paler and dull, circa 10 cm (4 in); leaf stalk very narrowly winged. *Flowers* Solitary or in small

clusters; flowers white, 3 cm (1.2 in), with twenty stamens and five petals.
Fruit Depressed globose, often indented at both ends, with a loose easily-removed thin rind, orange, fragrant, with a sweet pulp, 5–7.5 cm (2–3 in).

Range: Southern China to Vietnam.

Habitat: Cultivated as a fruit tree.

Varieties: The Clementine is a hybrid of the Tangerine and the Seville Orange.

Synonyms: *C. reticulata, C. nobilis.*

The Tangerine has the sweetest flesh of the citrus fruits, and is easily extracted from the rind or peel. An essential oil can be distilled from the rind.

p.231 **Lemon** *Citrus limon*

Description: Evergreen tree to 3–6 m (10–20 ft).
Crown Low, spreading, dense, often on several stems. *Bark* Coarsely fissured and greyish in old trees. *Shoot* Green, spotted with glands, angular when young but soon terete, with stout axillary spines, hairless. *Buds* Small. *Foliage* Leaves elliptic to broadly elliptic, apex acute, base wedge-shaped, margin with crenate or serrate teeth, lustrous dark green above, underside paler and dull, circa 10 cm (4 in) (to 15 cm (6 in)); leaf stalk narrowly winged, distinctly articulated at the junction with the blade. *Flowers* Solitary or in short sparse racemes; flowers white, of two types, hermaphrodite and male, with 25–40 stamens, petals five, white on the inside, flushed or streaked purple on the outside, carried throughout the year.
Fruit Oblong to ovoid, with a nipple-like apex, yellow, ripening from green, with 8–10 segments, 6.5–12.5 cm (2.6–4.9 in), rind rough to smooth, flesh acid, ripening throughout the year.

Range: Eastern Asia.

Habitat: Cultivated as a fruit tree.

Similar species: **Sweet Lime** *C. limetta* (p.231) is very similar, differing in the pure white flowers and the smaller greenish-yellow fruit. It has an insipid sweet flesh. It possibly derived as a mutation of the lemon.

This is the lemon of commerce, with its acid fruit rich in vitamin C. Its origin is lost in antiquity, having been cultivated for over 2000 years. It is tender, and only grows in the mildest regions.

p.232 **Citron** *Citrus medica*

Description: Evergreen small tree.
Shoot Angular when young, soon becoming round or terete, hairless with short stout axillary spines. *Buds* Small. *Foliage* Leaves elliptic-ovate to ovate-lanceolate, margin crenate or serrate, veins prominent on both sides; leaf stalk terete or with narrow margins but not winged. *Flowers* In short racemes, hermaphrodite or male, with many stamens set in clusters of four or more. *Fruit* Ovoid-cylindric, with a large nipple-like projection, rind rough, very thick and warty, ripening to yellow, with a pale green or yellow flesh which is sweetish or sharp, 15–25 cm (6–10 in).

Habitat: Cultivated as a fruit tree.

This is probably a progenitor of the lemon.

p.232 **Grapefruit** *Citrus paradisii*

Description: Evergreen tree, occasionally to 15 m (50 ft). *Crown* Rounded or conical, broad, with branches pendulous at the tips.
Shoot Angular, hairless with stout axillary spines. *Buds* Small. *Foliage* Leaves broad elliptic, apex subacute, base rounded or sometimes heart-shaped, midrib hairless, glossy green, 8–15 cm (3.1–6 in); leaf stalk broadly winged, to 1.5 cm (0.6 in), wings inversely heart-shaped (obcordate), tapering towards the base. *Flowers* In axillary clusters or terminal racemes; flowers to 5 cm (2 in), opening February to April, with 20–25 stamens. *Fruit* Depressed

globose to slightly pear-shaped, 10–15 cm (4–6 in) across; rind smooth, thick, pale yellow, pulp juicy, sharp to mild, with large coarse cells.

Range: Uncertain, possibly a hybrid which has arisen in cultivation.

Habitat: Cultivated as a fruit tree.

Similar species: **Shaddock** or **Pomelo** *C. grandis* (syn. *C. maxima*) (p.232) makes a less spiny tree. The shoots and midrib of the leaves are hairy, the leaf stalk less widely winged and the fruit to 25 cm (10 in) across. As the cells within the segments are smaller, the flesh is less grainy.

Ichang Lemon *C. ichangensis* (p.231) has even more pronounced winged leaf stalks, which are nearly as large as the leaf blade. The fruit is lemon shaped, and 7–10 cm (2.8–4 in). It is the hardiest *Citrus* species, surviving outdoors in southern England. It comes from northern central China.

This grapefruit is better able to withstand wind than most other citrus fruits.

---

p.230 **Orange** or **Sweet Orange** *Citrus sinensis*

Description: Evergreen tree to 10 m (33 ft).
Crown Rounded, dense, with horizontal branches. *Bark* Greyish. *Shoot* Green, with glands, angular when young but soon terete, with some slender flexible axillary spines. *Buds* Small. *Foliage* Leaves oblanceolate to ovate, apex acute, base wedge-shaped, lustrous dark green above with yellow spots where there are translucent glands, underside paler, to 15 cm (6 in); leaf stalk narrowly winged, wings oblanceolate, twice as long as wide. *Flowers* White, very fragrant, solitary or in short sparse racemes from February to April; flowers 3 cm (1.2 in) across, with five petals and about twenty stamens. *Fruit* Globose to short ovoid, orange or yellowish, ripening from green, with 10–13 segments, 7–9 cm (2.8–3.5 in), rind smooth, flesh sweet, ripening from October to June.

Range: Eastern China.

Habitat: Cultivated as a fruit tree.

Similar species: **Seville Orange** *C. aurantium* (p.230) can make a tree to 15 m (50 ft). It differs in the following respects. The leaves are 7.5–10 cm (3–4 in), broadly elliptic in outline with a sub-acute apex and wedge-shaped to rounded at the base. The wings or flanges on the leaf stalk are obovate in outline, tapering towards the wingless base. The fruit is sub-globose and flattened at both ends, with a thick rough rind and a bitter acid pulp in 10–12 segments. The core of the fruit is hollow when ripe. It is the traditional orange used in the manufacture of English marmalade. An oil used in perfumery (neroli oil) is distilled from the rind, whilst another essential oil, petitigrain, is obtained from the leaves and shoots.

Bergamot Orange *C. bergamia* (p.231) has leaves oblong-ovate with slightly winged leaf stalks. The flowers have ten stamens. The fruit is yellow-orange, with 10–15 segments and an inedible flesh. It is cultivated in Calabria for 'Oil of Bergamot' which is extracted from the thick rind. The oil is the flavouring in Earl Grey tea, and is also an essential ingredient in Eau de Cologne.

This is the commercial orange, with its sweet juicy flesh and only slightly bitter rind. The flowers and fruit are carried on the tree at the same time.

YELLOW-WOODS, *CLADRASTIS*
FAMILY LEGUMINOSAE

This genus has one species in North America and five in Asia from Japan, China to the eastern Himalayas. The leaves are pinnate, not toothed, and rather alternate along the rachis. The base of the leaf stalk is enlarged, enclosing the buds (of which there are two or more together). The flowers are pea-like, in hanging or spreading panicles and are followed by compressed pods. The wood is yellow. The descriptive scientific name is derived from the Greek and translates as 'brittle shoot'.

p.337 **Yellow-wood** *Cladrastis kentukea*

Description: Deciduous tree to 20 m (65 ft) with a bole
diameter to 50 cm (1.6 ft).
Crown Rounded with spreading branches.
Bark Grey and smooth, resembling *Fagus*.
Shoot Shiny dark, almost purplish, brown,
lacking a terminal bud, in the second year
greyer and dull. *Buds* Conic, dark brown
with naked hairy leaves, 4 mm (0.2 in),
enclosed in bulbous base of leaf stalk at
first. *Foliage* Leaves pinnate, 20–30 cm
(8–12 in), with seven or nine (rarely five or
eleven) spaced leaflets which are set
alternately along the rachis and tend to
increase in size towards the apex; leaflets
broad ovate, obovate to nearly rotund,
apex abruptly short with a slender point,
base broad wedge-shaped to nearly
rounded, with a distinct leaflet stalk of
6–8 mm (0.25–0.3 in), margin untoothed,
upper surface shiny green with impressed
midrib and about ten pairs of veins,
underside pale to whitish green with hairs
on the raised veins and midrib, 6–13 ×
3–7 cm (2.4–5.1 × 1.2–2.8 in); leaf stalk
and rachis round, green with dark brown
warts, base enlarged and enclosing the
bud; autumn colour yellow to gold.
Flowers In pendulous terminal clusters to
30 cm (12 in) in late spring, white, pea-
like, fragrant. *Fruit* In pendent narrow
flat oblong pods 5–8 cm (2–3.1 in),
ripening in autumn and falling unopened,
seeds two to six.

Range: Eastern USA from Virginia, North Carolina
and Georgia across to Oklahoma and north
to Indiana.

Habitat: Cultivated as an ornamental, in the wild
occurring in broadleaved forests on moist
soils.

Synonyms: *C. lutea, C. tinctoria*.

This tree rarely flowers in Britain but is an
attractive sight for the pleasant foliage and
bark. The leaves completely enclose the
bud in the base of the leaf stalk. They turn
golden-yellow in autumn. The Latin name
is derived from the Greek, meaning 'brittle

branch'. The common name comes from the colour of the wood of freshly felled trees, which is yellow, but ripens to light brown. A yellow dye can be made from the wood.

---

p.337   **Chinese Cladrastis** *Cladrastis sinensis*

Description: Deciduous tree to 12 m (39 ft), possibly taller, with a bole diameter to 40 cm (1.3 ft).
Crown Spreading. *Shoot* Green at first with rusty hairs. *Buds* Naked and small, several together (superposed) and hidden in the enlarged leaf base until autumn. *Foliage* Leaves pinnate, with 9–15 leaflets which are usually alternate along the round and hairy rachis; leaflets ovate-elliptic to oblong-lanceolate, apex acute or slender pointed, base rounded to wedge-shaped, margin untoothed, green and hairless above, underside grey-green or glaucous with rusty hairs on the midrib, 4.5–10 × 2–3.5 cm (1.8–4 × 0.8–1.4 in); leaf stalk enlarged at base and hiding buds. *Flowers* In erect much-branched conical panicles 12–30 cm (4.7–12 in) long, with showy pea-like flowers in July; petals pinkish purple or white, to 1 cm (0.4 in). *Fruit* Pod linear-oblong, persisting unopened for some time, 4–8 × 1 cm (1.6–3.1 × 0.4 in), with four to six seeds.
Range: Central China from Sichuan and Hubei south into Yunnan and west along the Himalayas to central Bhutan.
Habitat: Cultivated as an ornamental, in the wild occurring as a component of broadleaved forest.

This charming tree is most attractive in July when it is bedecked with the impressive flowers. These are more showy than in *C. lutea* as they are erect, not drooping. The smaller and more numerous leaflets, which are fairly even in size, distinguish it from *C. lutea* when it is not in flower.

Virgin's Bower, *Clematis*
Family Ranunculaceae

This is a large genus of woody climbers with a few herbaceous species. Some, especially the species featured here, can develop stems 15 cm (6 in) in thickness but they are only 'trees' by reason of their clambering over trees. The flowers have four or more sepals and a mass of stamens, but no petals. A number of single-seeded fruits or achenes develop, with the style elongating and becoming feathery-hairy to assist wind dispersal of the seed. The leaves are variable, usually trifoliate, pinnate or bi-pinnate, but occasionally simple; in one New Zealand species, they are dispensed with and photosynthesis is carried out by the green shoots. The leaves and buds are in opposite pairs on the shoots.

p.314 **Old Man's Beard** or **Traveller's Joy**
Clematis vitalba

Description: Deciduous climber 10–20 m (33–65 ft), occasionally developing stems to 15 cm (6 in) in diameter.
Crown Depends upon support.
Bark Brown, fibrous and stringy.
Shoot Ribbed, downy when young, ripening brown. *Buds* In opposite pairs.
Foliage Leaves 8–20 cm (3.1–8 in), pinnate with five leaflets but the basal pair sometimes trifoliate; leaflets ovate to lanceolate, apex acute, base rounded to heart-shaped with a short leaflet stalk, margin untoothed to coarsely toothed, variably downy on both surfaces, 2.5–10 cm (1–4 in). *Flowers* In panicles of 8–13 cm (3.1–5.1 in) in late summer, carried in the leaf axils; flowers dull white with four strap-like sepals, to 2 cm (0.8 in) across, with a faint aroma of almonds. *Fruit* Cluster of achenes forming a globular head which becomes a tufted ball when fully ripe; seeds with a long feathery plume-like style which acts as the dispersal agent.
Range: Widely distributed across Europe and Asia.
Habitat: Woods and hedgerows, especially on calcareous soils.
Varieties: Many species of *Clematis* are native or cultivated, although few are as vigorous as *C. vitalba*.

Similar species: *C. montana* from the Himalayas and west
China has flowers which are white to pinkish
in spring, before the trifoliate leaves.
C. armandii has leaves evergreen and
trifoliate, with oblong-lanceolate to ovate
leaflets 8–15 cm (3.1–6 in) which are
prominently three veined and a lustrous
green. The flowers are carried in dense
axillary clusters in spring. It is a native to
central and western China.

This climber only scrambles over other
plants, or in the absence of these over rocks
and boulders. It can swamp trees, especially
in young plantations, and can be a nuisance
on chalk sites. When it grows over a
vigorous support, stems 15–20 cm (6–8 in)
in thickness are produced. It is not showy
in flower, although not without charm, but
becomes more prominent from autumn
until well into the winter, as the fluffy hairs
on the styles spread out, giving an
appearance of a hoary beard.

CHANCE TREE, *CLERODENDRUM*
FAMILY VERBENACEAE

This is a large genus of mainly tropical and warm
temperate herbs, shrubs, climbers and trees. Only one
species is listed here.

---

p.171   **Chance Tree** *Clerodendrum trichotomum*

Description: Deciduous shrub or tree to 6 m (20 ft) with
a slender bole to 25 cm (10 in).
Crown Open, with tiered level branches,
sometimes with suckers from the roots.
Bark Brown, fissured with orange.
Shoot Green or grey-green with brownish
hairs and oval raised lenticels, becoming
shiny, buff and hairless in the second year,
brittle. *Buds* In opposite pairs, conical,
pointed, dark or chocolate brown, 2 mm
(0.1 in). *Foliage* Leaves ovate to oblong-
ovate, apex abruptly slender pointed, base
broad wedge-shaped to somewhat rounded,
margin wavy, entire or with faint rounded

teeth, upper surface matt green with erect simple hairs and slightly impressed veins, underside light green with raised veins which are covered with curly hairs, 5–22 × 4–12 cm (2–8.7 × 1.6–4.7 in); leaf stalk grooved, green, with a dense covering of curly hairs, 2–6 cm (0.8–2.4 in); autumn colour poor, crushed foliage with a foetid odour. *Flowers* In July to September, terminal on the current season's growths in cymes and strongly fragrant, calyx five lobed with the lobes forming ridges where they meet, pink or purple, slightly hairy, corolla with a slender tubular base circa 1.5 cm (0.6 in) which is pinkish, ovoid in bud, opening with five linear to obovate white reflexed petals 1–1.5 cm × 5–7 mm (0.4–0.6 × 0.2–0.3 in), stamens four, long projecting on slender filaments, anthers oval, chocolate brown, style slender with a small green pointed swelling, 4–5 cm (1.6–2 in). *Fruit* Globose drupe, bright blue, ripening to black, 6–10 mm (0.25–0.4 in), shown off by the persistent crimson calyx lobes which enlarge and become fleshy.

Range: Widely distributed in eastern Asia from Central China northeast to Manchuria, Korea, throughout Japan and south along the Ryukyus to Taiwan and the Philippines.

Habitat: Cultivated as an ornamental, in the wild occurring in woods and thickets.

Varieties: Var. *fargesii* occurs in Sichuan, west China. It differs in the leaves which are glossy green and nearly hairless on both sides, in the greyish almost hairless shoots and in the calyx lobes which are green at the time of flowering.

This delightful small tree is valued for its fragrant late-summer flowers and the even more spectacular fruits which are often turquoise, contrasting strongly with the crimson calyx lobes. It may sucker. The Scientific or Latin name is derived from the Greek *kleros* (chance or fortune) and *dendron* (tree) and refers to the name given to the first species found in the genus in Ceylon (Sri Lanka).

BLADDER SENNAS, *COLUTEA*
FAMILY LEGUMINOSAE

This small genus, which can be found from the
Mediterranean region south into Africa and east to China,
has pinnate leaves and pea-like flowers typical of the
Leguminosae family. The fruit, however, is not typical.
It is a thin-walled inflated bladder rather than a typical
legume pod and is similar to the (unrelated) fruits of
Koelreuteria and *Staphylea*.

---

p.337 **Bladder Senna** *Colutea arborescens*

Description: Deciduous shrub or small tree to 4–6 m
(13–20 ft).
Crown Dense, shrubby and much
branched. *Bark* Grey-green. *Shoot* Grey
or yellowish grey, slender, becoming
brown later. *Buds* Minute.
Foliage Leaves 7–15 cm (2.8–6 in),
pinnate with four to six pairs of short
stalked (1–2 mm (0.1 in)) oval leaflets
which are notched at the tip and rounded
at the base, margin untoothed, upper
surface grey-green, smooth, underside
paler, with stiff whitish hairs pressed
against the shoot, 1.2–2.5 × 1 cm (0.2–1
× 0.4 in); leaf stalk with dry lanceolate
stipules at the base, rachis grooved, green
with sparse white hairs; autumn colour
yellow. *Flowers* In racemes, carried in the
leaf axils as the shoot expands in early
summer, flowers pea-like, yellow, 2 cm
(0.8 in). *Fruit* Inflated bladder-like
translucent green, white or brown pod of
5–6 cm (2–2.4 in) with a short pointed
beak, containing a number of kidney
shaped brown seeds each on an individual
stalk of 2 mm (0.1 in).
Range: Mediterranean region and more widely in
southeast Europe.
Habitat: Dry, open situations.

Rarely making a tree, this is usually a large
shrub. It naturalized outside its native
range on disturbed banks, and is used in
gardens for the showy flowers and curious
bladder-like fruits.

DAISIES, COMPOSITAE (SYNONYM: ASTERACEAE)

This is a very large family containing over 21,000 species with a cosmopolitan distribution. In Europe, they are nearly all herbs or shrubs, and only one small tree is featured here (*Olearia paniculata*; p.863). The defining characters of the family are the daisy flower, which is a cluster of single flowers surrounded by a ring of 'petals', and the fruit which has a ring of hairs (a 'pappus') to assist wind distribution.

CABBAGE TREES, *CORDYLINE*
FAMILY AGAVACEAE

This genus comes from India south and east to New Zealand and contains 15 species. They are monocots, as indicated by the leaves which have parallel veins. The fragrant flowers have six lobes to the corolla and six stamens, and are carried in large terminal panicles. The fruit is a globose black berry and contains several seeds. The various species are used as amenity plants.

---

p.351 **Cabbage Tree** *Cordyline australis*

Description: Evergreen tree to 10–15 m (33–50 ft) with a stout stem.
Crown Composed of a few erect branches, with basal suckers. *Bark* Fawn-grey, rough from fine fissured, becoming furrowed with deep corky ridges. *Shoot* Stout, buried beneath the living or persistent dead leaves. *Buds* Hidden. *Foliage* Leaves spiral around the shoot, erect when young, drooping when dead and brown, linear to linear-lanceolate, tapering to a sharp slender point, margin untoothed, upper surface dark green, cupped and tough with many parallel veins, 30–90 × 2.5–8 cm (12–36 × 1–3.1 in). *Flowers* In large terminal panicles 60–120 × 30–60 cm (24–48 × 12–24 in); flowers creamy white, fragrant, 1 cm (0.4 in). *Fruit* Globose berry, white or bluish white, 6 mm (0.25 in), and containing many small black seeds.

Range: New Zealand.

Habitat: Cultivated as an ornamental in southern and western districts.

Synonyms: *Dracaena australis*.

Similar species: *C. indivisa* is similar, differing in the large leaves 0.9–1.8 m × 10–15 cm (2.9–5.9 ft × 4–6 in) which are green above and glaucous beneath. The fruit is purplish blue. It is also a native of New Zealand and only hardy in mild districts.

This has large sword-like leaves and a palm-like appearance. In cold districts, it gets cut back by frost.

DOGWOOD, CORNACEAE

This family includes the various segregate genera of *Cornus*, see *Benthamidia* (p.518), *Cornus* and *Swida* (p.1188). These are disparate in flower and fruit characters but uniform in vegetative ones. The family may also be used for a number of other genera which are otherwise placed in monotypic families (the only of these which is featured here is *Aucuba* (p.515) in the Aucubaceae).

CORNELS, *CORNUS*
FAMILY CORNACEAE

In the treatment adopted here, the genus *Cornus* is restricted to the typical Cornelian cherry group. This comprises four species centred on *C. mas*, which is the only one commonly encountered in cultivation. They are distinguished by the flowers being in dense umbels with a yellow involucre which falls away as they open in spring before the leaves, and the fruit being an oblong drupe. The flowers lack the large petal-like bracts of *Benthamidia*. The fruits have a tasty flesh which is used for culinary purposes. The alternative treatment is to use *Cornus* in the wide sense, including *Swida* and *Benthamidia*. The leaves of *Cornus* are in opposite pairs (except in two species of *Swida*) and have spaced veins which curve forwards parallel to the leaf margin; they are thus closer to the midrib at top and bottom of the leaf than in the centre. The hairs are often pressed down on the blade and attached in the centre. If a leaf is carefully torn in half, a rubber-like latex from the veins will keep the two halves attached.

p.144 **Cornelian Cherry** *Cornus mas*

Description: Deciduous tree or large shrub to 8–15 m
(26–50 ft) with a bole diameter to 30 cm
(1 ft).
Crown Spreading, often on several stems
and shrubby, less often on a single trunk.
Bark Grey-brown, becoming scaly.
Shoot Green or purplish pink for the first
two or three years, then dark brown or
grey-brown, with a dense covering of flat
grey hairs, slender. *Buds* In opposite
pairs, ovoid-pointed but flattened and
cylindrical from the side, beaked,
purplish or green with grey flat hairs,
2–5 mm (0.1–0.2 in). *Foliage* Oval to
elliptic with an abrupt tip, veins in three
to five pairs, prominent below and curve
forwards, margins entire, mid to dark
green above, shiny pale green beneath,
4–10 × 2–4 cm (1.6–4 × 0.8–1.6 in).
Flowers From buds on the bare twigs of
the previous season, in clusters of 10–25
flowers on a silvery hairy stalk; to 4 mm
(0.2 in), with four yellow bracts and four
stamens. *Fruit* Ripening in the first
autumn, ovoid, 1.5–2 cm (0.6–0.8 in),
but to 4 cm (1.6 in) in some forms
cultivated for fruit, pendulous, fleshy,
ripening through green to cherry red,
containing a single oblong seed.

Range: Southern Europe to western Asia.

Habitat: Banks and wood edges, especially on
calcareous soils.

Varieties: Two garden selections with variegated
foliage are 'Aurea Elegantissima', leaves
with a yellow or sometimes pink margin,
and 'Variegata' with creamy-white patches.

It was, before the introduction of *Hamamelis
mollis*, widely planted as a late-winter
flowering tree when its yellow flowers give
a strong haze to the bush or tree. The fruits
have a pleasant acid flavour when ripe and
can be used to make jams or syrups.
Selected forms cultivated in the Ukraine
have fruits 3.5–4 cm (1.4–1.6 in). The
wood is tough and was formerly used for
small domestic utensils.

HAZELS OR COBNUTS, *CORYLUS*
FAMILY BETULACEAE (CORYLACEAE)

The distinguishing feature of this small genus, which is widely distributed in the northern hemisphere, is the fruit. This is a large nut enclosed within a bony case and sitting, until ripe, within a leafy involucre or cup. The male catkins are formed in the autumn and exposed over winter. They expand in late winter and hang down. The female flowers are wind pollinated. They have a number of small, usually bright red, stigmas – and are quite attractive when viewed through a hand lens! The species of hazel divide into two groups on the basis of their stature and habit. *C. colurna* and its relatives make medium-to-large trees, but the larger part of the genus is composed of shrubs rather than true trees. This group can be divided on the basis of the involucre. In *C. avellana* and similar species, the involucre forms an open cup, with the nut visible, but in other species, it more resembles a glove or a sock and conceals the nut (although the involucre is always open at the tip).

p.190 **Hazel** or **Cobnut** *Corylus avellana*

Description: Deciduous shrub or rarely a small tree 8–10 m (26–33 ft) with a bole diameter to 40 cm (1.3 ft).
Crown Rounded, domed, usually on several stems. *Bark* Light brown, slightly peeling in young growths, becoming smooth and grey-brown in old stems. *Shoot* Pale brown with reddish or whitish lenticels, hairy with a short dense covering and a smaller number of long glandular hairs, becoming hairless and smooth in the second year. *Buds* Obovoid, rounded or bluntly pointed, with green scales. *Foliage* Rounded to obovate, base heart-shaped, apex slender pointed, margin lobed in the lower half and sharply serrate, downy, especially below, mid green, turning yellow in autumn, 5–10 × 4–8 cm (2–4 × 1.6–3.1 in); leaf stalk glandular hairy, 6–12 mm (0.25–0.5 in). *Flowers* On previous season's shoots in late winter; male catkins formed in autumn and exposed over winter, expanding after Christmas to 4–8 cm (1.6–3.1 in), yellow to lemon-yellow, pendulous and hairy under a lens; female

flowers from buds in central portion of
shoot, with only the 12–15 crimson-to-
purple stigmas exposed 1–2 mm (0.1 in).
Fruit Nut 1.5–2 cm (0.6–0.8 in), chestnut
brown, ripening in first autumn and
enclosed in a green-toothed leafy husk
which ripens to brown.

Range: Across Europe to Turkey and North Africa.
Habitat: Woodlands.
Varieties: 'Contorta' has the twigs twisted and curled.

This small tree or large bush is a frequent
understorey plant in woodlands across
Europe. It has been managed by coppicing
for centuries, whereby the plants are cut
down every 12–15 years for the pliant
shoots which are split to make hurdles. The
nut is edible and an important food for
squirrels and woodpeckers.

---

p.190 **Turkish Hazel** *Corylus colurna*

Description: Deciduous tree 15–25 m (50–80 ft) with a
bole diameter to 1 m (3.3 ft).
Crown Conical or columnar, regular, with
short spreading branches. *Bark* Ash-grey
or buff-brown, scaly in thin flecks when
young, in old trees in thicker plates and
fissured. *Shoot* Green-brown or brown in
first year with short pale hairs and longer
gland-tipped hairs, buff-brown, hairless
and starting to peel in second year, lenticels
few, boat-shaped. *Buds* Ovoid, pale brown.
Foliage Leaves round, oval or ovate, margin
lobulate with double bluntly-pointed teeth,
ciliate, apex short and slender pointed or
acute, base deeply heart-shaped, main veins
in 6–10 pairs, upper surface mid green,
sub-shiny, beneath light green, softly
downy on both sides, 7–13 × 6–14 cm
(2.8–5.1 × 2.4–5.5 in); leaf stalk downy
and glandular, grooved only at base, green
or with a pinkish tinge, 2.5–4 cm
(1–1.6 in); autumn colour yellow or brown.
Flowers Male catkins exposed over winter,
opening in late winter or early spring
before the leaves and expanding to 5–8 cm
(2–3.1 in), yellow or brownish yellow,

female flowers small, with red stigmas.
Fruit In clusters of three or more, husk
thick and rather fleshy with deep lobes,
greenish yellow, ripening to brown, covered
with down and green or reddish glandular
hairs; nut 1 cm (0.4 in), bright brown.

Range: Southeast Europe to west Asia Minor.

Habitat: Woodlands, planted as an amenity or street
tree over much of Europe.

Similar species: **Jacquemont Hazel** *C. jacquemontii* from
the western Himalayas has leaves, shoots
and husks without or with few glandular
hairs and leaves which are more obovate in
outline.

Chinese Hazel *C. chinensis* differs in the
darker colour of the down, more
persistently glandular downy shoots and
leaves which have fine and more even teeth
and are oblique at the base.

Turkish hazel has a regular habit, usually
broadly conical but less often columnar,
which together with its tolerance of a wide
range of sites makes it a valuable amenity
tree. It is fairly fast-growing tree and is
particularly attractive for the hanging
catkins in late winter and the bark.

p.190 **Filbert** *Corylus maxima*

Description: Deciduous shrub or rarely a small tree
8–10 m (26–33 ft) with a bole diameter to
25 cm (10 in).
Crown Rounded, domed, usually on several
stems. *Bark* Light brown, slightly peeling
on young growths. *Shoot* Pale brown,
glandular hairy, becoming hairless and
smooth in the second year. *Buds* Obovoid,
rounded or bluntly pointed, with green
scales. *Foliage* Rounded to obovate, base
heart-shaped, apex slender pointed, margin
with two rows of teeth, downy, especially
below, mid green, turning yellow in autumn,
5–12 × 4–10 cm (2–4.7 × 1.6–4 in); leaf
stalk glandular hairy, 6–12 cm (2.4–4.7 in).
Flowers On previous season's shoots in late
winter; male catkins formed in autumn and
exposed over winter, expanding after

Christmas to 5–8 cm (2–3.1 in), yellow to yellow-brown, pendulous; female flowers from buds in central portion of shoot, with only the 12–15 crimson to purple stigmas exposed 1–2 mm (0.1 in). *Fruit* Nut 1.5–2.5 cm (0.6–1 in), ovoid to oblong, light greenish brown to pale brown, ripening in first autumn, hidden within a tubular green or brown husk which at 4–5 cm (1.6–2 in) is twice as long as the nut and totally encloses it.

Range: Balkans, across to Turkey.

Habitat: Woodlands.

Varieties: Var. *purpurea* has the leaves and catkins deep reddish purple, and is not without charm.

This tree is widely cultivated for the tasty nuts. It is closely related to *C. avellana*, differing in the husk which is longer than the ripe nut and encloses it like a sock.

SMOKE TREES, *COTINUS* (SYNONYM: *RHUS* IN PART)
FAMILY ANACARDIACEAE

This is a genus of three species which has been treated as part of *Rhus* in the past. However, the hairy 'smoky' flowers and the simple leaves distinguish it from the compact inflorescence and pinnate leaves of *Rhus*.

---

p.128 **Venetian Sumach** *Cotinus coggygria*

Description: Deciduous shrub or small tree to 5–6 m (16–20 ft).
Crown Ovoid to domed, branching low and rather shrubby. *Bark* Fissured, grey-brown. *Shoot* Wood yellow. *Buds* Small, with several imbricate scales.
Foliage Leaves oval, rounded to obovate, apex rounded to slightly emarginate (notched), base rounded, not wedge-shaped, margin untoothed, veins parallel, hairless to softly downy, 3–8 cm (1.2–3.1 in); leaf stalk slender; autumn colour spectacular reds or yellows. *Flowers* In large loose terminal panicles, 15–20 cm (6–8 in) high and wide, giving the appearance of smoke and smothering the plant in June–July.

Fruit Small dry obovoid drupe, net-veined, 3–4 mm (0.1–0.2 in).

Range: Central and southern Europe east to the Himalayas and Northern China.

Habitat: Dry hillsides.

Varieties: 'Foliis Purpureis' is one of a number of selections with purple foliage, although fading back to green. In 'Notcutt's Variety' and 'Royal Purple', the foliage remains dark maroon-purple throughout the summer, turning red in autumn.

Synonyms: *Rhus cotinus*.

Similar species: *C. obovatus* (syn. *Rhus cotinoides*, *Cotinus americanus*) is the second tree-forming species in the genus. It has larger obovate leaves, to 13 cm (5.1 in), with a wedge-shaped base and makes a small tree to 9 m (29 ft). It comes from Tennessee, Alabama, Missouri, Arkansas, Oklahoma and eastern Texas, occurring on scattered limestone uplands.

This makes an attractive shrub, less often assuming tree-like proportions. The flowering panicles create a smoky haze over the plant. The autumn colour can be magnificent.

COTONEASTERS, *COTONEASTER*
FAMILY ROSACEAE

This is a large genus of perhaps 300 species (mainly shrubs) from the Old World. The leaves are alternate on the shoots and untoothed. The buds are rather small and nondescript. Spines are not present. The flowers have free styles with 10–20 stamens and are carried in cymes or small clusters, and occasionally singly. The petals may be spreading (white) or cup-shaped (pink). The fruit is a pome with one to five bony nutlets.

p.157 *Cotoneaster affinis*

Description: Deciduous or semi-evergreen small tree to 8 m (26 ft).
Crown Rounded, often on several stems. *Bark* Smooth, grey-brown. *Shoot* Slender, downy when young, then hairless.

Buds Small. *Foliage* Leaves elliptic, oblanceolate to obovate, apex acute or blunt, base rounded, margin untoothed, upper surface dull green, hairless, underside woolly, texture thin, 4–10 × 1.5–5 cm (1.6–4 × 0.6–2 in); leaf stalk 5–10 mm (0.2–0.4 in). *Flowers* In small compact hairy cymes of circa 15 small white flowers with mauve anthers. *Fruit* Cylindrical, purple then finally black, succulent, 1–1.2 cm × 6 mm (0.4–0.5 × 0.25 in), with two obovate nutlets.

Range: Western Himalayas.

Habitat: Cultivated as an ornamental, in the wild occurring in mixed open and rather dry forest.

Similar species: *C. bacillaris* has the leaves hairless except for some hairs on the midrib beneath.
C. gamblei has red fruit, turning finally purple, and carried in looser cymes.

This small tree or large shrub is one of a number of rather similar apomictic species from the Himalayas. They are attractive in flower, but the dark fruits make them less attractive in the autumn. The wood is strong and elastic.

---

p.156 **Tree Cotoneaster** *Cotoneaster frigidus*

Description: Semi-evergreen or tardily deciduous tree 8–15 m (26–50 ft) with a bole diameter to 30 cm (1 ft).
Crown Rounded, domed, usually on several stems. *Bark* Pale grey, smooth, becoming scaly and brown-grey or buff in old trees. *Shoot* Initially densely hairy but these soon lost, green in the first winter, then buff-brown. *Buds* Long conic, slightly curved, densely pale silky hairy, 3–5 mm (0.1–0.2 in). *Foliage* Elliptic, oval to obovate, tapered at both ends, margins untoothed, matt green above, beneath pale or whitish green with prominent midrib and secondary veins, at first densely white woolly but the hairs mainly lost by autumn, 8–15 × 4–5 cm (3.1–6 × 1.6–2 in); leaf stalk grooved, 1 cm (0.4 in). *Flowers* In clusters

5 cm (2 in) in diameter from axillary short shoots on previous season's and older shoots in early summer; flowers white, 8 mm (0.3 in) across, fragrant. *Fruit* Ripening to bright red in autumn, about 7 mm (0.3 in) across, containing two seeds.

Range: Himalayas.

Habitat: Cultivated in Europe as an ornamental, in the wild occurring in mixed valley forests.

This makes the largest cotoneaster, capable of attaining a bole diameter of 1 m (3.3 ft) in exceptional circumstances. The fruits provide a valuable source of food for birds over winter. It will grow on a wide range of soils.

---

p.156 **Waterer's Cotoneaster**
Cotoneaster × *watereri*

Description: Deciduous or semi-evergreen small tree to 7 m (23 ft) with a bole diameter of up to 60 cm (2 ft).
Crown Rounded, often on several stems, outer branches often pendent.
Bark Smooth, greyish. *Shoot* Dark grey-brown. *Buds* Small. *Foliage* Leaves narrow elliptic, apex acute to slender pointed, base wedge-shaped, margin untoothed, dark sub-shiny green, slightly rugose and hairless above, underside initially white haired, becoming hairless, with about twelve pairs of veins, 5–9 cm (2–3.5 in); leaf stalk 5–7 mm (0.2–0.3 in). *Flowers* In cymes of 30–50, creamy white.
Fruit Globose, scarlet, 8–9 mm (0.3–0.4 in); nutlets two to four.

Range: Garden hybrid.

Habitat: Cultivated as an ornamental.

Varieties: 'John Waterer' is the type form. 'Cornubia' makes a taller tree, sometime to 8–10 m (26–33 ft), with very abundant red fruits. In 'Salmon Spray', the fruits are pinkish orange.

Similar species: *C. salicifolius* (p.157) is an evergreen shrub to 5 m (16 ft). The leaves are strongly rugose or wrinkled and have recurved margins and a felted to thinly woolly underside (although sometimes more or less hairless by autumn).

C. lacteus has evergreen leaves obovate to broadly elliptic and somewhat shiny with impressed veins above but yellow hairy on the underside. The flowers, in cymes of about one hundred, have milky white petals, hence the specific name.

This is believed to be a hybrid of two diploid species, *C. frigidus* from the Himalayas and *C. salicifolius* from central China. The hybrid has occurred on a number of occasions, giving rise to several different forms.

HAWTHORNS, *CRATAEGUS*
FAMILY ROSACEAE

This is a large genus of mainly small trees from the northern hemisphere, especially North America. The leaves are variously lobed, usually coarsely so, less often only coarsely toothed. The leaf veins can assist in identification. In *CC. crus-galli, nigra* and × *persimilis* the veins end only in the tips of the lobes or teeth, whereas in the other species here listed the veins may end in sinuses between teeth or lobes as well as in the tips of the lobes. The flowers are carried in corymbs, or singly. They have five sepals and petals, with 5–25 stamens. The number of styles is important. In *CC. calycina*, × *lavallei* and *monogyna* there is only a single style and nutlet, whilst in *CC. azarolus, crus-galli, laevigata*, × *lavallei*, × *persimilis* and *sanguinea* there are usually two to three styles and nutlets, and *CC. nigra, pentagyna, submollis*, and *tanacetifolia* have four to five styles and nutlets. The fruits have a fleshy edible covering and contain one to five hard bony nutlets. The shoots are usually well armed with spines. In *CC. crus-galli*, × *lavallei*, × *persimilis* and *submollis*, the spines can be over 2.5 cm (1 in) in length.

p.270 **Azarole** *Crataegus azarolus*

Description: Deciduous tree 6–10 m (20–33 ft) with a bole diameter to 30 cm (1 ft).
Crown Rounded. *Bark* Fissured, becoming rugged. *Shoot* Clothed with short ash-white hairs, thorns short. *Buds* Small, rounded. *Foliage* Leaves obovate to rhombic, apex rounded, base wedge-shaped, margin with three or five deep narrow

oblong lobes which are bluntly lobed or
toothed at the apex, upper surface bright
green, with a weak pubescence which is
gradually lost, underside more hairy,
2.5–3.5(–5) × 1.5–3(–5) cm (1–1.4(–2) ×
0.6–1.2(–2)in); leaf stalk 1–2.5 cm
(0.4–1 in), stout; stipules sickle-shaped,
herbaceous, deeply toothed, 1–1.5 cm
(0.4–0.6 in). *Flowers* Inflorescence compact
corymb of flowers in June. Flowers white,
1.2 cm (0.5 in) across, stamens twenty,
styles two or three (rarely 1 or 4).
Fruit Globose, orange or yellow, but in
some forms white or red, with an apple-like
flavour, 2–2.5 cm (0.8–1 in).

Range: Mediterranean region east to Iran and Iraq.
Habitat: Rocky mountain slopes, or in hedgerows
and orchards.

This tree is cultivated in southeast Europe
for the fruits. It has become naturalized,
and thus its native distribution is obscure.
It is probably restricted as a wild plant to
southeast Europe, Crete, Cyprus and across
to Turkey and west Asia.

Sawtoothed Hawthorn *Crataegus calycina*

Description: Deciduous shrub or small tree to 11 m
(36 ft).
Crown Rounded. *Bark* Grey, brownish red
or purple. *Shoot* Hairless, purple-brown to
cinnamon-brown, with a few axillary spines
to 1.3 cm (0.5 in) or none, rarely with
spine-tipped lateral shoots. *Buds* Small,
rounded. *Foliage* Leaves ovate-rhombic to
broad ovate, apex acute or slender pointed,
base long, broad wedge-shaped, margin
with three to five (rarely seven or nine)
finely serrate lobes which extend up to two-
thirds to the midrib and have narrow acute
sinuses, dark green above, underside pale
green with hairs on the veins and in the
vein axils, 3–6(–8.5) × 3–5(–6.5) cm
(1.2–2.4(–3.3) × 1.2–2(–2.6) in); leaf stalk
hairy, 1–3.5 cm (0.4–1.4 in); stipules
sickle-shaped or oblong with an awl-like
apex. *Flowers* In lax hairless clusters of four

to nine in May/June; flowers 1.5–2 cm (0.6–0.8 in), with a single style and twenty red anthers. *Fruit* Oblong-cylindric to sub-globose, containing a single seed, ripening in autumn to light to dark red with spreading or erect calyx lobes, 6–13 × 5–10 mm (0.25–0.5 × 0.2–0.4 in).

Range: North and Central Europe from France, Belgium, Denmark and southern Norway east to Greece, Bulgaria and southern Russia.

Habitat: Understorey in deciduous woodland, less often in pine forest.

Varieties: Ssp. *calycina* covers those plants with erect calyx lobes to the oblong-cylindric fruits, ripening light red. Ssp. *curvisepala* has the fruit more ellipsoidal to sub-globose with deflexed lobes of the calyx, ripening darker red.

Similar species: *C. microphylla* (p.268) from the Crimea and also from the Caucasus region and northern Iran differs in the lobes of the leaves being sub-obtuse and the bright red fruit which is sub-globose and up to 1.5 cm (0.6 in) in length.

The single style and nut in the fruit and the general aspect of the foliage shows a relationship with *C. monogyna*. However, the fruit or haw is longer than it is broad and the margins of the leaves are finely toothed almost to the base of the lobes.

---

p.204 **Cockspur Thorn** *Crataegus crus-galli*

Description: Deciduous shrub or small tree to 10 m (33 ft).
Crown Broad rounded, often wider than high. *Bark* Grey and smooth, darkening with age and becoming cracked at the base. *Shoot* Grey-brown or purple-brown, hairless, with many purple spines up to 10 cm (4 in) in length. *Buds* Dark brown. *Foliage* Leaves obovate to oblong obovate, apex rounded to bluntly pointed, base wedge-shaped, margin sharply serrate with glandular teeth except untoothed at the base, not lobed, thick and rather leathery in

texture, upper surface dark green and somewhat lustrous, underside paler, hairless on both sides, 2–8 × 0.5–2 cm (0.8–3.1 × 0.2–0.8 in); leaf stalk 0.5–1.5 cm (0.2–0.6 in); autumn colour orange.
Flowers In hairless corymbs in May; flowers white, 1.5 cm (0.6 in); styles two or three, stamens ten (rarely twenty), pink or yellow. *Fruit* Red, globose with acute untoothed sepals, persisting through the winter, 1 cm (0.4 in); seeds two.

Range: Northeast North America.
Habitat: Cultivated as an ornamental.

The large thorns have a resemblance to the spurs of fighting cocks, standing out from the shoot at a right angle.

---

p.269 **Midland Hawthorn** *Crataegus laevigata*

Description: Deciduous tree to 12 m (39 ft) with a bole diameter to 60 cm (2 ft).
Crown Rounded, with a dense mass of twiggy branches. *Bark* Grey-brown to orange-brown or pink-brown, becoming cracked and fissured. *Shoot* Green-brown, hairless and shiny, becoming purplish grey-brown, slender. *Buds* Ovoid, rounded or slightly conic, dark brown, 3 mm (0.1 in). *Foliage* Leaves ovate to almost rounded in outline, apex rounded, base rounded to broad wedge-shaped, margin with one or two pairs of shallow forward lobes with acute sinuses and rounded apiculate teeth, glossy green above with indented (but raised) veins, underside whitish green, hairless or with faint axillary tufts, 1.5–6 × 2–5 cm (0.6–2.4 × 0.8–2 in), but usually less than 4 cm (1.6 in) each way; leaf stalk grooved, 1.3–2 cm (0.5–0.8 in); autumn colour yellow. *Flowers* In clusters of six to twelve, carried on the branches in May with the nearly fully expanded leaves; flowers white (or pink, *see* below), with two or three styles. *Fruit* Pumpkin-shaped, broader than long, rounded at the base and somewhat indented at the apex where the

triangular calyx lobes persist, 8 × 11 mm (0.3 × 0.4 in), with two or three seeds.

Range: Central and western Europe including Britain.

Habitat: Woodlands, especially on heavy soils.

Varieties: 'Paul's Scarlet' is a form (or possibly hybrid with *C. monogyna*) which has double pink flowers. It is not as attractive as common *C. monogyna* when laden with its creamy white blooms.

Synonyms: *C. oxycantha* in part.

This tree is much less common than *C. monogyna*, from which it is distinguished by the two or three styles and nutlets and the less lobed leaves. However, the two hybridize, as does *C. laevigata* with *C. calycina*.

---

p.204 **Hybrid Cockspur Thorn**
Crataegus × lavallei

Description: Tardily deciduous tree to 8–14 m (26–46 ft) with a bole diameter to 50 cm (1.6 ft).
Crown Domed, usually broader than tall, with spreading branches. *Bark* Smooth, dark grey, but becoming scaly and fissuring with age. *Shoot* Green with long loose pale hairs and small elliptic lenticels in the first year, ripening to greenish brown, shiny and nearly hairless by the second summer, and later becoming grey; thorns few but stout, 2.5–4 cm (1–1.6 in). *Buds* Bluntly pointed, small, green-brown, to 2 mm (0.1 in). *Foliage* Leaves alternate, obovate or elliptic, broadest above the middle, tapering to the acute apex and more gently towards the somewhat rounded base but which then narrows and is downward growing on the leaf stalk, margins finely serrate from the middle to the tip, usually entire for the basal half, upper surface lustrous deep green with stiff translucent or whitish hairs and slightly impressed veins, lower surface somewhat whitish green and sub-shiny, with a light covering of whitish hairs especially on the raised veins, usually

to 8 × 3 cm (3.1–1.2 in) (but sometimes to 11 × 6 cm (4.3 × 2.4 in)); leaf stalk without decurrent leaf less than 5 mm (0.2 in), but including the flange of the leaf base up to 1.5 cm (0.6 in). Autumn colour bronzy red in early winter, or leaves falling whilst still green. *Flowers* In elliptic corymbs 8–10 × 4–5 cm (3.1–4 × 1.6–2 in) of about ten to twenty opening in early summer (June); flowers to 2.5 cm (1 in); peduncle, flower stalks and receptacle white hairy; calyx lobes linear and toothed; petals five, white; stamens twenty, pinkish, styles one to three. *Fruit* Globose with the base tapering onto the stalk, ripening to orange-red with brown spots and green calyx lobes, 1.5–2 cm (0.6–0.8 in), persisting through the winter.

Range: Hybrid origin.

Habitat: Cultivated as an amenity tree.

Varieties: Cultivar 'Carrièrei' is the predominate, perhaps only, form in general cultivation. It originated from a later crossing of the two parent species.

Synonyms: *C. × carrièrei*.

This attractive tree is believed to have originated as a hybrid of the Mexican *C. stipulacea* with *C. crus-galli*. It makes a small tree and is most attractive when in flower, when the glossy young leaves are an effective background for the white flowers.

p.268 **May, Hawthorn** or **Quickthorn**
Crataegus monogyna

Description: Deciduous tree 10–16 m (33–53 ft) with a bole diameter to 0.3–1 m (1–3.3 ft).
Crown Rounded, ovoid, with dense twiggy branches which descend at the tips.
Bark Grey-brown and smooth in young trees, becoming pink-brown, fissured and scaly in old trees. *Shoot* Slender, green and pink, hairless, maturing to purplish red, often with sharp straight thorns 1–2.5 cm (0.4–1 in), orange-brown or grey in later years, spur shoots usually terminating in a thorn. *Buds* Ovoid, pointed, with green

and brown somewhat angular scales, 2–2.5 mm (0.1 in). *Foliage* Leaves somewhat rhombic or rhombic-ovate in outline, with two or three pairs of generally deep lobes which have parallel sides and form narrow acute sinuses, apex and tips of lobes with sharp triangular teeth, base very broad wedge-shaped or truncate, upper surface with a few scattered silky hairs, shiny green, underside whitish green, with hairs confined to the axils of the raised veins, 1.5–5 × 2–5 cm (0.6–2 × 0.8–2 in); leaf stalk grooved, 1–2 cm (0.4–0.8 in), with a pair of leafy sharp-toothed stipules to 2 cm (0.8 in) at the base, but on flowering, fruiting sprays the stipules are lanceolate to awl-like and entire; autumn colour yellow or pinky red. *Flowers* In corymbs with 9–18 flowers (in multiples of three) which terminate lateral branches in May, flowers white, 1–1.5 cm (0.4–0.6 in) across, scented, with a single style. *Fruit* Globose to obovoid, carmine red to maroon, with some white hairs, calyx persistent and set in a depression, 8–14 mm (0.3–0.6 in), containing a single seed 6–8 mm (0.25–0.3 in).

Range: Throughout Europe except Iceland east to western Asia.

Habitat: Woodlands, hedgerows, scrub.

Varieties: 'Stricta' is a form with initially ascending branches which have few side branches. As a young tree, it forms a narrow oval, but with age it broadens considerably. It is used as a street tree, but without the grace of the normal form.

The flowers are white, or occasionally pink tinged, and scented, clothing the arching branches in April or May and followed by the red or maroon haws. It hybridizes with other species of *Crataegus* wherever they meet, forming a complex number of intermediates. The pure species is characterized by the single style in the flowers and the single seed in the fruit. Hybrids with *C. laevigata* tend to have pink petals. The thorny nature and its tough constitution make it an excellent hedging plant.

p.271   **Black Hawthorn**   *Crataegus nigra*

Description: Deciduous tree to 6 m (20 ft) with a bole
diameter to 30 cm (1 ft).
Crown Rounded. *Bark* Purple-red,
ridged. *Shoot* Felted with grey down at
first, then soon hairless and purple by
autumn, spines to 1.2 cm (0.5 in), few or
absent. *Foliage* Leaves ovate to triangular,
acute, base wedge-shaped, margin with
7–11 sharply-serrate lobes, with the lower
ones extending half way to the midrib to
form narrow acute sinuses but shallower
towards the apex, texture thin, tomentose
on both surfaces and dull green, 4–8 ×
2.5–5.5 cm (1.6–3.1 × 1–2.2 in); leaf stalk
1–3 cm (0.4–1.2 in); stipules wide, ovate
to sickle-shaped with sharply-toothed
margins. *Flowers* Inflorescence in lax
corymbs of 10–20 flowers in April/May.
Flowers white but fading to pink,
1.2–1.7 cm (0.5–0.7 in) across, stamens
twenty, styles four or five, top of ovary
hairless. *Fruit* Globose or ovoid, shiny
black with green flesh, soft, 8–13 ×
9–11 mm (0.3–0.5 × 0.4 in).

Range: Hungary, Rumania and northern Balkans.
Habitat: Marshy open woodland.

This small tree is restricted to the Danube
River system and is marked by the lustrous
black fruits.

p.269   **Five-seeded Hawthorn**
Crataegus pentagyna

Description: Deciduous tree to 8 m (26 ft) with a bole
diameter to 30 cm (1 ft).
Crown Rounded, with arching branches.
Bark Pale brown, yellow-brown in fissures.
Shoot Sparsely woolly with cobwebby hairs,
then hairless and grey-brown, spines circa
1 cm (0.4 in). *Buds* Ovoid, rounded
pointed, dark brown, 2.5 mm (0.1 in).
Foliage Leaves rhombic-ovate to obovate,
apex acute, base wedge-shaped, margin
with three to seven irregular lobes which
are irregularly acute to obtuse toothed,

lower pair of lobes forming acute sinuses and extending two-thirds the way to the midrib, upper surface dark to olive-green and nearly hairless with impressed veins, underside pale with a thicker cobwebby indumentum which is long persistent, net-veined, 2–6 × 2–4 cm (0.8–2.4 × 0.8–1.6 in); leaf stalk usually less than 2 cm (0.8 in), hairy, grooved; stipules narrowly sickle-shaped, long slender pointed at the apex and untoothed or remotely toothed. *Flowers* Inflorescence in lax many flowered corymbs in late May or June. Flowers white, hairy, 1.2–1.5 cm (0.5–0.6 in) across, stamens twenty, styles three to five, sepals broadly triangular. *Fruit* Globose or ellipsoidal, dull blackish purple, 7–10 × 6–11 mm (0.3–0.4 × 0.25–0.4 in), seeds four or five.

Range: Eastern Europe from Hungary, Bulgaria, Rumania, the Ukraine and south to the northern Balkans and European Turkey.

Habitat: Open scrub or forest.

---

p.205 **Broad-leafed Cockspur Thorn**
Crataegus persimilis

Description: Deciduous tree 6–8 m (20–26 ft) with a bole diameter to 30 cm (1 ft).
Crown Rounded, domed, usually broader than tall, densely twiggy. *Bark* Grey, smooth, becoming fissured. *Shoot* Hairless and shiny, green in the first year but becoming light brown, chocolate brown or grey in subsequent seasons, lenticels elliptic, raised, pale brown; spines dark chocolate to purple, 1.5–2 cm (0.6–0.8 in), on strong branches. *Buds* Ovoid, green to shiny brown, 3 mm (0.1 in).
Foliage Leaves broadly ovate to rhombic, apex acute, base wedge-shaped, tapering onto the leaf stalk, margins simply toothed, slightly doubly, except for the basal 1–2 cm (0.4–0.8 in) which are entire, upper surface lustrous dark green with slightly impressed veins, hairless except along the veins, lower surface light or whitish matt green, veins raised, six to

nine pairs, with axillary tufts, 4–8 ×
3–6 cm (1.6–3.1 × 1.2–2.4 in); leaf stalk
grooved, hairless, 7–15 mm (0.3–0.6 in);
autumn colour brilliant orange through
red to crimson. *Flowers* In corymbs 5 cm
(2 in) across in late May/early June, flower
stalks densely greyish hairy, flowers 1.5 cm
(0.6 in) across with creamy-white petals,
blackish stamens and two styles. The sepals
are narrowly triangular, glandular and
somewhat hairy along the central groove.
Fruit Globose, red, 1.5 cm (0.6 in),
ripening in autumn and soon falling.

Range: Cultivated an an ornamental.

Habitat: Uncertain, but of North American origin or
parentage.

Synonyms: *C. prunifolia.*

This small tree is spectacular in its autumn
colour, when the glossy foliage turns from
green to orange, red and finally bright
crimson before falling. Its origin is clouded,
but it has been in cultivation since the 18th
century. It may be a hybrid between two
North American species, which arose either
in the wild or in cultivation. From
Cockspur Thorn (which is one possible
parent), the hairy inflorescence, broader
leaves and fruit falling soon after ripening
distinguish it. However, it shares with it
the sharp stout spines on vigorous shoots,
which are likened to the spurs of a fighting
cock. It is represented in cultivation by the
clone 'Prunifolia'.

---

p.271   **Red Hawthorn** *Crataegus sanguinea*

Description: Deciduous tree to 6 m (20 ft) with a bole
diameter to 30 cm (1 ft).
Crown Rounded. *Bark* Brown, becoming
fissured and scaly at the base.
Shoot Sparsely hairy at first, then soon
hairless and purple by autumn, with few or
no spines. *Buds* Globose, red, to 4 mm
(0.2 in). *Foliage* Leaves rhombic to ovate,
apex acute, base wedge-shaped, margin
with three to seven (one to three pairs) of
shallow lobes which are sharply and

sometimes doubly toothed, variously hairy
on both sides, especially in the vein axils
beneath, 5–8 × 4.5–6.5 cm (2–3.1 ×
1.8–2.6 in); leaf stalk 0.8–1.6 cm
(0.3–0.6 in); stipules coarsely toothed.
Flowers Inflorescence in hairless corymbs.
Flowers white, 1–1.5 cm (0.4–0.6 in)
across, sepals untoothed, stamens twenty
with pink or purple anthers, styles two to
five (mainly three). *Fruit* Globose, bright
red (but yellow in var. *chlorocarpa*),
0.8–1.2 cm (0.3–0.5 in), with five seeds.

Range: Central and eastern European Russia to 60
degrees north, east into Central Asia
(Kazakhstan) and Siberia.

Habitat: Open scrub or forest.

Similar species: *C. altaica* with globose yellow fruits and
with the lobes deeper, extending more
than half way to the midrib, is recorded
from southeast Russia and Kazakhstan.
The leaves may be larger, to 9 × 8 cm
(3.5 × 3.1 in) maximum, whilst the
anthers are white.

This makes a small tree or shrub.

p.205 **Downy Hawthorn** *Crataegus submollis*

Description: Deciduous tree 6–10 m (20–33 ft) with a
bole diameter to 30 cm (1 ft).
Crown Rounded with spreading branches,
on a short stem. *Bark* Grey-brown,
smooth but becoming scaly at the base.
Shoot Green-brown and lightly pilose at
first, becoming grey-brown in the second
year, with thorns on the spur shoots
5–8 cm (2–3.1 in). *Buds* Ovoid, green-
brown, shiny, 3 mm (0.1 in).
Foliage Leaves broadly ovate with an acute
apex, base wedge-shaped to subcordate,
margin lobulate with large triangular
double teeth, upper surface matt dark
green with pilose hairs pressed against the
shoot, undersurface light green and pilose,
especially on the four or five pairs of raised
veins, 6–10 × 5–10 cm (2.4–4 × 2–4 in);
leaf stalk with spaced brown glands,
grooved from the continuation of the

somewhat downward-growing leaf blade, green and white pilose, 3–3.5 cm (1.2–1.4 in); autumn colour red or orange.
Flowers In corymbs, flowers white, 2.5 cm (1 in) across, with ten stamens, set on pilose and lenticulate flower stalks.
Fruit Pear-shaped, 1–2 × 1.5 cm (0.4–0.8 × 0.6 in), hairy, ripening to orange-red and soon falling.

Range: Eastern North America from northeast USA and southeast Canada.

Habitat: Cultivated as an ornamental, in the wild occurring in thickets and open woods.

This small tree is often grown as *C. mollis*, which differs most obviously in having twenty stamens.

---

p.270   **Tansy-leafed Thorn**
Crataegus tanacetifolia

Description: Deciduous tree to 10 m (33 ft) with a bole diameter to 60 cm (2 ft).
Crown Rounded. *Bark* Purplish grey-brown or steely grey, smooth at first, then becoming scaly and flaking to reveal orange or orange-brown. *Shoot* Densely grey woolly at first, only slowly becoming hairless with some wool persisting through the first winter or for longer, grey, not or only lightly thorned.
Buds Rounded dome, grey and brown, 2 mm (0.1 in). *Foliage* Leaves rhombic or obovate in outline, rounded at the apex and long wedge-shaped at the base, margin deeply cut, almost to the midrib, into seven (or five) parallel-sided lobes which are acute at the apex with triangular slender-pointed glandular teeth (especially on the lower pair of lobes), sinuses acute, both surfaces persistently hairy, grey-green, 2.5–5 × 2.5–5 cm (1–2 × 1–2 in); leaf stalk to 1.3 cm (0.5 in); stipules curved, toothed. *Flowers* In June in rounded clusters of six to eight; flowers fragrant, white, 2.5 cm (1 in), ovary grey haired, styles five, stamens twenty, with red anthers. *Fruit* Globose, yellow or

infused with red, with some persistent wool, with the aroma and taste of an apple, 2–2.5 cm (0.8–1 in) across; subtended by one or more mossy bracts.

Range: Asia Minor and Syria.

Habitat: Cultivated as an ornamental.

Synonyms: *Mespilus tanacetifolia*.

Similar species: These include:

Oriental Hawthorn *C. laciniata* (syn. *C. orientalis*) (p.270), a related tree from southeast Spain, Sicily, the Balkans, Hungary and Rumania to the Ukraine, is usually a shrub but can make a tree to 10 m (33ft). The leaves are similar, but with jagged, non-glandular teeth at the tips of the lobes, with the stipules soon falling. The shoots soon lose their coating of hairs, revealing the blackish bark. The fruit is smaller, 1.5–2 cm (0.6–0.8 in), and is brick-red to orange-red. In var. *pojarkovae* from the Crimea, the fruit is pear-shaped and yellow-orange.

Heldreich's Hawthorn *C. heldreichii* (p.271) is a shrub, rarely small tree, from the mountains of southern Albania, central and southern Greece and Crete. It shares the woolly twigs but has small spines. The leaves are leathery in texture, broadly ovate with three to five wide acute and sparsely serrate lobes which extend to two-thirds the way to the midrib. The stipules are somewhat rounded to sickle-shaped with few teeth or untoothed margins. The styles are one to three, and the 7 mm (0.3 in) fruit is red, globose with erect or recurved sepals and one to three nutlets.

C. schraderiana, from the mountains of northern Greece and the Crimea, has the shoots less woolly, soon hairless and purple by autumn. The leaves are obovate to rhombic and leathery. They have three to five wide and sub-obtuse lobes which extend about half of the way to the midrib, forming narrow sinuses. The margins of the lobes are untoothed, or with one to three coarse teeth at the apex. The large stipules are semi-heart-shaped and serrate. The styles are two to four. The fruit is sub-globose and dark dull red-purple with two to four seeds.

This makes a neat small tree and is characterized by the glandular tips to the leaves and the mossy bract(s) beneath the fruit. The grey woolly leaves are neatly cut. It is an uncommon constituent of municipal plantings but deserves wider cultivation

JAPANESE CEDARS, *CRYPTOMERIA*
FAMILY TAXODIACEAE

This is a conifer genus of two species (although it is often with some justification treated as one species with two subspecies) from Japan and China. The leaves are awl-like and arranged in a helix around the shoot. The cones are terminal on the stronger shoots. They are globose, with several scales, each of which has a single hooked point with a number of small spines. It is considered that the scales are derived from the fusion of an ovuliferous scale (the hooked point) with the subtending bract scales (the smaller spines). Male cones are borne in the axils of leaves in spring and are clustered at the tips of the weaker shoots. The bark is somewhat stringy but not particularly thick and fibrous. Japanese Cedar has an excellent reddish timber.

p.57   **Fortune Cedar** *Cryptomeria fortunei*

Description: Evergreen tree 25–30 m (80–100 ft) with a bole diameter to 2 m (6.6 ft).
Crown Conical when young but becoming broader with age and eventually domed, rather open, branch ends rounded and billowing. *Bark* Red-brown, flaky in young trees but in old ones becoming fibrous and peeling in long stringy strips to reveal orange or bright orange-brown beneath.
Shoot Green for three or four winters, then red-brown, slender. *Buds* Green, enclosed in small leaves rather than bud scales. *Foliage* In pendent three-dimensional sprays with radial leaves; leaves light green to yellow-green, incurved, laterally compressed, with two bands of whitish green stomata on each face, to 2 cm (0.8 in); crushed foliage

with strong resin scent. *Flowers* On previous season's growths in late winter; male cones set singly in leaf axils but clusters of up to fifty terminating weak shoots, yellow-brown, 3–8 mm (0.1–0.3 in). *Fruit* Globose with a flatter base, ripen brown to dull brown in first autumn, with around twenty scales, 1–1.5 cm (0.4–0.6 in); scales shield-like, with a spreading dorsal prickle and five or six short triangular teeth to 2 mm (0.1 in), usually only two seeds per scale.

Range: Southern China from Zhejiang across to Sichuan.

Habitat: Cultivated in Europe as an ornamental, in China occurring in mixed forests.

Varieties: Forma *lobbii* has the foliage in rather stiff clusters which are bunched at the branch ends. The crown is regularly conical, but it is inferior to the 'wild' form.

Synonyms: *C. japonica* var. *sinensis*.

This tree is very similar to *C. japonica* and often treated as no more than a variety. It can be distinguished best by the more open habit with fresh green soft foliage which is more strongly pendent and often longer and by the smaller cones which have shorter points to the various prickles and only two seeds per scale. (The way to do this is to get an unopened cone and collect all the seeds as they fall out, then count the number of fertile scales.) It makes a larger tree than its Japanese cousin. Its native distribution is lost in the mists of cultivation, but was presumably along the lower slopes of the mountains bordering the southern side of the Yangtse River.

p.57 **Japanese Cedar** *Cryptomeria japonica*

Description: Evergreen tree to 30 m (100 ft) with a bole diameter to 1.5 m (5 ft).
Crown Conic when young, becoming more rounded with age, generally open with spaced branches which carry dense foliage.
Bark Red-brown or orange-brown,

exfoliating in small square flakes in young trees, becoming fibrous and relatively thick in old trees and peeling in long strips. *Shoot* Green for around two winters from the decurrent leaf bases, then red-brown once the leaves die and are later shed, rather slender. *Buds* Green with small and tightly clustered leaves rather than bud scales, 2–3 mm (0.1 in). *Foliage* In three-dimensional sprays, set radially around the shoot in five or six rows; leaves acicular to a rather soft point, flattened and incurved, mid to dark green with two bands of pale green or greenish-white stomata on each face, longest in middle of shoot, decreasing to both ends, up to 2 cm × 1.5 mm (0.8 × 0.1 in); crushed foliage with moderate resin scent. *Flowers* On previous season's growths in late winter; male cones singly from leaf axils near the tip of and terminating weaker shoots, in clusters of four to twenty, ovoid to oblong, green and yellow, shedding yellow pollen, 4–8 mm (0.2–0.3 in); female cones single at tips of shoots, ovoid, brownish green, with a cluster of bracts, 4 mm (0.2 in). *Fruit* Globose, green but ripening to brown in first autumn, with 20–30 scales, 1.5–2 cm (0.6–0.8 in); scales peltate (shield-like), with a dorsal recurved spine and three to five erect triangular teeth 3–4 mm (0.1–0.2 in), with three to five seeds per fertile scale.

Range: Yakushima and elsewhere in southern Japan.

Habitat: Cultivated in Europe as an ornamental, in the wild occurring on cool moist mountain slopes.

Varieties: 'Elegans' is a fixed juvenile selection. The foliage is spaced, long and soft. Unlike the normal adult form, the leaves are rounded in section, thus more comparable to most other conifers. They are bright green but in winter become attractively bronzed or red-brown, almost looking damaged but then turning green again in spring. It will cone, although is normally sterile, and can make a tree to 20 m (65 ft).

The wild origin of Japanese Cedar has partly been lost with its use throughout southern Japan as an important timber tree but the open stands on Yakushima Island, off the southern coast of Kyushu, are believed to be wild. It is one of the few conifers which will coppice or regrow from the base when cut down. It thrives on a wide range of sites. The foliage is similar to the juvenile foliage of *Taiwania* but softer and generally shorter.

CHINA FIRS, *CUNNINGHAMIA*
FAMILY TAXODIACEAE

This is a conifer genus with two or three species from China and Taiwan. The foliage resembles some *Araucaria* but the leaves have two broad bands of stomata on both sides and are toothed. They are arranged in a helix around the shoot but bent to make them spreading on either side. The cones are terminal on the stronger shoots and are globose. Male cones are borne in clusters at the tips of weaker shoots in spring. The bark is reddish brown, somewhat fibrous and of moderate thickness. China firs have an excellent reddish timber and are one of the few conifers which will coppice.

p.98 China Fir *Cunninghamia lanceolata*

Description: Evergreen tree 15–25 m (50–80 ft) with a bole up to 80 cm (2.6 ft) in diameter. *Crown* Conical when young, with whorled spaced branches, columnar in old trees with a pointed or rounded apex, often with persistent dead foliage which on dry sites can mar its appearance, usually with coppice sucker growth at base of the stem. *Bark* Reddish brown, thick and furrowed, fibrous but hard compared to *Sequoia* and *Sequoiadendron* bark. *Shoot* Light green for several years with decurrent leaf bases, then brown, slender. *Buds* Hidden in axils of the leaves. *Foliage* In spreading sprays, parted and pointing gently below the shoot with side foliage often curved down, widely parted above; leaves lanceolate, decurrent on shoot, evenly tapered from near the base to the acute tip, flat, upper surface shiny mid to dark green, often with some white waxy lines of stomata, lower surface with two whitish-green waxy bands of stomata, 3–7 cm × 4–5 mm (1.2–2.8 × 0.2 in); crushed foliage with a grassy smell.

Flowers Terminal on previous season's shoots in late spring; male cones clustered, yellow-brown; female cones green, globose. *Fruit* Ovoid-conic, truncate at base, rounded pointed at tip, green but ripening to brown, on short leafy shoots, 3–4 × 3–4 cm (1.2–1.6 × 1.2–1.6 in); scales ovate with a slender-pointed apex.

Range: Central and southern China from Zhejiang across to Sichuan and Yunnan and south into north Vietnam (but where it is probably planted).

Habitat: Cultivated in Europe as an ornamental, in the wild occurring in mixed forest or plantations on limestone and acidic soils.

Varieties: 'Glauca' is a selection with the foliage glaucous green, partly from more vivid stomatal bands but also from a waxy bloom which covers the leaves.

Synonyms: *C. sinensis*.

Similar species: *C. konishii* from Taiwan has shorter foliage on mature trees, to 2.5 cm × 2.5 mm (1 × 0.1 in), which is arranged radially and harder to the touch, and smaller cones to 2.5 cm (1 in).

Grown in a damp climate, this can be a most attractive tree but when planted on a site which dries out or in too dry an atmosphere, the persistent brown dead foliage seriously detracts. It is one of the few conifers which will make new growth either from the bole or the stump if cut back. Trees are usually surrounded by a number of such suckers at the base, whilst if the crown is cut back to the stem, the regrowth can be far more attractive than the original foliage, at least for a time. The original distribution of China fir is unclear, as it has been extensively planted throughout China for the valuable red-coloured timber.

CYPRESSES, CUPRESSACEAE

This family of conifers includes seventeen genera which are widely scattered in both hemispheres, although the northern hemisphere genera, especially *Juniperus* (p.756) and *Cupressus* contain most of the species. Except in juvenile plants, the leaves are scale-like and in decussate pairs, although the alternate pairs are usually of quite different sizes. In juvenile plants, however, the leaves are acicular or awl-like. In much of *Juniperus*, this juvenile phase is fixed and the leaves are often in whorls of three, or sometimes both pairs and threes and scale leaves! The fruit is a woody cone, but *Juniperus* is the exception with the scales becoming mealy or juicy and developing into a berry. The other sixteen genera have cones, which have peltate scales (shield-like) in *Chamaecyparis* (p.597) and *Cupressus*, but in most other genera the scales are hinged at the base (valvate). The seeds are small and usually winged. Members of this family require open sunny conditions and are often drought tolerant. The family is close to the Taxodiaceae and may have arisen from it. The whorled or decussate arrangement of the foliage is a convenient if not totally effective way of separating the two families (only *Metasequoia* (p.840) in Taxodiaceae fails!).

CYPRESSES, *CUPRESSUS*
FAMILY CUPRESSACEAE

Cupressus is a genus of around twenty evergreen conifers distributed in western North America south into Guatemala, in southern Europe and North Africa and west to China. The species are predominantly found on hot dry sites, and do not generally tolerate shade. The leaves are scale like, covering the fine shoots in decussate pairs, and persist for two or so years before turning brown. In some species, the scale leaves have free tips (*CC. cashmeriana, glabra*, × *leylandii, lindleyi* and *nootkatensis*), but in *CC. arizonica, macrocarpa, sempervirens, torulosa* and also sometimes in × *leylandii* the tips of the scale leaves are pressed down on the shoot. The scale leaves often have a large dorsal gland, especially in *CC. arizonica, goveniana, sempervirens* and in *C. glabra* where the gland is secreting white blobs of resin. The foliage is in flattened and usually pendent sprays in *CC. cashmiriana, × leylandii, lindleyi, nootkatensis* and *torulosa*, and in three-dimensional sprays in *CC. arizonica, glabra, goveniana, × leylandii, lindleyi, macrocarpa* and *sempervirens*. In juvenile plants, the leaves are longer and more awl-like. The male cones open over the autumn/winter period and are usually yellow. The female flowers are small, generally bluish, and have 5–25 or so ovules per fertile scale. At flowering time, the ovules can be clearly seen with a hand lens between the scales and illustrate the 'naked seed' character of gymnosperms. The cones ripen over two summers. Much of the enlargement occurs in the first summer but the seeds are not ripe and will not germinate if collected then. The cones have peltate scales and open by the scales shrinking. In *CC. arizonica, macrocarpa* and *sempervirens* the cones are over 2 cm (0.8 in) in diameter, whilst in *CC. cashmiriana, goveniana, × leylandii, lindleyi, nootkatensis* and *torulosa* they are less than 1.8 cm (0.7 in) in diameter, whilst *C. glabra* straddles this character, with cones 1.7–2.3 cm (0.7–0.9 in) in diameter. Cypresses have a good timber but are mainly planted as amenity trees. The number of ovules per scale, flowering time and time taken to ripen the cones are amongst the characters which distinguish *Cupressus* from *Chamaecyparis*.

---

p.42 **Arizona Cypress** or **Rough Bark Arizona Cypress** *Cupressus arizonica*

Description: Evergreen tree 10–20 m (33–65 ft) with a bole diameter of 50–90 cm (1.6–2.9 ft). *Crown* Conical in young trees, becoming rounded and domed. *Bark* Greenish brown with red flakes and finely fissured in young trees, becoming grey or grey-brown and furrowed with thick, somewhat stringy ridges on the trunk and main branches of old trees. *Shoot* Green and rather stiff for the first year, then red-brown. *Buds* Hidden in the scale leaves. *Foliage* In three-dimensional sprays; scale leaves grey-green, oval, apex acute, pointed, pressed down on the shoot in old trees but free in young ones and on vigorous growths, with usually conspicuous dorsal resin gland which does

not secrete blobs of white resin, 1.5–2 mm
(0.1 in), to 1 cm (0.4 in) on strong shoots;
crushed foliage with a musty smell
somewhat reminiscent of garlic.
Flowers On previous season's shoots in
autumn. *Fruit* Ripen in second year to
globose, grey, 2–2.5 cm (0.8–1 in); scales
6–12, with a prominent central prickle.

Range: Southwest Arizona east to southwest Texas
and south to Coahuila and Durango states
in northern Mexico.

Habitat: Cultivated in Europe as an ornamental, in
the wild occurring on dry valley sites, often
on limestone.

Varieties: None, but *see C. glabra.*

This tree is far less commonly planted that
C. glabra, from which it is distinguished by
the stringy bark and the grey-green foliage
without (or at most only a few) white flecks
of resin. It will grow on a wide range of
sites, including shallow chalk and
limestone ones.

---

p.44 **Bhutan Cypress** or **Kashmir Cypress**
Cupressus cashmeriana

Description: Evergreen tree 10–20 m (33–65 ft)
(–40 m(–130 ft)) with a bole diameter of
20–50 cm (0.7–1.6 ft), up to 2 m (6.6 ft).
Crown Conical, becoming wide spreading
in old trees or broad columnar.
Bark Smooth, red-brown, later stringy and
stripping in long flakes, then ridged.
Shoot Green for first year, then becoming
light red-brown and later darker red-brown
with a greyish tint, smooth, slender,
0.75–1 mm (0.1 in). *Buds* Hidden in axils
of the scale leaves. *Foliage* In hanging flat
sprays with a long axis of around 30 cm
(12 in) long and short (4–6 cm
(1.6–2.4 in)) flat side shoots, glaucous blue-
green, hard; leaves in decussate pairs (i.e.
with each pair at a right angle to those
above and below), acute with free outturned
bony tips, free tips about 1 mm (0.1 in) on
weaker side shoots, to 2.5 mm (0.1 in) on
the central axis of pendent shoots, with an

elliptic dorsal resin gland; crushed foliage resin scented with a hint of parsley.
Flowers On previous season's shoots in autumn; male cones small, yellow-brown, at ends of weak shoots, 6 mm (0.25 in); female cones small, violet-green.
Fruit Ellipsoidal, 1–1.3 cm (0.4–0.5 in) and glaucous blue-green to green-brown in first year, becoming globose, 1.8 cm (0.7 in), and ripening in the second season to brown or red-brown; scales ten, each with a central depression and a small acute reflexed prickle.

Range: West central Bhutan.

Habitat: Mixed forest on limestone outcrops, with *Tetracentron*, *Lithocarpus* and *Betula*.

Varieties: The commonest form in cultivation deriving from the original introduction, has very flat hanging blue sprays and makes a narrow columnar tree. Recently, material has been introduced from the wild populations on the Pele La in Bhutan, which are somewhat hardier than those in Britain.

Synonyms: *C. torulosa* var. *cashmeriana*, *C. himalaica*, *C. corneyana* misapplied.

This is a most attractive tree with its pendulous side shoots displayed on the spreading lateral branches.

---

p.42 **Smooth Cypress** or **Arizona Smooth Cypress** *Cupressus glabra*

Description: Evergreen tree 10–20 m (33–65 ft) with a bole diameter of up to 60 cm (2 ft).
Crown Ovoid or conical when young, regular conical in older trees.
Bark Reddish purple to purple, smooth but blistering in the fourth year as small circular scales are shed, revealing paler underbark, thin. *Shoot* Green for first year, changing to light red or red-brown and then to dark red-brown, 1.5 mm (0.1 in) thick. *Buds* Hidden in axils of the scale leaves. *Foliage* In dense three dimensional sprays with fine shoots emerging around the stems, blue-grey; leaves in decussate

pairs, apex acute with the free tip pointing forwards along the shoot, scales crowded, 1 mm (0.1 in) apart, with actively secreting dorsal resin gland in young foliage, on old foliage showing as dried specks of white resin; crushed foliage with resinous grapefruit scent. *Flowers* On previous season's shoots in late winter; male cones ovoid, yellow, 4 mm (0.2 in).
Fruit Globose, ripening in second autumn; one-year cones green or green-brown, full-size, second-year cones brown, 1.7–2.3 cm (0.7–0.9 in); scales with transverse forward-pointing prickle.

Range: Central Arizona, USA.

Habitat: Cultivated in Europe as an ornamental, in the wild found on dry rocky hillsides with other conifers.

Varieties: 'Pyramidalis' is the commonest form in cultivation and is as described above, but 'Hodgins' has a narrower habit.

Synonyms: *C. arizonica* var. *glabra*.

This small tree is frequently planted for the blue-grey foliage, which tends to emerge in early summer more silvery blue, and the neat conical habit. It tolerates a wide variety of sites and soils, being especially suited to chalk and limestone. It is closely related to *C. arizonica*, differing in the smooth purple and flaky (not fibrous), bark and the leaves having active resin glands or with white flecks of dried resin.

---

p.42 **Gowen Cypress** or **Californian Cypress**
Cupressus goveniana

Description: Evergreen tree 15–20 m (50–65 ft) with a bole diameter of up to 60 cm (2 ft).
Crown Columnar, or occasionally spreading. *Bark* Brown to grey, smooth in young trees but becoming rough and peeling in fine fibrous strips. *Shoot* Green for first year, becoming red-brown, later dark red-brown, slender, 1 mm (0.1 in) or less at tips. *Buds* Hidden in axils of the scale leaves. *Foliage* Widely spreading three-dimensional sprays; leaves in

decussate pairs, acute tips either pressed on or forwards close to the stem, dorsal resin gland fairly prominent on scale leaves on strong shoots but elsewhere absent, grey-green, 1–2 mm (0.1 in); crushed foliage has strong scent of citrinella. *Flowers* On previous season's shoots in late winter; male cones 3 mm, pale yellow; female cones 2 mm (0.1 in), pale green. *Fruit* Globose, ripening glossy dark brown in second autumn, 1.5 cm (0.6 in); scales six to eight with stout forward-pointing prickle.

Range: In the wild, it is restricted to two localities near Monterey County, California.

Habitat: In two low-elevation coastal groves, cultivated as an ornamental.

Varieties: **Mendocino Cypress** (var. *pygmaea*) makes a mature tree only 1 m (3.3 ft) high on particularly barren sands at Mendocino White Plains, hence the name; however, on more favoured localities in Mendocino and Sonoma counties, California, it grows to 30 m (100 ft), a vigour emulated in cultivation. It differs from the typical variety in darker foliage, shiny warted seeds and longer pointed scale leaves.

Similar species: **Santa Cruz Cypress** *C. abramsiana* is a related species from the Santa Cruz mountains where it occurs in *Pinus ponderosa* forest; it has larger cones to 3 cm (1.2 in).

This is one of the hardiest of cypresses.

---

p.45 **Leyland Cypress** *Cupressus* × *leylandii*

Description: Evergreen tree to 20–35 m (65–115 ft) with a bole diameter of up to 1 m (3.3 ft). *Crown* Columnar with a pointed apex and a leading shoot which is offset to one side; in coastal sites, it may be broader and conical. *Bark* Bark smooth, brown-green in young trees, becoming dark brown, shallowly ridged and flaking and later stringy. *Shoot* Green for the first winter, then pale red and later red-brown or greyish. *Buds* Hidden in axils of the scale leaves. *Foliage* In flat pendent sprays to about 30 cm (1 ft) long with short side shoots about 10 × 2 cm (4 × 0.8 in); leaves in decussate pairs, pointing forwards, apex acute and free or rounded and incurved, 2–10 mm (0.1–0.4 in), grey-green to bluish grey, resin glands faint or absent; crushed foliage with an earthy resinous scent, similar to *C. nootkatensis*.

Flowers On previous season's shoots in late winter; male cones 3 mm (0.1 in), yellow; female cones green, very flat and open, 4 mm (0.2 in) across. *Fruit* If present, ripen in the second year through green to brown with small spreading pointed dorsal prickle, about 1.5 cm (0.6 in).

Range: Cultivated hybrid.

Habitat: Only known in cultivation.

Varieties: As a sterile hybrid species, it is represented by several cultivars. 'Haggerston Grey' is the commonest one, having grey-green foliage and pointed scale leaves with free tips. Next most planted is 'Castlewellan', in which the foliage is a dull bronzy yellow. 'Robinson's Gold' has better-coloured foliage but is harder to propagate. 'Naylor's Blue' has grey-blue foliage and makes an attractive bluish tree, especially when festooned with drops of rain after a shower. Other clones include 'Leighton Green' (grey-green leaves and massed cones), 'Stapehill' (inclined to suffer in dry years and become very sparse), and 'Silver Dust' and 'Harlequin', two sports with creamy white or ivory white variegations.

Synonyms: × *Cupressocyparis leylandii*.

This very vigorous tree is a hybrid of two American cypresses but is sterile. Apart from the limited number of clones, it is produced by cuttings. It is closer to the *C. nootkatensis* parent, from which it also acquires hardiness. If *C. nootkatensis* is treated as a *Chamaecyparis nootkatensis*, the hybrid genus × *Cupressocyparis* has to be used for this tree. It makes a good specimen tree but is mainly used for hedges and screens, tolerating clipping well but growing a little too quickly!

p.43 **Mexican Cypress** *Cupressus lindleyi*

Description: Evergreen tree to 15–25 m (50–80 ft) with a bole diameter up to 1 m (3.3 ft).
Crown Conical and rather open when young, then columnar, usually narrow but sometimes with spreading branches.
Bark Rich brown, becoming shallowly fissured into spiralling spiral strips.
Shoot Pale green with a waxy bloom in first winter, subsequently turning light red-brown and then darkening with age, moderately slender, 1.5 mm (0.1 in).
Buds Hidden in axils of the scale leaves.
Foliage Set in hanging somewhat flattened sprays which are usually glaucous or bloomed with a waxy covering; leaves in decussate pairs, tips acute, free for end 1 mm (0.1 in), either incurved or at an acute angle to the shoot, 1.5–5 mm (0.1–0.2 in), dorsal resin gland indistinct; crushed foliage effectively scentless. *Flowers* On previous season's shoots in late winter; male cones yellow, 3–4 mm (0.1–0.2 in); female cones pale bluish green 2 mm (0.1 in).
Fruit Globose, glaucous blue in first year, ripening to brown in second year, about 1.5 cm (0.6 in), scales six to eight, with a small recurved dorsal prickle.

Range: Central and southern Mexico into northern Guatemala.

Habitat: Cultivated in Europe as an ornamental, in Mexico in dry open forest.

Varieties: Cultivars include 'Glauca Pendula', which has strongly glaucous foliage which is weeping at the branch ends. It is a fine selection, although such trees are common in central Mexico.

Similar species: **Cedar of Goa** *C. lusitanica* has been cultivated in Portugal since trees were planted at Bussaco, near Coimbra in 1634. The origin of these trees is a mystery, although the origin given was the Portuguese territory of Goa, on the west coast of India. Botanists subsequently identified it with Mexican Cypress, although as Mexico was a Spanish colony and the Portuguese and Spaniards were rivals in the 17th century, no satisfactory answer was

produced to explain its occurrence in
Portugal and to disprove the Indian origin.
Recent analysis using essential oils and
DNA is consistent with it not being related
to the cypresses of Mexico but to cypresses
from north-east India in Assam and
Darjeeling. The species has attained 30 m
(100 ft) with a bole diameter of 1 m (3.3 ft)
in Portugal, and has glaucous, pendent
foliage and glaucous cones with a broad
point terminated by a small prickle. It is
only known for certain from Portugal.

Bentham Cypress *C. benthamii* is a species
related to *C. lindleyi*, often as a variety, or as a
variety of *C. lusitanica*. It differs in the more
flattened sprays of foliage, and in characters
of the essential oils and DNA. It occurs in
north-east Mexico and is occasionally
cultivated.

Mexican Cypress makes a fast-growing tree
of reasonable hardiness and tolerant of a
wide range of sites. In Europe, it has long
been equated with *C. lusitanica* (which has
priority if the two are considered the same
species).

---

p.43 **Monterey Cypress** *Cupressus macrocarpa*

Description: Evergreen tree 20–30 m (65–100 ft) with a
bole diameter to 2.5 m (8 ft).
Crown Columnar in young trees, may remain
so in old trees but often becoming flat topped
with large spreading branches and
resembling *Cedrus*. *Bark* Pale brown, finely
ridged in young trees, becoming pink-brown
to pale grey with shallow cross ridges in old
trees. *Shoot* Green for the first winter, then
pale red-brown to brown as the scale leaves
die and then green-brown to brown as the
outer layer is shed as papery flakes.
Buds Hidden in the scale leaves. *Foliage* In
dense, three-dimensional sprays; scale leaves
green, with a triangular acute apex which is
pressed down on the shoot, dorsal resin gland
scarcely visible, 2 mm (0.1 in), to 1 cm
(0.4 in) on strong shoots; crushed foliage
with a resiny lemon scent. *Flowers* On

previous season's shoots in late spring; male cones yellow, 6 mm (0.25 in). *Fruit* Ripens in second year to brown, red-brown or grey, globular, 2–4 cm (0.8–1.6 in); scales 8–12, uneven, with an obscure central ridge.

Range: Cypress Point and Point Lobos, Monterey County, California.

Habitat: Cultivated in Europe as an ornamental, in the wild restricted to windswept coastal cliffs on two promontories.

Varieties: 'Lutea' has foliage which is yellow at first, then greener. It makes a more spreading tree than other forms and is more tolerant of salt sprays. It is the Monterey Cypress (*C. macrocarpa*) parent of the Leyland Cypress (*C. leylandii*) clone 'Castlewellan'. 'Goldcrest' is an upright form with golden-green foliage. Young plants, which have somewhat softer leaves with free tips, are sometimes sold as house plants. Like all cypresses, however, they need full light. 'Gold Cone', 'Gold Pillar' and 'Donard Gold' are similar selections. 'Pendula' has weeping tips to the horizontally spreading branches.

Synonyms: *C. lambertiana*.

This tree has a very restricted distribution in the wild but is widely planted as an ornamental tree, and for hedges (although for this use it has been displaced by its hybrid, *C. × leylandii*). It tolerates a wide range of sites, and is good for coastal conditions, especially the cultivar 'Lutea'. Like *C. sempervirens* and some other cypresses, it is susceptible to *Corynium* canker, caused by the fungus *Seiridium cardinale*. This infects the scale leaves and kills small portions of the crown, thus destroying their beauty. Occasionally, the fungus can grow down a stem and kill large branches or the entire tree.

---

p.45 **Nootka Cypress** *Cupressus nootkatensis*

Description: Evergreen tree 15–30 m (50–100 ft) with a bole diameter of up to 1 m (3.3 ft).
Crown Conical, varying from narrow to broad but remarkably regular, only rarely

columnar, the leading shoot is flexible and nods off to one side. *Bark* Brown or orange-brown, becoming fibrous and peeling in low stringy ridges. *Shoot* Green for first winter, then red and progressively pale red-brown later dark red-brown and smooth, moderately stout, 1.5 mm–2 cm (0.1–0.8 in). *Buds* Hidden in axils of the scale leaves. *Foliage* In very pendulous sprays which hang down either side of the main branches giving a curtain effect; sprays to 50 cm (20 in) with laterals to 11 × 3–5 cm (4.3 × 1.2–2 in); scale leaves in decussate pairs with the laterals slightly larger and keeled and the facial pair marginally smaller, acute with a bony point, slightly spreading forwards, rather dark green with a glaucous hint, pale somewhat yellow-green beneath, resin glands very faint or absent, 1.5–4 mm (0.1–0.2 in); crushed foliage with an earthy resinous smell which is sometimes equated to ox-eye daisies. *Flowers* On previous season's shoots in late winter; male cones 3 mm (0.1 in), yellow; female cones very open, to 4 mm (0.2 in) across, green. *Fruit* Globular but spiky due to the strong recurved dorsal prickles, taking two years to ripen; in first year 7 mm (0.3 in), violet-green; expanding during the second year to 1.2 cm (0.5 in) and ripening red-brown, scales four to six.

Range: Along the mountain ranges from south Alaska to northern California.

Habitat: Cultivated in Europe as an ornamental, occurring as a native tree on wet mountain sites in mixed conifer stands.

Varieties: No varieties but one cultivar is common. This is the Afghan hound tree, 'Pendula'. It has more fully pendulous branches, making a narrow, conical, gaunt tree with long pendent sprays of flat foliage carried on main branches which arch down from the trunk and up at the tips.

Synonyms: *Chamaecyparis nootkatensis*.

This tree is remarkable for the regular conical habit. It has been treated as a *Chamaecyparis* but does not fit well in that genus, differing in the cones taking two seasons to ripen, and other characters. It has hybridized in cultivation with three *Cupressus* to form hybrids but not with any *Chamaecyparis*. It tolerates a wide range of sites, including moist ones. The leaves and foliage sprays are very similar to those of *C. cashmeriana*, although slightly coarser.

p.43 ### Italian Cypress or Mediterranean Cypress *Cupressus sempervirens*

Description: Evergreen tree to 20 m (65 ft) with a bole diameter to 1.2 m (3.9 ft).

Crown Conical or spire-like in young trees, becoming columnar with spreading branches or retaining a close spire habit. *Bark* Grey-brown, developing shallow spiral scaly ridges. *Shoot* Green in first year, becoming red-brown in second and later brown; green shoots slender, 1 mm (0.1 in). *Buds* Hidden in axils of the scale leaves. *Foliage* In short somewhat flattened sprays which are arranged around the horizontal or erect shoots; leaves scale-like, in opposite pairs; on weak shoots acute, with a dorsal gland, pressed against the shoot, clothing it and making it smooth and round, 1 mm (0.1 in); on strong shoots, acute tips spread at a narrow angle, decurrent with up to 1.3 cm (0.5 in) to the next pair; crushed foliage scentless or with a light resinous aroma. *Flowers* On tips of previous season's shoots in late winter; male cones on weak shoots, ovoid, 2–3 mm (0.1 in), opening yellow; female cones small, globose and spiky, 4 mm (0.2 in), on tips of actively growing shoots. *Fruit* Ripens over two years, globose or globose-ovoid, greenish brown or grey-brown, 2.5–3.5 cm (1–1.4 in); scales with a blunt triangular dorsal rounded knob.

Range: Shores of the eastern Mediterranean across to northern Iran.

Habitat: Limestone areas, although happily growing on other well-drained soils.

Varieties: The typical variety is probably the less common form with horizontal spreading branches (var. *horizontalis*). In cultivation, the form with erect branches and a very narrow habit predominates; this is forma *stricta* and comes true (more or less) from seed.

The wild distribution of this tree is obscured by it having been planted widely throughout the Mediterranean region. It is almost certainly not native to Italy and occurs naturally no further west than Greece. It, and other, cypresses are suffering from a disease, *Corynium* canker, caused by the fungus *Seiridium cardinale*. This infects the scale leaves, girdling the shoot. A few of the infections grow down the stem and may girdle side branches, eventually causing the death (visible as brown or red-brown patches) of portions of the crown. It rarely kills the tree but can destroy its amenity value.

---

p.44 **West Himalayan Cypress**
Cupressus torulosa

Description: Evergreen tree 15–25 m (50–80 ft) with a bole diameter of 60 cm (2 ft).
Crown Conical as a young tree, becoming columnar, with spreading branches and drooping laterals. *Bark* Dull brown and smooth when young, soon developing shallow curling ridges; in old trees, becoming fibrous and peeling in strips. *Shoot* Light green from live leaf bases, becoming red-brown and then ageing to shiny mid brown, slender with green shoots 1–1.5 mm (0.1 in) diameter. *Buds* Hidden in axils of the scale leaves. *Foliage* Foliage in rather flattened pendent sprays; leaves scale-like, in decussate pairs at right angles, forming nearly round ultimate shoots; scales acute, with tips pressed against the shoot, 1.5 mm (0.1 in) long, with small vestigial dorsal resin gland; crushed foliage with a faint resin scent. *Flowers* On previous years shoots, opening in late winter; male cones terminal on weak shoots, with seven or eight pairs of scales, 4 mm (0.2 in), green and yellow; female cones terminal on stronger shoots, globose, with four or five pairs of scale, 3 mm (0.1 in), black and green, ovules naked between the scales at

pollination, visible as minute dots to naked eye or under a hand-lens. *Fruit* Ripens over two years; one-year cone, ovoid-globose with spreading rounded knob on scales, green and brown, 1 cm (0.4 in), (at this stage the cone is soft and resinous); mature cone, 1.5 cm (0.6 in), ripens woody to red-brown, with less-prominent rounded knobs.

Range: Northwest Himalayas from northwest India to central Nepal.

Habitat: Cultivated in collections in Europe, in the wild occurring on open hillsides, especially on limestone.

This makes an attractive cypress. It has been confused with related trees from southern Tibet (*C. gigantea*, which has stouter foliage shoots, blue-green foliage and makes a narrow upright tree to 10 m (33 ft) in cultivation but 30 m (100 ft) × 6 m (20 ft) in diameter in Tibet) and from Sichuan, China (*C. chengiana*, with flatter sprays of fresher green foliage).

TREE FERNS, CYATHEACEAE

The tree ferns, *Dicksonia*, p.664.

QUINCE, *CYDONIA*
FAMILY ROSACEAE

This genus consists of only the one widely cultivated species, although in the past it has been used as a repository for several taxa now given separate generic status (for example, the shrubby flowering quince or 'Japonica' which is in the genus *Chaenomeles*). The large pear-shaped or apple-shaped fruits with a deliciously fragrant flesh and the oblong, ovate to elliptic, untoothed leaves which are densely woolly on the underside, distinguish the genus. The flowers are single and carried on short leafy shoots.

---

p.129 **Quince** *Cydonia oblonga*

Description: Deciduous tree to 8 m (26 ft) with a bole diameter to 30 cm (1 ft).
Crown Rounded, dense and twiggy.

Bark Smooth and purplish grey, flaking in large plates to reveal orange beneath.
Shoot Initially covered with a loose white wool, becoming shiny dark green to purple by autumn and nearly hairless, slightly grooved, in later years dark chocolate brown with orange lenticels. *Buds* Ovoid but flattened against the shoot, pointed, red-brown with white hairs, 3 mm (0.1 in).
Foliage Leaves oval, nearly rounded in outline, or ovate, apex with a short blunt point, base broad wedge-shaped to truncate, margin untoothed, upper surface shiny green with slightly impressed veins, underside whitish green, with long greyish wool, becoming hairless, with raised veins, 5–10 × 4–9 cm (2–4 × 1.6–3.5 in); leaf stalk grooved, green or purplish pink, warty and initially woolly, 0.5–1.5 cm (0.2–0.6 in); autumn colour yellow.
Flowers Solitary, terminal on short shoots with two or three leaves, petals white or pink and cupped, 4–5 cm (1.6–2 in) across, in May. *Fruit* Pear-shaped or obovoid, or globose, apex rounded and indented with the persistent calyx, constricted and tapering to an indented base with a short stalk less than 1 cm (0.4 in), golden yellow, with a thin covering of white wool, 2.5–12 × 2–8 cm (1–4.7 × 0.8–3.1 in), delightfully fragrant.

Range: Cultivated throughout southern Europe and in North Africa but probably native to western Asia.
Habitat: Naturalized in hedges and woodland.
Synonyms: *Pyrus cydonia.*

The fragrance of a ripe quince can fill a room and is similar to that of Passion Fruit. They can be made into a preserve, with the word 'marmalade' deriving from the Portuguese name for quince jam. They are, however, astringent when raw. The large flowers are usually pink, and quite showy. The origin of the quince is obscured by cultivation and subsequent naturalization. It is believed to derive from western and central Asia. Apart from its fruit, quince is used as a rootstock onto which cultivated pears are grafted.

BROOMS, *CYTISUS*
FAMILY LEGUMINOSAE

This is a group of mainly shrubs from southern Europe, extending into North Africa and western Asia. In most species, the leaves are small and fleeting, with photosynthesis carried out through the green stems. However, in the small-tree species listed here, the leaves are trifoliate, resembling those of *Laburnum* (p.773), but hairy. The flowers are pea-like, but in *C. battandieri* they are in erect racemes (cf. pendulous in *Laburnum*). The fruit is a typical legume pod, opening explosively to scatter the seeds. It does not have the thickened sutures found in *Laburnum*.

p.308 | **Moroccan Broom** or **Pineapple Broom**
Cytisus battandieri

Description: Deciduous shrub or small tree to 6 m (20 ft).
Crown Rounded. *Bark* Green-brown, smooth. *Shoot* Initially white-silky, green for several years but hairless from the second year. *Buds* Ovoid, silky hairy. *Foliage* Leaves trifoliate, silky white hairy (sericeous) when young, becoming hairless above but remaining silky beneath; leaflets obovate, apex rounded or notched, base wedge-shaped with a short leaflet stalk, margin untoothed, leaflets 4–6 × 2.5–3 cm (1.6–2.4 × 1–1.2 in); leaf stalk grooved, silky, 1.5–3 cm (0.6–1.2 in); in autumn, colour poor. *Flowers* Terminal or lateral on short leafy shoots in mid-summer in dense golden yellow, erect or spreading racemes, deliciously scented of pineapple, on a silky white hairy stalk, 7–12 cm (2.8–4.7 in). *Fruit* Erect or spreading stiff legume 4–5 cm (1.6–2 in) long with six or seven seeds.

Range: Middle Atlas Mountains of Morocco.
Habitat: Cultivated as an ornamental, in the wild occurring on open hillsides.

This small tree or large shrub comes from around 1800 m (5900 ft) in the Middle Atlas Mountains of Morocco. It has trifoliate leaves, like those of *Laburnum*, but the flowers are in shorter erect racemes.

Dove Tree, Davidiaceae
(Synonym: Nyssaceae in part)

This is a monotypic family related to, and often included in, the Nyssaceae.

Dove Tree, *Davidia*
Family Davidiaceae

This is a monotypic genus currently treated as having two varieties. The leaves are lime-like in shape. The buds are reddish, conic. The flowers lack a corolla. They are in a cluster of many male flowers with a single (rarely two) egg-shaped ovary near the apex. They are subtended by two, rarely three, large bracts which flop down and appear like doves sitting in the tree. The bracts are of unequal size, gradually enlarging and colouring from green to creamy white. The fruit is a drupe with a thick green outer covering over the woody nut, and contains three to ten seeds. The roots are thick and fleshy.

---

p.238 **Dove Tree** or **Ghost Tree**
Davidia involucrata var. *vilmoriniana*

Description: Deciduous tree 10–20 m (33–65 ft) with a bole diameter to 80 cm (2.6 ft).
Crown Conic in young trees, but the branches tending to radiate out from a short bole so that older trees have rounded or domed crowns on spreading usually level branches. *Bark* Grey-brown or pale brown, soon finely fissured and flaking, in old trees becoming scaly at the base. *Shoot* Green, shiny and hairless with small linear lenticels in the first year, purplish grey-brown in later years. *Buds* Ovoid-conic, pointed, green to shiny deep red over winter, 5–10 mm (0.2–0.4 in). *Foliage* Leaves ovate, tapered to the slender-pointed, short bristle-like apex, base sub-cordate to heart-shaped, margin with broad triangular forward-directed teeth, upper surface matt green with the veins slightly impressed, underside glaucous pale green, hairless or with just the occasional long straight hair, with five to nine pairs of raised veins forwards at 45 degrees, 12–20 × 7–15 cm (4.7–8 × 2.8–6 in); leaf stalk hairless, grooved, yellow-green or pink,

6–15 cm (2.4–6 in); autumn colour yellow. *Flowers* Pendulous on long stalks in late spring (May), a globose head 2 cm (0.8 in) across of massed stamens, subtended by two or rarely three large leafy bracts; bracts unequal, at first erect but as they enlarge and turn from green to white or cream, they droop either side of the flower head, with the larger one 10–25 cm (4–10 in) long, the smaller 7–15 cm (2.8–6 in). *Fruit* Broad ovoid to long ovoid drupe 3–4 × 2–2.5 cm (1.2–1.6 × 0.8–1 in), purple or green, finally russet, fleshy coating which rots to reveal the hard ridged nut with three to five cells.

Range: China from west Hubei, Sichuan, south Gansu, Hunan, Guizhou and north Yunnan.

Habitat: Cultivated as an ornamental, in the wild occurring in mixed broadleafed forests on hillsides.

Varieties: The above description covers var. *vilmoriniana* which is the common form in cultivation. The typical form is var. *involucrata*. This differs most markedly in the leaves which are pale green, not glaucous, beneath and densely covered (especially on the veins) by long white hairs, giving a velvety feel. The fruits may also be oblate, i.e. rounded but flattened at the ends. It makes an equally fine tree, being predominant at the western end of the species range. Recent research has shown that var. *vilmoriniana* has one extra pair of chromosomes which will effectively prevent the two varieties interbreeding. It may therefore be more appropriate to treat them as two closely allied species. Var. *vilmoriniana* would then become *D. vilmoriniana*.

Synonyms: *D. vilmoriniana*.

In May, this tree is spectacular when covered with the large drooping white bracts, which are derived from modified leaves. The ovoid hard fruit hanging down from the branches on long stalks is also characteristic. At other times, it can be distinguished by the lime-like leaves and the ovoid-conic buds which have several scales (only two exposed scales in *Tilia*). The Dove Tree has fleshy roots and can be difficult to transplant, requiring attention to watering until the tree has been established for some time. The young leaves are frost tender. An alternative common name is 'Pocket Handkerchief Tree', which does not have the poetic ring of 'Dove Tree'.

DECAISNEA, *DECAISNEA*
FAMILY LARDIZABALACEAE

This genus comprises two species. The shoots are rather thick and pithy, covered with a grey waxy bloom and prominent buds during the winter. The leaves are pinnate, large and held out at stiff angles. The yellow-green flowers are in drooping panicles which terminate the new growths; they have six sepals but no petals. The fruit is a cylindrical follicle with many flattened dark-brown seeds in a latex-rich pulp.

---

p.325 **Decaisnea** *Decaisnea fargesii*

Description: Deciduous shrub or small tree to 8 m (26 ft) with a bole diameter to 20 cm (8 in). *Crown* Domed, rather sprawling and often on more than one stem. *Bark* Brown, rough. *Shoot* Stout, hairless, green with a waxy bloom when young, later brown. *Buds* Conical, pointed, glaucous, to 1.5 cm (0.6 in). *Foliage* Leaves pinnate, overall 60–90 cm (24–36 in), leaflets 13–25, ovate, slender-pointed tip, base rounded to wedge-shaped with a short stalk, margin entire, upper surface mid green with slightly impressed veins, hairless, lower surface rather glaucous green with raised veins, hairless, 7–15 × 5–10 cm (2.8–6 × 2–4 in); leaf stalk rounded, pink or yellow, with an enlarged base; autumn colour yellow. *Flowers* In drooping panicles which terminate the new growths, 30–50 cm (12–20 in), flowers with six yellow-green 3 cm (1.2 in) pointed sepals. *Fruit* Cylindrical pod 7–10 × 2–3 cm (2.8–4 × 0.8–1.2 in), dull blue with a thick covering of waxy bloom, containing many flat 1 cm (0.4 in) dark brown or blackish seeds set in a pulp with a milky sap.

Range: Western China from Yunnan, Sichuan, Guizhou and south into northern Vietnam.

Habitat: Cultivated as an ornamental, in the wild occurring in thickets on mountain slopes.

Similar species: *D. insignis* is similar but the fruit is greenish yellow or golden-yellow. It is found in the Himalayas from Nepal eastwards.

This small tree has bold foliage and is especially attractive when carrying the blue fruits. It is susceptible to spring frosts, even the trees in northern Vietnam.

TREE FERN, *DICKSONIA*
FAMILY CYATHEACEAE

Dicksonia is a genus of ferns which can make small to medium trees. The primary difference between ferns and all the other trees listed here is that ferns produce spores, not seeds. The leaves are large compound fronds, carried at the tops of the usually unbranched stems. There are about 25 species of *Dicksonia* in Australasia, Polynesia and Mexico. The genus *Cyathea* differs in the base of the fronds having shaggy brown scales, not woolly brown hairs as in *Dicksonia*.

---

p. 350 **Tree Fern** *Dicksonia antarctica*

Description: Evergreen tree 5–15 m (16–49 ft) with a single stem up to 60 cm (2 ft) in diameter.
Crown Monopodal, unbranched.
Bark Densely covered with the bases of old leaves and matted roots, brown.
Leaves Fronds to 2 m × 60 cm (6 × 2 ft), tri-pinnate or much divided, dark green, rachis greenish brown or green, sparsely covered with softly shaggy and silky hairs.
Flowers Spores carried on margins of leaves.
Range: South and east Australia, from Tasmania, New South Wales, Victoria and Queensland.
Habitat: Cultivated as an ornamental in the milder damper parts of western Europe.
Similar species: *Cyathea dealbata* differs in the more slender trunk to no more than 20 cm (8 in) diameter and in the larger leaves to 4 m (13 ft), which are bright green above and white or bright silver-grey beneath. It comes from New Zealand.

This is the hardiest tree fern and is only at home in the mildest Atlantic fringes of the British Isles. It can be slow growing.

PERSIMMONS OR EBONY, *DIOSPYROS*
FAMILY EBENACEAE

A very large genus of mainly tropical trees, best known for the black wood (ebony) and the fruit. It is distinguished by the four spreading sepals at the base of the fruit. These enlarge after the flowers on female trees have finished. The fruit contains a number of oblong, flattened seeds and is tasty when fully ripe. The leaves are untoothed, glossy green above and set alternately on the shoots, which do not form terminal buds.

---

p.153 **Persimmon** *Diospyros kaki*

Description: Deciduous tree to 14 m (46 ft).
Crown Rounded to columnar. *Bark* Fissures into squarrish scales. *Shoot* Initially downy. *Buds* Ovoid, downy. *Foliage* Leaves elliptic ovate, oblong-ovate to obovate, apex acute, base broad wedge-shaped, margin untoothed, upper surface becoming hairless and lustrous dark green, paler and hairy beneath, 7–20 × 4–9 cm (2.8–8 × 1.6–3.5 in); leaf stalk 1–1.5 cm (0.4–0.6 in); autumn colour red. *Flowers* Yellowish white; male flowers in threes 1 cm (0.4 in), with 16–24 stamens; female flowers 1.5–1.8 cm (0.6–0.7 in), with the styles divided to the base. *Fruit* Ovoid to depressed globose with a pointed apex, subtended by the large leafy and four lobed calyx, ripening orange to yellow, 3.5–7 cm (1.4–2.8 in).

Range: China and Japan, widely cultivated.
Habitat: Cultivated as a fruit tree.

This produces the Persimmon or Sharon fruit of commerce. The fruit is astringent until softened by overripening, when the flesh becomes sweet and juicy. It is a native to eastern Asia but widely cultivated and its original rather lost with time.

---

p.153 **Date Plum** *Diospyros lotus*

Description: Deciduous tree to 10–20 m (33–65 ft) with a bole diameter 30–50 cm (1–1.6 ft).
Crown Upright narrow dome to a rounded dome. *Bark* Black or dark pinkish grey,

becoming cracked into small squares.
Shoot Green, sparsely white hairy at first,
becoming brown or greyish brown and
hairless. *Buds* Conic, pointed, flattened,
green and brown, sparsely hairy, 6 mm
(0.25 in). *Foliage* Leaves oval-elliptic,
rounded with a short slender-pointed tip,
rounded to wedge-shaped at the base, margin
untoothed but wavy, upper surface sub-shiny
somewhat greyish green to lustrous deep
green and variably haired, underside pale
green with scattered white hairs, with dense
golden-brown hairs on the raised midrib and
veins, 6–18 × 2.5–5 cm (2.4–7.1 × 1–2 in);
leaf stalk grooved, sparsely hairy, green,
5–10 mm (0.2–0.4 in); autumn colour
yellow; crushed foliage with a curious smell.
Flowers In leaf axils of current season's shoots
in July, with four large green calyx lobes;
males two to three in a small cyme, female
flowers urn-shaped, solitary, 8–10 mm
(0.3–0.4 in), with yellow, green or reddish
petals. *Fruit* Globose, with a short pointed
tip, yellow or purplish, 1.5 cm (0.6 in), with
the large green four-pointed calyx at the base,
ripening to a fleshy juicy fruit in southern
climates with several oval dark-brown seeds.

Range: Asia, widely cultivated.

Habitat: Cultivated as an ornamental and for the
fruit, of uncertain wild origin.

This makes a small tree which is quite hardy
in northern Europe but does not ripen the
fruit. In the south, it is widely naturalized
and also cultivated. Its wild origin is
obscured by long-term cultivation, but I have
seen it both in the Forbidden City in Beijing
and in Buddhist monasteries in Bhutan.

---

p.153 **Persimmon** *Diospyros virginiana*

Description: Deciduous tree 15–20 m (50–65 ft), rarely
to 30 m (100 ft), with a bole diameter to
60 cm (2 ft).
Crown Columnar with a rounded top.
Bark Soon cracked into small squares,
brown or blackish. *Shoot* Green with white
hairs and small rounded lenticels, light buff-

brown in the second year. *Buds* Slender conical, sharp pointed, green, 3 mm (0.1 in). *Foliage* Leaves oval to elliptic, tapering to the acute to short slender-pointed apex, base wedge-shaped, margin untoothed but wavy, upper surface shiny dark green, underside pale whitish green with raised midrib, variously hairless or hairy, 6–15 × 4–7.5 cm (2.4–6 × 1.6–3 in); leaf stalk slightly winged or grooved from the decurrent base of the leaf, hairy, 1–1.5 cm (0.4–0.6 in); autumn colour yellow. *Flowers* Bell-shaped, fragrant and stalkless or almost so in the axils of the leaves, with four white lobes to the corolla, separate male and female trees, males in clusters of two or three flowers, female flowers solitary. *Fruit* Rounded or slightly flattened, 2–4 cm (0.8–1.6 in) across and set on the persistent four-lobed calyx, ripening to orange or purplish brown and juicy, containing four to eight large flat shiny brown seeds 2 cm (0.8 in).

Range: Southeastern USA from Connecticut south to Florida, across to eastern Texas and Iowa.

Habitat: Cultivated as an ornamental, in the wild favouring valley bottoms, hillsides and mixed forest.

The fruit is tasty when ripe and juicy but very astringent when immature due to the concentration of tannins.

DIPTERONIA, *DIPTERONIA*
FAMILY ACERACEAE

This genus consists of two species. It is related to *Acer*, sharing the opposite leaves and buds and the winged fruits. The distinguishing characters are the pinnate leaves (more than seven leaflets), the naked buds, the wing of the fruit encircling the nutlet and the more shrubby habit.

---

p.315 **Dipteronia** *Dipteronia sinensis*

Description: Deciduous shrubby tree 10–15 m (33–50 ft) with a bole diameter to 30 cm (1 ft). *Crown* Rounded, usually on several stems. *Shoot* Purple to purplish green, slender,

smooth, initially hairy but becoming hairless, with oval lenticels first becoming prominent on two-year-old shoots.
Buds In opposite pairs, naked, hairy, small.
Foliage Leaves pinnate, usually in three to five pairs, 20–40 cm (8–16 in); leaflets oblong-ovate to oblong-lanceolate, apex fairly long to long slender pointed, base rounded to wedge-shaped, margin with acute to bluntly pointed teeth near the apex but untoothed lower down, upper surface deep green, hairless, underside paler, hairless, except for tufts in the axils of the 10–11 pairs of raised veins, 7–10 × 2–4 cm (2.8–4 × 0.8–1.6 in); leaflets stalkless to stalked, especially the terminal one; autumn colour yellow. *Flowers* In erect terminal or axillary hairless panicles 15–30 cm (6–12 in) on 3–5 cm (1.2–2 in) stalks; flowers white, 2.5 mm (0.1 in) across, with eight stamens and five petals.
Fruit Two compressed nutlets which are connate or jointed at the base and encircled by a rounded to obovate wing, 2–2.5 × 1.7–2.3 cm (0.8–1 × 0.7–0.9 in); seed rounded in outline, 5 mm (0.2 in).

Range: China from Henan, Sichuan, Hubei, Shaanxi and Guizhou provinces.

Habitat: Cultivated as an ornamental; in the wild an understorey tree in broadleafed woodland.

Uncommon tree in cultivation, and is usually seen on several stems. The fruits are similar to those of *Ulmus* and *Ptelea* with their broad wing surrounding the nutlet, but the pinnate and opposite leaves clearly separate it.

DRAGON TREE, *DRACAENA*
FAMILY AGAVACEAE

This genus is similar to *Cordyline*, differing mainly in the fruits containing only a single seed.

---

p.351   **Dragon Tree** *Dracaena draco*

Description: Evergreen tree to 18 m (60 ft) with a thick bole.

Crown Unbranched until after first flowering, developing radiating branches every time it flowers. *Bark* Fluted and convoluted. *Shoot* Stout, hidden beneath the leaves, fallen leaves revealing dark-red resinous areas. *Buds* Not visible.

Foliage Leaves spirally arranged, arching or reflexed in dense rosettes, lanceolate with the base broadening and clasping the shoot, apex pointed, margin untoothed, glaucous green but tinged red at base, without an obvious midrib, 30–60 × 2.5–4 cm (12–24 × 1–1.6 in). *Flowers* In large much branched terminal panicles with flowers in groups of four or five; flowers greenish white.

Fruit Globose, orange-yellow to reddish orange single-seeded berry, 1.5 cm (0.6 in).

Range: Canary Islands, Madeira and Morocco.

Habitat: Cultivated as an ornamental in mild areas.

Similar species: Other species are sometimes grown in the mildest parts of the Mediterranean or in glasshouses and can make trees with time:

D. arborea, from tropical Africa. This has leaves to 1.5 m × 4–10 cm (5 ft × 1.6–4 in), with a distinct midrib on the underside and flowers in threes, creamy white, to 2 cm (0.8 in). It can attain 20 m (65 ft).

D. umbraculifera, an uncertain native of Mauritius, has leaves to 1 m (3.3 ft) by no more than 3 cm (1.2 in) which have a prominent midrib on both sides.

D. fragrans from tropical Africa has bright green leaves 0.5–1.5 m × 5–10 cm (1.6–5 ft × 2–4 in) with a prominent midrib beneath and very fragrant 1.5–2.5 cm (0.6–1 in) flowers.

This tree is the hardiest species of a large, mainly African genus, but is only hardy close to the Mediterranean.

DRIMYS, *DRIMYS*
FAMILY WINTERACEAE

This is a genus of around twenty species from South America north to Mexico, New Caledonia, Malaysia and eastern Australia. The fruits consist of a single whorl of carpels and have been used as a pepper substitute.

p.167 **Winter's Bark** *Drimys winteri*

Description: Evergreen tree to 20 m (65 ft) with a bole
diameter to 60 cm (2 ft).
Crown Conical and rather whorled when
young, becoming more open with age.
Bark Smooth, orange-brown, aromatic.
Shoot Light green or with a pinkish purple
hue, slightly hairy with dark glands at first,
green in the second year and remaining so for
several years, aromatic if scraped, smooth and
without the stipular scars seen in *Magnolia*.
Buds Ovoid with a long slender, sharply-
pointed beak, to 8 mm (0.3 in).
Foliage Leaves oblanceolate to oblong-ovate,
tapering to the narrow rounded apex and to
the wedge-shaped base, margin untoothed,
leathery in texture, upper surface sub-shiny,
smooth, underside bright glaucous white and
papillose when viewed through a hand-lens,
midrib green and raised only towards the
base, crushed foliage aromatic, 7–17 ×
2–6 cm (2.8–6.7 × 0.8–2.4 in); leaf stalk
with a shallow groove caused by ridges which
are decurrent from the leaf blade, warty,
green, 0.7–2.5 cm (0.3–1 in); leaves retained
for four years. *Flowers* In June in a fascicled
or umbellate inflorescence with several
fragrant ivory-white flowers to 4 cm (1.6 in)
on 2.5 cm (1 in) stalks. *Fruit* A compound
fleshy carpel with a number of seeds.

Range: Central-south Chile, and west Argentina.

Habitat: Cultivated as an ornamental, in the wild
occurring in woods and shrubberies.

The leaves resemble *Magnolia virginiana*
and the tree is related to the Magnolia
family; however, it can be quickly
distinguished by the absence of stipules
(compare the shoots). The bark has been
used as a spice and as a source of vitamin C
and it was in these roles that Captain
Winter, who accompanied Francis Drake
on his round-the-world trip in 1577–1580,
first collected it. Some accounts treat
Winter's Bark as extending throughout
South America into Mexico, but the plants
in the northern part of this range are
usually treated as separate species.

EBONY, EBENACEAE

This family consists of two mainly tropical genera. Only *Diospyros* (p.665) is occasionally cultivated in Europe.

EHRETIA, EHRETIACEAE
(SYNONYM: BORAGINACEAE IN PART)

This small family is sometimes included in the Boraginaceae.

EHRETIA, *EHRETIA*
FAMILY EHRETIACEAE

This is a genus of around 50 species.

p.201 Ehretia *Ehretia dicksonii*

Description: Deciduous tree 10–20 m (33–65 ft) with a bole diameter to 50 cm (1.6 ft).
Crown Spreading, variable. *Bark* Light brown, deeply furrowed. *Shoot* Green at first with stiff spreading whitish hairs, nearly hairless and brown by late summer, in the second year dark brown with pale striations or grey. *Buds* Small dark-brown broad-based cones, with light-brown hairs, 1 × 3 mm (0.1 in). *Foliage* Leaves broad elliptic, tapering to an acute and short slender-pointed apex, base wedge-shaped, margin with small very broad-based spreading teeth, upper surface scabrid (rough) due to stiff pointed white hairs, mid green and sub-shiny, underside light shiny green, similarly rough, veins raised, hairy, 10–25 × 5–10 cm (4–10 × 2–4 in); leaf stalk green, grooved, hairy (especially in the groove), 2–3 cm (0.8–1.2 in); autumn colour poor. *Flowers* In flattish panicles 5–10 cm (2–4 in) across in May–June, corolla 1 cm (0.4 in) across, white. *Fruit* Sub-globose drupe, 1.2 cm (0.5 in), greenish yellow.

Range: China and Taiwan.

Habitat: Cultivated as an ornamental.

Similar species: *E. ovalifolia* (syn. *E. thyrsiflora*) carries the fragrant flowers in August, in larger pyramidal panicles to 20 cm (8 in) across. The shoots are hairless, and the leaves have axillary tufts in the vein axils. It comes from China and Japan, with a closely related species extending into Australia.

The leaves are rough to the touch but the flowers can be attractive in season. As a young tree, it is susceptible to spring frost.

RUSSIAN OLIVE, ELAEAGNACEAE

This small family contains three genera, *Elaeagnus*, *Hippophäe* (p.738) and the shrubby North American *Shephardia*. The family is characterized by copious silvery scales. *Hippophäe* has separate male and female plants, whilst in *Elaeagnus* the flowers are perfect, i.e. containing functional male and female parts.

RUSSIAN OLIVES, *ELAEAGNUS*
FAMILY ELAEAGNACEAE

This is a small genus from the northern hemisphere. The flowers are tubular, fragrant and perfect. The plants are covered in silvery scales, including the flesh on the edible and tasty fruits, which are single-seeded drupes. The plants have nitrogen-fixing bacteria in the roots.

p.166 **Russian Olive** or **Oleaster**
Elaeagnus angustifolia

Description: Deciduous shrub to small tree, 6–12 m (20–39 ft) in height.
Crown Rounded. *Bark* Fissured.
Shoot Silvery grey with glistening scales, darker and hairless by the second year, occasionally spiny. *Buds* Small, ovoid, with few scales. *Foliage* Leaves lanceolate to narrow oblong, apex acute to bluntly pointed, base broad wedge-shaped, margin untoothed, upper surface dull green with scattered scales, underside silvered with

many scales, 2.5–9 × 1–1.5 cm (1–3.5 × 0.4–0.6 in); leaf stalk 5–8 mm (0.2–0.3 in). *Flowers* Fragrant, single or in twos or threes from the leaf axils in June, corolla bell-shaped with four spreading lobes, yellow on the inner surface, white and scaly on the outer surface, 1 cm (0.4 in). *Fruit* Oval drupe with a mealy sweet flesh, ripening to yellow, scaly, 1–1.5 cm (0.4–0.6 in).

Range: West and central Asia, widely naturalized or cultivated in central and southern Europe.

Habitat: Open sunny sites.

Similar species: Many other species of Russian Olive are cultivated and occasionally naturalized in parts of Europe but tend to be definite shrubs, not trees. They include evergreen species and hybrids as well as deciduous ones, some of which are spring flowering with the fruit ripening in the autumn; in others, the flowers open in the autumn and the fruit ripens over the winter. *E. commutata* from across northern North America has the leaves strongly silvery on both sides. It is also spring flowered. *E. pungens* from Japan is autumn flowered and evergreen.

This small tree has fragrant flowers and tasty fruits and has been cultivated for centuries. The silvery foliage makes it useful as a small landscape tree.

FIRE BUSH, *EMBOTHRIUM*
FAMILY PROTEACEAE

This genus comes from Central and Southern South America. The flowers have a tubular corolla which splits into four strap-like segments. The fruit is a woody follicle which contains many winged seeds.

p.167 **Fire Bush** *Embothrium coccineum*

Description: Evergreen or semi-evergreen tree to 15 m (50 ft) with a bole diameter to 30 cm (1 ft). *Crown* Variable from slender tall column to broad bush on several stems, frequently surrounded by suckers from the roots. *Bark* Purplish brown, dark, somewhat flaking in old trees. *Shoot* Green in the first year, hairless and shiny, becoming reddish brown in later years. *Buds* Terminal buds pinkish red, conical, to 1.5 cm (0.6 in), side buds ovoid, small. *Foliage* Leaves alternate, very variable from lanceolate, oblong-elliptic to obovate, tapering to a rounded or acute apex with a short abrupt point, base broad or narrow wedge-shaped, margins entire, upper surface dull mid green with raised veins, lower surface light, slightly bluish green with level veins, 5–15 × 0.7–3 cm (2–6 × 0.3–1.2 in); leaf stalk 3–10 mm (0.1–0.4 in); no autumn colour. *Flowers* In terminal and axillary racemes in May–June on a rachis 1.5 cm (0.6 in); flower stalks 2 cm (0.8 in), crimson-scarlet; perianth (undifferentiated sepals and petals) tubular with a bulbous tip 3–4 cm (1.2–1.6 in) long, opening into four segments which recurve and each have a stamen, ovary narrow with a long style, all parts crimson-scarlet to orange-scarlet, rarely yellow. *Fruit* Woody follicle (capsule splitting along its length and containing many seeds) to 3 cm (1.2 in); seeds winged.

Range: Chile and adjoining parts of The Argentine from 37 degrees south to Tierra del Fuego.
Habitat: Cultivated as an ornamental, in the wild occurring in forests or on exposed ridges.
Varieties: 'Norquinco Valley' is a selected hardier form.
Synonyms: *E. lanceolatum*.

This flamboyant tree requires an acidic soil. Apart from this, it is happy in sun or shade, although more floriferous in reasonable light. It varies in its hardiness depending upon seed origin, with the plants from the Argentinean part of the range (where the climate is drier and harsher than in Chile on the Pacific coast) tend to be hardier and semi-deciduous.

HEATHER, ERICACEAE

The heather family consists of over a hundred genera, characterized by the bell-shaped flowers. The fruit may be a capsule (*Erica* (p.675), *Oxydendrum* (p.866) and *Rhododendron* (p.1094)) or a berry (*Arbutus* (p.508)).

HEATHER, *ERICA*
FAMILY ERICACEAE

This genus contains a vast number of mainly shrubs. The leaves are in whorls, with the flowers bell-shaped and followed by a small capsule.

p.38 **Tree Heath** *Erica arborea*

Description: Evergreen bush, occasionally assuming tree-like proportions and growing to 6 m (20 ft).
Crown Rounded, on several stems.
Bark Fissured. *Shoot* Slender, hairy.
Buds Minute. *Foliage* Leaves in whorls of three, densely packed on the shoots, linear, grooved beneath, hairless, 3–6 mm (0.1–0.25 in). *Flowers* Clustered on short side shoots of the previous year at the ends of the twigs, opening in March and April, bell-shaped and fragrant, with a globose nearly white corolla 3 mm (0.1 in).
Fruit Small capsule which contains many fine seeds.

Range: Widely distributed from the south of Europe east to Asia Minor and the western Caucasus, in North Africa and then south through Ethiopia to central and east Africa.

Habitat: Dry sunny slopes.

Similar species: *E. australis* is usually only 2–3 m (6.6–10 ft) in height. It comes from Spain and Portugal and has pink flowers which open in April. The leaves are glandular, in whorls of four.

The small whorled linear leaves give this a mossy appearance.

LOQUAT, *ERIOBOTRYA*
FAMILY ROSACEAE

This is a genus of evergreen shrubs to small trees. It is allied to *Photinia*, differing in the larger three- or five-celled fruits. These are edible, with a sweet acid flavour. The leaves are leathery, with many parallel veins which extend to the leaf margins.

p.206 **Loquat** *Eriobotrya japonica*

Description: Evergreen tree or large shrub, 8–12 m
(26–39 ft), with a bole diameter to 40 cm
(1.3 ft).
Crown Rounded, usually broader than
high. *Bark* Dark grey-brown, fissuring.
Shoot Stout, densely hairy with buff- to
red-brown hairs which persist for three or
so years, then showing shoot as brown to
grey-brown. *Buds* Ovoid, green with
rufous hairs, 1 cm (0.4 in). *Foliage* Leaves
oblanceolate to elliptic, usually broadest
above the middle, tapering to an acute
apex, wedge-shaped at base, margin
untoothed and wavy to coarsely serrate
with rounded teeth, upper surface deep
lustrous green, corrugated with the veins
impressed and slightly hairy, underside
light green with a thin but dense covering
of pale and rufous hairs, veins raised, in
15–20 pairs, 15–30 × 7–13 cm (6–12 ×
2.8–5.1 in); leaf stalk stout, hairy, circa
1 cm (0.4 in); leaves retained three to
four years. *Flowers* In terminal erect
panicles 12–15 cm (4.7–6 in) high, with
individual flowers 2 cm (0.8 in), white,
stalks densely brown woolly, opening in
the autumn, fragrant. *Fruit* Obovoid or
pear-shaped but with a broad indented
apex which contains the hairy calyx and
is similar to the apex of *Mespilus*, hairy,
ripening from green to yellow in
spring/summer with sweet flesh, 3–6 cm
(1.2–2.4 in), seeds large, brown, 1.5 cm
(0.6 in).

Range: China.

Habitat: Cultivated as a fruit tree in southern
Europe and as an ornamental. Not hardy in
cold districts.

Synonyms: *Mespilus japonica*, *Photinia japonica*.

This makes a bold evergreen foliage tree
with tasty fruit (although rarely produced
in England) and white flowers which are
scented of hawthorns. It is believed to
originate from China, but has been
cultivated for a long time and its original
distribution lost.

ERIOLOBUS, *ERIOLOBUS* (SYNONYMS: *MALUS* IN PART)
FAMILY ROSACEAE

This genus of deciduous trees is often included in *Malus* but differs in the leaves being palmately lobed.

---

p.263 **Turkish Apple** *Eriolobus trilobatus*

Description: Deciduous tree 10–20 m (33–65 ft) with a bole diameter to 50 cm (1.6 ft).
Crown Columnar, with a pointed or rounded apex. *Bark* Dark brown, finely scaly in small plates which reveal orange beneath when they exfoliate. *Shoot* Green-brown to purple-grey and initially with white wool but which is largely lost by the autumn, lenticels few, small, in the second year grey-brown and somewhat shiny.
Buds Ovoid, apex rounded and white woolly, brown, 7 mm (0.3 in).
Foliage Leaves deeply cut like *Crataegus* or *Acer campestre*, three-lobed at the base with the side lobes widely spreading and sometimes subdivided, main lobe with large lobulate triangular teeth (sometimes trilobed itself), apex acute, base heart-shaped, margin with rounded teeth, upper surface shiny dark green, net-veined, veins impressed and with scattered black or dark-brown glands, underside whitish green with prominent raised hairy veins and midrib, 5–10 × 4–10 cm (2–4 × 1.6–4 in); leaf stalk grooved, pink or green, 3–6 cm (1.2–2.4 in); autumn colour good red.
Flowers In small terminal corymbs in June, with individual flowers white, 3.5 cm (1.4 in) across, with clawed woolly petals.
Fruit Globose or pear-shaped, erect, usually only one or three from each corymb, 1.5–2 cm (0.6–0.8 in), shiny red, yellow or green, somewhat woolly, with the persistent spreading calyx remaining at the top, on 2.5 cm (1 in) stalks.
Range: Northeast Greece, through Turkey to Syria, The Lebanon and northern Israel.
Habitat: Hedgerows.
Synonyms: *Malus trilobata*, *Crataegus trilobata*, *Pyrus trilobata*.

This makes an excellent erect branched tree
and is attractive both for the white flowers,
the curiously shaped leaves and the good
autumn colour. The leaves recall those of
Sorbus torminalis, as does the bark.

GUMS, *EUCALYPTUS*
FAMILY MYRTACEAE

Eucalyptus is a very large evergreen genus of around 500
species, all except five of which are confined in the wild to
Australia. They occur from high snow-covered slopes to dry
semi-deserts. Perhaps a hundred species are in cultivation in
Europe, but potentially many more could be cultivated.
Seventeen species are comprehensively treated here, so it is
not a genus where you can expect to identify every species.
The genus is characterized by the petals. These are fused to
form the operculum, which covers the flowers when they are
in bud. The operculum is shed as the flowers open. The floral
attraction is the massed stamens. The fruit is a woody capsule
which ripens a year after flowering. The very small seeds are
shed through valves in the disc which ends the fruit and
provides a useful feature to assist identification. Eucalypts
have two main types of leaves, juvenile and adult. The
juvenile leaves are usually produced, not just on young trees,
but also when the trees are cut or damaged. They are in
opposite pairs and tend to be more glaucous and broader and
often stalkless. The adult leaves are similar on both sides
(which is a distinguishing character) and give the appearance
of being alternate, as the pairs are displaced. This is best
shown by the transition leaves between the juvenile and
adult phases. The other character which is useful for dividing
the genus is the bark. In the gums, which are the commonest
group in cultivation, the bark exfoliates in sheets. The other
main group are the ashes which have a fibrous bark. Of the
species treated here, only *EE. botryoides, gomphocephala, resinifer*
and *robusta* have a fibrous bark, with the other species having
a shedding or exfoliating bark. Eucalypts resent disturbance
to the roots and are best planted out when young. They also
demand full sun.

Informal Key

FLOWERS/FRUITS
(i) **single:** *globulus*
(ii) **groups of 3:** *citriodora, dalrympleana, gunnii, johnstonii,*

tereticornis, urnigera, viminalis

(iii) **groups of 3–7:** *coccifera, maidenii* (sometimes up to 10), *tereticornis*

(iv) **groups of 5–12:** *botryoides* (6–10), *camuldulensis* (5–10), *gomphocephala* (6–8), *pauciflora* (7–12), *niphophila* (7+), *resinifer* (5–10), *robusta* (5–10)

Bangalay *Eucalyptus botryoides*

Description: Evergreen tree to 20 m (65 ft) with a bole diameter to 80 cm (2.6 ft).
Crown Rounded, tall dome. *Bark* Grey-brown and somewhat fibrous, with the strips remaining on the trunk and main branches. *Shoot* Green to pinky red. *Buds* Not visible, leaves alternate in the adult phase, but juvenile leaves opposite for three or four pairs. *Foliage* Adult leaves lanceolate to oval, slender-pointed apex, base wedge-shaped, veins faint to conspicuous with an intramarginal vein close to the untoothed margin, dark green, 10–14 × 3–6 cm (4–5.5 × 1.2–2.4 in); juvenile leaves broad lanceolate to ovate, thin with wavy margins and slender veins, on short leaf stalks, 5–8 × 3–4 cm (2–3.1 × 1.2–1.6 in). *Flowers* Umbels of six to ten on a stout stalk 7–10 × 3–4 mm (0.3–0.4 × 0.1–0.2 in); flower buds stalkless, compressed to give two ribs, 1–1.2 cm × 5–6 mm (0.4–0.5 × 0.2–0.25 in), operculum hemispherical with a bluntly pointed or apiculate tip. *Fruit* Cylindrical or barrel-shaped, not glaucous, opening by three or four triangular valves which are below to slightly above the rim, 7–9 mm (0.3–0.4 in) long and broad.

Range: Victoria and New South Wales, southeast Australia.

Habitat: Cultivated as a forest and ornamental tree in southern Europe, especially in Italy, Spain and Portugal.

This tree will grow on a wide range of sites but is particularly well adapted to sandy gravels and marshy soils. It is grown as a timber and shade tree.

p.126   **Red Gum** *Eucalyptus camuldulensis*

Description: Evergreen tree to 20–30 m (65–100 ft) with a bole diameter to 80 cm (2.6 ft). *Crown* Broad and spreading, with pendulous branchlets. *Bark* White, yellow or grey where the bark decorticates (exfoliates) in irregular patches. *Shoot* Grey to pinkish red. *Buds* Not visible, leaves alternate in the adult phase, but juvenile leaves opposite for three or four pairs. *Foliage* Adult leaves narrow lanceolate and sickle-shaped, apex elongated and slender pointed, base wedge-shaped, veins conspicuous with the intramarginal vein inside of the untoothed margin, leathery and glaucous to dull pale green, 6–15(–20) × 1–2.5 cm (2.4–6(–8) × 0.4–1 in), on a leaf stalk 1.5–2.5 cm (0.6–1 in); juvenile leaves broadly lanceolate to ovate, bluish with a waxy covering, 6–9 × 2.3–4 cm (2.4–3.5 × 0.9–1.6 in). *Flowers* Umbels of five to ten (rarely three or up to fifteen), on a stalk 1–2.5 cm (0.4–1 in); flower buds on a slender stalk to 1 cm (0.4 in), 6–10 × 4–5 mm (0.25–0.4 × 0.2 in), operculum rounded with a beaked apex or conical; stamens red. *Fruit* Hemispherical with a rim, 5–6 mm (0.2–0.25 in) long by 6–8 mm (0.25–0.3 in) wide with the disk domed with the four or five sharp triangular valves projecting and prominent.

Range: Australia, where it is widely distributed.

Habitat: Widely planted in warm temperate regions as a forest and ornamental tree.

Synonyms: *E. rostrata*.

Similar species: *E. ficifolia* has similar but much more showy red flowers. It is a smaller tree from Western Australia, unfortunately only hardy in the mildest districts.

This is one of the most widely cultivated of all forest trees, but is not hardy in northern climates. It will tolerate saline soils. The tree was first introduced into Italy in 1803 and is named after the (pre-Italian Unification) mini-state of Camuldula, near Naples.

p.126 Lemon-scented Spotted Gum
Eucalyptus citriodora

Description: Evergreen tree to 20–40 m (65–130 ft)
with a bole diameter to 80 cm (2.6 ft).
Crown Tall ovoid, with ascending branches.
Bark White to pinkish white, exfoliating
and smooth. *Shoot* Yellow-green.
Buds Not visible, leaves alternate in the
adult phase, but juvenile leaves opposite for
four or five pairs. *Foliage* Adult leaves
narrow or broad lanceolate, apex acute, base
wedge-shaped, veins moderately conspicuous
but intramarginal vein forming the
untoothed margin, crushed foliage with a
strong lemon scent, 10–25 × 1–4 cm (4–10
× 0.4–1.6 in); juvenile leaves oblong to
lanceolate, rough and bristly, 7–15 ×
3–6 cm (2.8–6 × 1.2–2.4 in).
Flowers Umbels of three, rarely five, on a
stalk 5–7 mm (0.2–0.3 in); flower buds on a
stalk, 1–1.2 cm × 7–8 mm (0.4–0.5 ×
0.3 in), operculum hemispherical.
Fruit Globose to sub-cylindrical or barrel-
shaped, contracted at the mouth before
opening out slightly at the rim, opening by
three or four triangular valves which are
below the rim, 1 cm (0.4 in) long and broad.

Range: Queensland, Australia.

Habitat: Cultivated as an ornamental tree in
southern Europe, especially in Italy, Spain
and Portugal.

The lemon-scented leaves are the principal
attraction of this tree.

p.124 Mount Wellington Peppermint
Eucalyptus coccifera

Description: Evergreen tree 15–25 m (50–80 ft) with a
bole diameter of up to 1.2 m (4 ft).
Crown Rounded, spreading, sometimes
shrubby. *Bark* White and smooth, then
darkening to grey before shedding in
longitudinal strips. *Shoot* Yellow or red-
brown, often with a waxy bloom. *Buds* Not
visible, leaves alternate in the adult phase,
but juvenile leaves opposite. *Foliage* Adult

leaves elliptic to lanceolate, apex uncinate (with a fine-hooked point), base wedge-shaped, margin untoothed, veins at an angle to the midrib, crushed leaves with a smell of peppermints, 5–10 × 1.5–2 cm (2–4 × 0.6–0.8 in); juvenile leaves broadly elliptic, heart-shaped at the base and stalkless, grey-green to glaucous, thin in texture, 2.5–5 × 1.5–3.5 cm (1–2 × 0.6–1.4 in). *Flowers* In umbels of four to seven (only in threes on Mount Wellington population), flowers on an angular stalk; flower bud club-shaped, ribbed or angled, glaucous, stalkless, operculum flattened, very uneven, wrinkled and warty. *Fruit* Funnel-shaped to obconical, usually glaucous, to 1.1 × 1.3 cm (0.4 × 0.5 in), disc broad with small valves.

Range: Tasmania, Australia.
Habitat: Cultivated as an ornamental.

This tree is one of a number whose adult leaves have a peppermint smell. In the wild, it ranges up to the tree line, where the plants are bushy, rather than tree-like, but at lower altitude, taller, but less-hardy forms occur.

p.123 **Broad-leaved Kindling Gum**
Eucalyptus dalrympleana

Description: Evergreen tree 20–35 m (65–115 ft) with a bole diameter to 1 m (3.3 ft).
Crown Conical, narrow. *Bark* Exfoliating in large irregular plates to reveal cream, which darkens through green, pink and grey to light brown. *Buds* Not visible, leaves alternate in the adult phase, but juvenile leaves opposite. *Foliage* Adult leaves lanceolate, sickle-shaped, acute apex, base wedge-shaped, margin untoothed but wavy, pale bluish green, 10–18 × 1.2–3 cm (4–7.1 × 0.5–1.2 in); juvenile leaves broad ovate to rounded in outline, heart-shaped, untoothed, stalkless and often clasping the stem, pale green, 4–6 cm (1.6–2.4 in). *Flowers* In three-flowered umbels, on a short slightly flattened stalk 3–6 mm (0.1–0.25 in); flower bud oval to cylindrical, stalkless or with a very short stalk,

operculum conical. *Fruit* Hemispherical or cupular, stalkless or sub-stalkless, 5–8 × 7–9 mm (0.2–0.3 × 0.3–0.4 in); disc convex with spreading projecting valves.

Range: Tasmania, New South Wales and Victoria, Australia.

Habitat: Cultivated as an ornamental tree.

This makes an attractive fast-growing tree of moderate hardiness. The mature tree is very similar to *E. viminalis* but the ovate-to-round juvenile leaves and the bark flaking in irregular plates distinguish it.

---

p.125 **Tasmanian Blue Gum** *Eucalyptus globulus*

Description: Evergreen tree 10–45 m (33–158 ft) with a bole diameter to 2 m (6.6 ft).
Crown Conic when young, becoming tall domed. *Bark* Smooth, exfoliating to show white and then maturing through fawn, pink and greenish grey to grey-brown before decorticating again, but persistent at the base in old trees. *Shoot* Square in section, often with a waxy bloom.
Buds Not visible, leaves alternate in the adult phase, but juvenile leaves opposite for many pairs. *Foliage* Adult leaves lanceolate to narrow lanceolate, sickle-shaped, tapering to an acute apex, base wedge-shaped, margin untoothed, blue-green, leathery with moderately conspicuous veins, 10–30 × 3–4 cm (4–12 × 1.2–1.6 in); juvenile leaves broad lanceolate to ovate with a heart-shaped base, stalkless and often clasping the stem, glaucous blue, 7–16 × 4–9 cm (2.8–6.3 × 1.6–3.5 in).
Flowers Solitary, on a short stalk; flower bud conical, ribbed, glaucous, 3 × 2 cm (1.2 × 0.8 in), operculum hemispherical.
Fruit Depressed globe, tapering into the stalk, four-ribbed and glaucous when first ripe, 1–1.5 × 1.5–3 cm (0.4–0.6 × 0.6–1.2 in); disc smooth, with three to six valves.

Range: Tasmania and Victoria, Australia.

Habitat: Cultivated in forestry and as an ornamental tree.

This makes a fast-growing tree and is used for timber production. In Britain, it is only reliably hardy in the southwest and in Ireland, where it has made 15 m (50 ft) in six years. However, it is much employed for its glaucous juvenile foliage in summer bedding schemes and, if not killed during the first winter, is a tree by the second autumn. It is easily distinguished by the large ribbed and warty fruit which is carried singly. It is mainly native to Tasmania but also occurs in one locality on the mainland of Australia.

---

p.127   **Tuart** or **Black Gum**
Eucalyptus gomphocephala

Description: Evergreen tree to 20–40 m (65–130 ft) with a bole diameter to 80 cm (2.6 ft). *Crown* Broad. *Bark* Finely fibrous and rather soft, grey or brown. *Shoot* Grey to pinkish red. *Buds* Not visible, leaves alternate in the adult phase, but juvenile leaves opposite for three or four pairs. *Foliage* Adult leaves lanceolate, slender-pointed apex, base wedge-shaped, margin untoothed, thick and leathery, dark green, 10–18 × 2–4 cm (4–7.1 × 0.8–1.6 in), on a leaf stalk 2–3 cm (0.8–1.2 in); juvenile leaves broadly lanceolate, bluish with a distinct leaf stalk, 5–7 × 4–5 cm (2–2.8 × 1.6–2 in). *Flowers* Umbels of six to eight (rarely only three), on a stalk 2–3.5 cm (0.8–1.4 in); flower buds stalkless, funnel-shaped with the operculum, which is domed to bluntly conical, wider than the base, 1–1.2 cm × 8–9 mm (0.4–0.5 × 0.3–0.4 in). *Fruit* Campanulate or bell-shaped and slightly angled, 1.3–2 × 1.1–1.5 cm (0.5–0.8 × 0.4–0.6 in), forming a rim with the three or four slightly-projecting valves.

Range: Western Australia, along the coast.

Habitat: Cultivated in forestry and for the stabilization of sand dunes.

This tree is well adapted to arid sites and will tolerate saline soils.

p.122 **Cider Gum** *Eucalyptus gunnii*

Description: Evergreen tree 20–30 m (65–100 ft) with a
bole diameter to 1 m (3.3 ft).
Crown Narrow conic or columnar in young
trees with a fuzzy halo when growing fast,
becoming domed in old trees. *Bark* Shed
in large flakes which reveal pale green to
creamy white, then changing to dark grey,
grey-brown or pinkish grey. *Shoot* Green or
pink-purple and warty in first winter, often
with a waxy white bloom, becoming green
and brown in second year, later pale brown.
Buds Not visible, leaves alternate in the
adult phase, but juvenile leaves opposite for
several pairs. *Foliage* In two main types;
juvenile leaves opposite, stalkless, crenulate,
broadly elliptic to rounded, green or
glaucous blue-green due to a waxy covering,
2.5–4.5 × 2–4 cm (1–1.8 × 0.8–1.6 in);
adult leaves alternate, pendulous, lanceolate
to ovate, green or glaucous, leathery, with
transparent glands, apex acute, base wedge-
shaped to rounded, 6–10 × 3–4 cm (2.4–4
× 1.2–1.6 in); leaf stalk wrinkled,
glandular, 2.5–3 cm (1–1.2 in); crushed
foliage with an aromatic curry scent.
Flowers In groups of three in leaf axils on
trees over five years old, opening in mid
summer; flower buds cylindrical to urn-
shaped with a pointed cap or operculum,
glaucous; flowers open by the loss of the
operculum, white, fluffy. *Fruit* Cylindrical,
ovoid to somewhat urn- or top-shaped,
ripening in following summer around the
time that the next flowers open, green,
stalkless, with a flat top which has four
sutures, 5 mm (0.2 in); seeds shed by the
opening of the sutures, small, brown.

Range: Tasmania and southeast Australia.

Habitat: Cultivated in Europe as an ornamental and
occasionally in forestry, in the wild
occurring in mountain forests.

Similar species: *E. archeri* is a related species, best
distinguished by the flower buds not being
glaucous, and the smaller, narrower leaves.
It makes a smaller tree.
E. glaucescens has pendent sickle-shaped
leaves to 15 × 1.8 cm (6 × 0.7 in) with an

acuminate tip and on a pink leaf stalk. The new foliage is glaucous but matures to dark green. Both *E. archeri* and *E. glaucescens* have flowers in groups of three.

This is probably the commonest Eucalypt in colder districts, tolerating short periods of frost to −18°C and longer periods down to −14°C. It is fast growing, capable of making 2 m (6.6 ft) or so a year. The juvenile foliage is usually an attractive glaucous blue and is sold in florists shops.

---

p.126 **Johnston's Gum** *Eucalyptus johnstonii*

Description: Evergreen tree 20–40 m (65–130 ft) with a bole diameter to 1 m (3.3 ft).
Crown Conical, narrow. *Bark* Exfoliating, orange-red to brownish green, scaly and persistent at the base. *Buds* Not visible, leaves alternate in the adult phase, but juvenile leaves opposite. *Foliage* Adult leaves ovate to lanceolate, acute apex, base wedge-shaped, margin with faint crenate teeth, lustrous green and leathery, 5–13 cm (2–5.1 in); juvenile leaves ovate to rounded in outline, stalkless, margin with shallow crenate teeth, glandular, lustrous green, 4–6 cm (1.6–2.4 in). *Flowers* In three-flowered umbels, on a short flattened stalk; flower bud cylindrical, stalkless, operculum flattened and beaked. *Fruit* Hemispherical or obconical (deltoid), stalkless, 0.8 × 1.3 cm (0.3 × 0.5 in); disc convex with projecting valves.

Range: Tasmania, Australia.

Habitat: Cultivated as an ornamental tree.

Synonyms: *E. muelleri.*

Similar species: *E. subcrenulata* makes a smaller tree with smaller leaves. The fruit is hemispherical to campanulate, to 6 × 9 mm (0.25 × 0.4 in), whilst the operculum is conical.
E. vernicosa is also closely related. It is shrubby and makes only a small tree. The leaves, both juvenile and adult, are in opposite pairs. They are broadly elliptic to oblong and less than 5 cm (2 in). The flowers and fruits may be solitary or in threes.

This makes a tall growing tree which is characterized by the glossy green leaves which have faint rounded or crenate teeth.

p.125 **Maiden's Gum** *Eucalyptus maidenii*

Description: Evergreen tree up to 40 m (130 ft).
Crown Tall dome. *Bark* Smooth and white or bluish white, exfoliating. *Buds* Not visible, leaves alternate in the adult phase, but juvenile leaves opposite for many pairs. *Foliage* Adult leaves narrow lanceolate to lanceolate, sickle-shaped, tapering to a slender apex, base wedge-shaped, margin untoothed, glossy green and leathery, circa 20 × 2.5 cm (8 × 1 in); juvenile leaves ovate to nearly rounded in outline, heart-shaped and clasping the stem, glaucous, 4–16 × 4–12 cm (1.6–6.3 × 1.6–4.7 in). *Flowers* In umbels of 3–7(–10) on a flattened stalk 1–1.5 cm (0.4–0.6 in); flower buds stalkless or on a short stalk, apex rounded with a short beak to broadly conical, 1.5 × 0.8 cm (0.6 × 0.3 in). *Fruit* Campanulate to conical, sub-stalkless and glaucous, with one or two ribs 8–10 mm (0.3–0.4 in) long 1–1.2 cm (0.4–0.5 in) broad, valves strongly projecting, partly fused to the thick smooth disc.

Range: Southeast Australia.
Habitat: Cultivated as a forest and ornamental tree.

This tree is grown in Italy, Spain and Portugal and tolerates heavy soils.

p.124 **Snow Gum** *Eucalyptus niphophila*

Description: Evergreen tree 10–25 m (33–80 ft) with a bole diameter to 60 cm (2 ft).
Crown Rounded, spreading, often shrubby. *Bark* Smooth, deciduous, white when recently exposed, maturing to grey-green before exfoliating again. *Shoot* Green or grey-green with a silvery glaucous bloom, becoming dark red to orange-red by winter, with a fresh coating of wax in the following year. *Buds* Not visible, leaves alternate in

the adult phase, but juvenile leaves opposite. *Foliage* Adult leaves lanceolate or oblong, not sickle-shaped, acute uncinate (with an abrupt hooked tip), base wedge-shaped, margin untoothed, veins curved at base and parallel to midrib, glossy grey-green and leathery, 6–10 cm (2.4–4 in); juvenile leaves green; new foliage mahogany-red to light brown. *Flowers* In umbels of seven or more flowers on a stout stalk to 1.6 cm (0.6 in); flower bud funnel-shaped, smooth, glaucous, stalkless, operculum flattened with a small conic beak. *Fruit* Globose to pear-shaped, stalkless; valves enclosed.

Range: Victoria and New South Wales, Australia.
Habitat: Cultivated as an ornamental tree.
Synonyms: *E. pauciflora* ssp. *niphophila*.

This makes a very attractive small tree. It is closely allied to *E. parviflora* (and sometimes treated as a subspecies) but comes from higher altitudes, up to the snow line. In the wild, it is restricted to circa 6 m (20 ft) and shrubby, but can grow taller in cultivation. It is the best Eucalypt for a small garden.

---

p.124 **Cabbage Gum** *Eucalyptus pauciflora*

Description: Evergreen tree 10–25 m (33–80 ft) with a bole diameter to 60 cm (2 ft).
Crown Rounded, spreading, often shrubby. *Bark* Smooth, deciduous, white when recently exposed, maturing to grey-green before exfoliating again. *Shoot* Dark red, shiny. *Buds* Not visible, leaves alternate in the adult phase, but juvenile leaves opposite for three to five pairs.
Foliage Adult leaves broadly lanceolate, sickle-shaped, acute apex, base wedge-shaped, margin untoothed, veins curved at base and parallel to the midrib, bright lustrous green and leathery, 6–15 × 1.2–3 cm (2.4–6 × 0.5–1.2 in); juvenile leaves ovate to almost rounded in outline, stalkless or short stalked, grey-green, thick and leathery, 2.5–6 × 1.2–3 cm (1–2.4 × 0.5–1.2 in). *Flowers* In umbels of seven to

twelve flowers on a stout stalk; flower bud funnel-shaped, smooth, glaucous or green, stalkless, operculum flattened with a small conic beak. *Fruit* Globose to pear-shaped, stalkless; valves enclosed.

Range: Tasmania, Victoria and New South Wales, Australia.

Habitat: Cultivated as an ornamental tree.

Synonyms: *E. coriacea.*

Similar species: *E. debeuzevillei* is similar, but easily separated when in flower or fruit, as these are both distinctly angled. It is from New South Wales.

This makes an attractive small tree, taller in cultivation than in the wild. It is inferior, as an ornamental tree, to *E. niphophila.*

p.127 **Red Mahogany** *Eucalyptus resinifer*

Description: Evergreen tree up to 40 m (130 ft) with a bole diameter to 1.2 m (4 ft).
Crown Tall dome. *Bark* Rough and very fibrous, persistent, with longitudinal fissures, reddish. *Buds* Not visible, leaves alternate in the adult phase, but juvenile leaves opposite for three or four pairs.
Foliage Adult leaves lanceolate, tapering to a slender apex, base wedge-shaped, margin untoothed, dark green on the upper surface, paler on the underside with inconspicuous veins, 10–16 × 2–3 cm (4–6.3 × 0.8–1.2 in); juvenile leaves lanceolate to ovate, shortly petiolate, 4–6 × 1.5–2 cm (1.6–2.4 × 0.6–0.8 in). *Flowers* In umbels of five to ten on a flattened or angular peduncle 1–1.5 cm (0.4–0.6 in); flower buds on distinct stalks, apex conical to beaked, two to three times as long as the tube, 1.2–1.7 cm × 5–6 mm (0.5–0.7 × 0.2–0.25 in). *Fruit* Ovoid to hemispherical, 5–8 mm (0.2–0.3 in) long and broad, disc domed, valves four, strongly projecting.

Range: Queensland and New South Wales, Australia.

Habitat: Cultivated as a forest and ornamental tree.

Similar species: *E. × trabutii* is similar but has the stalk to the flowers round or nearly so. It originated in Algeria but is believed to result from a cross of *E. camuldulensis* with *E. botryoides*.

This tree is grown in France, Italy, Spain and Portugal for its hardy heavy timber which has a fine grain.

---

p.127 **Swamp Mahogany** *Eucalyptus robusta*

Description: Evergreen tree 10–30 m (33–100 ft).
Crown Tall spreading dome. *Bark* Rough and somewhat fibrous, persistent, dark. *Buds* Not visible, leaves alternate in the adult phase, but juvenile leaves opposite for four or five pairs. *Foliage* Adult leaves lanceolate to oval, tapering to a long slender apex, base wedge-shaped, margin untoothed, dark shiny green on the upper surface, duller on the underside with moderately conspicuous veins, 10–18 × 4–8 cm (4–7.1 × 1.6–3.1 in); juvenile leaves broad lanceolate to elliptic lanceolate, petiolate, thick, to 11 × 7 cm (4.3 × 2.8 in). *Flowers* In umbels of five to ten on a flattened stalk 2–3.3 cm (0.8–1.3 in); flower buds on distinct stalks, operculum beaked, 1–2 cm × 7–1 mm (0.4–0.8 × 0.3–0.4 in). *Fruit* Cylindrical or urn-shaped, 1.2–1.5 × 1–1.2 cm (0.5–0.6 × 0.4–0.5 in), valves deeply enclosed or very slightly projecting.
Range: Eastern Australia.
Habitat: Cultivated as a forest and ornamental tree, growing in the wild in swampy sites, especially estuaries.

This tree is grown in France, Italy, Spain and Portugal. In the wild, it occurs in marshes and will tolerate brackish water.

---

p.126 **Forest Red Gum** *Eucalyptus tereticornis*

Description: Evergreen tree to 20 m (65 ft).
Crown Spreading, open. *Bark* Whitish to grey, exfoliating in large irregular flakes, smooth. *Buds* Not visible, leaves alternate in the adult phase, but juvenile leaves

opposite. *Foliage* Adult leaves narrowly lanceolate, tapering to the slender-pointed apex and usually sickle-shaped, base wedge-shaped, margin untoothed, leathery, green or becoming glaucous, 6–14(–22) × 1–2.5(–4) cm (2.4–5.5(–8.7) × 0.4–1(–1.6) in), on a leaf stalk 1–3 cm (0.4–1.2 in); juvenile leaves elliptic to broad lanceolate, 6–16 × 5–6 cm (2.4–6.3 × 2–2.4 in). *Flowers* Umbels of three to seven, on a peduncle 1–1.5 cm (0.4–0.6 in); flower buds on stalks 2–6 mm (0.1–0.25 in), cup shaped and 2–3 × 3–4 mm (0.1 × 0.1–0.2 in), operculum conical with a very short beaked point, reddish when new, fading to white or pale yellow at maturity. *Fruit* Hemispherical, slightly constricted at the apex, 6 mm (0.25 in), with four broadly triangular and distantly projecting valves.

Range: Eastern Australia from Victoria to Queensland and in Papua New Guinea.

Habitat: Cultivated as a forest and ornamental tree.

Synonyms: *E. umbellulatus.*

---

p.122 **Urn Gum** *Eucalyptus urnigera*

Description: Evergreen tree 15–35 m (50–115 ft) with a bole diameter of up to 1.2 m (4 ft). *Crown* Domed. *Bark* Smooth, pinkish, shedding to show white then darkening cream, grey, green and orange. *Shoot* Warty. *Buds* Not visible, leaves alternate in the adult phase, but juvenile leaves opposite. *Foliage* Adult leaves ovate to lanceolate, apex gently tapering, base rounded or wedge-shaped, margin untoothed, green to glaucous, 5–10 × 2–5 cm (2–4 × 0.8–2 in); juvenile leaves rounded in outline, notched or abruptly short pointed at the apex, glaucous, 2.5–4.5 cm (1–1.8 in) long and wide. *Flowers* In umbels of three-flowers on a stalk to 2.5 cm (1 in); flower bud urn-shaped, on distinct stalks, operculum flattened conic. *Fruit* Urn-shaped, to 1.8 × 1.1 cm (0.7 × 0.4 in), valves deeply recessed.

Range: Tasmania, Australia.

Habitat: Cultivated as an ornamental.

This tree is one of the hardiest of eucalypts. It resembles *E. gunnii*, but is easily separated by the stalked urn-shaped fruits which are set on a long common stalk.

---

p.123   **Ribbon Gum**   *Eucalyptus viminalis*

Description: Evergreen tree 20–35 m (65–115 ft) with a bole diameter to 1.2 m (4 ft). *Crown* Broad dome. *Bark* Shedding and hanging in long narrow strips off the trunk and main branches, white or yellow when first exposed, turning brown, at the base of the bole often persistent. *Shoot* Dark red, warty. *Buds* Not visible, leaves alternate in the adult phase, but juvenile leaves opposite for many pairs. *Foliage* Adult leaves narrow lanceolate, flat or wavy, tapering to an acute apex, base wedge-shaped, margin untoothed, pale green, with inconspicuous to moderately conspicuous veins, 10–18 × 1.5–2.5 cm (4–7.1 × 0.6–1 in); juvenile leaves lanceolate, stalkless and often clasping the stem, pale green, 5–10 × 1.5–3 cm (2–4 × 0.6–1.2 in); intermediate leaves up to 25 × 5 cm (10 × 2 in). *Flowers* In three flowered umbels, on a short angular stalk 3–6 mm (0.1–0.25 in); flower bud oval to cylindrical, stalkless or with a short stalk, 7 × 5 mm (0.3 × 0.2 in), operculum hemispherical or conical. *Fruit* Spherical, slightly tapering at the base, stalkless or sub-stalkless, 5–6 × 7–8 mm (0.2–0.25 × 0.3 in); disc convex with spreading projecting valves.

Range: Tasmania, South Australia, New South Wales and Victoria, Australia.

Habitat: Cultivated in forestry and as an ornamental tree.

Synonyms: *E. angustifolia*.

This is very similar to *E. dalrympleana* in the adult stage but differs in the lanceolate juvenile leaves and the bark shedding in strips, not irregular flakes. It secretes a sugary material from the bark and thus is also known as the Manna Gum.

GUTTA-PERCHA TREE, EUCOMMIACEAE

This is a monotypic family.

GUTTA-PERCHA TREE, *EUCOMMIA*
FAMILY EUCOMMIACEAE

This is a monotypic genus which is not known in the wild but has for centuries been cultivated for medicinal purposes in China. The leaves contain a latex and if they are carefully torn in half, strands can be seen across the fractured veins. The flowers are on separate male and female trees.

---

p.154 **Gutta-percha Tree** *Eucommia ulmoides*

Description: Deciduous tree 10–15 m (33–50 ft) with a bole diameter to 40 cm (1.3 ft).
Crown Broad domed with large spreading branches, rather conical when young.
Bark Pale grey, becoming cross-hatched with a network of deep dark-grey fissures and ridges. *Shoot* Hairless, green with small round brown lenticels at first, becoming light, slightly orange-brown in the second year. *Buds* Ovoid-conic, beaked, dark brown and hairy, 3 mm (0.1 in). *Foliage* Leaves elliptic to oblong-ovate, apex tapers to a long slender tip, base wedge-shaped, margin with large forward-pointing serrations which do not terminate the veins, upper surface deep lustrous green with impressed veins which loop around the margin, underside light shiny green, with a few whitish hairs on the raised veins, 7–18 × 3–10 cm (2.8–7.1 × 1.2–4 in); leaf stalk green, grooved, 1–3 cm (0.4–1.2 in); autumn colour negligible. *Flowers* Dioecious, with separate male and female trees. *Fruit* On female trees only, flat single seed with a wing, 2.5–3 × 1 cm (1–1.2 × 0.4 in), green and inconspicuous until ripening brown in autumn.

Range: China.

Habitat: Cultivated as an ornamental and in China as a medicinal plant, not known in the wild.

This is the only tree hardy in temperate regions which contains rubber. If a leaf is gently torn, the strands of rubber hold the two halves together. It is not now known in the wild, but is widely cultivated in China for the bark which is harvested and used for its medicinal properties. The fruits are very similar to those of the elms, hence the specific name, but are carried singly and only on the female trees; they are also thicker and inconspicuous until ripe. As with *Ginkgo* and several other trees from eastern Asia, it is now only known from cultivation but fossils are found in coal seams in Europe and formerly the genus was widespread.

EUCRYPHIA, EUCRYPHIACEAE

This is a monotypic family.

EUCRYPHIAS, *EUCRYPHIA*
FAMILY EUCRYPHIACEAE

This is a genus of five or six species from Chile and The Argentine and eastern Australia and Tasmania, plus several hybrids. The leaves may be pinnate (*see E. glutinosa*) or simple (*see EE. cordifolia* and *lucida*), or both simple and trifoliate on the same tree in the two hybrids *E.* × *intermedia* and *E.* × *nymansensis*. Most species are evergreen but *E. glutinosa* is deciduous, with large buds. The flowers are white in mid to late summer and have a large rounded knob of stamens. The fruit is a woody capsule.

p.173 **Ulmo** *Eucryphia cordifolia*

Description: Evergreen tree 5–20 m (16–65 ft) with a bole up to 50 cm (1.6 ft) in diameter. *Crown* Columnar. *Bark* Grey-brown, smooth, fissuring at base. *Shoot* Green in the first year and hairy with pale hairs, with a ring of hairs and a stipular scar at the nodes where the shoot is flattened, grooved between the decurrent leaf bases, in the second year dark brown or grey-brown, remaining hairy into the fifth year when the shoot is grey, slightly fissured with small oval raised lenticels. *Buds* In opposite pairs, ovoid or globose, densely hairy, pale brown, 4 mm (0.2 in). *Foliage* Leaves oblong with a broadly rounded apex, base subcordate, margin with gentle rounded undulations as teeth, blade cupped but with the margin curved down, stiff like thick card, upper surface dull sub-shiny green with a roughened surface, grey-downy but becoming hairless apart from hairs along the raised midrib, underside glaucous or whitish green, veins in circa 15 pairs, slightly raised with pale golden hairs, 4–8 × 2–4 cm (1.6–3.1 × 0.8–1.6 in); leaf stalk grooved, densely hairy, 5–10 mm (0.2–0.4 in); leaves persist up to four years. *Flowers* In the leaf axils of the current season's shoots in August to early September, single on a short 2–3 mm (0.1 in) extension of the shoot which is surrounded by a ring of bud scales (showing as scars in fruit), stalks 1–1.5 cm (0.4–0.6 in), hairy, opening widely with four white obovate 1.5–2 × 1–1.5 cm (0.6–0.8 × 0.4–0.6 in) petals, calyx lobes four, spreading, stamens many in a central rounded boss, ovary superior, conical, green, with circa 15 short stigmas. *Fruit* Oblong cylindrical capsule on a 2.5 cm (1 in) stalk, green at first, ripening brown in the second summer and splitting in many segments, 1.2–1.5 cm (0.5–0.6 in).

Range: Central Chile from the provinces of Valdivia, Llanquihue and Chiloe.

Habitat: Cultivated as an ornamental, in the wild occurring in warm temperate rain forests in central Chile.

This majestic tree requires a moist mild climate to flourish, such as is found in southwest England and Ireland. It does not tolerate dry sites, although it is able to thrive on chalk soils.

p.313 **Eucryphia** *Eucryphia glutinosa*

Description: Deciduous or semi-evergreen shrub or tree 4–8 m (13–26 ft), rarely to 15 m (50 ft), with a bole diameter to 30 cm (1 ft).

Crown Rounded, domed. *Bark* Smooth, grey-brown. *Shoot* Light green-brown in first winter, with slender scattered brown hairs pressed against the shoot, flexible, becoming mid brown with pale oval lenticels. *Buds* In opposite pairs, with a ridge around the shoot between the buds, long ovoid-conical, apex pointed to slender pointed, light green, to 1 cm (0.4 in). *Foliage* Pinnate or trifoliate, with three to seven leaflets, 4–8 × 5–7 cm (1.6–3.1 × 2–2.8 in); leaflets ovate to oval, stalkless (except for the terminal leaflet), with coarsely serrate margins, truncate bases and rounded to pointed tips, dark shiny green above, paler beneath, with white hairs on underside and rachis, 2.5–3 × 1.5 cm (1–1.2 × 0.6 in); rachis round, light green; autumn colour usually orange and red. *Flowers* In late summer from leaf axils on the current season's shoots, 5–7 cm (2–2.8 in) in diameter, with four white petals and a massed rounded boss of stamens with yellow anthers. *Fruit* Woody pear-shaped capsule which ripens brown in the following summer, 1.2–2 cm (0.5–0.8 in).

Range: Central Chile.

Habitat: Cultivated in Europe as an ornamental, in the wild occurring as an understorey element in temperate rainforest.

Synonyms: *E. pinnatifolia*.

This makes a delightful bush or small tree when laden with bloom in July and August. It requires an acidic soil and needs a cool moist soil for best effect.

---

p.313 **Rostrevor Eucryphia**
Eucryphia × *intermedia*

Description: Evergreen tree 12–17 m (39–55 ft) with a bole diameter to 70 cm (2.3 ft). *Crown* Columnar. *Bark* Grey-brown, smooth. *Shoot* Faintly grooved. *Buds* In opposite pairs. *Foliage* Leaves either simple or trifoliate; simple leaves oblong, apex rounded and abruptly short pointed, base rounded, margin ciliate and slightly toothed, to 6 cm (2.4 in); trifoliate leaflets with the middle one as above but the side pair smaller, stalkless and to 2.5 cm (1 in); leaflets dark green above, somewhat glaucous on the underside; leaf stalk hairy. *Flowers* Single or in pairs in late summer; flowers with four pure white, broad obovate, overlapping petals, 2.5–3 cm (1–1.2 in) across. *Fruit* Woody capsule.

Range: Hybrid which has arisen in cultivation.

Habitat: Cultivated as an ornamental.

Varieties: 'Rostrevor' is the original cross and most widely cultivated form.

This is a hybrid between the Chilean *E. glutinosa* (from which it inherits the tendency for leaves to have leaflets) and the Tasmanian *E. lucida* (which gives it the glaucous underside of the leaves). It first arose at Rostrevor, in Northern Ireland.

---

p.173 **Tasmanian Eucryphia** *Eucryphia lucida*

Description: Evergreen tree usually 6–8 m (20–26 ft) with a bole diameter of 30 cm (1 ft), but to 30 m (100 ft) in Tasmania.
Crown Columnar or spire-like, with slender short spreading branches. *Bark* Smooth, brown. *Shoot* Slender, green, warty and sticky in the first year, becoming brown in the third year. *Buds* In opposite pairs, ovoid, conic, green, 5 mm (0.2 in). *Foliage* Leaves oval or oblong, rounded at both ends, untoothed, lustrous warty green above with a pale midrib, beneath pale glaucous green, 4–7 × 1–2 cm (1.6–2.8 × 0.4–0.8 in).
Flowers Solitary on a pendulous 1.2 cm (0.5 in) stalk, white with four petals, and many yellow stamens, 2.5–5 cm (1–2 in) across. *Fruit* Woody cylindrical capsule 2 cm (0.8 in), splitting longitudinally.

Range: Tasmania.

Habitat: Cultivated as an ornamental, in the wild occurring in forests.

Varieties: 'Pink Cloud' has the flowers pale pink at the margins and red at the base, fading to white.

Similar species: *E. mulliganii* has smaller leaves and cup-shaped flowers only 1.5–2 cm (0.6–0.8 in) across, followed by capsules 1 cm (0.4 in) long. It is also a native of Tasmania and has made a narrow columnar tree to 7 m × 1 m (23 × 3.3 ft) in cultivation.

This is a small but attractive species, which is not common in cultivation.

---

p.313   **Nyman's Eucryphia**
Eucryphia × *nymansensis*

Description: Evergreen tree 12–25 m (39–80 ft) with a bole diameter to 70 cm (2.3 ft). *Crown* Columnar. *Bark* Pale brown and smooth with buff striations. *Shoot* Green and densely haired at first, ribbed, maturing to brown and becoming hairless. *Buds* In opposite pairs, ovoid-conic, light green, to 6 mm (0.25 in). *Foliage* Leaves mainly trifoliate but variable, with some simple (with only one leaflet); terminal leaflet oblong-ovate, apex acute, base wedge-shaped, margin with regular rounded (crenate) teeth, upper surface dark somewhat glossy green, underside pale green, variably hairy on both sides, especially the veins beneath, 4–9 × 2.5–4 cm (1.6–3.5 × 1–1.6 in); lateral leaflets spreading, stalkless on the leaf stalk, to 5 × 2 cm (2–0.8 in); leaf stalk pale green, densely haired, 1–2 cm (0.4–0.8 in). *Flowers* In August on hairy stalks; flowers with four pure white, irregular, overlapping petals, to 6 cm (2.4 in) across, stamens numerous, with yellow anthers. *Fruit* Woody capsule.
Range: Hybrid which has arisen in cultivation.
Habitat: Cultivated as an ornamental.
Varieties: 'Nymansay' is the predominant form in cultivation; it is derived from 'Nymans A'.

This is a hybrid between two Chilean species, *E. glutinosa* (from which it inherits the tendency for leaves to have leaflets) and *E. cordifolia* (giving it the dark green leaves which are hairy especially beneath). It first arose at Nymans, Sussex. It has inherited hardiness from the former parent and the ability to tolerate chalk from *E. cordifolia*.

SPINDLES, *EUONYMUS*
FAMILY CELASTRACEAE

This is a large genus of around 170–200 species. Most are shrubs rather than trees, and a few have a climbing habit. The leaves are in opposite pairs, with most species evergreen. The flowers are in cymes and carried at the base of the current season's shoots. The fruits ripen in the first autumn. They have three to five cells each with a single seed, and open to display the seeds which have a brightly coloured, often scarlet, covering. I used to consider this a rather pedestrian genus, but was impressed when I first saw the attractive trees of *E. bungeanus* which line the streets of Beijing near the Forbidden City and was enthralled to discover a spindle tree 25 m (80 ft) high in North Vietnam.

---

p.174 **Spindle** *Euonymus europaeus*

Description: Deciduous large shrub or tree 6–10 m (20–33 ft) with a bole diameter to 25 cm (10 in).
Crown Ovoid, spiky with ascending branches and rather shrubby. *Bark* Grey-brown, fissured. *Shoot* Green, flattened at the nodes and four angled, finely grey downy, remaining green and downy for two years and in the third year becoming brown in patches but becoming more rounded in the second year. *Buds* In opposite pairs, ovoid-conic, flattened against the shoot and rather angular, scales green and brown, slightly hairy, 2–4 mm (0.1–0.2 in).
Foliage Leaves narrow elliptic, less often obovate or ovate, tapering to an acute slender apex, base wedge-shaped, margin with fine regular triangular serrations, upper surface deep green, hairless, with the veins slightly impressed but the midrib slightly raised, underside pale to whitish green with a raised midrib, hairless, 2.5–8 × 1–3 cm (1–3.1 × 0.4–1.2 in); leaf stalk grooved, less than 1 cm (0.4 in); autumn colour pink-red. *Flowers* In May–June in small cymes of three to five (occasionally more) flowers with four yellowish-green petals and four stamens. *Fruit* Pendent, four lobed (but only if all four segments form fertile seeds), pink-red and 1.2–1.5 cm

(0.5–0.6 in) (but occasionally to 2 cm (0.8 in)) across, each segment opening along a central suture to reveal a single 6 mm (0.25 in) seed which has an orange outer layer but is white if this is removed.

Range: Throughout Europe except for the far north and far south.

Habitat: Hedgerows, scrub and woodland margins, especially (but not exclusively) on chalk and limestone soils.

Varieties: 'Red Cascade' is an excellent form in which the branches are pendant at the tips. Forma *albidus* has the fruits white. Var. *intermedius* has large more ovate leaves which may be rounded (not wedge-shaped), at the base, to 9 × 4 cm (3.5 × 1.6 in). It is reported from parts of Italy and Switzerland.

Similar species: **Broad-leafed Spindle** E. *latifolius* (syn. *E. europaeus* var. *latifolius*) (p.174), differs in the following respects: The leaves are oblong or elliptic and usually widest above the middle, to 16 cm (6.3 in). The buds are larger, 7–12 mm (0.3–0.5 in). The flowers are more numerous, with 4–12 in the cymes, and having four to five petals which are pink tinged. The fruits are 1.5–2 cm (0.6–0.8 in) across with the four lobes winged at the sutures or angles. It makes a smaller tree, rarely more than 6 m (20 ft), or a shrub. It is found from southern Germany and southern France across southern and eastern Europe to Turkey.

This is a delightful small tree in autumn when covered in the pinky red fruits and when these open to show the orange seeds. The wood is hard and is used in turnery. Traditionally, it was used for spindles, hence the common name.

p.174 **Japanese Spindle** *Euonymus japonicus*

Description: Evergreen shrub or small tree usually 3–5 m (10–16 ft) but up to 8 m (26 ft). *Crown* Spreading, domed. *Bark* Pale brown. *Shoot* Green for several years, stout. *Buds* In opposite pairs, long conic or spindle-shaped, sharp pointed, pale green,

1–2 cm (0.4–0.8 in). *Foliage* Oval to obovate, margins toothed, leathery, retained for one to two years, apex rounded, base wedge-shaped, glossy dark to mid green above, pale green beneath, five pairs of parallel veins, hairless, 2.5–7.5 × 2–4 cm (1–3 × 0.8–1.6 in); leaf stalk pale green, 1.5 cm (0.6 in). *Flowers* On current season's growths in early summer, greenish white, in clusters of 5–12. *Fruit* Globose, green, ripening to pink-purple over winter, 1 cm (0.4 in); opening by five segments to expose the orange-covered seeds.

Range: Japan.

Habitat: Cultivated in Europe as an ornamental and tolerant of seaside exposure.

This makes a small tree or, more usually, a large shrub. The fruits colour from November onwards, providing valuable winter colour.

BEECH AND OAK, FAGACEAE

The Fagaceae includes seven genera from both the northern and southern hemispheres. The fruit is a nut which is enclosed, or held, by a cupule. In *Quercus* (p.1054), the cupule is open at the top (with rare exceptions) but in the other commonly cultivated genera, the nut is enclosed. The flowers are wind pollinated. The members of this family are the dominant trees in certain floral zones.

BEECHES, *FAGUS*
FAMILY FAGACEAE

Beeches are distributed in North America south into Mexico, in Europe from southern Sweden and England across Europe to Turkey and the Caucasus and in eastern Asia from China, Japan, Korea, Taiwan and into northern Vietnam. The buds are spindle-shaped, pointed and rather large. The male flowers are in pendulous clusters. The fruits are a four parted cupule which includes two triangular nuts. On germinating, these have two large rather kidney-shaped cotyledons. Beeches have an excellent timber, although it is not durable in contact with the soil. In juvenile or clipped bushes, dead brown leaves remain attached which, with their ability to withstand clipping makes them useful for hedges.

---

p.131 **Engler Beech** *Fagus engleriana*

Description: Deciduous tree 10–15 m (33–50 ft) with a bole diameter to 30 cm (1 ft).
Crown Ovoid, becoming rounded.
Bark Smooth, silvery grey. *Shoot* Hairless, shiny dark brown with narrow oblong pale lenticels, grey or grey-brown in the third year. *Buds* Ovoid, bluntly pointed, dark chestnut brown, 4–6 mm (0.2–0.25 in).
Foliage Leaves elliptic to ovate, tapering to a slender-pointed apex, base wedge-shaped to broadly wedge-shaped, margin untoothed, wavy, upper surface sea-green, hairless, smooth, lower surface pale somewhat glaucous green with 10–14 pairs of very parallel and raised veins which stop before the margin, net-like between the veins, hairless apart from axillary tufts, 5–9 × 2.5–4 cm (2–3.5 × 1–1.6 in); leaf stalk faintly ridged, hairless, 0.5–1.5 cm (0.2–0.6 in); autumn colour russet. *Fruit* Woody cupule 1.5–2 cm (0.6–0.8 in), pendulous on a hairless 4–6 cm (1.6–2.4 in) stalk, opening along four sutures, outer surface somewhat hairy and with spaced linear-oblong or narrow spoon-shaped appendages which are initially green, then brown at the base, with those nearer the apex more linear and forking to give two to four points; nutlets in pairs, triangular, hairy, brown 1.4 cm × 6 mm (0.6 × 0.25 in).

Range: Central China.

Habitat: Cultivated as an ornamental, in the wild occurring in mixed woodlands.

Similar species: *F. lucida* from Hubei, China, has glossy green ovate leaves 5–10 × 2.5–6 cm (2–4 × 1–2.4 in) with the veins running out to form small teeth. The cupules have short deltoid appendages pressed on to the shoot. It makes a tree to 10 m (33 ft).

This is a most delightful tree with its sea-green foliage.

p.131 **Oriental Beech** *Fagus orientalis*

Description: Deciduous tree 20–35 m (65–115 ft) in
height with a bole diameter to 1 m (3.3 ft).
Crown Conic in young trees, becoming
ovoid and domed. *Bark* Smooth, silvery
grey. *Shoot* Green-brown and silky hairy at
first, becoming shiny brown, hairless with
oval buff or orange lenticels. *Buds* Spindle-
shaped, pointed, chestnut brown, 7–10 mm
(0.3–0.4 in). *Foliage* Leaves obovate, apex
rounded acute, tapered to the base which is
rounded or abruptly broad wedge-shaped,
margin untoothed, with around 9–10
(range 7–14) pairs of veins which turn away
from the margin, wavy, upper surface soon
hairless, lustrous medium to dark green
with slightly impressed veinlets and raised
midrib, underside light shiny green, with
slightly raised veins which are long hairy
especially in the axils, 6–11 × 3–6 cm
(2.4–4.3 × 1.2–2.4 in); leaf stalk densely
white pilose, round, 7–11 mm (0.3–0.4 in);
autumn colour yellow to brown.
Fruit Woody cupule 2.5 cm (1 in),
pendulous on a hairy 3–4 cm (1.2–1.6 in)
stalk, opens along four sutures, outer
surface hairy and with spaced linear-
oblong or narrow spoon-shaped appendages
which are initially green, then brown;
nutlets in pairs, triangular, 1.7 × 1.2 cm
(0.7 × 0.5 in).

Range: Eastern Balkans eastwards to across Turkey
to the Caucasus and Caspian forests of Iran.

Habitat: Woodlands, forming pure or mixed stands
with other broadleaved trees in sheltered
habitats.

Similar species: *F. taurica* is intermediate between *F.
sylvatica* and *F. orientalis*, having the cupule
characters of *orientalis* but the fewer veins of
sylvatica.

This tree is easily distinguished from *F.
sylvatica* by the larger number of leaf veins,
the smaller and blunter buds, the long and
slender pendulous stalks on the fruit and
the broader (not round and prickle-like)
appendages on the cupule. It makes an
elegant and vigorous tree.

p.131 **Beech** *Fagus sylvatica*

Description: Deciduous tree 20–35 m (65–115 ft) in
height with a bole diameter to 1.8 m
(5.9 ft).
Crown Conic in young trees, becoming
domed on radiating branches in open-
grown old trees, but in forest-grown trees,
tall domed on a long straight bole.
Bark Smooth, silvery grey, only slightly
roughened in old trees, rarely becoming
somewhat scaly and platy. *Shoot* Green-
brown and silky hairy at first, usually zig-
zagged from node to node, becoming dull
purple-brown, hairless with oval buff
lenticels. *Buds* Spindle-shaped, sharp
pointed, light brown, 1–2 cm (0.4–0.8 in).
Foliage Leaves oval to obovate, apex acute,
base wedge-shaped, margin with small
rounded teeth at the ends of the five to
seven pairs of veins, wavy, upper surface
soon hairless, sub-shiny medium to dark
green, underside light sub-shiny green,
with slightly raised veins which are hairy
especially in the axils, 6–10 × 4–7 cm
(2.4–4 × 1.6–2.8 in); leaf stalk densely
white pilose, grooved, 1 cm (0.4 in);
autumn colour yellow to orange-brown,
good, late; new foliage exquisite light
green. *Flowers* Male flowers in globose
1 cm (0.4 in) heads with the new foliage,
on pendent 2 cm (0.8 in) stalks, yellow
then brown; female flowers green, on a stiff
hairy stalk, in the axils of the upper leafs on
current season's shoots. *Fruit* Woody
cupule 2 cm (0.8 in) on a hairy 1 cm
(0.4 in) stalk, opens along four sutures,
outer surface hairy and with spaced reflexed
linear-pointed prickles; nutlets in pairs,
triangular, 2 × 1 cm (0.8 × 0.4 in).

Range: Western and southern Europe from
southern England and southern Sweden
south to the Pyrenees and across to the
Balkans and the Ukraine.

Habitat: Woodlands, forming pure or mixed stands
with conifers and other broadleaved trees.

Varieties: Many cultivars have been named. Forma
purpurea covers the forms selected for
purple foliage. The leaves of these have a

larger proportion of xanthocyanins which mask the green chlorophyll pigment. When young, they can look most attractive but they tend to become dull after a few weeks and are grossly overplanted. 'Asplenifolia' (syn. 'Heterophylla') is the Fern-Leafed Beech. This has narrow ovate to lanceolate leaves which are deeply cut with about six pairs of triangular lobes. 'Dawyck' is a form with a narrow upright habit of ascending branches. Forma *pendula* has pendulous branches, making a weeping mound. It can be very effective. 'Zlatia' is a tree found in Serbia, having the new foliage yellow, but soon turning normal dark green. The clonal name is from the Serbian word for 'gold'. Forma *latifolia* covers the plants with larger and broader leaves, which in the selection 'Prince George of Crete' may be 17×13 cm (6.7×5.1 in). These plants are similar to *F. orientalis* in some aspects, but the number of veins places them with *F. sylvatica*.

Similar species: *F. moesiaca* is a species from the Balkans which is intermediate between *F. sylvatica* and *F. orientalis*, having narrower and more wedge-shaped leaves with more veins than *sylvatica* but with the cupule bearing longer and softer prickles.

Beech makes a large tree which is adapted to both acidic sands and chalk or limestone downland. It needs freely drained soils, and does not tolerate waterlogging at the roots. It is native to parts of southern England, but elsewhere in the British Isles it has been planted, although frequently naturalized. It has an excellent timber, used for furniture, musical instruments, dowel and the sticks in ice lollies. It withstands clipping, and can be clipped as a 20 m (65 ft) tall tree if desired, but is not reliable about coppicing as an old tree. If it is necessary to reduce an old tree or hedge, it is prudent to tackle one side at a time, leaving a space of a year. Trimmed plants keep the brown foliage over winter, thus providing screening despite the deciduous nature of the leaves.

FIGS, *FICUS*
FAMILY MORACEAE

This is a very large genus, which is mainly tropical or warm temperate. Most species are trees, but some are climbers. The leaves have a milky sap and when young are enclosed by the stipule, which is soon shed. The flowers are in modified shoot tips, and have a small hole at the tip allowing insects involved in pollination to enter, breed and disperse. The fruits mature into the figs.

p.303 **Fig** *Ficus carica*

Description: Deciduous tree to 10–15 m (33–50 ft) with a bole diameter to 60 cm (2 ft).
Crown Broad and spreading, low.
Bark Pale grey, smooth but finely wrinkled. *Shoot* Stout, green with transverse stipular scars and finely downy in the first year, becoming brown with half-moon leaf traces, later grey.
Buds Conic, pointed with a slender-pointed tip, yellow-green, to 1.5 cm (0.6 in). *Foliage* Leaves ovate to rounded in outline, with three to five rounded-to-obovate lobes (but the occasional leaf unlobed) with deep rounded and narrow sinuses, apices rounded and with a small abrupt point, base truncate to subcordate, margin with small flat rounded teeth, upper surface rough with stiff hairs and raised veins, matt green, underside light green, downy, midrib, veins and veinlets raised, to 30 × 25 cm (12 × 10 in); leaf stalk stout, pale yellow-green, round, nearly hairless; autumn colour yellow.
Flowers Pear-shaped, hidden in the modified shoot tips which develop from lateral buds, green, with a small hole at the apex, containing a large number of hidden flowers. *Fruit* Pear-shaped to obovoid with a flattened apex, ripening to 5 cm (2 in), containing many seeds.

Range: Western Asia, but widely cultivated around the Mediterranean region.

Habitat: Cultivated for the fruit.

Varieties: 'Nottingham' is a selected form which will set fruit parthenocarpically, i.e. without being pollinated. It can thus be grown in climates outwith the range of the pollinating insect.

This is the fig of commerce and culinary use. The flowers are modified shoot tips, and in most forms involve a complex interaction between the plant and an insect which raises its brood within the flower. Two generations of fruits are produced each year, although in northern climates only those which develop in the autumn and can be overwintered are likely to ripen.

p.132 **Rubber Plant** *Ficus elastica*

Description: Evergreen tree to 20 m (65 ft) with a bole diameter to 50 cm (1.6 ft).
Crown Conical or columnar in young trees, rounded in old ones. *Bark* Grey.
Shoot Stout, purple-green with rings from the stipular scars at each leaf, later brown and rough, with a milky sap.
Buds Conical. *Foliage* Leaves elliptic, thick and leathery, apex rounded, with a short drip tip, base wedge-shaped to rounded, margin untoothed, glossy dark green above with close parallel veins, paler beneath, 15–25 × 10–15 cm (6–10 × 4–6 in); leaf stalk stout. *Fruit* Greenish yellow 1 cm (0.4 in) figs from lateral buds on old shoots.
Range: Southeast Asia.
Habitat: Cultivated as an ornamental, especially in northern climes as a house plant.

This is the common rubber plant. Whilst the trees can be tapped for rubber, the yield is low and not commercial compared with the Brazilian Rubber Tree, *Hevea brasiliensis*.

ALERCE, *FITZROYA*
FAMILY CUPRESSACEAE

This is a monotypic genus from Chile and bordering parts of The Argentine.

p.49 **Patagonian Cypress** *Fitzroya cupressoides*

Description: Evergreen tree to 15 m (50 ft) with a bole
diameter to 60 cm (2 ft).
Crown Conical to broad conical with pendent
shoot tips, often shrubby or on several stems
and clothed with foliage to ground level.
Bark Red-brown, becoming stringy and
shed in long strips, in old trees grey and
fissured. *Shoot* Green for the first winter,
then light red-brown, paler or grey with age,
slender, drooping. *Buds* Hidden in axils of
the scale leaves. *Foliage* In pendent open
three-dimensional sprays; leaves in whorls of
three, wide spreading with downward-
growing bases, apex with a small hook, dark
green with two short waxy silver bands of
stomata on each side, free portion to 4 mm
(0.2 in), downward-growing base 4–9 mm
(0.2–0.4 in); crushed foliage with a faint
resin scent. *Flowers* Terminal on previous
season's growths in late spring; male cones
cylindrical; female cones on shoot tips,
globose, 3–4 mm (0.1–0.2 in).
Fruit Globose, to 7 mm (0.3 in), composed
of three whorls each of three scales, only the
upper two whorls fertile, ripen from light
green to bright mid brown; scales open
widely, hinged at base, obovate with a
dorsal forward-pointing hook, 5 × 3.5 mm
(0.2 × 0.1 in).

Range: Southern Chile and adjoining Argentina,
from Valdivia south to the island of Chiloe.

Habitat: Cultivated in Europe as an ornamental, in
the wild occurring in cool cloudy and very
wet montane forests above *Nothofagus* forest.

Synonyms: *F. patagonica.*

This interesting tree has a graceful habit
with its pendulous shoots and a very
attractive peeling bark. It is very slow
growing in the wild, thereby producing a
very high-quality dense timber, known as
alerce. With the foliage in whorls of three
bluntly pointed needles it can only be
confused with some *Juniperus*, from which
the cones with valvate scales quickly
distinguish it. In an attempt to arrest its
destruction in the wild, this tree is subject

to the CITES agreement controls, which prohibit unauthorized trading of the timber.

FLACOURTIA, FLACOURTIACEAE

This is a mainly tropical family in which the temperate genera usually contain only one or a few species. The genera featured here are *Azara* (p.517), *Carrièrea* (p.564), *Idesia* (p.742) and *Poliothyrsis* (p.994).

ALDER BUCKTHORNS, *FRANGULA* (SYNONYMS: *RHAMNUS* IN PART)
FAMILY RHAMNACEAE

This genus is related to *Rhamnus* (and often included as a subgenus within *Rhamnus*) but differs in the flowers having five parts (mainly in fours in *Rhamnus*), the buds being naked (compared with many imbricate scales) and always alternate, and in the absence of spines (often but not always present in *Rhamnus*).

p.154 **Alder Buckthorn** *Frangula alnus*

Description: Deciduous shrub or small tree to 6 m (20 ft) with a bole diameter to 20 cm (8 in). *Crown* Rounded, usually on several stems. *Bark* Dark brown or blackish brown, when cut or blazed shows lemon-yellow beneath. *Shoot* Green at first and downy with pale brown hairs, becoming dark brown or purplish brown and variably hairy by autumn, grey-brown or dark grey to chocolate brown in second and third years. *Buds* Conic to ovoid-conic, naked, with exposed small hairy leaves instead of bud scales, to 5 mm (0.2 in). *Foliage* Leaves oval to obovate, tapering to a short acute point, base rounded to wedge-shaped, margin untoothed but somewhat wavy, upper surface sub-shiny dark green with impressed veins, underside pale sub-shiny green with eight to nine pairs of raised parallel veins which are somewhat downy, 3–7 × 2.5–4 cm (1.2–2.8 × 1–1.6 in); leaf stalk slender, grooved, yellow-green, hairy,

1.3–1.5 cm (0.5–0.6 in); autumn colour yellow. *Flowers* In the leaf axils of the current season's shoots, in clusters of two to ten, not showy. *Fruit* Singly or in pairs, globose with the calyx persisting as a rim at the base and the style as a short abruptly pointed prickle at the tip, ripening to 6–10 mm (0.25–0.4 in) from green to red then dark purple, juicy with two, rarely three oval pale-brown 5 mm (0.2 in) seeds.

Range: Britain and across central and northern Europe to Siberia, south to Morocco and Algeria in the Atlas Mountains but generally rare in the Mediterranean region.

Habitat: In scrub, thickets, hedgerows and as an understorey in moist, acid woods.

Synonyms: *Rhamnus frangula*.

This is more of a shrub than a tree. The wood produces a high grade charcoal which was used to make quality gun-powder. The fruits have purgative properties.

ASHES, *FRAXINUS*
FAMILY OLEACEAE

The ashes are a genus of perhaps 60 species of deciduous trees from the northern hemisphere. They are characterized by the fruit which is a slender samara with a terminal wing. The leaves are mainly, but not exclusively, pinnate. They are borne in opposite pairs, or in whorls of three (*see FF. angustifolia* and *oxycarpa*, although weaker shoots of these usually have paired buds). The buds of *F. excelsior* are black or very dark, but in other species they are brown. The flowers in most species are rather insignificant, without petals or beauty. However, in the *Ornus* group (*see F. ornus*), the flowers terminate leafy shoots in summer and are showy, with petals. Ashes have a high-quality timber. They need light, faring badly when heavily shaded.

Informal Key

NUMBER OF LEAFLETS PER LEAF
(i)   1: *angustifolia* 'Veltheimii', *excelsior* 'Diversifolia', *velutina*
(ii) 3–5: *velutina*
(iii) 5–9: *americana, latifolia, pennsylvanica, ornus, oxycarpa*
(iv) 7–19: *angustifolia* (7–13), *excelsior* (9–13), *oxycarpa* (7–19), *pallisiae* (5–13)

p.318 **White Ash** *Fraxinus americana*

Description: Deciduous tree 15–30 m (50–100 ft) with a bole diameter to 1 m (3.3 ft).

Crown Ovoid, becoming tall domed with open branching. *Bark* Finely fissured, brown, becoming grey and developing deep furrows and forking ridges. *Shoot* Olive-brown, smooth with few lenticels and flattened between the paired buds, usually hairless, becoming grey or brown later.

Buds In opposite pairs, broad ovoid, pointed, brown and hairy, with two pairs of bud scales exposed, 5 mm (0.2 in). *Foliage* Leaves oval, with five to nine leaflets which are slightly longer towards the tip, to 35 cm (14 in); leaflets oblong lanceolate, tapering to the acute and pointed apex, wedge-shaped or rounded and on a distinct petiolule of circa 7 mm (0.3 in) at the base, margin with small rather distant rounded teeth, upper surface matt green with 12–15 pairs of slightly impressed veins which do not generally run to a tooth, lower surface whitish green with raised veins and midrib, often white haired, 6–15 × 3–7 cm (2.4–6 × 1.2–2.8 in), terminal leaflet as above but more elliptic and on a longer leaflet stalk; leaf stalk and rachis faintly grooved, grasping the bud at the base; autumn colour purple or yellow.

Flowers In small purplish clusters before the leaves, not showy, usually separate male and female trees. *Fruit* Samara or winged cylindrical nutlet, green, ripening brown, with an apical wing, 2.5–5 cm (1–2 in).

Range: Eastern North America from Ontario and Newfoundland south to Florida, west to Texas and north to Minnesota.

Habitat: Cultivated as an ornamental, in the wild found on rich well-drained loams.

Synonyms: *F. alba.*

Similar species: **Biltmore Ash** *F. biltmoreana* (syn. *F. americana* var. *biltmoreana*) differs in the young shoots being downy and grey-brown, the terminal buds having apiculate tips, the leaflets being untoothed, very white and downy beneath with a hairy rachis. It may be the result of hybridization of *F. americana* with *F. pennsylvanica*.

This makes a large tree and has good autumn colour and bold foliage. The bark has been likened to that of Walnut (but the opposite buds will quickly distinguish non-fruiting trees).

---

p.317 **Narrow-leafed Ash** *Fraxinus angustifolia*

Description: Deciduous tree 15–30 m (50–100 ft) with a bole diameter to 1.1 m (3.6 ft).
Crown Tall irregular dome with dense billowing upcurved branches. *Bark* Dark grey to blackish grey, becoming deeply fissured into small squares, knobbly with age. *Shoot* Olive-green to olive-brown, maturing to buff-brown, hairless, in the second year green-grey. *Buds* In opposite pairs and in threes, ovoid, rounded to pointed, terminal bud ribbed and angled, dark brown, slightly hairy, 6 mm (0.25 in).
Foliage Leaves oval to obovate in outline, pinnate with 7–13 pairs of spaced leaflets; leaflets lanceolate to ovate-oblong, tapering to an acute or slender-pointed apex, base wedge-shaped to rounded, margin with sharp forward-pointing teeth, upper surface deep matt green, shiny green or bluish green, hairless with an impressed midrib, underside matt whitish green with a raised midrib, hairless but with dark glandular dots on the midrib, 3–9 × 0.8–2 cm (1.2–3.5 × 0.3–0.8 in); leaf stalk grooved, green with blackish dots, rachis grooved, as is the short (1–5 mm (0.1–0.2 in)) leaflet stalk, all hairless; autumn colour poor.
Flowers Small, without petals, before the leaves in axillary panicles, dioecious.
Fruit Samara or key, green ripening brown, 2–4.5 cm (0.8–1.8 in), oblong to lanceolate.
Range: Western Mediterranean region from west and central southern Europe and north Africa.
Habitat: Deciduous woods and river banks.
Varieties: 'Veltheimii' is a selection with the leaves reduced to a single leaflet. This is lanceolate in outline and with a blade up to 12 × 5 cm (4.7 × 2 in) on a leaf stalk 4–5 cm (1.6–2 in). The margin is very jagged and coarse cut with around five large saw-like

teeth, sometimes almost lobes and cut to the midrib. In other characters, it fits *F. angustifolia*, although it has been suggested as a possible hybrid. It is most easily separated from the single leaf form of *F. excelsior* by the bark. Var. *lentiscifolia* is a form with the leaves spreading, rather than pointing forwards as in the type, and more distantly set on the rachis, giving a leaf of up to 25 cm (10 in) in length.

This tree is distinct in the deeply fissured dark or blackish brown bark and the narrow leaves. It is allied to *F. oxycarpa*, differing in the bark, leaf characters and distribution.

---

p.316 **Ash** *Fraxinus excelsior*

Description: Deciduous tree 20–30 m (65–100 ft) with a bole diameter to 1 m (3.3 ft).
Crown Rounded, dome with an open habit of ascending branches. *Bark* Grey or pale grey-brown and smooth in young trees, becoming fissured into interwoven ridges in old trees, resembling Oak bark. *Shoot* Stout, green-brown, flattened at and wider behind the buds, grey-brown or grey-green in later years. *Buds* In opposite pairs, rounded except for the terminal buds which are conic, black or very dark, to 1 cm (0.4 in).
Foliage Leaves 20–35 cm (8–14 in) and pinnate with four to six pairs of leaflets, leaflets elliptic, tapering to a slender tip, base oblique and wedge-shaped, stalkless except for the terminal leaflet which has a stalk of circa 1 cm (0.4 in), margins with acute forward-pointing small teeth, upper surface matt green, lower surface with raised midrib and small side veins, hairless except for pale or light-brown hairs on the midrib, 5–12 × 2–3 cm (2–4.7 × 0.8–1.2 in); rachis round except grooved with reddish hairs between the pairs of leaflets; leaf stalk green, slightly grooved, to 7 cm (2.8 in); autumn colour poor, rarely yellow. *Flowers* On leafless shoots in late spring before the leaves, emerging from lateral buds on previous year's shoots behind the tips,

separate male and female flowers which are purplish and green, without petals. *Fruit* In dense panicles, green until autumn when ripening to brown, 3.5 cm (1.4 in), single-seeded samaras, with half the fruit being the twisted seed, the remainder the parallel-sided wing which has a terminal notch.

Range: Europe eastwards to the Caucasus.

Habitat: Forests, open hillsides and hedgerows.

Varieties: 'Jaspidea' is probably the best clone. This has the twigs yellow over winter, with the leaves yellowish when new. It forms a large tree with a broad-domed crown. Forma *diversifolia* is the single-leafed ash. In this form (which has arisen on several occasions) the leaves are reduced only to the single terminal leaflet (but possibly with a few twigs having leaves with three or even five leaflets). The leaflets may be 8–20 × 4–12 cm (3.1–8 × 1.6–4.7 in). The paired black buds allow certain identification of this form even when the fruits are not present. 'Pendula' is a selection which has entirely weeping branches, forming a broad umbrella crown from the height at which it is grafted or trained. 'Pendula Wentworthii' is a much better tree, with the main stems erect or sprawling and only the branchlets hanging. It can attain 15–20 m (50–65 ft), with a spread nearly as large.

Ash is a frequent tree and found at higher altitudes than most other large growing broadleaved trees. It has a very good and valuable timber, which is white and resilient. On poorer sites, however, this becomes yellow or stained and is less useful. The timber burns adequately when green, although (like other woods) it burns better still when dried. Although valuable in forestry, as an amenity tree, it is rather uninspiring, neither flowering nor colouring in the autumn, being late into leaf and supporting only a limited number of insects. The crown is open, thus casting only a light shade, but the roots tend to be shallow and it does not make a good companion or overstorey tree. The black buds are distinctive.

p.319 **Oregon Ash** *Fraxinus latifolia*

Description: Deciduous tree 15–25 m (50–80 ft) with a bole diameter to 80 cm (2.6 ft).
Crown Ovoid when young, becoming narrow in old trees, with dense foliage.
Bark Brown, finely fissured, in old trees grey or brown with deep forking fissures and scaly ridges. *Shoot* Olive-green to chocolate-brown with whitish star-shaped hairs, shiny and stout, in the second and later years grey.
Buds In opposite pairs, broad ovoid-conic, brown and hairy, with two or three pairs of bud scales exposed, 6 mm (0.25 in).
Foliage Leaves 15–30 cm (6–12 in) with five or seven (rarely nine) leaflets; leaflets oval, elliptic or oblong, narrowing to a slightly slender-pointed but broad tip, rounded to wedge-shaped (mainly on the terminal leaflet) at the base, margin mainly untoothed but with some small rounded teeth especially on the terminal leaflet, upper surface mid sub-shiny green, rugose with slightly impressed veins, underside light green with raised veins and whitish star-shaped hairs, 5–13 × 2–4 cm (2–5.1 × 0.8–1.6 in); leaf stalk to 5 cm (2 in), widely grooved and broadened at the base, stellate hairy, rachis grooved, hairy, leaflets except terminal one almost stalkless with 1 mm (0.1 in) stalks (the terminal one has a stalk to 2.5 cm (1 in) with a long decurrent leaf blade); autumn colour yellow. *Flowers* In small yellow or greenish clusters before the leaves, not showy, usually separate male and female trees.
Fruit Samara or winged slightly flattened nutlet, green, ripening brown, with a broad rounded wing which extends nearly to the base of the fruit, 3–5 cm (1.2–2 in).

Range: Western USA from Washington south to central California.

Habitat: Cultivated as an ornamental, in the wild found on rich wet soils beside streams.

Synonyms: *F. oregona*, *F. pennsylvanica* ssp. *oregona*.

This tree has been associated with *F. pennsylvanica* but it is quite different in aspect and easily separated by the stalkless lateral leaflets.

p.317   **Manna Ash** *Fraxinus ornus*

Description: Deciduous tree 15–25 m (50–80 ft) with a
bole diameter to 1 m (3.3 ft).
Crown Rounded, less often broad columnar
with a domed top, with spreading sinuous
branches. *Bark* Smooth, dark grey, weakly
fissured at base in old trees, where grafted
onto *F. excelsior* the contrast is striking.
Shoot Olive-green with some hairs,
flattened at the nodes, in the second year
with raised round orange lenticels, brown,
later grey-brown. *Buds* In opposite pairs,
rounded to squat with a short blunt point,
grey-brown to grey due to the coating of
hairs, 7 mm (0.3 in). *Foliage* Leaves
20–30 cm (8–12 in), pinnate with five to
nine leaflets; leaflets variable, from
lanceolate, oblong to obovate, apex acute to
rounded and abruptly slender pointed, base
wedge-shaped to broad wedge-shaped to
almost rounded, margin with fine rounded
teeth and usually wavy, upper surface dark
matt green with slightly impressed veins,
underside light green with slightly raised
veins and midrib, with brown hairs on the
lower half of the midrib and some
spreading out over the adjoining leaf blade,
5–10 × 2–4 cm (2–4 × 0.8–1.6 in); leaf
stalk grooved, rachis narrowly grooved,
both with some brown hairs, especially at
and above where the leaflets are attached,
leaflet stalks variable, from 0.5–1.5 cm
(0.2–0.6 in) on the same leaf; autumn
colour purplish, not strong. *Flowers* In
terminal and axillary panicles to 20 cm
(8 in) in May with the new leaves, dense
and abundant, petals narrow, white to
whitish cream, with a faint odour.
Fruit Narrow oblong samara or key, green
ripening brown, 1.5–2.5 cm (0.6–1 in) ,
with the seed in the lower half.

Range: Southern Europe to Asia Minor.

Habitat: Woodlands.

Varieties: Var. *rotundifolia* from southern Italy
(Calabria) and the Balkans differs in the
leaflets being only about 2.5 cm (1 in) in
length and broadly rhombic-elliptic. It
makes a smaller tree than typical Manna Ash.

The name Manna Ash refers to the sugar which can be obtained by making an incision in the bark. An alternative common name is Flowering Ash, as unlike *F. excelsior*, the flowers are large and showy. The leaves are variable, not just between trees (which is an acceptable practice) but between the leaflets of a single leaf (which is not!).

p.317 **Caucasian Ash** *Fraxinus oxycarpa*

Description: Deciduous tree 15–25 m (50–80 ft) with a bole diameter to 70 cm (2.3 ft).
Crown Ovoid in young trees but becoming rounded with radiating branches.
Bark Smooth, pale grey, lightly cracked at base with brown fissures. *Shoot* Shiny grey-green with small buff lenticels, slender, in the second and later years dark grey.
Buds In opposite pairs and in threes, with the nodes sometimes rather displaced, ovoid, rounded to pointed, terminal bud ribbed and angled, dark brown, slightly hairy, 6 mm (0.25 in). *Foliage* Leaves obovate in outline, pinnate with three to nine pairs of spaced leaflets; leaflets narrow lanceolate, tapering to a slender acute or slender-pointed apex, base wedge-shaped, margin with forward-pointing teeth ending in a hooked point, upper surface shiny dark green, hairless with an impressed midrib, underside matt green with a raised midrib which has white hairs on the lower half, especially on the side towards the leaf apex, 4–8 × 1–1.5 cm (1.6–3.1 × 0.4–0.6 in); leaf stalk flattened on top, pinkish or green, rachis grooved, as is the short (1–5 mm (0.1–0.2 in)) stalk, all hairless; autumn colour plum-purple. *Flowers* Small, without petals, before the leaves.
Fruit Samara or key, green ripening brown.
Range: Southeast Europe from the Balkans and Rumania across Turkey to the Caucasus region and Iran.
Habitat: Woodlands, also cultivated as a street and park tree.
Synonyms: *F. angustifolia* ssp. *oxycarpa*.

This tree is mainly cultivated as the clone 'Raywood' which was raised in Australia and selected for the better autumn colour. The crown is dense and leafy, although the leaflets are well spaced out on the leaves. Although most ashes will produce buds and leaves in threes (rather than in pairs), this aberration is the norm on vigorous shoots of this species.

p.316   **Pallis' Ash**   *Fraxinus pallisiae*

Description: Deciduous tree 15–30 m (50–100 ft) with a bole diameter to 80 cm (2.6 ft).
Crown Becoming rounded. *Bark* Brown, with pale fissures. *Shoot* Grey-green with long whitish hairs and a denser covering of short down, rather slender, in the second year grey. *Buds* In opposite pairs or in slightly displaced whorls of three, ovoid-conic, dark brown and hairy, with two or three pairs of bud scales exposed, 5 mm (0.2 in). *Foliage* Leaves with 5–13 leaflets, usually more than seven; leaflets oval, elliptic or lanceolate, almost stalkless on the rachis, at the tip tapering to an acute and narrow pointed apex, base rounded to wedge-shaped, margin with small rounded teeth, upper surface light green with slightly impressed veins, rough due to the short stiff hairs, underside light green with raised veins and densely hairy, texture rather stiff, 3.5–7 × 1.5–2.5 cm (1.4–2.8 × 0.6–1 in); leaf stalk to 5 cm (2 in), grooved, densely hairy, rachis grooved, hairy, leaflets stalkless with stalks of no more than 1 mm (0.1 in); autumn colour yellow.
Flowers Small, without petals, ovary hairy.

Range: Southeast Europe from Bulgaria, Rumania, Turkey, Serbia and the Ukraine.

Habitat: Woods.

Similar species: *F. holotricha* from southeast Europe differs in the shoots being hairy but with all the hairs of one length and in the leaflets having distinct petiolules to 8 mm (0.3 in) but being much less densely hairy.
F. sogdiana is similar but has hairless shoots and leaves. It comes from Turkestan and central west Asia.

Pallis' Ash is usually associated with
F. oxycarpa in the wild, which it resembles
in the spaced leaflets but differs in their
hairiness and in their being almost stalkless.

---

p.319 **Green Ash** or **Red Ash**
Fraxinus pennsylvanica

Description: Deciduous tree 15–20 m (50–65 ft) in height
with a bole diameter to 80 cm (2.6 ft).
Crown Ovoid as a young tree, developing a
tall domed crown. *Bark* Grey-brown, with
shallow reddish fissures, in old trees
becoming scaly, with a reddish inner layer.
Shoot Olive-brown, hairless or softly
downy, grey in later years. *Buds* In
opposite pairs, domed, golden brown,
4 mm (0.2 in). *Foliage* Leaves to 25 cm
(10 in), pinnate with five to nine (usually
seven) leaflets; leaflets ovate to oval,
tapering to a slender-pointed apex, base
rounded, margin with spaced fine rounded
minute teeth or untoothed, upper surface
matt green, somewhat hairy with dimpled
veins, underside light grey-green with
spaced hairs on the circa ten pairs of raised
veins, stalkless, 5–11 × 2.5–5 cm (2–4.3 ×
1–2 in); leaf stalk round, slightly clasping
bud at base, stalk and rachis grooved, hairy;
autumn colour yellow. *Flowers* On separate
male and female trees, green, insignificant,
before the leaves in spring. *Fruit* In
clusters, nutlet cylindrical, wing obovate,
extending back almost the full length of
the nutlet, 3–6 cm (1.2–2.4 in).

Range: North America from Nova Scotia to Alberta
and south to eastern Texas and Florida.

Habitat: Cultivated as an ornamental, in the wild
occurring in moist woodland sites alongside
streams.

This makes an interesting ash with reliable
autumn colour, forming a vigorous tree. It
is variable in the degree of pubescence, with
the hairless form sometimes being
separated as var. *subintegerrima*, but the
distinction is rather artificial in that most
plants fully fit neither end of the spectrum.

p.318   **Velvet Ash** or **Arizona Ash**
Fraxinus velutina

Description: Deciduous tree 10–15 m (33–50 ft) with a
bole diameter to 40 cm (1.3 ft).
Crown Ovoid to rounded, open.
Bark Dark grey to grey-brown, deeply but
finely fissured, scaly in old trees.
Shoot Grey and densely hairy in the first
year, then buff to grey and hairless, but in
var. *glabra* smooth, without hairs, green to
olive-brown in the first year and later grey;
flattened at the nodes. *Buds* In opposite
pairs, broad conic, mid to dark brown,
slightly hairy, 3 mm (0.1 in).
Foliage Leaves 15–20 cm (6–8 in), usually
pinnate with three to five leaflets but some
leaves simple; leaflets lanceolate, tapering
to the acute to slender-pointed apex, base
wedge-shaped and tapering down the stalk,
margin with few rounded to acute teeth,
upper surface mid matt green with a dense
velvety covering of short white hairs with
the midrib impressed, underside grey-green
with a thicker coating of velvety hairs and
raised veins and midrib (but *see* var. *glabra*
below), 2–10 × 2–4 cm (0.8–4 ×
0.8–1.6 in); leaf stalk grooved, rachis
narrowly grooved and enlarged where the
leaflets are attached, stalks grooved and
from 0.1–1.5 cm (0.1–0.6 in), either
velvety or hairless; autumn colour yellow.
Flowers Small, without petals, males
(yellowish) and females (greenish) on
separate trees, in small dense clusters before
the leaves. *Fruit* Narrow obovate samara
or key, green ripening brown in early
autumn, 2–3 cm (0.8–1.2 in), with the seed
in the lower half and the wing not
extending past the seed.

Range: North America from west Texas west to
southern California, north to Nevada and
Utah and south into northern Mexico.

Habitat: Cultivated as an ornamental, in the wild
occurring beside streams and where there is
access to water in otherwise desert
conditions.

Varieties: Var. *glabra* represents the hairless or bald
end of the range of variation. The leaflets

may be obovate with the terminal one larger or, as is usual for the species, all rather similar as regards size. The leaves tend to be of thinner texture. The shoot character is given above. There is a full range of intermediates between the type and this variety. Other varieties are var. *coriacea*, with the leaves more leathery and only moderately pubescent, and var. *toumeyi* in which the leaflets are serrate towards the apex and elliptic to lanceolate in shape.

Synonyms: *F. pennsylvanica* ssp. *velutina*.

This small tree grows better in the drier regions, such as East Anglia. It will tolerate alkaline soil conditions. It is variable in the degree of pubescence.

BROOMS, *GENISTA*
FAMILY LEGUMINOSAE

This is a genus of around ninety species from the Mediterranean region, extending into western Asia. The genus is closely related to the common brooms (*Cytisus*), differing in a number of technical characters. One species forms a tree.

---

p.346 **Mount Etna Broom** *Genista aetnensis*

Description: 'Evergreen' tree 10–15 m (33–50 ft) with a bole diameter to 40 cm (1.3 ft).
Crown Rounded, domed, twiggy, with pendent shoots. *Bark* Yellow-brown, slightly roughened. *Shoot* Slender, grey-green with some whitish silky hairs with narrow linear grooves, remaining green for two to three years, then becoming greenish brown. *Buds* Minute. *Foliage* Leaves rarely noticed and soon lost, photosynthesis carried out through the green shoots. *Flowers* On current year's growths in mid to late summer (July–August), single golden-yellow pea-like flowers at the tips of the shoots. *Fruit* Short spreading legume 1.2 cm (0.5 in) long with a sharp decurved point and containing two or three dark-brown seeds.

Range: Sicily and Sardinia.

Habitat: Mountain slopes.
Synonyms: *Spartium aetnensis*.

This small tree occurs on Mount Etna between 1000 m (3275 ft) and 2000 m (6550 ft). The flowers are fragrant and freely carried. It forms a spectacular tree of open habit. Although normally treated as, and appearing as, an evergreen, the leaves are fleeting and inconsequential. The evergreen coloration derives from the pendent green twigs, through which all photosynthesis is carried out.

GINKGO, *GINKGO*
FAMILY GINKGOACEAE

This a monotypic genus which is the sole survivor of an ancient group of plants midway between the ferns and the conifers. Its unique feature amongst the seed plants is that pollination is achieved by motile sperm. Fossil leaves dated as 200 million years old appear identical to the one surviving species. The broad flat but lobed leaves with an oily texture and many parallel veins serve to identify the genus.

p.352 **Ginkgo** or **Maidenhair Tree** *Ginkgo biloba*

Description: Deciduous tree 15–25 m (50–80 ft) with a bole diameter to 1.2 m (3.9 ft).
Crown Narrow columnar for many years, then spreading but often with erratic side branches and ultimately forming a broad spreading tree with an open habit.
Bark Grey-brown with corky ridges and shallow fissures in young trees, then the fissures widen with crossing ridges and the colour changes to dull grey, often becoming fluted with curious ridges appearing to 'grow' down the bark in old trees.
Shoot Green and hairless when young, shiny fawn then becoming greyer from the third year on. *Buds* Broadly conical or flattened ovoid, green to red-brown, 3 mm (0.1 in).
Foliage Leaves broadly fan shaped with a rounded apex which is notched in most leaves and variously indented (in juvenile plants often with three or more deep notches), base

broadly wedge-shaped and decurrent on the stalk, veins parallel, upper surface sub-shiny light green, underside slightly paler, somewhat oily texture to the leaf, blade 5–7 × 5–7 cm (2–2.8 × 2–2.8 in); leaf stalk half moon in section with a grooved upper surface, yellow-green; autumn colour beautiful golden-yellow for several weeks. *Flowers* On separate male and female trees. Male catkins in clusters on the short or spur shoots, yellow-green, cylindrical, 2–3 cm (0.8–1.2 in). Female catkins on a 4–5 cm (1.6–2 in) stalk. *Fruit* Ovoid, yellow-green with a thick oily fleshy covering which stinks, 2.5–4 cm (1–1.6 in); seed 2 cm (0.8 in), whitish, edible.

Range: Eastern China, widely cultivated in eastern Asia.

Habitat: Cultivated as an ornamental.

Varieties: Various selected habit forms are named but are of minor significance.

This tree is unique in its own Order and Family. Pollination is effected by motile sperm, unknown amongst trees but otherwise found in the ferns. It is recorded from throughout the northern hemisphere in the fossil record but only survived in the wild until recent times in one or two remote parts of eastern and possibly southwestern China. It is long lived, with the original 1762 tree at Kew in the best of health. For the first hundred or so years, the habit tends to be very narrow, only broadening later. The combination of the habit coupled with the tolerance to urban conditions and the brilliant autumn colour make it a desirable amenity tree for towns. However, male trees are often selected for these situations as the oily flesh of the nuts (which are only produced on female trees) emits a most unwelcome odour as it decays. The nuts themselves are edible and very tasty and used in Chinese cuisine. The foliage is produced on both long and short shoots, sometimes with a tree 'sulking' and only producing short shoots for a number of years, such as when conditions are not suitable.

BLACK LOCUSTS, *GLEDITSIA*
FAMILY LEGUMINOSAE

This is a genus of around 14 species with a rather unusual distribution. There are two or three species in eastern North America, one in the Caucasus region and others in India across China to Japan and south to the Philippines, which is a fairly common distribution for an ancient genus (for example, *Carya* omits the Caucasus region, *Pterocarya* is not found in North America). What makes *Gleditsia* unusual is the species in northeast Argentina, which is very closely related to species in China, despite apparently being separated for 60 million years! The species are variable in whether the leaves are pinnate or bi-pinnate, often on the same tree. There are stout, branched spines both on the branches and arising from the trunk, which develop from the upper of several buds in the leaf axils. The flowers are in small greenish racemes. The fruit is a pod with a sweet pulp but which does not split to release the seeds.

p.343 **Honey Locust** *Gleditsia triacanthos*

Description: Deciduous tree 15–25 m (50–80 ft) with a bole diameter to 80 cm (2.6 ft).
Crown Columnar, with rather level and spreading branches, in old trees becoming flat topped. *Bark* Blackish or purplish grey, rough, becoming scaly with long narrow ridges, often with clusters of three-pronged spines. *Shoot* Green in the first year, becoming brown then grey-brown with raised orange lenticels, in some forms with three pronged spines beside the buds which can be up to 20 cm (8in).
Buds Orange-brown flat cone just above the leaf base, 1 mm (0.1 in). *Foliage* Leaves 10–20 cm (4–8 in), both pinnate and bi-pinnate, and sometimes both on the same leaf; pinnate leaves with 7–18 pairs of leaflets but usually without a terminal one; leaflets oblong-lanceolate to ovate-lanceolate, apex rounded, abruptly short pointed, base rounded, margin with fine forward-pointing teeth, light to mid green above with sparse whitish hairs, underside light green with hairs on the raised midrib, 2.5–4 × 0.8–1.5 cm (1–1.6 × 0.3–0.6 in); bi-pinnate leaves with up to eight pairs of pinnae, each with circa 11 pairs of small

2 cm (0.8 in) leaflets; leaf stalk and rachis round, green hairy, with the base of the leaf stalk enlarged; autumn colour bright gold. *Flowers* On separate male and female flowers or trees; in short racemes or clusters at the base of the leaf bases in late spring, yellow-green, not showy. *Fruit* Flat dark-brown pod 15–40 cm (6–16 in) which is usually twisted and contains many flat dark-brown seeds set in a sweet edible pulp.

Range: Eastern North America from South Dakota, Ontario and Pennsylvania south to northern Florida and southeast Texas.

Habitat: Cultivated as an ornamental, in the wild occurring on river plains in mixed woodland.

Varieties: Forma *inermis* covers the plants without spines. Spines are a feature of the wild species, but spineless forms are propagated for amenity use. 'Sunburst' is an attractive, rather small growing form which has the leaves golden-yellow in spring, becoming yellow-green later.

This is a most attractive tree in the fresh pinnate or bi-pinnate foliage. The sweet pods are only produced in northern climates in hot summers. The remarkable spines are only a diagnostic character where they are present, as selections without spines have been made, especially for amenity use where the 5–20 cm (2–8 in) spines at eye level can be considered something of a hazard!

PAPAUMAS, GRISLINIACEAE (SYNONYM: CORNACEAE IN PART)

This is a monotypic family often included in the Cornaceae.

PAPAUMAS, *GRISLINIA*
FAMILY GRISLINIACEAE

This is a group of six species from New Zealand, Chile and southeast Brazil, which is sometimes placed in its own family. Only the following species is commonly cultivated in coastal regions of western Europe.

p.128 **Papauma** *Grislinia littoralis*

Description: Most often an evergreen sprawling shrub, but in milder western regions capable of making a tree to 20 m (65 ft) with a bole diameter of 1 m (3 ft) or so.
Crown Rounded, domed. *Bark* Furrowed, scaly, brown. *Shoot* Yellow green, rough, retaining some green for 3–5 years, but becoming fissured with brown linear lenticels. *Buds* Narrow conical, 2 mm (0.1 in). *Foliage* Leaves elliptic to ovate, tapering to the rounded blunt apex and wedge-shaped base, margin untoothed and undulate, leathery in texture, upper surface sub-shiny mid- to yellow-green with a raised midrib, underside pale green, glabrous, 5–11 cm (2–4.3 in) by 2–5 cm (0.8–2 in); petiole rough, 1.5–2 cm (0.6–0.8 in). *Flowers* On separate male and female trees; flowers yellow-green, not showy, produced in axillary racemes or panicles in mid-spring; male flowers with 5 small spreading petals and 5 anthers.
Fruit Oblong drupe 6 mm (0.2 in), ripening blue-black, with a single seed.

Range: New Zealand, from South Island and the southern part of North Island.

Habitat: Cultivated as an ornamental; in the wild occurring in moist forest or in the open.

This makes an excellent small tree for moister western regions. It can be treated as a hedge and will withstand Atlantic gales. It will also thrive on soils derived from chalk. Fruits are not often seen, as most gardens contain only a single clone, and both male and female plants are needed to produce fruit.

KENTUCKY COFFEE TREES, *GYMNOCLADUS*
FAMILY LEGUMINOSAE

This is a genus of five species, one in eastern North America and the rest in eastern Asia. The leaves are large, bi-pinnate, on stout shoots. The flowers are regular, not showy and in racemes or panicles, without the showy pea-shaped petal arrangement of most legumes. They lead to the large pods with comparably big seeds.

p.343 **Kentucky Coffee-tree** *Gymnocladus dioica*

Description: Deciduous tree 10–20 m (33–65 ft) in height
with a bole diameter to 70 cm (2.3 ft).
Crown Gaunt with open branching,
making a domed or columnar tree.
Bark Grey or grey-brown, developing
narrow scaly ridges. *Shoot* Very stout,
pale buff-brown, soon hairless with round
flat lenticels which have a darker spot,
glaucous bloomed over winter, in later
years grey-brown, then flaky, with a thick
reddish-brown pith. *Buds* Flat yellow-
brown or dark-brown dome set in a raised
ring just above the base of a leaf.
Foliage Leaves to 90 × 60 cm (36 × 24 in),
bi-pinnate except for two or four simple
pinnae at the base, pinnae in three to eight
pairs but the pairs usually displaced, each
pinnae with 6–14 leaflets, terminal
present or absent, leaflets ovate, tapering
to an acute or short slender-pointed tip,
base rounded on a 1–2 mm (0.1 in) stalk,
margin untoothed, upper surface matt
green, under side glaucous green, rather
net-veined with hairs on the slightly
raised midrib, leaflets 3–6 × 2–3.5 cm
(1.2–2.4 × 0.8–1.4 in); leaf stalk and
rachis flattened on top, green, enlarged at
the base and at the base of pinnae; autumn
colour yellow, new leaves pink, late.
Flowers On separate male and female trees;
female flowers in large conical panicles
20–30 cm (8–12 in) long by 7–10 cm
(2.8–4 in) wide, with individual flowers
1.5–2 cm (0.6–0.8 in) long, greenish
white with a narrow tube and four or five
spreading petals; male flowers in panicles
one-third as large. *Fruit* Large dark red-
brown pod 15–25 cm (6–10 in) long by
4–5 cm (1.6–2 in) broad, falling
unopened, containing several 2 cm (0.8 in)
round thick-coated seeds.

Range: Eastern North America from New York
across to Ontario, south to Oklahoma and
Minnesota.

Habitat: Cultivated as an ornamental, in the wild
occurring in moist valley sites with other
broadleaved trees.

Varieties: 'Variegata' is a form in which the leaves are
weakly spotted with creamy white and
pink.

Synonyms: *Guilandina dioica, Gymnocladus canadensis.*

This makes a very striking tree during the
summer with its enormous leaves composed
of 60–80 leaflets. In winter, the silhouette
is open, sparse, as is always indicated by
such large leaves. The fruit used to be
roasted as a substitute for coffee, although
uncooked seeds are poisonous. They are
coated with such a thick waxy case that
they need to be covered by their own depth
of boiling water, which is then allowed to
cool, before they will reliably germinate.
This softens the wax later, allowing the seed
to absorb water.

SNOWDROP TREES, *HALESIA*
FAMILY STYRACACEAE

Halesia is mainly found in eastern North America, with four
species, but also has a single species in southeast China. The
pendent white snowdrop flowers, which are produced on the
previous year's shoots, and the simple leaves with star-
shaped hairs show the relationship of this small genus with
the rest of the *Styrax* family. The most convenient
distinguishing character is the fruit. This has a woody
central core which contains the seeds. Around this there is a
stiff fleshy covering which is ridged with either two or four
wings. The pith is chambered, which separates *Halesia* from
Pterostyrax.

p.233   **Snowdrop Tree** or **Silverbell**
Halesia monticola

Description: Deciduous tree 10–20 m (33–65 ft) with a
bole diameter to 50 cm (1.6 ft).
Crown Columnar to broad conic.
Bark Light brown or grey with deep
orange or pink fissures, darker grey and
separating into loose plates in old trees.
Shoot Light brown with sparse star-shaped
hairs, hairless and greyer brown in the
second year, split shoot with a chambered
pith. *Buds* Ovoid-conic, pressed against

the shoot, scales green and brown, hairy, to 7 mm (0.3 in), superposed, with a small second bud in the base of the leaf stalk. *Foliage* Leaves ovate-oblong, tapering to the acute and somewhat slender-pointed apex, base rounded, margin with small forward-pointing hooked teeth, upper surface matt deep green with impressed veins, initially hairy but most hairs lost by autumn, beneath light green, hairy but soon becoming hairless, with prominent raised veins in about ten pairs, 12–20 × 5–10 cm (4.7–8 × 2–4 in); leaf stalk green, deeply grooved, circa 2.5 cm (1 in); autumn colour yellow. *Flowers* Hanging in May in small clusters from the buds on previous year's shoots, with white to pale-pink petals, 3 cm (1.2 in) across, on slender 2 cm (0.8 in) stalks. *Fruit* Obovoid nut with the style persistent at the apex, with four broad flange-like wings, 4–5 cm (1.6–2 in), green, ripening to brown.

Range: Southeast USA from North Carolina across to Arkansas and eastern Oklahoma.

Habitat: Cultivated as an ornamental, in the wild occurring in forests.

Varieties: Var. *vestita* covers the more westerly forms which are more densely haired. In other characters, it is similar to the type. Forma *rosea* covers those plants with pink or pink-tinged flowers; unfortunately, the pink is not sufficiently strong to make an improvement on the normal white flowered plants.

Synonyms: *H. carolina* var. *monticola*.

Similar species: **Carolina Snowdrop Tree** *H. carolina* differs in its smaller habit, rarely 10 m (33 ft), smaller flowers to only 2 cm (0.8 in), and close bark with small scales pressed against the shoot.
H. diptera is even smaller, rarely more than 5 m (16 ft). The fruits have only two wings.

This tree is grown for the bell-shaped flowers which hang down from the previous season's shoots in late spring. They are followed by the curious fruits which contain a cylindrical or spindle-shaped core but with four large linear wings or flanges.

WITCH HAZELS OR SWEET GUM, HAMAMELIDACEAE (SYNONYM: ALTINGIACEAE)

This family consists of a number of small genera, with only about three times as many species as genera. The genera treated here are *Hamamelis* (p.730), *Liquidambar* (p.792) and *Parrotia* (p.869). *Liquidambar* is sometimes placed in a separate family, the Altingiaceae. The family is related to the Platanaceae.

WITCH HAZELS, *HAMAMELIS*
FAMILY HAMAMELIDACEAE

This is a genus of five or six species from eastern North America, Japan and China. The flowers are strap-like, in either autumn or over winter, and are followed by the beaked capsules. The species are large shrubs rather than true trees. Witch hazel is distilled from the shoots of *H. virginiana*, with the other species widely cultivated for their fragrant flowers during the winter.

p.198 **Chinese Witch Hazel** *Hamamelis mollis*

Description: Deciduous shrub or small tree to 6–8 m (20–26 ft).
Crown Broad with ascending-spreading branches from or near ground level.
Bark Dark brown, rough. *Shoot* In the first year, pale buff-grey with a dense covering of buff and reddish brown star-shaped or fascicled hairs, sparsely hairy and sub-shiny in later years, slender.
Buds Long, ovoid, rounded at the apex, dark brown with a dense covering of pale hairs, 5–9 mm (0.2–0.4 in). *Foliage* Leaves broad obovate, apex rounded, short abrupt slender pointed, base heart-shaped, margin wavy but largely untoothed in the lower half, towards the apex with broad shallow teeth, upper surface matt green with scattered hairs pressed against the shoot, veins in five or six pairs, impressed and hairy, underside pale green with a dense covering of star-shaped or fascicled hairs,

including those on the prominently raised veins and midrib, 7–14 × 4–9 cm (2.8–5.5 × 1.6–3.5 in); leaf stalk slightly grooved, densely hairy, 5–10 mm (0.2–0.4 in); autumn colour yellow. *Flowers* From mid to late winter from flower buds along the lower portion of the leafless shoots, fragrant; the flower buds in clusters of four, set on a densely brown hairy stalk circa 2.5 mm (0.1 in), rounded, dark-brown hairy; individual flowers stalkless, opening with four strap-like rich golden-yellow straight petals to 2 cm × 2 mm (0.8 × 0.1 in), with red-brown hairy calyx lobes. *Fruit* Capsule with two valves, circa 1 cm (0.4 in), containing two jet-black oblong 5–7 mm (0.2–0.3 in) seeds.

Range: Central China.

Habitat: Cultivated as an ornamental.

Varieties: 'Coombe Wood' is the original introduction by Charles Maries to Veitch's Nursery in 1879. It is the commonest clone in cultivation, although 'Goldcrest', which flowers from February into March with the petals suffused red at the base, is also encountered.

Similar species: **Japanese Witch Hazel** *H. japonica* (p.198) differs in the light-brown buds and paler less-densely hairy twigs, the leaves being oval, ovate or obovate with a more pointed apex and wavy margins and smaller, 4–12 × 3–8 cm (1.6–4.7 × 1.2–3.1 in), with six to eight pairs of veins with light shiny green between the veins beneath and only sparsely hairy by autumn, the flowers only slightly fragrant and the petals crinkled (and thus not as attractive). It occurs throughout Japan. 'Sulphurea', with pale yellow petals, and 'Zuccariniana' with pale lemon-yellow petals are the two commonest clones. *H. mollis* and *H. japonica* have crossed in cultivation to produce *H. × intermedia* (p.198). These tend to retain the hairs on the leaves (inherited from *H. mollis*) but have leaves which are broadest at the middle, tapering to the acute apex and to the narrower wedge-shaped base which is rounded or subcordate where it joins the leaf stalk, and somewhat folded or crumpled petals. Named clones of this cross are common, such as 'Pallida', with petals of a soft sulphur-yellow, 'Jelena', with bright copper-orange petals, 'Advent', with the petals bright yellow, the first to bloom in December at the start of the season of Advent. **Virginian Witch Hazel** or original **Witch Hazel** *H. virginiana* (p.199) differs in the following respects: the shoot is at first downy but soon hairless and brown, darkening somewhat with age, the leaves are broad ovate, broad elliptic to obovate, somewhat shiny deep green above and soon hairless except for the hairs which persist along the veins, light green and only sparsely hairy beneath but with reddish glands on the midrib, leaf stalk slender, grooved, warty, to 2 cm (0.8 in). The most obvious character, however, is that it flowers in the autumn, with or just after the leaves have fallen. The petals are yellow, crinkled, to 1 cm (0.4 in). The leaves turn golden-yellow in autumn, usually making a stronger display than the flowers. It comes from eastern North America from Ontario to Nova Scotia and south to northern Florida and eastern Texas.

Ozark Witch Hazel *H. vernalis* comes from Missouri, Arkansas and Louisiana. It has foliage similar to *H. virginiana*, differing in the duller green leaves, suckering habit and flowering after Christmas, in the period January to March. The flowers have a strong odour. 'Sandra' is a named selection with the new foliage plum-purple and with vivid autumn colours; the flowers have cadmium-yellow petals.

H. mollis is valued for blooming during the winter, with the pleasantly fragrant flowers opening from December to February, dependent upon the weather. It has displaced *Cornus mas* as a winter-flowering shrub. *H. virginiana* (*see* above) was named by early settlers on account of the similarity of its foliage with *Corylus avellana*. This species is grown for the twigs and leaves from which witch hazel is extracted and used in eye and skin preparations.

Ivy, *HEDERA*
FAMILY ARALIACEAE

This genus contains about ten species of self-clinging climbers from Europe, the Canary Islands and North Africa east to Japan and Taiwan. They do not form trees, but can develop sizeable stems and by clambering over trees, give the appearance of being trees. The leaves are dimorphic, i.e. they appear in two different forms. On juvenile plants, they are palmately five lobed and self-clinging extension growth is made, but on adult plants, the leaves are ovate to oval, growth is slow and free-standing. The change on an individual shoot from juvenile to adult involves the switching off of some genes, a process which can only be reversed by the external application of a growth hormone.

p.133   **Ivy** *Hedera helix*

Description: Evergreen climber 10–20 m (33–65 ft) with stems occasionally to 30 cm (1 ft). *Crown* Shape mirrors that of the tree over which it is clambering but usually 1–2 m (3.3–6.6 ft) smaller. *Bark* Grey-brown, rough. *Shoot* Green at first and clothed with minute star-shaped hairs, then grey-brown, with light whitish grey roots which are used solely for support; mature fruiting shoots are light yellow-green and without support roots. *Buds* Flattened, ovoid-conic, pinky brown or light red-brown, to 3 mm (0.1 in). *Foliage* Produced in two main forms, but always thick and leathery: juvenile plants produce climbing or scrambling shoots which bear leaves with three or five deep or shallow lobes and a heart-shaped base, dark green above with pale-green veins, beneath pale green, size of leaves variable, from 3 × 4 cm (1.2 × 1.6 in) to 12 cm (4.7 in) each way, with a similarly variable leaf stalk; leaves on flowering/fruiting branches in full light obovate to rhombic with a short slender-pointed acuminate or acute tip and a rounded to wedge-shaped base, glossy light green above, paler beneath, unlobed but often cupped, 5–8 × 2.5–5 cm (2–3.1 × 1–2 in), leaf stalk stouter, 1.5–5 cm (0.6–2 in). *Flowers* In autumn from

mature shoots in full sunlight only; in a globose terminal cluster to 3 cm (1.2 in) across of radiating flowers, yellow-green, fragrant and visited by bees and moths.
Fruit Ripens over winter, changing from green to green-black with a violet hue, globose with a flattened apex and usually persistent style, 8 mm (0.3 in), on a stalk 1 cm (0.4 in); two to five seeds.

Range: From Britain and southern Scandinavia across Europe to Turkey, but replaced by other species in Spain and North Africa.

Habitat: Woodlands, rocky slopes, tolerant of great shade in the juvenile phase.

Varieties: Many cultivated forms, with variegated or leaves unusual for some other feature, are grown.

Similar species: *H. hibernica* from wetter western parts of Britain and the Atlantic coast of western Europe, is a closely related hexaploid species. This has often larger leaves but is reliably distinguished by the rays on the hairs of new shoots. These are arranged at varying angles to the shoot, whereas in *H. helix* the five to eight rays of each star-shaped hair are flat along the shoot surface.

This common climber clings to trees or rocks, or where these are absent, simply scrambles over the ground. It uses trees merely for support, to reach full sunlight. It is not parasitic and therefore does not harm trees. Unlike *Clematis* and *Lonicera*, the stems rarely throttle their support, being too loosely attached and in any event are too brittle. Therefore it does not directly harm trees, although it will compete with them for nutrients and sunlight. Only moribund trees are overgrown; in healthy trees, the ivy rarely grows over the foliage shoots, being restricted to the inner parts of the crown. It has considerable wildlife benefit, as the flowers in the autumn are an important source of nectar for butterflies, moths and bees, thereby providing food for birds which feed on these, whilst the berries ripen over the late winter period and are eaten by thrushes, blackbirds and other songbirds. It is a diploid.

MOUNTAIN HEMLOCK, *HESPEROPEUCE*
(SYNONYMS: *TSUGA* IN PART)
FAMILY PINACEAE

This genus comprises a single species of conifer from western North America. It has been (and frequently still is) included in *Tsuga*, but differs in the much longer cone with scales which are hairy (these are hairless in *Tsuga*) and purple when immature (not green) and which reflex back after shedding the seed, in the stouter and radially arranged leaves, which have stomata on both the upper and lower surfaces, and in the general appearance of the mature trees.

---

p.98 **Mountain Hemlock**
Hesperopeuce mertensiana

Description: Evergreen tree 15–30 m (50–100 ft) in height with a bole diameter of up to 1 m (3.3 ft).
Crown Narrow conical with a pointed top and a drooping leader, older trees becoming columnar conic with short horizontal branches. *Bark* Purplish brown to red-brown and smooth in young trees, becoming greyer and cracking into scaly ridges. *Shoot* Pale red-brown to pale orange-brown or yellow-brown, becoming brown and peeling in third or fourth year, with long fine brown hairs, slender, 2 mm (0.1 in), with peg-like leaf bases as in *Picea*. *Buds* Elliptic or spindle-shaped, pointed, pale brown, 3 mm (0.1 in). *Foliage* In pendent irregular sprays, soft, leaves arranged radially, beneath they are forwards along shoot or at an angle, at the side forwards, whilst those above the shoot curved upwards, rather crowded except on extension shoots where arrangement lax; leaves thick, linear with a bluntly-pointed apex and tapered, pressed against a short leaf stalk, margin entire, upper surface flat or angled, sometimes with a groove and with a single broad band of waxy stomata, bloomed green, grey-green or blue-grey, and a keeled lower surface which has a coalesced waxy band of stomata which are covered by a waxy

bloom, 0.6–2.5 cm × 1.5 mm (0.25–1 × 0.1 in); crushed foliage with a strong parsley scent. *Flowers* On previous season's growths in late spring; male cones pendulous, purplish blue with yellow pollen, 1 cm (0.4 in); female flowers initially erect. *Fruit* Oblong-cylindric, pendent when ripe in first autumn, changing from yellow-green or purple to dark brown, 2.5–8 × 1.5–2.5 cm (1–3.1 × 0.6–1 in); scales 40–80 per cone, oblong, apex rounded, opening very widely or reflexed, to 1 cm (0.4 in) in width.

Range: Pacific coast of western North America from Alaska south to British Columbia and then along both sides of the Rocky Mountains into central California on the west and northern Idaho on the east.

Habitat: Cultivated in Europe as an ornamental, in the wild in subalpine forests on acidic soils.

Varieties: Forma *argentea* covers the forms which have very glaucous foliage. These make slower-growing trees but are extremely attractive. 'Glauca' is also used as a name for these selections. Such plants occur in the wild within the normal variation of the species. Var. *jeffreyi* has more slender and flatter needles with fewer stomata which are more parted, at least beneath the shoot. It has been considered a hybrid with *Tsuga heterophylla*, for which there is no supporting evidence. Ssp. *grandicona* occurs in the southern part of the range, from Oregon into the Sierra Nevada of California. It differs in the cones being at the larger end of the spectrum, with fewer broader scales which are light brown when mature.

Synonyms: *Tsuga mertensiana*.

This makes a much better tree in cool northern climates. The thick but soft leaves are unique. In appearance they rather resemble *Picea breweriana*. The cone is somewhat intermediate between *Picea* and *Tsuga*, with many more scales than found in *Tsuga*. When open, the scales are spreading, or more usually fully reflexed.

WOODY MALLOWS, *HIBISCUS*
FAMILY MALVACEAE

A large genus of perhaps 200 species, including both woody and herbaceous plants. The flowers are characterized, as in the family, by the stamens forming a tube attached to the style.

---

p.302 **Woody Mallow** *Hibiscus syriacus*

Description: Deciduous shrub or small tree usually 3–4 m (10–13 ft) but capable of 6 m (20 ft). *Crown* Rounded, often on several stems. *Bark* Brown. *Shoot* Grey-green, hairy in the first year, later dark grey with ridges and knobbly from the short flowering side shoots. *Buds* Conical, minute with hair-like bud scales, 1 mm (0.1 in). *Foliage* Leaves variable, ovate in outline with three lobes or strongly toothed margins with triangular acute tips, base rounded to broad wedge-shaped, upper surface mid sub-shiny green with raised veins, underside light green with raised parallel veins and scattered star-shaped hairs and many clear dots, 4–10 × 3–7 cm (1.6–4 × 1.2–2.8 in); leaf stalk grooved with pale-brown hairs especially in the groove, 1 cm (0.4 in); autumn colour poor.
Flowers On the current year's shoots in late summer singly in leaf axils but clustered at the shoot tips, opening from cup-shaped to spreading, with five obovate petals and a central column with many white stamens and terminal stigmas, flowers 6–10 cm (2.4–4 in) across, of variable colour from white to purple. *Fruit* Woody capsule with five segments, covered in star-shaped hairs and subtended by the five large green leafy triangular calyx lobes, 2 × 1.5 cm (0.8 × 0.6 in).

Range: India to China, but widely cultivated.

Habitat: Cultivated as an ornamental.

Varieties: Many selected on flower colour. The single ones generally have more poise and are thus more attractive than the doubles.

This is a delightful small tree or shrub which is valuable for flowering profusely over a protracted period after mid-summer.

HORSE CHESTNUT, HIPPOCASTANACEAE

A small family which includes only *Aesculus* (p.481) and *Billia* (evergreen trees from tropical South America to Mexico).

SEA BUCKTHORNS, *HIPPOPHÄE*
FAMILY RHAMNACEAE

This genus consists of three species from Europe and central Asia as far east as western China. The flowers are on separate male and female plants, and are followed by berries with an acid juice which has been used to flavour sauces.

---

p.152 **Sea Buckthorn** *Hippophäe rhamnoides*

Description: Deciduous tree to 13 m (43 ft) or shrub, with a bole to 30 cm (1 ft) in diameter. *Crown* Usually rounded as a shrub but trees tend to have a slender columnar crown, with suckers from the roots. *Bark* Brown, with scaly ridges. *Shoot* Stiff and usually ending in a sharp point, densely covered with silvery-grey or brown-grey scales which persist for two to three years, then shoot brown or grey. *Buds* Domed, brown, 1 mm (0.1 in). *Foliage* Leaves linear, tapering to a slender acute point at the apex and a wedge-shaped base, margin untoothed, upper surface with a dense coating of silvery-grey scales over the green with a groove along the midrib, underside silvery white with brownish scales and a raised rounded midrib, 2.5–7.5 cm × 3–7 mm (1–3 × 0.1–0.3 in); leaf stalk grooved and covered in brownish scales, 2 mm (0.1 in); autumn colour poor. *Flowers* On separate male and female trees in April, wind pollinated, not showy. *Fruit* On female bushes only, orange- to amber-coloured globose to ovoid berries which are extremely juicy, 6–9 mm (0.25–0.4 in); containing a single ovoid seed.

Range: Britain and western Europe across the temperate areas of Asia to west China.

Habitat: Sandy or gravelly sites, and coastal dunes.

Similar species: *H. salicifolia* is found in the Himalayas beside rivers. The fruit is more yellow in colour, whilst the leaves are broader, less silvery and felted beneath.

This is well distinguished by the narrow silvery leaves and the orange-coloured berries. Because the juice in the berries is acidic, birds are very reluctant to eat them, thus they remain colourful on the bushes for long periods. It is pollinated by wind. Suckers are usually found in the vicinity of established bushes.

HOUHERIAS, *HOHERIA*
FAMILY MALVACEAE

This is a small genus of five species from New Zealand with the flowers white and mainly in small axillary cymes.

p.236 Houhere or Long-leafed Lacebark
Hoheria sexstylosa

Description: Evergreen tree or shrub to 12 m (39 ft). *Crown* Narrow upright when young, becoming ovoid to rounded. *Bark* Grey or grey-brown, rather smooth. *Shoot* Brown with star-shaped hairs, becoming less hairy. *Buds* Beaked, conic. *Foliage* Leaves lanceolate, tapering to the slender-pointed apex, base wedge-shaped, margin with coarse saw-like teeth which end in narrow bristle-like tips with rounded to scalloped sinuses, upper surface glossy green with raised veins, underside whitish green with purplish veins which have star-shaped hairs and are somewhat net-veined, 6–14 × 2–3 cm (2.4–5.5 × 0.8–1.2 in); leaf stalk purplish, star-shaped hairy, to 1.5 cm (0.6 in); juvenile plants have rounded ovate leaves circa 1.5 cm (0.6 in) in length, rarely to 2.5 cm (1 in). *Flowers* In July–August, in cymes of two to five or single, in the axils of the current season's shoots; flowers scented, white, with spreading petals, to 2 cm (0.8 in) across, with six or seven (only very rarely five) styles and carpels. *Fruit* Cluster of six or seven winged carpels each containing a single seed, pale green, circa 1 cm (0.4 in).

Range: New Zealand from both main Islands.

Habitat: Cultivated as an ornamental, in the wild occurring in clearings and forest margins.

Varieties: Var. *ovata* from the northern part of the South Isle of New Zealand has leaves which are broadly ovate to ovate and less than 8 cm (3.1 in) in length.

Synonyms: *H. populnea* var. *lanceolata*.

Similar species: *H. populnea* is also evergreen but has the leaves from broad ovate to elliptic, to 14 × 6 cm (5.5 × 2.4 in), and larger flowers to 2.5 cm (1 in) which are single or in axillary cymes of five to ten. The species is basically hairless, although with some star-shaped hairs on the new leaves and in the inflorescence. The best character is the number of styles or carpels (or wings of the fruit). These are five, rarely six. It occurs in the lowland forests of North Island.

H. angustifolia is the third evergreen species (although like the others it can be defoliated in hard winters). This has adult leaves to 3 × 1 cm (1.2 × 0.4 in) on 5 mm (0.2 in) leaf stalks, with rotund juvenile leaves of circa 8 mm (0.3 in). The styles and carpels are in fives, whilst the flowers are usually single. It occurs on South Island.

H. glabrata is a deciduous shrubby tree. It is more or less hairless, has a steely grey finely-cracked bark, ovate and heart-shaped leaves which have a slender-pointed apex and are 5–11 × 4–5 cm (2–4.3 × 1.6–2 in). The flowers are up to 4 cm (1.6 in) across, with 10–15 styles and carpels, but the fruits are almost unwinged. It comes from the wetter western side of South Island.

H. lyallii is closely related to *H. glabrata* in the 10–15 styles and carpels (but which are slightly winged in fruit). The leaves are also heart-shaped but rather lobulate. The main difference is that the leaves and shoots are covered in star-shaped hairs. It comes from the drier eastern side of the South Island.

Various hybrids between the species of *Hoheria* are known, such as 'Glory of Amlwch', which is believed to be *H. sexstylosa* × *H. glabrata*. This makes a small evergreen tree, hardy in the milder parts of Britain.

Like many species from New Zealand, there is a marked difference between the juvenile and adult foliage. The wings of the fruit stick out like the flights of an arrow or dart.

LORD HOWE'S PALMS, *HOWEIA* (SYNONYM: *HOWEA*)
FAMILY PALMAE

This genus comprises only two species.

---

p.348 **Sentry Palm** *Howeia forsteriana*

Description: Evergreen tree to 20 m (65 ft) with a slender bole.
Crown Monopodal with a single unbranched stem and a terminal rosette of erect to spreading leaves. *Bark* Grey, smooth, with leaf scars. *Foliage* Leaves pinnate to 5 m (16 ft); leaflets narrowly lanceolate, widely spaced, with a single rib and flat, green on both surfaces and scaly beneath; leaf stalk to 1.5 m (5 ft), erect, rarely arching, stout, not spined or toothed. *Flowers* Inflorescence pendent, with three to eight branches to 1 m (3.3 ft); flowers in threes with two male and one female, greenish brown. *Fruit* Narrowly ellipsoidal to ovoid, 4–6 cm (1.6–2.4 in), densely set.

Range: Lord Howe Island (between Australia and New Zealand).

Habitat: Cultivated as an ornamental.

Synonyms: *Kentia forsteriana*.

This makes a slender tree which can only be grown in the Mediterranean region outdoors, although used as a pot plant in colder climates.

IDESIA, *IDESIA*
FAMILY FLACOURTIACEAE

This is a monotypic genus from Japan and China. The leaves are large, but thick (cf. *Catalpa*), with one or two pairs of glands or extrafloral nectaries on the leaf stalk. The shoots are pithy whilst the side branches spread horizontally.

p.200 **Idesia** *Idesia polycarpa*

Description: Deciduous tree to 20 m (65 ft) with a bole
diameter to 50 cm (1.6 ft).
Crown With horizontally spreading
branches. *Bark* Grey-green and pinkish,
smooth with horizontal lenticels.
Shoot Grey-brown, thick, with a large pithy
core, hairless. *Foliage* Leaves ovate to
deltoid, apex short and slender pointed, base
heart-shaped to rounded-truncate, margin
with irregular hooked teeth, upper surface
dark green, hairless, underside glaucous
with thick veins, variably hairy, 10–20 ×
8–20 cm (4–8 × 3.1–8 in); leaf stalk scarlet,
with two oblong glands near the apex and
(especially in young trees) one or two pairs
midway along stalk, 12–30 cm (4.7–12 in).
Flowers Dioecious, with separate male and
female trees, in pendulous panicles in June
and July. *Fruit* Globose berry with many
small seeds, ripens to dark red, 8–10 mm
(0.3–0.4 in).

Range: Widespread in eastern Asia from Japan
(Honshu, Shikoku and Kyushu) south
along the Ryukyus to Taiwan and across
Korea and China to Sichuan and Yunnan.

Habitat: Cultivated as an ornamental.

Varieties: Var. *vestita* differs in the leaves being
densely downy beneath. It occurs (along
with the typical form) from Gansu south
through Sichuan to Yunnan.

The leaves resemble those of *Catalpa* or
Populus lasiocarpa, but can be distinguished
from both these by the pair (or more) of
large glands on the leaf stalk. These are
extrafloral nectaries, encouraging ants
which will then drive off caterpillars. The
fruits are showy, but only produced where
trees of both sexes are grown together.

HOLLIES, *ILEX*
FAMILY AQUIFOLIACEAE

The hollies are a very large genus of 400 or so species. Many
are tropical or warm temperate, forming trees and tall shrubs,
and less often carpeting shrubs. The genus is represented in

all the continents except Australia and Antarctica, and is also absent from western North America. The leaves are frequently spiny, especially on young trees, but the spines can be reduced to small teeth, and in mature trees out of the reach of herbivores the leaves may be untoothed except for terminal prickles. Most species are evergreen but some are deciduous. The fruit is a drupe (although often called a berry) with several, usually two or four, pyrenes or stony seeds.

---

p.265 **Highclere Holly** *Ilex × altaclerensis*

Description: Evergreen tree 10–20 m (33–65 ft) with a bole diameter to 60 cm (2 ft).
Crown Conical when young but becoming columnar with a domed top. *Bark* Grey, smooth, becoming silvery grey in old trees.
Shoot Glabrous, green or purple and remaining so for several years.
Buds Conical, green, scales hairy, to 4 mm (0.2 in). *Foliage* Oval or elliptic, dark glossy green above, paler matt or sub-shiny green below, with only a narrow hyaline margin, midrib pale green, either untoothed or with a few forward-pointing teeth, retained for two to four years, 8–14 × 4–8 cm (3.1–5.5 × 1.6–3.1 in); leaf stalk stout, 1–2 cm (0.4–0.8 in), green or purple. *Flowers* On previous season's shoots in spring from buds in leaf axils, dioecious; male flowers clustered, white or purple, fragrant, 6–8 mm (0.25–0.3 in), with four anthers but no stigmas; female flowers fewer, without anthers. *Fruit* On female bushes only, globose, ripening red in autumn and retained for varying periods over winter; berry 1–1.2 cm (0.4–0.5 in).

Range: Western Europe across to western Asia.

Habitat: Cultivated as an ornamental.

Varieties: Cultivars include 'Camelliifolia'(female), with large very lustrous untoothed leaves, 'Golden King' (also female!) but with spined leaves with a deep yellow marginal variegation, 'Hodginsii', (male) with purple shoots, toothed leaves and a metallic sheen to the upper leaf surface, 'Lawsoniana', a female form with marbled gold, yellow and green leaves, and 'Wilsonii', (female) but with broad yellow-green very glossy leaves.

This hybrid is the result of a cross between *I. aquifolium* and *I. perado* from Madeira, the Canary Islands and the Azores. It shows hybrid vigour, growing more vigorously than Common Holly.

p.264 **Holly** *Ilex aquifolium*

Description: Evergreen tree 10–25 m (33–80 ft) with a bole diameter to 1 m (3.3 ft).
Crown Conical in young trees, remaining so in those growing quickly but generally becoming columnar with a domed top.
Bark Grey, smooth, becoming silvery-grey in old trees. *Shoot* Glabrous, green or purple and remaining so for several years.
Buds Minute, conical, side buds often shortly stalked, green, 1 mm (0.1 in). *Foliage* Oval or elliptic, dark glossy green above, paler matt or sub-shiny green below, with a hyaline margin, 5–12 × 2–6 cm (2–4.7 × 0.8–2.4 in); shape varies between lower crown (and young trees) and upper crown, retained for two to four years; juvenile plants have large triangular teeth which end in a sharp bony point and which are wavy, often alternately pointing up and down; as the bush ages and especially in the upper crown, the leaves lose the teeth, usually only retaining the sharp terminal spine; leaf stalk stout, 1 cm (0.4 in), green. *Flowers* On previous season's shoots in spring from buds in leaf axils, dioecious; male flowers clustered, white, fragrant, 6–8 mm (0.25–0.3 in), with four anthers but no stigmas; female flowers fewer, without anthers. *Fruit* On female bushes only, globose, ripening red in autumn and retained for varying periods over winter; berry 6–10 mm (0.25–0.4 in), containing two to four seeds.

Range: Western Europe across to western Asia.
Habitat: Mainly in woodlands, also in hedgerows.
Varieties: Many cultivars are recorded, mainly differing in variegated foliage (e.g. 'Silver Queen', a male form!), but also including different leave colours (e.g. 'Flavescens', with leaves suffused yellow) and berry forms (e.g. 'Amber', with bronze-yellow berries).

Berries are only borne on female trees but males are necessary for pollination. Holly is very tolerant of site and conditions, withstanding dense shade as well as exposure. The berries are an important food for birds during the winter period.

p.264 **Himalayan Holly** *Ilex dipyrena*

Description: Evergreen tree to 12 m (39 ft) with a bole diameter to 50 cm (1.6 ft).
Crown Columnar. *Bark* Grey-brown, finely roughened. *Shoot* Green in the first year with small sparse lenticels, round or angled with ridges running down from the leaf bases, soon hairless, becoming grey-brown in blobs in the second year.
Buds Ovoid with angular purplish hairy scales to 4 mm (0.2 in) at the shoot tip, lateral buds rounded, 1 mm (0.1 in).
Foliage Leaves thick with a leathery texture, elliptic, ovate to broadly ovate, apex acute to a short sharp slender point, base rounded, margin entire to wavy and spinous with up to ten pairs of triangular needle-pointed teeth, upper surface deep lustrous green with an indented midrib and main veins, underside pale shiny green with a raised midrib, 6–11 × 2–4.5 cm (2.4–4.3 × 0.8–1.8 in); leaf stalk grooved, stout, purplish, 2–9 mm (0.1–0.4 in); leaves persist two years.
Flowers In axillary fascicles on previous season's growths, greenish white or purple, with ciliate calyx and corolla lobes, stamens (in male flowers) four, stigma (female flowers) disc-like. *Fruit* Globose to elliptic, 6–8 mm (0.25–0.3 in), ripening red, with two (rarely three) 6 × 4–5 mm (0.25 × 0.2 in) sculptured seeds (or pyrenes).
Range: Himalayas from Nepal eastwards through Sikkim, Bhutan, northeast India, northern Burma to southeast Tibet and Yunnan, China.
Habitat: Cultivated as an ornamental, in the wild occurring in mixed or evergreen oak forests or along hedgerows.

This tree is similar to *I. aquifolium*, with
which it shares the character of spiny leaves
on young trees and in the lower crown and
less or untoothed leaves in the upper crown.
The leaves are generally narrower, with a
more tapered apex and not as glossy. The
fruits (on female trees only) have only two
nutlets or pyrenes.

p.265   **Madeira Holly** *Ilex perado*

Description: Evergreen tree to 6–8 m (20–26 ft).
Crown Columnar. *Bark* Smooth, grey-
brown. *Shoot* Green and purple, round,
hairless, with small buff linear lenticels,
becoming rough in the second year where
the lenticels erupt as small pimples.
Buds Terminal bud conical, slender pointed
at the apex, green or purple, finely warty,
6 mm (0.25 in), lateral buds domed, 1 mm
(0.1 in). *Foliage* Leaves oval, rounded to
obovate, apex short and slender pointed,
base wedge-shaped to subcordate, margin
with scattered spine teeth especially towards
the leaf apex, less often spineless or regularly
spined, upper surface lustrous mid green,
smooth but with the veins showing clearly
as pale green, underside sub-shiny dull mid
green with a raised midrib, texture leathery,
6–10 × 3–6 cm (2.4–4 × 0.1–2.4 in); leaf
stalk grooved, green, 0.5–1.5 cm
(0.2–0.6 in); no autumn colour, leaves
persisting two years. *Fruit* Globose to
ellipsoidal, ripening red, 1 cm (0.4 in).
Range: Madeira, varieties on the Azores and Canaries.
Habitat: Woods.
Varieties: Var. *azorica* from the Azores has smaller
leaves, only 2.5–6 cm (1–2.4 in) in length,
varying from ovate, elliptic to rounded,
with none or few forward-pointing spines.
Var. *platyphylla* from the Canary Islands and
also Madeira has much larger leaves,
10–15 cm (4–6 in) but occasionally to 20 ×
6–11 cm (8 × 2.4–4.3 in).
Synonyms: *I. maderensis*.

This holly is one of the parents of the
I. altaclerensis group of hybrids.

p.265 **Perny Holly** *Ilex pernyi*

Description: Evergreen shrub or tree to 15 m (50 ft)
with a bole diameter to 30 cm (1 ft).
Crown Narrow columnar to conical, rounded
in old trees. *Bark* Grey-brown. *Shoot* Green
and densely short grey hairy for two winters,
then developing brown fissures, later brown.
Buds Conical with a slender-pointed apex,
green, hairy, 2 mm (0.1 in); male flowers in
clusters of seven, brown, rounded, 1.5 mm
(0.1 in); female flower buds single or paired,
brown, rounded on a short stalk, 1.5 mm
(0.1 in). *Foliage* Leaves spreading
pectinately either side of the shoot; basal part
square with a triangular apex, base squarrish
or subcordate, margin with a sharp spine at
each of five corners, occasionally with another
pair in the centre or only three, spines bony,
yellow with a brown tip, margin hyaline and
cupped, glossy mid to dark green above, pale
green beneath, 2–3 × 1.3–2 cm (0.8–1.2 ×
0.5–0.8 in); leaf stalk green, hairy, 3 mm
(0.1 in). *Flowers* In leaf axils on previous
season's growths, pale yellow.
Fruit Rounded oblong, broader than long,
nearly stalkless, bright sub-shiny red,
6–8 mm (0.25–0.3 in), with four seeds.

Range: Central and western China to Manipur in
eastern India.

Habitat: Cultivated in Europe as an ornamental, in
the wild occurring in open woodland.

Varieties: Var. *veitchii* has larger leaves, 4–5 cm
(1.6–2 in) in length.

This has remarkable leaves which are
mainly five-sided, each corner marked by a
long sharp spine. It makes a small tree,
usually very narrow columnar but
sometimes conical.

JACARANDA, *JACARANDA*
FAMILY SCROPHULARIACEAE

A genus of about 30 species from South America north to
Mexico. One species is widely planted in subtropical and
warm temperate parts of the world. The name derives from
the local Brazilian name for the first species to be described.

p.342 **Jacaranda** *Jacaranda mimosifolia*

Description: Deciduous tree 10–15 m (33–49 ft) with a
bole diameter to 50 cm (20 in).
Crown Spreading and rather flat topped.
Bark Fissured, brown. *Shoots* Stout,
brown, rough. *Buds* Ovoid, two to three
together in leaf axil. *Foliage* Leaves bi-
pinnate, to 30 cm (12 in), with about 16
pairs of opposite pinnae, each with 14–24
pairs of oval pinnules or small leaflets of
3–12 × 1–4 mm (0.1–0.5 × 0.05–0.2 in),
giving a fern-like appearance to the foliage,
light green. *Flowers* In spreading panicles
of about 50 before the leaves in early spring;
flowers tubular, foxglove-like, 2–3 cm
(0.8–1.2 in), lilac-purple with a paler inside
to the tube and silky hairy on the outside,
five stamens, with hairy filaments, calyx
small, triangular. *Fruit* Oblong capsule.

Range: The Argentine and Bolivia.

Habitat: Cultivated as an ornamental in the mildest
parts of Europe, in the wild coming from
seasonally dry subtropical areas.

Synonyms: *J. acutifolia* misapplied.

When in full flower, it can be stunning, but
it needs a warm temperate climate to produce
the best displays, and will tolerate a limited
degree of frost. The fern-like foliage and
spreading rounded habit give an attractive
tree which casts only a light shade.

JASMINES, *JASMINUM*
FAMILY OLEACEAE

This is a large genus of 200–450 species depending upon
interpretation. They mainly form climbers and shrubs,
rather than trees. The flowers are tubular with spreading
petals and are often fragrant. The fruit is a juicy berry.

---

p.309 **Winter Jasmine** *Jasminum nudiflorum*

Description: Deciduous scandent shrub capable of
scrambling to 5 m (16 ft).
Crown Depends upon support.
Shoot Glabrous, four-angled. *Buds* In

opposite pairs. *Foliage* Leaves trifoliate; leaflets oval, pointed at both ends, margin untoothed but with ciliate hairs when young, deep glossy green above.

Flowers On previous season's growths from over winter, from November to February, solitary, bright yellow, tube 2.5 cm (1 in), petal lobes in sixes, spreading 2–2.5 cm (0.8–1 m) across. *Fruit* Juicy berry.

Range: China.

Habitat: Cultivated as an ornamental.

Synonyms: *J. sieboldianum*.

Similar species: **Common Jasmine** *J. officinale* differs in the following respects. The leaves are pinnate, with five to nine leaflets which are 1.2–6.5 × 0.4–2.5 cm (0.5–2.6 × 0.2–1 in). The flowers are in terminal clusters of cymes, with each cyme consisting of three to five very fragrant white blooms with four or five lobes to the corolla. They are produced over an extended period from June to November. It can grow up to 13 m (43 ft) into trees and is found in the wild from the Caucasus region, east through Iran and Afghanistan to the Himalayas and China.

Wild Jasmine *J. fruticans* (p.309) is a semi-evergreen shrub to 2 m (6.6 ft) but sometimes scandescent and attaining 5 m (16 ft) or so. The leaves are trifoliate, with the leaflets narrow oblong to narrow obovate with a rounded or pointed apex and wedge-shaped base. The flowers are carried in cymes of three to five from June onwards and are yellow, with five lobes to the corolla. It is native from southern Europe, North Africa and the western parts of Asia.

This jasmine is valuable for flowering over the winter period. It is a shrub more than a tree but is capable of attaining 5 m (16 ft).

CHILEAN WINE PALM, *JUBAEA*
FAMILY PALMAE

This genus consists of only the one species.

p.348 **Chilean Wine Palm** *Jubaea chilensis*

Description: Evergreen tree 10–20 m (33–65 ft) with a stout bole up to 2 m (6.6 ft) in diameter. *Crown* Monopodal with a single stem which has a terminal rosette of numerous leaves, without basal suckers. *Bark* Elephant grey with rhombic ridges from the leaf base scars. *Foliage* Leaves pinnate, to 4 m (13 ft); leaflets many, circa 120 pairs, crowded and arranged in groups of two to five, green or silvery green, sharp pointed with a bifid or indented apex, stiff, to 70 × 3 cm (28 × 1.2 in); leaf stalk without spines or teeth, short; sheath open, fibrous. *Flowers* In pendent inflorescences to 1 m (3.3 ft) which arise from the axils of the lower leaves, with yellow flowers. *Fruit* Ovoid, yellow, 4 × 2.5 cm (1.6 × 1 in).

Range: Coastal central Chile.

Habitat: Cultivated as an ornamental.

This tree is planted as an ornamental in the Mediterranean region but is hardy as far north as the south coast of Devon. It was once very common in Chile but has been over-exploited for the sugary sap. This is collected by felling and cutting off the rosette of leaves. It used to be concentrated by boiling as for maple syrup or fermented.

WALNUT, JUGLANDACEAE

This family includes seven genera with about 60 species with pinnate leaves. The four genera treated here can be separated on the basis of the pith in the centre of one- or two-year shoots. In *Carya* (p.565) and *Platycarya* (p.988) it is solid, whilst in *Juglans* (p.750) and *Pterocarya* (p.1040) it is chambered.

WALNUTS, *JUGLANS*
FAMILY JUGLANDACEAE

Walnuts occur in the Americas, mainly in North America but extending well into South America, and in Asia. The leaves are pinnate. The shoots have a pith which is divided into a number of segments or chambers (cf. *Carya*), whilst the buds have scales (i.e. are not naked as in *Pterocarya*). The male catkins are unbranched, opening before or just in advance of the leaves. The fruit is a nut which is surrounded by a variably fleshy husk. The shoots provide a convenient character for separating the species at most times of the year. In *JJ. ailanthifolia* and *cinerea*, the shoots have glandular hairs which make them sticky, whilst *J. nigra* has downy but not sticky shoots and in *J. regia* the shoots are smooth and glabrous or without hairs. Walnuts are grown both for the tasty fruits and for the timber.

---

p.326 **Japanese Walnut** *Juglans ailanthifolia*

Description: Deciduous tree 10–20 m (33–65 ft) with a bole diameter to 70 cm (2.3 ft).
Crown Ovoid, gaunt in winter. *Bark* Grey-brown, striped, becoming shallowly fissured. *Shoot* Green with a thick coat of whitish sticky glandular hairs and white and brown linear lenticels, in the second year grey-brown, hairless, with large T-shaped traces from the leaf bases, pith chambered. *Buds* Ovoid-conical, with hairy scales, to 1.5 cm (0.6 in), lateral buds in tandem with the male cone buds. *Foliage* Leaves large, 40–100 cm (16–39 in), with 9–21 leaflets; leaflets oblong, tapering to a slender tip, base rounded, oblique, margin with small teeth, upper surface dark matt green, underside light green with whitish star-shaped hairs with 15–20 pairs of raised hairy veins, 10–20 × 4–7 cm (4–8 × 1.6–2.8 in); leaf stalk round, glandular hairy, rachis ridged between leaflets but grooved between the pairs; autumn colour yellow. *Flowers* In late spring, with the male catkins from buds formed in the leaf axils the previous year and the female flowers terminal on the current season's shoots; female flowers with large purple-pink stigmas, in racemes circa 15 cm (6 in) long with 12–20 flowers; male catkins 10–30 cm (4–12 in). *Fruit* Ovoid with a pointed apex, green with pale green markings and covered with sticky glandular hairs, 4 cm (1.6 in), with the seed rugose but not ridged except where the two halves meet, 2.5–3.5 cm (1–1.4 in).

Range: Hokkaido, Honshu, Kyushu, Shikoku,
Japan and in Sakhalin.

Habitat: Cultivated as an ornamental, in the wild
occurring in mixed broadleafed forests.

Varieties: Var. *cordiformis* is a cultivated form with a
thin smooth shell, with the nut heart-
shaped at the base, and is a garden form
selected for ease of access to the tasty
kernel.

Synonyms: *J. sieboldiana*.

Similar species: *J. mandshurica* is closely related but with
only 5–10 flowers in the female raceme and
with larger sub-globose or ovoid nut. The
nuts are 4.5–5.5 cm (1.8–2.2 in) long with
eight sharp ridges. It occurs in north China,
Korea and Pacific Russia but in central and
west China there is the almost
indistinguishable *J. cathayensis*.

This walnut has large leaves which are
sticky with glandular brown hairs and also
with white star-shaped hairs. The fruits are
in long racemes, and have a thick shell.

---

p.327 **Butter Nut** *Juglans cinerea*

Description: Deciduous tree to 20 m (65 ft) with a bole
diameter to 70 cm (2.3 ft).
Crown Usually broad and open on a short
bole with stout spreading branches.
Bark Light grey, smooth, becoming
furrowed with scaly ridges. *Shoot* Green,
stout and densely covered with sticky
glandular hairs in the first year with a hairy
band on the leaf scars, in the second year
hairless and smooth shiny grey-brown with
prominent deltoid scars from the old leaf
bases, pith chambered. *Buds* Ovoid, light
brown to pinkish, hairy, two or three
superposed (i.e. one above another in a leaf
axil), to 1.5 cm (0.6 in). *Foliage* Leaves
35–70 × 10–22 cm (14–28 × 4–8.7 in)
with 11–17 leaflets; leaflets ovate-
lanceolate to oblong-lanceolate, tapering to
a slender-pointed tip, base rounded and
stalkless on the rachis, margin ciliate and
with small forward teeth ending main veins
and often intermediate veins, upper surface

fresh to mid green, slightly hairy, underside
light to somewhat glaucous green, covered
with soft pale hairs especially on the raised
veins, 5–12 × 2–5 cm (2–4.7 × 0.8–2 in);
rachis and leaf stalk round and densely
glandular hairy, enlarged where attached to
the shoot; autumn colour yellow or brown.
Flowers Male catkins 5–8 cm (2–3.1 in);
female flowers in racemes of six to eight.
Fruit In three to fives in drooping clusters,
narrow ovoid with a long pointed apex,
fleshy covering hard with two ridges and
covered with red-brown sticky hairs; seed
with a thick shell, light brown with eight
ridges, flesh very oily.

Range: Eastern North America from Minnesota
and Quebec across to New Brunswick and
south to Georgia and Arkansas.

Habitat: Cultivated as an ornamental and
occasionally as a timber tree, in its native
area found in moist valley bottoms and
slopes in hardwood forests.

The nut is sweet and very oily, hence the
name butternut. It is similar to *J. nigra* but
the hairy pad between the leaf base and the
bud provide a constant distinguishing
character.

---

p.327 **Black Walnut** *Juglans nigra*

Description: Deciduous tree 15–35 m (50–115 ft) with a
bole diameter to 2 m (6.6 ft).
Crown Rounded or domed, sometimes
widely so. *Bark* Dark brown, occasionally
blackish or grey, with deep furrows and
crossing scaly ridges. *Shoot* Light brown
or greenish brown, finely hairy, becoming
grey in the second year and roughened by
the hardened lenticels, pith chambered,
light brown. *Buds* Rounded with a short
point but the terminal ones ovoid to conic,
grey-brown, hairy, often superposed (in
tandem), 0.3–1.2 cm (0.1–0.5 in).
Foliage Leaves 30–60 cm (12–24 in),
aromatic, with 9–23 leaflets; leaflets
lanceolate, oval or oblong, tapering to a
slender-pointed apex, base rounded to

broad wedge-shaped, oblique, usually with more of the blade towards the tip of the leaf, margin finely toothed with small triangular spaced and shallow points, upper surface shiny green, faintly brown hairy along the veins, more or less smooth, underside whitish green hairy all over but especially in tufts in the axils of the raised veins, 6–13 × 3–4 cm (2.4–5.1 × 1.2–1.6 in); leaf stalk round except near the base where shallowly grooved, hairy, leaflets usually not quite opposite, rachis round, hairy, leaflet stalk hairy, short, 1 mm (0.1 in) (to 2 cm (0.8 in) on the terminal leaflet); autumn colour yellow. *Flowers* In early spring, small, greenish, male catkins yellow, 5–10 cm (2–4 in), two to five female flowers from buds at branch tips. *Fruit* Smooth with a thick green or brown husk covering a thick shelled rugose nut, 3–5 cm (1.2–2 in), single or in pairs; nut edible and sweet flavoured.

Range: Eastern North America from southern New England south to Florida, west to Texas, north to South Dakota and just extending into southern Ontario, Canada.

Habitat: Cultivated as an ornamental, in the wild occurring as scattered trees in moist well-drained streamside sites.

Similar species: *J. microcarpa* (syn. *J. rupestris*), the Texan walnut, differs in the leaves being smaller, to 30 cm (12 in), and the leaflets soon becoming hairless. The male catkins are more slender and the fruit is much smaller (the smallest of all walnuts), in the range 1.2–2.5 cm (0.5–1 in), with a thin hairy husk. It is recorded from Kansas west to New Mexico and south into Texas and into northeast Mexico. In cultivation, it has made a neat tree to 20 × 0.6 m (65 × 2 ft).

The timber is of the highest quality, with a dark heartwood which is used for gunstocks and for its attractive grain. The nuts have a sweet flesh but the generally thick shell makes access difficult. Some trees, however, are recorded as having thinner shells. A black dye can be made from the husk.

p.326 **Walnut** *Juglans regia*

Description: Deciduous tree 15–25 m (50–80 ft) with a
bole diameter to 2 m (6.6 ft).
Crown Rounded dome with a short bole and
large radiating branches, taller and narrower
in woodland conditions. *Bark* Shiny grey in
young trees, smooth, becoming pale grey
with smooth ridges and deep wide fissures.
Shoot Stout with a chambered pith, shiny
green maturing to dark brown with sparse
hairs or hairless and long narrow lenticels in
the first year, later dark chocolate brown and
smooth. *Buds* Ovoid, pointed or rounded,
dark greyish black to black, with two bud
scales, 3–8 mm (0.1–0.3 in). *Foliage* 20–
45 cm (8–18 in), pinnate with five to nine
(rarely to 13) leaflets; leaflets oval, ovate or
oblong with a short 1 mm (0.1 in) stalk,
increasing in size towards the terminal leaflet,
apex rounded to a short triangular tip, base
rounded, margin untoothed except in young
trees, upper surface sub-shiny dull green,
hairless with raised veins, underside sub-
shiny light green veins prominently raised,
hairless except for whitish axillary tufts,
crushed leafs pungent, leaflets variable, up to
20 × 10 cm (8 × 4 in); leaf stalk green,
hairless, with a faint groove or rounded and
with two lateral flanges, base enlarged, rachis
round with dark brown rounded lenticels;
autumn colour poor. *Flowers* In spring with
the new leaves from axillary buds, male
catkins 5–10 cm (2–4 in), female catkins
terminal on the new shoots in clusters of two
to five. *Fruit* Globose with a thick green
smooth case which splits to expose the ovoid,
pointed rugose nut 4–5 cm (1.6–2 in).

Range: Southeast Europe eastwards across Central
Asia and along the Himalayas to southwest
China (Yunnan) and northern Burma.

Habitat: Open woodlands.

Varieties: 'Laciniata' has the leaves cut into deep
lobes. Various geographical varieties are
recorded from across its enormous range.

The origin of the walnut is lost as it has been
cultivated for centuries for the deliciously
tasty fruit used in confectionery and as a nut.

If picked in early summer before they become woody, they can be pickled. The timber is of a high quality, especially the dark heartwood, and trees are dug rather than felled as the best timber is that at the base where the roots join the trunk. It is the only species of walnut which has untoothed leaves (except on young trees where some teeth may be present) and in which the leaflets are markedly larger towards the terminal one. As a tree it requires an open site but does not like frosty conditions.

JUNIPERS, *JUNIPERUS* (SYNONYM: *SABINA*)
FAMILY CUPRESSACEAE

This is a genus of 50 or so species, ranging from carpeting shrubs to tall trees with a quality fragrant timber. The leaves are in pairs or whorls of three. In some species, the leaves are always awl-like or acicular (needle-like), and either jointed at the base (see *JJ. communis, drupacea, oxycedrus* and *rigida*) or decurrent on the shoot. However, in most species, the adult leaves are scale-like in pairs, but even these species often have some needle-like leaves (which are always decurrent on the shoot). The leaves in juvenile plants are always needle-like. The fruits develop into berries with either a dry mealy pulp or a more juicy bluish pulp, and contain one to a dozen seeds. Species with bluish, often glaucous bloomed, fruits are *JJ. chinensis, communis, rigida, thurifera, scopulorum* and *virginiana*. In *JJ. recurva* and *wallichiana* the fruits ripen black, whilst in *JJ. drupacea, excelsa, foetidissima, oxycedrus* and *phoenicea* they ripen to reddish brown. The relationship with the scales of a *Cupressus* cone are shown by some species, where the outline of the scales is evident, at least before the fruit is fully ripe. Juniper seeds are not winged and have a thick coat. They are intended to be eaten and to pass through the gut, which hastens germination (otherwise this takes up to five years).

The genus is sometimes treated as two or three genera. *Arceuthos* contains only the one species, *J. drupacea*, which has needle-like leaves 1–2.5 cm (0.4–1 in) and in which the three seeds in each fruit are fused together. In *Sabina*, the flowers are on short scaly shoots, the leaves are predominantly scale-like and are decurrent on the shoot. If these genera are accepted, *Juniperus* is left with about eight species characterized by the needle-like leaves which are jointed at the base and the stalkless female flowers which are borne in the axils of the leaves.

Junipers are used as amenity plants, and on a small scale for timber. The berries are also used to flavour gin.

Informal Key

FRUIT
(i) **single seed:** *drupacea* (3 but fused as 1), *recurva*, *wallichiana*
(ii) **1–3 seeds:** *chinensis* (1–4), *communis* (1–3), *drupacea* (three but fused as one), *foetidissima* (1–2, rarely 3), *oxycedrus* (3), *rigida* (1–3), *scopulorum* (2), *thurifera* (2–4), *virginiana* (1–2)
(iii) **3–9 seeds:** *chinensis* (1–4), *excelsa* (4–6), *phoenicea* (3–9), *thurifera* (2–4)

p.52 **Chinese Juniper** *Juniperus chinensis*

Description: Evergreen tree 15–20 m (50–65 ft) with a
bole diameter to 1 m (3.3 ft).
Crown Conical to columnar or erratic,
depending upon cultivar, usually dense.
Bark Brown, peeling in long narrow
twisted strips. *Shoot* Green for the first
winter or two, then red-brown or grey-
brown, later red-brown and peeling.
Buds Hidden in leaf axils. *Foliage* Both
juvenile and adult foliage often borne on
the same tree; juvenile leaves needle-like, in
threes or in pairs, lanceolate with a tapered
long slender bony point, decurrent on the
shoot, inner (abaxial) surface concave,
glaucous blue, outer (adaxial) surface
convex, mid green, 0.5–1 cm × 1 mm
(0.2–0.4 × 0.1 in); adult leaves in decussate
pairs, apex acute to slender pointed, pressed
against shoot, with a dorsal gland, grey-
green to fresh yellow-green, 1–1.5 mm
(0.1 in); crushed foliage resin scented.
Flowers On previous season's growths in
late winter or early spring, dioecious; male
cones ovoid, yellow to yellow-brown, 3 mm
(0.1 in); female cones with three pairs of
scales, pale glaucous green, 2 mm (0.1 in).
Fruit One-year cone lumpy, green, with
the scales visible and like a small *Cupressus*
cone, 5 mm (0.2 in); expanding and
ripening in the second year, becoming
globose or obovoid, scales still visible but
less obvious and more flesh-like, whitish
blue due to a thick glaucous wax, becoming
dark brown over the second winter,

6.7–8 mm (0.25–0.3 in), with one to four shiny brown ovoid seeds 4–5 mm (0.2 in).

Range: China from Inner Mongolia to south of the Yangtse and across to coastal sites on Honshu, Kyushu and Shikoku, Japan.

Habitat: Cultivated in Europe as an ornamental, in the wild occurring on dry hillsides or coastal sands.

Varieties: Many but mostly dwarf forms. Notable tree forms include 'Aurea', which has golden foliage and makes a narrow ovoid-columnar or conic tree. It is very attractive in April when laden with the yellow male cones. 'Columnaris' makes a very narrow cone. It has almost entirely juvenile foliage, although adult foliage may be produced and will show the plant to be male. 'Kaizuka' has entirely adult foliage and is female, usually laden with cones of varying ages. The foliage is bright green to yellow-green and carried in dense erratic sprays which give the tree an attractive but irregular appearance.

This tree is very common in cultivation, mainly as a small number of cultivars. It will withstand clipping and is capable of making new growth if cut back into bare wood provided sufficient live foliage remains elsewhere on the bush.

---

p.53 **Juniper** *Juniperus communis*

Description: Evergreen tree to 8 m (26 ft) and a bole to 20 cm (8 in) diameter or a spreading or sprawling shrub.
Crown Columnar to spreading, tips of branches often nodding. *Bark* Reddish brown, developing papery scales.
Shoot Pale brown or yellow-green or yellow-brown in first winter, becoming red-brown, then dark red-brown and smooth, slender. *Buds* Small, ovoid, with green scales, 2 mm (0.1 in). *Foliage* In prickly three-dimensional sprays with leaves in whorls of three; leaves linear-ovoid (needle-like), tapering to a sharp bony apex, jointed at base and not decurrent on the shoot,

inner surface cupped, with a broad waxy glaucous white stomata, outer surface convex, mid to yellow-green, without stomata, 1–2 cm × 1–2 mm (0.4–0.8 × 0.1 in); crushed foliage with a sweet citrus scent. *Flowers* On previous season's shoots in early summer, dioecious; male cones yellow, in leaf axils, 8 mm (0.3 in); female cones with three to eight scales, 2 mm (0.1 in). *Fruit* Ovoid or globose, green in the first year, then blue with a waxy glaucous bloom, ripening in the third year to black, 6–9 mm (0.25–0.4 in); one to three seeds.

Range: Very widely distributed in the northern hemisphere, throughout Europe and south into north Africa, east to the western Himalayas and north across Asia to Japan, and in North America from Canada but extending south down the Appalachian and Rocky Mountain chains.

Habitat: Chalk downland, dry hillsides and acid boggy peats in pine forests.

Varieties: Dwarf or prostrate forms are ssp. *nana* which rises no more than a few inches. In towns, selected forms, such as 'Hibernica', with a narrow columnar habit, are often planted.

Juniper is very variable in its habit, from narrow conical columns through sprawling shrubs to prostrate mats. It is very widely distributed and tolerates a wide range of sites, but needs reasonable to full light.

p.54 **Syrian Juniper** *Juniperus drupacea*

Description: Evergreen tree 10–15 m (33–50 ft) with a bole to 30 cm (1 ft) diameter.
Crown Narrow columnar or conical, with upright branches; old trees may become domed. *Bark* Orange-brown and grey, stripping to reveal red-brown beneath.
Shoot Shiny green for one to two years, turning pink-brown or red-brown and then grey-brown, slender, 1–1.5 mm (0.1 in).
Buds Minute, hidden in leaf axils.
Foliage Irregularly arranged, soft to very prickly; leaves in whorls of three, with the

whorls arranged at an angle, so that viewed from above, there are six rows of leaves, lanceolate and decurrent on shoot, tip slender pointed, mid shiny green on the convex outer surface, with two silvery green waxy bands of stomata on the concave inner side (forwards towards the shoot) on either side of the midrib, 1–1.5 cm (0.4–0.6 in) (to 2.5 cm (1 in)) × 2–4 mm (0.1–0.2 in); crushed foliage with a faint resinous smell. *Flowers* On the previous year's shoot in spring, dioecious; male cones on short leafy shoots, globular clusters of six to nine ovoid cones, opening yellow. *Fruit* Ovoid to sub-globose with six to nine fleshy scales whose outline remains visible on the fruit, brown or blackish blue with a pruinose waxy covering, seeds three, fused together, ripening in the second year, 2–2.5 cm (0.8–1 in).

Range: South Greece and across southern Turkey to northern Syria.

Habitat: Dry rocky slopes, tolerant of a wide range of sites in cultivation.

Synonyms: *Arceuthos drupaceae.*

This makes an unusual juniper with an attractive upright habit. It is mainly represented in cultivation by male trees.

p.50 **Grecian Juniper** *Juniperus excelsa*

Description: Evergreen tree to 25 m (80 ft) (but sometimes a prostrate shrub) with a bole diameter of up to 2.5 m (8 ft) in very old trees.
Crown Conic, becoming domed.
Bark Reddish-brown, smooth in young trees but soon peeling in flaky scales; in old trees fibrous and furrowed, peeling in long strips. *Shoot* Green in the first winter, then red-brown, later the leaf bases are shed and the shoot is smooth and purplish brown. *Buds* Hidden in leaf axils.
Foliage In two types; juvenile foliage and shaded portions of mature trees have needle-like grey-green leaves in threes; these have a sharp bony point and a dorsal

gland, with a free tip 1.5–3 mm (0.1 in); adult leaves scale-like in decussate pairs, ovate-rhombic with a tip pressed against shoot or just-free tip, with the ultimate branches round and 0.7–1 mm (0.1 in) in diameter; crushed foliage with a somewhat cat-like smell. *Flowers* On previous season's shoots in late spring; male cones green and yellow, 3–4 × 2–3 mm (0.1–0.2 × 0.1 in). *Fruit* Globose, ripening from purplish green or blue to purplish brown or purplish black in second autumn, 6–11 mm (0.25–0.4 in), with four to six fertile scales; about three to six seeds.

Range: Albania, Macedonia, Greece, Bulgaria, Turkey, Cyprus, Syria, Lebanon, the Crimea, Georgia, Azerbaijan and Turkmenia.

Habitat: Dry rocky slopes.

Similar species: *J. polycarpos* from Afghanistan, Armenia, Azerbaijan, Iran, Oman, Pakistan, Tadzhikistan, Turkey, Turkmenia and Uzbekistan differs in the thicker ultimate branches (1–1.3 mm (0.1 in)) which are more quadrangular, and the larger cones to 1.4 cm (0.6 in) with fewer (three or four) seeds.

This tree tolerates hot dry summer conditions.

p.50 **Stinking Juniper** *Juniperus foetidissima*

Description: Evergreen tree 10–15 m (33–50 ft) with a bole diameter to 1 m (3.3 ft).
Crown Narrow conic in young trees, becoming irregular, often domed, in old trees. *Bark* Smooth and red-brown with papery scales, in old trees grey, fibrous and furrowed with peeling ridges. *Shoot* Green in the first winter due to the decurrent leaf bases and four angled, then red-brown. *Buds* Hidden in leaf bases. *Foliage* In rather flat dense sprays; juvenile leaves linear, in threes; adult leaves scale-like, rhombic to ovate-rhombic, imbricate and decurrent with free backward-curved tips or pressed against shoot and an inconspicuous dorsal gland, grey-green to shiny yellow-green with two narrow marginal lines of

stomata, 2–5 mm (0.1–0.2 in); crushed foliage with a foetid smell. *Flowers* On previous season's shoots in late winter or spring, dioecious; male cones ovoid, 3 mm (0.1 in), yellow-brown; female cones sub-globose, blackish or dark violet-purple, with six scales, 3 mm (0.1 in).
Fruit Globose, ripening in the second year from glaucous blue-green to dark purple or violet, with usually two seeds (one to three), 8–10 mm (0.3–0.4 in).

Range: Albania, Macedonia, Greece, Turkey, Cyprus, Syria, Armenia, Georgia and the Crimea.

Habitat: Dry rocky hillsides.

This has a strong foetid smell to the crushed foliage. It makes a small tree, tolerant of summer heat and cold winters.

---

p.53 **Prickly Juniper** *Juniperus oxycedrus*

Description: Evergreen tree or shrub up to 15 m (50 ft) a bole diameter to 60 cm (2 ft).
Crown Conical to rounded. *Bark* Grey or reddish grey, becoming rough and scurfy. *Shoot* Whitish green or pale yellow-green in the first winter with narrow ridges decurrent behind the leaves and 1.5 mm (0.1 in) in diameter, becoming bright red-brown and rounded, smooth. *Buds* Hidden in leaves. *Foliage* Leaves in whorls of three, needle-like, pointing forwards, soft and lax but prickly; linear with a slender-pointed, very sharp bony apex, inner face concave with a single or two waxy whitish green bands of stomata, outer convex surface mid to dark matt green without stomata and with a narrow groove or ridge, 1–2.5 cm × 1–2 mm (0.4–1 × 0.1 in); crushed foliage has a grassy but resinous scent. *Flowers* On previous season's shoots in spring; male cones brownish, oblong-ovoid, 3 mm (0.1 in); female cones ovoid, pale green, 1 mm (0.1 in). *Fruit* Ovoid to globose, ripening dark reddish brown or violet-purple with a waxy bloom in second year, 5–10 mm (0.2–0.4 in), with usually three seeds.

Range: Southern Europe across to the Caucasus, Iraq and northern Iran.

Habitat: On dry stony mountain sides, with ssp. *macrocarpa* occurring on sandy dunes close to the sea.

Varieties: Ssp. *macrocarpa* has larger leaves to 2.5 cm × 2.5 mm (1 × 0.1 in) and larger cones 1.2–1.5 cm (0.5–0.6 in) across. It is restricted to maritime sites.

This makes a small tree, usually more of a shrub and on several stems. It is related to *J. communis*, which it largely replaces in southern Europe, and to *J. rigida*, differing in the larger and usually reddish-brown fruits.

p.50 Phoenician Juniper *Juniperus phoenicea*

Description: Evergreen shrub or tree to 10 m (33 ft), with a bole to 30 cm (1 ft).
Crown Conic, rounded in old trees, or prostrate on sea shores. *Bark* Grey-brown, peeling in narrow strips. *Shoot* Light green for first winter, then red-brown and later grey and flaking. *Buds* Hidden in scale leaves. *Foliage* In slender sprays; adult leaves rhombic-ovate with a dorsal gland, apex acute and pressed against shoot, grey-green, 1 mm (0.1 in); juvenile leaves in opposite pairs or threes, needle-like, incurved, slender pointed, 2.5 × 1 mm (0.1 × 0.05 in); crushed foliage with a faint resin scent. *Flowers* On previous season's shoots in late winter; male cones ovoid, 4 mm (0.2 in). *Fruit* Globose or ovoid, ripens to dark reddish brown in second year, shiny or slightly pruinose, 0.8–1.4 cm (0.3–0.6 in); three to six seeds, rarely nine, 7 × 3 mm (0.3 × 0.1 in).

Range: Shores of the Mediterranean and west to Portugal.

Habitat: Pine forest on rocky ground or sandy sea shores.

This makes a small tree or shrub, distinct in the red-brown cones which contain three or more seeds.

p.54 **Himalayan Weeping Juniper**
Juniperus recurva

Description: Evergreen tree 10–20 m (33–65 ft) with a
bole diameter 0.3–1 m (1–3.3 ft).
Crown Conical with pendent or weeping
branch tips, may become columnar in old
trees. *Bark* Orange-brown or grey-brown,
smooth and exfoliating in thin sheets on
young trees; on old trees, becoming
fibrous and furrowed. *Shoot* Green or
light green-brown for the first winter,
then brown as leaves die, later shedding
the leaf bases and becoming smooth and
red-brown. *Buds* Hidden in needle-like
leaves. *Foliage* In sprays which are
pendent at the tips and dry to the touch
(and also sharp!); leaves in whorls of three
which point forwards along the shoot,
lanceolate with a rounded base which is
decurrent on the shoot, gently tapered to a
sharp bony apex, grey-green or less often
blue-green with a waxy bloom on outer
surface, with a broad silvery waxy band of
stomata on the inner surface with broad
green margins, old leaves retained as
brown or orange-brown, 4–8 ×
0.7–1.5 mm (0.2–0.3 × 0.1 in); crushed
foliage with a parsley scent. *Flowers* On
previous season's shoots in late spring,
usually dioecious but occasionally
monoecious; male cones globose, light
yellow and green, 4 mm (0.2 in).
Fruit Globose or ovoid, ripening from
green to blackish purple in second year,
7–10 mm (0.3–0.4 in), containing a single
seed.
Range: Himalayas from Afghanistan to western
China.
Habitat: Cultivated in Europe as an ornamental, in
the wild found in a narrow band above *Picea*
and *Tsuga* and below *Abies*.
Varieties: Var. *coxii* is the Coffin Juniper from the
border between Burma and Yunnan. It has
bright green foliage which is 8–10 mm
(0.3–0.4 in) long.

This makes an attractive albeit rather slow-
growing tree.

p.53 **Temple Juniper** *Juniperus rigida*

Description: Evergreen tree to 8–15 m (26–50 ft) with a bole diameter to 50 cm (1.6 ft).
Crown Conical in young trees, becoming open and spreading with erect branches bearing pendulous shoots. *Bark* Grey or brown, dull, becoming peeling in long strips. *Shoot* Whitish green or pale yellow-green in the first winter with narrow ridges decurrent behind the leaves and 1.5–3 mm (0.1 in), becoming bright red-brown and rounded, smooth.
Buds Hidden in leaves. *Foliage* Leaves in whorls of three, needle-like, pointing forwards, soft and lax unless the spines are engaged; lanceolate, tapered to the base and to the slender-pointed, very sharp bony apex, inner face concave, angled with a narrow groove between the two waxy whitish green bands of stomata, outer convex surface mid to dark matt green without stomata and with a raised ridge, 1.2–2.5 cm × 2 mm (0.5–1 × 0.1 in); crushed foliage has a grassy scent.
Flowers On previous season's shoots in spring; male cones yellow. *Fruit* Globose, ripening purplish black in second year, 6–9 mm (0.25–0.4 in), with one to three seeds.

Range: Honshu, Shikoku and Kyushu, Japan, Korea and across China from Gansu to Manchuria.

Habitat: Cultivated in Europe as an ornamental.

Varieties: Ssp. *nipponica* is a prostrate form from high altitudes in Honshu and Hokkaido.

Similar species: *J. formosana* is a related species from Taiwan and across southern China. The leaves do not have the groove on the inner concave surface of the leaf. It forms a narrow-crowned small tree on limestone hillsides.

This small tree is allied to *J. communis* and *J. oxycedrus* but can be distinguished by the groove which runs along the inner or concave surface of the leaf. In cultivation it is a small sprawling tree with attractive drooping foliage.

p.51 **Rocky Mountain Juniper**
Juniperus scopulorum

Description: Evergreen tree 10–15 m (33–50 ft) with a
bole to 30 cm (1 ft).
Crown Spire like or conical when young,
becoming rounded domed. *Bark* Reddish
brown, becoming furrowed into peeling
strips or small flaking squares. *Shoot* Green
for one year, becoming brown and then
dark brown, slender, 1.5 cm (0.1 in).
Buds Hidden in axils of the scale leaves.
Foliage In short spreading or erect sprays,
consisting of many short flattened sections
irregularly arranged, ranging in colour
from pale grey-green to glaucous green or
silvery blue; leaves scale-like, in opposite
pairs; on strong shoots, decurrent with free
acute tips 1 mm (0.1 in) and 7 mm (0.3 in)
between pairs; on short shoots, linked with
pairs superimposed, incurved at tip, 1.5 cm
(0.1 in); crushed foliage with a slightly
oniony resinous strong scent. *Flowers* At
ends of previous season's shoots in late
winter, males and females on separate
trees; male cones globose, pale brown,
1.2–2 mm (0.1 in). *Fruit* Globose cone
with a soft, juicy, sweet, resinous flesh and
usually two seeds, ripening in the second
year, 6 mm (0.25 in).

Range: Western North America from British
Columbia south along the Rocky
Mountains to northern Mexico.

Habitat: Cultivated in Europe as an ornamental tree
or shrub, in the wild occurring in open
rocky hillsides or canyons, especially on
limestone or old lava flows.

Varieties: Several varieties are in commerce, the most
important being 'Skyrocket'. This makes a
narrow spire to 5–7 m × 30–50 cm (16–23
× 1–1.6 ft) crown diameter, with blue-grey
foliage. 'Springbank' is a small erect male
tree of columnar habit and is one of several
selections with silvery blue foliage.

Rare as a tree in cultivation, it is now
frequently planted as one of the selected
forms and will be more prominent in the
future.

p.51 **Spanish Juniper** *Juniperus thurifera*

Description: Evergreen tree 10–15 m (33–50 ft) in height
with a bole diameter of up 30 cm (1 ft).
Crown Ovoid-conical or conical, branches
upswept. *Bark* Dark brown, becoming
scaly and peeling in long strips.
Shoot Green in first winter, becoming dull
brown or grey-brown, slender.
Buds Hidden in axils of the scale leaves.
Foliage In short flat lateral sprays to 10 ×
4 cm (4 × 1.6 in), arranged at irregular
angles; scale leaves in similar decussate
pairs, decurrent on shoot, apex triangular,
free at the bony tip which may be spreading
or point forwards along the shoot, margins
entire or sometimes toothed, dorsal gland
prominent, secreting white resin on older
leaves, mid to dark green, 1–5 mm
(0.1–0.2 in); crushed foliage with a musty
resin smell. *Flowers* On previous season's
shoots. *Fruit* Globose but with the minute
prickles of the vestigial scales persisting,
pruinose, blue-green, ripening in the second
to dark purple, 7–8 mm (0.3 in), with
usually two to four seeds to 5 mm (0.2 in).

Range: Central, southern and eastern Spain south
into North Africa and in the Alps in
southeast France.

Habitat: Dry rocky mountainsides.

This small tree has a strong rather musty
scent to the crushed foliage. It is tolerant of
dry sites. It is also a rare ornamental in
specialist collections.

---

p.52 **Pencil Cedar** or **Eastern Red Cedar**
Juniperus virginiana

Description: Evergreen tree 10–20 m (33–65 ft) with a
bole diameter to 1 m (3.3 ft).
Crown Conical in young trees, becoming
columnar and usually retaining foliage to
the ground; old trees may become more
open. *Bark* Grey-brown or red-brown,
with spiral fibrous ridges which are
slightly stripping. *Shoot* Green or yellow-
green for first winter, then grey-brown and

later red-brown as the dead leaves are shed, slender. *Buds* Hidden in the scale or needle leaves. *Foliage* Adult foliage scale-like in decussate pairs, grey-green or dark grey, ovate, apex acute with the tip slightly free or pressed against shoot, small dorsal resin gland, 1–2 mm (0.1 in); juvenile leaves often partially retained at the base and tip of current season's shoots, in pairs, grey-green on the convex outer face and glaucous due to the waxy band of stomata on the inner concave face, 3–6 mm (0.1–0.25 in); crushed foliage with a fruity resin or soapy scent. *Flowers* On previous season's growths in late winter, dioecious; male cones yellow; female cones with four scales and two ovules, yellow-green, 1 mm (0.1 in). *Fruit* Ovoid, ripens in the first autumn to dark violet-blue or brownish violet with a thick glaucous waxy covering, 4–6 mm (0.2–0.25 in), with one or two seeds.

Range: Eastern North America from Maine across to southern Canada in Ontario and Quebec and south to central Texas and northern Florida.

Habitat: Cultivated in Europe as an ornamental, in the wild occurring in scattered small stands on limestone, from dry upland sites to swampy sites.

Varieties: A number of selected forms, including ones with narrow upright habits or more bluish foliage.

This is a common tree in cultivation, although without the charm of some of the other species, such as *J. recurva*. The small ovoid cones are sweet and juicy. It is similar to *J. chinensis* in some features, but the small cones ripen in one year and the juvenile leaves in pairs distinguish it.

Wallich Juniper *Juniperus wallichiana*

Description: Evergreen tree to 10–20 m (33–65 ft) with a bole diameter 0.3–1 m (1–3.3 ft). *Crown* Conical in young trees, becoming broad conical, branches pendent at tips in old trees stout and spreading. *Bark* Red-brown and grey-brown, smooth in young trees, but in old ones the bark becomes fibrous with the bright reddish brown underbark being revealed. *Shoot* Yellow-green in the first winter, then brown to red-brown, becoming smooth in the fourth or fifth year as the dead leaf bases are sloughed off, slender. *Buds* Hidden in axils of the scale leaves. *Foliage* In three-dimensional sprays with the lateral of the current season to 7×4 cm (2.8×1.6 in); adult scale leaves in equal pairs forming rounded tertiary shoots, oval with an abruptly short-pointed apex which is usually incurved and a dorsal oval resin gland, grey-green with flecks of resin, stomata in narrow whitish waxy bands at the margins between the scale leaves, 1.5 mm (0.1 in), juvenile leaves in whorls of three, needle-like with spreading slender tips ending in a bony point, at base with a concave outer face with no stomata and a convex decurrent inner face which has a broad band of waxy silvery white stomata, 3.5×1 mm (0.1×0.1 in); crushed foliage has a musty parsley scent. *Flowers* On previous season's shoots in late spring, on separate male and female plants. *Fruit* One-year cone ovoid, black and green, 7 mm (0.3 in), ripening to black berry in autumn of second year when enlarged to 1.3×1 cm (0.5×0.4 in), seed single, 8×7 mm (0.3×0.3 in), surrounded by a green fleshy coat.

Range: Himalayas.

Habitat: Cultivated in Europe as an ornamental, in the wild forming forests in dry inner valleys at 3000–4000 m (9850–13,100 ft) above sea level.

Synonyms: *J. indica* misapplied, *J. pseudosabina* misapplied.

The exact range of this tree is unclear because it is so often confused with *J. indica*, a shrubby species which attains no more than 60 cm (2 ft) but which has similar foliage and fruits. The best 'botanical' character which separates them is that *J. wallichiana* is spring flowering, whilst

J. indica flowers in the autumn. It makes a
neat ovoid tree in cultivation, but is much
more majestic in the wild, such as in Bhutan
where trees 20 m (65 ft) tall are found. Care
must be taken to avoid thinking that the
one-year berries are mature.

PRICKLY CASTOR-OIL TREE, *KALOPANAX*
FAMILY ARALIACEAE

This is a monotypic genus with lobed leaves, ivy-like fruits
and prickly stems.

---

p.303 **Prickly Castor-oil Tree**
Kalopanax septemlobus

Description: Deciduous tree 15–25 m (50–80 ft) with a
bole diameter to 60 cm (2 ft).
Crown Broad columnar, with rather spaced
and gaunt branching. *Bark* Brown or
grey-brown with thick interwoven purplish
ridges, spiny as a young tree with the bases
of the spines persisting. *Shoot* Stout, green
and slightly bloomed, with linear buff
lenticels, becoming green and brown with
raised lenticels in the second year, starting
to develop the sharp spined prickles or
thorns and grey or grey-buff in the third
year, cut or broken branches yield a brown
resinous fragrant gum. *Buds* Rounded
dome or broad cone, green. *Foliage* Leaves
palmately lobed, but see the variety below,
lobes five, rounded with a short slender-
pointed apex and acute sinuses, base
subcordate to truncate, margin with small
forward hooked teeth, upper surface dark
green with raised veins, underneath pale
green with scattered star-shaped hairs and
raised veins, 8–20 cm (3.1–8 in) each
way; leaf stalk round, green, yellowish or
red-brown, to 25 cm (10 in), with an
enlarged rather shovel-shaped base; autumn
colour yellow-green, poor. *Flowers* In
terminal umbels, white. *Fruit* Globose,
blue-black berry, remaining on the tree
after leaf fall, 5 mm (0.2 in), containing
two or three seeds.

Range: Throughout Japan, in the Kurile Islands, Sakhalin, Korea, Pacific Russia and the Ussuri region and in central and northern China.

Habitat: Cultivated as an ornamental, in the wild occurring in broadleaved forests.

Synonyms: *K. pictus*.

This tree is curious for the spines on the branches. The leaves are very variable in the degree of lobing, with some plants having them reduced to little more than cusps. In var. *maximowiczii*, the lobes are deep with rounded sinuses, and usually seven lobed.

KETELEERIA, *KETELEERIA*
FAMILY PINACEAE

This is a small genus of conifers from central and southern China and Taiwan, south into Vietnam and Laos, with from three to ten species. It is unique in the Pinaceae in the hypogeal germination of the seeds, in which the cotyledons remain underground with the first shoot bearing true leaves. It is also unusual in the family in being able to be coppiced. The leaves have a prominent ridge along the upper surface. The cone remains erect but does not disintegrate. It occurs in the wild in the warm temperate pine/oak forest zone.

---

p.67 **David's Keteleeria** *Keteleeria davidiana*

Description: Evergreen tree 10–15 m (33–50 ft) with a bole diameter to 50 cm (1.6 ft).
Crown Conical in young trees, later columnar, usually with a flat top in old trees. *Bark* Grey with a pinkish tinge, becoming fissured. *Shoot* Brown with dark brown hairs in first winter, later light brown. *Buds* Broad slightly pointed dome, brown, slightly resinous, 3–5 mm (0.1–0.2 in). *Foliage* Parted both above and below, pointing somewhat forwards and rather spaced (not dense) along the shoot; leaves lanceolate or linear, tip slender pointed, with a pungent apex, to bluntly pointed, base tapers to short (1 mm (0.1 in)) leaf stalk, upper surface fresh dark green with a raised midrib, lower surface

mid green with two green bands of stomata, 3–7 cm × 2.5–5.5 mm (1.2–2.8 × 0.1–0.2 in); crushed foliage with a grassy scent. *Flowers* From buds on previous season's growths in spring; male cones clustered from a single bud, yellow and brown, 1–1.5 cm (0.4–0.6 in); female cones erect, purplish red. *Fruit* Cylindrical or ovoid-cylindrical with the tips of the bracts just visible between the scales, remains erect and ripens in first autumn from green to brown, 8–12 × 3.5–6 cm (3.1–4.7 × 1.4–2.4 in); scales as long as or broader than long, free at the tips, 1.5–2 cm (0.6–0.8 in); seed brown, with a long papery wing.

Range: Central and northern China.

Habitat: Cultivated in Europe as an ornamental, in the wild occurring on dry hillsides in open pine and oak forest.

Similar species: **Fortune Keteleeria** *K. fortunei* differs in the nearly rounded in outline cone scales, which are cupped forwards without free tips in the unopened cones, the shorter leaves mainly less than 4 cm (1.6 in) and the hairless shoots. It occurs in eastern and southeastern China including Hong Kong. **Evelyn Keteleeria** *K. evelyniana* has leaves which are abruptly short pointed at the apex, weak hairy shoots and cones with the scales, longer than broad and free and spreading in the unopened cones (and more spreading when it opens). It comes from southwest China, with a closely related species (possibly synonymous) in southern Vietnam and Laos.

This is the hardiest species in the genus. It makes a small tree in cultivation but is not common.

PRIDE OF INDIA TREES, *KOELREUTERIA*
FAMILY SAPINDACEAE

This is a small genus from eastern Asia south to Fiji. The leaves are pinnate to bi-pinnate or tri-pinnate. The flowers are in large terminal panicles and are very showy. The fruits are a conical three-valved bladder, similar to *Colutea* and *Staphylea*.

p.320 **Pride of India** *Koelreuteria paniculata*

Description: Deciduous tree 10–20 m (33–65 ft) with a bole diameter to 50 cm (1.6 ft).
Crown Rounded dome, with ascending and spreading branches. *Bark* Brown or purple-brown with rough ridges and narrow orange fissures. *Shoot* Buff or pale coppery brown and shiny when young with small raised oval lenticels, in the second and later years dull light brown. *Buds* Conical, green and brown, 6 mm (0.25 in). *Foliage* Leaves pinnate to 4.5 mm (0.2 in), pink, reddish or yellowish when young, with the leaflets partially pinnate; leaflets in five or six pairs, ovate or oblong-ovate with deep lobulate lobes with rounded teeth, upper surface dark sub-shiny green with a raised midrib and scattered hairs, underside light green with raised hairy veins, to 8 × 5 cm (3.1 × 2 in); leaf stalk and rachis grooved, green or red, hairless, stalk 1 cm (0.4 in); autumn colour yellow. *Flowers* In large terminal pyramidal panicles 20–40 cm (8–16 in) high and wide in August, composed of many rich yellow flowers with four spreading strap-like petals 7 mm (0.3 in) and eight stamens on hairy filaments. *Fruit* Large papery inflated bladder with three valves, to 4–5 cm (1.6–2 in), with each section holding a single black or dark-brown pea-shaped seed.

Range: China, Japan and Korea.

Habitat: Cultivated as an ornamental, in the wild found in woods.

Varieties: 'Fastigiata' is a form with erect branches.

The large terminal panicles create a strong display in late summer, and are followed by the inflated bladders containing the seeds. It flowers better after long hot summers.

LABURNUMS, *LABURNUM*
FAMILY LEGUMINOSAE

This is a genus of three species of small trees or shrubs from central and southern Europe to Asia Minor. They have trifoliate leaves, pendulous or erect racemes of pea-shaped flowers and a pod which has thickened wings or sutures.

p.309   **Scotch Laburnum** *Laburnum alpinum*

Description: Deciduous tree 5–9 m (16–29 ft) (to 15 m
(50 ft)) with a bole diameter to 0.25–1 m
(0.8–3.3 ft).
Crown Rounded. *Bark* Purplish grey and
smooth, becoming fissured and flaking in
thick scales. *Shoot* Shiny, silvery-grey and
green, soon hairless, slender, then grey-
green and shiny remaining so for five or
more years. *Buds* Ovoid, green, enclosed
in the base of the leaf stalk which remains
attached as the leaf falls, 3 mm (0.1 in).
Foliage Leaves trifoliate; leaflets narrow
elliptic to obovate, apex acute with a short
aristate point, base wedge-shaped, margin
untoothed but ciliate, at least at first,
upper surface deep green with the midrib
indented, underside whitish green, nearly
hairless, 7–13 × 2.5–6 cm (2.8–5.1 ×
1–2.4 in); leaf stalk green, faintly grooved,
nearly hairless but with a few fascicled
hairs near the tip, with the base enlarged
and enclosing the bud, 3–6.5 cm
(1.2–2.6 in). *Flowers* In pendulous
racemes 10–15 cm (4–6 in) in late June
with many densely-packed 2 cm (0.8 in),
golden-yellow flowers set on 0.6–1.2 cm
(0.25–0.5 in) hairless or thinly hairy stalks.
Fruit Pod 4–7 cm (1.6–2.8 in), ripening
to light brown and constricted between the
seeds, with the top suture having three
knife-like wings or flanges (one on each
side and one along the suture); seed light
yellow-brown.

Range: Southern Alps in France, Switzerland,
Austria and extending south into northern
Italy, into the Balkans as far south as
Albania and into the Czech Republic.

Habitat: Damp sites.

Synonyms: *Cytisus alpinus.*

This has the flowers in larger and denser
racemes than found in *L. anagyroides*. The
leaves are generally larger and less hairy.
The most reliable distinction is in the
1 mm (0.1 in) wide wings or flanges along
the top of the pod.

p.309 **Common Laburnum** or **Laburnum**
Laburnum anagyroides

Description: Deciduous tree to 12 m (39 ft) with a bole
diameter to 1.4 m (4.6 ft).
Crown Open with ascending-arching
branches which splay out. *Bark* Smooth
dark green, becoming brown in old trees.
Shoot Grey-green with silky grey hairs
pressed against the shoot. *Buds* Ovoid,
grey-brown, hairy. *Foliage* Leaves
trifoliate; leaflets elliptic to elliptic-
obovate, apex bluntly pointed, base wedge-
shaped, margin untoothed, upper surface
grey-green, underside glaucous, with silky
hairs adpressed when young, 3–8 cm
(1.2–3.1 in); leaf stalk 2–6 cm
(0.8–2.4 in). *Flowers* In loose pendent
racemes in late spring, 10–30 cm
(4–12 in), shorter in older trees; flowers
2 cm (0.8 in), with golden-yellow petals.
Fruit Pod 4–6 cm (1.6–2.4 in) which has
downy hairs adpressed when young, almost
hairless by the time it ripens from green to
brown, with the upper suture unwinged;
seeds black.

Range: Widely spread in southern and central
Europe, cultivated elsewhere.

Habitat: Woods and scrub.

Synonyms: *Cystus laburnum*.

Similar species: *L. × watereri* (p.309) is the hybrid of
L. anagyroides with *L. alpinum*. It is
intermediate between the parents except
the racemes are more floriferous and longer.
As a consequence, it is more widely grown
where trees are selectively planted. The
pods tend to have fewer seeds than the
parent species. In the clone 'Vossii', the
racemes are up to 60 cm (23.6 in) in
length.

This is perhaps the commonest laburnum,
although in Britain it is generally displaced
by its hybrid (*see* above). The seeds and pods
are poisonous, although instances of
poisoning are extremely rare. The
heartwood is very hard and dark and has
been used as a substitute for ebony.

CRAPE MYRTLE, *LAGERSTROEMIA*
FAMILY LYTHRACEAE

This is a genus of around 50 species from eastern Asia but only one is common in cultivation. The leaves are variously arranged on the shoot, alternate, opposite or in whorls of three. The flowers are carried on the current season's growths in late summer and have six curiously crinkled showy petals.

---

p.146 **Crape Myrtle** *Lagerstroemia indica*

Description: Deciduous tree to 10 m (33 ft), or a shrub, with a bole diameter to 30 cm (1 ft). *Crown* Rounded. *Bark* Silky grey, smooth, underbark lighter. *Shoot* Four angled or ridged, hairless, slender, brown. *Buds* Alternate, opposite or in whorls of three along the same shoot, small. *Foliage* Leaves obovate or broad oval, apex rounded and abruptly short pointed, base rounded, not toothed, upper surface glossy green, paler beneath, hairless on both sides, 2.5–6 × 2–3.5 cm (1–2.4 × 0.8–1.4 in); leaf stalk short; autumn colour good. *Flowers* Terminal on the current season's shoots from July to September, in panicles 15–20 × 7–13 cm (6–8 × 2.8–5.1 in); flowers to 4 cm (1.6 in), with six obovate petals which have crinkled margins and are contracted at the base into a long stalk, mainly some shade of pink, less often white. *Fruit* Capsule.

Range: Northern China and Japan.

Habitat: Cultivated as an ornamental.

This makes a very attractive small tree. In Britain, it only flowers after the hottest and driest summers, but is suitable for conservatories.

LARDIZABALA, LARDIZABALACEAE

This is a small family which consists mainly of climbers with palmate leaves. However, *Decaisnea* (p.663) consists of large shrubs and small trees, with pinnate leaves. The family is characterized by the fruit which is a fleshy follicle with many embedded seeds.

Larches, *Larix*
Family Pinaceae

The larches are the largest and most widespread of the five genera of deciduous conifers. The leaves open bright green in early spring and normally give wonderful autumn tints. The shoots are of two kinds, long or extension shoots which bear helically arranged leaves only during the first growing season, and short shoots. These develop from the buds on the long shoots and may grow for several years, bearing short whorls of leaves. The male and female flowers are carried on the short shoots, after which they normally die, although occasionally a female cone will 'proliferate' and revert to vegetative growth for a single summer. Short shoots can revert and give rise to long shoots (especially if the tree is pruned). The cones are woody and erect, ripening in the first autumn. The genus divides into two sections on the basis of cone and leaf characters. In *LL. decidua, gmelinii, kaempferi, laricina* and *sibirica*, the cones are ovoid or globose with the bract scale shorter than the seed scale and normally not visible in the mature cone, and the leaves are flat, not keeled above; in this group, *LL. gmelinii* and *laricina* have only a few scales in the cone. In the other group, the cone is oblong or cylindrical with many scales and with prominent exerted bracts, and the leaves have four sides (i.e. are rhombic in section); this group includes *LL. griffithiana, occidentalis* and *potaninii*. Larches have an excellent timber and are widely used in forestry. They are also used as woodland landscape trees, and cast only a light shade.

---

p.99 **European Larch** *Larix decidua*

Description: Deciduous tree 20–40 m (65–130 ft) with a bole diameter to 1.5 m (5 ft).
Crown Conical when young but soon columnar conic, in old trees becoming wide spreading as a few large branches grow horizontally and then erect. *Bark* Grey and smooth in young trees but soon fissuring and reddish brown, becoming coarsely ridged and scaly in old trees. *Shoot* Shiny straw-yellow or yellow-brown (less often buff-pink or creamy) in first winter with many buds, then dull light brown, hairless, slender, on two-year and older shoots there are short spur shoots. *Buds* Small domes, wider than high, brown, to 1.5 × 2.5 mm (0.1 × 0.1 in), larger and ovoid on strong

shoots. *Foliage* Fresh green in early spring from buds on side buds and spur shoots with a rosette of 30–40 leaves, on long shoots leaves spirally set; leaves linear, soft with a rounded tip, green with two pale-green bands of stomata below, to 3.5 cm × 0.5–1 mm (1.4 × 0.1 in), turning bright yellow in autumn. *Flowers* On spur shoots which are two or more years old in early spring; male cones terminate a spur shoot on weak pendulous branches, yellow, 0.5–1 cm (0.2–0.4 in); female cones terminate spur shoots on stronger branches, erect, yellow to bright pink or red, 1 cm (0.4 in). *Fruit* Conic or cylindric, erect, ripen to brown in first autumn and persisting for a couple of years, 3.5–4.5 × 1.7–2 cm (1.4–1.8 × 0.7–0.8 in); scales rounded, erect, woody, to 1.5 cm (0.6 in) in width, bract visible between lower scales only, triangular, shorter than the seed scale.

Range: Central Europe from the Alps to the Carpathian Mountains.

Habitat: Mountain forests and in forestry plantations.

Varieties: Ssp. *polonica* is found in the Tatra Mountains in northwest Poland and adjoining Ukraine. It differs in the smaller ovoid-globular cones to 1.5 × 1.2 cm (0.6 × 0.5 in) which have more rounded and concave scales.

Synonyms: *L. europaea*.

This tree in one of the first into leaf in the spring and assumes rich yellow autumn colours in November. The one-year shoots give a yellow haze to plantations. It tolerates a wide range of sites, although it will not tolerate shade. It is a pioneer species, establishing quickly and coning at a young age, although capable of remaining around for a couple of centuries or more.

p.99 **Dahurian Larch** *Larix gmelinii*

Description: Deciduous tree to 15 m (50 ft) but up 30 m (100 ft) in continental climates with a bole diameter to 50 cm (1.6 ft).
Crown Conical when young but quickly becoming wide with heavy spreading

branches. *Bark* Red-brown, finely scaly, later fissured and scaly. *Shoot* Pink-brown, reddish brown or yellowish brown, usually hairless, becoming greyer. *Buds* Ovoid-globose, not (or scarcely) resinous, 2–3 mm (0.1 in). *Foliage* Radial and forward along the extension shoots, in rosettes of 20–35 on spur shoots, bright green; leaves linear, widest near the bluntly pointed or acute apex, soft, with two narrow bands of stomata on lower surface, 1.5–3 cm (0.6–1.2 in) (to 4. cm (1.6 in)) by 0.5–0.8 mm (0.1–0.3 in); autumn colour yellow. *Flowers* On spur shoots at least two years old from late winter to early spring; male cones yellow, 5–7 mm (0.2–0.3 in). *Fruit* Ovoid, shiny brown, 1.2–3 × 1–2 cm (0.5–1.2 × 0.4–0.8 in); scales 15–20, 4–7 mm (0.2–0.3 in) in width with a very small bract hidden.

Range: Eastern Siberia to northeast China.

Habitat: Cultivated in Europe as an ornamental, in the wild forming extensive forests on arctic plains, river valleys and low hills.

Varieties: Var. *olgensis*, from northeast China to the shores of the Pacific around Olga Bay, has pale-brown shoots which are densely covered with red-brown hairs and ovoid-oblong cones to 1.5–2.5 cm (0.6–1 in) which have 16–30 almost round scales which are squared at the tip and usually notched. It occurs on wet sites. Var. *japonica* comes from the Kurile Islands and Sakhalin (which were Japanese territory when it was named) and differs in the red-brown or reddish and slightly hairy one-year twigs and smaller (1–2 cm (0.4–0.8 in)) cones with 18–25 more pointed scales. More distinct is Prince Rupprecht Larch, *L. principis-rupprechtii* (var. *principis-rupprechtii*), which comes from northern China from near Beijing (Hebei province, Wutai shan) across to northern Korea. This has shoots which are straw-brown, yellow-brown or red-brown, hairless and with a thin waxy bloom and acute leaves to 3.5 cm (1.4 in). The cones are ovoid to elliptic and 2–4 cm (0.8–1.6 in) long by 2–2.5 cm (0.8–1 in); they have 25–45 scales which are notched

and ovate-oblong in shape. It makes a more
satisfactory tree in cultivation.

Synonyms: *L. dahurica.*

This tree is not adapted to a maritime
climate, often coming into leaf as early as
January. It makes a better tree in
continental climates where the seasons are
more dependable. It is the most variable of
the larches.

---

p.101 **Sikkim Larch** *Larix griffithiana*

Description: Deciduous tree 10–25 m (33–80 ft) with a
bole diameter to 60 cm (2 ft).
Crown Conical in young trees with slightly
ascending branches, becoming columnar
with the branches level except at the tips
and curtained with pendulous branchlets
60 cm (2 ft) long. *Bark* Purple-brown or
grey-brown, fissured with scaly ridges.
Shoot Straw-yellow, slightly purple and
pruinose at the tips in first winter and very
finely hairy, becoming more yellow-brown,
rough from ridges behind leaf bases.
Buds Domed with a short pointed apex
but more rounded on short shoots, red-
brown, slightly resinous, 2×3 mm ($0.1 \times$
0.1 in). *Foliage* Arranged spirally around
extension shoots and in rosettes of 30–40
on short shoots; leaves linear, apex subacute or bluntly pointed, fresh green
above, with two pale whitish bands of
stomata below, $2.5–4$ cm $\times 0.8–1.2$ mm
($1–1.6 \times 0.1$ in); autumn colour golden-
yellow. *Flowers* On short shoots in early
spring; male cones yellow, directed
forwards, $1–1.3$ cm $\times 7$ mm ($0.4–0.5 \times$
0.3 in); female cones purplish, erect, $3 \times$
1.5 cm (1.2×0.6 in). *Fruit* Cylindrical
but tapers to both ends, with prominent
and reflexed bracts, ripens in first autumn
from purplish brown to brown, $5–8 \times$
2.5 cm ($2–3.1 \times 1$ in); scales rounded,
$1–1.5$ cm ($0.4–0.6$ in) broad; bract scale
with the exposed portion triangular with
an apex acute, projecting $0.7–1.5$ cm
($0.3–0.6$ in).

Range: East Nepal along the Himalayas through Sikkim, Bhutan to northeast India and in adjacent southern Tibet.

Habitat: Cultivated in Europe as an ornamental, in the wild occurring on mountain slopes between the *Abies densa* forest and the treeline in somewhat dry sites.

Synonyms: *L. griffithii.*

Similar species: *L. speciosa* is a related species from west Yunnan and adjacent southeast Tibet. It differs in the longer broader leaves (to 5.5 cm (2.2 in) and up to 2 mm (0.1 in)), the hairless shoots and the shape of the cones, scales and bracts. It is treated as a variety (var. *speciosa*) by some authors.

This is one of the most beautiful of all the larches, with its pendent branchlets, large purplish cones and golden autumn colour.

---

p.100 **Japanese Larch** *Larix kaempferi*

Description: Deciduous tree to 30 m (100 ft) with a bole diameter to 80 cm (2.6 ft).
Crown Conical in young trees with gently rising branches and often a slightly wavy stem, becoming columnar with a conic apex in old trees with horizontal branches with pendent branchlets giving a dense twiggy crown. *Bark* Red-brown or purple-brown, initially smooth but soon fissuring and scaly with grey plates. *Shoot* Reddish purple in the first winter and often bloomed, sometimes hairy, greyer in later years, slender. *Buds* Domed or hemispherical, red-brown, resinous, 2 mm (0.1 in).
Foliage Radial or twisted to give a parting both above and below the shoot, on short or spur shoots in a rosette of 20–35 leaves, grey-green to bluish; leaves linear, apex bluntly pointed, base with ciliate hairs, rhombic in section, 3–4 cm (1.2–1.6 in) (on long extending shoots to 6 cm (2.4 in)) by 1 mm (0.1 in); autumn colour pale yellow to orange. *Flowers* On short shoots at least two years old in early spring; male cones domed, red-brown, opening to yellow, 0.5–1 cm (0.2–0.4 in); female cones erect, variously

but brightly coloured from purplish pink through red to yellow. *Fruit* Ovoid, erect, ripening shiny mid brown in first autumn, 2.5–3 × 2–2.5 cm (1–1.2 × 0.8–1 in); scales reflexed, stiff, thin and woody, bracts not visible or cusp just shows between seed scales at the base.

Range: Central Honshu, Japan.

Habitat: Cultivated as a forest and amenity tree in Europe, in Japan occurring in mixed coniferous forests on mesic (wet) sites.

Synonyms: *L. leptolepis.*

This tree is at its best in autumn when the leaves turn and fall and then in the distance when the purple colour of the one-year twigs gives a rich cast to a hillside. It grows faster than *L. decidua* and tolerates heavier soils.

---

p.102 **Tamarack** *Larix laricina*

Description: Deciduous tree to 20 m (65 ft) with a bole to 50 cm (1.6 in).
Crown Conical, slender. *Bark* Pinkish orange to dark red, smooth and thin in young trees, becoming scaly in old trees. *Shoot* Orange-brown with a pink-grey waxy bloom in the first winter with prominent ridges at the base of the fallen leaves, hairless, then dark brown. *Buds* Globose, red-brown, resinous, 1.5 mm (0.1 in). *Foliage* Leaves spiral on long shoots, in whorls of 15–30 on short shoots; leaves linear, rhombic (diamond-shaped) in section, keeled, apex bluntly pointed to acute, upper surface light to bluish or dark green with no (or a few) stomata, undersurface paler, with two bands of stomata, 2–3 cm × 0.5–1 mm (0.8–1.2 × 0.1 in). *Flowers* On spur shoots at least two years old; male cones yellow, small; female cones red, erect, to 1 cm (0.4 in). *Fruit* Ovoid or ovoid-globose with about 20 scales, ripening to light brown, 1.2–2 cm (0.5–0.8 in); scales round, striated, 8 mm (0.3 in) across, bracts just visible between the lower scales only.

Range: North America from Newfoundland and New England to the Yukon and Alaska.

Habitat: Boreal forests, including swampy sites.

This tree has a wide distribution in the wild, where it occurs on low hills and in muskeg or swamp sites. It shares the small cones with *L. gmelinii*, in which the scales are rhombic, not rounded.

---

p.102 **Western Larch** *Larix occidentalis*

Description: Deciduous tree 25 m (80 ft) or more in height with a bole diameter to 60 cm (2 ft). *Crown* Narrow conic when young, then columnar. *Bark* Red-brown to cinnamon-brown or purplish grey, scaly in young trees, becoming thick and deeply furrowed with platy ridges. *Shoot* Orange-brown in the first winter, then darker brown, initially hairy but soon hairless, brittle and stout. *Buds* Sub-globose, chestnut brown or reddish brown, resinous, 3 × 2 mm (0.1 × 0.1 in). *Foliage* Radial on long shoots and in rosettes of 30–40 on spur shoots; leaves linear, triangular in section, soft, dull to bright green with two bands of stomata beneath, 2–4 cm (0.8–1.6 in) but up to 6 cm (2.4 in) on extension shoots, by 0.5–1 mm (0.1–0.1 in); autumn colour yellow. *Flowers* On short shoots two or more years old in spring; male cones 0.8–1.5 cm (0.3–0.6 in), red and yellow. *Fruit* Cylindric with projecting bracts with a long erect or spreading cusp, ripening to purple-brown or red-brown in first autumn, 2.5–4.5 cm (1–1.8 in).

Range: Southeast British Columbia south to northern Oregon and inland across the Rocky Mountains to Idaho and northwest Montana.

Habitat: Cultivated in Europe as an ornamental, in the wild occurring on mountain slopes, either as pure stands or mixed with other conifers.

Triangular section of the leaves distinguishes this species from the other larches where the bract scales are prominent and projecting.

p.101 **Potanin Larch** *Larix potaninii*

Description: Deciduous tree 20–35 m (65–115 ft) with a bole diameter to 1 m (3.3 ft).
Crown Conic in young trees, becoming columnar with wide-spreading branches bearing pendulous branchlets.
Bark Purplish grey, scaly, developing long vertical fissures and ridges in old trees.
Shoot Orange-brown or reddish brown, hairless, with raised peg-like projections at base of leaves, in second year reddish brown with pale-brown fissures.
Buds Domed and rounded or weakly pointed, bright brown, 1–2 mm (0.1 in).
Foliage Spirally set on extension shoots, in rosettes of 20–40 on short shoots; leaves linear, bright green with two whitish bands beneath, 1.2–3.5 cm × 1–1.5 mm (0.5–1.4 × 0.1 in), turning rich golden-yellow in autumn. *Flowers* On short shoots at least two years old; male cones pale yellow, to 1 cm (0.4 in).
Fruit Cylindric or elliptical with projecting bracts, erect, ripening in first autumn from violet-purple to dark brown, mainly 3–5 × 1.5–2.5 cm (1.2–2 × 0.6–1 in); scales sub-rounded in outline, hairless on the exposed portion, to 1.2 cm (0.5 in) in width, bract scale erect or spreading with an acute tip, to 1.8 cm × 5 mm (0.7 × 0.2 in).

Range: South Gansu and Shaanxi south through to west Sichuan.

Habitat: Cultivated in Europe as an ornamental, in the wild occurring in ridges and mountain slopes.

Varieties: Var. *macrocarpa* from southwest Sichuan, northwest Yunnan and southeast Tibet has larger cones 5–7.5 × 2.5–3.5 cm (2–3 × 1–1.4 in) and stouter reddish-brown shoots.

This tree has a wide distribution in western China, and makes an attractive display with both the pendulous branchlets and the good golden autumn colour.

p.99 **Siberian Larch** *Larix sibirica*

Description: Deciduous tree 15–30 m (50–100 ft) with a
bole diameter to 50 cm (1.6 ft).
Crown Conical but becoming columnar.
Bark Orange-brown, becoming fissured,
scaly and light brown. *Shoot* Whitish
yellow or yellowish grey, initially hairy but
soon hairless, with raised peg-like
projections at base of leaves, in third year
grooves blackish brown. *Buds* Broadly
conic or domed, reddish brown, with free
scale tips, 1×2 mm (0.1×0.1 in).
Foliage Spirally set on extension shoots, in
rosettes of 20–40 on short shoots; leaves
pale green, 2.5–4 cm $\times$ 1 mm (1–1.6 $\times$
0.1 in), turning golden-yellow in autumn.
Flowers On short shoots at least two years
old; male cones pale yellow, to 1 cm
(0.4 in). *Fruit* Ovoid to sub-globose, erect,
ripening in first autumn from reddish or
rose to reddish brown, fading to grey-
brown, mainly 3–4.5 $\times$ 2.5 cm (1.2–1.8 $\times$
1 in); scales ovate to sub-rounded in
outline, hairy on the exposed portion, to
1.8 cm (0.7 in) in width.

Range: From northeast Russia across to the Lake
Baikal region of Siberia and south to the
Tien Shan in western Xinjiang, China.

Habitat: Cold taiga or dry boreal forest.

Synonyms: *L. russica*.

This tree needs a continental climate, with
a regular season, to flourish. In more
maritime climates, it breaks into growth
too early in the spring and is cut by frost.

LAUREL, LAURACEAE

This is a large family characterized by
spherical ethereal oil cells in the leaves,
which make crushed foliage delightfully
fragrant. The leaves are nearly always
simple, *Sassafras* (p.1126) being the
obvious exception. The fruit is a single-
seeded berry or drupe which is often
enclosed in a fleshy development of the base
of the flower (hypananthum).

PUKATEA, *LAURELIA*
FAMILY ATHEROSPERMATACEAE

This is genus of three species, two from South America and
one from New Zealand.

---

p.172   **Peruvian Nutmeg** *Laurelia sempervirens*

Description: Evergreen tree to 15 m (50 ft) with a bole
diameter 0.5–1 m (1.6–3.3 ft).
Crown Conic to columnar. *Bark* Smooth,
grey, aromatic. *Shoot* Four angled,
remaining green for several years. *Buds* In
opposite pairs, ovoid, light green, 4 mm
(0.2 in). *Foliage* Leaves narrowly elliptic,
apex bluntly acute, base wedge-shaped,
margin with shallow serrations, leathery in
texture, upper surface glossy green, paler
beneath and hairless, 4–8 cm (1.6–3.1 in);
leaf stalk grooved, 6 mm (0.25 in);
crushed leaves have a spicy aroma.
Flowers In leaf axils in clusters of three to
nine, various perfect or with separate male
and female flowers; on stalks 1–2 cm
(0.4–0.8 in); four stamens, with downy
filaments. *Fruit* Globose, opening to
release a cluster of achenes with long
brown hairs.

Range: Central to northern Chile and Peru.

Habitat: Cultivated as an ornamental, in the wild
occurring in forests, often with *Nothofagus
obliqua*.

Synonyms: *L. aromatica*.

Similar species: *L. serrata*, from central Chile and adjacent
parts of The Argentine, is closely allied. It
differs in the larger leaves which are more
strongly saw-toothed and which have the
midrib below coated with yellowish hair,
the stalks only 3 mm (0.1 in) and the
flowers having hairless filaments which are
shorter than the anthers. The timber has an
unpleasant smell, although the bark is
without odour.

Peruvian Nutmeg makes a small-to-
medium tree in cultivation. It has a
valuable but odourless timber. The fruit is
the source of Peruvian nutmegs.

LAURELS OR BAY LAURELS, *LAURUS*
FAMILY LAURACEAE

This genus consists of two species from southern Europe, the Canary Islands and the Azores, with aromatic leaves which are used in cooking. The fruit is a black drupe.

p.129	**Laurel, Bay Laurel, Poet's Laurel** or **Sweet Bay** *Laurus nobilis*
Description:	Evergreen tree to 20 m (65 ft) with a bole diameter to 60 cm (2 ft).
	Crown Conic or broad conic, becoming columnar with pointed or rounded apex. *Bark* Blackish grey, wrinkled but generally smooth, may become cracked at base in old trees. *Shoot* Matt green or purplish green and hairless in the first winter, becoming shiny green with pale brown lenticels in second and subsequent years, eventually brown. *Buds* Ovoid-conic, narrow, red, 5 mm (0.2 in), on a scaly stalk 1–3 mm (0.1 in).
	Foliage Lanceolate, or less often obovate, with a short slender-pointed apex, base wedge-shaped, margin finely crinkled, entire or faintly toothed with a hyaline strip, dark glossy green above, pale green beneath, veins raised on both sides, pale green, tertiary veins net-like, 5–13 × 2–5 cm (2–5.1 × 0.8–2 in); leaf stalk purplish, grooved above, rough, 0.3–1.2 cm (0.1–0.5 in); crushed foliage strongly aromatic. *Flowers* In clusters of two to four with stalked axillary buds on previous season's shoots in early spring; opening pale yellow, 1 cm (0.4 in) in diameter. *Fruit* Ovoid to obovoid berry, ripening from green to black in late autumn, containing a single seed, 1–1.5 cm (0.4–0.6 in).
Range:	Mediterranean region.
Habitat:	Evergreen forest and thickets.
Similar species:	*L. azorica* is closely related, differing in the generally larger leaves (8–13 × 5–8 cm (3.1–5.1 × 2–3.1 in)), which are downy beneath, and the downy shoots. It is native to the Azores and Canary Islands.

The leaves and twigs of this strongly aromatic tree are used in cooking. In ancient Greece and Rome, wreaths of laurel foliage were presented to victorious generals, or as a mark of respect to poets. The post of 'Poet Laureate' derives from this tradition. The degrees of Bachelor of Science, Arts, Education, etc. also owe their origin to this practice. The original Latin was *baccalaurus* or 'laurel berry', which became *bachelier* in French and then to 'bachelor'. French students still sit their baccalaureate as an entry exam for university.

LEGUME, LEGUMINOSAE (SYNONYM: FABACEAE)

This is a very large family. The unifying feature is the fruit, which is a typical pea or bean pod – laterally compressed, with an upper and lower suture and with the seeds spaced out and attached along one suture. The flowers are not quite as uniform. The typical flower is pea-like, with a large standard, two-wing petals and a lower pair of keel petals. However, a large part of the family does not have this form of flowers; instead, the flowers are regular with small petals and in globose heads, such as in *Acacia* (p.406). The leaves are almost invariably pinnate to bi-pinnate. The exceptions are the leaf-like stalks to the leaves of some *Acacia*, and *Cercis* (p.595) which has heart-shaped leaves. Another genus with simple leaves is *Bauhinia*, in which the leaves are cleft at the apex, but this shrubby climber is not common in Europe and is not featured here. The name Fabaceae is an alternative name and is quite valid. It is not technically a synonym. The family is generally split into three subfamilies, but these are sometimes treated as separate families. The subfamilies Caesalpinioideae (Caesalpiniaceae as a family) and Papilionoideae have typical pea flowers, whilst the subfamily Mimosoideae (or family Mimosaceae) have regular flowers in globose heads.

PRIVETS, *LIGUSTRUM*
FAMILY OLEACEAE

This genus consists of around 50 species of trees and shrubs from Europe east to Asia and south through Malaysia to Australia. The leaves are simple, untoothed and either evergreen or deciduous. The flowers are showy in terminal panicles, white with a tubular corolla and have two stamens. They have a strong fishy smell, due to trimethylamine, which is found unpleasant by many people and can taint the taste of honey. The fruit is a berry.

p.149 **Chenault's Privet** *Ligustrum chenaultii*

Description: Semi-evergreen tree to 12 m (39 ft) with a bole diameter to 30 cm (1 ft).
Crown Rounded or domed. *Bark* Smooth and grey, becoming ridged and rather scaly. *Shoot* Brown or greenish brown at first, hairless or minutely downy and flattened at the nodes, grey or grey-green in the second year. *Buds* In opposite pairs, ovoid, pointed, green and brown, 3 mm (0.1 in). *Foliage* Leaves lanceolate, tapering to the acute tip, base rounded to broad wedge-shaped, margin untoothed with a thin hyaline (translucent) strip, upper surface sub-shiny dark green, undersurface light sub-shiny green, covered with small green dots or glands, midrib raised, hairless, texture rather flaccid, 8–15 × 2.5–5 cm (3.1–6 × 1–2 in); leaf stalk grooved, green or purplish, 1.5–2 cm (0.6–0.8 in); little autumn colour. *Flowers* In large loose terminal panicles to 15 × 12 cm (6 × 4.7 in) in late summer (July–August), teardrop shaped in bud, opening with four slender white petals and two large yellow stamens, individual flowers to 4 mm (0.2 in) across, fragrant. *Fruit* Ovoid, dark violet or black with a waxy bloom, 0.6–1 cm (0.25–0.4 in).
Range: Yunnan, China.
Habitat: Cultivated as an ornamental, in the wild occurring in thickets.
Similar species: *L. compactum* from Yunnan west to the northwest Himalayas has rounded winter buds and generally smaller leaves which are more fully deciduous.

L. confusum from east Nepal eastwards to Assam has pale glossy hairless leaves which are 4–8 × 1–2.5 cm (1.6–3.1 × 0.4–1 in), set on downy shoots.

This tree loses its leaves over winter or may keep them in mild areas until the new growth starts in spring. It makes an attractive tree with its large terminal trusses of fragrant white flowers, followed by the bloomed berries. The leaves can be up to 25 cm (10 in). *L. chenaultii* is closely allied to *L. compactum* (*see* above) and may be only a long-leafed form.

---

p.148   **Chinese Privet**   *Ligustrum lucidum*

Description: Evergreen tree 10–20 m (33–65 ft) with a bole diameter to 50 cm (1.6 ft).
Crown Rounded, domed, often with several main stems radiating out from the top of a short trunk. *Bark* Grey-brown, smooth at first, then becoming fissured and slightly roughened. *Shoot* Initially green but light brown with only patches of green by first winter, with prominent oval lenticels, pale brown later, flattened either side of the buds on weaker shoots. *Buds* In opposite or nearly opposite pairs, conical, pointed, small, on a short stalk, 1–1.5 mm (0.1 in). *Foliage* In somewhat decussate pairs but twisted at the leaf stalk to give flattened sprays; leaves elliptic, oval or ovate, base wedge-shaped, apex short and slender pointed with a broad and down-turned tip, margins untoothed and, with the veins, hyaline (translucent), upper surface lustrous dark green, lower surface pale glaucous green with (under a hand-lens) white dots and large spaced brown glands, 7–15 × 3–6 cm (2.8–6 × 1.2–2.4 in); leaf stalk green or purple, 4–1.5 mm (0.2–0.1 in). *Flowers* Terminal on current season's growths in late summer or early autumn, in large spreading or erect panicles of many fragrant small white flowers, to 20 cm (8 in) high and 30 cm (12 in) across.

Fruit Oblong, 0.8–1.2 cm (0.3–0.5 in), bluish black or purplish and bloomed, containing a single seed.

Range: Central China.

Habitat: Cultivated in Europe as an ornamental, in the wild in woods.

Varieties: 'Excelsum Superbum' has leaves margined and mottled with deep yellow and creamy white. In 'Tricolor', the leaves have an irregular pink and white border. Both make small trees and are attractive in their bold variegated foliage.

This makes one of the most attractive evergreen trees, valuable for the late flowering. It is widely cultivated in all continents. The natural distribution has been obscured because it has been planted in China for a wax obtained from an aphid which feeds on it.

---

p.148 **Privet** *Ligustrum ovalifolium*

Description: Semi-evergreen or evergreen bush or small tree to 8 m (26 ft).
Crown Spiky. *Bark* Grey-brown, rough. *Shoot* Fawn-brown, hairless, sub-shiny, flattened at the nodes with decurrent ridges from the leaf bases. *Buds* In opposite pairs, ovoid, pointed, with paired scales which are acute or slender pointed at the apex, green and dark purplish brown, to 3 mm (0.1 in). *Foliage* Leaves oval or elliptic, tapering to an abruptly pointed apex and to a wedge-shaped base (but sometimes bluntly pointed at both ends), margin untoothed, upper surface dull to glossy green with four or five pairs of looping and slightly indented veins, underside fresh pale green, 2–10 × 1–5 cm (0.8–4 × 0.4–2 in); leaf stalk grooved, 0.3–1 cm (0.1–0.4 in). *Flowers* In erect terminal panicles in July, 5–10 × 5–10 cm (2–4 × 2–4 in); flowers crowded, dull white with a strong fragrance which many people find unpleasant. *Fruit* Globose shining black berry to 1 cm (0.4 in).

Range: Honshu, Shikoku and Kyushu, Japan.

Habitat: Cultivated as a hedging plant, in the wild occurring in thickets in coastal locations.

Varieties: 'Aureum' is a selection in which the leaves have a variable border of a rich golden-yellow. It makes a distinct improvement on the green form, provided they are not planted alternately in hedges.

Similar species: **Wild Privet** *L. vulgare* (p.149) is a sprawling generally deciduous shrub, rarely of even modest tree-like proportions. It is wild throughout much of Europe, especially on soils derived from limestone or chalk. The distinguishing features are the narrowly oval or lanceolate leaves and the minutely hairy shoots.

This is mainly grown as a hedging plant, for which it is fairly effective. However, overgrown hedges turn into belts of small shrubby semi-evergreen trees. It tolerates a wide range of soils.

SWEET GUMS, *LIQUIDAMBAR*
FAMILY HAMAMELIDACEAE

This genus occurs in eastern USA and south into Mexico, in the eastern Mediterranean region and in China and Taiwan. The leaves are generally lobed (and toothed) as in most *Acer* species but they are alternate on the shoots; thus the two genera can be distinguished even on leafless trees. The fruit is a mace-like cluster of carpels.

---

p.305 **Chinese Sweet Gum**
Liquidambar formosana

Description: Deciduous tree to 15 m (50 ft) with a bole diameter to 50 cm (1.6 ft).
Crown Ovoid or conic when young, becoming columnar. *Bark* Grey, smooth but becoming scaly. *Shoot* Green and hairy at first or hairless, becoming green-brown in the second year, then dark or chocolate brown. *Buds* Ovoid-conic, green, 5 mm (0.2 in). *Foliage* Leaves strongly three lobed, rarely with small additional basal lobes, lobes spreading widely, broad ovate-triangular, tapering to the tail-like apex,

sinuses more or less making a right angle, base rounded and deeply heart-shaped, margin with fine forward hooked teeth, upper surface matt green with the veins slightly proud, underside light sub-shiny green with raised veins, 8–16 × 10–20 cm (3.1–6.3 × 4–8 in); leaf stalk pink-purple, basal 5 mm (0.2 in) enlarged but the stipular scar within 2 mm (0.1 in) of the base (i.e. not at the top of the enlarged portion), 2.5–8 cm (1–3.1 in); autumn colour orange, red or purple.
Fruit Pendulous round cluster 4 cm (1.6 in) in diameter.

Range: Taiwan, eastern and central China and south into Indochina.

Habitat: Cultivated as an ornamental, in the wild occurring in mixed forests.

Synonyms: *L. acerifolia*.

This tree differs from *L. styraciflua* in the leaves having much broader and more solid-looking lobes. It is variable in the degree of hairiness, with var. *monticola* maintained for the forms which are entirely hairless.

p.305 **Oriental Sweet Gum**
Liquidambar orientalis

Description: Deciduous tree 10–30 m (33–100 ft) with a bole diameter to 50 cm (1.6 ft).
Crown Rounded to domed. *Bark* Dark orange-brown, becoming fissured into thick squarrish exfoliating plates. *Shoot* Slender, hairless, initially green, becoming red-brown. *Buds* Ovoid, glossy red-brown, with six outer scales. *Foliage* Leaves rounded in outline with five spreading lobes, shallowly heart-shaped at the base, 4–6 cm (1.6–2.4 in) wide and long; lobes ovate, rounded and slender pointed at the apex, forming acute sinuses which extend one-half to two-thirds of the way to the margin, margin with coarse teeth which end in small glands and sometimes lobulate, hairless on both sides; leaf stalk 2.5–5 cm (1–2 in). *Flowers* In globose heads with the new leaves, greenish.

Fruit Globose cluster 2–2.5 cm (0.8–1 in) across containing many beaked capsules, opening to shed one or two winged seeds.

Range: West and southwest Turkey and on the Greek Island of Rhodes.

Habitat: Mainly cultivated, preferring a hot sunny location.

Synonyms: *L. imberbe.*

This tree is cultivated for the fragrant resin, known as 'liquid storax', which is used in various medical preparations. It is obtained by cutting into the inner bark.

---

p.305 **Sweet Gum** or **Liquidambar**
Liquidambar styraciflua

Description: Deciduous tree 20–30 m (65–100 ft) with a bole diameter to 1 m (3.3 ft).
Crown Ovoid or conic when young, becoming columnar with a rounded or domed apex. *Bark* Grey, smooth or with corky wings when young, becoming fissured into small scales and in old trees rough with narrow deep scaly ridges. *Shoot* Green and sparsely white pilose with dark rounded lenticels when young, green-brown or grey-brown in the second year. *Buds* Ovoid-conic, shiny green with hairy tips to the scales, 5 mm (0.2 in). *Foliage* Leaves five lobed, rarely seven lobes with the lobes oblong-ovate to a slender-pointed apex and with deep acute sinuses, base subcordate or truncate, margin with small rounded forward-hooked teeth, resin scented when crushed, upper surface matt green with impressed veins which are slightly hairy, lower surface light shiny green, hairy, especially on the raised veins, 7–15 × 9–17 cm (2.8–6 × 3.5–6.7 in); leaf stalk grooved, green 6–15 cm (2.4–6 in), with a thickened base of circa 0.5–1 cm (0.2–0.4 in) having two dark scars where the stipules have fallen off; autumn colour scarlet or red. *Flowers* In pendent round heads, males small, 5–8 mm (0.2–0.3 in); females composed of many flowers, 1 cm

(0.4 in). *Fruit* Pendulous round cluster (2.5–3 cm (1–1.2 in) in diameter) of seed vessels which are beaked at the tips and open to release one or two black oval winged seeds 4 mm (0.2 in).

Range: Southeast USA from Connecticut across to Illinois and south to Texas and Florida, with a variety in northeast and eastern Mexico.

Habitat: Cultivated as an ornamental, in the wild occurring in moist valley sites, especially as a pioneer species following logging.

Varieties: Several selections for dependable autumn colour are available commercially but are not sufficiently distinct to be reliably identified without knowledge of their origin.

The leaves very closely resemble maples (*Acer*) and will always confuse those who do not learn that the first principle with any tree is to determine whether the leaves and buds are set alternately along/around the shoot or in opposite pairs (or whorls). The leaves are resin scented when crushed, which is not a feature of *Acer*. The fruit is similar to that of *Platanus*, to which it is closely related.

TULIP TREES, *LIRIODENDRON*
FAMILY MAGNOLIACEAE

This genus has a species in the eastern USA and a second one in southeastern China and northern Vietnam. The leaves are curiously truncate at the tip, with a prominent waist. The flowers are erect and tulip-like. The fruit is a cluster of carpels with dry winged seeds. The autumn colour is excellent and the genus is used for amenity plantings. It also produces a good timber.

---

p.283 **Chinese Tulip Tree** *Liriodendron chinense*

Description: Deciduous tree 15–25 m (50–80 ft) with a bole diameter to 80 cm (2.6 ft).
Crown Conic as a young tree, becoming columnar with a rounded or domed apex.
Bark Pale grey, smooth, becoming lightly fissured and ridged. *Shoot* Green and

smooth with a glaucous bloom when young, later yellow-green and shiny, with a stipular scar around the shoot between the leaf and the bud, in the second year brown, later grey-brown and lightly fissured. *Buds* Laterally flattened or rounded paddle-shaped, with a stipule covering the shoot apex or each leaf expanding during the growing season, in turn glaucous, green, to 2 cm (0.8 in). *Foliage* Leaves curiously shaped with four points, apex truncate and indented with a bluntly pointed sinus, base truncate, rounded or very broadly wedge-shaped, margin untoothed but with one pair of rounded triangular lobes and a deep rounded sinus which extends two-thirds the way to the midrib, upper surface sub-shiny to matt, slightly bluish green, hairless, cupped, underside glaucous green with a dense covering of minute papillae, veins hairless, raised, 7–22 × 8–22 cm (2.8–8.7 × 3.1–8.7 in); leaf stalk round, rough, stiff, yellow-green, 5–12 cm (2–4.7 in); autumn colour good yellow; new leaves folded over and enclosed in the stipule.
Flowers Flowers to 6 cm (2.4 in), terminal on the shoots in July, with three yellow-green sepals bent sharply downwards and five pale-orange petals. *Fruit* Woody cluster of carpels, ovoid-conic, pointed at the apex, ripening brown.

Range: Eastern China from Zhejiang and Hubei south in an arc around the coast to North Vietnam.

Habitat: Cultivated as an ornamental, in the wild occurring in mixed woodland.

Synonyms: *L. tulipiferum* var. *chinense*.

This tree is very similar to *L. tulipiferum*, with the usual character of the deeper waist to the leaves helpful but not conclusive, as epicormic shoots on *tulipiferum* often are more deeply indented. The best character requires a strong hand-lens, being the dense covering of papillae on the underside of the leaf. These give the leaf a silvery or glaucous cast.

p.283 **Tulip Tree** or **Yellow Poplar**
Liriodendron tulipiferum

Description: Deciduous tree 25–30 m (80–100 ft) tall
with a bole diameter to 1 m (3.3 ft).
Crown Columnar-conic in young trees,
becoming broad columnar or domed.
Bark Grey-brown or grey and shallowly
fissured in young trees, becoming grey or
somewhat silvery grey and furrowed, platy
scales in old trees and with orange-brown
fissures. *Shoot* Pale green in the first year
with small lenticels and a prominent ring
encircling the shoot just above each leaf
base or bud, hairless or loosely hairy, in the
second year glossy mid-to-dark brown,
later developing shallow grey-brown
fissures. *Buds* Oval, flattened, stalked,
glaucous green during the summer but
maturing to shiny red-brown, enclosed in
two scales which are the stipules to the
leaves, to 1 cm (0.4 in). *Foliage* Leaves
distinctively shaped with an indented or
truncate apex, broadly wedge-shaped to
subcordate base and two (rarely three) pairs
of acute pointed lobes, margins untoothed,
upper surface glossy mid green with
approximately five pairs of slightly raised
veins, lower surface glaucous green,
smooth, hairless except for brownish hairs
along the prominent raised veins, 7–20 ×
8–20 cm (2.8–8 × 3.1–8 in); leaf stalk
lumpy, rounded, enlarged at base, 5–10 cm
(2–4 in); autumn colour yellow-gold
excellent. *Flowers* On current season's
growths in mid summer, in bud ovoid-
conical, glaucous green, opening to cup
shaped with six erect greenish-white petals
with an orange or less often yellow-orange
or greenish-orange spot, 4–5 cm
(1.6–2 in), stamens long, 2–2.5 cm
(0.8–1 in) on stalks 2 cm (0.8 in).
Fruit Erect narrow ovoid-conical cone-like
structure with overlapping woody hinged
scales which persist, 4–5 cm (1.6–2 in).
Seed linear.

Range: Eastern North America from Nova Scotia
and extreme southern Ontario south to
northern Florida and Louisiana.

Habitat: Cultivated as an ornamental, in the wild
occurring in moist well-drained valley-
bottom sites.

Varieties: 'Aureomarginata' has the leaves margined
with zones of yellow and yellow-green.
'Aureopictum' has a central yellow blotch.
'Fastigiatum' has erect branches, making a
columnar tree. In f. *integrifolium*, the leaves
lack lateral lobes and thus are rectangular
in outline. It represents a persistent
juvenile phase. All these forms attain sizes
similar to normal trees.

This tree is unmistakable in the curiously-
shaped leaves. In autumn, these turn a
beautiful golden-yellow, giving the tree an
appearance of a poplar and thus one of its
common names. The flowers resemble
tulips, giving its other name. The roots are
fleshy and resent disturbance.

STONE OAKS OR LITHOCARPS, *LITHOCARPUS* (SYNONYM: *PASANIA*)
FAMILY FAGACEAE

This is a large genus, with between 100 and 300 species.
One species occurs in California, two in Japan but the main
distribution is from China, south through southeast Asia to
New Guinea and west along the Himalayas. The leaves are
evergreen, thick and untoothed. The male flowers are in
erect spikes, often with female flowers at the base of the
catkins. The erect male catkins, with twelve stamens and a
rudimentary ovary serves to distinguish *Lithocarpus* from
Quercus (where the male catkins are pendulous and have six
or less stamens). The fruit has a thick shell or pericarp. It is
this feature which give the genus its name, literally 'stone
seed'. Lithocarps make bold evergreen trees.

---

p.160 **Japanese Stone Oak** or **Tanoak**
Lithocarpus edulis

Description: Evergreen tree to 10 m (33 ft) or more with
a bole diameter to 30 cm (1 ft).
Crown Rounded with spreading branches
off a short bole, less often more upright.
Bark Smooth, grey-brown, finely fissured.
Shoot Green, slightly scaly, and grooved

and angled in the first year, in the second year green and brown with raised erupting oval whitish lenticels, with more brown in the third year. *Buds* Ovoid or domed, green, 30 cm (12 in), those at the shoot apex with a ring of awl-like scales. *Foliage* Leaves thick and chartaceous (card-like in texture), narrow elliptic to oblanceolate, tapering to a narrow rounded point, base long wedge-shaped, margin untoothed, upper surface shiny green, smooth with a pale-yellow midrib, underside with a silvery or golden sheen due to a covering of scales but without hairs, midrib and 9–11 pairs of veins raised, 7–16 × 2–7 cm (2.8–6.3 × 0.8–2.8 in); leaf stalk grooved, with the decurrent wings of the leaf blade extending half way down, yellow-green, hairless, 1.5–3 cm (0.6–1.2 in); no autumn colour. *Flowers* In erect simple spikes from buds in the leaf axils at the tip of previous year's shoots, with male flowers at the top and female flowers at the base in clusters of threes, spike circa 13 cm (5.1 in). *Fruit* In erect spikes 5–10 cm (2–4 in) which ripen in the second autumn, acorns in spaced clusters of three, long ovoid-conic with a pointed apex, shiny brown, with a thick shell, 2–2.5 × 1.2 cm (0.8–1 × 0.5 in), sitting in a shallow cup circa 5 mm (0.2 in) deep and which is fused to the adjoining cups, with conical pointed processes on the scales.

Range: Japan from south and west Honshu, Shikoku and Kyushu, and south along the Ryukyu Island chain.

Habitat: Cultivated as an ornamental, occurring in the wild in mixed temperate forest.

Similar species: *L. glaber* from Japan and east China differs in the leaves being silvery beneath due to a dense covering of down and having only six to eight pairs of veins. The shoot and fruiting spikes are also hairy, with a grey or yellowish down.

Synonyms: *Pasania edulis*, *Quercus edulis*.

This makes a small evergreen tree with dense glossy foliage.

p.160 **Henry's Stone Oak** or **Tanoak**
Lithocarpus henryi

Description: Evergreen tree to 10–20 m (33–65 ft) or
more with a bole diameter to 40 cm (1.3 ft).
Crown Rounded, becoming domed.
Bark Grey-brown, rough, becoming
fissured, scaly in old trees at the base.
Shoot Green and slightly downy when
young, strongly grooved and angled and
remaining so for two years, developing
brown fissures in the grooves in the third
year, with ridges persisting behind the leaf
bases. *Buds* Conic, with silvery down,
3 mm (0.1 in), with the terminal bud
having long pointed 7 mm (0.3 in) hairy
scales. *Foliage* Leaves thick and stiffly
leathery in texture, narrow elliptic or
lanceolate, tapering to a slender point, at
the base long wedge-shaped, margin
untoothed but rolled over slightly, upper
surface matt to shiny green, cupped or
folded along the midrib which is flat
except raised slightly towards the base,
underside pale slightly yellow-green, veins
in about 10 pairs, slightly raised and
spaced, midrib raised, 4–25 × 4–5 cm
(1.6–10 × 1.6–2 in); leaf stalk with a
slender groove and decurrent leaf base,
hairless, yellow-green, 2.5–3 cm
(1–1.2 in); no autumn colour.
Flowers Male flowers in erect, branched,
downy spikes at or near the shoot tips.
Fruit In stout spikes 10–20 cm (4–8 in),
acorns ovoid with a flattened rounded apex,
ripening in the second year, cup shallow,
with keeled scales.

Range: Western Hubei and eastern Sichuan, China.
Habitat: Cultivated as an ornamental, occurring in
the wild in mixed temperate forest.
Synonyms: *Quercus henryi*.
Similar species: *L. cleistocarpus* has leaves 7–20 × 2.5–6 cm
(2.8–8 × 1–2.4 in), greyish green with
9–12 pairs of veins but up to 30 ×
10–12 cm (12 × 4–4.7 in) in young trees.
The acorn is almost fully enclosed in the
cupule.
L. pachyphyllus also has the acorns enclosed
in the cupule but the cupules are fused

together into a bony mass, similar to a clump of barnacles. The leaves are 15–20 cm (6–8 in) long.

This makes a majestic evergreen tree with bold foliage.

HONEYSUCKLES, *LONICERA*
FAMILY CAPRIFOLIACEAE

This is a large genus. Most species are shrubs, generally small but with some assuming tree-like proportions. The genus is probably better recognized for the climbers. One species from each group is illustrated here. The leaves are opposite, sometimes becoming connate beneath the inflorescence. The flowers are either borne in pairs in the axils of the leaves on the current growths, or in whorls at the end of shoots, with the basic building number of the whorls being six (a pair of threes). The flowers are tubular and five lobed, but the lobes are often displaced with four upper ones and a large strap-like lower one. The fruit is a fleshy berry.

---

p.145 **Honeysuckle** or **Woodbine**
Lonicera periclymenum

Description: Deciduous climbing shrub, to 6 m (20 ft) or so. *Crown* Depending upon support. *Bark* Light brown, peeling. *Shoot* Purplish pink or green when young and hollow, maturing to light brown or orange-brown, hairless or downy, ribbed below the buds. *Buds* In opposite pairs, conical, brown. *Foliage* Leaves ovate, oval to obovate, never connate or joined at the base, apex pointed, less often bluntly pointed, base wedge-shaped, margin untoothed, ciliate when young, green above with sparse veins, glaucous beneath and variably downy but becoming hairless, 4–6 × 2.5–4 cm (1.6–2.4 × 1–1.6 in); petiolate except the upper most pairs which are nearly stalkless to completely stalkless. *Flowers* In a terminal cluster of three-flowered stalkless cymes but forming a tight whorl; flowers with a long glandular tube and two-lipped corolla, 4–5 cm (1.6–2 in), varying from yellow to white and reddish purple in

colour, fragrant. *Fruit* Globose juicy red
berry to 1 cm (0.4 in), in clusters.

Range: Across Europe and North Africa to Asia
Minor and the Caucasus region.

Habitat: Hedgerows, woods.

Similar species: *L. caprifolium* from southern Europe differs
primarily in the leaves beneath the whorls
of flowers being connate.
L. japonica is also a vigorous climber but it
belongs to a different, mainly shrubby,
subgenus. The flowers are produced in pairs
in the leaf axils of the current season's
shoots.

This climber has very wiry stems and can
cause damage in young plantations by
strangling trees. It belongs to a large group
of climbing species, characterized by the
flowers being in cymes of three.

---

p.145   **Fly Honeysuckle** *Lonicera xylosteum*

Description: Deciduous shrub to 3 m (10 ft) or so.
Crown Rounded. *Shoot* Grey-brown,
downy or hairy, hollow. *Foliage* Leaves
ovate to obovate, apex pointed to short and
slender pointed, base rounded to broad
wedge-shaped, margin untoothed, dark or
greyish green above and initially somewhat
hairy, underside hairy, 3–6 × 2.5–4 cm
(1.2–2.4 × 1–1.6 in); leaf stalk 6 mm
(0.25 in). *Flowers* In pairs in May–June on
previous season's shoots; on hairy stalks
1–2 cm (0.4–0.8 in) which are longer than
the leaf stalks; flowers white or yellow-
white, with a tube circa 1 cm (0.4 in).
Fruit Globose juicy dark red berry ripening
in late summer (August).

Range: Southeast England (but possibly only
naturalized) across Europe to western
Siberia and the Altai region.

Habitat: Understorey shrub in woodland.

Similar species: *L. maackii* can make a small tree to 6–8 m
(20–26 ft) with a stem which may be
30 cm (12 in) in diameter just above soil
level. It differs in the flower stalks being no
longer than, or shorter than, the leaf stalks.
The flowers are pure white when first

opening, changing to a yellow. It comes from north to northeast China.

This shrub is one of many shrubby honeysuckles, as shown by the flowers in axillary pairs.

LYONOTHAMNUS, *LYONOTHAMNUS*
FAMILY ROSACEAE

This is a genus with a single species restricted to a few islands off the California coast. The flowers and fruits place it in the Spiraeoideae or *Spiraea* subfamily of the Rosaceae.

---

p.314 **Lyonothamnus** *Lyonothamnus floribundus* var. *asplenifolius*

Description: Evergreen tree 10–15 m (33–50 ft). *Crown* Columnar, slender. *Bark* Red-brown, fibrous and stringy.
Shoot Glabrous, green when young, ripening to red-brown or brown. *Buds* In opposite pairs. *Foliage* Leaves bi-pinnate, 10–20 cm (4–8 in); three to nine leaflets, 5–11 × 1.2–2 cm (2–4.3 × 0.5–0.8 in), deeply divided into hatchet shaped or triangular segments which are curved on the lower side and nearly straight on the upper side, dark glossy green above, paler white to greyish green and downy beneath. *Flowers* In terminal paniculate corymbs 7–15 cm (2.8–6 in) across and holding many 6 mm (0.25 in) white flowers. *Fruit* A pair of glandular follicles, with each follicle containing four seeds.

Range: Santa Catarina and Santa Cruz Islands off the coast of southern California.

Habitat: Cultivated as an ornamental.

Varieties: Typical var. *floribundus* has simple, oblong-lanceolate leaves which are either minutely toothed or untoothed. It occurs on the same island chain off the coast of Los Angeles.

This is the only tree-like member of the Spiraea subfamily of the Rosaceae. It is an attractive evergreen tree, but only hardy in milder districts.

HENNA, LYTHRACEAE

This is a family of mainly herbs, most of which are tropical in origin. Only *Lagerstroemia* (p.776) is cultivated and woody.

MAACKIA, *MAACKIA*
FAMILY LEGUMINOSAE

This is a small genus of legumes with pinnate leaves. The leaflets are opposite, rather than tending to be alternate along the rachis as in the related *Cladrastis*. Other distinctions from *Cladrastis* are that the buds are single and not hidden in the base of the leaf stalk, whilst the twigs are not brittle. The inflorescence is erect, rather dense but not overtly showy.

---

p.337 **Amur Maackia** *Maackia amurensis*

Description: Deciduous tree 8–13 m (26–43 ft) with a bole diameter to 30 cm (1 ft).
Crown Rounded, domed on a short bole. *Bark* Brown, peeling. *Shoot* Buff-brown, downy with raised slit-like lenticels.
Buds Rounded, pale green to brown, 5 mm (0.2 in). *Foliage* Leaves pinnate with 7–11 leaflets which are set in opposite pairs along the rounded green rachis, leaflets ovate with a bluntly pointed tip, base rounded with a short 3 mm (0.1 in) leaflet stalk, upper surface dark green, beneath pale green and hairless, 4–7 × 3–4 cm (1.6–2.8 × 1.2–1.6 in); leaf stalk green, rounded, swollen at the base but not hiding the bud; autumn colour yellow. *Flowers* In clusters of three to seven dense erect racemes of 10–15 cm (4–6 in) in mid-to-late summer (July–August), flower pea-like, narrow, white and green, 1.2 cm (0.5 m).
Fruit Legume with slightly winged seam, hairy when immature, 5–7 cm (2–2.8 in), with three to six seeds.

Range: Northeast China and adjacent Maritime Russia.

Habitat: Cultivated as an ornamental, in the wild occurring in forests.

Varieties: Var. *buegeri* from Honshu and Hokkaido, Japan, differs in the leaves having hairs which are pressed against the leaf beneath and with acute to subobtuse leaflets.

Synonyms: *Cladrastis amurensis.*

This makes a small rounded tree which is useful for its mid to late summer flowers.

OSAGE ORANGE, *MACLURA*
FAMILY MORACEAE

This is a spiny small tree which, like other members of the Mulberry family, has a latex-like sap. Its leaves are also palatable to silkworms. It only includes the single species, although some authors include *Cudrania* from China south to Australia, which raises the number of species to six.

p.132 **Osage Orange** *Maclura pomifera*

Description: Deciduous tree 10–15 m (33–50 ft) with a bole diameter to 50 cm (1.6 ft).
Crown Irregular rounded or spreading.
Bark Grey or brown, with deep reddish-brown or orange fissures and scaly coarse ridges. *Shoot* Green, hairy and zig-zagged, maturing to hairless and brown, with short straight 1 cm (1.2 in) spines by the buds (especially at the base of the shoot).
Buds Small, brown. *Foliage* Leaves narrow ovate with a short slender-pointed apex, sometimes more lanceolate and long slender pointed, base rounded, margins untoothed, slightly wavy, upper surface shiny green, hairless, underside paler and thinly pilose (especially on the veins) or nearly hairless, 5–12 × 1.5–6 cm (2–4.7 × 0.6–2.4 in); leaf stalk hairy with a milky sap, 3–5 cm (1.2–2 in); autumn colour yellow. *Flowers* In dense rounded clusters to 2.5 cm (1 in), in June at the junction of previous year's wood with the base of the new shoots, yellow-green, male and female flowers on separate trees. *Fruit* Globose, wrinkled and warty, hard fleshy syncarp, green, ripening to orange, 9–13 cm (3.5–5.1 in) long and wide; flesh stringy, with a milky juice, inedible with many light-brown nutlets.

Range: Central USA from southwest Arkansas, east Oklahoma and eastern Texas.

Habitat: Cultivated as an ornamental and used in hedges, in the wild occurring in moist river-valley sites.

Synonyms: *Maclura aurantiaca*.

Similar species: **Cudrania** *Cudrania tricuspidata* (p.132) is closely allied, differing in the often three-lobed leaves which have fewer more prominent veins, and in flowering on the current season's shoots. It is native to China where it is used for feeding silkworms.

This tree is distinct in the glossy leaves, the short sharp spines and the large orange fruit, although without segments and internally more like a plane or raspberry fruit. Fruits are only produced where both male and female trees are grown together.

MAGNOLIA, MAGNOLIACEAE

This family has flowers in which the sepals and petals are normally very similar and the term 'tepal' has been coined to describe them. The family contains two subfamilies. The *Liriodendron* subfamily has just two species and is characterized by the fruit being a cluster of woody winged nutlets or samara which are shed to leave a persistent spindle-shaped axis. The *Magnolia* subfamily is a much larger group, consisting of up to twelve genera. In this group, the fruit consists of a series of follicles which are persistent on the axis. In *Michelia*, the flowers are borne in the leaf axils, whilst in *Magnolia* and *Manglietia* they are carried at the ends of the shoots. *Magnolia* has two ovaries per carpel, whilst in *Manglietia* there are four to six.

Species of *Manglietia* may be found in warmer western gardens but are not illustrated or described in detail here. The commonest is *Manglietia insignis*, which is an evergreen tree to 20 m (65 ft) with leathery oblong-elliptic leaves which are 10–20 cm (4–8 in) in length by 4–6.5 cm (1.6–2.6 in). and bluish beneath. It has fragrant flowers with 12 tepals, variously white, yellowish to rose-pink and comes from northeast India, northern Burma, western Yunnan and northern Vietnam. *Manglietia fordiana* has leaves 5–17 × 1.5–6.5 cm (2–6.7 × 0.6–2.6 in) and appears hardier. It comes from southern China and northern Vietnam where it makes a tree to 20 m (65 ft).

MAGNOLIAS, *MAGNOLIA*
FAMILY MAGNOLIACEAE

This is a large and ancient genus, with fossils dated as 110 million years old. The leaves are simple, usually with an intricate network of veins but without marginal teeth. They may be deciduous or evergreen. In most species, the new leaves are enclosed in the stipules which are attached to the leaf stalk, showing a pronounced stipular scar when they are shed. The stipular scar also shows as a ring around the shoot on the opposite side to the leaf and bud. However, in *M. grandiflora*, there is no stipular scar, which assists in separating this species from the other commonly cultivated evergreen species *M. delavayi*. The leaves are clustered into false whorls, i.e. restricted to a short length of the shoot near the tip of the season's growth, in MM. *fraseri*, *macrophylla*, *officinalis*, and *tripetala*. The leaves are glaucous beneath in some species, especially in *M. virginiana*. The flowers are terminal on the shoots, consisting of a number of sepals and petals, which as they are indistinguishable from one another, are known as tepals. However, in a few species, e.g. *tripetala*, there are three basal tepals which are much smaller than the others, spreading backwards and bent sharply. In nearly all species the flowers are held erect, but in *M. wilsonii* and its allies (section *Oyama Nakai*) they are pendent on a curved peduncle. The anthers are in a cluster above the tepals and below the cluster of carpels. The manner in which the anthers open is an important character in the classification of the genus. In subgenus *Magnolia*, the anthers open by splitting along the vertical face which is towards the carpels or axis of the flower. The species in this subgenus all flower with, or after, the leaves, and includes MM. *delavayi*, *fraseri*, *grandiflora*, *macrophylla*, *officinalis*, *tripetala*, *virginiana* and *wilsonii*. The second subgenus is *Yulania*. In this group, the anthers open by splitting along their sides. This subgenus includes species which flower on the bare branches (precocious flowering), including MM. *campbellii*, *kobus*, *salicifolia* and × *soulangiana*, and species which flower with the leaves, of which only *M. acuminata* is fully described. The fruit ripens in the first autumn and opens along a central suture to reveal two seeds which have a thin oily covering. The seeds hang out, attached by a slender thread and are designed to be eaten by birds and scattered. In most species, the fruits remain erect (although the larger ones cause the branch to bend down) but in *M. wilsonii* and its allies, they are pendent. Magnolias are mainly planted as amenity trees. They have a reasonable timber. In China, many are used for medicinal purposes, especially the bark of *M. officinalis*.

p.136 **Cucumber Tree** *Magnolia acuminata*

Description: Deciduous tree to 30 m (100 ft) with a bole diameter to 1 m (3.3 ft).
Crown Conic and open in young trees, becoming spreading or domed with age. *Bark* Smooth and brown to grey-brown at first, in older trees becoming fissured with narrow scaly forking ridges. *Shoot* Green at first but purplish brown by autumn, in the second year lighter brown to grey-brown and somewhat shiny. *Buds* Ovoid-oblong with a blunt rounded-to-pointed apex, white with silky hairs, to 1.5 cm (0.6 in). *Foliage* Leaves elliptic to broad ovate, apex rounded to acute (but not strongly slender pointed), base wedge-shaped to rounded, margin untoothed, upper surface light green to yellow-green, with the circa 10–14 pairs of veins slightly impressed and hairy, underside light whitish green with the veins prominent, generally lightly haired, especially on the veins, 8–25 × 5–11 cm (3.1–10 × 2–4.3 in); leaf stalk grooved, yellow-green, sparsely hairy, stipular scar restricted to the basal quarter, 2.5–4 cm (1–1.6 in); autumn colour yellow to russet. *Flowers* Terminal on leafy shoots in June, bell-shaped with yellow-green tepals, not showy unless seen from above. *Fruit* Cylindrical and likened to cucumbers but shocking-pink to red, 5–8 cm (2–3.1 in), with scarlet seeds.
Range: Eastern North America from Ontario across to New York, south to Florida, west to Louisiana and north to Missouri.
Habitat: Cultivated as an ornamental, in the wild occurring in damp stream-side sites.

Similar species: *M. cordata* is closely related and often treated as var. *subcordata*. It makes a smaller tree and differs in the bark not becoming furrowed even in old trees. The young shoots are downy, the leaves more rounded with wedge-shaped to rounded bases (rarely heart-shaped despite the Latin name) and the flowers are a deeper yellow. It occurs in the USA from North Carolina south to Georgia and Alabama. It is a better garden plant, flowering at a small size and usually having a further flush of flowers in the autumn.

Although the flowers are rather lost when seen from below (as the leaves are nearly fully expanded), this has been used in breeding schemes to try and obtain hardier forms which will flower on the bare branches and also to get yellow magnolias. It can be quite attractive when carrying the pink immature fruits.

p.134 **Campbell Magnolia** *Magnolia campbellii*

Description: Deciduous tree 15–25 m (50–80 ft) with a bole diameter to 1 m (3.3 ft).
Crown Ovoid as a young tree, in old ones becoming broadly domed. *Bark* Light grey or grey-brown, lightly fissured and finely wrinkled, only deeply fissured and scaly at the base of old trees. *Shoot* Stout, glaucous green in the first year, hairless except for some hairs in the stipular scars, becoming shiny in the second year but remaining green or part green and brown for several seasons. *Buds* Long narrow ovoid-conic and usually curved, glaucous green at the base with pale brown hairs at the tip, 1.5–4 cm (0.6–1.6 in). *Foliage* Leaves large and broad elliptic to elliptic, tapering to an acute apex, base broad wedge-shaped to rounded, margin untoothed with a hyaline down-turned rim, upper surface sub-glossy mid green, somewhat cupped along the midrib, underside glaucous green with circa 20 pairs of raised veins which do not run to the leaf margin, generally hairy below, more so when young, 15–33 × 8–15 cm (6–13 ×

3.1–6 in); leaf stalk scarcely grooved with the stipular scars restricted to the basal portion, pale golden-brown haired, 3–6 cm (1.2–2.4 in); autumn colour yellow, but sometimes dismal. *Flowers* Buds large, erect, ovoid, hairy, circa 8 cm (3.1 in), carried only on mature trees, terminating previous season's shoots, opening before the leaves to produce large cup shaped flowers 20–30 cm (8–12 in) across with 12–16 pink or white obovate tepals. *Fruit* Cone-like structures 15–20 cm (6–8 in) in length with many rounded carpels which each contain one or two seeds having a purple fleshy covering and black or dark-brown beneath.

Range: Himalayas from east Nepal east across Sikkim, Bhutan, northeast India, southeast Tibet and northern Burma to western Yunnan, China.

Habitat: Cultivated as an ornamental, in the wild occurring in the warm temperate zone in mixed forest with *Tsuga dumosa*, *Betula utilis* and other broadleaved trees.

Varieties: Ssp. *mollicomata* differs in having broad elliptic-to-obovate leaves and hairy flower stalks, with the flowers having a purplish tinge. It is recorded from western Yunnan, possibly as far west as eastern Bhutan.

This tree is spectacular when seen in full flower, sometime between February and May. However, the flowers are susceptible to frost damage, which often mars the display or totally destroys it. This tree requires a moist well-sheltered site, preferably with a good depth of loam. It is not suited to shallow chalk soils, exposed positions or dry locations. The typical form is that from Sikkim which has clear pink flowers and broad elliptic leaves. This suffers in that it only flowers after some 25–30 years, outwith most gardeners' patience! The white-flowered form is by far the commonest in both east Nepal and Bhutan, and is reported to flower at an earlier age, as do grafted plants. The subspecies *mollicomata* described above often will flower when only a decade or a dozen years from seed, but tends to have flowers which have a purplish hue or tinge. A large number of hybrid forms, especially between the two subspecies, are grown in gardens, such as 'Charles Raffil'.

p.138 **Delavay Magnolia** *Magnolia delavayi*

Description: Evergreen tree to 15 m (50 ft) with a bole diameter to 60 cm (2 ft).
Crown Domed. *Bark* Grey-brown and rough in young trees, later becoming thick and corky with fissures. *Shoot* Green with prominent oval raised lenticels in first year, later grey-brown, pith not chambered; stipular scars surround the shoot by each leaf base. *Buds* Long oval, pointed, green, hairy, side buds short, about 1 cm (0.4 in), terminal bud to 5 cm (2 in), enclosed by the stipule of the last leaf. *Foliage* Broad elliptic, leathery, base rounded, apex bluntly acute, veins yellow-green, prominent below, margins untoothed but wavy, glossy mid to dark green above, beneath glaucous pale green with a light to dense covering of curly light brown or grey hairs, 20–35 × 12–20 cm (8–14 × 4.7–8 in); leaf stalk stout with a thicker base, grooved above, pale green with light-grey hairs, 5–8 cm (2–3.1 in).
Flowers Terminal from large-domed buds at the ends of the current season's shoots in mid-summer, opening cup-shaped, to 18 cm (7.1 in), fragrant with nine fleshy creamy-white tepals, opening for a single day. *Fruit* Woody cone-like structure with many carpels, 10–20 × 5–6 cm (4–8 × 2–2.4 in), seeds scarlet.

Range: South and west Yunnan, China.

Habitat: Cultivated in Europe as an ornamental, in the wild occurring on open hillsides in dry valleys.

This tree is amongst the largest leafed hardy evergreen trees. It is tender in cold districts, whilst in milder ones it may be cut back to ground level by really severe winters, although usually regrowing from the base.

p.136 **Fraser Magnolia** *Magnolia fraseri*

Description: Deciduous tree around 15 m (50 ft) in height with a bole diameter to 50 cm (1.6 ft).

Crown Rather spreading, becoming broadly domed. *Bark* Light grey, smooth and thin, becoming scaly in old trees. *Shoot* Stout, golden or yellow-brown, hairless, in the second year becoming red or reddish brown and shiny, with pale whitish-grey lenticels. *Buds* Long narrow conic, glaucous, hairless, 1–3 cm (0.4–1.2 in). *Foliage* Leaves obovate and rather rhombic, broadest above the middle and then tapering to the bluntly pointed apex, at the base tapering to a pair of auricles, margin untoothed, upper surface sub-shiny mid green, underside glaucous whitish green with rather indistinct veins, 18–46 × 10–20 cm (7.1–18.1 × 4–8 in); leaf stalk flattened for the lower half between the stipular scars, rounded above, pale yellow-green; autumn colour russets. *Flowers* Carried at the end of current year's branches in late spring/early summer, 20–25 cm (8–10 in) across with six to nine cream-coloured tepals, fragrant. *Fruit* Cone-like structures 10–13 cm (4–5.1 in) in length with many rounded carpels, rose-red.

Range: Southeast USA from Virginia and West Virginia south to Georgia.

Habitat: Cultivated as an ornamental, in the wild occurring in moist valley sites in mountain hardwood forests.

Similar species: *M. pyramidata* is a related species (sometimes treated as a variety) from the costal plains of South Carolina to east Texas. It makes a small tree to 12 m (39 ft). The leaves are smaller, 18–25 cm (7–10 in). They are abruptly tapered to the narrow heart-shaped or auricled base. The flowers are 10–18 cm (4–7 in) across.

The fragrant flowers of this tree tend to be lost against the foliage, unless they can be viewed from above. The glossy red-brown twigs are quite distinctive.

p.138 **Evergreen Magnolia, Southern Magnolia** or **Bull Bay** *Magnolia grandiflora*

Description: Evergreen tree to 10–15 m (33–50 ft) in height with a bole diameter to 50 cm (1.6 ft).
Crown Columnar or conical, domed.
Bark Light brown, rough and scaly at the base. *Shoot* Stout, densely covered with buff to rufous hairs in the first year, then dark, almost blackish brown thereafter; stipular scars absent; pith chambered.
Buds Long ovoid-conic, pointed, with rufous hairs, 2–4 cm (0.8–1.6 in).
Foliage Leaves oval, broad elliptic to oblong-obovate, tapering to a short slender-pointed apex, base broad wedge-shaped to rounded, margin untoothed, texture thick and stiff, lustrous light green above and often wavy, underside with a dense covering of rufous hairs in the first year, thinning out in years two and three, with raised midrib, 13–25 × 5–10 cm (5.1–10 × 2–4 in); leaf stalk stout, rufous hairy, with two ridges, stipular scar in lower third only, 2–5 cm (0.8–2 in); leaves fall yellow in third autumn. *Flowers* Terminal on the current season's growths on stout rufous hairy stalks from June to September, 15–25 cm (6–10 in) across with nine or more creamy white tepals, strongly scented.
Fruit Ovoid-conic cone-like structure, yellow-green with rufous hairs, with the raised carpel apices, 7–10 × 4–5 cm (2.8–4 × 1.6–2 in).

Range: Coastal southeast USA from North Carolina to Florida and west to Texas.

Habitat: Cultivated as an ornamental, in the wild occurring in moist lowland valley sites with other broadleaved trees.

Varieties: 'Exmouth' has lanceolate to oval leaves which are narrower than usual. It forms an erect tree with upright branches, 'Goliath' is a selection with larger flowers, to 30 cm (12 in) across.

This is one of the hardiest and showiest of evergreens, with large glossy leaves and big, strongly-fragrant flowers. Despite its southern origin in the USA, it is surprisingly hardy, although in cold climates it is often grown against the wall of a house. It is a hexaploid, with six sets of chromosomes.

p.135 **Kobushi** *Magnolia kobus*

Description: Deciduous tree 12–18 m (39–60 ft) with a bole diameter to 70 cm (2.3 ft).
Crown Broadly conic. *Bark* Grey, smooth but finely roughened, becoming fissured at the base. *Shoot* Glabrous, maturing to light brown, new shoots with a slight aniseed scent when crushed. *Buds* Downy. *Foliage* Leaves obovate to broad obovate, thinly chartaceous (stiff like card), apex rounded to an abrupt short slender-pointed tip, base wedge-shaped, margin untoothed, upper surface hairless, dark green with slightly impressed veins, underside slightly hairy and shiny green, 6–15 × 3–7.5 cm (2.4–6 × 1.2–3 in); leaf stalk 1–1.5 cm (0.4–0.6 in). *Flowers* Before the leaves on the bare branches; flowers erect, remaining vase-shaped with the tepals not fully spreading, usually with a small leaf at the base and three small linear sepals (to 1.8 cm × 4 mm (0.7 × 0.2 in)) and six to nine obovate tepals which are white (or white with a flush of pink or purple at the base) and up to 10 cm (4 in). *Fruit* Cylindric, 7–10 cm (2.8–4 in).

Range: Japan, from Hokkaido, Honshu, Kyushu and Shikoku and also on Cheju Island off the coast of Korea.

Habitat: Cultivated as an ornamental, in the wild occurring in woodland.

Varieties: Var. *borealis* is sometimes used for the northern part of the species' range from Hokkaido and northern and western Honshu. It is said to differ in the larger leaves (to 18 × 8–10 cm (7.1 × 3.1–4 in)), slightly larger flowers which are tinged pink and to flower at a younger age. However, the consensus is that it is only a minor variant and not worth distinguishing.

Synonyms: *M. praecocissima*, *M. thurberi*.

Similar species: *M. stellata* is allied to *M. kobus* and often treated as var. *stellata*. It makes a small tree or shrub, differing in the shoots which are silky haired when young and more strongly aromatic and the narrow obovate to broad lanceolate leaves which are bluntly pointed to rounded at the apex and 6–10 cm (2.4–4 in) in length with leaf stalks less than 5 mm (0.2 in). The flowers are fragrant and open widely, with 12–18 similar tepals (but without a distinguishable set of three much smaller sepals) which are narrow oblong or strap-shaped to oblanceolate. It occurs on two sites in Honshu, Japan, but is widely cultivated. The flowers are usually white, but in 'Rosea' they are rosy pink. *M.* × *loebneri* (p.135) is the result of hybrid between *M. kobus* and *M. stellata*. It is, as expected, intermediate between the parents, with around a dozen tepals and narrow obovate leaves. It is mainly represented in cultivation by two clones: 'Leonard Messel', with 12 tepals which are purplish pink on the outer side and white on the inside, and 'Merrill' with more tepals but which are twice as wide as those of *M. stellata*.

This makes a very floriferous tree when mature but is slow to attain the flowering stage. The flowers are amongst the smallest in the genus and tend to remain vase-shaped. Crushed young shoots and leaves have a smell of aniseed but much milder than that displayed by *M. salicifolia*, from which it can be distinguished by the obovate leaves and stouter brown shoots and hairless buds.

---

p.137 **Big-leafed Magnolia**
Magnolia macrophylla

Description: Deciduous tree 10–20 m (33–65 ft) with a bole diameter to 40 cm (1.3 ft).
Crown Broad columnar or domed, with a gaunt open crown. *Bark* Light grey, smooth. *Shoot* Stout, green with white star-

shaped hairs, becoming dark brown after several years. *Buds* Conical, beaked, glaucous green with silvery hairs, 3 cm (1.2 in). *Foliage* Leaves in terminal whorls of five or six enormous leaves 35–80 cm (14–32 in) long by 15–25 cm (6–10 in) wide, obovate, apex acute to rounded, margin untoothed, tapers to a rounded and auricled (like ear lobes) base, upper surface matt green with 20–25 pairs of lateral veins, underside silvery glaucous with the veins raised, hairy; leaf stalk stout, hairy, green, with a flattened area on the upper side which shows the scars from the stipules; autumn colour poor. *Flowers* Terminal on current season's shoots in mid-summer (June–July), with nine creamy-white tepals, fragrant, stamens many, pale yellow, 16–30 cm (6.3–12 in) across. *Fruit* Elliptic cone-like structure, rose-red, ripening in autumn, 6–8 cm (2.4–3.1 in).

Range: North Carolina south to Georgia and west to Louisiana.

Habitat: Cultivated as an ornamental, in the wild occurring in moist valley sites in ravines under broadleafed forest.

This tree has the largest leaves of any magnolia, and in young trees they can be up to 1 m (3.3 ft) in length. The leaves are thin and easily damaged by strong winds. The large flowers are delightfully fragrant but tend to be produced only in the upper crown where, from below, they are hidden by the leaves.

---

p.136 **Chinese Large-leafed Magnolia**
Magnolia officinalis

Description: Deciduous tree to 15 m (50 ft) in height with a bole diameter to 50 cm (1.6 ft). *Crown* Conic when young, becoming rounded. *Bark* Light grey, wrinkled, becoming scaly at the base in old trees. *Shoot* Stout, fawn-coloured with dense short pale hairs. *Buds* Cylindric-conic, velvety with short brownish-golden hairs, 3 cm (1.2 in). *Foliage* Leaves in rosettes or whorls at the tips of the shoots, obovate with a rounded or deeply-notched apex, tapering to the wedge-shaped base, margin untoothed, cupped along the midrib, upper surface matt or sub-shiny mid green, hairless with circa 20 pairs of veins, underside light whitish green, softly hairy, veins raised, 20–50 × 10–25 cm (8–20 × 4–10 in); leaf stalk grooved in upper third, flat in lower two-thirds between the stipular scars, about 3 cm (1.2 in); autumn colour russets.

Flowers Carried in early summer at the end of the main shoots but hidden from below by the leaves, cupped shaped with 9–12 creamy white tepals and a strong fragrance of antiseptic, 15–20 cm (6–8 in) across. *Fruit* Oblong to ovoid cone-like structure, 10–13 cm (4–5.1 in).

Range: Central China from west Sichuan east to Anhui.

Habitat: Cultivated as an ornamental, rare in the wild.

Varieties: The plants with the leaf apex strongly notched are sometimes called var. *biloba*, although such leaves are often found on typical plants.

Similar species: **Japanese Big-leaf Magnolia** *M. hypoleuca* (syn. *M. obovata*) (p.136) is closely related. It is found throughout Japan and in the Kurile Isles to the north. It principally differs from *M. officinalis* in the shoots being hairless and light brown to purple-brown, with the cone-like fruit being pointed at the end, not flat topped. The leaves are obovate with a short acute apex. It is perhaps slightly more common in cultivation.

This tree has large fragrant flowers but, as with the other large-leaved species which flower at the end of the current season's growths after the leaves, they are hidden from below. The fragrance is best described as similar to antiseptic cream. In China, the bark of this and other species of Magnolia are boiled and used as a medicine and tonic. Removing the bark, however, kills the tree and for this reason wild trees are almost unknown. However, it is frequently found growing in monasteries.

p.135 **Willow-leafed Magnolia**
Magnolia salicifolia

Description: Deciduous tree 15–20 m (50–65 ft) in height with a bole diameter to 70 cm (2.3 ft).
Crown Slender columnar or conic with a rounded apex, becoming wider spreading in old trees. *Bark* Smooth, dark brown with pale shallow fissures. *Shoot* Slender, green with oval orange-brown erupting lenticels and hairless, remaining green (at least in part) for three or four years, then becoming brown, scraped bark with an aromatic scent of lemon verbena. *Buds* Ovoid, green or glaucous green, hairless, 1 cm (0.4 in).
Foliage Leaves oval to lanceolate, tapering gently towards the narrowed rounded or acute apex and more strongly to the broad wedge-shaped base, margin untoothed, upper surface dull green, hairless, underside glaucous green with fine down, midrib raised, 4–15 × 1.5–5 cm (1.6–6 × 0.6–2 in); leaf stalk grooved, stipular scar in lower third only, circa 2 cm (0.8 in); autumn colour yellow; crushed foliage with an aniseed scent. *Flowers* Buds ovoid-conic, pointed, covered in silky white hairs, 2–2.5 cm (0.8–1 in), flowers opening in April before the leaves without a small leaf at the base of the stalk, 7–10 cm (2.8–4 in) across with six pure-white tepals, the outer whorl of three oblong and pointed, 5 × 1.2 cm (2 × 0.5 in), the inner whorl obovate, shorter and broader. *Fruit* Rosy pink, 5–8 cm (2–3.1 in), seeds scarlet due to the fleshy covering.

Range: West Honshu and Kyushu, Japan.

Habitat: Cultivated as an ornamental, in the wild found in mountain forests.

Varieties: Var. *concolor* has broader leaves (to 8 cm (3.1 in)) and broader petals. It is in cultivation from Mt. Hakkoda, Honshu, Japan.

Synonyms: *Buergeria salicifolia*.

Similar species: M. *'Kewensis'* is a hybrid with M. *kobus*; it has the vegetative buds with a few silky hairs, the leaves narrowly obovate to elliptic, fragrant flowers and shoots.

M. × *proctoriana* covers the hybrids with *M. stellata*; these have leaves broader above the middle and silky haired growth buds, and flowers with 6–12 tepals.
M. biondii is a related species from central China, differing in the larger leaves to 18 × 7.5 cm (7.1 × 3 in) which are glossy above and larger tepals.

This small attractive tree is distinctive in the scent of the shoots and the crushed foliage. It is similar to *M. kobus* but can be distinguished by the absence of a small leaf at the base of the flower stalk, by the narrower leaves which are glaucous beneath and the more slender shoots.

---

p.134 **Saucer Magnolia** *Magnolia* × *soulangiana*

Description: Deciduous sprawling shrub to tree 8–12 m (26–39 ft) with a bole diameter to 40 cm (1.3 ft).
Crown Vase-shaped when young, becoming widely spreading or rounded. *Bark* Grey. *Shoot* Maturing to brown with narrow stipular scars, becoming flaking and later greyish. *Buds* Downy, cylindric pointed, to 1 cm (0.4 in), flower buds narrow ovoid pointed, about 2 cm (0.8 in). *Foliage* Leaves broad elliptic, oblanceolate to broad obovate, apex rounded with a short abrupt point, base wedge-shaped, margin untoothed, upper surface dark and usually glossy green, hairless, underside paler green with fine hairs on the midrib and main veins, 8–15(–20) × 3–12.5 cm (3.1–6 (–8) × 1.2–4.9 in); leaf stalk 0.7–3 cm (0.3–1.2 in), with small stipular scars at the base. *Flowers* Before the leaves on the bare branches; flowers erect, with around nine tepals but with the outer whorl of three generally half as long as the inner whorl, opening to goblet, cup or saucer shape and from white to purplish pink, depending upon cultivar, 15–25 cm (6–10 in) across. *Fruit* Cylindric, 10–20 cm (4–8 in).
Range: Hybrid arisen in cultivation.
Habitat: Cultivated as an ornamental.

Varieties: Innumerable cultivars, mainly shrubs and only slowly forming trees.

Similar species: The **Yulan** *M. denudata*, a parent of *M.* × *soulangiana*, has lemon-scented vase-shaped white or rosy-purple flowers with similar-sized tepals. It forms a shrub to a spreading small tree.

M. lilliiflora is the second parent. It is more of a shrub, with the stipular scars on the leaf stalk long and the base of the leaf decurrent. The flowers have three outer tepals which are smaller and more like sepals; these fall early. There are six main tepals which are white to deep purple and often bicoloured.

This is the result of the deliberate crossing of *M. denudata* with *M. lilliiflora*, both Chinese species. It is the commonest magnolia in gardens and is usually seen as a bush, rather than a tree. The predominant form has rather poor purplish pink flowers, but some, such as 'Lennei' (flowers pink) and 'Lennei Alba' (white) are much superior.

---

p.137   **Umbrella Tree** *Magnolia tripetala*

Description: Deciduous tree 10–20 m (33–65 ft) in height with a bole diameter to 50 cm (1.6 in).
Crown Becoming wide spreading with open branching. *Bark* Light grey, smooth, not fissured. *Shoot* Olive-brown, stout, becoming light brown and somewhat shiny in later years. *Buds* Long ovoid-conic, glaucous green, 3–4 cm (1.2–1.6 in).
Foliage Leaves arranged rather like the spokes of an umbrella, oblanceolate to elliptic but broadest above the middle, tapering to an acute apex, base wedge-shaped, margin untoothed, upper surface mid sub-shiny green with slightly impressed midrib, underside pale glaucous green, initially downy and remaining silky haired on the raised veins and midrib, 25–50 × 10–25 cm (10–20 × 4–10 in); leaf stalk with stipular scar extending two-thirds to three-

quarters of length, grooved near the top, 2.5–4 cm (1–1.6 in); autumn colour russet. *Flowers* Terminal on the current season's shoots in May–June and rather hidden from beneath by the leaves, 18–25 cm (7.1–10 in) across, six to nine tepals, creamy-white, to 12 × 5 cm (4.7 × 2 in), strongly but not pleasantly scented. *Fruit* Oblong, cone-like, rosy red, 6–10 cm (2.4–4 in).

Range: South central USA from Pennsylvania south to Georgia and west to Mississippi and Indiana.

Habitat: Cultivated as an ornamental, in the wild occurring in moist mountain-valley sites in hardwood forests.

Synonyms: *M. umbrella.*

This large-leafed Magnolia is better adapted to cultivation in Europe than most of the similar species, and flowers and fruits freely. However, as these are produced after the leaves have expanded, they are best where they can be seen from above. The common name refers to the resemblance of one year's growth of leaves to the spokes of a wheel, whilst the Latin name refers to the three larger outer tepals (or sepals), not to the full complement of tepals in any one flower.

p.137 **Sweet Bay** *Magnolia virginiana*

Description: Deciduous or evergreen tree to 10 m (33 ft) with a bole diameter to 30 cm (1 ft). *Crown* Ovoid, upright, often on several stems. *Bark* Smooth, grey-brown. *Shoot* Yellow-green, hairless, with oval narrow pale lenticels and stipular scars at the nodes, in the second or third year becoming chocolate brown in patches, only fully dark brown after four years and later becoming grey-brown, crushed bark fragrant. *Buds* Glaucous green, long conic, hairy at the tip, 1–2 cm (0.4–0.8 in). *Foliage* Leaves oval or oblong, rounded at both ends and untoothed, upper surface glossy green, smooth, underside glaucous whitish green, with fine white hairs pressed against shoot, 6–13 × 3–7 cm (2.4–5.1 × 1.2–2.8 in); leaf stalk with two scars from the stipules nearly to the base of the leaf, slightly hairy, green, 2–2.5 cm (0.8–1 in); autumn colour poor. *Flowers* Single on a thick green stalk of 2 cm (0.8 in) at the end of the current season's shoots from July until the autumn, fragrant with a rich sweet perfume, flowers with seven or eight obovate tepals with the inner whorl narrower, creamy white when young, becoming yellow or brown as they age, 7–8 cm (2.8–3.1 in) across. *Fruit* Ovoid cone-like structure with circa 15 carpels, green but ripening to red, with two seeds in each fertile carpel, 4–5 cm (1.6–2 in) when mature.

Range: In an arc around the coast of the eastern USA from New York and Massachusetts to Florida and southeastern Texas.

Habitat: Cultivated as an ornamental, in the wild found along streams, pond margins and at the edges of swamps.

Varieties: Var. *australis* applies to the evergreen forms from Florida and the Carolinas, where it may form a tree 20 m (65 ft) tall.

Synonyms: *M. glauca.*

This makes a small tree, with delightfully fragrant flowers carried in succession from mid-summer until autumn. It varies in whether it is deciduous (from the northern parts of its range) to evergreen.

p.139 **Wilson Magnolia** *Magnolia wilsonii*

Description: Deciduous tree 6–10 m (20–33 ft) with a bole diameter to 25 cm (10 in).
Crown Spreading, usually broader than tall and often on several stems. *Bark* Brown, roughened. *Shoot* Green, densely brown hairy at first but becoming sparse during the first year, with narrow elliptic brown lenticels, becoming mid brown in second year. *Buds* Narrow conical, green with brown hairs, to 1.5 cm (0.6 in).
Foliage Leaves oval, ovate-lanceolate to

oblong, apex pointed, acute, base rounded or somewhat subcordate, margin untoothed, upper surface matt dark green, soon hairless, underside somewhat glaucous green, densely covered with white hairs except along the midrib where they are brownish, veins prominent below, with 8–10 pairs reaching the margin, 8–15 × 3.5–7 cm (3.1–6 × 1.4–2.8 in); leaf stalk grooved, with the scar where the stipules initially covered the shoot tip, brown hairy, 2.5–3.5 cm (1–1.4 in); autumn colour russets. *Flowers* On leafy shoots in late spring or early summer (May–June), single, in bud pendulous, pear-drop or plumb-like shaped, opening 7–10 cm (2.8–4 in) across, cup-shaped with nine white incurved tepals, fragrant, stamens many, rich red or red-purple, 1.2 cm (0.5 in). *Fruit* Pendulous, cylindric-ovoid, 5–7 cm (2–2.8 in), with circa 30 carpels which ripen from green to purplish pink and open in early autumn to reveal the scarlet-coated seeds.

Range: Western China from West Sichuan to Yunnan.

Habitat: Cultivated as an ornamental, in the wild occurring in mixed mountain forests.

Similar species: *M. sieboldii* has obovate or obovate-oblong leaves which are proportionately wider with only seven to nine pairs of veins and pale or grey-brown shoots. It is more shrubby, but carries the flowers opening outwards, rather than pendulous. It comes from Japan and Korea, just extending into northeast China. *M. sinensis* from west Sichuan, China, has larger flowers 10–12 cm (4–4.7 in) across.

This is a beautiful spring-flower small tree. The pendent flowers are best viewed from beneath, but are also attractive when they hang down like the weight on a plumb line.

CRAB APPLES, *MALUS* (SYNONYM: *PYRUS* IN PART)
FAMILY ROSACEAE

This genus is important for containing the orchard apples (*M. domestica*). It consists of around 30 species, plus many hybrids and cultivars. The leaves are mainly elliptic in outline, with finely-toothed margins. Some species have the underside of the leaves distinctly woolly, including *MM. dasyphylla, domestica, spectabilis* and *tschonoskii*. The spur shoots may be spiny (*see MM. baccata, dasyphylla, hupehensis* and *sylvestris*), although most are not. The flowers are in umbel-like clusters, with 15–30 stamens and rounded anthers. The styles are united at the base. The fruit may be indented at the base, and the calyx may be shed from the developing fruit, leaving a circular depression (*see MM. baccata, florentina,* × *floribunda, hupehensis* and × *purpurea*), but in the other species the calyx persists into the ripe fruit. Fruit size can also be a good identifier, with fruits less than 1.2 cm (0.5 in) (mainly less than 1 cm (0.4 in)) in *MM. baccata, florentina,* × *floribunda* and *hupehensis,* and at least 1.5 cm (0.6 in) (mainly over 2 cm (0.8 in) and up to 10 cm (4 in)) in *MM. dasyphylla, domestica,* × *purpurea, spectabilis, sylvestris* and *tschonoskii*.

---

p.208 **Siberian Crab** *Malus baccata*

Description: Deciduous tree to 10–15 m (33–50 ft) with a bole diameter to 70 cm (2.3 ft).
Crown Usually low and spreading or rounded, but sometimes more erect and becoming ovoid. *Bark* Smooth, dark grey, becoming scaly at the base in old trees.
Shoot Slender, finely white haired when very young or hairless, brown to purple-brown with a thin wax layer by autumn, brown in later years; spur shoots thorn-like.
Buds Ovoid conic to conic, pointed to sharp, scales purple and brown with white hairs at the tips, 4 mm (0.2 in). *Foliage* Leaves ovate to elliptic-lanceolate, apex acute or slender pointed, base wedge-shaped or rounded, margin finely and sharply toothed, hairless and shiny green above, paler beneath and either hairless or with fine hairs on the midrib and veins, 3.5–8 × 1.5–5 cm (1.4–3.1 × 0.6–2 in); leaf stalk slender, 2–5 cm (0.8–2 in); autumn colour yellow.
Flowers In corymbs of three to seven on slender 2–3.5 cm (0.8–1.4 in) stalks in April; pink to deep pink in bud, opening pinkish white to ivory white or pure white and 4 cm (1.6 in) across; calyx hairless, constricted above the ovary, lobes lanceolate,

3–4 mm (0.1–0.2 in). *Fruit* Globose to ellipsoidal, bright red, less often yellow, with a thin flesh, indented at the base, 0.7–1 cm (0.3–0.4 in); calyx deciduous, leaving a small round scar in the fruit apex.

Range: Russia from eastern Siberia to the Pacific, south into Mongolia and northern China with varieties in the Himalayas and western China and in northern Japan and Korea.

Habitat: Cultivated as an ornamental, in the wild occurring in mixed forest.

Varieties: Var. *mandshurica* (*Malus mandshurica* from northern China northeast to Japan differs in the leaves and calyx being more hairy (especially on the inside of the lobes), in the larger leaves to 10 cm (4 in) which are more finely toothed (and sometimes untoothed at the base). Var. *himalaica* from southwest China (Yunnan, southwest Sichuan) along the Himalayas to Bhutan has flowers pink and makes a more upright tree. It is included here within *M. baccata*, but might be better treated as a separate species.

Synonyms: *Pyrus baccata*.

Similar species: *M. transitoria* (p.210) makes a small spreading tree with creamy white flowers in mid to late spring. These are followed by small rounded pea-like fruits (to 6 mm (0.25 in)) which ripen to yellow. The leaves are hairy and up to 5 cm (2 in) long, but variable in shape, often being lobed and nearly always toothed. It comes from northwest China, from Gansu and Sichuan.

This tree usually has pure white and very showy flowers on a low-spreading crown with the branches pendulous at their tips. However, trees from the Himalayan part of its range (*see* above as var. *himalaica*) have much deeper pink flowers, looking casually more like *M. floribunda*.

Danube Apple *Malus dasyphylla*

Description: Deciduous small tree to 8–12 m (26–39 ft). *Crown* Rounded or domed. *Shoot* White woolly when young, becoming brown and hairless, spur shoots somewhat thorny.

Foliage Leaves elliptic to ovate, apex short pointed, base rounded, margin with crenate teeth, upper surface dull green and soon hairless, underside densely white hairy, 3.5–11 × 2.5–5 cm (1.4–4.3 × 1–2 in); leaf stalk hairy, 1.5 cm (0.6 in). *Flowers* In small corymbs, white, 4 cm (1.6 in) across in May. *Fruit* Globose to sub-globose, indented at both ends with a persistent calyx, yellow or yellow and red, circa 4 cm (1.6 in) across on stalks circa 2.5 cm (1 in).

Range: Southeastern Europe from the Danube Basin and the northern Balkans, from Austria, Hungary, Romania, Bulgaria, Greece, Albania, Serbia and Croatia.

Habitat: Damp lowland woods.

This small tree is closely allied to the domestic apple (*M. domestica*) and is almost certainly involved in the parentage of that hybrid species. It differs in having some, at least, spiny spur shoots, in the smaller fruits, the hairless styles and smaller leaves.

---

p.207 **Apple** *Malus domestica*

Description: Deciduous tree 8–12 m (26–39 ft), rarely to 15 m (50 ft), with a bole diameter to 50 cm (1.6 ft).
Crown Rounded or domed. *Bark* Grey-brown or purplish grey, smooth but flaking in scales at the base on old trees.
Shoot White, woolly when young, becoming brown and hairless by autumn, spur shoots end in a bud, not thorny.
Buds Ovoid, white, woolly, 6 mm (0.25 in). *Foliage* Leaves elliptic-ovate, apex short pointed, base rounded to broad wedge-shaped, margin with crenate to sharp teeth, upper surface dull green and initially hairy, underside densely white hairy but less so by autumn, 4.5–13 × 3–7 cm (1.8–5.1 × 1.2–2.8 in); leaf stalk hairy, 2–3 cm (0.8–1.2 in); autumn colour poor. *Flowers* Corymbs of four to seven flowers in April–May, mainly on spur shoots; pink in bud, opening to pink or

white with a pink blush; stalks and calyx woolly, styles hairy at least at the base.
Fruit Sub-globose to ovoid-ellipsoid, indented at the base and at the apex with the persistent calyx, green, russet or red, 5–10 cm (2–4 in).

Range: Widely cultivated as a fruit tree.

Habitat: Known only in cultivation.

Varieties: Many clones, such as 'Cox's Orange Pippin' (best apple for flavour and taste) and 'Bramley's Seedling' (best cooking apple, although it becomes sweeter after Christmas).

Synonyms: *M. pumila* in part.

Similar Species: **Magdeburg Crab** *M.* '*Magdeburgensis*' (p.211) is a hybrid of *M. domestica*, probably with a double-flowered form of *M. sylvestris* (but some authorities suggest *M. spectabilis* as the other parent). It makes a rounded small tree, often broader than high. The flowers are borne in May, 4 cm (1.6 in) across, covering the branches, each flower with around a dozen petals. The fruits are yellow-green, about 3 cm (1.2 in) but not ornamental.

This is the garden or domestic apple and is very widely cultivated throughout the temperate regions of the world. It is an ancient hybrid, probably comprising the genes from several European to western and central Asian species. These include *M. sylvestris* (of which it is sometimes made a variety), from which it is best distinguished by the hairiness of the leaves, shoots and floral parts and *M. dasyphylla*. The name *M. pumila* is sometimes used for this species as a bit of a botanical catch-all. However, this name is of uncertain application but probably relates either to an ornamental cultivar or to a wild apple from western Asia.

---

p.208 **Italian Crab** *Malus florentina*

Description: Deciduous tree to 9 m (29 ft) with a bole diameter to 40 cm (1.3 ft).
Crown Upright with ascending branches, becoming rounded or domed at the top.

Bark Purple-grey, scaly or fissured at base and revealing orange. *Shoot* Slender, shaggy white haired when young, purple-brown to green-brown. *Buds* Ovoid-conic, sharp pointed, reddish brown with hairy scale margins, 3 mm (0.1 in). *Foliage* Leaves broadly ovate in outline with several lobes having sharp teeth, apex bluntly acute, base subcordate, rounded to truncate, upper surface deep green and at first hairy, underside paler and more persistently downy with white hairs, 3–6 cm (1.2–2.4 in); leaf stalk downy, 1–2.5 cm (0.4–1 in); autumn colour orange-scarlet. *Flowers* In lax corymbs in June 5–7 cm (2–2.8 in) across with five to seven pure white 2 cm (0.8 in) flowers on the short shoots; stalks downy, slender and purplish, 2–3 cm (0.8–1.2 in); calyx woolly, with narrow, pointed lobes. *Fruit* Broad ellipsoidal, red, with a deciduous calyx, 1–1.2 cm (0.4–0.5 in).

Range: Northern Italy across the Balkans to northern Greece.

Habitat: Woodland, rare.

Synonyms: *Crataegus florentina*.

The affinities of this tree are debatable. The leaves recall those of several *Crataegus*, but also a miniature version of *Sorbus torminalis*. As a consequence, it has been suggested as a hybrid of *Malus sylvestris* with either *Sorbus torminalis* or a *Crataegus*. There is nothing inherently implausible in such an origin. The Pomoideae subfamily is littered with hybrids between distantly related subgenera (or genera), and the genus *Sorbus* only holds as an entity for convenience, not on botanical characters. However, I am suspicious of the above origins and consider that it is more likely to be a relict species (as, for instance, *Mespilus germanica*). There is some merit in considering it as a separate genus, especially if the hybrid origin theory is accepted and the genus *Malosorbus* has been proposed. It is rare both in the wild and in cultivation, where it makes an attractive small tree with good autumn colour.

p.210 **Flowering Crab** *Malus × floribunda*

Description: Deciduous tree to 6 m (20 ft), rarely to 9 m (29 ft), with a bole diameter to 30 cm (1 ft).
Crown Spreading to rounded, dense and twiggy. *Bark* Grey-brown, becoming scaly. *Shoot* Slender, initially downy, later hairless, dark brown. *Buds* Ovoid, pointed. *Foliage* Leaves on flowering shoots narrow to broad ovate or oblong-ovate, apex slender pointed, base rounded or wedge-shaped, margin coarsely and sharply toothed, dull green and hairless above, paler and somewhat hairy beneath, 4–8 cm (1.6–3.1 in); leaf stalk 1.5–2.5 cm (0.6–1 in); leaves on strong or non-flowering shoots with deep, large teeth and sometimes three to five lobed. *Flowers* In corymbs of four to seven; rosy red in bud, opening to pale pink and 2.5–3 cm (1–1.2 in) across. *Fruit* Globose, yellow, with a depression where the calyx has fallen away, about 1 cm (0.4 in); stalks 2.5–3.5 cm (1–1.4 in).

Range: Cultivated in Japan.

Habitat: Known only in cultivation.

Similar species: **Hall's Crab** *M. halliana* (p.210) is similar and may be one of the parents of *M. × floribunda* (or a similar hybrid). The leaves are rolled up when in bud and first expanding (in *M. × floribunda* they are folded along the midrib), oval to ovate, less toothed and with a glandular midrib. The flowers are deep rose, on stalks 3–6 cm (1.2–2.4 in) and are followed by obovoid purple fruits. The shoots are dark purple in colour. It may have been an early introduction from China to Japan, but has not been found in the wild in China. However, in Kyushu, there occurs a very similar plant, but with white flowers with stalks only 2–2.5 cm (0.8–1 in) and elliptic to obovate leaves.

This small tree is very attractive with its massed pink and rosy-pink blooms in late April or May. It is probably a hybrid, with *M. baccata* being one possible parent.

p.209   **Hubei Crab** *Malus hupehensis*

Description: Deciduous tree 8–13 m (26–43 ft) with a
bole diameter to 30 cm (1 ft).
Crown Rounded, with spreading branches
and usually broader than high.
Bark Orange-brown or purple-brown,
smooth but becoming scaly at the base.
Shoot Olive-brown and white woolly in
the first year, becoming purplish grey and
hairless with oval orange lenticels, spur
shoots ending in a bud. *Buds* Conic,
chestnut-brown with white hairy margins,
3 mm (0.1 in). *Foliage* Leaves oval to
ovate, with a short slender-pointed tip,
base rounded to wedge-shaped, margin
regularly finely serrate with forward-
pointing teeth, upper surface mid green
with few spaced slightly indented veins,
underside shiny light green with raised
hairy veins, 5–10 × 3–6 cm (2–4 ×
1.2–2.4 in); leaf stalk grooved, woolly,
3–6 cm (1.2–2.4 in); autumn colour
yellow. *Flowers* With the leaves in April,
on short spur shoots which fork forming
one vegetative one bud and an umbel of
three to seven flowers; flowers pink or deep
pink in bud, opening white or pale pink,
3.25–4 cm (1.3–1.6 in) across, on woolly
2.5–4 cm (1–1.6 in) slender stalks, calyx
triangular-ovate, styles usually three.
Fruit Globose, hard, green or pinky-
green, 0.8–1 cm (0.3–0.4 in) across,
calyx deciduous in fruit, leaving a small
circular dark brown scar 2 mm (0.1 in)
across.

Range: Central and west China.

Habitat: Cultivated as an ornamental tree, in the
wild occurring in woods.

Synonyms: *Pyrus hupehensis, Malus theifera.*

This tree makes an attractive flowering
crab. It is a triploid, i.e. with three sets of
chromosomes, and comes true from seed
(apomictic). The crabs are like small hard
peas, distinctive in the soon deciduous
calyx which leaves a flat scar at the apex.

p.211 **Purple Crab** *Malus × purpurea*

Description: Deciduous tree to 8 m (26 ft) with a bole
diameter to 50 cm (1.6 ft).
Crown Rounded, rather open and often
losing the foliage by late summer, of very
limited beauty except when fleeting in
blossom. *Bark* Purple-grey, scaly at the
base. *Shoot* Slender, purplish.
Foliage Leaves ovate-lanceolate to elliptic,
apex acute, base rounded, margin toothed
and on strong shoots slightly lobed, upper
surface lustrous dark green, underside
paler and shiny with a dark purplish
midrib, 3–5 cm (1.2–2 in); new leaves
reddish purple. *Flowers* In corymbs of six
or seven in late April–May, ruby-red in
bud, opening to reddish purple, 4 cm
(1.6 in) across. *Fruit* Globose, dark red,
with a persistent or sometimes deciduous
calyx, 1.5–2.5 cm (0.6–1 in), on 2.5 cm
(1 in) stalks.

Range: Hybrid of garden origin.

Habitat: In horticulture only.

Varieties: The clones 'Aldenhamensis', 'Eleyi' and
'Lemoinei' are forms of this hybrid,
differing in flower colour, foliage or habit.
'Profusion' is a back cross with *M. sieboldii*,
with a better display of flowers and a better
constitution. *M. sieboldii* is a small shrub
(usually only 3 m (10 ft) but up to 6 m
(20 ft)) with oblong to lobed leaves and
flowers which are pink in bud but open
white. It is a native of Japan and Korea.

Synonyms: *Malus floribunda* var. *purpurea*.

The tree can be very attractive with the
purple new foliage and the ruby-red
flowers, but from May onwards it is in
decline. It arose as a cross between *M.
niedzwetzkyana* (a small tree from
Kazakhstan in central Asia whose leaves,
shoots and fruits are suffused with purple,
but which is otherwise similar to *M.
domestica*) and *M. × atrosanguinea*. *M. ×
atrosanguinea* is a hybrid of *M. halliana ×
M. sieboldii*.

p.211 **Chinese Crab** *Malus spectabilis*

Description: Deciduous tree to 6–13 m (20–43 ft), with a bole diameter to 60 cm (2 ft).
Crown Upright or rounded, with drooping branchlets. *Shoot* Initially downy, later hairless, dark brown. *Foliage* Leaves oval, obovate to almost rotund, apex with a short abrupt point, base rounded or wedge-shaped, margin with teeth pressed against shoot, upper surface shiny green, hairless, underside paler and downy when young, texture stiff like card (chartaceous), 5–8 × 3–5 cm (2–3.1 × 1.2–2 in); leaf stalk 0.6–2.5 cm (0.25–1 in). *Flowers* In corymbs of six to eight in April–May; deep rosy red in bud, opening to blush pink and 5.5–3 cm (2.2–1.2 in) across stalks downy, 2–3 cm (0.8–1.2 in). *Fruit* Globose, yellow, tapered at the base, calyx persistent at the apex, circa 2 cm (0.8 in); stalks 2–3 cm (0.8–1.2 in).

Range: North China.

Habitat: Not known in the wild.

Varieties: 'Riversii' is a form with deeper pink flowers with up to twenty petals.

This tree is not known in the wild and is probably an old Chinese garden selection. It has a tendency to produce flowers which are semi-double or double. In flower it is attractive, but has no great amenity at other times of the year.

p.207 **Crab Apple** or **Wild Crab** *Malus sylvestris*

Description: Deciduous tree 10–15 m (33–50 ft) with a bole diameter to 40 cm (1.3 ft).
Crown Rounded, domed, often dense with downward-curving branches. *Bark* Dark brown, becoming cracked and fissured into small squares. *Shoot* Green-brown or brown, hairless or at first loosely hairy with grey hairs, becoming grey-brown, lenticels oval, light brown, short spur shoots often ending in a thorn. *Buds* Ovoid to conic, dark brown with some whitish hairs, 3–5 mm (0.1–0.2 in). *Foliage* Leaves elliptic to

obovate, tapering to a short acute apex, base rounded to wedge-shaped, margin finely serrate with small rounded teeth, upper surface shiny dark green, nearly hairless and rather rugose, folded along the midrib and rather cupped, underside whitish green, hairless except for hairs on the raised veins, texture leathery, 3–7 × 2–4 cm (1.2–2.8 × 0.8–1.6 in); leaf stalk grooved, downy, green or crimson, 2–3 cm (0.8–1.2 in); autumn colour yellow, generally poor. *Flowers* In umbels of four to seven with the leaves, with white or pink petals, to 4 cm (1.6 in), stalks, receptacle and outside of calyx hairless or nearly hairless. *Fruit* Globose or oblate (wider than long) apple indented at both ends, green with russet markings, juicy but sour and with a rather rubbery texture, five celled, 2–3 × 2–4 cm (0.8–1.2 × 0.8–1.6 in); seeds light brown, ovoid, pointed and flattened, 6 × 4 mm (0.25 × 0.2 in); stalk short, hairy, less than 1 cm (0.4 in).

Range: Throughout Europe, including Britain.
Habitat: Hedgerows and old woodlands.

This small tree is probably one of the parents of the cultivated commercial or domestic apples, which have larger and tomentose leaves and shoots. It may have been planted as a fruit tree in the past before the domestic apple was developed and many of the naturalized populations may either be garden escapes or have introgression of genes from the cultivated apple.

p.209 **Chonosuki Crab** or **Pillar Crab**
Malus tschonoskii

Description: Deciduous tree 8–15 m (26–50 ft) with a bole diameter to 50 cm (1.6 ft).
Crown Narrow ovoid-conical to broad conical or flame-shaped, with ascending branches. *Bark* Grey-brown, smooth, becoming platy at the base in old trees. *Shoot* Green or purplish, densely white woolly when young but becoming hairless, with round raised pale brown lenticels, in

the second year green-brown with a greyish cast and some scattered wool. *Buds* Ovoid, rounded bluntly pointed, scales purple with patches of white wool, 4 mm (0.2 in). *Foliage* New leaves pinkish grey due to a dense covering of hairs which are largely lost above except along the midrib but remain covering the undersurface, ovate to broad ovate or rather oblong ovate, tapering to an acute apex, base rounded subcordate, margin with irregular triangular teeth, mid green above, light green beneath with 6–10 pairs of raised veins, 5–13 × 4–8 cm (2–5.1 × 1.6–3.1 in); leaf stalk round, white woolly, 2–3 cm (0.8–1.2 in), with small but soon lost ovate stipules at the base; autumn colour brilliant golds and scarlets. *Flowers* On spur shoots with the new leaves and in small erect umbels of four to six, opening white and to 2.5–3 cm (1–1.2 in) across but flushed rose in bud, three styles. *Fruit* Generally rather sparsely carried, globose with a persistent calyx, ripening from green to brownish yellow and purple, woolly when young, 2.5 cm (1 in) across, on a hairy stalk.

Range: Honshu, Japan.

Habitat: Cultivated as an ornamental, in the wild occurring as a rare woodland tree.

Synonyms: *Eriolobus tschonoskii*.

This tree has a narrow upright or pyramidal habit and develops exquisite autumn colours, thus making it very useful for street planting and in other confined spaces. It is not attractive in flower or fruiting, although the absence of the latter adds to its charm as a street tree. It was first collected by Chonosuki, a Japanese collector working for the Russian botanist Maximowicz in the late 19th century.

MALLOW, MALVACEAE

This is a large genus characterized by the stamens being attached to the style. The genera treated here are *Abutilon* (p.404), *Hibiscus* (p.737) and *Hoheria* (p.739).

MAITENS, *MAYTENUS*
FAMILY CELASTRACEAE

This is a large genus of mainly tropical distribution with fruits and seeds similar to *Euonymus*. Only *M. boaria* is both commonly cultivated and a sizeable tree.

---

p.173 **Maiten** *Maytenus boaria*

Description: Evergreen tree to 20 m (65 ft) with a bole diameter to 90 cm (2.9 ft).
Crown Oval or narrow rounded domed, with pendent branchlets. *Bark* Brown, smooth. *Shoot* Green on the underside, purple on the upper side for the first winter, then grey-brown, hairless. *Buds* Ovoid, dark brown, 1 mm (0.1 in).
Foliage Lanceolate, tapered to a slender acute tip, decurrent on the leaf stalk at the base, margins finely saw-toothed with a thin hyaline border, hairless, shiny mid green above, paler and matt beneath with slightly raised lateral veins, 0.5–6 × 0.6–2 cm (0.2–2.4 × 0.25–0.8 in); leaf stalk purple and green, 3–5 mm (0.1–0.2 in).
Flowers In leaf axils on previous season's shoot in spring, in clusters of two to eight, yellowish-white. *Fruit* Globular, green, 7 mm (0.3 in), containing two seeds each enclosed within a red seed coat.

Range: Southern South America, from Chile, The Argentine, Peru, Bolivia and Brazil.

Habitat: Cultivated in Europe as an ornamental, in the wild occurring in open pastures.

Synonyms: *M. chilensis.*

This tree makes a neat small evergreen, although the flowers and fruit have no great beauty. The foliage is attractive to cattle, hence the Latin name, meaning 'of cattle'.

MAHOGANY, MELIACEAE

This is a mainly tropical family, with *Toona* (p.1234) as the only genus hardy in Britain and western Europe, although *Melia* (p.836) is hardy in warmer countries.

BEAD TREES, *MELIA*
FAMILY MELIACEAE

This a genus of three species from the Old World tropics and warm temperate regions. The bi-pinnate leaves on stout shoots, naked buds and fruit which is a drupe, distinguish the genus.

p.343 **Bead Tree** *Melia azedarach*

Description: Deciduous tree to 15 m (50 ft) with a bole diameter to 40 cm (1.3 ft).
Crown Spreading, low and usually flat topped. *Bark* Dark brown to reddish brown, becoming furrowed in old trees. *Shoot* Stout, green and pithy. *Buds* Small, rounded. *Foliage* Leaves bi-pinnate, 25–80 cm (10–32 in) by half as wide; leaflets numerous, ovate to elliptic, apex acute to a slender point, base unequally wedge-shaped, margin toothed and sometimes wavy, upper surface dark green, paler beneath, hairless or somewhat hairy on the midrib and veins, 2–5 × 1–2 cm (0.8–2 × 0.4–0.8 in); rachis hairless or downy, slender; crushed foliage with a strong odour and a bitter taste. *Flowers* Fragrant, in loose axillary panicles 10–20 cm (4–8 in) on the young leafy shoots in spring; petals lilac, 2 cm (0.8 in) in diameter. *Fruit* Globose berry with a thin fleshy covering and containing three to five seeds, poisonous, drying wrinkled, yellow to cream, 1.5 cm (0.6 in) in diameter.

Range: Northern India across to central and southern China.

Habitat: Cultivated and naturalized as an ornamental in warm temperate and tropical climes.

This is widely planted and naturalized throughout the warm temperate and tropical regions of the world. The fruits are hard and are used to make rosaries, but are also poisonous. It is very attractive in spring when carrying the fragrant lilac flowers with the contrasting new foliage. It is very fast growing when young, but rather short lived.

MELIOSMA, *MELIOSMA*
FAMILY SABIACEAE

This is a genus from eastern Asia, where it extends as far north as Korea, and tropical regions of the Americas. The leaves may be either simple or pinnate, with a species in each grouping illustrated here. The shoots have naked buds. The white flowers have three larger outer petals and two smaller ones, but are small. However, they are carried in large heads and are fragrant (the scientific name is from the Greek for 'honey' (*meli*) and 'smell' (*osma*). The fruit is a single-seeded drupe.

p.236 **Gogun Tree** *Meliosma dilleniifolia*

Description: Large shrub to a deciduous tree to 10–15 m (33–50 ft) with a bole diameter to 50 cm (1.6 ft).
Crown Rounded. *Bark* Pale, corky.
Shoot At first with stiff rusty brown hairs, dark brown and largely hairless by winter, becoming striped with pale buff lines, with relatively large half-moon leaf traces.
Buds Naked, with furry brown miniature leaves, small (2–3 mm (0.1 in)).
Foliage Leaves simple, obovate or oblanceolate to elliptic, acute or short slender pointed at the apex, base long narrow wedge-shaped or attenuate, margin with fine awl-like teeth which terminate on the 15–22 pairs of parallel veins and with smaller teeth between, upper surface green with hairs pressed on shoot, underside paler with rust coloured hairs on the veins, 10–18 cm (4–7.1 in) (but sometimes to 25 cm (10 in)) by 4.5–10 cm (1.8–4 in). *Flowers* In stiffly erect panicles in July–August, 15–30 cm (6–12 in); flowers white, fragrant.
Fruit Black drupe, 6 mm (0.25 in).
Range: Himalayas east to Burma, with subspecies through western and northern China to Korea and Japan.
Habitat: Cultivated as an ornamental, in the wild occurring in moist temperate woodland.
Varieties: Three closely related species or subspecies are small trees, usually only 6 m (20 ft) or so. They differ as follows: ssp. *cuneifolia* (*M. cuneifolia*) has smaller, more simply-toothed leaves with axillary tufts and is mainly a

shrub to 5 m (16 ft). It comes from western China. Ssp. *flexuosa* (*M. flexuosa*, syn. *M. pendens*) has the flower panicles pendulous or pendent and the leaves are without axillary tufts. It occurs in central eastern China; ssp. *tenuis* (*M. tenuis*) has shoots darker and conical nodding flower panicles, whilst the leaves have axillary tufts. It occurs in southern Japan.

This small tree is rare in cultivation. The common name is taken from the Nepali name for the tree. The above subspecies are better represented in cultivation.

---

p.320 **Veitch's Meliosma** *Meliosma veitchiorum*

Description: Deciduous tree to 15 m (50 ft) with a bole diameter to 50 cm (1.6 ft).
Crown Columnar, and rather open with thick stiff branches. *Bark* Brown, rough, becoming platy. *Shoot* Stout, greenish brown in the first year, with orange raised lenticels, in the second year greyish buff. *Buds* Naked (without bud scales), conical and beaked, green or brown, 1 cm (0.4 in). *Foliage* Leaves pinnate with four or five pairs, which are larger towards the terminal leaflet, to 45 × 25 cm (18 × 10 in) (including 8–10 cm (3.1–4 in) leaf stalk), rachis pinky purple, round or slightly grooved; leaflets ovate to ovate-oblong, tapered to the acute tip, base rounded and somewhat decurrent on the short (3–5 mm (0.1–0.2 in)) stalk (but the terminal leaflet has a stalk to 5 cm (2 in)), margin untoothed, upper surface matt green, lower surface shiny light green with raised veins, leaflets 6–15 × 3–6 cm (2.4–6 × 1.2–2.4 in); autumn colour russets. *Flowers* In late spring in large terminal yellow or creamy white panicles which are up to 50 × 30 cm (20 × 12 in) and contain masses of small (6 mm (0.25 in)) flowers. *Fruit* Globose, violet, 1.5 cm (0.6 in).
Range: Sichuan, western China.
Habitat: Cultivated as an ornamental, in the wild occurring in mixed forests.

This rare tree has majestic bold foliage. The branches are stout, and in winter the tree has a rather gaunt appearance.

MEDLAR, *MESPILUS*
FAMILY ROSACEAE

This contains only the single species. It is allied to *Crataegus* and *Cotoneaster*. It is distinguished by the solitary large flowers which have five carpels and the large fruit with persistent spreading sepals.

---

p.206 **Medlar** *Mespilus germanica*

Description: Deciduous tree or shrub, 5–8 m (16–26 ft) (rarely to 18 m (60 ft)) with a bole diameter to 60 cm (2 ft).
Crown Generally low, with tangled spreading branches. *Bark* Grey-brown, fissuring into oblong scaly plates with lift at the margins. *Shoot* Densely white hairy when young, maturing to brown, often with stiff spines 0.5–2.5 cm (0.2–1 in). *Buds* Rounded. *Foliage* Leaves oval to lanceolate or oblong, apex rounded, abruptly short-pointed, margin untoothed or with minute teeth, upper surface dark yellow-green with impressed veins, somewhat hairy, underside paler with much denser hairs, 5–15 cm (2–6 in); leaf stalk very short. *Flowers* Single on terminal leafy shoots in May or June; flowers white, 2.5–6 cm (1–2.4 in) across; five petals, stamens 30–40, sepals with long triangular points. *Fruit* Obovoid or pear-shaped with the persistent sepals spreading from the dimpled apex; ripening to brown, 2–3 cm (0.8–1.2 in).

Range: Southeast Europe across western Asia to Iran, but naturalized in central Europe.
Habitat: Woodland, as an understorey small tree.
Varieties: Named fruiting clones only.

The fruit is astringent until softened ('bletted') by frost, by which time it has become palatable. The large persistent sepals and the single flowers provide easy clues to its identification, but otherwise it appears similar to many *Crataegus*.

DAWN REDWOOD, *METASEQUOIA*
FAMILY TAXODIACEAE

This contains only the single species. It is a deciduous conifer, most similar in general appearance to *Taxodium*, sharing foliage in two types of shoot. On persistent shoots, the leaves fall in the autumn, but on the more common deciduous shoots, there are no buds and the entire shoot is shed. It is distinguished, however, by the leaves, buds and cone scales being in opposite pairs. The winter shoots are unique in that each bud has a scar both above (from the deciduous shoot) and below (from the subtending leaf).

p.59 **Dawn Redwood**
Metasequoia glyptostroboides

Description: Deciduous tree to 15–30 m (50–100 ft) with a bole diameter to 80 cm (2.6 ft). *Crown* Conical, with old trees perhaps columnar, with ascending branches. *Bark* Orange-brown to red-brown, smooth in young trees but soon shedding thin papery flakes and then fibrous, on the bole the bark fissures with stringy ridges, often fluted. *Shoot* Brown, slender in the first year, becoming red-brown and stout in the second, with paired buds sticking out at right angles and with a scar above the bud from the deciduous shoot and below from the subtending leaf. *Buds* Ovoid, pale brown, 2 mm (0.1 in), on a short stalk, on previous season's shoots and also on older shoots. *Foliage* On flat deciduous shoots which are shed in autumn; leaves spreading widely on either side of the shoot, decurrent at base, linear, apex pointed, soft, blue-green or yellow-green above, paler beneath, 1.5–2.5 cm × 2–3 mm (0.6–1 × 0.1 in); autumn colour from yellow-brown through pink to red-brown. *Flowers* On previous season's shoots in late winter; male cones rare, in pendent panicles to 25 cm (10 in), yellow-brown. *Fruit* Ovoid, pointed, with decussate shield-like scales, green but ripening brown in first autumn, 2 cm (0.8 in), set on a 2–4 cm (0.8–1.6 in) long stalk.

Range: China in southern Hubei and southeast Sichuan.

Habitat: Cultivated in Europe as an ornamental, in the wild occurring in wet sites with broadleaved trees.

This tree was only found in the 1940s and introduced in 1948. It has attractive feathery foliage which assumes good autumn colours and is frequently planted as an ornamental. It tolerates a wide range of sites, quickly attaining 10 m (33 ft) but only maintaining fast growth on wet sites. Male cones are rare, but female cones are often produced after hot summers. These are normally only visible after the leaves have fallen, when they remain as small bobbles dangling for the branches in the upper crown.

BANANA SHRUBS, *MICHELIA*
FAMILY MAGNOLIACEAE

This is a genus of around 45 species from southeast Asia, closely related to *Magnolia*. However, it differs in the flowers being axillary, i.e. carried in the axils of leaves (not at the shoot tips as in *Magnolia*) and in the ovary being stalked. Also all the species are evergreen, whereas in *Magnolia* many are deciduous. They all have strongly fragrant flowers.

p.139 **Michelia** *Michelia doltsopa*

Description: Evergreen tree 8–25 m (26–80 ft) with a bole diameter to 60 cm (2 ft).
Crown Columnar to broad and rounded. *Bark* Grey-brown, smooth, becoming scaly. *Shoots* Shiny green for one to two years, then brown, with circular stipular scars at leaf bases. *Buds* Conical, greyish brown hairy. *Foliage* Leaves elliptic to oblong or oblanceolate, apex acute or slender pointed, base wedge-shaped or rounded, margin untoothed, upper surface dark green with impressed veins, hairless,

underside bluish with raised veins and initially densely hairy, leathery in texture and persisting for one to two years, 10–25 × 3.5–8 cm (4–10 × 1.4–3.1 in); leaf stalk 1.5–3 cm (0.6–1.2 in), with only a short stipular scar of 5–7 mm (0.2–0.3 in). *Flowers* Axillary, produced in spring often freely, white or pale yellow, 7.5–15 cm (3–6 in), with 12–16 oblanceolate tepals, very fragrant. *Fruit* A loose spike 7–12 cm (2.8–4.7 in) with spaced stalked carpels which are 1–1.5 × 0.7–1 cm (0.4–0.6 × 0.3–0.4 in), with one or two seeds.

Range: Eastern Himalayas from central Nepal east through Bhutan, northeast India, southeast Tibet to northern Burma and west Yunnan.

Habitat: Cultivated in mild moist areas as an ornamental, in the wild occurring in warm temperate broadleafed evergreen forest.

Similar species: Several other species of *Michelia* are occasionally cultivated. These include: *M. velutina* (p.139) has narrow lanceolate to elliptic leaves (17–25 × 3–6 cm (6.7–10 × 1.2–2.4 in)) which are slender pointed or long slender pointed at the apex and broad wedge-shaped at the base. The leaves are densely hairy at first above. The upper surface matures to mid sub-glossy green with scattered coarse hairs especially along the midrib. The undersurface is pale green with a light covering of stiff long pale hairs. The leaf stalk is 0.7–2 cm (0.3–0.8 in) in length, with a stipular scar of 3–5 mm (0.1–0.2 in). Both leaf stalks, buds and shoots are densely covered in pale golden brown hairs. The flowers have around 16 oblanceolate tepals, circa 3.5 cm × 7 mm (1.4 × 0.3 in), which are pale yellow but darken with age. The flowers open from August to October, with the fruits ripening to reddish pink in the following autumn. It originates from the warm temperate broadleafed forests of Sikkim, Bhutan and Arunachal Pradesh (India) and southeast Tibet.

M. figo makes a shrubby tree to 6 m (20 ft). This is best distinguished by the very short stalked or stalkless leaves, with a maximum leaf stalk length of 4 mm (0.2 in). The leaves are 3–8 × 2–4 cm (1.2–3.1 ×

0.8–1.6 in). The flowers are also smaller, circa 3 cm (1.2 in) in diameter, with only six creamy white or yellowish tepals, but are wonderfully fragrant. It comes from southeast China.

M. champaca, also from southern China, makes a tree to 10 m (33 ft) and has flowers to 4 cm (1.6 in) in diameter with 12 tepals. This has ovate to lanceolate leaves 10–15 × 3.5–8.5 cm (4–6 × 1.4–3.3 in). It is best distinguished by the leaf stalks, which have stipular scars running along at least half the 1–2.6 cm (0.4–1 in) length and are finely downy.

M. compressa makes a tree to 20 m (65 ft) and is native to southern Japan and the Ryukyu Islands. The leaves range from obovate-oblong to oblanceolate and are leathery, 5–10 × 2–4 cm (2–4 × 0.8–1.6 in), with glaucous undersides. The flowers are 3–4 cm (1.2–1.6 in) across with 12 tepals which are white with purplish bases. The leaf stalks are 2–3 cm (0.8–1.2 in) and without stipular scars. The buds, shoots and young leaves are all covered in brownish hairs.

M. yunnanensis from Yunnan, China, makes a small bushy tree. It has oblanceolate leaves which are shiny above with impressed veins and glaucous beneath, 4–8 × 1.5–3 cm (1.6–3.1 × 0.6–1.2 in). The leaf stalks are 4–5 mm (0.2 in) with a small stipular scar. The small white flowers have six tepals. The slender shoots, buds and new leaves have reddish-brown to golden brown hairs. This species has only recently been introduced but appears to be the hardiest species.

Michelia makes an attractive spring flowering tree for mild areas.

MULBERRY, MORACEAE

This is a large family whose members (except in one genus) have a milky sap. The genera treated here are *Broussonetia* (p.549), *Ficus* (p.706), *Maclura* (p.805) and *Morus* (p.844).

MULBERRIES, *MORUS*
FAMILY MORACEAE

This is a genus of a dozen or so species. It is best known as including the White Mulberry, which is the principal food of the silkworm larvae. The leaves are rather variable in outline on the same tree, ranging from simple and toothed to deeply three or five lobed. The flowers are small and scarcely noticeable. They are followed by the fruit (which in the case of the Black Mulberry is deliciously sweet with a tart taste when purple and ripe), which is a cluster of drupes enclosed in the enlarged sepals.

p.262 **White Mulberry** *Morus alba*

Description: Deciduous tree to 10–15 m (33–50 ft) with a bole diameter to 60 cm (2 ft).
Crown Rounded. *Bark* Grey-green to pinkish brown, rough and dull in young trees, becoming orange-brown in fissures in old trees. *Shoot* Slender, grey, finely hairy at first. *Buds* Ovoid, small. *Foliage* Leaves broad ovate to ovate, slender pointed, apex abruptly pointed or occasionally rounded and sometimes three lobed, base heart-shaped to rounded, margin coarsely toothed, texture thin, upper surface smooth or only slightly rough, glossy green, underside pale shiny green with raised hairy veins, size variable, from 7–20 × 5–12 cm (2.8–8 × 2–4.7 in); leaf stalk grooved, slightly hairy, 1.2–2.5 cm (0.5–1 in); autumn colour poor.
Flowers Small, not showy, in May in the leaf axils. *Fruit* Cluster of closely packed drupes, green, then ripening to white or pink, sweet but insipid, 1.2–2.5 cm (0.5–1 in).

Range: China.

Habitat: Cultivated as an ornamental and to feed silkworms for silk manufacture.

Varieties: 'Macrophylla', a cultivated form with large leaves. 'Pendula', a form with a pendulous habit.

This small tree is the preferred food plant for the silkworm. Otherwise it is inferior to the Black Mulberry (*M. nigra*).

p.262 **Black Mulberry** *Morus nigra*

Description: Deciduous tree to 10 m (33 ft) with a bole diameter to 50 cm (1.6 ft).
Crown Rounded rugged low dome.
Bark Orange-brown, more orange in the fissures, rough and scaly or stringy, often with burrs on the trunk. *Shoot* Stout, stiff, brown to purple grey and persistently hairy. *Buds* Ovoid-conic, stout, pointed, dark shiny purplish red-brown. *Foliage* Leaves broad ovate, apex abruptly pointed, base deeply heart-shaped, margin coarsely toothed and sometimes three lobed, texture thick, upper surface rough to the touch with short stiff hairs, dull green, underside pale green and hairy, especially on the raised veins, 8–12 × 6–8 cm (3.1–4.7 × 2.4–3.1 in) (rarely larger); leaf stalk grooved, stout, hairy, 1.5–2.5 cm (0.6–1 in); autumn colour poor.
Flowers Small, not showy, in May in the leaf axils. *Fruit* Oval cluster of drupes, green in early summer, ripening through purple-red to dark purple-black, juicy with a pleasant slightly acidic flavour, 2–2.5 cm (0.8–1 in).

Range: Uncertain, long cultivated.

Habitat: Cultivated as an ornamental and for the tasty fruit.

This tree has pleasant fruits which can either be eaten raw when ripe (at the risk of staining the fingers purple) or used to flavour apples and other fruits. The leaves have short stiff hairs affording a hard and rough feel and are not relished by the silkworm grub. The choice of this species as food plant was a major factor in the failure of King James I to establish a silk industry in England in the early 17th century. The origin of this tree is uncertain, although believed to be somewhere in the Orient or central Asia. It forms a small tree with a gnarled bole which appears old and venerable. However, stories of trees being as much as a hundred years old (or older) should only be accepted after several large brandies or glasses of malt scotch!

BANANA, MUSACEAE

This family includes two or three genera of
monocotyledons. Only *Musa* is seen in
cultivation. Technically, they are
herbaceous plants, as all growth is made
from the underground rhizome.

BANANA, *MUSA*
FAMILY MUSACEAE

This genus is composed entirely of herbaceous plants, and
grows, as with grasses, from the base. However, the leaf
sheaths form a tight cluster and make a pseudostem. The
leaves are large, with parallel side veins, whilst the fruits
have three carpels (most easily seen in the three longitudinal
segments of a banana). Both these features display its
membership of the monocotyledons.

p.350 **Banana** *Musa cavendishii*

Description: Evergreen plant usually 4–6 m (13–20 ft).
Crown On several stems which grow from
the rhizome. *Bark* Smooth, green,
actually the sheath of the leaves.
Foliage Leaves enormous, 1.2–2 m ×
40–60 cm (4–6.6 × 1.3–2 ft), oblong, apex
bluntly pointed to pointed, margin
untoothed but the many parallel veins
separate out when exposed to wind, giving
a tatty appearance, glaucous green with a
waxy bloom. *Flowers* Inflorescence
pendent spike to 1 m (3.3 ft), with white,
cream or yellow flowers and pinkish purple
bracts. *Fruit* Oblong fleshy fruit with
three segments, ripening yellow or yellow
and brown, 12–18 cm (4.7–7.1 in).

Range: Southeast Asia to northern Australia.

Habitat: Cultivated as an ornamental and for food.

Synonyms: *M. zebrina*.

Similar species: *M. basjoo* is a related species from the
Ryukyu Islands of Japan. It differs in the
leaves and false stems being green and
without a waxy bloom.

The banana is a familiar fruit, obtained
from sterile plants which will set fruits

without fertilization. It is not a woody plant, but a herb, growing from a rhizome. The false stems are soft and pithy. They flower and fruit once and then die, but are replaced by others from the rhizome.

MYOPORUM, MYOPORACEAE

This is a small family. *Myoporum* is the only tree genus and is cultivated in parts of southwestern Europe.

MYOPORUM, *MYOPORUM*
FAMILY MYOPORACEAE

This genus is from southeast Asia south through Australia to New Zealand and across the Pacific to Hawaii. Only the one species is cultivated in southwestern Europe.

p.133 **Myoporum** *Myoporum tenuifolium*

Description: Evergreen tree or shrub to 8 m (26 ft). *Crown* Rounded. *Bark* Grey-brown, finely fissuring. *Shoot* Green. *Foliage* Leaves oblanceolate to lanceolate, apex pointed, base wedge-shaped, margin untoothed or sometimes with a few teeth, upper surface glossy green with many translucent glands, hairless, 5–10(–17 cm) (2–4(–6.7 in)) by up to 5 cm (2 in); leaf stalk 0.5–1 cm (0.2–0.4 in). *Flowers* In axillary cymes of five to nine flowers, but occasionally single; flowers white with purple spotting and bell-shaped, with four stamens. *Fruit* Globose to ovoid slightly fleshy drupe which ripens purple, 7–9 mm (0.3–0.4 in).

Range: Australia and New Caledonia.

Habitat: Cultivated as an ornamental in the Iberian Peninsula.

This is a variable small tree. It has been used to give shelter in parts of Spain, Portugal and the Balearic Islands, and has become naturalized in places.

Bog Myrtle, Myricaceae

This is a rather uninteresting family of only three genera, with only one species (*Myrica faya*) making a small tree.

Bog Myrtles, *Myrica*
Family Myricaceae

This is a genus of around 50 species which usually have nitrogen-fixing bacteria. Nearly all are shrubs and only *M. faya* is described here.

p.152 Canary Islands Myrtle *Myrica faya*

Description: Evergreen shrub or small tree to 8 m (26 ft).
Crown Rounded, often shrubby.
Shoot Reddish brown due to a covering of small peltate hairs. *Foliage* Leaves oblanceolate, apex acute to bluntly pointed, base wedge-shaped, margin rolled down, untoothed, hairless, 4–11 cm (1.6–4.3 in).
Flowers Dioecious, axillary on the leafy part of the shoots, catkins branched.
Fruit Slightly fleshy drupe.

Range: Azores, Madeira, Canary Islands, also possibly native (otherwise naturalized) in central and southern Portugal.

Habitat: Dry broadleaved forest.

This is a shrubby tree from the Atlantic Islands but naturalized (or possibly) native in Portugal. It is related to the Bog Myrtle or Sweet Gale, *M. gale*, which has toothed leaves which have fragrant glands. This forms a shrub 1–2.5 m (3.3–8 ft) and is widely distributed.

Myrtle, Myrtaceae

This is a large family. It divides into two groupings, those genera in which the fruit is dehiscent, such as the capsule of *Eucalyptus* (p.678), and those in which the fruit is not dehiscent but usually fleshy, as in the berry of *Myrtus*. These two genera are the only ones featured here.

MYRTLES, *MYRTUS* (SYNONYM: *LUMA*)
FAMILY MYRTACEAE

This is a small genus of evergreen trees and shrubs. The leaves are opposite, untoothed and with fragrant glands. The flowers are produced in the leaf axils of the current season's shoots and are white, fragrant, with a mass of stamens. The fruit is berry-like, with a persistent calyx. The genus is sometimes split into several genera, with *M. luma* being the type of the genus *Luma* (in which genus the name is *Luma apiculata*, as botanical nomenclature does not allow tautology in naming, i.e. *Luma luma*).

p.146 **Myrtle** *Myrtus communis*

Description: Evergreen shrub or small shrubby tree to 4–5 m (13–16 ft).
Crown Conic, rounded in old age.
Bark Smooth, brown. *Shoot* Orange-brown, ridged, hairy, becoming more coppery in the second year and then peeling lightly, slender. *Buds* In opposite pairs, ovoid, pointed, grey woolly, 1 mm (0.1 in). *Foliage* Leaves ovate to lanceolate, tapering evenly to a long slender bristle tip, base rounded to broad wedge-shaped, margin untoothed, upper surface sub-shiny mid green, convex with a dimpled main vein, underside light shiny green with a raised midrib, more or less hairless but covered on both sides with transparent glands, fragrant when crushed, 3–4 × 1.2–2 cm (1.2–1.6 × 0.5–0.8 in); leaf stalk grooved, 2 mm (0.1 in); leaves fall yellow.
Flowers Globose in bud with pure white petals and contrasting triangular calyx lobes, opening to 2–3 cm (0.8–1.2 in) across with obovate petals 1 cm (0.4 in), massed stamens which have slender silky white long filaments and small yellow or brown anthers and a single persistent style, set singly on a slender green 2 cm (0.8 in) stalk in the axils of the current

season's growths. *Fruit* Rounded to oblong purple-black (rarely white or yellow) berry 1.2 cm (0.5 in), fleshy and containing many small seeds.

Range: Throughout the Mediterranean region, possibly not native but an early introduction from Turkey or Iran.

Habitat: Maqui, or scrub.

Varieties: Var. *leucocarpa* covers the forms with white berries.

This shrubby tree has long been associated with the goddess of love and is often used in wedding bouquets, especially for the pleasant fragrance of the flowers and leaves.

p.146 **Orange-bark Myrtle** *Myrtus luma*

Description: Evergreen tree 5–15 m (16–50 ft) with a slender bole up to 40 cm (1.3 ft) in diameter.
Crown Conic or columnar, slender on trees but broader when on several stems.
Bark Orange or cinnamon coloured, flaking, developing white streaks in old trees. *Shoot* Slender, reddish brown with curved pale hairs in the first year, becoming stout, generally hairless and ash-grey in later years. *Buds* In opposite pairs, conic, small, dark red or green, hairy, 1–2 mm (0.1 in). *Foliage* Leaves dense on the shoot and often curved up, simple, broad elliptic, tapering to a short apiculate sharp-pointed apex and a wedge-shaped or rounded base, upper surface dark shiny to sub-shiny green, hairless with scattered glands and an indented midrib, underside shiny light green with a raised hairy midrib, ciliate margins and scattered glands, 2–3 × 1–2 cm (0.8–1.2 × 0.4–0.8 in); leaf stalk grooved, pink, hairy, 2 mm (0.1 in); leaves kept two to three years. *Flowers* At the tips of the current season's shoots in late August to September, single (rarely double) in the leaf axils but clustered into pseudowhorls, stalks slender, circa 1 cm (0.4 in) with a smaller leaf at the base and two small

quickly deciduous bracts at the base of the ovary, flower in bud globose, opening to cup-shaped with four white or pink tinged cup shaped petals to 1 cm (0.4 in), calyx lobes ovate, four, green, stamens many, convoluted, stigma single, purplish pink. *Fruit* Globose, fleshy, three celled, dark purple, 1 cm (0.4 in).

Range: Chile and Argentina.

Habitat: Cultivated as an ornamental, in the wild occurring in temperate rain forests in central Chile and adjoining regions of The Argentine.

Synonyms: *Luma apiculata.*

This tree is spectacular with its bright orange or cinnamon-coloured bark which has a soft almost velvety feel when newly flaked. Unfortunately, it is only suitable for the milder parts of the country.

SOUTHERN BEECHES, *NOTHOFAGUS*
FAMILY FAGACEAE

The southern beeches are a genus of around 40 species from southern South America, Tasmania and eastern Australia, New Zealand, New Caledonia and New Guinea. They have fruits and nuts which are superficially very similar to *Fagus*. However, closer examination shows that there are three fruits in the *Nothofagus* cupules (except one species which has seven). Thus, whilst the end two nuts are triangular, as is a beech nut, the central one is flat. The cupule is much smaller, and less prickly than that of beech. The male flowers are solitary, or in threes, as opposed to the pendent globose heads of *Fagus*. The leaves are variable. Seven species are deciduous, and have leaves not dissimilar to *Fagus*, with distinct veins and a thin texture. Of this group, three are fully described and easily separated on the number of veins, with 3–5 pairs in *N. antarctica*, around 9 pairs in *N. obliqua* and 15–18 pairs in *N. nervosa*. The other 30 odd species in the genus are evergreen, with much smaller leaves, which are thick and leathery, and with few rather indistinct veins. Illustrated in this group are *N. betuloides* (teeth rounded), *N. dombeyi* (teeth serrate), *N. fusca* (teeth rounded scalloped), *N. menziesii* (teeth rounded) and *N. solandri* (margin untoothed). The scientific name means 'false beech'. The species are planted both as forest trees and for amenity.

p.241 **Antarctic Beech** *Nothofagus antarctica*

Description: Deciduous tree 10–15 m (33–50 ft) with a bole diameter to 40 cm (1.3 ft).
Crown Irregular, narrow upright or spreading tree, sometimes shrubby.
Bark Smooth and chocolate brown at first, becoming cracked at the base with pale brown fissures. *Shoot* Greenish grey with white hairs and buff oval lenticels in young shoots, becoming brown in the second year, slender. *Buds* Ovoid or globose, reddish brown, resinous, 5–6 mm (0.2–0.25 in).
Foliage Leaves oblong-ovate to deltoid, rounded or bluntly triangular at the apex, base rounded and then decurrent along the leaf stalk, margin toothed with the veins ending in triangular teeth and with four small rounded or triangular teeth between each vein end, upper surface shiny green, hairless or lightly hairy, underside light green, sub-shiny with three to five pairs of raised spaced veins, variably hairy, often balsam scented when young, 2–4.5 × 1.5–2.2 cm (0.8–1.8 × 0.6–0.9 in); leaf stalk grooved with decurrent leaf base, green, 5–7 mm (0.2–0.3 in); autumn colour yellow. *Flowers* In leaf axils of current season's growths in late spring.
Fruit Ovoid spreading or erect stalkless cupule to 7 × 7 mm (0.3 × 0.3 in) and rather four sided, with each segment having three or four large rounded scales with ciliate margins set one above another, green, ripening to brown, opening into four segments; seeds three, two triangular with a flattened central seed, light brown, 5 × 6 mm (0.2 × 0.25 in).

Range: Chile and adjacent Argentina from 36 degrees south to Tierra del Fuego.

Habitat: Cultivated as an ornamental, in the wild forming extensive subalpine forests.

Varieties: Var. *uliginosa* has the leaves hairy on both sides.

Synonyms: *Fagus antarctica*.

Similar species: *N. pumilio* occurs in the wild with *N. antarctica* and is a similar small tree. The most useful distinguishing character is that the five or six pairs of veins run out to an acute sinus in the leaf margin and that there are only two rounded teeth between each sinus.

This small tree is one of the hardiest of the southern beeches. The leaves are usually balsam scented, although not all people appear to be able to detect the scent.

p.242 **Coigüe de Magallanes**
Nothofagus betuloides

Description: Evergreen tree 15–20 m (50–65 ft) with a bole diameter to 80 cm (2.6 ft).
Crown Columnar with a conic apex, becoming rounded. *Bark* Smooth, grey-brown, developing horizontal oblong scales. *Shoot* Green, finely hairy and slender, shiny and sticky with resin, becoming dark green and shiny in the second year, then green-grey or shiny brown. *Buds* Ovoid-conic, flattened, green with a light orange-brown tip, shiny, 2 mm (0.1 in). *Foliage* Leaves ovate but often oblique and rather dense on the shoot, with a triangular apex, base rounded or wedge-shaped, margin with small rounded teeth, upper surface shiny dark green with a raised purplish midrib, underside light green except for the midrib, smooth, persisting for two years, 1.5–2.5 × 1–2 cm (0.6–1 × 0.4–0.8 in); leaf stalk grooved, hairless, 3 mm (0.1 in), with the chestnut brown ovate-lanceolate stipules persisting on either side of the leaf, to 4 mm (0.2 in); autumn colour dark green, turning yellow when falling. *Flowers* Male flowers pendent with bright red anthers. *Fruit* Ovate, with four valves, scales short and tooth-like.
Range: Chile and western Argentina from 40 degrees south down to Tierra del Fuego.
Habitat: Cultivated as an ornamental, in the wild forming pure stands on moist hillsides.
Synonyms: *Fagus betuloides*.

This tree is similar to *N. dombeyi* but has smaller and more densely set leaves which have blunt teeth.

p.242 **Coigüe** *Nothofagus dombeyi*

Description: Evergreen tree 15–25 m (50–80 ft) with a
bole diameter to 2 m (6.6 ft).
Crown Ovoid in young trees with ascending
branches and pendent shoot tips, becoming
broad conic and eventually domed in old
trees. *Bark* Blackish grey, smooth but
wrinkled in young trees, developing shallow
fissures which gradually produce peeling
strips or plates which reveal orange or red
beneath. *Shoot* Slender, green and brown
with brown lenticels and downy in first
winter, later pale or dark brown.
Buds Ovoid, green-brown, 1 mm (0.1 in).
Foliage In rather flat dense sprays; leaves
varying from oval to lanceolate, apex acute,
base wedge-shaped, margin irregularly and
somewhat doubly saw-toothed with small
forward teeth, sinuses acute, upper surface
dark sub-shiny green, underside light,
somewhat glaucous green, midrib
prominent on both sides, minutely downy
beneath, tertiary veins net-like, 2–4 ×
1–2.3 cm (0.8–1.6 × 0.4–0.9 in); leaf stalk
pale green, very finely downy. *Flowers* On
previous season's shoots; male flowers in
pendent catkins, mainly in threes, with dark
red stamens. *Fruit* Cupule four lobed, with
short tooth-like projections, 1–1.2 cm
(0.4–0.5 in), containing three seeds.
Range: Chile and adjoining western Argentina.
Habitat: Cultivated in Europe as an ornamental, in
the wild occurring in moist forests, often
with *N. obliqua* and *N. nervosa*.
Synonyms: *Fagus dombeyi*.

This makes a bold evergreen tree but can be
difficult to establish when young. The main
problem is that it appears incapable of
shedding surplus leaves as a response to
drought (following transplanting).

p.241 **Red Beech** *Nothofagus fusca*

Description: Evergreen tree 15–25 m (50–80 ft) with a
bole diameter to 1.5 m (5 ft).
Crown Slender columnar in young trees,

becoming domed in old ones. *Bark* Dark grey, smooth but later fissured and finely scaly. *Shoot* Slender, zig-zagged, purple with buff lenticels and downy in first winter, later more brown. *Buds* Long ovoid-conic, pointed, shiny brown, 2–3 mm (0.1 in). *Foliage* Sparse and spaced along the shoot, remaining on the tree over winter as a mixture of yellow, red and green; leaves ovate, base wedge-shaped, margin coarsely toothed with four to six pairs of scalloped forward-pointed teeth with rounded sinuses in which there is a very small tuft of hairs, and with occasional extra teeth, yellow-green or deep green, matt above, shiny beneath, midrib prominent on both surfaces, 2–4 × 1.5–3 cm (0.8–1.6 × 0.6–1.2 in); leaf stalk grooved, downy, 4–5 mm (0.2 in). *Fruit* Cupule four lobed, 1–1.2 cm (0.4–0.5 in), containing three seeds.

Range: New Zealand, from both North and South Isles.

Habitat: Cultivated in Europe as an ornamental, in the wild occurring in moist forests.

Synonyms: *Fagus fusca.*

This evergreen tree has a remarkably sparse and open crown with spaced foliage. It looks as if it should be tender, but has proved hardy north to Edinburgh.

p.243 **Silver Beech** or **Menzies Beech**
Nothofagus menziesii

Description: Evergreen tree to 20 m (65 ft) with a bole diameter to 70 cm (2.3 ft).
Crown Conic or bushed conic, broad, usually with many stems, narrow conic as a young tree. *Bark* Silvery white to purple-brown in young trees with thick bands of horizontal lenticels, may become shiny red-brown. *Shoot* Slender, densely hairy and brown in the first year, becoming grey-brown in the second year then shiny chocolate brown in the third, with few hairs remaining and rounded pale buff lenticels, slightly zig-zagged. *Buds* Conic, pink with whitish

hairs on the tips, 2 mm (0.1 in). *Foliage* In dense frondose sprays; leaves broad ovate to nearly rounded in outline with an acute apex and a rounded base, margin with rounded often paired teeth, upper surface shiny deep green, smooth and hairless except for hairs on the veins and some on the margin, cupped, underside light green, smooth and hairless except for a few hairs at the base and in two small deep pits at the base of the main lateral pair of veins, 0.6–1.5 × 0.5–1.5 cm (0.25–0.6 × 0.2–0.6 in); leaf stalk grooved, hairy, 2 mm (0.1 in); persisting into the second year. *Flowers* On current season's growths in late spring, male flowers at base of shoot in pendent clusters of anthers, female flowers towards the tip of the shoot, green. *Fruit* Ovoid, green, ripening brown, with swollen glands, 1 cm (0.4 in), containing three seeds.

Range: New Zealand from southern North Island and from South Island.

Habitat: Cultivated as an ornamental, in the wild occurring in woods and on mountain slopes where it may be restricted to a small shrub.

Synonyms: *Fagus menziesii*.

Similar species: **Cunningham Beech** or **Myrtle Beech** *N. cunninghamii* (p.243) is closely allied and is native to Tasmania. It differs most markedly in the absence of the pits on the leaf underside. The leaves are deltoid to ovate with a truncate base and more pointed apex. The teeth are more triangular and ciliate. The buds are shiny green ovate but blunt. The shoot is paler, brown and not shiny. The fruit is only 6–8 mm (0.25–0.3 in).

This tree has small evergreen leaves which have a pair of small pits filled with hairs on the lower part of the blade.

---

p.240 **Rauli** *Nothofagus nervosa*

Description: Deciduous tree 20–25 m (65–80 ft) with a bole diameter to 1 m (3.3 ft).
Crown Conic with whorled branching when young, becoming broadly conical

with ascending upper branches and pendulous lower ones in old trees.
Bark Grey-green and strongly marked by lenticels, in old trees dull greenish grey with broad dark fissures. *Shoot* Green and densely hairy at first with oval orange lenticels, hairless, smooth and shiny green-brown or dark brown in the second year with pale lenticels, rather slender.
Buds Narrow conical, pointed, four angled, bright red-brown or chestnut-brown, 1 cm (0.4 in). *Foliage* Leaves ovate-lanceolate or oblong-ovate, acute or rounded at the apex, base rounded, margins finely toothed with small triangular serrations and ciliate, upper surface matt green and corrugated with 15–18 pairs of impressed veins, underside light shiny green, pilose on the raised and parallel veins, 4–8 × 2–4 cm (1.6–3.1 × 0.8–1.6 in); leaf stalk grooved, with long pilose white hairs, purplish, 0.5–1 cm (0.2–0.4 in); autumn colour gold or crimson. *Flowers* Male flowers in pendent globular heads, 1 cm (0.4 in).
Fruit Ovoid, 1 cm (0.4 in), with four segments which are covered with filigree green scales; seeds three, one flattened and two triangular.

Range: Central Chile and adjoining regions of The Argentine.

Habitat: Cultivated as an ornamental and in commercial forestry, in the wild forming forests, either pure or with *N. obliqua*.

Synonyms: *N. procera*.

Similar species: *N.* × *alpina* is the hybrid between *N. nervosa* and *N. obliqua*, being largely intermediate in its characters such as vein number. It occurs with the parents in Chile and also is raised where seed is collected from mixed plantings of the parent species in cultivation.

This tree has a very high-quality timber which is similar in its properties to Beech (with the common name being the Spanish for Beech). It is very fast growing in cultivation but can be damaged by severe winters and unseasonable frosts, which cause bark lesions. The leaves with their

massed deeply impressed veins are
attractive.

---

p.240 **Roble Beech** *Nothofagus obliqua*

Description: Deciduous tree 20–30 m (65–100 ft) with a
bole diameter to 1 m (3.3 ft).
Crown Conical and slender in young trees,
becoming rather columnar with a domed
top and pendent outer branches in old trees,
occasionally irregular. *Bark* Smooth, grey-
brown at first but becoming shaggy as it
develops large scaly plates with wide buff
fissures in older trees. *Shoot* Greenish grey
with white hairs and pale oval lenticels in
young shoots, becoming grey-brown or
chocolate brown and sub-shiny in the
second year, slender. *Buds* Ovoid, light
brown, 5 mm (0.2 in). *Foliage* Leaves
oblong-ovate, rounded at both ends,
margin with six to nine lobulate projections
each with three or four small rounded or
triangular teeth and ciliate, upper surface
matt dark green and corrugated, with
sparse white hairs, underside glaucous pale
green with raised hairy veins, 4–8 ×
2–2.5 cm (1.6–3.1 × 0.8–1 in); leaf stalk
round, hairy, green, 3–7 mm (0.1–0.3 in);
autumn colour yellow and red. *Flowers* In
leaf axils of current season's growths in late
spring. *Fruit* Ovoid spreading or erect
cupule to 8 × 5 mm (0.3 × 0.2 in), with
erect oblong hairy scales, green, ripening to
brown, opening into four segments; seeds
three, two triangular with a flattened
central seed, pale brown, 7 mm (0.3 in).

Range: Central and southern Chile and adjacent
Argentina.

Habitat: Cultivated as an ornamental and in forestry,
in the wild forming extensive forests.

Roble is the Chilean name and means 'oak'
in Spanish, referring to the hard durable
timber. In cultivation this tree is hardy and
fast growing, thriving as far north as
Aberdeen in Scotland, and withstanding
drier and colder conditions than *N. nervosa*.
It quickly forms an attractive tree.

p.243 **Mountain Beech** *Nothofagus solandri* var. *cliffortioides*

Description: Evergreen tree 15–20 m (50–65 ft) with a bole diameter to 80 cm (2.6 ft).
Crown Conic, becoming rounded.
Bark Smooth green-brown with orange fissures, becoming scaly at the base.
Shoot Slender, grey-brown, hairy in the first year, becoming dark brown but the surface peeling to show green beneath.
Buds Oblong-conic, scales red-brown, 4 × 1 mm (0.2 × 0.1 in). *Foliage* Leaves oval to ovate, apex rounded to acute, base rounded, margin untoothed, upper surface cupped down at the sides but up at the tip, dull shiny green, rough under a hand-lens, underside whitish or glaucous green, covered with a close dense whitish down but even under a hand-lens appearing hairless with indistinct veins, persisting two to three years, 1.2–1.5 cm × 7–9 mm (0.5–0.6 × 0.3–0.4 in); leaf stalk grooved, white pilose, dark brown, 2 mm (0.1 in); autumn colour green, yellow when leaves eventually fall. *Flowers* Male flowers with red anthers, single or in threes. *Fruit* Ovate, 5–6 mm (0.2–0.25 in), with three valves which are much shorter than the seeds, scales ovoid, green with a purple-brown margin.

Range: New Zealand, from both North and South Islands.

Habitat: Cultivated as an ornamental, in the wild occurring in mountain forests.

Varieties: Typical var. *solandri* occurs at lower altitudes than the var. *cliffortioides* and has flat leaves which are more oval and blunt at the apex.

Synonyms: *Fagus cliffortioides*, *N. cliffortioides*.

This tree is the only *Nothofagus* which has entire leaves.

TUPELO, NYSSACEAE

This family contains two genera, *Nyssa* (p.860) and *Camptotheca*, from southern North America and eastern Asia. Only

Nyssa is commonly cultivated. *Davidia* (p.661) is often placed here but seems better treated as a monotypic family.

TUPELO, *NYSSA*
FAMILY NYSSACEAE

This is a genus of five species, three from eastern and southeastern USA, one in central and southern China and the other from southeast Asia. The leaves are generally untoothed and oval to obovate, colouring well in the autumn. The flowers are in axillary heads near the tips of the current season's growths and are on long stalks. They are either unisexual, or mainly male with a few female flowers and easily overlooked. The fruit is a single-seeded drupe, with usually two or four together on a long stalk.

p.219   **Chinese Tupelo** *Nyssa sinensis*

Description: Deciduous tree 10–15 m (33–50 ft) with a bole diameter to 40 cm (1.3 ft).
Crown Rounded, often on several stems and rather shrubby. *Bark* Smooth, grey-brown, becoming fissured at the base. *Shoot* Rich brown to yellow-brown in the first year and hairless with sparse lenticels, later brown to grey-brown. *Buds* Narrow ovoid, pink and green with hairy tips to the scales, to 5 mm (0.2 in).
Foliage Leaves elliptic to broad elliptic or slightly obovate, tapering to an acute or slight slender-pointed apex, base wedge-shaped to broad wedge-shaped or slightly rounded, margin untoothed, upper surface sub-shiny green with impressed pinkish veins, hairless, underside light shiny green with raised veins, 10–17 × 3–7 cm (4–6.7 × 1.2–2.8 in); leaf stalk faintly grooved, hairless, pink and yellow-green, 1.5–2 cm (0.6–0.8 in); autumn colour brilliant shades of red; new growths strongly reddish purple. *Fruit* Oblong berry 1.2 cm (0.5 in) long, ripening to blue-black.
Range: Central China.
Habitat: Cultivated as an ornamental, in the wild occurring in mixed forests.

This tree is less common than *Tupelo* in cultivation and does not grow as tall. In terms of autumnal beauty, however, it is even better.

p.219 **Tupelo** or **Black Gum** *Nyssa sylvatica*

Description: Deciduous tree 15–25 m (50–80 ft) with a bole diameter to 80 cm (2.6 ft).
Crown Conical to columnar with level or gently down-turned branches. *Bark* Grey or dark grey to brown, coarsely fissured into rectangular plates with irregular ridges, thick. *Shoot* Green at first but maturing to pale brown, hairless, in later years grey to dark brown. *Buds* Ovoid, tapering to a sharp pointed apex, with green and brown scales, to 7 mm (0.3 in). *Foliage* Leaves variable in shape, mainly elliptic to oblanceolate, apex acute to bluntly pointed, base wedge-shaped, margin untoothed or rarely with a few weak teeth, upper surface shiny mid green, usually hairless, smooth with rather indistinct lateral veins, underside pale green, midrib raised, 5–13 × 2.5–7.5 cm (2–5.1 × 1–3 in); leaf stalk grooved, pink, hairy, 1–1.5 cm (0.4–0.6 in); autumn colour scarlet, gold and deep bright red. *Flowers* Greenish, not showy, carried on long stalks in the leaf axils of the new foliage; with separate male and female trees. *Fruit* Elliptic berry 1–1.2 cm (0.4–0.5 in) long which ripens from green to blue-black, usually in pairs on a common stalk.
Range: Eastern USA from Maine south to Florida and across to Michigan and Texas, also occurring in Canada in southern Ontario and in northeast Mexico.
Habitat: Cultivated as an ornamental, in the wild occurring in moist sites in both broadleaved and pine forests.

This tree has spectacular autumn colour, creating a strong display as the glossy leaves change through scarlet and gold to bright deep red.

OLIVE, OLEACEAE

This family contains two dozen genera and around 900 species. Most have the leaves set in opposite pairs, although in *Jasminum* they may be helically set. Both simple and pinnate leaves are found. The fruit is a capsule (*Syringa*, p.1192), samara (*Fraxinus*, p.710), berry (*Jasminum*, p.748) or drupe (*Olea*, *Phillyrea*, p.877) in the genera listed here

OLIVE, *OLEA*
FAMILY OLEACEAE

This genus consists of around twenty species from the tropics and warm temperate regions of the Old World. The Common Olive, however, is the only one which is likely to be encountered, either gastronomically or in the flesh. The leaves are simple, evergreen, and in opposite pairs on hairy shoots. The flowers are white and carried in axillary decussately arranged panicles. The fruit is an ovoid to spherical drupe which ripens from green to black or dark blue.

p.147   **Olive** *Olea europaea*

Description: Evergreen tree to 15 m (50 ft) with a bole diameter to 1 m (3.3 ft) or more.
Crown Rounded, often spreading, on a short bole. *Bark* Silvery grey, becoming finely fissured, often fluted or with crossing ridges which create dark hollows.
Shoot Silvery grey due to a dense covering of scales, round in section or four-angled, becoming brown later. *Buds* In opposite pairs, small. *Foliage* Leaves lanceolate to narrow obovate, apex shortly pointed, base wedge-shaped, margin untoothed, leathery in texture, grey-green above, whitish and densely scaly beneath, 2–8 × 0.8–2 cm (0.8–3.1 × 0.3–0.8 in); leaf stalk short.
Flowers In many flowered axillary panicles on the current season's growths in July-August, fragrant, with four sepals and petals. *Fruit* Ovoid to globose drupe, ripening over 12 or more months from green to black or brown (rarely white), with an oily flesh, 1–3.5 cm (0.4–1.4 in).

Range: Widely cultivated throughout the
Mediterranean region, probably only truly
native to the east of the region, down into
Saudi Arabia.

Habitat: Open hillsides.

Varieties: Var. *sylvestris* is the wild form. It has much
smaller oval leaves and more pronouncedly
four-angled shoots which are spiny. It forms
a low spreading bush, especially on dry
rocky sites.

This is the olive used to make oil and
flavour cocktails or adorn pizzas. It is a
characteristic tree of the Mediterranean
region, giving a greyish tint to hillsides.

DAISY BUSHES, *OLEARIA*
FAMILY COMPOSITAE

This is a large genus from New Guinea, Australia and New
Zealand. Most of the 130 species are shrubs but a few are trees.
The species listed here is a small tree or large shrub, which is
grown in the warmer and wetter parts of western Europe.

p.166 Akiraho *Olearia paniculata*

Description: Evergreen small tree to 6–8 m (20–26 ft),
or a shrub.
Crown Ovoid. *Bark* Furrowed, grey-
brown and slightly lifting. *Shoot* Grey-
brown, hairy, angled. *Buds* Conic, narrow.
Foliage Leaves elliptic to ovate-oblong,
apex bluntly pointed, base broad wedge-
shaped to slightly heart-shaped, margin
untoothed, either flat or wavy, leathery,
upper surface shiny green and hairless,
underside with a thin layer of white to buff
hairs pressed against the shoot, 3–10 ×
2–4 cm (1.2–4 × 0.8–1.6 in); leaf stalk
grey-brown hairy, 5 mm (0.2 in).
Flowers In small branched axillary panicles
from October to November; flowers dull
white, sweetly fragrant. *Fruit* Seed like
that of a daisy or dandelion.

Range: New Zealand, from both North and South
Islands.

Habitat: Cultivated as an ornamental.

Synonyms: *O. forsteri.*

This makes a small tree in milder regions, with sweetly scented flowers in late autumn.

PRICKLY PEARS, *OPUNTIA*
FAMILY CACTACEAE

This is a large genus of cacti, in which the stems are in large segments covered with stout spines. Photosynthesis is carried out by the green parts of the stems. Most are shrubs, with a few running horizontally along the ground.

p.346 **Prickly Pear** *Opuntia ficus-indica*

Description: Evergreen sprawling shrub to 5 m (16 ft). *Crown* Rounded. *Bark* Brown, green for several years and spiny. *Shoot* Oval to oblong broad flat leaf-like stalks to the leaves which are in jointed sections of 20–50 cm (8–20 in) and covered with single or paired pale barbed spines to 5 cm (2 in). *Buds* Minute, in the small rounded knobs on the stem and margin.
Foliage Absent, represented by the jointed stem sections. *Flowers* Bright yellow with many petals and stamens, 7–10 cm (2.8–4 in), carried around the periphery of the jointed stem sections. *Fruit* Ovoid, ripening yellow, red or purple with a sweet flesh, 5–9 cm (2–3.5 in), covered in small spines.

Range: America.

Habitat: Cultivated as an ornamental and naturalized, used for hedging and for its fruit.

Similar species: *O. maxima* has the stem sections dull green with clusters of one to four pale or white 3 cm (1.2 in) spines.
O. monacantha has the stem sections bright green, with the yellow to dark reddish brown spines single or in pairs, to 4 cm (1.6 in).

This cactus makes a stock-proof fence, as well as providing tasty, if potentially prickly fruits.

Hop Hornbeams, *Ostrya*
Family Betulaceae (Synonym: Carpinaceae)

This is a genus of eight to ten species but only one species is native to Europe and common in cultivation. The leaves are like some *Carpinus* in having many pairs of parallel veins. The two main differences between *Carpinus* and *Ostrya* are that the male catkins of *Ostrya* are exposed over the winter period in an unexpanded state, whereas in *Carpinus* they are enclosed in buds, and the fruit is wholly enclosed in a bladder. This is a stage further than the section of *Carpinus* (*see CC. japonica* and *cordata*) which has the fruit hidden in folds of the bract but not sealed.

---

p.189 **Hop Hornbeam** *Ostrya carpinifolia*

Description: Deciduous tree 15–20 m (50–65 ft) with a bole diameter to 60 cm (2 ft).
Crown Broad conical, usually with a pointed apex but rounded in old trees.
Bark Smooth, grey-green, becoming fissured into coarse scaly or platy ridges which reveal orange-brown when they flake off. *Shoot* Green and sparsely pilose with light-brown oval lenticels when young, in the second year brown, later somewhat chocolate brown and shiny, slender.
Buds Conical or ovoid, green and shiny, 4 mm (0.2 in). *Foliage* Leaves elliptic or ovate, apex acute and short slender pointed, base rounded or subcordate, margin regularly but somewhat doubly serrate with acute or abruptly short-pointed teeth, upper surface matt green, underside light green, hairless except for pale hairs along the midrib and the 12–15 pairs of raised veins, 6–12 × 3–6 cm (2.4–4.7 × 1.2–2.4 in); stipules linear, not leafy and soon lost; leaf stalk shallowly grooved with light-coloured hairs, around 1 cm (0.4 in); autumn colour yellow. *Flowers* Male catkins exposed over winter, formed in mid summer in clusters of about three and opening in spring to 7 cm (2.8 in); female catkins terminating short leafy shoots, female flowers in pairs along the rachis. *Fruit* In pendent clusters from mid-summer when they are pale green or whitish, ripening brown in autumn,

containing 15–20 bladder-like fruits in a tight catkin, 4–5 × 2–2.5 cm (1.6–2 × 0.8–1 in), on a floppy hairy stalk 1.5 cm (0.6 in); individual fruit ovoid, sparsely hairy, 1.5–2 × 0.8–1 cm (0.6–0.8 × 0.3–0.4 in), containing a single ovoid-slender-pointed smooth flattened nutlet 6 × 3 mm (0.25 × 0.1 in).

Range: Southern Europe from southeast France across Asia Minor to the Caucasus.

Habitat: Woodlands.

Synonyms: *Carpinus ostrya* in part.

Similar species: **Ironwood** *0. virginiana* from the eastern states of the USA is similar but differs in the young shoots having glandular tipped hairs (in *C. carpinifolia* they are not glandular) and larger nutlets to 8 mm (0.3 in). On dry sites in cultivation, it tends to assume autumn colours rather early, often in late summer in Britain, and rarely makes such a large tree.

This tree has neatly cut foliage whilst the catkins provide a display from spring through till autumn. It is similar to *Carpinus*, differing in the seeds being fully enclosed in a bladder-like fruit (which mirrors that of the hop) and the male catkins being exposed over winter (as in the birches). The timber is similar to hornbeam.

SORREL TREE, *OXYDENDRUM*
FAMILY ERICACEAE

This genus contains only one species.

---

p.197 **Sorrel Tree** *Oxydendrum arboreum*

Description: Deciduous tree to 18 m (60 ft) with a slender bole of diameter to 50 cm (1.6 in), sometimes shrubby.
Crown Columnar, becoming broader at the domed top. *Bark* Brown or grey, initially with buff-orange fissuring, later developing narrow scaly ridges. *Shoot* Red-brown or purplish above and yellow-green beneath, hairless. *Buds* Narrow conic, yellow-green,

hairless, to 3 mm (0.1 in). *Foliage* Leaves elliptic to oblong-lanceolate, apex slender pointed, base wedge-shaped, margin with very finely serrate teeth or untoothed, shiny yellow-green to deep green above, paler beneath and slightly hairy (and sometimes bristly) on the veins, 10–20 × 4–9 cm (4–8 × 1.6–3.5 in); leaf stalk pinkish, 1.2–2.5 cm (0.5–1 in); sour to the taste; autumn colour red or scarlet. *Flowers* In terminal spreading or drooping panicles 15–25 cm (6–10 in) in length and consisting of several slender racemes in August–September; flowers bell-shaped, white, 6 mm (0.25 in). *Fruit* Dry woody capsule with five cells and containing many small seeds.

Range: Eastern USA from Pennsylvania and Maryland south to northern Florida and west to Louisiana and southern Indiana.

Habitat: Cultivated as an ornamental, in the wild occurring on moist oak or pine-dominated sites.

Synonyms: *Andromeda arborea.*

This tree flowers late in the summer and often is displaying its fall colours before flowering has finished. It requires a moist acidic soil. The flowers show a strong resemblance to those of *Pieris* and several other shrubby members of the Heather family.

CHRIST'S THORN, *PALIURUS*
FAMILY RHAMNACEAE

This is a genus of eight species from southeastern Europe across Asia to Japan. The shoots bear stipular spines; in most species they are straight but in *P. spina-christi* one is straight and its pair is curved. The fruit is dry with a circular wing.

---

p.152 **Christ's Thorn** *Paliurus spina-christi*

Description: Deciduous lax shrub or small tree to 3–4 m (10–13 ft) in height.
Crown Rounded. *Bark* Dark grey-brown.
Shoot Slender and flexible, zig-zagged, finely pilose at first, then hairless with pairs of

sharp spines which derive from the stipules; the longer spine is straight and 0.5–1 cm (0.2–0.4 in), the second one is shorter and curved. *Buds* Small, with two or three scales. *Foliage* Leaves broad ovate, asymmetrical, set on the shoot in two opposite vertical rows, strongly three veined at the base with the veins looping forwards towards the bluntly pointed or acute apex, base broad wedge-shaped, truncate or subcordate, margin finely glandular toothed or nearly untoothed, glossy green, hairless or slightly pilose on the veins, 2–5 × 1–4 cm (0.8–2 × 0.4–1.6 in); leaf stalk grooved, thinly pilose, 0.5–1.5 cm (0.2–0.6 in). *Flowers* In dense cymose clusters in the leaf axils, golden-yellow and showy. *Fruit* Disc-like with a central seed and a broad corky wing, 2–3.5 cm (0.8–1.4 in) across.

Range: Mediterranean region east to Iran.
Habitat: Hot dry hillsides or stream-side sites.

Tradition has it that this plant was used to make Christ's crown of thorns. Certainly, the twigs are sufficiently spiny. It is quite attractive in flower, and has curiously shaped discus like fruits.

PALMS, PALMAE (SYNONYM: ARECACEAE)

The palms are a large group of mainly tropical monocotyledons. The leaves may be pinnate with separate leaflets (*see Howeia* (p.741), *Jubaea* (p.749), *Phoenix* (p.878) and *Syagrus* (p.1191)), or palmate (with the leaves usually folded and ribbed, but only partly separated) (*see Chamaerops* (p.604), *Trachycarpus* (p.1238) and *Washingtonia* (p.1263)), but are invariably large. In many species, growth only occurs at a single terminal growing point, giving a tufted crown on long stems. As monocots, the plants are not capable of secondary thickening, with the thickness of the stem dependent upon the vigour of the plant at the time it was made. As a consequence, the stems can be thicker higher up the trunk than they are near the base.

PERSIAN IRONWOOD, *PARROTIA*
FAMILY HAMAMELIDACEAE

A monotypic genus with flaky bark that bears some resemblance to *Platanus*; the unlobed leaves and flowers before the leaves in spring distinguish it. The flowers are without petals, with their colour deriving from the massed stamens.

p.199 **Persian Ironwood** *Parrotia persica*

Description: Deciduous tree 10–20 m (33–65 ft) with a bole diameter to 60 cm (2 ft), or a rather tall sprawling bush.

Crown Wide spreading with level branches, less often upright domed. *Bark* Purplish brown to grey-brown and then flaking in large plates to reveal pink-buff and yellow, which gradually darkens through grey-green. *Shoot* Grey-green with sparse star-shaped hairs and small warts when young but becoming hairless by autumn, in the second year grey-brown with lenticels of the same colour. *Buds* Ovoid-conic, dark blackish brown, hairy, to 6 mm (0.25 in). *Foliage* Leaves obovate, oblong, elliptic to almost rounded in outline, rounded or acute at the apex, base wedge-shaped to rounded, margin wavy, usually with rounded teeth near the apex, upper surface glossy green initially star-shaped hairy but the hairs soon rubbing off except along the slightly impressed veins, underside shiny to matt light or slightly glaucous green, slightly hairy and more strongly so on the six to eight pairs of raised veins and in the vein axils at the base, 5–13 × 4–8 cm (2–5.1 × 1.6–3.1 in); leaf stalk slightly grooved, green, densely hairy, less than 1 cm (0.4 in); autumn colour a combination of red, orange and crimson before falling deep red. *Flowers* Flower buds ovoid in the leaf axils, 8 mm (0.3 in), with two brownish hairy bud scales, on a short bent stalk; flowers open in late winter in clusters 1.5 cm (0.6 in) across from January to March (depending upon season), with numerous deep-red stamens but without petals. *Fruit* Ovoid capsule, with a single shiny oblong seed in each cell.

Range: Northern Iran and Transcaucasus region.
Habitat: Cultivated as an ornamental, in the wild restricted to the forests around the Caspian Sea.
Synonyms: *Hamamelis persica*.

This tree has a bark which resembles that of London Plane. The leaves are very similar to some *Hamamelis*, especially *H. virginiana*, but the genus differs in not having any petals in the flowers. Despite this, they are attractive, making a display on the bear branches by the weight of red stamens.

VIRGINIA CREEPERS, *PARTHENOCISSUS*
FAMILY VITACEAE

This is a small genus of climbers from North America and Asia. Most species are self-clinging, with the tendrils having sticky pads. The leaves may be simple, trifoliate or palmate, and colour spectacularly in the autumn. The fruit is a berry.

---

p.303 **Japanese Creeper or Boston Ivy**
Parthenocissus tricuspidata

Description: Deciduous climber to 20 m (65 ft) developing a stem to 20 cm (0.7 ft). *Crown* Depends upon structure over which it clambers. *Bark* Brown, with paler fissures. *Shoot* Pale buff to grey-brown, slender, hairless, with tendrils opposite the leaves and buds. *Buds* Narrow conic, small. *Foliage* Variable, from broad ovate with a heart-shaped base with shallow to coarse teeth but not significantly lobed, through deeply three lobed to trifoliate with the terminal leaflet obovate; mature plants tend to have three-lobed leaves; hairless above, downy beneath, 5–20 cm (2–8 in) in length and breadth; autumn colour brilliant reds. *Flowers* In cymes on short lateral shoots with two leaves on the current season's growths; flowers yellow-green. *Fruit* Dark blue berry with a waxy bloom, 6–8 mm (0.25–0.3 in).
Range: Throughout Japan, Korea and in northern China.

Habitat: Cultivated as an ornamental, in the wild occurring on trees and rocks or as a ground-covering ivy in woodland.

Synonyms: *Ampelopsis tricuspidata.*

Similar species: **Virginia Creeper** *P. quinquefolia* (p.303) has digitately palmate leaves with five, or rarely only three, oval to obovate leaflets. It shares the feature of having sucker-like pads on the tendrils. It comes from eastern and central North America.

P. inserta also has palmate leaves but differs from both the above in the absence of sucker-like pads and thus can only clamber and twine but not self-attach. It has a similar distribution to *P. quinquefolia* and is confused with it in gardens.

This is a climber which attaches itself to walls, rocks and other trees by means of the sucker-like viscous pads on the tendrils.

EMPRESS TREES, *PAULOWNIA*
FAMILY SCROPHULARIACEAE

This is a small genus from eastern Asia, mainly China but south into northern Vietnam and Taiwan, with species native or cultivated in Korea and Japan. The leaves are large, thin and covered in hairs, often sticky. They are set in opposite pairs on the stout shoots, and fall without colouring in the autumn. The flowers are formed in panicles at the ends of the shoots in late summer, but do not open until mid spring the next year before the leaves flush. They are therefore conspicuous in bud over the winter period. The flowers are tubular, like thimbles or foxglove blooms, and delicately scented. The fruit is a capsule, opening along two sutures and containing many small-winged seeds. The genus shows considerable similarity to *Catalpa*, although they are placed in separate families. They are planted as amenity trees, but also have a good timber, and are fast growing.

p.141 **Paulownia** or **Foxglove Tree**
Paulownia tomentosa

Description: Deciduous tree 10–20 m (33–65 ft) with a bole diameter to 60 cm (2 ft).
Crown Rounded, open, usually broader than high. *Bark* Grey-brown or purple-grey

with grey striations in young trees, becoming smooth and grey in old trees. *Shoot* Stout and pithy, pale brown and hairy in the first year, becoming hairless with oval erupting pale buff lenticels, flattened at the nodes with round leaf traces. *Buds* In opposite pairs, flat domed, small, scarcely apparent, terminal buds missing.

Foliage Leaves large, ovate, apex acute to long slender pointed, base deeply heart-shaped, margin untoothed but on strong shoots with one or two pairs of small acute lobes, upper surface fresh green with soft pale hairs, beneath densely sticky glandular haired with raised rounded veins, 15–35 × 10–25 cm (6–14 × 4–10 in), but larger on coppiced shoots; leaf stalk hairy, stout, 10–15 cm (4–6 in); autumn colour nil, green until killed by frost. *Flowers* In terminal panicles forming in autumn, to 30 × 10 cm (12 × 4 in), with the flower buds globose, covered by the thick sepals which are densely fawn-brown tomentose on tomentose stalks; flowers opening in May, corolla bell-shaped, similar to the flowers of foxglove or *Catalpa*, violet to blue-purple, delightfully fragrant, 4–5 cm (1.6–2 in). *Fruit* Ovoid pointed, woody capsule, opening along two sutures, 4–5 cm (1.6–2 in); containing many small-winged seeds.

Range: Northern China, cultivated and first introduced from Japan.

Habitat: Cultivated as an ornamental, in the wild in mixed temperate forest.

Synonyms: *Bignonia tomentosa*, *P. imperialis*.

Similar species: *P. lilacina* has the shoots and leaf stalks covered with glandular hairs, unlobed leaves and paler, usually larger flowers. It is reported from western China and often treated as no more than a cultivar of *P. tomentosa*.

P. fortunei is much more distinct. This native of central China from Yunnan and Sichuan eastwards to the coast has young shoots with stellate (star-shaped) hairs, unlobed leaves which are smaller (15–20 × 13–15 cm (6–8 × 5.1–6 in)) and with the inflorescence consisting of almost stalkless cymes except at the base.

The flowers need a dark background to show them off to best effect, and preferably to be sited near stairs or a window where the delectable fragrance can be enjoyed. In maritime climates, the changeable nature of winters can cause the flowers to start to open, thus losing their winter hardiness, and are then killed by the next cold snap. The leaves are thin and soft, very liable to damage by strong winds.

AVOCADOS, *PERSEA* (SYNONYM: *MACHILUS*)
FAMILY LAURACEAE

This is a genus of around 150 species from the tropics and warm temperate regions. The fruit is a drupe with a fleshy outer layer. The main species encountered is the commercial Avocado, *P. americana*.

p.168 **Avocado** *Persea americana*

Description: Evergreen tree 7–18 m (23–60 ft) in height.
Crown Rounded to broad globose, often on several stems. *Bark* Grey-brown, aromatic. *Shoot* Green, maturing to brown, ridged, hairless. *Foliage* Leaves elliptic to ovate, apex short and slender pointed or acute, base wedge-shaped, margin untoothed, leathery and hairless, upper surface lustrous dark green, veins prominent, pinnate or three from the base, underside bluish-green, 10–20 cm (4–8 in); crushed foliage aromatic. *Flowers* In terminal panicles; flowers greenish and grey hairy, 2 cm (0.8 in). *Fruit* Obovoid or pear-shaped to globose berry, with a thick green or yellow wrinkled and warty or smooth skin, and a pale oily flesh around a large shiny seed.

Range: Central America.

Habitat: Cultivated as a fruit tree in the Mediterranean region.

Synonyms: *P. gratissima*.

Similar species: *P. ichangensis* (syn. *Machilus ichangensis*) is an evergreen and hardy tree from central China to southeast Tibet. It differs in the narrow leaves which vary from oblanceolate to ovate-lanceolate in shape and 13–24 × 2–4 cm (5.1–9.4 × 0.8–1.6 in). They are initially finely downy on both sides, becoming hairless, and are rather glaucous beneath. Flowers greenish yellow in slender panicles on silky haired stalks, and followed by small sub-globose berries.

This is the avocado of greengrocers. It has been cultivated for the oily flesh since before the time of Columbus.

CORK BARK TREES, *PHELLODENDRON*
FAMILY RUTACEAE

This is a genus of around ten species. The leaves are pinnate, in opposite pairs, hiding the buds in the enlarged base of the leaf stalk; they have a somewhat foetid smell. The bark becomes rather corky.

p.312 Amur Cork Tree *Phellodendron amurense*

Description: Deciduous tree to 10–15 m (33–50 ft) with a bole diameter to 70 cm (2.3 ft). *Crown* Spreading and rather gaunt. *Bark* Shallowly cross-fissured with pale buff fissures and dark-brown ridges, becoming corky in old trees. *Shoot* Dark coppery brown with raised oval lenticels in the first year, becoming greyer with age with horseshoe-shaped leaf traces. *Buds* In opposite pairs, domed, ridged, small, 1 × 2 mm (0.1 in), almost totally surrounded by base of leaf stalk. *Foliage* Leaves 25–40 cm (10–16 in), pinnate with 5–11 leaflets; leaflets oval to elliptic, tapering to a slender-pointed apex, base rounded to broad wedge-shaped, margin with small indentations, ciliate, upper surface matt green, with some glandular hairs along the impressed midrib, veins in circa 10 pairs, slightly impressed, underside whitish green, downy, with raised hairy midrib, 7–13 × 4–6 cm (2.8–5.1 × 1.6–2.4 in); leaf stalk grooved, hairy in the groove, to 10 cm (4 in), with a bulbous base which encloses the bud, rachis narrowly grooved, stalk hairy, 5–6 mm (0.2–0.25 in); autumn colour yellow. *Flowers* In terminal erect panicles on the current season's growths, to 8 cm (3.1 in), with separate male and female trees; flowers yellow-green. *Fruit* Globose, green, ripening to black with five cells, strong citrus scent, 1 cm (0.4 in).

Range: Northeast Asia from the Amur and Ussuri regions, north and northeast China, Korea and throughout Japan.

Habitat: Cultivated as an ornamental, in the wild occurring in mountain forests.

This tree is grown for the cork-like bark.

MOCK ORANGE, PHILADELPHACEAE (SYNONYM: HYDRANGEACEAE IN PART)

This family consists of two genera, *Deutzia* (with star-shaped hairs) and *Philadelphus* (simple hairs). Only one species is featured here, and this makes but a shrubby tree. In cultivation, there is a multiplicity of forms and hybrids, most of which are shrubs and grown for their fragrant flowers.

MOCK ORANGE, *PHILADELPHUS*
FAMILY PHILADELPHACEAE

This is a genus mostly of shrubs and mainly from Asia but with species in Europe and America. The leaves are simple, toothed, and in opposite pairs. The flowers are white, fragrant, and develop into the capsule, which has a large and persistent calyx.

p.172 **Mock Orange** *Philadelphus pubescens*

Description: Deciduous shrub or shrubby tree to 6 m (20 ft) or so.
Crown Vase-shaped, often on several stems.
Bark Glossy brown, paler in the fissures and becoming slightly fibrous.
Shoot Green and almost hairless when young, maturing to grey-brown to brown and finely ribbed with stipular scars at the

nodes. *Buds* In opposite pairs, rounded, small, purplish brown. *Foliage* Leaves ovate, up to 9 × 6 cm (3.5 × 2.4 in) but variable, apex short and slender pointed, base broad wedge-shaped to sub-rounded, margin with a few remote (towards the apex) spaced short teeth, upper surface dull green, sparsely hairy, beneath pale green with three to five main veins from near the base, with fairly dense covering of simple whitish hairs; leaf stalk hairy, 5–8 mm (0.2–0.3 in), enclosing the buds during the summer. *Flowers* In racemes in late June or July on shoots which develop from buds laid down in the previous year, usually with seven or nine flowers, with the lower two pairs in the upper leaf axils; flowers cupped, to 4 cm (1.6 in) across, fragrant, petals white, elliptic, acute, stamens yellow, calyx lanceolate, slender pointed, hairy, stalks hairy, 5–8 mm (0.2–0.3 in). *Fruit* Woody four-valved dry capsule which splits to release the many seeds.

Range: Southeastern USA from Tennessee to Alabama and Arkansas.

Habitat: Cultivated as an ornamental.

Similar species: *P. delavayi* has larger leaves, to 10 × 4.5 cm (4 × 1.8 in) on flowering shoots but up to 20 × 10 cm (8 × 4 in) on vigorous extension growths. It is a most beautiful species from west China (Yunnan, Sichuan) across to southeast Tibet and northern Burma.

P. coronarius is the 'Mock Orange' of gardens. It differs from *P. pubescens* in being almost (but not quite) hairless and the flowers yellowish white, with a heavy scent. The bark is peeling on one-year-old shoots. It makes a large shrub, to 4 m (13 ft) and occurs in the wild in southeast Europe across to Asia Minor.

P. inodorus is a small shrub 1.2–2 m (4–6.6 ft), with glossy leaves and solitary flowers with four overlapping petals, making the flower square in outline.

Many hybrids have been raised, primarily between *P. pubescens*, *P. coronarius* and *P. inodorus*, and include forms with both double and semi-double flowers.

This is usually the tallest or most tree-like of the many *Philadelphus* cultivated as garden shrubs. It will form a small tree 6 m (20 ft) or so in height, although usually needs regular pruning to obtain a single stem. It has been mistakenly given the common name 'syringa' in English, but is not related to the true genus *Syringa*.

PHILLYREA, *PHILLYREA*
FAMILY OLEACEAE

This is a genus of four species from Madeira to northern Iran. The leaves are evergreen, in opposite pairs. The flowers are white, in the leaf axils in spring, and followed by purplish single-seeded drupes.

p.175 **Phillyrea** *Phillyrea latifolia*

Description: Evergreen tree to 6–10 m (20–33 ft) with a bole diameter to 25 cm (10 in).
Crown Conical in young trees but becoming domed and often broader than high. *Bark* Smooth and blackish grey at first, becoming fissured with the ridges finally cracked into small squares.
Shoot Grey-brown and finely hairy at first, becoming dark grey, flattened around the leaves/buds, slender, stiff. *Buds* In opposite pairs, conical, green, with short hairs, 2.5 mm (0.1 in). *Foliage* In decussate pairs, variable in shape from ovate through elliptic to lanceolate, base rounded or wedge-shaped, apex rounded to acute, mid to dark glossy green above with a pale green main vein, beneath pale green with a paler vein with glandular dots, margins entire, serrate or dentate, 1.5–6 × 1–4 cm (0.6–2.4 × 0.4–1.6 in); leaf stalk pale green, finely hairy, 5–6 mm (0.2–0.25 in). *Flowers* In late winter or early spring from axillary buds on previous season's growth in short clusters; dull whitish or yellowish green, 2 mm (0.1 in). *Fruit* Rounded drupe, ripening to blue-black in first autumn, 6–10 mm (0.25–0.4 in).

Range: Mediterranean region across from southern Europe from Portugal, North Africa and western Asia.

Habitat: Evergreen woodland.

Synonyms: *P. media*.

Similar species: *P. angustifolia* is a related species which rarely makes a tree, usually less than 3 m (10 ft) in height. The leaves are linear, the flowers produced in late spring or early summer and the fruit has a pointed apex.

This relative of privet makes a slow-growing small tree. It is very variable in the shape and toothing of the leaves.

DATE PALMS, *PHOENIX*
FAMILY PALMAE

This genus of around 17 species is characterized by the large pinnate leaves. The fruit is a drupe, dry in some species (*see* PP. *canariensis* and *theophrastii*), but with a sweet flesh in the cultivated Date Palm, *P. dactylifera*.

p.347 **Canary Palm** *Phoenix canariensis*

Description: Evergreen tree 15–20 m (50–65 ft) with a bole diameter to 90 cm (2.9 ft) or more. *Crown* Monopodal with a single stem which has a terminal rosette of numerous leaves, without basal suckers. *Bark* Grey, rough with ridges which are broader than high from the leaf bases, but at first covered with the fibrous leaf sheaths and reddish brown. *Foliage* Leaves pinnate, to 6 m (20 ft); leaflets many, circa 150–200, crowded and set in opposite pairs or regularly in one rank or plane to the rachis, induplicate (folded upwards to give a V-shape in section), light to dark green, sharp pointed, stiff; leaf stalk with the lower leaves reduced to spines and with the first functional leaves smaller. *Flowers* In pendent inflorescences to 2 m (6.6 ft) which arise from the axils of the lower leaves; flowers creamy-yellow. *Fruit* Globose-ovoid, orange, wrinkled with a dry non-edible flesh, 3 cm (1.2 in).

Range: Canary Islands.

Habitat: Cultivated as an ornamental.

Similar species: *P. sylvestris* has a stem which is usually only 50 cm (1.6 ft) or less in diameter and is solitary. The leaves are grey-green, with the leaf stalk scars on the stem higher than they are wide. It is a native of India and is cultivated as an ornamental.

This tree makes a better amenity tree than the Date Palm, with its much stouter non-suckering trunk and larger rosettes with many leaves. The fruit, however, is inedible.

p.347 **Date Palm** *Phoenix dactylifera*

Description: Evergreen tree 15–30 m (50–100 ft) with a bole diameter of about 30 cm (1 ft). *Crown* Monopodal single stem which has a terminal rosette of 20–40 leaves, naturally often with suckers at the base but these are frequently removed. *Bark* Grey, rough with ridges which are as high or higher than wide from the leaf bases, but at first covered with the fibrous leaf sheaths and reddish brown. *Foliage* Leaves pinnate, to 4 m (13 ft); leaflets set in pairs forming an acute angle to the rachis and arranged in several ranks, induplicate (folded upwards to give a V-shape in section), bluish green with a white powdery wax above and rather glaucous beneath, sharp pointed, stiff, to 50 cm (20 in); leaf stalk with the lower leaves reduced to spines. *Flowers* In large spreading or pendent inflorescences towards the base of the rosette; flowers creamy yellow. *Fruit* Cylindric to ellipsoidal drupe with a sweet edible flesh, 2.5–8 cm (1–3.1 in); seed pointed and grooved.

Range: Middle East.

Habitat: Cultivated as an ornamental and as a food crop.

Similar species: **Cretan Palm** *P. theophrastii* (p.347) has similar foliage which is grey-green and is also suckering but differs in the dry inedible fruit which is 1.5 × 1 cm (0.6 × 0.4 in). It attains 10 m (33 ft) in height, with leaves 3–5 m (10–16 ft) in length. It occurs in the eastern region of the Greek island of Crete and also in a few groves in southern Turkey.

The date palm gives the tasty date. It provides a staple food for millions and is well adapted to hot dry situations. It is mainly grown in southern Europe close to the Mediterranean as a shade and ornamental tree, but in a small region of southeast Spain it is cultivated for the fruit. Most dates, however, come from the lands bordering the southern and eastern shores of the Mediterranean, especially North Africa.

PHOTINIAS, *PHOTINIA* (SYNONYMS: *STRANVAESIA, ARONIA*) FAMILY ROSACEAE

This is a large genus of trees and shrubs, allied to *Malus*, *Sorbus* and other genera of the apple subfamily of the Rosaceae. Many, but not all, species are evergreen. The new growth is often strongly coloured.

p.155 **Stranvaesia** *Photinia davidiana*

Description: Evergreen shrub or tree to 12 m (39 ft) with a bole diameter to 30 cm (1 ft). *Crown* Rounded, domed, in some forms prostrate or spreading. *Bark* Grey, smooth. *Shoot* Purple or green with white or grey hairs in the first winter, becoming grey but retaining the hairs for some years. *Buds* Ovoid-conic, beaked or pointed, purple-pink with the scales hairy on the outer margin, to 1 cm (0.4 in). *Foliage* Leaves semi-evergreen, most falling in late winter and turning red or orange; shape variable, from lanceolate, oblong, elliptic to oblanceolate, margins untoothed but sometimes wavy, abruptly tapered to a short pointed apex, base wedge-shaped, matt green above, weakly veined but with hairs along the midrib, beneath more or less hairless, 5–12 × 1–4 cm (2–4.7 × 0.4–1.6 in); leaf stalk 2–2.5 cm (0.8–1 in), grooved, hairy. *Flowers* From terminal buds on previous season's growths in mid-summer in hairy corymbs 5–10 cm (2–4 in)

across; flowers white, 6 mm (0.25 in).
Fruit Globose, ripening in first autumn to bright red, 6–10 mm (0.25–0.4 in).

Range: Central, southern and western China.
Habitat: Cultivated in Europe as an ornamental, in the wild found in mixed forests.
Synonyms: *Stranvaesia davidiana*.

This makes a small tree. The leaves assume attractive red and orange 'autumn' colours but in the spring (although a few are lost in the autumn).

---

p.155 **Giant Photinia** *Photinia serratifolia*

Description: Evergreen to 20 m (65 ft) with a bole diameter to 50 cm (1.6 ft).
Crown Rounded, domed, sometimes on several stems. *Bark* Grey-brown, wrinkled, becoming smooth, cracking at the base and exfoliating to reveal red-brown beneath. *Shoot* Stout, greenish brown with prominent vertical brown lenticels, usually hairless but in some forms densely whitish-grey woolly. *Buds* Ovoid-conic with an acute offset apex, greenish red, hairless, up to 2.5 cm (1 in). *Foliage* Leaves lanceolate to oblong or oblanceolate, margins finely serrate, apex acute, base wedge-shaped to rounded, lustrous dark green above, paler beneath, weakly veined and usually hairless except for some hairs along the midrib beneath, 10–20 × 4–8 cm (4–8 × 1.6–3.1 in); leaf stalk 2.5–4 cm (1–1.6 in), white hairy; new foliage emerges green, bronze or rich red. *Flowers* From terminal buds on previous season's growths in mid summer in large 10–18 cm (4–7.1 in) corymbs; flowers white, 1 cm (0.4 in), hawthorn scented. *Fruit* Globose, ripening in first autumn to red, 6 mm (0.25 in).
Range: Central, southern and western China and Taiwan.
Habitat: Cultivated in Europe as an ornamental, in the wild found in mixed forests.
Synonyms: *Photinia serrulata*, *Crataegus serratifolia*.
Similar species: **Red Tip Photinia** *P.* × *fraseri* (p.155) makes a small tree or large spreading shrub.

The leaves emerge strongly and brilliantly red tinted before maturing to deep green. They are smaller than in *P. serratifolia*, and the flowers are in smaller corymbs. It is a hybrid between *P. serratifolia* and *P. glabra* which is a shrubby species from Japan. It is frequently planted as a garden shrub for its new foliage. In this respect it attempts to rival the best forms of *Pieris formosana* but with the virtue of growing on chalky soils.

This makes a small to medium-sized tree, with glossy foliage and in late spring or early summer large clusters of small white flowers.

BAMBOOS, *PHYLLOSTACHYS*
FAMILY GRAMINEAE (SYNONYM: BAMBUSAE)

This is a large genus of bamboos. It is characterized by the stems being flattened above the nodes, with most other bamboos having round or terete stems. As monocotyledons, the stems are not capable of secondary thickening once formed. They grow from the base, with side twigs growing from the buds in the nodes.

---

p.350 **Bamboo** *Phyllostachys nigra*

Description: Evergreen multistemmed plant 6–8 m (20–26 ft) with stems 3–4 cm (1.2–1.6 in) in diameter.
Crown Rounded. *Shoot* Green or black, divided into a series of nodes, with the intervening portion flattened on alternate sides above the nodes, hollow between the nodes. *Buds* Underground, growing as an erect shoot covered by papery bracts. *Foliage* On two or three shoots growing from the nodes in the second and subsequent years, leaves narrow elliptic, slender pointed, base wedge-shaped, veins parallel, mid to dark green above, somewhat glaucous green beneath, 5–11 × 0.7–2 cm (2–4.3 × 0.3–0.8 in). *Flowers* Only produced at around thirty-year intervals. *Fruit* Grass-like, rarely seen.
Range: South and east China.
Habitat: Cultivated in Europe as an ornamental.

Varieties: 'Boryana' has the stems yellow when mature.

Synonyms: *Bambusa nigra*.

Similar species: *P. aurea* has the stems pale yellowish green with a swollen band around the nodes. It flowers on a cycle of approximately fifteen years.

This may be taken as indicative of the wide range of bamboos. These are woody grasses. Height and diameter growth is made in the first year, with the foliage being formed from buds on the nodes in the subsequent seasons. The height growth made by the extending shoots can be fast, as much as 30 cm (12 in) in 24 hours in temperate climates and more for the larger-growing tropical species. Many, but not all, bamboos flower at intervals, with the clumps dying after flowering or being severely reduced in their vigour. This is an important part of the ecology, allowing other plants to become established. The young shoots or culms are edible. They are soaked in a saline solutions and boiled.

SPRUCES, *PICEA*
FAMILY PINACEAE

The spruces are a large genus of around 40 species of evergreen conifer. They are widely distributed across the northern hemisphere, forming extensive forests in boreal and Alpine regions but extending as far south as the Tropic of Cancer in Taiwan and Mexico. The leaves are four sided or square in section, or variably flattened. In the species with flattened leaves, the stomata are in two whitish bands on the underside, although there may be some incomplete bands on the leaf upper surface: *PP. brachytyla, breweriana, glehnii, likiangensis, jezoensis* ssp. *hondoensis, omorika, orientalis, purpurea, sitchensis* and *spinulosa*. In the species with four-sided needles (one of these needles can be rolled between the fingers) the stomatal bands are more or less evenly distributed on all four sides (but some species are green and the bands are not distinct). In this group are: *PP. abies, alcockiana, asperata, engelmannii, glauca, koyamai, mariana, morrisonicola, obovata, pungens, schrenkiana, smithiana, torano* and *wilsonii*. In many species, the apex is bevelled, but in some it is very sharply pointed (feel *PP. asperata* (not all trees), *pungens, sitchensis* and *torano*), although young trees of all species have sharp needles. The shoot is prominently ridged, with the leaf sitting on an extension of the shoot which is called a pulvinus. Where leaves are naturally shed, the pulvinus remains as a short peg, but if the leaf is torn off, it comes away with the leaf. Female flowers are in spring and are erect, as in *Abies* and other members of the pine family. However, once pollination is accomplished, they become pendent. They ripen in the first autumn, and open to shed the winged seeds. In most species, the cones fall soon after shedding the seeds, but they remain intact. Spruces are very widely used in forestry, and as amenity trees. They have a good general-purpose white timber. Most do not tolerate coastal exposure or atmospheric pollution.

Informal Key

LEAF LENGTH
(i)   **<8 mm** (0.3 in): *orientalis*
(ii) **0.8–1.8 cm** (0.3–0.7 in): *asperata, glauca, glehnii, jezoensis* ssp. *hondoensis, koyamai, likiangensis, mariana, morrisonicola, purpurea, wilsonii*
(iii) **1.5–2.5 cm** (0.6–1 in): *abies, alcoquiana, brachytyla, breweriana, engelmannii, obovata, omorika, pungens, schrenkiana, sitchensis, spinulosa, torano*
(iv) **>2.5 cm** (1 in): *breweriana, engelmannii, pungens, schrenkiana, smithiana*

CONE LENGTH
(i)   **<5 cm** (2 in): *mariana, purpurea* (rarely to 5.5 cm (2.2 in))
(ii) **<8 cm** (3.1 in): *engelmannii, glauca, glehnii, jezoensis* ssp. *hondoensis, morrisonicola, omorika, wilsonii*
(iii) **5–12 cm** (2–4.7 in): *alcoquiana, asperata* (to 14 cm (5.5 in)), *brachytyla, koyamai, likiangensis, obovata, orientalis, pungens, schrenkiana, sitchensis, spinulosa, torano*
(iv) **>10 cm** (4 in): *abies, asperata, breweriana, likiangensis, smithiana*

CONE SCALES
(i)   **woody, usually stiff:** *abies, asperata, brachytyla, breweriana, glauca* (scarcely), *koyamai, mariana, morrisonicola, obovata, omorika, orientalis, schrenkiana, smithiana, spinulosa, torano, wilsonii*
(ii) **thin or papery, generally flexible:** *alcoquiana, engelmannii, glauca, glehnii, jezoensis* ssp. *hondoensis, likiangensis, pungens, purpurea, sitchensis*
(iii) **rhombic at the apex:** *abies, alcoquiana, asperata, brachytyla, engelmannii, jezoensis* ssp. *hondoensis, likiangensis, mariana, pungens, purpurea, sitchensis, spinulosa*

p.68 **Norway Spruce** *Picea abies*

Description: Evergreen tree 20–40 m (65–130 ft) with a
bole diameter of up to 1.2 m (4 ft).
Crown Conical in young trees, becoming
columnar with a conic or rounded top and
short level or pendent branches.
Bark Red-brown and finely flaky in young
trees, becoming purple or grey in old trees
and slightly scaly at the base. *Shoot* Red-
brown, golden-brown or orange-brown in
the first winter, becoming darker and less
bright in subsequent years, varying from
slender to stout, hairless or finely hairy.
Buds Ovoid-conical, red-brown or brown,
not or scarcely resinous, to 8 mm (0.3 in).
Foliage Parted beneath the shoot, spreading
at the side with the uppermost leaves
pressed down and pointing forwards, dark
green to grey green; leaves linear, curved
forwards, apex bluntly pointed, rhombic in
section with four bands of spaced white
waxy dots (stomata), 1.4–2.5 × 1 mm
(0.6–1 × 0.1 in); crushed foliage with a
sweet resin scent. *Flowers* On previous
season's growths in late spring; male cones
yellow, 1–1.5 cm (0.4–0.6 in); female cones
erect. *Fruit* Cylindrical, pendent, green or
red and ripening in the first autumn to
orange-brown or brown, 10–20 × 2.5–3 cm
(4–8 × 1–1.2 in), opening to 4 cm (1.6 in);
scales rhombic at the apex, thinly woody or
somewhat leathery, 1–2 cm (0.4–0.8 in) in
width.

Range: Europe from the Balkans north to southern
Scandinavia and from eastern France to
Romania and southeast Russia.

Habitat: Mountain forests in mixed or pure stands
but towards the northern part of the range
becoming lowland trees.

Varieties: A number of habit cultivars are recorded,
with perhaps 'Virgata' being notable (or
curious); this has long and generally
unbranched snake-like branches.

Synonyms: *P. excelsa*, *Pinus abies*.

Similar species: *P. alpestris* occurs in southeast Switzerland.
This has a greyish white bark, more densely
pubescent shoots, radially spreading shorter
(1–2 cm (0.4–0.8 in)) glaucous-green leaves

and stout heavy cones 7–14 cm (2.8–5.5 in) with rounded scales (thus similar to *P. smithiana* and *P. obovata*). It is often sunk in *P. abies* or treated as var. *alpestris* but probably represents a relict population which survived the last ice age. *P. × fennica* is found from northern Scandinavia east to the Urals and has hairy shoots, deep-green leaves and smaller cones with rounded but finely-toothed scales. It represents a hybrid population with characters from both *P. abies* and *P. obovata*.

This tree is very variable in cone and foliage characters. Some of this variability may be due to hybridization following the last Ice Age, when different populations expanded from their refuges. It is the common Christmas tree, a task for which it is not well suited as it too readily loses the needles, neither is it the traditional Christmas tree (which was *Abies alba*). At its best, it can be an imposing tree, but it is probably one of the less attractive spruces.

---

p.73 **Alcock Spruce** *Picea alcoquiana*

Description: Evergreen tree to 15–25 m (50–80 ft) with a bole diameter to 70 cm (2.3 ft). *Crown* Broad conical in young trees, becoming columnar and rather gaunt in old trees with the main branches spreading and rising strongly. *Bark* Purplish brown and finely flaky, in old trees grey and breaking into scaly plates at the base. *Shoot* White or pale buff-brown or pink-brown in first winter, pale orange-brown in later years, usually hairless, rough with prominent ridges, stout. *Buds* Globose or conical, rounded or pointed, purplish brown and thickly resinous, to 3 mm (0.1 in). *Foliage* Pointing forwards, slightly parted below, side leaves spreading, those above the shoot denser and rising, in very obvious 'tufts' as the leaves close to the buds are shorter, mid to somewhat yellow-green; leaves linear and slightly incurved, with a blunt and slightly bevelled bony point, square in section with four roughly equal sides, outer exposed surface with two faint bands of white dots (stomata), inner (facing shoot, and thus hidden) surface with two bluish-white waxy bands of stomata, 0.8–1.5 cm (0.3–0.6 in) (rarely to 2 cm (0.8 in)) by 1–1.5 mm (0.1 in); crushed foliage with an orangey resin scent. *Flowers* On previous season's shoots in late spring; male cones rosy red with yellow pollen, 1–1.5 cm (0.4–0.6 in). *Fruit* Narrowly ovoid, violet when young, ripening in the first autumn to reddish brown or brown, 6–12 × 3–5 cm (2.4–4.7 × 1.2–2 in); scales obovate to rhombic with a wavy and irregularly toothed margin, thin and flexible, to 1.5 cm (0.6 in) in width.

Range: Central Honshu, Japan.

Habitat: Cultivated in Europe as an ornamental, in Japan occurring in mixed mountain forests.

Varieties: Var. *reflexa* has shorter leaves and cones with entire scales which have an elongated reflexed apex. It occurs on the Akaishi Mountain range in Honshu.

Synonyms: *P. bicolor.*

Similar species: *P. shirasawae* is a related tree with a thin greyish bark which is flaky-scaly, with thicker and longer bluish needles and cones with rounded smooth obovate woody scales. It occurs on the Yatsugadake range in central Honshu with *P. koyamai* and probably started as a hybrid of *P. koyamai* with *P. alcoquiana*. It is sometimes named *P. alcoquiana* var. *acicularis.*

This makes a slow-growing tree. The synonym, *P. bicolor*, refers to the marked differences between the white inner side and green outer side of the quadrangular leaves.

p.68 **Dragon Spruce** *Picea asperata*

Description: Evergreen tree 10–15 m (33–50 ft), with a bole to 30 cm (1 ft).
Crown Conical when young, broad conical or columnar with age, with spreading branches. *Bark* Orange-brown and smooth

but in old trees purplish grey with moderately thick flaky scales. *Shoot* Stout, prominently ridged, pale yellow-brown or buff, becoming ash-grey with age, hairless or hairy. *Buds* Conical, pale brown, slightly resinous, 1 cm (0.4 in).

Foliage Spreading forwards at sides and curving upwards above the shoot, sparse or parted beneath, longest third or quarter of the way along the shoot, decreasing in length at both ends; leaves quadrangular, stout, bluish green, with three or four lines of stomata on each face, 1–1.8 × 1–2 mm (0.4–0.7 × 0.1 in), tapering towards sharp or bluntly pointed apex; crushed foliage with a moderate resinous aroma.

Flowers On previous season's growths; male cones cylindrical, pendulous, 1–1.5 cm (0.4–0.6 in), reddish with yellow pollen; female cones erect, purple.

Fruit Cylindrical, fawn brown or dull brown, 5–12 cm (2–4.7 in); scales rounded thin and woody, 0.8–1.6 cm wide (0.3–0.6 in).

Range: West China in Sichuan and southern Gansu

Habitat: Cultivated in Europe as an ornamental, although not common; in the wild, it forms extensive pure forests.

Varieties: Varieties include var. *ponderosa* with longer cones 12–16 cm (4.7–6.3 in) but this is only found in specialist collections.

Similar species: Several related species are sometimes considered as varieties, including *P. retroflexa* which has greyer bark, golden-yellow shoots and usually green foliage, and *P. aurantiaca* with orange shoots and wider cones.

This is a variable tree which is related to Norway Spruce. It grows happily on a wide variety of soils, including shallow soils over chalk.

p.77 **Sargent Spruce** *Picea brachytyla*

Description: Evergreen tree to 25 m (80 ft) with bole diameter to 90 cm (2.9 ft).

Crown Conical when young, becoming domed in old trees, with spreading branches and pendent laterals.

Bark Purplish grey and smooth in young trees, becoming cracked into squares or fissures and more reddish in colour. *Shoot* White, buff or yellow-brown, shiny and sometimes bloomed, becoming light brown in second and subsequent years, with a marked change between one year and older shoots, hairless or with sparse glandular hairs, slender. *Buds* Ovoid, bluntly pointed, chestnut brown, 5 mm (0.2 in), scales persist as a dark brown ring around base of shoots. *Foliage* Radial around the shoot and pointing forwards, somewhat pressed down above and parted beneath the shoot; leaves dark glossy green on the outer surface (with no stomata), with one or two bright silvery waxy bands of stomata on the inner surface, flattened or rhombic in section, apex acute and bevelled, 1.5–2 × 1.5–2 mm (0.6–0.8 × 0.1 in); crushed foliage with only a very faint resin smell. *Flowers* On previous season's growths; male cones pendulous, 1–2 cm (0.4–0.8 in), yellow; female cones erect, purple, terminal. *Fruit* Cylindrical or cylindric-ovoid, tapering to the blunt apex, purplish brown, 6–12 × 3 cm (2.4–4.7 × 1.2 in); scales rhombic, with thin woody tips.

Range: West China from Hubei, Sichuan, northwest Yunnan, northern Burma and possibly into northeast India and southern Tibet.

Habitat: Cultivated as an ornamental in Europe, in the wild forming an element in mixed conifer forest with *Abies* or with broadleaved trees.

Varieties: Var. *complanata* (*P. complanata*) has longer cones (8–15 cm (3.1–6 in)) with woody rounded scales, with longer leaves (2–2.5 cm (0.8–1 in)) and pruinose shoots.

Synonyms: *P. sargentiana*.

This is a very attractive tree both in the pendent habit of the lateral branches and in the dense leafy crown and the vividly glaucous foliage. It tolerates a wide variety of sites.

p.77 **Brewer Spruce** *Picea breweriana*

Description: Evergreen tree 10–20 m (33–65 ft) high
with a bole diameter of up to 50 cm (1.6 ft
Crown Columnar crown with spreading side
branches and pendent laterals.
Bark Smooth and grey, developing rounded
scales which flake off, exposing browner bark
but remaining basically smooth.
Shoot Pink-brown and hairy in first year,
becoming reddish brown in second and
subsequent seasons, slowly losing the hairs,
slender and flexible. *Buds* Ovoid, bluntly
pointed, red-brown, with acicular scales.
Foliage Spreading radially around the shoot,
especially on the long hanging laterals which
may be 1–2 m (3.3–6.6 ft) long; leaves dark
glossy green on the side away from the shoot
and with two whitish green waxy stomatal
bands on the inner face, two-sided, stiff,
1.5–3.5 × 1 mm (0.6–1.4 × 0.1 in), linear,
apex bluntly pointed; the leaves are on a
peg-like pulvinus 2 mm (0.1 in) long;
crushed foliage with a faint grassy aroma.
Flowers Flowers in late spring; male cones
globular, 1 cm (0.4 in), on the hanging
laterals, female cones cylindric, dark red,
confined to the tips of the spreading main
branches in the upper crown. *Fruit* Cone
cylindrical, slightly tapered at both ends,
10–15 × 2.5 cm (4–6 × 1 in), very resinous,
brown, scales rounded, 2 cm (0.8 in) across.

Range: Siskiyou Mountains, southwest Oregon and
northwest California where it is restricted
to a few mountain-top sites.

Habitat: Grown as an amenity tree.

It is very attractive in its dark columnar
crown and the curtain effect from the
weeping lateral shoots, making it unlike
any other spruce. It is occasionally confused
with *P. smithiana* but this has stout ash-
coloured shoots, longer and quadrangular
needles and broader cones. Young trees are
slow to develop the adult foliage, having
shorter more glaucous leaves. Native trees
in the Siskiyou Mountains are described as
having shorter cones (7–10 cm (2.8–4 in))
than those on trees cultivated in Europe.

p.71 Engelmann Spruce *Picea engelmannii*

Description: Evergreen tree 15–25 m (50–80 ft) with a bole diameter to 60 cm (2 in).
Crown Conical when young, becoming columnar in old trees, with declinate branches. *Bark* Red-brown, smooth and initially flaky in young trees, becoming cracked into hard squarrish grey-brown scales in old trees. *Shoot* Pale yellow-brown or pale orange-brown with blackish hairs in the first winter, becoming reddish-brown. *Buds* Ovoid to conic, with a pointed apex, chestnut brown, with small flecks of resin between the scales, 6 mm (0.25 in). *Foliage* Widely but not totally parted beneath the shoot, side leaves point slightly forwards, those above the shoot somewhat pressed down at the base and rising or imbricate along the shoot; leaves four-sided, tapering to a bony pointed apex, relatively soft and flexible, glaucous or bluish green with waxy lines of silvery white stomata on all four surfaces, 1.5–3 cm × 1–1.5 mm (0.6–1.2 × 0.1 in); crushed foliage initially with a sweet scent (likened to camphor) but soon giving way to a more foetid smell. *Flowers* On previous season's shoots in early summer; male cones yellow, 1–1.5 cm (0.4–0.6 in). *Fruit* Cylindric or ovoid-cylindric, ripening in first autumn to reddish brown or yellowish brown, 2.5–7.5 × 2–2.5 cm (1–3 × 0.8–1 in); scales thin and flexible, not woody, often wavy and irregularly toothed.

Range: Central British Columbia and Alberta (Canada) south to Arizona and New Mexico along the Rocky Mountains.

Habitat: Cultivated in Europe as an ornamental, in the wild occurring in montane forests, often with *Abies lasiocarpa*.

Varieties: 'Glauca' has bright blue-green leaves and is the commonest form in cultivation. In 'Fendleri', the branches are pendulous and also have bluish foliage.

Synonyms: *P. glauca* ssp. *engelmannii*.

Similar species: **Mexican Spruce** *P. mexicana* (p.71) from northeast Mexico is a closely related taxon. It has whitish scaly bark, and more radial leaves which are sparser on the shoot, stiffer but more slender, to 1 mm (0.1 in). It is sometimes treated as a subspecies, as ssp. *mexicana*.

This tree is similar to *P. pungens* in the cone but the foliage is much more lush and slender, and being flexible is softer to the touch.

---

p.73 **White Spruce** *Picea glauca*

Description: Evergreen tree 15–20 m (50–65 ft) with a bole diameter 50 cm (1.6 ft).
Crown Conical in young trees but becoming columnar, usually narrow and spire-like. *Bark* Pink-grey then ash brown, developing shallow cracks with scaly plates. *Shoot* Buff-white and sub-shiny in first winter, then pale yellow, brown or ash white, usually hairless. *Buds* Ovoid, pointed, light brown or chestnut brown with some white flecks of resin, 6 mm (0.25 in). *Foliage* Parted beneath the shoot with the side leaves spreading forwards with those above the shoot somewhat imbricate, on strong shoots all tending to curve upwards; leaves linear, curved forwards, tapered to a bony point, rhombic in section, bluish green with waxy silvery white lines of stomata on all four sides, 1–1.7 cm × 1 mm (0.4–0.7 × 0.1 in); crushed foliage with a sweet resin scent or more malodorous. *Flowers* On previous season's shoots in spring; male cones yellow, 1–2 cm (0.4–0.8 in). *Fruit* Long ovoid, tapering at both ends, with rounded thinly woody and finely toothed scales, usually resinous, ripening in first autumn to light brown and falling soon after, 2.5–6 × 1.5–2.5 cm (1–2.4 × 0.6–1 in); scales 0.8–1.2 cm (0.3–0.5 in) broad.

Range: Across Canada from the Atlantic to the Pacific, south into the USA from Maine to Minnesota, with isolated occurrences in Dakota, Wyoming and Montana.

Habitat: Cultivated in Europe as an ornamental and occasionally in forestry, in the wild occurring on a wide range of sites.

Varieties: With such a wide distribution, it has given several geographical forms. Var. *albertiana* is the form from Alberta and Montana in the northern Rocky Mountains. It has a more flaky bark, darker and usually hairy shoots, longer leaves to 2 cm (0.8 in) which are rounded at the tips and smaller more regularly ovoid cones 2.5–5 cm (1–2 in). The selection 'Conica' belongs to this variety. It makes a neat cone and is slow growing, but capable of attaining 5–7 m (16–23 ft). Var. *densata* from the Black Hills of Dakota has light green leaves and cylindrical cones 3–5 cm (1.2–2 in). Var. *porsildii* from northwest Canada and Alaska has a broader crown, more hairy shoots and a smoother bark with resin blisters.

Synonyms: *Abies canadensis*, *Picea alba*.

This makes a small and rather slow growing tree but is capable of withstanding severe conditions. It hybridizes with both *P. engelmannii* and *P. sitchensis* where their ranges meet.

---

p.75 **Glehn Spruce** or **Sakhalin Spruce**
Picea glehnii

Description: Evergreen tree 15–30 m (50–100 ft) with a bole diameter to 50 cm (1.6 ft).
Crown Narrow conical, becoming columnar. *Bark* Reddish brown or purple-brown in young trees and soon flaking, becoming rough with scaly irregular plates of grey-brown, purple-brown or dark grey in old trees.
Shoot Light yellow-brown or reddish brown in first winter with brown hairs mainly in the grooves, then grey-brown or purple-brown. *Buds* Ovoid to globose, rounded or bluntly pointed, chestnut brown, very slightly resinous, to 5 mm (0.2 in). *Foliage* Widely parted beneath the shoot, spreading forwards at 45 degrees at sides and imbricate at 30 degrees along the top of the shoot; linear but tapering to a sharp bony point or

bluntly pointed, dark green or blue-green, four-sided with lines of white stomata along each side but more on the inner side, 0.6–1.2 cm × 1.2–1.5 mm (0.25–0.5 × 0.1 in); crushed foliage resin scented. *Flowers* On previous season's shoots in late spring; male cones yellow, 1–2 cm (0.4–0.8 in). *Fruit* Ovoid-oblong to oblong-cylindric, ripening in the first autumn from purplish green or dark violet through purple-brown to brown, seed shed soon after opening, 3.5–8.5 × 2.5–4 cm (1.4–3.3 × 1–1.6 in); scales thin woody, flexible, obovate with an wavy usually erose (nibbled or toothed) margin, to 1.2 cm (0.5 in) in width.

Range: Southern Sakhalin (Pacific Russia), Hokkaido and northern Honshu, Japan.

Habitat: Cultivated in Europe as an ornamental, in the wild occurring on north-facing slopes on both acidic and ultra-basic (serpentine) rocks.

This tree is related to *P. mariana* and *P. orientalis*, sharing with them the very short leaves and similar cones.

---

p.72 **Hondo Spruce** *Picea jezoensis*
ssp. *hondoensis*

Description: Evergreen tree to 15–30 m (50–100 ft) by up to 1 m (3.3 ft) bole diameter.
Crown Conical in young trees, becoming broader in old trees and often gaunt with spreading-ascending spaced branches.
Bark Brown, rather smooth in young trees, becoming fissured and purplish grey or dark brown in old trees. *Shoot* Orange-brown or white in first winter, later more yellow-brown, hairless, relatively stout.
Buds Ovoid-conic, purplish brown, slightly resinous, to 7 mm (0.3 in).
Foliage Spreading widely and forwards below the shoot, leaves above loosely pressed down, dark green above, bluish green with contrasting shoot colour below; leaves linear, apex rounded or bluntly pointed and bevelled, flat in section, shiny and without stomata above, stomata in

two broad or one coalesced band beneath with a waxy covering, 1.2–1.8 cm × 1.5–2 mm (0.5–0.7 × 0.1 in); crushed foliage with a pungent resinous smell. *Flowers* On previous season's shoots in late spring; male cones yellow, 1.5–2 cm (0.6–0.8 in). *Fruit* Cylindrical, ripening in first autumn to pale reddish brown, 4–6.5 cm (1.6–2.6 in); scales thin but stiff, finely toothed.

Range: Central Honshu, Japan.

Habitat: Cultivated in Europe as an ornamental, in Japan occurring in mixed mountain forests.

Varieties: The typical ssp. *jezoensis* differs in the more sharply pointed leaves which are grey-white (not glaucous) beneath and pressed down flatter above the shoot, in the more slender (usually) white or white-grey shoots and in the scarcely resinous more rounded buds. The cones are lighter in colour ripening yellow-brown with thinner and more flexible scales. It occurs on Hokkaido (formerly Yezo), Japan, and across northeast Asia from Sakhalin, Korea, northeast China and adjacent Pacific Russia. It requires a continental climate, making growth too early in a maritime one and then being severely damaged by frost.

Synonyms: *P. hondoensis.*

Usually treated as a variety or subspecies of *P. jezoensis*, it may be better treated as a separate but related species (*see* above). It grows much better than *P. jezoensis* in maritime districts, but in more continental climates *P. jezoensis* does better. Both are closely related to *P. sitchensis*, as is shown by the papery thin scales on the cones. The Latin and common names refer to Hondo, an old name for Honshu.

---

p.69 **Koyama Spruce** *Picea koyamai*

Description: Evergreen tree 15–25 m (50–80 ft) with a bole diameter to 50 cm (1.6 ft).
Crown Conical in young trees with spiky branches, becoming columnar with a conical apex. *Bark* Brown, smooth but

soon flaking in young trees, becoming purple-grey or dark grey-brown and scaly in old trees. *Shoot* Golden-brown or orange-brown in the first year, sub-shiny, hairless or hairy in grooves (especially weaker shoots), then yellow-brown or purple-brown in second and later years. *Buds* Ovoid, with a rounded or bluntly pointed apex, purple, moderately thickly encrusted with resin which usually clouds white, to 6 mm (0.25 in). *Foliage* Widely parted or pointing along the shoot below, becoming more curved upwards at the sides and nearly erect above the shoot, length varies with the leaves longest one-third of the way along the season's growths, tapering to the base and apex; leaves with four nearly-equal sides and only slightly flattened, stout, linear, apex bluntly pointed to rounded and somewhat bevelled, light bluish green with lines of waxy white stomata on all four sides, 0.7–1.5 cm (0.3–0.6 in) (rarely to 2 cm (0.8 in) on young plants) by 1.5–2 mm (0.1 in); crushed foliage with a honey-like aroma. *Flowers* On previous season's shoots in late spring; male cones yellow, 1–1.5 cm (0.4–0.6 in). *Fruit* Ovoid-cylindrical or cylindrical, green or green-brown and ripening through pink-brown to dull brown, 4–10 × 3.5 cm (1.6–4 × 1.4 in); scales rounded and minutely toothed, to 1.2 cm (0.5 in) in width.

Range: Mount Yatsuga-dake in central Honshu, Japan.

Habitat: Cultivated in Europe as an ornamental, in the wild occurring in small groves on north facing slopes.

This tree is very rare in the wild, with only a few hundred trees known. It is well distinguished by the strongly (for *Picea*) resinous buds and the way in which the leaves are longest one-third of the way along a shoot and become shorter towards both the base and especially the tip of a season's growths. It makes a neat tree of moderate growth and is allied to *Picea asperata*.

p.74 **Lijiang Spruce** *Picea likiangensis*

Description: Evergreen tree to 20 m (65 ft) in height
with a bole diameter of up to 60 cm (2 ft).
Crown Conical in young trees, becoming
columnar to broad conical and eventually
with a rounded apex; branches spaced,
spreading and upswept at the tips or
curved upwards, base of branches on stem
often with tubercules. *Bark* Pale grey,
smooth, becoming cracked and scaly in old
trees. *Shoot* Buff-brown or pale yellow-
brown, hairless or more usually with
scattered hairs, ridged, becoming pale
grey-brown, moderately stout.
Buds Ovoid or ovoid-conic, apex blunt to
pointed, slightly resinous at base, brown or
whitish brown, 5–6 mm (0.2–0.25 in).
Foliage Spreading beneath the shoot and at
a wide angle or slightly forwards at the
side, those above the shoot curving
upwards to pointing forwards at 45
degrees; leaves rhombic in section, with a
slightly bevelled acute tip, upper surface
mid to blue green with two narrow bands
with one or two lines of waxy glaucous
stomata, underside glaucous blue with two
wide waxy stomatal bands of four or five
lines, 1.3–1.8 cm × 1.5 mm (0.5–0.7 ×
0.6 in); crushed foliage with a grassy or
lemon-resin scent. *Flowers* On previous
season's shoots in late spring; male cones
globular and purple-red at first, expanding
to 2–2.5 cm (0.8–1 in) and yellow, on
shoots throughout the crown; female cones
erect, rich purple or purple-red, 3–4 cm
(1.2–1.6 in), on vigorous shoots in upper
crown. *Fruit* Cylindrical or ellipsoidal,
pendent, bright purple-red during the
summer and ripening to bright brown in
first autumn, 7–15 × 2.5–3 cm (2.8–6 ×
1–1.2 in); scales rhombic or rounded
rhombic, margins wavy or pressed against
shoot and tight in the closed cone, firmly
papery, to 1.5 cm (0.6 in) in width.

Range: Northwest Yunnan and southern Sichuan
(China) across into southeast Tibet.

Habitat: Cultivated as an ornamental in Europe, in
the wild in montane forest in dry zones.

Varieties: Several taxa have been recorded as varieties but these are here listed under *P. purpurea*.
Synonyms: *Abies likiangensis, Picea yunnanensis.*

This tree is spectacular when carrying the massed male cones and the fewer but more strongly-coloured female cones. It thrives on a wide range of soils, but is perhaps most attractive on dry sandy soils, which stimulate precocious flowering. It is quite variable, both in habit and foliage colour, and also in cone characters, with forms with free papery scales and also ones with more rounded and tight scales. However, the combination of the two-tone leaves and the large and colourful cones distinguish it. Some forms develop large growths or tubercules at the base of the branches. This phenomenon also occurs in *P. sitchensis* and rarely in *P. abies*.

---

p.73 **Black Spruce** *Picea mariana*

Description: Evergreen tree 10–20 m (33–65 ft) in height with a bole diameter to 50 cm (1.6 ft).
Crown Conical when young, in old trees columnar, but the lower branches will layer if they touch the ground, and then form a ring of secondary stems. *Bark* Grey-brown and peeling into small flakes in young trees, becoming scaly and grey in old ones.
Shoot Yellow-brown and usually reddish hairy in the first winter, becoming brown or reddish brown or darker in later years, slender. *Buds* Ovoid, pointed, red-brown or brown, 3 mm (0.1 in). *Foliage* Rather radial and forwards around the shoot but denser above and thinner or parted below, bluish green; leaves linear, apex tapered to a bony point, quadrangular with lines of waxy stomata on all four sides, 1–1.3 cm (0.4–0.5 in) (rarely 0.6–1.8 cm (0.25–0.7 in)) by 0.7 mm (0.1 in); crushed foliage with a balsam or lemon balm scent.
Flowers On previous season's shoots in late spring; male cones yellow-brown, 1–1.5 cm (0.4–0.6 in). *Fruit* Ovoid, purple when

growing, ripening to dark purple or reddish to grey-brown (in the far north this may be in their second autumn) and remaining on the tree for two to three years, 2–3.5 × 1.5–2 cm (0.8–1.4 × 0.6–0.8 in); scales thin, woody, wrinkled, to 1 cm (0.4 in) in width.

Range: Across northern North America from Newfoundland to the Alaska coast.

Habitat: Cultivated in Europe as an ornamental, in the wild occurring on barren acid sands and in sphagnum bogs.

Synonyms: *P. nigra*.

This tree is unusual in its ability to layer the branches and can make a fairy ring of secondary stems. Layering may be an important method of regeneration in the northern part of its range, where the cones may be two years in ripening. Only *P. omorika* has similar persistent cones, and the two trees have produced a hybrid, *P. × mariorika*, which is intermediate between the parents.

---

p.69 **Taiwan Spruce** *Picea morrisonicola*

Description: Evergreen tree 10–20 m (33–65 ft) with a bole diameter to 50 cm (1.6 ft). *Crown* Conic in young trees, later columnar. *Bark* Brown or purplish grey with resin blisters, finely flaky, in old trees rough and scaly. *Shoot* Ash white or ash grey and slender in first winter with blackish dots, brown by three or four years. *Buds* Ovoid-conic, chestnut brown, shiny, 4 mm (0.2 in). *Foliage* Parted below the shoot, spreading at the sides and tightly imbricate above; leaves linear, slender, rhombic, apex tapers to a sharp bony point in young trees, to a more bluntly pointed or acute apex in old ones, grass green with a line or two of white dots of stomata on all four surfaces, 0.8–1.4 cm (0.3–0.6 in) (to 2 cm (0.8 in) on young plants) by 1–1.5 mm (0.1 in) (but only 0.7–1 mm (0.1 in) on young plants; crushed foliage faintly resin scented. *Flowers* On previous

season's shoots in spring; male cones yellow,
1–1.5 cm (0.4–0.6 in). *Fruit* Oblong,
ripens to brown, 5–7 × 2.5–3 cm (2–2.8 ×
1–1.2 in); scales obovate, rounded, pressed
against shoot, moderately woody.

Range: Taiwan on the central mountains.
Habitat: Cultivated in Europe as an ornamental, in
          the wild occurring in mixed forests.

This species is very closely related to
P. wilsonii and may be considered as a
vicarious species (i.e. 'in another place').
Young plants have rather lax and sharp-
pointed foliage, but in older trees the leaves
are densely arranged on the shoots and
acute or bluntly pointed.

---

p.69 **Siberian Spruce** *Picea obovata*

Description: Evergreen tree 15–20 m (50–65 ft) with a
              bole diameter to 60 cm (2 ft).
              Crown Conic, later columnar.
              Bark Purplish grey, finely flaky. *Shoot* Pale
              brown or buff-yellow, usually glandular
              hairy. *Buds* Ovoid, pointed, chestnut
              brown or brown, 5 mm (0.2 in).
              Foliage Parted beneath the shoot, pointing
              forwards at sides and imbricate above;
              leaves linear, apex tapered to a bony point,
              rhombic in section, fresh green with faint
              lines of white dots of stomata on all four
              sides, 1.3–2.3 cm × 0.7–1 mm (0.5–0.9 ×
              0.1 in); crushed foliage with a faint resin
              smell. *Flowers* On previous season's shoots
              in spring; male cones yellow, 1–1.5 cm
              (0.4–0.6 in). *Fruit* Cylindric-ovoid, ripens
              to brown, 5–11 × 2–3 cm (2–4.3 ×
              0.8–1.2 in); scales obovate, rounded,
              pressed against shoot, moderately woody.

Range: Northwest Europe across northern Asia to
           central Siberia.
Habitat: Woodlands.
Synonyms: *Picea abies* ssp. *obovata*.

This tree is very different from *P. abies* in
the smaller cone, with its tight (when
unopened) scales which are rounded and
woody, not as thin and flexible as in *P. abies*.

The more slender foliage and hairy shoots also distinguish it. However, where the two species meet in Scandinavia and northeastern Russia, hybrid swarms have been formed, with characters from both parent species. These are referred to *P. × fennica*, mainly distinguished by the more or less rhombic cone scales. The two species are presumed to have survived the last Ice Age in different parts of Eurasia, and to have met when both expanded their ranges as the ice melted.

p.76 **Serbian Spruce** *Picea omorika*

Description: Evergreen tree to 15–25 m (50–80 ft) with a bole to 60 cm (2 ft).
Crown Narrow columnar or spire-like crown, initially with spreading branches which soon become pendulous, arching out at the tips, giving a crown 1–3 m (3.3–10 ft) in diameter. *Bark* Bark orange-brown, reddish or purplish brown, finely flaky, becoming rough in old trees with thin scaly flakes. *Shoot* Orange-brown or pinkish brown, with similar or darker-coloured hairs, becoming dark purplish brown or black in subsequent years. *Buds* Conic or ovoid-conic, pointed, brown, slightly resinous, to 7 mm (0.3 in). *Foliage* Imbricate along the shoot above but spreading at the sides and parted beneath, but in the pendulous branches the leaves are pressed against the shoot at base, before curving erect; leaves flattened, dark glossy green without stomata on the outer surface, with two silvery green bands of waxy stomata beneath on the inner surface, 2–2.5 cm × 1–1.5 mm (0.8–1 × 0.1 in), apex rounded, abruptly short-pointed; crushed foliage only slightly resin scented. *Flowers* On previous season's growths; male cones globular, red, shedding yellow pollen in late spring; female cones clustered in upper crown on terminal shoots, pinkish red. *Fruit* Ovoid-conic, purplish blue whilst growing, ripening purplish brown, persisting on the tree for a year or so, 3–6.5

× 2 cm (1.2–2.6 × 0.8 in); scales thin, rigid, rounded, to 1.3 cm (0.5 in) in width.

Range: Valley of the Drina River in Bosnia-Herzegovina and Serbia.

Habitat: Mountain slopes, also much planted for ornament and in forest plots.

Varieties: 'Pendula', with strongly pendulous branches, is occasionally cultivated.

This is a very attractive tree with its remarkable narrow crown. This is not because the branches are shorter than in other spruces, but because they become pendulous, arching out only at the tips, which is believed to be an adaptation to minimize snow damage. It is extremely tolerant of sites and conditions.

p.75 **Caucasian Spruce** or **Oriental Spruce**
Picea orientalis

Description: Evergreen tree 20–40 m (65–130 ft), with a bole to 90 cm (2.9 ft).
Crown Conical in young trees, becoming dense and columnar in old trees with spreading or slightly pendent branches.
Bark Pink-grey and slightly roughened in young trees, becoming brown or grey-brown and cracked into rounded scales in old trees. *Shoot* Ridged, pale brown with short pale brown hairs on the ridges and leaf bases, becoming brown on older shoots. *Buds* Ovoid, bluntly pointed, brown with some white flecks of resin, 4 mm (0.2 in).
Foliage Pointing forwards all around the shoot at an angle of about 45 degrees, except parted below, dense with the leaves persisting for five to eight years; leaves very short, curved forwards, 6–8 × 1.5–2 mm (0.25–0.3 × 0.1 in), quadrangular or four-sided, dark shiny green with about six lines of scattered stomata along the centre of each surface, apex bevelled, rounded or bluntly pointed to acute; crushed foliage with a resinous fragrance. *Flowers* In spring on previous year's shoots; male cones throughout the crown in late spring, brick-red and showy, 1–2 cm (0.4–0.8 in), with

yellow pollen; female flowers erect, bright red-purple. *Fruit* Narrow spindle-shaped or cylindric-conical, tapered towards apex and more abruptly at base, 6–10 × 1.5–1.8 cm (2.4–4 × 0.6–0.7 in) (closed), scales rounded, broader than long, to 1.8 cm (0.7 in) wide, thin.

Range: Caucasus Mountains and northeast Turkey, around the eastern shore of the Black Sea.

Habitat: Cultivated as an ornamental in Europe, in the wild forming extensive pure forests, or occasionally with *Abies nordmanniana*.

Varieties: 'Aurea' is a garden selection in which the new foliage flushes creamy yellow through gold for six weeks, before becoming dark green. 'Skylands' is a new form which retains the yellow-gold colour, but loses the attractiveness of the male and female cones.

This is a very attractive spruce, both for the dense crown and in spring for the massed male cones.

---

p.71 **Colorado Spruce** or **Colorado Blue Spruce** *Picea pungens*

Description: Evergreen tree 15–30 m (50–100 ft) with a bole diameter to 60 cm (2 ft).
Crown Conical and spiky in young trees, becoming columnar and dense in old trees. *Bark* Red-brown to purplish grey, with scaly or peeling plates. *Shoot* Orange-brown to yellow-brown in first winter, stout, sub-shiny and hairless, then purplish brown or yellow-brown. *Buds* Conical to ovoid-conic, pale to chestnut brown, slightly or not resinous, scales free at the tips, often a ring of awl-like scales around the base, 6 mm (0.25 in). *Foliage* Parted beneath or with a few erratic leaves, at the side spreading and above the shoot either curved upwards or pointing forwards along the shoot at a wide angle; leaves curved, four-sided, rhombic and almost square in section, tapering to a sharp (pungent) bony tip, stomata in bands along all four sides, grey-green to vivid glaucous blue depending upon the quantity of wax

present but becoming greener after the first winter as the wax is washed off, 1.5–3 cm × 1.5 mm (0.6–1.2 × 0.1 in); crushed foliage with a sweet resin scent. *Flowers* On previous season's shoots in early summer; male cones cylindrical, yellow, 2–3 cm (0.8–1.2 in). *Fruit* Cylindric with soft papery scales which are wavy, rounded, and notched or toothed at the tips, ripening in first autumn to pale brown or whitish brown but only falling in second year, 5–10 × 3–4.5 cm (2–4 × 1.2–1.8 in).

Range: Wyoming, Idaho, Utah, Arizona, New Mexico and Colorado, USA.

Habitat: Cultivated in Europe as an ornamental, in the wild occurring in scattered small stands close to streams or on north-facing slopes.

Varieties: Clonal selections for glaucous foliage include 'Glauca', 'Koster', 'Hoopsii', 'Hoto', 'Spek' and 'Thomsen'. In all these, the new foliage especially tends to be silvery for a period.

This tree is predominantly cultivated as one of the selected blue forms and as a young tree can be spectacular. The blue wax is usually lost after a year or so with the leaves reverting to a more normal grey-green. The leaves fall after three or four years, revealing the red-brown branches which can contrast poorly with the glaucous foliage in unthrifty trees. Adelgid insects (aphids) can also cause unsightly defoliation.

---

p.74   **Purple-cone Spruce** *Picea purpurea*

Description: Evergreen tree to 25 m (80 ft) in height with a bole diameter to 60 cm (2 ft). *Crown* Conical in young trees, becoming columnar or broad conic, dense, with branches either spreading or strongly curved upwards at the tips. *Bark* Orange-brown, finely flaky with small papery scales, not (or scarcely) scaly at base. *Shoot* Pale buff-coloured, later ash brown, densely hairy, slender to moderately stout. *Buds* Ovoid or conic, chestnut brown, slightly resinous, mainly 3–4 mm

(0.1–0.2 in). *Foliage* In soft and flexible but prickly sprays, leaves widely parted beneath the shoot, at the side at right angles or forwards at 45 degrees, those above forward along the shoot (imbricate) or at an acute angle to the shoot, rhombic in section, dark shiny green above with a single line or sometimes no lines of waxy silvery stomata and a bevelled slender-pointed to rounded-pointed apex, beneath greyish or bluish green with two broad bands of waxy stomata, 0.6–1.5 cm × 1–1.8 mm (0.25–0.6 × 0.1 in); crushed foliage with a faint grassy resinous scent. *Flowers* On previous season's growths in mid-spring; male cones conical, light red, becoming paler on opening with yellow pollen, 1.5–2.5 cm (0.6–1 in); female cones erect, bright purple, 2 cm (0.8 in). *Fruit* Purple until ripening through purple-brown to mid to grey-brown in first autumn, ovoid, 2.5–4 cm (1–1.6 in) (rarely to 6 cm (2.4 in)) by 2 cm (0.8 in); scales rhombic, with a free wavy apex, papery and flexible.

Range: Northern Sichuan, east Qinghai and from south to central Gansu, China.

Habitat: Cultivated as an ornamental in Europe; in China it occurs in pure forests on moist mountain-sides.

Synonyms: *P. likiangensis* var. *purpurea*.

Similar species: **Balfour Spruce** *P. balfouriana* is a closely related species, which perhaps should be treated as a subspecies. It has similarly imbricate foliage but it is bluish grey and the side leaves tend to droop down, it has resinous buds and the larger cones (4–9 cm (1.6–3.5 in)) have more rounded or slender-pointed and tighter scales.

This is a very attractive tree, forming neat specimens. The cones are brightly coloured but are too small to create an effective display. It is related to *P. likiangensis* but easily distinguished by the bark, imbricate grey-green foliage and smaller cones. It is tolerant of a wide variety of sites. The plants from Sichuan make taller trees than those from Gansu.

p.70   **Schrenk Spruce** *Picea schrenkiana*

Description: Evergreen tree 15–20 m (50–65 ft) with a
bole diameter to 50 cm (1.6 in).
Crown Conical in young trees, remaining
conical and spire-like, or broadening to
columnar, retaining the branches to the
ground in open situations; branches
spreading or declinate with the laterals
pendent but relatively short. *Bark* Grey
and smooth in young trees, soon flaking,
becoming in old trees blackish grey and
scaly into small plates which exfoliate to
reveal orange-brown underbark. *Shoot* Pale
straw brown in first winter, becoming ash or
pale brown over several years with little
change between the years, usually hairless,
moderately stout, with the peg-like leaf base
(pulvinus) short. *Buds* Ovoid with a
rounded or bluntly pointed apex, brown,
not resinous, 7 mm (0.3 in). *Foliage* Rather
radial and pointing forwards around the
shoot, especially on the pendent laterals, but
denser and imbricate above and laxer
beneath; leaves linear and incurved towards
the shoot, abruptly tapered to a bony point,
about equally four-sided, grey-green with a
few lines of white waxy dots (stomata) on all
sides, 2–3 cm (0.8–1.2 in) (occasionally to
3.5 cm (1.4 in)) by 1–1.5 mm (0.1 in);
crushed foliage with faint resin scent.
Flowers On previous season's growths in late
spring; male cones 1.5–2.5 cm (0.6–1 in),
yellow. *Fruit* Cylindric-oblong, purplish
green when growing, ripening in first
autumn to purplish brown or dull brown,
6–10 × 2.5–3.5 cm (2.4–4 × 1–1.4 in);
scales rounded, woody.

Range: Tien Shan in Xinjiang, China and in
Kirgiziya (in former USSR).

Habitat: Cultivated in Europe as an ornamental, in
the wild occurring on moist north-facing
mountain slopes or in sheltered ravines
where snow lies.

Similar species: *P. tianchanica* or *P. schrenkiana* ssp.
tianchanica differs in the larger cones and
shorter thicker foliage (leaves 1.5–2 cm ×
1.4–2 mm (0.6–0.8 × 0.1 in)). It occurs in
the western Tien Shan, mainly in Kirgiziya.

This tree is close to *P. smithiana*, being in many ways intermediate between *P. smithiana* to the south, *P. wilsonii* to the east and *P. obovata* to the north. In cultivation, it forms a denser tree than *P. smithiana*, with shorter foliage and without the graceful pendent lateral branches.

p.72 **Sitka Spruce** *Picea sitchensis*

Description: Evergreen tree to 20–60 m (65–200 ft) with a bole diameter 0.5–2 m (1.6–6.6 ft). *Crown* Narrow conic and whorled in young trees, becoming broad columnar-conic with wide spreading branches; in old trees there are often tubercular growths from the main trunk around the base of the branches. *Bark* Purplish brown and thin in young trees, developing purplish-grey scaly concave plates at the base in old trees. *Shoot* White or buff and hairless in the first year, becoming orange-brown to grey-brown in later years. *Buds* Ovoid, rounded, light brown to red-brown, 2–10 mm (0.1–0.4 in). *Foliage* Rather parted beneath the shoot but may have some pointing vertically down, spreading at a right angle to the shoot at the sides with the upper leaves imbricate along the shoot; leaves linear, apex drawn out to a sharp bony point, flat rhombic in section, upper surface deep shiny green without stomata or with two narrow bands, below with two greyish green or bluish waxy bands, 2–2.5 cm × 1 mm (0.8–1 × 0.1 in); crushed foliage faintly resin scented. *Flowers* On previous season's growths in spring; male cones dark red, globular. *Fruit* Cylindric, ripens in first autumn to pale brown or nearly white, 5–10 × 3 cm (2–4 × 1.2 in); scales thin but stiff with an irregularly toothed margin.

Range: Coastal western North America from Alaska south to northern California.

Habitat: Cultivated in Europe as a major forest tree, in the wild occurring in pure or mixed stands within fifty miles of the coast in a moist fog belt.

This tree is very widely planted in western and upland parts of Europe where it makes a fast-growing and important timber tree on otherwise poor and windswept sites. It is attractive on its own when well grown with its rather glaucous foliage, but thousands of acres make for a rather monotonous landscape! As an amenity and Christmas tree, it loses out as the foliage is very pungent or sharp.

p.70 **Morinda Spruce** or **West Himalayan Spruce** *Picea smithiana*

Description: Evergreen tree 20–35 m (65–115 ft) with a bole diameter to 1.2 m (4 ft).
Crown Conical in young trees, soon columnar with horizontal spreading branches from which the lateral branches hang down. *Bark* Purplish grey and smooth in young trees, later flaking and grey-brown, in old trees grey and breaking in small hard scaly plates. *Shoot* Off-white or very pale brown, shiny and hairless (hairy in var. *nepalensis*) in the first winter, becoming dull and pale grey-brown, moderately stout, with a pulvinus of 1 mm (0.1 in). *Buds* Ovoid, pointed, pale brown, with variable amounts of resin, to 8 mm (0.3 in). *Foliage* Rather radial around the shoot but fewer beneath and more above, with all leaves pointing forwards and incurved, rather lax; leaves linear, apex tapered to a sharp bony point, rhombic in section with four faces and broadest in line with the shoot, grey-green with a few lines of waxy white dots or stomata on each face, 2.5–5 cm × 1–1.5 mm (1–2 × 0.1 in); crushed foliage with a sweet oil of orange resin scent. *Flowers* On previous season's shoots in late spring; male cones 2–3 cm (0.8–1.2 in), yellow. *Fruit* Cylindrical or spindle-shaped, tapered and bluntly pointed at both ends, green ripening to glossy mid- to dark brown in the first autumn, 10–20 × 4–5 cm (4–8 × 1.6–2 in); scales rounded and woody.

Range: Eastern Afghanistan to west Nepal.
Habitat: Cultivated in Europe as an ornamental, in the wild forming forests especially on northern aspects.
Varieties: Var. *nepalensis* occurs in west Nepal and has densely hairy shoots.
Synonyms: *P. morinda*.

This tree has the longest needles and largest cones of any spruce. It makes a tall column with gracefully pendent lateral shoots. It thrives on a wide range of soils but can be slow to establish as it is sensitive to frost whilst young.

p.76 **Sikkim Spruce** *Picea spinulosa*

Description: Evergreen tree 15–25 m (50–80 ft) with a bole diameter to 90 cm (2.9 ft).
Crown Conic in young trees, becoming domed in old ones with markedly pendulous branchlets. *Bark* Pink-grey, smooth, becoming scaly and then in old trees fissured. *Shoot* White to pale pinkish brown, hairless or sparsely hairy, becoming paler and ash grey on older shoots, of moderate thickness. *Buds* Ovoid, pointed, chestnut brown and slightly resinous, 7 mm (0.3 in), bud scales persist around the base of the shoot as a pale brown ring. *Foliage* Radial and pointing forwards around the pendent shoots, imbricate above and parted below on strong shoots and on young trees; leaves dark glossy green without stomata on outer surface, with one or two blue-green waxy bands of stomata on inner surface, flattened, apex acute, scarcely bevelled, 1.8–2.5 cm × 1–1.5 mm (0.7–1 × 0.1 in); crushed foliage only faintly resin scented.
Flowers On previous season's shoots; male cones pendulous, 2–2.5 cm (0.8–1 in), yellow; female cones erect, green or purplish green. *Fruit* Cylindrical, glossy brown, 7–11 cm (2.8–4.3 in); scales rhombic, thin, woody.
Range: Sikkim, Bhutan and northeast India.
Habitat: Cultivated as an ornamental in Europe, in

the wild forming extensive forests above *Pinus wallichiana* and below *Abies densa*.

Synonyms: *P. morindoides*.

The old plants in cultivation do not match the trees in the wild in Bhutan, where it forms a majestic tree to 40 m (130 ft). It thrives on a wide range of sites. It is allied to *P. brachytyla*, with which it shares the pendent shoots and leaves glaucous beneath, but differs in the more slender leaves, somewhat stouter shoots and larger buds.

---

p.71 **Tiger Tail Spruce** *Picea torano*

Description: Evergreen tree to 25 m (80 ft) with a bole diameter to 1 m (3.3 ft).
Crown Conical, becoming columnar. *Bark* Purplish brown or grey-brown, becoming scaly. *Shoot* Stout, pale yellow or pale reddish brown, hairless in first winter, later buff or pale orange.
Buds Ovoid-conic, chestnut brown, not resinous, 0.8–1.2 cm (0.3–0.5 in).
Foliage Rather radial around the shoot but fewer beneath and more curving upwards above; leaves rhombic with faint lines of stomata on all four sides, with a very sharp apex, dark green, 1.5–2 cm × 1.5–2 mm (0.6–0.8 × 0.1 in).
Flowers On previous season's growths in late spring; male cones reddish or yellow, 3–3.5 cm (1.2–1.4 in). *Fruit* Long ovoid, ripening in the first autumn from yellow-brown to red-brown or purplish brown, 8–12 × 4–5 cm (3.1–4.7 × 1.6–2 in); scales pressed on shoot, thin, 1.5–2.5 cm (0.6–1 in) wide.

Range: Central Honshu, Shikoku and Kyushu, Japan.

Habitat: Cultivated in Europe as an ornamental, in the wild forming occasional stands with other conifers and broadleaved trees.

Synonyms: *P. polita*.

This tree has the sharpest needles of any spruce.

p.69 **Wilson Spruce** *Picea wilsonii*

Description: Evergreen tree to 15–20 m (50–65 ft) with
a bole diameter to 40 cm (1.3 ft).
Crown Conical in young trees, later
columnar with spreading branches.
Bark Pink-brown or grey-brown, finely
flaky in young trees, scaly at the base in
old trees and in some trees becoming
flaky into large papery scales. *Shoot* Ash
grey or buff grey, hairless and usually
shiny, slender to stout. *Buds* Ovoid-
conic, bluntly pointed, brown, slightly
resinous, to 6 mm (0.25 in).
Foliage Spreading and angled forwards
below the shoot, upper leaves imbricate,
dark green; leaves linear, bluntly pointed,
rhombic in section with faint lines of
white dots (stomata) on each of the four
sides, 0.8–1.5 cm (0.3–0.6 in) (rarely to
1.8 cm (0.7 in)); crushed foliage with a
faint resin scent. *Flowers* On previous
season's shoots in late spring; male cones
yellow, 2–3 cm (0.8–1.2 in).
Fruit Oblong and rounded at both ends,
green, ripening in the first autumn to
dark brown and soon falling, 5–8 ×
2.5–4 cm (2–3.1 × 1–1.6 in); scales are
rounded, woody, 0.9–1.4 cm (0.4–0.6 in)
in width.

Range: Across northern China from northern
Sichuan and southern Gansu east through
Hubei and Shaanxi to Hebei and Shanxi.

Habitat: Cultivated in Europe as an ornamental, in
the wild forming pure stands or mixed
forest in mountain regions.

Synonyms: *P. watsoniana.*

This is a small and slow-growing tree,
making half the size of *P. abies*, although
reported to 50 m (165 ft) in China. The
leaves are slender with four sides, and are
easily rolled in the fingers. It is variable in
the thickness of the shoots, some plants
with slender shoots being named *P.
watsoniana*. These show similarities to *P.
morrisonicola*, which occurs on Taiwan. It
also is related to *P. obovata*, which is found
across northern Eurasia.

PICRASMA OR QUASSIAS, *PICRASMA*
FAMILY SIMAROUBACEAE

This is a genus of eight species from tropical America and eastern Asia but only the one is occasionally encountered in cultivation in Europe. The genus is characterized by the pinnate leaves and alternate naked buds. The fruit is a berry.

p.320 **Picrasma** *Picrasma quassioides*

Description: Deciduous tree to 10–12 m (33–39 ft) with a bole diameter to 50 cm (1.6 ft).
Crown Low, rounded, less often slender and upright. *Bark* Dark brown and finely roughened, ridged and light brown at base. *Shoot* Dark purplish brown with rounded deep orange lenticels in the first year, dark grey or blackish in later years, with large leaf traces. *Buds* Naked, globose, golden brown with the immature leaves folded over, 7 mm (0.3 in). *Foliage* Leaves 25–40 cm (10–16 in), pinnate with 7–13 spaced leaflets; leaflets ovate to lanceolate, apex slender pointed, base rounded to wedge-shaped, oblique, margin coarsely and irregularly serrate with rounded triangular teeth, upper surface matt green, with some brown glandular hairs, midrib ridged, underside shiny light green, hairless, midrib raised, 2.5–10 × 1.5–4.5 cm (1–4 × 0.6–1.8 in); leaf stalk flattened above, brown glandular hairy, green and pinkish, 2.5–4 cm (1–1.6 in), rachis hairy, leaflet stalk 2–6 mm (0.1–0.25 in); autumn colour orange to red, brilliant. *Flowers* In lax corymbs 8–15 cm (3.1–6 in) tall and wide in late spring, flowers greenish. *Fruit* Globose-ovoid berry with persistent calyx, ripening to red, 6–7 mm (0.25–0.3 in).
Range: Himalayas east across north China to Korea and Japan; down the Ryukyu to Taiwan.
Habitat: Cultivated as an ornamental, in the wild occurring in lowland woods.
Synonyms: *P. ailanthioides*.

This is grown for the very attractive autumn colour of the leaves. The Latin name refers to the very bitter bark.

PINE, PINACEAE

The pine family consists of around 200–250 species in eleven to thirteen genera. Genera described here are *Abies* (p.355), *Cedrus* (p.582), *Hesperopeuce* (p.735), *Keteleeria* (p.771), *Larix* (p.777), *Picea* (p.883), *Pinus* (p.913), *Pseudolarix* (p.1035), *Pseudotsuga* (p.1036) and *Tsuga* (p.1240). Genera not in cultivation (or very rare) are *Cathaya*, *Ducampopinus* and *Nothotsuga* (p.851). The family is defined by the cones, which have two seeds on each fertile and woody ovuliferous scale, which is subtended by a bract scale. The mature cones disintegrate to release the seeds in *Abies*, *Cedrus* and *Pseudolarix*, but in the other genera the cones open to shed the seeds (except in some *Pinus* where the cone falls to the ground and is opened by animals). The family exhibits a range of foliage arrangements on the shoot. In *Pinus*, the functioning leaves are restricted (except in seedlings) to the dwarf or short shoots which have a bundle or fascicle of 2–5 needles. Short shoots are also found in *Cedrus*, *Larix* and *Pseudolarix* (and to a limited extent around the internodal buds in *Hesperopeuce* and *Tsuga*), but these genera also have leaves on the long shoots. In *Abies*, *Hesperopeuce*, *Keteleeria*, *Picea*, *Pseudotsuga* and *Tsuga*, the foliage is only carried on long shoots.

PINES, *PINUS*
FAMILY PINACEAE

The pines are the largest genus of conifers, with around 110–120 species. They are widely distributed in the northern hemisphere, just extending to 1 degree south in Indonesia. The genus as interpreted here and in nearly all major accounts consists of three or so very different phylogenic units and if classification was starting again, these would be treated as separate genera. However, classification is for our understanding and convenience, and therefore the stability of treating them all as *Pinus* is more convenient. The unifying features of *Pinus* include the arrangement of leaves. In the seedling state, they are helical around the shoot, simple and saw-toothed. At this stage they show similarities to the leaves of most other members of the family. As the tree matures (and in most species this is by the second year) the juvenile simple leaves are reduced to non-photosynthesizing scale leaves. These can be seen on the new growths, although they are normally quickly shed. The foliage on mature pines is borne on short shoots which form in the axils of the scale leaves. The short shoots consist of two, three or five (rarely one or four, and up to six to eight in some Mexican species) leaves or needles and are collectively known as a fascicle (from the bundle of staves which surrounded the ceremonial axe of the ancient Roman Senate). The leaves of each fascicle form a perfect cylinder when put together, i.e. the two-needled pines have a cross-section which is a half circle, the three- and five-needled pines have leaves triangular in section. The fascicle is held together (at least initially) by a sheath. The long shoots expand in spring, initially erect and resembling candles. The fascicles then develop during the summer. Leaves are normally retained for three to five years, but with some exceptions (*see PP. aristata*, balfouriana and *longaeva*). The margins are often very finely saw-toothed and stomata are either in lines on all (three) faces or restricted to the inner faces. Each season's long shoots may have only a single node or be 'uninodal', but many species are 'multinodal', with two to four nodes on one season's long shoots. Multinodal species often also produce only uninodal shoots (especially on older or less healthy trees), so this is generally a useful character if the tree is multinodal but not informative if it is uninodal. Multinodal pines treated here include *PP. attenuata*, *banksiana*, *brutia*, *contorta*, *canariensis*, *echinata*, *elliotii*, *halepensis*, *muricata*, *patula*, *pinaster*, *pungens*, *radiata*, *rigida* and *taeda*.

The cones are produced on the long shoots. Female cones are located at the nodes or ends of the shoots, and may be in clusters. Male cones are concentrated in the basal portion of the shoots, replacing leaf fascicles. In mature trees, the bottom part of each shoot is bare of foliage (even if male cones are not produced). Pollen is shed as the shoots expand in the spring, but the female cones are not fertilized until the following spring, when the conelets expand to their mature characters. The part of the scale which is exposed on the one year conelet is known as the umbo. The cones ripen in the autumn/winter period of the second year, except in *P. pinea* (and a couple of rare Mexican species) when the process is delayed by a further twelve months. The cones mainly open by the scales separating to release the seeds, which usually have a wing to assist seed dispersal. The differences between the various groups are as follows: in the soft pines, there is a single vascular bundle in the leaves, the fascicle sheath is soon shed (by the autumn of the first year), the cones are generally soft and not very woody, the scales have a terminal umbo and the wood is uniform, soft and easily worked. Species illustrated in this group include *armandii*, *ayacahuite*, *cembra*, *flexilis*, *koraiensis*, *monticola*, *parviflora*, *peuce*, *strobiformis*, *strobus* and *wallichiana*. In the hard pines, there are two vascular bundles in each needle, and the sheath is usually persistent throughout the life of the fascicle, the cones are hard and woody, often not opening immediately upon ripening, with a dorsal umbo, and the wood has pronounced differences between the spring wood and the summer wood (making it less easily worked). Between these two groups are the piñon (or nut) pines and the foxtail pines. These have a single vascular bundle, but the sheath normally falls apart over two or three years, the cones have dorsal umbos but are not hard and woody, whilst the timber is soft. This group includes *PP. aristata*, *balfouriana*, *bungeana*, *cembroides*, *edulis*, *johannis*, *longaeva*, *monophylla* and *remota*. The seeds of most pines have a long functioning wing to assist in dispersal, but in large seeded pines (with edible seeds) the wing is shorter than the seed or almost absent, including *PP. armandii*, *bungeana*, *cembra*, *cembroides*, *coulteri*, *edulis*, *flexilis*, *johannis*, *koraiensis*, *monophylla*, *parviflora*, *pinea*, *sabiniana* and *strobiformis*. Pines are widely planted as forest, shelter and amenity trees. Some are also important producers of nuts, or tapped for resin.

Informal Key

LEAVES

(i) **single**: *monophylla*

(ii) **in fascicles of two** (the occasional fascicle of three is often present): *banksiana*, *brutia*, *cembroides*, *contorta*, *densiflora*, *echinata* (2–3 mixed together), *edulis*, *elliotii* (2–3 mixed together), *halepensis*, *heldreichii* var. *leucodermis*, *mugo*, *muricata*, *nigra*, *pinaster*, *pinea*, *pungens*, *remota* (2–3, rarely 4), *resinosa*, *sylvestris*, *tabuliformis*, *thunbergii*, *uncinata*

(iii) **in fascicles of three**: *attenuata*, *bungeana*, *canariensis*, *cembroides* (2–3), *coulteri*, *echinata* (2–3 together), *elliotii* (2–3 together), *engelmannii* (3–5), *hartwegii* (3–5), *johannis* (3–4), *jeffreyi*, *patula*, *ponderosa*, *radiata*, *rigida*, *sabiniana*, *taeda*

(iv) **in fascicles of five**: *aristata*, *armandii*, *ayacahuite*, *balfouriana*, *cembra*, *engelmannii* (3–5), *flexilis*, *hartwegii* (3–5), *koraiensis*, *longaeva*, *montezumae*, *monticola*, *parviflora*, *peuce*, *pseudostrobus*, *rudis*, *strobiformis*, *strobus*, *wallichiana*

p.115 **Bristlecone Pine** *Pinus aristata*

Description: Evergreen tree 3–15 m (10–50 ft) with a
bole diameter to 30 cm (1 ft).
Crown Broad conic with upswept branches
which are densely clothed with persistent
leaves. *Bark* Dark grey, smooth, becoming
reddish brown and fissured on old trees.
Shoot Red brown or orange-brown with
dense shaggy hairs, later grey-brown,
uninodal. *Buds* Ovoid with a conic pointed
apex and incurved free scales, dark red-
brown, to 1.2 cm (0.5 in). *Foliage* Leaves in
fascicles of five, dense, radial and pointing
forwards in the first year when the fascicles
are tight and curved and flecks of white
resin few, in the second and subsequent
years the needles separate slightly and many
more flecks of white resin are produced, may
be retained for 10–20 years, linear, curved,
apex bony and pointed, bright glossy green
with a groove on outer surface but no
stomata, on the inner two sides with two
blue-white bands of waxy stomata, margins
not toothed, 2–4 cm × 0.7 mm (0.8–1.6 ×
0.1 in); fascicle sheath grey and chestnut
brown, 1 cm (0.4 in) in first year, then
splitting and reflexed from second year
onwards; crushed foliage with a pungent
resin smell. *Flowers* On current season's
shoots in early summer; male cones yellow.
Fruit One-year conelet light brown, ovoid,
with spreading prickles; maturing in second
year to cylindric-ovoid, brown, with long
slender spreading or reflexed dorsal prickles
(to 6 mm (0.25 in)) on the scales, 4–10 ×
3–4 cm (1.6–4 × 1.2–1.6 in); scales to
1.3 cm (0.5 in) in width.

Range: Western Colorado, northern New Mexico
and northern Arizona.

Habitat: Cultivated in Europe as an ornamental,
occurring in the wild on high dry
mountain-sides with extreme conditions of
summer heat and winter cold.

Varieties: None, but *see P. longaeva*.

This tree thrives on the northeast coast of
Iceland. It is one of the foxtail pines (the
sparsely branched shoots with dense leaves

retained for a decade or more give the appearance of a fox's brush). It differs from *P. longaeva* in the occurrence of the resin flecks on the leaves. If a leaf is examined under a hand-lens, the narrow groove along the outer surface is apparent. Beneath this is a shallow resin canal. By the second year these often puncture, releasing the characteristic flecks of resin, whereas in *P. longaeva* the resin ducts are paired, smaller and deeper and set beneath two grooves. *P. balfouriana* rarely has resin flecks; the prickles on the cones are stouter and more persistent.

p.117 **Armand Pine** *Pinus armandii*

Description: Evergreen tree 15–25 m (50–80 ft) with a bole to 80 cm (2.6 in) diameter.
Crown Conical in young trees with whorled spaced branches, becoming columnar conic in old trees, or with a flat top. *Bark* Grey, smooth in young trees, becoming deeply cracked into small squarrish platy scales in old trees. *Shoot* Mid to olive-green in first year, green-brown or olive-brown with a grey tint in succeeding seasons, hairless or sometimes with a short scurfy pubescence when young, smooth but with triangular scales, stout; uninodal. *Buds* Cylindrical or ovoid, with a conic apex, brown, slightly white resinous, 1.5 cm (0.6 in).
Foliage Leaves in fascicles of five, arranged forwards along shoot and either stiff and radial or floppy and bending down, straight or kinked after 2 cm (0.8 in), soft, shiny green on outer face without stomata, bluish green with several waxy lines of stomata on the two inner faces, 8–20 cm × 1 mm (3.1–8 × 0.1 in); fascicle sheath brown, to 1.5 cm (0.6 in), lost in first autumn; crushed foliage with a grassy scent. *Flowers* On the current season's shoots in early summer; male cones at base of shoot, yellow, 1 cm (0.4 in); female cones stalked, erect. *Fruit* One-year conelet 2–3.5 cm (0.8–1.4 in) on 1.5–3 cm (0.6–1.2 in) stout stalk, erect or spreading, green-brown and like a miniature pineapple; mature cone ripens through green to pale

brown in autumn of second year and becomes
pendulous, 12–20 cm (4.7–8 in) (rarely
7–25 cm (2.8–10 in)) by 5–10 cm (2–4 in);
scales thick softly woody, 2.2–3.5 cm
(0.9–1.4 in) across; seeds large and wingless,
1.4 × 1 cm (0.6 × 0.4 in) with only a
rudimentary wing of 2 mm (0.1 in).

Range: Across central and northern China south to
Yunnan and northern Burma and into
southeast Tibet, with a variety or related
species on Taiwan.

Habitat: Cultivated as an ornamental in Europe, in
the wild from dry hillsides with oaks and
other pines.

Varieties: The wild population can be divided into
four taxa, three of which are in cultivation.
The typical form or subspecies comes from
northern China and has cones and foliage at
the shorter end of the range, with the leaves
more radial in arrangement and is much
slower growing, but hardier. More attractive
are the plants from the southwest of China,
with long pendent leaves and larger cones;
these make larger trees but are less hardy in
cold districts. Var. *mastersiana* has 9–12 cm
(3.5–4.7 in) cones with seeds 0.8–1.2 cm
(0.3–0.5 in) and short 8–15 cm (3.1–6 in)
leaves. Cultivated plants also differ in the
much finer shoots. It is found in Taiwan.

At its best this is one of the most attractive
soft pines, with its pendulous bluish-green
foliage. It is very similar in foliage characters
to *P. wallichiana* but easily distinguished by
the cones and the much larger seeds without
wings. The character sometimes given of
P. armandii having hairy shoots does not
hold, as most trees are hairless.

p.110   **Knobcone Pine** *Pinus attenuata*

Description: Evergreen tree to 15 m (50 ft) with a bole
diameter to 60 cm (2 ft).
Crown Conical in young trees but becoming
open with wide-spreading and ascending
branches. *Bark* Grey-brown, smooth in
young trees but becoming fissured with
shallow scaly ridges. *Shoot* Brown to

reddish brown and ridged in first year, stout, fissures expanding green in second year; multinodal. *Buds* Cylindrical with a pointed apex, chestnut brown with white resin, to 5 cm (2 in). *Foliage* Leaves in fascicles of three, radial and rather forwards along the shoot in the first year, then more spreading, flexible, grey-green with lines of white dots of stomata on all three sides, 8–20 cm × 1.5 mm (3.1–8 × 0.1 in); fascicle sheath brown and grey, about 1 cm (0.4 in), splitting in second year; crushed foliage resin scented. *Flowers* On current season's growths in late spring; male cones clustered at base of shoot, globular, pale yellow; female cones at internodes or terminal node, often two or three together. *Fruit* One-year conelet 3–4 cm (1.2–1.6 in), brown with spiky scales, spreading on 1.5–2 cm (0.6–0.8 in) stalks; expanding in second year and becoming long ovoid-conic, curved back along the shoot, with a number of the scales on the outer side bearing a stout triangular projection which ends in a short forward-pointing or spreading prickle, 9–20 × 5 cm (3.5–8 × 2 in), remaining unopened on the tree for some years.

Range: Southwest Oregon through California to northern Baja California, becoming less frequent in the south of its range.

Habitat: Cultivated in Europe as an ornamental, in the wild occurring in pure stands on poor rocky sites.

Synonyms: *P. tuberculata.*

This tree is related to *P. muricata* and *P. radiata*, differing in the ovoid-conic cone which has a score or so of triangular scales (each armed with a stout spine) on the outer side. As in these species, the cones remain closed until opened by a forest fire.

p.118 **Mexican White Pine** *Pinus ayacahuite*

Description: Evergreen tree 15–25 m (50–80 ft) with a bole diameter to 60 cm (2 ft).
Crown Conical when young, becoming columnar and later flat-topped.

Bark Smooth, ash grey, becoming fissured, grey-brown, rough and scaly in old trees.
Shoot Dark red-brown, hairy in first year, becoming medium brown or yellow-brown, moderately stout; uninodal.
Buds Cylindrical with a pointed apex, scales with free tips, slightly resinous, 1.5 cm (0.6 in). *Foliage* Leaves in fascicles of five, pendent and forwards along the shoot, slender, flexible, glossy mid green on outer face without stomata and bluish green on inner faces due to lines of waxy stomata, 10–20 cm × 0.8 mm (4–8 × 0.3 in), retained three to four years; fascicle sheath deciduous by first winter; crushed foliage with a citrus scent. *Flowers* On current season's growth; male cones at base of shoot, 1.5 cm (0.6 in); female flowers terminal, on a short stalk. *Fruit* One-year conelet cylindrical, on stout 1–1.5 cm (0.4–0.6 in) stalk; mature cone cylindrical, slightly curved, very resinous, with reflexed basal scales, yellow-brown, 20–40 cm (8–16 in), falling soon after seeds shed; seeds 0.7–1 cm (0.3–0.4 in) with a functional wing 3–4 cm (1.2–1.6 in).

Range: Southern Mexico, northern Guatemala and Honduras.

Habitat: Cultivated as an ornamental in Europe, in the wild it grows on well-drained mountain sites with other pines at high altitudes.

Similar species: *P. strobiformis* from northern Mexico and southwest USA has shorter bluer foliage, smaller cones (15–30 cm (6–12 in)) with larger seeds 1.5 cm (0.6 in) with only a rudimentary wing of less than 1 cm (0.4 in). *P. ayacahuite* var. *veitchii* is intermediate between *P. strobiformis* and *P. ayacahuite*, with seeds 1 cm (0.4 in), but with a 1–2 cm (0.4–0.8 in) wing and longer cones (to 45 cm (18 in)) with elongated tips to the scales. In England this has crossed with *P. wallichiana* to produce *P.* × *holfordiana*, which is intermediate between the parents.

Despite its southern origin, the tree is hardy in Britain and similar climates and is very attractive in the long weeping soft foliage and large cones.

p.115 **Foxtail Pine** *Pinus balfouriana*

Description: Evergreen tree 10–20 m (33–65 ft) with a bole diameter to 50 cm (1.6 in).
Crown Conical, becoming columnar-conic.
Bark Whitish grey, smooth, in old trees deeply furrowed into irregular ridges and reddish brown. *Shoot* Covered with reddish-brown hairs for several years, then pale brown and smooth; uninodal.
Buds Ovoid-conic, apex acute, pointed, scales free at tips, red-brown with whitish resin, 7 mm (0.3 in). *Foliage* Leaves in fascicles of five, radial around the shoot and pointing forwards in tight bundles in first year but becoming more open later, without any flecks of resin, linear, curved, apex with a yellow bony point, grey-green with lines of glaucous white stomata, 2–4.5 cm × 1 mm (0.8–1.8 × 0.1 in); fascicle sheath lost in first summer; crushed foliage with a marmalade smell. *Flowers* On current season's shoots in early summer.
Fruit Cylindrical but tapering towards the apex, ripening in second summer from purple-brown to reddish brown, 9–13 cm (3.5–5.1 in); scales with a small prickle.

Range: California, in two disparate populations, one in the northern coastal ranges, the other in the central Sierra Nevada.

Habitat: Cultivated in Europe as an ornamental, in the wild occurring in open forests where due to the poor dry conditions few other plants survive.

Varieties: Ssp. *austrina* is the southern population which is located in the Sierra Nevada only some 35 km (22 miles) from the populations of *P. longaeva*. From the typical form it differs in the cinnamon-brown bark, shorter cones less than 10 cm (4 in) and leaves with a waxy bloom on the inner surfaces.

This tree is closely related to *P. aristata* and *P. longaeva* and like them can retain the leaves for 10–20 years. It differs in the absence of any flecks of resin and the longer cylindrical cones with only a short small but stouter prickle.

p.107 **Jack Pine** *Pinus banksiana*

Description: Evergreen tree 15–20 m (50–65 ft) with a
bole diameter to 50 cm (1.6 ft).
Crown Conical when young but becoming
irregular and scruffy with branches
spreading and curving erratically.
Bark Orange-grey or red-brown, fissured
and scaly in old trees. *Shoot* Purple-brown
or olive-brown in first winter, then red-
brown or purple-brown, slender, flexible,
hairless; multinodal. *Buds* Cylindrical,
thickly encrusted with clouded grey resin,
to 1.5 cm (0.6 in). *Foliage* Leaves in
fascicles of two, spreading around the shoot
rather untidily as they are twisted and
divergent, yellow-green to mid green,
linear, apex pointed, lines of white dots of
stomata on both sides, 2–4 cm × 1 mm
(0.8–1.6 × 0.1 in); fascicle sheath persistent,
grey, 4–5 mm (0.2 in); crushed foliage with
a strong resin scent. *Flowers* On current
season's shoots in early summer; male cones
ovoid, 1.3 cm (0.5 in), yellow. *Fruit* One-
year conelet ovoid, pointing forwards along
the shoot, 1 cm (0.4 in); maturing to ovoid-
conic and brown in second autumn,
pointing forwards along shoot or spreading
at a right angle, usually curved either
forwards or backwards, smooth or somewhat
knobbly on the outer surface, often
remaining unopened for some years, 3–6.5
× 1.5–2 cm (1.2–2.6 × 0.6–0.8 in).

Range: Northern North America from
Newfoundland to the Northwest Territories
in Canada and south to northern Indiana
and New York state.

Habitat: Cultivated in Europe as an ornamental, in
the wild mainly occurring on sandy knolls.

Synonyms: *P. divaricata*.

This scrubby pine is closely related to *P.
contorta*. Both these species are expanding
their ranges from Ice Age refuges and
where they meet east of the Rocky
Mountains they hybridize. The forward or
spreading cones of *P. banksiana* serve to
distinguish it. The only other species which
has forward-pointing cones is *P. brutia*.

p.106 **Calabrian Pine** *Pinus brutia*

Description: Evergreen tree to 20–30 m (65–100 ft)
with a bole diameter to 1 m (3.3 ft).
Crown Conical in young trees, becoming
columnar and then domed in old ones.
Bark In young trees orange-red and flaking
in thin scales, at the base of old trees
becoming thick and orange with black
fissures. *Shoot* Olive-green to pale reddish
brown in first winter, hairless and slender,
becoming grey-brown and rough with small
pimples from leaf bases; uni-nodal or
multinodal. *Buds* Ovoid, pointed, brown,
scales free with reflexed tips and grey fringes,
not resinous, to 1.5 cm (0.6 in).
Foliage Leaves in fascicles of two (rarely in
threes) arranged radially and pointing
forwards along the shoot, yellow-green,
rather sparse, linear, pointed, slender, with
whitish dotted lines of stomata on both sides,
10–15 cm × 1 mm (4–6 × 0.1 in); fascicle
sheath persistent, dark brown 0.7–1.5 cm
(0.3–0.6 in); crushed foliage with an orangey
resin scent. *Flowers* On current season's
shoots in early summer; male cones ovoid,
7 mm (0.3 in). *Fruit* One-year conelet
ovoid; cones mature in second autumn, long
conic, spreading widely or pointing forwards
along the shoot, not reflexed, ripening bright
brown, 5–11 × 3.5–4.5 cm (2–4.3 ×
1.4–1.8 in) (closed); scales hard and woody,
smooth to slightly raised.

Range: Eastern Mediterranean region from
northeast Greece and Crete to the Lebanon,
Turkey and Crimea.

Habitat: Dry sunny hillsides, tolerant of summer
drought.

Varieties: Ssp. *eldarica* has smaller cones (5–8 cm
(2–3.1 in)) and shorter leaves (8–13 cm
(3.1–5.1 in)) and is occasionally
encountered. It is recorded in the wild from
Azerbaijan and Iraq east to Iran and
northern Pakistan, but probably
naturalized over much of this area.

Synonyms: *P. halepensis* var. *brutia*.

This tree is one of only two species of pine
with the cones not reflexed down the shoot

but is easily separated from *P. banksiana* by the sparse and longer foliage and large cones. It is more closely allied to *P. halepensis* but the larger spreading or forward cones and the comparatively stouter foliage and rough two- or three-year-old shoots distinguish it. It is one of the quirks of botanical naming that this tree, with its main distribution in the eastern Mediterranean region, especially Turkey, should have been named from a naturalized population on Calabria, southern Italy (Latin *brutium*), whilst *P. halepensis* with a predominantly western Mediterranean distribution should have been named from the small outlying population around Aleppo in Syria.

---

p.113 **Lacebark Pine** *Pinus bungeana*

Description: Evergreen tree 10–20 m (33–65 ft) with a bole diameter to 60 cm (2 ft).
Crown Conical or bushy in young trees, older ones becoming columnar, with long ascending branches. *Bark* Grey-green and smooth at first, then becoming scaly and exfoliating in flaky plates; these lift off to reveal the underbark which is creamy white or pale yellow, gradually darkening through green and olive-brown to reddish pink or purple, before lifting. *Shoot* Dull green or olive-green in first winter, becoming grey-green in subsequent years, hairless, stout; uni-nodal but there may be a short length of shoot formed above a cone. *Buds* Ovoid, pointed, scales with free tips, 1–1.2 cm (0.4–0.5 in).
Foliage Leaves in fascicles of three, radial around the shoot and pointing forwards, hard, stiff, linear, apex acute and bony, grey-green with lines of white dots of stomata on all three sides, 6–8 cm × 2–2.5 mm (2.4–3.1 × 0.1 in); fascicle sheath pale brown, 1–1.5 cm (0.4–0.6 in), shed during first winter; crushed foliage with a pungent resin scent. *Flowers* On current season's shoots in early summer; male cones yellow. *Fruit* One-year conelet

ovoid, brown, with spreading spines, 2 cm (0.8 in), on a 1 cm (0.4 in) green stalk; maturing to ovoid with spreading short dorsal spines, and ripening brown in second autumn, 4–7 × 3.5 cm (1.6–2.8 × 1.4 in); scales thick, not woody; seed 1 cm (0.4 in), with almost no wing.

Range: China from Hebei west to Shaanxi, possibly in Korea.

Habitat: Cultivated in Europe as an ornamental, in the wild occurring in scattered groves on dry hillsides.

Similar species: **Chilgoza Pine** *P. gerardiana* is closely related, differing in the leaves longer (5–12 cm (2–4.7 in)), the shoots which are brown or orange-brown for the first year or so before becoming olive-brown or grey-green and the larger cones (10–20 × 8–12 cm (4–8 × 3.1–4.7 in)) with seeds 2–2.5 cm (0.8–1 in). The bark is finely flaky with small oval or oblong scales and pink-grey with patches of green, yellow or brown but not as outstanding as that of *P. bungeana*. It comes from the northwest Himalayas.

This tree is remarkable for the bark, which flakes in a similar fashion to *Platanus*, but is even more beautiful. It is a slow-growing tree. It has been widely planted across northern China to Korea, with really old trees having an almost white bark.

---

p.111 **Canary Island Pine** *Pinus canariensis*

Description: Evergreen tree 20–40 m (65–130 ft) with a bole diameter to 1 m (3.3 ft).
Crown Conical in young trees, becoming spreading or domed in old trees, usually retaining some lower branches.
Bark Grey, red-brown or deep red, becoming fissured into scaly plates.
Shoot Light yellow or straw brown, becoming buff-brown; multinodal.
Buds Ovate or cylindrical, with a short abrupt pointed apex, light chestnut-brown, 2–4 cm (0.8–1.6 in).

Foliage Leaves in fascicles of three, radial forwards around the shoot and drooping, grass green to grey-green with lines of white stomata on all three surfaces, margins more strongly saw-toothed than in most other species, 12–30 cm × 0.5–1.3 mm (4.7–12 × 0.2–0.5 in); glaucous blue-green juvenile leaves often retained for many years, at least on some shoots; fascicle sheath light brown, persistent, 1–2 cm (0.4–0.8 in); crushed foliage with a resinous scent. *Flowers* On current season's shoots in late spring; male cones greenish yellow but opening to red-bronze, 1.5–3 cm (0.6–1.2 in).

Fruit One-year conelet spindle-shaped to ellipsoidal, greenish; expanding and ripening in the second year to greenish grey or greenish red and to ellipsoid-ovoid in outline (opening to broad ovoid or ovoid-conic), 9–20 × 5–8 cm (3.5–8 × 2–3.1 in), on a stalk 2 cm (0.8 in); scales woody, 1.5–2 cm (0.6–0.8 in) wide.

Range: Canary Islands of La Palma, Hierro, Tenerife and Gran Canaria.

Habitat: Upper slopes of the extinct volcanoes from 1200 m (3900 ft) to 2200 m (7300 ft).

This tree is unusual in the manner in which juvenile foliage (*see* introduction to *Pinus*) is produced even on old trees. In the Canary Islands, it occurs up to the winter snowline.

---

p.119 **Arolla Pine** or **Swiss Stone Pine**
Pinus cembra

Description: Evergreen tree to 20 m (65 ft) with a bole diameter to 1 m (3.3 ft).
Crown Conical, then narrow columnar, dense with short level branches.
Bark Dark grey, smooth in young trees, developing red-brown fissures and scaly ridges. *Shoot* Brown or red-brown with a dense covering of long brown hairs, later grey-brown, remaining hairy for three or four years, stout; uni-nodal. *Buds* Ovoid-conical, dark brown, with free scale tips, not resinous, 1.5 cm (0.6 in).

Foliage Leaves in fascicles of five, set radial around the shoot and pressed tightly forwards, becoming more spreading in the second year, linear, apex acute, yellowish, mid to dark glossy green on outer face without stomata, in two faces with a broad band of waxy silvery white stomata, 7–9 cm × 1 mm (2.8–3.5 × 0.1 in); fascicle sheath soon deciduous; crushed foliage resin scented. *Flowers* On current season's growth in early summer; male cones yellow, globular. *Fruit* One-year conelet green, globular; cone matures in second autumn to purple or brown, broad oblong-conic with incurved scales, falls unopened when ripe with the seeds scattered by birds and small mammals, 6–8 × 6 cm (2.4–3.1 × 2.4 in); seeds 1–2 cm (0.4–0.8 in), edible.

Range: Alps and Carpathian Mountains.

Habitat: Subalpine forests, either pure or with *Larix decidua*.

Similar species: **Siberian Stone Pine** *P. sibirica* is closely related, differing in the glossy buds, the stouter leaves which have three resin canals (one in each corner of the leaf, cf. only two in *P. cembra*) and the often larger cones. The seeds have a thinner shell. It occurs from the Urals across Siberia to the Altai Shan in Mongolia and Xinjiang in western China. It is also reported from the Kola Peninsula near where the Russian, Norwegian and Finnish borders meet.

This pine is one of a group of five species which drop the mature cones unopened. They are then broken up by birds and small mammals, which carry off the seeds, planting a few in suitable crevices. It is slow growing in cultivation. The stout and very hairy shoot and the small cones serve to distinguish it. The seeds are edible.

p.113 **Mexican Piñon** *Pinus cembroides*

Description: Evergreen tree usually 5–8 m (16–26 ft), but up to 18 m (60 ft), with a bole diameter to 50 cm (1.6 ft).
Crown Conical when young, becoming

rounded domed. *Bark* Smooth when young, silvery grey and scaly in old trees with red-brown fissures. *Shoot* Glaucous white or green-brown, becoming grey-brown, usually hairless but sometimes hairy, slender; uni-nodal. *Buds* Ovoid, with free scales, apex acute, light brown, slightly resinous, 5 mm (0.2 in).

Foliage Leaves in fascicles of two or three, rarely four, radial, forwards along shoot, fresh to medium green, two lines of whitish dots of stomata on outer face, more on inner two surfaces, margins not toothed, 3–6.5 cm × 1.2–1.6 mm (1.2–2.6 × 0.1 in); fascicle sheath brown, 7 mm (0.3 in), becoming reflexed through 270 degrees before falling; crushed foliage faint resin scented.

Flowers On current season's shoots in early summer; male cones yellow.

Fruit One-year conelets globose with small prickles; expanding to globose or sub-globose in the second year, ripening from bright green to reddish or yellowish brown, 2.5–4 × 3–5.5 cm (1–1.6 × 1.2–2.2 in); seed 1.4 cm (0.6 in), with a pink flesh, with no wing.

Range: Sierra Madre Occidental from the New Mexico and Arizona border south to central Mexico and in the Sierra Madre Oriental from Tamaulipas to Coahuila.

Habitat: Cultivated in Europe as an ornamental, in the wild occurring on dry rock slopes.

Varieties: Ssp. *orizabensis* differs in the leaves in bundles of three or four and broader, 1.5–2 mm (0.1 in). The cone is larger, to 6 × 7 cm (2.4–2.8 in). It occurs in Puebla, Tlaxcala and Veracruz states of central eastern Mexico and is sometimes treated as a separate species, *P. orizabensis*.

This tree is one of the piñon or pinyon pines, which is harvested in Mexico for the edible nuts it produces. It tolerates hot and very dry conditions, slowly making a medium-sized tree. Formerly, several very distinct species have been treated as varieties, such as *P. edulis*, *P. monophylla* and *P. remota*.

p.107 Shore Pine, Beach Pine or **Lodgepole Pine** *Pinus contorta* ssp. *contorta*

Description: Evergreen tree 15–25 m (50–80 ft) with a bole diameter to 1 m (3.3 ft).
Crown Bushy at first, then becoming conical when making rapid height growth, later domed. *Bark* Reddish brown or yellow-brown, becoming deeply fissured into darker squares and in old trees red-brown with short plates. *Shoot* Greenish brown, hairless and shiny in first winter, becoming orange-brown, stiff; uni-nodal or multinodal. *Buds* Cylindrical but tapered to a pointed apex, brown but densely covered by resin which soon clouds white, to 2.5 cm (1 in).
Foliage Leaves in fascicles of two, radial and pointing forwards about 45 degrees to the shoot, linear, straight, tapered to an acute bony apex, bluish green to deep green but in winter becoming yellow-green, lines of white dots of stomata on both sides, 4–5 cm × 1–1.5 mm (1.6–2 × 0.1 in); fascicle sheath persistent, brown, 7 mm (0.3 in); crushed foliage with an antiseptic resin scent. *Flowers* On current season's shoots in late spring; male cones massed in basal portion, yellow.
Fruit One-year conelet globose-ovoid, 1.5 cm (0.6 in), with spreading prickles; maturing in second autumn to long conic, oblique, brown, sometimes with heavier scales on the basal outer portion, 5 × 2.5 cm (2 × 1 in), remaining on the tree but mainly opening on maturity.

Range: From southeast Alaska to northern California within 100 miles of the Pacific coast.

Habitat: Cultivated in Europe in forestry and as an ornamental, in the wild occurring in coastal forests.

Varieties: Ssp. *latifolia* is the true Lodgepole Pine. It differs in the following characters: the bark is often scaly with small red-brown flakes; the crown is narrow conic and more open, with a straighter bole; the leaves are longer and usually twisted, 6–10 cm × 1.5 mm (2.4–4 × 0.1 in) and a brighter green colour; the cone is more long ovoid and coppery when freshly ripe, most cones remaining closed or largely closed on the tree awaiting a passing fire. This form is slower growing in cultivation, and only makes a tree to 20–25 m (65–80 ft). It occurs in the Rocky Mountains from Yukon (Canada) south to Colorado (USA) in an area where natural forest fires are common. Ssp. *murrayana* (Sierra Lodgepole Pine) occurs from Washington to Baja California (Mexico) along the western side of the Rocky Mountains. It has a thinner bark which is brown and scaly, rigid yellow-green leaves 5–8 cm (2–3.1 in) long by 1.3–2.2 mm (0.1 in) and cones which are symmetrical and open on maturity, and then fall.

This tree grows quickly on very inhospitable sites. On wet or waterlogged sites it can make special roots which will conduct oxygen to the root tips, allowing them to grow up to 15 cm (6 in) into the anaerobic zone. It often develops a basal bow, due to wind rocking young plants.

p.112 **Coulter Pine** *Pinus coulteri*

Description: Evergreen tree to 30 m (100 ft) with a bole diameter of up to 1 m (3.3 ft).
Crown Broad conic when young, becoming rounded and domed, with stout slightly ascending branches. *Bark* Grey in young trees, soon fissured to reveal red-brown or brown, in old trees becoming blackish or dark purple-brown with broad scaly ridges. *Shoot* Green-brown with a purplish bloom in the first winter, then grey-brown to brown, moderately stout; uni-nodal. *Buds* Cylindric or ovoid, with white and brown hairs pressed against shoot, lightly resinous, to 5 cm (2 in). *Foliage* Leaves in fascicles of three, stiff and spreading forwards radially around the shoot, often crinkled at the base, grey-green with dotted lines of white waxy stomata, apex acute with a sharp bony point, 20–30 cm

(8–12 in); fascicle sheath dark grey with a brown base, persistent but splitting in the second year, 1.5 cm (0.6 in); crushed foliage with a faint resinous smell.
Flowers On current season's growths in early summer; male cones dark purple with yellow pollen; female cones dark red-brown or pink. *Fruit* One-year conelet ovoid, like a prickly pineapple; cone matures in second year to ovoid-oblong, recurved on a stout stalk, light yellow-brown, 20–35 × 10 cm (8–14 × 4 in); scales terminating in a stout forward-pointing spine; seeds large, 2 cm (0.8 in), with a longer wing.

Range: Central and southern California into northern Baja California.

Habitat: Cultivated in Europe as an ornamental, in the wild found on dry rocky slopes and ridges.

The enormous cones may weight up to 2 kg (4.4 lb), and are armed with corresponding sharp spines. They may open on maturity but in cultivation are usually retained on the tree for several years. It will grow on a wide range of sites, including heavy clays. It is related to *P. sabiniana*, but that species has smaller cones with spreading or recurved spines and the wings of the seeds are shorter than the seeds.

p.103 **Japanese Red Pine** *Pinus densiflora*

Description: Evergreen tree 10–15 m (33–50 ft) with a bole to 50 cm (1.6 ft).
Crown Conical when young, becoming flat-topped when mature, with spreading branches. *Bark* On young trees and upper part of bole, reddish brown and flaking in small thin scales, at base of trunk grey-brown with orange-red fissures.
Shoot Pale brown or whitish green, rather slender and smooth; uni-nodal.
Buds Cylindrical with a conical apex, scales spreading and reflexed, to 1.5 cm × 5 mm (0.6–0.2 in). *Foliage* Leaves in paired fascicles, radial and forwards along the shoot at 40–45 degrees, bright or mid

green but yellow-green at acute apex, stomata in lines on all surfaces, 8–12 cm × 0.7–1.2 mm (3.1–4.7 × 0.1 in); fascicle sheath 8 mm (0.3 in). *Flowers* On current season's growth; male flowers at base of shoots, yellow-brown, 1–1.5 cm (0.4–0.6 in); female flowers at tips of shoots, purple-brown, shortly stalked. *Fruit* One-year conelet ovoid-globose, 1 cm (0.4 in), with pointed spines on umbos; mature cone ovoid-conic, rather smooth except where the small 1.5 mm (0.1 in) prickle on the umbo remains, pale brown, 5 × 3 cm (2 × 1.2 in) (closed); scales thin, to 1.5 cm (0.6 in) wide.

Range: Japan, Korea and adjacent areas of northeast China and Pacific Russia.

Habitat: Cultivated as an ornamental in specialist collections, in the wild forming extensive forest.

Varieties: Several cultivars are occasionally grown: 'Aurea' has foliage yellow-green in summer but becoming a bright, if harsh, yellow-gold over winter. 'Oculis-draconis' is a selection with two yellow spots on each leaf, with the effect being stronger after good summers; 'Pendula' has pendent side branches; 'Umbraculifera' forms a rounded dome-shaped or umbrella crown, to a maximum of 4 m (13 ft) high by 6 m (20 ft).

This tree is closely related to *P. sylvestris*, as best evidenced by the two-tone bark, but differs in the slender green leaves and the smoother cones.

p.109 **Shortleaf Pine** *Pinus echinata*

Description: Evergreen tree 15–25 m (50–80 ft) with a bole diameter to 60 cm (2 ft). *Crown* Conic, becoming columnar and open in old trees. *Bark* Very dark to nearly black, thin and scaly on young trees, but in older trees red-brown with scaly plates, with pockets of resin. *Shoot* Whitish green to green-brown in first winter, flexible and slender, darkening in the second year and in the third year losing the outer layer in thin small flakes to reveal orange-brown beneath; multinodal. *Buds* Cylindrical with a sharp pointed apex, chestnut-brown with flecks of white resin, 1 cm (0.4 in). *Foliage* Leaves in fascicles of both two and three on the same shoot, mainly arranged above the shoot and forwards, becoming more radial and spreading in the second year, flexible, grey-green or yellow-green with lines of white dots of stomata on both sides, 6–13 × 1–1.5 mm (2.4–5.1 × 0.1 in); fascicle sheath grey, to 1 cm (0.4 in); crushed foliage resin scented. *Flowers* On current season's growths in late spring; male cones clustered at base of shoot, pale purple. *Fruit* Conical to narrow ovoid, ripening in second autumn to dull brown and opening but remaining attached to the tree, 3–8 × 2–3 cm (1.2–3.1 × 0.8–1.2 in); scales thin, keeled with a small prickle.

Range: In a broad triangular swathe of eastern USA from southeast New York state to northern Florida and across to Texas.

Habitat: Cultivated in Europe as an ornamental and in forestry, in the wild occurring in pure stands on dry sandy sites.

This is the most widely distributed pine in the USA, being found in twenty-one of the southeastern states where it is an important forest tree. It is unusual amongst the hard pines in the mixed number of leaves in each fascicle on the shoots. The predominant number is two but there is a substantial proportion of threes. On most two-needled pines, it is possible to find a few three-needled bundles but rarely more than 2–3 per cent.

---

p.114 **Rocky Mountain Piñon** or **Colorado Piñon** *Pinus edulis*

Description: Evergreen tree 6–15 m (20–50 ft) with a bole diameter to 50 cm (1.6 ft). *Crown* Conical and compact in young trees, becoming irregular but rounded and domed in old ones. *Bark* Grey, smooth in young trees but becoming furrowed and reddish brown with scaly ridges in old trees. *Shoot* Buff in first winter, later grey-brown; uni-nodal. *Buds* Ovoid, apex pointed, shortly stalked, buff, 0.7–1 cm (0.3–0.4 in). *Foliage* Leaves in fascicles of two, radial around the shoot and curved forwards, linear with a slender-pointed bony apex, margin not toothed, grey-green lines of stomata on outer surface, inner surface bluish green more waxy on the lines of stomata, for the first two years the pairs are close together, becoming splayed in the third year and retained for three to nine years, 3–6 cm × 1 mm (1.2–2.4 × 0.1 in); fascicle sheath pale brown, splitting in second year to become reflexed through 90–150 degrees, then falling, 6 mm (0.25 in); crushed foliage with a sweet resin scent. *Flowers* On current season's shoots in early summer; male cones red-brown, ovoid, 7 mm (0.3 in). *Fruit* Globose or sub-globose with a flattened base, ripening in second season from green to yellow-brown or greenish tan, resinous, 3 × 4–7 cm (1.2 × 1.6–2.8 in) when open; four to six scales fertile, seed 1.1–1.4 cm (0.4–0.6 in), wingless, dark reddish brown.

Range: Colorado, eastern Utah, Arizona, New Mexico and western Texas.

Habitat: Cultivated in Europe as an ornamental, in the wild occurring in dry open foothills, often with *Juniperus*.

Synonyms: *P. monophylla* var. *edulis*, *P. cembroides* var. *edulis*.

This small tree tolerates very dry conditions. The seeds are large and edible, forming the piñons or pinyon nuts of commerce.

p.109 **Slash Pine** *Pinus elliotii*

Description: Evergreen tree to 30 m (100 ft) with a bole diameter to 80 cm (2.6 ft). *Crown* Conical in young trees, becoming columnar and domed. *Bark* Blackish grey, rough and fissured on young trees, but purplish brown and developing flattened scaly plates on old trees. *Shoot* Orange-brown, stout, becoming grey-brown; multinodal. *Buds* Cylindric with brown scales which are fringed with white hairs, 2 cm (0.8 in). *Foliage* Leaves in fascicles of both two and three, set radially around the shoot, stout, dark glossy green with lines of stomata dots on all three surfaces, 18–30 cm × 1 mm (7.1–12 × 0.1 in); fascicle sheath light brown, 1.5–2 cm (0.6–0.8 in). *Flowers* On current season's shoots in late spring; male cones up to 6 cm (2.4 in) in length. *Fruit* Ripens in second autumn to narrow ovoid and dark shiny brown, 6–15 × 3–4 cm (2.4–6 × 1.2–1.6 in) (closed), opening on maturity to 8–10 cm (3.1–4 in) and soon shed; scales with a short stout prickle.

Range: Southeast USA from southern South Carolina, Georgia, Florida, southern Alabama and southeast Louisiana.

Habitat: Cultivated in Europe as an ornamental, in the wild occurring in swampy sites and at the margins of ponds or on poorly drained sites.

This tree is fast growing in tropical and warm temperate climates. It is an important timber- and resin-producing tree, both in its native region and in commercial forestry in suitable climates. The name 'Slash' refers to its occurrence in the wild in swampy sites or 'slashes'.

---

p.120 **Apache Pine** *Pinus engelmannii*

Description: Evergreen tree 10–25 m (33–80 ft) with a bole diameter of 30–80 cm (1–2.6 ft). *Crown* Rounded or domed from an early age with spreading horizontal branches, tall domed in old trees. *Bark* Dark brown, rough and scaly in young trees, in older ones becoming furrowed into long narrow platy ridges. *Shoot* Exceptionally stout (one-year shoots 1.5–2 cm (0.6–0.8 in) in diameter), brown or yellow-brown, rough from the decurrent leaf bases; uni-nodal.

Buds Cylindrical with a conical pointed apex, reddish brown, scales with free tips, slightly resinous, to 4.5 cm (1.8 in).
Foliage Leaves in fascicles of five, three or, less often, four, stiffly held all around the shoot like a bottle-brush, grey-green, with dotted lines of white waxy stomata on all three sides, apex pointed, bony, 25–40 cm × 1.5 mm (10–16 × 0.1 in); fascicle sheath persistent, light brown or black, 2.5–4 cm (1–1.6 in) long; crushed foliage with a grassy scent. *Flowers* On current season's shoots in early summer. *Fruit* One-year conelet long ovoid to oblong, 3–4 cm (1.2–1.6 in), purple; mature cones asymmetrical, long conic, ripening to shiny yellow brown, 10–15 cm × 4 cm (4–6 × 1.6 in) (closed); scales with a raised, broad pyramidal, recurved point with a small sharp prickle.

Range: Mexico along the Sierra Madre Occidental from Zacatecas northwards to the USA border (extreme southwest New Mexico and southeast Arizona), and also in Nuevo Leon and Coahuila in northeast Mexico.

Habitat: Cultivated in Europe as an ornamental, in the wild occurring on dry mountain slopes or in moist valley sites.

Synonyms: *P. ponderosa* var. *macrophylla*.

The longest needles of any pines are found in **Longleaf Pine** (*P. palustris*) from southeast USA and in **Michoacan Pine** (*P. devoniana*, syn. *P. michoacana*) from central Mexico. These two species are rarely cultivated. *P. engelmannii* has the next longest leaves and is hardier. The predominant form in cultivation (and at least in northeast Mexico) has fascicles of five needles, but three or four are commoner in some parts of the range.

p.118   **Limber Pine** *Pinus flexilis*

Description: Evergreen tree 15 m (50 ft) or so with a bole to 50 cm (1.6 ft) diameter.
Crown Conical when young, becoming rounded in old trees once height growth

ceases. *Bark* Grey-white, smooth, becoming furrowed into scaly ridges and rectangular plates and dark brown.
Shoot Moderately stout but very flexible and capable of being tied into a knot, olive-green, hairless, taking on a greyish tinge with age; uni-nodal. *Buds* Cylindrical, pointed, brown with white resin, 1 cm (0.4 in). *Foliage* Leaves five in a fascicle, set radially around the shoot and pointing forwards especially in the first year, firm, dark green without stomata on outer surface, inner surfaces bluish with two waxy bands of stomata, margins not toothed, 5–12 cm × 1 mm (2–4.7 × 0.1 in); fascicle sheath to 2 cm (0.8 in), brown, lost over first winter; crushed foliage with a resinous turpentine scent.
Flowers On the current season's shoots in early summer; male cones yellow.
Fruit One-year conelets ellipsoidal, on a short stalk; cones ripen in second year, ovoid to cylindrical, 7–15 × 3.5 cm (2.8–6 × 1.4 in) yellow-brown, with thick soft scales 1.8 cm (0.7 in) wide; seeds 6–8 mm (0.25–0.3 in), with a wing to 1 cm (0.4 in).

Range: Western North America from British Columbia and Alberta south along the Rocky Mountains to California and New Mexico, also in Dakota and Nebraska.

Habitat: In Europe cultivated as an ornamental, in the wild found on dry rocky slopes, often as pure stands.

Synonyms: *P. reflexa*.

Similar species: **Whitebark Pine** *P. albicaulis* is similar but differs in the smaller cones (4–8 × 4–6 cm (1.6–3.1 × 1.6–2.4 in)) which do not open when ripe, but drop from the tree and are scattered by squirrels and birds, the leaves with stomata in lines on all three surfaces, the whitish grey smooth bark and the less pliant shoots.

This makes a small tree with a dense crown of dark green foliage. It is unusual in the flexibility of the shoots. It tolerates a wide range of sites, and in the wild often occurs on very windswept ridges where the habit is stunted.

p.106 **Aleppo Pine** *Pinus halepensis*

Description: Evergreen tree 15–20 m (50–65 ft) with a
bole diameter 50 cm (1.6 ft).
Crown Conical in young trees, becoming
rounded in old ones, sparse and light.
Bark Silvery grey and smooth in young
trees, becoming red-brown, fissured and
scaly in old trees; uni-nodal. *Shoot* Grey-
glaucous, with a slight waxy bloom in the
first year, slender, slightly hairy or hairless,
later brown-grey and smooth; uni-nodal or
multinodal. *Buds* Ovoid, brown with free
forward-pointing or reflexed scales, not
resinous, 1 cm (0.4 in). *Foliage* Leaves in
fascicles of two (rarely in threes), radial and
forwards along shoot, sparse, fresh green,
linear, apex acute, moderately stiff, lines of
whitish dots of stomata on both faces,
slender, retained two years, 6–11 cm ×
0.7 mm (2.4–4.3 × 0.1 in); fascicle sheath
dark grey, 3–4 mm (0.1–0.2 in); crushed
foliage with a grassy scent. *Flowers* On
current season's shoots in early summer.
Fruit Matures in second autumn to
oblong-conic, red-brown, reflexed down
the shoot to spreading widely but not at
right angles or forwards, persisting on the
tree, often unopened for several years, 5–12
× 2.5–3.5 cm (2–4.7 × 1–1.4 in); scales
fairy smooth, hard, woody but flexible, to
1.5 cm (0.6 in) in width.

Range: Mediterranean region from Syria and Israel,
Greece and west to Spain, Morocco and
Algeria.

Habitat: Dry hillsides.

This tree is related to *P. brutia* but has even
more slender and sparser foliage and also
smaller cones which are always pointing back
along the shoot to some extent. Its past and
present use for afforestation in areas with
severe summer droughts has resulted in the
original distribution being obscured. It has
also been planted in low elevation sites in
northeast Mexico. It is one of the quirks of
botany that it was named from an outlying
population in Aleppo, Syria, when its main
distribution is in the western Mediterranean.

p.121 **Hartweg Pine** *Pinus hartwegii*

Description: Evergreen tree 15–30 m (50–100 ft) with a
bole diameter to 80 cm (2.6 ft).
Crown Conical in young trees, becoming
columnar with a rounded or domed top.
Bark Rough and furrowed in young trees,
becoming thick and reddish brown with
large scaly plates in old trees. *Shoot* Brown,
slightly bloomed and rough in first year,
becoming dark red-brown or purplish
brown, scale leaves at base of leaf fascicles
persistent, red-brown, 1.5 cm (0.6 in); uni-
nodal. *Buds* Cylindrical, apex pointed,
scales free, bright light red-brown, with
flecks of whitish resin, to 2.5 cm (1 in).
Foliage Leaves in fascicles of three, four or
five, often on the same shoot, stiff, set
radially and forwards along the shoot, with
a bony point, shiny green, with lines of
dotted white stomata on all three faces,
9–15 cm × 0.7 mm (3.5–6 × 0.1 in);
fascicles sheath persistent, red-brown and
grey, to 2 cm (0.8 in); crushed foliage resin
scented. *Flowers* On current season's
growths in early summer. *Fruit* One-year
conelet oblong-ovoid, dark purple;
expanding to long ovoid or cylindric-ovoid,
often curved, and ripening in second
autumn to purplish black or very dark
brown, 7–17 cm (2.8–6.7 in), falling
leaving a few scales attached to the branch;
scales woody but thin, with a bulbous apex;
seeds 5 mm (0.2 in), black.

Range: Central and southern Mexico into
Guatemala and northwest El Salvador.

Habitat: Cultivated in Europe as an ornamental, in
the wild forming pure forests on the higher
mountain slopes.

Synonyms: *P. montezumae* var. *hartwegii*.

The stiff but rather slender leaves with the
purple cones distinguish this tree from its
nearest relatives. It is found on the high
volcanic peaks from central Mexico south
into El Salvador. It was first collected by,
and named after, Theodor Hartweg. He was
sent to Mexico in 1836 by the Royal
Horticultural Society to collect plants.

p.105 **Bosnian Pine** *Pinus heldreichii*
var. *leucodermis*

Description: Evergreen tree 10–20 m (33–65 ft) with a
bole diameter to 60 cm (2 ft).
Crown Conical when young, becoming
columnar with a conical top. *Bark* Smooth
grey in young trees, breaking into regular
small squares or rectangles and ash-grey in
old trees. *Shoot* Pale yellow-brown in first
year with a waxy bloom and softly hairy,
becoming ash-grey for a couple of years and
then pink-brown; uni-nodal. *Buds* Conical
with long acute tip, chestnut brown,
1.5–2.5 cm (0.6–1 in). *Foliage* Leaves in
fascicles of two which are held close together
radial and forward pointing and may by
retained for up to ten years, dark glossy
green, with stomata in lines on all surfaces,
stiff, sharply pointed, 7–9 cm × 1.2 mm
(2.8–3.5 × 0.1 in); fascicle sheath persistent
6 mm (0.25 in); crushed foliage with a
resinous scent. *Flowers* On shoots of the
current year in early summer; male cones
cylindric, at base of shoots, 1.5–2.5 cm
(0.6–1 in), pollen yellow; female cones
terminal, red. *Fruit* Conelet 1.8 cm
(0.7 in); mature cones rich cobalt-blue from
autumn of first year until fully ripe in
autumn of second year when they turn
orange-brown, ovoid-conic with a small
down-curved spine, 5–10 × 2.5 cm (2–4 ×
1 in) when closed, opening to 7 cm (2.8 in)
across; scales thin, 1.2 cm (0.5 in) wide.

Range: Balkans from Bulgaria across Serbia, Bosnia
to northern Greece and Albania and in
southwest Italy (Calabria).

Habitat: Dry limestone sites.

Varieties: Several dwarf forms are recorded. The
typical form, *P. heldreichii* (Heldreich Pine)
differs in having twigs which are brown in
the second year (not pruinose and ash-
white) and that the cones have flat outer
portions of the scales, with a short acute
prickle, and brown. It is also native to the
Balkans, from Albania, northern Greece
and Macedonia and Serbia. The two are
sometimes treated as conspecific, and thus
under the name *P. heldreichii*, or as two

separate species (with the possibility that *P. heldreichii*, which was named first, may be a hybrid of *P. leucodermis* and *P. nigra*).

Synonyms: *P. leucodermis.*

This makes a neat attractive tree in cultivation with its dense habit and dark green glossy foliage. The cones are beautiful in the second season when fully expanded.

---

p.111 **Jeffrey Pine** *Pinus jeffreyi*

Description: Evergreen tree 15–30 m (50–100 ft), with a bole diameter to 60 cm (2 ft).
Crown Conical when young, becoming columnar with a conical or domed top. *Bark* Black or dark grey, fairly smooth, becoming purplish brown and furrowed with scaly ridges. *Shoot* Stout, grey-green with a white waxy bloom, especially on vigorous shoots, becoming greyish brown or red-brown, resin from the shoot lemon scented; uni-nodal. *Buds* Conical or ovoid-conical, pointed at apex, chestnut brown with papery scales, to 3 cm (1.2 in). *Foliage* Leaves in fascicles of three, radial and pointing forwards, stiff, grey-green or bluish green with lines of stomata on all surfaces, 12–26 cm × 1.5–2 mm (4.7–10.2 × 0.1 in); fascicle sheath persistent, 8 mm (0.3 in); crushed foliage with a moderate resinous smell. *Flowers* On current year's shoots in early summer; male cones at base of shoot, 1.5 cm (0.6 in). *Fruit* One-year conelet long-conic, purplish brown; mature cone conical or ovoid-conic with a rounded base when closed but opening to a broad flat base 13–25 × 5–8 cm (5.1–10 × 2–3.1 in) (closed) to 15 cm (6 in) (open), light reddish brown, soon falling after seeds shed and leaving a few basal scales on the branch; scales with a raised apophysis with a recurved prickle.

Range: Western North America from southwest Oregon south through California and west Nevada to northern Baja California (Mexico).

Habitat: Cultivated as an ornamental in Europe, in the wild found on dry rocky slopes.

Synonyms: *P. ponderosa* var. *jeffreyi*.

This tree has bold foliage and makes a majestic specimen, although not long lived in cultivation. The scent of the resin in the shoots is from heptane, a hydrocarbon which in a purified state will run a car engine.

---

p.113 **Johan Piñon** *Pinus johannis*

Description: Evergreen tree to 6 m (20 ft) or a shrub on several stems, bole diameter to 20 cm (0.7 ft).
Crown Conical or rounded domed.
Bark Grey, becoming scaly. *Shoot* Green with brown ridges in the first year, later grey-green-brown, rough from old leaf bases; uni-nodal (rarely appearing multinodal due to lammas growth in cultivation). *Buds* Cylindrical or ovoid, light brown, non-resinous, scales free at the tips, 4 mm (0.2 in). *Foliage* Leaves in fascicles of three or four, less often five, radial and forwards along the shoot linear, apex with a long bony yellowish point, outer face glossy dark green without stomata, inner faces with lines of pale to glaucous stomata, margins not toothed, 3.5–6 cm × 1–1.5 mm (1.4–2.4 × 0.1 in); fascicle sheath persistent; light brown through first winter, 5 mm (0.2 in), by second winter splitting and reflexed through 270 degrees, then lost.
Flowers On current season's shoots in early summer. *Fruit* Ovoid globular, green and lumpy, ripening to brown, 2.5–4 × 2.5–3 cm (1–1.6 × 1–1.2 in), opening to 3–5 cm (1.2–2 in); seeds wingless, flesh white, 1.2 cm (0.5 in).

Range: Northeast Mexico from northeast Zacatecas, southern Coahuila and southern Nuevo Leon.

Habitat: Cultivated in Europe as an ornamental, in the wild found on dry to very dry mountain slopes with cacti.

This makes a small tree well adapted to extremely dry conditions.

p.119 **Korean Pine** *Pinus koraiensis*

Description: Evergreen tree to 20 m (65 ft) with a bole
diameter to 60 cm (2 ft).
Crown Conical in young trees, later broad
conical or broad columnar, in old trees
domed. *Bark* Dark grey, smooth,
developing fissures with scaly ridges, in old
trees reddish grey. *Shoot* Light brown with
a dense coat of short light-brown hairs,
becoming greyer in subsequent years,
moderately stout; uni-nodal.
Buds Cylindrical with a conical apex,
brown with white flecks of resin, 2 cm
(0.8 in). *Foliage* Leaves in fascicles of five,
spreading radially and pointing forwards
along the shoot at less than 45 degrees, may
hang down to some extent, linear, straight,
occasionally kinked, outer surface glossy
mid green without stomata, inner two
surfaces with a wide waxy bluish band of
stomata, 6–13 cm × 1 mm (2.4–5.1 ×
0.1 in); fascicle sheath soon deciduous;
crushed foliage with a parsley resin scent.
Flowers On current season's shoots in early
summer; male cones crimson, globular,
4 mm (0.2 in); female cones red.
Fruit One-year conelet 2–3 cm
(0.8–1.2 in); cone green, rarely purplish,
during the second summer, ripening to
brown, cylindro-conic with thick forward-
pointing scales (except as base where
reflexed), expanding to 9–14 × 5–6 cm
(3.5–5.5 × 2–2.4 in), falling unopened;
scales soft, not woody, very resinous; seed
1.2–1.6 × 0.7–1 cm (0.5–0.6 × 0.3–0.4 in),
with a rudimentary wing.
Range: Northeast Asia from Manchuria, Korea and
Pacific Russia and in Honshu and Shikoku,
Japan.
Habitat: Cultivated in Europe as an ornamental, in the
wild forming extensive pure or mixed forests.
Synonyms: *P. mandshurica.*

This makes a neat tree and has a very good-
quality timber. It is related to *P. armandii*,
but amply distinguished by the larger
green cones and the shoots which are
densely hairy.

p.115 **Ancient Pine** *Pinus longaeva*

Description: Evergreen tree to 10–15 m (33–50 ft) with
a bole to 0.5–1 m (1.6–3.3 ft) or more.
Crown Conical when young, becoming
broad and gnarled in old trees. *Bark* Grey
or whitish grey and smooth in young
trees, becoming reddish brown with
furrows and scaly ridges in ancient trees.
Shoot Red-brown or orange-brown,
becoming grey-brown after three or four
years, densely and persistently hairy for
several years, medium thickness, flexible;
uni-nodal. *Buds* Ovoid-conic, with a
slender-pointed tip, brown, 1 cm (0.4 in).
Foliage Leaves in tight fascicles of five
needles, arranged radially around the shoot
and persisting for ten to twenty years or
more, mid green on outer face without
stomata but with two narrow linear
grooves, silvery green due to the waxy
covering on the stomatal bands on the two
inner faces, 2.5–4.5 cm × 1–1.5 mm
(1–1.8 × 0.1 in), apex bluntly pointed,
margins not toothed, no flecks of resin on
first-year needles, some small flecks may
develop on older needles; fascicle sheath
persistent for first year, 5 mm (0.2 in),
opens and becomes reflexed in second year
and subsequently lost. *Flowers* On
current season's shoots; male cones at base
of shoot, brown, 1 cm (0.4 in); female
cones at tips. *Fruit* One-year conelet
ovoid, with small pointed prickles; mature
cone ovoid with a rounded base, 6–10 cm
(2.4–4 in), red-brown; scales with a
slender fragile prickle which is soon lost.

Range: White mountains of eastern California,
central Utah and southern Nevada.

Habitat: Cultivated in Europe as an ornamental, in
the wild found on barren mountains where,
due to the extreme of climate, other plants
cannot survive.

Synonyms: *Pinus aristata* var. *longaeva*.

Ancient Pine grows in the very
inhospitable White Mountains, with
extremes of temperature and a distinct
shortage of rain. Here the oldest living

trees have been found, dated as 4900 years old, and still alive! However, these ancient trees are gnarled specimens, with more dead branches than live foliage. They are aged by taking small cores of timber and counting the rings. Because of the dry conditions, dead branches are not decayed and the age of a tree can be established from samples taken from both living and attached dead portions. For long equated with *P. aristata*, Ancient Pine has recently been shown to be different, and closer to *P. balfouriana*. From *P. aristata* it differs in the following characters: the needles are shorter and do not develop white flecks of resin in the first year, although small flecks may develop thereafter; the cones are rounded at the base and the bristles on the scales are slender and very fragile. The flecks of resin difference is because there are two small resin canals along the outer surface of each needle (rather than one larger one closer to the surface in *P. aristata*) and less liable to burst. From *P. balfouriana* it differs in the long prickle on the smaller cones. With both species it shares the ability to retain the needles for many years, occasionally for thirty years or more.

p.114 **Single-leaf Piñon** *Pinus monophylla*

Description: Evergreen tree to 10 m (33 ft) (rarely to 20 m (65 ft)) with a bole to 50 cm (1.6 ft). *Crown* Conical in young trees, becoming domed. *Bark* Dark brown or grey, smooth, becoming dark grey, fissured and scaly. *Shoot* Light brown in the first year with scattered hairs, thereafter grey-green; uni-nodal. *Buds* Ovoid to cylindric with a rounded or pointed apex, scales free at tips, light brown, 0.7–1.5 cm (0.3–0.6 in). *Foliage* Leaves in a fascicle of one, or occasionally two, radial and pointing forwards, round (or half-moon when in pairs), curved forwards, broadest in lower third and tapering to a sharp pointed apex, grey-green to glaucous blue-green, especially in the first year due to a glaucous wax covering, stomata in 18–31 lines all around the leaf, persisting for four to twelve years, 3.5–6.5 cm × 1.5–3 mm (1.4–2.6 × 0.1 in); fascicle sheath light brown, 0.7–1.1 cm (0.3–0.4 in), some splitting in the first year but mainly in year two and becoming recurved through 270 degrees or more before falling in the third year; crushed foliage with a turpentine aroma. *Flowers* On current season's shoots in early summer; male cones yellow. *Fruit* One-year conelet globose; expanding to ovoid-conic, lumpy, ripening to light brown or yellow-brown, resinous, 5–8 × 5–6 cm (2–3.1 × 2–2.4 in), opening to 8 cm (3.1 in); scales softly woody, with a stout spreading protuberance on the scale; seed wingless, 1.7–2 cm × 8–9 mm (0.7–0.8 × 0.3–0.4 in), with a thin wall.

Range: From southern Idaho to southwest Utah, north central Nevada and central southern California.

Habitat: Cultivated in Europe as an ornamental, in the wild occurring on dry hillsides.

Synonyms: *P. cembroides* var. *monophylla*.

Similar species: **California Single-leaf Piñon**
P. californiarum differs in the narrower dark green leaves which have more than nine (to sixteen) resin canals, fewer lines of stomata and a shorter fascicle sheath 5–7 mm (0.2–0.3 in), and cones which are generally wider than long with flatter scales. It occurs mainly in southern California and northern Baja California in Mexico, but just extends into southern Nevada and western Arizona.

This tree is remarkable for the single leaves, although a few fascicles of two leaves are usually present. The single leaves are round or terete in section, although where fascicles of two leaves are present, each leaf is half-moon shaped in section. It forms a dense tree, tolerant of cold winters and hot dry summers. The seed is large, with a thin wall and a starchy edible flesh.

p.121 **Montezuma Pine** or **Mexican Rough Bark Pine** *Pinus montezumae*

Description: Evergreen tree to 20 m (65 ft) with a bole to 60 cm (2 ft).
Crown Conical in young trees, becoming rounded in old ones. *Bark* Reddish brown in young trees, soon scaly, in old trees dark grey and fissured into rough scaly plates. *Shoot* Stout, green-brown in first year, later reddish brown and in older branches grey-brown, rough due to the decurrent base of the fascicles, stout; uni-nodal. *Buds* Cylindrical, with a pointed apex, light chestnut brown, somewhat resinous, 1.5 cm (0.6 in). *Foliage* Leaves in fascicles of five, rarely four or six, pointing forwards along the shoot and pendulous, soft, mid green, with faint lines of stomata on all surfaces, 15–25 cm (6–10 in) (or 30 cm (12 in)) by 1–1.5 mm (0.1 in); fascicle sheath persistent, grey and chestnut brown, 2–2.5 cm (0.8–1 in); crushed foliage with a faint oniony smell. *Flowers* On current season's growths on early summer. *Fruit* One year conelet ovoid-conical; maturing in second autumn to light brown and shiny, ovoid or conical, 12–15 cm (4.7–6 in) long by 3–4 cm (1.2–1.6 in) (closed), to 7–10 cm (2.8–4 in) when open; scale hard and stiff, woody.

Range: Central Mexico, south to Guatemala.

Habitat: Cultivated as an ornamental in Europe, in the wild occurring in montane forests.

This is a very attractive tree with its spreading crown and pendent foliage. It is not all that common in cultivation, with many trees labelled as *P. montezumae* proving to be something else, frequently *P. rudis*, which differs in the blue-green and stiff foliage and the strong tendency for the live foliage to be restricted to a dome of foliage at the top of a long stem. The rough shoots amply ditinguish it from *P. pseudostrobus*, and are formed by the base of the leaf fascicles.

p.116   **Western White Pine** *Pinus monticola*

Description: Evergreen tree to 30 m (100 ft) with a bole
diameter to 1 m (3.3 ft).
Crown Narrow conical in young trees with
tiers of whorled branches, becoming
columnar with horizontal spreading
branches in old trees; uni-nodal.
Bark Grey, smooth and thin in young trees,
becoming cracked into square or rectangular
plates and dark grey with age. *Shoot* Grey-
green underneath a dense coating of rusty
brown hairs in the first winter, becoming
hairless, smooth, and grey-green or coppery
brown; uni-nodal. *Buds* Cylindrical with a
pointed apex, scales free at tips, chestnut
brown with some whitish resin, to 1.2 cm
(0.5 in). *Foliage* Leaves in fascicles of five,
radial and forwards along the shoot at an
acute angle, becoming more splayed in third
year, persisting for three or four years, grey-
green or bluish green, dotted lines of bluish
white or grey glaucous stomata on all three
faces but more on the inner two, 7–10 cm ×
1 mm (2.8–4 × 0.1 in); fascicle sheath lost
during the first year; crushed foliage with a
strong resin scent. *Flowers* On current
season's shoots in early summer; male cones
yellow. *Fruit* One-year conelet oblong, on a
long stalk; expanding to narrow conic and
ripening in second year from green to light
brown, very resinous, 13–35 cm (5.1–14 in)
(mainly 15–27 cm (6–10.6 in); scales softly
woody, seed 6 mm (0.25 in), with a wing
2.5 cm (1 in).

Range: Along both sides of the Rocky Mountains
south from British Columbia, to central
California in the west and to northwest
Montana.

Habitat: Cultivated in Europe as an ornamental, in
the wild occurring on mountain slopes in
mixed conifer forests.

This tree is distinguished by the rusty
brown hairs and the dotted lines of stomata
on all three faces of the leaves. Like *P.
strobus*, it is susceptible to White Pine
blister rust, a rust fungus which has an
alternate generation on currants (*Ribes*).

p.105 **Dwarf Mountain Pine** *Pinus mugo*

Description: Evergreen tree or shrub to 4 m (13 ft).
Crown Spreading or rounded with thick
ascending or decumbent branches.
Bark Grey, becoming scaly. *Shoot* Green-
brown in first winter, later brown, slender
but stiff, with prominent ridges behind
each fascicle, most noticeable in third and
fourth year as needles lost; uni-nodal.
Buds Cylindrical, apex pointed, resinous,
scales free at tips. *Foliage* Leaves in
fascicles of two, radial and forwards in
current season, spreading at right angles to
the shoot in second and third years, with
the pairs slightly spreading; leaves slightly
twisted, mid slightly greyish green with
lines of waxy stomata on both rounded and
flat surface, stiff, apex pointed, 3–8 cm ×
1–2.5 mm (1.2–3.1 × 0.1 in); fascicle
sheath persistent for two years then
splitting, grey at top, brown at base, 1 cm
(0.4 in); crushed foliage with a soapy
resinous scent. *Flowers* On current season's
growths in early summer; male cones
clustered at base of shoot. *Fruit* One-year
conelet ellipsoidal, brown, with spreading
prickles terminating all the scales, 1.5 cm
(0.6 in); mature cone symmetrical, ripening
in second autumn, ovoid, 2–6 ×
1.5–2.5 cm (0.8–2.4 × 0.6–1 in); prickles
on the scales usually lost.

Range: Mountains of Central Europe, south into
Italy and the Balkans.

Habitat: High mountains at or above the tree-line,
often forming dense impenetrable stands
with interlocking stems.

Varieties: Several named selections but not forming
trees. Var. *pumilio* shows introgression
(hybridization) with *P. uncinata* and has the
cones asymmetrical, with the scales larger
and convex on the outer side and flat or
concave on the inner (i.e. towards the shoot).

Synonyms: *P. montana*, *P. mughus*.

This is more of a shrub than a tree. It is
related to *P. uncinata*. It is frequently used
in urban landscaping schemes as a shrubby
evergreen ground cover.

p.110 **Bishop Pine** *Pinus muricata*

Description: Evergreen tree to 30 m (100 ft) with a bole
diameter of up to 1 m (3.3 ft).
Crown Conical or broad conical whilst
young, becoming either broadly domed
(var. *muricata*) or narrow tall domed (var.
borealis) with maturity. *Bark* Dark grey or
brown with reddish brown fissures and
parallel platy ridges. *Shoot* Orange-brown
or pink-brown in first winter, hairless of
faintly hairy and with streaks of white
resin, later pale brown to orange-brown,
moderately stout; multinodal.
Buds Cylindrical with a bluntly pointed or
conical apex, brown with white resin,
1.5–5 cm (0.6–2 in). *Foliage* Leaves in
fascicles of two, stiffly forwards and fairly
radial around the shoot, blue-green (var.
borealis) or grey-green (var. *muricata*) with
dotted lines of white stomata on both
surfaces, apex acute and bony, 10–18 cm ×
1.5 mm (4–7.1 × 0.1 in); fascicle sheath
persistent, reddish brown, 0.7–1.2 cm
(0.3–0.5 in); crushed foliage with a grassy
resin scent, more turpentine-like from the
cut shoot. *Flowers* On current season's
growths in early summer; male cones
yellow at base of nodes; female cones at
intermediate nodes or at tip of shoot, in
clusters of up to six. *Fruit* One year
conelet ovoid, short stalked, like a prickly
pineapple with prominent and spreading
prickles on the scales, brown, 2–2.5 cm
(0.8–1 in); ripen to dark brown or dull
orange-brown, ovoid-conic and oblique,
6–8 × 4–5 cm (2.4–3.1 × 1.6–2 in),
remaining unopened on the tree for several
decades; scales conical on the exposed
surface with a prominent pointed and
spreading spine, especially on the outer
scales.

Range: From seven sites in Baja, California, coastal
California and from the islands of Santa
Cruz and Santa Rosa just off-shore.

Habitat: Cultivated in Europe for forestry and as an
ornamental, in the wild occurring on low
dry hillsides in the fog belt.

Synonyms: *P. remorata*.

This is a very fast-growing species on dry acid soils, especially in the var. *borealis* from the two northern Californian populations. The cones may be retained for up to seventy years, eventually becoming incorporated within the trunk or branch. Seeds, however, may only remain viable for around twenty years. It is one of the serotinous pines which rely upon the occasional forest fire for regeneration. The cones require to be heated in a fire, then to get wet in a subsequent shower before they will open to release the seeds (onto a damp seed bed from which competing vegetation has been burnt off).

---

p.104 **Black Pine** *Pinus nigra* ssp. *nigra*

Description: Evergreen tree to 40 m (130 ft) with a bole diameter to 1 m (3.3 ft).
Crown Conical when young but soon columnar conic, with wide-spreading and tiered branches with dense foliage.
Bark Dark brown to green-black, soon fissuring in young trees and developing deep fissures and scaly ridges.
Shoot Yellow-brown, stout and hairless; uni-nodal. *Buds* Ovoid-conical to cylindric-conical, brown but with a dense grey coating of resin, to 2.5 cm (1 in).
Foliage Leaves in fascicles of two, radial around the shoot and pointing forwards, grey-green, dense and stiff, sharp pointed, linear, apex acute, with silvery white lines of dots (stomata) on both sides, 8–14 cm × 1.5–2 mm (3.1–5.5 × 01 in); fascicle sheath persistent, dark brown, 1–1.3 cm (0.4–0.5 in); crushed foliage resin scented.
Flowers On current season's shoots in early summer; male cones yellow. *Fruit* One-year conelet ovoid, 1.3 cm (0.5 in); maturing in second autumn to ovoid-conic, yellow-brown or brown, 5–8 × 2.5 cm (2–3.1 × 1 in); scales with a blunt ridge.

Range: Southern Austria to Romania and south into central Italy, Croatia, Slovenia, Bosnia and Serbia.

Habitat: Rocky mountain-sides.

Varieties: Var. *caramanica* differs in the bark being pink-grey to buff in old trees, the leaves 8–16 cm (3.1–6.3 in) and the yellower cones 5–10 cm (2–4 in) with thicker scales. It occurs in Turkey, Cyprus, Greece and Macedonia. Var. *pallasiana* from the Crimea has leaves 12–18 cm (4.7–7.1 in) and cones 6–11 cm (2.4–4.3 in) which are buff (not yellow) with thick scales. Var. *dalmatica* has shorter leaves, only 4–7 cm (1.6–2.8 in) and smaller cones 3.5–4.5 cm (1.4–1.8 in); it is found along the Dalmatian coast in Croatia.

Synonyms: *P. nigra* var. *austriaca*.

This tree belongs to the typical eastern subspecies of *P. nigra*. The foliage is dense and in more pronounced bunches, reflecting individual seasons' growths. The denser crown with the branches spreading and slightly downswept distinguish it from the western subspecies. It tolerates chalk and limestone soils.

Corsican Pine *Pinus nigra* var. *corsicana*

Description: Evergreen tree to 40 m (130 ft) with a bole diameter to 1.3 m (4 ft).
Crown Conical when young but soon columnar conic, with spreading and tiered branches. *Bark* Pink or grey and soon fissuring in young trees, becoming dark grey with deep furrows and scaly ridges. *Shoot* Yellow-brown or orange-brown in first winter, later yellow-brown, hairless; uni-nodal. *Buds* Cylindrical with a conical long-tapered apex, grey-brown with a grey coating of resin. *Foliage* Leaves in fascicles of two, radial around the shoot and pointing forwards, grey-green and moderately soft, rather spaced, linear, apex acute, with indistinct silvery white lines of dots (stomata) on both sides, 12–18 cm × 1.5 mm (4.7–7.1 × 0.1 in); fascicle sheath persistent, dark brown, 0.7–1.5 cm (0.3–0.6 in); crushed foliage resin scented. *Flowers* On current season's shoots in early summer; male cones yellow and purple;

female cones dull pink. *Fruit* One-year conelet ovoid, 1.3 cm (0.5 in); maturing in second autumn to ovoid-conic, slightly curved and yellow-brown or grey-brown, 5–9 × 3.5 cm (2–3.5 × 1.4 in); scales rather flat.

Range: Corsica, Calabria and Sicily.

Habitat: Rocky hillsides.

Varieties: Var. *cebennensis* differs in the softer leaves which are only 1–1.2 mm (0.1 in) wide and the smaller flatter cones 4–6 × 3 cm (1.6–2.4 × 1.2 in) which are purple-brown. It occurs in the Pyrenees and north and eastern Spain and the Cevennes in southern France. Var. *mauretanica* from southeast Spain, Morocco and northern Algeria has thicker leaves to 1.7 mm (0.1 in) and cones 5–7 cm (2–2.8 in).

Synonyms: *P. nigra* var. *maritima*, *P. nigra* var. *coricana*, *P. nigra* var. *calabrica*, *P. nigra* ssp. *laricio*.

This tree belongs to the western subspecies of *P. nigra*, ssp. *salzmannii*. It is extensively used for forestry on lowland sites in Britain, tolerating both sands, and chalk and limestone. It needs sufficient summer heat, otherwise it is susceptible to a fungal disease, *Brunchorstia destruens*, which causes severe dieback. The crown is always more open and less dense than the eastern subspecies.

p.119 **Japanese White Pine** *Pinus parviflora*

Description: Evergreen tree to 20 m (65 ft) in height with a bole diameter to 60 cm (2 ft). *Crown* Conical or broad conical, becoming rounded or flat topped in old trees. *Bark* Purplish grey, smooth, developing scales and at the base becoming cracked and fissured. *Shoot* Yellow-brown in first winter, becoming greyish brown, usually hairy but may be hairless, moderately slender; uni-nodal. *Buds* Cylindrical or ovoid, pointed, chestnut brown to pale brown, scales free at the tips, 1 cm (0.4 in). *Foliage* Leaves in fascicles of five, parted and twisted, mid green on outer surface with no stomata, on inner two surfaces with glaucous waxy band of stomata, giving overall glaucous or bluish colour, 2–6 cm × 1–1.5 mm (0.8–2.4 × 0.1 in); fascicle sheath lost by first winter; crushed foliage with a sweet resinous scent. *Flowers* On current season's growths in early summer; male cones pink-purple; female cones green or pink. *Fruit* One year conelet green; maturing through green to brown in autumn of second year, resinous, ovoid-oblong, 5–7 × 2.5–3 cm (2–2.8 × 1–1.2 in); scales rounded, soft woody; seeds 1–1.3 cm (0.4–0.5 in), with a rudimentary wing.

Range: Central Honshu south to Kyushu and Shikoku, Japan, with the variety in northern Honshu and southern Hokkaido and on a Korean island.

Habitat: Cultivated in Europe as an ornamental, in Japan occurring in temperate mixed forest.

Varieties: Var. *pentaphylla* differs in the seed wings being as long as the seeds, and in the less-tapered cones and more rounded cone scales. Cultivar selections include 'Blue Giant', with a regular habit and blue-grey leaves and 'Glauca', with a low spreading habit, bright bowed and twisted foliage and persistent cones.

Synonyms: *P. himekomatsu*, *P. pentaphylla*.

This tree is usually seen as a garden selection, most of which make only small trees to no more than 8 m (26 ft).

---

p.112 **Mexican Weeping Pine** *Pinus patula*

Description: Evergreen tree to 15 m (50 ft) in height with a bole diameter to 60 cm (2 ft). *Crown* Conical in young trees but soon becoming broad and rounded, with hanging cascades of pendulous foliage. *Bark* Yellowish red, thin and scaly in young trees and above 3–4 m (10–13 ft) in old trees, whilst at the base it becomes thick and fissured. *Shoot* Whitish green for first winter, often with a waxy bloom, becoming brown or reddish brown, slender, multinodal. *Buds* Cylindrical with a slender point, reddish brown, scales free but pointing forward, not resinous, 1–1.5 cm (0.4–0.6 in). *Foliage* Leaves in fascicles of three, rarely in fours or fives, arranged forwards and all drooping below the shoot, long, soft, slender, glossy fresh green with faint waxy lines of stomata on all faces, 15–30 cm × 1 mm (6–12 × 0.1 in); fascicle sheath persistent, grey at top and brown at base, to 1.8 cm (0.7 in); crushed foliage with a sweet resin scent. *Flowers* On current year's growths during the summer; males cones yellow. *Fruit* Conelet ovoid, with a small deciduous prickle; maturing in second summer to conical or long-conical, stalkless, yellow-brown to chestnut brown, persisting on the tree in an unopened state (serotinous), 6–10 × 3 cm (2.4–4 × 1.2 in).

Range: Eastern Mexico along the Sierra Madre Oriental from Tamaulipas to Oaxaca.

Habitat: Cultivated in Europe as an ornamental, in the wild forming forests in moist well-drained mountain sites, especially in cloud forest.

Similar species: **Gregg Pine** *P. greggii* from northeast Mexico, has bright green needles which are stiff and arranged all around the shoot and larger oblong-conic cones 7.5–13 cm (3–5.1 in) which are yellow-brown and irregular in shape. It is hardier than *P. patula*.

This most majestic tree is unfortunately not hardy in cold climates. In Britain it is hardy in the south and west. Young trees are less hardy than older ones, which may be as much because only the hardier individuals survive as due to a greater cold tolerance with age. It is extensively used in Africa for forestry plantations.

p.117 **Macedonian Pine** *Pinus peuce*

Description: Evergreen tree 15–30 m (50–100 ft) with a bole diameter of up to 1 m (3.3 ft). *Crown* Conical in young trees, becoming columnar with a conic apex, branches ascending in upper crown, then becoming level. *Bark* Grey-green and smooth, becoming cracked with red-brown fissures, in old trees breaking into short plates at the base. *Shoot* Green-brown in the first winter, hairless and shiny but sometimes with a waxy bloom, then grey-brown, stout; uni-nodal. *Buds* Cylindrical with a conical pointed apex, light brown with white resin, 1.5 cm (0.6 in).

Foliage Leaves in fascicles of five, radial and pointing forwards along shoot, more spreading in second and third years, linear, acute, grey-green, lines of white waxy dots of stomata on all three sides, although few on the somewhat shiny outer (convex) side, 7–11 cm × 0.6 mm (2.8–4.3 × 0.1 in); fascicle sheaths brown, 1–1.5 cm (0.4–0.6 in), shed during first autumn winter; crushed foliage with a resin or turpentine scent. *Flowers* On current year's shoots in early summer; male cones long ovoid, yellow. *Fruit* One-year conelet oblong; in second year green and resinous, ripening in second autumn to cylindrical but curved and red-brown to pale brown, 7–16 × 3.5–4 cm (2.8–6.3 × 1.4–1.6 in) (to 6 cm (2.4 in) when open); scales thin, not woody, incurved; seeds 6 mm (0.25 in) with a long wing 1.5–2 cm (0.6–0.8 in).

Range: Albania, Macedonia and Bulgaria.
Habitat: Mountain forests.

This tree is closely related to *P. wallichiana*. It differs in the shorter and more radial foliage and the smaller cones. It is tolerant of a wide range of sites, making steady but not fast growth.

p.108   **Maritime Pine** *Pinus pinaster*

Description: Evergreen tree 20–30 m (65–100 ft) with a bole diameter of up to 1.5 m (5 ft). *Crown* Conical in young trees, becoming domed on a tall bole in old trees, usually on a somewhat sinuous bole. *Bark* Orange-brown and fissured in young trees, then

becoming dark purple or rust-brown and deeply fissured with narrow rough ridges. *Shoot* Orange-brown or pink-brown, hairless, stout, later grey-brown; uni-nodal or sometimes multinodal.
Buds Cylindric-ovoid, apex bluntly pointed, red-brown with white margins to the free and reflexed scales, not resinous, to 3.5 cm (1.4 in). *Foliage* Leaves in fascicles of two, arranged radially around the shoot and somewhat forwards, stiff, grey-green, linear, tapering gently to the hard bony apex, lines of silvery white dots (stomata) on both sides, 10–25 cm × 2–2.5 mm (4–10 × 0.1 in); fascicle sheath blackish brown, persistent, 1.5–2.5 cm (0.6–1 in); crushed foliage with a grassy resin scent. *Flowers* On current year's shoots in late spring; male cones cylindrical, yellow-brown, 1.5 cm (0.6 in), the scale which sits on the shoot beneath the male cones is short, rounded and persistent, 2–3 mm (0.1 in). *Fruit* One-year conelet ovoid; maturing in second autumn to ovoid-conic, bright or red-brown and shiny, slightly curved, 8–20 × 4–6 cm (3.1–8 × 1.6–2.4 in) (closed), opening to 7–11 cm (2.8–4.3 in); scales hard and woody, with a prominent spreading pyramidal projection; seeds oval-oblong, 1 cm (0.4 in) with a 3 cm (1.2 in) long wing.

Range: From the Atlantic coast of France to Portugal east across the Mediterranean to Greece and in Morocco.

Habitat: Coastal sand dunes but in Morocco occurring at up to 2000 m (6550 ft).

Synonyms: *P. hamiltonii, P. maritima.*

A proportion of the cones may remain on the tree unopened for some time, requiring a forest fire to open them. It is widely tapped for resin, which traditionally was called 'naval stores'. This yields turpentine and rosin, which is used to make quality paper. The harvesting technique involves making V-shaped cuts through the bark, collecting the resin in a cup.

p.108 **Stone Pine** or **Umbrella Pine** *Pinus pinea*

Description: Evergreen tree 15–20 m (50–65 ft) with a
bole diameter to 1 m (3.3 ft).
Crown Conical in young trees but as height
growth slows down, that of the main
branches does not, creating a radiating
dome of heavy branches (likened to the
spokes of an umbrella). *Bark* Orange and
soon fissured in young trees, becoming
orange and pink-brown with deep furrows
and long flat scaly plates. *Shoot* Green-
brown and orange in first winter, later pale
orange-brown, moderately slender; uni-
nodal. *Buds* Ovoid, pointed, red-brown,
with free scales which are reflexed at the
tips, 1–2 cm (0.4–0.8 in). *Foliage* Leaves in
fascicles of two, radial around the shoot and
pointing strongly forwards, grey-green,
linear, with a bony apex, moderately stiff
and easily snapped if bent, with pale
whitish dotted lines of rather indistinct
stomata, 8–18 cm (3.1–7.1 in), rarely to
28 cm (11 in), by 1–2 mm (0.1 in); fascicle
sheath persistent, grey-brown, 8 mm
(0.3 in); crushed foliage oniony resin
scented; juvenile foliage is single leaved, not
in fascicles but stalkless on the shoot, blue-
grey and 4–6 cm (1.6–2.4 in) long; they are
often retained on young plants for several
years. *Flowers* On current season's shoots in
mid summer; male cones orange-brown.
Fruit Cones take three years to ripen, one-
year and two year conelets globose,
expanding in third summer to ovoid and
ripening from green to shining brown,
ovoid, knobbly, 8–15 × 6–10 cm (3.1–6 ×
2.4–4 in); scales rounded; seeds 2 cm
(0.8 in), without a wing.
Range: Mediterranean region, rarely far inland, and
on the southern coast of the Black Sea.
Habitat: Sandy and coastal sites.

The seeds are edible and have been a
delicacy since Roman times. As a
consequence it has been widely planted and
its original homeland has become obscured.
It is unusual in retaining the juvenile leaves
for four to six years or more.

p.111 **Ponderosa Pine** or **Western Yellow Pine**
Pinus ponderosa

Description: Evergreen tree 20–40 m (65–130 ft) with a
bole diameter to 1.5 m (5 ft).
Crown Conical at first, then narrow to broad
columnar conic. *Bark* Young trees have
purple-grey to dark brown bark with scaly
ridges, which become deeply fissured in old
trees with the ridges developing into broad
flat plates which shed scales and are
cinnamon-coloured, yellow-brown and pink.
Shoot Green-brown in first winter, stout and
hairless but not bloomed, becoming orange-
brown to dark red-brown; uni-nodal.
Buds Cylindrical with a pointed apex, red-
brown with variable amounts of resin,
2–5 cm (0.8–2 in) long, depending upon
how much elongation has taken place before
winter; male cones visible as ovoid side buds,
to 1 cm (0.4 in) *Foliage* Leaves in fascicles
of three, radially set around the shoot and
stiffly forwards, grey-green, linear, with a
bony point, lines of white dots of stomata on
all surfaces, 11–22 cm × 1.5 mm (4.3–8.7 ×
0.1 in); fascicle sheath persistent, brown,
1.2–1.6 cm (0.5–0.7 in); crushed foliage
with an oniony scent. *Flowers* On current
season's shoots in early summer; male cones
cylindrical, purple with yellow pollen,
starting to swell in autumn, 2.5–4 cm
(1–1.6 in); female cones purple or red.
Fruit One-year conelet ovoid, prickly with
reflexed spines, 2 cm (0.8 in); maturing
through purple in summer to purple-brown
or brown in second autumn, ovoid to ovoid-
conic, 6–16 × 3.5–5 cm (2.4–6.3 ×
1.4–2 in); scales thin with a reflexed prickle,
1.5–2 cm (0.6–0.8 in) wide; cone shed
within a year of ripening but leaving a
rosette of scales attached to the branch.

Range: British Columbia to northeast California
along the western flank of the Rocky
Mountains.

Habitat: Cultivated in Europe as an ornamental, in
the wild forming pure stands on open
hillsides.

Varieties: Ssp. *scopulorum* (*P. brachyptera*) occurs on the
drier eastern side of the Rocky Mountains

from eastern Montana to Arizona and New Mexico. The leaves are in bundles of two or three, shorter, to 7–15 cm × 1.5–1.8 mm (2.8–6 × 0.1 in) and more densely set. The cones are smaller, 6–9 cm (2.4–3.5 in) (rarely to 12 cm (4.7 in)), green when immature and ripening buff to brown with spreading prickles. Ssp. *washoensis* (*P. washoensis*) is close to ssp. *ponderosa*, differing in the shorter leaves 11–17 cm × 2 mm (4.3–6.7 × 0.1 in) and the cones which are smaller (5–8 cm (2–3.1 in)) but with more numerous scales and purple when immature. It occurs on the eastern side of the Rocky Mountains in west Nevada, northeast California and southeast Oregon.

Similar species: *P. benthamiana* has longer but less stout leaves 15–27 cm × 1.3–1.7 mm (6–10.6 × 0.1 in) and larger cones 8–13 × 4 cm (3.1–5.1 × 1.6 in), opening to 7–9 cm (2.8–3.5 in) with scales to 2.3 cm (0.9 in) in width, green when immature but ripening to buff-brown. It occurs along the Pacific coast ranges and Sierra Nevada from Washington to California. It is often included in *P. ponderosa*.

This makes a tall-growing tree in cultivation and is planted for the bold foliage. The expanded but not mature cones are attractive in their second summer.

p.120 **Smooth Bark Mexican Pine**
Pinus pseudostrobus

Description: Evergreen tree to 15–30 m (50–100 ft) with a bole diameter to 60 cm (2 ft). *Crown* Conical in young trees, becoming columnar and domed in old trees, usually losing the lower branches. *Bark* Yellowish brown, thin and smooth for several years, becoming thick, grey. *Shoot* Glaucous blue with a waxy bloom in the first winter or light brown or rust-brown, later brown or grey-brown, at first somewhat roughened by the ridges behind the leaf fascicles but soon smooth; uni-nodal. *Buds* Cylindric-conic, pointed, light brown with whitish resin, 1 cm (0.4 in). *Foliage* Leaves in fascicles of five, drooping forwards along and beneath the shoot, slender, fresh green with white dots of grey-white stomata in lines on all three surfaces, flexible, 20–30 cm × 0.7–0.9 mm (8–12 × 0.1 in); fascicles sheath grey or brown, persistent, 1.2–1.5 cm (0.5–0.6 in); crushed foliage with little scent. *Flowers* At base of current season's shoots in early summer. *Fruit* One-year conelet long conic; maturing in second autumn to ovoid or long-ovoid, light brown and somewhat shiny, 8–10 × 3–4 cm (3.1–4 × 1.2–1.6 in), opening to 5–7 cm (2–2.8 in), opening when ripe and then falling.

Range: Central Mexico from Jalisco to Vera Cruz and south to Guatemala.

Habitat: Cultivated in Europe as an ornamental and more widely in warm temperate countries as a forest tree, in the wild occurring in mountain forests.

This tree is rather tender and not common in cultivation. In warm temperate climates it is capable of fast growth and has a good timber.

---

p.106 **Table Mountain Pine** *Pinus pungens*

Description: Evergreen tree 15–20 m (50–65 ft) with a bole diameter to 60 cm (2 ft).
Crown Conic in young trees, becoming increasingly irregular and flat topped or rounded. *Bark* Dark brown, scaly with orange fissures, becoming deeply furrowed in old trees with thick platy ridges.
Shoot Green-brown to brown in the first winter, later grey to brown; multinodal.
Buds Cylindrical with a rounded pointed apex, pale brown with thick whitish resin, to 4 cm (1.6 in). *Foliage* Leaves in fascicles of two, radial and forwards around the shoot, becoming more spreading in the second year, twisted, stout and stiff, tapering to a sharp bony point, grey-green or yellow-green, with lines of white dots of stomata on both sides, 3–8 cm × 2 mm (1.2–3.1 × 0.1 in); fascicle sheath brown

and grey, persistent, less than 1 cm (0.4 in); crushed foliage has a lemony resin smell. *Flowers* On current season's shoots in late spring; male cones cylindric-ovoid, red-brown, 1.8 cm (0.7 in). *Fruit* One-year conelet ovoid, brown, with stout forward projecting prickles, 2 cm (0.8 in), on a stalk less than 1 cm (0.4 in); expanding in the second year and ripening to light or pale shiny brown, stalkless, with stout sharp forward curved prickles, remaining closed for some years, 5–9 × 3–4 cm (2–3.5 × 1.2–1.6 in).

Range: Appalachian Mountains from Pennsylvania to northeast Georgia.

Habitat: Cultivated in Europe as an ornamental, in the wild occurring on dry gravelly or rocky slopes, either in pure stands or mixed with other pines.

The small cones which are stout and sharply armed (pungent!) distinguish this tree.

---

p.110 **Monterey Pine** *Pinus radiata*

Description: Evergreen tree to 30 m (100 ft) or more with a bole diameter of 1–1.5 m (3.3–5 ft).
Crown Narrow conical in young trees with open whorls of branches until about two-thirds or three-quarters full height is obtained, then becoming broad with a domed crown and often billowing branches, dense and appearing black in the distance. *Bark* Purplish grey in young trees, progressively darkening to black or dark grey and becoming furrowed and thick with broad platy ridges. *Shoot* Grey-green or reddish brown in first year, later pale orangey brown or grey-brown, moderately stout, hairless; multinodal.
Buds Cylindrical with an abrupt rounded pointed apex, pale brown, not or slightly resinous, to 2 cm (0.8 in). *Foliage* Leaves in fascicles of three, radially and forwards around the shoot, grassy green, linear, slender and soft, lines of whitish dots of stomata on all three sides, 10–16 cm ×

0.8–1 mm (4–6.3 × 0.1 in); fascicle sheath pale brown, persistent, 1–1.3 cm (0.4–0.5 in); crushed foliage faintly resin scented. *Flowers* On current season's shoots in late winter or early spring; male cones bright yellow; *Fruit* One-year conelet ovoid, pale brown, on a stout recurved stalk, 2.2 × 1.8 cm (0.9 × 0.7 in); expanding in second year to green and ripen in second autumn to green-brown, gradually fading to light brown, ovoid, very oblique, usually with a score or so large rounded scales on the outer side but sometimes smooth, remaining closed on the tree for forty years, from 6 × 4 cm (2.4 × 1.6 cm) to 16 × 11 cm (6.3 × 4.3 in).

Range: California on three promontories (varieties from two islands off Baja California, Mexico).

Habitat: Cultivated in Europe for forestry and as an ornamental, in the wild restricted to five dry coastal sites where much of the precipitation is in the form of fog.

Varieties: Var. *binata* from Guadelupe Island off the coast of Baja California (Mexico) has leaves in pairs, only in threes on the strongest shoots. This small island variety also has about half the trees with smooth or symmetrical cones, which are only 6–9 cm (2.4–3.5 in) long. Var. *cedrosensis* has smaller (5–7 cm (2–2.8 in)) cones and also leaves in pairs; it comes from Cedros Island off the Baja Californian coast.

Synonyms: *P. insignis*.

In the wild it is restricted to three sites on the Californian coast, including Monterey, with the varieties on two islands further south. However, it has a reasonable timber and grows fast, and thus has been extensively planted in warm temperate areas in forestry. It is not a long lived tree, but in New Zealand has made 60 m (200 ft) in 37 years, and is especially tolerant of coastal conditions. The cones are retained for forty or so years on the branches (although the seeds probably only remain viable for twenty) and require a forest fire to open them.

p.113 **Papershell Piñon** *Pinus remota*

Description: Evergreen shrub or tree to 7 m (23 ft) with
a bole diameter to 30 cm (1 ft).
Crown Irregular domed in old trees.
Bark Grey-brown, becoming scaly.
Shoot Grey to green-brown in first winter,
hairless, slender, later greyer, uni-nodal.
Buds Cylindric-ovoid, chestnut brown with
dark brown scales with free spreading tips,
slightly resinous, 6 mm (0.2 in).
Foliage Leaves in fascicles of two or three,
less often four, radial and forwards at an
acute angle in the first year, later spreading
more widely like a bottle-brush, linear,
apex with a bony point, margins not
toothed, grey-green with dotted lines of
stomata on all three sides but more on inner
two sides, 3–5.5 cm × 1–1.8 mm (1.2–2.2
× 0.1 in); fascicle sheath light brown, soon
breaking up at the tip and becoming
reflexed through 90–180 degrees, then
falling; crushed foliage with a sweet
turpentine scent. *Flowers* On current
season's shoot in early summer. *Fruit* Sub-
globose, ripening to glossy yellow in second
autumn, 2–4 × 2–3.5 cm (0.8–1.6 ×
0.8–1.4 in) when closed, opening to
3–6 cm (1.2–2.4 in), with only five to seven
fertile scales; seed 1–1.6 cm (0.4–0.6 in)
with a shell only 1–3 mm (0.1 in) in
thickness, flesh pale pink.
Range: Mexico from Nuevo Leon north into
southwest Texas.
Habitat: Cultivated in Europe as an ornamental, in
the wild found on dry rocky slopes.
Synonyms: *Pinus cembroides* var. *remota*.

The case of the seed is the thinnest of any
pine. It is recorded from low altitudes and
well adapted to hot dry sites.

---

p.104 **Red Pine** or **Norway Pine** *Pinus resinosa*

Description: Evergreen tree 20 m (65 ft) in height with
a bole diameter to 90 cm (2.9 ft).
Crown Conic in young trees, becoming
irregular and domed. *Bark* Red-brown

with dark flaking scales on young trees and in the upper crown, lower bole with broad flat scaly plates of red-brown or grey.
Shoot Orange-brown to purplish brown, hairless, rough, uni-nodal. *Buds* Conic with red-brown scales, 2 cm (0.8 in).
Foliage Leaves in fascicles of two, set radially and forwards and bunched towards the tips of the shoots, brittle (snapping off when bent sharply), twisted and olive-green with lines of stomata dots on all three surfaces but mainly on the outer one, 10–17 cm × 1 mm (4–6.7 × 0.1 in); fascicle sheath pale brown, 1.5–2 cm (0.6–0.8 in), falling after two to four years; crushed foliage with a scent of lemon-balm. *Flowers* On current season's shoots in late spring; male cones red.
Fruit Ripens in second autumn to ovoid-conic and light shining brown, 4–6 × 2–3 cm (1.6–2.4 × 0.8–1.2 in) when closed, opening on maturity to 3.5–5 cm (1.4–2 in) and soon falling; scales without a prickle.

Range: Northeast North America from Newfoundland and Nova Scotia west to southeast Manitoba and south to Illinois and West Virginia.

Habitat: Cultivated in Europe as an ornamental, in the wild occurring on well-drained, mainly sandy sites.

This tree has a two-tone bark somewhat like that of *P. sylvestris* but without as much charm. The foliage appears similar to *P. nigra* but snaps when bent, whereas in *P. nigra* the needle may break but the two halves remain attached.

p.109 **Pitch Pine** *Pinus rigida*

Description: Evergreen tree to 20 m (65 ft) with a bole diameter to 70 cm (2.3 ft).
Crown Conic or ovoid in young trees, becoming more irregular and domed in old trees. *Bark* Dark grey or dark grey brown and fissured into parallel ridges, often with bunches of epicormic shoots on the bole.
Shoot Pale orange-yellow, hairless and ridged in the first winter, becoming pale red-brown

and then brown, rough from persistent scale leaf bases; multinodal. *Buds* Cylindric with a conical pointed apex, chestnut brown but thickly encrusted with white resin, 1–2 cm (0.4–0.8 in). *Foliage* Leaves in fascicles of three, set radially around the shoot like a bottle-brush, somewhat spaced, grey-green with lines of white dots of stomata on all three surfaces, stiff, 7–14 cm × 1 mm (2.8–5.5 × 0.1 in); fascicle sheath brown and grey, persistent, 8 mm (0.3 in); crushed foliage resin scented. *Flowers* On current season's shoots in late spring; male cones yellow, 3 cm (1.2 in). *Fruit* Ovoid-conic, ripening in second summer to yellow-brown or greyish brown, usually opening once ripe but persisting on the tree, 3–9 × 3–4 cm (1.2–3.5 × 1.2–1.6 in); scales with a spreading slender prickle 2 mm (0.1 in).

Range: Eastern North America from Maine to southeast Ontario and south to Georgia.

Habitat: Cultivated in Europe as an ornamental, in the wild occurring on open dry infertile sites.

Similar species: **Pond Pine** *P. serotina* is allied and sometimes treated as a variety or subspecies. It has a more southerly distribution and is found in the wild in swampy and low-lying flat wetland sites. It differs in the slender, flexible longer leaves, 15–20 cm (6–8 in) long, the subglobose to broadly ovoid matt yellow cones 6–9 × 5–7 cm (2.4–3.5 × 2–2.8 in), which are nearly spherical when open, and which may remain unopened on the tree for several years.

This tree is unusual amongst the pines in throwing epicormic shoots on the bole and cut trees may produce coppice growths although these rarely survive to fruit.

---

p.121   **Endlicher Pine** *Pinus rudis*

Description: Evergreen tree 15 m (50 ft) or so with a bole diameter to 1 m (3.3 in).
Crown Conical in young trees, but in old ones losing the lower branches and developing a domed umbrella-like top.
Bark Dark grey, very rough and becoming

almost black and deeply fissured into squarrish plates. *Shoot* Purple-brown, variably pruinose, later grey-brown, stout; uni-nodal. *Buds* Cylindric-conic, pointed, light reddish brown, 1.5 cm (0.6 in). *Foliage* Leaves in fascicles of five, pointing forwards along the shoot and hanging down, slender, grey-green or blue-green, with lines of white dots of stomata on all three surfaces, 10–16 cm (4–6.3 in) but to 25 cm (10 in), by 1 mm (0.1 in); fascicle sheath grey and brown, persistent, 2 cm (0.8 in); crushed foliage with a citrus scent. *Flowers* On current season's shoots in early summer. *Fruit* One-year conelets oblong, reddish purple; mature cones in second autumn long ovoid, slightly curved and tapering to apex, ripening from dark purple to dark brown, 7–13 cm (2.8–5.1 in); scales with a raised conical prickle.

Range: Central and northern Mexico.

Habitat: Cultivated in Europe as an ornamental, in the wild forming forests, either pure or mixed with other pine species, on the high mountains of Mexico.

Synonyms: *P. montezumae* misapplied; *P. montezumae* var. *rudis*; *P. hartwegii* in part.

Most of the older trees named *P. montezumae* in cultivation are this species. It is hardier than *P. montezumae* but less attractive, with stiffer leaves and a pronounced tendency to lose the lower branches.

---

p.112 **Digger Pine** *Pinus sabiniana*

Description: Evergreen tree to 20 m (65 ft) with a bole diameter of up to 60 cm (2 ft) .
Crown Conical in young trees, light and open, soon domed or irregular, with long whippy branches and ascending stems.
Bark Light grey, smooth on young trees and branches, breaking up into scaly plates and in old trees with deep reddish fissures and dark grey shaggy scaly ridges.
Shoot Whitish purple-brown with a waxy bloom in the first year, becoming greyer, moderately stout; uni-nodal. *Buds* Long

cylindrical with a pointed apex, pale brown; the buds may be several centimetres in length as they start extending in the autumn, with the male cones forming ovoid conical shiny pale brown buds on the base of the bud over winter. *Foliage* Leaves in fascicles of three, arranged stiffly forwards and around the shoot for the first year, then drooping, grey-green with dotted lines of stomata on all three surfaces, apex drawn out to a long bony point, 20–30 cm × 1.5 mm (8–12 × 0.1 in); fascicle sheath to 1.5 cm (0.6 in), brown or black, persistent at base but may split; crushed foliage with a citrus resin scent. *Flowers* On current season's growths in late spring; male cones yellow. *Fruit* One-year conelet globose, prickly, on a long stalk, purple; mature cone ripens to chocolate brown, ovoid to broad ovoid, on a long recurved stalk 15–25 cm (6–10 in) long; scales with a stout spreading, deflexed or S-shaped sharp claw; seeds 1–2.5 cm (0.4–1 in), with a wing half as long, edible.

Range: California.

Habitat: Cultivated in Europe as an ornamental, in the wild occurring on very dry ridges and low hill sites throughout California.

This tree has a light open crown. It does not like waterlogged sites, thriving in dry open situations, but is not hardy in northern continental Europe. It is odd in the buds making extension growth in the autumn. The large seeds are edible, albeit thick-shelled. The common name refers to the Digger tribe of Indians, to whom the seeds were an important source of food.

---

p.118 **Southwestern White Pine**
Pinus strobiformis

Description: Evergreen tree 15–20 m (50–65 ft) with a bole diameter to 1 m (3.3 ft).
Crown Conical in young trees with whorled branches, becoming columnar with age; uni-nodal. *Bark* Silvery grey, smooth and thin in young trees, greyish brown, rough and divided into small plates on old trees.

Shoot Shiny green in the first winter, becoming grey-green in later years, strongly ridged behind the leaf bases, hairless or with some reddish hairs; uni-nodal; somewhat flexible but not as flexible as *P. flexilis*. *Buds* Oblong-ovate to cylindrical, pointed, scales free, brown with whitish resin, 1–1.5 cm (0.4–0.6 in). *Foliage* Leaves in fascicles of five, radial, dense and tightly forwards but rather irregular in the first year, becoming more open in second year, dark to bluish green, with dotted lines of glaucous stomata on the two inner faces only, slender, 7–13 cm × 0.7–1 mm (2.8–5.1 × 0.1 in); fascicle sheath soon lost; crushed foliage with a resin scent. *Flowers* On current season's growths in early summer; male cones yellow-brown. *Fruit* One-year conelet ovoid; maturing through green to yellow-brown, 15–30 cm (6–12 in); scales thick, often recurved; seeds 1–1.5 cm (0.4–0.6 in), with a wing of less than 2 mm (0.1 in).

Range: Southwest Texas, southern New Mexico and Arizona south to Durango along the Sierra Madre Oriental in northern Mexico.

Habitat: Cultivated in Europe as an ornamental, in the wild occurring in mountain forests.

Synonyms: *P. ayacahuite* var. *brachyptera*.

This tree comes from a region of Mexico and southwest USA where the winters are cold and dry, with most rainfall during the summer months. The large seeds are edible.

---

p.116 **Eastern White Pine** or **Weymouth Pine**
Pinus strobus

Description: Evergreen tree 15–25 m (50–80 ft) with a bole diameter up to 2 m (6.6 ft). *Crown* Conical when young with spaced upswept branches, becoming domed and twiggy in old trees. *Bark* Dark grey and smooth in young trees, becoming furrowed with narrow scaly ridges and rough in old trees. *Shoot* Shoot slender, in first year shiny olive-brown, with small hairy ridges behind each fascicle, otherwise hairless, becoming smooth and olive-green or grey-brown;

uni-nodal. *Buds* Cylindric or ovoid, apex conical, slender pointed, mid to pale brown and resinous, with tight scales, to 1 cm (0.4 in). *Foliage* Leaves in fascicles of five, pointing forwards and close to shoot for first year, more spreading in second year and rarely lasting through the third year, slender, grey-green with two waxy bands of stomata on outer face, greyish white with a broad band of several lines of waxy stomata on inner faces, 8–10 cm (3.1–4 in), sometimes to 14 cm (5.5 in), by 0.7 mm (0.1 in); fascicle sheath soon lost; crushed foliage with a rather parsley-like smell. *Flowers* On the current season's shoots in early summer; male cones cluster at base of shoot, yellow. *Fruit* One-year conelet ellipsoidal, 2–3 cm (0.8–1.2 in); expanding and becoming pendulous in second season, green and ripening to bright brown, resinous, to 10–20 × 1.5–2 cm (4–8 × 0.6–0.8 in); scales softly woody, rounded, seeds with long wings.

Range: Eastern North America in a triangle from Newfoundland across to southeast Manitoba and south to northern Georgia.

Habitat: Cultivated in Europe as an ornamental and in forestry plantations, in the wild occurring in well-drained sandy soils in mixed forest.

Varieties: No botanical varieties but a few foliage or habit selections are occasionally encountered, such as 'Alba' ('Nivea') with whitish-green new foliage, 'Fastigiata' with a narrow habit formed by the branches ascending at 30 degrees to the trunk, 'Inversa', with pendulous branches, whilst in 'Pendula' the branches are horizontal but the side shoots are pendulous.

The timber is excellent, soft and yellowish and easily worked; in the past, the masts of sailing ships were often made from trunks of Eastern White Pine. However, the tree is susceptible to White Pine blister rust, caused by the fungus, *Cronatium ribicola*. This leads to the death of affected trees and forestry use has declined. The fungus has an alternate host state on currants (*Ribes* species). The disease has also devastated the species in its native range.

p.103 **Scots Pine** *Pinus sylvestris*

Description: Evergreen tree to 30 m (100 ft) in height
with a bole diameter to 1.5 m (5 ft).
Crown Conical in young trees, becoming
rounded in old ones when height growth
ceases. *Bark* In young trees and on the
upper bole of old trees red-brown or orange,
exfoliating in thin scales, at base of bole
deeply fissured with purple-grey ridges
which are shed in small thick scales.
Shoot Green-brown but dull pink-brown by
first winter, then grey-brown, slender; uni-
nodal. *Buds* Cylindric-ovoid with a
bluntly pointed tip, chestnut brown or dull
brown, slightly resinous to resinous, to
1 cm (0.4 in). *Foliage* Leaves in fascicles of
two, pointing forwards along shoot, more
spreading in second year, kept for two to
three years, often twisted, stout, blue-green
with lines of waxy white stomata on both
surfaces, stiff, 5–7 cm (2–2.8 in),
occasionally to 11 cm (4.3 in) on young
trees, by 1–2 mm (0.1 in); fascicle sheath
grey and brown, persistent, 5–8 mm
(0.2–0.3 in); crushed foliage with a sweet
resinous scent. *Flowers* On current season's
growths in late spring; male cones pale
lemon-yellow; female cones dark red to
brown. *Fruit* One-year conelet ovoid,
green; in second year expanding to become
ovoid-conic with a truncate base, ripening
from green to grey-brown or red-brown, on
a short slender stalk, 3–7 × 2–2.5 cm
(1.2–2.8 × 0.8–1 in); scales with a
prominent blunt dorsal knob or smooth.

Range: From Scotland, Spain and Norway across
northern Eurasia nearly to the Pacific Ocean
and south into Turkey and the Caucasus.

Habitat: Dry barren sands or peaty soils, mainly in
continental climates.

Varieties: The only botanical variety which can be
easily identified is var. *mongolica* from North
China, which has very resinous buds,
smooth grey-green shoots and yellow-grey-
green foliage. It is found in a few specialist
collections and in forest plots. Cultivars
include the very attractive 'Aurea'. In this
small tree the foliage turns golden from

December to early spring, especially well in cold years, but throughout the summer and autumn it is a normal blue-green. 'Edwin Hillier' ('Argentea') is a selection with bluish silver foliage. 'Fastigiata' makes a narrow erect tree with ascending branches.

Scots Pine has an enormous distribution. The Scottish populations are unusual in that they occur in a maritime climate, whereas elsewhere throughout its range, it occurs in areas with continental climates. With such a wide distribution it shows variation in a number of characters, with innumerable varieties named. It tolerates a wide range of sites, but is not happy for long on shallow soils over chalk. Grafted plants using scions from old trees, such as with the selected cultivars listed above, never form the typical adult tree basal bark but remain permanently in the upper-bole scaly, flaking bark phase.

---

p.103 **Chinese Red Pine** *Pinus tabuliformis*

Description: Evergreen tree 10–15 m (33–50 ft) with a bole diameter of 30 cm (1 ft).
Crown Conical in young trees, becoming flat topped with wide spreading branches in old trees. *Bark* In young trees and on upper trunk, red-brown or grey-pink, scaly in small flakes, in old trees at base scaly, fissured and grey-brown. *Shoot* Pale yellow-brown, hairless, becoming greyer, stout; uni-nodal. *Buds* Cylindric to ovoid, with a conic pointed apex and free scale tips, chestnut brown with some white resin, 2 cm (0.8 in). *Foliage* Leaves in fascicles of two, forwards and radial around the shoot, mid to dark glossy green with stomata in lines on all surfaces, slender, 9–15 cm × 1–1.5 mm (3.5–6 × 0.1 in); fascicle sheath 1.3 cm (0.5 in), persistent. *Flowers* On current year's shoots; male cones at base of shoot, 1–1.5 cm (0.4–0.6 in), yellow; female cones terminal, on a 1 cm (0.4 in) scaly stalk *Fruit* One-year conelet globose, with small forward-pointing prickles, brown; mature

cone in second year ovoid, dark brown and nearly smooth as small prickle is soon lost, 5 × 3.5 cm (2 × 1.4 in) (closed), opening to be globose; scales moderately thick, 1.5 cm (0.6 in) in width.

Range: Northern China.

Habitat: Cultivated as an ornamental in specialist collections in Europe, in the wild found in montane habitats.

Synonyms: *P. sinensis*.

This pine is related to *P. sylvestris* and *P. densiflora* in the flaky bark of the upper bole but it differs in the smoother more egg-shaped cones and the longer needles. It is suited to a wide variety of sites but is not a long-lived tree. The scientific or Latin name 'table-forming' refers to the flat top of mature trees, especially when they are grown in parks.

p.109 **Loblolly Pine** *Pinus taeda*

Description: Evergreen tree to 30–40 m (100–130 ft) with a bole diameter to 1 m (3.3 ft). *Crown* Conical in young trees, becoming rounded and domed with spreading branches. *Bark* Very dark brown and scaly in young trees, becoming blackish grey with deep scaly fissures or plates which expose the red-brown inner bark. *Shoot* Olive-brown, glossy, slender and glaucous in the first winter, then yellow-brown to red-brown; multinodal. *Buds* Cylindric-conic with red-brown scales which are free at the tips, resinous, to 1.3 cm (0.5 in). *Foliage* Leaves in fascicles of three, set radially around the shoot in the first year but drooping forwards later, slender, flexible and twisted, grey-green with lines of stomata dots on all three surfaces, 13–25 cm × 1–2 mm (5.1–10 × 0.1 in); fascicle sheath red-brown and grey-white, 1–2.5 cm (0.4–1 in); crushed foliage with a turpentine scent. *Flowers* On current season's shoots in late spring; male cones yellow. *Fruit* Ripens in second autumn to ovoid-conic and buff red-brown,

6–14 cm (2.4–5.5 in), opening on maturity but remaining attached to the tree; scales with a short stout prickle.

Range: In an arc across the southeast USA from southern New Jersey to Florida and west to central Texas.

Habitat: Cultivated in Europe as an ornamental, in the wild occurring on poorly drained to well-drained sites including abandoned farmland.

This is an important timber- and resin-producing tree in the southern USA and has also been used in forestry plantations elsewhere. The word 'Loblolly' can mean 'mud puddle' and refers to the trees frequent occurrence in wet depressions in its native range.

---

p.105 **Japanese Black Pine** *Pinus thunbergii*

Description: Evergreen tree to 25 m (80 ft) with a bole diameter to 60 cm (2 ft).
Crown Conical in young trees, developing in old tree a broader crown with erratic level branches which are upswept at the tips.
Bark Dark purplish grey, then black-grey with narrow fissures. *Shoot* Shiny green-brown in first winter, stout and hairless, later becoming browner to dark brown; uni-nodal. *Buds* Cylindrical or ovoid but tapering to a slender point, usually not resinous but with silky white scales, to 2.5 cm (1 in). *Foliage* Leaves in fascicles of two, set radially around the shoot and pointing forwards, shiny dark green, linear, stiff with a pointed bony tip, with grey-white dotted lines of stomata on both sides, 7–15 × 1.5–2 mm (2.8–6 × 0.1 in); fascicle sheath persistent, light grey-brown, 1–1.3 cm (0.4–0.5 in); crushed foliage with an orangey scent. *Flowers* On current season's shoots in early summer; male cones brown with yellow pollen, oblong, 1 cm (0.4 in); female cones normally solitary or in groups of two or three at shoot tips but in some cultivated forms they may be in clusters of up to fifty, replacing the male

cones along the basal portion of the shoot.
Fruit One-year conelet ovoid, red-brown to
purple; maturing to ovoid-conic in second
autumn and ripening to purple-brown or
blackish brown, 3–7 × 2.5–3 cm (1.2–2.8 ×
1–1.2 in); scales few, to 1.5 cm (0.6 in) in
width, thick and softly woody.

Range: Japan from the coastal areas of Honshu,
Shikoku and Kyushu and from Korea.

Habitat: Cultivated in Europe as an ornamental, in
the wild occurring in low-altitude coastal
forests.

Varieties: 'Occulo-draconis' is a selection which has
the leaves with a broad band of yellow or
creamy-white in the centre, mainly on one-
year-old leaves. The buds are resinous and
browner, without the silky-white scales
normally associated with this species.

Synonyms: *P. thunbergiana*.

This tree has a greater tolerance to salt
spray than other pines, occurring naturally
down to the shoreline. The silky white
margins to the bud scales and the cones
with few, rather thick and only softly
woody scales, provide key characters.

---

p.105 **Mountain Pine** *Pinus uncinata*

Description: Evergreen tree to 15–25 m (50–80 ft) with
a bole diameter to 60 cm (2 ft).
Crown Conical, becoming columnar and
eventually rounded domed in old trees.
Bark Grey-pink and quickly cracking into
small squares, becoming black as these
scales are shed. *Shoot* Orange-brown to
green-brown, shiny, hairless, becoming
brown with age, stout and stiff, rough from
ridges behind leaf fascicles; uni-nodal.
Buds Cylindric, with a rounded or pointed
apex, thickly encrusted with resin,
1.5–2 cm (0.6–0.8 in). *Foliage* Leaves in
fascicles of two, radial and closely pointing
forwards in first year, spreading in second
and subsequent years, kept up to five years,
dense, linear, apex acute, bony, grey-green
with lines of white dots (stomata) on both
sides, 4–6 cm × 1.5 mm (1.6–2.4 × 0.1 in);

fascicle sheath grey, 8 mm (0.3 in),
disintegrates in third year; crushed foliage
with a strong but mild resin scent.
Flowers On current season's shoots in early
summer. *Fruit* One-year conelet obovoid,
brown, 1 cm (0.4 in); expanding in second
year and ripening to dark brown, ovoid to
ovoid-oblong, oblique, outer scales have a
backward-pointing protuberant pyramidal
point which 'rests' on the scale below, 4–6
× 2–3 cm (1.6–2.4 × 0.8–1.2 in)

Range: Central Spain north through the Pyrenees
to the central and western Alps.

Habitat: Wet moorland sites.

Varieties: Var. *rotundata* has a shrubby habit and cones
with the scales rounded or hooded. It shows
introgression (introduction of genes by
hybridization) from *P. mugo*.

This tree hybridizes with *P. mugo* where
they meet.

---

p.117 **Blue Pine** *Pinus wallichiana*

Description: Evergreen tree to 20–30 m (65–100 ft)
with a bole diameter to 1.2 m (4 ft).
Crown Conical with spaced level branches
when young, remaining conical or columnar
when old or developing a wide-spreading
habit with large branches when grown in
the open. *Bark* Smooth, grey-green in
young trees, becoming dark grey or blackish
in old trees and cracked and fissured into
small scales. *Shoot* Hairless, olive-green and
moderately stout in first year, becoming
grey-green and smooth; uni-nodal.
Buds Cylindrical with an acute tip, 1.5 cm
(0.6 in), pale brown. *Foliage* Leaves in
fascicles of five, pointing forwards and
drooping down, slender, flexible, sometimes
kinked about 2 cm (0.8 in) from the base,
dull to vivid blue-green or occasionally
grey-green, 11–20 cm × 1 mm (4.3–8 ×
0.1 in); fascicle sheath soon reflexed and lost
over first winter; crushed foliage with a
strong resinous aroma. *Flowers* On current
season's shoots; male cones at base of shoot,
1 cm (0.4 in), pale yellow in early summer;

female cones terminal, on short stalk, erect.
Fruit One-year conelet on stout stalk
3–6 cm (1.2–2.4 in), erect, cylindrical,
green-purple; mature cones ellipsoidal,
often curved and very resinous, bluish-green
ripening to pale brown, pendent, 10–30 ×
3.5 cm (4–12 × 1.4 in) (closed), opening to
5–9 cm (2–3.5 in); scales to 2.5 cm (1 in)
wide; seed 0.6–1 × 0.4–6 cm (0.25–0.4 ×
0.2–2.4 in) with a long wing 1.5–3 ×
0.7–1 cm (0.6–1.2 × 0.3–0.4 in).

Range: Himalayas from eastern Afghanistan
through Pakistan, India, Nepal, Bhutan to
southern Tibet.

Habitat: Cultivated widely as an ornamental, in the
wild occurring in a wide range of habitats.

Varieties: There are no botanical varieties but the
species occurs naturally over a wide range of
sites. Trees from the western Himalayas
seem to have longer and more graceful
foliage than those from the eastern end.

Synonyms: *P. excelsa*, *P. griffithii*.

This is tolerant of a broad range of sites but
is especially suited to limestone soils. The
foliage is variable in the degree of blueness,
and more strongly developed in light shade.
It is similar in foliage characters to *P.
armandii* but easily distinguished by the
cone and seeds.

PISTACHIAS, *PISTACIA*
FAMILY ANACARDIACEAE

This is a genus of 11 species from the Mediterranean region
south into tropical East Africa, west across the Atlantic to
Mexico and the southern USA and east through Central Asia
to China and southeast Asia. The leaves vary from simple,
trifoliate to pinnate (often with equal numbers of leaflets).
The flowers are small and wind pollinated, with the sexes
separate. They are followed by single-seeded drupes which
are laterally compressed. In the illustrated species, the rachis
of the leaf is winged, the leaflets paired (i.e. without a
terminal leaflet) and the tree evergreen in *P. lentiscus*; but not
winged, and the trees deciduous and usually with an odd
number of leaflets in *PP. atlantica*, *terebinthus* and *vera*.
Pistachias make shrubs to small trees. The Pistachio nut is
widely cultivated in warm temperate regions.

p.321 **Large Terebinth** *Pistacia atlantica*

Description: Deciduous tree normally to 10 m (33 ft)
but occasionally to 20 m (65 ft), with a bole
to 1 m (3.3 ft) diameter.
Crown Broad. *Bark* Pale grey-brown,
fissured in old trees. *Shoot* Grey,
resiniferous. *Foliage* Leaves pinnate with
three to five pairs of leaflets, 10–15(–20) ×
5–12 cm (4–6(–8) × 2–4.7 in); leaflets
lanceolate, narrowly oblong or ovate-oblong,
apex bluntly pointed, without a sharp point
at the tip, base rounded to broad wedge-
shaped, margin untoothed, flat, upper
surface grey-green, drying to somewhat
glaucous green, hairless except possibly
along the veins and midrib, 3–10 × 2–5 cm
(1.2–4 × 0.8–2 in); leaf stalk flattened above
but not winged, hairless or minutely haired,
rachis narrowly winged. *Flowers* Dioecious,
with separate male and female trees,
appearing with the new foliage in spring;
male flowers in dense panicles, compact at
first but expanding to 10 cm (4 in), female
flowers on lax panicles. *Fruit* Ovoid to sub-
globose drupe which is only slightly
compressed, with a blue-black fleshy layer
when ripe, 6–7 mm (0.25–0.3 in).

Range: Throughout the Mediterranean region.
Habitat: Dry rocky hillsides.

This tree produces mastic and makes a
larger tree than *P. terebinthus*. The slightly
winged rachis to the leaves and the leaflets
not ending in a sharp point provides the
best means to separate it from *P. terebinthus*.

p.321 **Terebinth** or **Turpentine Tree**
Pistacia terebinthus

Description: Deciduous shrub or small tree to 10 m
(33 ft).
Crown Spreading. *Bark* Dark ash-grey,
rough, fissured in old trees. *Shoot* Grey,
resiniferous. *Buds* With several outer scales.
Foliage Leaves pinnate with two to four,
rarely to six, pairs of leaflets, usually with a
terminal one but sometimes this is much

reduced or wanting, mainly 10–20 × 5–10 cm (4–8 × 2–4 in) but sometimes larger or smaller; leaflets variable, oblong to ovate, on a short stalk, apex bluntly pointed, acute or slender pointed, always with a short abrupt point at the very tip, base rounded to broad wedge-shaped, margin untoothed, flat, upper surface lustrous green, hairless except possibly along the veins and midrib, underside paler, 2–6 × 0.8–3 cm (0.8–2.4 × 0.3–1.2 in); leaf stalk and rachis flattened above but not winged, hairless or somewhat hairy especially in the axils with the leaflets; new foliage reddish. *Flowers* Dioecious, with separate male and female trees, appearing with the new foliage in spring; male flowers in dense panicles 5–10 cm (2–4 in), female flowers on lax panicles. *Fruit* Ovoid drupe with a thin fleshy covering, red when young, maturing to black or blue-black, 5–7 × 5 mm (0.2–0.3 × 0.2 in).

Range: Throughout the Mediterranean region and east into southwest Asia.

Habitat: Dry rocky hillsides.

Synonyms: *P. palaestina*.

The coral-red young fruits can be very attractive.

p.321 **Mastic Tree** or **Lentisc** *Pistacia lentiscus*

Description: Evergreen shrub or small tree 4–8 m (13–26 ft) in height.
Crown Rounded, dense. *Bark* Greyish brown, pale, rough with lenticels.
Shoot Glabrous, warty. *Foliage* Leaves 5–10 × 3 cm (2–4 × 1.2 in), pinnate with two to four (rarely only one or up to seven) pairs of leaflets but no terminal leaflets, with the conspicuously winged rachis continuing into a short prickle; leaflets ovate, oblong or elliptic, leathery in texture, apex bluntly pointed to rounded with a short mucro, margin distinctly rolled down or curved down, untoothed, dark green and hairless on both sides, 1.2–4.5 × 0.6–1.8 cm (0.5–1.8 × 0.25–0.7 in); leaf stalk winged and

channelled above, less than 2 cm (0.8 in).
Flowers Dioecious, with separate male and
female plants, inflorescence a raceme,
1–3 cm (0.4–1.2 in). *Fruit* Globose drupe
with a thin fleshy layer which is red, then
ripens to black, 5 mm (0.2 in).

Range: Mediterranean region from Portugal and
the Atlantic Islands eastwards but absent
from Egypt, with a variety extending south
through East Africa to Tanzania.

Habitat: Dry rocky hillsides, sand dunes and
lowland pine forests.

Similar species: *P.* × *saportae* is a hybrid of *P. lentiscus* with *P. terebinthus*. It is more similar to *P. lentiscus* in foliage, differing in the flowers in panicles (not racemes) and in the more shrubby habit, and the longer leaf stalks to the leaves. It is sterile, and the fruits persist when *P. lentiscus* (and other *Pistacia*) have lost their fruits.

This small tree gives mastic.

---

p.322 **Pistacio** *Pistacia vera*

Description: Deciduous small tree to 8 m in height
(26 ft).
Crown Rounded. *Bark* Greyish-brown,
rough and shortly ridged. *Shoot* Grey.
Foliage Leaves pinnate with one or two,
rarely three, pairs of leaflets with a terminal
leaflet; leaflets broad ovate to oblong-ovate
or nearly round, thin but leathery in texture
with distinct net veining, apex bluntly
pointed or rounded with a short mucro,
margin untoothed, grey-green finely haired
at first on both sides, later hairless,
3.5–9 cm (1.4–3.5 in); leaf stalk and rachis
without a wing or with only a faint wing.
Flowers In long lax panicles 7–10 cm
(2.8–4 in). *Fruit* Ovoid-conic pointed
drupe with the fleshy layer easily separating
from the pale reddish-brown ripe fruit,
exposing the bony seed, 1.5–2.5 ×
0.6–1.2 cm (0.6–1 × 0.25–0.5 in).

Range: Central Asia.

Habitat: Cultivated as a fruit tree, in the wild
occurring in semi-desert zones.

This tree is grown for the tasty fruit, which is best eaten roasted but not bad as a flavouring for ice cream and on cakes. It is only produced where both male and female trees are present. As a fruit tree, it is often grafted onto *P. terebinthus*.

PITTOSPORUM, PITTOSPORACEAE

This family comprises nine genera, eight restricted to Australia or extending into Malaya, but with only *Pittosporum* more widely and common in cultivation.

PITTOSPORUMS, *PITTOSPORUM*
FAMILY PITTOSPORACEAE

This genus of approximately 200 species extends from the Canary Islands and Madeira across Africa to China and Japan, but most species are found in Australia and New Zealand. They are invariably evergreen. The leaf margin is wavy in *PP. eugenoides*, *tenuifolium* and *undulatum*, but straight and often slightly recurved in *PP. colensoi*, *crassifolium* and *tobira*. The flowers have five sepals, petals and stamens. The fruit is a woody to leathery capsule with two to five valves. The name *Pittosporum* refers to the resinous substance which surrounds the seeds. They are planted for amenity, including their fragrant flowers.

p.165 **Black Mapou** *Pittosporum colensoi*

Description: Evergreen shrub or tree to 9 m (29 ft).
Crown Rounded, somewhat vase-shaped in old trees. *Bark* Grey. *Shoot* Brown with small pale lenticels, loosely silky haired when young but soon hairless.
Buds Oblong to ovoid, bluntly pointed.
Foliage Leaves elliptic to obovate-oblong or elliptic-lanceolate, apex rounded and bluntly pointed to acute, base rounded to wedge-shaped, margin untoothed, glossy green above with a raised yellowish midrib, underside shiny pale green and net-veined, hairless except for some downy hairs when young, 4–10 × 2–5 cm (1.6–4 × 0.8–2 in); leaf stalk grooved, 1 cm (0.4 in).

Flowers Axillary, single or in small cymes towards the end of the shoots in spring, velvety purple or dark red with reflexed petals, 1.5 cm (0.6 in) across. *Fruit* Ovoid capsule with three valves, circa 5 mm (0.2 in); seeds black.

Range: New Zealand, from both South and North Islands.
Habitat: Cultivated as an ornamental, in the wild occurring in forest clearings.

This small tree is similar to *P. tenuifolium* in the flowers, but has larger and thicker leaves on stouter shoots.

---

p.165   **Karo** *Pittosporum crassifolium*

Description: Evergreen shrub or tree to 10 m (33 ft). *Crown* Ovoid. *Shoot* Covered with white- to buff-coloured hairs. *Buds* Ovoid, hairy. *Foliage* Leaves obovate to elliptic, apex acute, base wedge-shaped, margins untoothed and slightly recurved, thick and very leathery in texture, upper surface crackled and glossy green, hairy when young, underside with a thin whitish or buff covering of hairs, 5–7 cm (2–2.8 in) (rarely to 10 cm (4 in)) by up to 2.5 cm (1 in); leaf stalk 1.2–2.5 cm (0.5–1 in). *Flowers* In terminal umbels in spring; flowers maroon to dark purple, scented; male flowers in fives to tens, females in fives, or single or in pairs. *Fruit* Globose capsule with three or four valves, whitish or yellow hairy, 2–3 cm (0.8–1.2 in); seeds black.
Range: North Island, New Zealand.
Habitat: Cultivated as an ornamental, in the wild favouring stream sides and forest clearings.
Similar species: *P. ralphii* (p.165) makes a small tree or shrub to 4 m (13 ft). It is similar in the leaves having a white to buff dense covering of felt on their undersides (with similarly felty hairs on the leaf stalks, flower stalks and shoots) but the leaves are larger 7–12.5 × 2–2.5 cm (2.8–4.9 × 0.8–1 in) with non-curved-down margins (although they may be wavy) and the fruit which is ovoid-

pointed with three valves and smaller, circa
1.3 cm (0.5 in). It also comes from the
North Island of New Zealand.

This tree is tolerant of salt spray, making it
suitable for mild coastal areas.

---

p.164 **Tarata** or **Lemonwood**
Pittosporum eugenioides

Description: Evergreen tree to 12 m (39 ft) (but
sometimes a shrub) with a bole diameter to
60 cm (2 ft).
Crown Conical when young, becoming
rounded and spreading. *Bark* Grey,
rough, becoming slightly and finely scaly.
Shoot Glabrous, greenish, maturing to
dark purplish brown. *Buds* Ovoid,
pointed. *Foliage* Leaves elliptic, apex
rounded, base wedge-shaped, margin wavy,
upper surface glossy yellow-green to green
with a yellowish raised midrib, underside
paler, 10–15 × 2–4 cm (4–6 × 0.8–1.6 in);
leaf stalk slender, to 2 cm (0.8 in); crushed
foliage with a lemon scent. *Flowers* In
large terminal clusters on hairy stalks in
spring, creamy-white, with a heavy honey
scent, 1–1.5 cm (0.4–0.6 in).
Fruit Ovoid, pointed capsule with two or
three valves; seeds black.
Range: New Zealand, from both South and North
Islands.
Habitat: Cultivated as an ornamental, in the wild
occurring in forest clearings.
Varieties: 'Variegatum' has the leaves margined with
a crisp but variable band of creamy-white.

The fragrant flowers and leaves are used by
the Maori peoples as a scent and unguent
(ointment).

---

p.164 **Kohuhu** *Pittosporum tenuifolium*

Description: Evergreen tree 6–16 m (20–53 ft) in height
with a bole diameter to 1 m (3.3 ft).
Crown Ovoid, becoming domed on old
trees. *Bark* Dull grey, smooth.

Shoot Brown to chocolate brown in the first winter, later grey-brown but with a dark red-brown or chocolate underbark. *Buds* Ovoid, flattened, green and brown, to 3 mm (0.1 in). *Foliage* Obovate, oblong or elliptic, spaced and clustered in apical half of shoot, lower portion usually bare, tapered at both ends, margins untoothed but wavy, very glossy and light yellow-green above with a raised rounded midrib, underside very pale glossy green with net-like tertiary veins, 2.5–6 × 2–3 cm (1–2.4 × 0.8–1.2 in); leaf stalk grooved, yellow-green, 1.5 cm (0.6 in). *Flowers* In pairs or singly from large ovoid green and brown buds in leaf axils in spring, purple or chocolate purple, very fragrant (especially in the evening), with five cup-shaped petals 0.6–1.2 cm (0.25–0.5 in). *Fruit* Capsule, green but ripening to black, with three valves and thinly woody segments, 1.2 cm (0.5 in).

Range: New Zealand, on both North and South Island.

Habitat: Cultivated in Europe, in the wild occurring in forests.

Varieties: Several cultivars have been named, including 'Purpureum', with the leaves purple, and 'Silver Queen', with the leaves irregularly margined white.

The foliage of this small tree lasts well when cut. The flowers, whilst not showy, are attractive in detail with the chocolate-coloured or purple petals and excite the olfactory senses when they perfume the air in the evening.

---

p.165 **Tobira** *Pittosporum tobira*

Description: Evergreen shrub or tree to 10 m (33 ft). *Crown* Rounded, bushy, usually on several stems. *Foliage* Leaves narrow obovate, apex blunt to rounded, base wedge-shaped, margin untoothed and slightly recurved, leathery, glossy green above with a pale midrib, paler and hairless beneath, 4–10 ×

2–4 cm (1.6–4 × 0.8–1.6 in); leaf stalk short. *Flowers* In terminal simple or branched umbels 5–7 cm (2–2.8 in) across in spring, flowers cream-coloured, fading to yellowish, fragrant, 2.5 cm (1 in) across. *Fruit* Sub-globose woody or nearly woody capsule opening by three valves, 1.2 cm (0.5 in); seeds red.

Range: Honshu, Kyushu and Shikoku, Japan, south along the Ryukyu islands to Taiwan, and in south Korea and China.

Habitat: Cultivated as an ornamental.

Synonyms: *Euonymus tobira*.

The flowers have a scent-like orange blossom. It is not hardy in cold districts.

---

p.164 **Wavy Pittosporum** *Pittosporum undulatum*

Description: Evergreen shrub or tree to 20 m (65 ft). *Crown* Ovoid with a rounded top. *Bark* Grey. *Foliage* Leaves ovate-lanceolate to obovate, tapering to a slender acute or slender-pointed apex and to the wedge-shaped base, margin untoothed, wavy, leathery, upper surface dark glossy green, paler beneath, hairless, 7–15(–20) × 2.5–6 cm (2.8–6(–8) × 1–2.4 in). *Flowers* In terminal umbels 5–7 cm (2–2.8 in) across in spring to early summer; flowers white, fading to yellowish white, 1.2–2 cm (0.5–0.8 in). *Fruit* Obovoid, hairless capsule with two valves, ripening orange, 1–1.2 cm (0.4–0.5 in); seeds red-brown.

Range: Eastern Australia.

Habitat: Cultivated as an ornamental.

This tree is tolerant of salt spray and has been used to shelter orange groves. The orange coloured capsules are attractive over the winter period.

PLANE, PLATANACEAE

This family consists solely of the genus *Platanus* (p.986).

PLANES, *PLATANUS*
FAMILY PLATANACEAE

There are six or seven species of *Platanus*, one from the eastern Mediterranean region to Iran, one in southeast Asia and the others in North America and Mexico. However, the most important member is the hybrid, *P.* × *hispanica*, which is widely planted in temperate regions (and from China to Mexico). The leaves are large, palmately lobed (except in the anomalous species *P. kerrii* from southeast Asia) with the base of the leaf stalk enlarged and enclosing the bud. The flowers are in globose clusters, followed by the fruit which is a cluster of hairy achenes.

p.304 **London Plane** *Platanus* × *hispanica*

Description: Deciduous tree 20–40 m (65–130 ft) developing a bole 0.7–2 m (2.3–6.6 ft) or more in diameter.
Crown Tall domed to rounded and spreading on radiating branches.
Bark Changing through the year; in the upper crown brown and smooth, usually flaking in the autumn to shed sheets of bark and reveal creamy white beneath, at the base of the bole becoming thicker and scaly but not shedding. *Shoot* Initially hairy but soon hairless and becoming shiny, yellow-green on the underside and brownish above, in the second year reddish brown to grey; terminal buds absent.
Buds Ovoid to conic, apex rounded, enclosed in a single scale and hidden in the base of the leaf stalk during the summer, shiny and pinkish, to 1 cm (0.4 in).
Foliage Leaves variable in shape, mainly palmately lobed with five lobes based on three main veins from the base of the leaf, lobes ovate, with a few conical and abruptly short-pointed teeth and rounded scalloped margins, sinuses rounded, base heart-shaped to wedge-shaped, with or without some of the blade beneath the basal veins, densely greyish hairy when young, becoming hairless above and glossy green, and more or less hairless beneath and paler, texture card-like, fallen leaves not decaying readily but persistent, to 20 × 23 cm (8 ×

9.1 in); leaf stalk oval in section with an enlarged base which encloses the bud, variable in length, often with broad ovate and toothed stipules; autumn colour russets. *Flowers* Pendulous in separate male and female catkins 6–8 cm (2.4–3.1 in) with two to six globose heads; males yellow; females crimson.
Fruit Brown, rough and composed of many achenes (single-seeded winged fruits) which are coalesced into a globose head 2–3.5 cm (0.8–1.4 in) across, with light brown hairs, disintegrating in spring.

Range: Arisen in cultivation.

Habitat: Widely planted as an ornamental tree.

Varieties: 'Augustine Henry' is a form with the lower branches lax and rather pendulous, lighter green leaves and a smoother more freely flaking trunk. It is a very impressive tree. 'Pyramidalis' is a poorer form, although too widely planted as it is easier to strike from cuttings. This has a low bole which becomes scaly and almost fissured at the base and is loath to shed the bark. The habit is rounded, with radiating branches, and it forms only a medium but wide spreading tree.

Synonyms: *P.* × *acerifolia, P.* × *hybrida.*

This is almost certainly a hybrid between *P. orientalis* and *P. occidentalis* from eastern North America, from which it inherits the less-lobed leaves and immense vigour. It is a fertile hybrid and will seed itself onto river gravels and other suitable habitats. It therefore exists in a bewildering array of forms. It has been widely planted, including in urban situations in China!

p.304 **Oriental Plane** *Platanus orientalis*

Description: Deciduous tree 15–30 m (50–100 ft) with a bole diameter to 3 m (10 ft).
Crown Domed, broad and often layering, but in parts of its range narrow and upright. *Bark* Pinkish brown and shedding in large round plates, revealing yellow in cultivated northern trees, but in

hotter climates becoming almost snow white. *Shoot* Finely hairy and pinkish green or yellow-brown at first, later grey-brown. *Buds* Oblong-conic, red-brown, enclosed in the leaf stalk base and stipules during summer, 5 mm (0.2 in).
Foliage Leaves rounded in outline with three to five deep palmate lobes which extend two thirds the way to the midrib, lobes linear, acute at the apex, with deep rounded-acute sinuses, margin untoothed, coarsely serrate to lobulate, base wedge-shaped, card-like in texture, upper surface deep green, underside with raised hairy veins, 9–20 × 9–20 cm (3.5–8 × 3.5–8 in); leaf stalk with a swollen reddish base, round or flattened above, star-shaped hairy at first with stipules which encircle the strong shoots but are soon deciduous, 2–6 cm (0.8–2.4 in); autumn colour bronzy purple. *Flowers* In globose heads of three to six clusters, on a 3–8 cm (1.2–3.1 in) stalk. *Fruit* Pendent on stalks to 14 cm (5.5 in) with three to six globose heads to 2–2.5 cm (0.8–1 in) across with many single-seeded fruits (achenes).

Range: Greece, Bulgaria, Turkey, Cyprus and possibly further east.

Habitat: By streams or springs where summer water is accessible.

Varieties: The island populations of Crete and Cyprus are sometimes distinguished as var. *insularis* on the basis of the deeper lobing of their leaves.

The Oriental Plane is one of the parents of London Plane, differing in the more deeply lobed and finer leaves. It is extremely long lived.

PLATYCARYA, *PLATYCARYA* (SYNONYMS: *PETROPHILOIDES*; *FORTUNEA*)
FAMILY JUGLANDACEAE

This is a genus of two species from eastern Asia. The pith is solid, as in *Carya*, not chambered as in *Juglans* and *Pterocarya*.

p.325 **Platycarya** *Platycarya strobilaceae*

Description: Deciduous tree 5–10 m (16–33 ft) with a bole diameter of up to 30 cm (1 ft). *Crown* Rounded. *Bark* Brown, smooth or weakly fissured. *Shoot* Brown or yellow-brown, hairy when young, with a solid pith. *Buds* Ovoid, pointed, small, with scales. *Foliage* Leaves pinnate with 7–15 leaflets, 15–30 cm (6–12 in). Leaflets ovate to ovate-lanceolate, often sickle-shaped, apex slender pointed, base wedge-shaped and nearly stalkless on rachis, oblique, margin doubly serrate, loosely brown hairy when young but hairs only persisting in vein axils beneath, 4–10 × 1–3 cm (1.6–4 × 0.4–1.2 in). *Flowers* Male catkins erect, in clusters at shoot tips, 5–8 cm (2–3.1 in); female flower erect. *Fruit* Woody persistent cone-like structure erect at shoot tips on a distinct stalk, ovoid to oblong, around 3 cm (1.2 in); seeds flattened, winged nutlet, 5 mm (0.2 in).

Range: Across eastern Asia from Japan (not Hokkaido), Korea and Taiwan across China to Yunnan.

Habitat: Cultivated as an ornamental, in the wild found in open warm temperate hillsides.

Synonyms: *Petrophiloides strobilaceae.*

Similar species: *P. longipes* is the second species in the genus. It differs in having three to five (occasionally seven) leaflets, and smaller rounded fruits less than 2 cm (0.8 in). It is native to Guangxi and Guangdong provinces of China but may not be in cultivation.

This small tree is easily distinguished by the persistent cone-like fruit, when these are available, and the pinnate leaves, as well as by the solid pith in the shoots. It was first discovered as a fossil in the clay beds dating from the Eocene period in the London area. It was later found to be growing in Japan. In botany, a species named from living material takes precedence over one named from fossils, otherwise it would be *Petrophiloides strobilaceae.*

BIOTA, *PLATYCLADUS* (SYNONYM: *THUJA* IN PART)
FAMILY CUPRESSACEAE

This is a genus of one species which has been included in
Thuja and will still be found in most horticultural references
as *Thuja orientalis*. However, it is very clearly distinguished
from all true *Thuja* species by the cone, which has large
scales with a prominent hooked protuberance, the large and
unwinged seeds and the non-fragrant foliage.

p.48   **Biota, Chinese Thuja** or **Chinese
Arbor-vitae** *Platycladus orientalis*

Description: Evergreen tree 10–20 m (33–65 ft) with a
bole diameter to 60 cm (2 in).
Crown Conical in young trees, becoming
irregular, rounded and narrow domed with
the foliage mainly at the branch tips and
bare beneath. *Bark* Dull red-brown,
stripping in shallow, fibrous ridges.
Shoot Green for first winter, then becoming
pale brown as decurrent leaves die and then
red-brown as they are shed. *Buds* Hidden
in scale leaves. *Foliage* In flat sprays carried
erect and rather erratically, fresh green to
dull, dark green; leaves in opposite pairs
with only a slight difference between the
facial and lateral pairs, acute and bluntly
pointed with the tip of lateral leaves
pointing forwards along the shoot, with a
few white dots of stomata, 1.5–8 mm
(0.1–0.3 in); crushed foliage without a
scent. *Flowers* On previous season's growths
in spring; male flowers globular, red-brown,
1 mm (0.1 in); female flowers on a curved
stalk, spreading or slightly turned down,
yellow-green, with two to four fertile scales
each with one or two ovules, 2 mm (0.1 in).
Fruit Erect ovoid or flask-shaped, grey
bloomed but ripening in first autumn to
brown, 1.5–2 cm (0.6–0.8 in); scales
leathery with a recurved hooked prickle;
seed ovoid, 3 mm (0.1 in), wingless.

Range: Northern China southwest to northern
Yunnan, northeast Iran and possibly Korea.

Habitat: Cultivated in Europe as an ornamental, in
the wild occurring on dry valley sides in
full sun.

Varieties: Several dwarf forms but no significant tree forms.

Synonyms: *Biota orientalis*, *Thuja orientalis*.

This tree is often listed as a *Thuja* but shares few botanical characters with the members of this genus. It is easily distinguished by the large wingless seed, the cones with recurved hooked scales and the absence of scent in the foliage. Its native distribution is rather lost as it is widely planted as an amenity. It tolerates dry climates and dry situations, both hot and cold, and is the only tree which I have seen which grows in Beijing, London and Bangkok, to mention three disparate places! It will regenerate in cracks in old walls. Like many members of the cypress family (but not *Thuja*!) it does not like shady conditions.

PODOCARP, PODOCARPACEAE

This family consists of around fifteen genera. The male flowers are in catkins, whilst the female flowers have only a few bracts which ripen a single seed (and often only one per cone). The family is widely distributed in eastern and southern Asia south to Africa and Australia and New Zealand, and in the Americas from Mexico southwards. Genera treated here are *Podocarpus*, *Prumnopitys* (p.1010) and *Saxegothea* (p.1127).

PODOCARPS, *PODOCARPUS*
FAMILY PODOCARPACEAE

This is a large genus of conifers with around a hundred species, mainly tropical in distribution. The leaves are strap-like, with a prominent ridge along the midrib on the upper surface. The fruit is subtended by a fleshy growth which is intended to be eaten by birds as a means of distribution. In the past, *Podocarpus* has been treated in a very broad sense but recent investigations have shown the artificial nature of this. However, most of the segregate genera are tropical and are not found (or only very rarely) in cultivation, except *Prumnopitys*.

p.61   **Kusamaki** *Podocarpus macrophyllus*

Description: Evergreen tree to 15 m (50 ft) with a bole
diameter to 60 cm (2 ft), more usually as a
shrub.
Crown Columnar or conical with spreading
horizontal branches. *Bark* Ash-grey, rugose,
thick. *Shoot* Light green for two years,
before turning orange-brown. *Buds* Ovoid,
pointed, with free scales, chestnut brown,
small, 1.5–3 mm (0.1 in). *Foliage* Radial
around shoot and pointing forwards; leaves
flat, light green and sub-shiny above with a
ridge along the midrib and no stomata, pale
green with two broad bands of indistinct
stomata beneath, apex rounded to bluntly
pointed, leathery, 6–11 × 0.6–1 cm (2.4–4.3
× 0.25–0.4 in); juvenile leaves up to 17 ×
1.2 cm (6.7 × 0.5 in); crushed foliage with a
grassy smell. *Flowers* On previous year's
shoots; male cones in small clusters,
cylindrical, 3–3.5 cm (1.2–1.4 in).
Fruit Solitary cone with a reddish-purple
fleshy base and ovoid glaucous green seeds
1.2–1.5 cm (0.5–0.6 in) long.
Range: South Japan and eastern China.
Habitat: Cultivated in Europe as an ornamental, in
the wild occurring in mixed forest.
Varieties: 'Angustifolia' is named but the leaves are
scarcely any narrower!

This is slow growing but hardy in Britain.

p.61   **Chilean Totara** *Podocarpus nubigenus*

Description: Evergreen tree to 15 m (50 ft) with a bole
diameter to 1 m (3.3 ft).
Crown Ovoid, bushy. *Bark* Purplish brown,
peeling in strips. *Shoot* Green for three or
four years and becoming brown initially
between the decurrent leaf bases, grooved in
the first year and hairless. *Buds* Conic or
broad conic, with free green or brown scales,
to 4 × 6 mm (0.2–0.25 in). *Foliage* Radial
and rather spaced, those below partly
spreading or pointing along the shoot;
linear, tapered to the abrupt sharp-pointed
apex and wedge-shaped at the base with a

short stout leaf stalk 1 mm (0.1 in), upper surface dark matt green with a raised midrib, below with two silvery white waxy bands of stomata and a light green midrib, 1.5–4 × 3–5 mm (0.6–1.6 × 0.1–0.2 in); crushed foliage almost scentless. *Flowers* On previous season's shoots; male cone solitary or in clusters. *Fruit* On a 1.5–2 cm (0.6–0.8 in) stalk, receptacle 7 × 3 mm (0.3–0.1 in), seed 9 × 7 mm (0.4 × 0.3 in).

Range: South Chile, extending into Argentina.
Habitat: Cultivated in Europe as an ornamental.

This is a small tree except in moist wet regions where it flourishes.

p.61 **Willowleaf Podocarp** *Podocarpus salignus*

Description: Evergreen tree to 20 m (65 ft) with a bole diameter to 1 m (3.3 ft).
Crown Conical in young trees, becoming columnar, with whorled branches when young. *Bark* Red-brown and smooth in young trees, becoming fibrous and peeling in long strips. *Shoot* Green and smooth in the first winter, becoming brown in patches in the second year, somewhat shiny. *Buds* Broad and shallow or rounded, with free chestnut brown or green scales, 1 × 1–3 mm (0.1 × 0.1 in). *Foliage* In lax and pectinate sprays with the leaves pointing forwards to variable extents; leaves often clustered towards the tips of the shoots, linear or strap-like, tapered to a narrow acute apex, base tapered to a leaf stalk 3 mm (0.1 in), upper surface cupped, concave with a raised midrib, mid to dark glossy green, lower surface convex, pale green, 5–11 cm × 4–8 mm (2–4.3 × 0.2–0.3 in); crushed foliage with little scent. *Flowers* On previous season's shoots; male cone cylindrical. *Fruit* Fruit on a 2 cm (0.8 in) stalk, with a green or dark violet receptacle 5 mm (0.2 in) bearing one or two green seeds 8 × 4 mm (0.3 × 0.2 in).

Range: Central southern Chile.
Habitat: Cultivated in Europe as an ornamental, in the wild forming a minor constituent of *Nothofagus obliqua* forests.

This makes the most attractive of the hardy podocarps, with its long willow-like leaves.

---

p.62 **Totara** *Podocarpus totara*

Description: Evergreen tree to 20 m (65 ft) with a bole diameter to 1 m (3.3 ft).
Crown Broadly conical or ovoid, becoming irregular in old trees. *Bark* Brownish grey or orange-brown and peeling in young trees, becoming thick, stringy and usually deeply furrowed on old trees. *Shoot* Green or yellow-green and grooved in the first winter, becoming brown, red-brown or grey-brown in the second year. *Buds* Broad conic to rounded, with free scale tips, chestnut brown, 1–2 mm (0.1 in). *Foliage* Spaced and rather irregularly arranged on the shoot; lanceolate, tapered at both ends, acute to slender pointed, light green on both sides with two broad indistinct bands of stomata below, 1.3–3.5 × 3–4 mm (0.5–1.4 × 0.1–0.2 in); crushed foliage with little scent. *Flowers* On previous season's shoots in early summer; male cones cylindric, yellow and red, 1.5 cm (0.6 in). *Fruit* Cone with an orange-red or crimson receptacle 5 mm (0.2 in) bearing one or two green sub-globose seeds.

Range: New Zealand, throughout the North Island and in the northeast of South Island.

Habitat: Cultivated in Europe as an ornamental, in the wild forming forests.

Varieties: 'Aurea' has golden foliage.

Similar species: *P. hallii* is closely related, differing in the thinner, more papery bark and the leaves having a groove along the upper surface.

This makes a large tree in New Zealand, up to 40 m (130 ft) with a bole diameter to 3.5 m (11.5 ft). The timber is red and durable.

POLIOTHYRSUS, *POLIOTHYRSIS*
FAMILY FLACOURTIACEAE

This is a monotypic genus from China.

p.201 **Poliothyrsis** *Poliothyrsis sinensis*

Description: Deciduous tree 10–15 m (33–50 ft) with a
bole diameter to 40 cm (1.3 ft).
Crown Ovoid. *Bark* Smooth, grey-brown,
becoming deeply furrowed in old trees.
Shoot Grey, hairless, lightly fissured with
round buff lenticels in the first summer,
becoming brown in later years. *Buds* Conic
to ovoid-conic, pointed, brown or grey, hairy,
3 mm (0.1 in). *Foliage* Leaves ovate,
leathery, with a short slender-pointed apex,
rounded or rarely heart-shaped at the base,
margin with a hyaline band and blunt
triangular teeth which end in a brown gland,
upper surface sub-shiny mid green with three
or five main veins from the base, hairless,
underside light green, veins raised and with a
few pilose hairs, 5–10 × 3–7 cm (2–4 ×
1.2–2.8 in); leaf stalk grooved, pink-purple,
hairless, with two oval glands near the base of
the leaf; autumn colour poor. *Flowers* In
panicles which terminate the current season's
shoots in August and September, to 15 ×
7 cm (6 × 2.8 in), fragrant, flowers creamy-
or pale yellow, either male or female but both
on the same inflorescence, individually
6–8 mm (0.25–0.3 in) across with five ovate-
triangular petals, in bud ovoid pointed with
five ridges. *Fruit* Ellipsoidal capsule
1.5–2 cm (0.6–0.8 in) long with many
winged seeds.

Range: Hubei and Sichuan, China.

Habitat: Cultivated as an ornamental, in the wild
found in woods.

This makes a very attractive small tree
when covered with its fragrant late summer
flowers. The leaves are very stiff and
leathery, with a hyaline margin.

POPLARS, *POPULUS*
FAMILY SALICACEAE

This is a genus of around 35 species from the temperate
regions of the northern hemisphere, preferring wet or moist
soils. The main feature of *Populus* (as opposed to the similar
Salix) is that the flowers are wind pollinated and thus are

carried on the naked shoots before the leaves (which are broad and only rarely lanceolate), and the shoots have a terminal bud (in *Salix*, the tip of the shoot aborts) with all the buds having several helically arranged scales (single external scale in *Salix* buds).

Populus is divided into five distinct groups, although the hybrids in cultivation cut across these groups. In the section *Populus* (syn. *Leuce*) the leaves are coarsely toothed, often palmately lobed, and hairy beneath, the leaf stalks are laterally compressed to round, and the bracts of the catkin are fringed with long hairs. The bark is also smooth, at least in the upper crown, and usually grey-green, and suckers from the roots are very common. This section further divides into the white poplars (*alba* and × *canescens*) which have lobed leaves which are densely white or silvery haired, and the aspens (*tremula*) with leaves more rotund, coarsely toothed but not lobed, and soon hairless. Section *Leucoides* has a rough bark, large leaves which are hairy beneath and set on stout shoots, a scaly bark, and a hairy ovary. The leaves in this section are uniformly large, changing little between vigorous and short shoots. The leaf stalk is grooved. *P. lasiocarpa* belongs here. Section *Tacamahaca* consists of the balsam poplars, so named because of the sweet fragrance of their new leaves and from the viscid buds. The leaves are generally whitish beneath with a translucent or hyaline margin and have leaf stalks which are round or squarrish in section, not compressed. Species which belong here are *balsamifera*, *candicans*, *maximowiczii*, *simonii* and *trichocarpa*. Section *Aigeiros* has the leaves green on both sides but with a hyaline margin and usually broad at the base, but with a laterally compressed leaf stalk. The bark is furrowed. This group includes *P. nigra*, and is more important for the hybrids between *P. nigra* and *P. deltoides* (*P.* × *canadensis*). Hybrids between sections *Tacamahaca* and *Aigeiros* include *P.* × *berolinensis*. The final section is *Turanga*, which has shoots without a terminal bud, polymorphous leaves, hairy not viscid buds and a segmented disc (which is soon shed) in the flowers. *P. euphratica* is the original weeping willow and occurs from North Africa across to central Asia. It is naturalized in a small area of southeast Spain in Alicante province (near Elche) but is not further described here.

Informal Key

LEAVES
(i)   palmately lobed, white haired beneath: *alba*, × *canescens*
(ii) rounded, toothed, green and soon more or less glabrous beneath: *tremula*, × *canescens*

(iii) **whitish beneath:** *balsamifera*, × *berolinensis*, *candicans*, *maximowiczii*, *simonii*, *trichocarpa*

(iv) **large, green, but very hairy beneath:** *lasiocarpa*

(v) **green beneath, not conspicuously hairy:** *nigra*, × *canadensis*, × *berolinensis*

---

p.244 **White Poplar** or **Abele** *Populus alba*

Description: Deciduous tree 15–25 m (50–80 ft) (rarely 30–40 m (100–130 ft)) with a bole diameter to 1 m (3.3 ft).
Crown Broad columnar to domed, appearing greyish in the distance in summer, surrounded by suckers from the roots. *Bark* Of young trees and at the tops of older ones, grey-green to creamy white, smooth and pitted, at the base becoming black, furrowed and cracked. *Shoot* Vividly white woolly when new, showing green beneath as the hairs are lost, pale brown in the second year. *Buds* Ovoid, pointed, scales orange-brown with white hairs. *Foliage* Leaves variable depending upon where and when they are growing; on vigorous shoots, rather maple-like with three or five triangular lobes which have a few large teeth and a heart-shaped base, on less vigorous shoots they are broadly ovate to nearly round, blunt at the apex, rounded to heart-shaped at the base and with wavy, irregularly toothed margins but without a translucent border; initially densely white hairy on both sides, that above soon rubbing off to reveal the shiny deep green blade, remaining greyish white beneath, 6–12 cm (2.4–4.7 in); leaf stalk flattened, 3–4 cm (1.2–1.6 in); autumn colour yellowish. *Flowers* In early spring before the leaves; male catkins crimson and grey, expanding to 8 cm (3.1 in), with five to ten stamens; female catkins pale green. *Fruit* Catkins 8–10 cm (3.1–4 in).

Range: Europe from Germany south to Tunisia in North Africa and east through Asia Minor to Central Asia.

Habitat: Wet or well-watered sites.

Varieties: 'Pyramidalis' has narrow brown upright branches, rather like a broader Lombardy

Poplar. It differs in the leaves of short shoots becoming almost hairless by autumn. It has been treated as a separate species (*P. bolleana*) and represents the form from central Asia (Turkmenistan). 'Richardii' has the leaves dull yellow above and yellow-grey beneath.

Synonyms: *P. bolleana, P. nivea*.

This tree is very attractive for the silvery white hairs which are carried on the new growths and is widely planted as an amenity tree outwith its natural distribution. It is a parent (with *P. tremula*) of, and similar to, *P. × canescens*. The two trees can be distinguished by the leaves on long shoots on *P. alba* being lobed and white hairy, whilst those of *P. × canescens* have irregular serrate teeth and are grey hairy. A further distinction is in the bract which subtends the flowers of all poplars. In *P. alba*, it is toothed, whilst in *P. × canescens* it is deeply divided into narrow segments (laciniate).

p.247 **Balsam Poplar** *Populus balsamifera*

Description: Deciduous tree to 15–30 m (50–100 ft) with a bole diameter to 70 cm (2.3 ft). *Crown* Upright, usually with many suckers from the roots. *Bark* Light brown and smooth, maturing to grey and furrowed with flat scaly ridges and pinkish fissures. *Shoot* Terete or rounded, stout, brown. *Buds* Long ovoid-conic, sticky with yellowish resin which smells of balsam, to 2.5 cm (1 in). *Foliage* Leaves ovate to broad ovate, apex acute, pointed, base rounded to subcordate, margin sinuate (wavy) with rounded teeth but without a translucent border, upper surface dark shiny green, underside whitish or pale with conspicuous net veining, hairless or slightly (usually rusty) downy on the veins beneath, size variable, normally 7–13 × 4–7 cm (2.8–5.1 × 1.6–2.8 in), but up to 35 cm (14 in) on vigorous sucker shoots; leaf stalk rounded, 2–5 cm (0.8–2 in); new foliage with a strong balsam scent; autumn colour yellow to poor. *Flowers* Male catkins to 8 cm (3.1 in) in May. *Fruit* Catkins to 13 cm (5.1 in) with ovoid pointed light-brown hairless capsules to 8 mm (0.3 in) which open along two sutures.

Range: North America from Newfoundland to Alaska and south to Iowa and Pennsylvania, local south to Colorado on the east side of the Rocky Mountains.

Habitat: Cultivated as an ornamental tree, in the wild occurring on moist sites.

Synonyms: *P. tacamahaca.*

This tree has a strong balsam scent. It is not as common in cultivation as *P. trichocarpa*, or their mutual hybrid, 'Balsam Spire' (syn. 'TT32').

---

p.248 **Berlin Poplar** *Populus × berolinensis*

Description: Deciduous tree to 25 m (80 ft) with a bole diameter to 1 m (3.3 ft).
Crown Narrow columnar. *Bark* Dull grey, developing irregular pale buff fissures and narrow ridges. *Shoot* Slightly angular and hairy, yellowish brown, becoming yellowish grey. *Buds* Conic, resinous. *Foliage* Leaves rhombic ovate to broad ovate, apex slender pointed, base rounded or wedge-shaped, margin with fine serrate teeth and a narrow translucent border but not glandular, upper surface bright green with a whitish midrib, underside pale green to slightly whitish, 7–12 × 4–7 cm (2.8–4.7 × 1.6–2.8 in); leaf stalk rounded, downy at first, 2–5 cm (0.8–2 in). *Flowers* Catkins crimson, 4–7 cm (1.6–2.8 in), with about 15 stamens.

Range: Hybrid origin.

Habitat: Cultivated as a forest and ornamental tree.

Similar species: **Central Asian Balsam Poplar** *P. laurifolia* (p.249) is a balsam poplar from central Asia, from the Altai shan to Mongolia and northern China. It has strongly angular new shoots which are grey and downy in the grooves, narrow leaves which are greyish beneath with finely serrate glandular tipped teeth, and initially erect (then drooping) male catkins with numerous stamens.

This tree is a hybrid of *P. laurifolia* (*see* above) and *P. nigra* 'Italica'. It first arose in Berlin, but similar crosses have been made and released as forest trees. It is better adapted to continental climates, and is widely planted both in central Europe and in the prairies of North America. In Britain, the foliage is susceptible to a species of *Marssonina*, which causes premature leaf fall.

p.246 **Hybrid Black Poplar** *Populus* × *canadensis*

Description: Deciduous tree 20–45 m (65–150 ft) with a bole diameter to 2 m (6.6 ft).
Crown Columnar conic in young trees, becoming rounded domed on a long bole.
Bark Pale to dark grey, developing a regular network of fissures but without rounded knobs or burrs. *Shoot* Light brown, round or with angular ridges.
Buds Conic, sharp pointed, shiny green or glossy brown, to 2 cm (0.8 in).
Foliage Leaves broad ovate, apex slender pointed or shortly acute, base more or less truncate to broad wedge-shaped, margin ciliate with large rounded scalloped teeth and a translucent border, shiny dark green above, paler beneath, hairless, mainly around 8 cm (3.1 in) broad and long, but to 20 × 15 cm (8 × 6 in) on strong coppice shoots; leaf stalk flattened, usually with one or two glands, 2–6 cm (0.8–2.4 in); autumn colour yellowish; new foliage in spring reddish brown to orange in some clones.
Flowers In early spring; male catkins crimson; female catkins greenish yellow.
Fruit Shedding cottony seeds in June.
Range: Hybrid origin in cultivation.
Habitat: Widely planted, tolerating most soils but preferring moist ones.
Varieties: It exists as a number of named clones which are produced by cuttings. 'Serotina' is a male clone with the leaves emerging in late May when they are reddish brown. 'Serotina

Aurea' is a sport with golden green foliage. 'Robusta' also is a male clone. Mature trees have a narrower crown, and the foliage emerges earlier in spring. 'Regenerata' and 'Marilandica' are female clones.

Similar species: *P. deltoides* differs in the more strongly angled shoots, the more densely ciliate leaf margins, the male trees having flowers with 30–60 stamens and the capsules on female trees having three or four valves.

Synonyms: *P. × euramericana*.

This is a hybrid of *P. nigra* with the Eastern Cottonwood (*P. deltoides*) from eastern North America. It first arose in France in the middle of the 18th century but has been produced on many subsequent occasions. It has enormous hybrid vigour (heteroisis) and is widely planted, as one clone or another, in forestry. For urban areas, however, the branches are somewhat brittle, and the roots invasive, which is especially a problem on shrinkable clay soils.

p.248 **Balm of Gilead** *Populus candicans*

Description: Deciduous tree 15–20 m (50–65 ft) with a bole diameter to 50 cm (1.6 ft).
Crown Narrow conic, becoming broad columnar, surrounded by a ring of suckers from the roots. *Bark* Grey-green, smooth in young trees, becoming broadly fissured. *Shoot* Angular and downy when young but becoming rounded and hairless by the autumn when purple-brown to orange-brown, later brown. *Buds* Ovoid-to slender pointed, viscid and strongly fragrant of balsam, scales hairy, 1–1.3 cm (0.4–0.5 in). *Foliage* Broad ovate, apex acute and short slender pointed, base heart-shaped, margins with regular incurved teeth and ciliate whitish hairs when young but without a translucent border, upper surface sub-shiny green, lower surface whitish with conspicuous venation, strongly balsam scented especially when young or following rain, 5–15 × 4.5–12 cm (2–6 × 1.8–4.7 in); leaf stalk downy, terete,

3–7 cm (1.2–2.8 in). *Flowers* Female clone only, with catkins in early spring from lateral buds, pendent, 4–6 cm (1.6–2.4 in). *Fruit* Pendent catkin to 16 cm (6.3 in) with cottony seeds.

Range: Presumed eastern North America.

Habitat: Cultivated as an ornamental for the fragrant new foliage.

Varieties: 'Aurora' is a form in which the leaves show varying degrees of white or pink variegation. This is most strongly exhibited on the vigorous extension shoots from mid-summer onwards. Unfortunately, it is particularly susceptible to a bacterial canker.

Synonyms: *P. balsamifera* var. *candicans, P. × jackii.*

The origin of this tree is subject to debate and speculation. Only the female form is known and it apparently originated in, or came to prominence in, eastern North America in the early colonial period. It could be a form of *P. balsamifera* or a hybrid of that species with *P. deltoides*, which is *P. × jackii.* Unfortunately, it is subject to the bacterial canker noted above, which blights the branches and reduces vigour.

---

p.244 **Grey Poplar** *Populus × canescens*

Description: Deciduous tree 25–40 m (80–130 ft) with a bole diameter to 2 m (6.6 ft).
Crown Young trees conical, becoming broad and domed with maturity, surrounded by many suckers from the roots. *Bark* In young trees and upper crown of older ones, dark grey to silvery white, smooth except for deep triangular pits, in mature trees at the base becoming dark brown or blackish with a network of crossing ridges.
Shoot Covered in white wool when young but this soon rubbing off, revealing greyish green-brown. *Buds* Ovoid-conic, scales red-brown with white hairs at the base, hairless and yellow-brown at the tip. *Foliage* Leaves variable, from ovate to rounded in outline on short shoots, with big irregular and rather coarse teeth and a rounded to shallow heart-shaped base, to shallow five lobed on

vigorous shoots, with crinkled lobulate margins and a truncate base, margin without a translucent border; emerging silvery white due to a coating of hairs, but soon losing these above and changing to glossy grey-green above, underside from persistently hairy with greyish white hairs to almost hairless on the more rotund leaves, to 8 cm (3.1 in); leaf stalk hairy, flattened, to 5 cm (2 in). *Flowers* In early spring; males maturing greyish to reddish purple, shedding yellow pollen.

Range: Central Europe.

Habitat: Widely planted, tolerating dryish sites but at its best on damp ones.

This is a hybrid of *P. alba* with *P. tremula*, and in most respects is intermediate between them. However, the foliage shows the greater influence of *P. alba quid vide*, for the main distinctions. It is of much greater vigour than either parent, forming a larger tree. It is represented by a limited number of named clones. Because it suckers profusely from the roots, it forms a forest of subsidiary stems where these are not cut or grazed. By this means, it readily escapes from cultivation and becomes naturalized.

p.245 **Chinese Necklace Poplar**
Populus lasiocarpa

Description: Deciduous tree to 10–20 m (33–65 ft) with a bole diameter to 50 cm (1.6 in).
Crown Conical, or columnar, with slightly ascending branches. *Bark* Grey-brown or brown, fissuring and developing scaly ridges. *Shoot* Stout, green but becoming buff, with a dense covering of buff hairs which persist through several years. *Buds* Large, ovoid-conical with an acute apex, shiny green, hairy and somewhat sticky, to 1.5 cm (0.6 in). *Foliage* Leaves heart-shaped, rounded or bluntly acute at the tip, base deeply heart-shaped, margin with regular rounded incurved glandular teeth but without a translucent border, upper surface matt green with pale or pinkish veins, lower

surface light green with paler veins, densely hairy beneath, leaf blade enormous, to 35 × 25 cm (14 × 10 in); stipules lanceolate, soon lost; leaf stalk stout, rounded or terete, pink or green hairy, to 11 cm (4.3 in); autumn colour poor. *Flowers* Male catkins yellow, 20–25 cm (8–10 in), female flowers often carried at base of male catkins, opening before the leaves on leafless lateral shoots. *Fruit* In spaced strings of ovoid 'beads', green, ripening in mid summer to release cottony down with green 4 × 1 mm (0.2 × 0.1 in) seeds.

Range: Western China.

Habitat: Cultivated as an ornamental, in the wild occurring in mixed forests beside streams.

Similar species: **Wilson Poplar** *P. wilsoniana* has rounded and rather smaller leaves (to 22 cm (8.7 in)) which are rather bluish green. The shoots are soon hairless and olive-brown or purplish brown. It also comes from central and western China.

This is one of the most spectacular trees with its bold foliage which does not decrease in size as the tree grows older. It is also unique amongst the poplars in producing catkins which are polygamous, with male flowers at the base and female ones further up. It will, therefore, produce fertile seed from a single tree, which is just as well as it is reluctant to root from cuttings (but is also grafted onto other poplars). It is hardy as far north as Aberdeen and southern Sweden, although preferring a warmer climate.

---

p.249 **Maximowicz's Balsam Poplar**
Populus maximowiczii

Description: Deciduous tree to 20 m (65 ft) with a bole diameter to 60 cm (2 ft).
Crown Rounded, domed. *Bark* Smooth, yellowish on young trees, becoming grey and deeply fissured on old trees.
Shoot Round, slightly downy when young, green and reddish brown, maturing to grey-brown. *Buds* Long ovoid-conic, greeny

brown, sticky with resin which smells of balsam, 1.5–2.5 cm (0.6–1 in).

Foliage Leaves broad elliptic to broad ovate, apex tapers abruptly to a short broad tip which is twisted and points downwards, base rounded to heart-shaped, rather wedge-shaped on strong shoots, margin bluntly toothed with ciliate hairs but without a translucent border, somewhat leathery in texture, upper surface dull fresh green with impressed veins, underside whitish, downy along the veins on both surfaces at least initially, 7–13 × 6–12 cm (2.8–5.1 × 2.4–4.7 in); leaf stalk terete, 2–4 cm (0.8–1.6 in); autumn colour yellow.

Flowers Male catkins 5–10 cm (2–4 in), each flower with 30–40 stamens. *Fruit* Capsules ripening in autumn, short stalk, hairless, opening along three or four sutures.

Range: Northeast Asia from Manchuria, Korea, Pacific Russia and Japan.

Habitat: Cultivated as an ornamental tree, in the wild occurring on moist sites.

It makes an attractive small-to-medium poplar. It has been used to produce a variety of hybrid clones, such as 'Androscoggin', 'Geneva' and 'Oxford'.

p.246 **Black Poplar** *Populus nigra*

Description: Deciduous tree 20–30 m (65–100 ft) with a bole diameter to 1.5 m (5 ft).

Crown Rounded, with billowing branches. *Bark* Grey-brown, becoming deeply fissured with short broad ridges, often with burrs. *Shoot* Whitish or yellow-brown, slender, terete, becoming fawn-grey and shiny in the second year. *Buds* Narrow ovoid-conic, apex pointed and curved out from the stem at the tip but pressed against shoot at the base, waxy pale brown or chestnut brown, 7 mm (0.3 in). *Foliage* Leaves rhombic ovate on strong shots, more triangular or deltoid on weaker shoots, apex slender pointed, base wedge-shaped to truncate, margin with small forward-pointing teeth and a translucent or hyaline border but not ciliate, upper surface glossy green, underside pale green, hairless, 5–8 × 6–8 cm (2–3.1 × 2.4–3.1 in); leaf stalk flattened, without glands, 3–4 cm (1.2–1.6 in); autumn colour yellow; new foliage green or slightly bronze-green. *Flowers* In early spring; male catkins crimson before shedding the pollen, with 20–30 stamens, expanding to 6–7 cm (2.4–2.8 in); female catkins greenish, shorter. *Fruit* Catkins expand to 10–15 cm (4–6 in); capsules with two valves, ripening in early summer.

Range: Throughout much of Europe except the north, extending into Central Asia and in Tunisia in North Africa.

Habitat: Sides of rivers, but planted more widely.

Varieties: Ssp. *betulifolia* has deciduous hairs on the twigs and the leaf stalks are finely pubescent. It has more pronounced burrs on the trunk and a crown with somewhat sinuous arching major branches. Lombardy Poplar, cultivar 'Italica', has a narrow crown composed of erect branches. It is possibly of central Asia origin. It is a male clone, although a female form, 'Italica Feomina', with heavy ascending branches is occasionally encountered. 'Plantierensis' is a hybrid of 'Italica' and ssp. *betulifolia*, having an erect but broader crown than 'Italica' but initially rather downy shoots and leaves. Ssp. *afghanica* is a columnar tree which is a dominant landscape feature in southern Europe where it often develops a pale-coloured bark.

Black Poplar has a wide range, and consequently shows some variation. Subspecies *betulifolia* was originally distinguished from cultivated trees in America, before it was realized to be the native form in western Europe. The commonest form in cultivation is the Lombardy Poplar ('Italica'), introduced from (or via) northern Italy. Black Poplar used to be an important timber tree, but has largely been supplanted in this role by its hybrids with *P. deltoides* from the eastern USA. An aphid, *Pemphigus bursarinus*, produces spiral galls on the leaf stalks of *P. nigra* but not on the hybrids.

p.249 **Simon's Poplar** *Populus simonii*

Description: Deciduous tree to 10–15 m (33–50 ft) with
a bole diameter to 50 cm (1.6 ft),
occasionally larger.
Crown Narrow rounded dome. *Bark* Pale
grey-brown to whitish, becoming fissured
on old trees. *Shoot* Angular and hairless,
brown, becoming terete or rounded as they
mature and reddish brown. *Buds* Ovoid-
conic, resinous, 1.5 cm (0.6 in).
Foliage Leaves diamond (rhombic) or
obovate in outline, tapering to an acute or
abrupt slender-pointed apex and wedge-
shaped base, margin with small, regular
blunt teeth but without a translucent
border, upper surface dark green, paler
beneath, hairless, 5–12 × 3–9 cm (2–4.7 ×
1.2–3.5 in); leaf stalk rounded, 0.5–2.5 cm
(0.2–1 in). *Flowers* Male catkins with
eight stamens, 2–3 cm (0.8–1.2 in).
Range: Across northwest to north China.
Habitat: Cultivated as a forest and ornamental tree,
in the wild occurring on moist sites.
Varieties: 'Fastigiata' has the branches erect.
Synonyms: *P. przewalskii*.

This makes a small tree attractive for the
fresh green rhombic leaves which open in
early spring (and can be susceptible to
spring frosts).

p.245 **Aspen** *Populus tremula*

Description: Deciduous tree 15–25 m (50–80 ft) with a
bole diameter to 1 m (3.3 ft).
Crown Conic to columnar, open with rather
short slender branches, usually with suckers
from the roots. *Bark* Smooth greenish-grey
with large lenticels, becoming shallowly
ridged at the base in old trees. *Shoot* Olive-
brown, smooth and shiny at first, becoming
brown to grey-brown, but on flowering
shoots the ridge located behind the catkin
buds leaves the shoots knobbly. *Buds* Ovoid-
conic, shiny brown, 6 mm (0.25 in) (but *see*
male flower buds). *Foliage* Leaves rounded to
broad ovate to oval but wider than broad,

apex acute, base rounded to subcordate, margin with large rounded teeth and scalloped sinuses but without a translucent border, upper surface bluish green, woolly when young, veins slightly raised, underside glaucous to pale green, veins only slightly raised, 1.5–8 cm (0.6–3.1 in) long and broad; leaf stalk laterally compressed near the leaf blade, rounded towards the base, 4–8 cm (1.6–3.1 in); autumn colour yellow; new foliage usually coppery; foliage on sucker growths and juvenile trees strongly and rather persistently white hairy and more ovate to heart-shaped *Flowers* Dioecious; male flower buds ovoid, tapering to a short point, green and brown, 1–1.2 cm (0.4–0.5 in), set on a bulbous base, opening to 5–10 cm (2–4 in) in late winter or early spring and dull brown; female green. *Fruit* Catkins to 4 cm (1.6 in), ripening in May and shedding the cottony seeds.

Range: Across Europe including Britain east into Asia Minor and central Asia, also in Algeria in North Africa.

Habitat: Damp hillsides and woods.

Similar species: **Big-tooth Aspen** *P. grandidentata* is a related species from northeast North America, differing in the large coarse teeth and the initially grey hairy shoots and leaves. It is occasionally planted for timber, especially in Austria.

P. tremuloides from northern North America south into northern Mexico has more finely toothed leaves. 'Pendula' is a small ornamental urban tree with weeping branches and mainly juvenile leaves. *P. tremuloides* has been crossed with *P. × canescens*, with the hybrid being used in forestry in parts of Scandinavia.

Due to the way in which the leaf stalk is vertically flattened near the leaf blade, the unstable leaves flutter in the slightest breeze, giving it the name of 'quaking aspen'. The fluttering produces a strong rustle or rattle as the leaves are rather thick and card-like. Aspen is widely distributed across Eurasia, and is the common or main species of a group of related taxa, with closely related species in the Himalayas and China, whilst in North America, *P. tremuloides* extends from Canada south into northern Mexico. The group is characterized by the flattened leaf stalk, rounded toothed leaves which open coppery in colour and the suckering habit. Aspen has hybridized with *P. alba* to produce *P. canescens*.

p.247 **Western Balsam Poplar** or **Black Cottonwood** *Populus trichocarpa*

Description: Deciduous tree to 20–35 m (65–115 ft) with a bole diameter to 70 cm (2.3 ft). *Crown* Columnar conic with whorled branches. *Bark* Dark grey-green to yellow-grey, smooth until becoming shallowly fissured and dark grey. *Shoot* Slightly angular ridged at first but maturing to terete, initially downy, maturing to shiny reddish brown. *Buds* Long ovoid-conic, often slightly curved, red-brown but sticky with yellowish resin which smells of balsam, to 3 cm (1.2 in). *Foliage* Leaves long ovate to nearly oblong, apex shortly pointed to tapering to a slender point, base rounded to subcordate, margin finely and shallowly wavy toothed but without a translucent border, upper surface dark shiny green, underside somewhat oily and painted white or yellowish white with net veining and minute rusty hairs on the main veins, normally 7–15 × 5–10 cm (2.8–6 × 2–4 in), but up to 25 cm (10 in) on vigorous shoots; leaf stalk round, hairy, 2.5–5 cm (1–2 in); new foliage strongly balsam scented; autumn colour golden-yellow but the leaves retain their pale silvery backs. *Flowers* Male catkins reddish purple, 4–8 cm (1.6–3.1 in); female catkins lime green and shorter. *Fruit* Capsules round, hairy, light brown, opening along three sutures, 6 mm (0.25 in).
Range: Western North America from southern Alaska to Baja California, extending east into Alberta, Montana and South Dakota.
Habitat: Cultivated as a forest and ornamental tree, in the wild occurring on moist sites.

Varieties: 'Fritzi Pauley' is a selected clone, resistant to bacterial canker, which is used in forestry.

Similar species: 'Balsam Spire' is a hybrid of *P. trichocarpa* with *P. balsamifera*, and also makes an excellent fast-growing tree. Various other hybrids involving the disease resistance of *P. trichocarpa* are used in forestry. The best of those involving *P. deltoides* as the other parent are *P.* × *generosa*, and the recent Belgian clones 'Beaupré' and 'Boelare'.

This is perhaps the most attractive of the poplars, and with a delightful balsam scent. It is fast growing. It is allied to *P. balsamifera*, with the best distinguishing character (only available on female trees) being that the capsules of *P. trichocarpa* split open into three segments, not two as in *P. balsamifera*.

PROTEA, PROTEACEAE

This is a large family native mainly to the southern hemisphere and especially Australia. All the species are evergreen. The family is characterized by the calyx and corolla not being differentiated, but forming a calyx-tube which covers the bud and opens by up to four valvate segments, and in having four stamens. Only *Embothrium* (p.673) is featured here, but *Grevillea*, *Hakea* and *Telopea* are cultivated, although only making shrubs in northern Europe. *Grevillea robusta* can form a large tree in warm temperate areas. Its leaves are leathery and obovate in outline but divided into eleven or twelve pairs of pinnate segments. The flowers are in axillary racemes and orange-red. On mature trees they are carried in profusion in spring.

PLUMYEWS, *PRUMNOPITYS*
(SYNONYM: *PODOCARPUS* IN PART)
FAMILY PODOCARPACEAE

This genus consists of ten species, from South America, Costa Rica in the Caribbean and from Malaya south across the Pacific to New Zealand. The male catkin is a spike, as are the female flowers. The seeds do not sit on a fleshy foot or base as in *Podocarpus*, but become enclosed in a leathery fleshy layer which is edible.

p.62 **Andean Plumyew** *Prumnopitys andina*

Description: Evergreen tree to 20 m (65 ft) with a bole diameter to 80 cm (2.6 ft).
Crown Ovoid to conic, often on several stems. *Bark* Smooth but with horizontal wrinkles, grey, grey-brown or black, thin. *Shoot* Green for the first two years from the decurrent leaf bases, then dark brown or grey-brown, smooth. *Buds* Ovoid-conic, green with brown free scales, very small, 1 mm (0.1 in). *Foliage* Parted beneath the shoot, elsewhere rather radial and forwards or upswept; leaves linear, tapering to the base which is decurrent on the shoot, apex rounded, slender pointed, dark bluish green on both sides, 2–3 cm × 2 mm (0.8–1.2 × 0.1 in); crushed foliage with a resin scent. *Flowers* On short shoots from previous season's growths in spring; male cones in clusters of ten to twenty on a short shoot, cylindrical, 5 mm (0.2 in). *Fruit* Plum-like and surrounded by a thin fleshy, blue-black or yellowish-white layer which is edible and tasty, 2 × 1.4 cm (0.8 × 0.6 in).

Range: Chilean Andes and adjoining Argentina.
Habitat: Cultivated in Europe as an ornamental, in the wild occurring in temperate forests.
Synonyms: *Podocarpus andinus*.

This tree make a neat evergreen with its smooth, elephant-like trunk.

CHERRIES AND PLUMS, *PRUNUS*
(SYNONYMS: *AMYGDALUS*, *CERASUS*, *LAUROCERASUS*, *PADUS*)
FAMILY ROSACEAE

This is a very large and diverse genus of great economic importance. The perhaps 400 species are divided into five main subgenera which are sometimes treated as separate genera. The unifying feature is the fruit, which is a single-seeded drupe with a fleshy outer covering and inside a hard stone which contains the nut. The term 'stone fruits' refers to the commercial crop. Most species have a pair of large glands (extrafloral nectaries to feed ants and thus keep predators away) towards the junction of the blade or lamina with the leaf stalk. Subgenus *Prunus* has the axillary buds single, with a terminal bud, the leaves are convoluted in bud (i.e. the two halves are rolled inwards towards the midrib), the flowers are solitary or in clusters of up to four, the fruit is grooved along one side and contains a somewhat flattened stone. In the true plums, section *Prunus*, the flowers are stalked and the fruit bloomed with a sculptured stone (species featured are *PP. cerasifera, cocomila, domestica* and *spinosa*). In section *Armeniaca* the flowers are only very shortly stalked to almost stalkless, the fruit has a velvety covering of hairs and the stone is rather smooth (*see PP. armeniaca* and *brigantina*). In subgenus *Amygdalus*, the axillary buds are in threes, with the two laterals producing flowers, terminal buds are present, the leaves are conduplicate (i.e. folded along the midrib, not rolled) and the stone is grooved or pitted. The fruit is downy (except in the cultivated nectarines in *persica*), with a thick juicy flesh (*persica*) or dry and splitting (*dulcis*). In subgenus *Cerasus*, the leaves are conduplicate in bud, the flowers are clustered (rarely racemose or corymbose), the fruit is not grooved with a smooth more or less globose stone. It includes a group of shrubs, not treated here, with the buds in threes, and the main ornamental cherries with single buds. Species included here are *PP. avium, cerasus, incisa, mahaleb, sargentii, serrula, serrulata, subhirtella,* × *yedoensis*. In subgenus *Laurocerasus* the trees are evergreen and conduplicate in bud. The flowers are in racemes which do not have any leaves at the base. They are produced in the spring from the leaf axils. Species here include *PP. laurocerasus* and *lusitanica*. In subgenus *Padus* the leaves are deciduous, conduplicate and the flowers are carried on leafy racemes. This group includes *padus, serotina* and *virginiana*.

Informal Key

FLOWERS
(i) **on bare branches, solitary or in small clusters:** *armeniaca, brigantina, dulcis, incisa, persica, spinosa*
(ii) **primarily before the leaves but the young leaves expanding, solitary or in small clusters:** *avium, cerasifera, cerasus, cocomila, domestica, mahaleb, sargentii, serrula, serrulata, subhirtella,* × *yedoensis*
(iii) **on leafy shoots after or with the leaves, flowers in racemes:** *laurocerasus, lusitanica, padus, serotina, virginiana*

p.224 **Apricot** *Prunus armeniaca*

Description: Deciduous tree to 10 m (33 ft) with a bole
diameter to 40 cm (1.3 ft).
Crown Rounded, with generally tortuous
branches. *Bark* Greyish brown, finely
fissured. *Shoot* Maturing to glossy reddish
brown, hairless, terminal bud absent.
Buds Conical, small, purplish brown.
Foliage Leaves broad ovate to rounded,
rolled or convoluted in bud, apex abrupt
and short slender pointed, base rounded to
truncate, margin with fine bluntly pointed
serrate teeth to 1 mm (0.1 in), upper
surface shiny dark green, underside paler,
hairless or with axillary tufts beneath, 6–9
× 4–6 cm (2.4–3.5 × 1.6–2.4 in); leaf stalk
pinkish, with two glands, to 2.5 cm (1 in);
new foliage reddish. *Flowers* In spring
before the leaves on the previous season's
shoots, on short stalks to 9 mm (0.4 in),
singly but often crowded together on short
spur shoots; flowers pink or white, to 3 cm
(1.2 in) across, style and ovary hairy.
Fruit Globose, indentation at both ends
and grooved, short haired, reddish orange
or yellow flushed red, 3–4 cm (1.2–1.6 in)
(rarely larger); flesh ripens sweet and tasty,
separates from the stone which is smooth
with three ridges (one on each side of the
two halves of the woody stone and one
where they meet), brown.

Range: Northern China, widely cultivated.

Habitat: Orchards and gardens.

Synonyms: *Armeniaca vulgaris.*

Similar species: **Japanese Apricot** *P. mume* has leaves which
are ovate to elliptic, more or less twice as
long as wide, with a longer slender-pointed
apex, often doubly toothed and with some
hairs on both sides, and flowers which are
single or in pairs. The fruit has a stone
which is pitted and which does not separate
away from the flesh. It is also almost
inedible. It comes from southern Japan.

The Apricot has been cultivated for several
thousand years. It is almost certainly an
early introduction from China (where it has
been found wild in the north), but the

Latin name refers to a belief that it was an Armenian tree. The fruit is hairy, as in the Almond and Peach. From both of these, the smooth but ridged stone and the characteristic leaves easily distinguish it.

---

p.220 **Gean, Wild Cherry**, or **Mazzard**
Prunus avium

Description: Deciduous tree to 25 m (80 ft) with a bole diameter to 1.5 m (5 ft).
Crown Conical with spaced whorled branches when young, becoming rounded and dense in old trees. *Bark* Greyish pink to purplish red and shiny in young and small trees, peeling slightly with prominent horizontal light-brown bands of lenticels, becoming fluted with blackish or greyish fissures and scales. *Shoot* Hairless, with a thin greyish waxy layer, becoming shiny purplish brown to dark brown in the second year, terminal bud present.
Buds Ovoid, bluntly pointed, dark brown, to 5 mm (0.2 in). *Foliage* Leaves oblong-ovate to oval, folded in bud along the midrib, apex slender pointed, base wedge-shaped to rounded, margin with coarse sharp serrate teeth, hairless and dark green above, paler with hairs on the raised veins and midrib beneath but downy when young, 7–12 × 4–5 cm (2.8–4.7 × 1.6–2 in); leaf stalk slender, grooved, with two to five stalked glands, red above and yellow-green beneath, 2–3.5 cm (0.8–1.4 in); autumn colour pale yellow or red. *Flowers* Profuse in small clusters in April with the new leaves; flowers white, 2.5–3.5 cm (1–1.4 in), pendent on slender stalks 2–5 cm (0.8–2 in). *Fruit* Round, blackish red or yellow-red, sweet or bitter but not acidic, 2 cm (0.8 in); stone pale grey-brown, flattened, pointed ovoid.
Range: Throughout Europe except the far north, North Africa, southwest Asia and east across Russia as far as western Siberia.
Habitat: Mixed woods, especially Oak woods.
Varieties: 'Plena' is a form with double flowers. These persist on the tree for up to three weeks and

are copiously carried. It is sterile and makes a somewhat smaller tree.

Synonyms: *Cerasus avium*.

This makes a large attractive flowering tree, capable of growing nearly as large and as tall as Oak tree on heavy clay soils. It is the parent species of the cultivated sweet cherries. It is allied to *P. cerasus*, differing in the absence of suckers from the roots, and the sweet or bitter (but not acid) flesh and the leaves which are more coarsely toothed and hairy on the underside.

---

p.225 **Briançon Apricot** *Prunus brigantina*

Description: Deciduous small tree to 6 m (20 ft). *Crown* Rounded. *Shoot* Glabrous, glossy brown. *Foliage* Leaves ovate to elliptic, rolled or convoluted in bud, apex, slender pointed base truncate to subcordate, margin with bold and irregular serrate teeth, glossy green and hairless above, paler and hairy on the veins beneath, 5–8 × 2.5–5 cm (2–3.1 × 1–2 in); leaf stalk hairy, 1–2 cm (0.4–0.8 in). *Flowers* Almost stalkless in clusters of two to five with the leaves, white, circa 1.5 cm (0.6 in) across. *Fruit* Sub-globose with a slightly pointed apex, lenticellate, hairless, yellow, 2.5 cm (1 in); flesh sour.

Range: Maritime and Cottian Alps from southeast France and adjoining Italy.

Habitat: Hedgerows, copses.

Synonyms: *P. armeniaca* ssp. *brigantiaca*.

An oil is expressed from the seeds, huile de Marmote.

---

p.227 **Myrobalan Plum** or **Cherry Plum**
Prunus cerasifera

Description: Deciduous tree 8–12 m (26–39 ft) with a bole to 60 cm (2 ft) in diameter. *Crown* Upright when young but soon rounded and domed, often broader than high, with suckers from the roots. *Bark* Brown and smooth at first, becoming almost black or dark brown and fissured into shallow plates. *Shoot* Green for first winter, becoming brown, then grey-brown, initially slightly hairy but soon hairless, terminal bud absent. *Buds* Conical, dark brown, 1–2 mm (0.1 in). *Foliage* Leaves oval, elliptic or obovate, convoluted or rolled in bud, margins toothed, veins impressed above, upper surface glossy deep green, paler matt green beneath and downy on the veins, 4–6 × 2.5–3 cm (1.6–2.4 × 1–1.2 in); leaf stalk short. *Flowers* In late winter or early spring on previous season's shoots and on spur shoots from previous years; flowers 2 cm (0.8 in) in diameter, single or in small clusters on stalks to 1.5 cm (0.6 in); five petals, oval, pure white to pink in selected forms, 1 cm × 8 mm (0.4 × 0.3 in). *Fruit* Ripens in early autumn to red or purple, smooth, 2.5–3 cm (1–1.2 in), indented where the stalk joins, tasty.

Range: Uncertain, *see* below.

Habitat: Field margins and hedgerows, abandoned orchards.

Varieties: 'Pissardii' was selected in Iran in 1880 by the then Shah of Persia's gardener. It has flowers pink in bud, opening to rose or off-white and leaves which, when they open, are fresh ruby-red, although like many purple plants they darken as they mature and become less attractive. 'Nigra' is similar, with deeper flowers and somewhat better foliage. The two are easily separated when in flower, but less clear at other times of the year.

Synonyms: *P. domestica* var. *myrobalan*.

This tree is the first plum to open its flowers in spring. The flowers are very dependent upon the weather for the time of opening, which may range from mid January to mid April. The wild form, with brilliant white flowers contrasting with the fresh green new leaves, is far superior to the selected forms with pink flowers and purple foliage. It is often misidentified as *P. spinosa*, which is a smaller shrub or rarely a tree and which flowers in April before the leaves. Like *P. spinosa*, it suckers freely from the roots and has been used both for hedging and as a rootstock for other plums and almonds. Its origin is lost. It is almost certainly derived from *P. divaricata* (syn. *P. cerasifera* ssp. *divaricata*) which is a species ranging from the Balkans into central Asia. This differs only in the smaller (2 cm (0.8 in)) yellow fruit which does not have the stalk indented into the fruit, the leaves being more rounded at the base and the flowers being smaller.

p.220 **Sour Cherry** *Prunus cerasus*

Description: Deciduous tree 4–6 m (13–20 ft) with a bole diameter to 30 cm (1 ft).
Crown Flattened, spreading, with suckers from the roots. *Bark* Dull brown, smooth. *Shoot* Browny green, hairless, becoming purplish grey in the second year, terminal bud present. *Buds* Ovoid, dark brown, 4 mm (0.2 in). *Foliage* Leaves oval to elliptic with slender-pointed apex, in bud folded along the midrib, base wedge-shaped with an extrafloral nectary gland at the base, margin doubly serrate with the teeth ending in purplish glands, upper surface deep sub-shiny green, lower surface light green, shiny, generally hairless, 3–9 × 1.5–3.5 cm (1.2–3.5 × 0.6–1.4 in); leaf stalk grooved, purple and green, 1–2 cm (0.4–0.8 in); autumn colour red or orange, not strong. *Flowers* White, in small clusters on a stalk 2 cm (0.8 in); individual blooms 2–2.5 cm (0.8–1 in) across. *Fruit* Red or black, 1–2 cm (0.4–0.8 in).
Range: Europe.
Habitat: Cultivated as an orchard tree and widely naturalized, but origin unclear.
Varieties: 'Semperflorens' is a selection which produces further flushes of flowers from the new growths throughout the summer. The late flowers are produced singly from the axils of leaves.
Synonyms: *Cerasus vulgaris*.

This species makes a small tree or shrub. The suckering habit differentiates it from *P. avium*, which is a much larger growing tree with sweet fruits and larger leaves.

p.225 **Naples Plum** *Prunus cocomila*

Description: Deciduous small tree or shrub to 6 m (20 ft).
Crown Rounded. *Shoot* Hairless, spiny,
terminal buds absent. *Foliage* Leaves oval to
obovate, rolled or convoluted in bud, apex
rounded to bluntly pointed, base wedge-
shaped, margin with crenate teeth, hairless,
2.5–4 × 1.2–2.5 cm (1–1.6–0.5–1 in).
Flowers In clusters of two to four with the
new leaves; flowers white, 1 cm (0.4 in)
across. *Fruit* Oval to oblong, tapered to the
apex, ripening to yellow and tasty, circa 4 ×
2.5 cm (1.6 × 1 in).

Range: Southern Italy from Naples to Sicily and in
the southern Balkans.

Habitat: Hedgerows, copses.

This makes a small tree with a tasty fruit.

---

p.226 **Plum** *Prunus domestica*

Description: Deciduous tree 6–10 m (20–33 ft) with a
bole diameter to 30 cm (1 ft).
Crown Rounded, low, often surrounded by
suckers from the roots. *Bark* Grey-brown
or dull brown, becoming fissured.
Shoot Hairy when young, becoming
hairless, not spiny, dull brown, terminal
bud absent. *Buds* Ovoid, pointed.
Foliage Leaves elliptic to obovate, rolled in
bud, apex rounded to acute, base wedge-
shaped, margin with crenate teeth, upper
surface shiny dull to dark green, paler
beneath with hairs on the veins and midrib,
3–8 × 1.5–5 cm (1.2–3.1 × 0.6–2 in); leaf
stalk grooved, with two glands, hairy,
1–1.5 cm (0.4–0.6 in). *Flowers* Before the
leaves in early spring, from lateral buds on
previous seasons' growths and from short
spur twigs; flowers solitary or in twos to
threes, white, 2–3 cm (0.8–1.2 in), on
stalks 0.5–2 cm (0.2–0.8 in).
Fruit Obovoid to globose, often bloomed,
2–8 cm (0.8–3.1 in); flesh juicy, sweet;
stone brown, flattened with sharp-angled
ridges and slightly pitted, flesh usually
separating free.

Range: Caucasus but widely cultivated.

Habitat: Orchards, but spreading and naturalizing due to root suckers.

Varieties: The bullace, ssp. *institia* has the shoots more persistently downy and is often spined. The fruits are rounded to ellipsoidal, dark purple with a less flattened stone, to which the flesh clings. The leaves are hairy on both sides. The damson and Mirabelle plums are derived from it. The greengage, ssp. *italica*, is intermediate, with rounded 3–5 cm (1.2–2 in) fruits in which the flesh clings to the stone (which is neither flattened nor angular). The leaves are hairless above.

Synonyms: *Prunus communis.*

The Plum is extensively cultivated for the juicy fruit. It is a fertile hexaploid and is believed to have arisen as a hybrid between *P. cerasifera* (diploid) and *P. spinosa* (tetraploid).

---

p.226 **Almond** *Prunus dulcis*

Description: Deciduous small tree to 10 m (33 ft) with a bole diameter to 30 cm (1 ft).
Crown Broad and rather spiky. *Bark* Dark brown, smooth but becoming cracked and fissured at the base. *Shoot* Green and purple in the first year, becoming purplish brown, then grey, in wild plants often spiny, terminal bud present. *Buds* Ovoid, pointed, purplish brown, with white hairs on the scales, 5 mm (0.2 in).
Foliage Leaves oblong-lanceolate to ovate-lanceolate, folded along the middle in bud, apex acute, base rounded, margin finely crenate-serrate, folded along the indented midrib above and dark to yellow-green, underside pale green, hairless, 4–12 × 1.2–3 cm (1.6–4.7 × 0.5–1.2 in); leaf stalk glandular, to 2.5 cm (1 in). *Flowers* On the previous year's shoots in late winter or early spring, usually in pairs; flowers 2.5–5 cm (1–2in), petals rosy red to nearly white.
Fruit Ovoid-oblong, fleshy covering thin, green and hairy, splitting along one suture to expose the compressed and finely pitted nut, 3.5–6 cm (1.4–2.4 in).

Range: Southwest Europe, West Asia and North
         Africa.
Habitat: Dry hillsides, extensively cultivated.
Varieties: Var. *amara* covers the bitter almonds. They
         are used in cooking and confectionery,
         either as ground or an oil is extracted.
Synonyms: *P. communis*, *P. amygdalus*, *Amygdalus
         communis*, *A. dulcis*.

This small tree produces the almonds of
commerce and is widely cultivated in the
Mediterranean region for the fruits. In
colder climates, it is largely grown for the
attractive flowers. The fruit, as in all species
of *Prunus*, is a drupe, the dictionary
definition of which states 'a non-dehiscent
fleshy fruit'; however, this is the exception
which proves the rule, as the flesh slowly
and incompletely splits along one suture,
releasing the pitted stone. The kernel
contains varying amounts of hydrogen
cyanide or prussic acid. In the sweet
almonds, the quantity is modest and an
adult would have to eat several hundred
fresh kernels to take in a lethal dose (but
only a hundred or so for a child), a quantity
which is probably beyond most people's
capacity. However in the Bitter Almond
(var. *amara*), the quantity of prussic acid is
much greater and consuming only a few can
afford a lethal dose.

p.221 **Fuji Cherry** *Prunus incisa*

Description: Deciduous shrub or small tree to 10 m
         (33 ft) with a bole diameter to 40 cm
         (1.3 ft).
         Crown Rounded. *Shoot* Grey, hairless,
         slender. *Foliage* Leaves obovate to ovate,
         folded in bud, apex abruptly slender
         pointed, base rounded, margin doubly or
         trebly toothed with sharp serrate teeth
         3 mm (0.1 in) or longer, downy on both
         sides, 2.5–6.5 × 1.5–3 cm (1–2.6 ×
         0.6–1.2 in); leaf stalk slender and hairy
         with two purple glands, 0.6–1.2 cm
         (0.25–0.5 in). *Flowers* In clusters of two to
         four (or single) on a stalk to 2.5 cm (1 in);

flowers arising from a leaf-like deeply toothed bract with a slender stalk, white or pink, 1.2–2 cm (0.5–0.8 in). *Fruit* Ovoid, purplish black, juicy but with a bitter tasting flesh, 6 mm (0.25 in).

Range: Honshu, Japan.

Habitat: Cultivated as an ornamental.

Similar species: **Oshima Cherry** *P. speciosa* makes a tree to 12 m (39 ft). The leaves are singly or doubly toothed with bristle-tipped teeth. The flowers are in corymbose racemes on a stalk 2.5–7.5 cm (1–3 in), individual but set on 2.5 cm (1 in) stalks with an obovate bract 1.2 cm (0.5 in) which is fringed with glandular teeth. The flowers are white, fragrant, 2.5–4 cm (1–1.6 in). It is involved in the parentage of many of the Japanese cultivated cherries (Sato Zakura), *see under P. serrulata*. 'Umineko' and 'Snow Goose' are two hybrids between *P. incisa* and *P. speciosa*. They have white 3 cm (1.2 in) flowers which are set in stalked umbels and open in April with the green leaves. They have upright branches, making them suitable for streets and other places where space is limited. 'Umineko' is the Japanese name for the White-tailed Sea Eagle.

This makes a floriferous small tree.

---

p.229 **Cherry Laurel** or **Laurel**
Prunus laurocerasus

Description: Evergreen tree to 15 m (50 ft) with a bole diameter to 60 cm (2 ft), but more often a spreading sprawling multistemmed shrub. *Crown* Rounded, domed. *Bark* Dark grey-brown or black, with many lenticels. *Shoot* Pale green, hairless, in the first winter, then becoming grey-brown, terminal bud present. *Buds* Ovoid to conical, pointed, flattened except for the terminal one, green, 3 mm (0.1 in). *Foliage* In rather flat sprays with the large leaves arranged somewhat pectinately either side of the shoot; leaves oblong to lanceolate, folded in bud along the midrib, tapering to a short down-turned apex, base rounded or wedge-shaped, margin with fine forward-pointing teeth, less often entire, and rolled slightly, upper surface mid to dark glossy green with paler veins, underside light, sub-shiny green, leathery, retained two to three years, 8–20 × 3–8 cm (3.1–8 × 1.2–3.1 in); leaf stalk grooved, pale green, about 1.5 cm (0.6 in); crushed foliage with a bitter almond or cyanide smell. *Flowers* On previous season's shoots in late winter; in erect racemes 8–13 cm (3.1–5.1 in) long with thirty to forty creamy-white flowers with petals 4 mm (0.2 in). *Fruit* Conical to globose, growing green but ripening in the first autumn through red to blackish purple, 1–2 cm across (0.4–0.8 in), with a globose slightly keeled stone.

Range: Eastern Balkans and Turkey to the Caucasus in Georgia and Abkhazia.

Habitat: Forests or woodland settings, mainly as an understorey.

Varieties: Many cultivars are grown, such as 'Otto Luyken', which is a free-flowering selection with small leaves (only 10 × 2.5 cm (4 × 1 in)) and much used as a ground cover.

Synonyms: *Padus laurocerasus*, *Laurocerasus officinalis*.

With its bold glossy foliage it is widely planted both as a shrub and a ground cover. Commonly called 'laurel', it is not related to the true Laurel, *Laurus nobilis*. The fruit has a bitter taste and contains cyanides.

---

p.229 **Portuguese Laurel** *Prunus lusitanica*

Description: Evergreen shrub or occasionally a tree to 15 m (50 ft) with a bole diameter to 80 cm (2.6 ft).
Crown Young plants bushy, becoming rounded and domed, usually broader than high, and frequently on several stems.
Bark Black, smooth, sometimes fissuring at base. *Shoot* Pink-purple (upper side) or green (especially underside), smooth, hairless and shiny in first winter, then light brown to grey-brown but retaining small areas of green for a couple of years, terminal

bud present. *Buds* Ovoid-conic, pointed, purplish-pink, 5 mm (0.2 in).
Foliage Leaves ovate-oblong, folded along the midrib in bud, apex slender pointed, base rounded, glossy dark green above, pale sub-shiny beneath, margins with shallow rounded teeth, leathery, cupped with the sides of the blade curved upwards, 7–12 × 3–5 cm (2.8–4.7 × 1.2–2 in); leaf stalk 2 cm (0.8 in), grooved, pinkish purple, without glands; crushed foliage rather scentless. *Flowers* On previous season's shoot tips and leaf axils in early summer in erect or spreading spikes 15–25 cm (6–10 in) in length; flowers many, fragrant, 1–1.5 cm (0.4–0.6 in) in diameter, petals creamy white. *Fruit* Ovoid-conical, pointed, ripening from red or green to purple in early autumn, 0.8–1.3 cm (0.3–0.5 in).

Range: Spain and Portugal.
Habitat: Open woodlands.
Varieties: Ssp. *azorica* is a form from the Azores which has rather wide leaves and few flowered spikes.

This tree is rare in Spain and Portugal but widely planted as an attractive evergreen shrub. *Laurus nobilis* has rather similar leaves but these are aromatic when crushed and its flowers are in short stalked umbels.

---

p.221 **St Lucie Cherry** *Prunus mahaleb*

Description: Deciduous tree to 12 m (39 ft), or a shrub. *Crown* Spreading, rather open. *Bark* Grey-brown with rows of lenticels. *Shoot* Downy with greyish glandular hairs. *Buds* Ovoid, pointed. *Foliage* Leaves broad ovate to nearly circular, folded along the midrib in bud, apex short and pointed, base rounded to heart-shaped, margin with rounded teeth with short abrupt tips to 1 mm (0.1 in), smooth, glossy dark green and folded along midrib above, underside paler and slightly downy, especially on the midrib, 4–7 × 2–5 cm (1.6–2.8 × 0.8–2 in); leaf stalk with two glands, about 1.2 cm (0.5 in).

Flowers In clusters of 3–10 on a stalk 3–4 cm (1.2–1.6 in); flowers pure white, fragrant, 1.2–2 cm (0.5–0.8 in), on stalks circa 1.2 cm (0.5 in). *Fruit* Ovoid, black, with a thin bitter flesh, 0.8–1 cm (0.3–0.4 in)

Range: Central and southern Europe, from Belgium east to the Ukraine and into central Asia.

Habitat: Dry hillsides, thickets and in woods.

Varieties: 'Pendula' is a selection with pendent branches, giving a graceful wide-spreading small tree.

Synonyms: *Cerasus mahaleb.*

This small tree has fragrant flowers which perfume the area around a tree in late April–early May.

---

p.228 **Bird Cherry** *Prunus padus*

Description: Deciduous tree to 10–20 m (33–65 ft) with a bole diameter to 80 cm (2.6 ft).
Crown Conic in young trees, becoming domed with drooping branches, but in the selected varieties tending to be wider spreading. *Bark* Dark grey-brown, smooth, with an acrid smell. *Shoot* Dark brown, shiny, downy at first but then hairless. *Buds* Long ovoid-conic, pressed against the shoot, brown at the base and darker at the sharp apex. *Foliage* Leaves elliptic or obovate, folded in bud, apex rounded with a short slender tip to 1 cm (0.4 in), base rounded, margin with fine serrate teeth, upper surface with impressed veins and dull dark green, underside with 10–13 pairs of raised veins, paler either hairless or with axillary tufts, 7–13 × 4–7 cm (2.8–5.1 × 1.6–2.8 in); leaf stalk hairless, with two or more glands, 1.2–2 cm (0.5–0.8 in); autumn colour early, pale yellow to red. *Flowers* In spreading or drooping racemes 7–15 cm (2.8–6 in) which are on side shoots in late spring (May) with some (often small) leaves at the base; flowers white, fragrant, 1.5 cm (0.6 in) across. *Fruit* Spherical,

black with a harsh, bitter taste, 8 mm (0.3 in).

Range: Europe from Britain eastwards across northern Asia to Manchuria, Korea, Sakhalin and to the Japanese island of Hokkaido, but absent from the Mediterranean region, Balkans and southeast Russia.

Habitat: Cool temperate woodlands.

Varieties: Var. *commutata* occurs in Siberia to Manchuria. It comes into leaf much earlier, and flowers in Britain around the middle of April, some three weeks before the normal form. 'Albertii' is a cultivar with massed flowers in rather short racemes. 'Watereri' has the flowers in racemes to 20 cm (8 in), with more pronounced axillary tufts on the leaves beneath.

Synonyms: *Padus racemosa*.

Similar species: *P. maackii* is a small tree from northern China, Korea and adjoining parts of Pacific Russia. It is intermediate between the Bird Cherry group and the Cherry Laurel group in having the racemes without leaves but springing directly from the previous season's wood and in the deciduous leaves. The most striking character is the bark, which is shining amber to yellowish brown and smooth.

In Britain, this tree is much commoner (as a native) in the cooler and moister western and northern districts. In the wild, it occurs on a wide range of soils, but especially limestones.

---

p.225 **Peach** or **Nectarine** *Prunus persica*

Description: Deciduous tree to 8 m (26 ft) with a bole diameter to 40 cm (1.3 ft).
Crown Bushy, rounded. *Bark* Greyish brown, finely fissured. *Shoot* Smooth with angular ridges, reddish, hairless, terminal bud present. *Buds* Conical, small, purplish brown. *Foliage* Leaves lanceolate to narrow elliptic, folded along the midrib in bud, apex tapered, acute, base wedge-shaped, margin with fine serrate teeth,

upper surface shiny green, underside paler, more or less hairless, 5–15 × 2–4 cm (2–6 × 0.8–1.6 in); leaf stalk grooved, green or pink, usually with two glands, to 1.2 cm (0.5 in). *Flowers* In spring before the leaves on the previous season's shoots, on short stalks, single; flowers pink or white, to 2.5–3.5 cm (1–1.4 in) across, style and ovary hairy. *Fruit* Globose, indentation at both ends or shortly acute at the apex, grooved, shortly velvety hairy (but hairless in var. *nucipersica*), reddish orange or yellow flushed red, 4–8 cm (1.6–3.1 in); flesh ripens sweet and tasty, aromatic, does not separate from the stone which is deeply pitted but without the strong ridges, brown.

Range: Northern China, widely cultivated.

Habitat: Orchards and gardens, occasionally naturalized.

Varieties: Var. *nucipersica* is the Nectarine. It differs only in the fruit being smooth and totally hairless.

Synonyms: *Persica vulgaris*, *Amygdalus persica*.

The Peach makes a small tree which flowers after the Apricot. It differs from this species in the shoots having a terminal bud, the deeply pitted stone and the much longer lanceolate or narrow elliptic leaves. It has been cultivated for ages, and its true wild distribution is unknown, but almost certainly it was an early import into Persia along the Silk Route from China. In the valley of the Yarlung Tsangpo in southern Tibet, there are trees with the leaves of Peach but smaller fruits with a smoother, almost apricot stone.

p.222 **Sargent's Cherry** *Prunus sargentii*

Description: Deciduous tree 10–15 m (33–50 ft) with a bole diameter to 60 cm (2 ft).
Crown Rounded with the branches arising at an acute angle, especially when grafted onto a standard rootstock, seedling trees more ovoid. *Bark* Purple-brown, smooth between horizontal bands of pale brown

lenticels. *Shoot* Dark red, hairless, lenticels pale brown. *Buds* Conic or ovoid-conic, pointed, dark red. *Foliage* Leaves obovate to elliptic, folded in bud, apex abrupt and slender pointed, base rounded to subcordate, margin with sharp serrate teeth which are slender pointed or with a awn-like tip, upper surface glossy dark green, underside pale or somewhat glaucous, hairless, 8–13 × 4–7 cm (3.1–5.1 × 1.6–2.8 in); leaf stalk reddish with two glands, 1.5–3 cm (0.6–1.2 in); autumn colour scarlet to deep crimson in September; new foliage bronze-coloured. *Flowers* In stalkless umbels of two to six; flowers blush pink, 3–4 cm (1.2–1.6 in), on stalks 2.5–3 cm (1–1.2 in); calyx lobes untoothed, style hairless. *Fruit* Dark purple or black, 1 cm (0.4 in).

Range: Northern Honshu and Hokkaido, Sakhalin and Korea.

Habitat: Cultivated as an ornamental, in the wild occurring in forests.

Varieties: 'Rancho' is a selection with an upright habit.

Synonyms: *P. serrulata* var. *sachalinensis*.

Similar species: Hybrids with *P. sargentii* as one parent include:

P. × juddii (p.221), which probably has *P. × yedoensis* as the other parent. The new leaves are less strongly coloured than in *P. sargentii* but are hairless, whilst the flowers are whitish flushed deep pink, with glandular serrate calyx lobes and hairs at the base of the style. Two widely cultivated clones of this cross giving good autumn colours are 'Hillieri', forming a broad crowned tree with single blush-pink flowers on a slender hairy stalk and leaves which are hairy beneath, and 'Spire' (often incorrectly called 'Hillieri Spire'), with similar leaves, soft pink flowers but a narrow crown with upright branches. It is often used as a street tree. The parentage of both 'Hillieri' and 'Spire' is often ascribed to *P. sargentii* crossed with *P. incisa*. 'Accolade' is a small tree with *P. × subhirtella* as the second parent. It has semi-double flowers with 12–15 petals and serrate bronze-coloured calyx lobes.

This tree is attractive in spring with the blush flowers and the bronze-coloured new leaves, in early autumn assuming brilliant fall colours.

p.228 **Rum Cherry** *Prunus serotina*

Description:
Deciduous tree 15–20 m (50–65 ft) with a bole diameter to 70 cm (2.3 ft).
Crown Rather irregular, with spreading and ascending main branches and pendent branchlets. *Bark* Dark purplish grey to almost black, rough and peeling in small strips, in old trees thick and ridged.
Shoot Green, slender, with round fawn lenticels, becoming brown by autumn, terminal bud present. *Buds* Conic, pointed, green with a brown tip, 4 mm (0.2 in). *Foliage* Leaves oblong-obovate, obovate to oblanceolate, longitudinally folded along the midrib in bud, broadest above the middle, apex tapered or abruptly tapered to a short slender tip, base wedge-shaped and usually with a pair of dark brown glands at the base of the blade or forming small basal teeth, margin toothed with small forward-pointed raised teeth, upper surface lustrous deep green, smooth, lower side shiny pale green, smooth and hairless except for the raised midrib which has rufous hairs on the lower half, 8–12 × 3–5 cm (3.1–4.7 × 1.2–2 in); leaf stalk grooved, green with a pink base, 1 cm (0.4 in); autumn colour yellow. *Flowers* In spreading racemes 10–15 × 2 cm (4–6 × 0.8 in) on short leafy deciduous shoots in late spring or early summer, white, 8 mm (0.3 in). *Fruit* Round, ripening black, 8 mm (0.3 in), with persistent triangular abrupt and short-pointed calyx lobes.

Range:
North America from Nova Scotia south to Florida and west to Arizona and Dakota.

Habitat:
Cultivated as an ornamental and in pheasant coverts, in the wild occurring in woodland.

Synonyms:
Padus serotina.

Similar species:
P. salicifolia is occasionally cultivated. It differs in the leathery hairless leaves which are lanceolate and not widest above the

middle, and the larger fruit. It is found from Mexico south to Ecuador in South America.

The most distinctive feature of this tree is the line of rufous or orange hairs which lie on either side of the midrib on the lower side. It has naturalized in parts of Europe, usually forming an understorey element in woodland. The Latin name refers to the late leafing in the spring. The common name is attributed to the cherries having been used to flavour rum or brandy.

---

p.222 **Tibetan Cherry** *Prunus serrula*

Description: Deciduous tree 10–15 m (33–50 ft) with a bole diameter to 60 cm (2 ft).
Crown Rounded to broad domed, with arching branches. *Bark* Shining like polished mahogany, peeling in thin copper brown strips, with large horizontal bands of pale brown lenticels. *Shoot* Light brown and hairy, starting to peel after two to three years. *Buds* Ovoid, apex pointed, pressed onto the shoot, chestnut brown, 6–7 mm (0.25–0.3 in). *Foliage* Leaves lanceolate with a long tapered acute apex, folded in bud, base rounded, margin with fine regular serrate teeth, upper surface fresh to dark green, underside paler and downy, especially on the midrib and in the vein axils, or hairless, 5–10 × 1.2–3 cm (2–4 × 0.5–1.2 in); leaf stalk with several glands, 0.6–1.2 cm (0.25–0.5 in). *Flowers* In twos or threes (between one and four) with the new leaves in April, white, discrete!
Fruit Oval, red, about 1.2 cm (0.5 in).

Range: West Sichuan and northwestern Yunnan, China.

Habitat: Cultivated as an ornamental, in the wild occurring in mixed forest.

This tree is widely grown for the beautiful bark, which is displayed on the trunk, main branches and along the smaller branches. The flowers are small, attractive in their own way, but not making any display.

p.223 **Hill Cherry** or **Japanese Cherry**
Prunus serrulata

Description: Deciduous shrub or small tree to 10 m
(33 ft) with a bole diameter to 40 cm
(1.3 ft).
Crown Rounded, variable. *Bark* Brown,
with horizontal pale brown lenticels.
Shoot Hairy or hairless, light brown, shiny.
Buds Ovoid-conic, pointed, red-brown.
Foliage Leaves narrow ovate to oblong,
folded in bud, apex abrupt and short
pointed, base rounded, margin coarsely
toothed with less than 4 sharp serrate teeth
per centimetre being slender pointed or
drawn out into a bristle tip, hairless to
downy depending upon variety and
somewhat glaucous beneath, 7.5–12.5 ×
3–6.5 cm (3–4.9 × 1.2–2.6 in); leaf stalk
with glands, up to 3 cm (1.2 in); autumn
colour yellow-red, often poor. *Flowers* In
racemes of two to five with the new leaves;
flowers white to pink. *Fruit* Ovoid,
shining black.

Range: Japan and central China, as below.
Habitat: Cultivated as an ornamental.
Varieties: Var. *spontanea* has hairless leaves which are
copper to brown when young, grey-brown
bark and white 2.5–3.5 cm (1–1.4 in)
flowers which are in short-stalked
corymbose inflorescences. It occurs in
Honshu, Japan. Var. *pubescens* occurs in
Korea. The leaves are green or only slightly
bronzy when young and hairy, as are the
leaf stalks. The flowers are in long-stalked
corymbs. Var. *hupehensis* from Hubei,
central China, has the flowers before the
leaves, in almost stalkless clusters. About
three dozen clones or hybrids of Japanese
garden cherries (Sato Zakura) are
cultivated. A brief selection of the
commoner ones is given here.
'Amanogawa' has a very upright-branch
habit, making a narrow columnar tree to
6 m (20 ft), then splaying out. The flowers
are semi-double and pale pink. 'Kanzan' is
the commonest form in Britain. The
flowers are semi-double, pink with red
young foliage. As a young tree, the tree has

the branches ascending at about 45 degrees, but in old trees, they arch over. 'Kiku-shidare' ('Cheal's Weeping') has a pendulous habit with few drooping branches. It is always grafted onto a stem (usually of *P. avium*) and only grows slightly taller than the height of grafting. The flowers are fully double pink. 'Shirofugen' has an arching habit with pendulous branches. The flowers are deep rose-pink, fading to whitish dull pink, fully double, and open late in the season. 'Shirotae' has a spreading crown which is rarely taller than the height of grafting or training. The flowers are an intense white in colour, semi-double and hanging beneath the branches. They contrast effectively with the bright green new leaves. 'Taihaku' has the largest flowers, individually 6–8 cm (2.4–3.1 in) across when fully open. They are single, palest pink in bud but opening to pure white. It forms a moderately vigorous tree. 'Ukon' has flowers of a greenish yellow colour, fading to whitish. The habit is rather upright, then arching.

This is generally treated as a mixture of wild forms and ancient hybrids or selected clones. However, it provides a convenient name under which the majority of the Japanese cherries (which are mainly complex hybrids including *P. speciosa* and *P. sargentii* and others in their parentage can be considered. The names *P. lannesiana*, *P. jamasakura*, *P. verecunda* are also used for this group of trees.

---

p.227 **Sloe** or **Blackthorn** *Prunus spinosa*

Description: Deciduous shrub, rarely to 5 m (16 ft) with some pretensions to being a tree.
Crown Rounded, often broader than tall and spreading widely by suckers.
Bark Black, rough. *Shoot* Downy when young, becoming hairless and greyish, side branches ending in a sharp thorn, terminal bud absent. *Buds* Ovoid, pointed, small, in

twos or threes. *Foliage* Leaves obovate, elliptic to ovate, rolled in bud, apex acute to bluntly pointed, base wedge-shaped, margin with fine serrate teeth, dull green, paler and shiny beneath, hairy on both surfaces but may become hairless by autumn, 2–4.5 × 1.2–2 cm (0.8–1.8 × 1.5–0.8 in); leaf stalk 1 cm (0.4 in). *Flowers* Before the leaves in April, from lateral buds on previous season's growths and from short spur twigs; flowers solitary or in pairs, somewhat creamy white, about 1.5 cm (0.6 in), on stalks 5 mm (0.2 in). *Fruit* Spherical to globose, deep blue to purplish blue, with a thick waxy bloom, astringent to the taste, circa 1.2 cm (0.5 in), with the flesh adhering to the stone.

Range: Widespread in Britain and across Europe except the far north and northeast, extending into northern Asia.

Habitat: Hedgerows, copses.

Varieties: 'Plena' is a selection with double flowers.

Similar species: *P. ramburii* from southern Spain differs in the following respects. It is completely hairless. The branches become silvery grey. The leaves are smaller, 1.5–2.5 cm (0.6–1 in) and elliptic to linear oblong and glossier. The flowers are in clusters of twos or threes and appear with the leaves.

This shrubby tree has a very tough wood. The fruit, or sloe, is not palatable, but can be used to flavour gin. The flowers have a somewhat pinkish tinge to them when in bud, opening to creamy-white. In Britain they open in April, almost whatever the weather, whereas in *P. cerasifera* (which is often misidentified as Blackthorn) the flowers open from January to April depending upon the weather and, in the true form, are purest white.

---

p.224 **Rosebud Cherry** *Prunus × subhirtella*

Description: Deciduous tree 8–12 m (26–39 ft) with a bole diameter of up to 70 cm (2.3 ft). *Crown* Rounded but variable as it is represented by several cultivars, becoming twigny. *Bark* Smooth and shiny grey-brown, with prominent raised lenticels. *Shoot* Pale brown to reddish brown, shiny, hairy when young but more or less hairless by autumn, greyish in the second year, slender. *Buds* Ovoid, obtuse, shiny reddish brown, 3 mm (0.1 in).

Foliage Leaves oblong, ovate to obovate, folded in bud, apex slender pointed, base rounded, margin coarsely and usually doubly serrate toothed, upper surface hairless or thinly hairy, underside downy on the seven to ten pairs of veins and on the midrib, 4–8 × 2–4 cm (1.6–3.1 × 0.8–1.6 in); leaf stalk 6 mm (0.25 in), hairy; autumn colour poor purple.

Flowers In stalkless umbels of two to five; flowers some shade of pink, to 2 cm (0.8 in), carried on scarcely haired stalks 1 cm (0.4 in) or so in length.

Fruit Round, shiny black, 1 cm.

Range: Japan.

Habitat: Cultivated as an ornamental.

Varieties: Var. *ascendens* is the wild form, deriving from Japan and possibly also Korea and China. It differs in the larger narrower leaves to 12 cm (4.7 in) with 10–14 pairs of veins which are less doubly toothed. Var. *pendula* has a pendulous habit, but is otherwise as for var. *ascendens*. It occurs in several different cultivars, and forms mound-shaped weeping trees.

Similar species: 'Pandora' is a hybrid of *P. × subhirtella* with *P. × yedoensis*. It forms a vase-shaped tree and carries massed flowers in April. These are up to 3 cm (1.2 in) across, with pale pink petals and darker margins.

This tree is mainly represented in cultivation in Europe by the clone 'Autumnalis', which flowers intermittently in mild periods from autumn to spring and does much to brighten up the dark days of winter. The other forms flower in April to May. *P. subhirtella* is sometimes treated as a hybrid between its variety *pendula* (which is then treated as *P. pendula*) and *P. incisa*. The merit of this hypothesis is that it explains the smaller, less veined and much more incised leaves of *subhirtella* (including 'Autumnalis') when compared to the varieties *ascendens* and *pendula*.

---

p.228 **Virginian Bird Cherry** or **Choke Cherry**
Prunus virginiana

Description: Deciduous shrub or small tree to 6 m (20 ft) with a bole diameter to 20 cm (8 in). *Crown* Conic, forming thickets with root suckers. *Bark* Brown or grey, smooth but becoming scaly at the base. *Shoot* Grey or brown, slender and hairless, with a disagreeable odour and taste. *Foliage* Leaves broad elliptic to broad obovate, folded in bud, apex acute or rounded to a short abrupt tip of less than 1 cm (0.4 in), base rounded, margin with fine sharp serrate teeth, upper surface dark shiny green, underside paler with axillary tufts, 4–8(–12) × 1.5–4 cm (1.6–3.1(–4.7) × 0.6–1.6 in); leaf stalk slender, with two or more glands, 1.2–2 cm (0.5–0.8 in); autumn colour yellow. *Flowers* In racemes 7–15 cm (2.8–6 in) which are on side shoots in late spring (May) with some (often small) leaves at the base; flowers white, fragrant, 1 cm (0.4 in) across. *Fruit* Spherical, dark red or black, juicy with an astringent or bitter taste, 1 cm (0.4 in); stone large, rich in prussic acid.

Range: Northern North America from Newfoundland to British Columbia south to North Carolina and California.

Habitat: Cultivated or naturalized as an ornamental, in the wild found in forest margins and beside streams.

Varieties: 'Shubert' is a selection in which the leaves flush or open green but mature during the summer to deep reddish purple or brownish maroon.

Synonyms: *Padus rubra*, *Prunus nana*.

This makes only a small tree but it suckers freely and has become naturalized (and a pest) in parts of Europe.

p.224 **Yoshino Cherry** *Prunus × yedoensis*

Description: Deciduous tree 8–15 m (26–50 ft) with a
bole diameter of up to 70 cm (2.3 ft).
Crown Wide spreading with arching
drooping branches. *Bark* Dark brown,
lenticellate. *Shoot* Thinly downy at first.
Buds Ovoid, bluntly pointed.
Foliage Leaves ovate, elliptic-obovate to
obovate, folded in bud, apex slender
pointed, base rounded to broadly wedge-
shaped, margin with double and coarse
serrate teeth, dark green and hairless above,
on the underside softly downy on the veins
and midrib, 6–15 × 4–7 cm (2.4–6 ×
1.6–2.8 in); leaf stalk hairy. *Flowers* In late
March–April, and usually before the leaves,
in stalked racemes of five or six flowers;
flowers pale pink, fading, to 3.5 cm (1.4 in)
across, on hairy stalks. *Fruit* Round, shiny
black, 8 mm (0.3 in).

Range: Japan.

Habitat: Cultivated as an ornamental.

Varieties: 'Ivensii' is a form with white flowers and
weeping branches.

This hybrid between *P. speciosa* and
P. subhirtella occurs where they meet in
Japan. It makes an extremely attractive and
floriferous spreading tree.

GOLDEN LARCH, *PSEUDOLARIX* (SYNONYM: *CHRYSOLARIX*)
FAMILY PINACEAE

This genus comprises the one species from China. In foliage
it is similar to *Larix*, but the cone breaks up on maturity to
scatter both seeds and scales, as in *Abies* and *Cedrus*.

---

p.100 **Golden Larch** *Pseudolarix amabilis*

Description: Deciduous tree 15–25 m (50–80 ft) with a
bole diameter to 1 m (3.3 ft).
Crown Broad conic in young trees,
becoming very broad with large-spreading
and spaced branches. *Bark* Grey, rarely
purplish, becoming fissured and cracked
into plates. *Shoot* Light brown, pink-

brown or purple in the first winter and often pruinose, with small raised leaf bases, later grey. *Buds* Ovoid to conic, with the tips of the scale free, 2–3 mm (0.1 in). *Foliage* Spiral on long shoots and in rosettes of ten to thirty on short shoots; leaves linear, soft, fresh green above, lighter green beneath with two bands of stomata, 2–5.5 cm × 1.5–4 mm (0.8–2.2 × 0.1–0.2 in); autumn colour golden-orange. *Flowers* On short shoots at least two years old; male cones in clusters of ten to twenty-five, cylindrical, green or yellow. *Fruit* Ovoid, erect with a spiky outline from the large deltoid scales, green and glaucous to yellow-green when immature, ripening in the first autumn to brown and disintegrating to scatter the seeds and scales, 6–8 × 4–5 cm (2.4–3.1 × 1.6–2 in); scales 2.8–3.5 × 1.3–1.8 cm (1.1–1.4 × 0.5–0.7 in).

Range: From Jiangsu, Jiangxi, Zhejiang, Fujian and Hubei in southern China.

Habitat: Cultivated in Europe as an ornamental, in the wild occurring in mixed lowland forests.

Synonyms: *Chrysolarix amabilis*, *Pseudolarix kaempferi*.

This tree has one of the best and most reliable of autumn colours. It is hardy over southern and western Europe but can be slow to get established. The cones are deciduous, breaking up when ripe as in *Abies* and *Cedrus*, whilst the foliage is similar to *Larix*.

Douglas Firs, *Pseudotsuga*
Family Pinaceae

This genus comprises around half a dozen species (any number between four and twelve!). The leaves are soft, not dissimilar to many *Abies*, and set on a slight rise on the shoots. The buds are very distinctly conical and non-resinous. The cones are similar to *Picea*, erect at pollination and becoming pendent as they enlarge and ripen. However, the bract scale is large and three lobed, projecting between the scales and usually reflexed. *P. menziesii* is a widespread tree in western North America, occurring in various forms from

British Columbia to central Mexico, and has a high-quality timber. It is widely planted as a timber tree in Europe.

---

p.94 **Big Cone Douglas Fir**
Pseudotsuga macrocarpa

Description: Evergreen tree 15–20 m (50–65 ft), with a trunk diameter up to 50 cm (1.6 ft). *Crown* Columnar conic. *Bark* Smooth and grey in young trees, becoming thicker and scaly, then dark reddish brown and furrowed. *Shoot* Buff-brown, becoming greyer, slender, with short persistent hairs. *Buds* Conic to ovoid conic, pointed, chestnut brown, to 7 mm (0.3 in). *Foliage* Pointing forwards or at 90 degrees to the shoot both above and below it, with only a weak parting above; leaves rather laxly set, fresh green above, whitish green beneath with two waxy bands of stomata, linear, apex pointed, 3–5 cm × 1.5 mm (1.2–2 × 0.1 in); crushed foliage with a resinous smell. *Flowers* Flowers open in spring, male cones yellow, from buds on previous year's shoots, female flower greenish, terminal on shoots. *Fruit* Woody narrow ovoid cone, 10–17 cm (4–6.7 in) long by 4 cm (1.6 in) wide, with broad rounded scales to 4 cm (1.6 in) across; the bract scales are projecting with a long cusp (1.5 cm (0.6 in)) and two short triangular lobes (to 5 mm (0.2 in)).

Range: Southern California and northern Baja California.

Habitat: Planted, in the wild occurring on dry slopes and in canyons.

Far less common and not as thrifty in cultivation as Douglas Fir (*Pseudotsuga menziesii*), it is generally only seen in specialist collections. It is easily distinguished from *P. menziesii* by the longer and laxer needles which have a tapered point. It is closer, especially in the lax foliage, to the Japanese *P. japonica*, the Taiwanese *P. wilsoniana* and two west Chinese species, *P. forrestii* and *P. sinensis*, but these all have smaller cones with less prominent bracts.

p.94 **Douglas Fir** *Pseudotsuga menziesii*

Description: Evergreen tree usually 25 m (80 ft) but up
to 60 m (200 ft), with a bole diameter of up
to 1 m (3.3 ft).
Crown Conical in young trees with whorled
branches, becoming columnar and ragged
with spreading branches in old trees.
Bark Smooth grey-green with resin blisters
in young trees, becoming scaly and then
thick and corky in old trees with deep wide
furrows, reddish brown or grey brown.
Shoot Olive-green at first, becoming buff
and turning grey or grey-brown after first
winter, slender, with short hairs.
Buds Pointed ovoid-conical, reddish
brown, to 5 mm (0.2 in).
Foliage Spreading forwards or at a wide
angle, usually weakly parted above the
shoot. Leaves linear, dark green or glaucous
blue above (*see* below), with two whitish
green waxy bands beneath, soft, slender,
1.5–3 cm × 1–1.5 mm (0.6–1.2 × 0.1 in),
apex rounded, crushed leaves with a strong
fruit scent. *Flowers* Opening in spring,
male cones from buds on previous season's
shoots, yellow, female cones green-brown,
at ends of shoots, initially erect but droop
after pollination. *Fruit* Woody narrow
ovoid cone, 5–8 × 2.5–3 cm (2–3.1 ×
1–1.2 in), brown, scales rounded, to
2.5–3 cm (1–1.2 in), bract projecting and
longer than the scales, trident-shaped with
a long (4–6 mm (0.2–0.25 in)) cusp and
two triangular lobes (3 mm (0.1 in)).

Range: Western North America from British
Columbia south to central Mexico.

Habitat: Widely planted in forestry and as an
amenity tree.

Varieties: **Blue Douglas Fir**, ssp. *glauca*, has foliage
which is strongly glaucous blue especially
on the upper surface. The bark remains
scaly and dark grey or blackish, not
developing corky fissures. The cones are
generally smaller and narrower, at the
bottom end of the sizes given, with
spreading bracts. In Mexico, the trees are
not glaucous and have more slender pointed
foliage. Although often included within *P.*

menziesii, they are equally often referred to
P. guinieri and *P. macrolepis* and their
relationship with Douglas Fir is not settled.
These forms extend from northern Mexico
south to the Pico de Orizaba.

Synonyms: *P. taxifolia, P. douglasii.*

Douglas Fir has an excellent reddish timber
which is widely used in construction. It
tolerates most sites preferring moist acidic
soils with shelter. The Green form is very
fast growing, coming from the wetter
western side of the Rocky Mountains. Blue
Douglas Fir comes from the drier eastern
side, extending into Mexico and makes a
smaller tree more tolerant of dry sites and
liking sunnier conditions. Douglas Fir has
one more pair of chromosomes ($n = 13$) than
Big Cone and other Douglas firs ($n = 12$).

HOP TREES, *PTELEA*
FAMILY RUTACEAE

This is a small genus of trees and shrubs from North
America, characterized by the trifoliate leaves which have
translucent glands. The fruit is a winged samara.

p.308 ## Hop Tree *Ptelea trifoliata*

Description: Deciduous tree to 9 m (29 ft) with a bole
diameter to 15 cm (0.5 ft).
Crown Rounded. *Bark* Brownish grey with
paler fissures, thin, smooth or somewhat
scaly, bitter. *Shoot* Slender, brown, downy
and slightly warty. *Foliage* Leaves trifoliate,
rarely with five leaflets, 10–18 cm
(4–7.1 in); leaflets ovate to elliptic or
lanceolate, apex short slender pointed, base
wedge-shaped, margin with finely wavy
teeth or untoothed, upper surface shiny dark
green with tiny pellucid dots, paler and
sometimes downy below, 5–10 × 2–5 cm
(2–4 × 0.8–2 in); leaf stalk 5–10 cm
(2–4 in); autumn colour yellow. *Flowers* In
terminal corymbs 5–7 cm (2–2.8 in) across
in June–July; flowers greenish white, 1 cm
(0.4 in). *Fruit* Thin disc-like or rounded

samara with a papery thin greenish yellow or brown wings which are net-veined and a central seed, 2–2.5 cm across (0.8–1 in).

Range: North America from New York across to southern Ontario and south to Florida, Texas and into northern Mexico.

Habitat: Cultivated as an ornamental, in the wild occurring on dry rocky hillsides or in canyons.

The fruit is similar to that of Elm, although in a different family. They are bitter and were used to flavour beer, as a substitute for hops. It is a variable species, or group of species, with typical *P. trifoliata* restricted to the eastern USA.

WING NUTS, *PTEROCARYA*
FAMILY JUGLANDACEAE

This genus comes from the Caucasus, China and Japan, with around eight taxa. The leaves are large and pinnate, in some species with a winged rachis, in others with a round one. The buds are naked in most species, but in one species from Japan (*P. rhoifolia*) they are initially enclosed in a cap of scales which is soon shed. The buds are also superposed, with two or more in one leaf axil. The shoot has a septate or chambered pith, as in *Juglans* but not in *Carya*. The flowers are in pendent racemes, with the fruits being small nuts which have two wings (but in *P. paliurus*, which is rare in cultivation, the wings form a circular disc, as in *Paliurus*).

---

p.328 **Caucasian Wingnut** *Pterocarya fraxinifolia*

Description: Deciduous tree 20–35 m (65–115 ft) with a bole diameter to 2 m (6.6 ft).
Crown Conic in young trees, usually developing as a multistemmed tree with a broad rounded crown, sometimes on a single short bole with ascending branches, surrounded by suckers from the roots.
Bark Dull grey, developing a coarse network of shallow fissures and ridges.
Shoot Green and finely scaly when young, ripening to smooth and light to mid brown with oval pale lenticels, in later years grey-brown, pith chambered. *Buds* Naked,

miniature leaves with dark brown hairs exposed, on a short stalk, superposed to 3 cm (1.2 in). *Foliage* Leaves 20–50 cm (8–20 in), to 60 cm (24 in), pinnate with from 7–27 leaflets (mainly around 15–21); leaflets oblong to oblong-obovate, increasing in size up the leaf, tapering to an acute apex, base oblique, rounded or heart-shaped, margin with small rounded irregular teeth, upper surface matt green and smooth (veins raised under a hand-lens), underside light green with scattered black glands and brown scales on the lower part of the midrib, veins raised, hairless except for axillary tufts, 5–12 cm (2–4.7 in), occasionally to 20 cm (8 in), by 4–5 cm (0.8–1 in); leaf stalk grooved, green, enlarged at base, rachis round, leaflets on a 1 mm (0.1 in) stalk; autumn colour yellow. *Flowers* With the new foliage and opening in late spring, female flowers at tips of shoots in pendent 10–15 cm (4–6 in) racemes, male catkins yellow, 5–12 cm (1–4.7 in). *Fruit* In long pendent racemes 25–50 cm (10–20 in) with the single stalkless fruits spaced at the base but denser towards the tip, nut with the remains of the style and petals persisting near the tip, circa 1 cm (0.4 in), with two rounded wings, 2–2.5 cm (0.8–1 in) across, green but ripening to brown.

Range: Caucasus region and Caspian forests of northern Iran.

Habitat: Cultivated as an ornamental, in the wild occurring in damp woods and beside streams.

Varieties: Var. *dumosa* is a dwarf form with smaller leaflets, usually less than 8 cm (3.1 in), and a shrubby habit.

Synonyms: *Juglans fraxinifolia.*

This relative of Walnut shares with it the chambered pith. The leaves resemble *Juglans nigra* and other American species rather than *J. regia*, whilst the scientific name alludes both to the affinity with *Carya* and to the pair of wings on the nut. It thrives in damp locations, usually forming an extensive multistemmed clump.

p.328 **Hybrid Wingnut** *Pterocarya × rehderiana*

Description: Deciduous tree 25 m (80 ft) with a bole diameter to 1.5 m (5 ft).
Crown Conic in young trees, developing a stout bole with a broad rounded crown on large radiating branches, surrounded by suckers from the roots. *Bark* Dull grey, developing a coarse network of shallow fissures and ridges. *Shoot* Green with fine brown scales when young, ripening to smooth and shiny green with pale orange linear lenticels, in the second year greenish brown, later grey-brown, pith chambered. *Buds* Naked, with miniature leaves with dark brown hairs exposed, on a short stalk, superposed to 1.5 cm (0.6 in). *Foliage* Leaves 20–50 cm (8–20 in), pinnate with from 7–19 leaflets (mainly around nine); leaflets oblong to oblong-elliptic, increasing in size towards the top of the leaf, tapering to an acute apex, base oblique, rounded, margin with small rounded irregular spreading teeth, upper surface sub-shiny green and veins slightly raised, underside light green with scattered fascicled hairs especially on the raised veins and midrib, 8–16 × 2.5–5.5 cm (3.1–6.3 × 1–2.2 in); leaf stalk grooved and enlarged at base, raised above and with two slight lateral flanges, green, rachis grooved and narrowly winged except by lowest pairs of leaflets and with dense rufous hairs above the leaflets, leaflets more or less stalkless; autumn colour yellow. *Flowers* With the new foliage and opening in late spring, female flowers at tips of shoots in pendent 10–15 cm (4–6 in) racemes, male catkins yellow, in bud cylindric, 1 cm (0.4 in), red-brown. *Fruit* In long pendent racemes 25–50 cm (10–20 in); nut 8 mm (0.3 in), with two sickle-shaped tapered wings which are joined and rounded at the base, 2 cm (0.8 in) across, green ripening to brown.

Range: Cultivated hybrid.

Habitat: Cultivated as an ornamental as a fast-growing tree.

This is a hybrid of *P. fraxinifolia* with *P. stenoptera*. It is most similar to the *fraxinifolia* parent, but shows the influence of *stenoptera* in the narrowly leafy winged rachis and the longer and tapered wings to the nuts. It also shows hybrid vigour, growing extremely fast on suitable sites.

p.328 **Chinese Wingnut** *Pterocarya stenoptera*

Description: Deciduous tree 15–25 m (50–80 ft) in height with a bole diameter to 1 m (3.3 ft). *Crown* Rounded, with arching spreading branches. *Bark* Grey-brown with orange fissures, becoming cross-ridged at the base. *Shoot* Green with orange oval to linear lenticels, rufous pubescent at first, in the second year pale grey-brown to grey, with a slender chambered pith. *Buds* Naked, with exposed leaves which are covered with rufous hairs, usually two or three superposed with the largest furthest from the leaf, length depends upon maturity and degree of elongation as there is no fixed time when the bud is dormant. *Foliage* Leaves 20–35 cm (8–14 in), pinnate with 9–25 leaflets (although mainly 15–19); leaflets oblong to narrow oval (especially the terminal one), tapering to an acute apex and wedge-shaped base, margin with fine forward-pointing serrations, upper surface fresh green, hairy at first especially along the raised midrib, underside light green with tufts in the axils of the raised veins, stalkless, 5–10 × 2–4 cm (2–4 × 0.8–1.6 in); leaf stalk grooved, rachis grooved with two wide leafy (sometimes toothed) wings or flanges on either side and especially towards the tip, being decurrent from the base of the leaflets; autumn colour yellow. *Flowers* Male catkins in spring, 8 cm (3.1 in); female catkins to 20 cm (8 in). *Fruit* Nutlets with two forward-pointing narrow parallel-sided wings which form a V-shape.

Range: China from north to south, with a variety in Vietnam.

Habitat: Cultivated as an ornamental, in the wild occurring in woods.

Varieties: Var. *tonkinensis* from Yunnan and North
Vietnam has leaves with four to six pairs of
leaflets, i.e. the lower end of the above range.

This tree is very distinctive in the narrow
wings of the fruit. When growing well, the
leaves have wide wings on the rachis which
may be serrate. Unlike *P. fraxinifolia*, this
tree does not sucker from the roots. Any
suckers around a tree suggest it either is not
this species, or is grafted (which usually
bodes ill as the rootstock often takes over).

WINGED STYRAX, *PTEROSTYRAX*
FAMILY STYRACACEAE

This is a genus of four species, distributed from Japan across
China to Burma. The foliage is similar to *Halesia* but the
flowers are in many-flowered panicles, with the individual
flowers small, but with petals and other parts in fives and
with protuberant stamens; the pith is solid or continuous,
not chambered.

p.235   **Winged Storax** *Pterostyrax corymbosa*

Description: Deciduous tree 10–15 m (33–50 ft) with a
bole diameter to 25 cm (0.9 ft).
Crown Rounded, on a short bole.
Bark Grey or greyish brown. *Shoot* Green,
rough or scabrid with short hairs when
young but then smooth and shiny, buff to
yellow-brown in the second year, later grey-
brown with a thin easily-damaged slightly-
peeling outer layer which reveals green
beneath. *Buds* Ovoid-conic, slender,
purplish and scaly, 3 mm (0.1 in), in pairs or
threes in leaf axils. *Foliage* Leaves obovate
to almost rounded in outline, less often ovate
or elliptic, apex rounded and short slender
pointed, base wedge-shaped, margin with
spaced aristate and initially gland-tipped
teeth which spread at right angles to the
margin, upper surface initially with stellate
hairs, becoming matt green with spaced
glandular depressions, underside pale green
with scattered glands and five to seven pairs
of raised somewhat looped veins and midrib,

initially with stellate hairs and warty on the veins, 7–13 × 3–7 cm (2.8–5.1 × 1.2–2.8 in); leaf stalk with a shallow wide groove which is glandular, purple, 1–3 cm (0.4–1.2 in); autumn colour yellow.

Flowers In nodding one-sided corymbose or paniculate racemes 8–12 cm (3.1–4.7 in), flowers white, fragrant, 1–2 cm (0.4–0.8 in), five petals, scarcely joined at the base, ten stamens, joined together to form a tube at the base. *Fruit* Obovoid drupe, five-winged, star-shaped and villous haired with the base of the style persisting, 0.8–1.2 cm (0.3–0.5 in), enclosing one or two seeds.

Range: Southwestern Honshu, Shikoku and Kyushu, Japan, and across central China to Sichuan.

Habitat: Cultivated as an ornamental, in the wild occurring in mixed woodland.

Synonyms: *Halesia corymbosa.*

Similar species: *P. hispida* is closely related, differing in the following respects. The leaves are larger, 10–20 cm (4–8 in) (to 25 cm (10 in)) and 5–8 cm (2–3.1 in) (to 10 cm (4 in)) in width with long whitish hairs on the 8–12 pairs of veins beneath, especially in axillary tufts. The flowering panicles are longer, 10–20 cm (4–8 in). The fruit is obovoid, only 7–8 mm (0.3 in) long, with ten ribs (not winged) and bristly with a minute covering of star-shaped hairs. It has a similar distribution.

This small uncommon tree has curiously winged fruits and white fragrant flowers which are carried in early summer.

POMEGRANATE, PUNICACEAE

This family consists of the one genus with two species. The leaves have an apical nectary.

POMEGRANATES, *PUNICA*
FAMILY PUNICACEAE

This genus comprises two species, one widely cultivated and the other restricted to a few trees on the Island of Sokotra between Yemen and Eritrea.

p.151 **Pomegranate** *Punica granatum*

Description: Deciduous shrub or small tree to 8 m
(26 ft) with a bole diameter to 30 cm (1 ft).
Crown Rounded, somewhat spiky.
Bark Brown, flaking to reveal creamy white
or buff beneath. *Shoot* Four-angled, often
ending in a spine on young or shrubby
plants, hairless. *Buds* In opposite pairs or
sub-opposite, small. *Foliage* Leaves elliptic-
oblanceolate or narrow oblong, apex bluntly
pointed and often abruptly short-pointed,
base wedge-shaped, margin untoothed, 3.5–7
× 1–2.5 cm (1.4–2.8 × 0.4–1 in); leaf stalk
0.2–1 cm (0.1–0.4 in). *Flowers* Terminal or
axillary on current season's growths, single or
in small clusters; flowers scarlet-red and
fleshy, 3–4 cm (1.2–1.6 in) across, calyx red,
tube funnel-shaped, five to seven petal lobes,
crimpled, many stamens, yellow, attached to
the calyx tube. *Fruit* Globose berry-like
fruit with a leathery rind and crowned by the
persistent calyx, 4.5–7 cm (1.8–2.8 in) in
length and diameter, containing many seeds
each with a sweet fleshy pulp.

Range: Widely cultivated throughout the warm
temperate world, probably native to the
Iran–Afghanistan region.

Habitat: Cultivated, thriving in warm sunny climes.

Varieties: Var. *nana*, a dwarf form. In 'Plena' the
flowers are double.

The flowers are very attractive and are
produced from June into the autumn. In
cooler temperate regions, they do not
develop fruits, failing to ripen before being
destroyed by frosts. The tree is susceptible to
winter cold, especially when young. Its
origin is unclear, as it has been cultivated for
millennia. The generic name *Punica* refers to
the Carthage or Punic region of North
Africa, whence came Hannibal and his
elephants. The common name,
'pomegranate' derives from the Latin name
Pomum granatum, literally 'the apple with
grains', referring to the many grain-like
seeds. This in turn has given us 'grenade', for
a small throwable bomb, as the original ones
were reminiscent of pomegranate fruits.

PEARS, *PYRUS*
FAMILY ROSACEAE

This is a genus of around 20–35 species. They occur throughout Asia but most species are found around the Mediterranean in southeast Europe, North Africa and western Asia. The leaves are often rounded and glossy and less than twice as long as broad (*see PP. calleryana, communis* and *cordata*) or more lanceolate and more than twice as long as broad (*see PP. amygdaliformis, austriaca, nivalis* and *salicifolia*), but in some species and especially on young vigorous growths, they may be deeply lobed. The flowers are similar to most members of the apple family (Maloideae) but are distinctive in the styles being free (in all other genera they are united at least at the base). The fruit is rarely indented where the fruit is attached to the stalk and contains abundant grit cells. The calyx is lost or dropped from the top of the maturing fruit to leave a dimpled depression in *PP. calleryana* and *cordata*, but is persistent in the other species. In the past *Malus* and *Sorbus* were treated as part of *Pyrus*. The reliable distinguishing character is the free styles of *Pyrus*, which together with other slightly variable characters builds to a convincing case for separate genera and almost no serious botanist lumps them together. Pears are important fruit trees, as well as attractive amenity trees and have a good-quality timber.

p.158 **Almond-leafed Pear**
Pyrus amygdaliformis

Description: Deciduous small tree or shrub to 6 m (20 ft).
Crown Slender, with spreading branches.
Shoot Dull grey, somewhat woolly when young, sometimes spiny. *Foliage* Leaves variable, from narrow lanceolate to obovate, sometimes three lobed, apex acute to bluntly pointed, base wedge-shaped, less often rounded, margin usually without teeth, initially sparsely hairy but soon lost, shiny above, beneath with minute projections, 2.5–8 × 1–3 cm (1–3.1 × 0.4–1.2 in); leaf stalk 1.2–5 cm (0.5–2 in).
Flowers In corymbs of 8–12 in April; flowers white, 2.5 cm (1 in).
Fruit Globose, yellow-brown or tawny brown, 1.5–3 cm (0.6–1.2 in); calyx persistent.

Range: Central and eastern Mediterranean from Italy eastwards and north into Bulgaria.

Habitat: Dry rocky sites.

Similar species: *P. bourgaeana* makes a round crowned tree to 10 m (33 ft). It is found in Portugal, western Spain and Morocco where it is associated with seasonal streams. It differs in the leaves being crenulate (with small rounded teeth) and consistently rounded at the base. The leaves are smaller but broader, 2–4 × 1.5–3.5 cm (0.8–1.6 × 0.6–1.4 in). *P. caucasica* from eastern Greece, northern Turkey and the Crimea across to the Caucasus has untoothed leaves with cuspidate or tail-like apices. It forms a tall tree, to 25 m (80 ft), and has rather rounded-ovate leaves.

This small tree is mainly found in countries on the northern shores of the eastern Mediterranean.

Austrian Pear *Pyrus austriaca*

Description: Deciduous tree to 20 m (65 ft).
Crown Domed. *Shoot* Slightly hairy when young but becoming hairless and shiny reddish brown, then blackish, stout, sometimes spiny. *Foliage* Leaves lanceolate to obovate-lanceolate, apex acute, base wedge-shaped, margin with fine rounded-pointed teeth towards the apex, initially woolly but soon lost above, underside retaining yellow-grey wool, 6–9 × 2.5–5 cm (2.4–3.5 × 1–2 in); leaf stalk 1.5–6 cm (0.6–2.4 in). *Flowers* In hairy corymbs with the leaves; flowers white, styles more or less hairless. *Fruit* Pear-shaped or top-shaped, maturing to greenish brown, 2.5–5.5 cm (1–2.2 in); calyx persistent.

Range: Central Europe from Switzerland, Austria, the Czech Republic, Slovakia to western Russia.

Habitat: Open sites.

This tree is cultivated and may be naturalized in parts of the above distribution.

p.213 **Callery's Pear** *Pyrus calleryana*

Description: Deciduous tree to 12 m (39 ft) with a bole diameter to 30 cm (1 ft).
Crown Ovoid to conic, narrow, broadening with age. *Bark* Grey-brown, smooth, becoming scaly or finely fissured at base. *Shoot* White woolly when new, becoming hairless or almost hairless by autumn, green in first winter with small scattered round lenticels, then dark grey, without thorns. *Buds* Rounded to ovoid, with tips of the scale free, pink and grey, with a coating of grey wool, to 1 cm (0.4 in). *Foliage* Leaves ovate to broad ovate, apex acute to tail-like, base rounded or somewhat truncate, margin with fine crenate teeth, glossy green and hairless above, paler and initially hairy on the veins below, 4–8 × 3–5 cm (1.6–3.1 × 1.2–2 in); leaf stalk slender, 1–4 cm (0.4–1.6 in); autumn colour good but late.
Flowers Inflorescence in spring with the new leaves, composed of six to twelve white flowers to 2 cm (0.8 in) across; twenty stamens, two or three styles. *Fruit* Globose to broad obovoid, russet-brown with many pale lenticels, calyx deciduous, leaving a deep pit in which the remains of the styles can be seen, base indented, to 2 cm (0.8 in) in width and 1.5 cm (0.6 in) in length; stalks shiny brown, 2–3 cm (0.8–1.2 in).
Range: Southern and central China.
Habitat: Cultivated as an ornamental.

This tree is widely used as a street tree as the clone 'Chanticleer' which has a narrow crown. 'Bradford' is a similar selection, but wider in the crown.

---

p.212 **Common Pear** *Pyrus communis*

Description: Deciduous tree 12–25 m (39–80 ft) with a bole diameter to 1.3 m (4 ft).
Crown Conic and spiky when young, becoming rounded and domed on a long bole in old trees. *Bark* Brown or

blackish, becoming fissured into small square plates or scales. *Shoot* Glossy brown, with sparse whitish hairs when young but soon hairless, later grey-brown to brown, often with the spur shoots becoming thorny. *Buds* Ovoid to conic, pointed, red-brown, shiny, hairless or hairy at the tips, 7 mm (0.3 in). *Foliage* Leaves rounded-ovate to elliptic, apex rounded to short pointed, base rounded to subcordate, margin untoothed to very finely toothed, texture leathery, upper surface glossy green, underside pale green with raised midrib, 4–8 × 4–5 cm (1.6–3.1 × 1.6–2 in); leaf stalk grooved, oval in section, yellow-green, 1.5–4 cm (0.6–1.6 in); autumn colour usually poor, occasionally yellow or red. *Flowers* In small corymbs 5–7 cm (2–2.8 in) across, white, before the leaves. *Fruit* Pear-shaped to rounded, slightly indented at the base, calyx persistent, yellow-brown or russet with many small lenticels, 2.5–12 cm (1–4.7 in).

Range: Widely cultivated across Europe and west Asia.

Habitat: Cultivated as an orchard tree, wild or naturalized in hedgerows and woods.

Varieties: 'Beech Hill' is a selection with erect branches and few side shoots. It makes a narrow crowned tree. Var. *culta* covers the forms with larger fruits, generally more than 6 cm (2.4 in) and with a narrowed base.

Similar species: **Wild Pear** *P. pyraster* (p.213) is often included within *P. communis*. However, sometimes it is considered as a separate species which was one of the progenitors of *P. communis*. In this case, it covers the forms with fruits less than 6 cm (2.4 in).
P. syriaca from Cyprus and western Asia makes a round crowned tree to 10 m (33 ft), with spiny branches. The twigs are reddish brown and hairless when young, maturing to grey. The leaves are narrow ovate to ovate-lanceolate, only hairy when very young.

The orchard pears are included as var. *culta*. However, they are probably the result of hybridization and selected from this species and other species. The wild origin of *P. communis* is believed to be western Asia, with apparent wild trees in southern Europe being considered early garden escapes. The flesh is tasty and juicy, but quickly becomes overripe when it is fit for perry! *See P. pyraster above.*

p.212 **Plymouth Pear** *Pyrus cordata*

Description: Deciduous tree to 8 m (26 ft) or a shrub, with a bole diameter to 30 cm (1 ft).
Crown Upright with spreading branches. *Bark* Grey-brown. *Shoot* Purple, more or less hairless, spur shoots spiny.
Foliage Leaves ovate to ovate-lanceolate, apex rounded to a short slender cuspidate tip, base rounded to subcordate, margin with crenate or finely serrate teeth, densely haired on both surfaces when young, becoming hairless, 2.5–5.5 × 1.5–3.5 cm (1–2.2 × 0.6–1.4 in); leaf stalk slender, 2–5 cm (0.8–2 in). *Flowers* With the new leaves, in small hairy corymbs; flowers white, petals obovate-elliptic, 6–8 × 5–7 mm (0.25–0.3 × 0.2–0.3 in).
Fruit Globose to obovoid, shiny russet or red with many lenticels, calyx deciduous, 0.8–1.8 cm (0.3–0.7 in).

Range: Southwest England (Devon and Cornwall), western France to Spain and Portugal.

Habitat: Hedgerows, woods.

Similar species: Several European native species share the character of a deciduous calyx.
P. magyarica from Hungary has hairless leaves with aristate teeth, a hairless inflorescence and a fruit 1.5–2 cm (0.6–0.8 in) with few lenticels. It is a constituent of oak woodland.
P. rossica from central European Russia has a bark which peels in thin sheets and leaves which are broadly ovate with an untoothed margin and 3–7 × 2–6 cm (1.2–2.8 × 0.8–2.4 in). It has a somewhat compressed globose fruit 2–2.5 cm (0.8–1 in) which is densely lenticellate, and forms a tree up to 20 m (65 ft).

P. cossonii from Algeria has rounded oval to broad ovate hairless leaves which are usually wedge-shaped at the base (rarely so in *P. cordata*).

P. pashia from Afghanistan along the Himalayas to west China (Yunnan) has ovate to ovate-oblong leaves 5–10 cm (2–4 in) with fine rounded teeth and dense corymbs of white flowers. On young plants, the leaves are deeply lobed, but this is a juvenile feature only.

This makes a small tree. The fruit is pear-shaped but has a deciduous calyx and is much smaller than the cultivated pear.

p.159 **Snow Pear** *Pyrus nivalis*

Description: Deciduous tree 8–20 m (26–65 ft) with a bole diameter to 50 cm (1.6 ft).
Crown Rounded or domed. *Shoot* Densely silvery woolly when young, becoming hairless, and dark grey to almost black, stout, usually without spines.
Foliage Leaves obovate to oval, acute at the apex, base wedge-shaped and decurrent on the leaf stalk, margin untoothed or sparsely toothed towards the apex, initially densely silvery haired, soon shedding the hairs above and becoming greyish green, underside retaining the hairs and greyish, 5–9 × 3–4 cm (2–3.5 × 1.2–1.6 in); leaf stalk 1–2 cm (0.4–0.8 in). *Flowers* With the new foliage in dense white hairy corymbs; styles densely hairy at the base.
Fruit Sub-globose to globose, yellow-green with purplish lenticels, sweet when fully ripe, 3–5 cm (1.2–2 in); calyx persistent.

Range: South and south central Europe from Austria and Italy across the Balkans to Romania.

Habitat: Open sites in full sun or dry open woodland.

Similar species: **Oleaster-leafed Pear** *P. elaeagrifolia* (p.159) from southeast Europe (Albania, Bulgaria, Greece and Romania), from the Crimea (Ukraine) and Tunisia, makes a much smaller tree. The shoots are much more spiny, the fruits smaller (2–3 cm (0.8–1.2 in)) and the styles densely hairy to the middle.

Sage-leafed Pear *P. salvifolia* (p.158) may be a hybrid of *P. nivalis* with *P. communis*. It differs from *P. nivalis* in the longer leaf stalks 2–5 cm (0.8–2 in), spiny branches, entire lanceolate to elliptic leaves and the more or less hairless styles. It is recorded from Belgium to the Balkans, Romania and Russia, but as it is planted as a fruit tree (used to make perry), its origin and natural distribution is unclear.

This tree is showy when the new foliage first opens. It is one of the several species which has contributed to the Orchard Pear, *P. communis*.

---

p.159 **Willow-leafed Pear** *Pyrus salicifolia*

Description: Deciduous tree to 8 m (26 ft) with a bole diameter to 30 cm (1 ft).
Crown Rounded. *Bark* Silvery grey, cracking into small squares.
Shoot Densely silvery white hairy during the first year, becoming hairless, not spiny.
Buds Ovoid, white hairy. *Foliage* Leaves narrow elliptic to lanceolate, tapering gently to both ends, margin untoothed, new foliage covered in silvery-grey hairs, falling from the upper surface to reveal glossy green persisting beneath, 4–9 × 1–2 cm (1.6–3.5 × 0.4–0.8 in); leaf stalk slender, to 1.5 cm (0.6 in); autumn colour nil. *Flowers* In small dense white hairy corymbs, only observed with difficulty as hidden amongst silvery-grey new foliage.
Fruit Obovoid, green with brown lenticels, 2.5–4 cm (1–1.6 in); calyx persistent.
Range: Caucasus region to northern Iran.
Habitat: Cultivated as an ornamental.

This tree is mainly encountered in gardens as the weeping form, 'Pendula'. This has all the branches pendent at the tips and makes an attractive silvery-grey foliaged tree.

OAKS, *QUERCUS*
FAMILY FAGACEAE

This is a very large genus of around 500 species spread across the northern hemisphere and south in the Americas to Venezuela. Most species are evergreen, whilst half the total number are recorded from Mexico. The leaves are very variable, but often clustered towards the tip of the shoot. The flowers are wind pollinated, with the male catkins pendulous. Female flowers are separate and small. They are carried on the current season's shoots but may ripen in the first or second autumn. The seed or acorn sits in a cup or cupule. Oaks are important timber and amenity trees. Some have edible acorns.

The genus is divided into two subgenera, *Quercus* and *Cyclobalanopsis*. Subgenus *Cyclobalanopsis* is often treated as a separate genus and is characterized by the cupules having concentric rings of scales. The species are evergreen, and the leaves are either untoothed or have small forward pointing spiny teeth. Species featured here are *QQ. acuta, glauca* and *myrsinifolia*. Subgenus *Quercus* is divided into several sections. In section *Cerris*, the scales of the acorn cup are elongated, sometimes reflexed, whilst the leaves either have short triangular aristate teeth or rounded teeth. In most species, the acorns take two years to ripen. Species include *QQ. acutissima, alnifolia, cerris, coccifera, macrolepis, semecarpifolia, suber, trojana, variabilis* and the hybrid × *hispanica*. Section *Quercus* has the acorns with short scales pressed onto the cupule and leaves with rounded lobes, less often untoothed. The fruits ripen in the first autumn. Species include *QQ. alba, canariensis, dentata, faginea, frainetto, ilex, macranthera, petraea, pontica, pubescens, pyrenaica, robur, rotundifolia*. Section *Erythrobalanus* has the leaves with the lobes ending in an awn-like bristle (in the untoothed or unlobed species, the apex has a bristle tip). The lobes are often deep. The fruits usually take two years to ripen. Species include *QQ. coccinea, marilandica, palustris, phellos, rubra, velutina*.

Informal Key

LEAVES

(i) **unlobed, untoothed or with small shallow teeth towards the apex:** *acuta, alnifolia, glauca, ilex, myrsinifolia, phellos, semecarpifolia*

(ii) **regular shallow serrate teeth ending in aristate points:** *acutissima, macrolepis, trojana, variabilis*

(iii) **lobes, often deep, tapering to bristle teeth:** *coccinea, marilandica, palustris, rubra, velutina*

(iv) **rounded small to deep lobes which are either abruptly short pointed (mucronate) or untoothed:** *alba, canariensis, cerris, dentata, faginea, frainetto, × hispanica, macranthera, petraea, pontica, pubescens, pyrenaica, robur*

(v) **spine teeth:** *coccifera, ilex, rotundifolia, semecarpifolia, suber*

---

p.163 **Akagashi** or **Japanese Evergreen Oak**
Quercus acuta

Description: Evergreen tree to 15 m (50 ft) with a bole diameter to 70 cm (2.3 ft).
Crown Rounded, often rather shrubby.
Bark Dark grey, smooth yet wrinkled.
Shoot Initially densely covered with long red-brown wool which is soon shed, revealing dark brown hairless shoots.
Buds Conic, pale yellow. *Foliage* Leaves ovate-elliptic to oval, leathery in texture, apex tapering to an abrupt long slender-pointed and rounded tip, base wedge-shaped or rounded, margin untoothed, dark glossy green above, dull yellow-green beneath and initially floccose, with 8–13 pairs of veins, 8–20 × 3–6 cm (3.1–8 × 1.2–2.4 in); leaf stalk slightly flattened, not grooved, 2–4 cm (0.8–1.6 in).
Flowers Male catkins with 10–12 stamens.
Fruit Crowded on a spike 4–5 cm (1.6–2 in); cupule with ring-like growths, downy; acorn ellipsoidal, 2 cm (0.8 in).
Range: Honshu, Kyushu and Shikoku, Japan, Korea and into eastern China.
Habitat: Cultivated as an ornamental.
Synonyms: *Cyclobalanopsis acuta, Q. laevigata.*

This makes a slow-growing hardy evergreen bush to small tree.

---

p.266 **Asian Chestnut Oak** *Quercus acutissima*

Description: Deciduous tree 10–20 m (33–65 ft) in height with a bole diameter to 40 cm (1.3 ft).
Crown Conical in young trees, becoming rounded, not dense. *Bark* Dark grey, rough with deep ridges. *Shoot* Olive-brown with scattered star-shaped hairs,

becoming hairless and buff-brown in the second year. *Buds* Ovoid, bluntly pointed, green and brown, 2–3 mm (0.1 in).
Foliage Leaves narrow elliptic, oblong or obovate, apex acute, base broadly wedge-shaped, margin regularly serrate with triangular teeth which end in a long bristle or filament tip of 2–7 mm (0.1–0.3 in), upper surface lustrous green with slightly raised yellow-green veins, underside pale sub-shiny green with slightly raised net-like tertiary veins which are covered in pale hairs, side veins in 10–16 pairs, slightly raised, 10–20 × 2.5–5 cm (4–8 × 1–2 in); leaf stalk grooved, green, 0.7–1 cm (0.3–0.4 in); autumn colour russet.
Flowers Male catkins 10–15 cm (4–6 in).
Fruit Cup with dense broadly linear and slightly reflexed and downy scales, 2–3 cm (0.8–1.2 in) across, enclosing the lower one-third to one-half of the ellipsoidal to sub-globose 1.5–2 cm (0.6–0.8 in) acorn.

Range: Honshu, Shikoku and Kyushu, Japan, Korea, across central China to Yunnan and along the Himalayas to northwest India, south into Indochina.

Habitat: Cultivated as an ornamental, in the wild occurring on dry hillsides or in cool broadleaved forest.

Varieties: Ssp. *chienii* occurs in southeast China and has hairless leaves and smaller acorns with the cup having more slender scales. The Himalayan form, ssp. *roxburghii* has fruits at the larger end of the spectrum, but may not be in cultivation.

This tree has leaves similar in shape and texture to *Castanea*. From *Q. variabilis*, the sparsely haired to hairless leaves separate it; *Q. castaneifolia* has leaves with blunt, not bristle-tipped teeth.

---

p.279 **White Oak** *Quercus alba*

Description: Deciduous tree 10–20 m (33–65 ft) with a bole diameter to 60 cm (2 ft).
Crown Rounded, domed in old trees with radiating branches. *Bark* Dark grey,

fissuring into flat ridges with scales which lift away at the base, giving a shaggy appearance. *Shoot* Olive-brown, hairless or soon hairless, ridged, with pale orange oval lenticels, shiny grey-brown in the second year. *Buds* Ovoid, light brown with hairy scales, 3 mm (0.1 in). *Foliage* Leaves obovate with five to nine broad ovate rounded untoothed lobes with deep narrow rounded sinuses which extend one-third to two-thirds of the way to the midrib, base wedge-shaped, upper surface sub-shiny dark green with light rounded veins, underside glaucous green, soon hairless, veins raised and leaving the midrib at an acute angle, 10–23 × 5–15 cm (4–9.1 × 2–6 in); leaf stalk ribbed at the sides, hairless, 1–2.5 cm (0.4–1 in); autumn colour purple. *Fruit* Acorn ovoid, 1–3 cm (0.4–1.2 in) long and ripening in the first autumn; cup shallow and only enclosing the bottom quarter of the acorn, with warty and finely hairy scales, light grey.

Range: Eastern North America from Maine across to southern Quebec, Ontario and Minnesota south to Florida and Texas.

Habitat: Cultivated as an ornamental, in the wild forming pure stands on well-drained moist sites.

This tree belong to the same group of oaks as *Q. robur* and *Q. petraea*. However, in cultivation it does not grow as well as the species of red oaks from the same area of North America.

p.267 **Golden Oak of Cyprus** *Quercus alnifolia*

Description: Evergreen tree 6–10 m (20–33 ft) with a bole diameter to 70 cm (2.3 ft).
Crown Rounded, low dome, more upright in young trees. *Bark* Grey, becoming fissured. *Shoot* Green, maturing to brown, densely covered with grey hairs which are lost during the second year. *Buds* Minute, ovoid, hairy. *Foliage* Leaves obovate or sub-rounded in outline, less often ovate, apex rounded or short acute, base wedge-shaped,

broad wedge-shaped or rounded, margin shallow scalloped between acute abruptly short-pointed teeth towards the apex, less often the toothing is obscure or absent, texture thick and leathery and generally cupped with the upper surface convex and smooth, matt to shining dark green, underside golden or sometimes brown woolly with four to eight pairs of slightly raised veins, 1.5–6 × 1–5 cm (0.6–2.4 × 0.4–2 in) (but exceptionally up to 10 × 8 cm (4 × 3.1 in)); leaf stalk up to 1.2 cm (0.5 in), hairy. *Flowers* Male catkins clustered at shoot tips, slender, spreading or hanging, 5–8 cm (2–3.1 in). *Fruit* Acorn solitary or paired, narrowly obovate or cylindrical, but tapering towards the base and with an apiculate tip, 2–2.5 × 0.8–1.2 cm (0.8–1 × 0.3–0.5 in), ripening in the second year and enclosed at the base by the cup which has linear erect to recurved scales.

Range: Troodos Mountains of Cyprus.

Habitat: Igneous rocky slopes from 800–1600 m (2625–5250 ft), forming pure forest or mixed with *Pinus brutia* and occasionally *Cedrus brevifolia*.

This makes a small slow growing tree. Its chief attraction is the bright golden underside to the leaves and in this respect it compares with *Q. semecarpifolia* and *Chrysophylla chrysolepis*. It is placed in its own subsection of *Quercus* and is restricted in the wild to the main mountain range of Cyprus, although there is one record of a plant on the northern Kyrenia range. The leaves are retained for several years.

---

p.276 **Mirbeck Oak** *Quercus canariensis*

Description: Evergreen or semi-evergreen tree 20–30 m (65–100 ft) with a bole to 1 m (3.3 ft) or more in diameter.
Crown Conic or ovoid when young, becoming domed with heavy ascending branches in old trees. *Bark* Dark grey or blackish, deeply fissured into scaly, slightly

shaggy ridges. *Shoot* Grey-brown, initially hairy but soon hairless, sub-shiny for several years, later brown. *Buds* Conical and slightly ovoid, pointed, with white hairs at the apex, light brown, terminal buds with a ring of awl-like scales at the base, to 1 cm (0.4 in). *Foliage* Obovate to oblong-ovate, base wedge-shaped, rounded or subcordate, margin with 9–14 pairs of shallow rounded or triangular lobes with acute sinuses which decrease evenly in size towards the leaf apex, matt mid green above, beneath pale glaucous green, veins 8–14 pairs, prominent below with the midrib raised above, tertiary veins net-like, 10–19 × 5–10 cm (4–7.5 × 2–4 in); leaf stalk 1.5–3 cm (0.6–1.2 in), round. *Flowers* On current season's shoots in late spring; male catkins at base of shoot, pendent, yellow, 4 cm (1.6 in). *Fruit* Acorn ripens in the first autumn to about 2.5 cm (1 in), and is enclosed, for the lower third, in a cup which has flattened downy scales. It has a stalk of less than 1 cm (0.4 in).

Range: Spain, Portugal, Morocco and Algeria.
Habitat: Woodlands.
Synonyms: *Q. mirbeckii*.

This tree retains a few leaves throughout most winters, only losing them all during severe ones. Most, however, fall off sometime after Christmas. It is one of the more majestic oaks. Fertile seed is produced in cultivation, but this is usually hybridized with *Q. robur*, making an inferior specimen.

p.280 **Turkey Oak** *Quercus cerris*

Description: Deciduous tree 20–40 m (65–130 ft) with a bole diameter to 1–2 m (3.3–6.6 ft). *Crown* Conical when young and up to circa 15 m (50 ft), then becoming rounded, in very old trees forming an extensive dome. *Bark* Dull grey to somewhat silvery grey, becoming fissured at an early age and developing deep corky ridges with small rough plates. *Shoot* Grey-brown, grooved and hairy in the first year, becoming light brown or dark grey-brown later.

Buds Ovoid-conical, pale brown, with long linear whiskered stipules around both terminal and lateral buds, 4 mm (0.2 in), but with whiskers to 1.3 cm (0.5 in).

Foliage Leaves oblong-obovate in rough outline but variable in the depth of lobing, with the margin variously deeply toothed with large rounded blunt teeth, or deeply scalloped almost to the midrib or sometimes with acute teeth, apex rounded, base rounded to somewhat truncate, upper surface deep sub-shiny green, rough with spaced star-shaped hairs, underside whitish due to a dense low covering of hairs with 6–10 pairs of slightly raised veins, 5–14 × 3–6.5 cm (2–5.5 × 1.2–2.6 in); leaf stalk slightly grooved, whitish hairy, 1–2 cm (0.4–0.8 in); autumn colour russets, rather poor. *Flowers* Male catkins pendulous in early summer from leaf axils at the base of the current season's growths, 5–6 cm (2–2.4 in), crimson then dying off yellow-brown; female flowers small, one to five on short spur shoots to 2.5 cm (1 in) in axils of current year's growths. *Fruit* Cup mossy with many linear round curved and twisted scales (green ripening to brown), arranged forwards at the top and reflexed at the base and mainly outwards in the centre, 1.5–2.2 cm (0.6–0.9 in) across and enclosing the lower two-thirds of the ovoid, pointed 2.5–3 × 1.5 cm (1–1.2 × 0.6 in) acorn which ripens in the second autumn.

Range: Across southern Europe from southeast France eastwards and into Turkey, north into the Czech Republic and the Carpathian Mountains of Rumania.

Habitat: Woodland.

Varieties: Var. *austriaca* from southeast Europe has the leaves edged with regular triangular lobes, and are more grey beneath. Ssp. *tournefortii* is the form in Asiatic Turkey. It has leaves which are permanently grey haired beneath with 9–15 pairs of veins, a leaf stalk 2–4 cm (0.8–1.6 in) in length and a cup which is 2–3 cm (0.8–1.2 in) across. 'Variegata' is a garden selection with the leaves banded with white.

Synonyms: *Q. lanuginosa*.

This is a fast-growing oak, quickly forming a tall tree and then spreading to make a large one. It forms a large, often straight bole, but the timber lacks the medullary rays of *Q. robur* and its allies and is of little value. It readily hybridizes with *Q. suber* (*see Q.* × *hispanica*) where they meet. It can be distinguished from its relatives by the presence of the whiskered bud scales or stipules which are found around lateral as well as terminal buds, and often persist at the base of one-year shoots.

---

p.267 **Kermes Oak** or **Holly Oak**
Quercus coccifera

Description: Evergreen shrub or small tree to 6–10 m (20–33 ft) with a bole diameter to 50 cm (1.6 ft).
Crown Rounded, often spreading where grazed. *Bark* Dull grey, finely scaly in old trees. *Shoot* Yellowish brown with scurfy hairs, becoming grey-brown. *Buds* Ovoid with an acute apex, chestnut brown, 3 mm (0.1 in) . *Foliage* Ovate to oblong, base heart-shaped to rounded, thick and leathery, sharply spined and wavy, with a hyaline margin and hyaline reticulation, shiny deep green above, lustrous light green beneath, initially bronzed and hairy when young, retained one to two years, 1.5–4 × 1–3 cm (0.6–1.6 × 0.4–1.2 in); leaf stalk 3 mm (0.1 in), round.
Flowers On current season's growths in early summer; male catkins 3–5 cm (1.2–2 in). *Fruit* Ripening in second autumn, acorn 1.2–2.5 cm (0.5–1 in), with the lower half or third enclosed in the cup which is to 1.8 cm (0.7 in) across and has stiff spreading or reflexed scales.

Range: Western Mediterranean region from Spain, Portugal and Morocco across to Italy and perhaps eastwards where it meets *Q. calliprinos*.

Habitat: Maquis scrub.

Similar species: *Q. calliprinos* is a related species from the
eastern Mediterranean region, from Greece
through to Palestine. It is also known as the
Sindian Oak or Palestine Oak, and is
sometimes treated as a subspecies of
Q. coccifera. It differs in the larger leaves,
4–5 cm (1.6–2 in) in length, which are
more oblong in outline and the larger acorn
cups which are 2–3 cm (0.8–1.2 in) across
with longer scales. The acorn has a more
rounded apex. It makes a larger tree,
occasionally with a bole a metre or more in
diameter. The 'Great Trees of Mamre' are
believed to have belonged to this species
(*Genesis* XVIII).

This small oak will make a tree in the wild
but is usually found on sites either too dry
or where grazing pressure restricts it to a
shrub. It has very holly-like spiny leaves. It
used to be important for the dye 'grain' or
'scarlet grain'. This was obtained from the
Kermes insect which feeds on it.

---

p.282 **Scarlet Oak** *Quercus coccinea*

Description: Deciduous tree 20–25 m (65–80 ft) in
height with a bole diameter to 1 m (3.3 ft).
Crown Conic and dense when young,
becoming tall domed with a few
wandering large branches in the lower
crown. *Bark* Smooth, silvery-grey to dark
grey with warts, becoming fissured into
fine scaly ridges, inner bark reddish.
Shoot Olive-green or red-brown, shiny and
hairless in the first year, then shiny grey.
Buds Conic to ovoid-conic, chestnut
brown, 4–7 mm (0.2–0.3 in).
Foliage Leaves elliptic to oval in outline
but usually somewhat broadest towards the
apex which is acute, base wedge-shaped to
broad wedge-shaped or rounded, margin
with three or four pairs of large, rather
parallel sided, variously toothed lobes,
with two or three deep rounded sinuses,
with the middle pair of lobes usually
spreading widely on either side, teeth and
lobes tapering to a slender bristle tip of

1–2 mm (0.1 in), upper surface hairless, deep sub-shiny green and smooth, underside pale green with raised whitish veins, almost hairless, 7–20 × 5–20 cm (2.8–8 × 2–8 in); leaf stalk weakly grooved, scarcely or not enlarged at base, 2–5 cm (0.8–2 in), rarely to 8 cm (3.1 in); autumn colour usually excellent scarlet; new leaves yellowish in the spring.
Flowers Male catkins 6–8 cm (2.4–3.1 in) in May at end of previous year's shoots, female flowers on a short shoot in leaf axils of new growths, usually in threes or fours.
Fruit Cup on a 4 mm (0.2 in) stalk, top shaped and enclosing the lower half to a third of the acorn, with brown dense scales, circa 1.5 cm (0.6 in) across, acorn ovoid, 1.2–2.5 cm (0.5–1 in), ripening in the second autumn.

Range: Eastern USA from Maine south to Georgia and west to Mississippi and Indiana.

Habitat: Cultivated as an ornamental and in forestry, in the wild forming forests on poor soils, either in pure or mixed stands.

Varieties: 'Splendens' is a form selected for its autumn colour, but which also has rather longer leaf stalks, to 6–8 cm (2.4–3.1 in).

Scarlet Oak gives a more reliable autumn colour than other 'red' oaks. It usually starts to turn on one or two branches, then spreading across the entire crown. The habit is more upright and columnar than in *Q. rubra*. It can be distinguished from *Q. rubra* and other similar oaks in leaf by the rounded scalloping of the sinuses, especially by the large spreading central lobe.

---

p.279 **Daimio Oak** *Quercus dentata*

Description: Deciduous small tree 10–15 m (33–50 ft) with a bole diameter to 50 cm (1.6 ft).
Crown Rounded, usually rather gaunt with spaced branches. *Bark* Grey, becoming thick and deeply furrowed. *Shoot* Stout, grey-green with a covering of greyish star-shaped hairs and small rounded whitish lenticels, becoming hairless and brown in

the second year. *Buds* Conical, rounded, scales hairy and chestnut brown with a ring of awl-like scales at the base 1 cm (0.4 in). *Foliage* Leaves large with a card-like texture, obovate, broadest in upper half and narrowed to the rounded auricled base, apex acute and bluntly pointed, margin with rounded lobes and sinuses, ciliate, upper surface dark green, rough with scattered star-shaped hairs with more hairs on the veins and midrib, underside pale greyish green with a covering of star-shaped or fascicled hairs, veins in 4–10 pairs, well spaced, veins and midrib prominent, 18–35 × 10–18 cm (7.1–14 × 4–7.1 in); leaf stalk stout, grooved, green, densely hairy, 1–1.5 cm (0.4–0.6 in); autumn colour brown with the leaves retained over most of the winter. *Flowers* Female flowers axillary near the tip of the current season's growth. *Fruit* Cup, enclosing more than half the ovoid-globose 1.5–2 cm (0.6–0.8 in) acorn, has downy, linear, elongated, spreading or recurved scales to 1.2 cm (0.5 in). Fruit ripening in the first autumn.

Range: Throughout Japan from Hokkaido, Honshu, Shikoku and Kyushu, also in the southern Kurile Islands of Pacific Russia and on the mainland of northeast Asia from Korea and northeast China.

Habitat: Cultivated as an ornamental.

Synonyms: *Q. daimio*.

This tree has large leaves which resemble those of *Q. robur* in general shape and lobing but are substantially larger and hairy. It is inclined to suffer from spring frosts and usually does not make a good tree, with the crown tending to be rather gaunt.

---

p.276 **Portuguese Oak** *Quercus faginea*

Description: Semi-evergreen shrub to a tree to 20 m (65 ft) with a bole diameter of up to 80 cm (2.6 ft).
Crown Rounded. *Bark* Thick, grey or brown, developing large rectangular

scales. *Shoot* Grey or white hairy at first, slowly becoming hairless. *Buds* Ovoid, downy. *Foliage* Leaves ovate, elliptic to obovate-oblong, apex rounded to bluntly pointed, base variably heart-shaped, truncate or rounded, margin with 5–12 pairs of triangular forward-pointing teeth which terminate the main veins, at first with sparse star-shaped hairs but soon hairless and becoming shiny grey-green above, underside whitish grey, initially densely grey woolly or felted but becoming somewhat hairless or remaining woolly by autumn, 4–10 × 1.2–4 cm (1.6–4 × 0.5–1.6 in); leaf stalk hairy, 1 cm (0.4 in); leaves remaining through much of the winter period and rather tardily deciduous. *Fruit* Acorn ripening in the first autumn, oblong-ovoid, 2.5 cm (1 in), with the bottom third to a fifth enclosed in the hemispherical or urn-shaped cupule which has downy scales pressed against the shoot.

Range: Spain and Portugal.
Habitat: Woodlands.
Synonyms: *Q. lusitanica.*

This tree is very variable in its foliage. It is related to *Q. canariensis*, but is best distinguished by the felted and variably persistent wool on the underside of the leaves and shoots.

p.277 **Hungarian Oak** *Quercus frainetto*

Description: Deciduous tree 20–35 m (65–115 ft) with a bole diameter to 1.7 m (5.6 ft).
Crown Ovoid in young trees, becoming domed with a stout bole and radiating branches. *Bark* Pale grey to brown, becoming fissured with deep cracks and small short ridges. *Shoot* Grey-green with fascicled pale hairs and fine buff lenticels, in the second year buff-grey to grey. *Buds* Ovoid, pointed, pale brown with hairy scales, to 1 cm (0.4 in). *Foliage* Leaves obovate in outline (but on vigorous extension shoots more oval),

card-like in texture, apex rounded, base narrowed and broad wedge-shaped to slightly auricled, margin with about nine pairs of large lobulate teeth, increasing in size from the base to the broadest part and then decreasing, sinuses rounded, deep, extending half way to the midrib, upper surface sub-shiny dark green with a scattering of star-shaped hairs (densely so when young) making the leaf harsh to the touch, underside pale or whitish green, persistently down and soft to the touch, margins and veins raised, 10–25 × 6–14 cm (4–10 × 2.4–5.5 in); leaf stalk grooved, hairy, 0.6–2 cm (0.25–0.8 in); autumn colour russet. *Flowers* Similar to *Q. petraea*. *Fruit* Acorns produced in stalkless or short stalked clusters of two to four; acorn 1.5–2 cm (0.6–0.8 in), ovoid pointed, ripening in the first autumn, cupule enclosing the lower half, with oblong, blunt, downy and overlapping scales.

Range: Hungary, Romania, Balkans and southern Italy.

Habitat: Deciduous woodland.

Varieties: 'Hungarian Crown' refers to the form commonly grown in Britain.

Synonyms: *Quercus conferta*.

The leaves of this tree are usually regularly lobed and quite distinctive. It is a fast growing tree, making a large-domed crown in old trees. It is related to *Q. petraea*, differing most obviously in the leaves and hairy shoots.

p.163 **Thonp Oak** *Quercus glauca*

Description: Evergreen tree 10–15 m (33–50 ft) with a bole diameter to 50 cm (1.6 ft).
Crown Ovoid, becoming domed.
Bark Smooth, grey-brown. *Shoot* Olive-brown or slightly yellow-brown, at first with yellow hairs but becoming somewhat shiny, slightly ridged and grooved, with very small pale lenticels, in the second year grey-brown. *Buds* Ovoid, almost

globose, red-brown, often with a few wispy scales at the base, 3 mm (0.1 in). *Foliage* Leaves elliptic to elliptic-ovate or lanceolate, tapering to a short slender-pointer apex, base wedge-shaped, broad wedge-shaped or almost rounded, margin untoothed in the basal half to a third, with broad shallow acute teeth ending in a brown point and right-angled sinuses, with a hyaline border, card-like, upper surface mid green, sub-shiny, smooth, cupped along the midrib, underside glaucous green with pale silky hairs pressed on shoot and 8–12 pairs of raised veins and raised midrib, 7–15 × 2–5 cm (2.8–6 × 0.8–2 in); leaf stalk grooved, pink and yellow, hairless, 1–3 cm (0.4–1.2 in); leaves falling in the second autumn. *Flowers* Male catkins 4–6 cm (1.6–2.4 in), two to four female flowers on short axillary shoots. *Fruit* Acorn ellipsoidal with a conic apex, 1.5–2 × 1 cm (0.6–0.8 × 0.4 in), set in a cup 1–1.5 cm (0.4–0.6 in) across which encloses the lower half to a third, with six or seven concentric rings of scales and silky hairy.

Range: Japan from Honshu, Shikoku and Kyushu, south to Taiwan, across central and southern China to the eastern Himalayas (Nepal, Bhutan, Sikkim).

Habitat: Cultivated as an ornamental, in the wild occurring in warm temperate forest.

Synonyms: *Q. annulata*, *Cyclobalanopsis glauca*.

This is a rather uncommon small evergreen tree. With such a wide distribution, it is variable, and probably divisible into several subspecies. The common name used is based on the Bhutanese vernacular name.

---

p.280 **Spanish Oak** *Quercus × hispanica*

Description: Deciduous to semi-evergreen tree 15–35 m (50–115 ft) with a bole diameter of up to 2.5 m (8 ft).
Crown Domed, on radiating branches.
Bark Variable, from pale smooth corky

and fissured, creamy grey and somewhat corky or dark grey with deep blackish ridges and plates. *Shoot* Grey-brown, pale, densely hairy. *Buds* Red-brown, terminal with a ring of stipular scales which are absent from the laterals. *Foliage* Leaves oblong-elliptic, oval or somewhat ovate, apex acute, base wedge-shaped and often oblique, margin with three to nine pairs of triangular sharp teeth and sometimes with a wide deep sinuses around the centre of the leaf, upper surface glossy green after the silvery-grey hairs on the new leaves are lost, underside felted grey, 10–12 × 3–4 cm (4–4.7 × 1.2–1.6 in); leaf stalk 1 cm (0.4 in); leaves lost during harsh periods over winter or shed as the new foliage is produced in the spring. *Flowers* Male catkins crimson, opening to yellow, 4 cm (1.6 in). *Fruit* Acorn ripening in the second autumn, ovoid, 2–2.5 cm (0.8–1 in), with the bottom half or more enclosed in the hemispherical cupule. The cupule scales are hairy, reflexed at the base but erect at the top.

Range: Occurring where the two parent species meet.

Habitat: Cultivated or spontaneous.

Varieties: 'Lucombeana' is an early form of the hybrid, raised by Lucombe in about 1763. Other named forms include 'Diversifolia', 'Fulhamensis' and 'Ambrozyana'.

Synonyms: *Q. lucombeana*, *Q* × *crenata*.

This is a hybrid between *Q. cerris* and *Q. suber*. It occurs in southern France and Italy, and elsewhere where the two species meet in cultivation. It is vigorous and somewhat evergreen. As a fertile hybrid, it is very variable, particularly in second- or third-generation plants, or where backcrossing with either parent species has occurred. This is best demonstrated by the bark, which ranges from almost typical *Q. cerris* bark to thickly corky bark as in *Q. suber*. The leaves are tardily deciduous, usually only falling after severe weather in the New Year or as the buds flush in spring.

p.162 **Holm Oak** *Quercus ilex*

Description: Evergreen tree to 30 m (100 ft) with a bole diameter 1–2 m (3.3–6.6 ft).
Crown Columnar, ovoid to rounded in young trees, becoming domed in old trees, dense. *Bark* Black or brownish black and smooth in young trees, becoming cracked into small thin curling squares. *Shoot* Dull grey-brown to whitish grey with dense fawn or white hairs, slender, becoming grey-green or green-brown in second or third year. *Buds* Ovoid, rounded, brown, 1–2 mm (0.1 in). *Foliage* Evergreen, retained for one winter and shed in early summer of the second year; very variable in shape, on old trees mainly oval or ovate-lanceolate with entire margins but some broad oval with up to five pairs of forward-pointing small teeth, texture card-like, glossy green and hairless above, whitish grey beneath with a dense covering of hairs, 4–8 × 2–3 cm (1.6–3.1 × 0.8–1.2 in), leaf stalk 1–1.5 cm (0.4–0.6 in), hairy; on young trees and on basal shoots of old trees, leaves sharply toothed, thinner and less hairy beneath, to 4 cm (1.6 in) in width; new leaves in early summer, silvery white, then pale glossy yellow. *Flowers* With new foliage in early summer; male catkins pendent, pale golden-yellow, 4–7 cm (1.6–2.8 in), displayed against dark green of the old leaves. *Fruit* Acorn ovoid, brown, ripening from green in first autumn, bitter, in clusters of one to three, 1.5–2 cm (0.6–0.8 in), lower half to one-third in pale grey to fawn cup.
Range: Mediterranean region.
Habitat: Woods in dry situations, or coastal cliffs.

This tree is one of the hardiest evergreens and very tolerant of coastal conditions. It is, however, rather dull except for a few weeks in early summer when it both flowers and expands the new leaves and sheds the old ones. It tolerates a wide range of soils. It is very variable in the shape and texture of the leaves, with those on vigorous growths, especially coppice shoots, sometimes larger than the dimensions given above.

p.279   **Caucasian Oak**   *Quercus macranthera*

Description: Deciduous tree 15–30 m (50–100 ft) with a
bole diameter to 1 m (3.3 ft).
Crown Tall domed with an ascending head
of branches. *Bark* Grey-brown to purplish
grey, fissuring with coarse scaly flakes.
Shoot Stout and purplish brown with a
dense covering of long whitish hairs with
small round orange lenticels, lightly
fissured and nearly hairless in the second
year and then purplish grey. *Buds* Conic
or ovoid-conic, pointed, to 1.5 cm (0.6 in),
chestnut brown with whitish hairs and
slender hairy brown stipules to 2 cm
(0.8 in). *Foliage* Leaves obovate in outline,
apex rounded, base wedge-shaped, margin
with 7–11 rounded lobes which are larger
in the lower half and decrease towards the
apex, forming deep narrow rounded
sinuses, upper surface shiny green, sparsely
hairy and smooth but with the net-like
veinlets slightly impressed, underside pale
green with raised veins and covered with a
thin layer of hairs, 8–23 × 5–14 cm
(3.1–9.1 × 2–5.5 in); leaf stalk grooved,
hairy, yellow-green, to 2 cm (0.8 in);
autumn colour russet. *Flowers* Male
catkins 5–8 cm (2–3.1 in), hairy.
Fruit Acorn ovoid, 2.5 cm (1 in), enclosed
for the lower half in the cup which is
covered in downy, erect, lanceolate scales,
nearly stalkless.

Range: Northern Iran in the forests south of the
Caspian Sea and in the Caucasus and
Transcaucasus region.

Habitat: Cultivated as an ornamental, in the wild
occurring in deciduous forest.

This makes a bold tree with its large leaves.
These resemble leaves of *Q. canariensis* and
Q. frainetto, but the tree is easily separated
by the densely hairy shoots and the
undersides of the leaves and in the buds
having persistent stipules, whereas the
leaves of *Q. canariensis* are not hairy, and
those of *Q. frainetto* are only densely hairy
when young, and both have scarcely hairy
shoots.

p.278 **Valonia Oak** *Quercus macrolepis*

Description: Deciduous to semi-evergreen tree to 25 m
(80 ft) with a bole diameter of up to 0.8 m.
Crown Broad, spreading. *Bark* Grey,
fissured. *Shoot* Velvety. *Buds* Ovoid, with
long linear stipules. *Foliage* Leaves oblong
to oblong obovate, apex acute, base
rounded, truncate or subcordate, margin
with five to seven pairs of large acute teeth
which end in a bristle-like point which
terminate the veins, less often scarcely
toothed but the bristles terminating the
main veins, leathery in texture, upper
surface soon hairless and shiny green,
underside thinly and persistently hairy,
5–14 × 2.5–8 cm (2–5.5 × 1–3.1 in); leaf
stalk 1–4 cm (0.4–1.6 in); leaves falling in
autumn or spring. *Fruit* Acorn ripening
in the second autumn, ellipsoidal to ovoid,
to 4 cm (1.6 in), with the bottom half or
more enclosed in the hemispherical cupule.
The cupule scales are hairy, pressed against
the base of the cupule, reflexed above with
the top ring being long, erect and pressed
against the acorn, to 5 cm (2 in) across.

Range: Greece, Albania and across Turkey except
in the southeast.

Habitat: Woodland.

Synonyms: *Q. aegilops* ssp. *macrolepis*.

Similar species: *Q. ithaburensis* occurs in southeast Turkey,
Syria, the Lebanon and Palestine. It differs
in the much woodier scales on the cupule.

This tree used to be widely cultivated for
the acorn cupules which are a rich source of
tannin. It may also be native to southeast
Italy. The name *Q. aegilops* is sometimes
used, but the correct application of this
name is confused and could apply to half a
dozen different taxa.

p.282 **Blackjack Oak** *Quercus marilandica*

Description: Deciduous tree 10–20 m (33–65 ft) with a
bole diameter to 40 cm (1.3 ft).
Crown Open, spreading irregularly, low.
Bark Dark or black, becoming rough and

fissured into thick broad square plates.
Shoot Green with small oval lenticels in
the first year, initially hairy but soon
hairless, light brown or grey in later years,
rather stout. *Buds* Ovoid, rounded,
golden-brown hairy, 4 mm (0.2 in).
Foliage Leaves wedge-shaped, broadest
near the somewhat truncate tip onto which
is an ovate terminal lobe, lobes ending in
long bristles 2–4 mm (0.1–0.2 in), upper
surface lustrous mid green, hairless, with
the veins which end in the lateral or corner
lobes arising in the centre of the leaf,
underside golden-brown due to a covering
of hairs, veins slightly raised, 6–17 ×
5–10 cm (2.4–6.7 × 2–4 in); leaf stalk
grooved, with star-shaped hairs, 0.5–1 cm
(0.2–0.4 in); autumn colour russets, rarely
red. *Flowers* From buds along previous
year's shoots, female ones on 1.5 cm
(0.6 in) shoots with two flowers at the base.
Fruit Cup shortly stalked, rusty brown
haired with loosely overlapping scales,
enclosing half the elliptic, pointed
1.5–2 cm (0.6–0.8 in) acorn.

Range: Eastern USA from New Jersey across to
Michigan and Iowa, south to Texas and
Florida.

Habitat: Cultivated as an ornamental, in the wild
occurring on upland ridges and slopes.

Similar species: **Water Oak** *Q. nigra* is related but differs in
the leaves being rounded at the apex, with
fewer bristle tips and blue-green above, and
in the rounded acorn 1–1.5 cm (0.4–0.6 in)
long and broad which sits in a shallow
saucer-shaped cup. It has a similar
geographical distribution but occurs in
moist or wet locations, such as beside
streams. In cultivation it makes a tree to
18 m (60 ft) with a bole diameter to 90 cm
(2.9 ft) and a broad-domed crown.

This tree is remarkable for the leaves which
are broadest near the tip and taper to a
wedge-shaped or slightly rounded base. The
golden-haired underside makes them
attractive throughout the summer, although
the habit is poor and usually sprawling.

p.163 **Bamboo-leafed Oak** *Quercus myrsinifolia*

Description: Evergreen tree 12–18 m (39–60 ft) with a bole diameter to 50 cm (1.6 ft).
Crown Usually a bush on several stems, forming a rounded dense crown.
Bark Smooth, grey-brown, with fine orange fissures. *Shoot* Chocolate brown to dark brown and shiny, with oval buff lenticels which become hard and firm in the second year and make the shoot appear warty. *Buds* Ovoid, blunt, scales green with brown tips, 3 mm (0.1 in).
Foliage Leaves lanceolate, apex narrowed and short slender pointed, base wedge-shaped to rounded, margin untoothed at the basal half but serrate with shallow teeth ending in a short blackish point and small rounded sinuses towards the apex, with a hyaline strip, upper surface shiny deep green with the 10–16 pairs of slender and yellow-green veins which are slightly raised, underside blue-green and mildly glaucous, midrib raised, hairless on both sides, 5–12 × 1.5–3 cm (2–4.7 × 0.6–1.2 in); leaf stalk flattened above, yellow-green, 1–1.5 cm (0.4–0.6 in); leaves persist two years, rarely to four, years, new growth purplish red.
Flowers Two to four on a slender stalk.
Fruit Ripening in the first autumn, acorn narrow ovoid, 2–2.5 cm (0.8–1 in), set in a hemispherical cup which has seven to nine concentric rings of scales.

Range: Southern Japan from warmer parts of Honshu, Shikoku and Kyushu, across southern and eastern China and south into Laos.

Habitat: Cultivated as an ornamental, in the wild occurring in warm temperate forest.

Synonyms: *Cyclobalanopsis myrsinifolia.*

This makes a dense evergreen and, with *Q. glauca*, is the hardiest species of the subgenus (or genus) *Cyclobalanopsis* which is distinguished from other *Quercus* by the scales on the cupules being arranged in concentric rings.

p.282   **Pin Oak**   *Quercus palustris*

Description: Deciduous tree 20–25 m (65–80 ft) in
height with a bole diameter to 1 m (3.3 ft).
Crown Conic and slender with level
branches when young, becoming tall
domed in old trees with the lower
branches pendulous. *Bark* Dark silvery
grey and smooth, becoming darker and
purplish grey, old trees fissured with short
broad scaly ridges. *Shoot* Slender, pin-
like, green-brown with a coating of star-
shaped hairs when young, later
grey-brown. *Buds* Ovoid, rounded, broad,
light or grey brown, 3 mm (0.1 in).
Foliage Leaves rounded or oval in outline,
broadest at or just below the middle, apex
acute, base wedge-shaped to broad wedge-
shaped, margin with two or three pairs of
long parallel-sided, toothed lobes, with
usually two deep rounded sinuses, with
the middle pair of lobes spreading widely
on either side, teeth and lobes tapering to
a slender bristle tip of 2–4 mm
(0.1–0.2 in), upper surface deep lustrous
green with slightly raised and hairy veins,
underside pale sub-shiny green with raised
whitish veins and prominent fawn-
coloured axillary tufts, 7–13 × 5–10 cm
(2.8–5.1 × 2–4 in); leaf stalk slender,
weakly grooved, scarcely or not enlarged at
base, 3–5 cm (1.2–2 in); autumn colour
scarlet to crimson; new leaves yellowish in
the spring. *Flowers* Female flowers on a
short shoot in leaf axils of new growths,
usually in threes or fours. *Fruit* Cup on a
short stalk, saucer-shaped with brown
densely-pressed scales, enclosing the
quarter to a third of the acorn which is
almost round and 1.2 cm (0.5 in) across,
ripening in the second autumn.

Range: Eastern North America from Vermont,
southern Ontario and Iowa south to
Oklahoma and North Carolina.

Habitat: Cultivated as an ornamental and in forestry,
in the wild forming forests on wet or poorly
drained sites.

Similar species: **Northern Pin Oak** *Q. ellipsoidalis* has
almost stalkless acorns which are enclosed

for the lower third to a half in the cup and are ellipsoidal in shape, from 1.2–2 cm (0.5–0.8 in). It occurs to the east and south of the Great Lakes from southern Ontario across to North Dakota and south to Ohio and Missouri, on well-drained soils.

This tree has glossy leaves and characteristic tufts of pale brown- or fawn-coloured hairs in the vein axils beneath. The pendulous branches of the lower crown also give a habit which is recognizable in the distance when leafless. In the wild, it occurs in marshy places, which is the translation of the Latin name.

p.275 **Sessile Oak** or **Durmast Oak**
Quercus petraea

Description: Deciduous tree 20–30 m (65–100 ft) with a bole diameter to 2 m (6.6 ft).
Crown Domed, usually on a long bole with radiating branches. *Bark* Grey-brown, smooth but becoming finely fissured and in old trees cracked and ridged. *Shoot* Green-brown with small oval fawn lenticels, hairless, in the second year green-brown with a greyish cast. *Buds* Ovoid, globose or conical, light brown, 5 mm (0.2 in). *Foliage* Leaves obovate, less often broad elliptic, apex rounded acute, base narrowed, rounded, rarely auricled, margins with rounded lobes and narrow rounded sinuses, with the largest lobes in the centre of the leaf and decreasing to both ends, texture card-like, upper surface matt or sub-shiny dark green with slightly raised veins, underside pale or glaucous green with raised veins, hairless apart from axillary tufts, 8–14 × 4.5–8 cm (3.1–5.5 × 1.8–3.1 in); leaf stalk grooved, green, 1.5–2 cm (0.6–0.8 in); autumn colour purple or russets. *Flowers* Male flowers pendent, golden-brown, in late spring, from buds at the tip of previous year's shoots, 5–8 cm (2–3.1 in); female flowers near the tip of current season's shoots, in clusters of two

to six, stalkless. *Fruit* Acorn stalkless or on short peduncles.

Range: Britain, to 62°N in Norway and south to northwest Spain and northeast Portugal, east across Europe (but not southern Italy) to northern Greece, southwest Russia, The Crimea and western Poland.

Habitat: Woodlands, especially on light and acid soils, rarely on heavy clays.

Synonyms: *Q. sessiliflora.*

Similar species: *Q. dalechampii* from southeast Europe has hairless leaves on a leaf stalk 1.5–2 cm (0.6–0.8 in) with four to seven pairs of narrow irregular and subacute lobes and cupules which have diamond-shaped blunt scales which are strongly warty or tuberculated and very shortly downy. It may be the result of past hybridization of *Q. petraea* with *Q. pubescens.*

Q. iberica from the Transcaucasus region, has leaves with eight to ten pairs of lobes and which have a prominent axillary tuft of hairs beneath, and the fruits on a short stalk.

Q. mas from the Pyrenees and northern Spain, has leaves with up to ten pairs of forward-pointing lobes and fruiting stalks which are silky hairy.

Balkan Sessile Oak *Q. polycarpa* (p.275) has the leaves, buds and twigs hairless, whilst the leaves are 6–10 cm (2.4–4 in), somewhat leathery, elliptic with seven to ten regular pairs of shallow bluntly-pointed lobes. The cupule has acute, broad ovate scales which are strongly tuberculated, hairy and brown. It is a native of southeast Europe, extending into the Czech Republic.

Q. × rosacea covers the occasional hybrids between *Q. petraea* and *Q. robur*. These are intermediate between the two parent species, differing in the narrowed and subcordate base to the leaves and the 1–3 cm (0.4–1.2 in) penduncles.

Durmast Oak makes a better and taller timber tree than *Q. robur*, with which it occasionally hybridizes. The leaves are less liable to insect defoliation, giving a neater and denser crown. It is found generally on acid and well-drained soils.

p.161 **Willow Oak** *Quercus phellos*

Description: Deciduous tree to 25 m (80 ft) with a bole diameter to 1.2 m (4 ft).
Crown Columnar or with a broad domed head with many slender twiggy shoots.
Bark Smooth, grey-green with orange fissures, becoming purple-grey and platy.
Shoot Initially hairy, pale grey-green in the first year, becoming greyer, slender.
Buds Conic to ovoid-conic, red-brown, 2 mm (0.1 in). *Foliage* Leaves oblong-lanceolate, narrow, rounded to a short point or prickle at the apex, base narrow wedge-shaped, margin untoothed, often wavy, upper surface sub-shiny green, initially hairy but soon hairless, underside light green with a raised midrib, 5–11 × 0.7–2 cm (2–4.3 × 0.3–0.8 in); leaf stalk short, flat on top, slightly hairy, 2–4 mm (0.1–0.2 in); autumn colour yellow.
Fruit Acorn nearly round with a pointed apex, brown, maturing in the second autumn, 1–1.2 cm (0.4–0.5 in), set in a shallow cup.

Range: Eastern USA in a broad arc from New Jersey southwest to eastern Texas.

Habitat: Cultivated as an ornamental, in the wild occurring on alluvial bottom land sites.

Similar species: **Shingle Oak** *Q. imbricaria* differs in the oblong to oblong-lanceolate leaves which are larger, 8–15 × 2–5 cm (3.1–6 × 0.8–2 in), and in the slightly larger acorns (1.2–1.5 cm (0.5–0.6 in)) which are enclosed for the lower half to one-third in the cup.

Several natural hybrids of *Q. phellos* are found in specialist oak collections, such as *Q. × ludoviciana* (*Q. phellos* × *Q. falcata*), with leaves with two pairs of forward-pointing acute lobes, and *Q. × heterophylla* (*Q. phellos* × *Q. rubra*), with one to four pairs of spined teeth on either side of the leaf. *Q. × leana* (*Q. imbricaria* × *Q. velutina*) also has few large triangular lobes.

This tree has leaves which are narrow and similar to some *Salix*, turning yellow in the autumn. The twigs are slender and dense.

p.278 **Armenian Oak** or **Pontine Oak**
Quercus pontica

Description: Deciduous small tree to 10 m (33 ft) with a
bole diameter to 30 cm (1 ft).
Crown Rounded, rather bushy and on a
short bole with radiating stems. *Bark* Grey,
with smooth purplish patches, becoming
fissured. *Shoot* Shiny olive-brown, very
stout, angled, with narrow lenticels, in the
second and third years grey-buff or grey-
brown. *Buds* Ovoid-conic, with many
imbricate scales which form five-angled
ridges on the terminal shoot, scales green
with brown ciliate tips, 1–1.5 cm
(0.4–0.6 in). *Foliage* Leaves oval to obovate,
apex acute, tapered to a rounded base,
margin serrate with on each side 25–30
large triangular teeth with a forward-
pointing acute or aristate tip which
terminates the 16 or 17 pairs of main veins
(half of which branch), upper surface shiny
green and smooth except for the lower
midrib which is rounded and raised,
underside whitish or glaucous green with a
prominent midrib and veins which are hairy
at least towards their base, 10–30 ×
5–15 cm (4–12 × 2–6 in); leaf stalk stout,
grooved, hairless, green, 2 cm (0.8 in);
autumn colour russet. *Flowers* in late
spring; male catkins from buds on previous
year's shoots, 15–20 cm (6–8 in); female
flowers terminal on current season's
extension growth, stalkless, with 5 long
stigmas. *Fruit* Acorn in a cluster of two or
three, stalkless beside the shoot tip, ripening
in the first autumn, cup 1.2 cm (0.5 in) deep
by 1.5–2 cm (0.6–0.8 in) wide, with ovate-
lanceolate green and brown scales, enclosing
the lower third of the acorn; acorn ovoid,
hairy towards the apex, green, ripening to
reddish brown, 2.5–4 cm (1–1.6 in).

Range: Northeast Turkey through Armenia and
Georgia to Transcaucasus region of Russia.

Habitat: Cultivated as an ornamental.

Similar species: *Q. × hickelii* is the hybrid between this
species and *Q. robur*, having intermediate
characters but best distinguished by the
large leaves with circa 12–16 pairs of veins,

the somewhat auricled leaf base and the short leaf stalk.

This tree has remarkable leaves with their 16 or so pairs of parallel veins. It is similar to *Q. robur* in its flower and fruiting characters, and seed from cultivated trees will usually produce a hybrid between the two.

---

p.275 **Downy Oak** *Quercus pubescens*

Description: Deciduous tree 10–20 m (33–65 ft) with a bole diameter to 1 m (3.3 ft).
Crown Rounded, usually rather open.
Bark Dark grey, becoming deeply cracked into small square rough plates.
Shoot Green and densely grey downy, becoming brown or buff and shiny in later years. *Buds* Ovoid, blunt, light brown, 3 mm (0.1 in). *Foliage* Leaves obovate or obovate-lanceolate in outline, apex rounded or slightly notched, base broad wedge-shaped, margin with four to eight pairs of rounded untoothed lobes with deep narrow rounded sinuses extending approximately half way to the midrib, upper surface star-shaped hairy at first, grey-green and shiny with raised veins which point forwards at circa 45 degrees from the midrib, underside white or grey with a dense covering of hairs especially on the raised veins, 5–9 × 3.5–5 cm (2–3.5 × 1.4–2 in); leaf stalk grooved, hairy, 0.4–1.2 cm (0.2–0.5 in); autumn colour russet. *Fruit* Acorns stalkless or on a short stalk, single or up to four and ripening in the first autumn; cup enclosing lower half of the acorn 1.5 cm (0.6 in) and deep, with grey downy scales tightly pressed on the shoot; acorn ovoid, pointed.

Range: West France and north Spain across southern Europe to the Caucasus.

Habitat: Open warm hillsides on limestone or siliceous soils.

Varieties: Ssp. *palensis* from the Pyrenees and north Spain differs in the leaves being less lobed and less than 7 cm (2.8 in) long. The scales on the acorn cup are fused at the base and free towards the rim where they have cuspidate tips.

Synonyms: *Q. lanuginosa.*

Similar species: *Q. brachyphylla* has leaves elliptic to broadly elliptic, mainly 5–6 × 4–5 cm (2–2.4 × 1.6–2 in), with three or four blunt lobes and veins parting from the midrib at a wide angle. The scales of the acorn cup are swollen and ovate at the base, but linear and thin towards the rim. This small tree or shrub comes from Greece, western Turkey and various Aegean islands, especially Crete.

Q. congesta has larger leaves, to 13 cm (5.1 in), with six to eight pairs of lobes. The cup has linear-lanceolate scales which are not adpressed. It is recorded from Sicily, Sardinia and southern France.

Q. virgiliana has leaves to 16 cm (6.3 in) on a leaf stalk to 2.5 cm (1 in) and with the scales on the acorn cup loosely pressed together. In some forms from Italy, the acorns are rounded and sweet, edible. It occurs from Corsica and Sardinia across Italy and the Balkans to the Black Sea region.

This species is related to *Q. petraea* but differs in the marked pubescence of the leaves, shoots and acorn cups. It grows on warm open hillsides.

---

p.277   **Pyrenean Oak**   *Quercus pyrenaica*

Description: Deciduous tree to 20–25 m (65–80 ft) with a bole diameter of up to 80 cm (2.6 ft). *Crown* Domed, rather open. *Bark* Pale grey and deeply fissuring into small square scales. *Shoot* Densely star-shaped hairy with grey down when new, rather pendulous. *Buds* Ovoid-conic, pale brown with a ring of whiskered scales. *Foliage* Leaves obovate to broad oblong, apex rounded pointed, base long wedge-shaped, margin with four to eight pairs of veins and broad obovate lobes which extend half way to the midrib and which have coarse rounded teeth, upper surface more or less hairless and grey-green, underside densely and persistently white hairy, 10–20 × 4–11 cm (4–8 × 1.6–4.3 in);

leaf stalk downy, 0.6–2 cm (0.25–0.8 in).
Flowers Male flowers golden, pendent, in
late June. *Fruit* Acorn ripening in the first
autumn, oblong, with the bottom third
enclosed in the hemispherical cupule which
has downy, ovate lanceolate, acute scales
adpressed against the cup.

Range: Portugal, Spain and to northwest France,
and in Morocco.

Habitat: Woodland.

Varieties: 'Pendula' is a name sometimes used.
However, the species generally has pendent
branches and this name is possibly
redundant.

Synonyms: *Q. toza.*

This tree usually has pendulous shoots. The
leaves are variable in size and lobing. In
their hairiness, they show an affinity with
Q. macranthera, but this has more shallow-
lobed leaves and more persistent bud
stipules. Another ally is *Q. frainetto*, which
has more numerous, shallower and more
regular lobing to the leaves.

p.274 **English Oak** or **Pedunculate Oak**
Quercus robur

Description: Deciduous tree 15–35 m (50–115 ft) with a
bole diameter 0.7–3 m (2.3–10 ft) or more.
Crown Conical when young, becoming
widely domed when growing in the open and
often broader than tall, in plantations slender
domed. *Bark* Smooth and grey-green in
young trees, becoming progressively fissured
into ridges and furrows, often cross-fissured
into rectangular or hexagonal plates.
Shoot Grey-green or olive and at first
somewhat bloomed, becoming shiny by
autumn, lenticels small, oval and orange,
ridged behind the leaf bases, in the second,
and later years grey to grey-brown.
Buds Ovoid to ovoid-conic, rounded or
bluntly pointed at the apex, mid brown,
clustered at the tips of the shoots, to 5 mm
(0.2 in). *Foliage* Leaves of card-like texture,
obovate to obovate-oblong, usually broadest
in the upper two-thirds, rounded at the apex,

tapering to a narrowed and auricled base, margin with four to six pairs of large rounded lobes which are usually smaller in the basal half, with the rounded sinuses extending between a quarter and a half of the way to the centre, upper surface matt mid to somewhat shiny green but usually covered with honeydew and often with sooty moulds, some hairs on the veins, underside pale glaucous green with prominently raised veins and often with spangle galls, hairless, 4–12 × 2–6 cm (1.6–4.7 × 0.8–2.4 in); leaf stalk oval or grooved, light yellow-green, hairless, 4–7 mm (0.2–0.3 in), rarely to 1 cm (0.4 in); autumn colour yellow to russets, remaining green until late autumn; new flushes, especially during the summer often bronze or yellow-green. *Flowers* In late spring with the new leaves; male catkins pendulous from the terminal cluster of buds, brownish green to yellow-green, 2–4 cm (0.8–1.6 in); female flowers terminal on the first flush of growth. *Fruit* One to four, rarely to six, spreading on a slender stalk 2–10 cm (0.8–4 in), sometimes to 20 cm (8 in), cupule with triangular scales pressed on shoot, hairless or slightly downy, with a hairy rim to the cup, enclosing the lower quarter of the acorn; acorn long ovoid to oblong, rounded at both ends, with the cluster of hairy stigmas remaining as a small prickle at the apex and with a small circular scar or hilium at the base, pale bloomed green until ripening brown, 1.5–4 × 1.3–2 cm (0.6–1.6 × 0.5–0.8 in); knopper galls are star-shaped woody yellow-green galls and are often found attached to the acorns.

Range: Throughout Europe east to the Caucasus region.

Habitat: Woodlands, often forming pure forest, and hedgerows.

Varieties: 'Concordia' is the Golden Oak with leaves bright yellow for most of the growing season. It is a most beautiful tree but needs careful siting as it is inclined to be scorched by strong sunlight. Forma *fastigiata* has a narrow crown of upright branches. Its colloquial name is the Cypress Oak; both these two entities should not be confused with the Golden Oak of Cyprus, *Q. alnifolia*. Forma *pendula* covers the selections with weeping or pendulous branches. Forma *purpurascens* covers the plants whose new leaves and shoots are purple.

Synonyms: *Q. pedunculata*.

Similar species: Related species, which have been treated as subspecies or varieties of *Q. robur* at various times, include:

Q. brutia from southern Italy having the undersides of the leaves, the shoots and the stalks downy, with generally larger leaves with deeper lobing and with the scales of the cupule having free-spreading tips.

Q. haas from Asia Minor differs in the much larger leaves in the range 10–20 × 4–7 cm (4–8–1.6–2.8 in) with only three to five pairs of lobes, in the persistent thin covering of star-shaped hairs on the leaf underside and in the acorn being 4–5 cm (1.6–2 in) long, set in a cupule with hairy adpressed scales.

Balkan Pedunculate Oak *Q. pedunculiflora* (p.274) occurs from southeast Europe from Greece, Bulgaria and Romania across Asia Minor to the Caucasus region. The differences from *Q. robur* are that the leaves are somewhat glaucous above with a yellow-grey down on the underside, and the scales of the cupule are warty, closely pressed together and yellow downy, with the cupule enclosing the lower third of the acorn.

Q. thomasii from southern Italy has deeply lobed leaves, which, with the stalks, are hairless, and very shallow cupules which have the scales with free rather spreading tips.

This tree has very variable leaves which are characterized by the auricles or ear-lobes on either side at the base and the short leaf stalk. The degree of lobing of the leaves is variable, as is the length of the stalk and the size and shape of the acorn. It is related to *Q. petraea*, which has more obovate leaves with more regular lobing and a rounded to wedge-shaped (not auricled) base on a leaf stalk of at least 1 cm (0.4 in), and the acorns are stalkless or only very shortly stalked. *Q. robur* is better adapted to heavy soils than *Q. petraea*, although it will thrive on other sites. It is capable of regenerating into abandoned grassland, with the acorns often spread by jays and other large birds. They contain too much tannin for cattle and horses but are eaten by pigs. The timber is excellent, with great beauty, structural properties and durability. The large rays give oak planks a very distinctive appearance. *Q. robur* grows in a series of flushes, usually three but depending upon the season from two to four. All the buds flush in the spring, but extra flushes are usually only produced on the terminal bud. It supports a large number of insects, both caterpillars and aphids.

---

p.162 **Round-leafed Oak** *Quercus rotundifolia*

Description: Evergreen tree to 10 m (33 ft) or so. *Crown* Rounded. *Bark* As for *Q. ilex*. *Shoot* White due to the dense silvery hairs in the first year, then grey and becoming brown as the hairs are lost. *Buds* Ovoid, brown with white woolly hairs and a few long free bud scales, 1–2 mm (0.1 in). *Foliage* Juvenile foliage rotund or oval, margins with five or six pairs of sharp forward spines, rounded or shallowly subcordate at base, matt grey-green above, silvery white beneath due to a plastered layer of hairs, 1.8–3 × 1.5–2.2 cm (0.7–1.2 × 0.6–0.9 in); leaf stalk 2–3 mm (0.1 in), grey woolly; adult leaves oblong to elliptic, rounded at both ends, untoothed except for an abrupt short pointed tip, with five to eight pairs of veins, 1.5–5 cm (0.6–2 in). *Flowers* As for *Q. ilex*. *Fruit* As for *Q. ilex* but larger with a sweet flesh.

Range: Southern Spain and North Africa.

Habitat: Dry evergreen thickets.

Synonyms: *Q. ilex* var. *ballota*.

This tree is closely related to *Q. ilex*. The acorn, however, is larger and has a sweet flesh, whereas in *Q. ilex* the acorn has a bitter inedible flesh. The tree is grown for the fruits, which can be roasted as for sweet chestnuts.

p.281 **Red Oak** *Quercus rubra*

Description: Deciduous tree 20–25 m (65–80 ft) in height with a bole diameter to 1.5 m (5 ft). *Crown* Conic and rather whorled in young trees, becoming wide domed with large radiating branches on a short bole in old trees. *Bark* Smooth, silvery grey to dark grey, becoming fissured into scaly ridges, inner bark reddish. *Shoot* Yellow-green, shiny and slightly ribbed in the first year, later grey-brown. *Buds* Conic to ovoid-conic, chestnut brown, slightly hairy at the tip, 5–7 mm (0.2–0.3 in). *Foliage* Leaves elliptic in outline, apex slender pointed, base wedge-shaped to broad wedge-shaped, margin with three to five pairs of large lobes which are variously toothed and with deep or shallow rounded sinuses, teeth and lobes tapering to a slender bristle tip of 2–4 mm (0.1–0.2 in), upper surface hairless, deep sub-shiny green with raised veins, underside pale green with raised whitish veins and brown axillary tufts of hair, 7–20 × 5–14 cm (2.8–8 × 2–5.5 in) (on sprout shoots and young trees can be up to 30 × 20 cm (12 × 8 in)); leaf stalk grooved with a slightly enlarged base, 1–4 cm (0.4–1.6 in); autumn colour variable, mainly good red but some trees yellow or brown; new leaves yellowish for a spell. *Flowers* Male catkins slender, 5–8 cm (2–3.1 in) in May, female flowers on a short shoot in leaf axils of new growths, usually in pairs. *Fruit* Cup on a 1 cm (0.4 in) stalk, broad shallow saucer with an incurved rim and enclosing less than one-third of the acorn, with reddish-brown blunt overlapping scales, 1.5–1.8 cm (0.6–0.7 in) across, acorn ovoid, 1.5–2.8 cm (0.6–1.1 in), ripening in the second autumn.

Range: Eastern North America from south of the St. Lawrence River across to Minnesota and down to Oklahoma and Georgia.

Habitat: Cultivated as an ornamental and in forestry, in the wild forming pure stands.

Varieties: 'Aurea' is a selection in which the new foliage is clear yellow for a few weeks, before becoming green. It requires a site which has an evergreen background and shelter from spring frost.

Synonyms: *Q. borealis.*

Red Oak is one of the commonest American oaks in cultivation and makes a large spreading old tree. The radiating branches give it a distinctive open habit which is easily recognizable. The autumn colour is usually fairly good, but variable.

p.267 **Himalayan Oak** *Quercus semecarpifolia*

Description: Evergreen tree 15–25 m (50–80 ft) with a bole diameter to 1 m (3.3 ft).
Crown Columnar, with a domed apex and spreading level branches. *Bark* Buff-brown, becoming scaly in small rectangular plates. *Shoot* Green with a covering of short star-shaped hairs when young, becoming nearly hairless by autumn, with pale oval lenticels, in later years shiny and rough dark greenish brown. *Buds* Conic, brown, 3–6 mm (0.1–0.25 in).
Foliage Leaves in pseudo-whorls at the tips of the shoots, oblong to broad elliptic, leathery or card-like in texture, apex rounded, base rounded to heart-shaped, margin curved down and untoothed on mature foliage but leaves on young trees and epicormic shoots on the bole have wavy margins which end in sharp long aristate needle-like points to 2 mm (0.1 in), upper surface lustrous deep green with indented veins, initially with star-shaped hairs but becoming hairless, lower surface with a dense felt of golden to whitish hairs (but epicormic shoots and those on juvenile trees pale green and less densely haired), veins raised, 3–2 × 2–7 cm (1.2–0.8 × 0.8–2.8 in); leaf stalk grooved, stout, with golden hairs, 4–7 mm (0.2–0.3 in); leaves retained one to two years. *Flowers* Male catkins pendulous at the base of the shoots in early summer, yellow with a hairy rachis, 6–12 cm (2.4–4.7 in). *Fruit* Cupule circa 1.5 cm (0.6 in) across and 1 cm (0.4 in)

deep with a rim, enclosing the lower part of the acorn only; acorn sub-globose with a short pointed apex, 2–2.5 cm (0.8–1 in), ripening during the summer rains of the second year.

Range: Northwest Himalayas across to Sichuan and northwest Yunnan, Western China.

Habitat: Cultivated as an ornamental, in the wild occurring in dry woods, sometimes restricted to a shrub.

The tree has bold evergreen foliage which is golden below and is also attractive when carrying the pendent golden-yellow catkins. The acorns ripen during the summer monsoon period in its native habitat and germinate immediately.

---

p.161 **Cork Oak** *Quercus suber*

Description: Evergreen tree to 20 m (65 ft) with a bole diameter to 1.5 m (5 ft).
Crown Conical or rounded when young, becoming broad domed in old trees.
Bark Corky and grey-brown, becoming deeply fissured and ridged from the fourth year, underbark bright red-brown or pink.
Shoot Grey-brown with a close grey down, slender, becoming brown. *Buds* Ovoid-conic, chestnut brown, 3 mm (0.1 in).
Foliage Ovate, oval to oblong, margins with small forward-pointing spine teeth and downturned, base rounded, apex rounded or acute, with a short spine, midrib somewhat sinuous, bending towards each alternate side vein, hairless above except when very young and dark glossy green, whitish grey felted beneath, 2.5–6 × 1.5–4 cm (1–2.4 × 0.6–1.6 in); leaf stalk 0.7–1.5 cm (0.3–0.6 in), grey. *Flowers* On current season's growths in early summer.
Fruit Ripening in the first season (but *see* var. *occidentalis*); cup is 1.2–1.8 cm (0.5–0.7 in) wide with long spreading scales and encloses the lower half of the acorn, 1.5–3 cm (0.6–1.2 in).

Range: From Portugal, Spain and Morocco east to Croatia.

Habitat: Dry rocky hillsides.

Varieties: Var. *occidentalis* comes from the western fringe of its range along the Atlantic coastline of France, Spain, Portugal and Morocco. The leaves are shed as soon as the new flush has matured. It flowers in both spring and autumn, with the autumn flowering ripening in the following summer.

The thick spongy bark is harvested on a seven- to ten-year cycle to give cork, used as an insulating material and for plugging wine bottles. The leaves usually persist for two years.

---

p.279 **Trojan Oak** or **Macedonian Oak**
Quercus trojana

Description: Semi-evergreen or tardily deciduous tree to 20 m (65 ft) with a bole diameter to 60 cm (2 ft).
Crown Conical when young, becoming domed in old trees. *Bark* Grey-brown, fissured. *Shoot* Green-brown to grey by autumn with whitish star-shaped hairs, grey-brown or buff in later years.
Buds Low rounded, domed, green or brown, with a few wispy stipules remaining around the terminal bud only, 2 mm (0.1 in). *Foliage* Leaves oblong-obovate or ovate-oblong, tapering to an acute apex, base broad wedge-shaped or subcordate, rarely somewhat rounded, margin wavy with short broad triangular teeth which terminate the 6–12 pairs of veins and end in a bristle tip of circa 1 mm (0.1 in), upper surface sub-shiny fresh green with the midrib slightly raised, underside sub-shiny light green with veins raised and initially hairy, tertiary veins net-like, 4–9 × 2–5 cm (1.6–3.5 × 0.8–2 in); leaf stalk grooved, sparsely hairy, 2–5 mm (0.1–0.2 in); autumn colour green! *Fruit* Stalkless or almost stalkless, solitary, cup 1.5–2.2 cm (0.6–0.9 in), wide enclosing two-thirds of the acorn, with adpressed upper and

spreading ovate to slender-pointed lower scales (which are rounded at the tip and grey downy); acorn truncate at the tip, 2–4 cm (0.8–1.6 in), ripening in the second autumn.

Range: Southeast Italy (Apulia), southern Balkans (Albania, Montenegro, Macedonia, Greece) and western Turkey.

Habitat: Woodland.

Synonyms: *Q. macedonica.*

This tree was first named from the western Anatolian populations in the vicinity of Troy but is mainly distributed in the southern Balkans.

p.281 **Chinese Cork Oak** *Quercus variabilis*

Description: Deciduous tree to 15–20 m (50–65 ft) with a bole diameter to 70 cm (2.3 ft).
Crown Ovoid, becoming open with spreading and usually spaced branches.
Bark Thick and corky, pink-grey to grey-brown, with short deep fissures.
Shoot Olive-brown to light brown, nearly hairless and sub-shiny, becoming grey-brown after the first year. *Buds* Ovoid-conic, light brown, scales with hairy margins, 5 mm (0.2 in). *Foliage* Leaves narrowly oval to oblong, tapering to an acute and whiskered apex up to 1.3 cm (0.5 in), base long wedge-shaped, margin with forward pointing bristle-tipped teeth (with the slender bristles to 5 mm (0.2 in)) on broad flat bases with shallow rounded sinuses, upper surface deep shiny green with impressed and somewhat hairy veins, folded along the midrib, underside whitish green or pale grey, covered with a close felted layer of star-shaped hairs, with the 9–16 pairs of veins and midrib raised, 7–20 × 2.2–5 (2.8–8 × 0.9–2 in) (to 10 cm (4 in)); leaf stalk grooved, yellow-green, 1.5–3 cm (0.6–1.2 in); autumn colour russet. *Fruit* Acorn 1.3–2 cm (0.5–0.8 in), ovoid-globose, almost fully enclosed in the cup which has long curly reflexed scales, ripening in the second year.

Range: Central and west China, Korea and
southern Honshu, Kyushu and Shikoku,
Japan.

Habitat: Cultivated as an ornamental, in the wild
occurring in deciduous woodland.

This tree has a thick corky bark and in this
respect is similar to *Q. suber*. The leaves
show a greater affinity to *Q. acutissima*
(which comes from the same regions) but
can be distinguished by the leaves being
whitish and densely hairy beneath.

p.281 **Black Oak** or **Quercitron Oak**
Quercus velutina

Description: Deciduous tree 15–25 m (50–80 ft) with a
bole diameter of up to 1 m (3.3 ft).
Crown Conic with ascending branches in
young trees, becoming domed. *Bark* Grey
and smooth on young trees, becoming
blackish, thick and fissured with age, inner
bark yellow or orange, bitter.
Shoot Initially with brown star-shaped
hairs, becoming hairless. *Buds* Very
downy, 0.6–1.2 cm (0.25–0.5 in).
Foliage Leaves elliptic to obovate, apex
with a thin spine-like bristle, base wedge-
shaped, margin with three or four pairs of
ovate to triangular lobes which have several
bristly-like teeth and corresponding
shallow to deep rounded to acute sinuses,
upper surface shiny dark green and soon
hairless, underside paler, initially with
brown scurfy hairs which only regularly
persist in the axils of the prominent main
veins, hooded with a leathery texture, 8–15
× 30 cm (3.1–6 × 12 in) on young trees, by
half to two-thirds as wide; leaf stalk stout
with a broad base, yellow, 2.5–6 cm
(1–2.4 in); autumn colour dull red or
brown. *Fruit* Acorn ellipsoidal, maturing
in the second autumn, 1.5–2 cm
(0.6–0.8 in); cupule enclosing the lower
half of the acorn, with loosely imbricate
red-brown hairy scales.

Range: Eastern USA from Maine south to Florida,
west to central Texas and north to

Minnesota, just extending into Canada in southern Ontario.

Habitat: Cultivated as an ornamental, in the wild characteristic of dry sandy rocky ridges, rarely forming pure groves.

Varieties: 'Rubrifolia' is a selection with larger leaves, up to 35 cm (14 in).

Synonyms: *Q. tinctoria*.

This is similar to *Q. rubra*, but differs in the bark characters, the stouter leaf stalks and the more deeply lobed and firmer leaves. The first common name refers to the bark of mature trees, the second to quercitron dye, which is made by drying and then pounding the inner bark. This yellow pigment is also present in the acorns. The Latin name refers to the velvety wool on the new foliage and shoots.

BUTTERCUP, RANUNCULACEAE

This family contains mainly herbs and climbers and only *Clematis* (p.613) is featured here.

REHDERODENDRON, *REHDERODENDRON*
FAMILY STYRACACEAE

This is a genus of five to ten species, from China to Vietnam. The leaves are typical of the *Styrax* family, as are the fragrant white flowers. The fruit is a large woody structure containing several seeds, which takes several years to break down and allow the seeds to germinate.

p.235 **Red Pepo Tree** or **Rehderodendron**
Rehderodendron macrocarpum

Description: Deciduous tree 7–10 m (23–33 ft) with a bole diameter to 25 cm (0.8 ft).
Crown Rounded, on a short bole or bushy.
Bark Light brown, shallow ridged.
Shoot Slender, golden-brown or brownish purple, sparsely star-shaped haired, in the second year grey-brown to yellowish grey, later dark brown with paler fissures.

Buds Conic, pointed, with two scales, green or purplish, sparsely star-shaped hairy on the outside, 2 mm (0.1 in). *Foliage* Leaves oblong-ovate to oblong-lanceolate, tapering to a slender point or short slender-pointed apex, base wedge-shaped to broad wedge-shaped, margin with small remote teeth, upper surface light to mid green, hairless with impressed veins and midrib, underside lustrous light green, hairless except for some star-shaped hairs on the raised midrib, veins in 9–11 pairs, 7–13 × 3.5–5.5 cm (2.8–5.1 × 1.4–2.2 in); leaf stalk grooved with decurrent ridges which are continuations of the leaf margins, bright purplish pink, 0.7–1.5 cm (0.3–0.6 in); autumn colour yellow or pink and yellow. *Flowers* In cymes of four to eight in late spring from previous season's shoots, opening narrow funnel shape with five creamy-white to yellow-white petals 1.5–18 cm (0.6–7.1 in) long. *Fruit* Ellipsoidal woody structure with 7–10 ribs, ripening from red and purplish green to brown, 5–7 × 2.5–3 cm (2–2.8 × 1–1.2 in), with a woody outer layer and a fibrous inner layer, enclosing one (occasionally more) 4–5 cm × 5 mm (1.6–2 × 0.2 in) seed.

Range: West and central China and northern Vietnam.

Habitat: Cultivated as an ornamental, in the wild occurring in mixed woodland.

This small tree has attractive white flowers and large woody fruits which are red on the outer or exposed side. The leaf stalks are brightly coloured.

BUCKTHORN, RHAMNACEAE

This is a large family with perhaps 900 species in some fifty genera. Most are trees and shrubs, with some climbers and a few herbs. Genera listed here are *Frangula* (p.709), *Paliurus* (p.867), *Rhamnus* (p.1093) and *Ziziphus* (p.1271).

BUCKTHORNS, *RHAMNUS*
FAMILY RHAMNACEAE

This is a genus of over 100 species distributed throughout much of the world. The leaves are alternate, opposite or sub-opposite on the shoot and rather dull. The flowers are nondescript, and followed by juicy berries.

p.176 **Alaternus** *Rhamnus alaternus*

Description: Evergreen spreading shrub or small tree to 6 m (20 ft) with a bole diameter to 20 cm (0.7 ft).
Crown Rather sprawling to rounded, dense. *Bark* Pale brown, becoming ridged with light brown fissures. *Shoot* Green with short pale hairs, becoming brown in the second year and remaining hairy. *Buds* Ovoid on a short peg-like extension of the shoot, 2 mm (0.1 in). *Foliage* Leaves variable from linear lanceolate to oval or oblong, leathery, tapering to both ends, apex with a slender bristle-like tip, margin with three pairs of small forward teeth and a hyaline band, upper surface lustrous dark green, with raised veins, mainly three-veined from the base, underside shiny light green hairless except for some axillary tufts, 2–5 × 1.2–2.5 cm (0.8–2 × 0.5–1 in); leaf stalk hairy, grooved, less than 1 cm (0.4 in); no autumn colour. *Flowers* In small axillary umbel-like racemes of three or more small yellowish-green flowers, sometimes clustered at shoot tips. *Fruit* Globose with a small dimple with the remains of the style at the tip, pinkish purple, ripening to black, calyx a round rim beneath the fruit, 5–7 mm (0.2–0.3 in).
Range: Mediterranean region from Portugal and Morocco east to the Crimea.
Habitat: Dry rocky hillsides, in maquis.
Varieties: Var. *angustifolia* covers the very narrow-leafed forms, where the leaves may be only 4–10 mm (0.2–0.4 in) in width. 'Argenteovariegata' has the leaves margined with creamy-white patches. It can be effective but requires a mild

climate for best effect. In cold districts, it may be tender.

Synonyms: *Alaternus latifolia*.

The beauty and attractiveness of this plant lies not in its floral or fruit attributes but in the pleasing shiny-green evergreen foliage.

---

p.176 **Buckthorn** *Rhamnus catharticus*

Description: Deciduous shrub attaining tree-like proportions and up to 6 m (20 ft) in height. *Crown* Rounded. *Bark* Brown.
Shoot Slender, hairless, terminating in a sharp spine on lateral branches. *Buds* Scaly, alternate or in sub-opposite pairs, dark brown, long ovoid-conic. *Foliage* Leaves elliptic to ovate, apex acute to bluntly pointed, base rounded or subcordate, sometimes wedge-shaped, margin with crenate teeth, thin in texture and dull green above, paler green beneath and usually hairless, with three to five pairs of veins, 2.5–7 × 1.2–3.5 cm (1–2.8 × 0.5–1.4 in); leaf stalk 0.6–2.5 cm (0.25–1 in); autumn colour poor, sometimes yellowish.
Flowers Yellow-green, easily overlooked.
Fruit Sub-globose juicy berry with two seeds, purplish black, giving a purplish dye, 6 mm (0.25 in).

Range: Europe eastwards to west and north Asia.

Habitat: Chalk downland to sandy scrub.

This can look quite attractive in autumn when carrying a large crop of berries. These are purgative if ingested, hence the Latin name. The shoots bear a mixture of alternate and opposite buds.

RHODODENDRONS, *RHODODENDRON* (SYNONYM: *AZALEA*)
FAMILY ERICACEAE

This is a very large genus of around 800–1000 species from the northern hemisphere south across the equator into northern Australia where there are two species. Most species are found in the Sino-Himalayan region and in New Guinea. About three-quarters of the species are shrubs, with the rest shrubby trees to full trees (to 30 m (100 ft)). The leaves are in whorls at the shoot tips, evergreen to deciduous and of variable size (less than 1 cm (0.4 in) up to 1 m (39 in)). The flowers are terminal on the shoots, in racemes, less often single, and are very showy. The fruit is a woody capsule. The species are widely planted for amenity.

p.130 **Gurass** *Rhododendron arboreum*

Description: Evergreen tree 10–20 m (33–65 in) with a bole diameter to 1 m (3.3 ft).
Crown Rounded to columnar, often on several stems. *Bark* Brown or grey-brown, flaking in long slender plates on old trees. *Shoot* Green or red-brown for one or two years with whitish or greyish hairs, becoming brown or grey-brown, smooth as the outer bark is shed. *Buds* Ovoid-conical, pointed, pale green, with long awl-like free scales at the base, 1 cm (0.4 in); flower buds rounded, 1.5–2 cm (0.6–0.8 in). *Foliage* In whorls at the ends of shoots, kept for two to three years; narrowly to broadly elliptic or ovate, tapered to the acute apex, rounded or wedge-shaped at base, folded along the midrib with margins untoothed but rolled, leathery, upper surface matt green, initially floccose but soon hairless, underside with prominent pale yellow-green midrib, silvery to rusty brown due to a dense covering of hairs, 6.5–19 × 1.8–5.5 cm (2.6–7.5 × 0.7–2.2 in); leaf stalk grooved, 1–2 cm (0.4–0.8 in). *Flowers* On buds formed in previous summer, opening in late winter or early spring, in rounded heads of 10–20 blooms, corolla 3–5 cm (1.2–2 in) across, white, pink or red. *Fruit* Woody capsule 1.5–3 cm (0.6–1.2 in), ripening brown.
Range: Himalayas, from Kashmir east to southwest China, in the Nilgari Hills of southern India, and Sri Lanka.
Habitat: Cultivated in Europe as an ornamental, in the wild occurring in dry to moist forest on mountain sides or ridges.
Varieties: The three commonest subspecies can be distinguished by the hairs on the underside

of the leaves. In ssp. *arboreum* they are white to silvery. It occurs in the western part of the Himalayas. Ssp. *cinnamomeum* has a rufous outer layer of hairs and red-brown shoots. It occurs towards the top of the range in east Nepal to Sikkim. Ssp. *delavayi* has spongy white hairs, occurring from central Bhutan east into northern Burma and Yunnan.

This makes an impressive tree, especially in the Himalayas. It has been crossed with *R. ponticum* and other species to produce the 'Hardy Hybrids', which excel in their more reliable flowers less affected by frosts or early seasons, but lose much poise. The common name given above is the Nepali name, with this tree being Nepal's national flower. The underside of the leaf has a dense compacted layer of hairs, but in some forms there is an outer looser layer.

---

p.130 **Korlinga** *Rhododendron falconeri*

Description: Evergreen tree 10–18 m (33–60 ft) with a bole diameter to 80 cm (2.6 ft).
Crown Rounded, domed. *Bark* Purplish brown, scaly in thin exfoliating plates.
Shoot Green for one or two years initially with whitish hairs, stout, becoming brown and smooth as the outer bark is shed.
Buds Ovoid-conic, pointed, red-brown or green, scales often free at tips, to 2 cm (0.8 in). *Foliage* In whorls at the ends of shoots, kept for two to three years; broadly elliptic to obovate, rounded at both ends, untoothed, card-like, upper surface dark matt green with impressed veins (blistered), initially with a loose red-brown coat of hairs but soon hairless, underside with prominent midrib and main veins pale yellow-green midrib, rufous brown due to a dense thick woolly covering of hairs, 18–35 × 8–17 cm (7.1–14 × 3.1–6.7 in); leaf stalk round, stout, 2.5–5 cm (1–2 in). *Flowers* On buds formed in previous summer, opening in late winter or early spring, in rounded

heads of 15–20 blooms, corolla 4–5.5 cm (1.6–2.2 in) across, yellow, cream or pale (often wishy-washy) pink. *Fruit* Woody capsule 4 cm (1.6 in), ripening brown.

Range: From east Nepal to northeast India.

Habitat: Cultivated in Europe as an ornamental, in the wild occurring in moist forest dominated by *Abies densa* on mountain-sides or ridges.

Varieties: The form with more persistent hairs above and pink flowers is often treated as a separate subspecies but is only marginally distinguishable.

Similar species: *R. arizelum*, a related species from northeast India across Burma to West Yunnan and southeast Tibet, has very similar foliage, but the ovary and flower stalks do not have the characteristic glands found on *R. falconeri*.

This makes a majestic tree when covered with the yellow blooms, at other times the foliage is just excellent. The bark is variable, but at its best almost as good as *Abies squamata* or *Acer griseum*. The common name used here is the Nepali one, although this is also shared with a related species! In a genus of over 800 species, most do not have any common name.

p.130 **Rhododendron** *Rhododendron ponticum*

Description: Evergreen shrub or small tree to 10 m (33 ft) with stems to 15 cm (0.5 ft). *Crown* Rounded or spreading, usually on several stems which may be very contorted, rarely on a single tree-like stem. *Bark* Brown, flaking in thin scales when young, becoming rough and lightly ridged and scaly in old plants. *Shoot* Green and stout for the first winter, becoming brown in second year. *Buds* Ovoid-conical, slender pointed at the apex, scales green, 1 cm (0.4 in). *Foliage* In whorls at the tip half of the shoot with a bare lower portion; oblanceolate to elliptic lanceolate, tapered to both ends, apex acute, dark glossy green above, pale slightly yellow-green beneath, 10–20 × 2.5–6.5 cm (4–8 × 1–2.6 in); leaf stalk grooved, 1–2 cm (0.4–0.8 in), yellow-green. *Flowers* From terminal buds on previous season's shoots in early summer; in trusses of 8–20 on a rachis 3–6 cm (1.2–2.4 in); flowers light purple to rosy purple with greenish or brown spots on the upper lobe of the funnel-shaped corolla, 3.5–5 cm (1.4–2 in) across. *Fruit* Woody capsule which ripens to brown in first autumn, to 2.5 cm (1 in), splitting to release the fine seeds.

Range: Southeast Portugal, southwest Spain, southeastern Bulgaria across Turkey along the Black Sea coast to the Caucasus and also in the Lebanon.

Habitat: Shady woodlands or open hill sides in wetter localities.

Varieties: This has been crossed with related species, particularly some from North America to produce the 'Hardy Hybrids'. These have flowers of a wide range of colours, from white to darkest purple and are widely planted as garden shrub.

Synonyms: *R. ponticum* ssp. *baeticum*.

This tree has a remarkable natural distribution but in the Tertiary Period was more widespread (when it occurred in Ireland). It has recolonized much of the territory it lost, partly through its ability to naturalize but greatly aided by the attractive floral display.

SUMACHS, *RHUS*
FAMILY ANACARDIACEAE

This is a large genus of around 200 species, including trees, shrubs and climbers. The leaves are trifoliate or pinnate and set alternately on the shoots. The buds are naked and rounded. The flowers are small but set in dense terminal or axillary panicles. The fruits are often reddish and moderately showy, but the species are mainly planted for the brilliant autumn colour displayed by most species. They contain a sap which is tapped for the lacquer used as a black varnish in oriental countries. However, the sap can be toxic to some people, even when the leaves are only brushed or crushed.

p.323 **Potanin's Sumach** *Rhus potaninii*

Description: Deciduous tree 10–20 m (33–65 ft) with a
bole diameter to 80 cm (2.6 ft).
Crown Spiky with branches which ascend
and spread, usually on several stems,
becoming more rounded in old trees, with
suckers from the roots. *Bark* Grey-brown or
grey-pink, smooth or shallowly fissured.
Shoot Green with very short fine brown down
in the first year with very small oval pale
lenticels, becoming hairless and light brown-
grey or buff grey in second year, rather brittle
with a poisonous sap. *Buds* Entirely hidden
by the leaf base during the summer, ovoid,
densely white or brown hairy, 3–5 mm
(0.1–0.2 in), terminal bud absent, replaced
by a small scar when extension growth stops.
Foliage Leaves pinnate with seven, nine or
eleven oblong to oblong-lanceolate leaflets,
leaflets stalkless except for the terminal one,
all of fairly even size, apex short and slender
pointed, base tapered onto the rachis or
sometimes rounded, margin entire, glossy
green above with a few hairs, below light to
slightly glaucous green with 10–15
somewhat raised veins, hairless, leaf
including leaf stalk 20–35 × 15–25 cm
(8–14 × 6–10 in), leaflets 8–12 × 3–5.5 cm
(3.1–4.7 × 1.2–2.2 in); rachis rounded, pink
or green, softly white downy, only stalk to
terminal leaflet somewhat winged, space
between leaflets 3–5 cm (1.2–2 in), base of
leaf stalk enlarged and covering bud, with a
white poisonous sap, to 8 cm (3.1 in);
autumn colour good pink or crimson.
Flowers In conical 7–18 cm (2.8–7.1 in)
panicles terminating the shoots in early
summer, rachis downy, petals creamy white
and hairy, 3 mm (0.1 in), stamens dark
purple. *Fruit* Fruit ripens to red, downy,
5 mm (0.2 in), in dense heads.

Range: Across northern China from Gansu and
Hubei east to Shaanxi, Shanxi and Henan.

Habitat: Cultivated as an ornamental, in the wild
occurring in mixed forests.

The sap of this tree is poisonous to some
people, although other people appear

unaffected. It forms a suckering tree and is valuable for the rich autumn colour.

---

p.323   **Stag's Horn Sumach**   *Rhus typhina*

Description: Deciduous tree 5–10 m (16–33 ft) with a bole diameter to 25 cm (0.8 ft).
Crown Rounded, domed on a short bole, with suckers from the roots. *Bark* Grey-brown. *Shoot* Stout and densely covered with a thick velvety coat of brown hairs for three to four years. *Buds* Conical, light brown, hairy, enclosed in the base of the leaf stalk at first, 3 mm (0.1 in). *Foliage* Leaves pinnate 30–60 cm (12–24 in), with 13–27 leaflets; leaflets oblong-lanceolate, tapering towards the slender-pointed apex, base rounded, margin with rather regular triangular pointed teeth, upper surface sub-shiny green, hairy at first but soon hairless, with the veins slightly raised, underside glaucous green with hairs, especially along the raised veins and midrib, 4–10 × 0.8–2 cm (1.6–4 × 0.3–0.8 in); leaf stalk enclosing bud in the swollen base, with the rachis rounded and persistently white or brown pilose hairs, leaflets stalkless; autumn colour good reds and yellow. *Flowers* In large dense red panicles in early summer at the tips of the branches, usually with separate male and female trees. *Fruit* In dense pinkish-red clusters, to 12 × 4 cm (4.7 × 1.6 in), which persist on the plant, containing many small fruits which are covered with dense crimson hairs.

Range: Eastern North America from Ontario east to Nova Scotia, and south to South Carolina and Tennessee.

Habitat: Cultivated as an ornamental, in the wild occurring in light woodland and at the margins of fields.

Varieties: 'Dissecta' has the leaves beautifully cut, otherwise as for the species.

Synonyms: *Rhus hirta*.

Similar species: **Sumach** *R. coraria* (p.323) is usually a shrub only 2–3 m (6.6–10 ft) in height. It is most easily separated by the distantly winged rachis to the leaves. It is found throughout the Mediterranean region and east to Iran.

This small tree has large clusters of flowers and fruits which may persist for more than a year. The autumn colour is excellent. Its two drawbacks are that disturbed trees will sucker, throwing shoots through paved areas, shrubberies or lawns without distinction, and some people are allergic to the sap.

---

p.324 **Varnish Tree** *Rhus vernaciflua*

Description: Deciduous tree 15–20 m (50–65 ft) with a bole diameter to 80 cm (2.6 ft).
Crown Conical when young, becoming upright domed. *Bark* Dark grey with black diamond shapes which coalesce to form fissures, in old trees becoming somewhat flaky. *Shoot* Stout, pale grey, rough with orange-brown lenticels, with a poisonous sap. *Buds* Ovoid, terminal buds beaked, to circa 1 cm (0.4 in), chestnut brown. *Foliage* Leaves pinnate with three to nine pairs of spaced leaflets, 30–60 (–80) cm (12–24(–32)in) on leaf stalk to 25 cm (10 in); leaflets broad ovate, apex long and slender pointed, base oblique to heart-shaped and with a short stalk, margin untoothed, leathery, upper surface glossy fresh green and hairless, underside with velvet down, especially on the 16–30 pairs of leaflets, 10–20 × 5–10 cm (4–8 × 2–4 in); autumn colour red or crimson. *Flowers* In lax panicles to 25 × 15 cm (10 × 6 in) in the axils of the current season's shoots in the upper crown in July; flowers yellowish white. *Fruit* Glossy creamy brown to yellow flattened drupe to 8 mm (0.3 in).

Range: China east to India, but widely cultivated (and possibly native) throughout eastern Asia.

Habitat: Cultivated as an ornamental.

This is the varnish tree from which the black lacquer or varnish is obtained by tapping the trunk. The sap is poisonous. The original distribution is uncertain, as it has been cultivated for such a long period.

ROBINIAS, *ROBINIA*
FAMILY LEGUMINOSAE

This is a genus of four or five species which are restricted to eastern USA. The leaves are pinnate, with the base of the leaf stalk enclosing the buds. The shoots often have paired spines, which are derived from the stipules, on either side of the buds. The flowers are typical pea-flowers, and the fruit is a normal legume. The species are well adapted to sandy soils in dry climates (with their nitrogen-fixing bacteria) and become naturalized in these situations. Most species also sucker from the roots, often several metres from the parent tree.

p.338 **Robinia, Black Locust** or **False Acacia**
Robinia pseudoacacia

Description: Deciduous tree 15–25 m (50–80 ft) with a bole diameter of up to 2 m (6.6 ft). *Crown* Open domed, becoming rather flat topped in old trees, with suckers from the roots. *Bark* Dull grey, rough and thick with coarse forking ridges and deep furrows, in young trees much smoother and brown. *Shoot* Dark brown or reddish brown, ridged and hairless, on strong shoots with a pair of stout recurved spines at the nodes on either side of a bud, spines 0.3–2.5 cm (0.1–1 in), but on shoots in the upper crown, these are usually absent. *Buds* Small, naked, hidden in base of the leaf stalk until leaf fall. *Foliage* Leaves pinnate with four to nine pairs of leaflets, 15–30 cm (6–12 in); leaflets oval to oblong, apex rounded and slightly emarginate with a short bristle in the notched tip, base rounded with a short 2 mm (0.1 in) stalk, margin untoothed, upper surface dark blue-green to yellow-green, underside grey-green, both surfaces initially silky hairy but soon more or less hairless, 2.5–6 × 1.2–2 cm (1–2.4 × 0.5–0.8 in); leaf stalk enclosing the bud in the swollen base; autumn colour yellow. *Flowers* In June, in pendulous racemes 10–20 cm (4–8 in) which terminate the current season's growths; flowers pea-like, white fragrant. *Fruit* Narrow flat dark brown oblong pod with the upper suture winged and the lower one thickened, ripening in autumn but tardily opening to shed the 3–14 dark-brown flattened seeds.

Range: USA from Pennsylvania and Ohio south to northeast Alabama and in a band from southern Missouri to eastern Oklahoma.

Habitat: Cultivated as an ornamental and used in the stabilization of sandy soils and forest, in the wild occurring on dry to moist sands and rocky soils.

Varieties: 'Frisia' has leaves which are golden-yellow throughout the growing season, becoming greener when grown in shade. It makes a very attractive tree. It flowers as freely as the normal form, but these are lost against the leaves and difficult to notice. In 'Aurea' the leaves are only pale yellow in the spring, maturing to a lime-green colour. 'Pyramidalis' ('Fastigiata') has a narrow columnar habit with ascending branches. It is very like Lombardy Poplar in gross appearance. It is shy of flowering. 'Inermis' is a selection without spines, which is sometimes confused with 'Umbraculifera'. This makes a small tree with a dense mop-headed crown, and rarely flowers.

This makes a very fast-growing medium-sized tree. The thickly ridged and fissured bark quickly gives the appearance of an old tree. The white flowers are showy and fragrant, although this latter point is often lost as they are mainly carried at the top of the tree. It thrives on dry barren sandy soils, quickly throwing a series of suckers from the roots and spreading widely, and has a good-quality timber. These two characters have led to its being used in afforestation, particularly because as a legume it can fix atmospheric nitrogen. The timber is especially durable when used in contact with the soil, such as as fence posts. The spines are modified stipules, hence the reason for their being in pairs, one each side of a bud. The size of the spines is dependent upon the vigour of the branch, with the best spines produced by young trees and on root suckers and few or usually none on less-vigorous shoots in the crown. The branches are brittle, and liable to damage by storms.

---

p.338 **Clammy Locust** *Robinia viscosa*

Description: Deciduous tree to 10 m (33 ft) or so with a bole to 50 cm (1.6 ft) in diameter.
Crown Spreading, often shrubby, with suckers from the roots. *Bark* Dark brown and smooth, becoming fissured, with burrs. *Shoot* Dark brown, covered with clammy or sticky glandular hairs when young, spines small at some nodes, paired.
Buds Naked, hidden in swollen base of the leaf stalk during the summer.
Foliage Leaves pinnate, with 6–10 pairs of leaflets, 13–25 cm (5.1–10 in); leaflets oval or ovate, apex rounded with a small mucro, base rounded, margin untoothed, dark green above, beneath paler and hairy but becoming hairless, 2–5 × 1–2 cm (0.8–2 × 0.4–0.8 in); leaf stalk glandular.
Flowers In racemes 5–8 cm (2–3.1 in) on a glandular clammy peduncle; flowers 2 cm (0.8 in), not fragrant, petals pale rose but yellow at the base, calyx dark red.
Fruit Narrow oblong legume or pod which is covered in clammy glandular hairs, 5–8 cm (2–3.1 in); with several mottled brown and flattened seeds.

Range: Southeast USA from Virginia to Alabama.

Habitat: Cultivated as an ornamental, in the wild occurring in open forests or forming thickets.

Synonyms: *R. glutinosa.*

Similar species: *R. × ambigua* is its hybrid with *R. pseudoacacia*, being intermediate in characters. From *R. viscosa*, it inherits the pink flowers and variably glandular new growths, acquiring greater vigour from *R. pseudoacacia*. 'Decaisneana' is a handsome form of this hybrid.
Rose Acacia *R. hispida* is really a shrub but is often top worked (grafted on a stem or leg) on *R. pseudoacacia* to produce a small tree. The most obvious character is the dense crimson or purple bristles, maturing

to mid brown, which are glandular tipped.
The leaf stalk and calyx also have such
bristles. The flowers are the largest in the
genus, up to 3 cm (1.2 in), and deep rose in
colour. They are carried in clusters of 5–10
in 5–8 cm (2–3.1 in) racemes. It rarely sets
pods and spreads mainly by root suckers. It
is native to the southeast USA.

This small tree is of interest for the sticky
or clammy glandular hairs on the new
shoots, leaf stalks, flower stalks and fruit.

ROSE, ROSACEAE

This is a large family, with around 100
genera and over 3000 species. It is usually
divided into four subfamilies, centred
around the fruit characters of *Rosa* (fruit a
cluster of achenes or drupelets), *Malus* (fruit
a pome, with a cartilaginous core), *Prunus*
(fruit a fleshy drupe) and *Spiraea* (fruit
ripening as a number of follicles) but recent
work suggests that this may be a somewhat
artificial division. Of the genera featured
here, *Amelanchier* (p.501), *Cotoneaster*
(p.624), *Crataegus* (p.627), *Cydonia* (p.658),
Eriobotrya (p.675), *Eriolobus* (p.677), *Malus*
(p.823), *Mespilus* (p.839), *Photinia* (p.880),
Pyrus (p.1047) and *Sorbus* (p.1138) all
belong to the apple subfamily (Maloideae),
with *Prunus* (p.1011) in the Amygdaloideae
and *Lyanothamnus* (p.803) in the
Spireaoideae.

RUE, RUTACEAE

This is a large family of around 160 genera
and 1700 species. The leaves have very
characteristic pellucid or translucent gland
dots. Those featured here are *Citrus* (p.606),
with simple leaves, *Ptelea* (p.1039), with
trifoliate leaves, and three genera with
pinnate leaves, *Phellodendron* (p.874) and
Tetradium (p.1206) in which they are
opposite, and *Zanthoxylum* (p.1266) in
which they are alternate.

SABIA, SABIACEAE

This small family has three genera, but only *Meliosma* (p.837) is generally encountered.

WILLOW, SALICACEAE

This family contains two principal genera, *Salix* and *Populus* (p.995), and one or two small segregate genera which are often included within *Salix*. Both *Salix* and *Populus* are dioecious, normally with the male and female flowers (catkins) on separate plants. However, in *Populus*, the flowers are wind pollinated, in *Salix* pollination is by bees and other insects. *Populus* leaves are usually much broader, more ovate and large, whilst Willow leaves are often lanceolate, but there are exceptions! In *Populus*, there is generally a terminal bud, whilst in *Salix*, the shoot tip aborts. Both genera have a bias for wet or damp sites.

WILLOWS OR SALLOWS, *SALIX*
FAMILY SALICACEAE

The willows are a very large genus (with about 400 species) of woody plants, ranging in nature throughout the northern hemisphere and south into Africa and South America, and in size from prostrate subshrubs scarcely attaining 1 cm (0.4 in) to trees of 30 m (100 ft) or more. The genus is divided into numerous sections based on the floral characters, principally on characters such as the number of stamens and nectaries and whether the flowers are on leafless catkins before the leaves (see SS. *caprea*, *cinerea* ssp. *oleifolia*, *daphnoides*, *purpurea*, *viminalis* – rarely with the leaves – and *xerophila*), with the leaves as they flush (see SS. *alba*, *babylonica*, *elaeagnos*, *fragilis*, *matsudana*, × *sepulcralis* and *triandra* – rarely before the leaves), or in leafy short shoots after the leaves have matured (see SS. *borealis* and *pentandra*). The characters that allow a plant to be identified as a willow include the following: the leaves are generally lanceolate to oval and initially at least with stipules; the winter buds have only a single scale; the shoot tip aborts, so that the last resting bud will be seen (providing you are not examining a budless section of twig) to have two scars, one from the leaf stalk and a second smaller one from the shoot tip; the flowers are in separate male and female catkins, in most species from buds laid down on the previous season's shoots and opening before the leaves, but in others (e.g. *S. pentandra*) terminal on leafy shoots in early summer; the flowers have nectaries and are insect pollinated (whereas in *Populus* they are wind pollinated); the fruits ripen quickly and are a two- to four-valved capsule with minute seeds with woolly hairs to assist wind dispersal. Willows are important timber trees, with cricket bats being their most prized end product. The pliant shoots of some species are used in basketry. An active ingredient found in the bark is salicin, better known as aspirin (and now manufactured commercially) – convenient when the taxonomy of willows can be such a headache!

Informal Key

LEAVES

(i) **generally lanceolate, three or more times as long as broad:** *alba, babylonica, daphnoides, elaeagnos, fragilis, matsudana, purpurea,* × *sepulcralis, triandra, viminalis*

(ii) **generally oval or obovate, around twice as long as broad or broader:** *borealis, caprea, cinerea* ssp. *oleifera, pentandra, xerophila*

---

p.250 **White Willow** *Salix alba*

Description: Deciduous tree to 10–30 m (33–100 ft) with a bole to 1 m (3.3 ft) in diameter. *Crown* Ovoid-conic in young trees, becoming domed with ascending main branches bearing spreading or pendent twigs. *Bark* Grey-brown, deeply fissured. *Shoot* Grey-green with silky hairs pressed against shoot at first, becoming brown or olive and hairless in the second year, with two-year-old shoots usually tearing away from the branch if pulled, not snapping off at the base. *Buds* Long conic with a rounded apex, and dorsally compressed onto the twig, silky haired, yellow-green, 5 mm (0.2 in). *Foliage* Leaves lanceolate, tapering from the middle to a slender-pointed apex, more abruptly tapered to the narrow to broad wedge-shaped base, margin with fine regular teeth, upper surface covered with a silky sheen of silvery forward-pointing hairs pressed against shoot when new, retaining a light covering of hairs and giving a grey-green effect, almost smooth, underside glaucous with silky hairs and a raised rounded midrib, 5–10 × 0.5–1.5 cm (2–4 × 0.2–0.6 in); leaf stalk grooved, broadening at the base, with several glands near the blade which darken to blackish as the season progresses, 0.5–1 cm (0.2–0.4 in); autumn colour poor. *Flowers* On separate male and female trees in late April or early May with the leaves; male catkins pale yellow, 4–5 × 8 cm (1.6–2 × 0.3 in), with two yellow anthers; female catkins shorter, 3–4 cm × 4 mm (1.2–1.6 × 0.2 in). *Fruit* Broad flask-shaped capsules, ripening in July.

Range: Britain and across Europe to central Asia.

Habitat: Lowland moist sites, usually near rivers or streams.

Varieties: The silver willow, forma *argentea*, differs in having the leaves strongly covered with silky white hairs (with one cultivar name being 'Sericea' which means just that). It makes an effective display, and is also somewhat smaller in stature. Var. *britzensis* is a selection in which the one-year shoots become bright red sometime after Christmas. It is often grown as a coppiced shrub, but will make a tall tree and can be most attractive in February sunshine. The Cricket Bat Willow, var. *caerulea*, is a vigorous selection planted for the quality timber which is used to make the blanks for cricket bats. The habit is rather conical, with ascending branches, and the leaves are slightly larger than usual, to 11 × 1.5–2 cm (4.3 × 0.6–0.8 in), with fewer silky hairs, becoming hairless. The Golden Willow, var. *vitellina*, has the twigs yellow or orange-red when mature. It was formerly used in osier beds but is mainly grown for the winter colour of the twigs. It is one of the parents of *S.* × *sepulcralis* 'Chrysocoma'; *see also S.* × *rubens*, which is described under *S. fragilis*.

This fast-growing tree is attractive with its silvery foliage. In the past, the bark was used for tanning, and the wood for various purposes, including making the charcoal used in gunpowder. The wood is light and resilient, but not durable when exposed to alternations of wet and dry. In Britain, hybridization with *S. fragilis* has nearly destroyed the native population of *S. alba*, with wild trees being rare. The hybrid, *S. × rubens* (*see S. fragilis*) usually has larger leaves and a more pronounced tendency for the two-year shoots to 'crack' when bent. In pure *S. alba*, they are usually supple.

p.251 **Chinese Weeping Willow** *Salix babylonica*

Description: Deciduous tree 10–20 m (33–65 ft) with a bole diameter to 80 cm (2.6 ft).
Crown Ovoid in young trees but becoming rounded at the top and domed, with the second- or third-order branches pendulous and hanging as a curtain. *Bark* Smooth, dark green or greyish brown, smooth, becoming fissured after a few years and finally furrowed with rather thick ridges. *Shoot* Slender, green and white downy at the tips of branches, becoming hairless and shiny green further back, in the second year shiny brownish green or green with rounded erupting lenticels. *Buds* Ovoid, blunt, green or brown, 4 mm (0.2 in), the buds have a ridge behind and an indentation in front. *Foliage* Leaves lance-shaped or somewhat sickle-shaped, tapering gently to both ends but with a long slender twisted drip tip, margin with small-forward pointing or hooked teeth, new foliage white hairy but most hairs soon lost, with the upper surface becoming glossy green with a slightly raised rounded midrib, underside bluish green, 8–13 × 1.5–2 cm (3.1–5.1 × 0.6–0.8 in), stipules rounded and leafy at shoot tips only and soon lost; leaf stalk slightly grooved, green, persistently downy, 1 cm (0.4 in); no significant autumn colour. *Flowers* In the spring before the leaves on separate male and female trees, female flowers on short lateral shoots, 2.5 cm (1 in). *Fruit* Catkins.

Range: China.
Habitat: Cultivated as an ornamental.
Synonyms: *S. pendula*.

This is the original Weeping Willow but has been displaced by its hybrids with *S. alba* and *S. fragilis*, which are listed as *S. × sepulcralis*, which have greater vigour and more strongly coloured shoots over winter. The Latin name is taken from Psalm 137 where the Exiles record hanging their harps as they wept for Jerusalem. However, the willow in this case is *Populus euphratica* (*see* p.996). *S. babylonica* is one of the trees whose wild origins is lost. All the evidence points to China, and that it was taken along the Silk Route to western Asia and then on to Europe from early times.

Boreal Willow *Salix borealis*

Description: Deciduous small tree, or shrubby.
Crown Rounded, with thick erect stems.
Shoot Densely white tomentose when young, becoming less so. *Foliage* Leaves elliptic to rounded in outline-ovate, apex acute to short and slender pointed, base rounded wedge-shaped, margin deeply toothed with large glands, leathery, green to glaucous beneath with net veining and whitish hairs, drying to blackish, 2–7(–10) × 1–4 cm (0.8–2.8(–4) × 0.4–1.6 in).
Flowers After the leaves on leafy stalks; male catkins ovoid to oblong, yellow, 1.5–2.5 cm (0.6–1 in); female catkins 1.5–3 cm (0.6–1.2 in). *Fruit* Lax, 5–8 cm (2–3.1 in).
Range: Northern Scandinavia (Norway and Finland) across northern Russia.
Habitat: Wetlands.
Similar species: **Dark-leaved Willow** *S. nigricans* is a related but more shrubby species, usually less than 4 m (13 ft) in height. It has a much wider distribution across central and northern Europe, south to the Pyrenees and Corsica and east to Bulgaria. It differs in flowering before the leaves, in the more slender twigs which are less hairy, the rounded-ovate to lanceolate leaves which

are usually distinctly glaucous beneath except towards the tip which is green and much less markedly toothed or sub-entire with less prominent veins.

In Britain, *S. myrsinifolia* differs in the ovate leaves with sharp forward-pointing teeth, but is only found as a shrub.

This makes a small tree restricted to the far north.

p.252 **Goat Willow** *Salix caprea*

Description: Deciduous tree usually 8–12 m (26–39 ft) but up to 20 m (65 ft) with a bole diameter up to 1 m (3.3 ft).
Crown Domed, frequently on several stems. *Bark* Smooth, pale grey, developing orange fissures. *Shoot* Initially grey and downy, becoming hairless and deep reddish brown or yellow-green or nearly black, without ridges beneath the bark. *Buds* Ovoid, pointed, glossy red or chestnut brown, to 4 mm (0.2 in). *Foliage* Leaves ovate, oval or ovate-oblong, apex bluntly pointed to shortly pointed, base rounded to somewhat heart-shaped, margin with shallow crenate to sharp teeth, upper surface blistered with veinlets impressed, dark green to greyish green, initially hairy but soon hairless, underside with raised veins, glaucous grey and softly downy, 5–10 × 3–6 cm (2–4 × 1.2–2.4 in); leaf stalk hairy, dark red, 1 cm (0.4 in); stipules on vigorous shoots ear-like, acute with wavy toothed margins, often falling early. *Flowers* Before the leaves; male catkins ovoid to oblong, silvery but with yellow anthers, 3 cm (1.2 in); female catkins pale green, less showy. *Fruit* Lax, 3–7 cm (1.2–2.8 in), maturing in May–June.
Range: Throughout Europe.
Habitat: Widespread.
Varieties: 'Kilmarnock' and 'Weeping Sally' are two clones grown for their very pendulous habit. They only grow as tall as the stem onto which they are grafted. 'Kilmarnock' is male, 'Weeping Sally' female.

Similar species: *S. coaetanea* is a related shrub or small tree to 9 m (29 ft). It is sometimes treated as a variety of *S. caprea* (var. *sphacelata*). It differs in the shoots becoming hairless and dull brown, with darker red and more hairy buds. The leaves are usually somewhat narrow obovate-elliptic, densely silky haired on both surface when new but only remaining so on the underside. They are wedge-shaped at the base, acute at the tip, more or less untoothed and do not have stipules. The catkins open with the leaves, which is the meaning of 'coaetanea'. It is recorded from northern Scandinavia, the Scottish Highlands, the Alps and Russia.

This tree is very attractive for the pussy-willow catkins on the males in late winter or early spring. Although widespread, it usually shows some adulteration due to introgression (hybridization) by other willows. Pure *S. caprea* is difficult to root from cuttings, relying on seed for distribution. The seed is scattered by the wind in June. It is only viable for a short period of time, and depends upon a period of rain to germinate. Provided these conditions are met, it will grow on sand, gravel as well as richer and more permanently moist soils. The wood on two-year-old twigs is smooth beneath the bark.

p.253 **Rusty Sallow** or **Common Sallow**
Salix cinerea ssp. *oleifera*

Description: Deciduous tree 5–15 m (16–50 ft) with a bole diameter to 30 cm (1 ft), rarely much larger.
Crown Ovoid, usually as a tree but sometimes on several stems.
Bark Smooth, grey-brown, becoming pitted and then fissured brown.
Shoot Greenish grey-brown, densely covered with short pale hairs, becoming hairless and shiny green-brown by autumn, in the second year grey-brown, peeled bark with scattered striate ridges. *Buds* Ovoid, bluntly pointed, often with a flattened rim,

hairy, green or pink, 0.3–1 cm (0.1–0.4 in). *Foliage* Leaves variable but mainly obovate to broadly oblanceolate, apex rounded to a short acute point, base wedge-shaped, margin with small rounded forward irregular teeth and often wavy, sometimes untoothed, upper surface initially hairy but only remaining so on the raised main veins, dark shiny green with a finely blistered surface, underside glaucous blue with six to nine pairs of raised veins and covered all over with scattered short rufous hairs, 2–9 × 1–3 cm (0.8–3.5 × 0.4–1.2 in), occasionally larger (to 16 × 5 cm (6.3 × 2 in)); leaf stalk round, grey haired, with an enlarged base, to 1 cm (0.4 in); stipules half-moon shaped, usually persistent on late summer shoots when similar to leaf texture and colour but often shed early; autumn colour poor. *Flowers* In late winter or early spring before the leaves; male catkins with two pale yellow stamens, cylindrical or ovoid, 2–3 cm (0.8–1.2 in) (rarely to 5 cm (2 in)) by 0.6–1 cm (0.25–0.4 in); female catkins green, grey haired. *Fruit* Cluster of capsules each to 1 cm × 2.5 mm (0.4 × 0.1 in), containing many silky seeds.

Range: Western Europe, including Britain.

Habitat: Hedgerows, moist sites and disturbed land.

Varieties: Typical **Grey Sallow** *S. cinerea* ssp. *cinerea* differs in having grey hairy leaves with usually larger and more prominent stipules. It is restricted to wet sites but has a wider distribution across Europe and from eastern England. It rarely grows much taller than 6 m (20 ft).

Synonyms: *S. atrocinerea*.

Similar species: *S. pedicelallata* is an allied species from the Mediterranean region. It is most easily differentiated by the hairless ovary of the female catkins, and the larger leaves with 10–12 pairs of veins.

This small tree is one of the pussy-willows, so called for the soft yellow catkins on male plants before the leaves which act as harbingers of spring. It makes a small fast-growing tree.

p.255   **Violet Willow**   *Salix daphnoides*

Description: Deciduous tree 10–15 m (33–50 ft) with a bole diameter to 50 cm (1.6 ft).
Crown Upright as a young tree, becoming rounded or domed in old trees.
Bark Grey, smooth, with some fissuring in old trees. *Shoot* Initially with silky white hairs and shiny green, then developing a waxy glaucous bloom which often rubs off with time but may persist in patches especially below the buds, green-purple to shiny reddish brown.
Buds Ovoid, pressed against shoot, laterally compressed, crimson, hairless or with stiff hairs at the base, 5 mm (0.2 in).
Foliage Oblong to narrow obovate, apex acute, base wedge-shaped, margins with regular glandular teeth, upper surface dark lustrous green and initially silky hairy, beneath glaucous with net veining, 7–12 × 2–3 cm (2.8–4.7 × 0.8–1.2 in), occasionally wider or longer; stipules leafy, often persistent, ovate to slender pointed, to 1.2 × 5 mm (0.5–0.2 in); leaf stalk grooved, densely hairy, 0.7–2 cm (0.3–0.8 in). *Flowers* On previous season's shoots in late winter with silky hairs; male catkins cylindric, to 4 cm (1.6 in), with two stamens per flower; female catkins smaller. *Fruit* Narrow ovoid capsule 4 × 1.5 mm (0.2 × 0.1 in).

Range: Central Europe from France, Italy and the Baltic states east across to the Balkans.

Habitat: Moist sites but frequently planted for the male catkins and the waxy bloomed shoots.

Varieties: Ssp. *acutifolia* is a related willow which is often treated as a separate species. It differs in the narrower leaves which have more lateral veins (15 or more, compared to 8–12 pairs) and taper to the apex, and the slender and often pendent shoots. It occurs in Russia, extending east as far as central Asia.

This makes a neat small tree with strongly bloomed shoots and attractive silky catkins. However, for best twig effect, like other willows it can be hard pruned in spring.

p.254 **Hoary Willow** *Salix elaeagnos*

Description: Deciduous shrub or small tree rarely to
16 m (52 ft).
Crown Upright, shrubby. *Shoot* Slender,
covered with a grey or whitish felty down,
becoming hairless, yellowish to reddish
brown. *Buds* Yellowish. *Foliage* Leaves
erect or spreading around the shoot, linear-
lanceolate to narrow linear, tapering to both
ends, apex acute, margin recurved, finely
glandular toothed, above at first densely
woolly, becoming dark green and hairless
with impressed veins, underside
persistently blue-grey felted, veins raised
but obscured by the woolly hairs, 5–13 ×
0.3–2.2 cm (2–5.1 × 0.1–0.9 in); leaf stalk
short, to 5 mm (0.2 in); stipules usually
absent. *Flowers* With the leaves, erect, to
6 cm (2.4 in) on 1 cm (0.4 in) stalks.

Range: Central Europe from France and Spain east
to the Ukraine, from Italy in the south and
north to Poland, and in Asia Minor.

Habitat: Wet sites, near watercourses, particularly in
limestone areas.

Varieties: Ssp. *angustifolia* from southern France and
Spain has leaves at the narrow end, to no
more than 5 mm (0.2 in).

Synonyms: *S. incana.*

The slender hoary leaves distinguish this
tree, although it is also similar to *S.
viminalis*. From *S. viminalis*, it is best
distinguished by the finely toothed leaves
and the stamens which have the filaments
joined in their basal part. In *S. viminalis*,
they are free or separate, whilst the leaves
are coarser and shining silvery grey beneath.

p.250 **Crack Willow** *Salix fragilis*

Description: Deciduous tree 10–15 m (33–50 ft) with a
bole diameter to 1 m (3.3 ft).
Crown Broad and rounded in old trees with
spreading branches, more ovoid-conical when
young and growing vigorously. *Bark* Grey,
becoming coarsely and deeply fissured with
thick ridges, scaly when young. *Shoot* Grey-

green, ridged and thinly pubescent when young, becoming hairless, round and shiny olive-brown by autumn, brittle at the point of attachment of the mature shoots to the previous year's growth. *Buds* Long conic with a rounded or bluntly acute tip, dorsally compressed onto the twig, yellow-green, slightly hairy, 0.3–1 cm (0.1–0.4 in). *Foliage* Leaves lanceolate, tapering from the lower third to a half to the slender-pointed apex, broadly wedge-shaped to rounded at base, margin with a raised rim due to the coarse and unevenly glandular teeth, upper surface mid to dark shiny green, soon hairless, underside glaucous bluish white with fine silky hairs pressed onto shoot, tending to become hairless, veins in circa 20 weak pairs, 9–15 × 1.5–3 cm (3.5–6 × 0.6–1.2 in); leaf stalk grooved, lightly haired with several blackish glands near the junction with the leaf blade, 0.5–1.5 cm (0.2–0.6 in); stipules soon falling, only leafy on coppice shoots; autumn colour poor. *Flowers* Separate male and female trees, appearing with the leaves in April and May; male catkins cylindrical, 4–6 cm (1.6–2.4 in), pale yellow, with usually two, rarely three, golden-yellow anthers; female flowers similar. *Fruit* Broadly ovoid capsule 4–5 × 2.5 mm (0.2 × 0.1 in).

Range: From Norway south to England, Spain and Portugal and eastwards across Europe to Romania.

Habitat: Moist lowland fertile sites, often planted or spread by man.

Varieties: Var. *russelliana* makes a somewhat taller tree to 25 m (80 ft), with less brittle twigs and rather larger and narrow leaves, mainly 13–15 × 2–2.5 cm (5.1–6 × 0.8–1 in). It is the commonest form in England and Ireland but usually as a planted tree. Its origin is not known. Var. *decipiens* (syn. *S. decipiens*) is generally a lower growing form, usually only 5–7 m (16–23 ft) in height. The twigs are often stained reddish when young, maturing to yellow ochre. The leaves are fully hairless, to 9 × 2–3 cm (3.5 × 0.8–1.2 in). It is commoner on the continent.

Similar species: *S. × rubens* (p.250) is a hybrid of *S. fragilis* with *S. alba* and is common, perhaps commoner than pure *S. fragilis*. It is closest to *S. fragilis*, differing in having silky white hairs on the young leaves and the mature leaves being narrower and more gradually tapered. From *S. alba*, it differs in the larger leaves which become hairless. A bewildering array of intermediate forms arise when *S. × rubens* backcrosses with either parent.

The glossy and rather larger leaves which are less silky haired distinguish this tree from *S. alba*. The best character is the habit of the mature shoots snapping off cleanly just above their junction with the older shoot. This is best tested on the previous year's shoots, although the current ones will snap off after they have become woody and firm in late summer. Three-year old and older shoots normally do not snap. The broken pieces will root if they land in water or suitably moist soil, which is probably the function of the phenomenon as the fruit capsules tend to be sterile.

p.251 **Peking Willow** *Salix matsudana*

Description: Deciduous tree 10–15 m (33–50 ft) with a bole diameter to 50 cm (1.6 ft).
Crown Ovoid with sinuous erect branches bearing contorted erect or spreading foliage. *Bark* Smooth and shiny grey-brown, becoming pale grey and fissured.
Shoot Slender and greenish yellow in the first year with a dense covering of short down, in the winter shiny olive, later grey-green, contorted and tortuous.
Buds Ovoid-cylindric with a rounded apex, pale green, hairy, 2 mm (0.1 in).
Foliage Leaves narrowly lanceolate, broadest in lower third, gently tapering to a tail-like tip and a rounded or somewhat wedge-shaped base, margin finely serrate with small forward hooked teeth, upper surface cupped and shiny green with short white hairs pressed onto shoot especially along the slightly raised midrib,

undersurface bluish green, sparsely haired and with a prominently raised midrib, 4–10 × 0.6–1.6 cm (1.6–4 × 0.25–0.6 in); leaf stalk grooved, densely hairy, circa 5 mm (0.2 in); autumn colour poor.
Flowers With the leaves on short leafy shoots in spring, in cylindrical spikes 1.5–2.5 cm (0.6–1 in).

Range: Cultivated in China.

Habitat: Planted in parks and gardens.

Varieties: 'Pendula' is a female weeping form, less attractive than *S.* × *sepulcralis* 'Chrysocoma'.

S. matsudana is closely related to *S. babylonica* and included in it by some authorities. The species comes from northern China.

---

p.255 Bay Willow *Salix pentandra*

Description: Deciduous tree 10–20 m (33–65 ft), but sometimes a shrub, with a bole diameter to 80 cm (2.6 ft).
Crown Broad domed. *Bark* Grey or grey-brown, lightly fissured with orange.
Shoot Glossy olive-green when young, becoming brown to reddish by autumn, supple, hairless. *Buds* Ovoid-conic, pointed, glossy dark brown, 5 mm (0.2 in).
Foliage Leaves ovate-elliptic, oblanceolate or broad lanceolate, apex slender pointed, base rounded to broad wedge-shaped, margin with fine regular glandular teeth, thick, upper surface lustrous dark green, underside paler, hairless on both sides, 5–12 × 2–5 cm (2–4.7 × 0.8–2 in); leaf stalk with several stalkless apical glands, less than 1 cm (0.4 in); stipules small, soon falling.
Flowers In May or June on short leafy shoots; male flowers cylindrical, dense, yellow, 2–8 × 1–1.5 cm (0.8–3.1 × 0.4–0.6 in); female flowers shorter. *Fruit* Capsule to 1 cm (0.4 in), ripening in July.

Range: North England, north Wales, Scotland, Northern Ireland and across northern-central Europe to Asia, extending south only on high mountains such as the Pyrenees.

Habitat: Streamside sites and on moist soils.
Varieties: 'Patent Lumley' is a selection with large particularly glossy leaves and is the best ornamental form.

This tree is attractive in flower, at least in male plants, and in the glossy leaves. These are somewhat similar in appearance to those of the True Bay or Bay Laurel (*Laurus nobilis*).

---

p.253 **Purple Osier** *Salix purpurea*

Description: Deciduous bush or small tree to 5 m (16 ft). *Crown* Slender, upright and often on several stems. *Bark* Smooth and pale grey with a yellow inner bark which has a very bitter taste. *Shoot* Slender, flexible and hairless, glossy, often purplish where exposed and buff beneath. *Buds* Mixed on the shoot with some in opposite pairs, others alternate, long ovoid, pointed, dark red or yellow, 4 mm (0.2 in).
Foliage Leaves obovate-oblong to linear-oblanceolate, generally slender and 3–15 times as long as wide but broader above the middle, apex acute or slender pointed, base wedge-shaped or rounded, margin very finely toothed towards the apex, dark green above, pale or glaucous beneath, hairless except when very young when sometimes thinly hairy, 3–12 cm × 3–8 mm (1.2–4.7 × 0.1–0.3 in); leaf stalk short, less than 6 mm (0.25 in); stipules small and soon lost.
Flowers Before the leaves in spring in dense cylindrical catkins 1.5–4.5 cm (0.6–1.8 in); male catkins with the two purplish red stamens fused along the filament and appearing as a single stamen. *Fruit* Capsules ovoid, hairy.
Range: Widespread throughout Europe except the far north, North Africa and across temperate Asia to northern China.
Habitat: Wet places.
Varieties: Ssp. *lambertiana* is restricted to lowlands. It has broader leaves to 2 cm (0.8 in) which are serrate throughout.

This make a small shrubby tree, usually with several slender stems. It is one of several species used for osier production, producing long straight flexible slender canes.

p.251 **Weeping Willow** *Salix × sepulcralis* 'Chrysocoma'

Description: Deciduous tree 10–18 m (33–60 ft) with a bole diameter to 1.3 m (4 ft).
Crown Rounded with strongly weeping branchlets which grow vertically downwards. *Bark* Smooth and golden-green in young trees, maturing to grey-brown after several years and developing deep coarse ridges and fissures.
Shoot Slender, pendulous, green and downy at first but ripening to golden-green by mid-winter. *Buds* Narrowly ovoid, pressed onto shoot, green but brown by winter, with silky hairs, especially near the tip, 5 mm (0.2 in). *Foliage* Leaves narrowly lanceolate, gently tapering to a long tail-like tip and a wedge-shaped base, margin with small forward hooked teeth, upper surface matt to shiny deep green with silky white hairs especially when young and a slightly raised midrib, undersurface bluish green, silky haired and with a prominently raised midrib, 7–13 × 0.7–2 cm (2.8–5.1 × 0.3–0.8 in); leaf stalk grooved, hairy, with a few black glands, less than 1 cm (0.4 in); autumn colour poor. *Flowers* With the leaves on short leafy shoots in spring, not showy, mainly male but some female.
Range: Cultivated hybrid.
Habitat: Planted in parks and gardens.
Varieties: Typical *S. × sepulcralis* has branchlets which are brown or olive in colour and are less pendulous.
Synonyms: *S. chrysocoma*.
Similar species: *S. × pendulina* is the hybrid between *S. babylonica* and *S. fragilis*; it has leaves which are distinctly and somewhat irregularly serrate and much less hairy. It is occasionally encountered in collections as the cultivars 'Elegantissima',

'Pendulina' and 'Blanda', with the former pair strongly weeping but with 'Blanda' only lightly weeping.

This is the Common Weeping Willow. It is a cross of *S. alba* (var. *vitellina*) with *S. babylonica*, combining the golden shoots of the one and the pendulous branches of the other. It is believed to have arisen in Germany at Späth's nursery in the 1880s, since when it has been extensively planted. It is an excellent tree associated with water and large gardens, but not a wise choice for planting in small gardens (and especially not near houses where the subsoil is a shrinkable clay and the foundations are not exemplary). It suffers from an anthracnose disease, caused by the fungus *Drepanopeziza sphaeroides*, which affects the new shoots and leaves and can cause extensive loss of foliage and vigour.

p.255 **Almond-leafed Willow** *Salix triandra*

Description: Deciduous shrub or tree to 10 m (33 ft). *Crown* Rounded to erect. *Bark* Smooth, grey-brown at first but flaking in irregular patches to reveal orange-brown beneath. *Shoot* Shiny green-brown or reddish-brown, hairless, angled. *Buds* Conical, acute at the apex and pressed against the shoot, initially finely hairy, later hairless. *Foliage* Leaves lanceolate to oblong-lanceolate or elliptic, apex acute to slender pointed, base rounded or wedge-shaped, margin with serrate teeth, upper surface dark shiny green, underside glaucous or green, hairless on both sides, 4–11 cm (1.6–4.3 in) (rarely to 15 cm (6 in)) by 1.5–2.5 cm (0.6–1 in); leaf stalk glandular towards the apex, 1–1.5 cm (0.4–0.6 in); stipules ear-like, large and persistent with glandular serrations. *Flowers* With the leaves, less often just before the leaves and with a few through the summer, erect, cylindrical; males 3–8 cm (1.2–3.1 in), fragrant, with three stamens; female catkins shorter and more dense. *Fruit* Flask-shaped.

Range: Temperate Europe and Asia, not in far north and rare in the south.

Habitat: River banks.

Varieties: The typical form has the leaves green beneath, ssp. *discolor* applying to those forms with the leaves glaucous on the underside. It is commoner in the south and east of the range.

Synonyms: *S. amygdalina*

The male catkins, having three stamens, distinguish this small tree from other commonly cultivated or indigenous species. It is widely used in the production of osiers, to make canes for basketry. For this, the trees are coppiced or cut back to ground level each winter, throwing many erect shoots 2–3 m (6.6–10 ft) by autumn. The cut shoots are then either dried, boiled or soaked to remove the bark.

---

p.254 **Osier** or **Common Osier** *Salix viminalis*

Description: Deciduous shrub or tree to 10 m (33 ft). *Crown* Narrow upright or rounded, dense and leafy. *Bark* Grey, fissuring. *Shoot* Grey downy when young, maturing to glossy hairless yellow-green or olive-green, with the leaves and buds densely set on the shoot. *Buds* Ovoid, bluntly pointed or pointed, initially hairy but becoming hairless and yellow, brown or red. *Foliage* Leaves linear to oblanceolate, tapering gradually to a long slender-pointed tip, base narrow wedge-shaped, margin untoothed, rolled or recurved, often wavy, upper surface dull green and sparsely haired with many (20–35) pairs of lateral veins, underside silvery grey with a silky down and a prominent midrib, 10–25 × 0.5–2.5 cm (4–10 × 0.2–1 in); leaf stalk hairy, to 1 cm (0.4 in); stipules narrow lanceolate, soon falling. *Flowers* Before the leaves, rarely with them; catkins erect, to 2.5 × 2 cm (1 × 0.8 in); male flowers with yellow anthers and with free (not joined) filaments. *Fruit* Flask-shaped.

Range: Central and eastern Europe, from France to the central Balkans, occurring in Britain and western Europe but possibly only naturalized there.

Habitat: Wet and damp locations.

Similar species: *S. rossica* replaces it towards the east in Russia. It differs in the buds being more bluntly pointed, the leaves being rounded at the base and in floral details.

This has long been cultivated in osier beds for canes for basketry. It is debated as to whether it is indigenous to Britain and western Europe, or just widely naturalized. It makes a dense leafy plant, with some similarities to *S. elaeagnos*, differing (from *elaeagnos*) in the filaments being free (cf. partly fused in *elaeagnos*) and the different hairs on the underside of the leaves. As with most other willows, this tree hybridizes freely when grown with other species, both in the wild and in cultivation.

Finnmark Willow *Salix xerophila*

Description: Deciduous shrub or tree to 6 m (20 ft). *Crown* Erect. *Shoot* Dark grey-brown, dull, usually woolly, wood not striated. *Buds* Conical, angled, red-brown. *Foliage* Leaves oblanceolate or oblong, apex acute or with a short uncinate point, base rounded to broad wedge-shaped, margins untoothed, upper surface greyish with seven or eight pairs of curved veins, 3–5 × 1–1.8 cm (1.2–2 × 0.4–0.7 in); leaf stalk 6–8 mm (0.25–0.3 in); stipules absent. *Flowers* Before the leaves, catkins 1.5–3 cm (0.6–1.2 in); flowers with a deeply parted stigma and hairy filaments. *Fruit* Capsule beaked, 8 mm (0.3 in).

Range: Norway, northern Finland and across Russia to the Ural Mountains.

Habitat: Beside lakes and rivers.

Synonyms: *S. cinerascens*.

This is a small northern tree or shrub with a silvery appearance.

ELDERS, *SAMBUCUS*
FAMILY CAPRIFOLIACEAE

This is a genus of around 40 species, consisting of shrubs or small trees with pithy stems or herbaceous plants. The leaves are pinnate, with 3–11 leaflets and set in opposite pairs on the shoot. The flowers are in terminal umbels or panicles, and are followed by the juicy fruits which contain three to five nutlets. The soft pith is used for holding botanical specimens when cutting thin sections, whilst the flowers and fruits (but especially the flowers) make an excellent cordial. Raw fruits are poisonous (as is the foliage) but heating destroys the toxin.

p.315   **Elder** *Sambucus nigra*

Description: Deciduous shrub or small tree to 10 m (33 ft) with a bole diameter up to 50 cm (1.6 ft). *Crown* Rounded, often on several stems. *Bark* Light brown to greyish with fissures and furrows. *Shoot* Stout with a thick amorphous pith, green at first with raised lenticels, becoming grey or brown, starting to fissure in the second year. *Buds* In opposite pairs, conic, dark brown, 3 mm (0.1 in). *Foliage* Leaves 10–30 cm (4–12 in), pinnate with five to seven, rarely three or nine, leaflets ovate to oblong-elliptic, tapering to a slender point, base rounded, margin with fine forward-pointing serrations, upper surface dull matt green, underside pale whitish green, both sides with stiff sparse hairs and more hairy veins, 4.5–12 × 3–5 cm (1.8–4.7 × 1.2–2 in); leaflets with a short stalk 2 mm (0.1 in) except on the terminal leaflet to 1 cm (0.4 in), rachis and leaf stalk grooved, hairy; autumn colour poor. *Flowers* In flat-topped corymbs 10–25 cm (4–10 in) across at the end of the current season's shoots in June–July, flowers white, strongly scented. *Fruit* Globose berry with a persistent calyx and three to five seeds, ripening from green through to blackish purple in September, 5–6 mm (0.2–0.25 in), in large drooping clusters.

Range: Widely distributed throughout Europe, north Africa and western Asia.

Habitat: Woodlands and hedgerows, especially in damp places.

Varieties: Several horticultural varieties are cultivated, including 'Aurea', with leaves yellow-green, forma *laciniata*, with the leaves cut and divided into a filigree, and 'Marginata', with the leaves bordered with creamy white.

This is a common weed species, as which it is much maligned. It usually forms a shrub but trees to 10 m (33 ft) or more are occasionally encountered. The flowers can be used to make a delicately flavoured and scented cordial, whilst both the flowers and fruits are used to flavour wines and in alternative medicine. The thick pith is soft and is used to hold botanical specimens for sectioning.

p.315 **Red-berried Elder** *Sambucus racemosa*

Description: Deciduous shrub or small tree to 5 m (16 ft).
Crown Rounded. *Bark* Light brown. *Shoot* Stout, green at first with prominent lenticels, hairless, light brown by autumn, pith cinnamon-coloured. *Buds* In opposite pairs, ovoid, pointed, reddish, 5 mm (0.2 in). *Foliage* Leaves pinnate with five to seven sub-sessile leaflets 15–23 cm (6–9.1 in); leaflets ovate, elliptic to ovate-elliptic, tapering to a slender-pointed apex, base wedge-shaped, margin sharply and regularly toothed, hairless on both surfaces, 4–10 × 2–4 cm (1.6–4 × 0.8–1.6 in). *Flowers* Yellow-white, in terminal corymbs on the new growths in April, 4–7 cm (1.6–2.8 in) across. *Fruit* Globose scarlet berry, 5 mm (0.2 in); seed finely striated.

Range: Central Europe eastwards to west Asia and Siberia.

Habitat: Shady montane woods.

Varieties: 'Plumosa' is a selection in which the leaves are deeply toothed, giving a rather feathery appearance. In 'Plumosa Aurea', the foliage is an attractive golden colour.

This plant is similar to *S. nigra*, and most easily distinguished when in fruit. It also differs in the pith being brown or brownish, not white as in *S. nigra*.

SOAP BERRY, SAPINDACEAE

This is a large tropical and warm temperate family whose only hardy tree genus is *Koelreuteria* (p.772).

SASSAFRAS, *SASSAFRAS*
FAMILY LAURACEAE

This genus consists of three species, one each from eastern North America, China and Taiwan. The leaves are variable, often on the same shoot.

p.129 **Sassafras** *Sassafras albidum*

Description: Deciduous tree 15–20 m (50–65 ft) with a bole diameter to 50 cm (1.6 ft).
Crown Dense and ovoid as a young tree, becoming domed, usually with root suckers present under the canopy. *Bark* Light brown, deeply furrowed with narrow ridges. *Shoot* Light green to yellow-green with a light waxy bloom in the first year with darker round lenticels, hairless or hairy, bright shiny green with more prominent oval pale lenticels in the second and third years, remaining green for several years, fragrant if snapped or crushed. *Buds* Ovoid to obovoid, pointed at the apex, light green with hairy scales which are brown at the tips, 0.2–1.2 cm (0.1–0.5 in).
Foliage Leaves variable on the same shoot, oval to obovate with one or two shallow or deep lobes, apex rounded, blunt to faintly notched, base wedge-shaped to long wedge-shaped, margin untoothed, lobes rounded, with sinuses rounded and extending from one-quarter to four-fifths the distance to the midrib, upper surface deep matt to glossy green, hairless, underside glaucous or pale green with raised midrib and veins which

loop forwards around the leaf margin, hairless or variously hairy, 7–20 × 3–13 cm (2.8–8 × 1.2–5.1 in); leaf stalk flattened on top, green or purple-pink, 1.5–4 cm (0.6–1.6 in); autumn colour yellow, orange or red; crushed foliage aromatic. *Flowers* In spring, usually dioecious, greenish yellow. *Fruit* Elliptic bluish-black shiny berry 1 cm (0.4 in), containing a single seed and set in a red cup on a long red stalk; seed shiny brown.

Range: Eastern North America from southern Ontario across to Maine, south to central Florida, east to east Texas and north to Michigan.

Habitat: Cultivated as an ornamental, in the wild occurring on moist sandy soils and in forest clearings.

Varieties: Var. *molle* covers the plants with down on the leaf undersides and shoots. It occurs throughout the range of the species.

Synonyms: *Laurus albida*.

The leaves are most variable in their lobing, with the lobes compared to hands in mittens, especially applicable where there is a single side lobe resembling the 'thumb' and a larger mass for the 'gloved fingers'. The tree is aromatic. An oil extracted from the roots and bark is used to perfume soap, to make sassafras tea and to flavour beer. The leaves have a somewhat gummy and spicy taste, rather numbing the mouth.

PRINCE ALBERT'S YEW, *SAXEGOTHEA*
FAMILY PODOCARPACEAE

This is a monotypic genus, unusual in the Podocarpaceae in having unwinged pollen and fruits which consist of a number of seeds.

---

p.60 **Prince Albert's Yew** *Saxegothea conspicua*

Description: Evergreen tree 15–20 m (50–65 ft) with a bole diameter to 50 cm (1.6 ft).
Crown Conical or bushy in young trees, older trees may be slender conical or

remain bushy (especially in colder districts), branches pendent.

Bark Purple-brown, smooth and often fluted, becoming scaly in old trees and flaking to reveal red-brown. *Shoot* Purple, especially on the upper side on strong shoots in full sun, and green (underside and weaker shoots) in first winter, with ridges from the decurrent leaf base, hairless, becoming brown or dark brown in second or third year. *Buds* Rounded or globose enlargement of the shoot tip, green or purple, 1–2 mm (0.1 in). *Foliage* Whorled with five or six side shoots and a longer extending shoot from each branch tip; leaf arrangement rather irregular and somewhat sparse, parted below, pointing forwards or spreading at the sides, and erratic above but usually with a narrow parting, rather dry and noisy or rattling to the touch; narrow lanceolate, widest in lower third, apex acute, pointed, base rounded to a short purplish leaf stalk, upper surface with a raised midrib, sub-glossy green without stomata, underside with two silvery white bands of stomata and two flat light green margins, persists for three to six years, 1.5–3 cm × 2–4 mm (0.6–1.2 × 0.1–0.2 in); crushed foliage scentless. *Flowers* On previous season's shoots in early summer; male cones ovoid, in pairs at base of leaves. *Fruit* Globose or mace-like, 1.5 cm (0.6 in) across, composed of around 15 overlapping triangular pointed scales which are glaucous green and become fleshy when ripe, seeds carried only on the upper scales, fruit on a scaly leafless stalk 1–1.5 cm (0.4–0.6 in).

Range: Southern Chile and adjoining western Argentina.

Habitat: Cultivated in Europe as an ornamental.

This tree is yew-like in its foliage. However, the fruit shows it belongs to the quite different family Podocarpaceae, although even here it is unique in the pollen grains not having bladder-like wings. It was named for Prince Albert of

Saxe-Coburg-Gotha, Queen Victoria's consort. It thrives best in the milder and damper parts, being reduced to a small bush and needing woodland shelter in cold districts.

SCHIMA, *SCHIMA*
FAMILY THEACEAE

This is a genus of up to 15 species, although one revision has treated all the taxa as forms of one variable species. The flowers are Camellia-like, but the fruit is a woody capsule with the seeds winged along one side.

p.239 **Schima** *Schima argentea*

Description: Evergreen tree 10–15 m (33–50 ft) with a bole diameter to 50 cm (1.6 ft).
Crown Ovoid or columnar. *Bark* Smooth, brown, becoming cracked with pale greybrown fissures. *Shoot* Green and sparsely hairy in the first year with oval orange lenticels, becoming olive-brown and later browner. *Buds* Conical, with a slenderpointed apex, silky haired, 8 mm (0.3 in).
Foliage Leaves narrowly oval-lanceolate to oblanceolate or narrowly obovate, apex rather abruptly tail-like, base wedgeshaped, margin untoothed, texture cardlike, upper surface glossy green and finely net-veined, underside glaucous blue-green with sparse hairs and a raised midrib, 7–13 × 2–5 cm (2.8–5.1 × 0.8–2 in); leaf stalk ridged from the decurrent leaf base, downy, green, 1.5–2 cm (0.6–0.8 in); no autumn colour, leaves persisting two years.
Flowers Singly (rarely in pairs or threes) in the axils towards the tips of the current season's growth in late summer on 1.5–2.5 cm (0.6–1 in) hairy stalks, with a pair of notched obovate soon-falling bracts (7 × 2 mm (0.3 × 0.1 in) long) beneath the flower, the buds are globose and open to 3–4 cm (1.2–1.6 in) across and strongly fragrant, the five ivory-white obovate petals are joined at the base and contrast with the massed rounded knob of yolk-

coloured stamens. *Fruit* Globose woody capsule which has a flattened apex, hairy, ripening after one year, splitting into five sections, seeds flattened, with a narrow wing on one side.

Range: Yunnan, China and probably adjacent Burma and Vietnam.

Habitat: Cultivated as an ornamental, in the wild occurring in warm temperate forests.

Similar species: *S. khasiana* from northeast India across Yunnan to Vietnam differs in the larger leaves (12–17 × 4–7 cm (4.7–6.7 × 1.6–2.8 in)) which are green beneath and have toothed margins, in the larger flowers and in the pair of bracts beneath the flowers being almost 2 × 1 cm (0.8 × 0.4 in).

This can be a very attractive tree with its fragrant white Camellia-like flowers but is not hardy in cold districts. It requires a lime-free soil.

PEPPER TREES, *SCHINUS*
FAMILY ANACARDIACEAE

This is a genus of trees and shrubs from tropical and South America. The leaves are simple in some species but in *S. molle*, which is the more widely cultivated and a very attractive tree in warmer parts of Europe (and the rest of the World), the leaves are much divided. The fruit is a round, one-seeded drupe.

p.322 **Peruvian Pepper Tree** *Schinus molle*

Description: Evergreen tree to 15 m (50 ft) with a bole to 40 cm (1.3 ft).
Crown Round or spreading, with graceful drooping branchlets. *Bark* Light brown, scaly. *Shoot* Slender, brown, variously hairless or finely haired. *Foliage* Leaves drooping, narrowly oblong in outline with 10–20 pairs of stalkless leaflets, with or without a terminal leaflet, and with a milky sap; leaflets linear-lanceolate or narrow lanceolate, usually curved at the tip which is slender pointed, margin untoothed or finely toothed, more or less

hairless and yellow-green on both surfaces,
2–5 cm × 5–6 mm (0.8–2 × 0.2–0.25 in);
rachis flattened or with very narrow wings.
Flowers Dioecious, with separate male and
female trees; inflorescence is a lax terminal
or subterminal panicle 20–30 cm
(8–12 in) with numerous small flowers,
from April to August; flowers 3 mm
(0.1 in) across, with five yellowish-white
petals. *Fruit* In large drooping clusters
which hang down from the branchlets
throughout the crown; globose with a
single seed, rosy red to pink, outer layer
aromatic, juicy at first and resinous,
5–6 mm (0.2–0.25 in).

Range: Peru south to northern Argentina, South
America.

Habitat: Cultivated as an ornamental in southern
Europe.

Similar species: *S. terebinthifolius* (p.322) differs in the fewer
leaflets which are oblong-ovate, the rachis
being distinctly winged and the fruits
bright red and less than 5 mm (0.2 in). The
branch structure is more erect, without the
graceful pendent habit which is so
attractive in Peruvian Pepper Tree.

This tree is attractive especially in autumn
when carrying the fruits, whose
resemblance to peppercorns gives the
common name. The fruits also have a
peppery taste. The Latin name is taken
from the South American Indian vernacular
name, 'Molle', not from the Latin *mollis*,
which is soft (usually inferring softly
downy, which this tree is not).

UMBRELLA PINES, SCIADOPITACEAE (SYNONYM: TAXODIACEAE IN PART)

This is a monotypic family.

UMBRELLA PINES, *SCIADOPITYS*
FAMILY SCIADOPITACEAE

This is a monotypic genus, clearly differentiated by the
whorls of curious leaves at the shoot tips.

p.60 **Japanese Umbrella Pine**
Sciadopitys verticillata

Description: Evergreen tree to 20 m (65 ft) with a bole
diameter to 50 cm (1.6 ft).
Crown Conical and dense, usually clothed to
the ground. *Bark* Dark red-brown,
becoming fissured and peeling in vertical
strips. *Shoot* Mid to light brown in first
winter, becoming paler or more yellow-
brown, with brown scale leaves and rounded
pimples spirally arranged on the stout shoot.
The occasional side branch may originate
from these pimples, especially near the base
of the shoot. *Buds* Rounded half-moon to
globose, red-brown, not resinous, 3×5 mm
(0.1×0.2 in). *Foliage* Set in whorls splayed
out like the spokes of an umbrella, initially
terminating a current year's shoot but
persisting for three years, subtended by small
brown scale leaves similar to those along the
shoot; leaves linear, soft and flexible, apex
rounded and notched, dark glossy green with
a groove on the upper surface, flat below with
a wider white or yellowish groove in which
are located the stomata, $5–15$ cm $\times 3–4$ mm
($2–6 \times 0.1–0.2$ in); crushed foliage resin
scented. *Flowers* From buds in the terminal
whorl of previous season's leaves; male cones
in clusters of 10–15, yellow, 2.5 cm (1 in).
Fruit Ovoid, initially green but ripening
over two years to dark brown, $5–8 \times 3–5$ cm
($2–3.1 \times 1.2–2$ in); scales dimpled, softly
woody, flexible, five to nine seeds per scale,
flattened.

Range: Central Honshu, Kyushu and Shikoku,
Japan.

Habitat: Cultivated in Europe as an ornamental, in
the wild occurring in forests and tolerating
wet sites.

This tree is unlike any other in the foliage in
its umbrella-like spokes. Although restricted
to Japan, it has been found in fossils
throughout the northern hemisphere. The
leaves are believed to be two leaves fused
together along their length and are thus
somewhat analogous to the short shoot of
Pinus. The presence of the scale leaves along

the shoot and subtending the whorl of leaves is also reminiscent of *Pinus*, whilst the cone structure and texture suggests *Sequoiadendron*. If the leaves are snapped in half, separate vascular bundles can be seen in each half.

FOXGLOVE, SCROPHULARIACEAE

This is a large family, composed mainly of herbs. The only tree genus common in cultivation in Europe is *Paulownia* (p.871).

REDWOOD, *SEQUOIA*
FAMILY TAXODIACEAE

This is a monotypic genus, characterized by the rather yew-like foliage, very thick soft bark and small cones which ripen in the first autumn.

---

p.58 **Redwood, Coastal Redwood** or **Sequoia**
Sequoia sempervirens

Description: Evergreen tree 15–50 m (50–165 ft) with a bole diameter to 2 m (6.6 ft) in Europe. *Crown* Conical when young but quickly becoming columnar, with short spreading or slightly pendulous side branches with upswept tips, trunk often surrounded by coppice shoots at the base. *Bark* Red-brown, very thick and fibrous, developing deep furrows and ridges, very soft. *Shoot* Green for several years, becoming red-brown often somewhat irregularly, slender. *Buds* Green, ovoid, at the tips of strong branches, 4 mm (0.2 in). *Foliage* Arranged in flat spreading sprays with the shoots angled forwards; leaves increase in length towards middle of current season's growth and then taper off into the bud scales, with sprays having the longest foliage in the middle; central leaves are flattened, spreading either side of the shoot, linear with an acute apex and tapered at base and decurrent on the shoot, mid matt green above with a few stomata, beneath silvery green due to two waxy bands of stomata, to 2 cm × 2 mm (0.8

× 0.1 in); leaves at tips of shoots (and less so
at base) are more scale-like, pressed against
shoot with free tips, as short as 4 mm
(0.2 in); crushed foliage has a waxy or citrus
scent. *Flowers* At end of previous season's
shoots in late winter; male cones elliptic,
7–9 mm (0.3–0.4 in), yellow-brown in early
spring. *Fruit* Ripens in first autumn,
rounded oblong, pendulous, with around
twenty peltate scales, 1.5–3 cm (0.6–1.2 in).

Range: Coastal California from San Francisco north
to southwest Oregon.

Habitat: Planted as an ornamental in Europe, but in
the wild restricted to the fog belt along the
northern Californian coast.

Varieties: No botanical varieties but 'Adpressa' is a
cultivar occasionally grown in specialist
collections. This has short broad foliage
which is loosely pressed against the shoot.
The new foliage emerges creamy white,
before turning green.

Synonyms: *Taxodium sempervirens.*

This is a very fast-growing tree with an
excellent red timber. The tallest living tree,
but not the bulkiest, is a redwood in the
Redwood Creek grove, with a height of
114 m (375 ft). It requires a moist climate
for good growth, not liking prolonged
periods of dry sub-freezing temperatures
which will burn-off the foliage and may
cause dieback. However, as it is one of the
few conifers which will coppice (it regrows
from a cut stump), it usually reclothes itself
next summer. The genus is named after
Sequoiah, the son of a British trader and a
Cherokee squaw, and who invented an
alphabet for the Cherokee language.

WELLINGTONIA, *SEQUOIADENDRON*
(SYNONYMS: *SEQUOIA* IN PART, *WELLINGTONIA*)
FAMILY TAXODIACEAE

This is a monotypic genus which has been included in *Sequoia*.
However, it differs in the leaves being all awl-like (in *Sequoia*
only those directly below the cone are awl-like), and in the
larger cones which have more seeds and which take two full
years to ripen. The bark is very thick as in *Sequoia*, but firmer.

p.58 **Wellingtonia, Sierra Redwood** or
Big Tree *Sequoiadendron giganteum*

Description: Evergreen tree to 50 m (165 ft) with a bole
of up to 3 m (10 ft) in diameter.
Crown Conical, soon columnar conical,
with short spreading side branches.
Bark Red-brown, soon deeply fissured and
fibrous, soft and very thick. *Shoot* Green
for first year, becoming red-brown by
patches during the second year, slender.
Buds Hidden in axils of the scale leaves.
Foliage Arranged in rather hard sprays
rising above and around the shoots; leaves
spirally set, scale-like with long free tips to
6 mm (0.25 in), decurrent on the shoot at
base, shiny grey-green with scattered white
stomata visible under a hand-lens.
Flowers On previous season's shoot in
spring; male cones terminal, stalkless,
yellow; female cones green. *Fruit* Ovoid,
green and ripening to green or brown at
end of second summer, 4–5 cm (1.6–2 in).

Range: California, in the Sierra Nevada.

Habitat: Widely cultivated as an ornamental from
Spain to western Norway, in the wild
occurring on moist rocky soils with *Abies
concolor*.

Varieties: No botanical varieties, but there are a few
cultivars. Most spectacular is 'Pendulum'
which has a more or less erect central axis
from which totally pendulous shoots hang
down. As the stem is not quite erect, it can
produce some weird and character effects as
it snakes across a space, especially when
secondary leaders develop. However, it is
not to some people's liking! 'Glaucum' was
named for slightly more glaucous or waxy
foliage but has a very narrow habit.

Synonyms: *Sequoia gigantea, Wellingtonia giganteum*.

This is a fast-growing and vigorous tree and
is usually the tallest tree around, especially
in drier areas. This makes it susceptible to
lightning strikes, which usually kill the top
few metres but which can be more
spectacular! It is hardier than *Sequoia*, from
which it is distinguished by the scale-like
foliage and larger cones. Unlike *Sequoia*, it

cannot regrow from the stump if cut down and does not have a useful timber. It is susceptible to honey fungus, *Armillaria*.

QUASSIA, SIMAROUBACEAE

This is a small and rather disparate family of mainly tropical trees, with only *Ailanthus* (p.488) and *Picrasma* (p.912) as temperate tree genera.

ROUGH BINDWEED, SMILACACEAE (SYNONYM: LILIACEAE IN PART)

This small family is allied to the Lily family and sometimes included within it. Only *Smilax* is featured here.

ROUGH BINDWEEDS, *SMILAX*
FAMILY SMILACACEAE

This is a large genus of perhaps 200–300 species of climbing woody or herbaceous monocotyledons. It has wiry stems armed with many small hooked spines and tendrils, which scramble through vegetation and can make progress tedious! The leaves are ovate, with three to nine prominent veins. The fruit is a black or red berry.

p.166 **Rough Bindweed** *Smilax aspera*

Description: Evergreen scandent plant, capable of growing through small trees and shrubs to 6 m (20 ft).
Crown Depends upon support.
Shoot Green for several years then brown, armed with short stout and usually hooked spines, four to six angled and zig-zagged.
Foliage Leaves broad ovate to deltoid, apex acute or shortly slender pointed, base heart-shaped, sometimes truncate, margin with prickly teeth, with five to nine main veins which curve forwards and are somewhat parallel, 4–10 × 2–8 cm (1.6–4 × 0.8–3.1 in); leaf stalk hairless or with short spines, 0.6–2.5 cm (0.25–1 in).

Flowers In terminal or axillary racemes from 3–10 cm (1.2–4 in); flowers pale green and fragrant. *Fruit* Red, globose, 7 mm (0.3 in).

Range: From the Mediterranean region east to central Asia and south into India.

Habitat: Scrub or light woodland.

The wiry stems are armed with short yet sharp spines. Where it clambers through thickets and scrub, it can make access difficult.

PAGODA TREES, *SOPHORA* (SYNONYMS: *STYPHNOLOBIUM*)
FAMILY LEGUMINOSAE

This is a genus of around 50–80 species of trees and shrubs and a few herbaceous plants. The leaves are pinnate and enclose the bud in the base of the leaf stalk. The flowers are pea-like, and followed by a legume in which the pod is conspicuously constricted between the seeds. The cultivated tree treated here is now sometimes placed in a segregate genus *Styphnolobium*.

p.339 **Pagoda Tree** *Sophora japonica*

Description: Deciduous tree 15–25 m (50–80 ft) with a bole diameter to 80 cm (2.6 ft).
Crown Ovoid, becoming irregularly domed. *Bark* Dark brown or grey, with broad ridges or corrugations. *Shoot* Green for several years, hairless or downy when very young. *Buds* Minute, hidden in the enlarged base of the leaf stalk, 1 mm (0.1 in). *Foliage* Leaves pinnate, 15–25 cm (6–10 in) with 9–15 leaflets, leaflets ovate, narrow ovate to ovate-oblong, apex acute, base rounded, margins untoothed, dark matt green above and hairless, underside bluish or glaucous green with whitish adpressed hairs and a raised main vein, 3–6 × 2–3.5 cm (1.2–2.4 × 0.8–1.4 in); leaf stalk and rachis round, green, leaflets set in pairs or alternately on a hairy stalk of 2–3 mm (0.1 in), base of leaf stalk encloses the bud; no autumn colour. *Flowers* Terminal on

current season's growths of mature trees in August–September, in broad panicles 15–30 cm (6–12 in) high and wide, flowers pea-like, creamy white, 1.2–1.5 cm (0.5–0.6 in), calyx green, bell-shaped, shallowly toothed. *Fruit* Pod with one to six seeds, initially downy, soon hairless, 5–8 cm (2–3.1 in).

Range: Northern China.

Habitat: Cultivated as an ornamental, in the wild occurring in mixed woodland.

Varieties: 'Pendula' is a selection with weeping branches.

Synonyms: *Styphnolobium japonicum.*

This tree was described from Japan but is an early introduction from China. It makes a large and long-lived tree, which in hot summers can be covered in the white or creamy-white blooms, but does not bloom as a young tree.

ROWANS AND WHITEBEAMS, *SORBUS* (SYNONYMS: *ARIA, TORMINARIA, CORMUS*; *MICROMELES, PYRUS* IN PART) FAMILY ROSACEAE

This is a large grouping of species. It is divisible into five genera which are not closely related. However, taxonomy is for our convenience, not for that of plants, and it is more convenient to treat these groups as subgenera. This is because the groups hybridize rather freely, producing fertile offspring. The main groupings are the pinnate-leaved rowans (subgenus *Sorbus*) and the entire-leaved whitebeams (subgenus *Aria*, including here subgenus *Micromeles*). In both groupings, there are a number of sexual diploid species and a larger number of tetraploid (and a few triploid) apomictic species. In the apomictic species, the seed is produced vegetatively and is therefore identical to the mother parent. However, pollination is required for seed set (actually to support the developing seed, not to fertilize the seed). With tetraploids, fertile pollen is produced and therefore a single tree may set seed, but triploids require pollination by another tree to set seed. Most diploids also need pollination by another tree, although here the process is sexual and the offspring are genetically different from the parents, so isolated diploid trees often have few seed-bearing fruits. This is of some horticultural interest as the fertile fruits (i.e. those with seeds) are usually larger and more showy.

The other three groupings are monotypic, with a single, mainly European, species in each. In subgenus *Cormus*, the leaflets are pinnate as in subgenus *Sorbus* but the carpels are connate, always five and inferior (that is below the level of the calyx), compared to the three to five more or less fused and partly superior carpels in subgenus *Sorbus*. The only species is *S. domestica*. In subgenus *Torminaria*, the styles are in pairs and united for more than half their length, the two carpels are surrounded by a layer of stone cells and the leaves are sharply lobed. This consists of *S. torminalis*, with a second Turkish taxon which is usually treated as a variety but sometimes as a second species. The fifth grouping is subgenus *Chamaemespilus*, which only contains the shrubby *S. chamaemespilus* from central and southern Europe (this is a shrub to 2–3 m (6.6–10 ft) with pink erect petals and leaves which are simple, but only sparsely hairy). Between these five groupings there are a large number of natural and fertile hybrids, a few of which are diploids but most are apomictic tetraploids or triploids. The largest number of hybrid species derive from the *Aria* group crossed with either subgenus *Sorbus* or subgenus *Torminaria*, but some may contain genes from three different subgenera. These taxa of hybrid origin are clones which reproduce by seed and are apomictic.

The flowers of all *Sorbus* are in terminal corymbs which are composed of a few to many small side branches. The number of styles varies from two to five, with a similar number of carpels. There are two ovules in each carpel, although often only one develops. The fruit starts green but it ripens red, russet, white or yellow. In some species, particularly those with small leaflets, there is often a tendency for the fruit to start crimson and fade to white speckled pink. Generally, the fruit has a persistent calyx, but in some species here included in subgenus *Aria* (but often treated as a separate subgenus) the calyx is deciduous, falling off to leave a round depression in the fruit apex (*see S. alnifolia* and *S. folgneri*). *Sorbus* are mainly grown as amenity trees, although a liqueur is made from some fruits.

Informal Key

LEAVES
(i) **simple, toothed but not lobed, but without free leaflets:** *alnifolia, aria, bristoliensis, folgneri, graeca, hedlundii, megalocarpa, thibetica, vestita*
(ii) **simple, lobed, but without free leaflets:** *aria, arranensis, austriaca, devoniensis, intermedia, latifolia, mougeotii, torminalis, umbellata*

(iii) **pinnate, all leaflets roughly the same size:** *aucuparia, cashmiriana, commixta, domestica, esserteauiana, glabrescens, harrowiana, 'Joseph Rock', microphylla, oligodonta, rufopilosa, sargentiana, scalaris, vilmorinii*

(iv) **with 1–2 (rarely to 6) pairs of free leaflets at the base but the terminal portion one very much larger leaflet:** *hybrida, meinichii, thuringiaca*

FRUIT

(i) **russet or brown, usually with prominent lenticels:** *devoniensis, hedlundii, latifolia, megalocarpa, thibetica, torminalis, vestita*

(ii) **orange, red to vermillion, mainly without prominent lenticels:** *alnifolia, aria, arranensis, aucuparia, austriaca, bristoliensis, commixta, domestica, esserteauiana, folgneri, graeca, harrowiana, hybrida, intermedia, meinichii, mougeotii, sargentiana, scalaris, vilmorinii, thuringiaca*

(iii) **yellow:** *aucuparia, esserteauiana, 'Joseph Rock'*

(iv) **white to pink:** *cashmiriana, glabrescens, harrowiana, microphylla, oligodonta, rufopilosa, vilmorinii*

---

p.216 **Alder-leafed Whitebeam** *Sorbus alnifolia*

Description: Deciduous tree 10–15 m (33–50 ft) in height with a bole diameter to 30 cm (1 ft). *Crown* Ovoid or columnar, with ascending or ascending and then splayed branches. *Bark* Smooth, dark grey. *Shoot* Olive-brown, white hairy, becoming dark brown in later years. *Buds* Ovoid, reddish brown, 6 mm (0.25 in). *Foliage* Leaves ovate, apex short and slender pointed, base rounded, margin with rounded or acute teeth, somewhat doubly toothed or lobulate towards the apex, upper surface matt green and slightly persistently hairy, corrugated with the 6–12 pairs of parallel veins somewhat impressed, underside light green, lightly hairy with prominent veins, 4–10 × 2–7 cm (1.6–4 × 0.8–2.8 in); leaf stalk grooved, pilose, 1 cm (0.4 in); autumn colour apricot-pink or orange-scarlet. *Flowers* In small tight corymbs, white. *Fruit* Rounded to obovoid, bright red or deep pink with small dark lenticels, 0.8–1.5 cm

(0.3–0.6 in), with a dimple at the tip from where the calyx lobes have fallen.

Range: Widely distributed in eastern Asia from Japan, Korea, central, western and northeastern China and Maritime Russia.

Habitat: Cultivated as an ornamental, in the wild occurring in mixed forests as an understorey element.

Varieties: 'Skyline' is a selection with an upright ovoid crown of ascending branches raised from Chinese seeds.

Synonyms: *Micromeles alnifolia*.

This is an unusual whitebeam which is sometimes placed in the genus, *Micromeles* although its affinities lies closer to *S. aria* itself. The fruits are attractive but many will be small and sterile unless two or more clones are grown together to allow for cross-pollination.

---

p.214 **Whitebeam** *Sorbus aria*

Description: Deciduous tree 15–25 m (50–80 ft) with a bole diameter to 80 cm (2.6 ft).
Crown Broad conic in young trees, becoming domed or rounded domed in old trees with rather radiating branches.
Bark Smooth, grey in young trees, becoming scaly and fissured at the base in old trees. *Shoot* Green and densely coated with white matted hairs when young, maturing to green and brown and hairless or with a few hairs only remaining.
Buds Ovoid, pointed, green and brown with white hairs on the scale tips, 1 cm (0.4 in). *Foliage* Leaves elliptic to ovate, acute or bluntly pointed at the apex, base rounded to wedge-shaped, margin sharply serrate with the 8–13 (rarely to 15) pairs of veins ending in large acute teeth or small sharp lobules which are curved towards the apex, upper surface initially densely coated with white or silvery hairs which are soon shed to show shiny to dull yellow-green to dark green with the veins impressed, underside persistently silvery haired with raised veins, 6–12 × 3–8 cm

(2.4–4.7 × 1.2–3.1 in); leaf stalk initially white-hairy, 1–2 cm (0.4–0.8 in); autumn colour russet to yellow. *Flowers* In large white-haired corymbs 5–10 cm (2–4 in) across in May–June, flowers dull white, 1.3 cm (0.5 in) diameter, two styles, anthers cream or pink. *Fruit* Corymbs nearly hairless by autumn, fruit ovoid to sub-globose, longer than broad, scarlet-red with small scattered lenticels, usually woolly towards the base, 0.8–1.5 cm (0.3–0.6 in).

Range:
Southern England, Ireland (Galway) east across southern Germany to Transylvania and the northern Balkans and south through Italy, Corsica and Spain, also in the Atlas Mountains in Morocco but naturalized elsewhere.

Habitat:
In the open or in open woodland on base-rich sites, especially those derived from limestone and chalk, but also occurring on acid sandy soils, but not tolerating waterlogged conditions.

Varieties:
'Lutescens' is the most commonly planted form, selected for the vivid new foliage. 'Majestica' ('Decaisnea') has larger leaves which are oblong-elliptic, to 15 cm × 9 m (6 in × 29 ft) and rather more finely toothed than usual in the species. They become deep rather glossy green once the grey hairs on the upper surface of the leaf are lost. 'Cyclophylla' has almost round leaves. In 'Chrysophylla', the leaves are yellowish on the upper surface and narrower, elliptic to obovate.

Synonyms:
Crataegus aria, Pyrus aria, Aria nivea.

This is a very variable diploid species. The new foliage is silvery white or whitish grey, but the hairs on the upper side of the leaves are soon shed. The fruits are attractive, both visually and to birds. It is also very tough, tolerating harsh conditions provided there is adequate drainage. It is thus frequently planted as a landscape tree. Normally, 15 m (50 ft) is the mature height, but when drawn up in sheltered woodland, 30 m (100 ft) has been attained.

p.272 **Arran Whitebeam** *Sorbus arranensis*

Description: Deciduous tree 5–10 m (16–33 ft) with a
bole diameter to 30 cm (1 ft).
Crown Slender, conic to columnar.
Bark Grey or grey-brown. *Shoot* Grey-
brown, slender. *Buds* Ovoid-conic,
pointed, reddish brown, 1 cm (0.4 in).
Foliage Leaves elliptic to rhombic-elliptic,
apex acute, base wedge-shaped, margin with
oblong or oblong-lanceolate acute lobes
which extend about three-quarters the
distance to midrib or occasionally almost to
the midrib near the base, with teeth mainly
on the lower side of the lobe, upper surface
slightly hairy at first but maturing hairless,
dark and slightly shiny yellow-green,
underside greenish-grey hairy, but whiter
when young, seven to nine pairs of veins,
prominent below, 6–9 × 3–6 cm (2.4–3.5 ×
1.2–2.4 in); leaf stalk 1–2 cm (0.4–0.8 in);
autumn colour russet. *Flowers* In small
narrow corymbs in May–June, flowers dull
white, 1 cm (0.4 in), two styles, anthers
cream or pink, receptacle woolly.
Fruit Ovoid, scarlet with few inconspicuous
lenticels, 0.8–1 cm (0.3–0.4 in).
Range: Isle of Arran, off the west coast of Scotland.
Habitat: Scattered trees in moorland, planted as an
amenity tree.
Synonyms: *Pyrus arranensis, Sorbus intermedia* var.
arranensis.

This tree is one of a number of apomictic
taxa which derive from tetraploid members
of the *S. aria* group (in the case of *S.
arranensis* this is *S. rupicola* (p.272)) with *S.
aucuparia* which is diploid. They are found
from Norway across Europe to the Caucasus
region. They are generally triploid with
three sets of chromosomes, thus two-thirds
whitebeam and one-third rowan. As
triploids, they require pollination by a
related tree, but as apomicts they normally
breed true. However, occasionally hybrids
or back-crosses with *S. aucuparia* occur, and
this has happened on Arran, producing the
tetraploid *S. pseudofennica*, which has one or
two pairs of free leaflets at the base.

p.332 **Rowan** or **Mountain Ash** *Sorbus aucuparia*

Description: Deciduous tree 8–10 m (26–33 ft) but occasionally to 20 m (65 ft), with a bole diameter usually 30–60 cm (1–2 ft). *Crown* Mainly ovoid or conical, especially in young trees, often becoming rounded or irregular and spreading. *Bark* Grey or silvery grey, smooth and shiny, on old trees grey-brown and developing scaly ridges. *Shoot* Green at first with a loose floccous white indumentum and elliptic buff lenticels, becoming hairless and shiny, in the second year grey-brown or purplish grey. *Buds* Ovoid-conic, purplish, with dense white hairs which are often brown at the tip, not gummy, 1–1.7 cm (0.4–0.7 in). *Foliage* Leaves pinnate, with around 13–15 leaflets (occasionally 9–19), 20 × 12 cm (8 × 4.7 in); leaflets ovate-oblong, stalkless except for the terminal one, acute at the apex, base rounded, oblique, margin coarsely serrate with triangular teeth, upper surface matt green with slightly impressed veins and a few scattered white hairs, lower surface light green with prominent raised veins, white hairy, especially on the veins, 3–7 × 1.5–2.3 cm (1.2–2.8 × 0.6–0.9 in); rachis grooved (especially at the slightly hairy nodes where there are small peg-like projections) or round, green or purplish; leaf stalk round, 3 cm (1.2 in); autumn colour usually poor brown but sometimes yellow, orange, red or crimson, especially in moist montane environments. *Flowers* In large terminal erect or nodding corymbs in late spring, 10–15 cm (4–6 in) across on woolly stalks, flowers creamy white, 1 cm (0.4 in), with a disagreeable odour. *Fruit* Fruit oblate (shaped rather like a pumpkin with the two ends flattened), ripening by August from green through orange to scarlet with few inconspicuous lenticels, with the three or four woolly carpel apices protruding, 6–9 mm (0.25–0.4 in).

Range: Throughout Europe eastwards to Turkey and the Caucasus, and in North Africa from the Atlas Mountains.

Habitat: Woodlands as an understorey, in mountain areas occurring on open hillsides, much planted as an amenity tree.

Varieties: Commonly grown cultivars include: 'Asplenifolia', which has the leaves more deeply cut, with the teeth themselves often toothed, and more downy than usual; 'Beissneri', which has a narrow upright habit with yellow-green deeply cut leaves. This is best after rain as the bark on the trunk and branches shows coppery brown; 'Dirkenii', has the leaves yellow when young; 'Edulis', is a selection which has somewhat larger fruits (to 1 cm (0.4 in)) which are sour but not bitter and therefore more palatable for jellies, etc.; 'Fructu Luteo' (syn. 'Xanthocarpa'), has the fruits orange-yellow, and often lasting longer as birds find them less attractive; 'Sheerwater Seedling', has a narrow crown of ascending branches.

Similar species *S. sibirica* (probably better treated as subspecies *sibirica*) from Siberia and which is almost totally hairless.

S. maderensis, from a few mountain-top sites in Madeira, which has rusty coloured hairs on the buds and bloomed fruits. It is very close to the form of *S. aucuparia* from Calabria, Corsica and Sicily (ssp. *praemorsa*), which has the leaflets bluntly pointed at the apex and more parallel sided, with a shorter leaf stalk (less than 2 cm (0.8 in)).

Ssp. *glabrata* is a shrubby form which has less hairy leaflets which taper to an acute apex, hairless inflorescences and fruits longer than broad. It is recorded from Scandinavia, the Baltic region and northwest Russia and possibly the mountains of central Europe.

Synonyms: *Pyrus aucuparia.*

Rowan is a very common and widespread small tree, although in the right woodland conditions it can be drawn up to make 20 m (65 ft) or so. It is attractive for the flowers and fruits, although the latter may be quickly devoured by birds and often do not last to provide autumn colour in suburban gardens. Frequently called Mountain Ash (as it usually vies with *Betula pubescens* to be the last deciduous tree towards the treeline), it is not related or similar to the ashes differing in the alternative arrangement of the leaves, the flowers and the fruits. The word 'rowan' is probably of Norse origin.

---

p.217 **Austrian Whitebeam** *Sorbus austriaca*

Description: Deciduous tree to 10 m (33 ft) with a bole diameter to 30 cm (1 ft).
Crown Conic to rounded. *Bark* Grey to grey-brown, smooth. *Foliage* Leaves elliptic to broadly ovate, acute at the apex, base wedge-shaped or decurrent on the leaf stalk, margin with triangular acute lobes which extend one-third the distance to the midrib and have narrow, often overlapping sinuses, upper surface shiny mid to dark green, soon hairless, underside with a persistent covering of grey or dull whitish hairs and 8–11 raised veins, 8–13 × 4–7 cm (3.1–5.1 × 1.6–2.8 in). *Flowers* In small corymbs, creamy-white. *Fruit* Globose, red with many large lenticels, 1.3 cm (0.5 in) across.

Range: Austria east to the Carpathian Mountains in Romania and south into the Balkans.
Habitat: Montane woodland sites.

This tree is similar to *S. intermedia* in its foliage but appears to have more influence of the *S. aria* group in its make-up, as shown by the redder fruit colour and whitish grey hairs of the leaves.

---

p.217 **Bristol Gorge Whitebeam**
Sorbus bristoliensis

Description: Deciduous tree to 10 m (33 ft) with a bole diameter to 40 cm (1.3 ft).
Crown Ovoid or tall rounded dome., *Bark* Smooth, grey, becoming fissured at the base and scaly. *Shoot* Initially covered in a greyish white wool, which is lost by

autumn to reveal the shiny green shoot with round to elliptic pale lenticels, in the second year grey-brown, chocolate brown or red-brown. *Buds* Ovoid, pointed, red-brown at the tips, otherwise brownish green, 5 mm (0.2 in). *Foliage* Leaves obovate to a greater degree, ranging from broad to narrow obovate, oblong-obovate to rhombic-obovate, apex rounded to a short acute point, base wedge-shaped or slightly rounded, margin scarcely toothed in the lower half, with small lobes above the centre which become smaller towards the apex, maximum depth of lobes one-sixth way to the midrib, upper surface dull shiny green, smooth and soon hairless, underside with a dense covering of silvery white hairs all over, including on the eight to nine (rarely seven or ten) pairs of raised veins, 7–10 × 3.5–6 cm (2.8–4 × 1.4–2.4 in); leaf stalk grooved, green with a loose floccous covering of wool, 1.3–2.2 cm (0.5–0.9 in); autumn colour russets. *Flowers* In small corymbs which are loosely woolly, flowers creamy white with pink anthers and a woolly receptacle, in early summer (late May to June). *Fruit* Green and woolly whilst young, ripening to bright orange with a mixture of small and medium-sized lenticels especially towards the base of the fruit, longer than broad, 0.9–1.1 cm (0.4 in), although some infertile smaller ones always present in the truss.

Range: Bristol Gorge, England.

Habitat: Rocky woods and in scrub on carboniferous limestone.

Similar species: *S. karpatii* is one of several similar apomictic species or 'microspecies' from central Europe. It has more globose fruits which are cinnabar-red and dotted with small lenticels. In its native woodlands in Hungary, it makes a small tree to 5 m (16 ft).

This species is a triploid, i.e. with three sets of chromosomes, and includes chromosome sets from *S. aria* and *S. torminalis*. It is apomictic, and thus breeds true.

p.334 **Kashmir Rowan** *Sorbus cashmiriana*

Description: Deciduous tree to 6 m (20 ft) with a bole diameter to 25 cm (0.8 ft).
Crown Rounded dome. *Bark* Grey-brown. *Shoot* Reddish brown, fairly stout, hairless or soon hairless. *Buds* Ovoid-conic, reddish brown with rufous hairs on the scales tips and margins, to 1.4 cm (0.6 in). *Foliage* Leaves pinnate with 15–21 leaflets, to 23 cm (9.1 in); leaflets ovate-lanceolate or lanceolate, apex acute, margin coarsely toothed almost to the oblique or rounded base, grey-green, initially white hairy but usually soon hairless, non-papillose beneath, 3–5.5 × 1.5–2 cm (1.2–2.2 × 0.6–0.8 in); autumn colour early, pale yellow. *Flowers* In broad corymbs with large flowers 1 cm (0.4 in) across with pale pink petals, four or five styles, 3.5–4 mm (0.1–0.2 in).
Fruit Ovoid, soft and fleshy, pure white or with a faint pink flush on the calyx lobes, ripening in August and remaining until November when becoming bruised and brown, 1.5 × 1.3 cm (0.6 × 0.5 in); calyx lobes protuberant and fleshy; seeds 5 × 2.5 mm (0.2 × 0.1 in), brown.

Range: Kashmir region of the northwest Himalayas.

Habitat: Cultivated as an ornamental, in the wild occurring as an understorey shrub in *Cedrus deodara* and mixed forest.

Varieties: Several closely related taxa are found, including one with pale pink fruits, in Kashmir.

This small tree has the largest fruits of any of the glistening white-fruited species. They are more attractive on the bush after the leaves have fallen, remaining in sheltered localities until well into autumn. However, in exposed sites, they become bruised and turn an unattractive brown. The flowers are also amongst the largest in the genus, and are distinctive with their pale pink petals. It is an apomictic tetraploid species, coming true from seed.

p.333 **Japanese Rowan** *Sorbus commixta*

Description: Deciduous tree 8–18 m (26–60 ft) with a bole diameter to 40 cm (1.3 ft).
Crown Upright when young, becoming rounded or remaining columnar in woodland conditions. *Bark* Silvery grey, smooth with pale brown lenticels.
Shoot Green and pink brown with prominent raised oval buff lenticels at first hairless or thinly pubescent, grey-brown in the second and later years. *Buds* Narrow long conic, sharply pointed, shining red-green or red, non-sticky to very sticky with few rufous or no hairs, to 2 cm (0.8 in).
Foliage Leaves obovate in outline, 20–30 cm (8–12 in), pinnate with 13–17 leaflets; leaflets narrow or broad lanceolate to oblanceolate, tapering to the long slender-pointed apex, base wedge-shaped, oblique, stalkless, margin sharply serrate with forward-pointing teeth, upper surface sub-shiny deep green with impressed veins and cupped along the midrib, underside whitish to glaucous green, smooth with a raised midrib, slightly rufous hairy to hairless, 4–7 × 1–2.5 cm (1.6–2.8 × 0.4–1 in); leaf stalk and rachis finely grooved, hairless, pink or pink tinged; autumn colour in a sequence from yellow or purple to brilliant scarlet. *Flowers* In terminal corymbs 9–15 cm (3.5–6 in) across of small whitish flowers in late spring. *Fruit* Globose, shiny orange-red, 7–8 mm (0.3 in) across, often persisting and unpleasantly tasting.
Range: Throughout Japan, also in Korea and on Ullung-do, with a variety on Sakhalin.
Habitat: Cultivated as an ornamental, in the wild occurring in mixed mountain forests.
Varieties: 'Embley' is a selection for its autumn colour and narrow upright habit. It was mistakenly grown as *S. discolor* at one time and is found in some collections under this name, which rightly belongs to a white-fruited rowan from northern China similar to *S. glabrescens*. 'Serotina' is a selection from Korea, named for flushing, flowering and ripening the fruit somewhat later than is,

usual. Var. *sachalinensis* from Sakhalin, the Kurile Islands as well as Hokkaido, differs in the larger leaflets to 8–9 cm (3.1–3.3 in). Plants from the Korean island of Ullung-do also have larger leaflets.

Similar species: *S. randaiensis* from Taiwan has more numerous and more leathery narrower and longer leaflets, in up to ten pairs.

S. rufo-ferruginea is sometimes included as a variety of Japanese Rowan. It has a more restricted distribution in southern Japan, from Honshu, Shikoku and Kyushu, and generally occurring at greater elevations. The foliage, flowers and inflorescence are densely covered in rusty brown woolly hairs, whereas Japanese Rowan is hairless or very nearly so.

This rowan is used as a street tree for its upright habit and brilliant autumn colour. It is variable, with some forms much better than others. The leaves are smooth beneath, unlike *S. aucuparia* and its allies where under a 40–100× microscope they are densely papillose.

---

p.217 **French Hales** or **Devon Whitebeam**
Sorbus devoniensis

Description: Deciduous tree 10–18 m (33–60 ft) with a bole diameter to 70 cm (2.3 ft).
Crown Columnar to domed. *Bark* Brown, becoming scaly. *Shoot* Olive-brown and slightly grey and hairless, becoming greyer in the second and subsequent years with rounded pale lenticels. *Buds* Ovoid-conic, sharp pointed, pinky green-brown, 0.8–1.3 cm (0.3–0.5 in). *Foliage* Leaves ovate to oblong-ovate, apex acute or short slender pointed, base rounded, margin shallowly lobed (to a maximum of one quarter distance to midrib), upper surface slightly hairy at first, maturing to deep green, underside greenish grey hairy, seven to nine pairs of veins, prominent below, 7–11 × 4–8 cm (2.8–4.3 × 1.6–3.1 in); leaf stalk 1–3 cm (0.4–1.2 in); autumn colour russet. *Flowers* In large sparsely

woolly corymbs 5–10 cm (2–4 in) across in May–June, flowers dull white, two styles, anthers cream, receptacle woolly. *Fruit* Sub-globose, brownish orange to brown with numerous large lenticels, especially at the base, 1–1.5 cm (0.4–0.6 in).

Range: England from Devon and Eastern Cornwall and in southern Ireland from Kilkenny, Wexford and Carlow.

Habitat: Mixed woods or hedgerows.

Similar species: *S. subcuneata* is a small tree from northeast Devon and the northern coast region of Somerset. It has elliptic to rhombic-elliptic leaves which are wedge-shaped at the base with short triangular lobes in the upper two-thirds.

S. croceocarpa ('Theophrasta') is similar to French Hales and *S. latifolia* but has leaves which are doubly toothed, not lobed. It is occasionally cultivated, but is of uncertain origin.

This tree is perhaps the commonest *Sorbus* in Devon. It is an apomictic tetraploid derived from *S. aria* crossed by *S. torminalis*. Thus it is of similar origin to *S. latifolia*, from which it differs in the narrower less-lobed leaves which are rounded at the base and more acute. From its occurrence in southwest England and southern Ireland, it is believed to have survived the last Ice Age in a refuge somewhere in this region. Across Europe, there are a number of similar species derived from *S. torminalis* crossed either by *S. aria* or one of its relatives.

p.331 **Service Tree** *Sorbus domestica*

Description: Deciduous tree 15–25 m (50–80 ft) with a bole diameter to 1 m (3.3 ft).
Crown Tall domed with horizontal spreading branches. *Bark* Brown and orange or pale brown, breaking into rectangular scales and fissured at base. *Shoot* Silky haired and olive-green when young, maturing to dark brown above and

green beneath. *Buds* Ovoid, glossy, resinous green with many scales, 1 cm (0.4 in). *Foliage* Leaves to 25 cm (10 in), pinnate with 13–21 leaflets and somewhat pendent; leaflets oblong, acute to bluntly pointed at the apex and base, sharply serrate in upper three-quarters but untoothed at the base, upper surface dark yellow-green, underside paler and more persistently white hairy, 3–6 × 1 cm (1.2–2.4 × 0.4 in); autumn colour poor. *Flowers* In rounded corymbose to pyramidal inflorescences 10–14 cm (4–5.5 in) across with white flowers 1.3–1.8 cm (0.5–0.7 in) in diameter, five styles, receptacle white hairy. *Fruit* Pear- or apple-shaped, russet to green with red, with the flesh containing stone or grit cells, 2.5–3 cm (1–1.2 in).

Range: Southern Europe to the Caucasus and in Morocco and Algeria, also on cliffs in south Wales.

Habitat: Mixed broadleaved woodland.

Varieties: Apple-shaped fruits are sometimes treated as forma *pomifera* and pear-shaped fruits as forma *pyrifera*.

Synonyms: *Cormus domestica*.

This tree is similar in general foliage to Rowan (*S. aucuparia*) but differs in the fruit which is much larger and the five carpels fully fused together. The bark is also very different and distinctive, although similar to *S. torminalis*. It is not related to the Rowan group and is more reasonably placed in its own monotypic genus, *Cormus*. The fruits are either apple- or pear-shaped. When first ripe they are rather bitter but as they become 'bletted' or soften and start to rot, they become sweet and more pleasant to eat. The fruits contain stone or grit cells, as in the true pears or *Pyrus*.

---

p.332 **Esserteau's Rowan** *Sorbus esserteauiana*

Description: Deciduous tree circa 10 m (33 ft) in height with a bole diameter to 30 cm (1 ft). *Crown* Ovoid, upright or becoming spreading. *Bark* Smooth, grey-green, scaly at base in old trees. *Shoot* Stout pinky purple at first with a dense covering of whitish hairs, maturing to green-brown in the autumn and in later years grey-brown. *Buds* Ovoid, flattened, green or purple but with a coating of whitish hairs, 1 cm (0.4 in). *Foliage* Leaves to 30 × 15 cm (12 × 6 in), pinnate with five to nine pairs of lanceolate or lanceolate-oblong, somewhat leathery leaflets which are rounded at the base and taper to an acute or somewhat slender-pointed apex, margin with spaced small triangular spreading teeth, upper surface sub-shiny green with 12–16 pairs of impressed veins, hairless, underside light green but densely covered with white wool, veins raised, leaflets larger at the middle of the leaf, smaller to the apex and base, 4.5–8 × 1.5–2 cm (1.8–3.1 × 0.6–0.8 in); leaf stalk and rachis grooved, green or pinky green, white hairy, with large rounded and persistent stipules which have acute teeth and clasp the bud and shoot; new foliage delicately coppery coloured with neat impressed veins, autumn colour good red or orange. *Flowers* In terminal creamy white corymbs in May to 12 cm (4.7 in) across. *Fruit* Sub-globose, broader than long, 5 mm (0.2 in), late ripening to bright red or orange-yellow, showy.

Range: West Sichuan, China.

Habitat: Cultivated as an ornamental, in the wild occurring in mixed forests as an understorey element.

Varieties: 'Flava' is a form with the fruits orange-yellow or yellow.

Synonyms: *S. conradinae.*

This tree is related to Rowan (*S. aucuparia*), especially in the hairy buds and the generally red rounded or globose small fruits. It is easily distinguished by the large leafy stipules which persist until the leaves turn and fall in the autumn and the more majestic leaves (especially when unfolding in the spring). It is also related to *S. sargentiana*, but this has even larger leaflets and rounded red sticky buds.

p.214 **Folgner's Whitebeam** *Sorbus folgneri*

Description: Deciduous tree 10–18 m (33–60 ft) with a
bole diameter to 40 cm (1.3 ft).
Crown Ovoid, with initially ascending then
pendent branches. *Bark* Purplish brown,
fissured. *Shoot* Green-brown with a dense
covering of white wool at first, becoming
hairless and in the second year shiny purplish
brown, slender with small oval orange-brown
lenticels. *Buds* Conic, red-brown, pressed
against the shoot, to 5 mm (0.2 in).
Foliage Leaves elliptic to oblanceolate,
tapering to an acute apex and wedge-shaped
at the base, margin with irregular rather
rounded or acute teeth, upper surface initially
white woolly but then hairless, dark matt
green with 8–11 pairs of impressed veins,
underside persistently silvery white woolly
with raised hairy veins, 5–10 × 2–4.5 cm
(2–4 × 0.8–1.8 in); leaf stalk grooved, white
woolly, to 1 cm (0.4 in); autumn colour
orange, scarlet and crimson with the
underside remaining silvered. *Flowers* In
small corymbs 5–10 cm (2–4 in) across,
white, woolly. *Fruit* Oval to oblong with
rounded ends, calyx deciduous, leaving a
small depression, bright shiny red (yellow in
'Lemon Drop') with few lenticels, 1–1.2 cm
× 5–6 mm (0.4–0.5 × 0.2–0.25 in), seeds
oval light brown, 6 mm (0.25 in).

Range: Central and western China.

Habitat: Cultivated as an ornamental, in the wild
occurring in forests.

This small tree is very graceful, especially
when the wind lifts the foliage and shows
off the silvery undersides. *S. zahlbruckneri*
differs in the broader leaves scarcely silvered
beneath and fruits with a persistent calyx.
Photos 1–3 (*see* p.214) may be this species.

---

p.334 **White-fruited Rowan** *Sorbus glabrescens*

Description: Deciduous tree 8–15 m (26–50 ft) with a
bole diameter to 40 cm (1.3 ft).
Crown Narrow ovoid or columnar with
ascending branches. *Bark* Purple-grey,

smooth. *Shoot* Green-brown and initially white pilose, becoming hairless by early summer, grey-brown or purple-grey in the second year, rather stout. *Buds* Ovoid-conic, green but maturing to red over winter, with white and rufous hairs on the margins of the scales, 1–1.5 cm (0.4–0.6 in). *Foliage* Leaves to 26 cm (10.2 in) with 11–17 leaflets; leaflets more or less even in size, oval to obovate, rounded to a short acute or abruptly short-pointed apex, base rounded and usually oblique, margin serrate in the apical half only with small forward teeth, stalkless except for the terminal leaflet, upper surface sea-green or grey-green with a somewhat impressed midrib, underside whitish green, hairless with a raised midrib which may be slightly hairy towards the base, 2.5–5.5 cm (1–2.2 in) (mainly over 3.5 cm (1.4 in)) × 1–2.1 cm (0.4–0.8 in); leaf stalk purplish pink at base, grooved, rachis grooved, stipules small and soon falling; autumn colour late, orange or crimson-red. *Flowers* In conical panicles in late May or early June, white, with four or five 2.5 mm (0.1 in) styles. *Fruit* Globose, hard, white with a pink or purple flush to the calyx (and the stalks), 7–8 mm (0.3 in); seeds dark brown, 3–4.5 × 2.5 mm (0.1–0.2 × 0.1 in).

Range: Yunnan (and Sichuan?), China.

Habitat: Cultivated as an ornamental, in the wild occurring in mixed forests.

Synonyms: *S. hupehensis* misapplied.

This tree is often called *S. hupehensis* but this is a rarely seen species from Hubei in central northern China, which also has white fruits, but the twigs are much slenderer. Other closely related taxa are *S. oligodonta* and *S. carmesina* in preparation. The small hard fruits are usually untouched by birds and may persist into the New Year. With the purple stalks contrasting with the glistening white of the fruit, they can give the appearance of a cherry in flower from a distance. It is a tetraploid apomictic species.

p.214 **Grecian Whitebeam** *Sorbus graeca*

Description: Deciduous tree 10 m (33 ft) in height with a bole diameter to 40 cm (1.3 ft).
Crown Conic in young trees, becoming rounded. *Bark* Grey. *Shoot* Olive-brown with a loose woolly covering which is soon lost and few oval raised pale orange-brown lenticels, in the second and later years grey-brown. *Buds* Ovoid, bluntly pointed, green and brown with hairy margins to the scales, 0.5–1 cm (0.2–0.4 in). *Foliage* Leaves obovate to oval if subtending a bud (the ones in the inflorescence may be narrower, sometimes elliptic), broadest at or above the middle with a rounded rather fan-shaped upper half and a broad wedge-shaped base, margin simply toothed in the lower half, becoming more doubly toothed or lobulate at the apex with triangular teeth, upper surface shiny mid green, initially woolly but soon hairless except for reddish peg-like hairs on the veins, underside white woolly, with 7–12 pairs of raised veins, 5–10 × 3.5–7.5 cm (2–4 × 1.4–3 in); leaf stalk grooved, woolly, 2 cm (0.8 in); autumn colour russets. *Flowers* In terminal leafy corymbs in May, with leaves subtending the branches of the inflorescence. *Fruit* Globose, 1–1.2 cm (0.4–0.5 in), initially white floccose, then hairless, green until ripening scarlet, with few rounded lenticels.

Range: From Sicily across southeast and eastern central Europe to the Caucasus and south to Turkey, Lebanon and Iraq, and in Morocco and Algeria.

Habitat: Woodlands and thickets.

This is a widespread species complex, as it is reported to include both diploid and tetraploid forms. The diploids will breed sexually and thus vary.

p.331 **Harrow Rowan** *Sorbus harrowiana*

Description: Deciduous tree 4–10 m (13–33 ft) with a bole diameter to 30 cm (1 ft).
Crown Rounded domed, sometimes rather

sprawling. *Bark* Grey-brown, becoming scaly at the base in old trees. *Shoot* Shiny brown, stout (around 6–8 mm (0.25–0.3 in)) in the first year and hairless, becoming chocolate brown in the second year with long elliptic pale buff lenticels. *Buds* Narrow ovoid-long conic, sharp pointed, shiny green and purple-pink, with rufous hairs on the scale margins, 1.5–2.5 cm (0.6–1 in). *Foliage* Leaves pinnate, 20–30 cm (8–12 in), with two or three pairs of leaflets; leaflets oblong, apex rounded, base rounded, margin finely serrate, initially rufous pubescent, upper surface deep green, underside glaucous white and non-papillose, 9–17 × 3–5 cm (3.5–6.7 × 1.2–2 in); rachis round or slightly grooved, leaf stalk clasping the shoot and bud at the base but the stipules small, not leafy; autumn colour orange to red. *Flowers* In large corymbs, flowers small, with white petals, two or three styles. *Fruit* Globose, pink to white, fading to white, 8 mm (0.3 in).

Range: West Yunnan and adjacent northern Burma.

Habitat: Cultivated as an ornamental, in the wild found in open forests in the *Abies* zone, often as an epiphyte when young.

Synonyms: *Pyrus harrowiana*

Similar species: *S. insignis* is very distinct in the smaller leaves with four to six (but mainly six) pairs of leaflets which are smaller, only 6–9 × 1.5–2.5 cm (2.4–3.5 × 0.6–1 in) and less glaucous beneath, in the larger corymbs to 15 cm (6 in) across with maroon-red fruits 5–7 mm (0.2–0.3 in) and in the rounded buds. However, the best distinguishing character is in the large leafy stipules which clasp the shoots either side of the buds. These are rounded, serrate and up to 2 cm (0.8 in) across. It is recorded from east Nepal, Sikkim and to central Bhutan. A plant often cultivated as *S. insignis*, grown from Kingdon-Ward's collection 7746 from northeast India, appears to be an undescribed species, also occurring in northwest Burma or Myanmar. This differs from both Harrow Rowan and *S. insignis* in the leaves which are densely rusty hairy on the veins beneath and have eight to nine pairs of leaflets which are smaller, to around 5–6 × 1.5 cm (2–2.4 × 0.6 in), in the smaller ovoid, red-pink or garish pink fruits in large corymbs on long stalks, in the leaf stalk base clasping the very stout shoot but without the large leafy stipules and the rounded domed buds.

'Leonard Messel' is a hybrid of Harrow Rowan (probably with *S. aucuparia*), having 9–11 oblong leaflets to 11 × 2.8 cm (4.3 × 1.1 in) and pink fruits. 'Ghose' is another hybrid of this group (probably KW 7746 crossed with *aucuparia*), with seven to nine pairs of dull green leaflets and large clusters of carmine red fruits.

This has the most remarkable leaves of all rowans, with five or seven (rarely only three) enormous leaflets, usually 10–12 cm (4–4.7 in) long but occasionally up to 18 cm (7.1 in). It grows in the moist cloud forests along the high mountains of western Yunnan and northern Burma. It can be susceptible to spring frosts in cultivation. It is a diploid and seed raised from isolated trees is likely to produce hybrids (*see* the clone 'Leonard Messel').

---

p.215 **Hedlund's Whitebeam** *Sorbus hedlundii*

Description: Deciduous tree to 20 m (65 ft) with a bole diameter to 70 cm (2.3 ft).
Crown Ovoid in young trees, becoming domed. *Bark* Grey-brown, smooth, becoming scaly. *Shoot* Initially with a dense covering of white wool which rubs off as the shoot matures to brown, hairless in the second year. *Buds* Ovoid, pointed, pink or green, 1.5 cm (0.6 in).
Foliage Leaves elliptic, tapering to a short acute apex, base wedge-shaped to broad wedge-shaped, margin finely serrate or doubly serrate, upper surface loosely white or grey woolly but becoming rubbed off to reveal mid to dark glossy green with impressed veins, underside with 12–17

pairs of raised veins which are covered with golden-brown hairs (as are the secondary veins) in mature plants with a white to silvery white woolly covering of hairs between the veins, in juvenile plants all hairs white to silvery white, 12–25 × 5–15 cm (4.7–10 × 2–6 in); leaf stalk white woolly, 0.5–1.5 cm (0.2–0.6 in); stipules slender pointed, white woolly; autumn colour russet on upper surface, silvery white and brown on underside. *Flowers* Terminal in late spring on white woolly stalks, flowers creamy white, in corymbs 3–6 cm (1.2–2.4 in) across, three to five styles. *Fruit* Globose, in clusters of around a dozen, with a persistent calyx, rosy red and green, 1–1.5 cm (0.4–0.6 in).

Range: Eastern Himalayas from Nepal to Bhutan.

Habitat: Cultivated as an ornamental, in its native area found in moist mixed valley forests.

This species is related to *S. thibetica* and *S. vestita*, differing in mature plants from both in the rufous or golden-brown hairs on the veins beneath. From *S. vestita*, the 12–17 pairs of veins and the sharper toothing of the margins amply distinguish it. From *S. thibetica*, the critical characters are the three to five styles and carpels in the fruit. Juvenile plants do not have the brown hairs on the veins except when the leaves are very young and non-fruiting specimens can be difficult to distinguish from *S. thibetica*.

---

p.331 **Bastard Service Tree** *Sorbus hybrida*

Description: Deciduous tree 10–15 m (33–50 ft) with a bole diameter to 50 cm (1.6 ft).
Crown Ovoid when young, but becoming rounded or domed. *Bark* Smooth, grey, slightly fissured at the base. *Shoot* Green with white woolly hairs and round pale lenticels, becoming chocolate-brown with a grey film and the lenticels erupting in the second and third years. *Buds* Ovoid, blunt, green or brown with whitish hairs, 1 cm (0.4 in). *Foliage* Leaves elliptic to ovate-elliptic, with one or two pairs of free leaflets

at the base, elsewhere with rounded serrate lobes which decrease towards the rounded leaf apex, upper surface matt green with slightly impressed veins, lower surface with a greyish white wool covering the blade and the prominent veins, 7–12 × 5–8 cm (2.8–4.7 × 2–3.1 in); leaf stalk white woolly, 2–3 cm (0.8–1.2 in); turning russet colours in autumn. *Flowers* In 6–11 cm (2.4–4.3 in) wide terminal clusters in late spring, flowers white, 2 cm (0.8 in) across, with petals which are hairy on the inner side, three styles. *Fruit* Globose, ripens from green to scarlet in autumn, 1.2–1.5 cm (0.5–0.6 in).

Range: Southern and southwestern Sweden and Norway.

Habitat: Coastal woods.

Synonyms: *S. fennica*, *S. pinnatifida*.

This tree is one of the large number of apomictic hybrids between *S. rupicola* with *S. aucuparia*. These vary in the number of free leaflets at the base and the depth of the lobing. *S. rupicola* is a tetraploid member of the Whitebeam group, with obovate or oblanceolate leaves which are wedge-shaped at the base. It rarely makes a tree, usually being restricted to a shrub to 5 m (16 ft), and is local from Devon to the Scottish Highlands, north and west Ireland and Scandinavia.

---

p.272   **Swedish Whitebeam**   *Sorbus intermedia*

Description: Deciduous tree 10–15 m (33–50 ft) with a bole diameter to 60 cm (2 ft).
Crown Columnar conic or ovoid in young trees, becoming rounded domed when mature. *Bark* Grey or purplish grey and smooth, developing scaly fissures between broad flat areas in old trees. *Shoot* Green or purplish brown in the first year with a dense but loose covering of greyish-white woolly hairs, slender 2.5–4 mm (0.1–0.2 in), becoming hairless in the second year when the shoot is brown with a greenish tinge and a thin waxy peeling

layer of grey, lenticels oval, orange-brown.
Buds Ovoid, rounded, scales green to dark
red-brown, initially with grey woolly hairs,
to 8 mm (0.3 in). *Foliage* Leaves oval to
ovate, apex rounded pointed to acute, base
rounded to nearly truncate, margin with
five to seven large rounded, pointed toothed
lobes which decrease towards the tip of the
leaf where there are serrate teeth, sinuses
cleft, reaching approximately a quarter of
the way to the midrib, upper surface deep
glossy green, with slightly impressed veins,
hairless except for an initial covering of
greyish wool, undersurface densely grey-
white woolly, midrib and side veins raised,
blade 7–12 × 5–7 cm (2.8–4.7 × 2–2.8 in);
leaf stalk grooved above, green with greyish
wool, 1.8–3 cm (0.7–1.2 in); autumn
colour yellow, orange or red. *Flowers* In
terminal corymbs in May, 8–12 cm
(3.1–4.7 in) across with individual flowers
1.5–2 cm (0.6–0.8 in) diameter, stalks grey
woolly, petals dull white, anthers pale pink,
two or three styles. *Fruit* Initially woolly,
ripens from green to red in autumn, oval, to
1.5 × 1 cm (0.6–0.4 in), calyx persistent,
reflexed, woolly.

Range: Southern Sweden south along the southern
shore of the Baltic from Denmark to Poland
but naturalized in Britain.

Habitat: Woodlands or hedgerows, much planted as
an amenity tree.

Synonyms: *Pyrus intermedia*.

Swedish Whitebeam is very tolerant of
urban conditions and makes an excellent
tough tree for streets, parks and similar
sites. It has a neat habit and attractive
flowers. These are followed in autumn by
the red berries, whose display is often
foreshortened by bird predation. It is an
apomictic tetraploid, i.e. with four sets of
chromosomes. Consequently, all seeds
produce identical copies of the mother tree,
with little potential for any variation. It
probably originated as a cross between
S. aucuparia with *S. aria* (or a tetraploid
form such as *S. rupicola*) but may have
S. torminalis in its ancestry.

p.333 **Joseph Rock's Rowan** *Sorbus* 'Joseph Rock'

Description: Deciduous tree 8–15 m (26–50 ft) with a bole diameter to 40 cm (1.3 ft).
Crown Narrow columnar with ascending branches. *Bark* Smooth, grey-brown. *Shoot* Green-brown, hairless, with elliptic pointed orange raised lenticels, grey-brown in later years. *Buds* Narrow flattened conic or ovoid, green or brown, with brown hairs at the tips, to 1.5 cm (0.6 in). *Foliage* Leaves 10–17 cm (4–6.7 in) pinnate with mainly nine pairs of leaflets (from 7–10), leaflets more or less even in size, oblong-elliptic, tapered to the acute and slightly slender-pointed tip, rounded to the base, margin sharply serrate with teeth which taper to a fine acute point with narrow sinuses, upper surface matt green with impressed veins, underside pale green with rufous hairs especially along the raised midrib, 2.5–4 × 1–1.5 cm (1–1.6 × 0.4–0.6 in); leaf stalk and rachis grooved and faintly winged (with a strip of green leaf) between the leaflets, rufous haired, pink and green; autumn colour crimson and purple, contrasting well with the amber berries. *Flowers* In large corymbs in late spring, white, to 10 cm (4 in) across. *Fruit* Globular or ovoid, green but ripening through white to amber yellow by October, persisting for several weeks including after leaf fall, 9 mm (0.4 in).

Range: Northwest Yunnan.

Habitat: Cultivated as an ornamental, in the wild occurring in woodlands.

Similar Species: 'Pink Pearl' and 'Pearly King' are two selections of this species which differ in having fruits which are initially pink and fade to pearly white, with more rounded and open habits which spread wider than high. *S. pluripinnata* of cultivation is a tetraploid relative of 'Pearly King', but *see also S. scalaris.*

The main description refers to the clone 'Joseph Rock', which is likely to be named as *S. rockii.* This was introduced from China, possibly from Yunnan or Sichuan, by Joseph Rock, who was a plant collector in the 1920s until the 1950s. He was born in Austria but became an American citizen and spent most of his life in China, especially in Gansu and Yunnan. It is a most attractive tree, but inclined to get fireblight, a disease which affects members of the apple subfamily of the Rosaceae and is caused by the bacterium *Erwinia amylovora*.

p.218 **Service Tree of Fontainebleau**
Sorbus latifolia

Description: Deciduous tree 10–20 m (33–65 ft), with a bole diameter to 60 cm (2 ft).
Crown Ovoid to rounded. *Bark* Smooth, grey, becoming scaly at the base.
Shoot Green with long loose white hairs, becoming hairless and shiny, lenticels small, oval, pale, in the second year brown to grey-brown. *Buds* Ovoid, green with brown tips, hairy, 6 mm (0.25 in).
Foliage Leaves rounded ovate to broad ovate, apex acute, base rounded to broad wedge-shaped, margin doubly toothed with coarsely triangular large teeth or small lobules and small abruptly short-pointed teeth, upper surface lustrous dark green, wrinkled, hairy when new but soon hairless, underside with a persistent greyish white covering of hairs with 6–10 raised veins, 5–10 × 5–10 cm (2–4 × 2–4 in); leaf stalk grooved, with loose long whitish hairs, 1.5–2.5 cm (0.6–1 in); autumn colours russets. *Flowers* In corymbs 8 cm (3.1 in) across in late spring (May), petals creamy white, flowers 1.5 cm (0.6 in) across. *Fruit* Globose, dull reddish brown with large pale lenticels, 1.2 cm (0.5 in).
Range: Central France, south of Paris around Fontainebleau.
Habitat: Woodlands.

This is one of the apomictic species derived from *S. torminalis* crossed with a member of the *S. aria* group.

p.216 **Mupin Whitebeam** *Sorbus megalocarpa*

Description: Deciduous tree 5–10 m (16–33 ft) with a
bole diameter to 30 cm (1 ft).
Crown Broad. *Bark* Brown, rough and
finely peeling. *Shoot* Shiny brown with small
pale boat-shaped lenticels, in the second year
chocolate brown, duller in the third year with
the lenticels enlarging. *Buds* Ovoid-conic,
pointed, shiny green, 0.6–2 cm
(0.25–0.8 in). *Foliage* Leaves broad ovate to
elliptic or obovate, with an acute or short
abruptly pointed apex, base rounded to
wedge-shaped, margin with irregular and
somewhat double triangular teeth, card-like
in texture, upper surface matt green, soon
hairless except for tufts on the impressed
veins and with small peg-like dark glands on
the veins, underside pale green, veins (11–20
pairs) hairy and prominent, 10–20 ×
5.5–10 cm (4–8 × 2.2–4 in) (rarely to 25 ×
13 cm (10 × 5.1 in)); leaf stalk grooved,
green, hairy, 0.8–2.5 cm (0.3–1 in); autumn
colour russet or red. *Flowers* On the leafless
branches in terminal rounded corymbs
8–15 cm (3.1–6 in) across in late winter,
flowers with dull white or cream petals,
strongly scented. *Fruit* Ovoid, 2–3 × 2 cm
(0.8–1.2 × 0.8 in), russet brown, wrinkled.

Range: West China from Sichuan, Yunnan,
Guizhou and Hunan.

Habitat: Cultivated as an ornamental, in the wild
occurring in temperate mixed forest,
sometimes as an epiphyte.

Varieties: Var. *cuneata* differs in the leaves being only
11–14 cm (4.3–5.5 in) long with a short
leaf stalk of less than 1 cm (0.4 in) and
smaller fruits 1.5 × 1 cm (0.6 × 0.4 in). It
is restricted to west Sichuan province but is
more common in cultivation.

Similar species: *S. caloneura* has oval to oblong leaves which
are doubly toothed and 9–16 pairs of veins.
The flowers are produced with the new
leaves, but these flush whilst most plants are
still dormant. It is recorded from central
China south through Indo-China to Malaysia.
The fruit is 1 cm (0.4 in) in diameter, bronze
or brown with many large lenticels,
becoming deliciously sweet when fully ripe.

S. meliosmifolia is similar to *S. caloneura* but the ovate-elliptic leaves are regularly ridged and furrowed with 18–24 pairs of closely spaced parallel veins and may be 18 cm (7.1 in) in length. It occurs in west Sichuan, although a related species (*S. brevipetiolata* with very short leaf stalks) occurs in North Vietnam.

S. epidendron (p.216) forms a small upright tree which often grows, or starts life, as an epiphyte. The leaves are narrowly obovate to elliptic, with rounded to acute apices and wedge-shaped at the base, with 10–12 pairs of leaf veins. They are soon hairless above but usually persistently hairy beneath. The fruit is globose, greenish brown or green with many small lenticels. It occurs in Yunnan (China), northern Burma and north Vietnam.

These three species (*caloneura*, *meliosmifolia* and *epidendron*) all have a fruit in which the calyx falls off at maturity, leaving a neat rounded depression. In this respect, they are similar to *S. alnifolia* and *S. folgneri*.

This tree is remarkable for the large fruits it produces, which have been likened to partridges' eggs. The flowers appear before the leaves in late winter, and are surprisingly frost hardy.

Meinich's Rowan *Sorbus meinichii*

Description: Deciduous tree 5–10 m (16–33 ft) with a bole diameter to 30 cm (1 ft).
Crown Slender, conic to columnar with erect branches. *Bark* Grey or grey-brown, smooth. *Shoot* Grey-brown. *Buds* Ovoid, pointed, brown with whitish hairs, 1 cm (0.4 in). *Foliage* Leaves partly pinnate with four to six pairs of free leaflets at the base and a large lobed terminal portion; leaflets oblong, bluntly pointed or acute at the apex, narrowed at the base and downward growing on the rachis and sharply toothed, terminal leaflet often three lobed, coarsely toothed; autumn colour yellow to russet. *Flowers* In small corymbs in May–June,

flowers creamy white, 1 cm (0.4 in).
Fruit Rounded, scarlet with a bitter flesh,
1.2 cm. (0.5 in)

Range: Western Norway south of Bergen.
Habitat: Open hillsides.
Synonyms: *S. aucuparia* var. *meinichii*, *S. hybrida* var.
meinichii.

This tree is a tetraploid apomictic which
has three sets of *S. aucuparia* chromosomes
and a single set from the *S. aria* group.

---

p.335 **Small-leaf Rowan** *Sorbus microphylla*

Description: Deciduous tree to 10 m (33 ft) with a bole
diameter to 25 cm (0.8 ft).
Crown Rounded low dome. *Bark* Grey-
brown. *Shoot* Reddish brown with white
hairs when young but becoming hairless and
maturing to dark grey, slender (2.5–3 mm
(0.1 in)). *Buds* Conical, brown with hairy
tips to the scales. *Foliage* Leaves pinnate
with 10–12 pairs of leaflets (but sometimes
only 8 or up to 13), oblong-elliptic, 8–13 ×
2.5–3 cm (3.1–5.1 × 1–1.2 in), rachis
grooved, slightly white hairy; leaflets oblong
to oval, bluntly pointed and slender pointed
at the apex, base oblique and rounded or
broad wedge-shaped on one side, margin
sharply toothed except at the base, hairless or
white or brown hairy especially on the veins
beneath, 1.2–2.5 × 0.5–1 cm (0.5–1 ×
0.2–0.4 in); stipules usually non-leafy (dry)
and soon falling, lanceolate, 3–4 mm
(0.1–0.2 in); autumn colour variable.
Flowers In small lax cymes with two
branches each with 10–12 small white
flowers on short leafy shoots; petals
spreading with toothed margins, 2–3 mm
(0.1 in); five styles. *Fruit* Globose, white or
pink, 0.8–1.2 cm (0.3–0.5 in).

Range: Northwest India and scattered along the
Himalayas east through Nepal and Sikkim
to Bhutan.
Habitat: Cultivated as an ornamental, in the wild
occurring in montane forest dominated by
Abies.
Synonyms: *Pyrus microphylla*.

This small tree is similar to and often confused with *S. rufopilosa*. It has fewer larger leaflets and leaves but the best distinction is in the flowers, with the spreading white flowers of Small-Leaf Rowan differing from the smaller cup-shaped flowers with pinkish petals of *S. rufopilosa*. It is a tetraploid aggregate species, with many different but vaguely similar forms. It thrives best in a cool moist climate, being 'burnt off' (i.e. losing the leaves in summer) in hotter dry climates.

p.218 **Mougeot's Whitebeam** *Sorbus mougeotii*

Description: Deciduous shrub or tree 8–20 m (26–65 ft) with a bole diameter to 50 cm (1.6 ft). *Crown* Ovoid, domed in old trees. *Bark* Grey, roughened by lenticels. *Shoot* Olive-brown with a few pale oval lenticels, becoming bark brown. *Buds* Long ovoid, pointed, green with hairy brown tips to the scales, 1 cm (0.4 in). *Foliage* Leaves elliptic to obovate, tapering to the rounded acute apex, base wedge-shaped to rounded wedge-shaped, margin untoothed at base but from around the middle with triangular lobules extending one-quarter to one-fifth the way to the midrib with small teeth on the lobules, upper surface woolly at first, becoming hairless except for some persistent wool along the impressed veins, shiny dark green, underside covered in white wool, veins circa 10 pairs, parallel, prominent, 6–10 × 3–4 cm (2.4–4 × 1.2–1.6 in); leaf stalk grooved, green, woolly, 1.5 cm (0.6 in); autumn colour russet. *Flowers* In small terminal corymbs 5 cm (2 in) across in late spring, individual flowers white or creamy white, 1 cm (0.4 in). *Fruit* In clusters of 6–15 bright shiny red globose fruits, with some white wool remaining but without or with very few lenticels, to 1 × 1.2 cm (0.4–0.5 in).

Range: Central southern Europe from the Pyrenees, Alps and east to Austria, but with similar species in Britain and Ireland.

Habitat: Mountain forests and slopes.

This is one of the apomictic taxa which
have derived most of their genetic
material from the *S. aria* group (probably
S. graeca) but one-quarter (one set of
chromosomes) from *S. aucuparia*. In
Britain and Ireland, this entity is
represented by *S. anglica*.

---

p.334   **Kite-leaf Rowan** *Sorbus oligodonta*

Description: Deciduous tree 10–15 m (33–50 ft) with a
bole diameter to 50 cm (1.6 ft).
Crown Ovoid or columnar. *Bark* Grey or
purplish grey, smooth. *Shoot* Deep red,
soon hairless, somewhat slender.
Buds Ovoid-conic, reddish purple, with
rufous or white hairs on the tips and scale
margins, to 1.2 cm (0.5 in). *Foliage* Leaves
pinnate with 11–15 leaflets which increase
in size towards the terminal trio, thus
giving a 'kite' shape, to 17.5 cm (6.9 in);
leaflets obovate, bluish green on the upper
surface, somewhat glaucous and papillose
beneath, margin serrate, at least on the
upper half, soon hairless, 3–4.5 ×
1.5–2 cm (1.2–1.8 × 0.6–0.8 in); autumn
colour chocolate brown, then brilliant red-
orange. *Flowers* Inflorescence pyramidal in
shape, to 10 cm (4 in), flowers white,
petals soon reflexed. *Fruit* Rounded or
spherical, small and very hard with fleshy
calyx lobes, white with a crimson flush,
deeper pink or crimson in full sunlight,
7–8 mm (0.3 in), four or five carpels, styles
2 mm (0.1 in).

Range: Yunnan, West China.

Habitat: Cultivated as an ornamental, in the wild
found as an understorey element in mixed
forest.

Varieties: 'Rosea', 'Rufus', 'Pink Pagoda' and
'November Pink' were plants named when
this species was confused with *S. glabrescens*
and listed as *S. hupehensis*. They belong here
and probably all represent the same clone,
with the reported distinctions being due to
cultural differences, such as with the berries

being deeper pink when the tree is grown in full sunlight.

Synonyms: *S. pseudohupehensis* provisional name.

This tree is one of a cluster of tetraploid (i.e. with four sets of chromosomes) apomictic taxa. It is allied to *S. glabrescens*, which is the other member of this group illustrated here, differing in the kite-shaped leaves which are more strongly blue-green above, the much more slender shoots which give the tree a more delicate appearance (cf. the rather gaunt winter habit of *S. glabrescens*) and the pink fruits. The fruits often persist until well after Christmas, ripening late in November.

p.335 **Tsema Rowan** *Sorbus rufopilosa*

Description: Deciduous tree to 10 m (33 ft) with a bole diameter to 25 cm (0.8 ft).
Crown Rounded low dome. *Bark* Grey-brown. *Shoot* Light brown or pinky grey-brown, slender, soon hairless.
Buds Conical, pointed, red-brown or purplish red-brown, with a few rufous hairs, 4–6 mm (0.2–0.25 in).
Foliage Leaves pinnate with (12–)13–17 pairs of leaflets, oblong-elliptic, to 10 × 2–2.5 cm (4 × 0.8–1 in), rachis grooved; leaflets ovate-lanceolate, bluntly pointed or acute at the apex, base rounded or oblique, margin with 8–10 pairs of sharp teeth, with rufous hairs especially below and when young, (0.5–)0.9–1(–1.7 cm) × 4–6 mm ((0.2–)0.4(–0.7) × 0.2–0.25 in); stipules usually non-leafy (dry) and soon falling, lanceolate, 3–4 mm (0.2 in); autumn colour usually good with oranges and red. *Flowers* In cymes with three or four branches on long stalks, each with three or four flowers; petals pink, pointing forward in a cup-shape; three or four styles.
Fruit Globose, white or less often pink or with pink freckles, green before ripening, 6–9 mm (0.25–0.4 in); calyx lobes forming a prominent cone.

Range: Himalayas from Nepal east through
Sikkim, Bhutan to southeast Tibet.

Habitat: Cultivated as an ornamental, in the wild
occurring in cool moist montane forest
dominated by *Abies*.

This makes a delightful species with its
feathery fern-like foliage, with the many
small leaflets coalescing into an attractive
blur. It requires a moist site and is not well
suited to hot dry localities. It is a diploid
species. It is often confused with the *S.
microphylla* aggregate. It lacks a common
English name, so I have used the
Bhutanese name.

p.333 **Sargent's Rowan** *Sorbus sargentiana*

Description: Deciduous tree 8–16 m (26–52 ft) with a
bole diameter to 50 cm (1.6 ft).
Crown Conic when young, developing a
rounded head with radiating branches from
a short bole. *Bark* Yellow-brown with
large lenticels, becoming grey and smooth.
Shoot Olive-brown with large oval lenticels
and grey down in the first year, becoming
hairless and dark buff-brown to grey-brown
in later years. *Buds* Ovoid with a rounded
apex or ovoid-conic and more pointed,
gummy with resin, red or red and green, to
2 cm (0.8 in). *Foliage* Leaves to 35 cm
(14 in), pinnate with 9–11 leaflets; leaflets
oblong-lanceolate, longest towards the leaf
apex but the basal pairs and the terminal
three smaller, tapering to an acute apex
with a short slender point, base rounded,
oblique, margin with sharp aristate teeth
and small acute sinuses except for the basal
quarter which is untoothed, upper surface
matt green with impressed veins, underside
whitish green, sparsely hairy with
prominent raised midrib and 20–25 pairs
of parallel veins, 5–14 × 3.5–5 cm (2–5.5 ×
1.4–2 in); leaf stalk with a pair of large
leafy stipules attached at the base, faintly
grooved, green and pink, sparsely downy,
5–8 cm (2–3.1 in), stipules half-moon
shaped, with sharp triangular aristate teeth,

to 3 cm (1.2 in) wide by 2 cm (0.8 in) deep with texture and colour as for leaves; autumn colour brilliant scarlet and gold, late; new foliage mahogany coloured.
Flowers In large terminal corymbs of small whitish flowers in June. *Fruit* In large erect heads to 25 cm (10 in) across usually containing 200–500 fruits; fruit flattened globose, matt orange-scarlet, 6–8 mm (0.25–0.3 in) each way.

Range: West Sichuan, China.

Habitat: Cultivated as an ornamental, in the wild occurring in mixed temperate forests.

Similar species: *S. wilsoniana* has similar but less vivid buds and smaller leaves which are more generally woolly. It is found in central China but is uncommon in cultivation.

This is a spectacular tree, especially when laden with the enormous trusses of fruit, and then as the leaves assume their autumn colouring. The buds are sticky, as in a Horse Chestnut, but bright red or with bright red patches.

p.332 **Ladder Rowan** *Sorbus scalaris*

Description: Deciduous tree 8–12 m (26–39 ft) with a bole diameter to 50 cm (1.6 ft).
Crown Wide with arching-spreading branches from a short bole. *Bark* Smooth, grey-brown. *Shoot* Purplish brown with a dense covering of greyish hairs which persist into the second year, then buff-brown to grey-brown, finely fissuring.
Buds Ovoid-conic with a blunt apex, purplish but covered with greyish hairs, 1–1.5 cm (0.4–0.6 in). *Foliage* Leaves oblong in outline, tapering to the narrower apex, to 20 × 8 cm (8 × 3.1 in), pinnate with 8–16 pairs of closely set leaflets which give the appearance of the steps of a ladder; leaflets somewhat leathery, narrowly oblong, slightly broader at the base and rounded at both ends or somewhat acute at the apex, margin rolled over somewhat, finely toothed only towards the apex, upper surface deep sub-shiny green and soon

hairless, folded along the midrib with the veins impressed, underside whitish green, hairy with a prominently raised midrib, 2.5–7 × 0.6–1.3 cm (1–2.8 × 0.25–0.5 in); leaf stalk with a pair of large leafy stipules attached at the base, grooved, hairy, pink, circa 2 cm (0.8 in), rachis deeply grooved, stipules half-moon in shape, finely toothed, to 2 cm (0.8 in) across; autumn colour brilliant orange-yellow to red; new foliage bronze. *Flowers* In large terminal corymbs, 9–17 cm (3.5–6.7 in) across, of small whitish flowers in late May or early June. *Fruit* Globose, 6 mm (0.25 in), ripening through green and orange to scarlet.

Range: West Sichuan, China.

Habitat: Cultivated as an ornamental, in the wild occurring in mixed temperate forests.

Synonyms: *S. pluripinnata* in part.

This Chinese rowan is related to *S. aucuparia*, as the birds which strip the berries soon after they have ripened appreciate. It is easily distinguished by the large leafy stipules which persist on the extension and fruiting branches, although they tend to fall soon on sterile spur shoots. It is also closely related to *S. esserteauiana* and less closely to *S. sargentiana*, coming from the same part of west Sichuan. *S. pluripinnata* is botanically a synonym of *S. scalaris* but the plants often labelled as *pluripinnata* are a tetraploid relative of *S. rockii* 'Pink Pearl' (*see S.* 'Joseph Rock').

Tibetan Whitebeam *Sorbus thibetica*

Description: Deciduous tree 10–20 m (33–65 ft) with a bole diameter to 70 cm (2.3 ft).
Crown Upright in young trees but becoming broad conic or rounded and domed with age. *Bark* Smooth, dark grey, in old trees becoming fissured and platy. *Shoot* Stout, initially green and covered with dense white cobwebby hairs, lenticels small, round or oval, in the second year nearly hairless and dark brown. *Buds* Ovoid, bluntly pointed, green or

reddish purple, hairless or initially woolly, 7 mm (0.3 in). *Foliage* Leaves elliptic, broad elliptic to obovate, apex acute or rounded with a short acute tip, base wedge-shaped to rounded, margins sharply, irregularly and often doubly serrate, upper surface initially covered with a white cobwebby wool but soon hairless, veins impressed, underside silvery white or grey due to a dense persistent covering of hairs, with 11–15 (rarely up to 18 or down to 10) pairs of prominent veins, 10–20 × 8–15 cm (4–8 × 3.1–6 in); leaf stalk stout, grooved, green with white wool, 1.5–2 cm (0.6–0.8 in); upper surface of the leaves turning russet colours in the autumn with the underside remaining silvery. *Flowers* In erect terminal corymbs of 7–15 flowers on stout white woolly stalks, receptacle and calyx lobes white woolly, petals creamy white, anthers bright crimson, two or three styles. *Fruit* Rounded or ellipsoidal, 1–2 cm (0.4–0.8 in) long and wide, colour varies from orange with a reddish tinge, to yellow or russet, seed brown, flat.

Range: Himalayas from central Nepal east through Sikkim, Bhutan, northeast India, southeast Tibet, Burma and into Yunnan, China.

Habitat: Cultivated as an ornamental, in the wild occurring as a component of either mixed forest or of *Abies* forest.

Varieties: 'John Mitchell' (syn. 'Mitchellii') is the commonest form in cultivation. It has enormous leaves which may be nearly rounded in outline and up to 20 × 17 cm (8 × 6.7 in), with larger fruits 1.5–2 cm (0.6–0.8 in) long by 1.5–2.4 cm (0.6–0.9 in) wide. In this form, the tertiary veins join across between the lateral veins and form a ladder-like lattice.

Synonyms: *Sorbus cuspidata* misapplied.

Similar species: **Ward's Whitebeam** *S. wardii* (p.215) has broad elliptic to rather obovate, soon nearly hairless leaves, which on fruiting sprays are only 6–8 × 3–5 cm (2.4–3.1 × 1.2–2 in) (but on sterile shoots they may be 12 cm (4.7 in) in length) with 9–11 pairs of prominent parallel side veins. It occurs in northern Burma and western Yunnan.

This is a very variable tree and is
represented in cultivation by a number of
introductions from different parts of its
large range. The unifying feature is in the
number of styles and cells of the fruit,
which are two or three (in the same
inflorescence) (and which reliably
distinguish it from *S. vestita* and *S. hedlundi*
which have four or five styles and ovary
cells). The bold foliage can look especially
good in February if the leaves are allowed t
remain undisturbed beneath the tree, when
the persistent russet autumn colours show
on one half, whilst the others have the
silvery undersides showing.

---

p.273 **Thuringian Service Tree**
Sorbus thuringiaca

Description: Deciduous tree to 10–15 m (33–50 ft) with
a bole diameter to 40 cm (1.3 ft).
Crown Ovoid, dense. *Bark* Dull grey,
becoming shallowly cracked at the base.
Shoot Green-brown with a thin covering of
white woolly hairs, becoming grey-brown,
shiny with oval pale lenticels, stout.
Buds Ovoid-pointed, green with brown
fringes and white hairs, 1–1.5 cm
(0.4–0.6 in). *Foliage* Leaves oblong-
lanceolate with a rounded triangular apex
and with one to four pairs of free leaflets at
the base and decreasing lobulate margins
with acute teeth, free leaflets oblong to
ovate-lanceolate, acute at the apex with a
number of marginal teeth and a variable
base, upper surface initially hairy but soon
dark glossy green with impressed veins,
underside light green with raised veins and
a thin covering of white hairs, 10–15 ×
6–9 cm (4–6 × 2.4–3.5 in), with leaflets
3.5–4 × 1.5–2 cm (1.4–1.6 × 0.6–0.8 in);
leaf stalk grooved, white woolly; autumn
colour russets. *Flowers* In late spring in
large terminal corymbs 10–15 cm (4–6 in)
across with slightly hairy stalks and white
flowers. *Fruit* Ellipsoidal to globose with a
hairy apex and an indented base, green
when immature, ripening through orange

to red, with two carpels, 1–1.2 cm (0.4–0.5 in) high and wide.

Range: Central Europe.

Habitat: Cultivated as an ornamental.

Varieties: 'Fastigiata' is a selection which has a dense narrow upright ovoid crown. 'Leonard Springer' is a similar selection with more ovoid orange-red fruits which are larger than usual, to 1.5 cm (0.6 in).

Synonyms: *Pyrus thuringiaca*, *S. semipinnata*.

This is a hybrid grex between *S. aria* and *S. aucuparia*, mainly cultivated as one of the clones mentioned above. It occurs as occasional trees with the parents in the wild.

---

p.273 **Wild Service Tree** *Sorbus torminalis*

Description: Deciduous tree 15–25 m (50–80 ft) with a bole diameter to 1.3 m (4 ft).
Crown Ovoid or conic in young trees, becoming columnar and domed in old trees, with some suckers from the roots.
Bark Smooth dark brown and grey in young trees, fissuring and developing shallow scaly plates in mature trees.
Shoot Green to olive-brown, at first with a loose woolly coat but hairless and shiny by autumn with small round or oval buff lenticels, in the second year shiny brown, later dark brown to grey-brown.
Buds Globose to ovoid, shiny green with brown hairy tips, 4–6 mm (0.2–0.25 in).
Foliage Leaves ovate in outline, more like those of a *Crataegus* and characterized by a pair of wide spreading narrow triangular and acute basal lobes which extend four-fifths of the way to the midrib and form a deep acute sinus, with the next pair of lobes shorter, broader and pointing forwards at 45 degrees, then two or three triangular lobules of decreasing size to the acute or pointed apex, base broad rounded, truncate or subcordate, margin simply to doubly and irregularly serrate with triangular teeth, upper surface deep sub-shiny green, underside at first hairy, then

pale shiny green with raised slightly hairy veins with axillary tufts, 6–14 cm (2.4–5.5 in) long and wide; leaf stalk grooved, slightly hairy, 2.5–5 cm (1–2 in); autumn colour yellow, russet or crimson. *Flowers* In terminal corymbs 5–12 cm (2–4.7 in) across in June with white 1.2 cm (0.5 in) flowers on woolly stalks, two styles. *Fruit* Globose to obovoid, ripening from russet-green to brown, covered with many small lenticels and white woolly at the apex, 1–1.5 cm, (0.4–0.6 in); seed ovoid, 4 mm (0.2 in).

Range: Southern and Central Europe including southern England, east to Asia Minor, and in Morocco and Algeria.

Habitat: Mixed woodland, local.

Varieties: Var. *caucasica* (*S. orientalis*) differs in the only slightly lobed leaves with smaller fruits. It occurs in the Caucasus region, eastern Turkey and the Elburz Mountains of northern Iran.

Synonyms: *Torminaria torminalis*, *Crataegus torminalis*.

The leaves of this tree are quite unlike any other *Sorbus* and it would be better treated as a separate genus, except that apomicts (such as *S. latifolia* and *S. devoniensis*), which are derived from *S. torminalis* crossed with an apomict of the *Aria* group of *Sorbus* as the other parent are common both in the wild and in cultivation. Although seed is set, it is capable of suckering and in Britain at least, this is the prevalent form of propagation.

---

p.218 **Balkan Whitebeam** *Sorbus umbellata*

Description: Deciduous tree to 7 m (23 ft) with a bole diameter to 30 cm (1 ft).
Crown Conic to rounded, often rather shrubby. *Bark* Grey to grey-brown, smooth. *Shoot* Reddish brown with conspicuous lenticels, hairless.
Buds Rounded, hairless or downy, 5–7 mm (0.2–0.3 in). *Foliage* Leaves obovate to nearly round, apex rounded to almost truncate, rarely acute, base rounded to

wedge-shaped and usually untoothed, margin with deep jagged teeth or doubly toothed and almost lobulate, especially towards the apex, upper surface slightly glossy mid to dark green, soon hairless, underside with a persistent covering of vivid or silvery white hairs and five to eight raised veins, 4–7 × 4–7 cm (1.6–2.8 × 1.6–2.8 in). *Flowers* In small loose corymbs in late May or June to 8 cm (3.1 in) across, flowers pure white with pink anthers, two styles. *Fruit* Ovoid to globose, yellow, yellowish, or red, circa 1.5 cm (0.6 in).

Range: Balkans east across Turkey to the Caucasus and the Crimea.

Habitat: Woodland.

This tree is variable in its foliage and may include a cluster of tetraploid forms. It is usually confused to some extent with *S. graeca*, from which the more strongly silvery white undersides of the leaves and the fewer veins help to distinguish it.

p.215 **Himalayan Whitebeam** *Sorbus vestita*

Description: Deciduous tree 10–20 m (33–65 ft) with a bole diameter to 70 cm (2.3 ft).
Crown Conical in young trees, becoming broadened with age and finally irregularly domed. *Bark* Dark grey, smooth, developing fissures and then platy scales at the base. *Shoot* Stout, green but with a thick white wool in the first year, in the second year light somewhat shiny chestnut brown with scattered remnants of the wool, lenticels small, elliptic, pale.
Buds Ovoid, green or pinkish, with some white wool. *Foliage* Leaves thick, elliptic to oval, apex acute, base wedge-shaped, margins regularly crenate serrate, not or only slightly doubly toothed, veins in 6–11 (occasionally to 15) pairs, upper surface initially white woolly but this is soon lost, revealing dark glossy green, lower surface persistently white woolly (even after the leaves have fallen and are

lying on the ground over winter) with raised veins, 8–20 × 4–12 cm (3.1–8 × 1.6–4.7 in); leaf stalk 1.5 cm (0.6 in), stout, woolly; autumn colours russet on upper surface only. *Flowers* In large terminal corymbs 4–9 cm (1.6–3.5 in) across with individual flowers 1.3 cm (0.5 in); stalks and receptacle densely white woolly; sepals triangular, persistent; petals creamy-white, woolly at the base; twenty stamens; stigmas with three to five lobes; ovary woolly. *Fruit* Globular, ripens green or brown and green, with brownish spots or lenticels, 1.5–2 cm (0.6–0.8 in), flesh granular, seeds flat, light brown.

Range: Himalayas from Pakistan to Sikkim.

Habitat: Cultivated as an ornamental, in the wild occurring in montane forests with mixed broadleaves or with *Abies spectabilis* and taller growing *Rhododendron* species.

Synonyms: *S. cuspidata.*

This tree has very bold foliage, although not as impressive as in *S. hedlundii* and *S. thibetica*. It has crossed in cultivation with *S. aria* (the selection 'Wilfrid Fox' belonging here) to give trees with more sharply toothed and lobulate leaves with more (12–15) pairs of veins.

---

p.335 **Vilmorin Rowan** *Sorbus vilmorinii*

Description: Deciduous tree 4–8 m (13–26 ft) with a bole diameter to 30 cm (1 ft), but often shrubby with several stems.
Crown Rounded domed with spreading level branches. *Bark* Grey-brown, becoming scaly at the base in old trees. *Shoot* Grey-brown with short stiff hairs, becoming red-brown and hairless, slender. *Buds* Ovoid-conic, acute, deep red with rufous hairs, especially on the margins and apex, to 8 mm (0.3 in). *Foliage* Leaves pinnate, 12–15 cm (4.7–6 in), with 9–14 pairs of leaflets; leaflets oblong-elliptic to elliptic, apex rounded-acute with an apiculate tip, base rounded, margin finely

serrate in upper one-third to three-quarters, initially rufous pubescent, non-papillose beneath, 2–2.8 cm × 6–8 mm (0.8–1.1 × 0.25–0.3 in); rachis grooved; autumn colour deep red in late autumn. *Flowers* In lax corymbs to 10 cm (4 in) across, flowers 6–7 mm (0.25–0.3 in) across with white petals, three or four styles, 2.5 mm (0.1 in). *Fruit* Ovoid, ripening from deep crimson-pink and fading to white with pink flecks, slightly longer than broad, around 1–1.1 cm (0.4 in); calyx lobes fleshy, blunt; seeds dark brown, pear-shaped, 5 × 2.5 mm (0.2 × 0.1 in).

Range: Yunnan, West China.

Habitat: Cultivated as an ornamental, in the wild in open forests.

Similar species: *S. pseudovilmorinii* is closely allied to Vilmorin Rowan, differing in the smaller leaflets to a maximum of 2.3 cm (0.9 in), the smaller fruit which is 8–9 mm (0.3–0.4 in) long but as wide (at 1.1 cm (0.4 in)), in the smaller oblong-ovate seeds which are 3.5 × 2 mm (0.1 × 0.1 in), and in the longer and more slender styles 2.5–3 mm (0.1 in). Adjacent trees may have fruits initially maroon or whitish pink. It is common in Yunnan on the northern Cang Shan and on the Yulong Shan above Lijiang, and possibly further west in Yunnan. As a diploid, it is a sexual species and thus tends to show a greater degree of variation than the apomictic Vilmorin Rowan.

This makes an attractive small tree which thrives much better in cooler moist districts. The fruits are initially deep crimson when they first colour but gradually fade through pink to almost white. It is a tetraploid apomictic species, and thus breeds true from seed without risk of hybridization. It was introduced by Delavay in the later years of the 19th century, probably from the Cang Shan, although its exact wild origin is uncertain, as most of the plants in western Yunnan are the diploid *S. pseudovilmorinii* described above.

SPANISH BROOM, *SPARTIUM*
FAMILY LEGUMINOSAE

This is a monotypic genus allied to *Genista* but the round shoots are without spines.

---

p.346 **Spanish Broom** *Spartium junceum*

Description: Evergreen shrub or small tree to 5–6 m (16–20 ft), often shrubby.
Crown Rounded, domed, usually leafless but with photosynthesis carried out through the shoots. *Bark* Green-grey, smooth. *Shoot* Green or grey-green for one or two years, then becoming grey-brown, soft with a thick pith, smooth, cylindrical with sub-opposite buds, initially with silky white hairs but soon hairless. *Buds* Grey-brown, very small, in the axil of a scale-leaf, 1 mm (0.1 in).
Foliage Linear, green with a thick covering of silky white hairs, produced in spring but soon deciduous, 1.2–2 cm (0.5–0.8 in).
Flowers On terminal racemes 30–50 cm (12–20 in) on the current season's growth from mid summer onwards; flowers yellow, pea-like, 2.5 cm (1 in). *Fruit* Hairy pod 4–8 cm (1.6–3.1 in) long which ripens to black and contains 5–12 seeds.

Range: Southern Europe from Spain and Portugal across to the Crimea and Turkey and in North Africa.

Habitat: On dry sunny slopes.

This is more usually shrubby but can make a small tree. The shoots are rush-like, especially similar to the rush *Juncus effusus*. They can be macerated to yield a fibre capable of being spun into thread or woven

---

BLADDER NUT, STAPHYLEACEAE

This is a small family of five genera and around twenty-five species. The only genus represented in Europe is *Staphylea* (p.1181), although *Euscaphis japonica* (widely spread in eastern Asia) should be hardy in the warmer parts.

BLADDER NUTS, *STAPHYLEA*
FAMILY STAPHYLEACEAE

This is a genus of around ten species from the temperate regions of the northern hemisphere. The species are characterized by the pinnate leaves (trifoliate in one species) which are arranged in opposite pairs. The flowers are carried in the spring and are followed by the bladder-like fruits.

p.308   **Chinese Bladder-nut** *Staphylea holocarpa*

Description: Deciduous tree 6–15 m (20–50 ft) with a
bole diameter to 50 cm (1.6 ft).
Crown Ovoid. *Bark* Smooth, light grey-
brown, fissured in old trees. *Shoot* Green
or purplish, initially hairy but only
remaining so through the first year above
the pairs of buds, in the second year brown
or green and brown with buff striations.
Buds In opposite pairs, ovoid, pointed,
flattened, purple, hairy, 3 mm (0.1 in),
terminal bud missing. *Foliage* Leaves
trifoliate, to 13 cm (5.1 in) broad and long,
leaflets narrow oval, tapering to the acute
apex, base rounded to broad wedge-shaped
on the terminal leaflets, oblique and
unequal on the two laterals, margin with
forward-pointing fine serrations and
slightly downturned, upper surface matt
green to bloomed bluish green, shiny if
rubbed, with few or no hairs, underside
pale green with raised midrib and veins,
hairy along the veins only, 5–10 × 2–4 cm
(2–4 × 0.8 –1.6 in); leaf stalk with two
side grooves, pink and green, 2.5–9 cm
(1–3.5 in), lateral leaves on a stalk 2 mm
(0.1 in), terminal on a stalk 2–4 cm
(0.8–1.6 in); autumn colour poor.
Flowers In slender upright panicles in
April–May from buds on previous year's
growths, white to rose, 1.2 cm (0.5 in).
Fruit Inflated three-celled pear-shaped
capsule which tapers to the base, apex
pointed, 5 × 2.5 cm (2 × 1 in); seeds shiny,
grey-brown, 6 mm (0.25 in).
Range: Central and western China.
Habitat: Cultivated as an ornamental, in the wild
occurring in forests as an understorey.

Varieties: Var. *rosea* differs in the leaves being woolly beneath and in the large flowers.

Similar species: **Bladder-nut** *S. pinnata* (p.308) (from southeast France across Italy east through the Balkans to the Ukraine, and in southwest Asia from Turkey, Syria and the Transcaucasus region) differs in having leaves which are dull green and pinnate, with five or seven leaflets (only rarely only three) and flowers in terminal drooping panicles. It only grows as a shrub or small tree, to 6 m (20 ft).

This tree can be attractive when carrying the white or pink flowers in spring before the leaves expand. However, the flowers are susceptible to spring frosts. Perhaps the best tree in Europe is the one at the Gothenburg Botanic Garden, from seeds collected in Gansu, China.

STUARTIAS, *STUARTIA* (SYNONYM: *STEWARTIA*)
FAMILY THEACEAE

This is a genus of eight species of trees and shrubs from eastern USA and eastern Asia (especially China). The species are mainly deciduous, although one not treated here (*S. pteropetiolata*) is evergreen. The leaves are simple, toothed. The flowers are similar to *Camellia* but are borne on the current season's shoots in July and August. The fruit is a woody ovoid capsule, with five carpels each containing up to four seeds. Some species have exquisite peeling barks. The spelling *Stewartia* is an orthographic error.

p.239   **Deciduous Camellia**
Stuartia pseudocamellia

Description: Deciduous tree 10–15 m (33–50 ft) with a bole diameter to 50 cm (1.6 ft).
Crown Conical to slender ovoid.
Bark Smooth, orange-brown or purple-brown, peeling in small thin flakes to reveal orange below. *Shoot* Green or with a bronze tinge when young and slender, hairless or with a few scattered long hairs, in the second year reddish brown or with greyish streaks, later buff or brown.

Buds Flattened conical, green to reddish and shiny, 5 mm (0.2 in). *Foliage* Leaves elliptic to ovate-elliptic, apex acute to short slender pointed, base wedge-shaped, margin with few small forward-pointing teeth and ciliate hairs, upper surface mid to dark green, initially hairy, sub-shiny, veins impressed, lower surface shiny light green with long pilose hairs on the midrib, 6–11 × 2.5–5 cm (2.4–4.3 × 1–2 in); leaf stalk deeply grooved above with flanges from the decurrent leaf blade, silky hairy, green or pink, 1 cm (0.4 in); autumn colour yellow or red, variable. *Flowers* Carried singly in the leaf axils on short shoots, opening in mid-summer (late June to July), cup-shaped or saucer shaped to 8 cm (3.1 in) across, calyx lobes five, green, ovate, toothed and hairy, persistent, petals five, white, with crinkled toothed margins, stamens many in a central rounded knob, ovary conical, stiffly hairy. *Fruit* Conical pointed woody capsule to 2–2.5 × 1.5 cm (0.8–1 × 0.6 in), opening into five segments, seeds flattened, dark grown or black, with two narrow wings.

Range: Honshu, Shikoku and Kyushu, Japan and Korea.

Habitat: Cultivated as an ornamental, in the wild occurring in mountain forests.

Varieties: Var. *koreana* differs only in the flowers opening more widely, spreading almost flat like a saucer, whilst the Japanese plants tend to have more cup-shaped flowers.

Synonyms: *Stewartia pseudocamellia*.

This makes a small tree which is attractive for the white Camellia-like flowers. It requires an acidic or neutral soil. The autumn colour can be good, but is somewhat variable.

p.239 **Chinese Stuartia** *Stuartia sinensis*

Description: Deciduous tree 10–18 m (33–60 ft) with a bole diameter to 60 cm (2 ft).
Crown Columnar in young trees, becoming more spreading with age.

Bark Smooth, pink to grey or creamy orange, peeling and exfoliating in small translucent coiled strips and generally most attractive. *Shoot* Crimson-purple, with fine hairs when young.
Buds Conical, slender. *Foliage* Leaves elliptic to ovate-oblong, apex acute, base wedge-shaped, margin untoothed but with ciliate hairs, upper surface bright green and densely hairy when young, underside bright green but less hairy, 4–10 × 2–4.5 cm (1.6–4 × 0.8–1.8 in); leaf stalk hairy, 3–6 mm (0.1–0.25 in). *Flowers* Single in the leaf axils in July; flowers white, fragrant, 4–5 cm (1.6–2 in). *Fruit* Ovoid capsule, five-angled with five beaks at the apex; each carpel contains two seeds.

Range: Central and eastern China.
Habitat: Cultivated as an ornamental, in the wild occurring in woodland.

This is the most exquisite of the stuartias and one of the best of all trees for its bark. Its floral qualities are not commensurate with the bark, but are quite pleasing.

STORAX, STYRACACEAE

This is a family of mainly warm temperate trees and shrubs with a dozen genera and over 150 species. The leaves have star-shaped hairs, are without stipules and are simple and toothed. The cultivated genera with tree species include *Halesia* (p.728), *Pterostyrax* (p.1044), *Rehderodendron* (p.1091) and *Styrax*. *Sinojackia xylocarpa* is also cultivated but is really only a shrub. It differs from *Styrax* in the flowers having an inferior ovary.

STORAX, *STYRAX*
FAMILY STYRACACEAE

This is a large genus, with well over a hundred species. One species is native to southern Europe but most originate in the Americas and eastern Asia south to

Malaysia. The leaves are simple and toothed. The buds are superposed, i.e. with two or more in a leaf axil one above the other. The flowers are white, pendent with twice as many yellow stamens as there are lobes to the corolla. The ovary is superior, i.e. located above the point of attachment of the stamens and calyx. The fruit is a dry or fleshy drupe, which contains one or two seeds. The leaves are large, more or less all over 7 cm (2.8 in), and the flowers are in terminal racemes or panicles in *SS. hemsleyana* and *obassia*, but small, all less than 9 cm (3.5 in) and mainly less than 7 cm (2.8 in), with the flowers in small clusters of less than eight in *SS. japonica* and *officinalis*. The species are mainly grown for ornament, although a fragrant resin can be tapped by making incisions into the bark.

p.234 **Hemsley's Storax** *Styrax hemsleyana*

Description: Deciduous tree or large shrub, to 12 m (39 ft) with a bole diameter to 30 cm (1 ft). *Crown* Upright open crowned. *Bark* Grey-brown. *Shoot* Brown, initially with star-shaped hairs. *Buds* Narrow conic, superposed (i.e. two or more together). *Foliage* Leaves obovate or ovate, often unequal, apex acute to abruptly slender pointed, tapered to a narrow rounded base, margin with fine distant and peg-like teeth, upper surface pale green and hairless, with prominent veins, underside with star-shaped down, 7–17 × 5–9 cm (2.8–6.7 × 2–3.5 in); leaf stalk 0.6–1 cm (0.25–0.4 in), not enclosing the bud in the base. *Flowers* In terminal racemes or lightly branched downy panicles to 10–15 cm (4–6 in) in June; flowers white circa 2.5 cm (1 in) across. *Fruit* Ovoid, dry to thinly fleshy drupe, seed bright light brown, circa 1 cm (0.4 in).

Range: Central and western China.

Habitat: Cultivated as an ornamental, in the wild found in woodlands.

This makes a very attractive tree in June with its pure white and fragrant flowers, and later with its large foliage. It is similar to *S. obassia*, differing in the less hairy and narrower leaves and the buds not being enclosed in the base of the leaf stalk.

p.234 **Japanese Styrax** or **Snowbell Tree**
Styrax japonica

Description: Deciduous tree 10–15 m (33–50 ft) with a
bole diameter to 30 cm (1 ft).
Crown Columnar-conic with short
spreading or drooping branches.
Bark Fawn-grey, rough, in old trees grey,
furrowed orange with thick ridges.
Shoot Slender, green with brown star-
shaped hairs, becoming buff and shiny,
hairless in second year. *Buds* Ovoid-conic,
pressed against the shoot, buff, hairy,
superimposed (one above the other) in pairs
above the leaf traces, with only the upper
one flushing unless frosted or damaged,
2–4 mm (0.1–0.2 in). *Foliage* Leaves
broad elliptic or broad ovate and very
variable in size, tapering to a short slender-
pointed tip, base wedge-shaped and
decurrent on the leaf stalk, margins
untoothed, upper surface dull green,
hairless except for some hairs along the
four to seven pairs of veins which are raised
(even the tertiary ones), underside light
green, shiny, scattered star-shaped brown
hairs, veins raised near midrib but
impressed elsewhere, size varies from 1.5 ×
1 cm (0.6 × 0.4 in) (flowering shoot) up to
13 × 6 cm (5.1 × 2.4 in) (extension shoot);
leaf stalk grooved, star-shaped hairy, to
6 mm (0.25 in); autumn colour poor.
Flowers On short shoots of the current
season's growth with two to four leaves in
June, in pairs or up to six blooms at the
end of the shoot, pendent on long slender
hairless stalks 2.5–4.5 cm (1–1.8 in), calyx
cup-shaped with three to five green star-
shaped pubescent paddle-shaped lobes to
3 mm (0.1 in), five petals but united near
the base, snow-white, lobes ovate, pointed,
1.5 × 9 mm (0.6 × 0.4 in), four to six
stamens with yellow-ochre anthers 6 mm
(0.25 in). *Fruit* Pendent, ovoid, with
persistent calyx, 1.5 cm (0.6 in), with a
single light-brown seed.
Range: Japan, Korea and Central China.
Habitat: Cultivated as an ornamental, in the wild
occurring in mixed forests.

This is a most attractive tree when carrying the massed snow-white flowers which droop below every branch, even those in fairly dense shade. It is susceptible to spring frosts and requires a moist sheltered site for best effect, preferably one where the flowers can be seen from below.

p.234 **Big-leaf Storax** *Styrax obassia*

Description: Deciduous tree to 10–15 m (33–50 ft) with a bole diameter to 50 cm (1.6 ft).
Crown Columnar, somewhat open.
Bark Grey-brown or grey, rough, becoming shallow fissured. *Shoot* Green with a brown star-shaped indumentum but this soon rubs off, in the second year dark red-brown, peeling in the third year to become orange-brown. *Buds* In superposed pairs, rufous brown hairy, ovoid, concealed in expanded base of leaf stalk, to 1 cm (0.4 in).
Foliage Leaves variable, from small elliptic to almost rounded in outline, apex acute or short slender pointed, base rounded, margin entire or with a few spaced small aristate teeth in the upper part, matt green above with slightly impressed veins, whitish green and densely star-shaped hairy beneath with 4–10 pairs of raised main veins and net-like tertiary veins, from 5 × 3 cm (2 × 1.2 in) to 20 × 15 cm (8 × 6 in); leaf stalk slightly grooved, green, hairless, expanded and flattened over the enclosed buds, 1–2.5 cm (0.4–1 in). *Flowers* In terminal racemes on short shoots in mid summer, flowers white, fragrant, 2–3 cm (0.8–1.2 in) across.
Fruit Ovoid, 1–1.5 cm (0.4–0.6 in), with a persistent green calyx and a thin green covering with short brown hairs, containing a single brown seed.

Range: Throughout Japan, Korea and northeast China.

Habitat: Cultivated as an ornamental, in the wild occurring in mixed forests.

This tree is spectacular when in full flower but requires a moist situation on a good soil for best effect.

p.233 **Storax** *Styrax officinalis*

Description: Deciduous tree or large shrub, to 7 m
(23 ft).
Crown Rounded. *Bark* Grey, smooth.
Shoot Slender, buff to grey in the first
winter and covered with dense star-shaped
down, becoming light brown, hairless and
somewhat shiny. *Buds* Ovoid to obovoid
and sometimes on a stalk, apex bluntly
pointed, densely covered in buff-grey star-
shaped down, to 1 cm (0.4 in), superposed.
Foliage Leaves ovate to broad ovate, apex
rounded, base wedge-shaped or
occasionally heart-shaped, margin
untoothed, covered with a dense white- to
buff-coloured star-shaped down on both
sides but more persistently beneath,
5–9 cm (2–3.5 in); leaf stalk circa 1 cm
(0.4 in). *Flowers* In short terminal clusters
of three to eight in June; flowers white
fragrant, 3 cm (0.2 in) across with the
corolla divided into six to eight downy
segments. *Fruit* Globose drupe, 2 cm
(0.8 in), with the calyx remaining at base
and becoming woody.

Range: Eastern Mediterranean region from
southern Italy east to western Asia with
varieties in California and western Mexico.

Habitat: Hillsides and scrub.

This small tree has a remarkable
distribution, with varieties (var. *californica*
and var. *jaliscana*) in California and Jalisco,
western Mexico. It can be tapped by
wounding the bark to produce storax, a
resin used as a perfume, as incense and in
some medicinal preparations.

DOGWOODS, *SWIDA* (SYNONYMS: *CORNUS* IN PART,
THELYCRANIA)
FAMILY CORNACEAE

This is a genus of around 20 species, ranging from shrubs
to medium-sized trees. The leaves are typical of the
Cornaceae, except in two species they are alternate on the
shoot (*see SS. controversa* and *alternifolia*), not in opposite
pairs. The flowers are carried in the spring or early summer

in corymbs, lacking both bracts and bracteoles. The fruit is a single-seeded fleshy drupe. The name 'dogwood' derives from the manufacture of skewers or 'dogs' from shoots.

p.142 **Table Dogwood** *Swida controversa*

Description:
Deciduous tree generally to 10–15 m (33–50 ft), with a bole diameter to 30 cm (1 ft).
Crown Conical with tiered level branches.
Bark Grey with pinkish fissures, smooth, becoming ridged at the base.
Shoot Green, slightly hairy, with small raised lenticels, becoming purple or dark olive-brown in later years. *Buds* Terminal buds conical, green or purple with brownish hairs at the tip, to 4 mm (0.2 in), lateral buds minute.
Foliage Leaves alternate along the shoot, on short or flowering shoots forming a helical rosette, oval or ovate, tip rounded to a short slender point, base rounded or broadly wedge-shaped, margin untoothed, upper surface shiny mid green with parallel incurved veins, undersurface whitish with raised veins, sparsely hairy especially on the veins, 7–15 × 2–7 cm (2.8–6 × 0.8–2.8 in); leaf stalk grooved, hairless except at base, purple-pink or pale green, 3–5 cm (1.2–2 in); autumn colour not strong. *Flowers* In erect terminal flattened cymes above the level of the branches, 8–18 cm (3.1–7.1 in) across, composed of many 1 cm (0.4 in) white flowers, produced in mid to late summer (June–July). *Fruit* Blue-black or whitish blue, globose, 6 mm (0.25 in).

Range:
From Nepal along the Himalayas across China to Japan and Korea and south into northern Vietnam.

Habitat:
Cultivated as an ornamental, in the wild occurring in ravines or woodland.

Varieties:
'Variegata' has the leaves with a yellowish-white border.

Synonyms:
Cornus controversa.

Similar species:
C. alternifolia is the second species with alternate leaves. These are strongly tapered at both ends and usually smaller, in the

range 5–12 cm (2–4.7 in). The flowers are carried in smaller cymes 5–6 cm (2–2.4 in) across. It also has a form which has the leaves variegated white, named 'Argentea'.

This tree is one of only two species in the Cornaceae or Dogwood family which has the leaves arranged alternately along the shoot. The tiered level branching is characteristic.

---

p.142   **Large-leafed Cornel** *Swida macrophylla*

Description: Deciduous tree to 10–15 m (33–50 ft) with a bole diameter to 50 cm (1.6 ft). *Crown* Conical to rounded, with short spreading branches. *Bark* Dark grey, rough and fissured at base. *Shoot* Purplish pink in the first year and grooved, becoming green or green and brown in the second year, then grey. *Buds* In opposite pairs, conic to ovoid-conic, flattened, dark brown, 4 mm (0.2 in). *Foliage* Leaves ovate to ovate-elliptic, tapering to a narrow twisted point, base rounded to broad wedge-shaped, margin untoothed, upper surface shiny green with six or seven pairs of slightly impressed parallel veins, underside whitish green, with raised veins, 10–18 × 5–10 cm (4–7.1 × 2–4 in); leaf stalk grooved, yellow-green, 1–3 cm (0.4–1.2 in); autumn colour poor. *Flowers* In erect wide corymbs carried above the branches in June with opposite branching; flowers dull white, 1 cm (0.4 in). *Fruit* Globose, green, ripening blue, with persistent calyx and style, 4–6 mm (0.2–0.25 in).

Range: Himalayas from Nepal eastwards across China to Korea and Japan.

Habitat: Cultivated as an ornamental, in the wild occurring in moist temperate forests.

Synonyms: *Cornus macrophylla, C. brachypoda.*

This tree is very similar to *S. controversa*, but can be distinguished by the opposite buds, branches and branches of the inflorescence.

p.144 **Dogwood** *Swida sanguinea*

Description: Deciduous shrub or rarely of small tree
stature and up to 6 m (20 ft), with a bole
diameter to 20 cm (0.7 ft).
Crown Rounded, usually on several stems.
Bark Brown, finely roughened. *Shoot* Green
or pinkish on the upper side and green
below, with rough small white hairs,
remaining green for several years, flattened
by the paired buds. *Buds* In opposite pairs,
ovoid long conic, chocolate brown or dark
brown with pale hairs, to 1 cm (0.4 in).
Foliage Leaves ovate or elliptic, apex acute
and often downcurved as a drip tip, base
wedge-shaped or rounded, margin
untoothed, dark green and rough with stiff
short hairs and slightly impressed veins
above, beneath mid to light shiny green
with three or four pairs of rather parallel
raised veins which curve in at the tips, rough
with short whitish or brownish hairs, 4–8 ×
2–4 cm (1.6–3.1 × 0.8–1.6 in); leaf stalk
with two decurrent flanges from the leaf,
pink or green, hairy, circa 1 cm (0.4 in);
autumn colour purple to red. *Flowers* In
small terminal cymes from flower buds laid
down the previous year, opening in early
summer (June), 4–5 cm (1.6–2 in) across,
dull white, fragrant. *Fruit* Globose,
ripening from green to purplish black,
6–8 mm (0.25–0.3 in), with a single seed.

Range: Britain and southern Scandinavia to
Portugal and across Europe to Turkey.

Habitat: Hedgerows, open woodlands as an
understorey.

Synonyms: *Cornus sanguinea, Thelycrania sanguinea*.

This is usually found as a large shrub but
occasionally makes a small tree.

QUEEN PALMS, *SYAGRUS* (SYNONYM: *ARECASTRUM*)
FAMILY PALMAE

This is a genus of 32 species from South America, especially
Brazil. The species cultivated in Europe and in warm
temperate regions around the world is often placed in a
separate monotypic genus, *Arecastrum*.

p.348 **Queen Palm** *Syagrus romanzoffiana*

Description: Evergreen tree to 15 m (50ft) with a bole
diameter to 70 cm (2.3 ft).
Crown Monopodal, with a single stem and
a terminal rosette of leaves. *Bark* Smooth,
grey-brown, distinctly ringed.
Foliage Leaves pinnate, at first arching erect
but becoming pendent as further leaves are
produced, plumose, to 5 m (16 ft) or more;
leaflets to 1 m × 3 cm (39 × 1.2 in), carried
in several rows and in groups of one to five,
soft, green on both surfaces; leaf stalk not
toothed; sheath fibrous. *Flowers* Amongst
the lower leaves, pendulous, to 1 m (39 in),
subtended by a woody boat-shaped bract
(with another hidden in the leaf bases);
flowers creamy yellow, in threes with two
male and one female. *Fruit* Ovoid, yellow,
beaked, with fleshy covering, 2.5–4 cm
(1–1.6 in).

Range: Brazil to The Argentine.

Habitat: Cultivated as an ornamental in the
Mediterranean region.

Synonyms: *Arecastrum romanzoffiana*, *Cocos
romanzoffiana*.

This makes a very attractive palm for mild
areas.

LILACS, *SYRINGA*
FAMILY OLEACEAE

This genus occurs in the temperate regions of the Old
World, and contains around two dozen mainly shrubby
species. The species have opposite, simple and untoothed
leaves and bear showy flowers which are followed by woody
capsules. Many hybrid cultivars have been selected in
cultivation.

---

p.147 **Lilac** *Syringa vulgaris*

Description: Deciduous shrub, rarely tree-like in
proportions, to 7 m (23 ft) with a bole
diameter to 20 cm (0.7 ft).
Crown Rounded, usually on several stems.
Bark Brown, fissured into stringy scales.

Shoot Brown to grey, flattened between the decussate pairs of buds with slight ridges running down the shoot, hairless, terminal bud usually missing. *Buds* In opposite pairs, ovoid-conic, pointed, brown with green inner scales which are covered with glands, to 7 mm (0.3 in). *Foliage* Leaves ovate to broadly ovate, apex acute, base heart-shaped, margin untoothed, slightly leathery, yellow-green and hairless, 4–8(–12) × 3–8 cm (1.6–3.1(–4.7) × 1.2–3.1 in) in width; leaf stalk 2–3 cm (0.8–1.2 in). *Flowers* In dense, terminal, conical, leafless panicles from buds on previous season's shoots in April–May; flowers white to lilac or purple, fragrant, small, set on stalks and with a calyx which has minute gland-tipped down.

Fruit Flattened smooth beaked capsule which splits along two sutures, 1.5–2 cm (0.6–0.8 in).

Range: Balkan region.

Habitat: Scrub on rocky hillsides, widely cultivated as a garden plant.

Similar species: **Hungarian Lilac** *S. josikaea* (p.147) belongs to a different section of the genus, in which the shoot has a terminal bud and the flowers are carried on leafy shoots. The leaves are elliptic with a wedge-shaped base, whilst the flowers tend to be a deeper lilac in colour. It occurs in Transylvanian region of Romania and in the Carpathian Mountains in the Ukraine.

S. yunnanensis is one of a number of Chinese species which are cultivated in gardens. It makes a shrub to 6–7 m (20–23 ft), and has warty reddish shoots and large oval to obovate wedge-shaped leaves.

This makes a shrub with erect stems, but occasionally grows on a single stem. It has been grown in cultivation for many years and different forms, other than the basic lilac coloured flowers, have been selected. Whether these forms are an improvement is a matter of taste, but they all share an exquisite fragrance. When not in flower, the plant is somewhat dowdy in appearance.

TAIWANIA, *TAIWANIA*
FAMILY TAXODIACEAE

This genus consists of two taxa, one from Taiwan and the
other from central southern and southwest China and along
the border region with Burma. The foliage is similar to
Cryptomeria but the cone is very different. Most trees in
cultivation, however, are juvenile.

p.57   **Taiwania** *Taiwania cryptomerioides*

Description: Evergreen tree to 15 m (50 ft) in
cultivation, but to 60 m (200 ft) in the
wild, with a bole diameter of 30 cm (1 ft)
(or to 10 m (33 ft) in the wild).
Crown Conical or broad conical with
spreading branches or decurrent branches
with pendent laterals. *Bark* Grey-brown,
soon fibrous and peeling in long strips, in
old trees furrowed. *Shoot* Green for several
years with decurrent leaf bases, later red-
brown. *Buds* Ovoid, green, to 3 mm
(0.1 in). *Foliage* In spreading or drooping
three-dimensional sprays which are harsh
and prickly to the touch; leaves in juvenile
plants radial, acicular with a pungent bony
apex, laterally compressed and slightly to
moderately incurved, grey-green or
glaucous, with two white somewhat waxy
bands of stomata on each side, 0.6–2 cm
(0.25–0.8 in); foliage on mature trees scale-
like, incurved, triangular, to 4 mm (0.2 in);
crushed foliage with a faint grassy resinous
scent. *Flowers* On previous season's shoots
but not recorded in cultivation. *Fruit* Not
reported in cultivation.

Range: Taiwan.

Habitat: Cultivated in Europe as an ornamental, in
the wild occurring in mixed montane forest
in the warm to cool temperate zone.

Similar species: The genus is considered to include two
species by many botanists. The other taxon
is *T. flousiana*, which is much more glaucous
and with pendent foliage. This is recorded
from southwest Yunnan and along the
border with Burma, and also from central
China in southern Hubei and Guizhou
provinces. The main botanical difference

between the two taxa is in the number of scales in the mature female cone, with 15–21 in the Taiwan populations, and 21–39 in mainland populations.

This tree makes immense specimens in Taiwan. It is hardy (somewhat surprisingly considering it comes from astride the Tropic of Cancer at only 1800–2400 m (5900–7875 ft)) as far north as Aberdeen, but the best trees are reported in warmer and moister southwestern districts. It is very similar to *Cryptomeria* in the foliage, but harsher to the touch. The mature foliage is quite different, being scale-like, whilst the cones are like a small version of a *Tsuga* cone.

TAMARISK, TAMARICACEAE

This small family is represented in cultivation by the genus *Tamarix*.

TAMARISKS, *TAMARIX*
FAMILY TAMARICACEAE

This is a genus of around 50 species. They have small flowers and scale leaves and are generally rather difficult to identify! Many species are characteristic of dry regions, where they often occur near or in water.

p.38 **Tamarisk** *Tamarix gallica*

Description: Deciduous shrub or small tree to 8 m (26 ft) with a bole diameter to 20 cm (0.7 ft).
Crown Rounded, often on several arching stems. *Bark* Brown, becoming fissured and somewhat scaly and flaking.
Shoot Slender, round, yellow-green at first, becoming red or purple, in the second year brown. *Buds* Hidden in the leaf axils, minute. *Foliage* Leaves scale-like, overlapping the slender shoots but alternate or helically set, narrow ovate, with an acute incurved apex, hairless, light green, 1 mm

(0.1 in) on side shoots, but triangular, slender pointed and up to 4 mm (0.2 in) on strong shoots. *Flowers* In slender racemes 5–10 cm (2–4 in) in summer, each flower carried on a short stalk with a small basal non-leafy bract, petals whitish or pink, in fives, cupped and elliptic-ovate to 2 mm (0.1 in), deciduous (i.e. not persisting on the fruit), stamens in fives, style shorter than the petals. *Fruit* A small capsule containing numerous small seeds which have a tuft of hairs at one end.

Range: Atlantic seaboard from northwest France south to North Africa, common in coastal Britain as a maritime hedge but doubtfully native.

Habitat: Coastal situations, cultivated more widely.

Synonyms: *T. anglica.*

Similar species: The species of *Tamarix* are difficult to separate even with good flowering material. Part of the problem is the small size of the parts, partly their inherent ability to vary! They can be divided on the basis of the number of stamens, which are either in fives or fours, although occasional aberrant plants are encountered and the following notes should allow flowering plants to be identified with reasonable confidence.

The species with five stamens are: *T. africana* (p.39) which has a similar distribution to *T. gallica* but differs in the flowers mainly being carried on the previous year's shoots, and therefore borne earlier in the season (although some forms may fruit later on the current season's shoots). The petals are persistent on the capsule, and acute to slender pointed at the apex.

T. ramossisima (p.39), from southern Russia and Asia Minor, has flowers in racemes 5 cm (2 in) or longer, with the style tapering into the ovary and longer than the petals. It flowers on the current season's shoots in mid to late summer, making large plumose displays.

T. chinensis is close to *T. ramossisima* but flowers on the old wood earlier in the season; it is native to central and eastern Asia, where it occurs along dry rivers in semi-deserts but has become naturalized in parts of Europe.

T. canariensis from dry maritime localities in the western Mediterranean region and Portugal, mainly flowers in the summer. The flowers have a green leafy bract which is longer than the calyx and small obovate early-falling petals. The bark is reddish brown.

T. smyrnensis (p.39), from the Aegean region across southeast Europe to the southern Ukraine, also has reddish-brown bark. It differs from *T. gallica* in the ovate-rounded in outline strongly keeled petals.

Three species have the petals and sepals in fours:

In *T. dalmatica*, the bark is dark brown or blackish and the flowers are in solitary but broad racemes, 0.7–1 cm (0.3–0.4 in) in width, with the bracts longer than the calyx. It occurs in coastal marshes and riverine situations in the eastern Mediterranean.

T. parviflora (p.39) has brown to purple bark and flowers with bracts shorter than the calyx. It occurs in the Balkan peninsula and around the Aegean where it is found along river banks, and roadside hedges.

T. tetrandra (p.39) has a black bark and differs from *T. parviflora* in the bracts which are herbaceous, at least in the basal half of the raceme, and the larger flowers, with petals more than 2 mm (0.1 in) in length. It is a montane species from the Balkans and southeast Europe, occurring in damp localities.

The foliage is very similar to the scale leaves of Cypresses and Junipers but, when not carrying the flowers, the genus can be identified by the scale leaves being helically arranged on the shoot, not in opposite (decussate) pairs or threes. Tamarisks naturally occur in salty places, either in maritime situations or along watercourses in desert regions. In cultivation, however, they grow better in moist loams. They are fast growing, but only small shrubby trees.

YEW, TAXACEAE

This is a small family of five genera. The only ones commonly found in cultivation are *Taxus* (p.1201) and *Torreya* (p.1235). *See also* Cephalotaxaceae (p.590).

REDWOOD, TAXODIACEAE

This is a small family of nine genera and only seventeen species, from both hemispheres. The family is related to the Cupressaceae, and included in it by some authors. The leaves are set in a helix on the shoot, except in *Metasequoia* (p.840).

SWAMP CYPRESSES, *TAXODIUM*
FAMILY TAXODIACEAE

This is a genus of three related species from southeast USA and throughout most of Mexico. The shoots are of two types, deciduous ones which do not have buds but fall in late autumn, and persistent ones where only the leaves turn brilliant colours and fall. In the shoots, therefore, the species are similar to *Metasequoia*, but the leaves are arranged helically along the shoot, not in opposite pairs. The male cones expand as long catkins from late autumn onwards. The species are adapted to thriving in wet and waterlogged sites, and produce aerial roots, or 'pneumatophores' to allow the roots to breathe.

---

p.59 **Pond Cypress** *Taxodium ascendens*

Description: Deciduous tree to 15 m (50 ft) with a bole diameter to 60 cm (2 ft).
Crown Narrow conic in young trees, becoming columnar and domed, with short level branching. *Bark* Dull brown, fissured into short vertical ridges.
Shoot Slender, matures to red-brown in first autumn but green during the growing season, in second and later years red-brown, rough and stout. *Buds* Domed, slightly beaked, green-brown, and subtended by a small persistent scale leaf, arranged erratically but mainly spirally on the shoot,

1 mm (0.1 in). *Foliage* In two forms, persistent and deciduous shoots; leaves spirally arranged and scale-like or awl-like, pressed against shoot, bright green, 0.5–1 × 0.2 cm (0.2–0.4 × 0.1 in), turning brick-red to russet in late autumn before falling with the shoot; the shoots are usually erect ('ascending'). *Flowers* Male cones pendulous. *Fruit* Globose, ripening from green to brown during one season, 2.5–3 cm (1–1.2 in).

Range: Southern Virginia to Louisiana.

Habitat: Cultivated in Europe as an ornamental, in the wild occurring around ponds, not along river valleys.

Varieties: Forma *nutans* (also often treated as a cultivar) has the foliage nodding by autumn, although this may be a general feature of the species. The clone in general cultivation has a narrow conical or columnar crown.

Synonyms: *T. distichum* var. *nutans*.

This tree is related to Swamp Cypress (*Taxodium distichum*), occurring generally at lower altitudes and around ponds rather than along river valleys. It rarely produces 'knees'. The scale or awl-like leaves on the deciduous shoot serve to separate it from *T. distichum*. The deciduous shoots are ascending and arranged all around the shoot. The persistent shoots are, as in *T. distichum*, in clusters of two or three at the shoot tips.

p.59 **Swamp Cypress** or **Bald Cypress**
Taxodium distichum

Description: Deciduous tree to 30 m (100 ft) with a bole diameter to 1.5 m (5 ft).
Crown Conical in young trees, becoming columnar with long level branches and often rather flat topped in old ones, on wet sites may be surrounded by 'knees'.
Bark Dull pale brown or reddish brown, shallowly fissured and peeling in slender strips, in some trees deeply fluted.
Shoot Slender, mature to brown in first

autumn but green during the growing season, in second and later years red-brown, smooth and peeling with fine fibrous strips. *Buds* Globose, green-brown, arranged erratically but mainly spirally on the shoot, 1–1.5 mm (0.1 in). *Foliage* In two forms; on persistent shoots the leaves are spirally arranged and scale-like; on deciduous shoots they are linear, pale green, twisted to lie flat either side of the shoot and 1–2 cm × 2 mm (0.4–0.8 × 0.1 in), turning brick red to russet in late autumn before falling with the shoot. *Flowers* Male cones pendulous, lengthening from 5–20 cm (2–8 in) in late autumn but only shedding pollen in early spring. *Fruit* Globose, ripening from green to brown during one season, 2.5–3 cm (1–1.2 in), on a stalk 3 mm (0.1 in); scales spirally set, few, with a central thorn.

Range: Coastal southeast USA from New Jersey to Texas (except peninsular Florida) and up the Mississippi valley.

Habitat: Cultivated in Europe as an ornamental, in the wild occurring in low-elevation valley bottoms which are often flooded for periods each year.

Synonyms: *Cupressus distichum.*

Similar species: *Glyptostrobus pensilis* is similar but has shoots which remain green for the first winter and cones more similar to those of *Cryptomeria*. It comes from southern China and southern Vietnam.

Swamp Cypress will tolerate sites which are flooded for a period of the year. It will survive with the roots in 15 cm (6 in) or more of water permanently but grows only very slowly in these situations. Best growth is made where the soil is freely drained, although in these situations other trees may grow faster. When growing on permanently wet sites, aerial roots, 'knees' or pneumatophores are produced. These rise above the water level and enable breathing (both acquisition of oxygen and venting of carbon dioxide) to occur. *Metasequoia* does not produce 'knees', although the rare Chinese Swamp Cypress (*Glyptostrobus*) does.

YEWS, TAXUS
FAMILY TAXACEAE

The yews are a widespread genus of extremely similar trees. It has been said that the cultivar 'Adpressa' of Common Yew is more distinct than the average species! As a consequence, there is debate as to how many species are present, and where to draw the boundaries, especially in eastern Asia where yews extend from China through Vietnam and into Indonesia and the Philippines. The foliage is arranged helically but except on leading shoots is twisted and parted on either side of the shoot, which remains green for some time. The fruit is subtended by a large fleshy aril. The aril is the only part of yew which is not poisonous, all other parts being positively harmful to people, cattle and horses if eaten. Yew is not a conifer, as the fruit is not in a cone but is terminal on a shoot. The wood is extremely hard, as to be expected from a long-lived yet slow-growing tree. Yews are also very tolerant of shade and, once established, of dry conditions.

p.64 **Yew** *Taxus baccata*

Description: Evergreen tree 10–25 m (33–80 ft) with a bole diameter of up to 3 m (10 ft), but usually less than 1 m (3.3 ft).
Crown Broadly conical in young trees but quickly becoming broad columnar as the side branches grow outwards as quickly as height growth is made, when on several stems or old becoming domed.
Bark Purplish brown and smooth in young trees, developing scales which flake off to reveal red-brown, yellow or purple patches, often fluted and always thin.
Shoot Green from the decurrent leaf bases for at least two years, then brown in the third or fourth year, slender. *Buds* Ovoid, green, 2–3 mm (0.1 in).
Foliage Spreading flat and gently forwards either side of the shoot on shaded branches, on those in full light the leaves are more curving upwards, with a V-parting above; leaves linear, abruptly tapered at base, more gently to the acute or rounded pointed apex, upper surface deep green with a raised midrib and no stomata, lower surface with two pale to mid-green bands

of stomata, 2–3 cm (0.8–1.2 in) (rarely to 4 cm (1.6 in)) by 3 mm (0.1 in); crushed foliage with no scent. *Flowers* On previous year's shoots in late spring, dioecious; male cones clustered in leaf axils on underside of shoot, globose and yellow, to 4 mm (0.2 in), on a 3 mm (0.1 in) stalk. *Fruit* With the blackish seed exposed in a thin green cup when immature, with the cup or aril swelling in the first autumn to nearly enclose the seed and becoming red and juicy, 1 cm × 0.6 mm (0.4–0.25 in).

Range: Throughout Europe except the north, extending east to Iran and into north Africa (Morocco, Algeria).

Habitat: Forming pure forests on chalk downland and as a minor constituent of acid broadleafed woodland.

Varieties: Several cultivars are found, including ones with golden foliage. More distinct is the Irish Yew, 'Fastigiata'; this has erect foliage with all the leaves arranged radially, as on a leading shoot. It makes a very dense and dark crowned tree to 15 m (50 ft).

Yew is a very long-lived tree, but not necessarily slow growing. It is extremely shade tolerant, and one of the few plants which will grow beneath Beech. All parts, except the fleshy red aril around the seed, contain poisonous alkaloids. As little as 100–200 g (3.5–7.1 oz) of foliage is sufficient to kill a horse, yet deer seem to browse it with impunity. The aril which partly encloses the seed is sweet, almost sickly so, and contains little or no alkaloids. It is intended to be eaten, with the seed (poisonous if crushed) passing through the gut. The seed case is thick and resistant to gastric juices, with the seed germinating more readily if previously ingested by a bird. One of the constituents of Yew, taxol, shows great promise as an anticancer drug. The timber is strong and resilient, with a yellow sapwood and a red-brown heartwood. Traditional longbows were made from yew, cut so that the bow contained both sapwood (to give springiness) and heartwood (for strength).

p.64 **Japanese Yew** *Taxus cuspidata*

Description: Evergreen tree 8–20 m (26–65 ft) with a bole diameter 0.3–1 m (1–3.3 ft).
Crown Conical or spreading. *Bark* Red-brown. *Shoot* Green in first winter, becoming red-brown in second year but retaining patches of green into the third year, hairless. *Buds* Long ovoid, apex rounded, scales brown, 4 mm (0.2 in).
Foliage Parted below the shoot or somewhat radial, spreading more or less at a right angle at the sides and above the shoot, rather open; leaves linear with a raised midrib above, base rounded with a 2 mm (0.1 in) stalk, apex abruptly tapered to a pointed apex, dull dark green above without stomata, beneath with two pale matt-green bands of very small stomata, 1.5–3 cm × 2–4 mm (0.6–1.2 × 0.1–0.2 in); crushed foliage scarcely scented.
Flowers On previous season's shoots in late winter or early spring; male cones globose, pink-brown, 3 mm (0.1 in). *Fruit* Enclosed by a fleshy aril which ripens from green to red in first autumn, seed ovate, greenish.

Range: Japan, across Korea to China where it occurs in Manchuria south to Shandong and Jiangsu provinces.

Habitat: Cultivated in Europe as an ornamental, in the wild forming an understorey element in mixed forests.

This tree is tolerant of much colder winters than *T. baccata*, which makes it a useful evergreen for continental districts.

p.65 **Maire Yew** *Taxus mairei*

Description: Evergreen tree to 10 m (33 ft) with a bole diameter to 30 cm (1 ft).
Crown Broad conical to spreading.
Bark Brown, smooth, becoming slightly peeling in large platy flakes and red-brown. *Shoot* Green for first winter and hairless, then turns bright brown with some green, later dark brown with red-brown fissures. *Buds* Ovoid to long ovoid, apex rounded, pale or yellowish green, to 2.5 mm (0.1 in),

with rounded, not keeled scales.
Foliage Widely spreading or pectinate either side of the shoot and very sparse, around one leaf per centimetre on either side, sickle-shaped, apex tapered to a short abrupt point, upper surface shiny mid green with a raised midrib, lower surface pale matt yellowish green and concave, 1.5–3 cm × 3–3.5 mm (0.6–1.2 × 0.1 in); crushed foliage scarcely scented. *Flowers* On season's growths in late winter or early spring; male cones ovoid, 2–3 mm (0.1 in) on a stalk 2 mm (0.1 in). *Fruit* Aril green with a dark olive two-angled seed, 6–7 mm (0.25–0.3 in).

Range: Central and western China.

Habitat: Cultivated in Europe as an ornamental, in the wild occurring in mixed woods on limestone.

Synonyms: *T. celebica* misapplied.

The range of this tree is rather confused. The plants in cultivation are from west Sichuan, collected by Wilson in 1910. Rather similar plants have been found as far south as the Celebes and Sumatra in Indonesia and some botanists have equated them with this species.

TETRACENTRON, TETRACENTRONACEAE

This is a monotypic family from China, Vietnam, Burma, northeast India, Bhutan and east Nepal.

TETRACENTRON, *TETRACENTRON*
FAMILY TETRACENTRONACEAE

This is a monotypic genus.

p.237   Spur Leaf *Tetracentron sinense*

Description: Deciduous tree 15–25 m (50–80 ft) with a bole diameter to 1 m (3.3 ft).
Crown Conic in young trees, becoming ovoid to columnar with spreading branches. *Bark* Brown, ridged. *Shoot* Bright green or red, hairless, grey-brown in second year;

developing spur or short shoots to 4 cm
(1.6 in). *Buds* Narrow conic, red or green,
with a single bud scale, to 1.5 cm (0.6 in).
Foliage Leaves single on spur shoots; ovate
to slender pointed, tip long pointed,
twisted slightly, base heart-shaped, margins
with fine forward serrations, five to seven
veins from the base, impressed above and
prominent below, upper surface matt green,
paler beneath with a rough surface under a
hand-lens and reddish veins, 7–16 ×
5–12 cm (2.8–6.3 × 2–4.7 in); leaf stalk
grooved, reddish, with the stipules adnate
to the lower half, 2–4 cm (0.8–1.6 in).
Flowers In pendulous spikes 7–20 cm
(2.8–8 in) long from the spur shoots in
early summer, greenish and small, without
petals. *Fruit* A cluster of four laterally-
joined follicles which ripen in autumn to
green and release small whitish seeds.

Range: Central China south to northern Vietnam and
west across north Burma through Arunachal
Pradesh (India) to Bhutan and east Nepal.

Habitat: Cultivated in Europe as an ornamental, in
the wild occurring in temperate forests on
hillsides or ridges.

Varieties: Var. *himalense* has longer-tipped leaves and
more lax fruiting spikes. It represents the
form from the western part of the range,
from Bhutan and Nepal, but possibly
extending as far east as Yunnan.

This tree bears a great similarity in the
foliage to *Cercidiphyllum*, but this has leaves
and buds in opposite pairs and does not
have the single-leafed spur shoots, nor the
catkin-like fruit. The wood is unusual, as
unlike almost all other broadleaved trees, it
has no vessels but only tracheids for water
conduction. Thus it is more similar to
conifer timber, except that the tracheids are
considered more primitive.

ALERCE, *TETRACLINIS*
FAMILY CUPRESSACEAE

This is a monotypic genus from southeast Spain, Malta,
Algeria and Morocco. The leaves are in false whorls of four,

with a pair of larger and a pair of smaller leaves arranged decussately.

---

p.49 Alerce *Tetraclinis articulata*

Description: Evergreen tree 10–20 m (33–65 ft) with a bole diameter to 1 m (3.3 ft).
Crown Conic in young trees, becoming columnar. *Bark* Brown. *Shoot* Green or yellow-green and lined from the decurrent leaf bases, slender. *Buds* Hidden in leaf bases. *Foliage* In flat open sprays; juvenile leaves linear, in pairs; adult leaves in false whorls composed of two superimposed pairs, with the laterals decurrent along the shoot and very small facial leaves, tips free, acute; crushed foliage resin scented.
Flowers Terminal on previous season's shoots in spring; male cones globose, yellow. *Fruit* Globose but angled due to the four valvate scales, ripening from glaucous green to brown in the first autumn or winter when they are 2 cm (0.8 in), then opening to release the four to six seeds which have two unequal wings.

Range: Northern Algeria, Morocco, southeast Spain and Malta.
Habitat: Dry hillsides.
Synonyms: *Thuja articulata*, *Callitris quadrivalis*.

This tree is very tolerant of hot dry conditions and is planted in Mediterranean countries such as Cyprus. The cones have four large scales which are valvate and thus similar to *Thuja*, but the seeds have two large unequal wings, as in *Calocedrus*. It withstands clipping and can be used as a hedge.

EUODIAS, *TETRADIUM* (SYNONYM: *EUODIA* IN PART)
FAMILY RUTACEAE

This is a genus of around nine species. It has been included as part of *Euodia* in the past, but differs in the pinnate leaves and the terminal flowers with smooth shiny seeds. The leaves are in opposite pairs. The buds are naked. The flowers are produced in late summer.

p.312 **Euodia** *Tetradium daniellii*

Description: Deciduous tree 10–20 m (33–65 ft) with a bole diameter to 80 cm (2.6 ft).
Crown Broadly domed on a low trunk with radiating branches. *Bark* Smooth, dark grey with brown speckles.
Shoot Olive-brown, velvety with a fine down and elliptic whitish lenticels, in the second year grey-brown. *Buds* In opposite pairs, naked with the miniature leaves folded over the shoot tip and covered with silvery-brown hairs, 3 mm (0.1 in).
Foliage Leaves 20–35 cm (8–14 in), pinnate with 5–11 leaflets; leaflets ovate to ovate-oblong, tapering to a short slender-pointed tip, base rounded but wedge-shaped where it actually joins the short leaf stalk, margin with slight indentations which have a small round translucent oil gland, ciliate, strongly scented with a citrus-like odour, upper surface medium matt green with simple hairs, underside whitish green with simple whitish hairs, clusters of glands and raised veins with axillary tufts, 5–13 × 4–6 cm (2–5.1 × 1.6–2.4 in); leaf stalk rounded, hairy, pinkish with an enlarged base, rachis faintly grooved; autumn colour yellow.
Flowers Terminal on the current season's growth in early September, in conical heads 10–15 cm (4–6 in) across, small white flowers. *Fruit* Clusters of small circa 1 cm (0.4 in) capsules with a short beaked tip, containing five cells with one or two black seeds per cell.

Range: Central and northern China and Korea.
Habitat: Cultivated as an ornamental, in the wild occurring in woods.
Synonyms: *Euodia daniellii*, *E. hupehensis*.

The rather earthy scent (which is similar to that of *Ailanthus*), the naked buds and opposite pinnate leaves with small round oil glands, distinguish this tree. It is valuable for flowering late in the summer or early autumn but before autumn colours develop. The flowers are followed by the purplish fruits.

TEA, THEACEAE

This small family is characterized by the fleshy flowers, massed stamens and absence of stipules. *Camellia* (p.555) *Schima* (p.1129) and *Stuartia* (p.1182) are the genera treated here.

THUJAS, *THUJA*
FAMILY CUPRESSACEAE

This is a genus of four species, with one each in Japan and North Korea and adjacent northeast China, and two in North America. A fifth species from western China is believed to be extinct. The foliage is strongly aromatic and in decussate pairs, but the lateral pairs are large, with much smaller facial pairs. In *T. koraiensis* the underside of the foliage sprays is vividly glaucous, but in the other species it is green. The cones are valvate from the base, containing two or three small winged seeds on each of the thin fertile scales. The species are used for forestry and as ornamental trees. They withstand clipping and will tolerate very wet site conditions. The foliage, cones and seeds are quite different from *Platycladus*, although many works include this as a species of *Thuja*.

---

p.46 **Korean Thuja** *Thuja koraiensis*

Description: Evergreen tree to 10 m (33 ft) with a bole to a diameter of 20 cm (0.7 ft).
Crown Rounded conic, sometimes on several stems. *Bark* Pinkish brown, peeling in thin strips. *Shoot* Mid to pale green for first year, then red-brown, to 2.5 mm (0.1 in) diameter. *Buds* Hidden in axils of the scale leaves. *Foliage* In flat spreading aromatic sprays which are matt pale green above, and vivid silver beneath; leaves in opposite pairs with pronounced differences between the pairs; facial pairs (when viewed in the plane of the flat sprays) small, acute, with a faint dorsal gland; lateral pairs (those at sides) pointed, keeled, overlapping the facial pairs, on the underside there are waxy silver stomatal bands except for light green midrib; on strong shoots the tips may spread somewhat; scales from 2 mm (0.1 in) on laterals, up to 8 mm (0.3 in) on strongest

shoots; crushed foliage with a strong acetone or almondy scent. *Flowers* On previous year's shoots; male cones small black dots, 1 mm; female cones spreading, brown and black, 2 mm (0.1 in). *Fruit* Ovoid, erect with four pairs of valvate scales, yellow-green, ripening to brown in first autumn, 1 cm (0.4 in).

Range: North Korea and adjacent northeast China.
Habitat: Cultivated in Europe as an ornamental.

This is a small slow-growing tree which makes an excellent small specimen tree. It is remarkable for the vivid silvery undersides.

p.46 **White Cedar, Eastern White Cedar** or **Arborvitae** *Thuja occidentalis*

Description: Evergreen tree to 10–15 m (33–50 ft) with a bole to a diameter of 50 cm (1.6 ft). *Crown* Rounded conic, with billowing branches, more especially at the base. *Bark* Light red-brown or orange brown, fibrous and shedding, with interconnecting ridges. *Shoot* Mid to pale green for first year, then light red-brown, darkening with age, smooth, green portions 1–2 mm (0.1 in) in diameter. *Buds* Hidden in axils of the scale leaves. *Foliage* In flat spreading aromatic sprays which are matt or sub-shiny mid green above, becoming bronzy yellow-green over winter, and pale whitish green beneath; leaves in opposite pairs with pronounced differences between the pairs; facial pairs (when viewed in the plane of the flat sprays) small, acute, with a dorsal gland; lateral pairs (those at sides) pointed, keeled, overlapping the facial pairs; on strong shoots the tips may spread somewhat; scales 1.5–3.5 mm (0.1 in); crushed foliage with a sweet apple-like scent, rich in vitamin C. *Flowers* On previous year's shoots; male cones small black dots, 1 mm (0.1 in); female cones erect, pale green. *Fruit* Ovoid, erect with four or five pairs of valvate scales, yellow-green, ripening to brown in first autumn, 1 cm (0.4 in); scales smooth, only the two central pairs carrying seeds.

Range: Northeast USA and adjacent Canada.
Habitat: Cultivated in Europe as an ornamental, in the wild occurring in swamps and on limestone.
Varieties: It has given rise to a large number of dwarf forms. Tree forms are less frequent, but include 'Columbia', in which the new growths flush white and return to white over winter and which makes a narrow tree, and 'Fastigiata', with a conic or ovoid habit but which retains the foliage green over winter.

This is a small slow-growing tree which has been used for informal hedges. It tolerates a very wide range of sites, but is always slow growing. The old name Arborvitae or 'tree of life' dates from the use of an infusion of the bark and foliage to give protection against scurvy, being rich in vitamin C.

---

p.46 **Western Red Cedar** *Thuja plicata*

Description: Evergreen tree to 25–45 m (80–150 ft) with a bole to a diameter of 1.5 m (5 ft). *Crown* Columnar conic, with billowing branches which in old trees become pendulous with the lower ones layering to form a ring of new trees, never dense. *Bark* Red-brown with a purplish hue, fissured with the ridges exfoliating in strips, base often fluted. *Shoot* Dark green for first year, then red-brown, darkening purple with age, smooth, green portions slender, 1–2 mm (0.1 in) in diameter. *Buds* Hidden in axils of the scale leaves. *Foliage* In flat spreading aromatic sprays which are matt or shiny dark green above, and pale silvery green beneath; leaves in opposite pairs with pronounced differences between the pairs; facial pairs (when viewed in the plane of the flat sprays) small, acute, with a faint dorsal gland; lateral pairs (those at sides) pointed and often free at the incurved tip, keeled, overlapping the facial pairs; on strong shoots the tips spreading; scales 2.5–8 mm (0.1–0.3 in); crushed foliage with a sweet pineapple-like scent.

Flowers On previous year's shoots in early spring; male cones small black dots 1–2 mm (0.1 in), opening pale yellow; female cones erect, green-green.

Fruit Ovoid, erect with four or five pairs of valvate scales, yellow-green, ripening to brown in first autumn, 1–1.5 cm (0.4–0.6 in); scales with a small spreading terminal hook, only the central two or three pairs carrying seeds.

Range: Northwest USA and adjacent Canada from southeast Alaska down the west coast to northern California and also east of the Rocky Mountains in southeast British Columbia and northern Idaho.

Habitat: Cultivated in Europe as an ornamental, in the wild occurring in swamps and on moist acidic soil.

Varieties: No varieties but the following cultivars are frequently encountered: 'Aurea', with golden-yellow foliage; 'Fastigiata' with a narrow habit and thus suitable for low-maintenance hedging; and 'Zebrina', in which the foliage is banded with whitish yellow, making a conical tree.

Synonyms: *T. lobbii*, *T. gigantea*.

This is a tall fast-growing tree which is used in forestry as well as for specimen trees and clipped hedges. The foliage is strongly aromatic, even if only brushed. It tolerates a very wide range of sites.

HIBA, *THUJOPSIS*
FAMILY CUPRESSACEAE

This is a monotypic genus, allied to *Thuja* but differing in the almost globular cones with usually six (three pairs) fertile woody scales, each with three to five seeds, and in the coarser foliage.

---

p.47 **Hiba** *Thujopsis dolabrata*

Description: Evergreen tree to 20 m (65 ft) with a bole diameter of up to 60 cm (2 ft).
Crown Conic, in the open often with a skirt at the base, usually on several stems,

occasionally on a single stem with spreading upturned branches.

Bark Brown, becoming finely shredded into peeling grey or rich purplish red-brown strips to reveal orange beneath. *Shoot* Green for several years from the decurrent bases of the scale leaves, stout, 3 mm (0.1 in). *Buds* Naked, a cluster of immature scale leaves 2–3 mm (0.1 in). *Foliage* In firm spreading sprays, with laterals to 20×15 cm (8×6 in); leaves in decussate dissimilar pairs, facial leaves boat-shaped, with a rounded pointed free tip and a small indistinct gland, lateral pairs hatched-shaped, with a free forward-pointing tip, 0.4–1 cm (0.2–0.4 in), above shiny mid-green with few waxy stomata in hidden bands, beneath with equal areas of shiny mid-green and vivid glaucous silver due to waxy bands of stomata; crushed foliage with a faint resin scent. *Flowers* On previous season's growths in late spring; male cones ovoid, 2 mm (0.1 in), scales black with paler margins. *Fruit* Sub-globose, blue-green when growing, ripening in first autumn to brown, 1–2 cm (0.4–0.8 in); six to eight scales, thick and leathery or somewhat woody, with an acute upturned prickle.

Range: Japan, with var. *dolabrata* in southern Honshu, Kyushu and Shikoku, and var. *hondae* in northern Honshu and Hokkaido.

Habitat: Cultivated as an ornamental in Europe, in Japan occurring on moist valley slopes.

Varieties: Var. *hondae* differs in the smaller and dense scale leaves and in the cones not having the prominent prickle. 'Variegata' is a garden selection with creamy-white or pale-yellow patches on the foliage. It is inclined to revert and scarcely makes an impact.

Synonyms: *Thuja dolabrata*.

This tree usually retains the lower foliage and thus develops a dense skirt around the base of the trunk. It is related to *Thuja* and *Platycladus*, but the hard stout leaves and the leather cones distinguish it. It is widely used in Japanese forestry for the quality timber, although growth is slow.

Lime or Linden, Tiliaceae

This is a medium-sized family with around 50 genera and over 700 species, but the only tree genus of note is *Tilia*.

Limes, *Tilia*
Family Tiliaceae

This is a genus of around 30 species from the northern hemisphere, in North America extending south into Mexico but absent from the Pacific northwest, and in Eurasia as far south as Vietnam but absent from the Himalayas. The leaves are simple, generally ovate to rounded in outline, toothed but not really lobed (although coarsely lobulate in *T. mongolica*) with a somewhat heart-shaped and oblique base. In most species, there are stellate or fascicled hairs, and where these are dense, the lower leaf surface is silvered (*see TT. henryana, heterophylla, mandshurica, maximowicziana, oliveri, × petiolaris* and *tomentosa*). However, in *TT. cordata* and *platyphyllos* and their allies from the Crimea across to northeastern Asia, only simple hairs are usually present. Species with leaves green or bluish beneath but not silvery include *TT. americana, cordata, dasystyla, × euchlora, × europaea, mongolica* and *platyphyllos*. The shoots do not form terminal buds, with the shoot tip aborting when extension growth ceases. If a Lime shoot is carefully examined, a small scar will be noticed beside the end bud (in addition to the leaf trace, if it's winter!). The buds have a pair of scales. The flowers are in small cymes from the leaf axils of the current season's shoots and are fragrant. They have five whitish to yellowish petals and sepals. Most species have staminodes, which are petal-like scales derived from non-functional stamens, opposite the petals, but these are absent from *TT. cordata, dasystyla, × euchlora, × europaea* and *platyphyllos*. The species with staminodes have flowers with erect (i.e. pointing forwards) petals, whilst in those without staminodes, the petals are spreading. The main feature of the flowers is the large leafy and generally tongue-shaped bract. This is attached to the stalk for much of its length, appearing to act as an umbrella above the flowers. The fruit is generally globose, with up to three seeds. The wall of the fruit may be thin (as in *cordata* and allies) when it can be broken between the fingers, or thick walled (as in *tomentosa* and most other species) when something stronger than fingers or teeth is needed. When identifying limes, it is important to choose shoots from the outer crown which are capable of flowering. Epicormic shoots or those on young trees are unlikely to assist. This is particularly the case with *cordata* (where the character of the rather glaucous blue underside is only reliably shown on shoots, in full sun, which are sufficiently mature to flower). Limes are planted as amenity trees, for their timber and also give excellent honey. In the past, the fibrous bark or bast was used to make rope, and is the origin of an alternative name, basswood. Many species host large numbers of aphids, which produce copious honeydew.

p.257 **American Basswood** or **American Lime**
Tilia americana

Description: Deciduous tree 15–25 m (50–80 ft) with a bole diameter to 1 m (3.3 ft).
Crown Tall dome with upturned main branches and dense spreading or gently pendent side branches. *Bark* Dark brown or dark grey, smooth but becoming rough and fissured with scaly ridges in old trees. *Shoot* Bright glossy green or reddish, soon hairless, slender, maturing to dark brown. *Buds* Ovoid, pointed, bright shining green and hairless, laterally displaced, 8 × 5 mm (0.3 × 0.2 in). *Foliage* Leaves rounded ovate to broad ovate, little longer than wide, apex short, triangular and slender pointed, base heart-shaped to truncate, oblique, margin with coarse but variable sharp triangular teeth which are often large with a long point to 0.2 mm (0.1 in), upper surface dark green or yellowish green and hairless, underside glossy paler green with raised veins, hairless or with very sparse hairs and small tufts in vein axils, 7–15(–20) × 5–15(–18) cm (2.8–6(–8) × 2–6(–7.1) in); leaf stalk hairless, slender, 4–7 cm (1.6–2.8 in); autumn colour yellow or brown. *Flowers* In pendent cymes of 10–12, very variable in length from 5–15 cm (2–6 in) with the flowers clustered or widely spread; bract oblanceolate, attached by the lower half, pale green, hairless, 7–12 × 2–2.5 cm (2.8–4.7 × 0.8 in); flowers 1.2–1.5 cm (0.5–0.6 in) across, with yellowish white petals, fragrant, staminodes present.
Fruit Elliptic to rounded, pointed, thick

walled and covered in brown down, 0.8–1 × 0.5–0.7 cm (0.3–0.4 × 0.2–0.3 in).

Range: Northeastern USA and adjacent southern Canada in a square from New Brunswick west to southeast Manitoba, south to northeast Oklahoma and east to western North Carolina.

Habitat: Cultivated as an ornamental, in the wild occurring on moist valley soils and in broadleaved forests.

Varieties: 'Fastigiata' and 'Redmond' are two selections with narrow conical habits. 'Dentata' has the leaves deeply toothed and large, to 20 cm (8 in). 'Nova' is similar.

Synonyms: *T. glabra*, *T. canadensis*, *T. nigra*.

Similar species: *T. × moltkei* has been claimed as a hybrid with *T. × petiolaris* but is probably just a selection of *T. americana* (in which case it would be treated as 'Moltkei'). It has large leaves, normally 15–20 cm (6–8 in) long and wide, but can be distinguished by the thin covering of grey star-shaped hairs beneath but no axillary tufts.

T. 'Spectabilis' is similar, but the leaves are rather smaller. It has some star-shaped hairs on the twigs and buds. It is believed to be *T. americana* × *T. tomentosa*.

In its native range this is a valued timber tree, but is less thrifty in cultivation. Although the leaves are, generally, nearly hairless, towards the northern end of its range, some hairs are often present and epicormic or sprout shoots (and vigorous young trees) are often downy beneath. Plants from this part of the range are sometimes treated as *T. neglecta*, which also has the floral bract broadly elliptic, to 3.5 cm (1.4 in) in width and the fruit obovoid with an apiculate tip.

---

p.256 **Small-leafed Lime** *Tilia cordata*

Description: Deciduous tree 20–35 m (65–115 ft) with a bole diameter to 2 m (6.6 ft).
Crown Tall narrow dome with dense ascending branches but with the branch tips ultimately descending, becoming

somewhat irregular in outline. *Bark* Grey, smooth or with some fine brown fissures in young trees, becoming scaly and platy at the base in old trees and dark grey or brown. *Shoot* Green, initially hairy but soon largely hairless and shiny with oval buff-coloured lenticels in the first year, then red-brown to grey-brown. *Buds* Ellipsoid to ovoid or oblong and bluntly pointed, with two scales visible, green or dark red, shiny, and hairless, 7–8 × 3–4 mm (0.3 × 0.1–0.2 in). *Foliage* Leaves rounded to triangular ovate, apex shortly and abruptly slender pointed, base deeply heart-shaped to truncate, usually oblique, margin sharply and evenly (but on young trees and lower foliage may be somewhat doubly) serrate with acute and shortly pointed teeth, upper surface matt somewhat bluish green, more or less hairless, lower surface bluish or glaucous with raised veins which are hairy, especially with tufts of pale rufous or orange hairs in the axils, but with the tertiary veins obscure, 3–8 × 3–8 cm (1.2–3.1 × 1.2–3.1 in); leaf stalk yellow-green, round, slender, hairless, 2–4 cm (0.8–1.6 in); autumn colour yellow. *Flowers* In mid-summer (July and about ten days after *T. platyphyllos* and *T. × europaea*) in small spreading cymes held at or above the foliage level; bract narrow to broadly elliptic or sometimes oblanceolate, 3–6 × 1.3–2.5 cm (1.2–2.4 × 0.5–1 in); stalk 3.5–6 cm (1.4–2.4 in) with the bract attached for a quarter of its length; flowers fragrant, in clusters of 5–11, 1.5 cm (0.6 in) across, whitish cream with many spreading stamens, staminodes absent, petals strap-like, 6 mm (0.25 in), ovary with long white hairs. *Fruit* Elliptic or globose, not ribbed, with a thin wall and covered with a loose greyish-brown coat which is soon lost, 6–7 × 4 mm (0.25–0.3 × 0.2 in).

Range: From England, northern Spain and southern Norway and Sweden across Europe to the northwest Russia and the Caucasus.

Habitat: Woodlands, also planted as an amenity or forestry tree.

Varieties: 'Swedish Upright' is a narrow crowned selection. 'Rancho' and 'Greenspire' are two narrow conical forms.

Synonyms: *T. parviflora, T. ulmifolia.*

It is one of the parents of *T. × europaea*, and in some respects a better tree for urban areas but not for avenues. It forms a neat tree with a dense crown composed of the small leaves and produces few suckers. Honeydew is also usually less of a problem. The useful character of the leaves being glaucous bluish green on the underside is only well expressed on exposed shoots in the sun, those in shade or within the canopy not developing this glaucousness and being easily confused with *T. europaea*. The fertile fruits tend to be the elliptic ones ('lemon' shaped) whilst the globose ones tend to be infertile. It will grow on a wide range of sites. The timber is soft and white, making it suitable for turnery or for carving.

p.261 **Crimean Lime** *Tilia dasystyla*

Description: Deciduous tree 15–25 m (50–80 ft) with a bole diameter to 70 cm (2.3 ft).
Crown Ovoid-conical in young trees, becoming hemispherical in old trees with spreading branches. *Bark* Smooth, grey, becoming rough, ridged and fissured at the base. *Shoot* Green, hairless or with a few star-shaped hairs on the youngest parts, later green-brown. *Buds* Ellipsoid, sharply pointed, usually red, hairless, 5 mm (0.2 in).
Foliage Leaves broad ovate to ovate-triangular, tapering to a short slender-pointed apex, base heart-shaped to deeply heart-shaped, margin serrate with alternate large and small sharp triangular teeth which terminate in points 0.5–1 mm (0.1 in) and narrow acute sinuses, upper surface dark glossy green, with brown fascicled hairs on the impressed veins, beneath pale green with pale brown hairs on the raised veins, deeper brown axillary tufts and sometimes sparse star-shaped hairs on the minor veins, 7–12 × 5–10 cm (2.8–4.7 × 2–4 in); leaf stalk

green, hairless, about half as long as the blade (2–6 cm (0.8–2.4 in)); autumn colour yellow. *Flowers* Floral bract 5–7 × 1–1.5 cm (2–2.8 × 0.4–0.6 in), elliptic, stalked, pale yellowish green and hairless, stiff and sharply curved back from the inflorescence stalk; flowers in small cymes of two to four, staminodes absent, style variously hairy or woolly. *Fruit* Globose-ovoid, globose or elliptic, with a bluntly pointed apex, shallowly five ribbed, covered with dense white star-shaped hairs, 1 cm (0.4 in).

Range: Crimea region of the Ukraine.

Habitat: Woodlands.

Varieties: Ssp. *caucasica* differs in the teeth which are more uniform in size, being sharply triangular to slender pointed and ending in a slender aristate tip. The floral bracts are larger, and often wavy. It occurs in the Caucasus region, from northeast Turkey to Georgia and Armenia. This subspecies includes *T. begoniifolia* which is reported from the Caspian forests of northern Iran and said to differ in the larger leaves which are broader than long.

It is rare in cultivation except for a somewhat extreme form with larger leaves which has the tips of the marginal teeth up to 4 mm (0.2 in) in length. The plant usually is called *T. × euchlora*, which may be its hybrid with *T. cordata*. In the wild *T. dasystyla* occurs on limestone and volcanic cliffs.

---

p.261 **Caucasian Hybrid Lime** *Tilia × euchlora*

Description: Deciduous tree 15–20 m (50–65 ft) with a bole diameter to 80 cm (2.6 ft).
Crown Rounded-column with ascending main branches and an untidy mass of pendent lower branches. *Bark* Smooth, grey, developing fissures on old trees.
Shoot Lime-green with a fine down and brown lenticels in the first year, becoming deeper green and brown in the second year with the brown slowly predominating.
Buds Long ovoid-conic, shiny lime-green, to 8 mm (0.3 in). *Foliage* Leaves rounded

ovate but off-set, with a short triangular slender-pointed tip, base oblique, truncate to subcordate (often one side truncate and the other side subcordate), margin serrate with very regular small triangular teeth with a short aristate tip, upper surface deep glossy green with raised veins and hairless, underside pale green with raised veins, hairless except for tufts of light-brown single or double hairs in the vein axils, 5–10 cm (2–4 in) long and broad (but to 15 cm (6 in) on sucker growths); leaf stalk round or faintly grooved, hairless, 2.5–5 cm (1–2 in); autumn colour yellow. *Flowers* In late July, in cymes of five to seven; floral bract narrow oblanceolate, widest in the middle and tapered to both ends, downward growing almost to the base of the stalk to which it is attached for half its length, 6–8 × 1.5 m (2.4–3.1 × 0.6 in); flowers yellow, to 1.5 cm (0.6 in), staminodes absent. *Fruit* Ovoid, tapering to both ends but narrower and more pointed at the apex, pale green with brown hairs and with five linear ribs, 6–9 mm (0.25–0.4 in).

Range: Uncertain.

Habitat: Cultivated as an ornamental.

Synonyms: *T. cordata* × *T. dasystyla*?

This tree is believed to have been raised from seed collected in the Crimea and is probably a hybrid of *T. cordata* with *T. dasystyla* or possibly with its subspecies *caucasica*. It is planted as an amenity tree, and advocated as an alternative to *T.* × *europaea*. To the extent that the foliage does not get afflicted by aphids and honeydew, it is an improvement but as the tree matures the lower branches droop untidily and there are better limes.

---

p.256 **Common Lime** *Tilia* × *europaea*

Description: Deciduous tree 20–45 m (65–150 ft) with a bole diameter to 2 m (6.6 ft).
Crown Tall dome with billowing branches, usually with a proliferation of epicormic and basal sucker shoots. *Bark* Dull grey

and smooth in young trees, becoming
fissured with shallow ridges and brown,
often with burrs and a mass of sprouts.
Shoot Green and soon hairless, with oval
brown lenticels, becoming grey-brown or
pale brown, rarely reddish brown, in the
first winter onwards. *Buds* Ovoid,
pointed, green or reddish brown, hairless
except for a fringe of simple hairs on the
margins of the scales, 6 mm (0.25 in).
Foliage Leaves broad ovate to nearly
rounded, tip triangular, slender pointed,
base truncate to subcordate, margin with
narrow triangular aristate teeth, upper
surface matt deep green, often becoming
shiny due to honeydew, underside matt
green, with raised veins, hairless except for
pale golden-brown tufts on the veins,
especially in the axils, 6–15 × 6–12 cm
(2.4–6 × 2.4–4.7 in); leaf stalk round,
green, 2.5–5 cm (1–2 in); autumn colour
yellow but often leaves lost early from a
fungal disease. *Flowers* In spreading or
pendent very fragrant cymes of 4–10 in
July, bract lanceolate, rounded at the tip,
8–11 cm (3.1–4.3 in) and more or less as
long as the flower cluster, with the stalk
pressed onto the shoot from near the base
to half way along, sepals and petals
yellowish white, staminodes absent.
Fruit Broad ovoid with a small blunt
point, densely hairy, only faintly ribbed,
with a tough coat, 8 mm (0.3 in).

Range: Origin uncertain but European.
Habitat: Cultivated as an ornamental.
Varieties: 'Pallida' is a selection of conical habit with
leaves yellowish green beneath (hence
'pallid'). The bole is fluted or with rounded
knobs, and with one to four main vertical
stems, the twigs are reddish and hairless
with rounded or ellipsoidal shining scarlet
buds 8–9 × 4–6 mm (0.3–0.4 ×
0.2–0.25 in). The leaves are 7–10 cm
(2.8–4 in) across, with a characteristic
oblique truncate base. The floral bract is
5–13 × 1–2 cm (2–5.1 × 0.4–0.8 in), widest
in the middle and tapering to both ends.
The flowers are pendulous, usually in
clusters of seven to nine. The fruit usually

has a small apical protuberance. In Germany it is known as 'Kaiserlinde', in the Netherlands as 'Koningslinde', and it is an improvement on the normal clones of *T.* × *europaea*. 'SvarteLinde' and 'Hatfield Tall' have more cylindrical boles with few basal sprouts and with a hemispherical crown on three to five divergent limbs. The young twigs are green to dull crimson, with ovoid, bluntly pointed buds 0.9–1.2 × 5–6 mm (0.4–0.5 × 0.2–0.25 in) and dull crimson. The leaves are 8–10 cm (3.1–4 in) across with an asymmetrically heart-shaped base, and rarely may have some star-shaped hairs on the minor veins. The floral bract is 4–11 × 1.7–2.7 cm (1.6–4.3 × 0.7–1.1 in), parallel sided with a rounded apex. The flowers are in clusters of two to four and the fruit does not have an apical protuberance. In 'Wratislavensis', the new leaves are yellow.

Synonyms: *T.* × *vulgaris*.

The above description covers the taxon. However, it is clearly a natural hybrid of *T. cordata* and *T. platyphyllos* and is in the main represented in gardens by a small number of clones, which are individually described above. The statement 'cultivated as an ornamental' may appear unlikely to those who have had to put up with the masses of honeydew which falls from this tree, or who have taken a natural dislike to the abundant basal suckers and epicormic shoots. The latter partly explains its preponderance in cultivation, since in the 17th century it was the easiest lime to propagate, as a coppiced tree would produce masses of basal suckers which could be layered. Unfortunately, some customs die hard, although it does have merit as an avenue tree. The honeydew is caused by sap-sucking aphids which find the proportion of sugars to proteins not to their liking, thus voiding the excess sugars as fine droplets. These fall onto the leaves, onto cars and pavements, etc. where they are colonized by sooty moulds. Many trees have such aphids, but few in such devastating numbers.

p.258 **Henry's Lime** *Tilia henryana*

Description: Deciduous tree 10–15 m (33–50 ft) by 30 cm (1 ft).
Crown Domed. *Bark* Light grey, fissured *Shoot* Star-shaped hairy when young, becoming nearly hairless and yellow-brown. *Bud* Ovoid, hairy or hairless. *Foliage* Leaves broad ovate to ovate, shortly tapered to an acute apex, base rounded, truncate or subcordate and usually oblique, margin with very prominent and distinctive hair-like teeth which usually extend for 2–3 mm (0.1 in) upper surface white when new due to a covering of star-shaped hairs but becoming more or less hairless and shiny green, underside covered by a thin dull brownish star-shaped pubescence, 5–13 × 4–14 cm (2–5.1 × 1.6–5.5 in). Leaf stalk 2–4 cm (0.8–1.6 in), star-shaped hairy. *Flowers* Numerous, 20–50 on long (10–15 cm (4–6 in)) pendulous cymes, whitish, with staminodes. Bract up to 15 × 1.2–2 cm (6 × 0.5–0.8 in), star-shaped hairy. *Fruit* Ellipsoid to obovoid, prominently five ribbed and warty, 0.8–1 × 0.4–0.6 cm (0.3–0.4 × 0.2–0.25 in).

Range: China on the mountains along the Yangtse River system from Hubei to Jiangxi.

Habitat: Cultivated as an ornamental, in the wild occurring as scattered trees.

Similar species: *T. tuan* has rather similar leaves, which are whitish hairy beneath with small axillary tufts. The teeth, however, are not drawn out into long bristles; the basal part of the leaf is untoothed, with only small distinct teeth towards the more slender tip. The flowers are in cymes of 15–20 and the fruit sub-globose with a thick shell. It comes from central west China (Sichuan, Hubei and Yunnan).

This is a rare tree which does not grow as large in cultivation as the other Chinese limes, although reported to attain upwards of 25 m (80 ft) in the wild. It is very remarkable for the long drawn-out tips to the otherwise rather small teeth.

p.261 **White Basswood** *Tilia heterophylla*

Description: Deciduous tree to 25 m (80 ft) with a bole
diameter to 80 cm (2.6 ft).
Crown Dense with ascending branches,
forming a narrow and often broad conical
crown. *Bark* Grey, smooth, becoming
fissured with scaly ridges. *Shoot* Green and
star-shaped hairy at first, but becoming red-
brown above by autumn, in the second and
subsequent years brown to grey-brown.
Buds Ovoid to ovoid-conic, bluntly pointed
and laterally flattened, shiny green with the
scale tips brown and star-shaped hairs, 0.9–1
× 0.5 cm (0.4 × 0.2 in). *Foliage* Leaves
broadly ovate, apex triangular with a short
slender-pointed tip, base asymmetrical, from
truncate to subcordate but the two sides
nearly in a straight line, margin with
relatively even and closely spaced broad
triangular teeth which end in a slender
aristate point 1 mm (0.1 in), upper surface
dark green with spaced star-shaped hairs at
first, veins slightly raised, palmate at the
base and with three to five lateral pairs,
underside greyish white to silvery white,
depending upon the extent and density of
the star-shaped hairs over the blade and
raised veins (with the star-shaped hairs
having 12–16 radiating limbs), with some
brownish hairs on the veins and in the axils,
7–19 × 6–14 cm (2.8–7.5 × 2.4–5.5 in); leaf
stalk round, slender but enlarged at both
ends, with some brownish hairs, to 7 cm
(2.8 in); autumn colour yellow. *Flowers* In
cymes in mid-summer; bract narrowly
elliptic to oblanceolate, narrowed to a
1.5–2 cm (0.6–0.8 in) stalk or stalkless on
the shoot, green, leafy and nearly hairless,
10–14 × 1.5–3.5 cm (4–5.5 × 0.6–1.4 in);
inflorescence attached to the lower two-
fifths; flowers fragrant, large, in clusters of
three to eight, five petals, yellow-white,
staminodes present. *Fruit* Pumpkin-shaped
(broader than long) to almost perfectly
spherical, with a thick wall, slightly
indented at both ends with a persistent style
base at the tip, with five rounded ridges and
shallow grooves, covered with grey-brown

star-shaped hairs, 0.7–1 × 0.9–1 cm (0.3–0.4 × 0.4 in).

Range: Eastern USA from New York and Pennsylvania south to Florida and across to Arkansas and Missouri.

Habitat: Cultivated as an ornamental, in the wild occurring in moist upland hardwood forests.

Synonyms: *T. alba*, in part.

Similar species: *T. michauxii* and *T. monticola* are two segregates of *T. heterophylla* which are confused in cultivation. *T. michauxii* has much larger leaves, to 30 × 18 cm (12 × 7.1 in), which are green beneath but with a covering of star-shaped hairs. It may be derived from hybridization between *T. heterophylla* and *T. americana*. Plants matching these characters have been found in a broad swathe of eastern USA from Pennsylvania to Arkansas, south to Georgia and northwest to Ohio. *T. monticola* is recorded from the Appalachians from Virginia, Tennessee and North Carolina and has leaves which are silvery white beneath. By most authorities, it is treated as an extreme variation of *T. heterophylla*.
T. caroliniana has leaves which have a thin covering of rust-coloured hairs on the leaf underside (although these are usually soon rubbed off) and a bark which is furrowed with orange fissures and scaly ridges. The shoots have a mixture of both long and short star-shaped and tufted hairs and are often brown. The buds are small, ovoid, 4–5 × 2–3 mm (0.2 × 0.1 in) with a dense covering of short star-shaped hairs. The leaves are small, 7–9 × 4–6 cm (2.8–3.5 × 1.6–2.4 in), ovate with a truncate to broad wedge-shaped base with widely spaced curved triangular teeth, and variably hairy. The floral bract is oblong with rounded ends, 5–8 × 1–1.5 cm (2–3.1 × 0.4–0.6 in), with 10–15 flowers in the rather compact inflorescence. The flowers have staminodes, and the fruit is spherical, 5–7 mm (0.2–0.3 in) with brown star-shaped down. It occurs from North Carolina and Florida west to Texas and Oklahoma.

This tree has leaves silvery white to greyish white beneath. It is most easily confused with *T. oliveri*, from which the hairy shoots and different fruit shape distinguish it.

---

p.259 **Manchurian Lime** *Tilia mandshurica*

Description: Deciduous tree 15–20 m (50–65 ft) with a bole diameter to 50 cm (1.6 ft).
Crown Hemispherical with spreading and arching branches. *Bark* Dark grey, smooth but becoming fissured. *Shoot* Green when young with greyish white or brownish star-shaped hairs. *Buds* Ovoid or ellipsoid, with greyish white or pale brown star-shaped hairs, 6–7 × 4 mm (0.25–0.3 × 0.2 in). *Foliage* Leaves round to broadly ovate, apex short and slender pointed, base heart-shaped, oblique, margin with coarse long pointed triangular teeth (which are sometimes indistinct lobes) with stout tips 2 mm (0.1 in), upper surface dark green and sparsely hairy at first, underside grey or white tomentose with dense star-shaped hairs which extend into the axils of the raised veins but without separate axillary tufts, 8–15 × 7–14 cm (3.1–6 × 2.8–5.5 in); leaf stalk stout, star-shaped hairy, 3–7 cm (1.2–2.8 in); autumn colour yellow. *Flowers* In pendent widely branched cymes of 7–15; bract lanceolate, 7–10 × 1.5–3 cm (2.8–4 × 0.6–1.2 in), almost stalkless, sparsely star-shaped hairy above, beneath the dense white or brown star-shaped hairs; flowers 1–1.2 cm (0.4–0.5 in), staminodes present.
Fruit Globose, with five indistinct ribs most obvious at the base, thick walled, star-shaped hairy, with a dense and even covering of pale-brown star-shaped hairs.

Range: Northeast China, Pacific Russia and Korea.

Habitat: Cultivated as an ornamental, in the wild occurring on moist valley soils and in broadleafed forests.

Varieties: The Korean plants are often treated as ssp. *megaphylla*.

This tree resembles *T. tomentosa*, differing in the more coarsely toothed and larger leaves which are brownish tomentose. It is also related to *T. oliveri*, but this has silvery white undersides to the leaves, much shorter serrations and hairless or nearly hairless twigs.

---

p.260 **Maximowicz Lime** *Tilia maximowicziana*

Description: Deciduous tree 15–25 m (50–80 ft) in height with a bole diameter to 70 cm (2.3 ft).
Crown Columnar, becoming domed at the top in old trees. *Bark* Grey, smooth, becoming fissured. *Shoot* Yellow-green with small round lenticels and initially star-shaped hairy, becoming hairless by autumn and green-brown, then grey-brown, stout. *Buds* Green, ovoid, blunt, with brownish star-shaped hairs, 1–1.2 cm × 7–8 mm (0.4–0.5 × 0.3 in). *Foliage* Leaves rounded to ovate with a short abrupt slender-pointed apex, heart-shaped to truncate and oblique at the base, margin with small low triangular serrations which end in a short aristate or bristly tip to 1 mm (0.1 in) but entire at the base, upper surface covered in star-shaped pubescent hairs which persist longest on the veins, deep rather matt green, underside with matted white star-shaped hairs all over and with reddish-brown hairs on the raised main veins and in axillary tufts, three to five veins (and weakly seven) at the base, with the main pair ascending at 45 degrees and branching, 6–17 × 5–13 cm (2.4–6.7 × 2–5.1 in); leaf stalk round, thicker at both ends, covered at least initially with star-shaped hairs which are white except near the base of the leaf where they are green, 3–7 cm (1.2–2.8 in); autumn colour yellow. *Flowers* In pendent cymes with 10–20 flowers; bract oblong or oblanceolate, 7–10 × 1–2 cm (2.8–4 × 0.4–0.8 in), on a stalk 3–9 mm (0.1–0.4 in), joined to the stalk for the lowest one-third to one-quarter, yellow-green, star-shaped hairy; peduncle stalk 3–4 cm (1.2–1.6 in); pedicels 1 cm (0.4 in) with large lenticels; flowers large, sepals and petals 7–9 mm (0.3–0.4 in), staminodes

present, stamens 60–70. *Fruit* Oblong to globose, rounded at the ends and weakly five ridged, greyish star-shaped pubescent, 0.8–1 cm (0.3–0.4 in).

Range: Central to North Honshu and Hokkaido, Japan.

Habitat: Cultivated as an ornamental, in the wild found in mixed forests.

Similar species: *T. chinensis* is similar in the leaves having star-shaped hairs and usually prominent axillary tufts but the leaves are thinly tomentose with translucent, white or pale-brown hairs (which may give the leaf a rusty bloom). Other points of difference are the more sharply serrate leaves and the shoots which quickly become hairless. The flowers are carried two to four together on a stalk which does not extend beyond the oblong stalkless or shortly stalked 7–9 cm (2.8–3.5 in) bract. The fruit is globose to obovoid, with prominent thick and somewhat sinuous ribs and a thick wall, and covered in dense white star-shaped hairs. It occurs in mixed forests in western China from Gansu south through Sichuan to Yunnan.

T. intonsa is very close to *T. chinensis*, of which it is sometimes treated as subspecies *intonsa*. It comes from west Sichuan and has densely grey woolly leaves and shoots and flowers in cymes of one to three.

T. nobilis, also from west Sichuan, has the leaves almost hairless except for axillary tufts and larger, 15–20 × 11–15 cm (6–8 × 4.3–6 in), with 7–15 flowers on a long stalk. The shoots are bright green, and the buds large and glossy.

This lime is well distinguished by the combination of brownish hairs in the axils of the leaves and along the veins together with the silvery white matt of star-shaped hairs.

---

p.260 **Mongolian Lime** *Tilia mongolica*

Description: Deciduous tree 10–20 m (33–65 ft) with a bole diameter to 50 cm (1.6 ft).
Crown Ovoid or upright narrow dome with ascending branches. *Bark* Grey-

brown, smooth. *Shoot* Green-brown to glossy red or brown in the first year and initially somewhat hairy but soon hairless, grey-brown or green grey-brown in subsequent years. *Buds* Rounded or flattened globose, shiny green, with two scales visible, 3–4 mm (0.1–0.2 in). *Foliage* Leaves broadly ovate to deltoid and almost symmetrical, apex slender pointed, base truncate to subcordate, margin often three lobed and with a small number of large coarse triangular teeth which have abrupt short-pointed tips to 1 mm (0.1 in), upper surface dark matt or glossy green, hairless, beneath pale somewhat bluish-glaucous green with prominent hairy veins and tufts in the axils or hairless, 4–7 × 4–7 cm (1.6–2.8 × 1.6–2.8 in); leaf stalk round, slender, shiny yellow-green or red, hairless, 2–4 cm (0.8–1.6 in); autumn colour yellow. *Flowers* In lateral spreading or erect cymes in leaf axils on current year's growths in July; floral bract narrow elliptic, pale green, wavy margined and hairless, with the inflorescence joined at the lower one-third, 3–4 cm × 8 mm (1.2–1.6 × 0.3 in); flowers mainly 6–10 but up to 30, petals creamy white, oblong, cupped forwards, 30–40 stamens yellow, staminodes present, ovary globose with a long (3 mm (0.1 in)) style. *Fruit* Ellipsoid to obovoid, tapering to the blunt apex where there is a scar from fallen style, thin walled, 4–6 × 3 mm (0.2–0.25 × 0.1 in).

Range: From Mongolia across northern China across to Pacific Russia.

Habitat: Cultivated as an ornamental, in the wild occurring in woodland.

The coarse toothing and, on young plants, the three or five lobes to the leaves, make this one of the most easily identified of the limes. It makes a generally small tree and is used as a tree to line streets in urban areas. In woodland areas, however, with shelter it can gain heights of 20 m (65 ft) or more.

p.259 **Oliver's Lime** *Tilia oliveri*

Description: Deciduous tree 15–25 m (50–80 ft) with a bole diameter to 80 cm (2.6 ft).
Crown Ovoid in young trees, becoming domed with spreading branches. *Bark* Light grey with brown zones beneath side branches, smooth, only becoming fissured in old trees. *Shoot* Green, shiny and hairless in the first season (rarely with sparse star-shaped hairs), becoming brown above and remaining green or green mottled brown beneath, in the third year grey-brown. *Buds* Ovoid, almost globose, with a rounded apex, shiny green, hairless, 3–7 mm (0.1–0.3 in).
Foliage Leaves broad ovate to almost rounded in outline, apex with an abrupt short point, base oblique and deeply heart-shaped, margin with relatively small acute teeth ending in a forward curved aristate gland, upper surface deep matt or sub-shiny green, initially hairy but soon hairless except where slightly impressed beside the main veins, very finely rugose, underside silvery white with a dense plastered layer of star-shaped hairs with seven or eight pairs of raised veins which have brown dots towards the base but without axillary tufts, texture leathery, 6–13 × 6–11 cm (2.4–5.1 × 2.4–4.3 in); leaf stalk faintly grooved, hairless except near the top and base where it is swollen and haired, scattered brown dots or glands in the groove, 3–8 cm (1.2–3.1 in); autumn colour yellow.
Flowers In cymes of 7–20 flowers; bract stalkless at the base, star-shaped haired, oblanceolate with a rounded apex, 5–12 × 1–1.5 cm (2–4.7 × 0.4–0.6 in); staminodes present. *Fruit* Globose, ellipsoidal or obovoid, with an apiculate tip and slightly ribbed, warty with a thick shell, and covered with greyish white hairs, 8–9 mm (0.3–0.4 in).

Range: Central China.

Habitat: Cultivated as an ornamental, in the wild occurring in mixed forests.

This tree is similar to *T. tomentosa* in the silvery underside of the leaves, with a thin plastered layer of hairs. However, it can be easily distinguished by the hairless and green shoots.

---

p.259 **Pendent Silver Lime** *Tilia × petiolaris*

Description: Deciduous tree 20–35 m (65–115 ft) with a bole diameter to 1.2 m (3.9 ft).
Crown Tall dense dome with ascending sinuous branches and pendent or weeping side branches, often grafted at 2 m (6.6 ft) in old trees. *Bark* Grey or rather silvery grey and smooth in young trees, becoming grey or dark grey and fissured with shallow ridges.
Shoot Green and covered with short star-shaped white hairs at first, in the second and later years green with shallow brown fissures.
Buds Ovoid, blunt, green with a covering of white star-shaped hairs, 6 mm (0.25 in).
Foliage Leaves rounded or rounded ovate, apex ending in a short triangular point, base oblique and heart-shaped, margin serrate with broad triangular teeth which end in a forward-pointing aristate tip, upper surface deep matt green, soon nearly hairless, underside somewhat bluish white due to dense covering of plastered whitish star-shaped hairs, veins raised, with white and rufous hairs, 6–15 × 5–12 cm (2.4–6 × 2–4.7 in); leaf stalk only slightly shorter than the blade (excluding tip), round, hairless except at base and near leaf blade, 4–8 cm (1.6–3.1 in); autumn colour yellow.
Flowers In pendent very fragrant cymes of 4–8 in late July, bract obovate, rounded at the tip, 6–10 cm (2.4–4 in) and more or less as long as the flower cluster, with the peduncle adpressed from near the base to half way along, sepals and petals creamy white when young, then golden-yellow, stamens brown, staminodes present, ovary ribbed.
Fruit Globose, with five grooves and rounded ridges, warty, 0.8–1 cm (0.3–0.4 in).
Range: Origin uncertain.
Habitat: Cultivated as an ornamental.
Synonyms: *T. americana* 'Pendula'.

This is a very attractive tree, especially in its hanging branchlets which hold the leaves so that, as they flutter in the wind the silvery underside is flashed. Its origin is enigmatic, but the best opinion is that it is a hybrid of *T. tomentosa*, differing in the larger and differently textured leaves and the much longer leaf stalks. It was first distributed as *T. americana* 'Pendula'. It produces viable fruit but the seeds do not normally germinate as they lack a gibberellic acid, one of the plant-growth regulators. The flowers contain a sugar which some bees, especially bumble bees are unable to assimilate. It is not uncommon to find them intoxicated beneath the trees when in flower. This also happens with other limes to a degree, even with *T. × europaea* on occasions, and the effect may be more severe in dry years.

---

p.257 **Large-leafed Lime** *Tilia platyphyllos*

Description: Deciduous tree 20–40 m (65–130 ft) with a bole diameter to 1 m (3.3 ft).
Crown Ovoid in young trees, becoming broadly columnar with a rounded top or with a wide-spreading hemispherical crown in mature open-grown trees, rarely with basal suckers or epicormic shoots.
Bark Dark grey, smooth at first but soon finely fissured, in old trees becoming ridged, fissured and grey-brown.
Shoot Green at first with sparse to dense stellate and long pale simple hairs, becoming reddish brown or greenish brown over winter with the hairs persisting in some measure into the second year, lenticels small, rounded, brown, scars from the stipules at the base of the leaf stalk or either side of the bud. *Buds* Ellipsoid to ovoid, bluntly pointed, green or dark green, variously hairy, with three scales visible, 7–8 × 5 mm (0.3 × 0.2 in). *Foliage* Leaves broad ovate to oblong-ovate, apex short and slender pointed, base obliquely subcordate to heart-shaped, margin ciliate at first, with regular rounded abruptly short-pointed teeth with small acute sinuses or with alternate larger and smaller teeth, upper

surface mid matt green, variably hairy above depending upon subspecies but soon hairless, with indented secondary and tertiary veins, underside light green and hairy all over but especially on the circa ten pairs of raised veins, 6–15 × 7–13 cm (2.4–6 × 2.8–5.1 in); leaf stalk round, green, hairy, 2–5 cm (0.8–2 in), with two yellow-green stipules which are soon lost, leaving scars on the shoot; autumn colour yellow. *Flowers* In cymes of three to five, rarely one or two, or up to six, in the leaf axils on side shoots in mid-summer; floral bract narrow oblong or oblanceolate with a rounded apex, pale or yellow-green, hairy along the veins above but almost hairless beneath 5–12 × 1–2 cm (2–4.7 × 0.4–0.8 in); inflorescence attached one-third the way along the bract, usually not exceeding the bract; flowers pendent, fragrant, 1.5–2 cm (0.6–0.8 in) across, whitish yellow when young, fading golden-yellow, sepals five, enclosing a rounded flower bud, petals triangular, stamens many but staminodes absent, ovary white woolly. *Fruit* Usually globose but ranging from ellipsoid to obovoid, ripening through green to brown, usually with five narrow white downy ribs, 0.8–1 cm (0.3–0.4 in).

Range: England across Europe to Asia Minor.

Habitat: Woodlands, but planted as an ornamental.

Varieties: 'Rubra' is a selection in which the one-year twigs are red over winter (not to be confused with the subspecies described below). 'Corallina' is similar. In 'Aurea', the shoots are golden-yellow. 'Laciniata' has the leaves smaller than usual and jaggedly and irregularly toothed. Ssp. *platyphyllos* from central Europe has the upper surface of the leaves more or less hairless and the hairs on the lower surface are mainly confined to the veins. In western and northern Europe from Britain in the west to southwest Russia is ssp. *cordifolia*. This subspecies has hairs on the upper surface of the leaves and is more generally hairy beneath, on the leaf stalks and shoots. Ssp. *pseudorubra* from the Balkans, Hungary, Romania, and the Ukraine differs in the leaves being nearly hairless, of firmer texture with the teeth ending in bristle tips. It is sometimes treated as a species, *T. rubra*, but the name *T. rubra* is a synonym of typical *T. platyphyllos* (i.e. it is not applicable to this entity).

Synonyms: *T. rubra, T. officinarum, T. grandifolia.*

This makes a strong growing tree and has a superior form to *T.* × *europaea*. It is variable with three subspecies recognised as described above. In the typical form, the leaves are generally hairy and soft to the touch. In southeast Europe, they become progressively more hairless, this form being ssp. *pseudorubra*.

---

p.258 **Silver Lime** *Tilia tomentosa*

Description: Deciduous tree 20–30 m (65–100 ft) with a bole diameter to 1 m (3.3 ft).
Crown Ovoid pointed in young trees, becoming rounded and domed, dense, with steeply ascending branches.
Bark Smooth, grey-green with striations, becoming grey with shallow network of low flat ridges. *Shoot* Buff or silvery due to a dense covering of star-shaped hairs, which if scraped off show green beneath, in second and subsequent years grey.
Buds Ovoid, pointed, with silvery brown star-shaped hairs, 5 mm (0.2 in).
Foliage Leaves round or ovate in outline and rather thick, with a short triangular apex, base oblique and subcordate, margin with fairly regular and large triangular or broad triangular teeth which end in a short blunt point, upper surface initially coated with silvery hairs which soon rub off to show sub-shiny deep green with slightly raised veins, underside star-shaped hairy and silvery tomentose with raised veins, 4–13 × 4–11 cm (1.6–5.1 × 1.6–4.3 in); leaf stalk silvery-brown hairy, 2.5–4 cm (1–1.6 in); autumn colour yellow. *Flowers* In cymes of 3–10 in late summer (July), pendent and very fragrant, bract oblanceolate 4.5–6 ×

1.5–2 cm (1.8–2.4 × 0.6–0.8 in) on a stalk 0.3–1 cm (0.1–0.4 in), longer than the inflorescence which is attached at the basal one-third only, flowers whitish yellow with narrow obovate petals, short brown stamens, staminodes present.
Fruit Ovoid-pointed with white hairs and slightly warted with five small ridges, 0.8–1 cm (0.3–0.4 in).

Range: Hungary and the Balkans across to southwest Russia and northwest Turkey.
Habitat: Woods.
Synonyms: *T. alba*, *T. argentea*.

This is the only European Silver Lime and makes a strong-growing and densely crowned tree. The nectar contains a sugar which bumble bees are unable to digest, leading to their intoxication. It is closely related to *T. × petiolaris* but this hybrid has thinner leaves which are less downy, much longer leaf stalks (from half as long as the blade up to as long) and a fruit which is depressed-globose, not ovoid and pointed.

CHINESE MAHOGANY, *TOONA* (SYNONYM: *CEDRELA* IN PART)
FAMILY MELIACEAE

This is a small genus of around half a dozen species from China south to northern Australia. Only *T. sinensis* is common in cultivation.

p.336 **Chinese Cedar** or **Chinese Mahogany**
Toona sinensis

Description: Deciduous tree 15–25 m (50–80 ft) with a bole diameter to 0.7 m (2.3 ft).
Crown Open, upright and rather gaunt due to the spaced branches, often with suckers from the roots. *Bark* Smooth coppery grey on young trees, becoming shaggy with coarse peeling pinkish grey flakes. *Shoot* Stout, coppery green and slightly hairy in the first year, becoming grey-buff or pinkish grey or pinkish brown, stripped bark and foliage has a

distinctive pungent aroma. *Buds* Broad ovoid and squat, slightly slender pointed, green with rufous hairy tips to the scales, 5 × 6 mm (0.2 × 0.25 in). *Foliage* Leaves 50–70 × 30–40 cm (20–80 × 12–16 in), pinnate with 10–24 leaflets, usually in an even number, leaflets oblong-ovate, tapering to the slender-pointed tip, base rounded to sub-cordate, somewhat oblique, margin with small forward triangular teeth with the weak later veins ending as a tuft of hairs in the sinus just in front of the tooth, upper surface sub-shiny dark green with scattered hairs on the slightly raised veins, underside light green with many pairs of veins, hairy mainly on the veins, 6–20 × 4–7 cm (2.4–8 × 1.6–2.8 in); leaf stalk round, hairy, rachis slightly ribbed above, stalk grooved, pink, hairy, circa 1.5 cm (0.6 in); usually remaining green until killed by frost in autumn. *Flowers* In terminal fragrant panicles 30–50 cm (12–20 in) across in July, white. *Fruit* Capsule 2.5 cm (1 in), with winged seeds.

Range: North and west China.

Habitat: Cultivated as an ornamental.

Synonyms: *Cedrela sinensis*.

The pungent aroma of the foliage is distinctive, although recalling that of *Ailanthus altissima* (which differs in the bark and the leaves having entire leaflets except for one to three large teeth) and, like that tree, suckering from the roots. The new foliage of *Toona* is picked as a vegetable in northern China, and has a distinctive oniony flavour.

NUTMEG TREES, *TORREYA* (SYNONYM: *TUMION*)
FAMILY TAXACEAE

This is a genus of around half a dozen species, two from the USA, one from Japan and the rest in China. The leaves are relatively long and spine-toothed, arranged in two spreading ranks on either side of the persistently green shoot. The fruit is an olive-like drupe.

p.65 **California Nutmeg Tree**
Torreya californica

Description: Evergreen tree to 10–20 m (33–65 ft), with
a bole to 0.5 m (1.6 ft).
Crown Conical when young, becoming
broadly conical or columnar with spreading
spaced branches. *Bark* Red-brown, flaky,
dividing into narrow scaly ridges in old
trees when brown or ash grey. *Shoot* Green
for one to three years before pale brown or
red-brown and then dark brown, slender,
hairless, with decurrent leaf bases.
Buds Conical or pointed ovoid, green,
3–5 × 2 mm (0.1–0.2 × 0.1 in). *Foliage* In
sprays with the leaves widely parted beneath
the shoot, pointing forwards at the side and
in two or three ranks above the shoot, with a
wide groove between the opposite ranks;
leaves usually paired either side of the shoot,
flattened, concave on upper surface and
slightly on lower surface, linear but tapering
to sharp and drawn-out tip, base rounded,
mid shiny green without stomata above,
beneath with pale green with indistinct
waxy white-green bands of stomata, 3–5 cm
(1.2–2 in) (rarely to 8 cm (3.1 in)) by
3–4 mm (0.1–0.2 in); crushed foliage with a
pungent resinous aroma. *Flowers* On
previous year's shoots, males and females on
separate trees; males from ovoid-conical
buds formed in leaf axils (including those of
previous years), globose, 1 cm (0.4 in);
female flowers from buds at tips of shoots.
Fruit Obovoid to globose-obovoid, green
with purple strips, with fleshy seed coat
containing a single seed, 2.5–4 cm
(1–1.6 in), taking two years to ripen.
Range: Central and northern California.
Habitat: Cultivated in Europe in specialist
collections, in the wild restricted to moist
valley-bottom sites.
Varieties: 'Spreadeagle' is a ground-hugging form,
probably the result of a cutting from a side
shoot which failed to make a leader.

This is a medium to large tree and tolerates
a wide range of sites provided the soil is
sufficiently moist. It will withstand dense

shade. The common name refers to the resemblance of the fruits to those of the commercial nutmeg. It is similar to *T. nucifera*, differing most markedly in the longer needles which point forwards, the conical buds and the larger globose fruit.

p.65 **Naya** or **Japanese Nutmeg Tree**
Torreya nucifera

Description: Evergreen tree to 10 m (33 ft). with a bole to 30 cm (1 ft).
Crown Conical when young, becoming columnar and flat topped, with spreading branches with age, rather open habit.
Bark Pinkish brown, finely ridged.
Shoot Green for two to three years before red-brown and then dark brown, slender, hairless, with decurrent leaf bases.
Buds Ovoid, bluntly pointed, red-brown, 2 mm (0.1 in). *Foliage* In flat sprays, with the leaves widely parted either side of the shoot and arched downwards; leaves flattened, concave on upper surface and very flat on lower surface, gently tapering from near base to sharp and drawn-out tip, base rounded, mid shiny green without stomata above, beneath with three pale-green bands and two waxy white-green bands of stomata, 2–3 cm × 4 mm (0.8–1.2 × 0.2 in); crushed foliage with a moderately pungent resinous aroma. *Flowers* On previous year's shoots, males and females on separate trees; males from conical buds formed in leaf axils, 1 cm (0.4 in); female flowers from buds at tips of shoots.
Fruit Ellipsoidal, green with fleshy seed coat containing a single seed, 2.5 cm (1 in), taking two years to ripen.
Range: Japan, from southern Honshu, Shikoku and Kyushu.
Habitat: Cultivated in Europe in specialist collections, in the wild restricted to moist valley-bottom sites.

This is a small tree which tolerates a wide range of sites provided the soil is sufficiently moist, and will withstand dense shade.

CHUSAN PALM, *TRACHYCARPUS*
(SYNONYM: *CHAMAEROPS* IN PART)
FAMILY PALMAE

This is a small genus of around six species from China, Vietnam, Thailand, northern India to Nepal, with large palmate leaves. Only *T. fortunei* is common in cultivation.

p.349 **Chusan Palm** or **Windmill Palm**
Trachycarpus fortunei

Description: Evergreen tree to 15 m (50 ft) with a bole diameter to 30 cm (1 ft).
Crown Monopodal with a single unbranched stem and a terminal erect to pendent rosette of leaves. *Bark* Covered with reddish brown fibrous leaf sheaths, underbark grey, ringed with ridges from the leaf bases. *Foliage* Palmate, round, to 1.25 m (4 ft) in diameter, stiff and divided to the middle or nearly to the base into spreading or drooping segments which have a single rib, dull green above, paler below; leaf stalk to 1 m (3.3 ft), stout, with inconspicuous spines. *Flowers* Amongst the leaves, arching out, on a stout yellowish stalk, with several thin bracts on the inflorescence which is shorter than the leaves; flowers golden-yellow.
Fruit Globose to kidney-shaped, fleshy with a bluish covering, 1.2 cm (0.5 in).

Range: China to North Burma and into North Vietnam; cultivated in part of this region.

Habitat: Cultivated as an ornamental and for the fibres.

Synonyms: *Chamaerops fortunei*.

Similar species: *T. martinianus* differs in the leaves being more regularly and neatly divided, only about half way to the midrib, and in their being glaucous beneath. The leaf sheaths are soon shed, making the stem naturally smooth. The fruit is oblong-ovoid, with a longitudinal groove. It comes from the Himalayas from Nepal east to Burma and possibly Yunnan in China.
T. takil from northwest India has less-divided leaves and fibres more closely pressed onto the trunk.

The Chusan Palm is similar to *Chamaerops*, differing in the monopodal habit (although in var. *surculosa* suckering occurs) and in the much smaller spines on the leaf stalk. It is the hardiest palm, occurring in sheltered coastal sites as far north as northeast England and further north on the milder west coast. The fibrous leaf sheaths form an unwoven cloth. In China, this is stripped from the stems and used to make raincoats, leaving the trunks bare. The natural occurrence is masked by long-term planting.

TROCHODENDRON,
TROCHODENDRONACEAE

This is a monotypic family.

TROCHODENDRON, *TROCHODENDRON*
FAMILY TROCHODENDRONACEAE

This is a monotypic genus.

---

p.237 **Trochodendron** *Trochodendron aralioides*

Description: Evergreen tree 15–20 m (50–65 ft) with a bole diameter to 70 cm (2.3 ft).
Crown Conic in young trees, becoming broader with age. *Bark* Brown, smooth, very finely fissured. *Shoot* Green with small sparse oval orange lenticels, remaining green or yellow-green but in the fourth and fifth years turning brown by degrees.
Buds Ovoid-conic, acute, scales green and brown, to 1.3 cm (0.5 in). *Foliage* Leaves oval, obovate to rhombic-obovate and tending to be whorled at the shoot tips, abruptly tapered to a slender-pointed apex, base broad wedge-shaped, margin entire at the base but from around half way almost to the tip with rounded forward teeth, thick with a leathery texture, upper surface sub-shiny green, slightly folded along the midrib, underside sub-shiny yellow-green, 6–12 × 2–7 cm (2.4–4.7 × 0.8–2.8 in); leaf stalk grooved, green, long and around three-

quarters length of leaf blade, 2–10 cm (0.8–4 in); leaves kept for three or four years, falling yellow in fourth autumn. *Flowers* In erect terminal racemes in April, flowers without sepals and petals, comprising a vivid or yellowish-green disk with numerous stamens. *Fruit* Depressed globose or spinning-top-shaped capsule with 5–10 carpels each topped by a short recurved persistent style, 7–10 cm (2.8–4 in); seeds linear, 4–6 mm (0.2–0.25 in).

Range: Honshu, Shikoku and Kyushu, Japan, in south Korea and south along the Ryukyus to Taiwan.

Habitat: Cultivated as an ornamental, in the wild occurring in mountain forests.

This tree has an ivy-like appearance. It is allied to *Tetracentron*, and together placed in their own Order, sharing wood anatomy very similar to the conifers as they rely upon tracheids for water conduction and do not have vessels. Trochodendron is found in the wild in the warm temperate zone and appears tender but is actually much hardier.

HEMLOCKS, *TSUGA*
FAMILY PINACEAE

This is a genus of ten species from North America and eastern Asia. With the removal of *Hesperopeuce* and *Nothotsuga* (not in general cultivation) the genus becomes uniform in character. The leaves are flattened, often silvery beneath and, under a hand lens, either finely toothed (*see TT. canadensis, chinensis, dumosa* and *heterophylla*) or untoothed (*see TT. caroliniana, chinensis, diversifolia* and *sieboldii*). The shoots are nodding to pendent at the tips, which allows the shade-tolerant seedlings to grow through competing forest. The cones are small, with few scales. The species are used in forestry and as amenity trees.

p.95 **Eastern Hemlock** *Tsuga canadensis*

Description: Evergreen tree to 30 m (100 ft) with a bole to 1 m (3.3 ft) in diameter.
Crown Conical in young trees with a drooping leader, becoming broad conical

with long slender horizontal branches which droop at the tips and usually on several stems. *Bark* Orange-brown and purplish grey, smooth in young trees but becoming fissured and scaly on the ridges. *Shoot* Yellow-brown in first winter, later buff and then brown, with short pale brown or golden-brown hairs, slender, 1 mm (0.1 in). *Buds* Ovoid-conic, brown, 1.5 mm (0.1 in). *Foliage* In flat soft pendent sprays, leaves widely parted and pointing forwards beneath, those above the shoot somewhat raised but widely parted with a few short leaves lying along the shoot and revealing the glaucous underside; leaves widest near base, tapering from the rounded base to the bluntly rounded-pointed apex, margin with small forward teeth, upper surface matt or sub-shiny without stomata, underside with two narrow bands of waxy whitish-green stomata, a yellowing narrow midrib and two broad flat pale green margins, 0.6–1.8 cm × 2–2.5 mm (0.25–0.7 × 0.1 in); crushed foliage with a lemony slightly resinous scent. *Flowers* On previous season's growth in late spring; male cones yellow, 3–5 mm (0.1–0.2 in). *Fruit* Elliptic or oblong-ovoid, green and ripening to light brown, pendent, 1.5–2 × 1 cm (0.6–0.8 × 0.4 in); scales rounded with a rounded tip, papery, 8 mm (0.3 in) in width.

Range: In a triangle from New England across to southern Ontario and east Minnesota and south to northern Alabama.

Habitat: Cultivated in Europe as an ornamental, in the wild occurring in mixed forests on acid soils on moist ravines or rock outcrops.

This tree is closely related to *T. heterophylla* but can be distinguished by the line of short leaves which are pressed along the shoot above, revealing the waxy white stomatal bands, the shorter hairs on the shoot, the leaves being broader near the apex and tapering to the tip and the lemony scent of crushed foliage. In cultivation it has given rise to a host of dwarf forms, used in rockeries and as ground cover. In the wild, it is a component of mixed forest, using its great shade tolerance to slowly attain the canopy as a single-stemmed tree. In cultivation it tends to fork onto several stems.

---

p.96 **Carolina Hemlock** *Tsuga caroliniana*

Description: Evergreen tree to 15 m (50 ft) with a bole diameter to 40 cm (1.3 ft).
Crown Conical or ovoid, with spreading branches which may droop at the tips.
Bark Red-brown with yellow resin blisters in young trees, becoming fissured into broad flat scaly ridges. *Shoot* Red-brown above and orange-brown beneath in first winter, becoming darker red-brown later, with pale to black hairs in grooves which persist into the third winter, moderately slender, 1.5–2 mm (0.1 in). *Buds* Ovoid, rounded with a blunt point, brown, slightly resinous, 2 mm (0.1 in). *Foliage* In flat spreading sprays, or with tips nodding, with spaced leaves which are widely parted and slightly forwards below with the occasional leaf pointing downwards, with those above rising in ranks to give a narrow parting but broken by a few erect leaves; leaves linear, with a blunt rounded apex, tapering to the slender base which is pressed against the short adpressed leaf stalk, margins entire, upper surface mid to dark, sub-shiny green without stomata, underside with two waxy white bands of very small stomata, a yellow-green midrib and two mid green margins, 0.5–1.9 cm × 1.5–2 mm (0.2–0.7 × 0.1 in); crushed foliage with a citrus resin scent.
Flowers On previous season's growths in late spring; male cones sub-globular, yellow. *Fruit* Ovoid to elliptic, pendent at maturity, ripening from green or purple-green to light brown or red-brown, 2–3.5 × 1 cm (0.8–1.4 × 0.4 in), opening to 1.5–2.5 cm (0.6–1 in); scales pointed, opening widely, papery and fragile.
Range: Southern Appalachians from southwest Virginia to northwest Georgia, USA.

Habitat: Cultivated in Europe as an ornamental, in the wild occurring on dry rocky slopes and cliffs.

This tree is more closely related to *T. chinensis* and the other eastern Asiatic species, sharing the absence of teeth on the leaf margins and the general character and format of the shoots, than it is to *T. canadensis* and *T. heterophylla*.

---

p.96 **Chinese Hemlock** *Tsuga chinensis*

Description: Evergreen tree 10–20 m (33–65 ft) with a bole diameter to 60 cm (2 ft).
Crown Conical and spiky when young but with nodding stiff branch tips, becoming domed, usually clothed to the ground.
Bark Orange-brown, dark, with flakes of grey-green. *Shoot* Buff or pale whitish brown in first winter, shiny, more or less hairless with lines of blackish hairs in grooves, in second year brown fissures replace the grooves and in third and later years these expand, leaving narrow strips of shiny original bark. *Buds* Globose, dark red, slightly resinous, 1–1.5 cm (0.4–0.6 in), often with a tuft of forward-pointing leaves or on a short length of shoot. *Foliage* Rather lax, evenly pointing forwards at 45–60 degrees to the shoot, widely spreading beneath the shoot, widely parted above, in three to four lengths with the shortest above the shoot; leaves linear, apex rounded, slightly notched, margins entire or faintly toothed especially near apex, base abruptly tapered into short (1 mm (0.1 in)) leaf stalk, above dark glossy green, grooved and without stomata, below flat, with two bands of waxy white stomata and a midrib and two broad margins of mid green, 0.7–2.6 cm × 2–3 mm (0.3–1 × 0.1 in); crushed foliage with a grassy smell. *Flowers* On previous season's shoots in late spring; male cones 3–5 mm (0.1–0.2 in), yellow or purple. *Fruit* Ovoid-oblong, light green, ripening in first autumn to glossy light brown, 1.5–2.5 × 1.3–2.2 cm (0.6–1 × 0.5–0.9 in); scales circular,

convex, with a rounded, truncate or retuse apex, to 1 cm (0.4 in) in width.

Range: Central China from Yunnan and Sichuan east to Zhejiang and with a related species or variety on Taiwan.

Habitat: Cultivated in Europe as an ornamental, in the wild occurring in mixed mainly coniferous forest.

Varieties: Var. *tchekiangensis* has the cone scales circular but with a wedge-shaped base and two auricles and the leaves more tapered with brighter stomatal bands beneath. In var. *oblongisquamata* the cone scales are obovate-oblong, whilst in var. *robusta* the cones are larger, to 4 cm (1.6 in), and the scales thicker.

Synonyms: *Abies chinensis*.

Similar species: *T. formosana* (syn. *T. chinensis* var. *formosana*) has grey furrowed bark, yellow shoots and cones with scales half-moon in shape with finely-toothed margins. It is the Taiwan form of Chinese Hemlock.

This tree is uncommon in cultivation. In the slightly toothed margins, especially found on young plants, it resembles *T. dumosa*, *T. heterophylla* and *T. canadensis*, but the leaves are never as silvery beneath as in these trees.

p.97 **Northern Japanese Hemlock**
Tsuga diversifolia

Description: Evergreen tree to 15 m (50 ft) in height with a bole diameter to 50 cm (1.6 ft). *Crown* Broad conical or a low dome on several stems. *Bark* Dark orange-brown with shallow pink fissures and small scaly ridges. *Shoot* Orange or orange-brown in first winter, becoming browner and duller, finally pale brown, initially finely pubescent but very soon hairless with shallow fissures between the decurrent leaf bases, stiff, 2 mm (0.1 in). *Buds* Ovoid to ovoid-conic with a rounded apex, reddish brown, 1.5–2 mm (0.1 in). *Foliage* In stiff sprays with the leaves sparse and pointing downwards beneath the shoot, spreading forwards at the sides and above, rather spaced; leaves linear with smooth margins, apex rounded, notched, base with distinct leaf stalk 1–2 mm (0.1 in) which is pressed onto the shoot, shiny mid green above without stomata, beneath with two broad silvery white waxy bands of stomata, a narrow yellow-green midrib and two narrow rounded pale-green margins, 0.8–1.8 cm (0.3–0.7 in); crushed foliage with a light resin scent. *Flowers* On previous season's shoots in late spring; male cones red, shedding yellow pollen. *Fruit* Narrow ovoid, pendent on a bent stalk, 2–2.5 × 1.2 cm (0.8–1 × 0.5 in), ripening shiny brown; scales oblong with a rounded exposed portion, to 1 cm (0.4 in) in width.

Range: Japan from central and northern Honshu and rarely in Kyushu.

Habitat: Cultivated in Europe as an ornamental, in the wild occurring on cool mountain slopes with mixed conifers.

This makes an attractive small tree with a low-spreading crown. It tolerates a wide range of sites but is best on acidic ones. It is similar to *T. sieboldii*, differing in the shoots which are initially hairy and orange in colour and the shiny brown cone scales.

p.97 **Himalayan Hemlock** *Tsuga dumosa*

Description: Evergreen tree to 25 m (80 ft) with a bole up to 1.5 m (5 ft) diameter.
Crown Conical in young trees, becoming broad and domed in old trees. *Bark* Pink brown and scaly in young trees, becoming dark brown, fissured and scaly in old trees. *Shoot* White brown, becoming shiny buff or pinkish brown by winter and somewhat darker with age, initially with some pale-brown to blackish hairs but these are soon lost. *Buds* Globose, chestnut brown, 3 mm (0.1 in). *Foliage* Parted beneath and at the sides and slightly forwards, those above the shoots rising in two or three ranks, with a wide V-groove above the shoot, lax; leaves glossy dark green above and grooved,

beneath with two (sometimes accrescent into one) silvery white waxy stomatal band, broadest near base, tapering to blunt apex, margin near apex with fine saw-teeth (visible under hand-lens only), 0.8–2.8 cm × 1.5–2.5 mm (0.3–1.1 × 0.1 in); crushed foliage with a mild resinous scent. *Flowers* On previous season's growths; male cones 3–5 mm (0.1–0.2 in), yellow, lateral on shoots; female cones terminal on side or short side shoots throughout the crown, purplish green. *Fruit* Ovoid, opening to broad ovoid, with 20–25 scales, ripening to dull brown, 2–2.5 × 1–1.3 cm (0.8–1 × 0.4–0.5 in) when closed, opening to 2 cm (0.8 in); scales rounded, thin, woody.

Range: Himalayas from northwest India east through Nepal, Sikkim, Bhutan, northeast India, northern Burma, north and west Yunnan and Sichuan (China) to northern Vietnam.

Habitat: Cultivated in specialist collections in mild wet western areas of Europe, in the wild occurring in montane forests.

Synonyms: *T. brunoniana*, *T. yunnanensis*.

This is an attractive tree but which requires a moist and rather sheltered site for its best growth. It is tolerant of a wide variety of soils. It is more closely allied to the two North American species, *T. canadensis* and *T. heterophylla*, with which it shares the saw-like margins of the leaves.

---

p.95 **Western Hemlock** *Tsuga heterophylla*

Description: Evergreen tree 20–40 m (65–130 ft) in height with a bole diameter of up to 1.5 m (5 ft).
Crown Narrow conical when young, becoming broader, leader and tips of laterals pendent. *Bark* Purple-brown and smooth in young trees, becoming red-brown or grey-brown and developing furrows and broad scaly ridges; cutting the bark exposes red inner bark. *Shoot* Buff or yellow-brown in first winter, becoming

darker brown, very slender and flexible, 1–1.5 mm (0.1 in), with long soft golden-brown hairs which persist for several years. *Buds* Globose to ovoid-conic, pale brown, very small, 1–1.5 mm (0.1 in), laterals on a short spur shoot. *Foliage* In fairly flat pendent sprays, leaves widely parted beneath the shoot and pointing forwards, those above the shoot rising, with a parting between the opposite ranks; leaves linear, tapered to both ends, apex bluntly pointed, upper surface of leaves matt, mid green without stomata, grooved, lower face with one (coalesced) or two silvery white waxy stomatal bands and pale-green margins and midrib, margins finely toothed, of mixed lengths from 0.6–2.3 cm × 2–2.5 mm (0.25–0.9 × 0.1 in); crushed foliage with parsley or hemlock scent. *Flowers* On previous year's growths in late spring; male cones crimson, 3–5 mm (0.1–0.2 in). *Fruit* Ovoid, green, ripening to brown in first autumn, 1.5–2.5 cm (0.6–1 in); scales oblong, rounded, to 7 mm (0.3 in) in width.

Range: Western North America from southeast Alaska to northern California along the Pacific or western side of the Rocky Mountains, and from southeast British Columbia to northern Idaho on the eastern or inland side.

Habitat: Cultivated as an ornamental and used in forestry in Europe, in the wild occurring in moist acid bottom lands or lower slopes in coniferous temperate rainforest.

Varieties: No botanical varieties and remarkably few cultivars. The only tree one is 'Laursen's Column', which makes a narrow crowned columnar tree with ascending stems.

This makes a most beautiful tree with its matt green soft foliage and pendent shoots. It is extremely tolerant of shade and also of acid sands. It will grow on a wide range of sites but on exposed ones is likely to be cut by the wind or frost. The inner bark has been used to make a coarse bread. The timber is pale yellow-white and is also an excellent source of pulp for the paper industry.

p.97 **Southern Japanese Hemlock**
Tsuga sieboldii

Description: Evergreen tree to 15 m (50 ft) with a bole diameter to 60 cm (2 ft).
Crown Broadly conic, open, often on several stems, with nodding branch tips.
Bark Dark grey, smooth at first but later cracking into small squares. *Shoot* Buff to straw-brown with small red-brown ridges behind the leaf bases on underside, darker above in first year, older shoots gradually paler and greyer, slender, 1.5 mm (0.1 in).
Buds Elliptic to ovoid, bluntly pointed, pale reddish-brown, 1.5–2 mm (0.1 in).
Foliage Spreading in flat sprays, leaves beneath the shoot widely parted on either side and curved down, those at the side spreading and slightly forwards, with the upper ranks much shorter and widely parted; leaves linear, apex rounded, notched, at base tapered into 2 mm (0.1 in) leaf stalk pressed on shoot, margins entire, dark glossy green above without stomata, beneath with two pale whitish or whitish green waxy bands of stomata and pale-green margins, 0.7–2.2 cm × 2–3 mm (0.3–0.9 × 0.1 in); crushed foliage resin scented. *Flowers* On previous season's shoots in late spring; male cones 3–5 mm (0.1–0.2 in), yellow. *Fruit* Ovoid, ripening from green-purple to lustrous brown in first autumn, pendent, 2–2.5 × 1–1.5 cm (0.8–1 × 0.4–0.6 in) (closed) or 1.5–2 cm (0.6–0.8 in) (open); scales with rounded exposed apex 0.8–1.2 cm (0.3–0.5 in) in width.

Range: Southern Japan from southern Honshu, Kyushu, Shikoku and Yakushima.

Habitat: Cultivated as an ornamental in Europe, in the wild occurring in mixed forests on wet hillsides.

This tree is closely related to *T. diversifolia* but differs in the much paler hairless shoot and the less-white leaf undersides. It is also close to *T. chinensis*, which has hairy shoots and pale green to greenish white leaf undersides.

ELM, ULMACEAE

This is a small family of around 16 genera and 140 species. The three main genera in cultivation are *Ulmus* and *Zelkova* (p.1268), with pinnate venation, and *Celtis* (p.588), in which the leaves are strongly three-veined at the base. In *Celtis* and *Zelkova*, the fruit is a drupe, whilst in *Ulmus* it is a samara. Species of the genera *Pteroceltis*, *Hemiptelea*, *Planera* and *Aphanathe* are occasionally encountered in specialist collections.

ELMS, *ULMUS*
FAMILY ULMACEAE

This is a medium-sized genus, with perhaps 30 species. The leaves are simple, usually very oblique at the base and doubly toothed, but in *UU. canescens* and *parvifolia* the toothing is single and regular. The upper surface of the leaves may be rough or scabrid in *UU. glabra*, *japonica* and *procera*, but is smooth in the other species of the genus. The flowers in most species are carried in the spring before the leaves, but in the autumn in *U. parvifolia*. The fruit is a samara with a wide thin wing. Elms are very tolerant of coastal exposure. Many sucker freely and were moved around by prehistoric tribes who used them to mark their territories. The foliage provides good fodder for cattle, and formerly elms were extensively lopped for this purpose. In recent years, they have been devastated by Dutch elm disease. This is a fungal disease, which is spread by elm bark beetles. The disease kills the trees, making them suitable breeding sites for the bark beetles. When the new brood matures, they fly off to other elms, carrying the fungal spores with which they inoculate a new tree, starting the cycle again.

p.194 **Grey Elm** *Ulmus canescens*

Description: Deciduous tree 10–15 m (33–50 ft). *Crown* Broad, spreading. *Bark* Fissured. *Shoot* Grey-brown, round, occasionally with corky ridges, initially thinly pilose but usually hairless by autumn. *Buds* Broad ovoid, scale bluntly pointed or rounded, bark brown, hairy, 3–5 cm (1.2–2 in).

Foliage Leaves ovate-elliptic, apex shortly acute to broadly pointed, base subcordate and very unequal, margin with blunt close wavy teeth, upper surface initially soft hairy, hairless at maturity, bright green, underside with 12–18 pairs of prominent parallel veins which have grey axillary tufts in the axils, 4.5–9 × 2.5–5 cm (1.8–3.5 × 1–2 in); leaf stalk hairy, stout, to 7 mm (0.3 in). *Flowers* Brownish red in small rounded clusters in February–March. *Fruit* Obovoid winged samara or nutlet, 2 × 1.5 cm (0.8 × 0.6 in); wing pale with a deep notched overlapping apex, seed reddish.

Range: Italy east along the northern shores of the Mediterranean to Israel, north to Romania and Turkey.

Habitat: Rocky slopes and ravines.

Synonyms: *U. minor* ssp. *canescens*.

This small tree is allied to the *U. minor* group, being best distinguished by the dense white down on young shoots and leaves, the rounded blunt teeth and the 12–16 or 18 pairs of veins.

---

p.193 **Wych Elm** *Ulmus glabra*

Description: Deciduous tree 20–30 m (65–100 ft) with a bole diameter to 1 m (3.3 ft) or more. *Crown* Young trees ovoid or columnar conic, developing a broad domed crown with radiating main branches in old trees. *Bark* Smooth and silvery grey for several years, then becoming dull and fissuring with black cracks, still later grey-brown and developing an interconnecting network of ridges. *Shoot* Brown with small pale lenticels and stout in first winter, initially hairy, later grey-brown. *Buds* Ovoid-conic, sharp pointed, chocolate brown with long hairs, 6–8 mm (0.25–0.3 in). *Foliage* In rather flat zig-zag sprays; leaves oval to obovate, base oblique and very unequal, apex with a slender point or with three or more points or coarse triangular lobes across the broad shoulder of the leaf, margin coarsely and doubly toothed, upper surface very rough to the touch with 14–20 impressed secondary veins, dull green, beneath finely downy and paler, 8–18 × 4–10 cm (3.1–7.1 × 1.6–4 in); leaf stalk stout, short, less than 6 mm (0.25 in).

Flowers From axillary buds on previous season's shoots in late winter; in dense, stalkless clusters of purplish red.

Fruit Expanding in spring to become showy pale green bunches with a thin wing 2.5 cm (1 in) across with an apical notch and a small flat seed, ripening to brown and shed in mid-summer.

Range: Throughout Europe except for the far north and into western Asia.

Habitat: Woodland, hedgerows, exposed ground and seasides.

Varieties: Ssp. *montana* covers the trees found in northern England, Scotland and Scandinavia. These do not have the shouldered lobes or large triangular teeth, rather they are narrower and tend to be more equal at the base. 'Camperdown' is a pendulous selection which forms a curtain of weeping branches. The winter silhouette is wonderful, with a contorted mass of twisting branches above the graft union. 'Pendula' has pendent branches which arch down at 45 degrees. It makes a taller and broader tree than 'Camperdown'.

Synonyms: *U. campestre* in part; *U. montana*.

This tree has a Latin name which translates as 'smooth' or (as usually implied) 'hairless' yet has very rough leaves (they are covered with short stiff hairs on the upper surface and downy beneath). The explanation is that the Latin name refers to the bark, which remains smooth for several years, and does not have the corky flanges found in some other species.

p.194 **Dutch Elm** *Ulmus × hollandica*

Description: Deciduous tree 15–30 m (50–100 ft) with a bole diameter to 1.5 m (5 ft).
Crown Upright dome to rounded dome with large radiating branches. *Bark* Grey-

brown at first and rather smooth, soon becoming fissured and developing either broad ridges or small scales. *Shoot* Brown or dull brown, initially with long hairs but becoming hairless by autumn. *Buds* Ovoid, red-brown, shiny, to 1 cm (0.4 in). *Foliage* Leaves oval, ovate or elliptic, apex abrupt and short slender pointed, base narrowed and rounded or heart-shaped on one side and wedge-shaped in the other, margin more or less doubly toothed, upper surface smooth, shiny rich green and more or less hairless, underside paler with raised, hairy veins, 10–15 × 8 cm (4–6 × 3.1 in); leaf stalk stout, yellow-green to pink, hairy, 1–2 cm (0.4–0.8 in); autumn colour yellow. *Flowers* Dark red, in late March–April. *Fruit* In late spring, obovate with a notched wing, 2 cm (0.8 in).

Range: Western Europe, especially the Low Countries and eastern England.

Habitat: Woods and hedgerows.

Varieties: 'Vegeta' is perhaps the best form, making a vigorous domed tree with the branches ascending.

This tree is a hybrid of *U. glabra* with the *U. minor* complex. It makes a fast-growing vigorous tree, but due to its mixed parentage, is variable between the many different forms in cultivation.

p.193 **Japanese Elm** *Ulmus japonica*

Description: Deciduous tree 15–20 m (50–65 ft) with a bole diameter to 60 cm (2 ft) . *Crown* Rounded, domed in old trees with pendulous branches. *Bark* Brown, ridged and furrowed. *Shoot* Ashen grey with white hairs and small fissures in the first year, becoming brown or grey-brown later, sometimes with corky wings or ridges. *Buds* Ovate, pointed, chestnut brown, to 6 mm (0.25 in). *Foliage* Leaves oval, obovate, elliptic or rather rhombic in outline, very oblique at the rounded base with up to 1 cm (0.4 in) difference, apex drawn out to a short slender point, margin regularly doubly serrate with rather rounded teeth, upper surface sub-shiny green with the 12–20 pairs of veins impressed, otherwise smooth, underside light green, hairy especially on the raised and parallel veins, size variable from 2.5 × 2 cm (1–0.8 in) up to 12 × 6.5 cm (4.7 × 2.6 in); leaf stalk rounded, green, white hairy, about 1–2 cm (0.4–0.8 in); autumn colour russets. *Fruit* obovate, hairless, 1–1.6 cm (0.4–0.6 in), with the seed towards the apex.

Range: Throughout Japan, but rare.

Habitat: Cultivated as an ornamental, in the wild occurring in woodlands.

Synonyms: *U. davidiana* var. *japonica*.

This tree is very tolerant of Dutch elm disease. It makes a tree similar in aspect to *U. glabra*.

---

p.195 **Fluttering Elm** or **European White Elm**
Ulmus laevis

Description: Deciduous tree 15–35 m (50–115 ft) with a bole diameter to 1.5 m (5 ft).
Crown Open wide-spreading dome.
Bark Brownish grey and smooth in young trees, becoming deeply furrowed with broad ridges. *Shoot* Dark red-brown, at first clothed with grey down.
Buds Conical, pointed, small, dark orange-brown. *Foliage* Leaves round to oval or obovate, tapering to a short slender-pointed apex, base very oblique with the outer side markedly longer with two or three pairs of extra veins, margin with double incurved teeth, veins 12–19 pairs, upper surface smooth, rarely with some stiff hairs, bright green, underside paler with raised veins and grey hairs, 6–13 × 3–7 cm (2.4–5.1 × 1.2–2.8 in); leaf stalk hairy, 3–6 mm (0.1–0.25 in). *Flowers* In clusters in early spring on stalks three to six times as long as the flowers.
Fruit Obovate with a notched apex and ciliate margin, 1–1.2 cm (0.4–0.5 in); pendent on long slender stalks.

Range: Eastern France eastwards to the Volga region of Russia and south into the Caucasus.

Habitat: Rich soils in river valleys.

Synonyms: *U. effusa*, *U. pedunculata*.

The long slender stalks easily separate this tree when in flower or fruit and cause the flowers and fruits to flutter in the slightest breeze. The leaves are very oblique, more so than in other elms with two or three extra pairs of veins on one side.

---

p.194 **Smooth Elm** or **European Field Elm**
Ulmus minor

Description: Deciduous tree 20–30 m (65–100 ft) with a bole diameter to 1.2 m (3.9 ft).
Crown Conical when young but becoming rounded and domed in old trees.
Bark Silvery-grey and smooth in young trees, then fissuring and finally deeply fissured with long thick ridges.
Shoot Glossy brown in first year and initially downy, later grey-brown.
Buds Long ovoid, shiny dark red, 2–4 mm (0.1–0.2 in). *Foliage* Oval or ovate or elliptic, base very oblique with one side rounded and the other wedge-shaped, apex slender pointed, margin doubly toothed, upper surface shiny green, hairless, lower surface paler green, hairy in vein axils and along midrib, veins 10–13 pairs, 4–12 cm (1.6–4.7 in), mainly 6–8 × 2.5–5 cm (2.4–3.1 × 1–2 in); leaf stalk 5 mm (0.2 in), hairy. *Flowers* On previous season's growths in early spring, in dense rounded heads (to 1 cm (0.4 in)) of purplish-red flowers. *Fruit* Flat with a wide papery wing all around, oval to obovate and notched at the top, hairless, 1.2–1.5 cm (0.5–0.6 in).

Range: Western Europe and North Africa across to southwest Asia.

Habitat: Lowland woods.

Varieties: The following British elms are variously treated as varieties or separate micro-species. Cornish Elm (var. *cornubiensis*) has a narrow habit with ascending spaced branches set in a fan-shape at the top of the trunk. It occurs in southwest England and southwest Ireland. Wheatley or Jersey Elm (var. *sarniensis*) has an ovoid-conical habit with a single stem. It originated on the Channel Islands. Lock Elm (var. *plotii*) from central England has a more broadly conical crown.

Synonyms: *U. carpinifolia*, *U. campestre*.

This makes a neat tree. It is related to *U. procera*, which has leaves rough above and hairy all over beneath. Different forms are treated either as varieties or separate species. In Britain, several of these were introduced by Belgic tribes in the Iron Age and were used as boundary markers, so there is a different 'species' corresponding to each tribe. The foliage of elm was also very important as fodder for cattle, both cut and dried as winter food but also to provide fresh leaves when dry periods in summer caused the grass to stop growing.

---

p.195 **Chinese Elm** *Ulmus parvifolia*

Description: Deciduous tree, but semi-evergreen in warm climates, to 10–18 m (33–60 ft) with a bole diameter to 60 cm (2 ft).
Crown Domed with spreading branches, dense. *Bark* Mottled grey-brown, becoming scaly and shedding to reveal orange to red-brown inner bark.
Shoot Slender, slightly zig-zagged, with close grey hairs. *Buds* Conical, small, less than 2 mm (0.1 in). *Foliage* Leaves set in two rows along the shoot, elliptic, ovate to oblong, apex acute, base rounded or oblique with one side wedge-shaped, margin with regular triangular teeth, rather thick in texture, upper surface glossy dark green and hairless, underside paler shiny green with whitish hairs especially on the rather indistinct veins, 2–5 × 1–2 cm (0.8–2 × 0.4–0.8 in); leaf stalk 2–6 mm (0.1–0.25 in); autumn colour red or purple,

or remaining green until frosts kill the leaves. *Flowers* In September–October in leaf axils, greenish. *Fruit* Elliptic with broad flat pale yellow wing, ripening in autumn, 1 cm (0.4 in).

Range: Central and eastern China, Taiwan, Korea and southern Japan (Honshu, Shikoku and Kyushu).

Habitat: Cultivated as an ornamental.

Synonyms: *U. chinensis.*

This tree has a very attractive bark and small glossy leaves which are regularly, if bluntly, toothed. In mild climates, the leaves remain green until cut by frost. It is the only commonly encountered elm which flowers in the autumn.

p.193 **English Elm** *Ulmus procera*

Description: Deciduous tree up to 30 m (100 ft) with a bole diameter to 1 m (3.3 ft) or more. *Crown* Ovoid or conic in young trees, becoming tall domed, with suckers from the roots. *Bark* Dark brown and soon fissured with crossing ridges or small squarrish plates. *Shoot* Slender, reddish brown or brown, with long persistent hairs in first winter, later becoming hairless and smooth, but with some shoots developing corky wings. *Buds* Ovoid, pointed, dark brown, scales with silky white hairs on outer surface, 2–3 mm (0.1 in).
Foliage Rounded ovate to oval, apex short pointed, margins doubly and coarsely sharp toothed, base oblique, rough above and dark green, below paler with whitish hairs especially along the midrib and the 10–12 pairs of lateral veins, 4–10 × 3.5–7 cm (1.6–4 × 1.4–2.8 in); leaf stalk finely hairy, 5 mm (0.2 in). *Flowers* On previous season's shoots in late winter or early spring, dark red, small.
Fruit Enclosed by a flat, hairless, rounded, papery wing which is notched at the apex, 1.2 cm (0.5 in).

Range: Southern England.

Habitat: Fields and hedgerows.

The origins of English Elm are rather enigmatic. The species (if that is the right determination) has evidently flourished as a consequence of the enclosures of common land from the 17th century onwards. The reasons lie in the vigorous suckering nature and the good-quality timber on an upright crown. Trees were planted in the new hedges for timber (which was reserved for the landowner) and when felled, the suckers ran riot. However, whether it was common before then is uncertain. It is almost always sterile, with the seed hollow, and therefore is probably of hybrid origin.

Unfortunately, the ravages of Dutch elm disease (caused by the fungus *Ophiostoma ulmi*) have largely removed all the mature trees, leaving only the suckers to survive for a decade or two.

p.195 **Siberian Elm** *Ulmus pumila*

Description: Deciduous tree (but sometimes tardily deciduous in warm climates) to 10–18 m (33–60 ft) with a bole diameter to 60 cm (2 ft).

Crown Rounded domed with open spreading branches. *Bark* Grey, becoming cracked into small squares and furrowed, brown-orange in the cracks. *Shoot* Grey, at first hairy but soon hairless, slightly zig-zagged with the side branchlets arranged in a herring-bone fashion, moderately slender. *Buds* Ovoid, glossy brown, small.

Foliage Leaves narrowly elliptic to ovate-lanceolate, acute to slender pointed at the apex, base regularly rounded, not oblique, margin coarsely toothed, usually with three or four teeth to each slight lobule, thickened in texture, dark green and hairless above, paler beneath and sometimes hairy on the 10–12 pairs of parallel veins, 2–5 × 1.2–2.5 cm (0.8–2 × 0.5–1 in); leaf stalk stout, hairy, 2–4 mm (0.1–0.2 in); autumn colour yellow. *Flowers* In spring, greenish. *Fruit* Rounded flat samara ripening in the spring with a broad wing which is notched at the apex, 1–1.5 cm (0.4–0.6 in).

Range: Central Asia from Turkmenistan across Siberia to Mongolia, China and Korea, south into Tibet.

Habitat: Cultivated as an ornamental, especially for its drought tolerance; in the wild occurring in dry regions along river banks.

Varieties: Var. *arborea* (*U. pinnato-racemosa*) has longer pointed leaves and more downy shoots. It occurs in western Siberia.

Synonyms: *U. humilis, U. microphylla.*

This tree is very similar in leaf to *U. parvifolia*, differing in being spring flowering and in the coarse toothing of the leaves. It has a degree of resistance to Dutch elm disease, although I have seen it affected by this disease at the Potala Palace in Lhasa, Tibet.

CALIFORNIAN HEADACHE TREE, *UMBELLULARIA*
FAMILY LAURACEAE

This is a genus of two species but only one is occasional in cultivation. The foliage is very strongly aromatic, giving a headache to those who sniff it too enthusiastically.

---

p.168   **Californian Laurel** or **Californian Headache Tree** *Umbellularia californica*

Description: Evergreen tree 15–25 m (50–80 ft) with a bole diameter to 80 cm (2.6 ft).
Crown Conical when young, becoming rounded and domed in old trees.
Bark Dark brown, thin, becoming fissured into small tight scaly plates and grey-brown. *Shoot* Green for the first winter, initially minutely downy but this is soon shed, becoming green with brown fissures, then dark greenish brown.
Buds Ovoid or ovoid-conical, pointed, green, on a short stalk, to 3 mm (0.1 in) but most only 1 mm (0.1 in).
Foliage Lanceolate or oblong-lanceolate, leathery, tapered to both ends, medium to dark shiny green above with a pale green

flat midrib, beneath light green with a prominent midrib, margins untoothed, 5–12 × 1.8–3.5 cm (2–4.7 × 0.7–1.4 in); leaf stalk green, 5 mm (0.2 in); crushed (and brushed) foliage strongly aromatic with a rich fruity more-ish scent.

Flowers In terminal and axillary umbels each 2 cm (0.8 in) across in mid spring before the new leaves; individual flowers yellow-green, 6 mm (0.25 in) with a six-parted calyx but without petals.

Fruit Ellipsoidal or round berry, ripening from green to purple, 2–2.5 cm (0.8–1 in), with a single brown seed and a thin pulp, calyx persistent at base.

Range: Central Oregon south along the coastal ranges of California and also in the interior range of central California.

Habitat: Cultivated in Europe as an ornamental, in the wild occurring in moist valley bottoms or on ridges.

This makes a neat evergreen tree which is closely related to *Laurus*. The plant is aromatic with a most delightful fruity scent. Unfortunately, heavy indulgence usually results in a splitting, albeit brief, headache and even unconsciousness. Some cases of dermatitis have also been blamed on the volatile fragrant oil in the foliage.

VERBENA, VERBENACEAE

This is a large family of which only *Clerodendrum* (p.614) and *Vitex* (p.1262) are featured here.

GUELDER ROSES, *VIBURNUM*
FAMILY CAPRIFOLIACEAE

This is a large genus, most of whose species are shrubs but occasionally making small trees. The leaves are simple, toothed. If a leaf is carefully torn in half, the latex in the veins will hold the leaves together, as in *Eucommia* and genera in the Cornaceae. The flowers are fragrant, and followed by the fruits which are red, blue or black single-seeded drupes. The species are used for amenity.

p.175 **Wayfaring Tree** *Viburnum lantana*

Description: Deciduous shrub or small tree to 6 m
(20 ft).
Crown Rounded, bushy. *Bark* Brown.
Shoot Covered with dense star-shaped pale
down, stipular ridge at nodes. *Buds* In
opposite pairs, naked, without scales but
with exposed miniature leaves with star-
shaped down. *Foliage* Leaves broadly ovate
to oblong, apex acute and short pointed or
blunt, base heart-shaped, margin finely
toothed, upper surface shiny green with
impressed veins, at first velvety but soon
hairless, underside white woolly with raised
veins, 5–12 × 3–10 cm (2–4.7 × 1.2–4 in);
leaf stalk hairy, 1.2–3 cm (0.5–1.2 in);
autumn colour red. *Flowers* In terminal
domed cymes on leafy shoots in May–June,
usually with seven branches; flowers white,
6 mm (0.25 in). *Fruit* Oblong, flattened,
maturing from green to red and ripening to
black when the flesh is juicy, 8 mm (0.3 in);
seed striated, pale.

Range: Southern and central Europe from northern
England east to the Caucasus and south
into North Africa.

Habitat: Rocky places, verges and hedges.

This makes a small tree or large shrub.

---

p.175 **Guelder Rose** *Viburnum opalus*

Description: Deciduous shrub or small tree to 6 m
(20 ft).
Crown Rounded, bushy. *Bark* Light
brown. *Shoot* Hairless, smooth and
ridged, pale brown, stipular ridge at
nodes. *Buds* In opposite pairs, ovoid,
pointed, reddish, 5 mm (0.2 in).
Foliage Leaves broad ovate to rounded in
outline but broken by three (less often
four or five) deep lobes, lobes ovate,
coarsely toothed, sinuses rounded, base
more or less truncate, upper surface deep
green and hairless, veins slightly
impressed, underside paler and variously
hairy, 5–10 cm (2–4 in) long and wide;

leaf stalk with two glands near the junction with the leaf blade and two thin linear stipules at the base, 1.2–2.5 cm (0.5–1 in); autumn colour red. *Flowers* In terminal cymes 5–7 cm (2–2.8 in) across on leafy shoots in June, with white sterile ray flowers 2 cm (0.8 in) across set around the perimeter of the inflorescence with fertile flowers clustered in the centre; flowers white with yellow anthers. *Fruit* Globose, nearly round, maturing to glistening red and persisting after leaf fall, 8 mm (0.3 in); seed striated, pale.

Range: Throughout Europe east to the Caucasus and central Asia and south into North Africa.

Habitat: Woods, thickets and in hedges.

Varieties: Selected forms include 'Xanthocarpum' with golden-yellow fruits, and forms with a greater proportion of sterile ray flowers.

This is an attractive large shrub, at its best in autumn.

---

p.141 **Laurustinus** *Viburnum tinus*

Description: Spreading evergreen shrub or less often a spreading tree to 7 m (23 ft).
Crown Rounded dome. *Bark* Brown.
Shoot Pink on upper surface and green beneath in first winter, later becoming brown over several seasons, hairless or with a few long hairs, lenticels oval. *Buds* In opposite pairs, flattened linear, green with black hairs, 2–3 mm (0.1 in).
Foliage Ovate to oblong, margins entire, rounded at base, tapering to acute apex, veins curve forwards, four or five pairs, matt mid green above pale green beneath with tufts of pale brown hairs in vein axils, retained two or three years, 4–10 × 1.5–4 cm (1.6–4 × 0.6–1.6 in); leaf stalk pink or red, 2 cm (0.8 in). *Flowers* In cymes 5–10 cm (2–4 in) across; flowers white, 6 mm (0.25 in) across, five petals, united at the base, five stamens, opening over winter. *Fruit* Ovoid, tapering to the attenuated persistent calyx, 7 × 4 mm (0.3

× 0.2 in), deep blue, finally black, with a single seed, ripening in late autumn.

Range: Southern Europe, primarily around the Mediterranean, and in north Africa.

Habitat: Maquis scrub.

This is usually seen as a spreading shrub in northern countries where it is cultivated for the winter flowers.

GRAPE, VITACEAE

This is a family of around eight hundred species. They are mainly climbers, using tendrils (sometimes with adhesive pads) to gain support. Only *Parthenocissus* (p.870) is featured here, as it occasionally makes a stem of almost tree-like proportions.

CHASTE TREES, *VITEX*
FAMILY VERBENACEAE

This is a large and mainly tropical genus of around 250 species.

---

p.312 **Chaste Tree** *Vitex agnus-castus*

Description: Deciduous shrub, rarely tree-like, to 4 m (13 ft).
Crown Rounded, shrubby. *Shoot* Four-angled and hairy when young, becoming round, dull brown. *Buds* In opposite pairs, small. *Foliage* Leaves palmately compound with five to seven narrow lanceolate leaflets; leaflets acute at the apex, wedge-shaped at the base with a short stalk, untoothed, green or grey and finely haired above, white tomentose beneath, 2–12 cm × 0.3–1.8 cm (0.8–4.7 × 0.1–0.7 in); leaf stalk slender, hairy, 2–7 cm (0.8–2.8 in). *Flowers* In erect terminal much branched inflorescences 7–20 cm (2.8–8 in) from June to December; flowers lilac, purple or less often white. *Fruit* Globose, 3 mm (0.1 in), with three or four seeds.

Range: Mediterranean region and southern Europe.

Habitat: Gravelly sites, such as dunes or along stream beds, usually moist sites.

Similar species: *V. negundo* from India to China is similar, differing in the flowers being in spaced clusters on the spikes and the leaves being variously toothed.

This makes a large shrub rather than a tree but is a common and distinctive plant.

PETTICOAT PALMS, *WASHINGTONIA*
FAMILY PALMAE

This is a genus of two species. The old leaves hang down to form a 'petticoat' beneath the crown.

---

p.349 **Petticoat Palm** *Washingtonia filifera*

Description: Evergreen tree 10–20 m (33–65 ft) with a stout bole 60–90 cm (2–2.9 ft) in diameter. *Crown* Monopodal with a single untapered stem which has a terminal rosette of numerous leaves with the old, dead ones hanging down like a thatch or petticoat, without basal suckers. *Bark* Grey, smooth but with horizontal lies and vertical ridges. *Foliage* Leaves palmate but with a short length of stem between each pair of leaflets (costapalmate), with a blade 0.9–1.5 m (2.9–5 ft) in diameter which is split into about fifty narrow, folded, singly-ribbed leathery segments which are grey-green, with a protrusion at the junction of the leaf blade with the leaf stalk, with hanging segments which are separated by filaments; leaf stalk spined. *Flowers* In erect inflorescences which arise from the axils of the lower leaves, with white or creamy flowers. *Fruit* Ovoid, wrinkled, with a thin sweet edible pulp, 1 cm (0.4 in), on pendent inflorescences.

Range: Southern California, Western Arizona and in northern Baja California (Mexico).

Habitat: Cultivated as an ornamental.

Similar species: **Mexican Fan Palm** *W. robusta* has a trunk which is tapered from a swollen base. The leaves are brilliant green with a tawny brown patch on the underside by the protrusion at the junction of the leaf blade and leaf stalk. Mature plants do not have the filaments characteristic of Petticoat Palm but this does not hold for juvenile plants.

Livistona australis has similar leaves which are up to 1.75 m (5.7 ft) in diameter with about seventy segments which are cleft at the apex which hangs down. The bole is brown, whilst the leaf stalk is spined along the full length. It is native to Eastern Australia but cultivated in the Mediterranean region as an ornamental. *L. decipiens* differs most markedly in the leaf stalk only being spined towards the base.

This is cultivated as an ornamental. It is characterized by the hanging dead older leaves which form a skirt beneath the rosette. The leaves have many filaments or threads.

WINTER'S BARK, WINTERACEAE

This small family is related to the Magnolia family, differing in the carpels which are in a whorl, not in a helix. It is considered as possibly the most primitive family of broadleaves. Only *Drimys* (p.669) is treated here.

WISTERIA, *WISTERIA*
FAMILY LEGUMINOSAE

This is a genus of climbers, from southeast USA and eastern Asia. The leaves are pinnate. The flowers are pea-like, in pendulous racemes. The fruit is a hairy pod or legume.

p.339 **Wisteria** *Wisteria sinensis*

Description: Deciduous climber capable of attaining 10–15 m (33–50 ft) up trees.
Crown Depends on support. *Bark* Brown.
Shoot Twining in an anti-clockwise

direction, grey-brown, at first silky hairy.
Buds Ovoid, pointed, dark red-brown.
Foliage Leaves pinnate, with 11 leaflets,
25–30 cm (10–12 in); leaflets elliptic to
ovate, apex acute, rich green above, hairy
beneath especially on the midrib, 3–10 ×
1.2–3 cm (1.2–4 × 0.5–1.2 in). *Flowers* In
long pendent racemes on short leafy shoots;
flowers opening progressively from the
base, petals violet to purplish blue,
fragrant. *Fruit* Pendent pod, green,
covered in velvety down, 7–15 cm
(2.8–6 in), containing two or three seeds.

Range: Central and northern China.
Habitat: Cultivated as an ornamental, grown on
trees or houses, occasionally trained as a
free-standing shrub or small tree on a stem.
Varieties: Several garden selections.
Similar species: *W. floribunda* differs in having 11–19
leaflets, and in the stems which twine
clockwise around supports. It is native to
Honshu, Shikoku and Kyushu, Japan.

This flamboyant climber is capable of
growing to the top of tall trees, once
established.

YUCCAS, *YUCCA*
FAMILY AGAVACEAE

This is a genus of around 30 species. The leaves are bayonet-
like. The flowers are terminal, in large erect panicles or
racemes.

---

p.351 **Spanish Bayonet** *Yucca aloifolia*

Description: Evergreen tree to 8 m (26 ft).
Crown Ovoid, on a number of erect little
branched stems which are terminated by
rosettes of leaves. *Bark* Brown, rough,
fissured and scaly. *Shoot* Stout, little
branched with persistent dead leaves.
Foliage Leaves lance or bayonet-like, with a
long sharp pointed brown spine, margin
with fine teeth, thick and stiff, upper
surface grooved, dull green without
noticeable veins, 30–50 × 2.5–4.5 cm

(12–20 × 1–1.8 in); stalkless on the shoot. *Flowers* In broad upright compact panicles; flowers bell-shaped, white, with fleshy pointed sepals. *Fruit* Cylindrical berry, with six angled ridges, with a bitter-sweet juicy pulp but becoming dry and ripening to dark purple or black, with many flat black seeds, 7.5–10 cm (3–4 in).

Range: Southeast USA from North Carolina to Alabama and in the West Indies, but always near the coast.

Habitat: Cultivated as an ornamental, in the wild occurring on coastal sands.

This tree has an edible fruit, whilst the flowers can be used as a salad or cooked. It has become naturalized in parts of the Mediterranean region. The fibres in the bark and leaves can be used to make rope. It is tolerant of salt and coastal exposure.

TOOTHACHE TREES, *ZANTHOXYLUM* (SYNONYM: *XANTHOXYLUM*)
FAMILY RUTACEAE

This is a large genus of around 250 species from all continents except Europe and Antarctica. The leaves are pinnate, with glandular dots typical of the Rutaceae. There are stout spines on the shoot and trunk. The fruits are capsules which split along two sutures to show the shiny black or blue seeds; these remain attached by slender threads, and await being eaten by birds. The fruits of some species have a spicy or peppery taste, and are used as the strong spice in the Sichuan style of Chinese cookery. They have a numbing influence upon teeth when chewed, hence the name toothache trees.

---

p.324 **Japanese Toothache Tree**
Zanthoxylum ailanthioides

Description: Deciduous tree 10 m (33 ft) or more with a bole diameter to 50 cm (1.6 ft). *Crown* Spreading widely on a short bole. *Bark* Smooth, grey, with persistent spines which have a conical oval base, later becoming knobbly as the spine tips are lost. *Shoot* Stout, green with a waxy white bloom, oval whitish lenticels, small round dimples, sparse hairs and small hooked spines which are stout at the base, becoming brown and green in the second year with large deltoid or kidney-shaped traces from the fallen leaves, shiny buff-brown from year three with persistent spines. *Buds* Domed or rounded with two or three warty green scales, 2–3 mm (0.1 in), superposed. *Foliage* Leaves 25–80 cm (10–32 in), pinnate with 7–23 leaflets; leaflets largest in the middle to upper third of leaf, ovate or ovate-lanceolate, slender pointed at the apex, rounded or subcordate and oblique at the base, margin with fine rounded projections interspersed by a translucent gland, upper surface fresh green with an impressed midrib which is slightly glandular, underside glaucous whitish green with a prominent raised midrib, both sides showing scattered translucent glands when held up to the light, 5–15 × 3–4 cm (2–6 × 1.2–1.6 in); leaf stalk and rachis with a fine groove, enlarged at base, yellow-green to purplish; autumn colour yellow. *Flowers* In terminal cymes 8–15 cm (3.1–6 in) across from the current season's growths in autumn, individual flowers minute yellow-green. *Fruit* Leathery follicle which splits to release the black seeds.

Range: Japan from Honshu, Shikoku and Kyushu, south along the Ryukyu Islands to Taiwan, and on the mainland from south Korea and eastern China.

Habitat: Cultivated as an ornamental, in the wild occurring in woodlands.

Synonyms: *Fagara ailanthioides.*

Similar species: *Z. simulans* (p.324) makes a shrubby tree 3–6 m (10–20 ft) in height. The bark is brown with curious knobbles which develop from the broad flat spines which are 0.6–2 cm (0.25–0.8 in) in length on the one-year-old shoots. The leaflets are in three to five pairs, and usually armed with spines both on the shiny upper surface, along the midrib beneath and along the rachis, especially where the leaflets are attached.

The fruit ripens to reddish. It comes from northern and central China.

The seeds of several *Zanthoxylum* taxa are used as spices, and if chewed release an agent which numbs the mouth. This is an uncommon species in cultivation.

ZELKOVAS, *ZELKOVA* (SYNONYM: *ABELICEA*)
FAMILY ULMACEAE

This is a small genus with one species each in Crete, the Caucasus and Japan, and two in China, whilst a sixth species was only discovered in Sicily in 1991. The leaves are elm-like, but are more simply toothed. The fruit is a small drupe. *Zelkovas* can get Dutch elm disease where the outbreak is severe.

p.192 Cretan Zelkova *Zelkova abelicea*

Description: Deciduous tree to 15 m (50 ft) (or a shrub) with a bole diameter to 60 cm (2 ft). *Crown* Domed. *Bark* Grey. *Shoot* Slender, densely white downy or hairy when young. *Buds* Small. *Foliage* Leaves oblong-ovate to ovate, bluntly pointed at the apex, base variable, heart-shaped, truncate or rounded, margin with three to six pairs of coarse deep blunt lobes, upper surface dark sub-shiny green with slightly impressed veins, either hairless or with hairs pressed onto shoot, underside paler, usually softly hairy with prominent veins, 1.2–4.5 × 0.6–3.5 cm (0.5–1.8 × 0.25–1.4 in); leaf stalk short, less than 3 mm (0.1 in); stipules bluntly pointed, linear, soon falling, to 3 × 1 mm (0.1 × 0.1 in); autumn colour poor. *Flowers* Male flowers in dense clusters, hermaphrodite flowers single, not showy. *Fruit* Sub-globose, irregularly, deeply rugose, slightly hairy, green, 5–6 mm (0.2–0.25 in).

Range: Crete, doubtfully recorded from northern Cyprus.

Habitat: Mountains, in open forests.

Synonyms: *Z. cretica, Quercus abelicea*.

This small tree has been reported from northern Cyprus but considerable doubt exists on the veracity of this record. It is allied to *Z. carpinifolia*, from which the smaller number of marginal lobules or large teeth provide the best distinguishing character. In *Z. abelicea*, they are mainly four or five, but can be up to six or as few as three, whilst in *Z. carpinifolia*, there are 9–11. The smaller leaves and hairy shoots provide another convenient, if not totally reliable, character.

---

p.192 **Caucasian Elm** *Zelkova carpinifolia*

Description: Deciduous tree 15–35 m (50–115 ft) with a bole diameter to 2 m (6.6 ft).
Crown Ovoid with a rounded top, set on a large number of erect stems which splay out at the top. *Bark* Greenish grey or buff, smooth, then flaking in small circular scales to leave orange patches beneath. *Shoot* Green-brown, slender, with whitish hairs which remain into the second summer, becoming shiny brown, gently zig-zagged. *Buds* Ovoid, rounded, brown, hairy, 2 mm (0.1 in), usually two or three side by side.
Foliage Leaves oblong-elliptic, apex rounded to bluntly pointed, base rounded or subcordate, oblique, margin with rounded teeth which end in a small point, side veins forking, with one half running out to the point and the other to the acute sinus, net-veined, upper surface deep green, and rough with simple whitish stiff hairs, underside light green with 7–11 pairs of raised hairy veins, 3–9 cm × 1.5–4 cm (1.2–3.5 × 0.6–1.6 in); leaf stalk wrinkled with white hairs, 3–5 mm (0.1–0.2 in); autumn colour brown to orange-brown. *Flowers* In leaf axils of the current season's growths, not showy.
Fruit Ovoid ribbed green stalkless nutlet 5–6 mm (0.2–0.25 in).

Range: Iran, eastern Turkey, Georgia and Armenia.
Habitat: Cultivated as an ornamental, in the wild occurring in mixed broadleafed forests.

Varieties: *Z. 'Vershaffeltii'* is a small tree with acute triangular serrate leaves. It is probably a selection of Caucasian Elm.
Synonyms: *Z. crenata*.

Similar species: *Z. sicula* is known only from a single site in southeast Sicily where some 200 individuals were discovered as recently as 1991. It differs in the larger leaves from 1–5 × 0.5–3.5 cm (0.4–2 × 0.2–1.4 in), with 6–8 acute lobes and longer leaf stalks, 1–4 mm (0.1 in).

This tree is characteristic in the many erect stems which resemble organ pipes or a Besom Broom. It comes from the forests around the Caspian Sea, especially on the southern Iranian side. It occasionally suffers from Dutch elm disease.

---

p.192 **Keaki** *Zelkova serrata*

Description: Deciduous tree 10–25 m (33–80 ft) with a bole diameter to 60 cm (2 ft).
Crown Broad with wide spreading branches which only ascend slightly, domed in old trees. *Bark* Smooth, grey or pale grey, with prominent pink, brown or orange lenticels, becoming flaking in old trees and revealing orange beneath.
Shoot Slender, greenish brown with large oval lenticels, with silky white hairs at first but becoming hairless, in the second year light brown to grey-brown.
Buds Ovoid with a bluntly pointed apex, brown, 1 mm (0.1 in), minute.
Foliage Leaves ovate lanceolate to ovate or lanceolate, apex tapered to an acute point, base rounded, often slightly oblique, margin with around nine (6–13) large coarse serrations, teeth triangular, forwards, with an abrupt short-pointed tip, upper surface sub-shiny dark green with short hairs, lower surface shiny light green and hairy on the raised midrib and veins, 3–12 × 1.5–4 cm (1.2–4.7 × 0.6–1.6 m); leaf stalk round, hairy, 7 mm (0.3 in); autumn colour attractive assemblage of yellows, pinks and orange.

Flowers On short shoots in late spring, green and of no ornamental value, male flowers in leafless axils at the base of the shoot with two or more flowers together, female flowers in axils of leaves towards the shoot tip, solitary. *Fruit* Rounded or heart-shaped nutlet, green, 4–5 mm (0.2 in).

Range: Honshu, Shikoku and Kyushu, Japan, in Korea and northeast China and Taiwan.

Habitat: Cultivated as an ornamental, in the wild occurring in lowland and mountain forests.

Synonyms: *Z. keaki*, *Z. acuminata*.

This is the commonest Zelkova in cultivation, although the largest and oldest trees belong to *Z. carpinifolia*. The two are easily separated by the triangular and slender-pointed teeth of *Z. serrata*, cf. the rounded teeth of *Z. carpinifolia*).

JUJUBA, *ZIZIPHUS*
FAMILY RHAMNACEAE

This is a genus of around 50 species. The leaves have three or more prominent basal veins. The stipules are modified into thorns, of which one is straight and the other hooked. The fruit is a globose or oblong drupe, with up to four seeds. In some species this is edible.

p.177 **Jujuba** *Ziziphus zizyphus*

Description: Deciduous large shrub or small tree to 10 m (33 ft) in height.
Crown Rounded. *Bark* Dark grey-brown. *Shoot* Slender and flexible, zig-zagged, hairless but with pairs of sharp spines which derive from the stipules, but these often missing on flowering shoots; the longer spine, which may be 3 cm (1.2 in), is straight but the second one is shorter and curved. *Buds* Small, with two or few scales. *Foliage* Leaves narrowly oblong or ovate, asymmetrical, set distichously on the shoot, strongly three-veined at the base with the veins looping forwards towards the bluntly pointed to subacute

apex, base oblique, wedge-shaped to rounded, margin with crenate teeth, glossy green and hairless above, slightly hairy beneath, 2–7 × 1–3 cm (0.8–2.8 × 0.4–1.2 in); leaf stalk 1–5 mm (0.1–0.2 in). *Flowers* In short dense axillary clusters, stalks and sepals hairless or only sparsely pilose, petals yellow-green. *Fruit* Ovoid or oblong drupe which ripens to reddish-brown or black, 1.5–3 cm (0.6–1.2 in).

Range: Southeast Europe to south and east Asia.
Habitat: Cultivated as a fruit tree, possibly native.
Synonyms: *Rhamnus zizyphus*, *Z. jujuba*.
Similar species: **Lotus Jujuba** *Z. lotus* (p.177) is truly native in Europe from Portugal east to southern Greece and Turkey and south through North Africa to Arabia. It is a much smaller plant, rarely making a tree. It differs in the globular fruit which is 1–1.5 cm (0.4–0.6 in) in length and dark yellow, in the more broadly oblong leaves and the fertile or flowering twigs usually being spiny.
Z. spina-christi makes a taller tree, to 14 m (46 ft), and is usually evergreen. It also has globose fruits, but unlike *Z. zizyphus* and *Z. lotus*, the stalks and calyx in the flower are densely haired. It is possibly native to Cyprus, and certainly wild in Syria east to northern India and south through Egypt to Ethiopia and Somalia.
Z. mauritiana (p.177) is also cultivated for the edible fruit and makes a shrub or small tree. The shoots and undersides of the broad elliptic leaves are white or rusty haired. It has globose or oblong fruits to 2.5 cm (1 in).

This small tree is grown for the edible fruit. It is believed to be a native of southern Asia, but as with most fruit trees, the precise origin tends to get lost with time. Tautology (stating the same thing twice) is not permitted in botanical naming (although zoologists permit it); although the genus and species names are nearly the same, the difference is held to be sufficient to satisfy the rules.

Part III

Appendices

GLOSSARY

accrescent increasing in size with age

achene small, dry, 1 seeded fruit which does not open

acicular needle shaped, e.g. leaves of *Picea* and some *Juniperus*

acuminate Tapering to a fine point

adnate united with another organ, e.g. stamens adnate on the style in Malvaceae

adpressed pressed down onto or against

adventitious buds which arise other than in the axil of a leaf, or roots which form on a stem or leaf

alternate arising singly at a node, cf. opposite and whorled

anther pollen producing part of a stamen

apiculate with a small point

apomictic reproducing asexually, usually by seeds formed without normal sexual fusion of the male (pollen) and female (ovule) DNA, more fully described in the *Sorbus* introduction on p.1138 a plant reproducing by apomixis is an apomict

apophysis in *Pinus*, the exposed part of a cone scale

aril a growth from the point of attachment of a seed to the ovary which partly or wholly covers the seed, *see Taxus*

aristate tipped by a bristle or awn

attenuate drawn out or elongated, usually to a fine point

auricle ear-like lobes at the base, of a leaf or petal

awn slender, stiff bristle

axil upper angle between two structures, such as leaf axil between a leaf and the shoot, vein axil the angle formed between two veins on a leaf

berry fleshy fruit containing one or more seeds set in a pulp

bi-pinnate doubly pinnate, bi or bis meaning two or twice

bract modified and usually reduced leaf, usually found in the flowers and fruits or at the base of a shoot

acicular

acuminate

adpressed

aristate

auricle

doubly pinnate

calyx outer whorl of a flower, composed of sepals

capsule dry opening fruit with more than one carpel

carpel unit in the female part of a flower containing ovules and a style

catkin inflorescence of single sexed flowers with overlapping bracts which each subtend a flower without petals, usually pendulous but not always

ciliate fringed with hairs on the margin

cladode branch which takes on the function and appearance of a leaf, with the leaves usually vestigial

clone all the plants derived from the vegetative propagation of one individual

conduplicate folded along the length, *see Prunus*

conic cone shaped

connate united into one unit

convoluted rolled up longitudinally, *see Prunus*

coppice to regrow if cut down

cordate heart shaped at the base

corolla inner whorl of a flower, containing the petals

corymb flat topped or convex flower cluster in which the outer flowers open first

cotyledon primary leaf of an embryo

crenate toothed with shallow rounded teeth

crenulate finely crenate

cupule bracts united at the base of a fruit or group of fruits, *see Quercus*

cuneate wedge-shaped at base; tapering evenly to the petiole

cyme convex or flat topped flower cluster in which the inner flowers open first and the other flowers are carried on later opening branches towards the base of the cluster

declinate branch which arches out and down from the main stem and is turned up at the tip

decorticate shedding the outer bark, e.g. *Eucalyptus* and *Platanus*

decumbent horizontal but becoming erect or semi-erect at the tip

decurrent running down the structure on which it sits, e.g. a leaf decurrent on a stem such as in *Cupressus*

decurved curved downwards or backwards

decussate in pairs with each succeeding pair at a right angle to the previous pair, e.g. *Cupressus*

deflexed bent back or down

dehiscent opening to release its contents

deltoid triangular, D-shaped with curved basal angles

dentate toothed with prominent outward pointing teeth

deltoid

depressed pressed down

digitate compound leaf where the leaflets arise at one point, like the fingers or digits of a hand, also called palmately compound, e.g. *Aesculus*

digitate

dioecious male and female flowers on different plants, i.e. in two houses

diploid having two sets of chromosomes

distichus arranged oppositely in two superposed ranks

drupe fruit in which the seed is enclosed in a hard stony layer but surrounded by a fleshy layer, e.g. *Prunus*, but the 'berry' of an *Ilex* is also technically a drupe

emarginate notched at the tip

emarginate

entire without teeth or lobes

epicormic shoot developing from a dormant bud on a trunk or branch

epigeal mode of germination of a seed where the cotyledons are raised above the ground and carry out initial photosynthesis, e.g. *Fraxinus*, cf. hypogeal

epiphyte a plant using another plant as a support and deriving its nutrients and water from debris, rain water and the atmosphere, but not parasitic

false whorl appearing as if whorled but not in a true whorl, e.g. leaf clusters of *Rhododendron* and *Quercus* which are often concentrated towards the tips of the shoot and not neatly spread out along the shoot

fascicle dense bundle

fastigiate with erect branches

filament stalk of a stamen, carrying the anther at the top

floccose with loose woolly flocks of soft hairs

follicle a dry fruit or carpel which opens along one seam or suture

frondose in fern-like sprays

gland secreting organ on a leaf, shoot, flower, hair or bristle

glaucous covered with a white or blue-white waxy bloom

globose like a ball or globe

haploid having one set of chromosomes

hexaploid having six sets of chromosomes

hyaline translucent margin

hybrid plant produced by crossing parents belonging to different named groups or taxa (i.e. species, subspecies, etc.). Hybrids may have hybrid vigour or heterosis where the genes of the two parents are sufficiently different.

hypogeal mode of germination of a seed where the cotyledons remain in the seed coat and are not involved in photosynthesis, e.g. *Quercus* and *Juglans*, cf. epigeal

imbricate overlapping, often used of bud scales and to describe the foliage of conifers such as *Picea*

impressed sunken below the surface

incised with deep narrow sinuses or 'spaces' between the teeth or lobes of a leaf

indehiscent not splitting or opening

indumentum covering of hairs

inflorescence flowering part of a plant

internode space on a branch between the nodes or joints

involucre two or more bracts which subtend a flower

lanceolate shaped like a lance, often used of leaves which are broadest below the middle and three or more times as long as wide

lanceolate

lenticel raised breathing pore on the surface of a shoot, bark or fruit

linear long and narrow, with parallel sides

linear

lobulate weakly lobed, i.e. projections stronger than toothed or doubly toothed, but not developed into lobes

midrib primary vein or central rib of a leaf, the continuation of the leaf stalk

lobular

monoecious male and female parts carried on the same individual plant but on different flowers

monopodal with one growing point, applied especially to palms where there is often only one growth bud, but also used where side branching is weak and the main stem is strongly dominant

monotypic one type, applied to a genus which contains only a single species, or family only one genus

mucro short abrupt point at the tip

node joint on a branch, or the point where a leaf or bud is attached

mucro, mucronate

ob- a prefix indicating inverse, usually indicating broadest above the middle

obconical conical but attached at the narrow end

oblanceolate lanceolate but broadest above the middle

oblique unequal-sided at the base (of a leaf or cone)

oblique

obovate ovate but broadest above the middle

obovoid egg-shaped but broadest above the middle

obtuse spreading at an angle of more than 90 degrees

obovate

operculum cap on the flowers of *Eucalyptus* which is formed from the petals and shed as the flower opens

opposite two leaves or buds which as a pair are at one point along a shoot but on different sides of the shoot

ovate egg-shaped in outline (i.e. flat), broadest below the middle

ovoid egg-shaped, three dimensional, broadest below the middle

ovuliferous bearing the eggs or ovules

ovate

palmate with lobes spreading out from a point at or near the base of the leaf, e.g. *Platanus*. Sometimes called palmatelifid (lobes reaching less than half way to the midrib) or palmatelisect (lobes reaching more than half way to the midrib).

palmately veined principal lateral veins arising at a single point off the midrib or main vein of a simple leaf near the base of the blade or lamina, e.g. *Acer* or *Platanus*, cf. pinnately veined. Small lateral veins may occur further up the midrib.

palmate

panicle a branched or compound raceme

paniculate like a panicle

papillose bearing small blunt or nipple-like
protuberances

pectinate

pectinate spreading in regular rows like
the teeth of a comb

peltate shield-like, with the stalk
attached not at the margin

perianth collective term for the calyx
and corolla (the 'showy'
parts of a flower) especially
used when the differences
between the calyx (sepals) and corolla
(petals) are not obvious

perula scales (modified from leaves) which protect
a bud, plural perulae

petal segment of the inner whorl of a flower

petiolate with a petiole or leaf stalk

petiole leaf stalk

phloem conducting tissue in the bark, also in the
leaf stalk, particularly used to distribute
food to the roots

photosynthesis conversion of water and carbon dioxide in
the leaf utilising energy from light to
produce sugars, i.e. the way in which plants
make food

phyllode a leaf stalk which has taken on the form and
function of a leaf

pilose with long soft straight hairs

pinna individual free part of a compound leaf or
pinnate leaf, plural pinnae

pinnate

pinnate compound leaf with the leaflets
carried on either side of the
rachis

pinnately principal lateral veins
veined arising along the length
of the midrib or main
veins of a simple leaf, e.g
Crataegus, cf. palmately
veined where they arise at
one point

pinnatifid with lobes arising along the length of the
leaf, i.e. not restricted to a point at or near
the base of the leaf, e.g. *Sorbus thuringiaca*.
Pinnatisect is similar, but the lobes are
more deeply cut almost to the midrib

pinnule smallest division of a bi-pinnate or tri-
pinnate leaf

plumose feathery

pome fleshy fruit of apple and related genera

pruinose bloomed or covered with a waxy powder

pulvinus swollen region at the base of a leaf, see especially *Picea*

raceme inflorescence consisting of stalked flowers set along one axis

rachis axis of a pinnate (e.g. *Sorbus*) or bi-pinnate leaf or a fruit (e.g. *Abies*). Can also be spelt rhachis

receptacle the tip or expanded portion of an axis which bears the flower parts

recurved curved or bent downwards

reflexed bent sharply downwards from the base

retuse rounded and slightly noted at the tip

rhizome horizontal underground or surface stems which acts as a food store

rugose wrinkled, of a leaf especially with impressed veins

samara winged nutlet, e.g. *Acer*, *Fraxinus*

sepal segment of the outer whorl of a flower

serrate with saw-like teeth which point forwards

sinus recess or bay between lobes or teeth

spindle-shaped widest at the middle and narrowed towards the ends

stamen pollen producing part of a flower comprising a stalk or filament and an anther

staminode infertile stamen, often becoming petal-like, e.g. *Tilia*

stellate star-like, particularly referring to branched hairs which have a central stalk and radiating arms

stigma portion at the tip of the style which receives pollen

stipule an appendage, usually in pairs, at the base of a leaf, sometimes falling early and leaving two scars, sometimes modified into spines, e.g. *Robinia*

stoma very small breathing pore in a leaf

stomata plural of stoma

strobile small cone-like structure, used especially of *Alnus* and *Betula* fruits

style slender stalk between the ovary and the stigma

sub- prefix indicating beneath or not fully

sub-entire not fully entire, i.e. with some teeth or partly lobed

sub-globose not quite globose

sub-obtuse not quite obtuse

sub-opposite leaves or buds which are nearly in opposite pairs but the pairs are displaced somewhat

serrate

subcordate   not fully cordate, but with some indentation at the base

subsessile   nearly sessile but with a slight stalk

subtending   used of any structure which is located in the axil of another structure, e.g. a bud is subtended by a leaf

superposed   one on top of another, used especially of buds where more than one occurs in the same leaf axil

suture   line of splitting

syncarp   fleshy aggregate fruit, such as a raspberry

tepal   segment of the calyx and corolla of *Magnolia* where it is not easy to distinguish between sepals and petals

terete   more or less cylindrical, round in cross-section and not grooved

tetraploid   having four sets of chromosomes

tri-   three, as in three sets of chromosomes (triploid) or thrice pinnate (tripinnate)

tomentose   with dense woolly hairs

tracheid   water conducting cells in the wood

truncate   abruptly cut off at the tip or base

tubercule   wart-like growth

umbel   inflorescence in which the pedicels all arise at the same point

umbellate   like an umbel

umbo   prickle on the exposed portion of a cone of *Pinus*

uncinate   with a fine hook at the tip

valvate   hinged at the base, with the segments meeting at the edges but not overlapping

vascular -bundle   water-carrying bundle in a leaf, including phloem and xylem elements

whorl   three or more structures arising at the same node

xylem   wood, especially when it is capable of conducting water

PICTURE CREDITS

All pictures have been researched and supplied via The Frank Lane Picture Agency Ltd. FLPA would like to thank Jean and David Hosking, Rosemary Foulger, Diane McKay, Marcus Webb, and the contributing photographers and photo agencies. With a special thank you to Martin B. Withers.

Cover photograph: Horse Chestnut in full flower, Silvestris. Spine photograph: Conkers on branch, Maurice Nimmo.

The positions of the photographs on each page of the colour section is indicated as follows:
t = top; um = upper middle; m = middle; lm = lower middle; b = bottom

L. Batten p133t4; p244t6; p264t4; p321m2; p346m2; p350m2; R. Bird p99t3; p266t2; B. Borrell p105lm2; p151m4; p161b3; p224t3; p225b2; p230b2; p231b2; p303t4; H.D. Bandl p68t5; p105lm1; M. Clark P347m1; Garden Matters p73m2; M. Hagman p75t2; p92b2; p93t3; D. Hall p59t2; p66t1; p71m4; p75b3; p79t1; p91b1; p116b1; p131b1; p153b1; p169m1; p188b1,4; p234m2; p252t3; p291m2; p298m2; p305b1; p310t4; p320t1; p326t1; A.R. Hamblin p250t6; p314m3; Harry Smith Col. p38t1; p40b1; p51t2,b3; p54t2,3; p59b1; p73t2; p89t2; p101t3,b2; p105um3; p106m4; p111t1; p123b2,3; p124b2; p126b2; p127m1,3; p128m4; p130t4; p132t2,m2; p133t2; p137m1; p138t3; p141b3; p142t3; p143t2; p145b2; p146t2,m3,b4; p148t5; p155t1; p156t5; p157t2; p158t1; p160t4; p161t3,b1; p162b2; p163m3; p164t2, b1,2,3; p165b1; p166b2; p167b2; p169m5; p173m2,b3; p176t2,b2; p177; p183m2; p184m3; p185m2,3; p186t2; p194t; p197m2,b1; p198t1; p199t1; p201b4; p202t2,3; p206b2; p208t4; p209t2,b2; p211t2,m4; p216t3,b3; p218t3; p219t2; p223t3,4,7,8; p224t1,2,m4,5; p228m3; p230t2,m2; p231m2; p232m2; p233t4; p234t2,b1; p235b4; p243m2; p246b2; p249b2; p253b2; p255t5,b1; p257t6; p259t2; p263b1; p270t1,3; p271t; p274t; p275m; p276t5,b1; p278t3; p282b1; p284b2; p289m3; p296t; p302t; p308t2; p309t1; p313t2,m4,b5; p314b1,2; p316b1; p317b2; p322t2; p323t; p324m; p325t1; p328m1,2; p330t,b3; p331t3,4; p333t1,2,m5,b3; p334t2; p335t2; p336b2; p338t2; p342t3,m1; p344t; p345m1,2; p346t3; p347t2,b1,2; p348b; p351t4; P. Heard p264t5; M. Hollings p227t5; E. & D. Hosking p38m1,b3; p42m4; p43t1; p46b5; p50t1; p56t3,b3; p58b1; p60b1; p61m1; p67t1; p68t2,b1; p71m1; p77b1; p80b1; p81b3; p82t1; p93b1,b3; p99t1,2; p100b1; p101b1; p102b1;

p238t3,6,b2; p241t3; p246b4; p251m2,b2; p253t3,b4;
p254m1,2; p255t4,m1; p257t3; p258t1,3,4; p260b1;
p261t1,2,m2,b1; p262t1; p265b2; p267b2,4; p270t2;
p272t4,b5; p273b2,3,4; p278t1,2,4; p279m1,b1,2;
p280b1; p281m4; p282t4,m2,b2; p284t2,3; p286t1,2;
p289t3,4,m2; p293b5,7; p294t1,3,4; p295t1,5; p296m,
b4,5,6; p297t1; p299t1,5,6; p300t2,b1; p301m4; p302m2;
p303t1,3; p306m4,5,b1; p307b2; p308b4; p309m1;
p310t2; p312b1; p313t3; p314t3; p315b1,2; p319b2,3;
p320t3; p321b1,2,3,4; p322t1,m1,2; p323b1,3,5;
p327t2,b2,3; p328t1,3; p329t2,4; p330m1,b2; p331b1,2;
p332t4; p335b4; p336t1; p338m6,b2; p339t4,b1,2;
p340b1,4; p341m; p342t1,2,4,m2; p343t3,b1,2; p344m,b;
p345t1,b; p346t2,b; p348t1,3,4,m1,2,3; p349t3,b2;
p351t2,m3,b1; M. Newman p72b3; M. Nimmo p38b2,b4;
p40t4,5; p41b3; p43m2; p45t1,3,b1,3,4; p46b4; p47b4;
p52t3,5,b1,2; p53t2; p54b2; p55m3,b2; p57m1,2;
p58t2,4,b2; p59m1,b3; p60t4; p64t1,3,4; p66t3,4,b3;
p67t4; p68t3; p69t1; p70b2,3; p72b5; p73m3; p74t4,5;
p76t4; p77t4,b3,5; p78t4,6; p79b3,5,6; p80t2; p81b1,5;
p82t2,3,b3; p85t3; p86b2; p91t5; p94t1,b2; p95b4;
p98t2,4; p99t5; p100b2; p103t4; p105b1; p107b2,3;
p108t3; p110t2,m2,b1,2,3; p111b2; p112t2; p113t4;
p115t2; p116t2,b2,3; p117b3; p118t2; p119t3,4,b2;
p122t2; p124m2; p128t2,5,m3; p129m3; p130m2,m4;
p131b3; p134t5; p138b2; p142t5; p143um3,lm2;
p146b2,3; p148b2; p149b1; p151m2,3; p158t3; p167b1;
p170b3; p174t3; p175t3; p176b1; p178t4,5,6; p179t1,5;
p187t4,5; p193b2,3; p198t2,m2,b4; p199b1,4; p202m2;
p203m1; p206b3; p211m2; p212t2,4; p214t3; p216t1;
p217m3; p219b2; p220t3,4; p222t2; p223t1; p226t3,b2,3;
p227b3; p228t2,3; p229t2,5; p233t1; p234m5; p238t5,b3;
p239b1; p240b3; p244t4,5,b3; p246t2; p247t2,b2,4;
p248t2,b2,3,4; p250t4,m2,4; p252t6; p253t4; p254t3;
p256t4; p262b2; p265t2,3,4; p268b4; p269t4; p272b2;
p273b5; p275t5; p278b2; p282t2; p283b2,4; p287t2;
p304t3,4,b2; p305b5; p309b2; p310b5; p313b3,4; p314t4;
p316t2,3,5; p317m2; p320t2,5; p326b2,3,4; p328t2,4;
p329m3,4; p332t2; p336t4,5; p338m2,3; p339t6; p343t2;
p352t4,5; Panda Photo p263t1; p343t6; P. Perry p56t2;
p104t2; p114t2; p171t2; p219b3; p285t2; p293b3;
p303b2; p305b3; p352t3; F. Polking p68t1; p332t5;
Premaphotos p64t6; p96t1; p112t3; p114t4; p145b3;
p154b3; p176b3; p228b1; p255b2,3; p268b3; p341t,b1,2;
p348t2; H. Rice p60b3; p175b4; p273t1; p300t4;
p305m2; p333b1; I. Rose p122t4; p178b5; M. Rose
p106b3; p125t4; p126m2; p250t1; p332t1; p347t1; Royal
Bot. Gardens p49t2; p61b2,4; p62b4,5,6; p200b6;
K. Rushforth p38t3,t4; p41t1,2; p42m1,2,3,b2; p43t2;

p44t2,3,4,5,b1; p45b2; p47t2,3,m4,b2,3; p48t1,2,3,4,5;
p49t1,b2; p50t2,3,m1,2; p51t1,b2; p52b3; p53b1,2,3;
p54b1,3,4; p55t1,m1,b1; p56t4,b4; p57t2,3; p59t3,m2;
p60b2; p61t1,b1,3; p62t1,b1,2,3; p63t1,2,3,4,b1;
p65t1,2,m5; p66b1; p67b1; p68b2,3; p69t3,b1; p70b1;
p71t2,b1; p72b4; p74t2,3,b1,2,3,4,5; p75t1,b4; p77t5,b4;
p78b1; p79t2,3; p80b3; p81t1,3; p82t4; p83t1,2,b1,2,3,4;
p84t1,2,ml,2,3,4,b2,3,4; p85t5,b1,2; p86t1,b3,4;
p87t3,4,5,6,ml,b1,2,4; p88t1,2,3,b1; p89t1,4,b1,2,3,4;
p90t1,3,4,b1,2; p91t3,b2; p92t1,2,m1,b1; p93t1,2,m1,3,
b4; p94t2; p95t2; p96t3,4,b1,2; p97t3,4,m1,2,3;
p98b1,2,3; p99m1; p101t1,2,4; p102t2,4; p103b1,2,3;
p105um2,4; p106t1,2,b1; p109lm1,2; p111m3,b4,5;
p112m4,b2; p113um1,2,lm1,2,b1; p117t2; p118m1,2,b1;
p120t2,3,4,b1,2; p121t1,2,3,m,b1,2; p122t5; p123t2,b1;
p124t1,2,3,m4; p126t; p128b1,2; p129t3,4,m2;
p130m1,3; p132b; p134t6; p135m1,b1; p136t3,m1,2,b2,3;
p137t1,2,3,b3; p138t1,2,4,5; p139t1,3,4,m1,b1,2;
p140m2,b; p141t2,3,m2,3,4; p142t1,4,b1,2,3; p143t1,3;
p146t1,b1; p147t1,2; p148t1,2,4,b1; p149t1; p150t1,2,3,
b1,2,3,4; p152t3,b1; p153m2,4,b2; p155t2,m1,2,3,4,b1;
p156t4,6; p157t1; p159b3; p160t1,2,3,5,m1,b1;
p164t1,3,4; p165t1,4,um1; p166m; p167t3,4,b3; p169t2,l
m,b1,2; p170m1,2; p171t4; p172t1,2,b2,3; p173t1,2,3,
m1,3,b4; p174m2; p175b2; p176t1; p178t1,b1,3;
p179b2,3; p180t2,m1; p182t1,m5,6,b1; p183t1,2,3,b2;
p184m1,b1,2; p185t,m4; p186t1,4,5,b2; p187b2;
p188m2,b2; p189t2,b5; p190b1; p191m3; p192m3,b2,3;
p193m; p194m1; p195m3; p197m1,3,4,5; p198m1;
p199b3; p200t1,2,b3,4; p201t2,3,b1,3; p202b2,3,4;
p203b1,2; p204b2,3; p206t2,4; p207b1,2,3,4,5; p208b2;
p210t2,b; p212t1; p214m2,3,b1,3; p215t1,2,um1,3,5,
m1,2,b1,2; p216m1,2,b1,2,4; p217t1,2,3,b1,2;
p218m1,2,3; p219t1,b4; p220b2; p221t1,2,3; p222t3,b4;
p223t2; p225m1,b1,3; p226b1; p228m2; p231t1,2,m1;
p232t1; p233t2; p234t1,b2; p235t4,b1,2,3; p236; p237;
p238t2; p239t1,2,m1,2,4,5,b2; p240t1,2,4,b4; p241t5,b;
p242t1,b4; p243t,m1,3,4,b1,2; p244t1,2,3,b4; p245 b2,4;
p246t1,4; p248t1; p249m3,b3; p251t2,3,m1; p252t5;
p253t1,2,5; p255m2; p257b3; p258t5,b; p259t1,3,m1,2;
p260t1,2,3; p261m1; p263b2,4,5; p264t7,b; p265m;
p267t1,2,m1,2,3,4; p268t1,2; p269b3; p270m1,2,
b1,2,3,4,5; p271b1,2,3; p272t1,2,3; p273t2; p277t2,3,4,5,
b2; p278b3,4; p281t1,2,3,m1,3,b; p282m1; p283b6;
p285t5,b; p286b2; p287b; p288t2; p290t1,2,b; p291m5,b;
p292t3; p293t,m; p295t3,m1,3,b2; p298b2; p299t2,3,4;
p300t1,3,m1,2,b2; p301t1,2,m5,b3,4; p302m1; p303m3,
b3; p307b3; p308t1,ml1,2,mr2,b1,2,3; p309t2; p310t1,3;
p311t1,2,3,m1,b2; p312t1,2,3,m3; p313t1,m1,2,3,b1;

p314m1,2; p315t2; p316t1; p318t1; p320m1,2,3,4,5,b1,2; p323m1,b2,6,7; p324t4,b1,2,3; p325t2,b; p326t2,3,4; p327b1; p328b1,2,3; p329tl,trl,,3,5; p330m2; p331m1,2; p332m,b1,2; p333m3; p334t1,3,ml,2,3,b1,2; p335m1,2,3; p336t3,b3; p337t4,m,b1,2; p338t1; p339t3,5; p340t3,4; p342b1,2,3; p343t5,m2; p346t1,4; p349m2,4,5; p350t1,2,3,4; p351t1,m1; A.D. Schilling p112m3; p130t1,2,3; p139m2; p168b2; p229t3; p240t3; p261b4; p290t3; p298t3; p313b2; Silvestris p38m3; p39t1; p46m1,2,b2; p50b1; p51b1; p53m1; p68t4; p71m2; p76t2; p78t3,5,m3; p79b2; p81b4; p82b2; p91t1; p116b4; p119t1; p125t2,5; p128t4; p129t2; p131m2,b4,5; p133t3; p135t4; p144t1,b3; p147b2; p149b2; p152b2,3; p153t1; p154b1; p157b2; p161b4; p162t2,3; p165t5; p166t2,b3; p174t1; p175b5; p176t4; p179t2,4; p180b1,2,3; p181t2,3,4; p182m2,3,4; p186t3; p189b2,3; p190t2,m2,4, b2; p191t2,m1; p198b3; p199t2; p206t5; p207t3; p245t3; p250t3,b3; p253b3; p254t4; p255t3,m3; p256t3,5; p257t4,5; p262t2,3; p263t2; p266t3; p269t1,2; p274b2,6; p275b1,2; p276b2; p279m4; p280t2,5; p281m2,5; p282t3; p285t4; p287t4,5; p291m3; p297t3,4; p308mr1; p309b1; p310t5,b2; p312b2; p317m3,6; p319b4; p321m1; p326b1; p328t5; p337lm2; p338m1,4,5; p339b3; p340t1,2,b2,3; p343ml; p347b3; p349t1,2; p351m2,b2; M.J. Thomas p53t3; p227b2,4; p246b3; p264t3; p275t2; p291m6; R. Tidman p145t3; p268b5; J. Tinning p144b1; p226t5; Van Hoey Smith p56b2; p65b2; p71b2; p98b4; p115m2; p119m2; VanNostrand p351t3; D. Warren p303t2; L. West p102t1; p143um2; p289b3; A. Wharton p103t5; p145t2; p207t1; p229t4; p256b2; p272b4; p333b2; J. Watkins p213b3; Wildlife Matters p39b1; p96t2; p122b; p143b1; p151b1; p153b3; p163m2; p165t2; p198b1; p309b4; R. Wilmshurst p38b1; p66b2; p67t2; p99t4; p104t5; p105b2; p131b2; p175m3,b3; p193t1; p247t1; p250m1,3; p258t2; p280t3,4; p303b1; p310b1,3; p315m5; p347t3; p352t2; Dr A. Wilson p212b2; W. Wisniewski p64t5; p174t2; p207t2; p226t4; p232b3; p264t6; p310b4; M.B. Withers p40t2,6; p41m1,2,3,4,b1,2,4; p42t1,b1,3; p43m1,3,b1; p44t1; p46t1,2,b1,3,6; p47t1,m1,2,b1; p49b1,3; p52t1,2,4; p53t1; p54t1; p55m2; p57b1; p58t3; p59t1; p60t1,3; p64t2; p65m1,2,3,4,6; p66t2,m1; p69t2,m1,2,3,b2; p70t1; p71t1,m3; p72t1,2; p73t1,m1,b1; p74t1; p75b2; p76t1,3,b1,2,3; p77t1,2,3; p78t1,2,m1,2; p80t1,b4; p81t2; p82b1; p84b1; p85t2,m1; p87t1,2; p89t3; p91t2,4; p93b2; p94b1,3,4; p95t1,b1,3,5; p97t1,2,b1,2; p98t1,3; p99m2; p100t1,3; p102t3; p103t1; p104t4,b1; p105t1,2; p107t1,2,b1,4,5,6; p108t1; p109t1,b1; p110t1,ml; p111m1,2 p112t1,m2,b1; p113t3; p114t1,3; p115m1,b1,2; p116t1; p117t1,3,b2,4;

LOCATION PHOTOGRAPHS

The habit photographs on the following pages were taken at these locations:
38 *Tamarix smyrnensis*, Isoria, NE Spain; 44 *Cupressus cashmiriana*, Drukyel dzong, NW Bhutan; 51 *Juniperus thurifera*, Isoria NE Spain; 54 *J. drupacea*, Parnon, Greece; *J. recurva*, Ziben shan, Nu shan, W Yunnan, China; 56 *Araucaria columnaris*, Lisbon, Portugal; *A. heterophylla*, Dalat, South Vietnam; 74 *Picea likiangensis*, Yarlung Tsangpo Valley, SE Tibet; 80 *Abies pinsapo*, Grazalema, S Spain; 83 *A. vejarii*, Caon de Jame, Coahuila, NE Mexico; 87 *A. delavayi*, Cang Shan, above Dali, W Yunnan, China; 97 *Tsuga dumosa*, Jele La, W Bhutan; 101 *Larix griffithiana*, 1. Merak, E Bhutan; 2. Pasum Tso, SE Tibet; 4. Sengor, E Bhutan; 104 *Pinus nigra* var. *corsicana*, Mt Cinto, Corsica, France; 105 *P. mugo*, Spain; *P. uncinata*, Pyrenees, Spain; 111 *P. ponderosa*, Arizona, United States; 113 *P. cembroides*, Galeana, Nuevo Leon, NE Mexico; *P. johannis*, NE Mexico; 119 *P. cembra*, Tatra Mountains, Poland; 120 *P. engelmannii*, Galeana, NE Mexico; 121 *P. hartwegii*, Nevada de Columa, Jalisco, W Mexico; *P. rudis*, Cerro Potosi, Galeana, NE Mexico; 130 *Rhododendron falconeri*, 1. Pele La, W Bhutan; 3. Yotong La, Bhutan; 138 *Magnolia delavayi*, Red Camellia Temple, Lijiang, W Yunnan; 139 *Michelia doltsopa*, Dochu La, Bhutan; *M. velutina*, Koray La, E Bhutan; 150 *Acer laevigatum*, Sapa, N Vietnam; 161 *Quercus suber*, S Spain; 162 *Q. ilex*, Spain; 181 *Betula pendula*, Heide, Germany; 191 *Celtis australis*, Mallorca, Spain; 196 *Arbutus undeo*, Massif des Maures, Provence, France; 206 *Eriobotrya japonica*, Dali, Yunnan, China; 215 *Sorbus hedlundii*, Sengor, E Bhutan; *S. thibetica*, Ziben shan Nushan, W Yunnan, China; 267 *Quercus semecarpifolia*, Dochu La, W Bhutan; 278 *Q. macrolepsis*, Peloponnese, Greece; 290 *Acer campbellii*, Dudh Khari Valley, E Nepal; 321 *Pistacia atlantica*, Israel; *P. terebinthus*, Greece; 340 *Ceratonia siliqua*, Crete; 347 *Phoenix dactylifera*, Israel.

INDEX

Numbers in **bold** refer to colour plates (pp.38–352). The circle preceding English names of trees makes it easy for you to keep a record of the trees you see. The authority for each tree species has been added to the Latin and family names.

A

○Abele 997
Abelicea see *Zelkova*
Abies Miller 355
  alba Miller 78, 357
  alba var. *nebrodensis*
    Lojacono-Pojéro 387
  amabilis Douglas ex
    Forbes 90, 358
  apollinis Link 362
  balsamea (L.)Miller 93,
    359
  bifida Siebold &
    Zuccarini 374
  bifolia Murray 383
  borisii-regis Mattfeld
    358
  bornmuelleriana
    Mattfeld 389
  brachyphylla
    Maximowicz 380
  bracteata (D. Don)
    Nuttall 89, 360
  brevifolia Henry 401
  canadensis Miller 893
  cephalonica Loudon 78,
    358, 361
  chengii Rushforth 86,
    363
  chensiensis van Tieghem
    84, 364
  chensiensis ssp. *salouensis*
    (Bordéres-Rey &
    Gaussen)Rushforth
  chinensis Franchet 1244
  cilicica (Antoine &
    Kotschy)Carrière 79,
    365
  concolor (Gordon)
    Hildebrand 82, 366

delavayi Franchet 87,
  367
delavayi var. *fabri*
  (Masters)Hunt 371
delavayi var. *forrestii*
  (C.C.Rogers)Jackson
  375
densa Griffith 87, 369
equi-trojani Aschers &
  Sintensis 390
fabri (Masters)Craib 87,
  370
fargesii Franchet 88,
  363, 372
fargesii var. *sutchuenensis*
  Franchet 372
faxoniana Rehder &
  Wilson 371
firma Siebold &
  Zuccarini 84, 373
forrestii C.C.Rogers 86,
  374
fraseri (Pursh)Poiret 93,
  376
gamblei Hickel 392
georgei Orr 375
grandis (Douglas ex D.
  Don)Lindley 82, 377
hirtella (H.B.K.)Lindley
  397
holophylla Maximowicz
  84, 378
homolepis Siebold &
  Zuccarini 85, 379
kawakamii (Hayata)Ito
  92, 380
koreana Wilson 91, 381
lasiocarpa (Hooker)
  Nuttall 93, 383
likiangensis Franchet
  898

lowiana (Gordon)
Murray 367
magnifica Murray 81,
384
mariesii Masters 90,
386
mariesii var. *kawakamii*
Hayata 381
marocana Trabut 394
minensis (Bordéres-Rey
& Gaussen)Rushforth
371
nebrodensis (Lojacono-
Pojero)Mattei 78,
387
nephrolepis (Trautvetter)
Maximowicz 91,
388, 403
nobilis Douglas ex D.
Don 395
nordmanniana (Steven)
Spach 79, 389
numidica De Lannoy ex
Carrière 80, 390
pectinata (Lambert)
Lambert & De
Candolle 358
pichta Forbes 399
pindrow Royle 85, 391
pinsapo Boissier 80, 393
procera Rehder 81, 394
recurvata Masters 85,
395
religiosa (H.B.K.)
Schlechtendal 83,
397
sachalinensis (Schmidt)
Masters 92, 398
salouenensis Bordéres-
Rey & Gaussen 365
semenovii Fedschenko
399
sibirica Ledebour 92,
399
sikokiana Nakai 382
spectabilis (D. Don)
Spach 89, 400
spectabilis var. *densa*
(Griff.)Silba 370

squamata Masters 88,
401
subalpina Engelmann
383
× *suntense* Brickell 302,
405
sutchuenensis (Franchet)
Rehder & Wilson
372
taxifolia Desfontaines
358
tazaotana Cozar ex H.
del Villar 394
veitchii Lindley 91, 402
veitchii var. *sikokiana*
(Nakai)Kusaka 382
vejarii Martinez 83, 403
venusta (Douglas)Koch
361
webbiana Lindley 401
Abutilon Miller 405
ochsenii Philippi 406
vitifolium (Cavanilles)
Presl 302, 405
◯Acacia 406
◯ Blackwood 345, 409
◯ False 1102
◯ Rose 338, 1104
Acacia L. 406
cyanophylla Lindley
345, 406
cyclops A. Cunningham
ex De Candolle 344,
409
dealbata Link 340, 407
decurrens var. *dealbata*
(Link)F.v.Mueller
408
farnesiana L. 341, 411
karoo Hayne 341, 410
longifolia (Andrews)
Willdenow 345,
408
mearnsii De Wild 341,
408
melanoxylon R. Brown
345, 409
pycnantha Bentham
344, 411

retinodes see rhetinodes

rhetinodes Schlechtendal 344, 410

Acer L. 412

amplum Rehder 285, 413

argutum Maximowicz 299, 414

barbatum Michaux 470

barbinerve Maximowicz 299, 415

buergerianum Miquel 295, 416

caesium Wallich ex Brandis 433

caesium ssp. *giraldii* (Pax)Murray 433

campbellii Hooker f. & Thomson ex Hiern 290, 417

campbellii ssp. *flabellatum* (Rehder) Murray 418

campbellii ssp. *oliverianum* (Pax) Murray 454

campestre L. 287, 419

capillipes Maximowicz 300, 420

cappadocicum Gleditsch 284, 421

cappadocicum ssp. *lobelii* (Tenore)Murray 443

carpinifolium Siebold & Zuccarini 169, 422

caudatum Wallich 298, 423

caudatum ssp. *ukurunduense* (Trautetter & Meyer) Murray 479

cissifolium (Siebold & Zuccarini)K. Koch 307, 424

cissifolium ssp. *henryi* (Pax)Murray 439

crataegifolium Siebold & Zuccarini 293, 425

creticum L. 472

dasycarpum Ehrhenberg 469

davidii Franchet 169, 427

diabolicum Blume & K. Koch 288, 428

distylum Siebold & Zuccarini 169, 429

eriocarpum Michaux 469

fabri Hance 442

flabellatum Rehder 418

floridanum (Chapman) Pax 470

forrestii Diels 300, 430

ginnala Maximowicz 297, 431

giraldii Pax 292, 432

granatense Boissier 296, 433

grandidentatum Nuttall 471

griseum (Franchet)Pax 306, 434

grosseri Pax 436

grosseri var. *hersii* (Rehder)Rehder 300, 436

heldreichii Orphanides ex Boissier 291, 437

henryi Pax 307, 438

hersii Rehder 436

hyrcanum Fischer & Meyer 296, 439

italicum Lauche 455

italum Lauther 455

japonicum Thunberg 294, 440

japonicum var. *microphyllum* Seismeyer 473

laetum C.A. Meyer 422

laetum var. *truncatum* (Bunge)Regel 477

laevigatum Wallich 150, 441

laxiflorum Pax 431

leucoderme Small 470

lobelii Tenore 284, 442

longipes Franchet ex Rehder 414

longipes ssp. *amplum* (Rehder)de Jong 414

macrophyllum Pursh 288, 444

maximowicziana Miquel 306, 445

maximowiczii Pax 293, 446

miyabei Maximowicz 287, 447

mono Maximowicz 286, 448

monspessulanum L. 296, 449

morifolium Koidzumi 421

negundo L. 314, 450

nigrum Michaux f. 470

nikoense Maximowicz 445

nikoense var. *grisea* Franchet 435

oblongum Wallich ex De Candolle 150, 451

obtusifolium Sibthorp & Smith 295, 452

oliverianum Pax 290, 453

opalus Miller 292, 454

opalus ssp. *hispanicum* (Pourret)Murray 434

opalus var. *hyrcanum* (Fischer & Meyer) Rehder 440

orientale Miller 472

palmatum Thunberg ex Murray 293, 455

papilio King 424

pectinatum Wallich ex Nicholson 301, 457

pectinatum ssp. *forrestii* (Diels)Murray 431

pectinatum ssp. *maximowiczii* (Pax) Murray 447

pensylvanicum L. 301, 459

pensylvanicum ssp. *rufinerve* (Siebold & Zuccarini)Wesmael 467

pictum hort., not Thunberg 449

platanoides L. 285, 460

pseudoplatanus L. 291, 462

pseudosieboldianum (Pax) Komarov 294, 464

reticulatum Champion 442

rubescens Hayata 421

rubrum L. 289, 465

rufinerve Siebold & Zuccarini 301, 467

saccharinum L. 289, 468

saccharum Marsh 289, 469

schwerinii Pax 428

sempervirens L. 295, 471

serrulatum Hayata 454

shirasawanum Koidzumi 294, 472

sieboldianum Miquel 465

skutchii Rehder 471

spicatum Lambert 298, 479

stachyophyllum Hiern 169, 473

sterculiaceum Wallich 288, 429

syriacum Boissier & Gaillardot 453

tataricum L. 297, 475

tataricum var. *ginnala* (Maxim.) Maximowicz 432

tegmentosum ssp. *rufinerve* (Siebold & Zuccarini) Murray 467

tetramerum Pax 474

trautvetteri Medwediew 291, 438

trifidum Hooker & Arnott 417

triflorum Komarov **306**, 475

trilobatum Lambert 450

truncatum Bunge **286**, 477

ukurunduense Trautvetter & Meyer **298**, 478

urophyllum Maximowicz 447

vanvolxemii Masters 480

veitchii Schwerin 428

velutinum Boissier var. *vanvolxemii* (Masters) Rehder **292**, 479

villosum Wallich 429

wilsonii Rehder **290**, 418

Aceraceae Jussieu 411–412, 667

Aesculus L. 481

arguta Buckley 484

× *carnea* Hayne **310**, 481

flava Solander **311**, 483

glabra 483

hippocastanum L. **310**, 484

indica (Camb.)Hooker **311**, 486

octandra Marsh 483

pavia L. **311**, 487

× *plantierensis* André 482

turbinata Blume 485

Agavaceae Endlicher 488, 617, 668, 1265

○Agave 488

Ailanthus Desfontaines 488

altissima (Miller) Swingle **336**, 488

glandulosa Desfontaines 489

vilmoriniana Dode 489

○Aka-shide **188**, 561

○Akagashi **163**, 1055

○Akiraho **166**, 863

○Alaternus **176**, 1093

Alaternus latifolia Miller 1094

○Albizia, Plume **342**, 491

Albizia Durazzini 490

julibrissin Durazzini **342**, 490

lebbeck (L.)Bentham 491

lophantha Bentham **342**, 491

Albizzia Bentham 490

○Alder **178**, 492, 494

○ Common 494

○ Green **180**, 499

○ Grey **179**, 495

○ Italian **178**, 492

○ Oriental **179**, 497

○ Red **180**, 497

○ Sitka 500

○ Speckled **180**, 498

○Alerce 49, 707, 1205–1206

○Almond 226, 1019

Alnobetula viridis (Chaix) Schur. 500

Alnus L. 492

alnobetula K. Koch 500

cordata Desfontaines **178**, 492

glutinosa (L.)Gaertner **178**, 494

incana (L.)Moenchen **179**, 495

maximowiczii Callier 500

oregona Nuttall 498

orientalis Decaisne **179**, 497

rubra Bongard **180**, 497

rugosa (Duroi)Sprengel **180**, 498

sinuata (Regel)Rydberg 500

subcordata Meyer 493

viridis (Chaix)De Candolle **180**, 499

Altingiaceae Lindley 730

Amelanchier Medikus 501

canadensis (L.)Medikus **203**, 503

× *grandiflora* Rehder
202, 501, 503
laevis Wieg. 202, 502
lamarckii F.-N.
Schroeder 503
lamarkii 202
ovalis Medikus 502
rotundifolia (Lambert)
Dum-Cours. 203,
502
spicata (Lambert)K.
Koch 203, 504
Ampelopsis tricuspidata
Siebold & Zuccarini
871
Amygdalus see Prunus
Amygdalus communis L.
1020
dulcis Miller 1020
persica L. 1026
Anacardiaceae Lindley
504, 623, 977,
1098, 1130
Andromeda arborea L. 867
○Apple 207, 826
○ Crab 207
○ Danube 825
○ Turkish 263, 677
○Apricot 224, 1013
○ Briançon 225, 1015
○ Japanese 1013
Aquifoliaceae Bartling
504, 742
Araliaceae Jussieu 504,
733, 770
Araucaria Jussieu 505
araucana (Molina)K.
Koch 56, 505
columnaris (Forster)
Hooker 56, 507
cookii R. Brown ex Don
507
excelsa R. Brown 508
heterophylla (Salisbury)
Franco 56, 508
imbricata Pavion 506
Araucariaceae Henkel &
Hochstetter
504–505

○Arborvitae 1209
○ Chinese 990
Arbutus L. 508
andrachne L. 196, 509
× *andrachnoides* Link
197, 509
hybrida Ker-Gawler 510
menziesii Pursh 197,
510
procera Douglas 511
unedo L. 196, 511
Arceuthos drupaceae
(Labillardière)
Antoine 760
Arecaceae C.H. Schulz 868
Arecastrum (Drude)Beccari
1191
romanzoffiana (Chamisso)
Beccari 1192
Aria see Sorbus
Aria nivea Host 1142
Armeniaca vulgaris Lambert
1013
○Ash 316, , 713
○ Arizona 720
○ Biltmore 711
○ Caucasian 317, 717
○ Green 319, 719
○ Manna 317, 716
○ Mountain 1144
○ Narrow-leafed 317,
712
○ Oregon 319, 715
○ Pallis' 316, 718
○ Red 719
○ Velvet 318, 720
○ White 318, 711
○Aspen 245, 1007
○ Big-tooth 1008
Asteraceae Dumort 617
Atherospermataceae 512,
786
Athrotaxis D. Don 512
cupressoides D. Don 55,
513
laxiflora Hooker 55,
513
selaginoides D. Don 55,
514

◯Aucuba **170**, 515
  Aucuba Thunberg 515
    japonica Thunberg **170**, 515
  Aucubaceae J. Agardh 515
  Austrocedrus Florin & Boutelje 516
    chilensis (D. Don)Florin & Boutelje **47**, 516
◯Avocado **168**, 873
  Azalea see Rhododendron
◯Azara 517
◯ Small-leafed **177**, 517
  Azara Ruiz & Pavon 517
    microphylla Hooker f. **177**, 517
◯Azarole **270**, 627

B

◯Balm of Gilead **248**, 1001
◯Bamboo **350**, 518, 882
  Bambusa see Phyllostachys
  Bambusa nigra Loddiges 883
  Bambusae 518, 882
◯Banana **350**, 846
◯Banana Shrub 841
◯Bangalay 679
◯Basswood, American **257**, 1214
◯ White **261**, 1223
◯Bead Tree **343**, 836
◯Bean Tree 576
◯ Indian **140**, 577
◯Beech **131**, 701, 704
◯ Antarctic **241**, 852
◯ Cunningham **243**, 856
◯ Engler **131**, 702
◯ Menzies 855
◯ Mountain **243**, 859
◯ Myrtle 856
◯ Oriental **131**, 703
◯ Red **241**, 854
◯ Roble **240**, 858
◯ Silver **243**, 855
◯ Southern 851

Benthamidia Spach 518
  capitata (Wallich)Hara **143**, 518
  florida (L.)Spach **143**, 520
  kousa (Hance)Hara **143**
  kousa var. *chinensis* Osbourne 521
  nuttallii (Audubon) Moldenke **143**, 522
Betula L. 524
  aetnensis Rafinesque 541
  alba L. 541, 545
  albo-sinensis Burk. **184**, 525
  alleghseniensis Britton **186**, 526
  austrosinensis Chun ex L.C. Li **185**, 528
  bhojpattra Wallich 548
  celtiberica Rothmaler & Vasconcellos 545
  ermanii Chamisso **185**, 529
  grossa Siebold & Zuccarini **186**, 530
  jacquemontii Spach **184**, 531
  jinpingensis P.C. Li 528
  lenta L. 533
  litvinowii Doluhanov 545
  lutea Michaux 527
  mandshurica (Regel) Nakai **182**
  mandshurica var. *japonica* (Miquel)Rehder 534
  mandshurica var. *szechuanica* Schneider 546
  maximowiczii Pax **183**, 536
  medwediewii Regel **183**, 537
  nigra L. **185**, 538
  papyrifera Marsh **183**, 539
  pendula Rothwell **181**, 540

platyphylla Sukaczew 535, 541

platyphylla var. *szechuanica* (Schneider)Rehder 546

populifolia Marsh 181, 542

pubescens Ehrhart 182, 543

resinifera (Regel)Britton 535

szechuanica (Schneider) Jansson 182, 546

ulmifolia Siebold & Zuccarini 531

utilis D. Don 184, 547

utilis ssp. *jacquemontii* (Spach)Kitamura 532

utilis var. *jacquemontii* (Spach)Winkler 532

utilis var. *sinensis* (Franchet)Winkler 526

verrucosa Ehrhart 541

viridis Chaix 500

Betulaceae Gray 492, 523–524, 558, 620, 865

○ Big Tree 1135

○ Bignonia 549

Bignonia see Campsis and Paulownia

Bignonia radicans L. 557

tomentosa Thunberg 872

Bignoniaceae Jussieu 549, 557, 576

○ Bindweed, Rough 166, 1136

○ Biota 48, 990

Biota see Platycladus

Biota orientalis (L.f.) Endlicher 991

○ Birch 523, 524

○ Black 538

○ Brown 543

○ Canoe 539

○ Cherry 533

○ Chinese Red 184, 525

○ Downy 543

○ Erman's 185, 529

○ Grey 181, 542

○ Himalayan 184, 547

○ Himalayan White 531

○ Jacquemont 184, 531

○ Japanese 182, 534

○ Japanese Cherry 186, 530

○ Manchurian 534

○ Maximowicz 183, 536

○ Medwediew's 183, 537

○ Monarch 536

○ Paper 183, 539

○ River 185, 538

○ Sichuan 182, 546

○ Silver 181, 540

○ South China 185, 528

○ Sweet 533

○ White 182, 543

○ Yellow 186, 526

○ Bitternut 329

○ Black Cottonwood 1009

○ Black Mapou 981

○ Blackthorn 1031

○ Bladder Senna 337, 616

○ Bladder-nut 308, 1180–1182

○ Chinese 308, 1181

○ Bog Myrtle 848

Boraginaceae Jussieu 671

○ Box 151, 552

○ Balearic 151, 552

○ Broom 660, 721

○ Moroccan 308, 660

○ Mount Etna 346, 721

○ Pineapple 660

○ Spanish 346, 1180

Broussonetia L'Heritier ex Ventanat 549

kazinoki Siebold & Zuccarini 549

papyrifera (L.)Ventanat 263, 549

○ Buckeye 481

○ Ohio 483

○ Red 311, 487

○ Texas 484
○ Yellow 311, 483
○Buckthorn 176, 1092–1094
○ Alder 154, 709
○ Sea 152, 738
Buddleja L. 550
  alternifolia Maximowicz 551
  colvilei Hooker f. & Thomson 170, 551
  davidii Franchet 170, 550
  variabilis Hemsley 551
Buddlejaceae Wilhelm 550
Buergeria see Magnolia
Buergeria salicifolia Siebold & Zuccarini 818
○Bull Bay 813
○Butter Nut 327, 752
○Buttercup 1091
○Butterfly Bush 170, 550
Buxaceae Dumort 551
Buxus L. 551
  balearica Lambert 151, 552
  sempervirens L. 151, 552

C

○Cabbage Tree 351, 617
Cactaceae Jussieu 553, 864
○Cactus 553
Callitris see Tetraclinis
Callitris quadrivalis Ventenat 1206
Calocedrus Kurz 554
  decurrens (Torrey)Florin 47, 554
○Camellia 238, 555
○ Deciduous 239, 1182
Camellia L. 555
  japonica L. 238, 555
  × *williamsii* W.W. Smith 556
Campsis Loureiro 557

grandiflora (Thunberg) K. Schum 557
  radicans (L.)Seemen 314, 557
Caprifoliaceae Jussieu 558, 801, 1124, 1259
○Carob 340, 593
Carpinaceae 558, 865
Carpinus L. 558
  betulus L. 187, 558
  cordata Blume 560
  duinensis Scop. 562
  fargesii Franchet 561
  japonica 189, 560
  laxiflora (Siebold & Zuccarini)Blume 188, 561
  orientalis Miller 187, 562
  ostrya L. 866
  tschonoskii Maximowicz 188, 562
  turczaninowii Hance 188, 563
  yedoensis Maximowicz 563
Carrièrea Franchet 564
  calycina Franchet 200, 564
Carya Nuttall 565
  alba K. Koch 572–573
  amara Nuttall 567
  aquatica (Michaux f.) Nuttall 329, 567
  cordiformis (Wangenheim)K. Koch 329, 566
  glabra (Miller)Sweet 330, 567
  illinoensis 569
  illinoinensis (Wangenheim)K.Koch 330, 568
  laciniosa (Michaux f.) Loudon 330, 570
  ovalis (Wangenheim) Sargent 568
  ovata (Miller)K.Koch 329, 571

pecan (Marsh)Engler &
    Graebner 569
porcina (Michaux f.)
    Nuttall 568
sulcata Nuttall 571
tomentosa (Poiret)Nuttall
    329, 572
○Cashew Nut 504
Castanea Miller 573
    chrysophylla Hooker 606
    sativa Miller **266**, 574
Castanopsis see Chrysophylla
Castanopsis chrysophylla
    Hooker 606
○Castor-oil Tree, Prickly
    303, 770
Casuarina Adanson 575
    cunninghamiana Miquel
        576
    equisetifolia J.R. & G.
        Forster **38**, 575
    glauca Sprengel 576
    littoralis Salisbury 576
    torulosa Aiton 576
    verticillata Lamark 576
Casuarinaceae R. Brown
    575
○Catalpa, Farges **141**, 579
○   Hybrid **140**, 578
○   Northern **140**, 581
○   Yellow **140**, 580
Catalpa Scopoli 576
    bignonioides Walter **140**,
        577
    × *erubescens* Carrière
        140, 578
    fargesii Bureau **141**,
        579
    × *hybrida* Spaeth 579
    kaempferi Siebold 580
    ovata G. Don **140**, 580
    speciosa Engelmann
        140, 581
    vestita Diels 580
○Cedar 582
○   Atlas **66**, 582
○   Chilean **47**, 516
○   Chinese **336**, 1234
○   Cyprus **66**, 584

○   Deodar 585
○   Eastern Red 767
○   Eastern White 1209
○   Fortune 57, 640
○   Incense **47**, 554
○   Japanese 57, 640–641
○   Pencil **52**, 767
○   Smooth Tasmanian **55**,
        513
○   Tasmanian **55**,
        512–513
○   Western Red **46**, 1210
○   White **46**, 1209
○Cedar of Goa 652
○Cedar of Lebanon **66**, 586
Cedrela see Toona
Cedrela sinensis Jussieu
    1235
Cedrus Trew 582
    atlantica (Endlicher)
        Manetti ex Carrière
        66, 582
    brevifolia (Hooker f.)
        Henry **66**, 584
    deodara (Roxburgh)
        G. Don **67**, 585
    libani Richard **66**, 586
    libani ssp. *atlantica* 583
    libani ssp. *brevifolia* 585
    libani var. *atlantica*
        (Endlicher)Hooker f.
        583
    libani var. *brevifolia*
        Hooker f. 585
Celastraceae R. Brown
    587, 699, 835
Celtis L. 588
    australis L. **191**, 588
    caucasica Willdenow
        589
    occidentalis L. **191**, 589
    tournefortii Lambert
        191, 589
Cephalotaxaceae Pilger
    590
Cephalotaxus Siebold &
    Zuccarini 590
    drupacea Siebold &
        Zuccarini 592

fortunei Hooker f. **63**, 591

harringtonia (Forbes) K. Koch **63**, 592

harringtonia var. *drupacea* (Siebold & Zuccarini)Koidzumi 592

sinensis (Rehder & Wilson)Li 592

Cerasus see Prunus

Cerasus avium (L.)Moenchen **1011**, 1015

mahaleb (L.)Miller 1024

vulgaris Miller 1017

Ceratonia L. 593

siliqua L. **340**, 593

Cercidiphyllaceae Engler 594

Cercidiphyllum Siebold & Zuccarini 594

japonicum Siebold & Zuccarini **171**, 594

magnificum Nakai 595

Cercis L. 595

siliquastrum L. **128**, 596

Chamaecyparis Spach 597

formosensis Maximowicz **41**, 597

henryae Li 603

lawsoniana (Murray) Parlatore **40**, 598

nootkatensis (D. Don) Spach 655

obtusa (Siebold & Zuccarini)Endlicher **41**, 600

pisifera (Siebold & Zuccarini)Endlicher **41**, 601

taiwanensis Masamune & Suzuki 601

thyoides (L.)Britton, Sterns & Poggenberg **40**, 603

Chamaerops L. 604 *see also Trachycarpus*

fortunei Hooker 1238

humilis L. **349**, 604

○Chance Tree **171**, 614
○Chaste Tree **312**, 1262
○Cherry 1011
○ Bird **228**, 1024
○ Choke 1034
○ Cornelian **144**, 619
○ Fuji **221**, 1020
○ Hill 1030
○ Japanese **223**, 1030
○ Oshima 1021
○ Rosebud **224**, 1032
○ Rum **228**, 1028
○ Sargent's **222**, 1026
○ Sour **220**, 1017
○ Spire **221**
○ St Lucie **221**, 1023
○ Tibetan **222**, 1029
○ Virginian Bird **228**, 1034
○ Wild 1014
○ Yoshino **224**, 1035
○Chestnut, Golden 605
○ Spanish 574
○ Sweet **266**, 573–574
○Chinkapin, Golden **160**, 605

Chrysolarix amabilis Moore 1036

Chrysolepis Hjelmqvist 605

chrysophylla (Hooker) Hjelmqvist **160**, 605

○Citron **232**, 608
○Citrus Fruit 606

Citrus L. 606

aurantium L. **230**, 610

bergamia Risso & Poiteau **231**, 610

deliciosa Tenore **230**, 606

grandis (L.)Osbeck **232**, 609

ichangensis Swingle **231**, 609

limetta Risso **231**, 607

limon (L.)Burman **231**, 607

maxima (Burman) Merrill 609

medica L. **232**, 608
nobilis Loureiro 607
paradisii Macfeyden
232, 608
reticulata Blanco 607
sinensis (L.)Osbeck **230**,
609
○ Cladrastis, Chinese **337**,
612
Cladrastis Rafinesque 610
amurensis Ruprecht &
Maximowicz 805
kentukea (Dumont de
Courset)Rudd **337**,
611
lutea (Michaux)
K. Koch 611
sinensis Hemsley **337**,
612
tinctoria Rafinesque 611
Clematis L. 613
armandii Franchet 614
montana De Candolle
614
vitalba L. **314**, 613
Clerodendrum L. 614
trichotomum Thunberg
171, 614
○ Cobnut 620
Cocos see Syagrus
Cocos romanzoffiana
Chamisso 1192
○ Coffee-tree, Kentucky
343, 727
○ Coigüe **242**, 854
○ de Magallanes **242**,
853
Colutea L. 616
arborescens L. **337**, 616
Compositae Giseke 863
Cordyline Commerson ex
R.Brown 617
australis (Forster f.)
Hooker f. **351**, 617
indivisa (Forster
f.)Steudal 618
○ Cork Bark Tree 874
○ Cork Tree, Amur **312**,
874

Cormus see Sorbus
Cormus domestica (L.)Spach
1152
Cornaceae Dumort 518,
618, 725, 1188
○ Cornel 618
○ Himalayan 143, 518
○ Japanese 143, 521
○ Large-leafed 142, 1190
○ Pacific 143, 522
Cornus L. 518, 618, 1188
alternifolia L.f. 1189
brachypoda C.A. Meyer
1190
capitata Wallich 519
controversa Hemsley
1189
florida L. 521
kousa var. *chinensis*
Osbourne 522
macrophylla Wallich
1190
mas L. **144**, 619
nuttallii Audubon 523
sanguinea L. 1191
Corylaceae 620
Corylus L. 620
avellana L. **190**, 620
chinensis Franchet 622
colurna L. **190**, 621
jacquemontii Decaisne
622
maxima Miller **190**,
622
Corynabutilon see Abutilon
Corynabutilon vitifolium
(Cavanilles)Kearney
406
Cotinus Miller 623
americanus Nuttall 624
coggygria Scopoli **128**,
623
obovatus Rafinesque 624
○ Cotoneaster, Tree 156, 625
○ Waterer's 156, 626
Cotoneaster Medikus 624
affinis Lindley 157,
624
bacillaris Lindley 625

frigidus Wallich 156,
625
salicifolius Franchet
157, 626
× *watereri* Exell 156,
626
◯ Crab Apple 823, 832
◯ Crab, Chinese 211, 832
◯   Chonosuki 209, 833
◯   Flowering 210, 829
◯   Hall's 210, 829
◯   Hubei 209, 830
◯   Italian 208, 827
◯   Magdeburg 211, 827
◯   Pillar 833
◯   Purple 211, 831
◯   Siberian 208, 824
◯   Wild 832
Crataegus L. 627
altaica (Loudon)Lange
637
aria L. 1142
azarolus L. 270, 627
calycina Peterman 628
× *carrièrei* Vauvel ex
Carrière 632
crus-galli L. 204, 629
florentina Zuccagni 828
heldreichii Boissier 271,
639
laciniata Ucria 270,
639
× *lavallei* Herincq ex
Lavalle 204, 631
laevigata (Poiret)De
Candolle 269, 630
microphylla K. Koch
268, 629
monogyna Jacques 268,
632
nigra Waldstein &
Kitaibel 271, 634
orientalis Pallas ex
Bieberstein 639
oxycantha L. 631
pentagyna Waldstein &
Kitaibel 269, 634
persimilis Sargent 205,
635

prunifolia (Lambert)
Persoon 636
sanguinea Pallas 271,
636
schraderiana Ledebour
639
serratifolia Desfontaines
881
submollis Sargent 205,
637
tanacetifolia (Lambert)
Persoon 270, 638
torminalis L. 1176
trilobata Poiret 677
Cryptomeria D. Don 640
fortunei Hooi. ex Otto &
Dietrich 57, 640
japonica (L.f.)D. Don
57, 641
japonica var. *sinensis*
Siebold 641
◯ Cucumber Tree 136, 808
Cudrania tricuspidata
(Carrière)Lavallé
132, 806
Cunninghamia R. Brown
643
konishii Hayata 644
lanceolata (Lambert)
Hooker. 98, 643
sinensis Rich 644
Cupressaceae Bartling
516, 554, 597, 645,
707, 756, 990,
1205, 1208, 1211
Cupressocyparis see *Cupressus*
Cupressus L. 597
abramsiana Wolf 650
arizonica Greene 42,
646
arizonica var. *glabra*
Woodall 649
benthamii Endlicher 653
cashmeriana Royle ex
Carrière 44, 647
corneyana misapplied
648
× *Cupressocyparis*
leylandii (Jackson &

Dallimore)Dallimore 651

distichum L. 1200

formosensis (Maximowicz) Henry 598

glabra Sudworth 42, 648

goveniana Gordon 42, 649

himalaica Silba 648

lambertiana hort. 654

lawsoniana Murray 599

× *leylandii* Jackson & Dallimore 45, 650

lindleyi Klotz 43, 652

lusitanica Miller 652

macrocarpa Hartweg ex Gordon 43, 653

nootkatensis D. Don 45, 654

obtusa (Siebold & Zuccarini)K. Koch 601

pisifera (Siebold & Zuccarini)K. Koch 602

sempervirens L. 43, 656

thyoides L. 603

torulosa D. Don 44, 657

torulosa var. *cashmeriana* (Royle ex Carrière) Kent 648

Cyathea dealbata (Forster) Swartz 664

Cyatheaceae Kaulf. 658, 664

Cyclobalanopsis see Quercus

Cyclobalanopsis acuta (Thunberg)Oersted 1055

glauca (Thunberg) Oersted 1067

myrsinifolia (Blume) Oersted 1073

Cydonia Miller 658

oblonga Miller 129, 658

○Cypress 597, 645
○   Arizona 42, 646
○   Arizona Smooth 648
○   Bald 1199
○   Bentham 653
○   Bhutan 44, 647
○   Californian 649
○   Gowen 42, 649
○   Hinoki 41, 600
○   Italian 43, 656
○   Kashmir 647
○   Lawson 40, 598
○   Leyland 45, 650
○   Mediterranean 656
○   Mexican 43, 652
○   Monterey 43, 653
○   Nootka 45, 654
○   Patagonian 708
○   Pategonian 49
○   Pond 59, 1198
○   Rough Bark Arizona 646
○   Santa Cruz 650
○   Sawara 41, 601
○   Smooth 42, 648
○   Swamp 59, 1198–1199
○   Taiwan 41, 597
○   West Himalayan 44, 657
○   White 40, 603

Cystus see Laburnum

Cystus laburnum L. 775

alpinus Miller 774

Cytisus Desfontaines 660

battandieri Maire 308, 660

D

○Daisy 617

○Daisy Bush 863

○Date Plum 665

Davidia Baillon 661

involucrata Baillon 238

involucrata var. *vilmoriniana* (Dode) Wanger 661

vilmoriniana Dode 662

Davidiaceae Takhtadjan 661

Decaisnea Hooker f. &
        Thomson 663
    fargesii Franchet 325,
        663
    insignis (Griffith)Hooker
        & Thompson 664
Dendrobenthamia see
    Benthamidia
○Deodar 67, 585
    Dicksonia 664
        antarctica Labillardière
            350, 664
    Diospyros L. 665
        kaki L.f. 153, 665
        lotus L. 153, 665
        virginiana L. 153, 666
○Dipteronia 315, 667
    Dipteronia Oliver 667
        sinensis Oliver 315, 667
○Dogwood 144, 618,
        1188, 1191
○   Flowering 143, 520
○   Table 142, 1189
○Douglas Fir 94, 1036,
        1038
○   Big Cone 94, 1037
○   Blue 1038
○Dove Tree 238, 661
    Dracaena Vandelli ex L.
        668
        arborea (Willdenow)
            Link 669
        australis Forster f. 618
        draco L. 351, 668
        fragrans (L.)Ker-Gawler
            669
        umbraculifera 669
○Dragon Tree 351, 668
○Drimys 669
    Drimys J.R & G. Forster f.
        669
        winteri J.R & G. Forster
            167, 670

E

    Ebenaceae Guerke 665,
        671

○Ebony 665, 671
○Ehretia 201, 671
    Ehretia P. Browne 671
        dicksonii Hance 201,
            671
        ovalifolia Hasskarl 672
        thyrsiflora (Siebold &
            Zuccarini)Nakai
            672
    Ehretiaceae Lindley 671
    Elaeagnaceae De Candolle
        672
    Elaeagnus L. 672
        angustifolia L. 166, 672
        commutata Rehder 673
        pungens Thunberg 673
○Elder 315, 1124
○   Box 314, 450
○   Red-berried 315, 1125
○Elm 1249
○   Caucasian 192, 1269
○   Chinese 195, 1255
○   Dutch 194, 1251
○   English 193, 1256
○   European Field 1254
○   European White 1253
○   Fluttering 195, 1253
○   Grey 194, 1249
○   Japanese 193, 1252
○   Siberian 195, 1257
○   Smooth 194, 1254
○   Wych 193, 1250
    Embothrium J. R. & G.
        Forster 673
        coccineum J. R. & G.
            Forster 167, 673
        lanceolatum Ruiz &
            Pavón 674
○Empress Tree 871
    Erica L. 675
        arborea L. 38, 675
        australis L. 675
    Ericaceae Jussieu 508,
        674–675, 866, 1094
    Eriobotrya Lindley 675
        japonica (Thunberg)
            Lindley 206, 676
    Eriolobus (De Candolle)
        Roemer 677

trilobatus (Poiret)
Roemer **263**, 677
tschonoskii (Maximowicz)
Rehder 834
Eucalyptus L'Heritier 678
angustifolia Desfontaines
692
archeri Maiden &
Blakely 685
botryoides Smith 679
camuldulensis Dehnhardt
126, 680
citriodora Hooker **126**,
681
coccifera Hooker f. **124**,
681
coriacea Schauer 689
dalrympleana Maiden
123, 682
debeuzevillei Maiden 689
ficifolia Müller 680
glaucescens Maiden &
Blakely 685
globulus Labillardière
125, 683
gomphocephala De
Candolle **127**, 684
gunnii Hooker f. **122**,
685
johnstonii Maiden **126**,
686
maidenii Müller **125**,
687
muelleri T.B.Moore, not
Miquel nor Naudin
686
niphophila Maiden &
Blakely **124**, 687
pauciflora Sieber **124**,
688
pauciflora ssp. *niphophila*
Johnson & Blaxell
688
resinifer Smith **127**, 689
robusta Smith **127**, 690
rostrata Schlechtandal
680
subcrenulata Maiden &
Blakely 686

tereticornis Smith **126**,
690
× *trabutii* Vilmorin ex
Trabut 689
umbellulatus Chapman,
not Domin 691
urnigera Hooker f. **122**,
691
vernicosa Hooker f. 686
viminalis Labillardière
123, 692
Eucommia Oliver 693
ulmoides Oliver **154**,
693
Eucommiaceae Engler
693
○Eucryphia **313**, 695
○ Nyman's **313**, 698
○ Rostrevor **313**, 696
○ Tasmanian **173**, 697
Eucryphia Cavanilles 694
cordifolia Cavanilles
173, 694
glutinosa (Poeppig &
Endlicher)Baillon
313, 695
× *intermedia* Bausch
313, 696
lucida (Labillardière)
Baillon **173**, 697
mulliganii Hooker f. 697
× *nymansensis* Bausch
313, 698
pinnatifolia Gay 696
Eucryphiaceae Engler 694
○Euodia **312**, 1207
Euodia see *Tetradium*
Euodia daniellii (Benn)
Hemsley 1207
hupehensis Dode 1207
Euonymus L. 699
europaeus L. **174**, 699
europaeus var. *latifolius*
(L.)Miller 700
japonicus Thunberg
174, 700
latifolius (L.)Miller
174, 700
tobira Thunberg 985

F

Fabaceae Lindley 788
Fagaceae Dumort 573,
    605, 701, 798, 851,
    1054
Fagara see Zanthoxylum
Fagara ailanthioides
    (Siebold &
    Zuccarini)Engler
    1267
Fagus L. 701
    antarctica Forster 852
    betuloides Mirbel 853
    dombeyi Mirbel 854
    engleriana Seemen 131,
        702
    fusca Hooker f. 855
    lucida Rehder &
        Wilson 702
    moesiaca (Maly)Czeczot
        705
    orientalis Lipsky 131,
        703
    sylvatica L. 131, 704
    taurica Poplov 703
○False Cypress 597
○Fan Palm, European 349,
    604
    Ficus L. 706
    carica L. 303, 706
    elastica Roxburgh ex
        Hornemann 132,
        707
○Fig 303, 706
○Filbert 190, 622
○Fir, Delavay 87
○   Algerian 80, 390
○   Balsam 93, 359
○   Bornmueller 389
○   Bristlecone 360
○   Caucasian 389
○   Cheng 86, 363
○   China 98, 643
○   Cilician 79, 365
○   Delavay 367
○   European Silver 357
○   Faber 87, 370
○   Farges 88, 372

○   Flaky 88, 401
○   Forrest 86, 374
○   Fraser 93, 376
○   Gamble 392
○   Giant 377
○   Grand 82, 377
○   Greek 78, 361
○   Hedgehog 393
○   Himalayan 400
○   Khinghan 91, 388
○   Korean 91, 381
○   Low's 367
○   Manchurian 84, 378
○   Maries 90, 386
○   Mayr 398
○   Min 85, 395
○   Momi 84, 373
○   Needle 378
○   Nikko 85, 379
○   Noble 81, 394
○   Nordmann 79, 389
○   Pacific 90, 358
○   Pindrow 85, 391
○   Red 81, 384
○   Sacred 83, 397
○   Sakhalin 92, 398
○   Salween 84, 364
○   Santa Lucia 89, 360
○   Shensi 364
○   Shikoku 382
○   Siberian 92, 399
○   Sicilian 78, 387
○   Sikkim 87, 369
○   Silver 78, 355, 357
○   Spanish 80, 393
○   Subalpine 93, 383
○   Taiwan 92, 380
○   Veitch 91, 402
○   Vejar 83, 403
○   Webb 89, 400
○   West Himalayan 391
○   White 82, 366
○Fire Bush 167, 673
    Fitzroya Hooker f. ex
        Lindley 707
    cupressoides (Molina)
        Johnston 49, 708
    patagonica Lindley 708
○Flacourtia 709

Flacourtiaceae De Candolle 517, 564, 709, 741, 994

○Flowering Maple 404, 405

Fortunea see Platycarya

○Foxglove 1133

○Foxglove Tree 871

Frangula Miller 709
  alnus Miller 154, 709

Fraxinus L. 710
  alba Marsh 711
  americana L. 318, 711
  americana var. *biltmoreana* (Beadle) J.Wright 711
  angustifolia Vahl 317, 712
  angustifolia ssp. *oxycarpa* (Willldenow)Franco & Rocha Alfonso 717
  biltmoreana Beadle 711
  excelsior L. 316, 713
  holotricha Koehne 718
  latifolia Bentham 319, 715
  oregona Nuttall 715
  ornus L. 317, 716
  oxycarpa Willldenow 317, 717
  pallisiae Wilmott 316, 718
  pennsylvanica Marsh 319, 719
  pennsylvanica ssp. *oregona* (Nuttall) G.N. Miller 715
  pennsylvanica ssp. *velutina* (Torrey) G.N.Miller 721
  sogdiana Bunge 718
  velutina Torrey 318, 720

○French Hales 217, 1150

G

○Gean 220, 1014

Genista L. 721
  aetnensis (Bivona)De Candolle 346, 721

○Ghost Tree 661

○Ginkgo 352, 722

Ginkgo L. 722
  biloba L. 352, 722

Ginkgoaceae Engler 722

Gleditsia L. 724
  triacanthos L. 343, 724

Glyptostrobus pensilis (Staunton)Koch 1200

○Goat Horn Tree 200, 564

○Gogun Tree 236, 837

○Golden Oak of Cyprus 267, 1057

○Golden Wreath 345, 406

Gramineae 518, 882

○Grape 1262

○Grapefruit 232, 608

Grislinia Forster f. 725
  littoralis (Raoul)Raoul 128, 726

Grisliniaceae (Wangerin) Takhtadjan 725

○Guelder Rose 175, 1259, 1260

Guilandina see Gymnocladus

Guilandina dioica L. 728

○Gum 678
○ Black 684, 861
○ Broad-leaved Kindling 123, 682
○ Cabbage 124, 688
○ Cider 122, 685
○ Forest Red 126, 690
○ Johnston's 126, 686
○ Lemon-scented Spotted 126, 681
○ Maiden's 125, 687
○ Red 126, 680
○ Ribbon 123, 692
○ Snow 124, 687
○ Tasmanian Blue 125, 683
○ Urn 122, 691

○Gurass 130, 1095

○Gutta-percha Tree 154, 693

Gymnocladus Lambert 726
  canadensis Lambert 728
  dioica (L.)K. Koch 343,
    727

H

○Hackberry 191, 588–589
Halesia Ellis ex L. 728
  carolina 729
  carolina var. *monticola*
    Rehder 729
  corymbosa 1045
  diptera 729
  monticola (Rehder)
    Sargent 233, 728
Hamamelidaceae R.
    Brown 730, 792,
    869
Hamamelis L. 730
  × *intermedia* Rehder
    198, 731
  japonica Siebold &
    Zuccarini 198, 731
  mollis Oliver 198, 730
  persica De Candolle 870
  vernalis Sargent 732
  virginiana L. 199, 732
○Hawthorn 627, 632
○ Black 271, 634
○ Crimean 268, 629
○ Downy 205, 637
○ Five-seeded 269, 634
○ Heldreich's 271, 639
○ May 268, 632
○ Midland 269, 630
○ Oriental 270, 639
○ Red 271, 636
○ Sawtoothed 628
○Hazel 190, 620
○ Chinese 622
○ Jacquemont 622
○ Turkish 190, 621
○Headache Tree,
    Californian 1258
○Heather 674–675
Hedera L. 733
  helix L. 133, 733

hibernica (Kirchner)Bean
    734
○Hemlock 1240
○ Carolina 96, 1242
○ Chinese 96, 1243
○ Eastern 95, 1240
○ Himalayan 97, 1245
○ Mountain 98, 735
○ Northern Japanese 97,
    1244
○ Southern Japanese 97,
    1248
○ Western 95, 1246
○Henna 804
Hesperopeuce Lemmon 735
  mertensiana (Bongard)
    Rydberg 98, 735
Heyderia see *Calocedrus*
Heyderia decurrens (Torrey)
    K. Koch 555
○Hiba 47, 1211
Hibiscus L. 737
  syriacus L. 302, 737
○Hickory 565
○ Bitternut 566
○ Red 568
○ Shagbark 329, 571
○ Shellbark 330, 570
○ Water 329, 567
Hicoria see *Carya*
Hippocastanaceae De
    Candolle 481, 738
Hippophaë L. 738
  rhamnoides L. 152, 738
  salicifolia D. Don 738
Hoheria Cunningham 739
  angustifolia Raoul 740
  glabrata Sprague &
    Summerhayes 740
  lyallii Hooker f. 740
  populnea A.
    Cunningham 740
  populnea var. *lanceolata*
    Hooker f. 740
  sexstylosa Collett 236,
    739
○Holly 264, 504, 742,
    744
○ Highclere 265, 743

○   Himalayan **264**, 745
○   Madeira **265**, 746
○   Perny **265**, 747
○ Honeysuckle **145**, 558, 801
○   Fly **145**, 802
○ Hop Tree **308**, 1039
○ Hornbeam **187**, 558
○   Chonosuki's **188**, 562
○   Hop **189**, 865
○   Japanese **189**, 560
○   Oriental **187**, 562
○   Sawa 560
○   Turczaninow's **188**, 563
○ Horse Chestnut **310**, 481, 484, 738
○   Indian **311**, 486
○   Japanese 485
○   Red **310**, 481
○ Houhere **236**, 739
○ Houheria 739
    Howea see Howeia
    Howeia Beccari 741
      forsteriana (Moore & Mueller)Beccari **348**, 741
    Hydrangeaceae 875

I

○ Idesia **200**, 741–742
    Idesia Maximowicz 741
      polycarpa Maximowicz **200**, 742
    Ilex L. 742
      × *altaclerensis* (Loudon) Dallimore **265**, 743
      aquifolium L. **264**, 744
      dipyrena Wallich **264**, 745
      maderensis Lambert 746
      perado Aiton **265**, 746
      pernyi Franchet **265**, 747
○ Ironwood 866
○   Persian **199**, 869
○ Ivy **133**, 733
○   Boston 870

J

○ Jacaranda **342**, 747–748
    Jacaranda Jussieu 747
      acutifolia misapplied 748
      mimosifolia **342**, 748
○ Japanese Creeper **303**, 870
○ Jasmine 748
○   Common 749
○   Wild **309**, 749
○   Winter **309**, 748
    Jasminum L. 748
      fruticans L. **309**, 749
      nudiflorum Lindley **309**, 748
      officinale L. 749
    Jubaea Kunth 749
      chilensis (Molina)Baillon **348**, 750
○ Judas Tree **128**, 595, 596
    Juglandaceae A. Rich. ex Kunth 565, 750, 988, 1040
    Juglans L. 750
      ailanthifolia Carrière **326**, 751
      cinerea L. **327**, 752
      cordiformis Wangenheim 567
      fraxinifolia Lambert 1041
      illinoinensis Wangenheim 569
      laciniosa Michaux f. 571
      mandshurica Maximowicz 752
      microcarpa Berlandier 754
      nigra L. **327**, 753
      ovata Miller 572
      regia L. **326**, 755
      rupestris Engelmann 754
      sieboldiana Maximowicz 752
○ Jujuba **177**, 1271

○ Indian 177, 1272
○ Lotus 177, 1272
○ Juniper 53, 756, 758
○ Chinese 52, 757
○ Grecian 50, 760
○ Himalayan Weeping 54, 764
○ Phoenician 50, 763
○ Prickly 53, 762
○ Rocky Mountain 51, 766
○ Spanish 51, 767
○ Stinking 50, 761
○ Syrian 54, 759
○ Temple 53, 765
○ Wallich 768

Juniperus L. 756
  chinensis L. 52, 757
  communis L. 53, 758
  drupacea Labillardière 54, 759
  excelsa Bieberstein 50, 760
  foetidissima Willdenow 50, 761
  formosana Hayata 765
  indica misapplied 769
  oxycedrus L. 53, 762
  phoenicea L. 50, 763
  polycarpos K. Koch 761
  pseudosabina misapplied 769
  recurva Buchanan-Hamilton ex D. Don 54, 764
  rigida Siebold & Zuccarini 53, 765
  scopulorum Sargent 51, 766
  thurifera L. 51, 767
  virginiana L. 52, 767
  wallichiana Hook. & Thomson ex Parlatore 768

K

Kalopanax Maximowicz 770
  pictus (Thunberg) Nakai 771
  septemlobus (Thunberg) Koidzumi 303, 770
○ Karo 165, 982
○ Karoo 341, 410
○ Katsura 171, 594
○ Keaki 192, 1270
Kentia see *Howeia*
Kentia forsteriana Moore & Mueller 741
○ Keteleeria, David's 67, 771
○ Eveyln 772
○ Fortune 772
Keteleeria Carrière 771
  davidiana (Bertram) Beissner 67, 771
  evelyniana Masters 772
  fortunei (Murray) Carrière 772
○ Kobushi 135, 814
Koelreuteria Laxmann 772
  paniculata Laxmann 320, 773
○ Kohuhu 164, 983
○ Korlinga 130, 1096
○ Kusamaki 61, 992

L

○ Laburnum 773, 775
○ Common 309, 775
○ Scotch 309, 774
Laburnum Medikus 773
  alpinum (Miller) Berchtold & Presl 309, 774
  anagyroides Medikus 309, 775
  × *watereri* (Kirchner) Dippel 309, 775
○ Lacebark, Long-leafed 739
Lagerstroemia L. 776
  indica L. 146, 776
○ Larch 777
○ Dahurian 99, 778

○ European **99**, 777
○ Golden **100**, 1035
○ Japanese **100**, 781
○ Potanin **101**, 784
○ Siberian **99**, 785
○ Sikkim **101**, 780
○ Western **102**, 783
○Lardizabala 776
Lardizabalaceae Decaisne
  663, 776
Larix Miller 777
  dahurica Turczaninow
    ex Trautvetter 780
  decidua Miller **99**, 777
  europaea Lambert & De
    Candolle 778
  gmelinii (Ruprecht)
    Ruprecht **99**, 778
  griffithiana (Lindley &
    Gordon)Carrière
    101, 780
  griffithii Hooker f. &
    Thomson 781
  kaempferi (Lambbert)
    Carrière **100**, 781
  laricina (du Roi)Koch
    102, 782
  leptolepis (Siebold & Zuc-
    carini)Gordon 782
  occidentalis Nuttall **102**,
    783
  potaninii Batalin **101**,
    784
  russica (Endlicher)
    Sabine ex Trautvetter
    785
  sibirica Ledebour **99**, 785
  speciosa Cheng & Fu
    781
Lauraceae Jussieu 785,
  787, 873, 1126,
  1258
○Laurel 785, 787, 1021
○ Bay **129**, 787
○ Californian **168**, 1258
○ Cherry **229**, 1021
○ Poet's 787
○Portuguese **229**, 1022

Laurelia Jussieu 786
  aromatica Poiret 786
  sempervirens (Ruiz &
    Pavon)Tulasne **172**,
    786
  serrata Bertero 786
Laurocerasus see *Prunus*
Laurocerasus officinalis
  Roemer 1022
Laurus L. 787
  albida Nuttall 1127
  azorica (Seub.)J. Franco
    787
  nobilis L. **129**, 787
○Laurustinus **141**, 1261
Leguminosae Jussieu 406,
  490, 593, 595, 610,
  616, 660, 721, 724,
  726, 773, 788, 804,
  1102, 1137, 1180,
  1264
○Lemon **231**, 607
○ Ichang **231**, 609
○Lemonwood 983
○Lentisc 979
Libocedrus see *Austrocedrus*
    and *Calocedrus*
Libocedrus chilensis D. Don
  517
  decurrens Torrey 555
Ligustrum L. 789
  chenaultii Hickel **149**,
    789
  compactum Brandis 789
  confusum 790
  lucidum Aiton f. **148**,
    790
  ovalifolium Hasskarl
    148, 791
  vulgare L. **149**, 792
○Lilac **147**, 1192
○ Hungarian **147**, 1193
Liliaceae Jussieu 1136
○Lime 1213
○ American 1214
○ Caucasian Hybrid
    261, 1218
○ Common **256**, 1219
○ Crimean **261**, 1217

○ Henry's **258**, 1222
○ Large-leafed **257**, 1231
○ Manchurian **259**, 1225
○ Maximowicz **260**, 1226
○ Mongolian **260**, 1227
○ Oliver's **259**, 1229
○ Pendent Silver **259**, 1230
○ Silver **258**, 1233
○ Small-leafed **256**, 1215
○ Sweet **231**, 607
○ Linden 1213
Liquidambar 794
  Liquidambar L. 792
    acerifolia Maximowicz 793
    formosana Hance **305**, 792
    imberbe Aiton 794
    orientalis Miller **305**, 793
    styraciflua styraciflua L. **305**, 794
  Liriodendron L. 795
    chinense (Hemsley) Sargent **283**, 795
    tulipifera L. **283**, 797
    tulipifera var. *chinense* Hemsley 796
  Lithocarpus Blume 798
    cleistocarpus (Seemen) Rehder & Wilson 800
    edulis (Makino)Nakai 160, 798
    glaber (Thunberg)Nakai 799
    henryi (Seemen)Rehder & Wilson 160, 800
    pachyphyllus 800
  Livistona australis (R. Brown)Martius 1264
    decipiens Beccari 1264
○ Locust 593

○ Black 724, 1102
○ Clammy 338, 1104
○ Honey 343, 724
  Loganiaceae C. Martius 550
  Lonicera L. 801
    caprifolium L. 802
    japonica Thunberg 802
    maackii (Ruprecht) Maximowicz 802
    periclymenum L. 145, 801
    xylosteum L. 145, 802
○ Loquat 206, 675–676
  Luma see Myrtus
  Luma apiculata (De Candolle)Burret 851
○ Lyonothamnus 314, 803
  Lyonothamnus A. Gray 803
    floribundus var. *asplenifolius* (Greene) Brandegee 314, 803
  Lythraceae J. St.-Hilaire 776, 804

M

○ Maackia, Amur 337, 804
  Maackia Ruprecht 804
    amurensis (Ruprecht & Maximowicz) K. Koch 337, 804
  Machilus see Persea
  Machilus ichangensis Rehder & Wilson 873
  Maclura Nuttall 805
    aurantiaca Nuttall 806
    pomifera (Rafinesque) Schneider 132, 805
○ Madroño 197, 510
○ Magnolia, Big-leafed 137, 815
○ Campbell 134, 809
○ Chinese Large-leaf 136, 816
○ Delavay 138, 811
○ Evergreen 138, 813

○ Fraser 136, 812
○ Japanese Big-leaf 136, 817
○ Loebner's 135, 815
○ Saucer 134, 819
○ Southern 813
○ Willow-leafed 135, 818
○ Wilson 139, 822
   Magnolia L. 807
     denudata Desrousseaux 820
     'Kewensis' cultivar 818
     acuminata L. 136, 808
     biondii 819
     campbellii Hooker f. & Thomson 134, 809
     cordata Michaux 809
     delavayi Franchet 138, 811
     fraseri Walter 136, 812
     glauca L. 822
     grandiflora L. 138, 813
     hypoleuca Siebold & Zuccarini 136, 817
     kobus De Candolle 135, 814
     × *loebneri* Kache 135, 815
     macrophylla Micheaux 137, 815
     obovata Thunberg 817
     officinalis Rehder & Wilson 136, 816
     praecocissima Koidzumi 814
     × *proctoriana* Rehder 819
     pyramidata Bartram 812
     salicifolia (Siebold & Zuccarini) Maximowicz 135, 818
     sieboldii K. Koch 823
     sinensis (Rehder & Wilson)Stapf 823
     × *soulangiana* Soulange-Bodin 134, 819

     thurberi Parsons ex Robinson 814
     tripetala L. 137, 820
     umbrella Desrousseaux 821
     virginiana L. 137, 821
     wilsonii (Finet et Gagnepaine)Rehder 139, 822
   Magnoliaceae Jussieu 795, 806–807, 841
○ Mahogany 835
○   Chinese 1234
○   Red 127, 689
○   Swamp 127, 690
○ Maidenhair Tree 722
○ Maiten 173, 835
○ Mallow 404, 834
○   Chilean 302, 405
○   Woody 302, 405, 737
   Malus Miller 823
     baccata (L.)Borkhausen 208, 824
     dasyphylla Borkhausen 825
     domestica Borkhausen 207, 826
     florentina (Zuccagni) Schneider 208, 827
     × *floribunda* Siebold ex Van Houtte 210, 829
     floribunda var. *purpurea* Barbier 831
     halliana Koehne 210, 829
     hupehensis (Pampanini) Rehder 209, 830
     'Magdeburgensis' 211, 827
     pumila in part, not Miller 827
     × *purpurea* (Barbier) Rehder 211, 831
     spectabilis (Aiton) Borkhausen 211, 832
     sylvestris (L.)Miller 207, 832

theifera Rehder 830
transitoria Schneider 210, 825
trilobata (Poiret) Schneider 677
tschonoskii (Maximowicz) Schneider 209, 833
Malvaceae Jussieu 404, 737, 739, 834
○ Maple 411–412
○ Amur 297, 431
○ Ash-leafed 450
○ Balkan 296, 439
○ Bearded 299, 415
○ Big-leafed 444
○ Bigtooth 471
○ Birch-leafed 169, 473
○ Black 470
○ Broad 285, 413
○ Campbell 290, 417
○ Canyon 471
○ Cappadocian 284, 421
○ Chalk 470
○ Chosen 306, 475
○ Cretan 295, 471
○ Cyprus 452
○ David's 169, 427
○ Deep-veined 299, 414
○ Devil's 428
○ Fan-leafed 418
○ Field 287, 419
○ Florida 470
○ Flying Moth 451
○ Forrest's 300, 430
○ Full Moon 294, 440
○ Giraldi's 292, 432
○ Green Bark 437
○ Hawthorn-leaf 425
○ Heldreich's 291, 437
○ Henry's 307, 438
○ Hers' 300, 436
○ Honshu 301, 467
○ Hornbeam 169, 422
○ Horned 288, 470
○ Italian 292, 454
○ Japanese 293, 455
○ Keijo 294, 464
○ Kyushu 300, 420
○ Lime-leafed 169, 429

○ Lobel's 284, 442
○ Maximowicz's 293, 446
○ Miyabe 287, 447
○ Mono 286, 448
○ Montpelier 296, 449
○ Mountain 298, 479
○ Nikko 306, 445
○ Norway 285, 460
○ Oliver 290, 453
○ Oregon 288, 444
○ Paperbark 306, 434
○ Red 289, 465
○ Red-bud 291, 438
○ Shandong 286, 477
○ Shirasawa 294, 472
○ Silver 289, 468
○ Skutch 471
○ Smooth 441
○ Smoothbark 150, 441
○ Spanish 296, 433
○ Striped 459
○ Sugar 289, 469
○ Syrian 295, 452
○ Tail-leaf 298, 423
○ Tartar 297, 475
○ Three-flowered 476
○ Trautvetter's 438
○ Trident 295, 416
○ Ukurundu 298, 478
○ Uri 293, 425
○ Van Volxem's 292, 479
○ Vine-leafed 307, 424
○ Wilson's 290, 418
○ Wongka 301, 457
○ Mapou, Black 165
○ Mastic Tree 321, 979
○ May 268, 632
Maytenus Molina 835
boaria Molina 173, 835
chilensis De Candolle 835
○ Mazzard 1014
○ Medlar 206, 839
Melia L. 836
azedarach L. 343, 836
Meliaceae Jussieu 835–836, 1234

○Meliosma, Veitch's **320**, 838

Meliosma Blume 837
  dilleniifolia (Wight & Arnott)Walpers **236**, 837
  veitchiorum Hemsley **320**, 838

○Mespilus, Snowy **202–203**, **501–503**

Mespilus L. 839
  amelanchier L. 502
  germanica L. **206**, 839
  japonica Thunberg 676
  tanacetifolia Lambert 639

Metasequoia Hu & Cheng 840
  glyptostroboides Hu & Cheng **59**, 840

○Michelia **139**, 841

Michelia L. 841
  champaca L. 843
  compressa (Maximowicz) Sargent 843
  doltsopa Buchanan-Hamilton ex De Candolle **139**, 841
  figo (Loureiro)Sprengel 842
  velutina De Candolle **139**, 842
  yunnanensis Franchet 843

Micromeles see Sorbus

Micromeles alnifolia (Siebold & Zuccarini) Koehne 1141

○Mimosa 407

Mimosa see Acacia

Mimosa longifolia Andrews 409

○Mockernut **329**, 572

Moniniaceae in part 512

○Monkey Puzzle **56**, **504–505**

○Moosewood **301**, 459

Moraceae Link 549, 706, 805, 843–844

Morus L. 844

  alba L. **262**, 844
  nigra L. **262**, 845
  papyrifera L. 549

○Mulberry 843–844
○ Black **262**, 845
○ Paper **263**, 549
○ White **262**, 844

Musa L. 846
  basjoo Siebold 846
  cavendishii Paxton **350**, 846
  zebrina Planchon 846

Musaceae Jussieu 846

Myoporaceae R. Brown 847

○Myoporum **133**, 847

Myoporum Banks & Solander 847
  tenuifolium G. Forster **133**, 847

Myrica L. 848
  faya Aiton **152**, 848

Myricaceae Blume 848

Myrtaceae Jussieu 678, 848–849

○Myrtle **146**, 848–849
○ Canary Islands **152**, 848
○ Crape **146**, 776
○ Orange-bark **146**, 850

Myrtus L. 849
  communis L. **146**, 849
  luma Molina **146**, 850

N

○Naya **65**, 1237
○Nectarine **225**, 1025

Negundo see Acer

Negundo aceroides Moenchen 451
  cissifolium Siebold & Zuccarini 425

○Nettle Tree **191**, 588

Nothofagus Blume 851
  × *alpina* (Poeppig & Endlicher)Oersted 857

antarctica (Forster)
  Oersted 241, 852
betuloides (Mirbel)Blume
  242, 853
cunninghamii (Hooker f.)
  Oersted 243, 856
dombeyi (Mirbel)Blume
  242, 854
fusca (Hooker f.) 241,
  854
menziesii (Hooker f.)
  Oersted 243, 855
nervosa (Philippi)Dim.
  & Mil. 240, 856
obliqua (Mirbel)Blume
  240, 858
procera (Poeppig &
  Endlicher)Oersted
  857
solandri (Hooker f.)
  Oersted 243, 859
solandri var. *cliffortioides*
  (Hooker f.)Poole
  859
◯Nutmeg Tree 1235
◯ California 65, 1236
◯ Japanese 1237
◯Nutmeg, Peruvian 172,
  786
Nyssa L. 860
  sinensis Oliver 219, 860
  sylvatica Marsh 219,
    861
Nyssaceae Dumort 661,
  859–860

O

◯Oak 701, 1054
◯ Armenian 278, 1078
◯ Asian Chestnut 266,
    1055
◯ Balkan Pedunculate
    274, 1083
◯ Balkan Sessile 275,
    1076
◯ Bamboo-leafed 163,
    1073
◯ Black 281, 1090
◯ Blackjack 282, 1071
◯ Caucasian 279, 1070
◯ Chinese Cork 281,
    1089
◯ Cork 161, 1087
◯ Daimio 279, 1063
◯ Downy 275, 1079
◯ Durmast 1075
◯ English 274, 1081
◯ Henry's Stone 160,
    800
◯ Himalayan 267, 1086
◯ Holly 1061
◯ Holm 162, 1069
◯ Hungarian 277, 1065
◯ Japanese Evergreen
    1055
◯ Japanese Stone 160,
    798
◯ Kermes 267, 1061
◯ Macedonian 1088
◯ Mirbeck 276, 1058
◯ Northern Pin 1074
◯ Pedunculate 1081
◯ Pin 282, 1074
◯ Pontine 1078
◯ Portuguese 1064
◯ Pyrenean 277, 1080
◯ Quercitron 1090
◯ Red 281, 1085
◯ Round-leafed 162,
    1084
◯ Scarlet 282, 1062
◯ Sessile 275, 1075
◯ She 38, 575
◯ Shingle 1077
◯ Spanish 280, 1067
◯ Thonp 163, 1066
◯ Trojan 279, 1088
◯ Turkey 280, 1059
◯ Valonia 278, 1071
◯ Water 1072
◯ White 279, 1056
◯ Willow 161, 1077
◯Old Man's Beard 314,
  613
Olea L. 862
  europaea L. 147, 862

Oleaceae Hoffmannsegg &
    Link 710, 748, 789,
    862, 877, 1192
Olearia Moenchen 863
    forsteri (Hooker f.)
        Hooker f. 864
    paniculata (J.R. & G.
        Forster)Druce 166,
        863
○Oleaster 672
○Olive 147, 862
○   Russian 166, 672
○Opoponax 341, 411
Opuntia Miller 864
    ficus-indica L. 346, 864
    maxima Miller 864
    monacantha
        Hawksworth 864
○Orange 230, 609
○   Bergamot 231, 610
○   Mandarin 606
○   Mock 172, 875
○   Osage 132, 805
○   Seville 230, 610
○   Sweet 609
○Osier 254, 1122
○   Common 1122
○   Purple 253, 1119
Ostrya Scopoli 865
    carpinifolia Scopoli 189,
        865
    virginiana (Miller)
        K. Koch 866
Oxydendrum De Candolle
    866
    arboreum (L.)De
        Candolle 197, 866

P

Padus see Prunus
Padus laurocerasus Miller
    1022
    racemosa Lambert 1025
    rubra Miller 1034
    serotina (Ehrhart)
        Borkhaussen 1028
○Pagoda Tree 339, 1137

Paliurus Miller 867
    spina-christi Miller 152,
        867
○Palm 868
○   Canary 347, 878
○   Chusan 349, 1238
○   Cretan 347, 879
○   Date 347, 878–879
○   Lord Howe's 741
○   Mexican Fan 1263
○   Petticoat 349, 1263
○   Queen 348,
        1191–1192
○   Sentry 348, 741
○   Windmill 1238
Palmae Jussieu 604, 741,
    749, 868, 878,
    1191, 1238, 1263
○Papauma 128, 725–726
Parrotia C.A. Meyer 869
    persica (De Candolle)
        C.A. Meyer 199, 869
Parthenocissus Planchon
    870
    inserta (Kerner)Fritsch
        871
    quinquefolia
        (L.)Planchon 871
    tricuspidata (Siebold &
        Zuccarini)Planchon
        303, 870
Pasania see Lithocarpus
Pasania edulis (Makino)
    Oersted 799
○Paulownia 141, 871
Paulownia Siebold &
    Zuccarini 871
    fortunei (Seemen)
        Hemsley 872
    imperalis Siebold &
        Zuccarini 872
    lilacina Sprague 872
    tomentosa (Thunberg)
        Steudel 141, 871
Pavia see Aesculus
○Peach 225, 1025
○Pear 1047
○   Almond-leafed 158,
        1047

○ Austrian 1048
○ Callery's 213, 1049
○ Common 212, 1049
○ Oleaster-leafed 159, 1052
○ Plymouth 212, 1051
○ Sage-leafed **158**, 1053
○ Snow 159, 1052
○ Wild **213**, 1050
○ Willow-leafed 159, 1053
○Pecan 330, 568
○Pepo Tree, Red 235, 1091
○Pepper Tree 1130
○ Peruvian 322, 1130
○Peppermint, Mount Wellington 124, 681

Persea Miller 873
   americana Miller **168**, 873
   gratissima Gaertner f. 873
   ichangensis (Rehder & Wilson)Kostermans 873
Persica see Prunus
Persica vulgaris Miller 1026
○Persimmon **153**, 665–666
Petrophiloides see Platycarya
   strobilaceae (Siebold & Zuccarini)Reid & Chandler 989
Phellodendron Ruprecht 874
   amurense Ruprecht 312, 874
Philadelphaceae D. Don 875
Philadelphus L. 875
   coronarius L. 876
   delavayi L. Henry 876
   inodorus L. 876
   pubescens Loiseleur-Deslongchamps 172, 875
○Phillyrea 175, 877

Phillyrea L. 877
   angustifolia L. 878
   latifolia L. 175, 877
   media L. 878
○Phirphiri 150, 451
Phoenix L. 878
   canariensis Chabaud 347, 878
   dactylifera L. 347, 879
   sylvestris (L.)Roxburgh 879
   theophrastii Greuter 347, 879
○Photinia, Giant 155, 881
○ Red Tip 155, 881
Photinia Miller 880
   davidiana (Decaisne) Cardot 155, 880
   × *fraseri* Dress 155, 881
   japonica (Thunberg) Franchet & Savatier 676
   serratifolia (Desfontaines) Kalkman 155, 881
   serrulata Lindley 881
Phyllostachys Siebold & Zuccarini 882
   aurea (Carrière)A. & C. Rivière 883
   nigra (Loddiges)Monro 350, 882
Picea Link 883
   abies (L.)Link 68, 885
   abies ssp. *obovata* (Ledebour)Hulten 900
   alba 893
   alcoquiana (Veitch ex Lindley)Carrière 73, 886
   alpestris Brügger ex Stein 885
   asperata Master 68, 887
   aurantiaca Masters 888
   balfouriana Rehder & Wilson 905

bicolor (Maximowicz) Mayr 887
brachytyla (Franchet) Pritzel 77, 888
breweriana S. Watson 77, 890
engelmannii (Parry) Engelmann 71, 891
excelsa Link 885
glauca (Moenchen)Voss 73, 892
glauca ssp. *engelmannii* (Engelmann)Taylor 891
glehnii (Schmidt) Masters 75, 893
hondoensis Mayr 895
jezoensis (Siebold & Zuccarini)Carrière 894
jezoensis ssp. *hondoensis* (Mayr)P. Schmidt 72, 894
koyamai Shirasawa 69, 895
likiangensis (Franchet) Pritzel 74, 897
likiangensis var. *purpurea* (Masters)Dallimore & Jackson 905
mariana (Mill.)Brittan, Spong & Poggenberg 73, 898
mexicana Martinez 71, 891
morinda Link 909
morindoides Rehder 910
morrisonicola Hayata 69, 899
nigra (Aiton)Link 899
obovata Ledebour 69, 900
omorika (Pancic)Purkyne 76, 901
orientalis (L.)Link 75, 902
polita (Siebold & Zuccarini)Carrière 910

pungens Engelmann 71, 903
purpurea Masters 74, 904
retroflexa Masters 888
sargentiana Rehder & Wilson 889
schrenkiana Fischer & Meyer 70, 906
schrenkiana ssp. *tianchanica* (Ruprecht)Bykov 906
shirasawae Hayashi 887
sitchensis (Bongard) Carrière 72, 907
smithiana (Wallich) Boisier 70, 908
spinulosa (Griffiths) Henry 76, 909
tianchanica Ruprecht 906
torano (K. Koch)Koehne 71, 910
watsoniana Masters 911
wilsonii Masters 69, 911
yunnanensis hort. 898
○ Picrasma 320, 912
Picrasma Blume 912
ailanthioides Planchon 912
quassioides (D. Don) Bennett 320, 912
○ Pignut 330, 567
Pinaceae Lindley 355, 582, 735, 771, 777, 883, 913, 1035–1036, 1240
○ Pine 913
○   Aleppo 106, 938
○   Ancient 115, 944
○   Apache 120, 935
○   Armand 117, 917
○   Arolla 119, 926
○   Beach 929
○   Bishop 110, 950
○   Black 104, 951
○   Blue 117, 976

○ Bosnian **105**, 940
○ Bristlecone **115**, 916
○ Calabrian **106**, 923
○ Canary Island **111**, 925
○ Chile 505
○ Chilgoza 925
○ Chinese Red **103**, 972
○ Cook **56**, 507
○ Corsican 952
○ Coulter **112**, 930
○ Digger **112**, 967
○ Dwarf Mountain **105**, 949
○ Eastern White **116**, 969
○ Endlicher **121**, 966
○ Foxtail **115**, 921
○ Gregg 955
○ Hartweg **121**, 939
○ Jack **107**, 922
○ Japanese Black **105**, 974
○ Japanese Red **103**, 931
○ Japanese Umbrella **60**, 1132
○ Japanese White **119**, 953
○ Jeffrey **111**, 941
○ King Billy **55**, 514
○ King William 514
○ Knobcone **110**, 918
○ Korean **119**, 943
○ Lacebark **113**, 924
○ Limber **118**, 936
○ Loblolly **109**, 973
○ Lodgepole 929
○ Longleaf 936
○ Macedonian **117**, 955
○ Maritime **108**, 956
○ Mexican Rough Bark 947
○ Mexican Weeping **112**, 954
○ Mexican White **118**, 919
○ Michoacan 936
○ Monterey **110**, 962
○ Montezuma **121**, 947

○ Mountain **105**, 975
○ Norfolk Island **56**, 508
○ Norway 964
○ Pitch **109**, 965
○ Pond 966
○ Ponderosa **111**, 959
○ Red **104**, 964
○ Scots **103**, 971
○ Shore **107**, 929
○ Shortleaf **109**, 932
○ Siberian Stone 927
○ Slash **109**, 934
○ Smooth Bark Mexican **120**, 960
○ Southwestern White **118**, 968
○ Stone **108**, 958
○ Swiss Stone 926
○ Table Mountain **106**, 961
○ Umbrella 958, 1131
○ Western White **116**, 948
○ Western Yellow 959
○ Weymouth 969
○ Whitebark 937
○ Pink Siris **342**, 490
○ Piñon, California Single-leaf 946
○ Colorado 933
○ Johan **113**, 942
○ Mexican **113**, 927
○ Papershell **113**, 964
○ Rocky Mountain **114**, 933
○ Single-leaf **114**, 945
Pinus L. 913
abies L. 885
albicaulis Engelmann 937
aristata Engelmann **115**, 916
aristata var. *longaeva* (Bailey) Little 944
armandii Franchet **117**, 917
attenuata Lemmon **110**, 918

ayacahuite Ehrenberg 118, 919

ayacahuite var. *brachyptera* Shaw 969

ayacahuite var. *veitchii* (Roezl)Shaw 920

balfouriana Jeffrey ex Murray 115, 921

banksiana Lambert 107, 922

benthamiana Hartweg 960

brutia Tenor 106, 923

bungeana Zuccarini 113, 924

californiarum Bailey 946

canariensis C. Smith 111, 925

cembra L. 119, 926

cembroides Zuccarini 113, 927

cembroides var. *edulis* (Engelmann)Voss 934

cembroides var. *monophylla* (Torrey & Fremont) Voss 946

cembroides var. *remota* Little 964

contorta Douglas 107, 929

coulteri D. Don 112, 930

densiflora Siebold & Zuccarini 103, 931

devoniana Lindley 936

divaricata (Aiton) Dum.Cours. 922

echinata Miller 109, 932

edulis Engelmann 114, 933

elliotii Engelmann 109, 934

engelmannii Carrière 120, 935

excelsa Wallich ex D. Don, not Lambert 977

flexilis James 118, 936

gerardiana Wallich ex D. Don 925

greggii Engelmann ex Parlatore 955

griffithii McClelland 977

halepensis Miller 106, 938

halepensis var. *brutia* (Tenore)Henry 923

hamiltonii Tenore 957

hartwegii Lindley 121, 939, 967

heldreichii Christ var. *leucodermis* (Antoine) Markgraf ex Fitschen 105, 940

himekomatsu Miyabe & Kudo 954

insignis Douglas ex Loudon 963

jeffreyi Greville & Balfour 111, 941

johannis M.F. Robert 113, 942

koraiensis Siebold & Zuccarini 119, 943

leucodermis Antoine 941

longaeva Bailey 115, 944

mandshurica Ruprecht 943

maritima Miller 957

michoacana Martinez 936

monophylla Torrey & Fremont 114, 945

monophylla var. *edulis* (Engelmann)M.E. Jones 934

montana Miller 949

montezumae Lambert 121, 947, 967

montezumae var. *hartwegii* (Lindley)Engelmann 939

montezumae var. *rudis* (Endlicher)Shaw 967

monticola Douglas 116, 948

mughus Scopoli 949

mugo Turra 105, 949

muricata D. Don 110, 950

nigra Arnold 104, 951

nigra ssp. *laricio* (Poiret)Maire 953

nigra var. *austriaca* (Hoess)Aschers & Graebner 952

nigra var. *calabrica* (Louden)Schneider 953

nigra var. *corsicana* Louden 952

nigra var. *maritima* (Aiton)Melville 953

palustris Miller 936

parviflora Siebold & Zuccarini 119, 953

patula Schlectendal & Chamisso 112, 954

pentaphylla Mayr 954

peuce Grisebach 117, 955

pinaster Aiton 108, 956

pinea L. 108, 958

ponderosa Douglas 111, 959

ponderosa var. *macrophylla* (Engelmann) Shaw 936

pseudostrobus Lindley 120, 960

pungens Lambert 106, 961

radiata D. Don 110, 962

reflexa Engelmann 937

remorata Mason 950

remota (Littel)Bailey & Hawksworth 113, 964

resinosa Aiton 104, 964

rigida Miller 109, 965

rudis Endlicher 121, 966

sabiniana Douglas 112, 967

serotina Michaux 966

sibirica du Tour 927

sinensis Lambert 973

strobiformis Engelmann 118, 920, 968

strobus L. 116, 969

sylvestris L. 103, 971

tabuliformis Carrière 103, 972

taeda L. 109, 973

thunbergiana Franco 975

thunbergii Parlatore 105, 974

tuberculata Gordon 919

uncinata Miller ex Mirbel 105, 975

wallichiana Jackson 117, 976

◯Pistachia 977

Pistacia L. 977

  atlantica Desfontaines 321, 978

  lentiscus L. 321, 979

  palaestina (Boissier) Kotschy 979

  × *saportae* Burnat 980

  terebinthus L. 321, 978

  vera L. 322, 980

◯Pistacio 322, 980

Pittosporaceae R. Brown 981

◯Pittosporum 981

◯   Wavy 164, 985

Pittosporum Banks ex Gaertner 981

  colensoi Hooker f. 165, 981

  crassifolium A. Cunningham 165, 982

  eugenioides A. Cunningham 164, 983

  ralphii Kirk 165, 982

  tenuifolium Gaertn. 164, 983

  tobira (Thunberg)Aiton 165, 984

undulatum Ventanat
164, 985
◯Plane 985–986
◯ London 304, 986
◯ Oriental 304, 987
Platanaceae Dumort
985–986
Platanus L. 986
× *acerifolia* (Aiton)
Wildenow 987
× *hispanica* Munchen-
hausen 304, 986
× *hybrida* Brotero 987
orientalis L. 304, 987
◯Platycarya 325, 988–989
Platycarya Siebold &
Zuccarini 988
longipes Wu 989
strobilaceae Siebold &
Zuccarini 325, 989
Platycladus Spach 990
orientalis (L.f.)Franco
48, 990
◯Plum 226, 1018
◯ Cherry 1015
◯ Date 153
◯ Myrobalan 227, 1015
◯ Naples 225, 1018
◯Plum Yew 63, 590, 592,
1010
◯ Andean 62, 1011
◯ Fortune 63, 591
◯Podocarp 991
◯ Willowleaf 61, 993
Podocarpaceae Endlicher
991, 1010, 1127
Podocarpus L'Héritier ex
Persoon 991 *see also*
Prumnopitys
andinus Endlicher 1011
hallii Kirk 994
macrophyllus (Thunberg)
D. Don 61, 992
nubigenus Lindley 61,
992
salignus D. Don 61, 993
totara D. Don ex
Lambert 62, 994
◯Poliothyrsis 201, 995

Poliothyrsis Oliver 994
sinensis Oliver 201, 995
◯Pomegranate 151,
1045–1046
◯Pomelo 609
◯Poplar 995
◯ Balsam 247, 998
◯ Berlin 248, 999
◯ Black 246, 1005
◯ Central Asian Balsam
249, 999
◯ Chinese Necklace 245,
1003
◯ Grey 244, 1002
◯ Hybrid Black 246,
1000
◯ Maximowicz's Balsam
249, 1004
◯ Simon's 249, 1007
◯ Western Balsam 247,
1009
◯ White 244, 997
◯ Wilson 1004
◯ Yellow 797
Populus L. 995
alba L. 244, 997
balsamifera L. 247, 998
balsamifera var. *candicans*
(Aiton)Gray 1002
× *berolinensis* Dippel
248, 999
bolleana Lauche 998
× *canadensis* Moenchen
246, 1000
candicans Aiton 248,
1001
× *canescens* (Aiton)Smith
244, 1002
× *euramericana* Dode
1001
grandidentata Michaux
1008
× *jackii* Sargeant 1002
lasiocarpa Oliver 245,
1003
laurifolia Ledebour
249, 999
maximowiczii Henry
249, 1004

nigra L. 246, 1005

nivea Wesmael 998

przewalskii Maximowicz 1007

simonii Carrière 249, 1007

tacamahaca Miller 999

tremula L. 245, 1007

trichocarpa Hooker 247, 1009

wilsoniana 1004

◯Prickly Pear 346, 864

◯Pride of India 320, 772–773

◯Privet 148, 789, 791

◯   Chenault's 149, 789

◯   Chinese 148, 790

◯   Wild 149, 792

◯Protea 1010

Proteaceae Jussieu 673, 1010

Prumnopitys Philippi 1010

andina (Poepel ex Endlicher)Laubenfels 62, 1011

Prunus L. 1011

amygdalus Batsch 1020

armeniaca L. 224, 1013

armeniaca ssp. *brigantiaca* (Villars) Dippel 1015

avium L. 220, 1014

brigantina Villars 225, 1015

cerasifera Ehrhart 227, 1015

cerasus L. 220, 1017

cocomila Tenore 225, 1018

communis (L.)Arcang, not Hudson 1019–1020

domestica L. 226, 1018

domestica var. *myrobalan* L. 1016

dulcis (Miller)Webb 226, 1019

incisa Thunberg 221, 1020

× *juddii* Anderson 221, 1027

laurocerasus L. 229, 1021

lusitanica L. 229, 1022

maackii Ruprecht 1025

mahaleb L. 221, 1023

mume Siebold & Zuccarini 1013

nana Du Roi 1034

padus L. 228, 1024

persica (L.)Batsch 225, 1025

ramburii Boissier 1032

salicifolia Kunth 1028

sargentii Rehder 222, 1026

serotina Ehrhart 228, 1028

serrula Franchet 222, 1029

serrulata Lindley 223, 1030

serrulata var. *sachalinensis* (F.Schmidt)Wilson 1027

speciosa (Koidzumi) Ingram 1021

spinosa L. 227, 1031

× *subhirtella* Miquel 224, 1032

virginiana L. 228, 1034

× *yedoensis* Matsumuara 224, 1035

Pseudolarix Gordon 1035

amabilis (Nelson)Rehder 100, 1035

kaempferi (Lambert) Gordon 1036

Pseudotsuga Carrière 1036

douglasii (Lindley) Carrière 1039

macrocarpa (Vasey)Mayr 94, 1037

menziesii (Mirbel)Franco 94, 1038

taxifolia (Poiret)Brittan 1039

Ptelea L. 1039

trifoliata L. **308**, 1039

Pterocarya Kunth 1040
  fraxinifolia (Lambert)
    Spach **328**, 1040
  × *rehderiana* Schneider
    328, 1042
  stenoptera C.DC **328**,
    1043

Pterostyrax Siebold &
    Zuccarini 1044
  corymbosa **235**, 1044
  hispida Siebold &
    Zuccarini 1045

○Pukatea 786

Punica L. 1045
  granatum L. **151**, 1046

Punicaceae Horan 1045

Pyrus L. 823, 1047, 1138
  amygdaliformis Villier
    158, 1047
  aria L. 1142
  arranensis (Hedlund)
    Druce 1143
  aucuparia (L.)Gaertner
    1145
  austriaca Kerner 1048
  baccata L. 825
  bourgaeana Decaisne
    1048
  calleryana Decaisne
    213, 1049
  caucasica Federov 1048
  communis L. **212**, 1049
  cordata Desvaux **212**,
    1051
  cossonii Rehder 1052
  cydonia L. 659
  elaeagrifolia Pallas **159**,
    1052
  harrowiana Bean 1157
  hupehensis Pampanini
    830
  intermedia Ehrhart
    1161
  magyarica Terpô 1051
  microphylla (Wenzig)
    Hooker 1166
  nivalis Jacques **159**,
    1052

pashia D. Don 1052
pyraster Burgsd. **213**,
    1050
rossica Danilov 1051
salicifolia Pallas **159**,
    1053
salvifolia De Candolle
    158, 1053
syriaca Boissier 1050
thuringiaca Ilse 1175
trilobata (Poiret)De
    Candolle 677

Q

○Quassia 912, 1136

Quercus L. 1054
  abelicea Lambert 1268
  acuta Thunberg **163**,
    1055
  acutissima Carruthers
    266, 1055
  aegilops ssp. *macrolepis*
    (Kotschy)Camus
    1071
  alba L. **279**, 1056
  alnifolia Poech **267**,
    1057
  annulata Smith 1067
  borealis Micheaux 1086
  brachyphylla Kotschy
    1080
  brutia Tenore 1083
  calliprinos Webb 1062
  canariensis Willdenow
    276, 1058
  cerris L. **280**, 1059
  coccifera L. **267**, 1061
  coccinea Muenchhausen
    282, 1062
  conferta Kitaibel 1066
  congesta Presl 1080
  × *crenata* Lambert 1068
  daimio K. Koch 1064
  dalechampii Tenore
    1076
  dentata Thunberg **279**,
    1063

edulis Makino 799

ellipsoidalis E. J. Hill 1074

faginea Lambert 276, 1064

frainetto Tenore 277, 1065

glauca Thunberg 163, 1066

haas Presl 1083

henryi Seemen 800

× *heterophylla* Michaux 1077

× *hickelii* Camus 1078

× *hispanica* Lambert 280, 1067

iberica Bieb. 1076

ilex L. 162, 1069

ilex var. *ballota* (Desfontaines)A.DC 1084

imbricaria Michaux 1077

ithaburensis Decaisne 1071

laevigata Blume 1055

lanuginosa Lambert 1061, 1080

× *leana* Nuttall 1077

lucombeana Sweet 1068

× *ludoviciana* Sargeant 1077

lusitanica Webb 1065

macedonica De Candolle 1089

macranthera Fischer & Meyer 279, 1070

macrolepis Kotschy 278, 1071

marilandica Muenchhausen 282, 1071

mas Thore 1076

mirbeckii Durieu 1059

myrsinifolia Blume 163, 1073

nigra L. 1072

palustris Muenchhausen 282, 1074

pedunculata Ehrhart 1083

pedunculiflora K. Koch 274, 1083

petraea (Mattfeld) Lieblein 275, 1075

phellos L. 161, 1077

polycarpa Schur. 275, 1076

pontica K. Koch 278, 1078

pubescens Willdenow 275, 1079

pyrenaica Willdenow 277, 1080

robur L. 274, 1081

× *rosacea* Bechstein 1076

rotundifolia Lambert 162, 1084

rubra L. 281, 1085

semecarpifolia Smith 267, 1086

suber L. 161, 1087

thomasii Tenore 1083

tinctoria Michaux 1091

toza De Candolle 1081

trojana Webb 279, 1088

variabilis Blume 281, 1089

velutina Lambert 281, 1090

virgiliana (Tenore) Tenore 1080

◯Quickthorn 632

◯Quince 129, 658

R

Ranunculaceae Jussieu 613, 1091

◯Rauli 240, 856

◯Redwood 58, 1133, 1198

◯ Coastal 1133

◯ Dawn 59, 840

◯ Sierra 1135

◯Rehderodendron 1091

Rehderodendron Hu 1091

macrocarpum Hu 235,
1091
Rhamnaceae Jussieu 709,
738, 867, 1092–
1093, 1271
Rhamnus L. 709, 1093
alaternus 176, 1093
catharticus L. 176, 1094
frangula L. 710
◯Rhododendron 130,
1094, 1097
Rhododendron L. 1094
arboreum Smith 130,
1095
arizelum Balfour &
Forrest 1097
falconeri Hooker f. 130,
1096
ponticum L. 130, 1097
ponticum ssp *baeticum*
(Boissier & Reuter)
Handel-Mazzetti
1098
Rhus L. 623
× *ambigua* Poiret 1104
coraria L. 323, 1100
cotinoides Nuttall 624
cotinus L. 624
hirta (L.)Sudworth
1100
potaninii Maximowicz
323, 1099
typhina L. 323, 1100
vernaciflua Stokes 324,
1101
◯Robinia 338, 1102
Robinia L. 1102
glutinosa Sims 1104
hispida L. 338, 1104
pseudoacacia L. 338,
1102
viscosa Ventenat 338,
1104
Rosaceae Jussieu 501,
624, 627, 658, 675,
677, 803, 823, 839,
880, 1011, 1047,
1105, 1138
◯Rose 1105

◯Rowan 332, 1138, 1144
◯ Esserteau's 332, 1152
◯ Harrow 331, 1156
◯ Japanese 333, 1149
◯ Joseph Rock's 333,
1162
◯ Kashmir 334, 1148
◯ Kite-leaf 334, 1168
◯ Ladder 332, 1171
◯ Meinich's 1165
◯ Sargent's 333, 1170
◯ Small-leaf 335, 1166
◯ Tsema 335, 1169
◯ Vilmorin 335, 1178
◯ White-fruited 334,
1154
◯Rubber Plant 132, 707
◯Rue 1105
Rutaceae Jussieu 606,
874, 1039, 1105,
1206, 1266

S

◯Sabia 1106
Sabiaceae Blume 837,
1106
Sabina see Juniperus
Salicaceae Mirbel 995,
1106
Salix L. 1106
alba L. 250, 1107
amygdalina L. 1122
atrocinerea Brotero
1113
babylonica L. 251, 1109
borealis Fries 1110
caprea L. 252, 1111
chrysocoma Dode 1120
cinerascens Andersson
1123
cinerea L. ssp. *cinerea*
1113
cinerea L. ssp. *oleifera*
Macreight 253,
1112
coaetanea (Hartmann)
B. Flod 1112

daphnoides Villars 255, 1114

elaeagnos Scopoli 254, 1115

fragilis L. 250, 1115

incana Schrank 1115

matsudana Koidzumi 'Tortuosa' 251, 1117

myrsinifolia Salisbury 1111

nigricans Smith 254, 1110

pedicelallata 1113

pendula Moenchen 1110

× *pendulina* Wenderoth 1120

pentandra L. 255, 1118

purpurea L. 253, 1119

rossica Nasarow 1123

× *rubens* Schrank 250, 1117

× *sepulcralis* Simonk 'Chrysocoma' 251, 1120

triandra L. 255, 1121

viminalis L. 254, 1122

xerophila 1123

○ Sallow 1106
○   Common 1112
○   Grey 1113
○   Rusty 253, 1112

Sambucus L. 1124

nigra L. 315, 1124

racemosa L. 315, 1125

Sapindaceae Jussieu 772, 1126

○ Sassafras 129, 1126
○   Black 512

Sassafras Nees & Ebermaier 1126

albidum (Nuttall)Nees 129, 1126

Saxegothea Lindley 1127

conspicua Lindley 60, 1127

○ Schima 239, 1129

Schima Reinwardt ex Blume 1129

argentea Pritzel 239, 1129

khasiana Dyer 1130

Schinus L. 1130

molle L. 322, 1130

terebinthifolius Raddi 322, 1131

Sciadopitaceae 1131

Sciadopitys Siebold & Zuccarini 1131

verticillata (Thunberg) Siebold & Zuccarini 60, 1132

Scrophulariaceae Jussieu 747, 871, 1133

○ Sequoia 1133

Sequoia Endlicher 1133 *see also Sequoiadendron*

gigantea Descaisne 1135

sempervirens (D. Don) Endlicher 58, 1133

Sequoiadendron Buchholz 1134

giganteum (Lindley) Buchholz 58, 1135

○ Service Berry 501
○ Service Tree 331, 1151
○   Bastard 331, 1159
○   Thuringian 273, 1174
○   Wild 273, 1175
○ Service Tree of Fontaine-bleau 218, 1163
○ Shaddock 232, 609
○ Silk Tree 490
○ Silverbell 728

Simaroubaceae De Candolle 488, 912, 1136

○ Sloe 227, 1031

Smilacaceae Ventenat 1136

Smilax L. 1136

aspera L. 166, 1136

○ Smoke Tree 623
○ Snowbell Tree 1186
○ Snowdrop Tree 233, 728
○   Carolina 729
○ Soap Berry 1126

Sophora L. 1137
  japonica L. 339, 1137
Sorbus L. 1138
  alnifolia (Siebold & Zuccarini)K. Koch 216, 1140
  aria (L.)Crantz 214, 1141
  arranensis Hedlund 272, 1143
  aucuparia L. 332, 1144
  aucuparia var. *meinichii* Lindeb. ex Hartman 1166
  austriaca (G. Beck) Hedlund 217, 1146
  bristoliensis Wilmott 217, 1146
  caloneura (Stapf)Rehder 1164
  cashmiriana Hedlund 334, 1148
  commixta Hedlund 333, 1149
  conradinae Koehne 1153
  croceocarpa Sell 1151
  cuspidata (Spach) Hedlund 1173, 1178
  devoniensis E.F. Warburg 217, 1150
  domestica L. 331, 1151
  epidendron Handel-Mazzetti 216, 1165
  esserteauiana Koehne 332, 1152
  fennica (Kalm)Fries 1160
  folgneri Rehder 214, 1154
  glabrescens (Cardot) Handel-Mazzetti 334, 1154
  graeca (Spach)Kotschy 214, 1156
  harrowiana (Bean) Rehder 331, 1156
  hedlundii Schneider 215, 1158

  hupehensis Schneider 1155
  hybrida L. 331, 1159
  hybrida var. *meinichii* Hartmann 1166
  insignis (Hooker) Hedlund 1157
  intermedia (Ehrhart) Persoon 272, 1160
  intermedia var. *arranensis* (Hedlund)Rehder 1143
  'Joseph Rock' 333, 1162
  karpatii Boros 1147
  latifolia (Lambert) Persoon 218, 1163
  megalocarpa Rehder 216, 1164
  meinichii (Hartman) Hedlund 1165
  meliosmifolia 1165
  microphylla Wenzig emend. Rushforth 335, 1166
  mougeotii Soyer-Willemet & Godron 218, 1167
  oligodonta (Cardot) Handel-Mazzettii 334, 1168
  pinnatifida hort. 1160
  pluripinnata (Schneider) Koehne 1172
  pseudohupehensis McAllister provisional name 1169
  pseudovilmorinii McAllister 1179
  randaiensis Hayata 1150
  rufo-ferruginea (Schneider)Schneider 1150
  rufopilosa Schneider 335, 1169
  rupicola (Syme)Hedlund 272
  sargentiana Koehne 333, 1170

scalaris Koehne 332,
1171
semipinnata Hedlund
1175
subcuneata Wilmott
1151
thibetica (Cardot)
Handel-Mazzettii
215, 1172
thuringiaca (Ilse)Fritsch
273, 1174
torminalis (L.)Crantz
273, 1175
umbellata (Desfontaines)
Fritsch 218, 1176
vestita (G. Don)
Loddiges 215, 1177
vilmorinii Schneider
335, 1178
wardii Merrill 215,
1173
wilsoniana Schneider
1171
○ Sorrel Tree 197, 866
○ Spanish Bayonet 351,
1265
Spartium L. 1180
aetnensis Bivona 722
junceum L. 346, 1180
○ Spindle 174, 587, 699
○   Broad-leafed 174, 700
○   Japanese 174, 700
○ Spruce 883
○   Alcock 73, 886
○   Balfour 905
○   Black 73, 898
○   Brewer 77, 890
○   Caucasian 75, 902
○   Colorado 71, 903
○   Colorado Blue 903
○   Dragon 68, 887
○   Engelmann 71, 891
○   Glehn 75, 893
○   Hondo 72, 894
○   Koyama 69, 895
○   Lijiang 74, 897
○   Mexican 71, 891
○   Morinda 70, 908
○   Norway 68, 885

○   Oriental 902
○   Purple-cone 74, 904
○   Sakhalin 893
○   Sargent 77, 888
○   Schrenk 70, 906
○   Serbian 76, 901
○   Siberian 69, 900
○   Sikkim 76, 909
○   Sitka 72, 907
○   Taiwan 69, 899
○   Tiger Tail 71, 910
○   West Himalayan 908
○   White 73, 892
○   Wilson 69, 911
○ Spur Leaf 237, 1204
Staphylea L. 1181
holocarpa Hemsley 308,
1181
pinnata L. 308, 1182
Staphyleaceae Lindley
1180–1181
Stewartia see Stuartia
Stewartia pseudocamellia
Maxim. 1183
○ Storax 233, 1184, 1188
○   Big-leaf 234, 1187
○   Hemsley's 234, 1185
○   Japanese 234, 1186
○   Winged 235, 1044
○ Stranvaesia 155, 880
Stranvaesia see Photinia
Stranvaesia davidiana
Decaisne 881
○ Strawberry Tree 196,
508, 511
○   Cyprus 196, 509
○   Hybrid 197, 509
○ Stuartia, Chinese 239,
1183
Stuartia L. 1182
pseudocamellia Maximo-
wicz 239, 1182
sinensis Rehder &
Wilson 239, 1183
Styphnolobium see Sophora
Styphnolobium japonicum
(L.)Shott 1138
Styracaceae Dumort 728,
1044, 1091, 1184

◯Styrax, Winged 1044
  Styrax L. 1184
    hemsleyana Diels 234,
      1185
    japonica Siebold &
      Zuccarini 234, 1186
    obassia Siebold &
      Zuccarini 234, 1187
    officinalis L. 233, 1188
◯Sumach 323, 1098, 1100
◯ Potanin's 323, 1099
◯ Stag's Horn 323, 1100
◯ Venetian 128, 623
◯Sweet Bay 137, 787, 821
◯Sweet Gum 305, 730,
      792, 794
◯ Chinese 305, 792
◯ Oriental 305, 793
  Swida Opiz 1188
    controversa (Hemsley)
      Sojak 142, 1189
    macrophylla (Wallich)
      Sojak 142, 1190
    sanguinea (L.)Opiz 144,
      1191
  Syagrus Martius 1191
    romanzoffiana
      (Chamisso)Glassman
      348, 1192
◯Sycamore 291, 462
  Syringa L. 1192
    josikaea Jacquin f. ex
      Reichenbach 147,
      1193
    vulgaris L. 147, 1192
    yunnanensis Franchet
      1193

T

◯Taiwania 57, 1194
  Taiwania Hayata 1194
    cryptomerioides Hayata
      57, 1194
    flousiana Gaussen 1194
◯Tamarack 102, 782
  Tamaricaceae Link 1195
◯Tamarisk 38, 1195

  Tamarix L. 1195
    africana Poiret 39,
      1196
    anglica Webb 1196
    canariensis Wildenow
      1197
    chinensis Loureiro 1196
    dalmatica Baum 1197
    gallica L. 38, 1195
    parviflora De Candolle
      39, 1197
    ramosissima Ledebour
      39, 1196
    smyrnensis Bunge 39,
      1197
    tetrandra Pallas ex Bieb.
      39, 1197
◯Tangerine 230, 606
◯Tanoak 798, 800
◯Tarata 164, 983
  Taxaceae Gray 1198,
      1201, 1235
  Taxodiaceae Warming
      512, 640, 643, 840,
      1131, 1133–1134,
      1194, 1198
  Taxodium Rich 1198
    ascendens Brongiart 59,
      1198
    distichum (L.)Richards
      59, 1199
    distichum var. *nutans*
      (Aiton)Sweet 1199
    sempervirens D. Don
      1134
  Taxus L. 1201
    baccata L. 64, 1201
    celebica misapplied 1204
    cuspidata Siebold &
      Zuccarini 64, 1203
    mairei (Lem. & Lev.)
      S.Y. Hu ex Liu 65,
      1203
◯Tea 1208
◯Terebinth 321, 978
◯ Large 321, 978
  Tetracentron Oliver 1204
    sinense Oliver 237,
      1204

Tetracentronaceae van
    Tieghem 1204
Tetraclinis Masters 1205
    articulata (Vahl)Masters
        49, 1206
Tetradium Loureiro 1206
    daniellii (Benn)Hartley
        312, 1207
Thea see Camellia
Theaceae D. Don 555,
    1129, 1182, 1208
Thelycrania see Swida
Thelycrania sanguinea
    (L.)Fouret 1191
○ Thorn, Broad-leafed
        Cockspur 205, 635
○   Christ's 152, 867
○   Cockspur 204, 629
○   Hybrid Cockspur 204,
        631
○   Tansy-leafed 270, 638
○ Thuja 1208
○   Chinese 990
○   Korean 46, 1208
Thuja L. 1208
    articulata Vahl 1206
    dolabrata L.f. 1212
    gigantea Nuttall 1211
    koraiensis Nakai 46,
        1208
    lobbii hort. ex Gordon
        1211
    occidentalis L. 46, 1209
    orientalis L.f. 991
    plicata D. Don 46,
        1210
Thujopsis Siebold &
    Zuccarini 1211
    dolabrata (L.f.)Siebold &
        Zuccarini 47, 1211
Tilia L. 1213
    alba Aiton 1224, 1234
    americana L. 257, 1214
    americana 'Pendula'
        1230
    argentea De Candolle
        1234
    canadensis Michaux
        1215

caroliniana Miller
    1224
chinensis Maximowicz
    1227
cordata Miller 256,
    1215
cordata × *Tilia dasystyla*
    1219
dasystyla Steven 261,
    1217
× *euchlora* K. Koch
    261, 1218
× *europaea* L. 256,
    1219
glabra Ventenat 1215
grandifolia Ehrhart
    1233
henryana Szyszylowicz
    258, 1222
heterophylla Ventenat
    261, 1223
intonsa Rehder &
    Wilson 1227
mandshurica Ruprecht
    & Maximowicz 259,
    1225
maximowicziana
    Shirasawa 260,
    1226
michauxii Nuttall
    1224
× *moltkei* Späth ex
    Schneider 1215
mongolica Maximowicz
    260, 1227
monticola Sargent 1224
nigra Borghausen
    1215
nobilis Rehder &
    Wilson 1227
officinarum Crantz
    1233
oliveri Szyszylowicz
    259, 1229
parviflora Ehrhart 1217
× *petriolaris* Hooker f.
    259, 1230
platyphyllos Scopoli
    257, 1231

rubra De Candolle 1233

'Spectabilis' 1215

tomentosa Moenchen **258**, 1233

tuan Szyszylowicz 1222

ulmifolia Scopoli 1217

× *vulgaris* Hayne 1221

Tiliaceae Jussieu 1213

○ Tobira **165**, 984

Toona (Endlicher)Roemer 1234

sinensis (Jussieu)Roemer **336**, 1234

○ Toothache Tree 1266

○ Japanese **324**, 1266

Torminaria see Sorbus

Torminaria torminalis (L.) 1176

Torreya Arnott 1235

californica Torrey **65**, 1236

nucifera (L.)Siebold & Zuccarini **65**, 1237

○ Totara **62**, 994

○ Chilean **61**, 992

Trachycarpus Wendland 1238

fortunei (Hooker)H. Wendland **349**, 1238

martinianus (Wallich) H. Wendle 1238

takil Beccari 1238

○ Traveller's Joy 613

○ Tree Fern **350**, 664

○ Tree Heath **38**, 675

○ Tree of Heaven **336**, 488

○ Trochodendron **237**, 1239

Trochodendron Siebold & Zuccarini 1239

aralioides Siebold & Zuccarini **237**, 1239

Trochodendronaceae Prantl 1239

○ True Cedar 582

○ Trumpet Vine **314**, 557

Tsuga Carrière 1240 *see also Hesperopeuce*

brunoniana (Wallich) Carrière 1246

canadensis (L.)Carrière **95**, 1240

caroliniana Engelmann **96**, 1242

chinensis (Franchet) Pritzel **96**, 1243

chinensis var. *formosana* (Hayata)Li 1244

diversifolia (Maximowicz) Masters **97**, 1244

dumosa (D. Don) Endlicher **97**, 1245

formosana Hayata 1244

heterophylla (Rafinesque)Sargent **95**, 1246

mertensiana (Bongard) Carrière 736

sieboldii Carrière **97**, 1248

yunnanensis 1246

○ Tuart **127**, 684

○ Tulip Tree **283**, 795, 797

○ Chinese **283**, 795

Tumion see Torreya

○ Tupelo **219**, 859–861

○ Chinese **219**, 860

○ Turpentine Tree 978

U

Ulmaceae Mirbel 588, 1249, 1268

○ Ulmo **173**, 694

Ulmus L. 1249

campestre L. 1251, 1255

canescens Melville **194**, 1249

carpinifolia Suckow 1255

chinensis Persoon 1256

davidiana var. *japonica*
(Rehder)Nakai 1253
effusa Willdenow 1254
glabra Hudson 193,
1250
× *hollandica* Miller
194, 1251
humilis Gmelin 1258
japonica (Rehder)
Sargent 193, 1252
laevis Pallas 195, 1253
microphylla Persoon
1258
minor Miller 194, 1254
minor ssp. *canescens*
(Melville)Brow. &
Ziel. 1250
montana Stokes 1251
parvifolia Jacques 195,
1255
pedunculata Fougeroux
1254
procera Salisbury 193,
1256
pumila L. 195, 1257
Umbellularia (Nees)
Nuttall 1258
californica (Hooker &
Arnott)Nuttall 168,
1258
◯ Umbrella Tree 137, 820

V

◯ Varnish Tree 324, 1101
◯ Verbena 1259
Verbenaceae J. St-Hilaire
614, 1259, 1262
Viburnum L. 1259
lantana L. 175, 1260
opalus L. 175, 1260
tinus L. 141, 1261
◯ Virgin's Bower 613
◯ Virginia Creeper
870–871
Vitaceae Jussieu 870,
1262
Vitex L. 1262

agnus-castus L. 312,
1262
negundo L. 1263

W

◯ Walnut 326, 750, 755
◯   Black 327, 753
◯   Japanese 326, 751
Washingtonia Wendland
1263
filifera (J.J. Linden)
Wendland 349,
1263
robusta Wendland 1263
◯ Wattle 406
◯   Cyclops 344, 409
◯   Golden 344, 411
◯   Green 341, 408
◯   Silver 340, 407
◯   Swamp 344, 410
◯   Sydney Golden 345,
408
◯   Willow 406
◯ Wayfaring Tree 175, 1260
◯ Wellingtonia 58,
1134–1135
Wellingtonia see
Sequoiadendron
Wellingtonia giganteum
Lindley 1135
◯ Whitebeam 214, 1138,
1141
◯   Alder-leafed 216, 1140
◯   Arran 272, 1143
◯   Austrian 217, 1146
◯   Balkan 218, 1176
◯   Bristol Gorge 217,
1146
◯   Devon 1150
◯   Folgner's 214, 1154
◯   Grecian 214, 1156
◯   Hedlund's 215, 1158
◯   Himalayan 215, 1177
◯   Mougeot's 218, 1167
◯   Mupin 216, 1164
◯   Swedish 272, 1160
◯   Tibetan 215, 1172

○ Ward's **215**, 1173
○ Willow 1106
○ Almond-leafed **255**, 1121
○ Bay **255**, 1118
○ Boreal 1110
○ Chinese Weeping **251**, 1109
○ Crack **250**, 1115
○ Dark-leaved **254**, 1110
○ Finnmark 1123
○ Goat **252**, 1111
○ Hoary **254**, 1115
○ Peking **251**, 1117
○ Violet **255**, 1114
○ Weeping **251**, 1120
○ White **250**, 1107
○ Wine Palm, Chilean **348**, 749–750
○ Wing Nut 1040
○ Wingnut, Caucasian **328**, 1040
○ Chinese **328**, 1043
○ Hybrid **328**, 1042
○ Winter's Bark **167**, **670**, 1264
Winteraceae Lindley 669, 1264
○ Wisteria **339**, 1264
Wisteria Nuttall 1264
floribunda (Willdenow) De Candolle 1265
sinensis (Sims)Sweet **339**, 1264
○ Witch Hazel **199**, **730**, 732
○ Chinese **198**, 730
○ Hybrid **198**, 731
○ Japanese **198**, 731
○ Ozark 732
○ Virginian 732
○ Woodbine 801

X

Xanthoxylum see Zanthoxylum

Y

○ Yellow-wood **337**, 610–611
○ Yew **64**, 1201
○ Japanese **64**, 1203
○ Maire **65**, 1203
○ Prince Albert's **60**, 1127
Yucca L. 1265
aloifolia L. **351**, 1265
○ Yulan 820

Z

Zanthoxylum L. 1266
ailanthioides Siebold & Zuccarini **324**, 1266
simulans Hance **324**, 1267
○ Zelkova, Cretan **192**, 1268
Zelkova Spach 1268
abelicea (Lambert) Boissier **192**, 1268
acuminata Planchon 1271
carpinifolia (Pallas) K. Koch **192**, 1269
crenata Spach 1270
cretica Spach 1268
keaki (Siebold) Maximowicz 1271
serrata (Thunberg) Makino **192**, 1270
sicula G. di Pasquale, G. Garti & P. Quezel 1270
Ziziphus Miller 1271
lotus (L.)Lambert **177**, 1272
mauritiana **177**, 1272
spina-christi 1272
ziziphus **177**, 1271

QUICK REFERENCE GUIDE

• **For a leafy specimen:**
Use the photographs. Their ordering is explained according to 'key' leaf characters on pp.29–32.

• **For fruits:**
Use the fruit key on pp.33–7 to shorten the number of photographs to be consulted.

• **If you know the genus but not the species:**
Look through the *genus* introductions in Part II, and *family and species descriptions* (pp.353–1272). Check the tree's features against the photographs and text. Part II is alphabetical by Latin or scientific name. Pages 25–8 explain the text section.

• **If you know the common name or an alternative name:**
Use the index (pp.1290–335) and turn to the photographs and text.

• The **glossary** is on pp.1275–82.